Lifespan Development

Lifespan Development

Seventh Edition

Denise **Boyd**

Houston Community College System

Helen **Bee**

PEARSON

Boston   Columbus   Indianapolis   New York   San Francisco   Upper Saddle River
Amsterdam   Cape Town   Dubai   London   Madrid   Milan   Munich   Paris   Montreal   Toronto
Delhi   Mexico City   São Paulo   Sydney   Hong Kong   Seoul   Singapore   Taipei   Tokyo

Editor-in-Chief: Dickson Musslewhite
Acquisitions Editor: Amber Chow
Editorial Assistant: Alex Stravrakas
VP, Director of Marketing: Brandy Dawson
Senior Marketing Manager: Jeremy Intal
Marketing Assistant: Frank Alarcon
Director, Project Management Services: Lisa Iarkowski
Senior Managing Editor: Linda Behrens
Project Manager: Shelly Kupperman
Program Manager: Diane Szulecki
Procurement Manager: Mary Fischer
Procurement Specialist: Diane Peirano
Cover Designer: Kathryn Foot

Digital Media Project Manager: Caitlin Smith
Full-Service Project Management: Jeanine Furino,
    Cenveo® Publisher Services
Printer/Binder: R. R. Donnelley and Sons
Cover Printer: Lehigh-Phoenix Color/Hagerstown
Cover Image: to come
Cover Art: Background Image: © irish1983 / Alamy;
Silhouette Images (left to right): © Philipp Kammerer /
Alamy; © Robert Adrian Hillman / Alamy; © Philipp
Kammerer / Alamy; © Oleksii Telnov / Alamy;
© fotoshoot / Alamy; © Bogusław Mazur / Alamy;
© Bogusław Mazur / Alamy.
Text Font: 10/12.5 Minion

Credits and acknowledgments borrowed from other sources and reproduced, with permission, in this textbook appear on the appropriate page of appearance.

Library of Congress Cataloging-in-Publication Data
Boyd, Denise Roberts.
 Lifespan development / Denise Boyd, Houston Community
College System, Helen Bee. -- 7th Edition.
    pages cm
 Includes bibliographical references and index.
 ISBN-13: 978-0-13-380566-6 (alk. paper)
 ISBN-10: 0-13-380566-2 (alk. paper)
1. Developmental psychology. I. Bee, Helen L., II. Title.
BF713.B435 2014
155--dc23
                        2013039922

10 9 8 7 6 5 4 3 2 1

Student Edition
ISBN 10:   0-13-380566-2
ISBN 13: 978-0-13-380566-6
Books à la Carte
ISBN 10:   0-13-377364-7
ISBN 13: 978-0-13-377364-4

This book is dedicated to my husband, Jerry Boyd,
in appreciation for the help and support he provided to me
while I was preparing the seventh edition of
Lifespan Development.

Brief Contents

List of Features

Contents

Contents

Contents

Preface

Having taught human development for many years, I know that teaching a course in lifespan development is one of the most difficult assignments an instructor can face. You must deal with the challenge of getting through all the necessary descriptive material in a single semester. At the same time, you have to cover theories of development, some of which are among the most complex and important theories in the behavioral sciences. In preparing this seventh edition of *Lifespan Development*, I hoped to support lifespan development instructors by producing a textbook that thoroughly addresses the basic facts of development, makes the more abstract material about theories understandable to students, and motivates them to read the book by presenting information in a way that is both engaging and relevant to real-world applications of developmental science.

New to the Seventh Edition

Following are some highlights of this new edition:

- **In-text references to MyVirtualLife and MyPsychLab video series.** At the beginning of each chapter, students are prompted to relate the material in the chapter to *MyVirtualLife*, an engaging online simulation tool that allows users to raise a virtual child to live their own virtual lives. Once the virtual child has been raised, the students shift to exploring simulated outcomes of important life decisions such as career selection. New icons prompt students to access the exciting new MyPsychLab video series.

- **DSM-5 updates.** Discussions of mental health issues have been updated to conform to DSM-5 terminology and diagnostic criteria.

- **New and expanded coverage of atypical development and mental health.** This edition includes new information on these important mental health topics:
  - Reactive attachment disorder (Chapter 6)
  - Autism spectrum disorders (Chapter 6)
  - Disruptive mood dysregulation disorder (Chapter 8)
  - Childhood-onset conduct disorder (Chapter 10, Chapter 12)
  - Adolescent-onset conduct disorder (Chapter 12)
  - Bipolar disorder (Chapter 13)
  - Complicated grief (Chapter 19)

- **Improved art program.** A number of new figures have been added to this edition, while other figures and tables have been revised and updated with new illustrations.

LEARNING OBJECTIVES. The numbered learning objective questions are now more prominent in the seventh edition. These objectives are listed in the chapter opener, called out in their corresponding sections, and repeated in the chapter summary to facilitate student review. In addition, the Instructor's Manual and Test Bank correspond to these learning objectives, allowing you to assess your students' knowledge of key educational objectives.

TEST YOURSELF BEFORE GOING ON. The end of each section now contains brief quizzes with multiple-choice, true/false, fill-in-the-blank, and critical thinking questions for students to test their knowledge before moving on to the next section. The answers to these questions are provided at the back of the text.

CHAPTER TEST. A 25-question multiple-choice practice test now appears at the end of every chapter. The answers are provided at the back of the text, allowing students to assess their knowledge and prepare for course quizzes and exams.

INTEGRATED MyPsychLab RESOURCES. Throughout the text, we have placed MyPsychLab icons indicating where students can go to find web-based videos, simulations, and expanded information on particular topics. Many more resources are available in addition to those highlighted in the text, but the icons draw attention to some of the most high-interest materials available on www.MyPsychLab.com.

👁 **Watch** the **Video** in **MyPsychLab**

✳ **Explore** the **Concept** in **MyPsychLab**

◉ **Simulate** the **Experiment** in **MyPsychLab**

✓ **Study** and **Review** in **MyPsychLab**

UPDATED RESEARCH.

- Genetic basis of neurodevelopmental disorders (Chapter 3)
- Language development in hearing infants of deaf parents (Chapter 5)
- Predictive validity of infant IQ tests (Chapter 5)
- Paternal influences on social development (Chapter 6)
- Genetics of hand dominance (Chapter 7)
- Insecure attachment and preschoolers' self-esteem (Chapter 8)
- Individual differences in the effects of spanking (Chapter 8)
- Cultural influences on the development of children's real and ideal selves (Chapter 10)
- Shifts in academic goals and their effects on children's achievement at the transition to middle school (Chapter 11)
- "Americanized" behavior as a source of conflict between immigrant teens and their parents (Chapter 12)
- Neurological basis of gender differences in responses to emotion-provoking stimuli (Chapter 13)
- Personality and career satisfaction (Chapter 14)
- Brain aging and image processing (Chapter 15)
- Effects of chronic disease on brain aging (Chapter 15)
- Terminal decline (Chapter 17)
- Depression among immigrant elders (Chapter 18)
- Effects of experience on information processing speed among the elderly (Chapter 18)
- Influence of young celebrities' deaths on their popularity among young adults (Chapter 19)

Themed Essays

NO EASY ANSWERS. The *No Easy Answers* essays introduce students to the idea that there are many questions for which developmental psychologists cannot provide definitive answers. For example, the essay in Chapter 15 deals with hormone therapy and discusses the benefits and potential risks of this therapy. Students are asked to take a stand on whether they feel that, due to the risks involved, hormone therapy should be a last resort or that, since no medical treatment is entirely free of risk, women should feel free to take hormone therapy to help relieve some of their menopausal symptoms.

I developed these discussions in response to my own students' continuing difficulty in understanding that psychology is not a science that can offer straightforward recipes for perfect behavioral outcomes. My hope is that, by reading these discussions, students will become more sensitive to the complexity of human development and more tolerant of the ambiguities inherent in the behavioral and social sciences.

NO EASY ANSWERS

The Pros and Cons of Hormone Therapy

Most of the physical symptoms and effects of menopause—including hot flashes, thinning of the vaginal wall, and loss of vaginal lubrication—can be reduced by taking estrogen and progesterone (hormone therapy [HT]). Moreover, in the 1990s, physicians thought that HT would protect women against heart disease and dementia. Thus, they commonly prescribed HT for women who complained of menopausal symptoms such as hot flashes.

Everything changed in 2002, with the publication of the results of the Women's Health Initiative (WHI), a longitudinal placebo-controlled study of HT (Writing Group for the Women's Health Initiative Investigators, 2002). These results included alarming evidence showing that long-term use of either estrogen alone or combined estrogen–progesterone hormone replacement therapy significantly increased the risk of both breast and ovarian cancers (Chlebowski et

al., 2003). There was also evidence of increased incidence of cardiovascular disease among study participants who already had it (Grady et al., 2002; Hulley et al., 2002). The evidence suggesting that HT might seriously harm women's health was so strong that the WHI was immediately terminated; all of the study's participants who had been given HT were advised to stop taking it (Writing Group for the Women's Health Initiative Investigators, 2002). Consequently, the number of women who take HT declined dramatically soon after these results were published (Udell, Fischer, Brookhart, Solomon, & Choudhry, 2006).

To date, the accumulated evidence indicates that the only consistent benefits associated with hormone replacement therapy are the reduction of hot flashes and protection against osteoporosis (Kaur, 2012). As a result of the most recent findings, the American College of Obstetricians and Gynecologists recommends that women be extremely cautious about entering into any regi-

men of hormone therapy. Physicians recommend that treatment be symptom specific. For example, if a woman's main complaint is vaginal dryness, then the best treatment for her is a vaginal cream. Finally, doctors recommend that women undergoing any kind of treatment for menopausal symptoms see their doctors regularly and follow their instructions with regard to cancer screenings (e.g., mammograms) (Szymanski & Bacon, 2008).

YOU DECIDE

Decide which of these two statements you most agree with and think about how you would defend your position:

1. *Due to the risks involved, hormone therapy should be a last resort for menopausal women who have hot flashes and other symptoms.*

RESEARCH REPORT. These essays provide detailed accounts of specific research studies. For example, Chapter 5 discusses research on early gestural language in the children of deaf parents, and Chapter 17 examines research on mild cognitive impairment and Alzheimer's disease. "Critical Analysis" questions appear at the end of each feature to help students assess the research and make connections between the research study and their daily lives.

DEVELOPMENTAL SCIENCE. *Developmental Science* essays explore practical applications of developmental theory and research. For example, the *Developmental Science in the Classroom* essay in Chapter 5 discusses the importance of reading to toddlers. Likewise, *Developmental Science in the Clinic* in Chapter 11 examines crisis intervention for pregnant teenagers, and *Developmental Science at Home* in Chapter 6 addresses choosing a day-care center. Each of these essays opens with a brief real-life vignette and concludes with "Reflection" questions.

Supplements for the Instructor

We have designed a collection of instructor resources for this edition that will help you prepare for class, enhance your course presentations, and assess your students' understanding of the material. These are available only to qualified instructors using the text. Please contact your local publishing representative for more information.

- **MyVirtualLife.** Raise your child. Live your life. MyVirtualLife is two simulations in one. The first simulation allows students to raise a child from birth to age 18 and monitor the effects of their parenting decisions over time. In the second simulation, students make first-person decisions and see the impacts of those decisions on their simulated future self over time. By incorporating physical, social, emotional, and cognitive development throughout the entire lifespan, MyVirtualLife helps students think critically as they apply their course work to their own virtual life. You can access MyVirtualLife within MyPsychLab or as a standalone product.

- **MyPsychLab (ISBN: 0133771725).** Available at www.MyPsychLab.com, MyPsychLab is an online homework, tutorial, and assessment program that truly engages students in learning. It helps students better prepare for class, quizzes, and exams—resulting in better performance in the course. It provides educators a dynamic set of tools for gauging individual and class performance:

  - **Customizable.** MyPsychLab is customizable. Instructors can choose what a course looks like by easily turning homework, applications, and more on and off.

- **Blackboard single sign-on.** MyPsychLab can be used by itself or linked to any course management system. Blackboard single sign-on provides deep linking to all new MyPsychLab resources.

- **Pearson eText and chapter audio.** As with the printed text, with the eText, students can highlight relevant passages and add notes. The Pearson eText can be accessed through laptops, iPads, and tablets. Download the free Pearson eText app to use on tablets. Students can also listen to their text with the audio eText.

- **Assignment calendar and gradebook.** A drag-and-drop assignment calendar makes assigning and completing work easy. The automatically graded assessment provides instant feedback and flows into the gradebook, which can be used in MyPsychLab or exported.

- **Personalized study plan.** Students' personalized plans promote better critical thinking skills. The study plan organizes students' study needs into sections, such as Remembering, Understanding, Applying, and Analyzing.

- **MyPsychLab margin icons.** Margin icons guide students from their reading material to relevant videos and activities. To package MyPsychLab with the student text, use ISBN 0133815854.

- **Class preparation tool.** Available for instructors within MyPsychLab, this exciting instructor resource makes lecture preparation easier and less time-consuming. MyClassPrep collects the very best class preparation resources—art and figures from our leading texts, videos, lecture activities, classroom activities, demonstrations, and much more—in one convenient online destination. You can search through MyClassPrep's extensive database of tools by content topic or by content type. You can select resources appropriate for your lecture, many of which can be downloaded directly; or you can build your own folder of resources and present from within MyClassPrep.

- **Instructor's Manual (ISBN: 0133771598).** The Instructor's Manual has been thoroughly revised and reorganized to be even more user friendly. Each chapter has the following resources: "At-a-Glance" grids, showcasing key supplemental resources available for instructors and students by chapter; a Chapter Overview; a list of the numbered Learning Objectives; and a complete Key Terms table, with page references. Each chapter also offers an extensive, detailed, and fully integrated Teaching Notes section with Discussion Launchers, Feature Box Activities, lists of available media to use in the classroom, Classroom Activity ideas, and Critical Thinking Questions. The Teaching Notes are closely tied to the numbered learning objectives from the text so you can easily connect the content of this manual to the corresponding learning objectives. For instructors looking to expand upon the textbook content, each chapter closes with an optional relevant Lecture Enhancer.

- **Test Bank (ISBN: 0133771490).** The Test Bank is composed of approximately 2,000 fully referenced multiple-choice, short-answer, and essay questions. The test questions are tied to the numbered learning objectives from the text, allowing you to assess knowledge of specific skills, as well as APA Learning Outcomes. In addition, questions may be viewed by level of difficulty and skill type. This supplement is also available in MyTest, a computerized Test Bank version that allows for easy creation of polished hard-copy tests.

- **MyTest (ISBN: 0133771504).** The Test Bank is also available via MyTest, a powerful assessment generation program that helps instructors easily create and print quizzes and exams. Questions and tests can be authored online, allowing instructors ultimate flexibility and the ability to efficiently manage assessments anytime, anywhere. For more information, go to www.PearsonMyTest.com or MyPsychLab, at www.MyPsychLab.com.

- **PowerPoint presentations (ISBN: 0133805719).** The lecture slides include both a detailed lecture outline with select art from the text and a set of slides containing the complete art program from the book. The PowerPoint lecture slides are available for download via the

Pearson Instructor's Resource Center (www.pearsonhighered.com) and on the MyPsychLab platform (www.MyPsychLab.com).

Video Resources for Instructors

The development video series in MyPsychLab engages students and brings to life a wide range of topics spanning the prenatal period through the end of the lifespan. This video collection contains a rich assortment of updated video clips for each chapter, including new sketchnote-style tutorials as well as cross-cultural footage and applied segments featuring real students sharing their experiences. Many of these video segments are tied to quizzes or writing prompts and can be assigned through MyPsychLab.

Print and Media Supplements for the Student

- *MyPsychLab* (ISBN: 0133771725). With this exciting new tool, students are able to self-assess using embedded diagnostic tests and instantly view results along with a customized study plan.

  The customized study plan will focus on the student's strengths and weaknesses, based on the results of the diagnostic testing, and present a list of activities and resources for review and remediation, organized by chapter section. Some study resources intended for use with portable electronic devices are made available exclusively through MyPsychLab, such as key terms flashcards and optimized video clips. Students will be able to quickly and easily analyze their own comprehension level of the course material and study more efficiently, leading to exceptional exam results! An access code is required and can be purchased at www.pearsonhighered.com or at www.MyPsychLab.com.

- *MyVirtualLife.* Raise your child. Live your life. MyVirtualLife is two simulations in one. The first simulation allows students to raise a child from birth to age 18 and monitor the effects of their parenting decisions over time. In the second simulation, students make first-person decisions and see the impact of those decisions on their simulated future self over time. By incorporating physical, social, emotional, and cognitive development throughout the entire lifespan, MyVirtualLife helps students think critically as they apply their course work to their own virtual life. You can access MyVirtualLife within MyPsychLab or as a standalone product.

- *CourseSmart eTextbook* (ISBN: 0133771547). CourseSmart offers students an online subscription to *Lifespan Development*, seventh edition, at up to a 60% savings. With the CourseSmart eTextbook, students can search the text, make notes online, print out reading assignments that incorporate lecture notes, and bookmark important passages. Ask your Pearson sales representative for details or visit www.coursesmart.com.

Supplementary Texts

Contact your Pearson representative to package any of these supplementary texts with *Lifespan Development*, seventh edition:

- *Current Directions in Developmental Psychology* (ISBN: 0205597505). This exciting reader includes more than 20 articles from the American Psychological Society that have been carefully selected for the undergraduate audience and taken from the very accessible *Current Directions in Psychological Science* journal. These timely, cutting-edge articles allow instructors to bring their students a real-world perspective about today's most current and pressing issues in psychology. The journal is discounted when packaged with this text for college adoptions.

- *Twenty Studies That Revolutionized Child Psychology* by Wallace E. Dixon, Jr. (ISBN: 0130415723). Presenting the seminal research studies that have shaped modern developmental psychology, this brief text provides an overview of the environment that gave rise to each study, its experimental design, its findings, and its impact on current thinking in the discipline.

- *Human Development in Multicultural Contexts: A Book of Readings* (ISBN: 0130195235). Written by Michele A. Paludi, this compilation of readings highlights cultural influences in developmental psychology.

- *The Psychology Major: Careers and Strategies for Success* (ISBN: 0205684688). Written by Eric Landrum (Idaho State University), Stephen Davis (Emporia State University), and Terri Landrum (Idaho State University), this 160-page paperback provides valuable information on career options available to psychology majors, tips for improving academic performance, and a guide to the APA style of research reporting.

Acknowledgments

No one ever accomplishes much of anything alone. I would like to thank a number of people for providing me with the support I needed to complete this project. First and foremost, my husband, Jerry Boyd; my sons, Matt and Chris Boyd; my daughter-in-law, Lindsay Boyd; my daughter, Marianne Meece; my son-in-law, Michael Meece; and my grandchildren, Mackenzie, Madeleine, and Noah Meece, are my most important cheerleaders. Likewise, a number of my colleagues at Houston Community College acted as sounding boards for various ideas as I was preparing the seventh edition.

The seventh edition was supervised by Amber Chow, who provided many ideas and words of encouragement. And, of course, developmental editors are essential to the process.

TO OUR REVIEWERS: Finally, I would like to thank the many colleagues who served as reviewers on both the seventh edition and prior editions of *Lifespan Development* for their thought-provoking comments and criticisms as well as their willingness to take time out of their busy schedules to help me improve this book.

Reviewers of the Seventh Edition

Willow Aureala, Hawaii Community College

Karen Banks, George Mason University

Ellen Cotter, Georgia Southwestern State University

Sarah D'Elia, George Mason University

Deborah Decker, Dixie State College

Annie Dunn, Montgomery College

Shawn Talbot, Kellogg Community College

Past Reviewers

Judi Addelston, Valencia Community College

Jeffrey Arnett, University of Maryland

Cynthia Avens, Daytona Beach Community College

Barbara E. Baker, Nashville State Tech

Ted Barker, Okaloosa-Walton College

Saundra Y. Boyd, Houston Community College

Troy E. Beckert, Utah State University

Laura Hess Brown, State University of New York at Oswego

Wanda Clark, South Plains College

Barbara DeFilippo, Lane Community College

Tara Dekkers, Northwestern College

Julie Felender, Fullerton College

Tina Footen, Boise State University

Loren Ford, Clackamas Community College

Tony Fowler, Florence-Darlington Technical College

Kathleen V. Fox, Salisbury State University

Lynn Haller, Morehead State University

Debra L. Hollister, Valencia Community College

Scott L. Horton, University of Southern Maine

Suzy Horton, Mesa Community College

Terry R. Isbell, Northwestern State University

Alisha Janowsky, University of Central Florida

Shabana Kausar, Minnesota State University

Dr. William Kimberlin, Lorain County Community College

John S. Klein, Castleton State College

Paul Kochmanski, Erie Community College—South Campus

David D. Kurz, Delmar College

Billie Laney, Central Texas Community College

Kathryn Levit, George Mason University

Susan Magun-Jackson, University of Memphis

April Mansfield, Long Beach City College

Carrie M. Margolin, The Evergreen State College

Joseph A. Mayo, Gordon College

Donna Mesler, Seton Hall University

Alan C. Miller, Santa Fe Community College

James E. Oliver, Henry Ford Community College

Regina K. Peters, Hawkeye Community College

Linda Petroff, Central Community College

Laura Pirazzi, San Jose State University

Jeanine Pontes-Boelter, Sonoma State University

Lynn Poulson, Snow College

Joe E. Price, San Diego State University

Celinda Reese, Oklahoma State University

Paul Roodin, State University of New York at Oswego

Jonathan Schwartz, Yeshiva University

Lynn Shelley, Westfield State College

Rosalind Shorter, Jefferson Community College

Stephanie Stein, Central Washington University

Kevin Sumrall, Montgomery College

Mojisola Tiamiyu, University of Toledo

Ashton Trice, James Madison University

Stephen Truhon, Winston-Salem State University

Patricia Riely Twaddle, Moberly Area Community College

Bradley M. Waite, Central Connecticut State University

John D. Williams, Brookhaven College

Eugene H. Wong, California State University—San Bernardino

Rebecca M. Wood, Central Connecticut State University

Virginia V. Wood, University of Texas—Brownsville

Pauline Davey Zeece, University of Nebraska at Lincoln

—Denise Boyd

c h a p t e r 1

Basic Concepts and Methods

The last time you saw a relative or friend whom you hadn't seen for a while, perhaps you remarked on how much or how little the person had changed. About a child, you may have said: "Sally's grown so much since the last time I saw her." About an older person: "Uncle Julio looks much more frail than he did at Grandpa's birthday party." Such comments suggest that we humans are natural observers of the ways in which we change with age. But we also notice characteristics that seem to stay the same over time. We might say,

LEARNING OBJECTIVES

AN INTRODUCTION TO HUMAN DEVELOPMENT

1.1 What ideas about development were proposed by early philosophers and scientists?

1.2 What is the lifespan perspective?

1.3 What major domains and periods do developmental scientists use to organize their discussions of the human lifespan?

KEY ISSUES IN THE STUDY OF HUMAN DEVELOPMENT

1.4 How do developmentalists view the two sides of the nature–nurture debate?

1.5 What is the continuity–discontinuity debate?

1.6 How do the three kinds of age-related change differ?

1.7 How does consideration of the contexts in which change occurs improve scientists' understanding of human development?

RESEARCH METHODS AND DESIGNS

1.8 What are the goals of scientists who study human development?

1.9 What descriptive methods do developmental scientists use?

1.10 What is the primary advantage of the experimental method?

1.11 What are the pros and cons of cross-sectional, longitudinal, and sequential research designs?

1.12 Why is cross-cultural research important to the study of human development?

1.13 What are the ethical standards that developmental researchers must follow?

"Sally's always been such a sweet child," or "Uncle Julio's mind is as sharp as ever." And our powers of observation don't stop with simple descriptions. We also come up with theories to explain our observations. Perhaps you've said something like, "Sally's parents are great role models. That's probably why she's so well behaved," or "Grandpa and Uncle Julio are both pretty sharp for their age. I guess they have good genes." As these observations suggest, the developmental pathway that each person follows results from the person's own characteristics, the choices that others make for her in childhood, and the decisions that she makes for herself in adulthood. These interactive effects are the driving theme behind *MyVirtualLife*, an online simulation that allows you to raise a child to adulthood and then adopt a first-person perspective to make decisions in adulthood.

In this introductory chapter, you will learn how the science of human development came into being. You will also learn about the key issues in the scientific study of development. When you finish reading the chapter, you will be acquainted with the research designs and methods that developmentalists use.

An Introduction to Human Development

The field of **human development** is the scientific study of age-related changes in behavior, thinking, emotion, and personality. Long before the scientific method was used to study development, though, philosophers offered explanations for differences they observed in individuals of different ages. In the 19th century, the scientific methods used by early pioneers in the study of human behavior were applied to questions about age-related change. Nevertheless, the term *development* was largely confined to childhood during the early years. However, in the second half of the 20th century, behavioral scientists began to acknowledge that important age-related changes occur across the entire human lifespan. Their efforts led to useful ways of categorizing important issues in the study of development and revealed a wealth of data suggesting that human development is a highly complex process.

Philosophical and Scientific Roots

LO 1.1   What ideas about development were proposed by early philosophers and scientists?

human development the scientific study of age-related changes in behavior, thinking, emotion, and personality

Early philosophers based their ideas about development on spiritual authorities, general philosophical orientations, and deductive logic. In the 19th century, though, people who wanted to better understand human development turned to science.

This page from the *Hoenshel's Complete Grammar*, published in 1895, illustrates the influence of the doctrine of original sin on education and child rearing. Statements that promote religious and moral principles are embedded in this exercise on verbs. The idea was that the goals of teaching grammar to children and shaping their spiritual development could be, and should be, accomplished simultaneously.

> **LESSON XXXII.**
>
> **VERBS.— REVIEW.**
>
> 1. Name the mode of each verb in these sentences:
>   1. Bring me some flowers.
>   2. I must not be careless.
>   3. Who is the King of Glory ?
>   4. Can that be the man ?
>   5. The pupils have recited well.
>   6. Passionate men are easily irritated.
>   7. Do not walk so fast.
>   8. The prize cannot be obtained without labor.
>   9. Idleness often leads to vice.
>   10. Live for something.
>   11. In all climates, spring is beautiful.
>   12. I would have gone if I had known that I was needed.
>   13. If we would seem true, we must be true.

ORIGINAL SIN, THE BLANK SLATE, AND INNATE GOODNESS Typically, philosophers' inquiries into the nature of development focused on why babies, who appear to be quite similar, grow up to vary widely. They were particularly concerned with the moral dimensions of development. For example, the Christian doctrine of *original sin*, often attributed to 4th-century philosopher Augustine of Hippo, taught that all humans are born with a selfish nature. To reduce the influence of this inborn tendency toward selfishness, Augustine taught, humans must seek spiritual rebirth and submit themselves to religious training. Thus, from this perspective, developmental outcomes, both good and bad, result from each individual's struggle to overcome an inborn tendency to act immorally when doing so somehow benefits the self.

By contrast, 17th-century English philosopher John Locke drew upon a broad philosophical approach known as *empiricism* when he claimed that the mind of a child is a *blank slate*. Empiricism is the view that humans possess no innate tendencies and that all differences among humans are attributable to experience. The blank-slate view suggests that adults can mold children into whatever they want them to be. Therefore, differences among adults can be explained in terms of differences in their childhood environments rather than as a result of a struggle to overcome any kind of inborn tendencies, as the original-sin view proposed.

Different still was the *innate goodness* view proposed by 18th-century Swiss philosopher Jean-Jacques Rousseau. He claimed that all human beings are naturally good and seek out experiences that help them grow (Crain, 2011). Rousseau believed that children need only nurturing and protection to reach their full potential. Developmental outcomes are good when a child's environment refrains from interfering in her attempts to nurture her own development. In contrast, outcomes are poor when a child experiences frustration in her efforts to express the innate goodness with which she was born. Thus, the innate-goodness and original-sin approaches share the view that development involves a struggle between internal and external forces. In contrast to both, the blank-slate view sees the child as a passive recipient of environmental influences.

EARLY SCIENTIFIC THEORIES The 19th century saw an explosion of interest in how scientific methods might be applied to questions that previously had been thought to belong within the domain of philosophy. Charles Darwin, for example, became well known for his suggestion that the wide variety of life-forms that exist on the Earth evolved gradually as a result of the interplay between environmental factors and genetic processes. Moreover, Darwin proposed that studying children's development might help scientists better understand the evolution of the human species. To that end, Darwin and other like-minded scientists kept detailed records of their own children's early development (called *baby biographies*), in the hope of finding evidence to support the theory of evolution (Dewsbury, 2009). These were the first organized studies of human development.

G. Stanley Hall of Clark University used questionnaires and interviews to study large numbers of children. His 1891 article "The Contents of Children's Minds on Entering School" represented the first scientific study of child development (White, 1992). Hall agreed with Darwin that the milestones of childhood were similar to those that had taken place in the development of the human species. He thought that developmentalists should identify **norms**, or average ages at which developmental milestones are reached. Norms, Hall said, could be used to learn about the evolution of the species as well as to track the development of individual children.

Arnold Gesell's research suggested the existence of a genetically programmed sequential pattern of change (Gesell, 1925; Thelen & Adolph, 1992). Gesell used the term **maturation** to describe such a pattern of change. He thought that maturationally determined development occurred, regardless of practice, training, or effort (Crain, 2011). For example, infants don't have to be taught how to walk. Because of his strong belief that many important developmental changes are determined by maturation, Gesell spent decades studying children and developing norms. He pioneered the use of movie cameras and one-way observation devices to study children's behavior. His findings became the basis for many **norm-referenced tests** that are used today to determine whether individual children are developing at a rate that is similar to

Charles Darwin, who fathered 10 children, initiated the scientific study of childhood. He used the same scientific methods that led to the discoveries on which he based his theory of evolution to make and record daily observations of his children's development.

norms average ages at which developmental milestones are reached

maturation the gradual unfolding of a genetically programmed sequential pattern of change

norm-referenced tests standardized tests that compare an individual child's score to the average score of others her age

that of other children of the same age. Such tests help early educators find ways of helping young children whose development lags behind that of others.

The Lifespan Perspective

LO 1.2   What is the lifespan perspective?

Psychologists once thought of adulthood as a long period of stability followed by a short span of unstable years immediately preceding death. This view has changed because, for one thing, it has become common for adults to go through major life changes, such as divorce and career shifts. There has also been a significant increase in life expectancy in the industrialized world. At the beginning of the 20th century, Americans' life expectancy at birth was only 49 years. By the century's end, the expected lifespan of someone born in the United States was about 76 years. As a result, older adults now constitute a larger proportion of the U.S. population than ever before. In fact, adults over the age of 100 are one of the most rapidly growing age groups in the industrialized world.

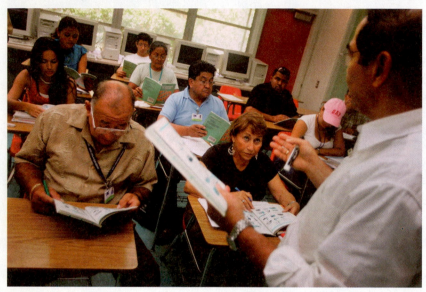

The lifespan perspective recognizes that important changes occur throughout life.

The changes outlined above have led to the adoption of the **lifespan perspective**, the idea that important changes occur during every period of development and that these changes must be interpreted in terms of the culture and context in which they occur (Baltes, Reese, & Lipsitt, 1980). Thus, understanding change in adulthood has become just as important as understanding change in childhood, and input from many disciplines is necessary to fully explain human development. This new perspective emphasizes these key elements:

- *Plasticity:* Individuals of all ages possess the capacity for positive change in response to environmental demands.

- *Interdisciplinary research:* Research from different kinds of disciplinary perspectives (e.g., anthropology, economics, psychology) is needed to fully understand lifespan development.

- *Multicontextual nature of development:* Individual development occurs within several interrelated contexts (e.g., family, neighborhood, culture).

Paul Baltes (1939–2006) was a leader in the development of a comprehensive theory of lifespan human development (Baltes, Staudinger, & Lindenberger, 1999; Lerner, 2008). Baltes emphasized the positive aspects of advanced age. He pointed out that, as human beings age, they adopt strategies that help them maximize gains and compensate for losses. He cited the example of concert pianist Arthur Rubinstein, who was able to outperform much younger musicians well into his 80s (Cavanaugh & Whitbourne, 1999). Rubinstein reported that he maintained his performance capacity by carefully choosing pieces that he knew very well (maximizing gain) and by practicing those pieces more frequently than he had at earlier ages (compensating for the physical losses associated with age). You will read more about Baltes's theories and his research in Chapters 17 and 18.

The Domains and Periods of Development

LO 1.3   What major domains and periods do developmental scientists use to organize their discussions of the human lifespan?

Scientists who study age-related changes often group them in three broad categories, called *domains of development*. The **physical domain** includes changes in the size, shape, and characteristics of the body. For example, developmentalists study the physiological processes associated with puberty. Also included in this domain are changes in how individuals sense and

lifespan perspective   the current view of developmentalists that important changes occur throughout the entire human lifespan and that these changes must be interpreted in terms of the culture and context in which they occur; thus, interdisciplinary research is critical to understanding human development

physical domain   changes in the size, shape, and characteristics of the body

perceive the physical world, such as the gradual development of depth perception over the first year of life.

Changes in thinking, memory, problem solving, and other intellectual skills are included in the **cognitive domain**. Researchers working in the cognitive domain study topics as diverse as how children learn to read and why some memory functions deteriorate in old age. They also examine the ways in which individual differences among children and adults, such as intelligence-test scores, are related to other variables in this domain.

The **social domain** includes changes in variables associated with the relationship of an individual to others. For instance, studies of children's social skills fall into the social domain, as does research on individual differences in personality. Individuals' beliefs about themselves are also usually classified within the social domain.

Using domain classifications helps to organize discussions of human development. We need to remember, however, that the three domains do not function independently. For instance, when a girl goes through puberty—a change in the physical domain—her ability to think abstractly (cognitive domain) and her feelings about potential romantic partners (social domain) change as well.

Developmental scientists also use a system of age-related categories known as *periods of development*. The first of these, the *prenatal period*, is the only one that has clearly defined biological boundaries at its beginning and end: It begins at conception and ends at birth. The next period, *infancy*, begins at birth and ends when children begin to use language to communicate, a milestone that marks the beginning of *early childhood*. Thus, while infancy begins at birth for all children, its end point can vary from one child to another. A social event—the child's entrance into school or some other kind of formal training—marks the transition from early to *middle childhood*. Consequently, cultures vary to some degree with regard to when early childhood ends and middle childhood begins. For example, children must be enrolled in school beginning at age 4 in Scotland but not until age 8 in a few states in the United States.

By contrast, a biological milestone, puberty, signals the end of middle childhood and the beginning of *adolescence*. Again, the timing of this transition varies across individuals. And when does adolescence end? One way of answering this question is by noting the legal boundaries that different cultures set for the end of adolescence and the beginning of *early adulthood*. For instance, a person must be 18 years of age to join the military without parental permission in the United States. By contrast, the age of majority for military service is 15 in Laos, 16 in the United Kingdom, 17 in Nicaragua, 19 in Algeria, 20 in South Korea, 21 in Brazil, and 22 in Afghanistan (*CIA World Factbook*, 2013). Even within a single culture, such as the United States, legal adulthood is defined differently for different activities: 16 for driving, 17 or 18 for criminal accountability, 18 for signing contracts, 21 for buying alcohol, and 24 for economic independence with regard to college financial aid. Such variations highlight the social and psychological, rather than biological, nature of the transition to adulthood, the complexities of which have led some researchers to propose a new period of development called *emerging adulthood* that encompasses the late teens and early 20s.

The transition from early to *middle adulthood*, generally thought to occur around age 40, is even more arbitrary. The timing of biological milestones that are associated with middle age, such as menopause, varies widely from one person to another. Thus, there is no clear physical boundary between early and middle adulthood, and social boundaries are rapidly changing. For instance, childbirth, once thought of almost exclusively as an early-adulthood event, is becoming increasingly common among middle-aged women. Likewise, *late adulthood*, though customarily described as beginning at age 60, is not distinguished by any biological or social events that clearly distinguish a middle-aged adult from an older adult.

Despite the difficulties involved in defining the various periods of development, these periods can still serve as a useful system for organizing the study of development. We have organized this textbook around them. For our purposes, the first two years after birth constitute infancy. Early childhood is defined as the years between ages 2 and 6. Our chapters on middle childhood discuss development between the ages of 6 and 12. Adolescence is defined as the years from 12 to 18, and early adulthood as those between 18 and 40. Finally, the period from 40 to 60 is middle adulthood, and the years from 60 to the end of life are late adulthood.

cognitive domain changes in thinking, memory, problem solving, and other intellectual skills

social domain change in variables that are associated with the relationship of an individual to others

Answers to these questions can be found in the back of the book.

1. Write the name of the philosopher who is associated with each view of development.
   (1) original sin _Augustine_
   (2) blank slate _John Locke_
   (3) innate goodness _Jean-Jacques Rousseau_

2. What did each of these early researchers do?
   (1) Charles Darwin _kept baby biographs_
   (2) G. Stanley Hall _1st scientific study of children_
   (3) Arnold Gesell _est. norms for phy. maturation_

3. The view that development from conception to death should be studied from multiple disciplinary perspectives is known as the _lifespan perspective_.

4. Give an example from the text of development in each domain.

Domain	Example
Physical	Puberty
Cognitive	Memory
Social	Ind. diff to personality

5. Fill in the milestones that mark the beginning and ending of each major period of development:

Period	Beginning Milestone	Ending Milestone
Prenatal	Conception	Birth
Infancy	Birth	Language
Early childhood	Language	School Entrance
Middle childhood	School Ent.	Puberty
Adolescence	Puberty	18yrs
Early adulthood	18yrs	40yrs
Middle adulthood	40 yrs	60yrs
Late adulthood	60yrs	Death

CRITICAL THINKING

6. What are the child-rearing implications of the original-sin, blank-slate, and innate-goodness views of development?

Key Issues in the Study of Human Development

Several key issues cut across all the domains and periods of development. These include the relative contributions to development of biological and environmental factors and the presence or absence of stages. In addition, one researcher might propose that a specific change is common to all human beings, while another might propose that it occurs under some conditions but not others. Researchers debate, too, the degree to which the settings in which development occurs contribute to developmental outcomes.

Nature versus Nurture

LO 1.4   How do developmentalists view the two sides of the nature–nurture debate?

Some early developmentalists thought of change as resulting from *either* forces outside the person *or* forces inside the person. The debate about the relative contributions of biological processes and experiential factors to development is known as the **nature–nurture debate**. In struggling with this important issue, psychologists have moved away from either/or approaches toward more subtle ways of looking at both types of influences. For example, the concept of *inborn biases* is based on the notion that children are born with tendencies to respond in certain ways. Some of these inborn biases are shared by virtually all children. For instance, the sequence in which children acquire spoken language—single words precede two-word sentences, and so on—is virtually identical in all children, no matter what language they are learning (Pinker, 2002). Moreover, babies seem to be equipped with a set of behaviors that entice others to care for them, including crying, snuggling, and, very soon after birth, smiling, and they appear to be delighted when their efforts to arouse interest in others are successful.

Other inborn biases may vary from one individual to another. Even in the early days of life, for example, some infants are relatively easy to soothe when they become distressed, while others are more difficult to manage. Whether these inborn patterns are coded in the genes, are created by variations in the prenatal environment, or arise through some combination of the

nature–nurture debate   the debate about the relative contributions of biological processes and experiential factors to development

two, the basic point is that a baby is not a blank slate at birth. Babies seem to start life prepared to seek out and react to particular kinds of experiences.

Thinking on the nurture side of the issue is also more complex than in the past. For example, modern developmentalists have accepted the concept of *internal models of experience*. The key element of this concept is the idea that the effect of an experience depends not on its objective properties but rather on the individual's *interpretation*—the meaning that the individual attaches to that experience. For instance, suppose a friend says, "Your new haircut looks great; it's a lot nicer when it's short like that." Your friend intends to pay you a compliment, but you also hear an implied criticism ("Your hair used to look awful"), and your reactions, your feelings, and even your relationship with your friend are affected by how you interpret the comment—not by what your friend meant or by the objective qualities of the remark.

Continuity versus Discontinuity

LO 1.5   What is the continuity–discontinuity debate?

Another key issue in the study of human development is the *continuity–discontinuity* issue. The question is whether age-related change is primarily a matter of amount or degree (the *continuity* side of the debate) or of changes in type or kind (the *discontinuity* side). For example, generally speaking, do you have more or fewer friends than you did when you were in elementary school? If you're like most other people, you have fewer (see Chapter 14). But do age differences in the number of friends people have really capture the difference between friendship in childhood and adulthood? Isn't it also true that friendship itself is different in childhood and adulthood? For example, mutual trust is a characteristic of adult and teen friendships but is not a feature of friendship prior to age 10 or so (see Chapter 10). Thus, the continuous aspect of friendship is that people of all ages have peer relationships, and the discontinuous aspect of friendship is that the characteristics of friendship itself vary by age.

Another way of approaching the continuity–discontinuity question is to think of it in terms of *quantitative* and *qualitative* change. A **quantitative change** is a change in amount. For instance, children get taller as they get older. Their heights increase, but the variable of height itself never changes. In other words, height changes continuously; it has continuity from one age to the next. Alternatively, a **qualitative change** is a change in characteristic, kind, or type. For example, puberty is a qualitative change. Prior to puberty, humans are incapable of reproduction. After puberty, they can reproduce. Therefore, postpubescent humans possess a characteristic that prepubescent humans do not: the capacity to reproduce. In other words, postpubescent and prepubescent humans are qualitatively different, and changes in the capacity to reproduce are discontinuous in nature. Later in life, another qualitative change in reproductive capacity occurs when women go through menopause and lose the capacity for reproduction.

Of particular significance to developmental theories is the idea that, if development consists only of additions (continuous, quantitative change), then the concept of **stages**—qualitatively distinct periods of development—is not needed to explain it. However, if development involves reorganization or the emergence of wholly new strategies, qualities, or skills (discontinuous, qualitative change), then the concept of stages may be useful. As you'll learn in Chapter 2, an important difference among theories of development is whether they assume that development occurs in stages or is primarily continuous in nature.

Three Kinds of Change

LO 1.6   How do the three kinds of age-related change differ?

Have you ever thought about the difference between taking your first steps and your first date? Clearly, both are related to age, but they represent fundamentally different kinds of change. Generally, developmental scientists think of each age-related change as representing one of three categories.

Normative age-graded changes are universal—that is, they are common to every individual in a species and are linked to specific ages. Some universal changes (like a baby's first step) happen because we are all biological organisms subject to a genetically programmed maturing

quantitative change a change in amount

qualitative change a change in kind or type

stages qualitatively distinct periods of development

normative age-graded changes changes that are common to every member of a species

The biological clock obviously constrains the social clock to some extent at least. Virtually every culture emphasizes family formation in early adulthood because that is, in fact, the optimal biological time for child rearing.

process. The infant who shifts from crawling to walking and the older adult whose skin becomes progressively more wrinkled are following a plan that is an intrinsic part of the physical body, most likely something in the genetic code itself.

However, some changes are universal because of shared experiences. A social clock also shapes all (or most) lives into shared patterns of change (Helson, Mitchell, & Moane, 1984). In each culture, the **social clock**, or *age norms*, defines a sequence of "normal" life experiences, such as the right time to go out on a first date, the appropriate timing of marriage and childbearing, and the expected time of retirement.

Age norms can lead to **ageism**—prejudicial attitudes about older adults, analogous to sexism or racism (Iverson, Larsen, & Solem, 2009). In U.S. culture, for example, older adults are very often perceived as incompetent. Many are denied opportunities to work because employers believe that they are incapable of carrying out required job functions. Thus, social expectations about the appropriate age for retirement work together with ageism to shape individual lives, resulting in a pattern in which most people retire or significantly reduce their working hours in later adulthood.

Equally important as a source of variation in life experience are historical forces, which affect each generation somewhat differently. Such changes are called **normative history-graded changes**. Social scientists use the word *cohort* to describe a group of individuals who are born within some fairly narrow span of years and thus share the same historical experiences at the same times in their lives. Within any given culture, successive cohorts may have quite different life experiences (see the *Research Report*).

Finally, **nonnormative changes** result from unique, unshared events. One clearly unshared event in each person's life is conception; the combination of genes each individual receives at conception is unique. Thus, genetic differences—including physical characteristics such as body type and hair color as well as genetic disorders—represent one category of individual differences. Characteristics influenced by both heredity and environment, such as intelligence and personality, constitute another class of individual differences.

Other individual differences result from the timing of a developmental event. Child-development theorists have adopted the concept of a **critical period**—the idea is that there may be specific periods in development when an organism is especially sensitive to the presence (or absence) of some particular kind of experience.

Most knowledge about critical periods comes from animal research. For baby ducks, for instance, the first 15 hours or so after hatching is a critical period for the development of a following response. Newly hatched ducklings will follow any duck or any other moving object that happens to be around them at that critical time. If nothing is moving at that critical point, they don't develop any following response at all (Hess, 1972).

The broader concept of a sensitive period is more common in the study of human development. A **sensitive period** is a span of months or years during which a child may be particularly responsive to specific forms of experience or particularly influenced by their absence. For example, the period from 6 to 12 months of age may be a sensitive period for the formation of parent–infant attachment.

In studies of adults, an important concept related to timing has been that of on-time and off-time events (Neugarten, 1979). The idea is that experiences occurring at the expected times for an individual's culture or cohort will pose fewer difficulties for the individual than will off-time experiences. Thus, being widowed at 30 is more likely to produce serious life disruption and distress than would being widowed at 70.

social clock a set of age norms defining a sequence of life experiences that is considered normal in a given culture and that all individuals in that culture are expected to follow

ageism prejudicial attitudes about older adults that characterizes them in negative ways

normative history-graded changes changes that occur in most members of a cohort as a result of factors at work during a specific, well-defined historical period

nonnormative changes changes that result from unique, unshared events

critical period a specific period in development when an organism is especially sensitive to the presence (or absence) of some particular kind of experience

sensitive period a span of months or years during which a child may be particularly responsive to specific forms of experience or particularly influenced by their absence

Atypical development is another kind of individual change. **Atypical development** (also known as *abnormal behavior*, *psychopathology*, or *maladaptive development*) refers to deviation from a typical, or "normal," developmental pathway in a direction that is harmful to an individual. Examples of atypical development include intellectual disability, mental illness, and behavioral problems such as extreme aggressiveness in children and compulsive gambling in adults.

Contexts of Development

LO 1.7   How does consideration of the contexts in which change occurs improve scientists' understanding of human development?

To fully understand human development, we must understand the context in which it occurs. For instance, a child grows up in a number of separate, but related, contexts: her neighborhood and school, the occupations of her parents and their level of satisfaction in these occupations, her parents' relationships with each other and their own families, and so on.

A good example of research that examines such a larger system of influences is Gerald Patterson's work on the origins of delinquency (Granic & Patterson, 2006). His studies show that parents who use poor discipline techniques and poor monitoring are more likely to have noncompliant children. Once established, such a behavior pattern has repercussions in other areas of the child's life, leading to both rejection by peers and difficulty in school. These problems, in turn, are likely to push the young person toward delinquency (Dishion, Patterson, Stoolmiller, & Skinner, 1991; Vuchinich, Bank, & Patterson, 1992). So a pattern that began in the family is maintained and made worse by interactions with peers and with the school system.

However, we have to keep in mind that all the various contexts interact with each other and with the characteristics of the individuals who are developing within them. Along these lines, some developmentalists have found the concepts of *vulnerability* and *resilience* to be useful (Bowman, 2013). According to this view, each child is born with certain vulnerabilities, such as a tendency toward emotional irritability or alcoholism, a physical abnormality, an allergy, or whatever. Each child is also born with some protective factors, such as high intelligence, good physical coordination, an easy temperament, or a lovely smile, that tend to make her more resilient in the face of stress. These vulnerabilities and protective factors then interact with the child's environment, so the

atypical development development that deviates from the typical developmental pathway in a direction that is harmful to the individual

The settings in which children grow up and adults age contribute to the developmental process. How do you think these older adults' experiences differ from those of people their age who live in industrialized cultures?

same environment can have quite different effects, depending on the qualities the child brings to the interaction.

The combination of a highly vulnerable child and a poor or unsupportive environment produces by far the most negative outcomes (Horowitz, 1990). Either of these two negative conditions alone—a vulnerable child or a poor environment—can be overcome. A resilient child in a poor environment may do quite well, since she can find and take advantage of all the stimulation and opportunities available; similarly, a vulnerable child may do quite well in a highly supportive environment in which parents help the child overcome or cope with her vulnerabilities. The "double whammy"—being a vulnerable child in a poor environment—leads to really poor outcomes for the child. The characteristics of the larger society in which a child's family and neighborhood are embedded matter as well. The term *culture* has no commonly agreed-on definition, but in essence it describes some system of meanings and customs, including values, attitudes, goals, laws, beliefs, moral guidelines, and physical artifacts of various kinds, such as tools, forms of dwellings, and the like. Furthermore, to be called a culture, a system of meanings and customs must be shared by some identifiable group, whether that group is a subsection of some population or a larger unit, and must be transmitted from one generation of that group to the next (Betancourt & Lopez, 1993; Cole, 1992). Culture shapes not only the development of individuals but also ideas about what normal development is.

For example, researchers interested in middle and late adulthood often study retirement: why people retire, how retirement affects their health, and so on. But their findings do not apply to older adults in nonindustrialized cultures, where adults gradually shift from one kind of work to another as they get older rather than give up work altogether and enter a new phase of life called "retirement." Consequently, developmentalists must be aware that retirement-related phenomena do not constitute universal changes. Instead, they represent developmental experiences that are culturally specific.

One final aspect of the context within which an individual's development occurs involves gender. Two individuals can be quite similar with regard to their individual characteristics and the environment within which they grow up. However, if one is female and the other male, they will experience the interaction between their characteristics and their environment differently. As you will learn in a Chapter 11, for example, the effects of the earliness or lateness with which a child goes through puberty depend on gender. Thus, early and late puberty have different meanings for boys and girls.

test yourself before going on ✓ Study and Review in MyPsychLab

Answers to these questions can be found in the back of the book.

1. Aspects of infants' appearance that motivate adults to care for them are examples of a(n) ___Inborn___ ___bias___.

2. Developmental stages are often a feature in the theories of developmentalists who emphasize ___qualitative___ changes.

3. Give an example from the text of each type of change in the chart below:

Type of Change	Example
Normative age-graded	Babys crawling
Normative history-graded	Older People who grew in dreat Depression
Nonnormative	Genetic influang

4. (Critical/sensitive) periods are more common in animal research than in studies with humans.

5. What is the "double whammy" described in the text?
vulnerable child in a poor environment

CRITICAL THINKING

6. How do your culture's behavioral expectations for 20-year-olds, 40-year-olds, and 60-year-olds differ?

Research Methods and Designs

The easiest way to understand research methods is to look at a specific question and the alternative ways we might answer it. For example, older adults frequently complain that they have more trouble remembering people's names than they did when they were younger. Suppose we wanted to find out whether memory really declines with age. How would we go about answering this question?

The Goals of Developmental Science

LO 1.8 **What are the goals of scientists who study human development?**

Researchers who study human development use the scientific method to achieve four goals: to describe, to explain, to predict, and to influence human development from conception to death. To *describe* development is simply to state what happens. In attempting to describe human development, for example, we might make a descriptive statement such as "Older adults make more memory errors than young and middle-aged adults." To test whether this statement meets its descriptive goal, we could simply measure memory function in adults of various ages.

Explaining development involves telling why a particular event occurs. To generate explanations, developmentalists rely on *theories*—sets of statements that propose general principles of development. Students often say that they hate reading about theories; they just want the facts. However, theories are important because they help us look at facts from different perspectives. For example, "Older adults make more memory mistakes because of changes in the brain that happen as people get older" is a statement that attempts to explain the fact of age-related memory decline from a biological perspective. Alternatively, we could explain memory decline from an experiential perspective and hypothesize that memory function declines with age because older adults don't get as much memory practice as younger adults do.

Useful theories produce *predictions* or *hypotheses*, that researchers can test, such as "If changes in the brain cause declines in memory function, then elderly adults whose brains show the most change should also make the greatest number of memory errors." To test this hypothesis, we would have to measure some aspects of brain structure or function as well as memory function. Then we would have to find a way to relate one to the other. Alternatively, we could test the experiential explanation by comparing the memories of older adults who presumably get the most memory practice, such as those who are still working, to the memories of those who get less practice. If the working adults do better on tests of memory, the experiential perspective gains support. Moreover, if both the biological and the experiential hypotheses are supported by research, we have far more insight into age-related memory decline than we would have from either kind of hypothesis alone. In this way, theories add tremendous depth to psychologists' understanding of the facts of human development and provide them with information they can use to influence development.

Finally, developmental scientists hope to use their findings to *influence* developmental outcomes. Let's say, for example, that an older adult is diagnosed with a condition that can affect the brain, such as a stroke. If we know that brain function and memory are related, we can use tests of memory to make judgments about how much the stroke has damaged the patient's brain. In addition, because developmental scientists know that experience affects memory, they can design training programs that occupational therapists can implement to help the patient recover memory functions that have been impaired by the stroke (see *No Easy Answers* on page 12).

Descriptive Methods

LO 1.9 **What descriptive methods do developmental scientists use?**

A researcher who is interested in age and memory ability must decide how to go about finding relationships between variables. To developmentalists, *variables* are characteristics that vary from person to person, such as physical size, intelligence, and personality. When two or more variables vary together, there is some kind of relationship between them. The hypothesis that

---

naturalistic observation the process of studying people in their normal environments

case study an in-depth examination of a single individual

laboratory observation observation of behavior under controlled conditions

memory declines with age involves two variables—memory and age—and suggests a relationship between them. There are several ways of identifying such relationships.

NATURALISTIC OBSERVATION When psychologists use **naturalistic observation** as a research method, they observe people in their normal environments. For instance, to find out more about memory in older adults, a researcher could observe older adults in their homes or workplaces. Such studies provide developmentalists with information about psychological processes in everyday contexts.

The weakness of naturalistic observation, however, is *observer bias*. For example, if the researcher who is observing older adults is convinced that most of them have poor memories, he is likely to ignore any behavior that goes against this view. Because of observer bias, naturalistic observation studies often use "blind" observers who don't know what the research is about. In most cases, for the sake of accuracy, researchers use two or more observers so that the observations of each observer can be checked against those of the other(s).

Naturalistic observation studies are limited in the extent to which the results can be generalized. In addition, naturalistic observation studies are very time-consuming. They must be repeated in a variety of settings so that researchers can be sure people's behavior reflects development and not the influences of a specific environment.

CASE STUDIES A **case study** is an in-depth examination of a single individual. To test the hypothesis about memory and age, we could use a case study comparing one individual's scores on tests of memory in early and late adulthood. Such a study might tell us a lot about the stability or instability of memory in the individual studied, but we wouldn't know if our findings applied to others.

Still, case studies are extremely useful in making decisions about individuals. For example, to find out whether a child has an intellectual disability, a psychologist would conduct an extensive case study involving tests, interviews of the child's parents, behavioral observations, and so on. Case studies are also frequently the basis of important hypotheses about unusual developmental events, such as head injuries and strokes.

LABORATORY OBSERVATION **Laboratory observation** differs from naturalistic observation in that the researcher exerts some degree of control over the environment. Suppose, for instance, that you volunteer to participate in a study in which you will have to take a computerized intelligence

Psychologists who conduct case studies gather detailed information about a single individual. Their data often include the results of psychological tests.

test. You go to the computer laboratory where the study will take place, and a researcher carrying a folder marked "Test Key" sits down with you in front of a computer. As she begins to explain the test's instructions, another person comes to the door and tells her that she must go to another room to take an important phone call. In her haste to leave, the researcher leaves the folder on the table next to the computer. A hidden video camera records your behavior while you are out of the room. (Do you think you would peek?) When the researcher returns, you complete the test that you believed was the purpose of the study. Later, the researcher and her colleagues will analyze the tapes of participants' responses in order to determine the frequency with which cheating occurs under such conditions. (Research ethics also requires that they inform you of the deceptive aspects of their study, as you will learn later.) As you can see, observing cheating behavior under controlled conditions offers many advantages over trying to identify and track it in an actual classroom.

SURVEYS Have you ever been questioned about which brand of soda you prefer or which candidate you plan to vote for in the next election? If so, then you have participated in a **survey**, a study in which researchers use interviews and/or questionnaires to collect data about attitudes, interests, values, and various kinds of behaviors. Surveys allow researchers to quickly gather information. They can also be used to track changes over time.

The value of any survey depends entirely on how representative the *sample* of participants is of the researcher's *population* of interest. A **population** is the entire group about which the researcher is attempting to learn something; a **sample** is a subset of that group. Thus, when voters are asked which candidate they prefer, the concept of interest is all the people who will vote in the election. The sample includes only the people who are actually questioned by the researchers. If the sample is not a **representative sample**—that is, if it does not include the same proportions of males, females, Democrats, Republicans, and so forth, as the actual voting population does—then the survey's results will be inaccurate. Moreover, survey participants are sometimes influenced by the perceived *social desirability* of their answers. If they think that they should answer a question in a certain way to please the researchers, then they may not give truthful answers. Thus, whenever you hear a news report about a survey, you should remember that to judge whether the survey is valid, you need to know something about how the sample of participants was recruited and how the questions were asked.

CORRELATIONS A **correlation** is a relationship between two variables that can be expressed as a number ranging from −1.00 to +1.00. A zero correlation indicates that there is no relationship between the two variables. A positive correlation means that high scores on one variable are usually accompanied by high scores on the other. The closer a positive correlation is to +1.00, the stronger the relationship between the variables. Two variables that change in opposite directions have a negative correlation, and the nearer the correlation is to −1.00, the more strongly the two are connected.

To understand positive and negative correlations, think about the relationship between temperature and the use of air conditioners and heaters. Temperature and air conditioner use are positively correlated. As the temperature climbs, the number of air conditioners in use goes up. Conversely, temperature and heater use are negatively correlated. As the temperature decreases, the number of heaters in use goes up.

If we wanted to know whether age is related to memory, we could use a correlation. We would need to administer memory tests to adults of varying ages and calculate the correlation between test scores and ages. If we found a positive correlation between age and the number of memory errors people made—if older people made more errors—then we could say that our hypothesis had been supported. Conversely, if we found a negative correlation—if older people made fewer errors—then we would have to conclude that our hypothesis had not been supported.

Useful as they are, though, correlations have a major limitation: They do not indicate *causal* relationships. For example, even a high positive correlation between memory errors and age would tell us only that memory performance and age are connected in some way. It wouldn't tell us what caused the connection. It might be that younger adults understand the test instructions better. In order to identify a cause, we have to carry out experiments (see *Developmental Science at Home* on page 14). ✳ **Explore** the **Concept** *Correlations Do Not Show Causation* in **MyPsychLab**.

survey a data-collection method in which participants respond to questions

population the entire group that is of interest to a researcher

sample a subset of a group that is of interest to a researcher who participates in a study

representative sample a sample that has the same characteristics as the population to which a study's findings apply

correlation a relationship between two variables that can be expressed as a number ranging from −1.00 to +1.00

The Experimental Method

LO 1.10 What is the primary advantage of the experimental method?

An **experiment** is a study that tests a causal hypothesis. Suppose, for example, that we think age differences in memory are caused by older adults' failure to use memory techniques, such as repeating a list mentally in order to remember it. We could test this hypothesis by providing memory-technique training to one group of older adults and no training to another group. If the trained adults got higher scores on memory tests than they did before training and the no-training group showed no change, we could claim support for our hypothesis.

A key feature of an experiment is that participants are assigned *randomly* to one of two or more groups. In other words, chance determines which group each participant is placed in. The groups then have equal amounts of variation with respect to characteristics such as intelligence, personality traits, height, weight, and health status. Consequently, none of these variables can affect the outcome of the experiment.

Participants in the **experimental group** receive the treatment the experimenter thinks will produce a particular effect, while those in the **control group** receive either no special treatment or a neutral treatment. The presumed causal element in the experiment is called the **independent variable**, and the characteristic or behavior that the independent variable is expected to affect is called the **dependent variable**. ⊙→ **Simulate** the **Experiment** *Distinguishing Independent and Dependent Variables* in **MyPsychLab**.

In a memory-technique training experiment like the one suggested above, the group that receives the memory training is the experimental group, and the one that receives no instruction is the control group. Memory-technique training is the variable that we, the experimenters, think will cause differences in memory function, so it is the independent variable. Performance on memory tests is the variable we are using to measure the effect of the memory technique training. Therefore, performance on memory tests is the dependent variable.

Experiments are essential for understanding many aspects of development. But two special problems in studying child or adult development limit the use of experiments. First, many of the questions researchers want to answer have to do with the effects of particular unpleasant or stressful experiences on individuals—abuse, prenatal influences of alcohol or tobacco, low birth weight, poverty, unemployment, widowhood. For obvious ethical reasons, researchers cannot manipulate these variables. For example, they cannot ask one set of pregnant women to have two alcoholic drinks a day and others to have none. To study the effects of such experiences, they must rely on nonexperimental methods, such as correlations.

experiment a study that tests a causal hypothesis

experimental group the group in an experiment that receives the treatment the experimenter thinks will produce a particular effect

control group the group in an experiment that receives either no special treatment or a neutral treatment

independent variable the presumed causal element in an experiment

dependent variable the characteristic or behavior that is expected to be affected by the independent variable

Second, the independent variable that developmentalists are often most interested in is age itself, and researchers cannot assign participants randomly to age groups. They can compare 4-year-olds and 6-year-olds in their approach to some particular task, such as searching for a lost object, but the children differ in a host of ways other than their ages. Older children have had more and different experiences. Thus, unlike psychologists studying other aspects of behavior, developmental psychologists cannot systematically manipulate many of the variables they are most interested in.

To get around this problem, researchers can use any one of a series of strategies, sometimes called *quasi-experiments*, in which they compare groups without assigning the participants randomly. Quasi-experiments are studies in which researchers compare members of naturally occurring groups that differ in some dimension of interest, such as children whose parents choose to place them in day-care programs and children whose parents keep them at home. Such comparisons have built-in problems because groups that differ in one way are likely to differ in other ways as well. Compared with parents who keep their children at home, parents who place their children in day care are generally poorer, are more likely to be single parents, and tend to have different values or religious backgrounds. If researchers find that the two groups of children differ in some fashion, is it because they have spent their days in different environments or because of these other differences in their families? Researchers can make such comparisons a bit easier if they select comparison groups that are matched on those variables the researchers think might matter, such as income, marital status, or religion. But a quasi-experiment, by its very nature, will always yield more ambiguous results than will a fully controlled experiment.

Designs for Studying Age-Related Changes

LO 1.11 What are the pros and cons of cross-sectional, longitudinal, and sequential research designs?

In addition to deciding which method to use, developmental scientists must also determine how to incorporate age into their research design. There are three general strategies for doing so: (1) study different groups of people of different ages, using a **cross-sectional design**; (2) study the same people over a period of time, using a **longitudinal design**; (3) combine cross-sectional and longitudinal designs in some fashion, in a **sequential design**.

CROSS-SECTIONAL DESIGNS Figure 1.1 is a good example of a cross-sectional study in which researchers examined age differences in people's ability to recognize facial expressions. As you can see, younger adults outperformed those who were older in identifying anger. If these findings fit the researchers' hypothesis, they might be tempted to conclude that the ability to identify anger in facial expressions declines with age. But we cannot say this conclusively based on the cross-sectional data because these adults differ in both age and cohort. Thus, the age differences in this study might reflect, for example, differences in education and not changes linked to age or development. Influences of this kind lead to **cohort effects**, findings that result from historical factors to which one age group in a cross-sectional study has been exposed.

Furthermore, cross-sectional studies cannot tell us anything about sequences of change with age or about the consistency of individual behavior over time because each participant is tested only once. Still, cross-sectional research is very useful because it can be done relatively quickly and can reveal possible age differences or age changes.

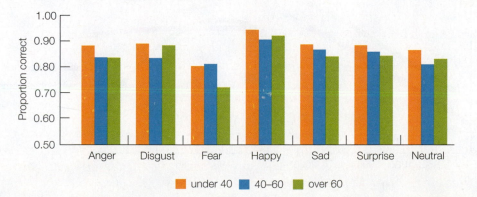

under 40   40–60   over 60

cross-sectional design a research design in which groups of people of different ages are compared

longitudinal design a research design in which people in a single group are studied at different times in their lives

sequential design a research design that combines cross-sectional and longitudinal examinations of development

cohort effects findings that result from historical factors to which one age group in a cross-sectional study has been exposed

Figure 1.1 An Example of a Cross-Sectional Design

In this cross-sectional study, researchers compared the ability to recognize various kinds of facial expressions across young adult, middle-aged adult, and older adult groups. This study is cross-sectional because it measured the same variable at the same time in people of different ages.

(*Source:* Figure 1, "Age Differences in Recognition of Emotion in Lexical Stimuli and Facial Expressions," by Derek M. Isaacowitz et al., from *Psychology and Aging*, Vol. 22 (1), pp. 147–159, Mar. 2007, American Psychological Association. Reprinted by permission.)

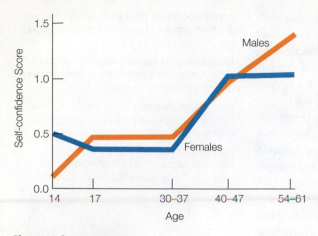

Figure 1.2 An Example of a Longitudinal Design

These results are from a classic study in Berkeley and Oakland, California, of a group of participants born either in 1920 or in 1928. They were tested frequently in childhood and adolescence, as well as three times in adulthood. Here you can see the sharp rise in self-confidence that occurred for both men and women in this group in their 30s—a pattern that may reflect a shared personality change, triggered by the common experiences of the social clock.

(*Source:* Adapted from Figures 1 and 2, p. 228, "As Time Goes By: Change and Stability in Personality Over Fifty Years," from *Psychology and Aging*, 1 (3), pp. 220–232, Haan, N. et al. Copyright © 1986 by the American Psychological Association. Adapted by permission.)

Figure 1.3 An Example of a Cross-Sequential Design

These findings illustrate the strengths of the cross-sequential design. Researchers tested more than 700 women in 1983, 1986, 1993, and 2003. Among the 700 were some women who were born during the "Baby Boom" (1946 to 1964) and some who were born earlier ("Preboomers"). Panel (a) shows that the tendency of women in both cohorts to describe themselves as "feminine" increased across all four testing points, but (b) shows that women's perceptions of conflict within their marriages remained stable across age for Preboomers but declined dramatically among Baby Boomers.

(*Source:* Adapted from Figure 1a, p. 950, Figure 6b, p. 953, from "Social Role and Birth Cohort Influences on Gender-Linked Personality Traits in Women: A 20-Year Longitudinal Analysis," by S. Kasen, et al., *Journal of Personality and Social Psychology*, 91 (5), Nov. 2006, pp. 944–958. Copyright © 2006 by the American Psychological Association. Adapted by permission.)

LONGITUDINAL DESIGNS Longitudinal designs seem to solve the problems presented by cross-sectional designs because they follow the same individuals over a period of time. Such studies allow psychologists to look at sequences of change and at individual consistency or inconsistency over time. And because longitudinal studies compare performance by the same people at different ages, they get around the obvious cohort problem.

A few well-known longitudinal studies have followed groups of children into adulthood or groups of adults from early to late adult life. One of the most famous of these is the Berkeley/Oakland Growth Study (see Figure 1.2) (Eichorn, Clausen, Haan, Honzik, & Mussen, 1981). Perhaps equally famous is the Grant study of Harvard men (Vaillant, 1977). This study followed several hundred men from age 18 until they were in their 60s. Such studies are extremely important in the study of human development, and you'll be reading more about them in later chapters.

Despite their importance, longitudinal designs have several major difficulties. One is that they typically involve giving each participant the same tests again and again. Over time, people learn how to take the tests. Such *practice effects* may distort the measurement of any underlying developmental changes.

Another significant problem is that some participants drop out, die, or move away. As a general rule, the healthiest and best educated participants are most likely to stick it out, and that fact biases the results, particularly if the study covers the final decades of life. Each succeeding set of test results comes from proportionally more and more healthy adults, which may give the appearance of less change or less decline than actually exists.

Longitudinal studies also don't really get around the cohort problem. For example, both the Grant study and the Berkeley/Oakland Growth Study observed and tested participants born in the same decade (1918–1928). Even if both studies showed the same pattern of change with age, we wouldn't know whether the pattern was unique to that cohort or reflected more basic developmental changes that would be observed in other cultures and other cohorts.

SEQUENTIAL DESIGNS One way to avoid the shortcomings of both cross-sectional and longitudinal designs is to use a sequential design. One group might include 25- to 30-year-olds and the other 30- to 35-year-olds. We would then test each group several times over a number of years. In a sequential study, each testing point beyond the initial one allows researchers to make two types of comparisons. Age-group comparisons provide them with the same kind of information as a cross-sectional study. Comparison of each group to itself at an earlier testing point allows the researchers to collect longitudinal evidence at the same time.

Sequential designs also allow for comparisons of cohorts. If both groups demonstrate similar age-related patterns of change over time, researchers can conclude that the developmental pattern is not specific to any particular cohort. Finding the same developmental pattern in two cohorts provides psychologists with stronger evidence than either cross-sectional or longitudinal data alone. For example, Figure 1.3 illustrates a sequential study in which Baby Boomer

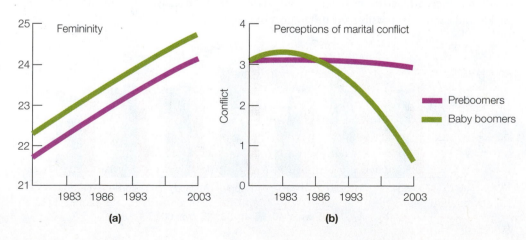

women who were born between 1946 and 1964 were compared to women born during the 1930s and early 1940s. Across four testing points, the two groups' self-perceptions of femininity increased in parallel fashion, suggesting a true developmental change. By contrast, the relationship between age and reported frequency of marital conflict was different in each cohort, a finding which suggests that historical factors may have caused the two groups to vary in either actual marital conflict or in their perceptions of what constitutes conflict.

ethnography a detailed description of a single culture or context

research ethics the guidelines researchers follow to protect the rights of animals used in research and humans who participate in studies

Cross-Cultural Research

LO 1.12 Why is cross-cultural research important to the study of human development?

Increasingly common in human development are studies comparing cultures or contexts, a task that researchers approach in several ways. For example, an **ethnography** is a detailed description of a single culture or context, based on extensive observation. Often the observer lives in the culture or context for a period of time, perhaps as long as several years. Each ethnographic study is intended to stand alone, although sometimes we can combine information from several different studies to see whether similar developmental patterns exist in the various cultures or contexts.

Alternatively, investigators may attempt to compare two or more cultures directly, by testing children or adults in each of the cultures with the same or comparable measures. Sometimes this involves comparing groups from different countries. Sometimes the comparisons are between subcultures within the same country; for example, increasingly common in the United States is research involving comparisons of children or adults living in different ethnic groups or communities, such as African Americans, Hispanic Americans, Asian Americans, and European Americans.

Cross-cultural research is important to the study of human development for two reasons. First, developmentalists want to identify universal changes—that is, predictable events or processes experienced by individuals in all cultures. Developmentalists don't want to make a general statement about development—such as "Memory declines with age"—if the phenomenon in question happens only in certain cultures. Without cross-cultural research, it is impossible to know whether studies involving North Americans and Europeans apply to people in other parts of the world.

Second, one of the goals of developmentalists is to produce findings that can be used to improve people's lives. Cross-cultural research is critical to this goal as well. For example, developmentalists know that children in cultures that emphasize the community more than the individual are more cooperative than children in more individualistic cultures. However, to use this information to help all children learn to cooperate, they need to know exactly how adults in such cultures teach their children to be cooperative. Cross-cultural research helps developmentalists identify specific variables that explain cultural differences. See Table 1.1 (page 18) for a comparison of various research methods and designs.

Ethnographers often interact in everyday settings with members of the cultures they study.

Research Ethics

LO 1.13 What are the ethical standards that developmental researchers must follow?

Research ethics are the guidelines researchers follow to protect the rights of animals used in research and humans who participate in studies. Ethical guidelines are published by professional organizations such as the American Psychological Association, the American Educational Research Association, and the Society for Research in Child Development. Universities, private foundations, and government agencies have review committees that make sure all research the institution sponsors is ethical. Guidelines for animal research include the requirement that animals be protected from unnecessary pain and suffering. Further, researchers must demonstrate that the potential benefits of their studies to either human or animal populations will be greater than any potential harm to animal subjects. ⊙➔ **Simulate** the **Experiment** *Ethics in Psychological Research* in **MyPsychLab**.

TABLE 1.1 Research Methods and Designs

Method	Description	Advantages	Limitations
Naturalistic observation	Observation of behavior in natural settings	Participants behave naturally	Researchers' expectations can influence results; little control over conditions
Case studies	In-depth study of one or a few individuals using observation, interviews, or psychological testing	In-depth information; important in the study of unusual events	Results may not generalize beyond the case that is studied; time-consuming; subject to misinterpretation
Surveys	Interviews, questionnaires used to gather information quickly	Accurate information about large groups; track changes	Validity limited by sample representativeness; responses influenced by questions, social desirability
Correlational studies	Determination of mathematical relationship between two variables	Assess strength and direction of relationships	Cannot demonstrate cause and effect
Experiments	Random assignment of participants to control and experimental groups; manipulation of independent (causal) variable	Identification of cause–effect relationships	Results may not generalize to nonresearch settings; many variables cannot be studied in experiments
Cross-sectional designs	Participants of different ages studied at one time	Quick access to data about age differences	Ignores individual differences; cohort effects
Longitudinal designs	Participants in one group studied several times	Track developmental changes in individuals and groups	Time-consuming; findings may apply only to the group that is studied
Sequential designs	Study that combines both longitudinal and cross-sectional components	Cross-sectional and longitudinal data relevant to the same hypothesis	Time-consuming; different attrition rates across groups
Cross-cultural research	Research that either describes culture or includes culture as a variable	Information about universality and culture specificity of age-related changes	Time-consuming; difficult to construct tests and methods that are equally valid in different cultures

Ethical standards for research involving human participants address the following major concerns:

- **Protection from harm:** It is unethical to do research that may cause participants permanent physical or psychological harm. Moreover, if the possibility of temporary harm exists, researchers must provide participants with some way of repairing the damage. For example, if the study will remind subjects of unpleasant experiences, such as rape, researchers must provide them with counseling.

- **Informed consent:** Researchers must inform participants of any possible harm and have them sign a consent form stating that they are aware of the risks of participating. In order for children to participate in studies, their parents must give permission after the researcher has informed them of possible risks. Children older than 7 must also give their own consent. If the research takes place in a school or day-care center, an administrator representing the institution must consent. In addition, both children and adults have the right to discontinue participation in a study at any time. Researchers are obligated to explain this right to children in language they can understand. ⊙ Watch the Video *Before Informed Consent: Robert Guthrie* in **MyPsychLab**.

- **Confidentiality:** Participants have the right to confidentiality. Researchers must keep the identities of participants confidential and must report their data in such a way that no particular piece of information can be associated with any specific participant. The exception to confidentiality is when children reveal to researchers that they have been abused in any way by an adult. In most states, all citizens are required to report suspected cases of child abuse.

- **Knowledge of results:** Participants, their parents, and the administrators of institutions in which research takes place have a right to a written summary of a study's results.
- **Deception:** If deception has been a necessary part of a study, participants have the right to be informed about the deception as soon as the study is over.

test yourself before going on ✓ **Study** and **Review** in **MyPsychLab**

Answers to these questions can be found in the back of the book.

1. The goals of developmental science are to ___describe___, ___Explain___, ___Prediet___, and ___to influence Human dev___ age-related changes.

2. Match each research method with its definition.
   - ___C___ (1) Manipulated independent variable
   - ___d___ (2) Behavior observed in controlled settings
   - ___b___ (3) In-depth study of single individual
   - ___e___ (4) Behavior observed in typical settings
   - ___A___ (5) Mathematical relationship between two variables
       - **(a)** Correlation
       - **(b)** Case study
       - **(c)** Experiment
       - **(d)** Laboratory observation
       - **(e)** Naturalistic observation

3. List the advantages and disadvantages of each method of studying age-related change.

Method	Advantages	Disadvantages
Cross-sectional	Quick access to data	Ignores ind. diff.
Longitudinal	Track dev. changes	Time Consuming
Sequential		

4. What are two reasons cross-cultural research is important?
   - (1) _____
   - (2) _____

5. Explain what researchers must do to meet ethical standards in each area listed in the table.

Issue	What Researchers Must Do
Protection from harm	
Informed consent	
Confidentiality	
Knowledge of results	
Deception	

CRITICAL THINKING

6. Researchers have found a positive correlation between a mother's age at the birth of her child and the child's later IQ: Very young mothers have children with lower IQs. How many explanations of this correlation can you think of?

7. Suppose a cross-sectional study of sex-role attitudes reveals that adults between the ages of 20 and 50 have the most egalitarian attitudes, while teenagers and adults over 50 have more traditional attitudes. How might cohort differences influence your interpretation of these results?

SUMMARY

An Introduction to Human Development (pp. 2–6)

LO 1.1 What ideas about development were proposed by early philosophers and scientists?

- The philosophical concepts of original sin, innate goodness, and the blank slate have influenced Western ideas about human development. Darwin studied child development to gain insight into evolution. G. Stanley Hall published the first scientific study of children and introduced the concept of norms.

LO 1.2 What is the lifespan perspective?

- Today's developmentalists recognize that change happens throughout life. The lifespan perspective includes the notions that plasticity exists throughout the lifespan, that information from a variety of disciplines is needed to understand development, and that development occurs in multiple contexts.

LO 1.3 What major domains and periods do developmental scientists use to organize their discussions of the human lifespan?

- Theorists and researchers group age-related changes into three broad categories: the physical, cognitive, and social domains. They also refer to the major periods of development: prenatal, infancy, early childhood, middle childhood, adolescence, early adulthood, middle adulthood, and late adulthood.

Key Issues in the Study of Human Development (pp. 6–10)

LO 1.4 How do developmentalists view the two sides of the nature–nurture debate?

- Historically, developmentalists have debated nature versus nurture, but now they believe that every developmental change is a product of both.

LO 1.5   What is the continuity–discontinuity debate?

- The continuity–discontinuity debate centers on whether change is a matter of amount or degree (continuous, quantitative change) or a matter of type or kind (discontinuous, qualitative change). Some aspects of development, such as height, are continuous and change quantitatively, while others, such as reproductive capacity, are discontinuous and change qualitatively. Developmental theorists who focus on qualitative changes usually propose explanations of psychological development that include stages.

LO 1.6   How do the three kinds of age-related change differ?

- Normative age-graded changes are those that are experienced by all human beings. Normative history-graded changes are common to individuals who have similar cultural and historical experiences. Genetic factors and the timing of experiences are two important causes of nonnormative changes in development.

LO 1.7   How does consideration of the contexts in which change occurs improve scientists' understanding of human development?

- The contexts of development include both individual variables and the settings in which development occurs (e.g., family, neighborhood, culture). Individual traits and contexts interact in complex ways to influence development.

Research Methods and Designs (pp. 11–19)

LO 1.8   What are the goals of scientists who study human development?

- Developmental psychologists use scientific methods to describe, explain, predict, and influence age-related changes and individual differences.

LO 1.9   What descriptive methods do developmental scientists use?

- Case studies and naturalistic observation provide a lot of important information, but it usually isn't generalizable to other individuals or groups. Correlational studies measure relationships between variables. They can be done quickly, and the information they yield is more generalizable than that from case studies or naturalistic observation.

LO 1.10   What is the primary advantage of the experimental method?

- To test causal hypotheses, it is necessary to use experimental designs in which participants are assigned randomly to experimental or control groups.

LO 1.11   What are the pros and cons of cross-sectional, longitudinal, and sequential research designs?

- In cross-sectional studies, separate age groups are each tested once. In longitudinal designs, the same individuals are tested repeatedly over time. Sequential designs combine cross-sectional and longitudinal comparisons.

LO 1.12   Why is cross-cultural research important to the study of human development?

- Cross-cultural research helps developmentalists identify universal factors and cultural variables that affect development.

LO 1.13   What are the ethical standards that developmental researchers must follow?

- Ethical principles governing psychological research include protection from harm, informed consent, confidentiality, knowledge of results, and protection from deception.

KEY TERMS

ageism (p. 8)

atypical development (p. 9)

case study (p. 12)

cognitive domain (p. 5)

cohort effects (p. 15)

control group (p. 14)

correlation (p. 13)

critical period (p. 8)

cross-sectional design (p. 15)

dependent variable (p. 14)

ethnography (p. 17)

experiment (p. 14)

experimental group (p. 14)

human development (p. 2)

independent variable (p. 14)

laboratory observation (p. 12)

lifespan perspective (p. 4)

longitudinal design (p. 15)

maturation (p. 3)

naturalistic observation (p. 12)

nature–nurture debate (p. 6)

nonnormative changes (p. 8)

normative age-graded changes (p. 7)

normative history-graded changes (p. 8)

norm-referenced tests (p. 3)

norms (p. 3)

physical domain (p. 4)

population (p. 13)

qualitative change (p. 7)

quantitative change (p. 7)

representative sample (p. 13)

research ethics (p. 17)

sample (p. 13)

sensitive period (p. 8)

sequential design (p. 15)

social clock (p. 8)

social domain (p. 5)

stages (p. 7)

survey (p. 13)

CHAPTER TEST ✓ Study and Review in MyPsychLab

Answers to all the Chapter Test questions can be found in the back of the book.

1. You are a developmentalist whose research shows that 8-year-olds' thinking is completely different from that of 4-year-olds. You probably subscribe to a developmental theory that emphasizes _____ changes.
   a. nonnormative
   b. normative history-graded
   c. continuous
   d. qualitative

2. Which domain of development does the research in question 1 focus on?
   a. Cognitive
   b. Social
   c. Physical
   d. Emotional

3. In an experiment, what do we call the group of participants who receive no treatment?
   a. Experimental group
   b. Control group
   c. Independent variable
   d. Dependent variable

4. Children get taller as they get older. This is an example of _____ change.
   a. continuous, quantitative
   b. discontinuous, qualitative
   c. continuous, qualitative
   d. discontinuous, quantitative

5. In which of the following research designs is one group of subjects studied at different points in their lives?
   a. Cross-sectional
   b. Ethnographic
   c. Longitudinal
   d. Cross-cultural

6. Which of the following best describes contemporary psychologists' views on human development?
   a. Human development is complete by age 18.
   b. Human development begins at conception and continues throughout the lifespan.
   c. Human development begins slowly at birth and accelerates as we age.
   d. Human development begins at birth, becomes stable in early adulthood, and declines in old age.

7. In survey research, a _____ faithfully reflects the characteristics of the whole group of people, or _____, being studied.
   a. representative population; sample
   b. survey sample; population
   c. representative sample; population
   d. survey population; sample

8. Which of the following best describes the goals of developmental science?
   a. To understand and explain social norms
   b. To explain, record and influence human differences
   c. To describe, explain, predict, and influence development
   d. To study cohort effects across cultures

9. A researcher wants to study how exposure to toxic chemicals affects a developing human fetus. Which type of research would be best suited for this in terms of both methodology and research ethics?
   a. Case study
   b. Quasi-experimentation
   c. Naturalistic observation
   d. Experimentation

10. Which of the following statements is true of people who were born at the end of the 20th century?
    a. Their life expectancy is 76 years.
    b. Most will live 30 or more years longer than their parents.
    c. Few, if any, will live to be 100 years old.
    d. Their life expectancy is double that of people born near the end of the 19th century.

11. Which type of research design is intended to avoid the shortcomings of both cross-sectional and longitudinal studies by combining features of both?
    a. Correlational study
    b. Sequential design
    c. Longitudinal case study
    d. Cross-longitudinal design

12. Judgments about individual adults' lives based on rigid applications of the social clock can lead to _____.
    a. ageism
    b. early death
    c. increased social support for the elderly
    d. unrealistically optimistic expectations for older adults' health and well-being

13. Which type of study is helpful for understanding development within the context of a particular culture?
    a. Longitudinal
    b. Experiment
    c. Ethnography
    d. Case study

14. Michael, age 16, has recently gained a considerable amount of weight but has not grown any taller. His father experienced a similar pattern of growth when he was a teenager. Theorists who suggest that Michael's growth pattern was inherited from his father emphasize the _____nature_____ side of the nature–nurture debate. Those who suggest that Michael's growth reflects behaviors that he has learned from his father emphasize the _____nurture_____ side.
    a. nurture; nature
    b. nature; nurture

15. Nearly all adults who were children living in Saigon when the U.S. armed forces left Vietnam in 1975 report that their lives were changed by those events. This exemplifies which of the following?
    a. Normative critical periods
    b. Normative age-graded changes
    c. Nonnormative life events
    d. Normative history-graded changes

16. Philosopher John Locke characterized the mind of a child as _____.
    a. innately good
    b. the product of evolution
    c. corrupted by original sin
    d. a blank slate

17. Leigh is counting the number of aggressive acts that occur during a preschool class. She is using the _____ method to study aggression in young children.
    a. interdisciplinary observation
    b. naturalistic observation
    c. laboratory observation
    d. behavioral observation

18. Dr. Jones is studying children's selection of toys in a laboratory setting in which there are an equal number of "boy" and "girl" toys. In one condition, children are placed in the laboratory in mixed-gender groups. In the other, they are placed in the laboratory in single-gender groups. The independent variable in the experiment is _____.
    a. the toys that each child chooses to play with
    b. the gender of each child
    c. "boy" and "girl" toys
    d. mixed- and single-gender groups

19. Charlie was born with a chromosomal error that causes intellectual disabilities. Which method would be best for examining how this condition affects Charlie's development?
    a. Experiment   c. Correlation
    b. Case study   d. Quasi-experiment

20. According to the discussion of vulnerability and resilience in the text, which child has the greatest probability of a poor developmental outcome?
    a. A child born with a mild birth defect
    b. A child growing up in an impoverished environment
    c. A child with a mild birth defect who is growing up in an impoverished environment
    d. A child with a mild birth defect who is growing up in an impoverished environment with a parent who is addicted to drugs

21. Which of the following best describe the ideas of the philosopher Jean-Jacques Rousseau about human development?
    a. It is the result of an individual's efforts to overcome inborn tendency toward selfishness.
    b. It involves an individual's effort to fulfill his or her inborn potential.
    c. Environmental influences determine its outcome.
    d. It follows the same course as human evolution.

22. Which of the following best defines *sensitive period*?
    a. The time when the tension between nature and nurture is resolved in an organism's development
    b. A time of psychological fragility, usually due to some type of loss such as the death of a spouse, termination of employment, deterioration due to aging, etc.
    c. The period of time during which developmental norms for physical development are reached or achieved
    d. A specific period in development when an organism is particularly responsive to specific forms of experience or particularly influenced by their absence

23. *Psychopathology* and *abnormal behavior* are alternative terms for _____.
    a. normative age-graded changes
    b. critical difference effects
    c. placebo effects
    d. atypical development

24. You are taking part in a survey that asks about your attitudes toward physical punishment of children. Even though you believe that spanking is sometimes necessary, you answer that you are opposed to any sort of physical punishment. Which of the following terms best describes why you answered the way that you did?
    a. Randomness   c. Experimenter bias
    b. Sample representation   d. Social desirability

25. Which of the following is an example from this text of an inborn bias?
    a. The sequence of motor development varies from one child to another.
    b. Male infants show a propensity toward aggression.
    c. Children's speech begins with single words before proceeding onto sentences.
    d. The same methods of soothing work with almost all infants.

To 👁 **Watch** ✳ **Explore** ⏩ **Simulate** ✅ **Study** and **Review** and experience MyVirtualLife go to MyPsychLab.com

chapter 2

Theories of Development

As you may have learned from raising your own "child" in *MyVirtualLife*, parents of infants have to make many decisions that have consequences for their children's physical and cognitive development: *Do I have to buy special, "educational" toys for* *him? What kind of music should I expose her to? Is it okay for a baby to watch television?* For example, when 7-month-old Zeke started crawling, his parents quickly learned that they would have to begin paying a lot more attention to what was on their floors. To their horror, Zeke

LEARNING OBJECTIVES

PSYCHOANALYTIC THEORIES

2.1 What are the main ideas of Freud's psychosexual theory?

2.2 What is the conflict associated with each of Erikson's psychosocial stages?

2.3 What are the strengths and weaknesses of psychoanalytic theory?

LEARNING THEORIES

2.4 How did Watson condition Little Albert to fear white, furry objects?

2.5 How does operant conditioning occur?

2.6 In what ways does social-cognitive theory differ from other learning theories?

2.7 How do the learning theories explain development?

COGNITIVE THEORIES

2.8 How does cognitive development progress, according to Piaget?

2.9 How did Vygotsky use the concepts of scaffolding and the zone of proximal development to explain cognitive development?

2.10 How does information-processing theory explain the findings of developmental psychologists such as Piaget and Vygotsky?

2.11 What are some of the important contributions of the cognitive theories?

BIOLOGICAL AND ECOLOGICAL THEORIES

2.12 How do behavior geneticists explain individual differences?

2.13 What kinds of behaviors are of interest to ethologists and sociobiologists?

2.14 What is the main idea of Bronfenbrenner's bioecological theory?

COMPARING THEORIES

2.15 What assumptions do the three families of theories make about development?

2.16 On what criteria do developmentalists compare the usefulness of theories?

2.17 What is eclecticism?

discovered a dead cockroach midway through his first solo excursion across the living room. Before they could snatch it away, Zeke crushed the bug's dried-out body in his hand. He was just about to start licking the insect's shattered remains out of his palm when his mother scooped him up and carried him off to the kitchen sink for a thorough scrubbing of the contaminated appendage. What is it about infants that makes them want to put things, even disgusting and potentially harmful things like dead insects, into their mouths?

As you learned in Chapter 1, developmental psychologists use theories to formulate hypotheses, or testable answers, to "why" questions about behaviors such as these. At the broadest level are three very broad families of theories—*psychoanalytic theory*, *learning theory*, and *cognitive-developmental theory*. Theories that deal with the biological foundations of development and interactions between these and the environment extend developmentalists' understanding of age-related changes beyond the explanations that the three major theories provide. Thus, the most comprehensive explanations of developmental phenomena often include ideas from the psychoanalytic, learning, and cognitive approaches as well as those derived from biological and contextual theories.

This chapter will introduce you to the three major families of theories. These theories will come up again and again as you make your way through this text. This chapter will also acquaint you with other theoretical trends in the field of human development, and you will learn how developmental psychologists compare theories.

Psychoanalytic Theories

One way of explaining why babies often put things in their mouths would be to suggest that infants derive more physical pleasure from mouthing objects than from manipulating them with other parts of their bodies. Such an approach would most likely belong to the family of **psychoanalytic theories**, a school of thought that originated with Viennese physician Sigmund Freud (1856–1939). Psychoanalytic theorists believe that developmental change happens because internal drives and emotions influence behavior.

Freud's Psychosexual Theory

LO 2.1   What are the main ideas of Freud's psychosexual theory?

Freud derived most of his ideas about development from his work with the childhood memories of adults with serious mental disorders. One of his most important conclusions was that behavior is governed by both conscious and unconscious processes. The most basic of these unconscious processes is an internal drive for physical pleasure that Freud called the *libido*. He believed the libido to be the motivating force behind most behavior.

Freud also argued that personality has three parts. The **id** operates at an unconscious level and contains the libido—a person's basic sexual and aggressive impulses, which are present at birth. The **ego**, the conscious, thinking part of personality, develops in the first 2 to 3 years of life. One of the ego's jobs is to keep the needs of the id satisfied. For instance, when a person is hungry, the id demands food immediately, and the ego is supposed to find a way to obtain it. The **superego**, the portion of the personality that acts as a moral judge, contains the rules of society and develops near the end of early childhood, at about age 6. Once the superego develops, the ego's task becomes more complex. It must satisfy the id without violating the superego's rules.

psychoanalytic theories theories proposing that developmental change happens because of the influence of internal drives and emotions on behavior

id in Freud's theory, the part of the personality that comprises a person's basic sexual and aggressive impulses; it contains the libido and motivates a person to seek pleasure and avoid pain

ego according to Freud, the thinking element of personality

superego Freud's term for the part of personality that is the moral judge

The Repressed-Memory Controversy

Freud claimed that hidden memories of traumatic events suffered in childhood, such as sexual abuse, often lie hidden away, or *repressed*, in a person's unconscious and cause emotional distress that can lead to mental illness. Consequently, Freud thought that the goal of psychotherapy was to uncover such events and help individuals learn to cope with them. Memory researchers have found that some people who were abused as children forget the events for long periods of time, just as Freud predicted. However, most people retain vivid memories of traumatic childhood events (Baddeley, 1998; Lindsay & Read, 1994). Moreover, perpetrators of abuse are more likely to forget the incidents than are their victims (Taylor & Kopelman, 1984).

Memory experts also point out that therapists who suggest the possibility of repressed memories risk creating false memories in their clients' minds (Ceci & Bruck, 1993). However, repression does sometimes occur, and discovery of a repressed memory does sometimes improve a person's mental health. Thus, mental health professionals face a dilemma: Should they ignore the possibility of a repressed memory or risk creating a false one?

Therapists address the dilemma by obtaining training in techniques that can bring out repressed memories but don't directly suggest that such memories exist. For example, when clients believe they have recalled a repressed event, therapists help them look for concrete evidence. In the end, however, both therapist and client should recognize that they must often rely on flawed human judgment to decide whether a "recovered" memory was really repressed or was invented in the client's mind.

YOU DECIDE

Decide which of these two statements you most agree with and think about how you would defend your position:

1. *If I thought that I had recovered a repressed memory of childhood abuse, I would prefer to have a skeptical therapist who would educate me about research findings showing that such memories are rarely forgotten.*

2. *If I thought that I had recovered a repressed memory of childhood abuse, I would prefer to have a supportive therapist who would help me search for evidence of the abuse.*

The ego is responsible for keeping the three components of personality in balance. According to Freud, a person experiences tension when any of the three components is in conflict with another. For example, if a person is hungry, the id may motivate her to do anything to find food, but the ego—her conscious self—may be unable to find any. Alternatively, food may be available, but the ego may have to violate one of the superego's moral rules to get it. In such cases, the ego may generate *defense mechanisms*—ways of thinking about a situation that reduce anxiety (see *No Easy Answers*). ✺ **Explore** the **Concept** *The Id, Ego, and Superego* in **MyPsychLab**.

Many of Freud's patients had memories of sexual feelings and behavior in childhood. This led Freud to believe that sexual feelings are important to personality development. Based on his patients' childhood memories, Freud proposed a series of **psychosexual stages** through which a child moves in a fixed sequence determined by maturation (see Table 2.1, p. 26). In each stage, the libido is centered on a different part of the body. In the infant, the focus of the drive for physical pleasure is the mouth; the stage is therefore called the *oral stage*. As maturation progresses, the libido becomes focused on the anus (hence, the *anal stage*), and later on the genitals (the *phallic stage* and eventually the *genital stage*).

Optimum development, according to Freud, requires an environment that will satisfy the unique needs of each period. For example, the infant needs sufficient opportunity for oral stimulation. An inadequate early environment will result in *fixation*, characterized by behaviors that reflect unresolved problems and unmet needs. Thus, as you might guess from looking at the list of stages in Table 2.1, emphasis on the formative role of early experiences is a hallmark of psychoanalytic theories.

Freud's most controversial idea about early childhood is his assertion that children experience sexual attraction to the opposite-sex parent during the phallic stage (ages 3 to 6). Freud borrowed names for this conflict from Greek literature. Oedipus was a male character who was involved in a romantic relationship with his mother. Electra was a female character who had a similar relationship with her father. Thus, for a boy, the Oedipus complex involves a conflict between his affection for his mother and his fear of his father; for a girl, the Electra complex pits her bond with her father against her anxiety over the potential loss of her mother's love. In both genders, the complex is resolved by abandoning the quest to possess the opposite-sex parent in favor of identification with the same-sex parent. In other words, the phallic stage reaches a successful conclusion when boys develop a desire to be like their fathers and when girls begin to view their mothers as role models.

psychosexual stages Freud's five stages of personality development through which children move in a fixed sequence determined by maturation; the libido is centered in a different body part in each stage

TABLE 2.1 Freud's Psychosexual Stages

Stage	Approximate Ages	Focus of Libido	Major Developmental Task	Some Characteristics of Adults Fixated at This Stage
Oral	Birth to 1 year	Mouth, lips, tongue	Weaning	Oral behavior, such as smoking and overeating; passivity and gullibility
Anal	1 to 3 years	Anus	Toilet training	Orderliness, obstinacy or messiness, disorganization
Phallic	3 to 6 years	Genitals	Resolving Oedipus/Electra complex	Vanity, recklessness, sexual dysfunction or deviancy
Latency*	6 to 12 years	None	Developing defense mechanisms; identifying with same-sex peers	None
Genital	12 years	Genitals	Achieving mature sexual intimacy	Adults who have successfully integrated earlier stages should emerge with sincere interest in others and mature sexuality

*Freud thought that the latency period is not really a psychosexual stage because libido is not focused on the body during this period; therefore, fixation is impossible.

Erikson's Psychosocial Theory

LO 2.2   What is the conflict associated with each of Erikson's psychosocial stages?

Many of Freud's critics accepted his assertion that unconscious forces influence development, but they questioned his rather gloomy view that childhood trauma nearly always leads to emotional instability in adulthood. Later theorists, known as *neo-Freudians*, proposed ideas that built on the strengths of Freud's theory but tried to avoid its weaknesses. **Watch** the **Video** *Introduction to Human Development: Erik Erikson* in **MyPsychLab**.

Erik Erikson (1902–1994) is the neo-Freudian theorist who has had the greatest influence on the study of development (Erikson, 1950, 1959, 1980, 1982; Erikson, Erikson, & Kivnick, 1986; Evans, 1969). Erikson thought development resulted from the interaction between internal drives and cultural demands; thus, his theory refers to **psychosocial stages** rather than to psycho*sexual* ones. Furthermore, Erikson thought that development continued through the entire lifespan. **Explore** the **Concept** *Erikson's Stages of Psychosocial Development* in **MyPsychLab**.

In Erikson's view, to achieve a healthy personality, an individual must successfully resolve a crisis at each of the eight stages of development, or *crises*, as summarized in Table 2.2. The key idea underlying Erikson's theory is that each new crisis is thrust on the developing person because of changes in social demands that accompany changes in age. Moreover, each crisis is defined by a pair of opposing possibilities. Successful resolution of a crisis results in the development of the characteristic on the positive side of the dichotomy. A healthy resolution, however, does not mean moving totally to the positive side. For example, an infant needs to have experienced some mistrust in order to learn to identify people who are not trustworthy. But healthy development requires a favorable ratio of positive to negative.

According to Erikson, the four childhood stages form the foundation of adult personality. The outcome of the first stage, *trust versus mistrust* (birth to 1 year), depends on the reliability of the care and affection infants receive from their primary caretaker. During the second stage, *autonomy versus shame and doubt*, children aged 1 to 3 express their independence. To help children resolve this crisis, caretakers must encourage them to function independently with regard to self-care skills, such as dressing themselves. In the third stage, *initiative versus guilt*, 3- to 6-year-olds begin to develop a sense of social initiative. In order to do so, a child needs opportunities to interact with peers during this stage. During the fourth stage, *industry versus inferiority*, children focus on acquiring culturally valued skills. In order to emerge from this stage with a sense of industry, children need support and encouragement from adults.

Erikson's description of the transition from childhood to adulthood, the *identity versus role confusion* stage, has been particularly influential. He argued that, in order to arrive at a mature

psychosocial stages Erikson's eight stages, or crises, of personality development in which inner instincts interact with outer cultural and social demands to shape personality

TABLE 2.2 Erikson's Psychosocial Stages

Approximate Ages	Stage	Positive Characteristics Gained and Typical Activities
Birth to 1 year	Trust versus mistrust	Hope; trust in primary caregiver and in one's own ability to make things happen (secure attachment to caregiver is key)
1 to 3 years	Autonomy versus shame and doubt	Will; new physical skills lead to demand for more choices, most often seen as saying "no" to caregivers; child learns self-care skills such as toileting
3 to 6 years	Initiative versus guilt	Purpose; ability to organize activities around some goal; more assertiveness and aggressiveness (Oedipus conflict with parent of same sex may lead to guilt)
6 to 12 years	Industry versus inferiority	Competence; cultural skills and norms, including school skills and tool use (failure to master these leads to sense of inferiority)
12 to 18 years	Identity versus role confusion	Fidelity; adaptation of sense of self to pubertal changes, consideration of future choices, achievement of a more mature sexual identity, and search for new values
18 to 30 years	Intimacy versus isolation	Love; persons develop intimate relationships beyond adolescent love; many become parents
30 years to late adulthood	Generativity versus stagnation	Care; people rear children, focus on occupational achievement or creativity, and train the next generation; turn outward from the self toward others
Late adulthood	Integrity versus despair	Wisdom; person conducts a life review, integrates earlier stages and comes to terms with basic identity; develops self-acceptance

sexual and occupational identity, every adolescent must examine his identity and the roles he must occupy. He must achieve an integrated sense of self, of what he wants to do and be, and of his appropriate sexual role. The risk is that the adolescent will suffer from confusion arising from the profusion of roles opening up to him at this age.

Erikson's adulthood stages are not strongly tied to age. In the first, the young adult builds on the identity established in adolescence to confront the crisis of *intimacy versus isolation*. Erikson hypothesized that an individual's capacity for intimacy is dependent upon a positive resolution of the identity crisis (Erikson, 1963). Many young people, Erikson thought, make the mistake of thinking they will find their identity in a relationship, but in his view, it is only those who have already formed (or are well on the way to forming) a clear identity who can successfully enter this fusion of identities that he called *intimacy*. Young adults whose identities are weak or unformed will remain in shallow relationships and will experience a sense of isolation or loneliness.

The middle and late adulthood crises are shaped by the realization that death is inevitable. Middle-aged adults confront the crisis of *generativity versus stagnation*, which is "primarily the concern in establishing and guiding the next generation" (Erikson, 1963, p. 267). The rearing of children is the most obvious way to achieve a sense of generativity. Doing creative work, giving service to an organization or to society, or serving as a mentor to younger colleagues can help a midlife adult achieve a sense of generativity. Failing that, a self-absorbed, nongenerative adult may feel a sense of stagnation. Finally, older adults experience *ego integrity versus despair*. The goal of this stage is an acceptance of one's life in preparation for facing death in order to avoid a sense of despair.

Adhering to group norms regarding which clothes are "in" and "out" is one of the ways that Erikson says teenagers begin to construct a sense of identity that distinguishes them from their parents.

Evaluation of Psychoanalytic Theories

LO 2.3 What are the strengths and weaknesses of psychoanalytic theory?

Psychoanalytic theories such as Freud's and Erikson's, summarized in Table 2.3, have several attractive aspects. Most centrally, they highlight the importance of a child's earliest relationships with caregivers.

TABLE 2.3 Psychoanalytic Theories

Theory	Main Idea	Evaluation	
		Strengths	**Weaknesses**
Freud's psychosexual theory	Personality develops in five stages from birth to adolescence; in each stage, the need for physical pleasure is focused on a different part of the body.	Emphasizes the importance of experiences in infancy and early childhood; provides psychological explanations for mental illness.	Sexual feelings are not as important in personality development as Freud claimed.
Erikson's psychosocial theory	Personality develops through eight life crises across the entire lifespan; a person finishes each crisis with either a good or poor resolution.	Helps explain the role of culture in personality development; important in lifespan psychology; useful description of major themes of personality development at different ages.	Describing each period in terms of a single crisis is probably an oversimplification.

Furthermore, they suggest that a child's needs change with age, so parents and other caregivers must continually adapt to the changing child. One implication is that we should not think of "good parenting" as an unchanging quality. Some people may be very good at meeting the needs of an infant but less capable of dealing with teenagers' identity struggles. The child's eventual personality and her overall mental health thus depend on the interaction pattern that develops in a particular family. The idea of changing needs is an extremely attractive element of these theories because more and more of the research in developmental psychology is moving developmentalists toward just such a conception of the process.

Psychoanalytic theory has also given psychologists a number of helpful concepts, such as the unconscious, the ego, and identity, which have become a part of everyday language as well as theory. Moreover, psychologists are taking a fresh look at Freud's ideas about the importance of defense mechanisms in coping with anxiety (e.g., Malone, Cohen, Liu, Vaillant, & Waldinger, 2013). Freud is also usually credited with the invention of psychotherapy, which is still practiced today. An additional strength of the psychoanalytic perspective is the emphasis on continued development during adulthood found in Erikson's theory. His ideas have provided a framework for a great deal of new research and theorizing about adult development. The major weakness of psychoanalytic theories is the fuzziness of many of their concepts. For example, how could researchers detect the presence of the id, ego, superego, and so on? Without more precise definitions, it is extremely difficult to test these theories, despite their provocative explanations of development.

test yourself before going on ✓ Study and Review in MyPsychLab

Answers to these questions can be found in the back of the book.

1. Psychoanalytic theories share the belief that _____ and _____ _____ shape development.

2. Write "F" for each concept or term that belongs to Freud's theory, and "E" for each that belongs to Erikson's theory.

   _____(1) psychosocial
   _____(2) psychosexual
   _____(3) id, ego, superego
   _____(4) eight stages from birth to death
   _____(5) five stages from birth to adolescence
   _____(6) libido is driving force behind development

   _____(7) development consists of a series of crises
   _____(8) young child is attracted to the opposite-sex parent
   _____(9) defense mechanisms
   _____(10) interaction between internal drives and cultural demands

CRITICAL THINKING

3. In which of Erickson's psychological stages would you place yourself? Does Erikson's description of it correspond to the challenges and concerns you are confronting?

Learning Theories

Psychologist John Watson (1878–1958) offered ideas about human development that were very different from those of Freud. Watson believed that, through manipulation of the environment, children could be trained to be or do anything (Jones, 1924; Watson, 1930). To refer to this point of view, Watson coined the term **behaviorism**, which defines development in terms of behavior changes caused by environmental influences. As Watson put it,

> Give me a dozen healthy infants, well-formed, and my own specified world to bring them up in and I'll guarantee to take any one at random and train him to become any type of specialist I might select—doctor, lawyer, merchant, chief, and yes, even beggerman and thief, regardless of his talents, penchants, abilities, vocations, and race of his ancestors. (1930, p. 104)

Watson's views represent a way of thinking about development that is common to all of the **learning theories**. These theories assert that development results from an accumulation of experiences. As you will see, however, each of the learning theories has a distinctive way of explaining how experience shapes development.

Classical Conditioning

LO 2.4   How did Watson condition Little Albert to fear white, furry objects?

Watson based many of his ideas about the relationship between learning and development on the work of Russian physiologist and Nobel Prize Winner Ivan Pavlov (1849–1936). Pavlov discovered that organisms can acquire new signals for existing responses (behaviors). The term **classical conditioning** refers to this principle. Each incidence of learning begins with a biologically programmed stimulus–response connection, or *reflex*. For example, salivation happens naturally when you put food in your mouth. In classical conditioning terms, the food is the *unconditioned (unlearned, natural) stimulus*; salivating is an *unconditioned (unlearned, natural) response*.

Stimuli presented just before or at the same time as the unconditioned stimulus are those that are likely to be associated with it. For example, most foods have odors, and to get to your mouth, food has to pass near your nose. Thus, you usually smell food before you taste it. Food odors eventually become *conditioned (learned) stimuli* that elicit salivation. In effect, they act as a signal to your salivary glands that food is coming. Once the connection between food odors and salivation has been established, smelling food triggers the salivation response even when you do not actually eat the food. When a response occurs reliably in connection with a conditioned stimulus in this way, it is known as a *conditioned (learned) response*. For Watson, Pavlov's principles of classical conditioning held the key to understanding human development. He viewed developmental change as nothing more than the acquisition of connections between stimuli and responses. To prove his point, Watson set out to show that he could use the principles of classical conditioning to cause an infant to develop a new emotional response to a stimulus. Watson's hapless subject, 11-month-old "Little Albert," was exposed to loud noises while he played with a white rat, a stimulus that had fascinated him when it was first introduced. As a result of the pairing of the rat with the noises, however, Albert learned to fear the rat so thoroughly that he cried hysterically at the mere sight of the rodent. Moreover, he generalized his fear of the rat to other white, fuzzy objects such as a rabbit, a fur coat, and a Santa Claus mask. 💥 **Explore** the **Concept** *Classical Conditioning of Little Albert* in **MyPsychLab**.

As you might guess, Watson's experiment would be regarded as unethical by today's standards. Moreover, few developmentalists would agree with Watson's assertion that classical conditioning explains all of human development. Yet the Little Albert experiment demonstrated that classical conditioning may indeed be the source of developmental changes that involve emotional responses. For this reason, classical conditioning continues to have a place in the study of human development. It is especially important in infancy. Because a child's mother or father is present so often when nice things happen, such as when the child feels warm, comfortable, and cuddled, the mother and father usually serve as conditioned stimuli

behaviorism the view that defines development in terms of behavior changes caused by environmental influences

learning theories theories asserting that development results from an accumulation of experiences

classical conditioning learning that results from the association of stimuli

Systematic Desensitization

Dr. Rawlins is a psychologist who works in a large urban school district. When confronted with a child who exhibits *school refusal*, Dr. Rawlins begins by determining whether there is a concrete reason for the child to refuse to go to school, such as the fear of being bullied. If such a reason is found, she works with the child's teachers and school administrators to address the problem. In most cases of school refusal, however, children do not want to go to school because they feel anxious in the school setting (Kauffman, 2005).

The mechanisms at work in John Watson's experiment with Little Albert hold the key to helping children overcome school refusal. Psychologists speculate that, among children who refuse to go to school, the neutral stimulus of school has become associated with stimuli that naturally provoke anxious responses in children.

Consequently, psychologists reason that children's fear of school can be unlearned through the same stimulus–response mechanism that produced it. Thus, like many other psychologists, Dr. Rawlins uses a technique called *systematic desensitization* to help children with school refusal learn to respond to the school setting differently (Kauffman, 2005; Wolpe, 1958). She begins by teaching the child how to control his respiration rate and muscular contractions in order to achieve a state of physical relaxation. Afterward, Dr. Rawlins helps him learn to "switch on" his relaxation response in connection with each step in the sequence of events that are involved in getting to and staying in school. For example, he will first learn to intentionally relax while getting ready for school. Next, he will practice intentionally relaxing while waiting for the bus and then while he is on the bus. Once at school, the therapist will encourage him to initiate his relaxation response in front of the school entrance. The final step will be to learn to intentionally relax in the classroom and to initiate the relaxation response whenever he experiences feelings of anxiety during the school day. As a result, the child will learn to associate going to school with the relaxation responses rather than with anxiety.

REFLECTION

1. *How could systematic desensitization be used to help a child who was bitten by a dog overcome her subsequent fear of all dogs?*
2. *What actions on the part of parents, teachers, or peers might prevent a child with school refusal from benefiting from systematic desensitization?*

---

for pleasant feelings, a fact that makes it possible for the parents' presence to comfort a child. Moreover, classical conditioning is the basis of several useful therapies for anxiety problems (see *Developmental Science in the Classroom* above).

Skinner's Operant Conditioning

LO 2.5   How does operant conditioning occur?

Another behavioral approach to development may be found in a set of learning principles known collectively as **operant conditioning**, a term coined by B. F. Skinner (1904–1990), the most famous proponent of this theory (Skinner, 1953, 1980). Operant conditioning involves learning to repeat or stop behaviors because of the consequences they bring about. **Reinforcement** is anything that follows a behavior and causes it to be repeated. **Punishment** is anything that follows a behavior and causes it to stop.

A *positive reinforcement* is a consequence (usually involving something pleasant) that follows a behavior and increases the chances that the behavior will occur again. For example, if you buy a scratch ticket and win $100, you will probably be more willing to buy another ticket in the future than you would if you hadn't won the money.

Negative reinforcement occurs when an individual learns to perform a specific behavior in order to cause something unpleasant to stop. For example, coughing is an unpleasant experience for most of us, and taking a dose of cough medicine usually stops it. As a result, when we begin coughing, we reach for the cough syrup. The behavior of swallowing a spoonful of cough syrup is reinforced by the cessation of coughing.

Positive and negative reinforcement often interact in complex ways in real-life contexts. For example, most people understand that paying attention to a preschooler's whining is likely to increase it—an example of positive reinforcement. However, parents learn to attend to whining preschoolers because whining is irritating, and responding to it usually makes it stop. In other words, like taking cough syrup for an annoying cough, the parents' behavior of responding to whining is negatively reinforced by its consequence—namely, that the child *stops* whining.

In contrast to both kinds of reinforcement, punishment stops a behavior. Sometimes punishments involve eliminating nice things—taking away TV or video-game privileges, for example. However, punishment may also involve unpleasant things such as scolding. Like reinforcement, however, punishment is defined by its effect. Consequences that do not stop behavior can't be properly called punishments.

operant conditioning learning to repeat or stop behaviors because of their consequences

reinforcement anything that follows a behavior and causes it to be repeated

punishment anything that follows a behavior and causes it to stop

An alternative way to stop an unwanted behavior is **extinction**, which is the gradual elimination of a behavior through repeated non-reinforcement. If a teacher succeeds in eliminating a student's undesirable behavior by ignoring it, the behavior is said to have been *extinguished*.

Such examples illustrate the complex manner in which reinforcements and punishments operate in the real world. In laboratory settings, operant-conditioning researchers usually work with only one participant or animal subject at a time; they needn't worry about the social consequences of behaviors or consequences. They can also control the situation so that a particular behavior is reinforced every time it occurs. In the real world, *partial reinforcement*—reinforcement of a behavior on some occasions but not others—is more common. Studies of partial reinforcement show that people take longer to learn a new behavior under partial reinforcement conditions; once established, however, such behaviors are very resistant to extinction.

Most parents try to use consequences to change their children's behavior. Few realize that, in many cases, they may actually be strengthening those behaviors. Consider the example of a father whose 3-year-old son repeatedly demands attention while the father is fixing dinner. The first three, or five, or seven times the child says "Dad" or tugs at the father's pants leg, the father ignores him. But after the eighth or ninth repetition, with the child's voice getting whinier each time, the father can't stand it anymore: "All right! What do you want?" The parent thereby creates a pattern of partial reinforcement that encourages the child to be even more demanding. In effect, the child becomes like a gambler who deposits token after token in a slot machine, knowing that he will eventually hit the jackpot. Thus, parents may have more success in changing children's behavior if they administer an appropriate consequence the first time an unwanted behavior occurs.

Laboratory research involving animals was important in the development of Skinner's operant conditioning theory.

Bandura's Social-Cognitive Theory

LO 2.6 In what ways does social-cognitive theory differ from other learning theories?

Learning theorist Albert Bandura (b. 1925), whose ideas are more influential among developmental psychologists than those of the conditioning theorists, argues that learning does not always require reinforcement (1977b, 1982, 1989). Learning may also occur as a result of watching someone else perform some action and experience reinforcement or punishment. Learning of this type, called **observational learning**, or **modeling**, is involved in a wide range of behaviors. For example, observant school children learn to distinguish between strict and lenient teachers by observing teachers' reactions to the misbehaviors of children who are risk takers—that is, those who act out without having determined how teachers might react. Observant children, when in the presence of strict teachers, suppress forbidden behaviors such as talking out of turn and leaving their seats without permission. By contrast, when they are under the authority of lenient teachers, these children may display just as much misbehavior as their risk-taking peers. **Explore** the **Concept** *Bandura's Study on Observational Learning* in **MyPsychLab**.

Bandura points out that what an observer learns from watching someone else will depend on two cognitive elements: what she pays attention to and what she is able to remember. Moreover, to learn from a model, an observer must be physically able to imitate the behavior and motivated to perform it on her own. Because attentional abilities, memory, physical capabilities, and motivations change with age, what a child learns from any given modeled event may be quite different from what an adult learns from an identical event (Grusec, 1992).

extinction the gradual elimination of a behavior through repeated nonreinforcement

observational learning, *or* **modeling** learning that results from seeing a model reinforced or punished for a behavior

Modeling is an important source of learning for both children and adults. What behaviors have you learned by watching and copying others?

As children, according to Bandura, we learn not only overt behavior, but also ideas, expectations, internal standards, and self-concepts, from models. At the same time, we acquire expectancies about what we can and cannot do—which Bandura (1997) calls *self-efficacy*. Once those standards and those expectancies or beliefs have been established, they affect the child's behavior in consistent and enduring ways. For example, you'll learn in Chapter 12 that self-efficacy beliefs influence our overall sense of well-being and even our physical health.

Evaluation of Learning Theories

LO 2.7 How do the learning theories explain development?

Several implications of learning theories, summarized in Table 2.4, are worth emphasizing. First, learning theories can explain both consistency and change in behavior. If a child is friendly and smiling both at home and at school, learning theorists would explain this behavior by saying that the child is being reinforced for it in both settings. It is equally possible to explain why a child is happy at home but miserable at school. We need only hypothesize that the home environment reinforces cheerful behavior but the school setting does not.

Learning theorists also tend to be optimistic about the possibility of change. Children's behavior can change if the reinforcement system—or their beliefs about themselves—change. So, problem behavior can be modified.

TABLE 2.4 Learning Theories

Theory	Main Idea	Evaluation	
		Strengths	**Weaknesses**
Pavlov's classical conditioning	Learning happens when neutral stimuli become so strongly associated with natural stimuli that they elicit the same response.	Useful in explaining how emotional responses such as phobias are learned.	Explanation of behavior change is too limited to serve as comprehensive theory of human development.
Skinner's operant-conditioning theory	Development involves behavior changes that are shaped by reinforcement and punishment.	Basis of many useful strategies for managing and changing human behavior.	Humans are not as passive as Skinner claimed; the theory ignores hereditary, cognitive, emotional, and social factors in development.
Bandura's social-learning theory	People learn from models; what they learn from a model depends on how they interpret the situation cognitively and emotionally.	Helps explain how models influence behavior; explains more about development than other learning theories do because of addition of cognitive and emotional factors.	Does not provide an overall picture of development.

The great strength of learning theories is that they seem to give an accurate picture of the way in which many behaviors are learned. It is clear that both children and adults learn through conditioning and modeling. Furthermore, Bandura's addition of mental elements to learning theory adds further strength, since it allows an integration of learning models and other approaches.

However, the learning theorists' approach is not really developmental; it doesn't tell us much about change with age, either in childhood or in adulthood. Even Bandura's variation on learning theory does not tell us whether there are any changes with age in what a child can learn from modeling. Thus, learning theories help developmentalists understand how specific behaviors are acquired but do not contribute to an understanding of age-related change.

test yourself before going on   **Study** and **Review** in **MyPsychLab**

Answers to these questions can be found in the back of the book.

1. Pavlov's experiments addressed (classical/operant) conditioning; Skinner's dealt with (classical, operant) conditioning.

2. A consequence that causes a behavior to be repeated is a _____; one that stops a behavior is a _____.

3. According to Bandura, what four factors explain why learning from a model is not an automatic process?

4. Eight-year-old Rodney does not believe he can learn how to hit a baseball. According to Bandura, Rodney has low _____ with regard to this behavior.

CRITICAL THINKING

5. Can you describe instances in your everyday life when your behavior is affected by classical conditioning, operant conditioning, and observational learning? How do you use these same principles to affect others' behavior?

Cognitive Theories

The group of theories known as **cognitive theories** emphasize mental aspects of development such as logic and memory. Have you ever watched a baby throw things out of her mother's shopping cart? No matter how many objects the baby drops, she watches each one intently as if she has no idea where it's going to land. Why do babies engage in repetitive actions of this kind? One reason might be that they use their motor skills (throwing things) and senses (watching them) to build mental pictures of the world around them. Thus, infants drop objects and watch them fall until they have learned all they can from this behavior; then they move on to a more mature way of interacting with the world.

cognitive theories theories that emphasize mental processes in development, such as logic and memory

Piaget's Cognitive-Developmental Theory

LO 2.8   How does cognitive development progress, according to Piaget?

One of the most influential theories in the history of developmental psychology is that of Swiss developmentalist Jean Piaget (1896–1980). Originally educated as a natural scientist, Piaget spent six decades studying the development of logical thinking in children. Because of the popularity of Watson's views, psychologists in the United States paid little attention to Piaget's work. During the late 1950s, however, American developmentalists "discovered" Piaget. Developmental psychologists in the United States then began to focus on children's thinking more than on how environmental stimuli influenced their behavior.

Piaget was struck by the fact that all children seem to go through the same sequence of discoveries about their world, making the same mistakes and arriving at the same solutions (Piaget, 1952, 1970, 1977; Piaget & Inhelder, 1969). For example, all 3- and 4-year-olds seem to think that if water is poured from a short, wide glass into a taller, narrower one, there is then more water because the water level is higher in the narrow glass than it was in the wide glass. In contrast, most 7-year-olds realize that the amount of water has not changed. To explain such age differences, Piaget proposed several concepts that continue to guide developmental research.

Piaget based many of his ideas on naturalistic observations of children of different ages on playgrounds and in schools.

Using Piaget's terminology, we would say this infant is assimilating the object to her grasping scheme.

A pivotal idea in Piaget's model is that of a **scheme**, an internal cognitive structure that provides an individual with a procedure to follow in a specific circumstance. For example, when you pick up a ball, you use your picking-up scheme. Piaget proposed that each of us begins life with a small repertoire of sensory and motor schemes, such as looking, tasting, touching, hearing, and reaching. As we use each scheme, it becomes better adapted to the world; in other words, it works better. During childhood and adolescence, mental schemes allow us to use symbols and think logically. Piaget proposed three processes to explain how children get from built-in schemes such as looking and touching to the complex mental schemes used in childhood, adolescence, and adulthood.

Assimilation is the process of using schemes to make sense of experiences. Piaget would say that a baby who grasps a toy is *assimilating* it to his grasping scheme. The complementary process is **accommodation**, which involves changing the scheme as a result of some new information acquired through assimilation. When the baby grasps a square object for the first time, he will accommodate his grasping scheme; the next time he reaches for a square object, his hand will be more appropriately bent to grasp it. Thus, the process of accommodation is the key to developmental change. Through accommodation, we improve our skills and reorganize our ways of thinking.

Equilibration is the process of balancing assimilation and accommodation to create schemes that fit the environment. To illustrate, think about infants' tendency to put things in their mouths. In Piaget's terms, they assimilate objects to their mouthing scheme. As they mouth each one, their mouthing scheme changes to include the instructions "*Do* mouth this" or "*Don't* mouth this." The accommodation is based on mouthing experiences. A pacifier feels good in the mouth, but a dead insect has an unpleasant texture. So, eventually, the mouthing scheme says it's okay to put a pacifier in the mouth, but it's not okay to do the same with a dead insect. In this way, an infant's mouthing scheme attains a better fit with the real world.

Piaget's research suggested to him that logical thinking evolves in four stages. During the *sensorimotor stage*, from birth to 18 months, infants use their sensory and motor schemes to act on the world around them. In the *preoperational stage*, from 18 months to about age 6, youngsters acquire symbolic schemes, such as language and fantasy, that they use in thinking and communicating. Next comes the *concrete operational stage*, during which 6- to 12-year-olds begin to think logically and become capable of solving problems such as the one illustrated in Figure 2.1.

scheme in Piaget's theory, an internal cognitive structure that provides an individual with a procedure to use in a specific circumstance

assimilation the process of using a scheme to make sense of an event or experience

accommodation changing a scheme as a result of some new information

equilibration the process of balancing assimilation and accommodation to create schemes that fit the environment

Figure 2.1   A Conservation Task

In one of the problems Piaget devised, a child is shown two glasses of the same size filled with equal amounts of liquid. Next, the researcher pours one glass of liquid into a taller, thinner glass and asks the child if the two glasses still contain the same amount of liquid. A preoperational thinker will say that one glass now contains more liquid than the other and will base his answer on appearance. "This glass has more because the liquid is higher now." A concrete operational thinker will say that the two still contain the same amount of liquid because no liquid was added or taken away from either.

TABLE 2.5 Piaget's Cognitive-Developmental Stages

Approximate Ages	Stage	Description
Birth to 18 months	Sensorimotor	The baby understands the world through her senses and her motor actions; she begins to use simple symbols, such as single words and pretend play, near the end of this period.
18 months to 6 years	Preoperational	By age 2, the child can use symbols both to think and to communicate; by the end of this stage he develops the abilities to take others' points of view, classify objects, and use simple logic.
6 to 12 years	Concrete operational	The child's logic takes a great leap forward with the development of new internal operations, such as conservation and class inclusion, but is still tied to the known world; by the end of the period, he can reason about simple "what if" questions.
12 years	Formal operational	The child begins to manipulate ideas as well as objects; she thinks hypothetically and, by adulthood, can easily manage a variety of "what if" questions; she greatly improves her ability to organize ideas and objects mentally.

The last phase is the *formal operational stage*, in which adolescents learn to think logically about abstract ideas and hypothetical situations.

Table 2.5 describes these stages more fully; you will read about each of them in detail later in the text. For now, it is important to understand that in Piaget's view, each stage grows out of the one that precedes it, and each involves a major restructuring of the child's way of thinking. It's also important to know that research has confirmed Piaget's belief that the sequence of the stages is fixed. However, children progress through them at different rates. In addition, some individuals do not attain the formal operational stage in adolescence or even in adulthood. Consequently, the ages associated with the stages are approximations.

Vygotsky's Sociocultural Theory

LO 2.9   How did Vygotsky use the concepts of scaffolding and the zone of proximal development to explain cognitive development?

Lev Vygotsky's **sociocultural theory** asserts that complex forms of thinking have their origins in social interactions rather than in the child's private explorations, as Piaget thought. According to Vygotsky, children's learning of new cognitive skills is guided by an adult (or a more skilled child, such as an older sibling), who structures the child's learning experience—a process Vygotsky called *scaffolding*. To create an appropriate scaffold, the adult must gain and keep the child's attention, model the best strategy, and adapt the whole process to the child's developmental level, or *zone of proximal development* (Landry, Garner, Swank, & Baldwin, 1996; Rogoff, 1990). Vygotsky used this term to signify tasks that are too hard for the child to do alone but that he can manage with guidance. For example, parents of a beginning reader provide a scaffold when they help him sound out new words.

Vygotsky's ideas have important educational applications. Like Piaget's, Vygotsky's theory suggests the importance of opportunities for active exploration. But assisted discovery would play a greater role in a Vygotskian than in a Piagetian classroom; the teacher would provide the scaffolding for children's discovery, through questions, demonstrations, and explanations (Tharp & Gallimore, 1988). To be effective, the assisted discovery processes would have to be within the zone of proximal development of each child.

Information-Processing Theory

LO 2.10   How does information-processing theory explain the findings of developmental psychologists such as Piaget and Vygotsky?

The goal of **information-processing theory** is to explain how the mind manages information (Munakata, 2006). Theorizing about and studying

sociocultural theory Vygotsky's view that complex forms of thinking have their origins in social interactions rather than in an individual's private explorations

information-processing theory a theoretical perspective that uses the computer as a model to explain how the mind manages information

Developmental psychologist Lev Vygotsky hypothesized that social interactions among children, such as the 2-year-old boy and girl playing here, are critical to both cognitive and social development.

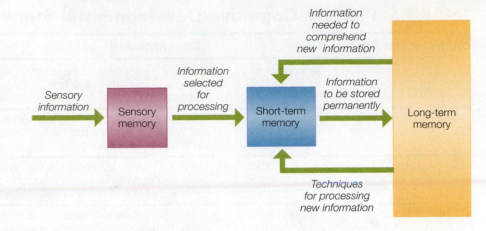

Figure 2.2   The Information-Processing System

Information-processing research on memory is based on the assumption that information moves into, out of, and through the sensory, short-term, and long-term memories in an organized way.

memory processes are central to information-processing theory. Most memory research assumes that the human memory is made up of multiple components. The idea is that information moves through these components in an organized way (see Figure 2.2). The process of understanding a spoken word serves as a good example. First, you hear the word when the sounds enter your *sensory memory*. Your experiences with language allow you to recognize the pattern of sounds as a word. Next, the word moves into your *short-term memory*, the component of the memory system where all information is processed. Thus, short-term memory is often called *working memory*. Knowledge of the word's meaning is then called up out of *long-term memory*, the component of the system where information is permanently stored, and placed in short-term memory, where it is linked to the word's sounds to enable you to understand it.

According to the information-processing model, children presented with problems such as Piaget's conservation tasks process the information they need to solve such problems in their short-term memories. As you will learn in Chapter 7, a great deal of research has shown that younger children's short-term memories are both more limited in capacity and less efficient than those of older children (Kail, 1990, 2008). Consequently, some developmentalists have used information-processing theory to explain Piaget's stages. Their theories are called **neo-Piagetian theories** because they expand on Piaget's theory rather than contradict it (Case, 1985, 1997). As you'll learn in Chapter 7, according to neo-Piagetians, older children and adults can solve complex problems like those in Piaget's research because they can hold more pieces of information in their short-term memories at the same time than younger children can (Kail 1990, 2008).

Evaluation of Cognitive Theories

LO 2.11   What are some important contributions of the cognitive theories?

Research based on cognitive theories, especially the work of Piaget, has demonstrated that simplistic views, such as those of the conditioning theorists, cannot explain the development of the complex phenomenon that is logical thinking. Moreover, since his work was first published in the 1920s Piaget's research findings have been replicated in virtually every culture and in every cohort of children. Thus, not only did he formulate a theory that forced psychologists to think about child development in a new way, he also provided a set of findings that were impossible to ignore and difficult to explain. In addition, he developed innovative methods of studying children's thinking that continue to be important today (see the *Research Report* on page 38).

Nevertheless, Piaget turned out to be wrong about some of the ages at which children develop particular skills. As you will see in later chapters, researchers have found that children develop some intellectual skills at earlier ages than Piaget's findings suggested. Furthermore, Piaget was probably wrong about the generality of the stages themselves. Most 8-year-olds, for example, show concrete operational thinking on some tasks but not on others, and they are more likely to show complex thinking on familiar tasks than on unfamiliar tasks. Thus, the whole process seems to be a great deal less stagelike than Piaget proposed.

At present, there is insufficient evidence to either support or contradict most of Vygotsky's ideas (Crain, 2011). However, studies have shown that children in pairs and groups do produce

neo-Piagetian theory   an approach that uses information-processing principles to explain the developmental stages identified by Piaget

more sophisticated ideas than individual children who work on problems alone (Tan-Niam, Wood, & O'Malley, 1998). Moreover, researchers have found that young children whose parents provide them with more scaffolding during the preschool years exhibit higher levels of achievement in elementary school than peers whose parents provide less support of this kind (Neitzel & Stright, 2003). Thus, future research may support the conclusion that Vygotsky's theory constitutes an important contribution to a full understanding of human development.

In contrast to Vygotsky's theory, the information-processing approach to cognitive development has received a great deal of empirical support (Birney & Sternberg, 2011). These findings have helped to clarify some of the cognitive processes underlying Piaget's findings. This approach, furthermore, has greatly enhanced developmentalists' understanding of human memory. Critics, however, have pointed out that much information-processing research involves artificial memory tasks such as learning lists of words. Therefore, say critics, research based on the information-processing approach doesn't always accurately describe how memory works in the real world. Consequently, as Piaget did, information-processing theorists may underestimate children's capabilities with regard to real-world tasks.

Piagetians claim that information-processing theory emphasizes explanations of single cognitive tasks at the expense of a comprehensive picture of development. Finally, critics of both cognitive theories say that they ignore the role of emotions in development. The cognitive theories are summarized in Table 2.6.

test yourself before going on   **Study** and **Review** in **MyPsychLab**

Answers to these questions can be found in the back of the book.

1. Piaget defined _____ as cognitive structures that provide a procedure to follow in a specific situation.

2. Match each term with its definition:
   _____ **(1)** assimilation
   _____ **(2)** accommodation
   _____ **(3)** equilibration
   - **(a)** changing a scheme in response to new information
   - **(b)** adapting schemes to the real world
   - **(c)** incorporating new information into an existing scheme

3. According to Vygotsky, a child's _____ includes tasks that the child cannot do alone but can accomplish with the help of an adult or older child.

4. Information-processing theorists (expand on/contradict) Piaget's ideas about cognitive development.

CRITICAL THINKING

5. What are the pros and cons of educating parents and teachers about Piaget's stages of cognitive development? That is, to what extent might parents and educators who learn about Piaget's stages overestimate or underestimate children's abilities?

TABLE 2.6 Cognitive Theories

Theory	Main Idea	Evaluation	
		Strengths	**Weaknesses**
Piaget's theory of cognitive development	Reasoning develops in four universal stages from birth through adolescence; in each stage, the child builds a different kind of scheme.	Helps explain how children of different ages think about and act on the world.	Stage concept may cause adults to underestimate children's reasoning abilities; there may be additional stages in adulthood.
Information-processing theory	The computer is used as a model for human cognitive functioning; encoding, storage, and retrieval processes change with age, causing changes in memory function; these changes happen because of both brain maturation and practice.	Helps explain how much information people of different ages can manage at one time and how they process it; provides a useful framework for studying individual differences in people of the same age.	Human information processing is much more complex than that of a computer; the theory doesn't provide an overall picture of development.
Vygotsky's sociocultural theory	Emphasizes linguistic and social factors in cognitive development.	Incorporates group learning processes into explanations of individual cognitive development.	Insufficient evidence to support most ideas.

Piaget's Clever Research

Piaget devised several creative strategies for testing children's cognitive development. Probably the most famous of all Piaget's clever techniques is his method for studying *conservation*, the understanding that matter does not change in quantity when its appearance changes. One of Piaget's best known problems is illustrated in Figure 2.1 on pg. 34. Piaget began by showing the child two containers with equal amounts of liquid. Next, he poured the contents of one of them into a new container of a different shape to determine whether children understood that the quantity of liquid remained the same regardless of its appearance. In a similar problem, Piaget began with two balls of clay of equal size; he showed them to a child and let the child hold and manipulate them until she agreed that they had the same amount of clay. Then in full view of

the child, Piaget rolled one of the balls into a sausage shape. Then he asked the child whether there was still the same amount of clay in the sausage and the ball or whether one had more. Children of 4 and 5 consistently said that the ball contained more clay; children of 6 and 7 consistently said that the shapes still had the same amount. Thus, the older children understood that the quantity of clay was conserved even though its appearance changed.

In conversations with children about the problems he devised, Piaget was always trying to understand how the child thought rather than trying to see whether the child could come up with the right answer. So he used an investigative method in which he asked probing follow-up questions such as "How did you figure that out?" to discover the child's logic. In the early

days of Piaget's work, many American researchers were critical of this method, since Piaget did not ask precisely the same questions of each child. Still, the results were so striking, and so surprising, that they couldn't be ignored. And when stricter research techniques were devised, more often than not, the investigators confirmed Piaget's observations.

CRITICAL ANALYSIS

1. *To what extent were Piaget's methods influenced by children's language skills?*

2. *How might older children's more highly developed capacity for reflecting on and explaining their thought processes have influenced Piaget's inferences about younger children's capacity for logical thinking?*

Biological and Ecological Theories

Theories that propose links between physiological processes and development represent one of the most important trends among developmentalists in the 21st century (Parke, 2004). Some of these theories focus on individual differences, while others deal with universal aspects of development. Moreover, all of them, to varying degrees, address the manner in which environmental factors interact with physiological processes.

Behavior Genetics

LO 2.12   How do behavior geneticists explain individual differences?

Behavior genetics focuses on the effect of heredity on individual differences. Traits or behaviors are believed to be influenced by genes when those of related people, such as children and their parents, are more similar than those of unrelated people. Behavior geneticists have shown that heredity affects a broad range of traits and behaviors, including intelligence, shyness, and aggressiveness.

Furthermore, the contributions of heredity to individual differences are evident throughout the lifespan. For example, researchers in the Netherlands have been studying a number of variables in identical and fraternal twins for several decades (Netherlands Twin Register, 2013). As you'll learn in Chapter 3, identical twins are particularly important in genetic research because they have exactly the same genes. As you can see in Figure 2.3, the Dutch researchers have found that IQ scores of identical twins are more strongly correlated than those of fraternal (nonidentical) twins from early childhood until middle age. Interestingly, too, such findings show that the environment affects IQ scores as well but that its effects may be transient. This conclusion is suggested by the fact that the IQ scores of fraternal twins are more strongly correlated in childhood, when they are living together, than in adulthood, when they do not share the same environment.

Behavior geneticists also study how individuals' genetic makeup influences the environments in which they are developing, a phenomenon that could occur via either or both of two routes. First, the child inherits his genes from his parents, who also create the environment in which he is growing up. So a child's genetic heritage may predict something about his environment. For example, parents who themselves have higher IQ scores are not only likely to

behavior genetics the study of the role of heredity in individual differences

pass their "good IQ" genes on to their children, they are also likely to create a richer, more stimulating environment for those children.

Second, each child's unique pattern of inherited qualities affects the way she behaves with other people, which in turn affects the way adults and other children respond to her. A cranky or temperamentally difficult baby may receive fewer smiles and more scolding than a placid, even-tempered one; a genetically brighter child may demand more personal attention, ask more questions, or seek out more complex toys than would a less bright child (Saudino & Plomin, 1997). Furthermore, children's interpretations of their experiences are affected by all their inherited tendencies, including not only intelligence but also temperament or pathology (Plomin, Reiss, Hetherington, & Howe, 1994).

Ethology and Sociobiology

LO 2.13 What kinds of behaviors are of interest to ethologists and sociobiologists?

The relationship between individuals and the settings in which they develop is the emphasis of *ecological theories*—perspectives that view development as resulting from the degree to which genes help or hinder individuals' efforts to adapt to their environments. One such theory, known as **ethology**, focuses on the study of animals in their natural environments. Ethologists emphasize genetically determined survival behaviors that are assumed to have evolved through natural selection. For example, nests are necessary for the survival of young birds. Therefore, ethologists say, evolution has equipped birds with nest-building genes.

Likewise, the young of many species are vulnerable to predators. Consequently, their genes direct them to form a relationship with a more mature member of the species very early in life. One such relationship results from a process called *imprinting*, in which newborns of some species learn to recognize the characteristics of a protective organism within the first hours of life. Ethologist Konrad Lorenz (1903–1989) studied imprinting among animals extensively (Lorenz, 1935). He learned that young ducklings and geese, for example, imprint on any moving object to which they are exposed during the critical period for imprinting (24 to 48 hours after hatching). In fact, one of the best-known images in the field of ethology is that of Lorenz himself being followed by several goslings who had imprinted on him.

Similarly, ethologists believe that emotional relationships are necessary to the survival of human infants (Bowlby, 1969, 1980). They claim that evolution has produced genes that cause humans to form these relationships. For example, most people feel irritated when they hear a newborn crying. Ethologists say the baby is genetically programmed to cry in a certain way, and adults are genetically programmed to get irritated when they hear it. The caretaker responds to a crying baby's needs in order to remove the irritating stimulus of the noise. As the caretaker and infant interact, an emotional bond is created between them. Thus, genes for crying in an irritating manner increase infants' chances of survival.

Sociobiology is the study of society using the methods and concepts of biological science. When applied to human development, sociobiology emphasizes genes that aid group survival. Sociobiologists claim individual humans have the best chance for survival when they live in groups. Therefore, they claim, evolution has provided humans with genetic programming that helps us cooperate.

To support their views, sociobiologists look for social rules and behaviors that exist in all cultures. For example, every society has laws against murder. Sociobiologists believe that humans are genetically programmed to create rules based on respect for other people's lives. Evolution has selected these genes, they claim, because people need to respect each other's lives and to be able to cooperate.

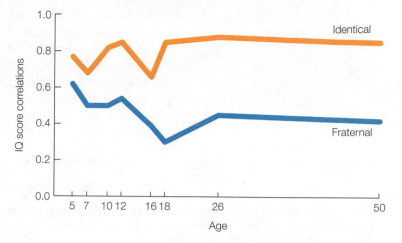

Figure 2.3 IQs of Fraternal and Identical Twins

This figure illustrates the combined findings of several longitudinal and cross-sectional studies of Dutch twins (Posthuma, de Geus, & Boomsma, 2003). You will notice that in childhood, when fraternal twins share the same environment, their IQ scores are more strongly correlated than in adulthood, when they presumably no longer live together. By contrast, the IQ scores of identical twins are even more strongly correlated in adulthood than during the childhood years. This pattern suggests conclusions about both heredity and environment. Specifically, at least with regard to IQ scores, the influence of heredity appears to increase with age, while that of the environment declines.

ethology a perspective on development that emphasizes genetically determined survival behaviors presumed to have evolved through natural selection

sociobiology the study of society using the methods and concepts of biology; when used by developmentalists, an approach that emphasizes genes that aid group survival

Lorenz found that once a gaggle of newly hatched geese had imprinted on him, they followed him wherever he went.

Critics of ethology and sociobiology claim that these theories underestimate the impact of the environment. Moreover, these theories are difficult to test. How, for example, can researchers test ethological theorists' claim that infant–caregiver attachment is universal because it has survival value? Finally, critics say that these theories ignore the fact that societies invent ways of enhancing whatever behaviors might be influenced by universal genetic programming. For instance, as sociobiologists hypothesize, genes may be involved in the universal prohibition of murder, but societies invent strategies for preventing it. Moreover, these strategies differ across societies and in their effectiveness.

Bronfenbrenner's Bioecological Theory

LO 2.14   What is the main idea of Bronfenbrenner's bioecological theory?

bioecological theory   Bronfenbrenner's theory that explains development in terms of relationships between individuals and their environments, or interconnected contexts

Another approach gaining interest in developmental psychology is that of Urie Bronfenbrenner (1917–2005). Bronfenbrenner's **bioecological theory** explains development in terms of relationships between people and their environments, or *contexts*, as Bronfenbrenner calls them (Bronfenbrenner, 1979, 1993). Bronfenbrenner attempted to classify all the individual and contextual variables that affect development and to specify how they interact.

According to Bronfenbrenner, the contexts of development are like circles within circles (see Figure 2.4). The outermost circle, the *macrosystem* (the cultural context), contains the values and beliefs of the culture in which a child is growing up. For example, a society's beliefs about the importance of education exist in the cultural context.

The next level, the *exosystem* (the socioeconomic context), includes the institutions of the culture that affect children's development indirectly. For example, funding for education exists in the socioeconomic context. The citizens of a specific nation may strongly believe that all children should be educated (cultural context), but their ability to provide universal education may be limited by the country's wealth (socioeconomic context).

The *microsystem* (the immediate context) includes those variables to which people are exposed directly, such as their families, schools, religious institutions, and neighborhoods. The *mesosystem* is made up of the interconnections between these components. For example, the specific school a child attends and her own family are part of the microsystem. Her parents' involvement in her school and the response of the school to their involvement are part of the mesosystem. Thus, the culture a child is born into may strongly value quality education. Moreover, her nation's economy may provide ample funds for schooling. However, her own education will be more strongly affected by the particular school she attends and the connections—or lack thereof—between her school and her family. Thus, the child's immediate context may be either consistent with the cultural and socioeconomic contexts or at odds with them.

Finally, the child's genetic makeup and developmental stage—her *biological context*—also influence her development. For example, a student who hasn't mastered the skill of reading isn't likely to benefit from an enriched literature program. Thus, her culture, the socioeconomic situation, the school she attends, and her own family may all be geared toward providing a quality education. However, her ability to benefit from it will be determined by the degree to which her education fits her individual needs.

Bronfenbrenner's bioecological theory provides a way of thinking about development that captures the complexity of individual and contextual variables. To date, its greatest contribution to developmental psychology has been its emphasis on the need for research examining interactions among these variables (Lerner, Lewin-Bizan, & Warren, 2011).

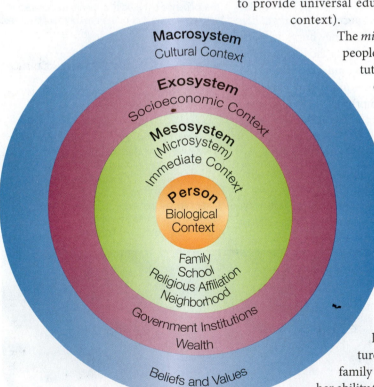

Figure 2.4 Bronfenbrenner's Contexts of Development

Bronfenbrenner's ecological theory proposes that people are exposed to interconnected contexts that interact in complex ways to influence development.

Bronfenbrenner's bioecological theory has helped researchers better understand how families moderate the effects of potentially damaging experiences, such as living in a refugee camp (like the Mayukwayukwa Camp feeding center for malnourished children in Zambia), on children's development.

test yourself before going on ☑ Study and Review in MyPsychLab

Answers to these questions can be found in the back of the book.

1. Match each theoretical approach to its emphasis:

   _____ (1) behavior genetics

   _____ (2) ethology

   _____ (3) sociobiology

       (a) genetic traits that aid group survival

       (b) relative effects of heredity and environment on individual differences

       (c) genetic traits that aid individual survival

2. According to Bronfenbrenner, the values of the culture in which a child is growing up are part of the _____, cultural institutions are part of the _____, and a child's parents are part of the _____.

CRITICAL THINKING

3. Like the learning theories you read about earlier in the chapter, behavior genetics, ethology, sociobiology, and bioecological theories consider the role of the environment in development to varying degrees. But what are some of the important differences between learning theories and the perspectives that are described in this section?

Comparing Theories

After learning about theories, students usually want to know which one is right. However, developmentalists don't think of theories in terms of right or wrong but instead compare theories on the basis of their assumptions and how useful they are in promoting understanding of development. Today's developmentalists often don't adhere to a single theory but take an approach that taps the strengths of each of the major theoretical perspectives.

Assumptions about Development

LO 2.15 What assumptions do the three families of theories make about development?

When we say that a theory assumes something about development, we mean that it holds some general perspective to be true. We can think of a theory's assumptions in terms of its answers to three questions about development.

One question addresses the *active or passive* issue: *Is a person active in shaping his own development, or is he a passive recipient of environmental influences?* Theories that claim a person's actions on the environment are the most important determinants of development are on the active side. Cognitive theories, for example, typically view development this way. In contrast, theories on the passive side, such as those of Pavlov and Skinner, maintain that development results from the environment acting on the individual.

As you learned in Chapter 1, the *nature versus nurture* question—*How do nature and nurture interact to produce development?*—is one of the most important in developmental psychology. All developmental theories, while admitting that both nature and nurture are involved in development, make assumptions about their relative importance. Theories claiming that biology contributes more to development than does environment are on the nature side of the question. Those that view environmental influences as most important are on the nurture side. Other theories assume that nature and nurture are equally important, and that it is impossible to say which contributes more to development.

You may also recall from Chapter 1 that the *continuity versus discontinuity* issue is a source of debate among developmentalists. Here, the question is *Does development happen continuously or in stages?* Theories that do not refer to stages assert that development is a stable, continuous process. Stage theories, on the other hand, emphasize change more than stability. They claim that development happens in leaps from lower to higher steps.

For the three major families of theories you have read about in this chapter, Table 2.7 lists the assumptions each individual theory makes regarding these issues. Because each theory is based on different assumptions, each implies a different approach to studying development. Consequently, research derived from each theory tells us something different about development. Moreover, a theory's assumptions shape the way it is applied in the real world.

For example, a teacher who approached instruction from the cognitive perspective would create a classroom in which children could experiment to some degree on their own. He would also recognize that children differ in ability, interests, developmental level, and other internal characteristics. He would believe that structuring the educational environment is important, but would assume that what each student ultimately learns will be determined by his own actions on the environment.

Alternatively, a teacher who adopted the learning perspective would guide and reinforce children's learning very carefully. Such a teacher would place little importance on ability differences among children. Instead, she would try to accomplish the same instructional goals for all children through proper manipulation of the environment.

TABLE 2.7 How Theories Answer Three Questions about Development

Theories	Active or Passive?	Nature or Nurture?	Stability or Change?
Psychoanalytic Theories			
Psychosexual theory	Passive	Nature	Change (stages)
Psychosocial theory	Passive	Both	Change
Learning Theories			
Classical conditioning	Passive	Nurture	Stability (no stages)
Operant conditioning	Passive	Nurture	Stability
Social-learning theory	Active	Nurture	Stability
Cognitive Theories			
Cognitive-developmental theory	Active	Both	Change
Sociocultural theory	Active	Both	Change
Information-processing theory	Active	Both	Both

Usefulness

LO 2.16 On what criteria do developmentalists compare the usefulness of theories?

Developmentalists also compare theories with respect to their usefulness. You should be aware that there is a fair amount of disagreement among psychologists on exactly how useful each theory is. Nevertheless, there are a few general criteria most psychologists use to evaluate the usefulness of a theory.

One approach is to assess a theory's ability to generate predictions that can be tested using scientific methods. For example, as you learned earlier in this chapter, one criticism of Freud's theory is that many of his claims are difficult to test. In contrast, when Piaget claimed that most children can solve concrete operational problems by age 7, he made an assertion that is easily tested. Thus, Piaget's theory is viewed by many developmentalists as more useful in this sense than Freud's. Vygotsky, learning theorists, and information-processing theorists also proposed many testable ideas. By contrast, according to some developmental psychologists, current biological and ecological theories are weak because they are difficult to test (Thomas, 2005).

Another criterion by which to judge the usefulness of a theory is its *heuristic* value—the degree to which it stimulates thinking and research. In terms of heuristic value, Freud's and Piaget's theories earn equally high marks. Both are responsible for an enormous amount of theorizing and research on human development, often by psychologists who strongly disagree with them. In fact, all of the theories in this chapter are important heuristically.

Yet another way of evaluating a theory's usefulness is in terms of practical value. In other words, a theory may be deemed useful if it provides solutions to problems. Based on this criterion, the learning and information-processing theories seem to stand out because they provide tools that can be used to influence behavior. A person who suffers from anxiety attacks, for example, can learn to use biofeedback, a technique derived from conditioning theories, to manage anxiety. Similarly, a student who needs to learn to study more effectively can get help from study skills courses based on information-processing research.

Ultimately, of course, no matter how many testable hypotheses or practical techniques a theory produces, it has little or no usefulness to developmentalists if it doesn't explain the basic facts of development. Based on this criterion, learning theories, especially classical and operant conditioning, are regarded by many developmentalists as somewhat less useful than other perspectives (Thomas, 2005). Although they explain how specific behaviors may be learned, they cannot account for the complexity of human development, which can't be reduced to connections between stimuli and responses or between behaviors and reinforcers.

As you can see, the point of comparing theories is not to conclude which one is true. Instead, such comparisons help to reveal the unique contribution each can make to a comprehensive understanding of human development.

Eclecticism

LO 2.17 What is eclecticism?

Today's developmental scientists try to avoid the kind of rigid adherence to a single theoretical perspective that was characteristic of theorists such as Freud, Piaget, and Skinner. Instead, they emphasize **eclecticism**, the use of multiple theoretical perspectives to explain and study human development (Parke, 2004). The interdisciplinary nature of the study of human development you read about in Chapter 1 is reflected in this trend as well.

To better understand the eclectic approach, think about how ideas drawn from several sources might help us better understand a child's disruptive behavior in school. Observations of the child's behavior and her classmates' reactions may suggest that her behavior is being rewarded by the other children's responses (a behavioral explanation). Deeper probing of the child's family situation may indicate that her acting-out behavior may be an emotional reaction to a family event such as divorce (a psychoanalytic explanation).

The interdisciplinary nature of today's developmental science also contributes to eclecticism. For instance, an anthropologist might suggest that the rapid-fire communication media found in almost every home nowadays (e.g., television) require children to develop attention

eclecticism the use of multiple theoretical perspectives to explain and study human development

strategies that differ from those that are appropriate for classroom environments. As a result, children today exhibit more disruptive behavior in school than children in past generations because of the mismatch between the kinds of information delivery to which they are accustomed and those which are found in school.

By adopting an eclectic approach, developmentalists can devise more comprehensive theories from which to derive questions and hypotheses for further research. In other words, their theories and studies may more closely match the behavior of real people in real situations.

test yourself before going on  ☑ **Study** and **Review** in **MyPsychLab**

Answers to these questions can be found in the back of the book.

1. Write "A" by each theory that views individuals as active in their own development and "P" by each that views individuals as passive.

_____ (1) psychosexual
_____ (2) operant conditioning
_____ (3) information processing
_____ (4) social-learning
_____ (5) cognitive-developmental
_____ (6) sociocultural
_____ (7) classical conditioning
_____ (8) psychosocial

2. A theory that fails to generate testable hypotheses or practical applications but stimulates debate and research has _____ value.

3. What is the main advantage of an eclectic approach to explaining age-related changes?

CRITICAL THINKING

4. Which of the many theories in this chapter do you find to be most useful to your own efforts to understand development? What are the theory's assumptions, and how do they compare to the criteria for usefulness? Finally, what other theories could be used along with them to broaden your understanding of development?

SUMMARY

Psychoanalytic Theories (pp. 24–28)

LO 2.1 What are the main ideas of Freud's psychosexual theory?

- Freud emphasized that behavior is governed by both conscious and unconscious motives and that the personality develops in steps: The id is present at birth; the ego and the superego develop in childhood. Freud proposed psychosexual stages: the oral, anal, phallic, latency, and genital stages.

LO 2.2 What is the conflict associated with each of Erikson's psychosocial stages?

- Erikson proposed that personality develops in eight psychosocial stages over the course of the lifespan: trust versus mistrust; autonomy versus shame and doubt; initiative versus guilt; industry versus inferiority; identity versus role confusion; intimacy versus isolation; generativity versus stagnation; and integrity versus despair.

LO 2.3 What are the strengths and weaknesses of psychoanalytic theory?

- Psychoanalytic concepts, such as the unconscious and identity, have contributed to psychologists' understanding of development. However, these theories propose many ideas that are difficult to test.

Learning Theories (pp. 29–33)

LO 2.4 How did Watson condition Little Albert to fear white, furry objects?

- Classical conditioning—learning through association of stimuli—helps explain the acquisition of emotional responses. Watson used these principles to condition a fear of white rats in an infant called "Little Albert," who generalized his fear to other white, furry objects.

LO 2.5 How does operant conditioning occur?

- Operant conditioning involves learning to repeat or stop behaviors because of their consequences. However, consequences often affect behavior in complex ways in the real world.

LO 2.6 In what ways does social-cognitive theory differ from other learning theories?

- Bandura's social-cognitive theory places more emphasis on mental elements than other learning theories do and assumes a more active role for the individual.

LO 2.7 How do the learning theories explain development?

- Learning theories provide useful explanations of how behaviors are acquired but fall short of a truly comprehensive picture of human development.

Cognitive Theories (pp. 33–38)

LO 2.8 How does cognitive development progress, according to Piaget?

- Piaget focused on the development of logical thinking. He discovered that such thinking develops across four childhood and adolescent stages: the sensorimotor, preoperational, concrete operational, and formal operational stages. He proposed that movement from one stage to another is the result of changes in mental frameworks called *schemes*.

LO 2.9 How did Vygotsky use the concepts of scaffolding and the zone of proximal development to explain cognitive development?

- Vygotsky's sociocultural theory has become important to developmentalists' attempts to explain how culture affects development.

LO 2.10 How does information-processing theory explain the findings of developmental psychologists such as Piaget and Vygotsky?

- Information-processing theory uses the computer as a model to explain intellectual processes such as memory and problem solving. It suggests that there are both age differences and individual differences in the efficiency with which humans use their information-processing systems.

LO 2.11 What are some of the important contributions of the cognitive theories?

- Research has confirmed the sequence of skill development Piaget proposed but suggests that young children are more capable of logical thinking than he believed. Information-processing theory has been important in explaining Piaget's findings and memory processes.

Biological and Ecological Theories (pp. 28–41)

LO 2.12 How do behavior geneticists explain individual differences?

- Behavior geneticists study the influence of heredity on individual differences and the ways in which individuals' genes influence their environments.

LO 2.13 What kinds of behaviors are of interest to ethologists and sociobiologists?

- Ethologists study genetically determined traits and behaviors that help animals adapt to their environments. Sociobiologists emphasize the genetic basis of behaviors that promote the development and maintenance of social organizations in both animals and humans.

LO 2.14 What is the main idea of Bronfenbrenner's bioecological theory?

- Bronfenbrenner's bioecological theory has helped developmental psychologists categorize environmental factors and think about the ways in which they influence individuals.

Comparing Theories (pp. 41–44)

LO 2.15 What assumptions do the three families of theories make about development?

- Theories vary in how they answer three basic questions about development: Are individuals active or passive in their own development? How do nature and nurture interact to produce development? Does development happen continuously or in stages?

LO 2.16 On what criteria do developmentalists compare the usefulness of theories?

- Useful theories allow psychologists to devise hypotheses to test their validity, are heuristically valuable, provide practical solutions to problems, and explain the facts of development.

LO 2.17 What is eclecticism?

- Developmentalists who take an eclectic approach use theories derived from all the major families, as well as those of many disciplines, to explain and study human development.

KEY TERMS

accommodation (p. 34)

assimilation (p. 34)

behavior genetics (p. 38)

behaviorism (p. 29)

bioecological theory (p. 40)

classical conditioning (p. 29)

cognitive theories (p. 33)

eclecticism (p. 43)

ego (p. 24)

equilibration (p. 34)

ethology (p. 39)

extinction (p. 31)

id (p. 24)

information-processing theory (p. 35)

learning theories (p. 29)

neo-Piagetian theory (p. 36)

observational learning, *or* modeling (p. 31)

operant conditioning (p. 30)

psychoanalytic theories (p. 24)

psychosexual stages (p. 25)

psychosocial stages (p. 26)

punishment (p. 30)

reinforcement (p. 30)

scheme (p. 34)

sociobiology (p. 39)

sociocultural theory (p. 35)

superego (p. 24)

CHAPTER TEST ✔ **Study** and **Review** in **MyPsychLab**

Answers to all the Chapter Test questions can be found in the back of the book.

1. Erikson's dilemma of *trust versus mistrust* is associated with which of these age ranges?
   a. 2–3 years
   b. birth to 1 year
   c. 30–60 years
   d. 18–30 years

2. Which of the following is *not* a goal of developmental theories?
   a. to explain age-related changes
   b. to predict age-related changes
   c. to control age-related changes
   d. to describe age-related changes

3. According to Erikson, which factor is generally considered to be an essential aspect of a school-age child's psychosocial development?
   a. learning to control bodily sensations or developing shame if unsuccessful
   b. being treated lovingly and predictably by caregivers and learning to trust
   c. acquiring skills that are deemed important by the child's culture
   d. becoming purposeful, goal oriented, and assertive, which leads to conflicts with parents

4. During which of Piaget's stages does the child learn to reason logically about hypothetical situations?
   a. sensorimotor
   b. preoperational
   c. concrete operations
   d. formal operations

5. Information is actively processed in the _____ _____ component of the information-processing system.
   a. sensory memory
   b. short-term memory
   c. episodic memory
   d. semantic memory

6. Neo-Piagetians' explanations of cognitive development employ concepts from Piaget's theory of cognitive development and _____.
   a. Bandura's learning theory
   b. Vygotsky's sociocultural theory
   c. Erikson's theory of psychosocial development
   d. information-processing theory

7. Which of the following is true of Vygotsky's sociocultural theory?
   a. It has less empirical support than Freud's theory of psychosexual development.
   b. It has more empirical support than information-processing theory.
   c. There is insufficient evidence to either support or contradict most of the theory.
   d. It has more empirical support than Piaget's theory.

8. Both Freud's psychoanalytic theory and Skinner's operant conditioning theory _____.
   a. claim that we are passive recipients of environmental influences
   b. are cognitive theories
   c. assert that nurture has a larger impact on development than nurture does
   d. suggest that we are active in shaping our own development

9. Seven-year-old Bethany saw some money on the kitchen table. She really wanted to take it so she could buy some candy, but her conscience kept her from doing so. According to Freud, which components part of Bethany's personality interacted to tempt her to take the money?
   a. ego and superego
   b. id and ego
   c. superego and id
   d. none of the above

10. Which of the following best defines Erikson's concept of *ego integrity*?
    a. the need to believe that one's life has been worthwhile
    b. the need to resolve a midlife crisis
    c. a sense of needing to make up for one's shortcomings
    d. a sense of wanting to give back to society and future generations

11. Which of the following features of Piaget's theory of cognitive development has been strongly supported by research?
    a. the ages at which children transition from one stage to the next
    b. the sequence of cognitive development
    c. the contribution of unconscious processes to cognitive development
    d. the role of modeling in cognitive development

12. Which theorist developed a model of the interactive contexts in which children develop?
    a. Bronfenbrenner
    b. Lorenz
    c. Vygotsky
    d. Bandura

13. The idea that certain human behaviors have developed and persisted in order to ensure survival of the species is drawn from which of the following?
    a. ethology
    b. classical conditioning
    c. nativism
    d. behaviorism

14. Which of the following statements is true regarding operant conditioning theory?
    a. Our own choices and behaviors are the primary contributors to our development; biology plays only a small role.
    b. Our environment provides us with consequences for our actions, and those consequences determine our future behavior.
    c. Developmental stages unfold according to a biological sequence.
    d. Development results primarily from social interactions.

15. Which of the following theorists proposed a theory of observational learning?
    a. B. F. Skinner
    b. Albert Bandura
    c. Erik Erikson
    d. Ivan Pavlov

16. When first presented with a drinking cup, 8-month-old Lucy attempted to suck the liquid out. Which of Piaget's concepts explains Lucy's behavior?
    a. assimilation
    b. accommodation
    c. cognition
    d. equilibration

17. Erikson is to psychosocial as Freud is to _____.
    a. psychological
    b. psychosexual
    c. psychoanalytic
    d. psychomotor

18. Based on his research, Piaget concluded that the capacity for logical thinking _____.
    a. is an inborn characteristic of humans that is fully developed by age 6
    b. exists only in adults
    c. develops in four stages
    d. varies widely from one individual to another

19. Alicia was bitten by a dog at age 4. Even though she is now an adult, Alicia still starts to sweat and her heart begins to race every time she sees a dog. According to classical conditioning, Alicia's physical response to dogs is a(n) _____.
    a. conditioned response
    b. contextual response
    c. assimilative response
    d. psychosocial response

20. Four-year-old Mark eagerly bit into a lemon wedge. In response to the lemon's sour taste, he said, "Yuck!" Mark never bit into another lemon wedge. Skinner would say that the lemon's taste functioned as a _____ for Mark's lemon-eating behavior.
    a. reflex
    b. reinforcement
    c. context
    d. punishment

21. Which of the following reinforcement schedules produces behaviors which are difficult to extinguish?
    a. interval
    b. fixed
    c. partial
    d. continuous

22. Which of the following is true of research examining children's memories?
    a. Vygotsky's concept of the zone of proximal development is applicable only to the memory of infants.
    b. Piaget overestimated the memory abilities of younger children.
    c. Younger children's short-term memories are more limited in capacity than those of older children.
    d. Older children's sensory memories are more fully developed than those of younger children.

23. According to Bandura, which of the following terms best describes the expectancies we acquire about what we can and cannot do?
    a. self-evidence
    b. self-monitoring
    c. self-efficacy
    d. self-evaluation

24. "Social interactions are the most important contributors to a child's cognitive development." Which of the following theorists would most likely have supported this statement?
    a. Piaget
    b. Bronfenbrenner
    c. Vygotsky
    d. Freud

25. According to the principles of Piaget's theory of cognitive development, _____ shape our responses to new information.
    a. schemes
    b. reinforcements
    c. emotions
    d. genes

To 👁 **Watch** ✳ **Explore** ◉ **Simulate** ✅ **Study** and **Review** and experience **MyVirtualLife** go to MyPsychLab.com

chapter 3

Prenatal Development and Birth

Today, news of an impending birth is cause for celebration, but it hasn't always been that way. In years past, high rates of maternal and infant mortality caused people in most cultures to delay celebrations and even the naming of the child until long after her birth. Thankfully, most mothers and babies survive and flourish these days, and, as a result, pregnancies and births are seen as important decision points in both parents' and children's lives. "What should I eat?" the mother-to-be wonders. Family and

LEARNING OBJECTIVES

CONCEPTION AND GENETICS

3.1 What are the characteristics of the zygote?

3.2 In what ways do genes influence development?

GENETIC AND CHROMOSOMAL DISORDERS

3.3 What are the effects of the major dominant, recessive, and sex-linked diseases?

3.4 How do trisomies and other disorders of the autosomes and sex chromosomes affect development?

PREGNANCY AND PRENATAL DEVELOPMENT

3.5 What are the characteristics of each trimester of pregnancy?

3.6 What happens in each stage of prenatal development?

3.7 How do male and female fetuses differ?

3.8 What behaviors have scientists observed in fetuses?

PROBLEMS IN PRENATAL DEVELOPMENT

3.9 How do teratogens affect prenatal development?

3.10 What are the potential adverse effects of tobacco, alcohol, and other drugs on prenatal development?

3.11 What risks are associated with teratogenic maternal diseases?

3.12 What other maternal factors influence prenatal development?

3.13 How do physicians assess and manage fetal health?

BIRTH AND THE NEONATE

3.14 What kinds of birth choices are available to expectant parents?

3.15 What happens in each of the three stages of labor?

3.16 What do physicians learn about a newborn from the Apgar and Brazelton scales?

3.17 Which infants are categorized as low birth weight, and what risks are associated with this status?

friends ask her, "What do you think about midwives?" and "Will the baby be born in a birthing center or a hospital?" and "Are you planning a medication-free delivery?" (No doubt you will encounter such questions when you plan the birth of your "child" in *MyVirtualLife*.) It helps to know what long-term consequences the child may experience as a result of the prenatal and birth choices that her parents make.

The technological advances that have reduced maternal and fetal mortality rates have transformed the subjective and social experience of pregnancy from one of fear and dread to one of joy and anticipation. These advances have also been accompanied by innovations that have allowed researchers and parents-to-be to gain insight into prenatal developmental processes that were shrouded in mystery just a few decades ago. As you explore this chapter, you will become acquainted with some of these insights and, we hope, gain a greater appreciation for the amazing process of prenatal development.

MyVirtualLife

What decisions would you make while raising a child? What would the consequences of those decisions be?

Find out by accessing MyVirtualLife at www.MyPsychLab.com to raise a virtual child and live your own virtual life.

Conception and Genetics

The first step in the development of an individual human being happens at conception, when each of us receives a combination of genes that will shape our experiences throughout the rest of our lives.

The Process of Conception

LO 3.1   What are the characteristics of the zygote?

Ordinarily, a woman produces one *ovum* (egg cell) per month from one of her two ovaries, roughly midway between menstrual periods. If the ovum is not fertilized, it travels from the ovary down the *fallopian tube* toward the *uterus*, where it gradually disintegrates and is expelled as part of the menstrual fluid. However, if a couple has intercourse during the crucial few days when the ovum is in the fallopian tube, one of the millions of sperm ejaculated as part of each male orgasm may travel the full distance through the woman's vagina, cervix, uterus, and fallopian tube and penetrate the wall of the ovum.

CHROMOSOMES, DNA, AND GENES As you probably know, every cell in the human body contains 23 pairs of **chromosomes**, or strings of genetic material. However, sperm and ovum, collectively called **gametes**, contain 23 single (unpaired) chromosomes. At conception, chromosomes in the ovum and the sperm combine to form 23 pairs in an entirely new cell called a **zygote**.

Chromosomes are composed of molecules of **deoxyribonucleic acid (DNA)**. Each chromosome can be further subdivided into segments, called **genes**, each of which influences a particular feature or developmental pattern. A gene controlling some specific characteristic always appears in the same place (the *locus*) on the same chromosome in every individual of the same species. For example, the locus of the gene that determines whether a person's blood is type A, B, or O is on chromosome 9.

DETERMINATION OF SEX Twenty-two pairs of chromosomes, called *autosomes*, contain most of the genetic information for the new individual. The twenty-third pair, the *sex chromosomes*, determines the sex. One of the two sex chromosomes, the *X chromosome*, is one of the largest chromosomes in the body and carries a large number of genes. The other, the *Y chromosome*, is quite small and contains only a few genes. Zygotes containing two X chromosomes develop into females, and those containing one X and one Y chromosome develop into males. Since the cells in a woman's body contain only X chromosomes, all her ova carry X chromosomes. Half of a

chromosomes strings of genetic material in the nuclei of cells

gametes cells that unite at conception (ova in females; sperm in males)

zygote a single cell created when sperm and ovum unite

deoxyribonucleic acid (DNA) chemical material that makes up chromosomes and genes

genes pieces of genetic material that control or influence traits

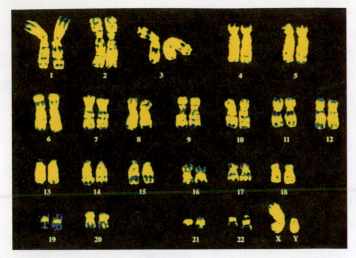

Each cell in the human body has 23 pairs of chromosomes in its nucleus. The 23 single chromosomes in a female gamete, or egg, combine with the 23 single chromosomes in a male gamete, or sperm, to create a new, genetically unique array of 23 pairs of chromosomes that contain all of the instructions that are needed to guide the development of a human being from conception forward and which will influence him or her throughout life.

gonads sex glands (ovaries in females; testes in males)

man's sperm contain X chromosomes; the other half contain Y chromosomes. Consequently, the sex of the new individual is determined by the sex chromosome in the sperm. ⊙ **Watch** the **Video** *Prenatal Development: A Preference for Sons* in **MyPsychLab**.

How do chromosomal differences become physical differences between males and females? Sometime between 4 and 8 weeks following conception, the *SRY* gene on the Y chromosome signals the male embryo's body to begin secreting hormones called *androgens*. These hormones cause male genitals to develop. If androgens are not present, female genitals develop no matter what the embryo's chromosomal status is. Likewise, female embryos that are exposed to androgens, either via medications that the mother is taking or a genetic disorder called *congenital adrenal hyperplasia*, can develop male-appearing external genitalia. Development of the **gonads**—testes in males and ovaries in females—also depends upon the presence or absence of androgens. Prenatal androgens also influence the developing brain and may play a role in the development of sex differences in cognitive functioning and in the development of sexual orientation (Lippa, 2005). (We will explore these topics in greater detail in later chapters.)

MULTIPLE BIRTHS In most cases, human infants are conceived and born one at a time. However, in about 4 out of every 100 births, more than one baby is born, usually twins. Two-thirds of twins are *fraternal twins*, or twins that come from two sets of ova and sperm. Such twins, also called *dizygotic twins* (meaning that they originate from two zygotes), are no more alike genetically than any other pair of siblings, and need not even be of the same sex.

The remaining one-third of twins are *identical twins* (*monozygotic*, or arising from one zygote). Identical twins result when a single zygote, for unknown reasons, separates into two parts, each of which develops into a separate individual. Because identical twins develop from the same zygote, they have identical genes. Research involving identical twins is one of the major investigative strategies in the field of behavior genetics (see *Research Report*).

Over the past 30 to 40 years, the annual number of multiple births has increased about 76% in the United States (Martin et al., 2012). One reason for the increase is that more women over 35 are giving birth for the first time. Two factors underlie the association between multiple births and maternal age (Reynolds, Schieve, Martin, Jeng, & Macaluso, 2003). First, for reasons that researchers don't yet understand, women are far more likely to naturally conceive twins and other multiples after age 35. Second, women over 35 are more likely than younger women to experience difficulty becoming pregnant and, thus, are more likely to be treated with fertility-enhancing drugs. Women of all ages who use these drugs are more likely to deliver multiples than women who conceive naturally.

The X chromosomes are quite large and carry thousands of genes. In contrast, the Y chromosome is very small and carries little genetic information. The mismatch between the genetic material on the X and Y chromosomes leaves males more vulnerable to some genetic disorders than females are. That's because if a female has a harmful gene on one of her X chromosomes, it is likely to be balanced by a corresponding gene on her other X chromosome that either blocks or minimizes the effects of the harmful gene.

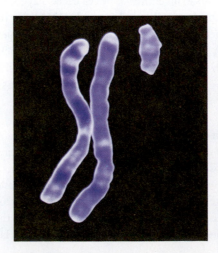

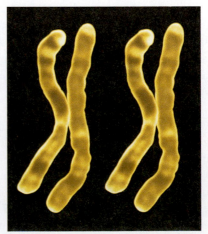

Twins in Genetic Research

Researchers interested in the role of heredity in human development have been comparing identical and fraternal twins since the earliest days of developmental psychology. The logic is this: If identical twins (whose genes are exactly the same) who are raised apart are more similar than fraternal twins or non-twin siblings (whose genes are similar but not identical) who are raised together, heredity must be important in the trait being studied. For example, intelligence test scores are more strongly correlated in identical twins than in fraternal twins or non-twin siblings, even when the identical twins are raised in different families (Bouchard & McGue, 1981). Such findings are taken to be evidence for the heritability of intelligence. Developmentalists have also studied emotional characteristics in identical and fraternal twins. Identical twins, whether raised together or apart, have been found to be more similar than fraternal twins on measures of emotionality, activity, and sociability (Bergeman et al., 1993).

Taken together, the findings of these studies point to strong genetic components in both intelligence and emotional characteristics. However, what these studies reveal about environment may be even more significant. If psychological characteristics such as intelligence, emotionality, activity, and sociability were determined solely by heredity, identical twins would be *exactly* alike, and researchers would find correlations of +1.00. The correlations that twins researchers have found are less than +1.00, even for identical twins who grow up in the same home.

To see the point more clearly, think about blood type. An individual's blood type *is* determined by the genes. Thus, identical twins always have the same blood type; that is, there is a correlation of 1.00, a perfect correlation, between the blood types of identical twins. Identical-twin studies offer strong evidence that psychological traits, though clearly influenced by heredity, are not determined by the genes to the same extent as physical traits such as blood type.

CRITICAL ANALYSIS

1. *Fraternal twins are no more genetically similar than non-twin siblings, yet the IQs of fraternal twins are more strongly correlated than those of non-twin brothers and sisters. What explanations can you think of to explain this difference?*

2. *The term environment is extremely broad. What are some of the individual variables that comprise an individual's environment?*

How Genes Influence Development

LO 3.2   In what ways do genes influence development?

At conception, the genes from the father contained in the sperm and those from the mother in the ovum combine to create a unique genetic blueprint—the **genotype**—that characterizes the new individual. The **phenotype** is the individual's whole set of actual characteristics. For example, you can easily see that a woman has brown eyes, which are part of her phenotype. Her genotype, though, can't be so easily determined. In many cases, you have to know her parents' and offsprings' eye color to find out whether she carries genes for another eye color, because complex rules govern the way genotypes influence phenotypes.

DOMINANT AND RECESSIVE GENES The simplest genetic rule is the **dominant–recessive pattern**, in which a single dominant gene strongly influences phenotype. (Table 3.1 lists

genotype the unique genetic blueprint of each individual

phenotype an individual's particular set of observed characteristics

dominant–recessive pattern a pattern of inheritance in which a single dominant gene influences a person's phenotype but two recessive genes are necessary to produce an associated trait

TABLE 3.1 Genetic Sources of Normal Traits

Dominant Genes	Recessive Genes	Polygenic (Many Genes)
Freckles	Flat feet	Height
Coarse hair	Thin lips	Body type
Dimples	Rh-negative blood	Eye color
Curly hair	Fine hair	Skin color
Nearsightedness	Red hair	Personality
Broad lips	Blond hair	
Rh-positive blood	Type O blood	
Types A and B blood		
Dark hair		

(*Source:* Tortora & Grabowski, 1993.)

several normal phenotypical traits and indicates whether they arise from dominant or recessive genes.) People whose chromosomes carry either two dominant or two recessive genes are referred to as *homozygous*. Those with one dominant and one recessive gene are said to be *heterozygous*.

If a child receives a single dominant gene for a trait from one parent, the child's phenotype will include the trait determined by that gene. In contrast, a child's phenotype will include a recessive trait only if she inherits a recessive gene from both parents. For example, geneticists have found that the curliness of hair is controlled by a single pair of genes (see Figure 3.1). The gene for curly hair is dominant; therefore, if a man has curly hair, his genotype includes at least one gene for curly hair, and half of his sperm carry this gene. Conversely, straight hair is recessive, so a straight-haired man's genotype must include two straight-hair genes for his phenotype to include straight hair. Geneticists also know that the only kind of hair type a straight-haired father can pass on to his children is straight hair because all his sperm carry recessive, straight-hair genes. ✳ **Explore** the **Concept** *Dominant and Recessive Traits* in **MyPsychLab**.

In addition, human geneticists have learned that both dominant and recessive genes differ in *expressivity*, meaning that the degree to which any gene influences phenotypes varies from person to person. For example, all individuals who have the gene for curly hair don't have equally curly hair. So, even when a child receives a dominant gene for curly hair from her father, the amount and type of curl in her hair probably won't be exactly the same as his.

Blood type is also determined by a dominant–recessive pattern of inheritance. Because a person must have two recessive genes to have type O blood, the genotype of every person who has this type is clear. However, the genotype of people with type A or B blood is not obvious because types A and B are dominant. Thus, when a person's phenotype includes either type A or type B blood, one of her blood-type genes must be for that type, but the other could be for some other type. However, if a type A father and a type B mother produce a child with type O, each of them carries a gene for type O, because the child must receive one such gene from each parent to have the type O phenotype.

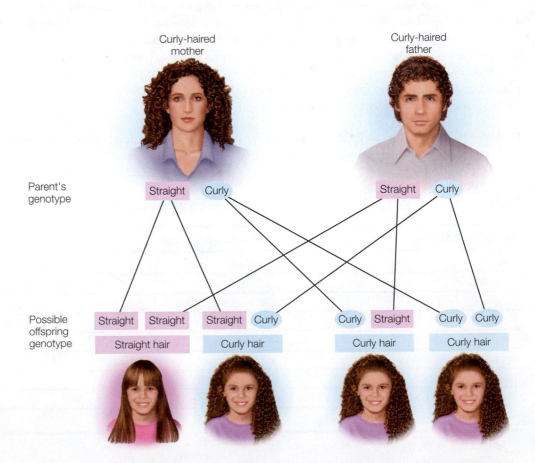

Figure 3.1 **The Genetics of Hair Type**

Examples of how the genes for curly and straight hair pass from parents to children.

POLYGENIC INHERITANCE With **polygenic inheritance**, many genes influence the phenotype. There are many polygenic traits in which the dominant–recessive pattern is also at work. For example, geneticists believe that children get several genes for skin color from each parent (Barsh, 2003). Dark skin is dominant over light skin, but the skin colors also blend together. Thus, when one parent is dark skinned and the other is fair skinned, the child will have skin that is somewhere between the two. The dark-skinned parent's dominant genes will ensure that the child will be darker than the fair parent, but the fair-skinned parent's genes will prevent the child from having skin as dark as that of the dark-skinned parent.

Eye color is another polygenic trait with a dominant–recessive pattern (Liu et al., 2010). Scientists don't know for sure how many genes influence eye color. They do know, however, that these genes don't cause specific colors. Instead, they cause the colored part of the eye to be dark or light. Dark colors (black, brown, hazel, and green) are dominant over light colors (blue and gray). However, blended colors are also possible. People whose chromosomes carry a combination of genes for green, blue, and gray eyes can have blue-gray, green-blue, or blue-green eyes. Likewise, genes that cause different shades of brown can combine their effects to make children's eye-color phenotypes different from those of their brown-eyed parents.

OTHER TYPES OF INHERITANCE Recent technological advances have enabled geneticists to study the impact of *genomic imprinting* on development. A genomic imprint is a chemical label that identifies each gene in a person's body as having come from his father or mother. Scientists don't yet fully understand the process of genomic imprinting and how it affects development. It could be that genomic imprints "turn on" an atypical developmental process or "turn off" a normal one. Alternatively, the imprints may evoke responses in other genes or tissues in the developing individual's body that set the process of atypical development in motion. Some studies suggest that age-related deterioration of genomic imprints may be particularly important in diseases that appear later in life, including several kinds of cancer, Type II diabetes, and heart disease (Jirtle & Weidman, 2007; Ribarska, Klaus-Marius, Koch, & Schulz, 2012).

Studies involving genetic material that is found in the mitochondria, rather than the nucleus, of a woman's eggs have gained importance in recent years as well. In *mitochondrial inheritance*, children inherit genes that are carried in structures called *mitochondria*, which are found in the fluid that surrounds the nucleus of the ovum before it is fertilized. Consequently, mitochondrial genes are passed only from mother to child. Geneticists have learned that several serious disorders, including some types of blindness, are transmitted in this way (Levy & Marion, 2011).

MULTIFACTORIAL INHERITANCE Many physical traits are influenced by both genes and environment, a pattern known as **multifactorial inheritance**. Height is one example. Many genes contribute to a child's height and rate of growth. However, if he is ill, poorly nourished, or emotionally neglected, a child may be smaller than others his age even though he carries genes that should result in his being taller than his peers. Thus, when a child is shorter than 97% of his agemates, doctors try to determine whether he is short because of his genes or because something is causing him to grow poorly (Jospe, 2011; Tanner, 1990).

As discussed in Chapter 1 and in *Research Report* on page 9, psychological traits such as intelligence and personality are influenced by both heredity and environment. Thus, they result from multifactorial inheritance. Similarly, many *neurodevelopmental disorders*, a group of conditions in which individuals' neurological development follows an atypical pattern, result from multifactorial inheritance (Zeidán-Chuliá et al., 2013). Neurodevelopmental disorders include conditions such as *attention-deficit/hyperactivity disorder* (American Psychiatric Association, 2013). (You will read more about this disorder in Chapter 9.)

polygenic inheritance a pattern of inheritance in which many genes influence a trait

multifactorial inheritance inheritance affected by both genes and the environment

Answers to these questions can be found in the back of the book.

1. Match each term with its definition.

_____ (1) chromosomes
_____ (2) heterozygous
_____ (3) zygote
_____ (4) phenotype
_____ (5) gametes
_____ (6) genes
_____ (7) dizygotic
_____ (8) homozygous
_____ (9) mitochondria
_____ (10) genotype

(a) cells that unite at conception
(b) strings of genetic material
(c) pieces of genetic material that control or influence traits
(d) describes twins that develop from two fertilized ova
(e) individuals whose chromosomes carry either two dominant or two recessive genes for a given trait
(f) DNA-bearing structures outside the nucleus of the ovum
(g) an individual's particular set of observed characteristics
(h) an entirely new cell formed when sperm and ovum unite to form 23 pairs of chromosomes
(i) individuals whose chromosomes carry one dominant and one recessive gene for a given trait
(j) the unique genetic blueprint of each individual

2. Define and give examples of each pattern of inheritance

Inheritance	Description
Dominant–recessive	
Polygenic	
Multifactorial	

CRITICAL THINKING

3. In what ways have genetic and environmental influences interacted to influence your development?

Genetic and Chromosomal Disorders

Did you know that the chances that a pregnancy will end with the birth of a healthy baby are about 97%? Of the 3% of births in which the health of a newborn is impaired or seriously threatened, about 30% are the result of harmful genes or errors in the process of early development that have altered a child's chromosomal makeup (CDC, 2005).

Genetic Disorders

LO 3.3 What are the effects of the major dominant, recessive, and sex-linked disorders?

Many disorders appear to be transmitted through the operation of dominant and recessive genes (see Table 3.2). *Autosomal disorders* are caused by genes located on the autosomes (chromosomes other than sex chromosomes). The genes that cause *sex-linked* disorders are found on the X chromosome.

AUTOSOMAL DISORDERS Most disorders caused by recessive genes are diagnosed in infancy or early childhood. For example, a recessive gene causes a baby to have problems digesting the amino acid phenylalanine. Toxins build up in the baby's brain and cause intellectual disability. This condition, called *phenylketonuria (PKU)*, is found in about 1 in every 12,000 to 17,000 babies (Levy & Marion, 2011). If a baby consumes no foods containing phenylalanine, however, he will not develop intellectual disability. PKU babies can't have milk and some other foods, so early diagnosis is critical. For this reason, most states require all babies to be tested for PKU soon after birth.

Like many other recessive disorders, PKU is associated with ethnicity. Caucasian babies are more likely to have the disorder than infants in other groups. Similarly, West African and African American infants are more likely to have *sickle-cell disease*, a recessive disorder that causes red blood cell deformities (Raj & Bertolone, 2010). In sickle-cell disease, the blood can't carry enough oxygen to keep the body's tissues healthy. However, with early diagnosis and antibiotic treatment, more than 90% of children diagnosed with the disease survive to adulthood (Maakaron, 2013).

Almost one-half of West Africans have either sickle-cell disease or *sickle-cell trait* (Levy & Marion, 2011). Persons with sickle-cell trait carry a single recessive gene for sickle-cell disease, which causes a few of their red blood cells to be abnormal. Thus, doctors can identify carriers of the sickle-cell gene by testing their blood for sickle-cell trait. Once potential parents know they carry the gene, they can make informed decisions about future childbearing. In the United States, about 1 in 500 African Americans has sickle-cell disease, and 1 in 12 has sickle-cell trait (Maakaron, 2013). The disease and trait also occur more frequently in individuals of Mediterranean, Caribbean, Indian, Arab, and Latin American ancestry than in those of European ancestry (Maakaron, 2013).

About 1 in every 3,000 babies born to Jewish couples of Eastern European ancestry has another recessive disorder, *Tay-Sachs disease*. By the time she is 1 to 2 years old, a Tay-Sachs baby is likely to have severe intellectual disability and be blind. Very few survive past the age of 3 (Ierardi-Curto, 2013).

Many disorders caused by dominant genes, such as *Huntington's disease*, are usually not diagnosed until adolescence or adulthood (Levy & Marion, 2011). This disorder causes the brain to deteriorate and affects both psychological and motor functions. Until recently, children of those with Huntington's disease had to wait until they became ill themselves to know for sure that they carried the gene. There is now a blood test to identify the Huntington's gene. Thus, people who have a parent with this disease can now make informed decisions about their own childbearing, as well as prepare themselves to live with a serious disorder when they get older.

SEX-LINKED DISORDERS   Most sex-linked disorders are caused by recessive genes (see Figure 3.2). One fairly common sex-linked recessive disorder is *red-green color blindness*. People with this disorder have difficulty distinguishing between the colors red and green when these colors are adjacent. About 1 in 800 men and 1 in 400 women have this disorder. Most learn ways of compensating for the disorder and thus live perfectly normal lives.

A more serious sex-linked recessive disorder is *hemophilia*. The blood of people with hemophilia lacks the chemical components that cause blood to clot. Thus, when a person with hemophilia bleeds, the bleeding doesn't stop naturally. Approximately 1 in 5,000 baby boys is born with this disorder, which is almost unknown in girls (Zaiden, 2013).

About 1 in every 4,000 males and 1 in every 8,000 females have a sex-linked disorder called *fragile-X syndrome* (Jewell, 2009). A person with this disorder has an X chromosome with a "fragile," or damaged, spot. Fragile-X syndrome can cause intellectual disability that becomes progressively worse as a child gets older (Jewell, 2009).

TABLE 3.2   Some Genetic Disorders

Autosomal Dominant Disorders	Autosomal Recessive Disorders	Sex-Linked Recessive Disorders
Huntington's disease	Phenylketonuria	Hemophilia
High blood pressure	Sickle-cell disease	Fragile-X syndrome
Extra fingers	Cystic fibrosis	Red-green color blindness
Migraine headaches	Tay-Sachs disease	Missing front teeth
Schizophrenia	Kidney cysts in infants	Night blindness
	Albinism	Some types of muscular dystrophy
		Some types of diabetes

(*Sources:* Amato, 1998; Tortora & Grabowski, 1993.)

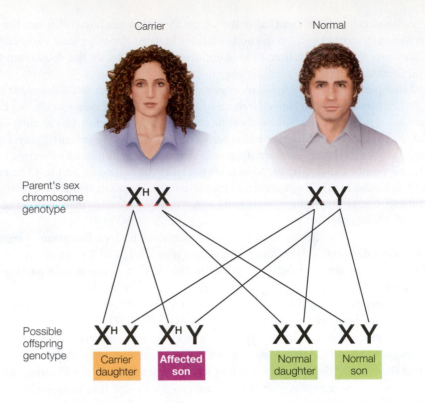

Figure 3.2 Sex-Linked Inheritance

Compare this pattern of sex-linked transmission of a recessive disease (hemophilia) with the pattern shown in Figure 3.1.

Carrier

Normal

Parent's sex chromosome genotype

X^H X

X Y

Possible offspring genotype

X^H X

Carrier daughter

X^H Y

Affected son

X X

Normal daughter

X Y

Normal son

Chromosomal Errors

LO 3.4 How do trisomies and other disorders of the autosomes and sex chromosomes affect development?

A variety of problems can occur when a child has too many or too few chromosomes, a condition referred to as a *chromosomal error*, or *chromosomal anomaly*. Like genetic disorders, these errors are distinguished by whether they involve autosomes or sex chromosomes.

TRISOMIES A *trisomy* is a condition in which a child has three copies of a specific autosome. The most common is *trisomy 21*, or *Down syndrome*, in which the child has three copies of chromosome 21. Roughly 1 in every 800–1,000 infants is born with this abnormality (Chen, 2010). These children have intellectual disability, distinctive facial features, undersized brains, and are at high risk for other physical abnormalities such as heart defects (Chen, 2010).

This child shows the distinctive facial features of a child with Down syndrome.

The risk of bearing a child with trisomy 21 is greatest for mothers over 35. Among women aged 35–39, the incidence of Down syndrome is about 1 in 385 births. Among those over 45, it is as high as 1 in 30 births (Chen, 2010).

Scientists have identified children with trisomies in the 13th and 18th pairs of chromosomes as well (Best & Gregg, 2009; Chen, 2009). These disorders have more severe effects than trisomy 21. Few trisomy 13 or trisomy 18 children live past the age of 1 year (Levy & Marion, 2011). As with trisomy 21, the chances of having a child with one of these disorders increase with a woman's age.

SEX-CHROMOSOME ANOMALIES A second class of anomalies is associated with the sex chromosomes. The most common is an XXY pattern, called *Klinefelter's syndrome*, which occurs in 1 out of every 500 males (Levy & Marion, 2011). Affected boys usually look no different than their peers but have underdeveloped testes and, as adults, very low sperm production. Many have language and learning disabilities. At puberty, these boys experience both male and female changes. For example, their penises enlarge, and their breasts develop.

A single-X pattern (XO), called *Turner's syndrome*, may also occur. Individuals with Turner's syndrome are anatomically female but show stunted growth. They are also at higher risk than others of having malformations of internal organs such as the heart and kidneys (Levy & Marion, 2011). Without hormone therapy, most individuals with Turner's syndrome do not menstruate or develop breasts at puberty. Nevertheless, about 10% experience normal puberty and have little or no difficulty conceiving children and carrying them to term (Levy & Marion, 2011). Many others can achieve successful pregnancies with the aid of donor ova.

test yourself before going on ✓ Study and Review in MyPsychLab

Answers to these questions can be found in the back of the book.

1. Most autosomal recessive disorders are diagnosed in (childhood/adulthood), while most autosomal dominant disorders are diagnosed in (childhood/adulthood).

2. Red-green color blindness is a(n) _____ disorder that is (more, less) common in males than in females.

CRITICAL THINKING

3. In your view, what are the advantages and disadvantages of genetic counseling for couples who want to have a child but are concerned about genetic or chromosomal disorder that runs in one or both of their families?

Pregnancy and Prenatal Development

Pregnancy is a physical condition in which a woman's body is nurturing a developing embryo or fetus. *Prenatal development*, or *gestation*, is the process that transforms a zygote into a newborn. Thus, the process that ends with the birth of a baby involves two sets of experiences: those of the pregnant woman, and those of the developing zygote, embryo, and fetus.

The Mother's Experience

LO 3.5   What are the characteristics of each trimester of pregnancy?

Pregnancy is customarily divided into trimesters—three periods of 3 months each (see Table 3.3).

FIRST TRIMESTER   Pregnancy begins when the zygote implants itself in the lining of the woman's uterus (also called the *womb*). The zygote then sends out chemical messages that cause the woman's menstrual periods to stop. Some of these chemicals are excreted in her urine, making it possible to diagnose pregnancy within a few days after conception. Other chemicals cause physical changes, such as breast enlargement. **Watch** the **Video** *Period of the Zygote* in **MyPsychLab**.

The *cervix* (the narrow, lower portion of the uterus, which extends into the vagina) thickens and secretes mucus that serves as a barrier to protect the developing embryo from harmful organisms that might enter the womb through the vagina. The uterus begins to shift position and put pressure on the woman's bladder, causing her to urinate more often. This and other symptoms, like fatigue and breast tenderness, may interfere with sleep. Another common early symptom of pregnancy is *morning sickness*—feelings of nausea, often accompanied by vomiting, that usually occur in the morning.

Prenatal care during the first trimester is critical to prevent birth defects, because all of the baby's organs form during the first 8 weeks. Early prenatal care can identify maternal conditions, such as sexually transmitted diseases, that may threaten prenatal development. Doctors and nurses can also urge women to abstain from using drugs and alcohol early in prenatal development, when such behavior changes may prevent birth defects. **Watch** the **Video** *Prenatal Development: Pregnancy and Prenatal Care* in **MyPsychLab**.

TABLE 3.3   Milestones of Pregnancy

Trimester	Events	Prenatal Care	Serious Problems
First trimester: From first day of last menstrual period (LMP) to 12 weeks	Missed period Breast enlargement Abdominal thickening	Confirmation of pregnancy Calculation of due date Blood and urine tests (and other tests, if needed) Monthly doctor visits to monitor vital functions, uterine growth, weight gain, sugar and protein in urine	Ectopic pregnancy Abnormal urine or blood tests Increased blood pressure Malnutrition Bleeding Miscarriage
Second trimester: From 12 weeks after LMP to 24 weeks after LMP	Weight gain "Showing" Fetal movements felt Increased appetite	Monthly doctor visits continue Ultrasound to measure fetal growth and locate placenta	Gestational diabetes Excessive weight gain Increased blood pressure Rh incompatibility of mother and fetus Miscarriage 13 to 20 weeks Premature labor 21 weeks
Third trimester: From 25 weeks after LMP to beginning of labor	Weight gain Breast discharge	Weekly visits beginning at 32nd week Ultrasound to assess position of fetus Treatment of Rh incompatibility if needed Pelvic exams to check for cervical dilation	Increased blood pressure Bleeding Premature labor Bladder infection

(*Sources:* Hobbs & Ferth, 1993; Kliegman, 1998; Tortora & Grabowski, 1993.)

Early prenatal care can also be important to the pregnant woman's health. For example, a small number of zygotes implant in one of the fallopian tubes instead of in the uterus, a condition called *ectopic pregnancy*. Early surgical removal of the zygote is critical to the woman's future ability to have children.

About 15% of pregnancies end in miscarriage, or *spontaneous abortion*. From the woman's point of view, an early miscarriage is similar to a menstrual period, although feelings of discomfort and blood loss are usually greater. Medical care is always necessary after a miscarriage because the woman's body may fail to completely expel the embryo.

SECOND TRIMESTER During the second trimester of pregnancy, from the end of week 12 through week 24, morning sickness usually disappears, resulting in increases in appetite. The pregnant woman gains weight, and the uterus expands to accommodate a fetus that is growing rapidly. Consequently, the woman begins to "show" sometime during the second trimester. She also begins to feel the fetus's movements, usually at some point between the 16th and 18th weeks.

At monthly clinic visits, doctors monitor both the mother's and the baby's vital functions and keep track of the growth of the baby in the womb. Ultrasound tests are usually performed, and the sex of the baby can be determined by the 12th week. Monthly urine tests check for *gestational diabetes*, a kind of diabetes that happens only during pregnancy. Women who have any kind of diabetes, including gestational diabetes, have to be carefully monitored during the second trimester because their babies may grow too rapidly, leading to premature labor or a baby that is too large for vaginal delivery. The risk of miscarriage drops in the second trimester. However, a few fetuses die between the 13th and 20th weeks of pregnancy.

THIRD TRIMESTER At 25 weeks, the pregnant woman enters her third trimester. Weight gain and abdominal enlargement are the main experiences of this period. In addition, the woman's breasts may begin to secrete a substance called *colostrum* in preparation for nursing.

Most women begin to feel more emotionally connected to the fetus during the third trimester (DiPietro, 2010). Individual differences in fetal behavior, such as hiccuping or thumb-sucking, sometimes become obvious during the last weeks of pregnancy. These behaviors may be observed during ultrasound tests that produce increasingly clear images of the fetus. In addition, most women notice that the fetus has regular periods of activity and rest.

Monthly prenatal doctor visits continue in the third trimester until week 32, when most women begin visiting the doctor's office or clinic once a week. Monitoring of blood pressure is especially important, as some women develop a life-threatening condition called *toxemia of pregnancy* during the third trimester. This condition is signaled by a sudden increase in blood pressure and can cause a pregnant woman to have a stroke.

Prenatal Development

LO 3.6 What happens in each stage of prenatal development?

In contrast to the trimesters of pregnancy, the three stages of prenatal development are defined by specific developmental milestones and are not of equal length. Moreover, the entire process follows two developmental patterns, which you can see at work in the photographs in Table 3.4. With the **cephalocaudal pattern**, development proceeds from the head down. For example, the brain is formed before the reproductive organs. With the **proximodistal pattern**, development happens in an orderly way from the center of the body outward to the extremities. In other words, structures closer to the center of the body, such as the rib cage, develop before the fingers and toes.

THE GERMINAL STAGE The first 2 weeks of gestation, from conception to *implantation*, constitute the **germinal stage**. During this stage, cells specialize into those that will become the fetus's body and those that will become the structures needed to support its development. Cell division happens rapidly, and by the 4th day, the zygote contains dozens of cells.

On day 5, the cells become a hollow, fluid-filled ball called a *blastocyst*. Inside the blastocyst, cells that will eventually become the embryo begin to clump together. On day 6 or 7, the blastocyst comes into contact with the uterine wall, and by the 12th day, it is completely buried in the uterine tissue, a process called **implantation**. Some of the cells of the blastocyst's outer wall combine with cells of the uterine lining to begin creating the **placenta**, an organ that allows oxygen, nutrients, and other substances to be transferred between the mother's and baby's blood. The placenta's specialized structures bring the mother's and baby's blood close to each other without allowing them to mix.

Like the zygote, the placenta secretes chemical messages (hormones) that stop the mother's menstrual periods and keep the placenta connected to the uterus. Other placental hormones allow the bones of the woman's pelvis to become more flexible, induce breast changes, and increase the mother's metabolism rate. At the same time, the blastocyst's inner cells begin to specialize. One group of cells will become the **umbilical cord**, the organ that connects the embryo to the placenta. Vessels in the umbilical cord carry blood from the baby to the mother and back again. Other cells will form the *yolk sac*, a structure that produces blood cells until the embryo's blood-cell-producing organs are formed. Still others will become the **amnion**, a fluid-filled sac in which the baby floats until just before it is born. By the 12th day, the cells that will become the embryo's body are also formed.

THE EMBRYONIC STAGE The **embryonic stage** begins at implantation, approximately 2 weeks after conception, and continues until the end of week 8. By the time many women first suspect a pregnancy, usually 3 weeks after conception, the embryo's cells are starting to specialize and come together to form the foundations of all the body's organs. For example, the cells of the nervous system, the **neurons**, form a structure called the *neural tube*, from which the brain and spinal cord will develop. A primitive heart and the forerunners of the kidneys also develop during week 3, along with three sacs that will become the digestive system.

In week 4, the end of the embryo's neural tube swells to form the brain. Spots that will become the eyes appear on the embryo's head, and its heart begins to beat. The backbone and ribs become visible as bone and muscle cells move into place. The face starts to take shape, and the endocrine system begins to develop.

By week 5, the embryo is about 1/4 inch long, 10,000 times larger than the zygote. Its arms and legs are developing rapidly. Five fingers are visible on its hands. Its eyes have corneas and lenses, and its lungs are beginning to develop.

cephalocaudal pattern growth that proceeds from the head downward

proximodistal pattern growth that proceeds from the middle of the body outward

germinal stage the first stage of prenatal development, beginning at conception and ending at implantation (approximately 2 weeks)

implantation attachment of the blastocyst to the uterine wall

placenta a specialized organ that allows substances to be transferred from mother to embryo and from embryo to mother, without their blood mixing

umbilical cord an organ that connects the embryo to the placenta

amnion a fluid-filled sac in which the fetus floats until just before it is born

embryonic stage the second stage of prenatal development, from week 2 through week 8, during which the embryo's organ systems form

neurons specialized cells of the nervous system

TABLE 3.4   Milestones in Prenatal Development

Stage/Time Frame	Milestones
GERMINAL — Day 1: Conception  Sperm and egg	Sperm and ovum unite, forming a zygote containing genetic instructions for the development of a new and unique human being.
Days 10 to 14: Implantation 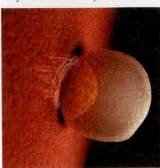 Zygote	The zygote burrows into the lining of the uterus. Specialized cells that will become the placenta, umbilical cord, and embryo are already formed.
EMBRYONIC — Weeks 3 to 8: Organogenesis 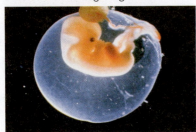 6-week embryo	All of the embryo's organ systems form during the 6-week period following implantation.
FETAL — Weeks 9 to 38: Growth and organ refinement	The fetus grows from 1 inch long and 1/4 ounce, to a length of about 20 inches and a weight of 7–9 pounds. By week 12, most fetuses can be identified as male or female. Changes in the brain and lungs make viability possible by week 24; optimum development requires an additional 14 to 16 weeks in the womb. Most neurons form by week 28, and connections among them begin to develop shortly thereafter. In the last 8 weeks, the fetus can hear and smell, is sensitive to touch, and responds to light. Learning is also possible.

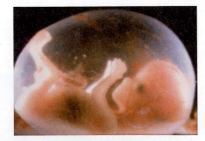
12-week fetus

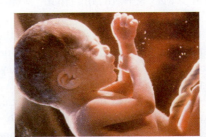
14-week fetus

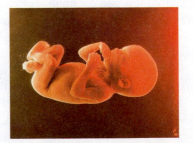
Well-developed fetus (age not given)

(*Sources*: Kliegman, 1998; Tortora & Grabowski, 1993.)

In week 6, the embryo's brain begins to produce patterns of electrical activity and it moves in response to stimuli. During week 7, embryos begin to move spontaneously (Joseph, 2000). They have visible skeletons and fully developed limbs. The bones are beginning to harden and the muscles are maturing; by this point, the embryo can maintain a semi-upright posture. The eyelids seal shut to protect the developing eyes. The ears are completely formed, and x-rays can detect tooth buds in the jawbones.

During the last week of the embryonic stage, week 8, the liver and spleen begin to function. These organs allow the embryo to make and filter its own blood cells. Its heart is well developed and efficiently pumps blood to every part of the body. The embryo's movements increase as the electrical activity in its brain becomes more organized. Connections between the brain and the rest of the body are also well established. The embryo's digestive and urinary systems are functioning. By the end of week 8, **organogenesis**—the technical term for organ development—is complete.

THE FETAL STAGE   The final phase is the **fetal stage**, which begins at the end of week 8 and continues until birth. The fetus grows from a weight of about 1/4 ounce and a length of 1 inch to a baby weighing about 7 pounds and having a length of about 20 inches, who is ready to be born. In addition, this stage involves refinements of the organ systems that are essential to life outside the womb (see Table 3.5). ⊙ **Watch** the **Video** *Fetal Development* in **MyPsychLab**.

A few babies born as early as week 20 or 21 survive. By the end of week 22, 20% to 33% of babies have attained **viability**, the ability to live outside the womb (Kyser, Morriss, Bell, Klein, & Dagle, 2012). Remaining in the womb just 1 week longer, until the end of week 23, increases a baby's chances of survival to 38% to 58%. By the end of week 24, 58% to 87% survive. The extra weeks probably allow time for lung function to become more efficient. In addition, most premature babies today are treated with drugs that accelerate lung development. As a result, survival rates of even the earliest-born preemies have greatly increased since the turn of the 21st century (Kyser et al., 2012).

THE FETAL BRAIN   As you learned earlier, the foundational structures of all of the body's organ systems are formed during the embryonic stage. Yet most of the formation and fine-tuning of the brain take place during the fetal stage. Recall that neurons, the specialized cells of the nervous system, begin developing during the embryonic stage in week 3. But the pace of neural formation picks up dramatically between the 10th and 18th weeks, a process known as *neuronal proliferation*.

Between the 13th and 21st weeks, the newly formed neurons migrate to the parts of the brain where they will reside for the rest of the individual's life (Johnson, 2011). While migrating, neurons consist only of **cell bodies**, the part of the cell that contains the nucleus

organogenesis the process of organ development

fetal stage the third stage of prenatal development, from week 9 to birth, during which growth and organ refinement take place

viability the ability of the fetus to survive outside the womb

cell body the part of a neuron that contains the nucleus and is the site of vital cell functions

TABLE 3.5   Milestones of the Fetal Stage

Period	What Develops
Weeks 9–12	Fingerprints; grasping reflex; facial expressions; swallowing and rhythmic "breathing" of amniotic fluid; urination; genitalia appear; alternating periods of physical activity and rest
Weeks 13–16	Hair follicles; responses to mother's voice and loud noises; 8–10 inches long; weighs 6 ounces
Weeks 17–20	Fetal movements felt by mother; heartbeat detectable with stethoscope; lanugo (hair) covers body; eyes respond to light introduced into the womb; eyebrows; fingernails; 12 inches long
Weeks 21–24	Vernix (oily substance) protects skin; lungs produce surfactant (vital to respiratory function); viability becomes possible, although most born now do not survive
Weeks 25–28	Recognition of mother's voice; regular periods of rest and activity; 14–15 inches long; weighs 2 pounds; good chance of survival if born now
Weeks 29–32	Very rapid growth; antibodies acquired from mother; fat deposited under skin; 16–17 inches long; weighs 4 pounds; excellent chance of survival if delivered now
Weeks 32–36	Movement to head-down position for birth; lungs mature; 18 inches long; weighs 5–6 pounds; virtually 100% chance of survival if delivered
Week 37	Full-term status; 19–21 inches long; weighs 6–9 pounds

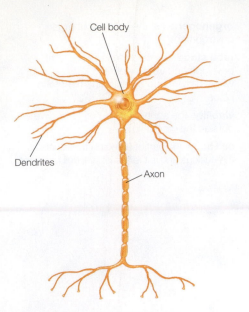

Figure 3.3 Parts of the Neuron

The structure of a single developed neuron. The cell bodies are the first to be developed, primarily between weeks 12 and 24. Axons and dendrites develop later, especially during the final 12 weeks, and continue to increase in size and complexity for several years after birth.

synapses tiny spaces across which neural impulses flow from one neuron to the next

axons taillike extensions of neurons

dendrites branchlike protrusions from the cell bodies of neurons

glial cells the "glue" that holds neurons together to give form to the structures of the nervous system

and in which all the cell's vital functions are carried out (see Figure 3.3). Once they have reached their final destinations in the fetal brain, the neurons begin to develop connections. These connections—tiny spaces between neurons across which neural impulses travel from one neuron to the next—are called **synapses**. Several changes in fetal behavior signal that the process of synapse formation is underway. For instance, the fetus exhibits alternating periods of activity and rest and begins to yawn (Walusinski, Kurjak, Andonotopo, & Azumendi, 2005; see Figure 3.4). When observed, these changes tell physicians that fetal brain development is proceeding normally.

Synapse formation requires the growth of two neuronal structures. **Axons** are taillike extensions that can grow to be several feet in length. **Dendrites** are tentaclelike branches that extend out from the cell body (see Figure 3.3). Dendrite development is thought to be highly sensitive to adverse environmental influences such as maternal malnutrition and defects in placental functioning (Dieni & Rees, 2003).

Simultaneously with neuronal migration, **glial cells** begin to develop. These cells are the "glue" that hold the neurons together to give shape to the brain's major structures. The brain now begins to assume a more mature appearance, which can be observed using *magnetic resonance imaging* (*MRI*) and other modern technologies that you will read more about later in the chapter (see Figure 3.5).

Sex Differences

LO 3.7 How do male and female fetuses differ?

Because prenatal development is strongly influenced by maturational codes that are the same for both males and females, there are only a few sex differences in prenatal development. One finding is that male fetuses are more responsive to touch, while female fetuses appear to be more responsive to sounds (Arabin, 2008; Groome et al., 1999). Interestingly, early studies suggested that male fetuses, on average, are more physically active than females (e.g., DiPietro, Hodgson, Costigan, & Johnson, 1996). However, more recent findings suggest that there are no sex differences in fetal activity levels (e.g., DiPietro et al., 2004). Thus more research is needed before developmentalists will know whether the sex differences in children's activity level you'll read about in later chapters begin in the womb.

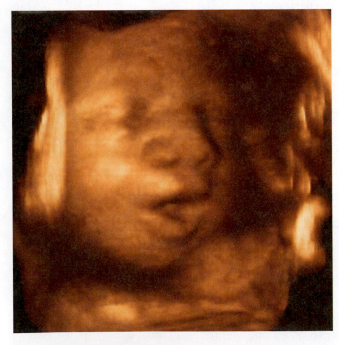

Figure 3.4 Fetal Yawning

Fetal yawning appears between the 10th and 15th week. Its presence signals the beginning of sleep stages in the fetal brain.

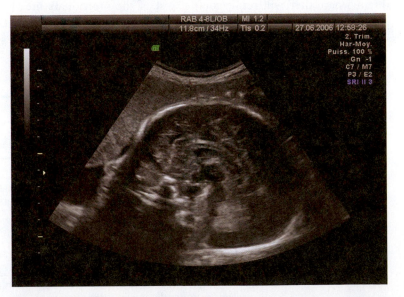

Figure 3.5 A Normal Third-Trimester Fetal Brain

Glial cells that develop during the last few months of prenatal development hold neurons together and give form and structure to the fetal brain.

(*Source:* Brown, Estroff, & Barnenott, 2004.)

Researchers have linked sex differences in prenatal hormones to cross-gender variations in spatial ability, verbal ability, physical aggression, and communication skills later in life (Auyeung, Lombardo, & Baron-Cohen, 2013; Cohen-Bendahan, van de Beek, & Berenbaum, 2004; Knickmeyer & Baron-Cohen, 2006). These hormonal differences may also contribute to sex differences in skeletal development (Tanner, 1990). Female infants are about 1–2 weeks ahead in bone development at birth, even though newborn boys are typically longer and heavier. Female superiority in skeletal development persists through childhood and early adolescence, allowing girls to acquire many coordinated movements and motor skills, especially those involving the hands and wrists, earlier than boys. The gap between the sexes gets wider every year until the mid-teens, when boys catch up and surpass girls in general physical coordination.

Boys are more vulnerable to all kinds of prenatal problems. Many more boys than girls are conceived—from 120 to 150 male embryos to every 100 female ones—but more of the males are spontaneously aborted. At birth, there are about 105 boys for every 100 girls. Male fetuses also appear to be more sensitive to variables such as marijuana and maternal stress, which may negatively affect prenatal development (Bethus, Lemaire, Lhomme, & Goodall, 2005; Wang, Dow-Edwards, Anderson, Minkoff, & Hurd, 2004).

Prenatal Behavior

LO 3.8   What behaviors have scientists observed in fetuses?

In recent years, techniques such as ultrasound imaging have provided researchers with a great deal of information about fetal behavior. Thus, in recent years, the number of research studies examining fetal behavior has increased significantly. These studies have revealed some rather remarkable findings, some of which are shown in Figure 3.6.

For one thing, researchers have discovered that the fetus can distinguish between familiar and novel stimuli by the 32nd or 33rd week (Sandman, Wadhwa, Hetrick, Porto, & Peeke, 1997). In one

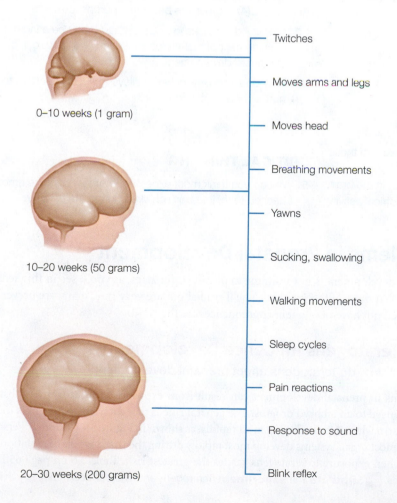

0–10 weeks (1 gram)

10–20 weeks (50 grams)

20–30 weeks (200 grams)

Twitches

Moves arms and legs

Moves head

Breathing movements

Yawns

Sucking, swallowing

Walking movements

Sleep cycles

Pain reactions

Response to sound

Blink reflex

Figure 3.6 Correlations between Fetal Behavior and Brain Development

Researchers have discovered numerous correlations between fetal brain development and behavior.

(*Source:* Walusinski, Kurjak, Andonotopo, & Azumendi, 2005.)

study, pregnant women recited a short children's rhyme out loud each day from week 33 through week 37. In week 38, researchers played a recording of either the rhyme the mother had been reciting or a different rhyme and measured the fetal heart rate. Fetal heart rates dropped during the familiar rhyme but not during the unfamiliar rhyme, suggesting that the fetuses had learned the sound patterns of the rhyme recited by their mothers (DeCasper, Lecaneut, Busnel, Granier-DeFerre, & Maugeais, 1994).

Evidence for fetal learning also comes from studies in which newborns appear to remember stimuli to which they were exposed prenatally. In a classic study of prenatal learning, pregnant women read Dr. Seuss's classic children's story *The Cat in the Hat* out loud each day for the final 6 weeks of their pregnancies. After the infants were born, they were allowed to suck on special pacifiers that turned a variety of sounds off and on. Each kind of sound required a special type of sucking. Researchers found that the babies quickly adapted their sucking patterns in order to listen to the familiar story, but did not increase their sucking in order to listen to an unfamiliar story (DeCasper & Spence, 1986). In other words, babies preferred the sound of the story they had heard *in utero* (in the womb).

Stable individual differences in behavior are also identifiable in fetuses. For example, studies have shown that very active fetuses tend to become infants who are very active (DiPietro, Ghera, & Costigan, 2008). Moreover, these children are more likely to be labeled "hyperactive" by parents and teachers. In contrast, fetuses that are less active than average are more likely to become children who have intellectual disability (Accardo et al., 1997).

test yourself before going on ☑ **Study** and **Review** in **MyPsychLab**

Answers to these questions can be found in the back of the book.

1. Label each item on the list as characteristic of the (A) first, (B) second, or (C) third trimester of pregnancy.
   _____(1) ectopic pregnancy
   _____(2) weekly doctor visits
   _____(3) fetal movement felt
   _____(4) breast enlargement
   _____(5) premature labor
   _____(6) ultrasound to locate placenta

2. In which stage (germinal, embryonic, or fetal) does each of these milestones of prenatal brain development occur?
   _____(1) migration of neurons to lifelong positions in the brain
   _____(2) brain begins to produce patterns of electrical activity
   _____(3) neural tube swells to form the brain
   _____(4) synapses between neurons form

3. Prenatal differences in _____ _____ may be a factor in the development of male/female differences in physical, cognitive, and social development.

4. Why do some researchers believe that it is important to establish norms for prenatal behavior?

CRITICAL THINKING

5. Why do you think most expectant mothers become emotionally attached to their unborn children during the third trimester?

Problems in Prenatal Development

Prenatal development is not immune to outside influences, as you'll see in this section. Keep in mind that most of the problems you'll read about are very rare, many are preventable, and many need not have permanent consequences for the child.

How Teratogens Influence Development

LO 3.9 How do teratogens affect prenatal development?

Deviations in prenatal development can result from exposure to **teratogens**—substances that cause damage to an embryo or fetus. The general rule is that each organ system is most vulnerable to harm when it is developing most rapidly, as shown in Figure 3.7 (Moore & Persaud, 1993). Because most organ systems develop most rapidly during the first 8 weeks of gestation, this is the period when exposure to teratogens carries the greatest risk. Table 3.6 on page 65 lists several teratogens. ◉ **Simulate** the **Experiment** *Teratogens and Their Effects* in **MyPsychLab**.

teratogens substances, such as viruses and drugs, that can cause birth defects

As Figure 3.7 suggests, there are *critical periods* in both the embryonic and fetal stages when certain body systems are especially sensitive to teratogens. If drugs or infections interfere with development during a critical period, a particular body structure will not form properly. For example, researchers found that Japanese people whose mothers were pregnant with them when the atomic bombs were dropped on Hiroshima and Nagasaki at the end of World War II in 1945 varied greatly in how they responded to the environmental hazard posed by the bombs' radioactive fallout (Schull & Otake, 1997). Many of those who were in the 8th to 15th week, during the period of rapid neuronal formation and the beginning of neuronal migration, were born with irreversible intellectual disability. Those who were exposed between the 16th and 25th week did not have higher-than-expected rates of intellectual disability, but they did exhibit higher levels of seizure disorders than individuals who were further along in prenatal development at the time of the bombings. Fetuses that were beyond the 25th week in gestational age did not show any degree of elevation in the rates of intellectual disability or seizure disorders.

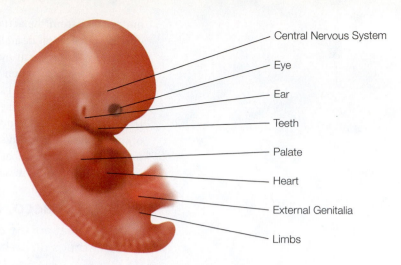

Figure 3.7 **The Timing of Teratogen Exposure**

Teratogens have the most impact on these body systems during the embryonic and early fetal phases of prenatal development. (3–15 weeks)

Despite the trends that were found among Hiroshima and Nagasaki survivors, remarkably, many individuals who experienced prenatal exposure to radiation, even during the critical periods, were born without defects of any kind. Such cases demonstrate that many factors contribute to the effects that a particular teratogen has on prenatal development. Two such factors are the duration and intensity of teratogen exposure. A single, brief exposure to even the most powerful teratogen may have little or no impact on development. However, if a single exposure is particularly intense—that is, if the "dose" of the teratogen is high—then it may be sufficient to cause damage. Among the Japanese atomic bomb survivors, the farther a person's

TABLE 3.6 Some Important Teratogens and Their Effects

Teratogen	Possible Effects on Fetus
Maternal Diseases	
Cancer	Fetal or placental tumor
Toxoplasmosis	Brain swelling, spinal abnormalities
Chicken pox	Scars, eye damage
Parvovirus	Anemia
Hepatitis B	Hepatitis
Chlamydia	Conjunctivitis, pneumonia
Tuberculosis	Pneumonia or tuberculosis
Drugs	
Inhalants	Problems similar to those of fetal alcohol spectrum disorder; premature labor
Accutane/vitamin A	Facial, ear, heart deformities
Streptomycin	Deafness
Penicillin	Skin disorders
Tetracycline	Tooth deformities
Diet pills	Low birth weight

(*Sources:* Amato, 1998; Kliegman, 1998.)

mother was from the actual impact sites of the two bombs, the less likely he or she was to develop intellectual disability or a seizure disorder. However, exposures of low intensity may be harmful if they occur over an extended period. For this reason, special precautions must be taken by pregnant women who are likely to be exposed to even minimal doses of radiation or other potentially harmful substances that are a part of their everyday working environments.

Finally, researchers have hypothesized that fetuses vary widely in their susceptibility to teratogens. These differences are thought to arise from genes that moderate or block the effects of some kinds of harmful substances. For instance, studies involving various strains of laboratory mice have shown that some strains are completely immune to teratogens that cause serious facial deformities in others (Syska, Schmidt, & Schubert, 2004).

Drugs, Tobacco, and Alcohol

LO 3.10   What are the potential adverse effects of tobacco, alcohol, and other drugs on prenatal development?

Any drug, including many whose safety we take for granted (e.g., antibiotics), can be teratogenic. That is why doctors always ask women of childbearing age whether they might be pregnant before prescribing medication for them. Unless a drug is absolutely necessary to a woman's health, doctors recommend avoiding drugs of any kind during pregnancy. However, sorting out the effects of drugs (prescription and nonprescription, legal and illegal) on prenatal development has proven to be an immensely challenging task, because many pregnant women take multiple drugs. Other factors, such as maternal stress, lack of social support, or poverty and poor prenatal care, also often accompany illegal drug use and alcohol consumption during pregnancy (Eaton et al., 2013; Johnson, Nusbaum, Bejarano, & Rosen, 1999). Nevertheless, several drugs seem to affect infant development, independent of other variables.

PRESCRIPTION AND OVER-THE-COUNTER DRUGS You may have heard about the thalidomide tragedy that occurred in the 1960s. The drug involved was a mild tranquilizer that doctors prescribed to pregnant women who were experiencing severe symptoms of morning sickness. Sadly, the drug caused serious malformations of the limbs in thousands of fetuses that were exposed to it (Vogin, 2005).

Some pregnant women must take drugs in order to treat health conditions that may be threatening to their own life and to their unborn child's life. For instance, pregnant women with epilepsy must take antiseizure medication because the seizures themselves are potentially harmful to the unborn child. Other drugs that pregnant women may have to risk taking, even though they can be harmful, include medications that treat heart conditions and diabetes, those that control asthma symptoms, and some kinds of psychiatric drugs. In all such cases, physicians weigh the benefits of medication against potential teratogenic effects and look for a combination of drug and dosage that will effectively treat the mother's health condition while placing her unborn child at minimal risk.

In contrast to prescription drugs, most people, pregnant or otherwise, take over-the-counter medicines on a casual, as-needed basis without consulting a doctor. Many of these drugs, such as acetaminophen, are safe for pregnant women unless taken to excess (Organization of Teratology Information Specialists, 2005). However, experts advise pregnant women to discuss the medicines they usually take with physicians at the outset of their pregnancies. These discussions should deal with both drugs and any vitamins or supplements that the pregnant woman usually takes. Their doctors will advise them as to which of the substances are safe and which are risky. Often, too, physicians can suggest safer alternatives. Typically, most look to older drugs that have been thoroughly tested (Vogin, 2005).

ILLEGAL DRUGS Significant numbers of pregnant women the world over take various illegal drugs. The drug most frequently used is marijuana. The infants of marijuana smokers weigh less, on average, than infants of nonsmokers (Marroun et al., 2009). Moreover, at age 6, children who experience prenatal exposure to marijuana are shorter on average than 6-year-olds whose mothers did not use marijuana during pregnancy and tend to have lower IQ scores (Cornelius, Goldschmidt, Day, & Larkby, 2002; Goldschmidt, Richardson, Willford, & Day, 2008).

Both heroin and methadone, a drug often used in treating heroin addiction, can cause miscarriage, premature labor, and early death (Brockington, 1996). Further, 60–80% of babies born to heroin- or methadone-addicted women are addicted to these drugs as well. Addicted babies have high-pitched cries and exhibit withdrawal symptoms, such as irritability, uncontrollable tremors, vomiting, convulsions, and sleep problems. These symptoms may last as long as 4 months.

The degree to which heroin and methadone affect development depends on the quality of the environment in which babies are raised. Babies who are cared for by mothers who continue to be addicted themselves usually don't do as well as those whose mothers stop using drugs or who are raised by relatives or foster families (Schuler, Nair, & Black, 2002). By age 2, most heroin- or methadone-addicted babies in good homes are developing normally.

Use of cocaine, in either powder or "crack" form, by pregnant women is linked to many kinds of developmental problems in their children (Gowen, 2011). However, most cocaine-using pregnant women are poor and abuse multiple substances, making it difficult to separate the effects of cocaine from those of poverty and other drugs. Studies that separate the effects of all such factors suggest that cocaine alone has no long-term effects on cognitive or social development (Dharan & Parviainen, 2009). However, cocaine can lead to pregnancy complications, such as disruption of placental function and premature labor, that may adversely affect the developing fetus (Gowen, 2011).

Children with fetal alcohol spectrum disorder have distinctive features.

TOBACCO The correlation between smoking during pregnancy and an infant's birth weight has been well documented by researchers. Infants of mothers who smoke grow more slowly in the womb and are on average about half a pound lighter at birth than infants of nonsmoking mothers (Gowen, 2011; Mohsin, Wong, Bauman, & Bai, 2003). Prenatal exposure to tobacco may also have long-term effects on children's development. Some studies suggest that there are higher rates of learning problems and antisocial behavior among children whose mothers smoked during pregnancy (Minnes, Lang, & Singer, 2011).

ALCOHOL In the face of mounting evidence documenting the detrimental effects of alcohol on prenatal development, the safest course for pregnant women is to drink no alcohol at all. For example, researchers have found that 6-year-olds who were prenatally exposed to alcohol are smaller than their non-alcohol-exposed peers (Cornelius et al., 2002). In fact, studies show that alcohol can even adversely affect an ovum prior to ovulation or during its journey down the fallopian tube to the uterus. Likewise, a zygote can be affected by alcohol even before it has been implanted in the uterine lining (Dharan & Parvainen, 2009).

Mothers who are heavy drinkers or alcoholics are at significant risk of delivering infants with *fetal alcohol spectrum disorder* (*FASD*). These children are generally smaller than normal, with smaller-than-typical brains. They frequently have heart defects and hearing losses, and their faces are distinctive, with a somewhat flattened nose and often an unusually long space between nose and mouth (Levy & Marion, 2011). As children, adolescents, and adults, they are shorter than normal and have smaller heads, and their intelligence test scores indicate mild intellectual disability. ◉ **Watch** the **Video** *Fetal Alcohol Damage* in **MyPsychLab**.

Maternal Diseases

LO 3.11 What risks are associated with teratogenic maternal diseases?

Several viruses pass through the placental filters and attack the embryo or fetus directly. For example, *rubella*, or *German measles*, causes a short-lived mild reaction in adults but may be deadly to a fetus. Most infants exposed to rubella in the first trimester show some degree of hearing impairment, visual impairment, and/or heart deformity (Gowen, 2011). Because the possible effects of rubella are so severe, doctors now recommend that all women of childbearing age be vaccinated against the disease (American College of Obstetrics and Gynecology [ACOG], 2002). However, the vaccine may also be teratogenic. For this reason, the American

College of Obstetrics and Gynecology suggests that women wait at least 1 month after receiving the vaccine before they begin trying to conceive.

HIV, the virus that causes AIDS, is one of many sexually transmitted organisms that can be passed directly from mother to fetus. The virus may cross the placenta and enter the fetus's bloodstream, or the infant may contract the virus in the birth canal during delivery. Only about a quarter of infants born to HIV-infected mothers become infected, although scientists don't yet know how to predict which infants will contract the virus (Springer, 2010). Transmission appears to be more likely when the mother has AIDS than when she is HIV positive but not yet ill (Abrams et al., 1995). In addition, HIV-positive pregnant women who take the drug AZT have a markedly lower risk of transmitting the disease to their children—as low as 8% (Springer, 2010).

Infants who acquire HIV from their mothers typically become ill within the first 2 years of life (Springer, 2010). The virus weakens children's immune systems, allowing a host of other infectious agents, such as the bacteria that cause pneumonia and meningitis, to attack their bodies. Even children who remain symptom free must restrict their exposure to viruses and bacteria. For example, HIV-positive children cannot be immunized with vaccines that utilize live viruses, such as the polio vaccine (Rivera & Frye, 2010).

Other sexually transmitted diseases (STDs), including *syphilis*, *genital herpes*, *gonorrhea*, and *cytomegalovirus*, cause a variety of birth defects. Unlike most teratogens, the bacterium that causes syphilis is most harmful during the last 26 weeks of prenatal development and causes eye, ear, and brain defects. Genital herpes is usually passed from mother to infant during birth. One-third of infected babies die, and another 25–30% experience blindness or brain damage. Thus, doctors usually deliver the babies of women who have herpes surgically. Gonorrhea, which can cause the infant to be blind, is also usually transmitted during birth. For this reason, doctors usually treat the eyes of newborns with a special ointment that prevents damage from gonorrhea.

A much less well-known sexually transmitted virus is *cytomegalovirus* (*CMV*), which is in the herpes group. As many as 60% of *all* women carry CMV, but most have no recognizable symptoms. Of babies whose mothers are infected with CMV, 1–2% become infected prenatally or from breast feeding (Schleiss, 2010). About 2,500 babies born each year in the United States display symptoms of CMV and have a variety of serious problems, including deafness, central nervous system damage, and intellectual disability (Schleiss, 2010).

Other Maternal Influences on Prenatal Development

LO 3.12   What other maternal factors influence prenatal development?

Other maternal characteristics that can adversely affect prenatal development include the mother's diet, her age, and her mental and physical health.

DIET Some specific nutrients are vital to prenatal development (Christian & Stewart, 2010). One is folic acid, a B vitamin found in beans, spinach, and other foods. Inadequate amounts of this nutrient are linked to neural tube defects, such as *spina bifida* (Lewis, 2011). The potential negative effects of insufficient folic acid occur in the very earliest weeks of pregnancy, before a woman may know she is pregnant. So it is important for women who plan to become pregnant to obtain at least 400 micrograms of this vitamin daily, the minimum required level.

It is also important for a pregnant woman to take in sufficient overall calories and protein to prevent malnutrition. A woman who experiences malnutrition during pregnancy, particularly during the final 3 months, has an increased risk of delivering a low-birth-weight infant who will have intellectual difficulties in childhood (Mutch, Leyland, & McGee, 1993). In addition, researchers have recently identified prenatal malnutrition, along with a variety of obstetrical complications, as an important risk factor in the development of mental illnesses in adulthood (Xu et al., 2009).

The impact of maternal malnutrition appears to be greatest on the developing nervous system—a pattern found in studies of both humans and other mammals. For example, rats whose protein intake has been substantially restricted during the fetal and early postnatal periods show a pattern of reduced brain weight and capacity for learning (Wang & Xu, 2007). In human studies of cases in which prenatal malnutrition has been severe enough to cause the death of the fetus or newborn, effects similar to those seen in the rat studies have been observed. That is, these infants had smaller brains and fewer and smaller brain cells (Georgieff, 1994). Moreover, studies of adults whose mothers were malnourished during pregnancy suggest that the detrimental effects of prenatal malnutrition can persist throughout the lifespan (Susser, St. Clair, & He, 2008).

AGE Have you heard sensationalized media reports about women giving birth in their 50s and even into their 60s? Such late-in-life births are very rare, but it is true that the average age at which women give birth for the first time has increased over the past few decades. In 1970, the average age at which a woman delivered her first child was 21.4 years in the United States. By contrast, in 2010, the average was 25 years (Martin et al., 2012).

In most cases, older mothers have uncomplicated pregnancies and deliver healthy babies, but the risks associated with pregnancy do increase somewhat as women get older (Martin et al., 2005). Their babies are also at greater risk of weighing less than 5.5 pounds at birth, a finding that is partly explained by the greater incidence of multiple births among older mothers. Still, infants born to women over the age of 35, whether single or multiple birth, are at increased risk of having problems such as heart malformations and chromosomal disorders.

At the other end of the age continuum, when comparing the rates of problems seen in teenage mothers with those among mothers in their 20s, almost all researchers find higher rates among the teens. However, teenage mothers are also more likely to be poor and less likely to receive adequate prenatal care, so it is very hard to sort out the causal factors (Martin et al., 2005). Nevertheless, researchers have found higher rates of adverse pregnancy outcomes even among middle-class teenage mothers who received good prenatal care (Chen, Wen, et al., 2007).

Reproductive technology has enabled women who are well past their childbearing years to give birth. After 10 years of fertility treatments, this Romanian woman gave birth to her daughter just shy of her 67th birthday.

CHRONIC ILLNESSES Chronic illnesses such as heart disease, diabetes, and lupus can also affect prenatal development negatively (Ross & Mansano, 2010). Thus, one of the most important goals of the new specialty of *fetal-maternal medicine* is to manage the pregnancies of women who have such conditions in ways that will support the health of both mother and fetus. For example, pregnancy often makes it impossible for a diabetic woman to keep her blood sugar levels under control. In turn, erratic blood sugar levels may damage the fetus's nervous system or cause it to grow too rapidly (Gowen, 2011). To prevent such complications, a fetal-maternal specialist must find a diet, a medication, or a combination of the two that will stabilize the mother's blood sugar but will not harm the fetus. Similarly, fetal-maternal specialists help women who have epilepsy balance their own need for anticonvulsant medication against possible harm to the fetus.

ENVIRONMENTAL HAZARDS A number of substances found in the environment may have detrimental effects on prenatal development. For example, women who work with mercury (e.g., dentists, dental technicians, semiconductor manufacturing workers) are advised to limit their exposure to this potentially teratogenic substance (March of Dimes, 2010). Consuming large amounts of fish may also expose pregnant women to high levels of mercury (because of industrial pollution of the oceans and waterways). Fish may also contain elevated levels of another problematic industrial pollutant known as polychlorinated biphenyls, or PCBs. For these reasons, researchers recommend that pregnant women limit their consumption of fish, especially fresh tuna, shark, swordfish, and mackerel (March of Dimes, 2010).

Pregnant women are advised to avoid several other environmental hazards (March of Dimes, 2010):

- *Lead*, found in painted surfaces in older homes, pipes carrying drinking water, lead crystal glassware, and some ceramic dishes
- *Arsenic*, found in dust from pressure-treated lumber

- *Cadmium*, found in semiconductor manufacturing facilities
- *Anesthetic gases*, found in dental offices, outpatient surgical facilities, and hospital operating rooms
- *Solvents*, such as alcohol and paint thinners
- *Parasite-bearing substances*, such as animal feces and undercooked meat, poultry, or eggs

MATERNAL EMOTIONS Some psychologists have suggested that maternal emotions can affect prenatal development. They argue that stressful psychological states such as anxiety and depression lead to changes in body chemistry. In a pregnant woman, these changes result in both qualitative and quantitative differences in the hormones and other chemicals that may affect the fetus. Some studies have shown an association between maternal stress hormones and reduced rates of fetal growth (e.g., Kivlighan, DiPietro, Costigan, & Laudenslager, 2008). ◉ **Watch** the **Video** *Maternal Stress and Cognitive Delay* in **MyPsychLab**.

Fetal Assessment and Treatment

LO 3.13 How do physicians assess and manage fetal health?

Ultrasonography has become a routine part of prenatal care in the United States because of its usefulness in monitoring fetal growth. (Ultrasound images are produced by the echoes that result from bouncing sound waves off of internal tissues.) Other tests, including *chorionic villus sampling (CVS)* and *amniocentesis*, can be used to identify chromosomal errors and many genetic disorders prior to birth (see Figure 3.8). With CVS, cells are extracted from the placenta and used in a variety of laboratory tests during the early weeks of prenatal development. With amniocentesis, which is done between weeks 14 and 16 of a woman's pregnancy, a needle is used to extract amniotic fluid containing fetal cells. Fetal cells filtered out of the fluid are then tested in a variety

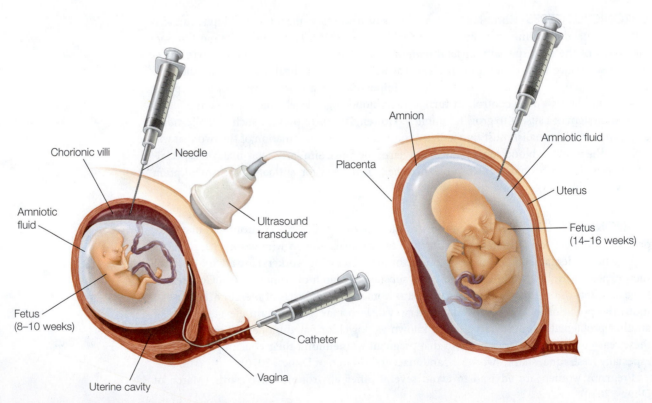

Figure 3.8 **Two Methods of Prenatal Diagnosis**

In chorionic villus sampling (left), placental cells are extracted through a hollow needle inserted in the mother's abdomen. These cells can then be used in a variety of laboratory analyses to determine whether the fetus is healthy. In amniocentesis, a similar technique is used to extract cells from the fluid that surrounds the fetus. These cells are used to create a chromosomal map that can help physicians identify several different kinds of birth defects.

of ways to diagnose chromosomal and genetic disorders. Both tests are associated with an increased risk of miscarriage. CVS is used most often when a medical condition in the mother necessitates early diagnosis of fetal abnormalities (Springer, 2010). In general, amniocentesis carries a lower risk of miscarriage and fetal injury than CVS does. Thus, it is usually the preferred prenatal diagnostic technique and is routinely recommended as a screening tool for Down syndrome and other chromosomal abnormalities in pregnant women over age 35.

Many laboratory tests use maternal blood, urine, and/or samples of amniotic fluid to help health-care providers monitor fetal development. For example, the presence of a substance called *alpha-fetoprotein* in a pregnant woman's blood is associated with a number of prenatal defects, including abnormalities in the brain and spinal cord. Doctors can also use a laboratory test to assess the maturity of fetal lungs (Springer, 2010). This test is critical when doctors have to deliver a baby early because of the mother's health.

Fetoscopy involves insertion of a tiny camera into the womb to directly observe fetal development. Fetoscopy makes it possible for doctors to correct some kinds of defects surgically (Springer, 2010). Likewise, fetoscopy has made such techniques as fetal blood transfusions and bone marrow transplants possible. Specialists also use fetoscopy to take samples of blood from the umbilical cord. Laboratory tests performed on fetal blood samples can assess fetal organ function, diagnose genetic and chromosomal disorders, and detect fetal infections (Springer, 2010). For example, fetal blood tests can help doctors identify a bacterial infection that is causing a fetus to grow too slowly. Once diagnosed, the infection can be treated by injecting antibiotics into the amniotic fluid (so that they will be swallowed by the fetus) or into the umbilical cord (Springer, 2010).

Researchers have examined how prenatal diagnosis affects parents-to-be. For instance, parents whose unborn children are diagnosed with fragile-X syndrome report feelings of sadness, guilt, and powerlessness after learning of the diagnosis (Xuncià et al., 2010). However, specialists in fetal medicine suggest that the negative emotional effects of prenatal diagnosis can be moderated by providing parents-to-be with counseling and specific information about treatment at the time the diagnosis is made, rather than waiting until after the birth. 👁 **Watch** the **Video** *Prenatal Development: Genetic Counseling* in **MyPsychLab**.

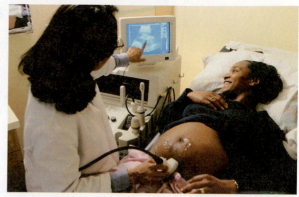

During the second trimester of pregnancy, ultrasound tests allow doctors to identify the fetus's sex, to diagnose fetal deformities and growth problems, and to determine the fetus's position in the uterus.

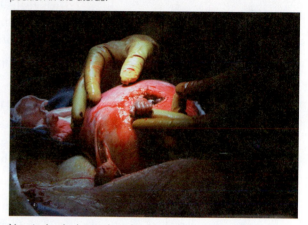

New technologies such as fetoscopy have led to the development of prenatal treatment strategies, including surgery, for correcting birth defects. A photographer snapped this amazing photo showing the tiny hand of a 21-week-old fetus grasping the finger of the surgeon who had just completed an operation to correct a serious malformation of the fetus's spine.

test yourself before going on   ☑ **Study** and **Review** in **MyPsychLab**

Answers to these questions can be found in the back of the book.

1. In most cases, teratogens are most harmful during the _____ period of prenatal development.

2. Describe the potentially harmful effects of each substance in the table development.

Drug	Effect
Heroin	
Cocaine	
Marijuana	
Tobacco	
Alcohol	

3. Match each disease and maternal factor with its potentially harmful effect on prenatal development. (Diseases can have more than one harmful effect.)

   _____ (1) rubella

   _____ (2) HIV

   _____ (3) syphilis

   _____ (4) genital herpes

   _____ (5) cytomegalovirus

   (a) blindness

   (b) AIDS

   (c) death

   (d) heart defects

   (e) brain damage

   (f) deafness

   (g) intellectual disability

4. (CVS/amniocentesis) is done during the first trimester; (CVS/amniocentesis) is done during the second.

CRITICAL THINKING

5. With the advent of antiretroviral drugs, the rate of mother-to-fetus transmission of HIV has been greatly reduced. Do you think that these findings justify mandatory testing and treatment of pregnant women who are at high risk of having HIV/AIDS?

Birth and the Neonate

Once gestation is complete, the fetus must be born—an event that holds some pain as well as a good deal of joy for most parents.

Birth Choices

LO 3.14 What kinds of birth choices are available to expectant parents?

In most places around the world, tradition dictates how babies are delivered. However, in industrialized countries, especially the United States, hospital deliveries became routine in the second half of the 20th century. Today, however, parents in such societies have several choices about who will attend their baby's birth, whether medication will be used to manage the physical discomforts of labor and delivery, and where the birth will take place.

THE LOCATION OF BIRTH AND BIRTH ATTENDANTS One choice parents must make is where the baby is to be born. In most of the industrialized world, women deliver their babies in specialized maternity clinics. However, in the United States, there are four alternatives in most communities:

- A traditional hospital maternity unit
- A birth center or birthing room located within a hospital, which provides a more homelike setting for labor and delivery and often allows family members to be present throughout
- A free-standing birth center, like a hospital birth center except that it is located apart from the hospital, with delivery typically being attended by a midwife rather than (or in addition to) a physician
- The mother's home

More than 99% of babies in the United States are born in hospitals (Martin et al., 2012). Thus, much of what researchers know about out-of-hospital births comes from studies in other countries. For example, in the Netherlands, 30% of all deliveries occur at home (EURO-PERISTAT Project, 2008). Home deliveries are encouraged for uncomplicated pregnancies during which the woman has received good prenatal care. When these conditions are met, with a trained birth attendant present at delivery, the rate of delivery complications or infant problems is no higher than for hospital deliveries.

Certified nurse-midwives are registered nurses who have specialized training that allows them to care for pregnant women and deliver babies. *Certified midwives* have training in midwifery but are not nurses. Instead, most received training in other health-care professions, such as physical therapy, before becoming certified midwives. In Europe and Asia, nurse-midwives and certified midwives have been the primary caretakers of pregnant women and newborns for many years. By contrast, in the United States, physicians provide prenatal care and deliver babies for 92% of women (Martin et al., 2012).

In the developing world, tradition determines where a baby is born and who attends the birth. Hospital deliveries are common in the United States, but many hospitals offer parents the option of delivering their babies in nonsurgical settings such as the birthing room pictured here.

DRUGS DURING LABOR AND DELIVERY One key decision for expectant mothers concerns whether to use drugs during labor and delivery. *Analgesics* may be given during labor to reduce pain. *Sedatives* or *tranquilizers* can be administered to reduce anxiety. *Anesthesia*, when used, is usually given later in labor to block pain, either totally (general anesthesia) or in certain portions of the body (local anesthesia such as an epidural).

Studying the causal links between drug use during labor and delivery and the baby's later behavior or development has proven to be difficult. First, it's clear that nearly all drugs given during labor pass through the placenta, enter the fetal bloodstream, and may remain there for several days. Not surprisingly, then, infants whose mothers have received any type of drug are typically slightly more sluggish, and spend more time sleeping in the first few weeks than do infants of mothers who do not receive anesthetics during labor and delivery (Gowen, 2011).

Second, there are no consistently observed effects from analgesics and tranquilizers beyond the first few days, and only hints from a few studies of long-term effects of anesthesia (Rosenblith, 1992). Given such contradictory findings, only one specific piece of advice seems warranted: If you are a new mother who received medication during childbirth, bear in mind that your baby is also drugged, and that this will affect her behavior in the first few days. If you allow for this effect and realize that it will wear off, your long-term relationship with your child is likely to be unaffected.

Nevertheless, many women choose to avoid drugs altogether. The general term *natural childbirth* is commonly used to refer to this particular choice. Natural childbirth involves several components. First, a woman selects someone, usually the baby's father, to serve as a labor coach. *Prepared childbirth classes* psychologically prepare the woman and her labor coach for the experience of labor and delivery. For example, they learn to use the term *contraction* instead of *pain*. Further, believing that her baby will benefit from natural childbirth provides the woman with the motivation she needs to endure labor without the aid of pain-relieving medication. Finally, relaxation and breathing techniques provide her with behavioral responses that serve to replace the negative emotions that typically result from the physical discomfort of contractions. Aided by her coach, the woman focuses attention on her breathing rather than on the pain. ◉ **Watch** the **Video** *Drug-Free Deliveries* in **MyPsychLab**.

Many fathers take prenatal classes like this one so that they can provide support to their partners during labor.

The Physical Process of Birth

LO 3.15 What happens in each of the three stages of labor?

Labor is typically divided into three stages (see Figure 3.9). Stage 1 covers the period during which two important processes occur: dilation and effacement. The cervix (the opening at the bottom of the uterus) must open up like the lens of a camera (*dilation*) and also flatten out (*effacement*). At the time of delivery, the cervix must normally be dilated to about 10 centimeters (about 4 inches).

Customarily, stage 1 is itself divided into phases. In the *early* (or *latent*) phase, contractions are relatively far apart and typically are not too uncomfortable. In the *active* phase, which begins when the cervix is 3 to 4 centimeters dilated and continues until dilation has reached 8 centimeters, contractions are closer together and more intense. The last 2 centimeters of dilation are achieved during a phase usually called *transition*. It is this phase, when contractions are closely spaced and strong, that women typically find the most painful. Fortunately, transition is also ordinarily the shortest phase. ◉ **Watch** the **Video** *Birth and the Newborn: Labor* in **MyPsychLab**.

There is a great amount of variability from one woman to another in the length of each phase of labor. In fact, among women delivering a first child, stage 1 may last as few as 3 hours or as many as 20 (Biswas & Craigo, 1994; Kilpatrick & Laros, 1989). Generally speaking, however, all three phases are longer among women delivering a first child than among those delivering a second child.

At the end of the transition phase, the mother will normally have the urge to help the infant emerge by "pushing." When the birth attendant (physician or midwife) is sure the cervix is fully dilated, she or he will encourage this pushing, and stage 2 of labor, the delivery, begins. The baby's head moves past the stretched cervix, into the birth canal, and finally out of the mother's body. Most women find this part of labor markedly less distressing than the transition phase because at this point they can assist the delivery process by pushing. Stage 2 typically lasts less than an hour and rarely takes longer than 2 hours. Stage 3, also typically quite brief, is the delivery of the placenta (also called the *afterbirth*) and other material from the uterus.

CESAREAN DELIVERIES Sometimes it is necessary to deliver a baby surgically through incisions made in the abdominal and uterine walls. There are several situations that justify the use of this

cesarean section (c-section) delivery of an infant through incisions in the abdominal and uterine walls

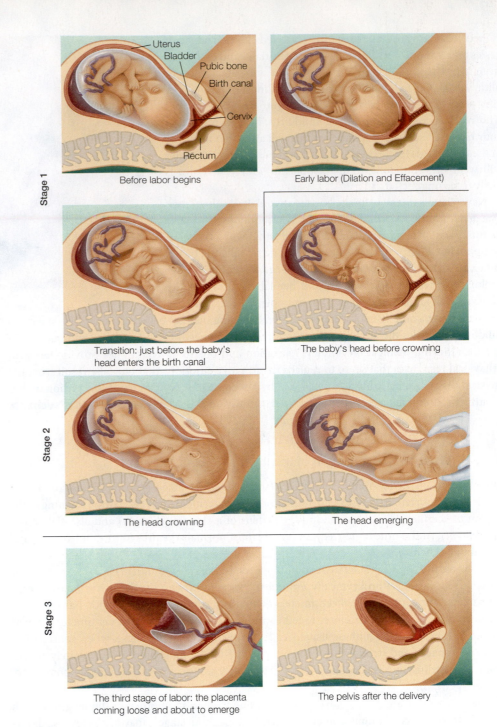

Stage 1

Before labor begins

Early labor (Dilation and Effacement)

Transition: just before the baby's head enters the birth canal

The baby's head before crowning

Stage 2

The head crowning

The head emerging

Stage 3

The third stage of labor: the placenta coming loose and about to emerge

The pelvis after the delivery

Figure 3.9 The Three Stages of Labor

The sequence of steps during delivery is shown clearly in these drawings.

operation, called a **cesarean section** (or **c-section**). A *breech presentation*, in which an infant's feet or bottom is delivered first, represents one of the most compelling reasons for a c-section because it is associated with collapse of the umbilical cord (ACOG, 2001). Other factors that call for the procedure include fetal distress during labor, labor that fails to progress in a reasonable amount of time, a fetus that is too large to be delivered vaginally, and maternal health conditions that may be aggravated by vaginal delivery (e.g., cardiovascular disease, spinal injury) or may be dangerous to a vaginally delivered fetus (e.g., herpes). Thus, in many situations, cesarean sections prevent maternal and fetal complications and, no doubt, save lives. Predictably, surveys show that 99% of childbirth-related maternal deaths occur in the developing nations of the world in which lack of access to high-quality medical care restricts cesarean rates to 2% to 5% of all births (Beukens, Curtis, & Alayon, 2003; World Health Organization, 2010; Wylie & Mirza, 2008).

Despite the benefits of cesarean delivery, many observers claim that the current rates of such births in the developed nations of the world are too high (Chaillet et al., 2007). During the 1960s, about 5% of births in the United States were by cesarean delivery (Martin et al., 2009). Today, just over 32% of all deliveries in the United States involve a cesarean section, as do about 26% of those in Canada (Hanley, Janssen, & Greyson, 2010; Martin et al., 2012). Rates of cesarean delivery in Latin America, East Asia, and the Middle East are similar to those in North America (Lumbiganon et al., 2010; Villar et al., 2006). In Europe, cesarean rates vary from a low of 14% in the Netherlands to a high of 38% in Italy (EURO-PERISTAT Project, 2008).

One factor that spurred increases in cesarean rates in developed nations from the 1960s to the 1980s was the increased popularity of postbirth surgical sterilization as a means of contraception (Placek, Taffel, & Moien, 1983). Women who choose to have a *tubal ligation*, an operation in which the fallopian tubes are surgically closed, immediately after birth often undergo a cesarean delivery. During those same decades, the number of older women giving birth began to increase dramatically, a phenomenon that is still continuing (Martin et al., 2012). As you learned earlier, older women are more likely to conceive twins and other multiples. In such cases, surgical delivery almost always increases the odds in favor of the babies' postnatal health.

BIRTH COMPLICATIONS During the process of birth, some babies go into *fetal distress*, signaled by a sudden change in heart rate. In most cases, doctors don't know why a baby experiences fetal distress. One known cause is pressure on the umbilical cord. For example, if the cord becomes lodged between the baby's head and the cervix, each contraction will push the baby's head against the cord. The collapsed blood vessels can no longer carry blood to and from the baby. When this happens, the baby experiences **anoxia**, or oxygen deprivation. Anoxia can result in death or brain damage, but doctors can prevent long-term effects by acting quickly to surgically deliver infants who experience distress (Gowen, 2011).

Infants may also dislocate their shoulders or hips during birth. Some experience fractures, and in others, nerves that control facial muscles are compressed, causing temporary paralysis on one side of the face. Such complications are usually not serious and resolve themselves with little or no treatment.

If a laboring woman's blood pressure suddenly increases or decreases, a cesarean delivery may be indicated. In addition, some women's labor progresses so slowly that they remain in stage 1 for more than 24 hours. This can happen if the infant's head is in a position that prevents it from exerting enough pressure on the cervix to force it open. In such cases, surgery is indicated because continuing labor can cause permanent damage to the mother's body.

After birth, most women require a period of a month or so to recover. During this time, the mother's body experiences a variety of hormonal changes, including those required for nursing and for returning to the normal menstrual cycle. A few women experience a period of depression after giving birth (a potential problem that you will read more about in the chapters on early adulthood). However, most recover quickly, both physically and emotionally, from the ordeal of pregnancy and birth.

Assessing the Neonate

LO 3.16   What do physicians learn about a newborn from the Apgar and Brazelton scales?

During the first month of life, a baby is referred to as a **neonate**. The health of babies born in hospitals and birthing centers, as well as most who are delivered at home by professional midwives, is usually assessed with the *Apgar scale* (Apgar, 1953). The baby receives a score of 0, 1, or 2 on each of five criteria, listed in Table 3.7. A maximum score of 10 is fairly unusual immediately after birth, because most infants are still somewhat blue in the fingers and toes at that stage. At a second assessment, usually 5 minutes after birth, however, 85–90% of infants score 9 or 10. A score of 7 or better indicates that the baby is in no danger. A score of 4, 5, or 6 usually means that the baby needs help establishing normal breathing patterns; a score of 3 or below indicates a baby in critical condition.

Health professionals often use the *Brazelton Neonatal Behavioral Assessment Scale* to track a newborn's development over about the first 2 weeks following birth (Brazelton, 1984).

anoxia oxygen deprivation experienced by a fetus during labor and/or delivery

neonate term for babies between birth and 1 month of age

TABLE 3.7 The Apgar Scale

Indicator	Score		
	0	1	2
Heart beats per minute	0	< 100	> 100
Respiration	Absent	Weak cry	Strong cry
Muscle tone	Limp	Some degree of muscle contraction indicated by flexed arm and leg joints	All joints of arms and legs strongly flexed
Reflexive response when feet exposed to stimuli	None	Some	Crying; withdrawal of feet from stimulus
Color of lips, palms, soles of feet	Blue	Pink with bluish edges	Pink

low birth weight (LBW) newborn weight below 5.5 pounds

A health professional examines the neonate's responses to stimuli, reflexes, muscle tone, alertness, cuddliness, and ability to quiet or soothe herself after being upset. Scores on this test can be helpful in identifying children who may have significant neurological problems. (See *Developmental Science in the Clinic*.)

Low Birth Weight and Preterm Birth

LO 3.17 Which infants are categorized as low birth weight, and what risk are associated with this status?

Classification of a neonate's weight is another important factor in assessment. All neonates below 2,500 grams (about 5.5 pounds) are classified as having **low birth weight (LBW)**. Most LBW infants are *preterm*, or born before the 38th week of gestation. The proportion of LBW infants is particularly high in the United States, where 12% of newborns are preterm and 8% of newborns weigh less than 2,500 grams (Martin et al., 2012). Multiple fetuses are especially likely to result in preterm birth. ⊙ **Watch** the **Video** *Birth and the Newborn: Premature Births and the Neonatal Intensive Care Unit* in **MyPsychLab**.

However, it is possible for an infant to have completed 37 weeks or more of gestation and still be an LBW baby. In addition, some preterm babies weigh the typical amount for their gestational age, while others are smaller than expected. These *small-for-date neonates* appear to have experienced slow fetal growth and, as a group, have poorer prognoses than do infants who weigh an appropriate amount for their gestational age.

DEVELOPMENTAL SCIENCE IN THE CLINIC

Singing to Preterm Infants

Dana works as a nurses' aide in the neonatal intensive care unit of a large hospital. All of the infants in Dana's unit were born prematurely and have serious medical conditions. She has noticed that many parents sing to these newborn babies. In her training program, Dana learned that premature infants are more sensitive to stimulation than full-term infants are. As a result, she wonders whether the NICU staff should discourage parents from singing.

The use of music by NICU staff and parents to support the development of preterm infants is an active area of research in the emerging field of *music therapy* (Stewart, 2009). Studies in this domain have shown that exposing LBW babies to music in the NICU makes important contribu-

tions to LBW babies' development (Loewy, Stewart, Dassler, Telsey, & Homel, 2013; Standley, 2002). One early study found that preterm newborns in a neonatal intensive care nursery who were sung to three times a day for 20 minutes over a 4-day period ate more, gained weight faster, and were discharged from the hospital earlier than infants who were not sung to (Coleman, Pratt, Stoddard, Gerstmann, & Abel, 1997). Remarkably, too, the physiological functioning of babies who were sung to (as measured by variables such as oxygen saturation levels in their bloodstreams) was superior. However, the greatest effect of parents' singing and babies' reactions to it may be communication of a mutual "I love you" message that helps

to establish a lasting emotional bond between parent and child, a bond that is equally important for preterm and full-term infants (Bergeson & Trehub, 1999). Thus, Dana should encourage parents who are so inclined to sing to the fragile babies in her NICU.

REFLECTION

1. *How could the research on singing to preemies be put into practice in neonatal intensive care units in nondisruptive ways?*

2. *If you were responsible for helping parents of newborns understand the value of singing to their babies, how would you explain the relevant research to them?*

Compared to other infants, LBW infants display markedly lower levels of responsiveness at birth and in the early months of life. Those born more than 6 weeks early also often have *respiratory distress syndrome* (also referred to as *hyaline membrane disease*). Their poorly developed lungs cause serious breathing difficulties. In 1990, physicians began treating this problem by administering surfactant (a chemical that makes it possible for the lungs to exchange oxygen and carbon dioxide in the blood) to preterm neonates, and this therapy has reduced the rate of death among very-low-birth-weight infants (Kyser et al., 2012).

With adequate parental and educational support, the majority of LBW babies who weigh more than 1,500 grams (about 3 pounds) and who are not small-for-date neonates catch up to their peers within the first few years of life, although they do so at widely varying rates (see *No Easy Answers*) (Hill, Brooks-Gunn, & Waldfogel, 2003). But those below 1,500 grams remain smaller than normal and have significantly higher rates of long-term health problems, lower intelligence-test scores, and more problems in school (Child Trends Data Bank, 2012).

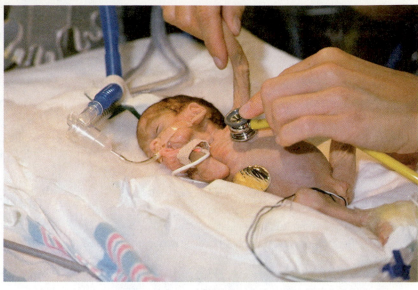

LBW infants' chances of survival are better when they receive care in a neonatal intensive care unit.

test yourself before going on   ✓ **Study** and **Review** in **MyPsychLab**

Answers to these questions can be found in the back of the book.

1. Which of the drugs that women take during the birth process enter the fetus's body?

2. Number these events in the order in which they occur during the birth process.
   - _____(a) delivery of the placenta
   - _____(b) flattening out of the cervix
   - _____(c) cervix dilated to about 10 centimeters
   - _____(d) contractions are far apart
   - _____(e) woman has the urge to push
   - _____(f) the newborn's entire body emerges from the womb

3. Immediately after birth, health-care professionals use the _____ _____ to assess the newborn's condition.

4. Most low-birth-weight newborns who weigh more than _____ and are not _____ catch up to their peers during the first few years of life.

CRITICAL THINKING

5. What three pieces of advice would you give a pregnant friend after reading this chapter?

SUMMARY

Conception and Genetics (pp. 49–54)

LO 3.1 What are the characteristics of the zygote?

- At conception, the 23 chromosomes from the sperm join with the 23 chromosomes from the ovum to make up the set of 46 that will be reproduced in each cell of the new individual.

LO 3.2 In what ways do genes influence development?

- Geneticists distinguish between the genotype (the pattern of inherited genes) and the phenotype (the individual's observable characteristics). Genes are transmitted from parents to children according to complex rules that include the dominant–recessive pattern, the polygenic pattern, and multifactorial inheritance.

Genetic and Chromosomal Disorders (pp. 54–57)

LO 3.3 What are the effects of the major dominant, recessive, and sex-linked diseases?

- Dominant disorders are usually manifested in adulthood. Huntington's disease, a fatal affliction of the nervous system, is one such disorder. Recessive disorders affect individuals earlier in life, often leading to intellectual disability and/or early death. These disorders include phenylketonuria, Tay-Sachs disease, cystic fibrosis, and sickle-cell disease. Hemophilia and fragile-X syndrome are serious sex-linked disorders that affect males far more often than females; fragile-X syndrome can cause progressive intellectual disability.

LO 3.4 How do trisomies and other disorders of the autosomes and sex chromosomes affect development?

- Abnormal numbers of chromosomes and damage to chromosomes cause a number of serious disorders, including Down syndrome. Sex-chromosome anomalies may affect sexual development and certain aspects of intellectual functioning.

Pregnancy and Prenatal Development (pp. 57–64)

LO 3.5 What are the characteristics of each trimester of pregnancy?

- During the first trimester, a woman experiences morning sickness, breast enlargement, and fatigue. As the woman's abdomen enlarges during the second trimester, her pregnancy becomes noticeable. She feels fetal movements for the first time and experiences an increase in her appetite. During the third trimester, the woman gains weight and may experience breast discharge in preparation for nursing.

LO 3.6 What happens in each stage of prenatal development?

- During the germinal phase, from conception to the end of week 2, the zygote travels down the fallopian tube to the uterus and implants itself in the uterine wall. During the embryonic phase, from week 3 through week 8, organogenesis occurs. From week 9 through the end of pregnancy, the fetal stage, the fetus grows larger, and the structure and functioning of the various organs is refined.

LO 3.7 How do male and female fetuses differ?

- Male fetuses may be more active than their female counterparts. They also develop more slowly and are more vulnerable to most of the potentially negative influences on prenatal development.

LO 3.8 What behaviors have scientists observed in fetuses?

- The fetus is responsive to stimuli and appears to learn in the womb. Prenatal temperamental differences (for example, activity level) persist into infancy and childhood, and some aspects of the prenatal sensory environment may be important to future development.

Problems in Prenatal Development (pp. 64–71)

LO 3.9 How do teratogens affect prenatal development?

- Teratogens exert greater effects on development during critical periods when specific organ systems are developing. The duration and intensity of exposure to a teratogen, as well as variations in genetic vulnerability, also contribute to teratogenic effects.

LO 3.10 What are the potential adverse effects of tobacco, alcohol, and other drugs on prenatal development?

- Drugs such as alcohol and tobacco appear to have harmful effects on a developing fetus, often resulting in lower birth weights and learning and behavior difficulties. The effects of drugs depend on the timing of exposure, the dosage, and the quality of the postnatal environment.

LO 3.11 What risks are associated with teratogenic maternal diseases?

- Some diseases contracted by a mother may cause abnormalities or disease in the child. These include rubella, AIDS, syphilis, gonorrhea, genital herpes, and CMV.

LO 3.12 What other maternal factors influence prenatal development?

- If a mother has poor nutrition, her fetus faces increased risks of stillbirth, low birth weight, and death during the first year of life. Older mothers and very young mothers face increased risks, as do their infants. Long-term, severe depression or chronic physical illnesses in the mother may also increase the risk of complications of pregnancy or difficulties in the infant.

LO 3.13 How do physicians assess and manage fetal health?

- Techniques such as fetoscopy, ultrasonography, chorionic villus sampling, and amniocentesis are used to diagnose chromosomal and genetic disorders, and along with laboratory tests identify problems in fetal development. A few such problems can be treated prior to birth with surgery and/or medication.

Birth and the Neonate (pp. 71–77)

LO 3.14 What kinds of birth choices are available to expectant parents?

- In the United States, most babies are delivered by physicians. For uncomplicated, low-risk pregnancies, delivery at home or in a birthing center is as safe as hospital delivery.

LO 3.15 What happens in each of the three stages of labor?

- The normal birth process has three parts: dilation and effacement, delivery, and placental delivery. Most drugs given to the mother during delivery pass through to the infant's bloodstream and have short-term effects on infant responsiveness and feeding patterns.

LO 3.16 What do physicians learn about a newborn from the Apgar and Brazelton scales?

- Doctors, nurses, and midwives use the Apgar scale to assess a neonate's health immediately after birth and the Brazelton Neonatal Behavioral Assessment Scale to track a newborn's development over the first 2 weeks of life.

LO 3.17 Which infants are categorized as low birth weight, and what risks are associated with this status?

- Neonates weighing less than 2,500 grams are designated as having low birth weight. The lower the weight, the greater the risk of significant lasting problems, such as low intelligence-test scores or learning disabilities.

KEY TERMS

amnion (p. 59)

anoxia (p. 75)

axons (p. 62)

cell body (p. 61)

cephalocaudal pattern (p. 59)

cesarean section (c-section) (p. 73)

chromosomes (p. 49)

dendrites (p. 62)

deoxyribonucleic acid (DNA) (p. 49)

dominant–recessive pattern (p. 51)

embryonic stage (p. 59)

fetal stage (p. 61)

gametes (p. 49)

genes (p. 50)

genotype (p. 51)

germinal stage (p. 59)

glial cells (p. 62)

gonads (p. 49)

implantation (p. 59)

low birth weight (LBW) (p. 76)

multifactorial inheritance (p. 53)

neonate (p. 75)

neurons (p. 59)

organogenesis (p. 61)

phenotype (p. 51)

placenta (p. 59)

polygenic inheritance (p. 53)

proximodistal pattern (p. 59)

synapses (p. 62)

teratogens (p. 64)

umbilical cord (p. 59)

viability (p. 61)

zygote (p. 49)

CHAPTER TEST ✔ Study and Review in MyPsychLab

Answers to all the Chapter Test questions can be found in the back of the book.

1. The process by which the basic structures of an embryo's organs, organ systems, and body parts are completed is _____.
   a. conception
   b. prenatal development
   c. organogenesis
   d. implantation

2. A child's father has type AB blood, and his mother has type O. Which statement is true about the child's phenotype for blood type?
   a. It could be either A, B, or O.
   b. It is definitely type AB.
   c. It could be either A or B.
   d. Cannot be predicted from the information given.

3. Which part of the neuron is believed to be sensitive to adverse environmental influences?
   a. axons
   b. glial cells
   c. cell bodies
   d. dendrites

4. _____ are the tiny spaces where impulses from one neuron are passed on to the next.
   a. Axons
   b. Dendrites
   c. Synapses
   d. Cell bodies

5. What is the difference between gametes and all other body cells?
   a. Gametes contain 23 single chromosomes; body cells contain 23 pairs of chromosomes.
   b. Body cells have 46 pairs of chromosomes; gametes have 23 pairs of autosomes.
   c. Gametes contain 46 chromosomes; other body cells contain 23 pairs of chromosomes.
   d. Gametes contain genes from both parents; body cells contain genes from just one.

6. Which statement or set of statements is true about the X and Y chromosomes?
   a. The Y chromosome is one of the largest cells in the body; the X chromosome is the smallest.
   b. Harmful genes are usually found on the X chromosome; genes on the Y chromosome usually offset the harmful ones on the X chromosome.
   c. SRY genes on the Y chromosome control prenatal sexual development.
   d. The X chromosome is present only in the female body; the Y chromosome is found only in the male body.

7. The chromosomes of monozygotic twins are _____.
   a. identical
   b. very similar
   c. no more alike than those of non-twin siblings
   d. more influenced by the mother's than the father's chromosomal makeup

8. Which pattern(s) of inheritance influences normal psychological traits such as intelligence and personality?
   a. dominant/recessive
   b. polygenic and dominant/recessive
   c. polygenic and multifactorial
   d. polygenic and mitochondrial

9. What is the prognosis for children born with trisomy 21?
   a. They rarely live past adolescence.
   b. They have severe psychological disorders and must usually be institutionalized.
   c. They are predisposed to respiratory disorders such as cystic fibrosis.
   d. They have intellectual disability but can learn many skills if given appropriate instruction.

10. According to the text, when do most pregnant women feel fetal movements for the first time?
    a. during the process of implantation
    b. between the 16th and 18th weeks
    c. just prior to birth
    d. at about the same time as the mature cells appear in the fetus's bones

11. Which of the following disease-causing microorganisms is found in 60% of women, most of whom have no symptoms?
    a. flu
    b. rubella
    c. cytomegalovirus
    d. HIV

12. Luisa was excited when she learned from a book on prenatal development that the baby she was carrying had just developed the ability to move in response to external stimuli. In which stage of development was Luisa's baby?
    a. germinal
    b. implantation
    c. fetal
    d. embryonic

13. Carmelita has smoked an average of one pack of cigarettes per day throughout her pregnancy. How is this likely to affect her child at birth?
    a. The infant is likely to be born with physical deformities.
    b. The infant will have an elevated risk for intellectual disability and deafness.
    c. The research is unclear as to the effects of smoking on fetuses.
    d. The infant may weigh less than average at birth.

14. Researchers have linked lack of dietary folic acid to a birth defect called _____.
    a. spina bifida
    b. congenital neuropathy
    c. developmental apraxia
    d. febrile seizures

15. Huntington's disease is an _____ disorder that is usually diagnosed in _____.
    a. autosomal dominant, childhood
    b. autosomal recessive, adulthood
    c. autosomal dominant, adulthood
    d. autosomal recessive, childhood

16. Which of the following is true regarding the first trimester of pregnancy?
    a. All three stages of prenatal development occur prior to the end of the first trimester.
    b. Most people can easily tell that the woman is pregnant.
    c. There are usually no unpleasant symptoms.
    d. The woman gains more weight than in the second and third trimesters.

17. Rolf has brown eyes, even though one of his biological parents has blue eyes. Genes for blue eyes are part of Rolf's _____.
    a. genotype
    b. phenotype
    c. genotype and phenotype
    d. Cannot be determined from the information given.

18. Which of the following organisms can be transmitted to an infant during the birth process?
    a. HIV
    b. diabetes
    c. rubella
    d. malnutrition

19. Studies of prenatal behavior suggest that _____.
    a. there are few differences from one fetus to the next
    b. learning can occur prior to birth
    c. there are no correlations between prenatal and postnatal behavior
    d. fetuses do not respond to sounds

20. Gloria has just found out that she is pregnant. Which of these statements corresponds most closely to the advice her doctor gave her about drinking alcohol?
    a. "An occasional beer or glass of wine is acceptable, but don't overdo it."
    b. "Don't drink at all until your third trimester."
    c. "There is no level of drinking that is considered safe at any time during pregnancy."
    d. "Alcohol is dangerous only during the first trimester."

21. Which of the following is caused by a recessive gene and affects Caucasians more frequently than it affects members of other groups?
    a. phenylketonuria
    b. Tay-Sachs disease
    c. Color blindness
    d. Sickle-cell disease

22. When researchers have examined the relationship between maternal emotions and prenatal development, the most consistent finding has been that _____.
    a. there is no link between maternal emotions and the development of the infant
    b. infants whose mothers were anxious or depressed are more likely to be anxious or depressed as adults
    c. stressful psychological states, such as anxiety or depression, lead to spontaneous abortion or fetal death
    d. fetuses of severely distressed mothers tend to grow more slowly

23. Hong was born 10 weeks early, with a birth weight that was appropriate for his gestational age. Which statement is true regarding Hong's future development?
    a. His prognosis is better than that of a full-term baby with low birth weight.
    b. If he develops breathing problems, his risk for delayed development will increase.
    c. His prognosis would be better if he were female rather than male.
    d. All of the above are true.

24. The risks of cesarean delivery include _____.
    a. uterine prolapse and urinary incontinence later in life
    b. excessive blood loss
    c. fetal anoxia
    d. fetal joint dislocations

25. Which of the following is true about the findings of twin research?
    a. Heredity influences many psychological traits.
    b. Environment has no influence on most psychological traits.
    c. Studies of identical twins raised apart suggest that environment more strongly influences most traits than heredity does.
    d. The findings are inconclusive.

To 👁 **Watch** ✳ **Explore** ◉ **Simulate** ✔ **Study** and **Review** **and experience MyVirtualLife go to MyPsychLab.com**

chapter 4

Physical, Sensory, and Perceptual Development in Infancy

Babies appear to be constantly on the go, manipulating objects with their hands, looking at them, feeling them, tasting them, and making sounds with them. At times, such activities seem purposeless, but they provide just the kind of skill practice and information infants need for both physical and cognitive development. Considering the energy it takes to keep up with infants' level of activity, it's little wonder their parents seem to be exhausted much of the time.

LEARNING OBJECTIVES

PHYSICAL CHANGES

4.1 What important changes in the brain take place during infancy?

4.2 How do infants' reflexes and behavioral states change?

4.3 How do infants' bodies change, and what is the typical pattern of motor skill development in the first 2 years?

HEALTH AND WELLNESS

4.4 What are the nutritional needs of infants?

4.5 How does malnutrition affect infants' development?

4.6 What are infants' health-care and immunization needs?

INFANT MORTALITY

4.7 What have researchers learned about sudden infant death syndrome?

4.8 How do infant mortality rates vary across groups?

SENSORY SKILLS

4.9 How do infants' visual abilities change across the first months of life?

4.10 How do infants' senses of hearing, smell, taste, touch, and motion compare to those of older children and adults?

PERCEPTUAL SKILLS

4.11 How do researchers study perceptual development in infants?

4.12 How do depth perception and patterns of looking change over the first 2 years?

4.13 How do infants perceive human speech, recognize voices, and recognize sound patterns other than speech?

4.14 What is intermodal perception?

4.15 What arguments do nativists and empiricists offer in support of their theories of perceptual development?

In this chapter, you will read about the processes through which a relatively unskilled newborn becomes a 2-year-old who can move about efficiently, respond to a variety of sensory stimuli, and accurately perceive the world around her. You will also learn about important variations across individuals and groups. The first topic we will tackle involves changes in infants' bodies and how their health can be maintained. We will deal with important decisions that parents must make in this domain, including issues surrounding infant feeding like those you will encounter as you raise your "child" in *MyVirtualLife*. Finally, we will move on to an exploration of infants' sensory and perceptual abilities.

Physical Changes

What comes to mind when you think about the first 2 years of life? If you take the time to reflect, you will realize that, apart from prenatal development, this is the period during which the greatest degree of physical change occurs. Although their senses work well, newborns have very limited physical skills. In contrast, 2-year-olds not only can move about independently, but they can also feed themselves and, to the dismay of many parents, get themselves into all kinds of precarious situations. Nevertheless, a 2-year-old still has a long way to go before she reaches physical maturity. But her brain is racing ahead of the rest of her body—a developmental pattern that accounts for the typical "top-heavy" appearance of toddlers.

synapses connections between neurons

synaptogenesis the process of synapse development

pruning the process of eliminating unused synapses

The Brain and Nervous System

LO 4.1 What important changes in the brain take place during infancy?

The brain and the nervous system develop rapidly during the first 2 years. Figure 4.1 shows the main structures of the brain. At birth, the midbrain and the medulla are the most fully developed. These two parts, both in the lower part of the skull and connected to the spinal cord, regulate vital functions such as heartbeat and respiration, as well as attention, sleeping, waking, elimination, and movement of the head and neck—all actions a newborn can perform at least moderately well. The least-developed part of the brain at birth is the cortex, the convoluted gray matter that wraps around the midbrain and is involved in perception, body movement, thinking, and language.

SYNAPTIC DEVELOPMENT You'll recall from Chapter 3 that all brain structures are composed of two basic types of cells: neurons and glial cells. Millions of these cells are present at birth, and **synapses**, or connections between neurons, have already begun to form (Johnson, 2011). Synapse development results from growth of both dendrites and axons (look back at Figure 3.3 on page 62). **Synaptogenesis**, the creation of synapses, occurs rapidly in the cortex during the first few years after birth, quadrupling the overall weight of the brain by age 4 (Johnson, 2011). However, synaptogenesis is not smooth and continuous. Instead, it happens in spurts.

Typically, each synaptic growth spurt generates many more connections between neurons than the individual actually needs. Thus, each burst of synaptogenesis is followed by a period of **pruning** in which unnecessary pathways and connections are eliminated (Huttenlocher, 1994). For example, each muscle cell seems to develop synaptic connections with several motor neurons (nerve cells that carry impulses to muscles) in the spinal cord. As the infant works to gain control over his movements, some of these connections are used repeatedly, while others are ignored. Soon, the unused connections die off, or get "pruned" by the system. Once the pruning process is completed, each muscle fiber is connected to only one motor neuron.

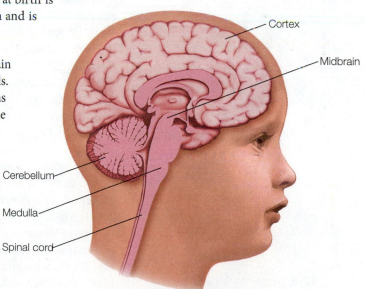

Figure 4.1 Parts of the Brain

The medulla and the midbrain are largely developed at birth. In the first 2 years after birth, it is primarily the cortex that develops, with each neuron going through an enormous growth of dendrites and a vast increase in synapses.

TV for Tots: How Much Is Too Much?

Surveys show that 90% of babies in the United States watch television and other forms of video entertainment every day, typically 60 to 120 minutes per day (Zimmerman, Christakis, & Meltzoff, 2007). Moreover, on average, infants are exposed to about 5 hours of background television per day, most often while they are playing or eating (Lapierre, Piotrowski, & Linebarger, 2012). There is no doubt that infants enjoy watching television, but is there a dark side to television watching in the early years of life?

The studies of researcher Dimitri Christakis and his colleagues show that excessive television watching in the first 3 years of life is linked to reduced social interactions between infants and caregivers as well as attention-deficit/hyperactivity disorder in the school-age years (Christakis et al., 2009; Christakis, Zimmerman, DiGiuseppe, & McCarty, 2004). Their studies support the official recommendation of the American Academy of Pediatrics (AAP) that parents prohibit television watching for children under age 2 (AAP, 1999). The AAP's policy assumes that television watching interferes with social activities that enhance infants' development and may adversely affect brain development. When research results and recommendations come from authoritative sources like the AAP, they are often unquestioned by the public. But are such claims justified?

As you learned in Chapter 1, correlation does not prove causation. The AAP's policy is based entirely on correlational data. Moreover, studies have shown that toddlers can acquire new vocabulary and even social skills from watching high-quality programs such as *Sesame Street* (Huston & Wright, 1998). Thus, some developmentalists suggest that parents focus on quality when selecting television programs for their toddlers to watch and, at the same time, limit the total amount of time that they allow their children to watch television.

YOU DECIDE

Decide which of these two statements you most agree with and think about how you would defend your position:

1. *I agree with the AAP's recommendation that children under age 2 shouldn't watch television at all.*

2. *I think that the AAP's recommendation goes too far. There is a place for television in the lives of toddlers.*

This cycle of synaptogenesis followed by pruning continues through the lifespan. With each cycle, the brain becomes more efficient. Consequently, a 1-year-old actually has denser dendrites and synapses than an adult does, but the 1-year-old's network operates far less efficiently than that of the adult. However, efficiency comes at a price. Because infants have more unused synapses than adults, they can bounce back from a host of insults to the brain (e.g., malnutrition, head injury) much more easily than an adult. Neuroscientists use the term **plasticity** to refer to the brain's ability to change in response to experience.

Developmentalists see several important implications in the cyclical synaptogenesis–pruning feature of neurological development. First, it seems clear that brain development follows the old dictum "Use it or lose it." A child growing up in a rich or intellectually challenging environment will retain a more complex network of synapses than one growing up with fewer forms of stimulation. The evidence to support this proposal comes from several kinds of research, including work with animals. For example, in a classic study, William Greenough and his colleagues found that rat infants reared in highly stimulating environments have a denser network of neurons, dendrites, and synaptic connections in adulthood than rats not raised in such settings (Greenough, Black, & Wallace, 1987). Animal studies also show that enriched environments help the young brain overcome damage caused by teratogens such as alcohol (Hannigan, O'Leary-Moore, & Berman, 2007).

In addition, as mentioned earlier, the brains of infants possess greater plasticity than those of older children and adults. Paradoxically, though, the period of greatest plasticity is also the period in which the child may be most vulnerable to major deficits—just as a fetus is most vulnerable to teratogens during the time of most rapid growth of any body system (Uylings, 2006). Thus, a young infant needs sufficient stimulation and order in his environment to maximize the early period of rapid growth and plasticity (de Haan, Luciana, Maslone, Matheny, & Richards, 1994). A really inadequate diet or a serious lack of stimulation in the early months may thus have subtle but long-range effects on the child's later cognitive progress. Some have even argued that watching too much television in the early months may impede brain development, as discussed in *No Easy Answers*.

Finally, new information about the continuation of synaptogenesis and pruning throughout the lifespan has forced developmental psychologists to change their ideas about the links between brain development and behavior. If the brain were almost completely organized by age 2, as most developmentalists believed until recently, it would seem logical to assume that whatever developments occurred after that age were largely the product of experience. But

plasticity the ability of the brain to change in response to experience researchers now know that changes in psychological functioning are linked to changes in the brain throughout the entire human lifespan.

MYELINIZATION Another crucial process in the development of neurons is the creation of sheaths, or coverings, around individual axons, which insulate them from one another electrically and improve their conductivity. These sheaths are made of a substance called myelin; the process of developing the sheath is called **myelinization** or *myelination*.

The sequence of myelinization follows both cephalocaudal and proximodistal patterns (which are defined in Chapter 3). For example, nerves serving muscle cells in the neck and shoulders are myelinized earlier than those serving the abdomen. As a result, babies can control their head movements before they can roll over. Myelinization is most rapid during the first 2 years after birth, but it continues at a slower pace throughout childhood and adolescence. For example, the parts of the brain that are involved in vision reach maturity by the second birthday (Lippé, Perchet, & Lassonde, 2007). By contrast, those that govern motor movements are not fully myelinized until a child is about 6 years old (Todd, Swarzenski, Rossi, & Visconti, 1995).

Other structures take even longer to become myelinized. For example, the **reticular formation** is the part of the brain responsible for keeping your attention on what you're doing and for helping you sort out important and unimportant information. Myelinization of the reticular formation begins in infancy but continues in spurts across childhood and adolescence. In fact, the process isn't complete until a person is in her mid-20s (Spreen, Risser, & Edgell, 1995). Consequently, during the first 2 years, infants improve their ability to focus on a task. Likewise, a 12-year-old is much better at concentrating than an infant but is still fairly inefficient compared to an adult.

Reflexes and Behavioral States

LO 4.2   How do infants' reflexes and behavioral states change?

Changes in the brain result in predictable changes in babies' reflexes, sensory capacities, and patterns of waking and sleeping. In fact, such changes—or their lack—can be important indicators of nervous system health.

REFLEXES Humans are born with many **adaptive reflexes** that help them survive. Some, such as automatically sucking any object that enters the mouth, disappear in infancy or childhood. Others protect us against harmful stimuli over the whole lifespan. These include withdrawal from a painful stimulus and the opening and closing of the pupil of the eye in response to variations in brightness. Weak or absent adaptive reflexes in neonates suggest that the brain is not functioning properly and that the infant requires additional assessment.
 Watch the **Video** on *The Newborn's Reflexes* in **MyPsychLab**.

The purposes of **primitive reflexes**, so called because they are controlled by the less sophisticated parts of the brain (the medulla and the midbrain), are less clear. For example, if you make a loud noise or startle a baby in some other way, you'll see her throw her arms outward and arch her back, a pattern that is part of the Moro, or startle, reflex. Stroke the bottom of her foot and she will splay out her toes and then curl them in, a reaction called the Babinski reflex. By 6 to 8 months of age, primitive reflexes begin to disappear. If such reflexes persist past this age, the baby may have some kind of neurological problem (Adolph & Berger, 2011).

BEHAVIORAL STATES Researchers have described five different states of sleep and wakefulness in neonates. Most infants move through these states in the same sequence: from deep sleep to lighter sleep and then to alert wakefulness and fussing. After they are fed, they become drowsy and drop back into deep sleep. The cycle repeats itself about every 2 hours.

Infants' sleep patterns change over the first few months as the neurological systems that synchronize their bodily functions with the

myelinization (myelination) a process in neuronal development in which sheaths made of a substance called myelin gradually cover individual axons and electrically insulate them from one another to improve the conductivity of the nerve

reticular formation the part of the brain that regulates attention

adaptive reflexes reflexes, such as sucking, that help newborns survive

primitive reflexes reflexes, controlled by "primitive" parts of the brain, that disappear during the first year of life

This 4-week-old baby is using the inborn adaptive reflex of sucking.

colic an infant behavior pattern involving intense daily bouts of crying totaling 3 or more hours a day

light/dark cycle of the world outside the womb, or *circadian rhythms*, mature. Neonates sleep as much as 80% of the time, as much in the daytime as at night (Sola, Rogido, & Partridge, 2002). By 8 weeks of age, the total amount of sleep per day has dropped somewhat, and signs of day/night sleep rhythms become evident. Babies of this age begin to sleep through two or three 2-hour cycles in sequence without coming to full wakefulness and thus are often said to have started to "sleep through the night." By 6 months, babies are still sleeping a bit over 14 hours per day, but sleep is more regular and predictable. Most have clear nighttime sleep patterns and nap during the day at more predictable times.

Of course, babies vary a lot around these averages. Moreover, cultural beliefs play an important role in parents' responses to infants' sleep patterns (Cole & Packer, 2011). For example, parents in the United States typically see a newborn's erratic sleep cycle as a behavior problem that requires "fixing" through parental intervention (Harkness, 1998). As a result, they focus a great deal of attention on trying to force babies to sleep through the night. In contrast, European parents are more likely to regard newborns' patterns of sleeping as manifestations of normal development and tend to expect babies to acquire stable sleep patterns naturally, without parental intervention, during the first 2 years.

Infants have different cries for pain, anger, and hunger. The basic cry, which often signals hunger, usually has a rhythmical pattern: cry, silence, breath, cry, silence, breath, with a kind of whistling sound often accompanying the in-breath. An anger cry is typically louder and more intense, and the pain cry normally has a very abrupt onset—unlike the other two kinds of cries, which usually begin with whimpering or moaning.

Cross-cultural studies suggest that crying increases in frequency over the first 6 weeks and then tapers off (Gahagan, 2011). Surveys suggest that 15–20% of infants develop **colic**, a pattern involving intense bouts of crying totaling 3 or more hours a day, for no immediately apparent reason such as hunger or a wet diaper. To be diagnosed with colic, an infant must have manifested symptoms for at least 3 weeks (Gahagan, 2011). Neither psychologists nor physicians know why colic begins or why it stops without any intervention. However, they do know that drugs and home remedies such as chamomile tea are of no help and can be dangerous. Thus, physicians typically counsel parents to avoid their use (Gahagan, 2011). There is no doubt that colic is a difficult pattern to live with, but the good news is that it does go away.

On average, neonates are awake and alert for a total of only 2 to 3 hours each day, and this time is unevenly distributed over a 24-hour period. In other words, the baby may be awake for 15 minutes at 6:00 a.m., another 30 minutes at 1:00 p.m., another 20 minutes at 4:00 p.m., and so on. Over the first 6 months, advances in neurological development enable infants to remain awake and alert for longer periods of time as their patterns of sleeping, crying, and eating become more regular.

Growth, Motor Skills, and Developing Body Systems

LO 4.3   How do infants' bodies change, and what is the typical pattern of motor skill development in the first 2 years?

Did you know that half of all the growing you would ever do in your life happened before you were 2 years old? In other words, a 2-year-old's height is approximately half of what it will be when she reaches physical maturity—a remarkable rate of growth, considering that the second half will be spread over a period of 10 to 12 years. But infants' bodies don't just change in size. Many qualitative changes, such as those that involve motor skills, happen during this period as well. As you read about them, recall from Chapter 3 that physical development proceeds from the head downward (*cephalocaudal* pattern) and from the center of the body outward (*proximodistal* pattern). 👁 **Watch** the **Video** *Motor Development in Infants and Toddlers: Karen Adolph* in **MyPsychLab**.

GROWTH AND MOTOR SKILLS Babies grow 10–12 inches and triple their body weight in the first year of life. By age 2 for girls and about 2½ for boys, toddlers are half as tall as they will be as adults. This means a 2- to 2½-year-old's adult height can be reliably predicted by doubling his or her current height. But 2-year-olds have proportionately much larger heads than do adults—which they need in order to hold their nearly full-sized brains.

TABLE 4.1 Milestones of Motor Development in the First 2 Years

Age (in months)	Gross Motor Skills	Fine Motor Skills
1	Stepping reflex; lifts head slightly	Holds object if placed in hand
2–3	Lifts head up to 90-degree angle when lying on stomach	Begins to swipe at objects in sight
4–6	Rolls over; sits with support; moves on hands and knees ("creeps"); holds head erect while in sitting position	Reaches for and grasps objects
7–9	Sits without support; crawls	Transfers objects from one hand to the other
10–12	Pulls self up and walks grasping furniture; then walks alone; squats and stoops; plays pat-a-cake	Shows some signs of hand preference; grasps a spoon across palm but has poor aim when moving food to mouth
13–18	Walks backward, sideways; runs (14–20 months); rolls ball to adult; claps	Stacks two blocks; puts objects into small container and dumps them out
19–24	Walks up and down stairs, two feet per step; jumps with both feet off ground	Uses spoon to feed self; stacks 4 to 10 blocks

(*Sources:* Capute et al., 1984; Den Ouden et al., 1991; Levine, 2011; Overby, 2002.)

Children acquire an impressive array of motor skills in the first 2 years. *Gross motor skills* include abilities such as crawling that enable the infant to get around in the environment. *Fine motor skills* involve use of the hands, as when a 1-year-old stacks one block on top of another. Table 4.1 summarizes developments in each of these areas over the first 24 months. ◉ **Watch** the **Video** *Infancy: Infant Fine Motor Development across Cultures* in **MyPsychLab**. ◉ **Watch** the **Video** *Toddlerhood: Gross Motor Development across Cultures* in **MyPsychLab**.

Throughout infancy, girls are ahead of boys in some aspects of physical maturity. For example, the separate bones of the wrist appear earlier in girls than in boys (Tanner, 1990). This means that female infants may have a slight advantage in the development of fine motor skills, such as self-feeding. Typically, boys are more physically active and acquire gross motor skills faster than girls do.

EXPLAINING MOTOR SKILL DEVELOPMENT Despite gender differences in the rate of physical development, the sequence of motor skill development is virtually the same for all children, even those with serious physical or mental disabilities. Children with intellectual disabilities, for example, move through the various motor milestones more slowly than normal children do, but in the same sequence. Such consistencies support the view that motor development is controlled by an inborn biological timetable (Thelen, 1995).

Esther Thelen (1941–2004) suggested that the inborn timetable for motor skills development interacts with other aspects of physical development (Thelen, 1995). She often cited the disappearance of the *stepping reflex*, the tendency for very young infants to attempt to take steps when they are placed in an upright position with their feet touching a flat surface, at 4 months of age as an example of her **dynamic systems theory**, the notion that several factors interact to influence development. Thelen noted that infants gain a proportionately substantial amount of weight at about the same time that they no longer show the stepping reflex. Consequently, claimed Thelen, infants no longer exhibit the stepping reflex because their muscles are not yet strong enough to handle the increased weight of their legs. True walking, according to Thelen, emerges as a result of both a genetic plan for motor skills development and a change in the ratio of muscle strength and weight in infants' bodies. This latter change is strongly influenced by environmental variables, especially nutrition. Thus, the streams of influence that are incorporated into dynamic systems theory include inborn genetic factors and environmental variables, such as the availability of adequate nutrition.

Wayne Dennis's (1960) classic early study of children raised in Iranian orphanages presaged Thelen's theory. His work demonstrated that babies who were routinely placed on

dynamic systems theory the view that several factors interact to influence development

The striking improvements in motor development in the early months are easy to illustrate. Between 6 and 12 months of age, babies progress from sitting alone, to crawling, to walking.

their backs in cribs learned to walk eventually, but about a year later than babies in less restrictive settings. Research involving infants living in normal environments supports the notion that experience influences motor development. In one such study, very young babies who were given more practice sitting were able to sit upright longer than those without such practice (Zelazo, Zelazo, Cohen, & Zelazo, 1993). Opportunities to practice motor skills seem to be particularly important for young children who have disorders such as cerebral palsy that impair motor functioning (Kerr, McDowell, & McDonough, 2007). Consequently, developmentalists are fairly certain that severely restricting a baby's movement slows down acquisition of motor skills, and many are beginning to accept the idea that a baby's movement experiences in normal environments may also influence motor skill development.

Cross-cultural research provides further support for the notion that experience influences motor development. More than 50 years ago, developmental scientists discovered that African infants, especially those born in rural areas, reach some motor milestones earlier than babies in other parts of the world, a phenomenon that was called *African infant precocity* (e.g., Geber & Dean, 1957). Subsequent studies found that a pattern of traditional cultural practices that both intentionally and coincidentally promote motor development was the most likely explanation for these findings (Berry, Poortinga, Segall, & Dasen, 2002). For instance, African mothers in traditional settings engage in activities that specifically target muscular and motor development. These activities include vigorous massage of babies' muscles and manipulation of their extremities in ways that mimic motor actions such as walking. African mothers also encourage infants to practice motor skills such as sitting up (Super, 1976). Coincidentally, mothers carry infants on their backs, a practice that promotes development of the head and trunk muscles. However, African infant precocity does not persist into early childhood, probably because parental practices that encourage motor development in young children differ less across cultures than they do for infants (Lynn, 1998).

DEVELOPING BODY SYSTEMS During infancy, bones change in size, number, and composition. Changes in the number and density of bones in particular parts of the body are responsible for improvements in coordinated movement. For example, at birth, the wrist contains a single mass of cartilage; by 1 year of age, the cartilage has developed into three separate bones. The progressive separation of the wrist bones is one of the factors behind gains in fine motor skills over the first 2 years. Wrist bones continue to differentiate over the next several years until eventually, in adolescence, the wrist has nine separate bones (Tanner, 1990).

The process of bone hardening, called *ossification*, occurs steadily, beginning in the last weeks of prenatal development and continuing through puberty. Bones in different parts of the body harden in a sequence that follows the typical proximodistal and cephalocaudal patterns. Motor development depends to a large extent on ossification. Standing, for example, is impossible if an infant's leg bones are too soft, no matter how well developed the muscles and nervous system are.

The body's full complement of muscle fibers is present at birth, although the fibers are initially small and have a high ratio of water to muscle (Tanner, 1990). In addition, a newborn's muscles contain a fairly high proportion of fat. By 1 year of age, the water content of an infant's muscles is equal to that of an adult's, and the ratio of fat to muscle tissue has begun to decline (Tershakovec & Stallings, 1998). Changes in muscle composition lead to increases in strength that enable 1-year-olds to walk, run, jump, climb, and so on.

The lungs also grow rapidly and become more efficient during the first 2 years (Kercsmar, 1998). Improvements in lung efficiency, together with the increasing strength of heart muscles, give a 2-year-old greater *stamina*, or ability to maintain activity, than a newborn. Consequently, by the end of infancy, children are capable of engaging in fairly long periods of sustained motor activity without rest (often exhausting their parents in the process!).

Answers to these questions can be found in the back of the book.

1. Match each term with its definition
   _____(1) synaptogenesis
   _____(2) pruning
   _____(3) plasticity
   _____(4) adaptive reflexes
   _____(5) primitive reflexes

   (a) reflexes that disappear during the first year of life
   (b) the process of synapse development
   (c) the brain's capacity to change in response to experience
   (d) reflexes that help infants survive
   (e) the elimination of unused synapses

2. Esther Thelen's dynamic systems theory proposes that two types of influences work together to shape motor development. What are these influences?
   (a) _____
   (b) _____

CRITICAL THINKING

3. Animal research plays a prominent role in developmentalists' understanding of early physical development. What problems arise in generalizing from the results of laboratory studies of animals to infants who are developing in the real world?

Health and Wellness

Babies depend on the adults in their environments to help them stay healthy. Specifically, they need the right foods in the right amounts, and they need regular medical care.

Nutrition

LO 4.4 What are the nutritional needs of infants?

After several decades of extensive research in many countries, experts agree that, for most infants, breastfeeding is substantially superior nutritionally to formula feeding (Krebs & Primak, 2011). Breastfeeding is associated with a number of benefits (Wagner, 2009). For one, breast milk contributes to more rapid weight and size gain. On average, breastfed infants are also less likely to suffer from such problems as diarrhea, gastroenteritis, bronchitis, ear infections, and colic, and they are less likely to die in infancy. Breast milk also appears to stimulate better immune-system function. For these reasons, physicians strongly recommend breastfeeding if it is at all possible, even if the mother can nurse for only a few weeks after birth or if her breast milk must be supplemented with formula feedings (Krebs & Primak, 2011).

Surprisingly, though, there are situations in which breast milk is not sufficient to meet babies' nutritional needs. For instance, preterm babies' intestinal tracts are not as mature as those of full-term infants. As a result, preterm babies require special formulas that contain amino acids and fats that full-term infants' bodies can manufacture on their own (Krebs & Primak, 2011). However, these babies also need the immunological benefits of breast milk. Thus, physicians typically recommend feeding preterm babies expressed breast milk that has been fortified with the proteins, fats, vitamins, and minerals their bodies need (O'Connor et al., 2008). ⊙ **Watch** the **Video** *Birth and the Newborn: Breastfeeding Practices across Cultures* in **MyPsychLab**.

There are also cases in which breastfeeding is impossible. For example, drugs are often present in the breast milk of mothers who are substance abusers or who depend on medications to maintain their own health. Many of these drugs can negatively affect infant development. Consequently, doctors recommend that these women avoid breastfeeding. In such cases, babies who are fed high-quality infant formula, prepared according to the manufacturer's instructions and properly sterilized, usually thrive on it (Tershakovec & Stallings, 1998).

Up until 4 to 6 months, babies need only breast milk or formula accompanied by appropriate supplements (Krebs & Primak, 2011). For example, pediatricians usually recommend iron supplements for most babies over 4 months of age and vitamin B12 supplements for infants whose nursing mothers are vegetarians (Tershakovec & Stallings, 1998). Likewise, doctors may recommend supplemental formula feeding for infants who are growing poorly.

There is no evidence to support the belief that solid foods encourage babies to sleep through the night. In fact, early introduction of solid food can interfere with nutrition. Pediatricians usually recommend withholding solid foods until a baby is at least 6 months old. The first solids should be single-grain cereals, such as rice cereal, with added iron. Parents should introduce a baby to no more than one new food each week. By following a systematic plan, parents can easily identify food allergies (Krebs & Primak, 2011).

Malnutrition

LO 4.5 How does malnutrition affect infants' development?

Malnutrition in infancy can seriously impair a baby's brain because the nervous system is the most rapidly developing body system during the first 2 years of life. *Macronutrient malnutrition* results from a diet that contains too few calories. Macronutrient malnutrition is the world's leading cause of death among children under the age of 5 (Krebs & Primak, 2011).

When the calorie deficit is severe, a disease called *marasmus* results. Infants with marasmus weigh less than 60% of what they should at their age, and many suffer permanent neurological damage from the disease. Most also suffer from parasitic infections that lead to chronic diarrhea. This condition makes it very difficult to treat marasmus by simply increasing an infant's intake of calories. However, a program of dietary supplementation with formula combined with intravenous feedings and treatment for parasites can reverse marasmus (Krebs & Primak, 2011).

Some infants' diets contain almost enough calories but not enough protein. Such diets lead to a disease called *kwashiorkor*, which is common in countries where infants are weaned too early to low-protein foods. Kwashiorkorlike symptoms are also seen in children who are chronically ill because of their bodies' inability to use the protein from the foods they eat. Like marasmus, kwashiorkor can lead to a variety of health problems as well as permanent brain damage (Krebs & Primak, 2011).

The goal of nutritional support programs for low-income mothers and children, such as the WIC program in the United States, is to prevent infant malnutrition. These programs may save taxpayers money in the long run, because malnutrition interferes with early brain development, thereby increasing the likelihood of learning problems and the need for special education services later in childhood.

Growth-rate studies of poor children in the United States suggest that a small number of them suffer from macronutrient malnutrition (Tanner, 1990). In addition, a small proportion of infants have feeding problems, such as a poorly developed sucking reflex, that place them at risk for macronutrient malnutrition (Wright & Birks, 2000). However, most nutritional problems in industrialized societies involve *micronutrient malnutrition*, a deficiency of certain vitamins and/or minerals. For example, infants who are still getting most of their calories from milk after the age of 12 months frequently develop *iron-deficiency anemia* (Krebs & Primak, 2011). Such deficiencies, although most common among low-income families, are found in children of all economic levels. Anemia is a serious threat to infants' future development in the cognitive and social domains as well as in the physical domain (Panepinto & Scott, 2011). Thus, health-care professionals typically screen all infants for signs of anemia and recommend iron supplements when it is diagnosed. Furthermore, public health officials support efforts to educate parents about the micronutritional needs of infants and children.

Health Care and Immunizations

LO 4.6 What are infants' health-care and immunization needs?

Infants need frequent medical check-ups. Much of well-baby care may seem routine, but it is extremely important to development. For example, during routine visits to the doctor's office or health clinic, babies' motor skills are usually assessed. An infant whose motor development is less advanced than expected for his age may require additional screening for developmental problems such as intellectual disabilities (Levine, 2011).

An important element of well-baby care is vaccination of the infant against a variety of diseases. Although immunizations later in childhood provide good protection, the evidence suggests that immunization is most effective when it begins in the first month of life and continues through childhood and adolescence (Levine, 2011). Even adults need occasional "booster" shots to maintain immunity.

In the United States, the average baby has seven respiratory illnesses in the first year of life (Smith, 2011). Interestingly, research in a number of countries shows that babies in day-care centers have about twice as many infections as those reared entirely at home, with those in small-group day care falling somewhere in between, presumably because babies cared for in group settings are exposed to a wider range of germs and viruses (Collet et al., 1994; Hurwitz, Gunn, Pinsky, & Schonberger, 1991; Lau, Uba, & Lehman, 2002). In general, the more people a baby is exposed to, the more often she is likely to be sick.

Neuropsychologists have suggested that the timing of respiratory illnesses that can lead to ear infections is important (Waseem & Aslam, 2010). Many note that infants who have chronic ear infections are somewhat more likely than their peers to have learning disabilities, attention disorders, and language deficits during the school years (Asbjornsen et al., 2005; Roberts et al., 2004). These developmental scientists hypothesize that, because ear infections temporarily impair hearing, they may compromise the development of brain areas that are essential for language learning during the first 2 years of life (Spreen et al., 1995). Thus, most pediatricians emphasize the need for effective hygiene practices in day-care centers, such as periodic disinfection of all toys, as well as prompt treatment of infants' respiratory infections.

As recently as 1992, only 55% of children in the United States had received the full set of immunizations—a schedule that includes three separate injections of hepatitis vaccine, four of diphtheria/tetanus/pertussis (DTP), three of influenza, three of polio, and one each of measles/rubella and varicella zoster virus vaccines (Committee on Infectious Diseases, 1996). In 1995, an intensive media campaign sponsored by the federal government and the AAP was put into place. As a result, the U.S. vaccination rate for these diseases rose to the current rate of more than 90% by 1999 (National Center for Health Statistics [NCHS], 2013). However, in recent years, the percentage of children who receive the complete DTP and polio series has begun to decline. Thus, public health officials believe that continued educational efforts, both in the media and by health-care professionals who work directly with infants and their families, are necessary to prevent further declines in immunization rates.

test yourself before going on ☑ Study and Review in MyPsychLab

Answers to these questions can be found in the back of the book.

1. In what situations is breastfeeding *not* recommended?

2. Label each case of malnutrition as (A) macronutrient malnutrition, (B) micronutrient malnutrition, (C) kwashiorkor, or (D) marasmus.
   (1) Jerome's diet is deficient in calcium and vitamin C.
   (2) Because she doesn't get enough to eat, 8-year-old Nala's weight is equivalent to that of an average 4-year-old.
   (3) George's diet is so low in protein that he is at risk of permanent brain damage.
   (4) This type of malnutrition is the world's leading cause of death among children under age 5.

3. Why is the statement "Healthy babies don't need to go to the doctor" false?

CRITICAL THINKING

4. How would you go about raising public awareness of the dangers of micronutrient malnutrition and the importance of early immunizations?

Infant Mortality

Researchers formally define **infant mortality** as death within the first year after birth. In the United States, 6 babies out of every 1,000 die before age 1 (MacDorman, Hoyert, & Mathews, 2013). The rate has been declining steadily for the past several decades (down from 30 per 1,000 in 1950), but the United States continues to have a higher infant mortality rate than other industrialized nations. Almost two-thirds of these infant deaths occur in the first month of life and are directly linked to either congenital anomalies or low birth weight (MacDorman et al., 2013).

infant mortality death within the first year of life

sudden infant death syndrome (SIDS) a phenomenon in which an apparently healthy infant dies suddenly and unexpectedly

Sudden Infant Death Syndrome

LO 4.7   **What have researchers learned about sudden infant death syndrome?**

After the death of a spouse, the death of a child, especially when the death is unexpected, is the most distressing source of bereavement possible for most adults (see *Developmental Science in the Clinic*). Parents' questions about the cause of their child's death are a natural part of the grief process. In the case of the loss of an infant, few parents find the answers they are looking for because most deaths after the first month of life are caused by *SIDS*. **Sudden infant death syndrome (SIDS)**, in which an apparently healthy infant dies suddenly and unexpectedly, is the leading cause of death in the United States among infants between 1 month and 1 year of age (Task Force on Sudden Infant Death Syndrome, 2005). Physicians have not yet uncovered the basic cause of SIDS. But there are a few clues. For one thing, it is more common in the winter, when babies may be suffering from viral infections that cause breathing difficulties. In addition, babies with a history of *apnea*—brief periods when their breathing suddenly stops—are at increased risk of dying from SIDS (Burnett & Adler, 2009). Episodes of apnea may be noticed by medical personnel in the newborn nursery, or a nonbreathing baby may be discovered by her parents in time to be resuscitated. In such cases, physicians usually recommend using electronic breathing monitors that will sound an alarm if the baby stops breathing again while asleep.

SIDS is also most frequent among babies who sleep on their stomachs or sides, especially on a soft or fluffy mattress, pillow, or comforter (Task Force on Sudden Infant Death Syndrome, 2005). The AAP, along with physicians' organizations in many other countries, recommends that healthy infants be positioned on their backs to sleep. Soon after the introduction of this recommendation in 1992, the AAP, together with the National Institute of Child Health and Human Development (NICHD) and agencies of the federal government, initiated the *Safe to Sleep* campaign, in which public health officials use informative materials such as the poster in Figure 4.2, on page 93, to educate parents about the need to place infants on their backs rather than on their stomachs to sleep. Since the campaign began, SIDS death rates have been reduced by more than 50% (NICHD, 2013).

Another important contributor is smoking by the mother during pregnancy or by anyone in the home after the child's birth. Babies exposed to such smoke are about four times as likely to die of SIDS as are babies with no smoking exposure (CDC, 2006b).

DEVELOPMENTAL SCIENCE IN THE CLINIC

When an Infant Dies

Morgan recently lost her 2-month-old son to SIDS. After the baby's death, she was determined to continue living as normal a life as possible, despite the overwhelming grief she felt. To that end, she went back to work immediately after the funeral and kept up all of her social activities. She also forced herself to attend family gatherings, even though she feared having to talk about the experience. To her dismay, her co-workers and relatives kept their distance from her, almost as if they didn't know what to say to her about her child's death. Morgan was torn between the relief she felt over not having to talk too much about what had happened and a desperate need for others to somehow acknowledge her loss.

When she discussed her concerns with a professional counselor, Morgan learned that her experiences are typical of parents who have lost an infant. The counselor explained that, when an older child dies, parents, family members, and the child's friends build reminiscences on their overlapping relationship histories with the child. They share anecdotes about the child's personality, favorite activities, and so on. Such devices help everyone in the child's relationship network release the child psychologically, a process that helps the child's parents deal with their own profound grief. But with an infant, there is little or no relationship history to draw on. As a result, grieving parents often have a greater need for support from family, friends, and health professionals than even they themselves realize (Vaeisaenen, 1998). Thus, health professionals have compiled a few guidelines that can be useful to family members or friends in supporting parents who have lost an infant (Wong, 1993):

- Don't try to force bereaved parents to talk about their grief or the infant if they don't want to.
- Always refer to the deceased infant by name.
- Express your own feelings of loss for the infant, if they are sincere.
- Follow the parents' lead in engaging in reminiscences about the baby.
- Discourage the parents from resorting to drugs or alcohol to manage grief.

- Assure grieving parents that their responses are normal and that it will take time to resolve the emotions associated with losing an infant.
- Don't pressure the parents to "replace" the baby with another one.
- Don't offer rationalizations (e.g., "Your baby's an angel now") that may offend the parents.
- Do offer support for the parents' own rationalizations.
- Be aware that the infant's siblings, even those who are very young, are likely to experience some degree of grief.

REFLECTION

1. *If you were one of Morgan's co-workers or relatives, how do you think you would behave toward her in everyday situations?*

2. *What sort of "mental script" could you develop from the recommendations above that would be helpful to friends and relatives of a person who has lost a child?*

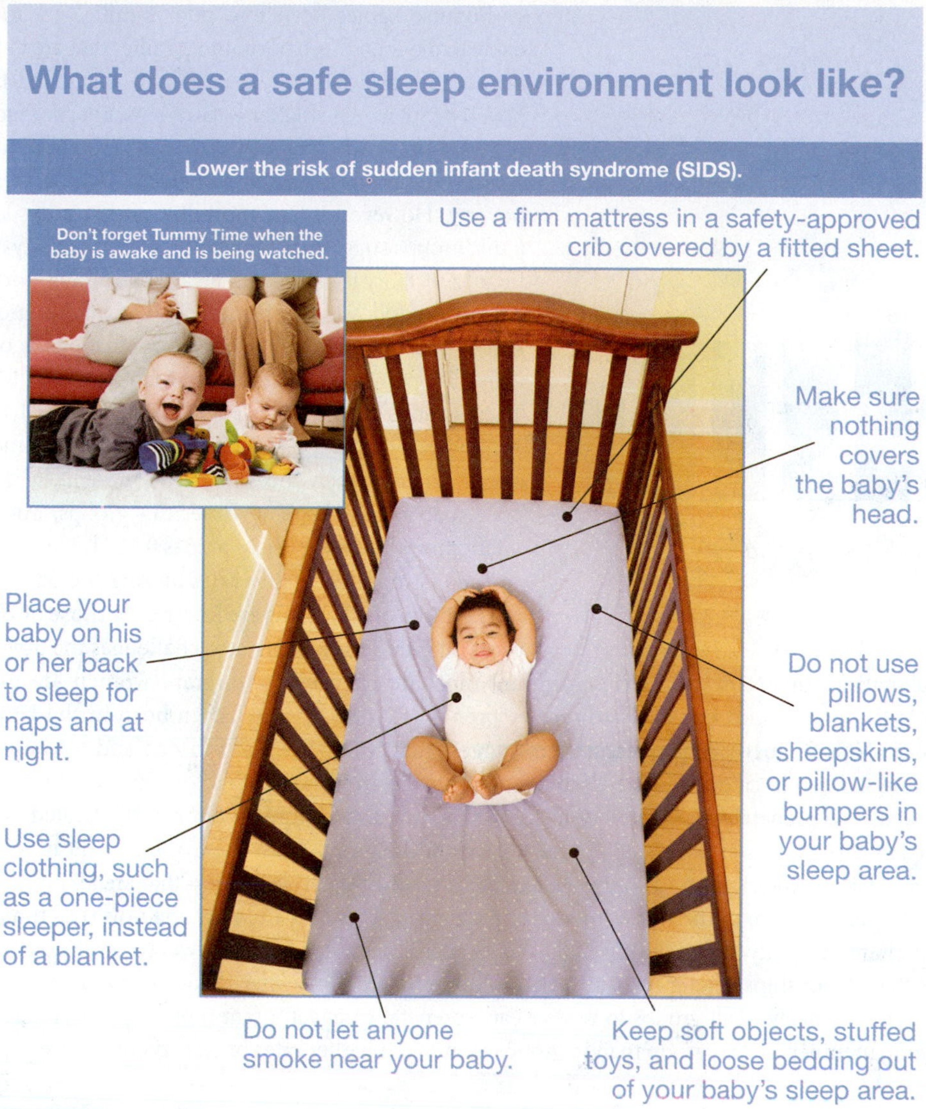

What does a safe sleep environment look like?

Lower the risk of sudden infant death syndrome (SIDS).

Don't forget Tummy Time when the baby is awake and is being watched.

Use a firm mattress in a safety-approved crib covered by a fitted sheet.

Make sure nothing covers the baby's head.

Place your baby on his or her back to sleep for naps and at night.

Do not use pillows, blankets, sheepskins, or pillow-like bumpers in your baby's sleep area.

Use sleep clothing, such as a one-piece sleeper, instead of a blanket.

Do not let anyone smoke near your baby.

Keep soft objects, stuffed toys, and loose bedding out of your baby's sleep area.

Figure 4.2 The *Safe to Sleep* Campaign

Since the *Safe to Sleep Campaign* began in 1994 as a joint project of the American Association of Pediatrics, the National Institute for Child Health and Human Development, and several government agencies, the SIDS death rate has declined by 50%. The campaign features brochures and other educational materials with illustrations such as this one.

(*Source:* Adapted from www.nichd.nih.gov/SIDS)

Imaging studies of the brains of infants at high risk for SIDS, such as those who display apnea in the early days of life, suggest that myelination progresses at a slower rate in these children than in others who do not exhibit such risk factors (Carolan, 2009; Morgan et al., 2002). Babies' patterns of sleep reflect these neurological differences and also predict SIDS risk. Infants who show increasingly lengthy sleep periods during the early months are at lower risk of dying from SIDS than babies whose sleep periods do not get much longer as they get older (Cornwell & Feigenbaum, 2006). Likewise, autopsies of babies who have died from SIDS have revealed that their brains often show signs of delayed myelination and deficiencies in the neurotransmitter serotonin (Duncan et al., 2010).

Group Differences in Infant Mortality

LO 4.8 How do infant mortality rates vary across groups?

Infant mortality rates, including deaths attributable both to congenital abnormalities and to SIDS, vary widely across ethnic groups in the United States, as shown in Figure 4.3 (Mathews & MacDorman, 2010). Rates are lowest among Chinese American infants; about 3 of every 1,000 such infants die each year. Among White babies, the rate is 5.6 per 1,000. The groups with the highest rates of infant death are African Americans (13.6 per 1,000), Native Hawaiians (9 per 1,000), and Native Americans (8.3 per 1,000). One reason for these differences is that infants in these groups are two to three times more likely to suffer from congenital abnormalities and low birth weight—the two leading causes of infant death in the first month of life—than babies in other groups. Furthermore, SIDS is also two to three times as common in these groups.

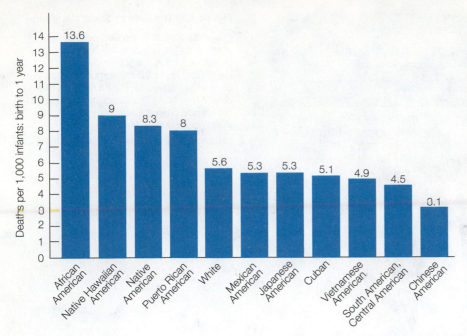

Figure 4.3 **Group Differences in Infant Mortality**

As you can see, infant mortality rates vary widely across U.S. ethnic groups.

(*Source:* MacDorman & Atkinson, 1999; Mathews & MacDorman, 2010.)

Because babies born into poor families are more likely to die than those born into families that are better off economically, some observers have suggested that poverty explains the higher rates of infant death among Native Americans (including Native Hawaiians) and African Americans, the groups with the highest rates of poverty. However, infant mortality rates among Hispanic groups suggest that the link between poverty and infant mortality is complex. The average infant mortality rate among Mexican American, Cuban American, and South and Central American populations is only about 5.4 per 1,000 (Mathews & MacDorman, 2010). These groups are almost as likely to be poor as African Americans and Native Americans. By contrast, Americans of Puerto Rican ancestry are no more likely to be poor than other Hispanic American groups, but the infant mortality rate in this group is 8 per 1,000.

Interestingly, mortality rates among the babies of immigrants of all groups are lower than those of U.S.-born infants. This finding also challenges the poverty explanation for group differences in infant mortality, because immigrant women are more likely to be poor and less likely to receive prenatal care than are women born in the United States (NCHS, 2010). Many researchers suggest that lower rates of tobacco and alcohol use among women born outside the United States may be an important factor.

Access to prenatal care is another factor that distinguishes ethnic groups in the United States (NCHS, 2010). As you can see in Figure 4.4, two of the groups with the highest infant mortality rates, African Americans and Native Americans, are also two of the groups that are least likely to obtain prenatal care in the first trimester of pregnancy. Thus, the links among poverty, ethnicity, and infant mortality may be partly explained by access to prenatal care. However, as we noted earlier, the relationships among all these variables are complex. Notice that Mexican American women are the least likely of all groups to receive early prenatal care, yet infant mortality rates are lower among members of this group than in groups with much higher rates of early prenatal care.

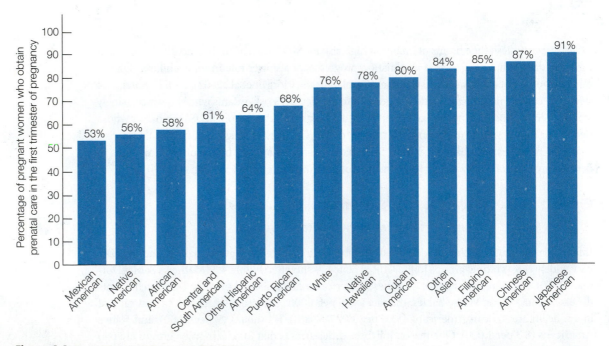

Figure 4.4 **Early Prenatal Care and Ethnicity**

Wide disparities exist across ethnic groups with regard to access to prenatal care.

(*Source:* National Center for Health Statistics (NCHS) (2006, 2010).)

Answers to these questions can be found in the back of the book.

1. Write Y next to risk factors for SIDS and write N next to characteristics that are not risk factors for SIDS.

   _____ **(1)** sleeping on the stomach

   _____ **(2)** history of sleep apnea

   _____ **(3)** summer birth

   _____ **(4)** mother smoked during pregnancy

   _____ **(5)** exposure to secondhand smoke

   _____ **(6)** family history of lung cancer

   _____ **(7)** sleeping on a firm mattress with no pillow

2. Number these groups in accordance with their rates of early prenatal care, with 1 indicating the highest percentage receiving care.

   _____ **(1)** Native Americans

   _____ **(2)** White Americans

   _____ **(3)** Chinese Americans

   _____ **(4)** Mexican Americans

   _____ **(5)** Japanese Americans

   _____ **(6)** African Americans

CRITICAL THINKING

3. Generate your own hypothesis to explain group differences in infant mortality. What kind of information would you need to test your hypothesis?

Sensory Skills

When we study sensory skills, we are asking what information the sensory organs receive. Does the structure of the eye permit infants to see color? Are the structures of the ear and the cortex such that a very young infant can discriminate among different pitches? The common theme running through all of what you will read in this section is that newborns and young infants have far more sensory capacity than physicians or psychologists have thought, even as recently as a few decades ago.

visual acuity how well one can see details at a distance

tracking the smooth movements of the eye to follow the track of a moving object

Vision

LO 4.9 How do infants' visual abilities change across the first months of life?

If you have ever had the chance to spend some time with a newborn, you probably noticed that, while awake, she spent a lot of time looking at things. But what, exactly, can a newborn see, and how well does she see it? The usual standard for **visual acuity** in adults is "20/20" vision. This means that you can see and identify something 20 feet away that the average person can also see at 20 feet. A person with 20/100 vision, in contrast, has to be as close as 20 feet to see something that the ordinary person can see at 100 feet. In other words, the higher the second number, the poorer the person's visual acuity. At birth, the infant's acuity is in the range of 20/200 to 20/400, but it improves rapidly during the first year as a result of synaptogenesis, pruning, and myelination in the neurons that serve the eyes and the brain's vision processing centers. Experts believe that most children reach the level of 20/20 vision by about 6 months of age (Lewis, 2011). It's difficult to determine an infant's true visual acuity, however, because children can't be tested with conventional eye exams until they are old enough to respond verbally to the examiner, typically at 4 to 5 years of age.

Researchers have established that the types of cells in the eye (cones) necessary for perceiving red and green are clearly present by 1 month (and perhaps are present at birth); those required for perceiving blue are probably present by then as well (Bornstein et al., 1992). Thus, infants can and do see and discriminate among various colors. Indeed, researchers have determined that infants' ability to sense color, even in the earliest weeks of life, is almost identical to that of adults (Pereverzeva, Hui-Lin Chien, Palmer, & Teller, 2002).

The process of following a moving object with your eyes is called **tracking**, and you do it every day in a variety of situations. You track

Newborns are pretty nearsighted and can focus very well at about 8 to 10 inches—just the distance between a parent's face and the baby's eyes when the baby is held for feeding.

the movement of other cars when you are driving; you track as you watch a friend walk toward you across the room; a baseball outfielder tracks the flight of the ball so that he can catch it. Because a newborn infant can't yet move independently, a lot of her experiences with objects are with things that move toward her or away from her. If she is to have any success in recognizing objects, she has to be able to keep her eyes on them as they move; she must be able to track. Classic research by Richard Aslin (1987) and others shows that tracking is initially fairly inefficient but improves quite rapidly. Infants younger than 2 months show some tracking for brief periods if the target is moving very slowly, but somewhere around 6 to 10 weeks a shift occurs, and babies' tracking becomes skillful rather quickly.

Hearing and Other Senses

LO 4.10 How do infants' senses of hearing, smell, taste, touch, and motion compare to those of older children and adults?

As you learned in Chapter 2, babies can hear long before they are born. However, like vision, hearing improves considerably in the early months of life. The other senses follow a similar course.

HEARING Although children's hearing improves up to adolescence, newborns' **auditory acuity** is actually better than their visual acuity. Research evidence suggests that, within the general range of pitch and loudness of the human voice, newborns hear nearly as well as adults do (Ceponiene et al., 2002). Only with high-pitched sounds is their auditory skill less than that of an adult; such a sound needs to be louder to be heard by a newborn than to be heard by older children or adults (Werner & Gillenwater, 1990). Another basic auditory skill that exists at birth but improves with age is the ability to determine the location of a sound. We know that newborns can judge at least the general direction from which a sound has come because they will turn their heads in roughly the right direction toward some sound. Finer-grained location of sounds, however, is not well developed at birth. For example, in classic research, Barbara Morrongiello observed babies' reactions to sounds played at the midpoint between the two ears, the *midline*, and then sounds coming from varying degrees away from the midline. Among infants 2 months old, it takes a shift of about 27 degrees off midline before the baby shows a changed response; among 6-month-olds, only a 12-degree shift is needed; by 18 months, discrimination of a 4-degree shift is possible—nearly the skill level seen in adults (Morrongiello, 1988; Morrongiello, Fenwick, & Chance, 1990).

SMELLING AND TASTING The senses of smell and taste are intricately related in infants, just as they are in adults. Consider the fact that if you cannot smell for some reason (for example, because you have a cold), your taste sensitivity is also significantly reduced. The taste buds on the tongue detect taste and register four basic flavors: sweet, sour, bitter, and salty. The mucous membranes of the nose register smell, which has nearly unlimited variations.

As you can guess from this expression on this boy's face, infants possess a well-developed sense of taste.

Newborns appear to respond differentially to all four of the basic flavors (Crook, 1987). Some of the clearest demonstrations of this come from an elegantly simple set of early studies by Jacob Steiner (Ganchrow, Steiner, & Daher, 1983; Steiner, 1979). Newborn infants who had never been fed were photographed before and after flavored water was put into their mouths. By varying the flavor, Steiner could determine whether the babies reacted differently to different tastes. Steiner found that babies responded quite differently to sweet, sour, and bitter flavors. Newborns can also taste *umami*, the characteristic flavor that comes from adding monosodium glutamate (MSG) to food and which is typical of high-protein foods that are high in glutamates (e.g., meat, cheese). Generally, newborns express pleasure when researchers test them for umami sensitivity (Nicklaus, Boggio, & Issanchou, 2005). Some researchers speculate that newborns' preferences for umami-flavored and sweet foods explain their attraction to breast milk, a substance that is naturally rich in sugars and glutamates.

SENSES OF TOUCH AND MOTION The infant's senses of touch and motion may well be the best developed sense of all. Certainly these senses are sufficiently well developed to get the baby fed. If you think back to the discussion of reflexes earlier in the chapter, you'll realize that the rooting reflex relies on a touch stimulus to the cheek, while the sucking reflex relies on touch in the mouth. Babies appear to be especially sensitive to touches on the mouth, the face, the hands, the soles of the feet, and the abdomen, with less sensitivity in other parts of the body (Reisman, 1987).

test yourself before going on ✓ Study and Review in MyPsychLab

Answers to these questions can be found in the back of the book.

1. (Visual, auditory) acuity is better at birth than (visual, auditory) acuity.
2. What taste sensations do newborns prefer, and how do their preferences relate to nutritional needs?

CRITICAL THINKING

3. In what ways do babies' sensory skills contribute to the development of parent-infant relationships?

Perceptual Skills

When we turn to studies of perceptual skills, we are asking what the individual does with the sensory information—how it is interpreted or combined. Researchers have found that very young infants are able to make remarkably fine discriminations among sounds, sights, and feelings, and they pay attention to and respond to patterns, not just to individual events.

Studying Perceptual Development

LO 4.11 How do researchers study perceptual development in infants?

Babies can't talk and can't respond to ordinary questions, so how are we to decipher just what they can see, hear, or discriminate? Researchers use three basic methods that allow them to "ask" a baby about what he experiences (Bornstein, Arterberry, & Mash, 2011). In the **preference technique**, devised by Robert Fantz (1956), the baby is simply shown two pictures or two objects, and the researcher keeps track of how long the baby looks at each one. If many infants shown the same pair of pictures consistently look longer at one picture than the other, this not only tells us that babies see some difference between the two but also may reveal something about the kinds of objects or pictures that capture babies' attention.

Another strategy takes advantage of the processes of **habituation**, or getting used to a stimulus, and its opposite, **dishabituation**, responding to a somewhat familiar stimulus as if it were new. Researchers first present the baby with a particular sight, sound, or object over and over until he habituates—that is, until he stops looking at it or showing interest in it. Then the researchers present another sight, sound, or object that is slightly different from the original one and watch to see whether the baby shows renewed interest (dishabituation). If the baby does show renewed interest, you know he perceives the slightly changed sight, sound, or object as "different" in some way from the original. **Watch** the **Video** *Infancy: Habituation* in **MyPsychLab**.

The third option is to use the principles of *operant conditioning*, described in Chapter 2. For example, an infant might be trained to turn her head when she hears a particular sound, with the sight of an interesting moving toy used as a reinforcement. After the learned response is well established, the experimenter can vary the sound in some systematic way to see whether or not the baby still turns her head.

Looking

LO 4.12 How do depth perception and patterns of looking change over the first 2 years?

One important question to ask about visual perception is whether the infant perceives his environment in the same way as older children and adults do. Can he judge how far away an object is by looking at it? Does he visually scan an object in an orderly way? Developmentalists

preference technique a research method in which a researcher keeps track of how long a baby looks at each of two objects shown

habituation a decline in attention that occurs because a stimulus has become familiar

dishabituation responding to a somewhat familiar stimulus as if it were new

In an experiment using a "visual cliff" apparatus, like the one used by Gibson and Walk, Mom tries to entice her baby out onto the "cliff" side. But because the infant can perceive depth, he fears that he will fall if he comes toward her, so he stays put, looking concerned.

believe that infants' patterns of looking at objects tell us a great deal about what they are trying to gain from visual information.

DEPTH PERCEPTION One of the perceptual skills that has been most studied is depth perception. An infant needs to be able to judge depth in order to perform all kinds of simple tasks, including judging how far away an object is so that he can reach for it, how far it is to the floor if he has ideas about crawling off the edge of the couch, or how to aim a spoon toward a bowl of chocolate pudding.

It is possible to judge depth by using any (or all) of three rather different kinds of information. First, *binocular cues* involve both eyes, each of which receives a slightly different visual image of an object; the closer the object is, the more different these two views are. In addition, of course, information from the muscles of the eyes tells you something about how far away an object may be. Second, pictorial information, sometimes called *monocular cues*, requires input from only one eye. For example, when one object is partially in front of another one, you know that the partially hidden object is farther away—a cue called *interposition*. The relative sizes of two similar objects, such as two telephone poles or two people you see in the distance, may also indicate that the smaller-appearing one is farther away. *Linear perspective* (like the impression that railroad lines are getting closer together as they get farther away) is another monocular cue. Third, *kinetic cues* come from either your own motion or the motion of some object: If you move your head, objects near you seem to move more than objects farther away (a phenomenon called *motion parallax*). Similarly, if you see objects moving, such as a person walking across a street or a train moving along a track, closer objects appear to move over larger distances in a given period of time.

How early can an infant judge depth, and which of these cues does he use? This is still an active area of research, so the answer is not final. The best conclusion at the moment seems to be that kinetic information is used first, perhaps by about 3 months of age; binocular cues are used beginning at about 4 months; and linear perspective and other pictorial (monocular) cues are used last, perhaps at 5 to 7 months (Bornstein, 1992; Yonas, Elieff, & Arterberry, 2002).

In a remarkably clever early study, Eleanor Gibson and Richard Walk (1960) devised an apparatus called a visual cliff. You can see from the photograph that it consists of a large glass table with a sort of runway in the middle. On one side of the runway is a checkerboard pattern immediately below the glass; on the other side—the "cliff" side—the checkerboard is several feet below the glass. The baby could judge depth here by several means, but it is primarily kinetic information that is useful, since the baby in motion would see the nearer surface move more than the farther surface. If a baby has no depth perception, she should be equally willing to crawl on either side of the runway, but if she can judge depth, she should be reluctant to crawl out on the cliff side. ⊚ **Simulate** the **Experiment** *The Visual Cliff* in **MyPsychLab**.

Since an infant had to be able to crawl in order to be tested in the Gibson and Walk procedure, the original subjects were all 6 months old or older. Most of these infants did not crawl out on the cliff side but were quite willing to crawl out on the shallow side. In other words, 6-month-old babies have depth perception.

What about younger infants? The traditional visual cliff procedure can't give us the answer, since the baby must be able to crawl in order to "tell" us whether he can judge depth. With younger babies, researchers have studied kinetic cues by watching babies react to apparently looming objects. Most often, the baby observes a film of an object moving toward him, apparently on a collision course. If the infant has some depth perception, he should flinch, move to one side, or blink as the object appears to come very close. Such flinching has been observed in 3-month-olds (Yonas & Owsley, 1987). Most experts now agree that this is about the lower age limit of depth perception.

WHAT BABIES LOOK AT In the first 2 months, a baby's visual attention is guided by a search for meaningful patterns (Bornstein et al., 2011). Babies scan the world around them until they

Langlois's Studies of Babies' Preferences for Attractive Faces

Studies on infant perception point toward the conclusion that many perceptual rules are built-in. One such rule appears to be a preference for attractive faces. In the first study in a classic series of experiments, Langlois and her colleagues (1987) tested 2- to 3-month-olds and 6- to 8-month-olds. Each baby was shown color slides of adult Caucasian women, of whom half were rated by adult judges as attractive and half as unattractive. On each trial, the baby was shown two slides simultaneously, with each face approximately life-size, while the experimenter peeked through a hole in the screen to count the number of seconds the baby looked at each picture. Each baby saw some attractive/attractive pairs, some unattractive/unattractive pairs, and some mixed pairs. With mixed pairs, even

the 2- and 3-month-old babies consistently looked longer at the attractive faces. Several later studies, including some in which pictures of individuals of different races were used, produced similar findings (Langlois, Roggman, & Rieser-Danner, 1990; Langlois, Ritter, Roggman, & Vaughn, 1991).

Later research extended Langlois's findings. These studies showed that infants prefer to look at images of other infants and animals that have been rated as attractive by adults (Quinn, Kelly, Lee, Pascalis, & Slater, 2008; Van Duuren, Kendall-Scott, & Stark, 2003). It is hard to imagine what sort of learning experiences could account for such preferences in a 2-month-old. Instead, these findings raise the possibility that there is some inborn template for the "correct" or "most

desired" shape and configuration for members of our species and that we simply prefer those who best match this template.

CRITICAL ANALYSIS

1. *If there is an inborn template against which faces are compared, how might such a template affect adults' interactions with others?*

2. *How would researchers determine the degree to which attractiveness affects adults' perceptions of infants' faces? Why would such research be unable to tell us whether the concept of attractiveness is inborn?*

---

come to a sharp light–dark contrast, which typically signals the edge of some object. Once she finds such an edge, the baby stops searching and moves her eyes back and forth across and around the edge. Motion also captures a baby's attention at this age, so she will look at things that move as well as things with large light-dark contrast. Between 2 and 3 months, the cortex has developed more fully, and the baby's attention seems to shift from *where* an object is to *what* an object is. Babies this age begin to scan rapidly across an entire figure rather than getting stuck on edges. As a result, they spend more time looking for patterns.

One early study that illustrates this point particularly well comes from the work of Albert Caron and Rose Caron (1981), who used a habituation procedure. The babies were first shown a series of pictures that shared some particular relationship—for example, a small diamond positioned above a larger diamond (small over big). After the baby stopped being interested in these training pictures (that is, after he habituated), the Carons showed him another figure (the test stimulus) that either followed the same pattern (small over big) or followed some other pattern such as a large triangle above a smaller one (big over small). If the baby had really habituated to the pattern of the original pictures, he should show little interest in stimuli that followed the small-over-big pattern. ("Ho hum, same old boring small over big thing"), but he should show renewed interest stimuli that followed the big-over-small pattern ("Hey, here's something new!"). Caron and Caron found that 3- and 4-month-old children did precisely that. So even at this early age, babies find and pay attention to patterns, not just specific stimuli.

Although there is little indication that faces are uniquely interesting patterns to infants—that is, babies do not systematically choose to look at faces rather than at other complex patterns—babies clearly prefer some to others. They prefer attractive faces (an intriguing result, discussed in *Research Report*). They also prefer their mother's face from the earliest hours of life, a finding that has greatly surprised psychologists, although it may not surprise you.

Beyond the issue of preference, we also have the question of just what it is that babies are looking at when they scan a face. Before about 2 months of age, babies seem to look mostly at the edges of faces (the hairline and the chin), a conclusion buttressed by the finding by Pascalis and his colleagues (1995) that newborns could not discriminate Mom's face from a stranger's if the hairline was covered. After 4 months, however, covering the hairline did not affect the baby's ability to recognize Mom. In general, babies appear to begin to focus on the internal features of a face, particularly the eyes, at about 2 to 3 months.

Listening

LO 4.13 How do infants perceive human speech, recognize voices, and recognize sound patterns other than speech?

Newborns recognize their mother's voice and by 1 month of age can discriminate between syllables such as *ba* and *pa*.

When we turn from looking to listening, we find similarly intriguing indications that very young infants not only make remarkably fine discriminations among individual sounds but also pay attention to patterns. Early studies established that as early as 1 month, babies can discriminate between speech sounds like *pa* and *ba* (Trehub & Rabinovitch, 1972). Studies using conditioned head-turning responses have shown that by perhaps 6 months of age, babies can discriminate between two-syllable "words" like *bada* and *baga* and can even respond to a syllable that is hidden inside a string of other syllables, like *tibati* or *koba ko* (Gerken & Aslin, 2005). Research also indicates that infants can rapidly learn to discriminate between words and nonwords in artificial languages researchers invent strictly for the purpose of such experiments (Aslin, Saffran, & Newport, 1998).

Even more striking is the finding that babies are actually better at discriminating some kinds of speech sounds than adults are. Each language uses only a subset of all possible speech sounds. Japanese, for example, does not use the *l* sound that appears in English; Spanish makes a different distinction between *d* and *t* than occurs in English. It turns out that up to about 6 months of age, babies can accurately discriminate all sound contrasts that appear in any language, including sounds they do not hear in the language spoken to them. At about 6 months of age, they begin to lose the ability to distinguish pairs of vowels that do not occur in the language they are hearing; by age 1, the ability to discriminate nonheard consonant contrasts begins to fade (Polka & Werker, 1994).

Newborns also seem to be able to discriminate between individual voices. DeCasper and Fifer (1980) found that the newborn can tell the mother's voice from another female voice (but not the father's voice from another male voice) and prefers the mother's voice. Moreover, there is a correlation between gestational age and maternal voice recognition: Premature infants are less likely to recognize their mother's voice than are babies born at term (DeRegnier, Wewerka, Georgieff, Mattia, & Nelson, 2002). Thus, *in utero* learning appears to be responsible for newborns' preference for the maternal voice.

Combining Information from Several Senses

LO 4.14 What is intermodal perception?

If you think about the way you receive and use perceptual information, you'll realize that you rarely have information from only one sense at a time. Psychologists have been interested in knowing how early an infant can combine such information. Even more complex, how early can a baby learn something via one sense and transfer that information to another sense (for example, recognize solely by feel a toy he has seen but never before felt)? This skill is usually called **intermodal perception**.

Research findings show that intermodal perception is possible as early as 1 month and becomes common by 6 months (Rose & Ruff, 1987). Moreover, research comparing these skills in children born prematurely and those born at term suggests that prenatal maturational processes play an important role in their development (Espy et al., 2002).

Research also suggests that intermodal perception is important in infant learning. One group of researchers found that babies who habituated to a combined auditory-visual stimulus were better able to recognize a new stimulus than infants who habituated to either the auditory or the visual stimulus alone (Bahrick & Lickliter, 2000). For example, suppose you played a videotape of someone singing for one baby, played the videotape without the sound for

intermodal perception formation of a single perception of a stimulus that is based on information from two or more senses

another, and played an audio recording of the song for a third. Research suggests that the first baby would recognize a change in either the singer (visual stimulus) or the song (auditory stimulus) more quickly than would either of the other two infants.

In older infants, intermodal perception can be readily demonstrated, not only between touch and sight but between other modalities such as sound and sight. For instance, in several delightfully clever early experiments, Elizabeth Spelke (1979) showed that 4-month-old infants can connect sound rhythms with movement. She showed babies two films simultaneously, one depicting a toy kangaroo bouncing up and down and the other a donkey bouncing up and down, with one of the animals bouncing at a faster rate. Out of a loudspeaker located between the two films, the infant heard a tape recording of a rhythmic bouncing sound that matched the bounce pattern of one of the two animals. In this situation, babies showed a preference for looking at the film showing the bounce rate that matched the sound.

An even more striking illustration of the same basic process comes from the work of Jeffrey Pickens (1994). He showed 5-month-old babies two films side by side, each displaying a train moving along a track. Then out of a loudspeaker he played engine sounds of various types, such as that of an engine getting gradually louder (thus appearing to come closer) or gradually fainter (thus appearing to be moving away). The babies in this experiment looked longer at a picture of a train whose movement matched the pattern of engine sounds. That is, they appeared to have some understanding of the link between the pattern of sound and the pattern of movement—knowledge that demonstrates not only intersensory integration but also a surprisingly sophisticated understanding of the accompaniments of motion.

Explaining Perceptual Development

LO 4.15 What arguments do nativists and empiricists offer in support of their theories of perceptual development?

The study of perceptual development has been significant because it has been a key battleground for the dispute about nature versus nurture. **Nativists** claim that most perceptual abilities are inborn, while **empiricists** argue that these skills are learned.

There are strong arguments for a nativist position on perceptual development. As researchers have become more and more clever in devising ways to test infants' perceptual skills, they have found more and more skills already present in newborns or very young infants: Newborns have good auditory acuity, poor but adequate visual acuity, and excellent tactual and taste perception. They have at least some color vision and at least rudimentary ability to locate the source of sounds around them. More impressive still, they are capable of making quite sophisticated discriminations from the earliest days of life, including identifying their mother by sight, smell, or sound.

On the other side of the ledger, however, we find evidence from research with other species that some minimum level of experience is necessary to support the development of the perceptual systems. For example, animals deprived of light show deterioration of the whole visual system and a consequent decrease in perceptual abilities (Hubel & Weisel, 1963). Likewise, animals deprived of auditory stimuli display delayed or no development of auditory perceptual skills (Dammeijer, Schlundt, Chenault, Manni, & Anteunis, 2002).

We can best understand the development of perceptual skills by thinking of it as the result of an interaction between inborn and experiential factors. A child is able to make visual discriminations between people or among objects within the first few days or weeks of life. The specific discriminations she learns and the number of separate objects she learns to recognize, however, will depend on her experience. A perfect example of this is the newborn's ability to discriminate her mother's face from a very similar woman's face. Such a discrimination must be the result of experience, yet the capacity to make the distinction must be built in. Thus, as is true of virtually all dichotomous theoretical disputes, both sides are correct. Both nature and nurture are involved.

Even though this 7-month-old is not looking at this toy while he chews on it, he is nonetheless learning something about how it ought to look based on how it feels in his mouth and in his hands—an example of intermodal perception.

nativists theorists who claim that perceptual abilities are inborn

empiricists theorists who argue that perceptual abilities are learned

Answers to these questions can be found in the back of the book.

1. _____ devised the preference technique to study perceptual development in infants.

2. Infants can discriminate among (more, fewer) speech sounds than adults.

3. What did the visual cliff experiment show?

4. Intermodal perception is possible as early as _____ month(s).

5. Label these statements as consistent with the (A) nativist or (B) empiricist view of perceptual development.

_____ (1) Perceptual skills are inborn.
_____ (2) Perceptual skills are learned.
_____ (3) The development of perceptual skills depends on experience.
_____ (4) Newborns can make perceptual discriminations.

CRITICAL THINKING

6. If the empiricists are correct, and much of early perceptual learning depends on experience, what kinds of objects and activities do you think would be helpful in supporting an infant's visual and auditory perceptual development?

SUMMARY

Physical Changes (pp. 83–89)

LO 4.1 **What important changes in the brain take place during infancy?**

• Changes in the nervous system are extremely rapid in the first 2 years. In most parts of the brain, development of dendrites and synapses reaches its first peak between 12 and 24 months, after which "pruning" of synapses occurs. Myelinization of nerve fibers also occurs rapidly in the first 2 years.

LO 4.2 **How do infants' reflexes and behavioral states change?**

• Adaptive reflexes include such essential responses as sucking; primitive reflexes include the Moro (startle) and Babinski reflexes, which disappear within a few months. Neonates move through a series of states of consciousness in a cycle that lasts about 2 hours.

LO 4.3 **How do infants' bodies change, and what is the typical pattern of motor skill development in the first 2 years?**

• During infancy, bones increase in number and density; muscle fibers become larger and contain less water. Stamina improves as the lungs grow and the heart gets stronger. Motor skills improve rapidly in the first 2 years, as the baby moves from "creeping" to crawling to walking to running and becomes able to grasp objects.

Health and Wellness (pp. 89–91)

LO 4.4 **What are the nutritional needs of infants?**

• Breastfeeding has been shown to be better for a baby nutritionally than formula feeding.

LO 4.5 **How does malnutrition affect infants' development?**

• Macronutrient malnutrition results from a diet that contains too few calories, while micronutrient malnutrition is caused by a diet that has sufficient calories but lacks specific nutrients, vitamins, or minerals.

LO 4.6 **What are infants' health-care and immunization needs?**

• Babies need regular check-ups and a variety of immunizations. Prompt treatment of respiratory infections is also crucial.

Infant Mortality (pp. 91–95)

LO 4.7 **What have researchers learned about sudden infant death syndrome?**

• Sudden infant death syndrome is the most common cause of death between 1 month and 1 year of age in the United States. Risk factors for SIDS include sleeping on the stomach, sleep apnea, and exposure to tobacco smoke before and after birth.

LO 4.8 **How do infant mortality rates vary across groups?**

• African American, Hawaiian American, and Native American children are more likely to die in the first year of life than those in other U.S. racial groups. Poverty seems a likely explanation, but the relationship between low income and infant mortality is complex.

Sensory Skills (pp. 95–97)

LO 4.9 **How do infants' visual abilities change across the first months of life?**

• Color vision is present at birth, but visual acuity and visual tracking skill are relatively poor at birth and then develop rapidly during the first few months.

LO 4.10 **How do infants' senses of hearing, smell, taste, touch, and motion compare to those of older children and adults?**

• Basic auditory skills are more fully developed at birth; acuity is good for the range of the human voice, and the newborn can locate at least the approximate direction of sounds. The sensory capacities for smelling, tasting, and the senses of touch and motion are also well developed at birth.

Perceptual Skills (pp. 97–102)

LO 4.11 **How do researchers study perceptual development in infants?**

• In the preference technique, researchers track how long babies look at each of a pair of stimuli. Habituation involves exposing babies to stimuli until they are no longer interested in them. The purpose is to see whether the babies will then respond to a new stimulus that is only slightly different from the original one (dishabituation). By using operant conditioning, researchers train babies to perform behaviors such as turning their heads in response to specific stimuli. Then the researchers vary the stimulus slightly; if babies do not respond as they have been trained to do, then the researchers know that they can tell the difference between the original and the new stimulus.

LO 4.12 How do depth perception and patterns of looking change over the first 2 years?

- Depth perception is present in at least rudimentary form by 3 months. Babies initially use kinetic cues, then binocular cues, and finally pictorial (monocular) cues by about 5 to 7 months. Visual attention appears to follow definite rules, even in the first hours of life. Babies can discriminate the mother's face from other faces, and the mother's voice from other voices, almost immediately after birth.

LO 4.13 How do infants perceive human speech, recognize voices, and recognize sound patterns other than speech?

- From the beginning, babies appear to attend to and discriminate among speech contrasts present in all possible languages;

by the age of 1 year, the infant makes fine discriminations only among speech sounds salient in the language he is actually hearing. By 6 months, babies also attend to and discriminate among different patterns of sounds, such as melodies or speech inflections.

LO 4.14 What is intermodal perception?

- Studies show that infants can learn something via one sense and transfer it to another sense—a skill known as intermodal perception. The capacity for intermodal perception develops before birth and matures across the first few months of life.

LO 4.15 What arguments do nativists and empiricists offer in support of their theories of perceptual development?

- A central issue in the study of perceptual development continues to be the nativism–empiricism controversy. Many basic perceptual abilities, including strategies for examining objects, appear to be built into the system at birth or to develop as the brain develops over the early years. But specific experience is required both to maintain the underlying system and to learn fundamental discriminations and patterns.

KEY TERMS

adaptive reflexes (p. 85)
auditory acuity (p. 96)
colic (p. 86)
dishabituation (p. 97)
dynamic systems theory (p. 87)
empiricists (p. 101)

habituation (p. 97)
infant mortality (p. 91)
intermodal perception (p. 100)
myelinization (p. 85)
nativists (p. 101)
plasticity (p. 84)

preference technique (p. 97)
primitive reflexes (p. 85)
pruning (p. 83)
reticular formation (p. 85)
sudden infant death
  syndrome (SIDS) (p. 92)

synapses (p. 83)
synaptogenesis (p. 83)
tracking (p. 95)
visual acuity (p. 95)

CHAPTER TEST   ✓ Study and Review in MyPsychLab

Answers to all the Chapter Test questions can be found in the back of the book.

1. Which of the following require input from only one eye?
   a. linear cues
   b. kinetic cues
   c. monocular cues
   d. binocular cues

2. What is the name of the process in which sheaths that speed neural transmissions develop around the axons?
   a. lateralization
   b. myelinization
   c. synaptogenesis
   d. pruning

3. Infants recognize the difference between speech sounds such as *ba* and *pa* as early as _____ month(s) of age.
   a. 1
   b. 6
   c. 12
   d. 18

4. According to this chapter, which of these statements is true regarding the nutritional needs of a preterm infant?
   a. Breast milk alone is sufficient.
   b. A formula that includes acids and fats that preterm babies' bodies cannot manufacture is sufficient.

   c. Optimal nutrition for preterm infants includes breast milk and a formula that includes acids and fats that preterm babies' bodies cannot manufacture.
   d. A formula that is supplemented with iron is sufficient.

5. Newborns' auditory skill is poorer than that of adults with

   _____.

   a. Low-pitched sounds
   b. High-pitched sounds
   c. Sounds played at very low volumes
   d. Sounds that are within the general range of pitch and loudness of the human voice

6. An infant exhibits habituation to a stimulus when she

   _____.

   a. shows signs of boredom such as quickly looking away from the stimulus when it is presented
   b. smiles at the stimulus
   c. looks directly at the stimulus
   d. looks at the stimulus for a long period of time

7. Which of these factors does *not* increase the risk of sudden infant death syndrome?
   a. prenatal exposure to tobacco
   b. sleep position
   c. delayed myelination
   d. increasingly lengthy sleep periods during the early months of life

8. Dr. Adwala is using the preference technique to study infant perception. His study will involve presenting two stimuli to infants and tracking _____.
   a. the babies' emotional responses to each stimulus
   b. the babies' motor responses to each stimulus
   c. how the babies' eyes move from one stimulus to the other
   d. how long the babies look at each stimulus

9. The reticular formation regulates _____.
   a. auditory perception
   b. attention
   c. memory functions
   d. body temperature

10. Studies by Gibson and Walk revealed that 6-month-old infants can _____.
    a. discriminate between angles of different sizes
    b. recognize their mothers' faces
    c. perceive depth
    d. see as well as an adult with 20/20 vision

11. A _____ deficiency would be classified as macronutrient malnutrition; a _____ deficiency would be classified as micronutrient malnutrition.
    a. protein, calcium
    b. calcium, protein
    c. iron, calcium
    d. calorie, protein

12. What is another name for the Moro reflex?
    a. pain withdrawal
    b. sucking
    c. pupil dilation
    d. startle

13. According to this chapter, there is a correlation between the frequency of ear infections in infancy and later learning disabilities, because ear infections _____.
    a. damage the brain
    b. interfere with hearing and language development
    c. cause delays in infants' motor development
    d. reduce an infant's appetite

14. Thelen's dynamic systems theory explains _____.
    a. the disappearance of reflexes in infancy
    b. the development of depth perception in the first 6 months of life
    c. the effects of television on the developing brain
    d. the development of auditory perception in infants and toddlers

15. A child's ability to walk up and down stairs requires which type of motor skills?
    a. nonlocomotive
    b. both gross and fine
    c. fine
    d. gross

16. Which group has the lowest infant mortality rate?
    a. Mexican Americans
    b. Chinese Americans
    c. African Americans
    d. Puerto Rican Americans

17. Which statement is true regarding synaptogenesis and pruning?
    a. Both continue throughout the lifespan.
    b. Synaptogenesis is completed in infancy, but pruning continues throughout the lifespan.
    c. Synaptogenesis continues throughout the lifespan, but pruning is completed in infancy.
    d. Both are completed in infancy.

18. Signs of a day/night sleep pattern in the first few weeks of life are a manifestation of _____.
    a. the strategies that parents use to get babies to sleep through the night
    b. the establishment of circadian rhythms
    c. parents' acceptance of babies' natural patterns of sleep and wakefulness
    d. babies' increasing interest in the world around them

19. When do infants develop the capacity for intermodal perception?
    a. prior to birth
    b. in the first month
    c. in the first 6 months
    d. in the first year

20. Which statement about infants' taste preferences is true?
    a. Infants first display taste preferences at about 6 months of age.
    b. Newborns prefer sweet tastes.
    c. The sense of taste is not present in preterm babies.
    d. Infants cannot taste umami.

21. The synaptogenesis/pruning cycle increases the _____ of the infant's brain.
    a. efficiency
    b. complexity
    c. responsiveness
    d. plasticity

22. When the bottom of its foot is stroked, a baby responds by splaying out its toes, then curling them under. Which reflex is this?
    a. Babinski
    b. Nisod
    c. Moro
    d. Bronfenbrenner

23. Which infant may have some type of neurological problem?
    a. Two-month-old Abby is still not sleeping through the night.
    b. Four-month-old Raj still exhibits the Moro reflex.
    c. Six-month-old Michael refuses to eat solid foods.
    d. Ten-month-old Navida still exhibits the Babinski reflex.

24. What is the name of the process of creating new synapses which happens very quickly in the first couple years after birth?
    a. synaptomiosis
    b. synaptic pruning
    c. myelinization
    d. synaptogenesis

25. Which statement about experience and motor skill development is true?
    a. Infants who are deprived of opportunities for movement develop motor skills more slowly.
    b. Infants who watch their older siblings or parents demonstrate motor skills develop more rapidly.
    c. There is no correlation between experience and motor skill development.
    d. Special instructional programs can speed up motor skill development.

To 👁 **Watch** ✳ **Explore** ⊙ **Simulate** ✓ **Study** and **Review**
and experience MyVirtualLife go to MyPsychLab.com

chapter 5

Cognitive Development in Infancy

When the "child" you are raising in *MyVirtualLife* begins to speak, you are likely to find that her first words are among the most exciting events of infancy. The acquisition of language enables a child to become a full-fledged member of the human community. But what does a baby need to achieve this critical milestone?

Advertisements for books, videos, and expensive toys often make parents wonder whether they're providing their infant with the stimulation needed for optimum

LEARNING OBJECTIVES

COGNITIVE CHANGES

5.1 What are the milestones of Piaget's sensorimotor stage?

5.2 How have other theorists challenged Piaget's explanation of infant cognitive development?

5.3 What does research tell us about infants' understanding of objects?

LEARNING, CATEGORIZING, AND REMEMBERING

5.4 What kinds of learning are infants capable of?

5.5 How does categorical understanding change over the first 2 years?

5.6 How does memory function in the first 2 years?

THE BEGINNINGS OF LANGUAGE

5.7 What are the behaviorist, nativist, and interactionist explanations of language development?

5.8 What are some environmental influences on language development?

5.9 How do infants' sounds, gestures, and understanding of words change in the early months of life?

5.10 What are the characteristics of toddlers' first words?

5.11 What kinds of sentences do children produce between 18 and 24 months of age?

5.12 What kinds of individual differences are evident in language development?

5.13 How does language development vary across cultures?

MEASURING INTELLIGENCE IN INFANCY

5.14 How is intelligence measured in infancy?

language development. But the influence of experience on language development and on cognitive development in general is most evident in cases in which a rather dramatic disruption in environmental support—malnourishment, child abuse, lead poisoning, and the like—impedes intellectual development. Researchers have known for some time that extraordinary amounts of intellectual stimulation do little, if anything, to enhance cognitive development in healthy infants (Bruer, 1999). As to what is actually required, anxious parents may rest easy. According to Bruer (1999), research shows that, in order to fulfill their intellectual potential, babies require caretakers who respond to all of their needs and who avoid narrowly focusing on a specific developmental outcome, such as increasing the odds that an infant will be able to get high scores on intelligence tests when she starts school.

In this chapter, you will learn about Piaget's explanation of the universal changes in thinking that happen in the first 2 years of life as well as the ways in which other theorists explain Piaget's research findings. You will also read about learning and memory during these years and about the beginnings of language. Individual differences in intelligence among infants will be discussed as well.

Cognitive Changes

The remarkable cognitive advances that happen in infancy are highly consistent across environments. Of course, 2-year-olds are still a long way from cognitive maturity, but some of the most important steps toward that goal are taken in the first 2 years of life.

Piaget's View of the First 2 Years

LO 5.1   What are the milestones of Piaget's sensorimotor stage?

Piaget assumed that a baby *assimilates* incoming information to the limited array of schemes she is born with—looking, listening, sucking, grasping—and *accommodates* those schemes based on her experiences. He called this form of thinking *sensorimotor intelligence*. Thus, the **sensorimotor stage** is the period during which infants develop and refine sensorimotor intelligence. (See Table 5.1 on page 107.)

SENSORIMOTOR STAGE In Piaget's view, a newborn who is in substage 1 (roughly 0–1 month) of the sensorimotor stage is entirely tied to the immediate present, responding to whatever stimuli are available. She forgets events from one encounter to the next and does not appear to plan. Substage 2 (from roughly 1 to 4 months) is marked by the beginning of the coordinations between looking and listening, between reaching and looking, and between reaching and sucking that are such central features of the 2-month-old's means of exploring the world. The technique that distinguishes substage 2, **primary circular reactions**, refers to the many simple repetitive actions seen at this time, each organized around the infant's own body. For example, the baby may accidentally suck his thumb one day, find it pleasurable, and repeat the action. ⊙ **Watch** the **Video** *The Sensorimotor Stage* in **MyPsychLab**.

In substage 3 (from about 4 to 8 months), the baby repeats some action in order to trigger a reaction outside her own body, a **secondary circular reaction**. The baby coos and Mom smiles, so the baby coos again to get Mom to smile again. These initial connections between body actions and external consequences seem to be simple, almost mechanical, links between stimuli and responses. However, in substage 4, the 8- to 12-month-old baby shows the beginnings of understanding causal connections, at which point she moves into exploratory high gear. One consequence of this new drive to explore is **means–end behavior**, or the ability to

sensorimotor stage Piaget's first stage of development, in which infants use information from their senses and motor actions to learn about the world

primary circular reactions Piaget's phrase to describe a baby's simple repetitive actions in substage 2 of the sensorimotor stage, organized around the baby's own body

secondary circular reactions repetitive actions in substage 3 of the sensorimotor period, oriented around external objects

means–end behavior purposeful behavior carried out in pursuit of a specific goal

TABLE 5.1 Substages of Piaget's Sensorimotor Stage

Substage	Average Age	Primary Technique	Characteristics
1	0–1 month	Reflexes	Use of built-in schemes or reflexes such as sucking or looking. Primitive schemes begin to change through very small steps of accommodation. Limited imitation, no ability to integrate information from several senses.
2	1–4 months	Primary circular reactions	Further accommodation of basic schemes, as the baby practices them endlessly—grasping, listening, looking, sucking. Beginning coordination of schemes from different senses, so that the baby now looks toward a sound and sucks on anything he can reach and bring to his mouth. But the baby does not yet link his body actions to results outside his body.
3	4–8 months	Secondary circular reactions	The baby becomes much more aware of events outside her own body and makes them happen again in a kind of trial-and-error learning. Scientists are unsure, however, whether babies this young understand the causal links yet. Imitation may occur, but only of schemes already in the baby's repertoire. Beginning understanding of the "object concept" can also be detected in this period.
4	8–12 months	Coordination of secondary schemes	Clear intentional means–end behavior. The baby not only goes after what he wants, but he may combine two schemes to do so, such as moving a pillow aside to reach a toy. Imitation of novel behavior occurs, as does transfer of information from one sense to the other (cross-modal perception).
5	12–18 months	Tertiary circular reactions	"Experimentation" begins, in which the infant tries out new ways of playing with or manipulating objects. Very active, very purposeful trial-and-error exploration.
6	18–24 months	Beginning of mental representation	Development of use of symbols to represent object or events. The child understands that the symbol is separate from the object. As a result, infants in this stage are able to solve problems by thinking about them. Moreover, deferred imitation becomes possible, because it requires ability to represent internally the event to be imitated.

keep a goal in mind and devise a plan to achieve it. Babies show this kind of behavior when they move one toy out of the way to gain access to another. The end is the toy they want; the means to the end is moving the other toy.

In substage 5 (from about 12 to 18 months), exploration of the environment becomes more focused, with the emergence of **tertiary circular reactions**. In this pattern, the baby doesn't merely repeat the original behavior but tries out variations. He may try out many sounds or facial expressions to see if they will trigger Mom's smile, or he may try dropping a toy from several heights to see if it makes different sounds or lands in different places. At this substage, the baby's behavior has a purposeful, experimental quality. Nonetheless, Piaget thought that the baby does not yet have mental symbols to stand for objects.

The ability to manipulate mental symbols, such as words or images, marks substage 6, which lasts from roughly 18 months to 24 months of age. This new capacity allows the infant to generate solutions to problems simply by thinking about them, without the trial-and-error behavior typical of substage 5. As a result, means–end behavior becomes far more sophisticated than in earlier stages. For example, a 24-month-old who knows there are cookies in the cookie jar can figure out how to get one. Furthermore, she can find a way to overcome just about any obstacle placed in her path (Bauer, Schwade, Wewerka, & Delaney, 1999). If her parents respond to her climbing on the kitchen counter in pursuit of a cookie by moving the cookie jar to the top of the refrigerator, the substage 6 toddler's response will likely be to find a way to climb to the top of the refrigerator. Thus, changes in cognition are behind the

tertiary circular reactions the deliberate experimentation with variations of previous actions that occurs in substage 5 of the sensorimotor period

Four-month-old Andrea may be showing a secondary circular reaction here, shaking her hand repeatedly to hear the sound of the rattle.

After babies acquire object permanence, they become fascinated with activities that involve putting objects into containers that partially or fully obscure the objects from view. This fascination goes far beyond toys such as the shape sorter pictured here and extends to all kinds of things that hold objects and can be opened and closed—purses, closets, drawers, cabinets, shopping bags, garbage cans, pet crates, and a wide variety of other things that parents probably don't want their babies to get into.

common impression of parents and other caregivers that 18- to 24-month-olds cannot be left unsupervised, even for very short periods of time.

OBJECT PERMANENCE You know that this book continues to exist even when you are unable to see it—an understanding that Piaget called **object permanence**. In a series of studies, many of which involved his own children, Piaget discovered that babies acquire this understanding gradually during the sensorimotor period. According to his observations, replicated frequently by later researchers, the first sign that a baby is developing object permanence comes at about 2 months of age (in substage 2). Suppose you show a toy to a child of this age and then put a screen in front of the toy and remove the toy. When you then remove the screen, the baby will show some indication of surprise, as if he knows that something should still be there. The child thus seems to have a rudimentary expectation about the permanence of an object. But infants of this age show no signs of searching for a toy that has fallen over the side of the crib or that has disappeared beneath a blanket or behind a screen. 👁 **Watch** the **Video** *Infancy: Object Permanence across Cultures* in **MyPsychLab**.

In substage 3 (at about 6–8 months), however, babies will look over the edge of the crib for dropped toys or on the floor for food that was spilled. (In fact, babies of this age may drive their parents nuts playing "dropsy" from the high chair.) Infants this age will also search for partially hidden objects. If you put a baby's favorite toy under a cloth but leave part of it sticking out, the infant will reach for the toy, which indicates that in some sense she "recognizes" that the whole object is there, even though she can see only part of it. But if you cover the toy completely with the cloth or put it behind a screen, the infant will stop looking for it and will not reach for it, even if she has seen you put the cloth over it.

This behavior changes again between 8 and 12 months, in substage 4. Infants of this age will reach for or search for a toy that has been covered completely by a cloth or hidden by a screen. Thus, by 12 months, most infants appear to grasp the basic fact that objects continue to exist even when they are no longer visible. However, substage 4 infants' understanding of where a hidden object might be found is limited by the **A-not-B error**. This flaw in logic leads infants to look for an object in the place where it was last seen (position A) rather than in the place to which they have seen a researcher move it (position B) (Flavell, 1963). In substage 5, infants' searching strategies are somewhat more logical. For instance, if they see a researcher hide an object in her hand and immediately move the hand behind screen A, dropping the object out of view, they will persist in searching for the object in the researcher's hand just as substage 4 infants do. However, if they see the researcher move a hidden object from behind screen A to behind screen B, they will immediately look for it behind screen B. This error is not resolved until substage 6. Thus, infants' full understanding of the behavior of objects and their connections to the spaces in which they appear and can possibly appear does not emerge until near the end of the second year of life.

IMITATION Piaget also studied infants' ability to imitate the actions of others. He observed that as early as the first few months of life, infants could imitate actions they could see themselves make, such as hand gestures. But he found that they could not imitate other people's facial gestures until substage 4 (8–12 months). This second form of imitation seems to require some kind of intermodal perception, combining the visual cues of seeing the other's face with the kinesthetic cues (perceptions of muscle motion) from one's own facial movements. Piaget argued that imitation of any action that wasn't already in the child's repertoire did not occur until about 1 year and that **deferred imitation**—a child's imitation of some action at a later time—was possible only in substage 6, since deferred imitation requires some kind of internal representation.

Challenges to Piaget's View

LO 5.2 How have other theorists challenged Piaget's explanation of infant cognitive development?

Many studies since Piaget's time have suggested that he underestimated the cognitive capacity of infants. By changing the methods used to measure object permanence, for instance,

object permanence the understanding that objects continue to exist when they can't be seen

A-not-B error substage 4 infants' tendency to look for an object in the place where it was last seen (position A) rather than in the place to which they have seen a researcher move it (position B)

deferred imitation imitation that occurs in the absence of the model who first demonstrated it

researchers have found that younger infants better understand object movements than Piaget suggested (Thomas, 2005). Moreover, studies have shown that imitation appears at younger ages than Piaget's research implied.

OBJECT PERMANENCE In Piaget's studies of object permanence, infants were judged as having object permanence if they moved a blanket in order to retrieve a hidden object. You may recall from Chapter 4 that infants are unable to grasp and move objects in this way until they are 7 to 8 months old. Thus, Piaget's methods made it impossible to tell whether younger infants failed to exhibit object permanence because they were physically unable to perform the task of moving the blanket (Birney & Sternberg, 2011).

Thanks to the advent of computers, researchers have been able to measure infants' understanding of objects in ways that do not depend on motor skill development. In many post-Piagetian studies of object permanence, researchers use computer technology to keep track of how infants' eyes respond when researchers move objects from one place to another. These "looking" studies have demonstrated that babies as young as 4 months show clear signs of object permanence if a visual response rather than a reaching response is used to test it (Baillargeon, 2004). Moreover, many studies have examined how infants respond to a moving object that temporarily disappears behind a screen (Hespos & Baillargeon, 2008). In these studies, most 5-month-olds immediately looked to the other side of the screen when the moving object disappeared behind it and were delighted when it reappeared. These findings indicate that infants are holding some kind of representation of the hidden object in mind when it is behind the screen—and this is the essence of object permanence. Nevertheless, such studies typically show that younger infants' understanding of object permanence is tied to the specific experimental situation. By contrast, babies who are nearing or past their first birthday understand object permanence sufficiently to use it across all kinds of situations, such as when they playfully hide objects from themselves and delight in "finding" them.

Findings like these have sparked renewed discussion of the nature-versus-nurture issue (e.g., Baillargeon, 2008; Kagan, 2008; Müller & Giesbrecht, 2008). Piaget assumed that a baby came equipped with a repertoire of sensorimotor schemes, but his most fundamental theoretical proposal was that the child constructed an understanding of the world based on experience. In contrast, more recent theorizing suggests that the development of object permanence is more a process of elaboration than one of discovery. Newborns may have considerable awareness of objects as separate entities that follow certain rules (Valenza, Leo, Gava, & Simion, 2006). Certainly, all the research on the perception of patterns suggests that babies pay far more attention to relationships between events than Piaget's model supposed. Still, no one would argue that a baby came equipped with a full-fledged knowledge of objects or a well-developed ability to experiment with the world.

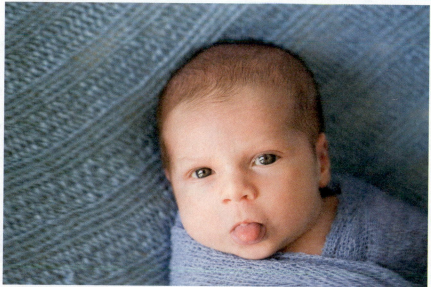

IMITATION With respect to imitation, Piaget's proposed sequence has been supported (Anisfeld, 2005). Imitation of someone else's hand movement or an action with an object seems to improve steadily, starting at 1 or 2 months of age; imitation of two-part actions develops much later, perhaps around 15–18 months (Poulson, Nunes, & Warren, 1989). Yet there are two important exceptions to this general confirmation of Piaget's theory: Infants imitate some facial gestures in the first weeks of life, and deferred imitation seems to occur earlier than Piaget proposed.

Several researchers have found that newborn babies will imitate certain facial gestures—particularly tongue protrusion, as shown in Figure 5.1 (Anisfeld, 2005; Meltzoff & Moore, 1977). This seems to happen only if the model sits with his tongue out, looking at the baby for a fairly long period of time, perhaps as long as a minute. But the fact that newborns imitate at all is striking—although it is entirely consistent

Figure 5.1 Imitation in Newborns

Although researchers still disagree on how much newborns will imitate, everyone agrees that they will imitate the gesture of tongue protrusion.

with the observation that quite young babies are capable of tactile–visual intermodal transfer, or perception.

Most studies of deferred imitation also support Piaget's model. However, some research indicates that infants as young as 6 weeks of age can defer imitation for at least a few minutes (Bremner, 2002). Moreover, studies show that babies as young as 6 months can defer imitation for 10 minutes or so (Goertz et al., 2011). By 9 months, infants can defer their imitation for as long as 24 hours (Herbert, Gross, & Hayne, 2006; Meltzoff, 1988). By 14 months, toddlers can recall and imitate someone's actions as much as 2 days later (Hanna & Meltzoff, 1993).

These findings are significant for several reasons. First, they make it clear that infants can and do learn specific behaviors through modeling, even when they have no chance to imitate the behavior immediately. In addition, these results suggest that babies may be more skillful than Piaget thought. Clearly, too, more abilities than he suggested may be built in from the beginning and develop continuously, rather than in stages, throughout infancy (Courage & Howe, 2002).

Alternative Approaches

LO 5.3   What does research tell us about infants' understanding of objects?

The many challenges to Piaget's characterization of infant thinking discussed above have led some developmental researchers to investigate object permanence within the more general context of infants' understanding of what objects are and how they behave. Researchers use the term **object concept** to refer to this understanding. The most thorough and clever work on the development of the object concept has been done by Elizabeth Spelke and her colleagues (Spelke & Hespos, 2001). Spelke believes that babies are born with certain built-in assumptions that guide their interactions with objects. One of these is the assumption that when two surfaces are connected to each other, they belong to the same object; Spelke calls this the connected-surface principle. For instance, you know that all sides of your textbook are connected together in a single, solid object.

In Spelke's early studies of this phenomenon (e.g., Spelke, 1982), she first habituated some 3-month-old babies to a series of displays of two objects; she habituated other babies to the sight of one-object displays. Then the babies were shown two objects touching each other, such as two square blocks placed next to each other so that they created a rectangle. Under these conditions, the babies who had been habituated to two-object displays showed renewed interest, clearly indicating that they "saw" this display as different, presumably as a single object. Babies who had seen the one-object displays during habituation showed no renewed interest.

In later experiments, Spelke (1991) used the **violation-of-expectations method**, a research strategy in which an infant is habituated to a display that depicts the movement of an object and then is shown another display in which the object moves in a way that goes against what the infant expects to happen. These studies demonstrated that babies as young as 2 and 3 months old are remarkably aware of what kinds of movements objects are capable of. In the habituation phase of the procedure, two-month-old babies watched as Spelke rolled a ball behind a screen. A wall behind the screen stopped the ball's motion. A few seconds after the ball disappeared behind the screen, Spelke removed the screen so that the infants could see the ball resting against the wall. After the infants were habituated to this series of events, Spelke varied the procedure by placing two walls, one behind the other, behind the screen. She showed the babies the ball rolling behind the screen as she had before. When Spelke lifted the screen, the infants saw the ball resting against the first wall. Predictably, the infants showed little interest in this variation because it was so similar to the one they had watched during the habituation phase. Next, Spelke rolled the ball behind the screen as before, but this time she moved the ball so that it rested against the second wall before lifting the screen. As a result, from the infants' perspective, when Spelke lifted the screen, the ball appeared to have rolled through the first wall and stopped against the second one, a physically impossible outcome. Spelke reported that the infants showed sharply renewed interest in the impossible outcome, suggesting that very young infants' understanding of the rules governing relations among objects was more fully developed than Piaget's theory argues.

object concept an infant's understanding of the nature of objects and how they behave

violation-of-expectations method a research strategy in which researchers move an object in one way after having taught an infant to expect it to move in another

Other researchers, such as Renée Baillargeon (1994; Baillargeon, Li, Ng, & Yuan, 2009), argue that knowledge about objects is not built in, but that strategies for learning are innate. According to this view, infants initially develop basic hypotheses about the way objects function—how they move and how they connect to one another. Then these early basic hypotheses are quite rapidly modified, based on the baby's experience with objects. For example, Baillargeon finds that 2- to 3-month-old infants are already operating with a basic hypothesis that an object will fall if it isn't supported by something, but they have no notion of how much support is required. By about 5 months of age, this basic hypothesis has been refined, so they understand that the cube in Figure 5.2(a) is less likely to topple over than the cube in Figure 5.2(b) is (Baillargeon, 1994).

However, other psychologists question Baillargeon's conclusions. For example, developmental psychologist Leslie Cohen and his associates have conducted similar experiments with 8-month-olds and argue that infants respond to the stimuli used in such studies on the basis of novelty, rather than because of an understanding of stable and unstable block arrangements (Cashon & Cohen, 2000). Such varying interpretations demonstrate just how difficult it is to make inferences about infants' thinking from their interactions with physical objects.

Research has also examined the degree to which infants can make practical use of their understanding of objects and object movements. For example, several studies have shown that 2-year-olds experience difficulty when they are required to use this understanding to search for a hidden object (Keen, 2003). In one study, 2-, 2.5-, and 3-year-olds were shown a sequences of events similar to those Spelke used in her experiments with two-month-olds and responded in exactly the same way as younger infants to impossible outcomes such as a ball rolling through one wall and coming to rest on another behind it (Berthier, DeBlois, Poirier, Novak, & Clifton, 2000). Next, a board in which there were several doors took the place of the screen; however, the barrier protruded several inches above this board (see Figure 5.3). Across several trials, children were shown the ball rolling behind the board and were asked to open the door behind which they thought the ball would be found. Even though the children could clearly see behind which door the barrier was placed in every trial, none of the 2-year-olds and only a few of the 2.5-year-olds were able to succeed on this task, in contrast to the large majority of 3-year-olds. Developmentalists interpret such results to mean that young infants' understanding of objects is the foundation upon which the object concept is gradually constructed and applied to real-world interaction with objects over the first 3 years of life (Keen et al., 2008).

Figure 5.2 Object Stability Perception
Renée Baillargeon's research suggests that 5-month-olds realize that the cube in Figure 5.2(a) is more stable than the one in Figure 5.2(b).

test yourself before going on ✓ Study and Review in MyPsychLab

Answers to these questions can be found in the back of the book.

1. Number the milestones of the sensorimotor stage in the order in which they occur.

    _____ **(a)** means–end behavior

    _____ **(b)** object permanence

    _____ **(c)** deferred imitation

    _____ **(d)** A-not-B error

2. In contrast to the research strategies that Piaget used, contemporary computerized methods of studying object permanence do not rely on infants' _____ _____ development.

3. _____ argued that babies are born with built-in assumptions about objects.

CRITICAL THINKING

4. How would you explain an infant's habit of throwing things out of her crib to a parent who viewed it as misbehavior that needed to be corrected?

Figure 5.3 Toddlers' Understanding of Object Movement

Researchers use devices such as this one to find out whether toddlers can predict that a moving object will be stopped by the barrier that protrudes above the wall of doors. Children younger than 3 typically fail to identify the door behind which the object will be found.

Learning, Categorizing, and Remembering

Generally, the term *learning* is used to denote permanent changes in behavior that result from experience. From the first moments following birth, infants exhibit evidence of learning—that is, environmental forces change their behaviors. However, infants also actively organize their interactions with these forces, as research examining categorization and memory clearly shows.

Conditioning and Modeling

LO 5.4   What kinds of learning are infants capable of?

Learning of emotional responses through classical conditioning processes may begin as early as the first week of life. For example, in classic research, pediatrician Mavis Gunther (1955, 1961) found that inexperienced mothers often held nursing newborns in ways that caused the babies' nostrils to be blocked by the breast. Predictably, the babies reflexively turned away from the breast in response to the sensation of smothering. During future nursing sessions, babies who had experienced the smothering sensation while nursing at their mother's right breast refused to nurse on the right side; babies who had associated the smothering sensation with the left breast displayed the opposite pattern of refusal. Gunther hypothesized that classical conditioning was at work in such cases. She developed an intervention based on principles of stimulus–response learning to help babies "unlearn" the response of turning away from the breast they had learned to associate with the sensation of smothering.

Newborns also clearly learn by operant conditioning. For example, music therapists have discovered that the use of *pacifier-activated lullaby* (PAL) systems in neonatal intensive care units improves preterm infants' sucking reflexes, which, in turn, causes them to gain weight more rapidly (Cevasco & Grant, 2005; Yildiz & Arikan, 2012). These systems reward infants with music whenever they suck on specially designed pacifiers. At the least, the fact that conditioning of this kind can take place in preterm infants means that whatever neurological wiring is needed for operant learning is present before birth. Results like these also tell developmentalists something about the sorts of reinforcements that are effective with very young children; it is surely highly significant for the whole process of mother–infant interaction that the mother's voice is an effective reinforcer for virtually all babies.

Infants can also learn by watching models, especially in the second year. In one study, 10- and 12-month-olds were randomly assigned to two learning groups (Provasi, Dubon, & Bloch, 2001). "Observers" first watched an adult demonstrate how to find a toy by lifting the lids of various containers and then were allowed to play with the containers. "Actors" played with the containers on their own. Researchers found that observers were more proficient at finding the toy than actors in both age groups. However, the effect was much more pronounced among the older infants. Moreover, by 14 months, infants distinguish between successful and unsuccessful models and, like older children and adults, are more likely to imitate those who succeed at an attempted task (Zmyj, Buttelmann, Carpenter, & Daum, 2010).

Schematic Learning

LO 5.5   How does categorical understanding change over the first 2 years?

Schematic learning is the organizing of experiences into expectancies, or "known" combinations. These expectancies, often called schemas, are built up over many exposures to particular experiences. Once formed, they help the baby to distinguish between the familiar and the unfamiliar.

One kind of schematic learning involves categories. Research suggests that by 7 months of age, and perhaps even earlier, infants actively use categories to process information (Elsner, Jeschonek, & Pauen, 2013). For example, a 7-month-old is likely to habituate to a sequence of 10 animal pictures and, if the next picture is of another animal, will not show surprise or look

schematic learning organization of experiences into expectancies, called schemas, that enable infants to distinguish between familiar and unfamiliar stimuli

at it any longer than the first 10. If, however, researchers show the baby a picture of a human after 10 animal pictures, the baby will look surprised and gaze at the picture longer. The same thing is likely to happen if researchers show an infant several pictures of humans and then switch to an animal picture.

Such findings suggest that infants build and use categories as they take in information. However, categorical organization as a cognitive tool is clearly not well developed in 7-month-olds. For one thing, infants of this age clearly do not understand the difference between lower-level and higher-level categories. "Dogs" and "animals," for example, can both be thought of as categories, but the higher-level one ("animals") includes the lower-level one. Thus, categories such as "animals" are referred to as *superordinates*. Researchers have found that infants respond to superordinate categories before they display reactions to basic-level categories (Pauen, 2002). In other words, 7- or 8-month-olds view "animals" and "furniture" as different categories, but not "dogs" and "birds." By contrast, 12-month-olds appear to understand both types of categories.

Still, 12-month-olds don't yet know that basic-level categories such as "dogs" and "birds" are nested within the superordinate category "animals." The concept that smaller categories are nested within larger ones, or *hierarchical categorization*, is demonstrated to some degree by 2-year-olds (Diesendruck & Shatz, 2001). However, full understanding of this kind of categorization is not typical until age 5 or so and is linked to language development and experiences with using words as category labels (Malabonga & Pasnak, 2002; Omiya & Uchida, 2002).

Memory

LO 5.6 How does memory function in the first 2 years?

An ingenious series of studies by Carolyn Rovee-Collier and her colleagues has shown that babies as young as 3 months of age can remember specific objects and their own actions with those objects over periods as long as a week (Rovee-Collier & Cuevas, 2009). A researcher first hangs an attractive mobile over a baby's crib, as shown in Figure 5.4, and watches to see how the baby responds, noting how often he kicks his legs while looking at the mobile. After 3 minutes of this "baseline" observation, a string is used to connect the mobile to the baby's leg, so that each time the baby kicks his leg, the mobile moves. Babies quickly learn to kick repeatedly in order to make this interesting action occur. Within 3–6 minutes, 3-month-olds double or triple their kick rates, clearly showing that learning has occurred. The researcher next tests the baby's memory of this learning by coming back some days later and hanging the same mobile over the crib but not attaching the string to the baby's foot. The crucial issue is whether the baby kicks rapidly at the mere sight of the mobile. If the baby remembers the previous occasion, he should kick at a higher rate than he did when he first saw the mobile, which is precisely what 3-month-old babies do, even after a delay of as long as a week.

Such findings demonstrate that a young infant is more cognitively sophisticated than developmentalists (and Piaget) had supposed. At the same time, these studies support Piaget's view that infants show systematic gains in the ability to remember over the months of infancy. Two-month-olds can remember their kicking action for only 1 day, 3-month-olds can remember it for over a week, and 6-month-olds can remember it longer than 2 weeks.

However, early infant memories are strongly tied to the specific context in which the original experience occurred (Barr, Marrott, & Rovee-Collier, 2003; Patel, Gaylord, & Fagan, 2013). Even 6-month-olds do not recognize or remember the mobile if the context is changed even slightly—for example, by hanging a different cloth around the crib in which the infant is tested. However, Rovee-Collier and her colleagues have also learned that lost infant memories can be "reactivated" with the use of cues that remind the baby of the association between a behavior, such as kicking, and a stimulus, such as a mobile (Bearce & Rovee-Collier, 2006). Thus, babies do remember more than Piaget believed, but their memories are highly specific. With age, their memories become less and less tied to specific cues or contexts.

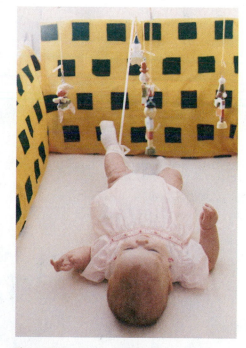

Figure 5.4 Rovee-Collier's Study of Infant Memory

This 3-month-old baby in one of Rovee-Collier's memory experiments will quickly learn to kick her foot in order to make the mobile move. Several days later, she will remember this connection between kicking and the mobile.

(*Source:* Rovee-Collier, 1993, 131.)

Answers to these questions can be found in the back of the book.

1. During the second year, infants begin to imitate models they view as _____.

2. Organization of experience into expectancies is called _____ learning.

3. Rovee-Collier's research showed that _____ is important in infant memory.

CRITICAL THINKING

4. In what ways do conditioning, modeling, categorical learning, and memory contribute to the development of social relationships between infants and their caregivers?

The Beginnings of Language

Most of us think of "language" as beginning when the baby uses her first words, at about 12 months of age. But all sorts of important developments precede the first words. Before we look at these developments, though, we'll look at the various theoretical perspectives that try to explain them.

Theoretical Perspectives

LO 5.7 What are the behaviorist, nativist, and interactionist explanations of language development?

The nature–nurture debate is alive and well in discussions of language development. The child's amazing progress in this domain in the early years of life has been explained from both behaviorist and nativist points of view and as part of the larger process of cognitive development.

THE BEHAVIORIST VIEW In the late 1950s, B. F. Skinner, the scientist who formulated operant conditioning theory, suggested a behaviorist explanation of language development (Skinner, 1957). He claimed that language development begins with **babbling**. While babbling, babies accidentally make sounds that somewhat resemble real words spoken by their parents. Parents hear the wordlike sounds and respond to them with praise and encouragement, which serve as reinforcers. Thus, wordlike babbling becomes more frequent, while utterances that do not resemble words gradually disappear from babies' vocalizations. Skinner further hypothesized that parents and others respond to grammatical uses of words and do not respond to nongrammatical ones. As a result, correct grammar is reinforced and becomes more frequent, but incorrect grammar is extinguished through nonreinforcement.

At first glance, Skinner's theory might appear to make sense. However, systematic examination of the interactions between infants and parents reveals that adults do not reinforce babies' vocalizations in this manner. Instead, parents and others respond to all of a baby's vocalizations, and even sometimes imitate them—a consequence that, according to operant conditioning theory, should prolong babbling rather than lead to the development of grammatical language. Skinner's mistake was that his theory was not based on observations of language development but rather on his assumption that the principles of operant conditioning underlie all human learning and development.

THE NATIVIST VIEW Have you ever heard a child say "I breaked it" instead of "I broke it" or "foots" instead of "feet"? Such utterances are the biggest challenge of all for behaviorists' explanations of language development because there is no way that they could be acquired through imitation. Moreover, when parents correct these errors, children often persist in using them, or they further *overregularize* them (e.g., "I broked it" or "feets"). Linguist Noam Chomsky used examples such as these to refute Skinner's theory (Chomsky, 1959). Chomsky argued that the only possible explanation for such errors was that children acquire grammar rules before they master the exceptions to them. Further, Chomsky proposed a nativist explanation for

babbling the repetitive vocalizing of consonant-vowel combinations by an infant

language development: Children's comprehension and production of language are guided by an innate language processor that he called the **language acquisition device (LAD)**, which contains the basic grammatical structure of all human language. In effect, the LAD tells infants what characteristics of language to look for in the stream of speech to which they are exposed. Simply put, the LAD tells babies that there are two basic types of sounds—consonants and vowels—and enables them to properly divide the speech they hear into the two categories so that they can analyze and learn the sounds that are specific to the language they are hearing. Chomsky supported the existence of the LAD with evidence compiled over hundreds of years by field linguists, which demonstrated that all human languages have the same grammatical forms. He also argued that the LAD is species specific—that is, nonhuman species do not have one and, therefore, cannot learn grammatical language.

Another influential nativist, Dan Slobin (1985a, 1985b), proposes that babies are preprogrammed to pay attention to the beginnings and endings of strings of sounds and to stressed sounds—a hypothesis supported by research (e.g., Morgan, 1994). Together, these operating principles would help explain some features of children's early grammars. In English, for example, the stressed words in a sentence are normally the verb and the noun—precisely the words that English-speaking children use in their earliest sentences. In Turkish, on the other hand, prefixes and suffixes are stressed, and Turkish-speaking children learn both very early. Both of these patterns make sense if we assume that the preprogrammed rule is not "verbness" or "nounness" or "prefixness" but "pay attention to stressed sounds."

THE INTERACTIONIST VIEW Clearly, nativist explanations like those of Chomsky and Slobin are more consistent than Skinner's view with both research findings and our everyday communication experiences with young children. Even so, some theorists cite research that demonstrates the rule-governed nature of young children's utterances to support a third approach. They argue that children's language follows rules because it is part of the broader process of cognitive development. Moreover, their explanations of language development include both internal and external factors. These theorists are known as **interactionists**.

Two common threads run through the interactionists' theories. First, infants are born with some kind of biological preparedness to pay more attention to language than to other kinds of information. Second, the interactionists argue that, rather than having a neurological module that is specific to language (i.e., an LAD), the infant's brain has a generalized set of tools that it employs across all of the subdomains of cognitive development. These tools allow infants to extract general principles from all kinds of specific experiences, including those that they have with language. Consequently, some interactionists argue that the nativists have paid too little attention to the role that the social context plays in language development (Tomasello, 1999), while others point out that nativist theories fail to capture the degree to which language and cognition develop interdependently (Bowerman, 1985).

One prominent proponent of this view, Melissa Bowerman, puts the proposition this way: "When language starts to come in, it does not introduce new meanings to the child. Rather, it is used to express only those meanings the child has already formulated independently of language" (1985, 372). Even more broadly, Lois Bloom argues that from the beginning of language, the child's intent is to communicate, to share the ideas and concepts in his head. He does this as best he can with the gestures or words he knows, and he learns new words when they help him communicate his thoughts and feelings (1993, 1997, 2004).

One type of evidence in support of this argument comes from the observation that it is children and not mothers who initiate the majority of verbal exchanges (Bloom, 1997). Further evidence comes from studies showing links between achievements in language development and the child's broader cognitive development. For example, symbolic play, such as drinking from an empty cup, and imitation of sounds and gestures both appear at about the same time as the child's first words, suggesting some broad "symbolic" understanding that is reflected in a number of behaviors. In children whose language is significantly delayed, both symbolic play and imitation are usually delayed as well (Bates, O'Connell, & Shore, 1987; Ungerer & Sigman, 1984).

language acquisition device (LAD) an innate language processor, theorized by Chomsky, that contains the basic grammatical structure of all human language

interactionists theorists who argue that language development is a subprocess of general cognitive development and is influenced by both internal and external factors

Gestures are just one of several skills in infants' repertoire of communicative skills.

A second example occurs later. At about the point at which two-word sentences appear, we also see children begin to combine several gestures into a sequence in their pretend play, such as pouring imaginary liquid, drinking, and then wiping the mouth. Those children who are the first to show this sequencing in their play are also the first to show two- or three-word sentences in their speech (e.g., McCune, 1995; Shore, 1986).

Influences on Language Development

LO 5.8 What are some environmental influences on language development?

Developmentalists better understand now how the environment influences language development than they did when Skinner and Chomsky began their historic debate in the 1950s. Moreover, the increasing emphasis on the interactionist approach has led researchers to examine the kinds of environmental influences to which children are exposed during different phases of language development. For example, adults and older children speak differently to infants than they do to preschoolers, a way of speaking that researchers call **infant-directed speech (IDS)**, also known as *motherese* or *parentese*. This pattern of speech is characterized by a higher pitch than that exhibited by adults and children when they are not speaking to an infant. Moreover, adults speaking to infants and young children also repeat a lot, introducing minor variations ("Where is the ball? Can you see the ball? Where is the ball? There is the ball!"). They may also repeat the child's own sentences but in slightly longer, more grammatically correct forms—a pattern referred to as an expansion or a recasting. For example, if a child said "Mommy sock," the mother might recast it as "Yes, this is Mommy's sock," or if a child said "Doggie not eating," the parent might say "The doggie is not eating."

Developmentalists believe that IDS influences language development to some degree (Cristia, 2013). For one thing, babies as young as a few days old can discriminate between IDS and adult-directed speech and that they prefer to listen to IDS, whether it is spoken by a female or male voice (Cooper & Aslin, 1994; Pegg, Werker, & McLeod, 1992). This preference exists even when the IDS is being spoken in a language other than the one normally spoken to the child. Janet Werker and her colleagues (1994), for example, have found that both English and Chinese infants prefer to listen to infant-directed speech, whether it is spoken in English or in Cantonese (one of the major languages of China). Other studies by Werker indicate that IDS helps infants identify the sounds in their mothers' speech that are specific to the language that they are learning (e.g., the English schwa, the Spanish rolled *r*) by emphasizing those sounds more than others (Werker et al., 2007). ◉ **Watch** the **Video** *Child Directed Speech* in **MyPsychLab**.

Infant-directed speech may also be important to grammar development. The quality of IDS that seems particularly attractive to babies is its higher pitch. Once the child's attention is drawn by this special tone, the very simplicity and repetitiveness of the adult's speech may help the child to pick out repeating grammatical forms. Children's attention also seems to be drawn to recast sentences. For example, Farrar (1992) found that a 2-year-old was two or three times more likely to imitate a correct grammatical form after he heard his mother recast his own sentences than when the mother used that same correct grammatical form in her normal conversation. Experimental studies confirm this effect of recastings. Children who are deliberately exposed to higher rates of specific types of recast sentences seem to learn the modeled grammatical forms more quickly than do those who hear no recastings (Nelson, 1977).

Developmentalists also know that children whose parents talk to them often, read to them regularly, and use a wide range of words in their speech differ from children whose parents do not. These children begin to talk sooner, develop larger vocabularies, use more complex sentences, and learn to read more readily when they reach school age (MacWhinney, 2011). Thus, the sheer quantity of language a child hears is a significant factor.

Finally, poverty is related to language development. By age 30 months, the difference in vocabulary between poor and better-off children is already substantial, and the gap widens

infant-directed speech (IDS) the simplified, higher-pitched speech that adults use with infants and young children

over the early childhood and school years (Horton-Ikard & Weismer, 2007). Similarly, Catherine Snow (1997) found that 4-year-old children reared in poverty use shorter and less complex sentences than do their better-off peers. Many factors no doubt contribute to these differences, but the richness and variety of the language a child hears is obviously highly significant. Of all these factors, being read to less often may be one of the most critical (Robb, Richert, & Wartella, 2009). (See *Developmental Science in the Classroom* below.)

Early Milestones of Language Development

LO 5.9   How do infants' sounds, gestures, and understanding of words change in the early months of life?

From birth to about 1 month of age, the most common sound an infant makes is a cry, although she also produces other fussing, gurgling, and satisfied sounds. Over the next few months, the number of ways in which a baby can express herself expands tremendously. Although some of these may seem to be of little consequence, each of the early milestones of language development makes a unique contribution to the language skills that all healthy children achieve in the first few years of life. ◉ **Watch** the **Video** *Toddlerhood: Language Development* in **MyPsychLab**.

FIRST SOUNDS AND GESTURES   At about 1 or 2 months, a baby begins to make some laughing and **cooing** vowel sounds. Sounds like this are usually signals of pleasure and may show quite a lot of variation in tone, running up and down in volume or pitch. Consonant sounds appear at about 6 or 7 months, frequently combined with vowel sounds to make a kind of syllable. Babies of this age seem to play with these sounds, often repeating the same sound over and over (such as *babababababa* or *dahdahdah*). This sound pattern, called babbling, makes up about half of babies' noncrying sounds from about 6 to 12 months of age (Mitchell & Kent, 1990).

Any parent can tell you that babbling is a delight to listen to. It also seems to be an important part of the preparation for spoken language. For one thing, infants' babbling gradually acquires some of what linguists call the *intonational pattern* of the language they are hearing—a process one developmental psychologist refers to as "learning the tune before the words" (Bates et al., 1987). At the very least, infants do seem to develop at least two such "tunes" in

cooing making repetitive vowel sounds, particularly the *uuu* sound

---

DEVELOPMENTAL SCIENCE IN THE CLASSROOM

The Importance of Reading to Toddlers

Greg is a certified early childhood educator. When he was pursuing his degree, he assumed that he would be teaching kindergarteners, so he developed an impressive repertoire of strategies for teaching preliteracy skills to 4- and 5-year-olds. However, the only job he was offered after graduation required him to spend half of each day teaching a group of 2-year-olds from low-income homes. Now he is wondering how he can utilize his preliteracy training with such young children.

Greg might be surprised to learn that 2-year-olds enjoy and benefit from many of the same preliteracy activities as older preschoolers. For instance, a classic series of studies by G. J. Whitehurst and his colleagues suggests that interactive reading can have powerful effects on a toddler's language development. In their first study, Whitehurst's team of researchers trained

some parents to read picture books to their toddlers and to interact with them using a strategy Whitehurst calls *dialogic reading*, which involves the use of questions that can't be answered by pointing (Whitehurst et al., 1988). For example, a parent reading a story about Winnie the Pooh might say, "There's Eeyore. What's happening to him?" Other parents were encouraged to read to their children but were given no special instructions about how to read. After a month, the children who had experienced dialogic reading showed a larger gain in vocabulary than did the children in the comparison group.

Whitehurst later replicated this study in day-care centers for poor children in both Mexico and New York City and in a large number of Head Start classrooms (Valdez-Menchaca & Whitehurst, 1992; Whitehurst et al., 1994; Whitehurst, Fischel, Crone, & Nania, 1995).

Greg can put Whitehurst's findings to work in his classroom by engaging in dialogic reading with his young pupils. In the process, he will be providing an important bridge between spoken and written language for children who will face the developmental task of acquiring literacy in just a few short years.

REFLECTION

1. *What would you say to a person who claimed that reading to an infant or a toddler is a waste of time because of their limited language skills?*

2. *If a toddler doesn't want to be read to, do you think his parents or teachers should try to get him interested in books? If so, how do you think they should go about it?*

their babbling. Babbling with a rising intonation at the end of a string of sounds seems to signal a desire for a response; a falling intonation requires no response.

A second important aspect is that when babies first start babbling, they typically babble all kinds of sounds, including some that are not part of the language they are hearing. But at about 9 or 10 months, their sound repertoire gradually begins to narrow down to the set of sounds they are listening to, with the nonheard sounds dropping out (Oller, 1981). Findings like these do not prove that babbling is necessary for language development, but they certainly make it look as if babbling is part of a connected developmental process that begins at birth.

Another part of that process appears to be a kind of gestural language that develops at around 9 or 10 months. At this age, babies begin "demanding" or "asking" for things, using gestures or combinations of gestures and sound. A 10-month-old baby who apparently wants you to hand her a favorite toy may stretch and reach for it, opening and closing her hand while making whining or whimpering sounds. Interestingly, infants of this age use gestures in this way whether they are exposed to spoken language or sign language (see *Research Report*). At about the same age, babies enter into those gestural games much loved by parents: "pat-a-cake," "soooo big," and "wave bye-bye" (Bates et al., 1987).

WORD RECOGNITION Recent research has shown that babies are already storing individual words in their memories at 6 months of age (Tincoff & Jusczyk, 2012). By 9 or 10 months, most can understand the meanings of 20–30 words; this ability to understand words is known as **receptive language**. In the next few months, the number of words understood increases dramatically. In one investigation, researchers asked hundreds of mothers about their babies' understanding of various words. Reportedly, 10-month-olds understood an average of about 30 words; for 13-month-olds, the number was nearly 100 words (Fenson et al., 1994).

receptive language comprehension of spoken language

RESEARCH REPORT

Early Gestural Language in the Children of Deaf Parents

Gestures play an important communicative role in the lives of babies, both hearing and deaf (Goldin-Meadow, 2002). Gestural language is especially important for deaf children, who are likely to be quite limited in their ability to acquire speech. Moreover, studying how deaf children acquire sign language can provide developmentalists with insight into the process of language development in hearing children.

Deaf children of deaf parents are a particularly interesting group to study. The children do not hear oral language, but many are exposed to language—sign language. And these children show the same early steps in language development as do hearing children. Deaf children show a kind of "sign babbling" that emerges between 5 and 7 months of age, much as hearing children begin to babble sounds in these same months (Takei, 2001). Then, at 8 or 9 months of age, deaf children begin using simple gestures, such as pointing, which is just about the same time that we see such gestures in hearing babies of hearing parents. At about 12 months of age, deaf babies seem to display their first referential signs (that is, signs in which a gesture appears to stand for some object or event)—for example, signaling that they want a drink by making a

motion of bringing a cup to the mouth (Petitto, 1988).

Researchers have also studied an equally interesting group—hearing children of deaf parents. These babies are exposed to sign language from their parents and to hearing language from their contacts with others in their world, including TV, teachers, other relatives, and playmates. Among such children, proficiency in sign language develops hand-in-hand with spoken language skills, with growth in one form of communication supporting the other (Kanto, Huttunen, & Laakso, 2013). In other words, the more experience that such infants have with sign language, the more rapidly they develop spoken language. Moreover, researchers have found that hearing infants of deaf parents achieve milestones in the two forms of language at about the same time. In one study, involving a small sample of nine babies, the first sign appeared at an average age of 8 months, the first referential sign at 12.6 months, and the first spoken word at 12.2 months (Folven & Bonvillian, 1991). In another study, researchers found that hearing babies of deaf parents exhibited hand movements while babbling that were very similar to those of babies of hearing par-

ents; remarkably, too, these hand movements were quite distinct from the infants' attempts to imitate their parents' sign language (Petitto et al., 2001). What is striking here is that the first referential signs and the first spoken words appear at such similar times and that the spoken words appear at such a completely normal time, despite the fact that these children of deaf parents hear comparatively little spoken language.

This marked similarity in the sequence and timing of the steps of early language in deaf and hearing children provides strong support for the argument that a baby is somehow primed to learn language in some form, be it spoken or gestural.

CRITICAL ANALYSIS

1. *Why do comparisons of deaf and hearing children of deaf parents support the view that language development is strongly influenced by an inborn plan of some kind?*

2. *In your view, what are the benefits and risks associated with being a hearing child of deaf parents?*

But how do babies separate a single word from the constant flow of speech to which they are exposed? Many linguists have proposed that a child can cope with the monumentally complex task of word learning only because he applies some built in biases or constraints (Archibald & Joanisse, 2013; Räsänen, 2012). For example, the child may have a built-in assumption that words refer to objects or actions but not both.

Learning a language's patterns of word stress may also help babies identify words. Recent research suggests that infants discriminate between stressed and unstressed syllables fairly early—around 7 months of age—and use syllable stress as a cue to identify single words (Yu & Ballard, 2007). For example, first-syllable stress, as in the word *market*, is far more common in English than second-syllable stress, as in the word *garage*. Thus, when English-learning infants hear a stressed syllable, they may assume that a new word is beginning. This strategy would help them single out a very large number of individual English words.

All this information reveals a whole series of changes that seem to converge by 9 or 10 months: the beginning of meaningful gestures, the drift of babbling toward the heard language sounds, imitative gestural games, and the first comprehension of individual words. It is as if the child now understands something about the process of communication and is intending to communicate to adults.

This little girl probably hasn't yet spoken her first words, but chances are she already understands quite a few. Receptive language develops before expressive language.

The First Words

LO 5.10   What are the characteristics of toddlers' first words?

If you have ever studied another language, you probably understood the language before you could produce it yourself. Likewise, a 9- to 10-month-old infant understands far more words than she can say. **Expressive language**—the ability to produce, as well as understand and respond to, meaningful words—typically appears at about 12 or 13 months (Levine, 2011). The baby's first word is an event that parents eagerly await, but it's fairly easy to miss. A word, as linguists usually define it, is any sound or set of sounds that is used consistently to refer to some object, action, or quality. This means that a child who uses *ba* consistently to refer to her bottle is using a word, even though it isn't considered a word in English.

Often, a child's earliest words are used in specific situations and in the presence of many cues. The child may say "bow-wow" or "doggie" only in response to such promptings as "How does the doggie go?" or "What's that?" Typically, this early word learning is very slow, requiring many repetitions for each word. In the first 6 months of word usage, children may learn as few as 30 words. Most linguists have concluded that this earliest word-use phase involves learning each word as something connected to a set of specific contexts. What the child has apparently not yet grasped is that words are symbolic—they refer to objects or events.

Very young children often combine a single word with a gesture to create a "two-word meaning" before they use two words together in their speech. For example, a child may point to his father's shoe and say "Daddy," as if to convey "Daddy's shoe" (Bates et al., 1987). In such cases, meaning is conveyed by the use of gesture and body language combined with a word. Linguists call these word-and-gesture combinations **holophrases**, and children use them frequently between 12 and 18 months of age.

Between 16 and 24 months, after the early period of very slow word learning, most children begin to add new words rapidly, as if they have figured out that things have names. Developmentalists refer to this period as the **naming explosion**. In this period, children seem to learn new words with very few repetitions, and they generalize these words to many more situations. According to one large cross-sectional study based on mothers' reports, the average 16-month-old has a speaking vocabulary of about 50 words; for a 24-month-old, the total has grown to about 320 words (Fenson et al., 1994). For most children, the naming explosion is not a steady, gradual process; instead, longitudinal studies suggest that vocabulary "spurts" begin at about the time the child has acquired 50 words (e.g., Goldfield & Reznick, 1990).

expressive language the ability to use sounds, signs, or symbols to communicate meaning

holophrases combinations of gestures and single words that convey more meaning than just the word alone

naming explosion the period when toddlers experience rapid vocabulary growth, typically beginning between 16 and 24 months

Most observers agree that the bulk of new words learned during this early period of rapid vocabulary growth are names for things or people: *ball, car, milk, doggie, he*. Action words tend to appear later (Gleitman & Gleitman, 1992). One study involving a large group of children suggested that as many as two-thirds of the words children knew by age 2 were nouns, and only 8.5% were verbs (Fenson et al., 1994). Some studies suggest that infants cannot consistently associate words with actions until about 18 months of age (Casasola & Cohen, 2000). However, studies in which researchers expose infants to languages that they have never heard before suggest that the fact that nouns occur more frequently than verbs in natural speech is an important factor. In such studies, infants demonstrate a remarkable ability to distinguish between object names and other types of words, based on the frequency with which object names occur in a stream of speech (Hochmann, Endress, & Mehler, 2010). Thus, infants may learn nouns before verbs due to a built-in strategy that says something like "Learn the most frequent types of words first and then concentrate on the others."

The First Sentences

LO 5.11 What kinds of sentences do children produce between 18 and 24 months of age?

Research suggests that sentences appear when a child has reached a threshold vocabulary of around 100 to 200 words (Fenson et al., 1994). For most children, this threshold is crossed between 18 and 24 months of age.

The first sentences have several distinguishing features: They are short, generally two or three words, and they are simple. Language development researcher Roger Brown coined the term **telegraphic speech** to refer to this pattern (Brown & Bellugi, 1964). Nouns, verbs, and adjectives are usually included, but virtually all grammatical markers (which linguists call **inflections**) are missing. At the beginning, for example, children learning English do not normally use the *-s* ending for plurals or put the *-ed* ending on verbs to make the past tense.

It is also clear that even at this earliest stage children create sentences following rules—not adult rules, to be sure, but rules nonetheless. They focus on certain types of words and put them together in particular orders. They also manage to convey a variety of different meanings with their simple sentences.

For example, young children frequently use a sentence made up of two nouns, such as *Mommy sock* or *sweater chair* (Bloom, 1973). The child who says "Mommy sock" may mean either *This is Mommy's sock* or *Mommy is putting a sock on my foot* (Bloom, 1973). Thus, to understand what a child means by a two-word sentence, it is necessary to know the context in which it occurred.

Individual Differences in Language Development

LO 5.12 What kinds of individual differences are evident in language development?

The sequences of development of language you've read about, and which are shown in Table 5.2, are accurate on the average, but the speed with which children acquire language skill varies widely. One factor influencing this rate is the number of languages to which a child has daily exposure (see *No Easy Answers* on page 121). There also seem to be important style differences.

DIFFERENCES IN RATE Some children begin using individual words at 8 months, others not until 18 months; some do not use two-word sentences until 3 years or even later. The majority of children who talk late eventually catch up. One study found that 97% of late-talking infants' language development was within the average range by age 6, about the time that most children enter school (Ellis & Thal, 2008). Most of those who do not catch up are children who also have poor receptive language (Ellis & Thal, 2008). This group appears to remain behind in language development and perhaps in cognitive development more generally. In practical terms, this means that if your child—or a child you care for—is significantly delayed in understanding as well as speaking language, you should seek professional help to try to diagnose the problem and begin appropriate intervention.

telegraphic speech simple two-word sentences that usually include a noun and a verb

inflections additions to words that change their meaning (e.g., the *s* in *toys*, the *ed* in *waited*)

TABLE 5.2 Language Development in the First 2 Years

Age	Milestone
2–3 months	Makes cooing sounds when alone; responds with smiles and cooing when talked to
20 weeks	Makes various vowel and consonant sounds with cooing
6 months	Babbles; utters phonemes of all languages
8–9 months	Focuses on the phonemes, rhythm, and intonation of language spoken in the home; has receptive vocabulary of 20 to 30 words
12 months	Expressive language emerges; says single words
12–18 months	Uses word-gesture combinations combined with variations in intonation (holophrases)
18–20 months	Uses two-word sentences (telegraphic speech); has expressive vocabulary of 100 to 200 words

Language Development across Cultures

LO 5.13   How does language development vary across cultures?

Studies in a wide variety of language communities, including Turkish, Serbo-Croatian, Hungarian, Hebrew, Japanese, a New Guinean language called Kaluli, German, and Italian, have revealed important similarities in language development (Maitel, Dromi, Sagi, & Bornstein, 2000). Babies the world over coo before they babble; all babies understand language before they can speak it; babies in all cultures begin to use their first words at about 12 months.

NO EASY ANSWERS

One Language or Two?

Knowing two languages is clearly a social and economic benefit to an adult. However, research suggests that there are cognitive advantages and disadvantages to growing up bilingual (Bialystok, 2007; Morales, Calvo, & Bialystok, 2013). In preschool and school-age children, bilingualism is associated with a clear advantage in metalinguistic ability, or the capacity to think about language (Bialystok, Shenfield, & Codd, 2000; Mohanty & Perregaux, 1997). This advantage enables bilingual children to more easily grasp the connection between sounds and symbols in the beginning stages of learning to read if the languages being learned (e.g., Spanish and English) are similar in this regard (van der Leij, Bekebrede, & Kotterink, 2010; Oller, Cobo-Lewis, & Eilers, 1998).

On the negative side, bilingual infants' receptive and expressive vocabularies are as large as those of monolingual infants, but the words they know are divided between two languages (Patterson, 1998). Consequently, they are behind monolingual infants in word knowledge no matter which language is considered, a difference that persists into the school years. In addition, children growing up in bilingual homes in which two languages vary greatly in how they are written (e.g., English and Chinese) may acquire reading skills in both languages more slowly than peers in monolingual homes (Bialystok, Majumder, & Martin, 2003).

Research indicates that bilingual children who are equally fluent in both languages encounter few, if any, learning problems in school (Vuorenkoski, Kuure, Moilanen, & Peninkilampi, 2000). However, most children do not attain equal fluency in both languages (Hakansson, Salameh, & Nettelbladt, 2003). As a result, they tend to think more slowly and know fewer words in the language in which they have less fluency (Chincotta & Underwood, 1997; Sheng, Bedore, Pena, & Fiestas, 2013). When the language in which they are less fluent is the language in which they are schooled, they are at risk for learning problems (Anderson, 1998; Thorn & Gathercole, 1999). Therefore, parents who choose bilingualism should probably take into account their ability to fully support children's acquisition of fluency in both languages.

Clearly, the advantages in adulthood of being bilingual are substantial and may outweigh any disadvantages experienced in childhood. Thus, bilingual parents need to balance the various advantages and disadvantages of bilingualism, as well as their long-term parenting goals, to reach an informed decision about the kind of linguistic environment to provide for their babies.

YOU DECIDE

Decide which of these two statements you most agree with and think about how you would defend your position:

1. *Parents who are fluent in more than one language should raise their children to be bilingual.*

2. *Parents who speak more than one language should decide on which language to speak most often in the home, and they should ensure that their children become fully fluent in that language.*

Moreover, holophrases appear to precede telegraphic speech in every language, with the latter beginning at about 18 months. However, the specific word order that a child uses in early sentences is not the same for all children in all languages. In some languages, a noun/verb sequence is fairly common; in others, a verb/noun sequence may be heard. In addition, particular inflections are learned in highly varying orders from one language to another. Japanese children, for example, begin very early to use a special kind of marker, called a *pragmatic marker*, that tells something about the feeling or the context. In Japanese, the word *yo* is used at the end of a sentence when the speaker is experiencing some resistance from the listener; the word *ne* is used when the speaker expects approval or agreement. Japanese children begin to use these markers very early, much earlier than children whose languages contain other types of inflections.

Most strikingly, there are languages in which there seems to be no simple two-word-sentence stage in which the children use no inflections. Children learning Turkish, for example, use essentially the full set of noun and verb inflections by age 2 and never go through a stage of using uninflected words. Turkish-speaking children's utterances are simpler than those of adults, just as they are in every other language group; however, they are rarely ungrammatical (Aksu-Koc & Slobin, 1985; Maratsos, 1998).

test yourself before going on  ☑ **Study** and **Review** in **MyPsychLab**

Answers to these questions can be found in the back of the book.

1. (Behaviorists, Nativists) emphasize the role of the environment in language development.

2. _____ _____ _____ is the simplified, higher-pitched speech that adults use with infants and young children.

3. Number these milestones of language development in the order in which they occur.

_____(a) telegraphic speech

_____(b) cooing

_____(c) babbling

_____(d) first words

_____(e) holophrases

_____(f) naming explosion

4. In what ways do children's first sentences vary across cultures?

CRITICAL THINKING

5. What would you say to someone who claimed that speaking to infants in "babytalk" interferes with their language development?

Measuring Intelligence in Infancy

intelligence the ability to take in information and use it to adapt to the environment

Bayley Scales of Infant Development the best-known and most widely used test of infant "intelligence"

LO 5.14 How is intelligence measured in infancy?

As you will learn in Chapter 7, psychologists have designed many instruments that measure children's and adults' **intelligence**—an ability to take in information and use it to adapt to the environment. However, it is quite difficult to create a test that can effectively measure intelligence in infants. Tests that measure intelligence in infancy, including the widely used **Bayley Scales of Infant Development**, measure primarily sensory and motor skills (Bayley, 1969, revised 1993 and 2006). For example, 3-month-old infants are challenged to reach for a dangling ring; older babies are observed as they attempt to put cubes in a cup (9 months) or build a tower of three cubes (17 months). Some more clearly cognitive items are also included; for example, uncovering a toy hidden by a cloth is a test item used with 8-month-old infants to measure an aspect of object permanence.

Bayley's test and others like it have proven to be helpful in identifying infants and toddlers with serious developmental delays (Dezoete, MacArthur, & Tuck, 2003; Gardner et al., 2006; Komur, Ozen, Okuyaz, Makharoblidze, & Erdogan, 2013). However, scales that measure development in the first 2 years tend to underestimate later rates of impairment in such children (Spittle et al., 2013). Similarly, infant tests, including the Bayley Scales, have not been nearly as useful for forecasting later IQ scores or school performance as many had hoped. For example, the typical correlation between a Bayley test score at 12 months old and an intelligence test score at 4 years old is only about .20 to .30 (e.g., Bee et al., 1982)—hardly substantial enough to

At 22 months, Katherine would clearly pass the 17-month item on the Bayley Scales of Infant Development that calls for the child to build a tower of three blocks.

be used for predicting intellectual performance at later ages. On the whole, it appears that what is being measured on typical infant intelligence tests is not the same as what is tapped by the commonly used childhood or adult intelligence tests (Colombo, 1993). The most recent version of the test, the Bayley-III (Bayley, 2006), includes items that address cognitive and language development in addition to those that assess sensory and motor skills. Future research will determine whether it is better than previous versions of the test at predicting future intellectual performance.

test yourself before going on   **Study** and **Review** in **MyPsychLab**

Answers to these questions can be found in the back of the book.

1. Infant intelligence tests measure primary (cognitive and language skills; sensory and motor skills).

2. Infant intelligence tests tend to (underestimate, overestimate) later rates of impairment.

CRITICAL THINKING

3. Think of contrasting "nature" and "nurture" explanations for individual differences in the kinds of sensory and motor skills that infant intelligence tests measure.

SUMMARY

Cognitive Changes (pp. 106–111)

LO 5.1   What are the milestones of Piaget's sensorimotor stage?

- Piaget described a sensorimotor infant as beginning with a small repertoire of basic schemes, from which she moves toward symbolic representation in a series of six substages. The milestones of this stage include primary, secondary, and tertiary circular reactions as well as object permanence, means–end behavior, and deferred imitation.

LO 5.2   How have other theorists challenged Piaget's explanation of infant cognitive development?

- Research suggests that Piaget underestimated infants' capabilities, as well as the degree to which some concepts may be wired into the brain.

LO 5.3   What does research tell us about infants' understanding of objects?

- Developmentalists such as Spelke and Baillargeon have studied object permanence within the context of infants' global understanding of objects. Their research shows that Piaget underestimated how much younger infants know about objects and their movements.

Learning, Categorizing, and Remembering (pp. 112–114)

LO 5.4   What kinds of learning are infants capable of?

- Within the first few weeks of life, babies are able to learn through classical conditioning, operant conditioning, and observation of models. By 14 months, they recognize the difference between

successful and unsuccessful modeled behaviors and are more likely to imitate models they view as competent.

LO 5.5   How does categorical understanding change over the first 2 years?

- From an early age, infants use categories to organize information. The sophistication of these categories, and an understanding of how they relate to each other, increases over the first 2 years of life.

LO 5.6   How does memory function in the first 2 years?

- Three- and 4-month-old infants show signs of remembering specific experiences over periods of as long as a few days or a week, a sign that they must have some form of internal representation well before Piaget supposed they do.

The Beginnings of Language (pp. 114–122)

LO 5.7   What are the behaviorist, nativist, and interactionist explanations of language development?

- Behaviorist theories of language development claim that infants learn language through parental reinforcement of wordlike sounds and correct grammar. Nativists say that an innate language processor helps them learn language rules. Interactionists say that language development is a subprocess of cognitive development.

LO 5.8   What are some environmental influences on language development?

- High-pitched infant-directed speech (IDS) helps infants learn language by attracting their attention to the simple, repetitive, and expanded expressions that adults use. The amount of verbal interaction that takes place between infants and mature speakers is another influence. Poverty is associated with language development as well.

LO 5.9   How do infants' sounds, gestures, and understanding of words change in the early months of life?

- Babies' earliest sounds are cries, followed at about 2 months by cooing, then at about 6 months by babbling. At 9 months, babies typically use meaningful gestures and can understand a small vocabulary of spoken words.

LO 5.10   What are the characteristics of toddlers' first words?

- The first spoken words, usually names for objects or people, typically occur at about 1 year, after which toddlers add words slowly for a few months and then rapidly.

LO 5.11   What kinds of sentences do children produce between 18 and 24 months of age?

- Simple two-word sentences appear in children's expressive language at about 18-24 months.

LO 5.12   What kinds of individual differences are evident in language development?

- The rate of language development varies from one child to another. Children who are late talkers typically catch up with their peers by the time they enter school.

LO 5.13   How does language development vary across cultures?

- Early word learning seems to follow similar patterns in all cultures. However, the word order of a child's telegraphic speech depends on which language he is learning.

Measuring Intelligence in Infancy (pp. 122–123)

LO 5.14   How is intelligence measured in infancy?

- Infant intelligence tests are not strongly related to later measures of intelligence. The addition of cognitive items to the most widely used infant intelligence test, the *Bayley Scales of Intellectual Development-III*, may strengthen the relationship between infant measures and those that are administered in later years.

KEY TERMS

A-not-B error (p. 108)

babbling (p. 114)

Bayley Scales of Infant Development (p. 122)

cooing (p. 117)

deferred imitation (p. 108)

expressive language (p. 119)

holophrases (p. 119)

infant-directed speech (IDS) (p. 116)

inflections (p. 120)

intelligence (p. 122)

interactionists (p. 115)

language acquisition device (LAD) (p. 115)

means–end behavior (p. 106)

naming explosion (p. 119)

object concept (p. 110)

object permanence (p. 108)

primary circular reactions (p. 106)

receptive language (p. 118)

schematic learning (p. 112)

secondary circular reactions (p. 106)

sensorimotor stage (p. 106)

telegraphic speech (p. 120)

tertiary circular reactions (p. 107)

violation-of-expectations method (p. 110)

CHAPTER TEST   ✓ Study and Review in MyPsychLab

Answers to all the Chapter Test questions can be found in the back of the book.

1. According to Piaget, what kind of thinking is developed and refined during infancy?
   a. sensory accommodations
   b. schematic motor learning
   c. primary sensory reactions
   d. sensorimotor intelligence

2. Which statement about deferred imitation is true?
   a. A 14-month-old can defer imitation for up to a week.
   b. Nine-month-olds can defer their imitation for as long as 24 hours.
   c. Deferred imitation doesn't happen until at least 18 months of age.
   d. The longest that a child under 14 months of age can defer imitation is 3–4 hours.

3. According to this chapter, what happens when an infant's vocabulary reaches 50 words?
   a. She begins to speak in sentences.
   b. She adds intonations to her speech that show she can distinguish between statements and questions.
   c. A vocabulary growth spurt begins.
   d. Her speech becomes more understandable.

4. What researcher demonstrated the importance of contextual cues in infant memory?
   a. Piaget   c. Spelke
   b. Baillargeon   d. Rovee-Collier

5. In infants between the ages of 12 and 18 months, single words combined with gestures and intonation function as sentences. These utterances are called _____.
   a. holophrases   c. overregularizations
   b. telegraphic speech   d. overextensions

6. In an experiment, a researcher finds that infants given sweet liquids suck more rapidly than infants who are given non-sweet liquids This demonstrates that infant learning is influenced by _____.
   a. delayed gratification
   b. deferred gratification
   c. classical conditioning
   d. operant conditioning

7. Which of the following theorists proposed that a structure in the brain called the language acquisition device (LAD) is responsible for the similarities in language development that have been found in infants around the world?
   a. Melissa Bower
   b. B. F. Skinner
   c. Noam Chomsky
   d. Dan Slobin

8. _____ learning from repeated exposure to particular experiences results in the development of "known" combinations of activities, or expectancies.
   a. Observational
   b. Sensorimotor
   c. Schematic
   d. Linguistic

9. Inflections are _____.
   a. grammatical markers
   b. changes in pitch
   c. the special features of language that adults use when they speak to infants
   d. informal rules for turn-taking that speakers follow

10. Scores on infant intelligence tests do not predict scores on tests later in childhood very well because _____.
   a. infant tests rely on babies' sensory and motor skills
   b. it is impossible to measure intelligence in infants
   c. all infants are equally intelligent
   d. they do not have appropriate norms

11. Most children who talk later than others _____.
   a. have some type of intellectual disability
   b. catch up with their peers by the time they enter school
   c. progress slowly through Piaget's sensorimotor stage
   d. come from homes with insufficient linguistic stimulation

12. Which term refers to the words that an infant understands?
   a. expressive language
   b. receptive language
   c. grammatical language
   d. infant-directed speech

13. The A-not-B error refers to an infant's _____.
   a. lack of object permanence
   b. inability to identify the source of a sound
   c. tendency to look for a hidden object where it was last seen
   d. inability to exhibit deferred imitation

14. According to Piaget, which of the following behaviors indicate that an infant is nearing the end of the first stage of cognitive development?
   a. means–end behavior
   b. primary circular reactions
   c. deferred imitation
   d. object permanence

15. The rapid increase in vocabulary growth that occurs between 16 and 24 months is called _____.
   a. the naming explosion
   b. telegraphic speech
   c. overextension
   d. verbal representation

16. According to this chapter, intelligence is _____.
   a. the ability to take in and use information to function within a particular environment
   b. the ability to function well within one's family
   c. the ability to rapidly solve problems
   d. the ability to use information and solve problems across a variety of cultures

17. With regard to culture and language development, which statement is *false*?
   a. Cooing, babbling, and holophrases appear in the same order in all cultures.
   b. In young infants in all cultures, receptive vocabulary is larger than expressive vocabulary.
   c. Turkish infants do not exhibit telegraphic speech.
   d. The word order in infants' telegraphic speech is the same in all cultures.

18. In which substage did Piaget find that infants develop means–end behavior?
   a. substage 1
   b. substage 2
   c. substage 3
   d. substage 4

19. Infant intelligence tests are poor predictors of later intellectual performance because they primarily measure
   a. cognitive skills such as object permanence
   b. sensory and motor skills
   c. individual differences in rates of language development
   d. the effects of early educational experiences such as daycare attendance

20. Lucy discovered that by kicking the side of her crib, she could cause the mobile that is mounted on it to shake. Since then, she kicks the side of the crib every time her parents put her to bed and squeals with joy when she sees the mobile shaking. Lucy's behavior fits Piaget's notion of a _____.
   a. primary circular reaction
   b. secondary circular reaction
   c. tertiary circular reaction
   d. sensorimotor circular reaction

21. _____ argue that language development is a subprocess of general cognitive development.
   a. Learning theorists
   b. Nativists
   c. Interactionists
   d. Cognitive developmentalists

22. Which of the following items are included in the Bayley-III scales of infant intelligence but were not included in earlier versions?
   a. items that assess motor skills
   b. items that assess sensory skills
   c. items that assess cognitive and language development
   d. items that assess sensorimotor intelligence

23. _____ cite research showing that children's language errors follow rules in support of their theories of language development.
   a. Interactionists
   b. Nativists
   c. Both interactionists and nativists
   d. Neither interactionists nor nativists

24. Chun Lee surprised his mother when he climbed to the top shelf of the pantry in search of a cookie when she wasn't looking. Chun Lee's behavior is consistent with substage _____ of the sensorimotor stage.

a. 6   c. 4

b. 5   d. 3

25. Which statement about infant memory is *false*?

a. Infant memories are strongly tied to the context in which they occurred.

b. Infants younger than 3 months of age do not form memories.

c. Lost infant memories can be reactivated with contextual cues.

d. Memory abilities improve dramatically over the first 6 months.

To 👁 **Watch** ✳ **Explore** ◎ **Simulate** ✔ **Study** and **Review** and experience MyVirtualLife go to MyPsychLab.com

chapter 6

Social and Personality Development in Infancy

I nfancy is the period during which parents and children experience more physical closeness than at any other time in development. Proximity is pleasurable for both parents and babies, but it is also practical. For one thing, a mother or father usually has to carry out other duties while simultaneously caring for a baby. For another, keeping babies close by helps parents protect them from harm. Practical considerations aside, proximity contributes to the development of strong emotional bonds between infants and caregivers. Physical closeness

LEARNING OBJECTIVES

THEORIES OF SOCIAL AND PERSONALITY DEVELOPMENT

6.1 How do Freud's and Erikson's views of personality development in the first 2 years differ?

6.2 What are the main ideas of attachment theory?

ATTACHMENT

6.3 How does synchrony affect parent–infant relations?

6.4 What are the four phases of attachment and the behaviors associated with them?

6.5 What are the four attachment patterns that Ainsworth discovered?

6.6 What variables might affect a parent's ability to establish an attachment relationship with an infant?

6.7 What are the long-term consequences of attachment quality?

6.8 In what ways do patterns of attachment vary across cultures?

PERSONALITY, TEMPERAMENT, AND SELF-CONCEPT

6.9 On which dimensions of temperament do most developmentalists agree?

6.10 What are the roles of heredity, neurological processes, and environment in the formation of temperament?

6.11 How do the subjective self, the objective self, and the emotional self develop during the first 2 years?

EFFECTS OF NONPARENTAL CARE

6.12 Why is it difficult to study the effects of nonparental care on development?

6.13 What might be the effects of nonparental care on physical and cognitive development?

6.14 What does research suggest about the risks of nonparental care with respect to social development?

6.15 What variables should be taken into account in interpretations of research on nonparental care?

MyVirtualLife

What decisions would you make while raising a child? What would the consequences of those decisions be?

Find out by accessing MyVirtualLife at www.MyPsychLab.com to raise a virtual child and live your own virtual life.

provides parents with many opportunities to comfort and show affection for infants. It also allows them to interact by exchanging smiles, frowns, or silly faces. Thus, it is little wonder that, by the time they are a few months old, infants begin to be distressed when they are separated from their caregivers, a phenomenon you will probably experience while raising your "child" in *MyVirtualLife*.

In the context of frequent physical contact, interactions between infants and the social world around them lay the foundations of development in the social/personality domain that are the topics of this chapter. We will first review the ideas proposed by the psychoanalytic theorists about the first 2 years along with those of theorists who take a different approach. Next, you will read about the process of attachment. The infant's emerging personality and sense of self come next, followed by a discussion of the effects of nonparental care on infants' development.

Theories of Social and Personality Development

Psychologists have used all of the theoretical perspectives you learned about in Chapter 2 to formulate hypotheses about infant social and personality development. However, the two most influential perspectives on these issues are the psychoanalytic and the ethological perspectives.

Psychoanalytic Perspectives

LO 6.1 How do Freud's and Erikson's views of personality development in the first 2 years differ?

You may remember from Chapter 2 that Freud proposed a series of psychosexual stages, extending from birth through adolescence, during which individuals attempt to satisfy certain basic drives in different ways. In the oral stage, from birth to age 2, infants derive satisfaction through the mouth. Freud further believed that the weaning process should be managed in such a way that the infant's need to suck is neither frustrated nor overgratified. The consequences of either, Freud claimed, would be fixation at this stage of development. Fixation would manifest itself, in Freud's view, in oral behaviors such as nail biting and swearing.

Freud also emphasized the *symbiotic* relationship between the mother and young infant, in which the two behave as if they were one. He believed that the infant did not understand herself to be separate from her mother. Thus, another result of a gratifying nursing period followed by a balanced weaning process, Freud thought, was the infant's development of a sense of both attachment to and separation from the mother.

Erikson went beyond Freud's view. Nursing and weaning are important, he conceded, but they are only one aspect of the overall social environment. Erikson claimed that responding to the infant's other needs by talking to him, comforting him, and so on, was just as important. He proposed that the first 2 years comprise a period during which the infant learns to trust the world around him or becomes cynical about the social environment's ability to meet his needs—the *trust versus mistrust* stage.

One of the best-known studies in developmental psychology demonstrated that Erikson's view of infant development was more accurate than Freud's (Harlow & Zimmerman, 1959). In this study, infant monkeys were separated from their mothers at birth. The experimenters placed two different kinds of "surrogate" mothers in their cages. The monkeys received all their feedings from a wire mother with a nursing bottle attached. The other mother was covered with soft terrycloth. The researchers found that the monkeys approached the wire mother only when hungry. Most of the time, they cuddled against the cloth mother and ran to it whenever they were frightened or stressed. Subsequent studies with human infants correlating maternal feeding practices with infant adjustment suggested that the infant's social relationships are not based solely on either nursing or weaning practices (Schaffer & Emerson, 1964).

Harlow's ingenious research demonstrated that infant monkeys became attached to a terry-cloth-covered "mother" and would cling to it rather than to a wire mother that provided them with food.

Adoption and Development

Most people who adopt a child assume that if they provide enough love and support, the child will develop both cognitively and emotionally pretty much the way their biological child would. However, adoptive parents need to take into account the child's circumstances prior to the adoption in order to form a realistic set of expectations. Children adopted before the age of 6 months, who have no history of institutionalization or abuse, are generally indistinguishable from nonadopted children in security of attachment, cognitive development, and social adjustment (Rutter et al., 2010). This is true whether adoptive parents and children are of the same or different races and/or nationalities (Juffer & Rosenboom, 1997).

In contrast, children who are adopted later, who have histories of abuse and/or neglect, or who have lived in institutions for long periods tend to have more problems, both cognitive and emotional, than nonadopted children (Juffer, van IJzendoorn, & Palacios, 2011; Merz & McCall, 2010; Tottenham et al., 2010). For example, infants who are institutionalized for many months

typically lack opportunities for forming attachments. As a result, they are at risk of developing *reactive attachment disorder*, a condition that seriously impairs an individual's capacity for forming social relationships (American Psychiatric Association, 2013). Children with this disorder are irritable and difficult to comfort. Most rarely show signs of positive emotional states, such as smiling. Many of these children also experience episodes of extreme fear. One study found that 91% of children who had been adopted after being abused, neglected, or institutionalized exhibited symptoms of reactive attachment disorder and other types of emotional problems even after having been in their adoptive families for an average of 9 years (Smith, Howard, & Monroe, 1998). Not surprisingly, parents of such children reported experiencing more parenting-related stress than did parents of either adoptees from more positive backgrounds or biological children (Mainemer, Gilman, & Ames, 1998). Consequently, people who adopt such children should expect that parenting them will not be easy.

The task of raising high-risk children can be made more manageable with parent training (Juffer, van IJzendoorn, & Bakermans-Kranenburg, 2008). Thus, adoptive parents should take advantage of any training offered by the institutions through which an adoption is arranged or look for training elsewhere, perhaps at a local community college. Finally, at the first sign of difficulty, adoptive parents should seek help from a social worker or psychologist who specializes in treating children. Therapists can help with everyday tasks such as toilet training and can teach parents strategies for dealing with behavior that reflects severe emotional disturbance, such as self-injury.

YOU DECIDE

Decide which of these two statements you most agree with and think about how you would defend your position:

1. *Raising an adopted child differs little from raising one's own biological child.*

2. *Raising an adopted child is more complex than raising one's own biological child.*

Ethological Perspectives

LO 6.2 What are the main ideas of attachment theory?

The *ethological perspective*, described in Chapter 2, claims that all animals, including humans, have innate predispositions that strongly influence their development. Thus, the ethological approach to social and personality development proposes that evolutionary forces have endowed infants with genes that predispose them to form emotional bonds with their caregivers, an approach known as **attachment theory**. Consequently, in contrast to the psychoanalysts, ethologists view the infant's capacity for forming social relationships as highly resistant to environmental forces such as variations in the quality of parenting. However, ethologists do claim that the first 2 years of life constitute a sensitive period for the formation of such relationships. They say that infants who fail to form a close relationship with a caregiver before the age of 2 are at risk for future social and personality problems (see the *No Easy Answers* box).

Because ethologists hypothesize that early emotional bonds influence later social and personality development, ethological perspectives have been very influential in the study of development in this domain across the entire lifespan. In John Bowlby's terminology, infants create different *internal models* of their relationships with parents and other key adults (Bowlby, 1969). These models include such elements as the child's confidence (or lack of it) that the attachment figure will be available or reliable, the child's expectation of rebuff or affection, and the child's sense of assurance that the other is really a safe base for exploration. The internal model begins to be formed late in the child's first year of life and becomes increasingly elaborated and better established through the first 4 or 5 years. By age 5, most children have a clear internal model of the mother (or other primary caregiver), a self model, and a model of relationships. Once formed, such models shape and explain experiences and affect memory and attention. Children notice and remember experiences that fit their models and miss or forget experiences that don't match. As Piaget might say, a child more readily *assimilates* data that fit the model. More importantly, the model affects the child's behavior: The child tends to

attachment theory the view that infants are biologically predisposed to form emotional bonds with caregivers and that the characteristics of those bonds shape later social and personality development

recreate, in each new relationship, the pattern with which he is familiar. This tendency to recreate the parent–infant relationship in each new relationship, say Bowlby and other ethologists, continues into adulthood. For this reason, ethologists believe that, for example, poor communication between adult romantic partners may result from maladaptive communication patterns that developed between one of the individuals and his or her early caregivers.

test yourself before going on

✓ **Study** and **Review** in **MyPsychLab**

Answers to these questions can be found in the back of the book.

1. Classify each of the following statements as consistent with (A) Freud's, (B) Erikson's, or (C) the ethological view of infant development.

_____(1) Feeding is the basis of attachment.

_____(2) Responsive caregivers help the infant develop a sense of trust.

_____(3) An infant whose needs are not met may become cynical.

_____(4) Infants satisfy their desire for pleasure with their mouths.

_____(5) Infants create internal models of social relationships.

_____(6) Harlow's infant monkeys preferred cloth mothers to those that had fed them.

_____(7) Infants are biologically predisposed to develop emotional bonds with caregivers.

CRITICAL THINKING

2. How would learning theorists' explanations of early social relationships and their influences on later relationships differ from those of the psychoanalysts and the ethologists?

Attachment

Somehow, in the midst of endless diaper changes, food preparation, baths, and periods of exhaustion that exceed anything they have ever experienced before, the overwhelming majority of parents manage to respond to their infants in ways that foster the development of an **attachment** relationship. An attachment is an emotional bond in which a person's sense of security is bound up in the relationship. As the research discussed in the *No Easy Answers* feature suggests, a child need not be biologically related to his or her parents in order to develop such a relationship. In fact, the development of attachment relationships depends on the quantity and quality of the interactions that take place between infants and parents. To understand attachment between parent and infant, it is necessary to look at both sides of the equation—at both the parents' bond to the child and the child's attachment to the parents. 👁 **Watch** the **Video** *Attachment in Infants* in **MyPsychLab**.

The Parents' Attachment to the Infant

LO 6.3 How does synchrony affect parent–infant relations?

Contact between mother and infant immediately after birth does not appear to be either necessary or sufficient for the formation of a stable long-term bond between them (Wong, 1993). What is essential is the opportunity for mother and infant to develop a mutual, interlocking pattern of attachment behaviors, called **synchrony** (Moore, 2007). Synchrony is like a conversation. The baby signals his needs by crying or smiling; he responds to being held by quieting or snuggling; he looks at the parents when they look at him. The mother, in turn, enters into the interaction with her own repertoire of caregiving behaviors.

The father's bond with the infant, like the mother's, seems to depend more on the development of synchrony than on contact immediately after birth. Aiding the development of such mutuality is the fact that fathers seem to have the same repertoire of attachment behaviors as do mothers. In the early weeks of the baby's life, fathers touch, talk to, and cuddle their babies in the same ways that mothers do (George, Cummings, & Davies, 2010; Parke & Tinsley, 1981).

After the first weeks of the baby's life, however, signs of a kind of specialization of parental behaviors begin to emerge. Fathers spend more time playing with the baby, with more physical roughhousing; mothers spend more time in routine caregiving and also talk to and smile at the baby more (Lamb & Lewis, 2011). These differences in parental behaviors may have a biological basis (Atzil, Hendler, Zagoory-Sharon, Winetraub, & Feldman, 2012). When mothers observe

attachment the emotional tie to a parent experienced by an infant, from which the child derives security

synchrony a mutual, interlocking pattern of attachment behaviors shared by a parent and child

or interact with their infants, their bodies release *oxytocin*, a hormone that is correlated with empathy, the desire for physical closeness with another person for whom one feels affection, and physical relaxation. By contrast, watching and interacting with babies stimulates *vasopressin* in fathers, a hormone that is linked to arousal, aggression, and physical activity.

By 6 months, infants display distinctive patterns of responding to these mother-father differences (Feldman, 2003). Signs of positive emotional states, such as smiling, appear gradually and subtly when babies are interacting with their mothers. In contrast, babies laugh and wriggle with delight in short, intense bursts in interactions with their fathers. This isn't a matter of babies' preference for one parent or the other. Instead, such results mean that infants recognize the same behavioral differences in mothers and fathers that developmental scientists do when they observe parental behavior. In fact, some researchers have noted that measures of attachment behaviors based on typical mother–infant interactions may cause researchers to inappropriately conclude that fathers are less involved with babies than mothers and, therefore, less important to infants' development (Lewis & Lamb, 2003). To the contrary, research clearly indicates that babies benefit tremendously when both kinds of interaction are available to them. Moreover, longitudinal research has demonstrated that infants whose fathers do not engage them in typical father-infant play activities in the early months of life are at risk of developing behavior problems such as excessive aggressiveness later in childhood (Ramchandani et al., 2013).

Some developmentalists point out that cultural bias may also distort interpretations of the results of studies of the father-infant relationship, almost all of which include only North American or European families (Celia, 2004). The few studies of paternal behavior that have been done in other cultural settings indicate that father involvement is beneficial to infants' development regardless of cultural context. However, the elements of father involvement that benefit infants are not the same in every culture. For example, in cultures that value gender equality, *paternal control*, a pattern in which fathers interrupt and redirect infants' behavior in line with cultural expectations for the child's age and gender, hinders infants' social development (e.g., Feldman & Masalha, 2010). By contrast, in cultures with strong patriarchal traditions and distinctive role prescriptions for mothers and fathers, such as some Middle Eastern societies, paternal control positively influences infants' social development (e.g., Feldman & Masalha, 2010). Thus, it appears that judgments about and interpretations of paternal behavior must consider the cultural context in which the behavior occurs.

Fathers engage in physical play with infants more often than mothers do.

The Infant's Attachment to the Parents

LO 6.4   What are the four phases of attachment and the behaviors associated with them?

Like the parent's bond to the baby, the baby's attachment emerges gradually and is based on her ability to discriminate between her parents and other people. As you learned in Chapters 3 and 4, an infant can recognize her mother's voice prior to birth. By the time the baby is a few days old, she recognizes her mother by sight and smell as well (Cernoch & Porter, 1985; Walton, Bower, & Bower, 1992). Thus, the cognitive foundation for attachment is in place within days after birth.

Cross-cultural studies suggest that the impact of paternal behaviors on children's development depends on the cultural context in which the behavior occurs.

ESTABLISHING ATTACHMENT Bowlby suggested four phases in the development of the infant's attachment (Bowlby, 1969). Bowlby and other ethologists claim that these phases appear over the first 24 to 36 months of life in a fixed sequence that is strongly influenced by genes present in all healthy human infants. The infant exhibits a distinctive set of attachment-related behaviors and interaction patterns in each phase:

- *Phase 1: Nonfocused orienting and signaling (birth to 3 months).* Babies exhibit behaviors, such as crying, smiling, and making eye contact, that draw the attention of others and signal their needs. They direct these signals to everyone with whom they come into contact.

stranger anxiety expressions of discomfort, such as clinging to the mother, in the presence of strangers

separation anxiety expressions of discomfort, such as crying, when separated from an attachment figure

social referencing an infant's use of others' facial expressions as a guide to his or her own emotions

- *Phase 2: Focus on one or more figures (3 to 6 months).* Babies direct their "come here" signals to fewer people, typically those with whom they spend the most time, and are less responsive to unfamiliar people.

- *Phase 3: Secure base behavior (6 to 24 months).* True attachment emerges. Babies show "proximity-seeking" behaviors such as following and clinging to caregivers whom they regard as "safe bases," especially when they are anxious, injured, or have physical needs such as hunger. Most direct these behaviors to a primary caregiver when that person is available and to others only when the primary caregiver, for some reason, cannot or will not respond to them or is absent (Lamb, 1981).

- *Phase 4: Internal model (24 months and beyond).* An internal model of the attachment relationship allows children older than 2 to imagine how an anticipated action might affect the bonds they share with their caregivers (van IJzendoorn, 2005). The internal model plays a role in later relationships with early caregivers (i.e., adult children and their parents) and in other significant relationships (i.e., romantic partnerships) throughout life.

ATTACHMENT BEHAVIORS Once a child has developed a clear attachment, at about 6 to 8 months of age, several related behaviors also begin appearing. *Stranger anxiety* and *separation anxiety*, attachment behaviors that are rare before 5 or 6 months, rise in frequency until about 12 to 16 months, and then decline. Infants express **stranger anxiety** with behaviors such as clinging to their mothers when strangers are present. **Separation anxiety** is evident when infants cry or protest being separated from the mother. The research findings are not altogether consistent, but fear of strangers apparently emerges first. Separation anxiety starts a bit later but continues to be visible for a longer period. Such an increase in fear and anxiety has been observed in children from a number of different cultures, and in both home-reared children and children in day care in the United States. 👁 **Watch** the **Video** *Toddlerhood: Separation Anxiety across Cultures* in **MyPsychLab**.

Another attachment behavior is **social referencing** (Carver & Cornew, 2009). Infants use cues from the facial expressions and the emotional tone of voice used by their attachment figures to help them figure out what to do in novel situations, such as when they are about to be examined by a health-care provider (Flom & Bahrick, 2007; Kim, Walden, & Knieps, 2010). Babies this age will first look at Mom's or Dad's face to check for the adult's emotional expression. If Mom looks pleased or happy, the baby is likely to explore a new toy with more ease or to accept a stranger with less fuss. If Mom looks concerned or frightened, the baby responds to those cues and reacts to the novel situation with equivalent fear or concern.

Social referencing also helps babies learn to regulate their own emotions. For example, an infant who is angry because an enjoyable activity is no longer available may use his caregiver's pleasant, comforting emotional expressions to transition himself into a more pleasant emotional state. By contrast, a baby whose caregiver responds to his anger with more anger may experience an escalation in the level of his own angry feelings. Most developmentalists think that the quality of the emotional give-and-take in interactions between an infant and his caregivers is important to the child's ability to control emotions such as anger and frustration in later years (Cole, Martin, & Dennis, 2004). 👁 **Watch** the **Video** *Infancy: Social Referencing* in **MyPsychLab.**

Separation anxiety signifies the formation of a true attachment relationship between an infant and her primary caregiver. Once the parent has actually left, this child will probably respond positively to her temporary caregiver.

Variations in Attachment Quality

LO 6.5 What are the four attachment patterns that Ainsworth discovered?

Virtually all babies seem to go through the four phases of attachment first identified by Bowlby, but the quality of the attachments they form differs from one infant to the next.

SECURE AND INSECURE ATTACHMENTS Variations in the quality of the first attachment relationship are now almost universally described using Ainsworth's category system (Ainsworth, Blehar, Waters, & Wall, 1978). The Ainsworth system distinguishes between secure attachment and two types of insecure attachment, which psychologists assess using a procedure called the *Strange Situation*.

The Strange Situation consists of a series of eight episodes played out in a laboratory setting, typically with children between 12 and 18 months of age. The child is observed in each of the following situations:

- With the mother
- With the mother and a stranger
- Alone with the stranger
- Completely alone for a few minutes
- Reunited with the mother
- Alone again
- With the stranger again
- Reunited with the mother

Ainsworth suggested that children's reactions in these situations—particularly to the reunion episodes—showed attachment of one of three types: **secure attachment**, **insecure/avoidant attachment**, and **insecure/ambivalent attachment**. More recently, developmentalists have suggested a fourth type: **insecure/disorganized attachment** (Main & Solomon, 1990). The characteristics of each type are listed in Table 6.1.

Whether a child cries when he is separated from his mother is not a helpful indicator of the security of his attachment. Some securely attached infants cry then, and others do not; the same is true of insecurely attached infants. It is the entire pattern of the child's response to the Strange Situation that is critical, not any one response. These attachment types have been observed in studies in many different countries, and secure attachment is the most common pattern in every country. ⏭ **Simulate** the **Experiment** *Attachment Classifications in the Strange Situation* in **MyPsychLab**.

STABILITY OF ATTACHMENT CLASSIFICATION When a child's family environment or life circumstances are reasonably consistent, the security or insecurity of her attachment also seems to remain consistent, even over many years (Hamilton, 1995; Wartner, Grossman, Fremmer-Bombik, & Suess, 1994; Weinfield & Egeland, 2004). However, when a child's circumstances change in some major way—such as when the parents divorce or the family moves—the security of the child's attachment may change as well. In one classic study, developmentalists followed a group of middle-class White children from age 1 to age 21 (Waters, Treboux, Crowell, Merrick, & Albersheim, 1995). Those whose attachment classification changed over this long

secure attachment a pattern of attachment in which an infant readily separates from the parent, seeks proximity when stressed, and uses the parent as a safe base for exploration

insecure/avoidant attachment a pattern of attachment in which an infant avoids contact with the parent and shows no preference for the parent over other people

insecure/ambivalent attachment a pattern of attachment in which the infant shows little exploratory behavior, is greatly upset when separated from the mother, and is not reassured by her return or efforts to comfort him

insecure/disorganized attachment a pattern of attachment in which an infant seems confused or apprehensive and shows contradictory behavior, such as moving toward the mother while looking away from her

TABLE 6.1 Categories of Secure and Insecure Attachment in Ainsworth's Strange Situation

Category	Behavior
Secure attachment	Child readily separates from caregiver and easily becomes absorbed in exploration; when threatened or frightened, child actively seeks contact and is readily consoled; child does not avoid or resist contact if mother initiates it. When reunited with mother after absence, child greets her positively or is easily soothed if upset. Clearly prefers mother to stranger.
Insecure/avoidant attachment	Child avoids contact with mother, especially at reunion after an absence. Does not resist mother's efforts to make contact, but does not seek much contact. Shows no preference for mother over stranger.
Insecure/ambivalent attachment	Child shows little exploration and is wary of stranger. Greatly upset when separated from mother, but not reassured by mother's return or her efforts at comforting. Child both seeks and avoids contact at different times. May show anger toward mother at reunion, and resists both comfort from and contact with stranger.
Insecure/disorganized attachment	Dazed behavior, confusion, or apprehension. Child may show contradictory behavior patterns simultaneously, such as moving toward mother while keeping gaze averted.

(*Sources:* Ainsworth et al., 1978; Carlson & Sroufe, 1995; Main & Solomon, 1990.)

interval had nearly all experienced some major upheaval, such as the death of a parent, physical or sexual abuse, or a serious illness. Research on the impact of domestic violence on attachment stability yields similar results. Securely attached infants are at risk of becoming insecurely attached preschoolers if the level of domestic violence in their homes increases across the early years of life (Levendosky, Bogat, Huth-Bocks, Rosenblum, & von Eye, 2011).

The fact that the security of a child's attachment can change over time does not refute the notion of attachment as arising from an internal model. Bowlby suggested that for the first 2 or 3 years, the particular pattern of attachment a child shows is in some sense a property of each specific relationship. For example, studies of toddlers' attachments to mothers and fathers show that some infants are securely attached to one parent and insecurely attached to the other (Minzi, 2010). It is the quality of each relationship that determines the security of the child's attachment to that specific adult. If the relationship changes markedly, the security of attachment may change, too. But, Bowlby argued, by age 4 or 5, the internal model becomes more a property of the child, more generalized across relationships, and thus more resistant to change. At that point, the child tends to impose the model on new relationships, including relationships with teachers or peers.

ATTACHMENT AND AUTISM SPECTRUM DISORDERS Influenced by Bowlby's theory of attachment, developmentalists once believed that **autism spectrum disorders (ASD)**, a group of disorders that impair an individual's ability understand and engage in the give-and-take of social relationships, result from a disturbance in the attachment process caused by insensitive parenting. However, despite their difficulties with synchrony, most infants with ASDs are securely attached to their caregivers (Rutgers et al., 2004). Moreover, contemporary research suggests that ASDs have neurological origins (American Psychiatric Association, 2013). Consequently, today's developmental scientists believe that ASDs are caused by a variety of interactive biological and environmental factors rather than a flawed attachment process. (By the way, there is no evidence that vaccines increase a child's risk of developing autism spectrum disorders (Orenstein et al., 2012).)

Clinicians use a three-category system to describe the severity of an individual's ASD (American Psychiatric Association, 2013). Children with *Level 1 ASD* have very limited or nonexistent language skills, display *stereotypic behaviors* such as hand-flapping and rocking, and have a severely limited range of interests. Most also have intellectual disabilities. Those with *Level 2 ASD* are capable of some degree of verbal communication and have mild degrees of cognitive impairment. However, most have difficulty looking at situations from other people's perspectives and often utter repetitive words or phrases that are inappropriate for the situations in which they occur. As a result, children with Level 2 ASD have a limited capacity for normal conversations and social interactions. Finally, children with *Level 3 ASD* have age-appropriate language and cognitive skills. As a result, most are not diagnosed with the disorder until later in childhood. In preschool or kindergarten, the unusual behaviors of children with Level 3 ASD set them apart from typically developing children. Some become intensely focused on memorizing things that have little meaning to them, such as bus schedules. Others engage in obsessive-compulsive behaviors, such as counting and recounting the number of squares on a tile floor. By school age, their inability to form friendships like those of other children their age is also quite apparent.

Treatments such as intensive social skills training and behavior modification for stereotypical behaviors can reduce the impact of ASD symptoms on children's lives. Such treatments are most successful when they are implemented during the first three years of life (Cohen, Amerine-Dickens, & Smith, 2006; Konstantareas, 2006; Luiselli & Hurley, 2005). Furthermore, training parents to whom infants and children are securely attached to administer such treatments in the home may improve the symptoms of ASD (Bearss, Johnson, Handen, Smith, & Scahill, 2013).

Caregiver Characteristics and Attachment

LO 6.6 What variables might affect a parent's ability to establish an attachment relationship with an infant?

Researchers have found that several characteristics of caregivers influence the attachment process. These characteristics include the caregivers' emotional responses to the infant, their marital and socioeconomic status (SES), and their mental health.

EMOTIONAL RESPONSIVENESS Studies of parent–child interactions suggest that one crucial ingredient for secure attachment is *emotional availability* on the part of the primary caregiver (Biringen, 2000). An emotionally available caregiver is one who is able and willing to form an emotional attachment to the infant. For example, economically or emotionally distressed parents, or those who have psychological or medical health problems, may be so distracted by their own problems that they can't invest emotion in the parent—infant relationship (Cassibba, van IJzendoorn, & Coppola 2012). Such parents may be able to meet the baby's physical needs but unable to respond emotionally.

Contingent responsiveness is another key ingredient of secure attachment (Blehar, Lieberman, & Ainsworth, 1977). Parents who demonstrate contingent responsiveness are sensitive to the child's cues and respond appropriately. They smile when the baby smiles, talk to the baby when he vocalizes, pick him up when he cries, and so on (Ainsworth & Marvin, 1995). Infants of parents who display contingent responsiveness in the early months are more likely to be securely attached at age 12 months (George et al., 2010). They are also less likely to exhibit behavior problems and emotional difficulties later in childhood (Marwick et al., 2013; Nuttall et al., 2012).

A low level of parental responsiveness thus appears to be an ingredient in any type of insecure attachment. However, each of the several subvarieties of insecure attachment is affected by additional distinct factors. For example, if the mother rejects the infant or regularly withdraws from contact with her, the baby is more likely to show an avoidant pattern of attachment, although the pattern also seems to occur when the mother is overly intrusive or overly stimulating toward the infant (Isabella, 1995). An ambivalent pattern is more common when the primary caregiver is inconsistently or unreliably available to the child. A disorganized pattern seems especially likely when the child has been abused, and in families in which either parent had some unresolved trauma in his or her own childhood, such as abuse or a parent's early death (Cassidy & Berlin, 1994; Main & Hesse, 1990).

MARITAL STATUS Researchers have found that infants whose parents are married are more likely to be securely attached than babies whose parents are either cohabiting or single (e.g., Rosenkrantz, Aronson, & Huston, 2004). However, the effects of marital status may be due to other characteristics of parents who choose to marry, cohabit, or remain single. Married parents typically have more education and are less likely to be poor than parents in the other groups.

Marital conflict poses risks for the development of attachment. Researchers have found that 6-month-olds who are exposed to parental arguments, especially those in which parents are verbally aggressive toward each other, are more likely to display signs of emotional withdrawal than babies who are not so exposed (Crockenberg, Leerkes, & Lekka, 2007). Emotional withdrawal on the part of the infant interferes with synchrony, thereby lessening the chances that she will develop a secure attachment to her primary caregiver.

MENTAL HEALTH Psychiatric illness, especially depression, is another caregiver characteristic that appears to be related to attachment quality (Murray et al., 1999; Teti, Gelfand, Messinger, & Isabella, 1995). Research suggests that depression diminishes a mother's capacity to interpret and respond to important infant signals such as crying (Quitmann, Krison, Romer, & Ramsauer, 2012). Thus, infants of mothers who have depression are at increased risk of developing insecure attachments as well as later emotional problems (Goodman & Brand, 2009; Quitmann et al., 2012). They also are at increased risk of developing psychiatric illnesses themselves in adulthood (Maki et al., 2004).

Of course, there are many mothers with depression who are just as sensitive and responsive to their babies' needs as mothers who do not have depression. And, as you might expect, infants whose mothers with depression exhibit sensitive parenting behaviors are less likely to display long-term negative effects than babies of less sensitive mothers with depression (Quitmann et al., 2012). In other words, when mothers with depression exhibit the same kinds of parenting behaviors as most mothers who are not depressed, their emotional status doesn't appear to have negative effects on their babies' development.

Studies involving many mothers with panic disorder have shown that these mothers, like mothers with depression, exhibit behaviors that may interfere with synchrony (Warren et al., 2003).

Long-Term Consequences of Attachment Quality

LO 6.7 What are the long-term consequences of attachment quality?

As we noted earlier, attachment theory proposes that early emotional relationships shape later ones. Thus, researchers have examined the links between Ainsworth's classification system and a wide range of other behaviors in infants, children, adolescents, and adults. Dozens of studies show that children rated as securely attached to their mothers in infancy are later more sociable, more positive in their behavior toward friends and siblings, less clinging and dependent on teachers, less aggressive and disruptive, more empathetic, and more emotionally mature in their interactions in school and other settings outside the home (Brumariu & Kerns, 2010; Shaver & Mikulincer, 2012).
👁 **Watch** the **Video** *Emotion Regulation in Early Childhood* in **MyPsychLab**.

Adolescents who were rated as securely attached in infancy or who are classed as secure on the basis of interviews in adolescence are also more socially skilled, have more intimate friendships, are more likely to be rated as leaders, and have higher self-esteem and better grades (Kobak, Zajac, & Smith, 2009; Woodhouse, Ramos-Marcuse, Ehrlich, Warner, & Cassidy, 2010). Those with insecure attachments—particularly those with avoidant attachments—not only have less positive and supportive friendships in adolescence but also are more likely to become sexually active early and to practice riskier sex (Carlson, Sroufe, & Egeland, 2004).

Quality of attachment in infancy also predicts sociability and relationship quality in adulthood (Fraley, Roisman, Booth-LaForce, Owen, & Holland, 2013; Thompson, 2008). Developmentalists have also found that an adult's internal model of attachment affects his or her parenting behaviors (Steele, Hodges, Kaniuk, Hillman, & Henderson, 2003). For example, mothers who are themselves securely attached are more responsive and sensitive in their behavior toward their infants or young children (Hammond, Landry, Swank, & Smith, 2000). Attachment history affects parental attitudes as well. Some studies have shown that parents with a history of insecure attachment are more likely to view their infants negatively (Pesonen, Raikkonnen, Strandberg, Kelitikangas-Jarvinen, & Jarvenpaa, 2004). Such parents may also lack confidence in their ability to perform effectively in the parenting role (Huth-Bocks, Levendosky, Bogat, & von Eye, 2004).

Examinations of the long-term consequences of quality of attachment suggest that both psychoanalysts and ethologists are correct in their assumption that the attachment relationship becomes the foundation for future social relationships. Certainly, it appears to be critical to the relationship most similar to it—the relationship an individual ultimately develops with her or his own child.

Cross-Cultural Research on Attachment

LO 6.8 In what ways do patterns of attachment vary across cultures?

Studies in a variety of countries support Ainsworth's contention that some form of "secure base behavior" occurs in every child, in every culture (van IJzendoorn & Sagi-Schwartz, 2008). But there is also some evidence suggesting that secure attachments may be more likely in certain cultures than in others. The most thorough analyses have come from classic research by Dutch psychologists who examined the results of 32 separate studies in eight different countries. Figure 6.1 presents the percentage of babies classified in each category for each country (van IJzendoorn & Kroonenberg, 1988). It is important to avoid overinterpreting the information in this figure, because in most cases there are only one or two studies from a given country, normally with quite small samples. The single study from China, for example, included only 36 babies. Still, the findings are thought-provoking. The most striking thing about them is their consistency. In each of the eight countries, secure attachment is the most common pattern, found in more than half of all babies studied.

In all the countries van IJzendoorn studied, infants typically have one caregiver, usually the mother. What would researchers find in a culture in which the child's early care was more communal? To find out, developmentalists studied a group of people called the Efe, who forage in the forests of Zaire (Tronick, Morelli, & Ivey, 1992). The Efe live in camps, in small groups of perhaps 20 individuals, each group consisting of several extended families, often brothers and their wives. Infants in these communities are cared for communally in the early months and years of life. They are carried and held by all the adult women and interact regularly with many

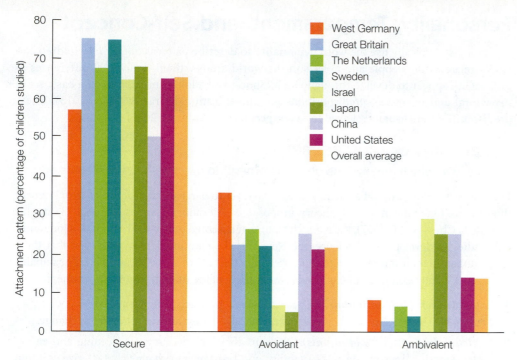

Figure 6.1 Cross-Cultural Comparisons of Attachment Categories

Although the percentage of infants in each of the attachment categories varies somewhat across cultures, secure attachment is the most common type of relationship between infants and caregivers in all societies. (*Source:* Based on Table 1 of van IJzendoorn & Kroonenberg, 1988, pp. 150–151.)

different adults. If they have needs, they are tended to by whichever adult or older child is nearby; they may even be nursed by women other than the mother, although they normally sleep with the mother. The researchers reported two things of particular interest about early attachment in this group. First, Efe infants seem to use virtually any adult or older child in their group as a safe base, which suggests that they may have no single central attachment. But, beginning at about 6 months, the Efe infants nonetheless seem to insist on being with their mother more and to prefer her over other women, although other women continue to help with caregiving responsibilities. Thus, even in an extremely communal rearing arrangement, some sign of a central attachment is evident, though perhaps less dominant.

At the moment, the most plausible hypothesis is that the same factors involving mother–infant interaction contribute to secure and insecure attachments in all cultures and that these patterns reflect similar internal models. But more study of long-term outcomes for individuals in the various categories is needed before researchers will know whether this is correct.

test yourself before going on ☑ Study and Review in MyPsychLab

Answers to these questions can be found in the back of the book.

1. Fill in the table below with information about the four phases of attachment proposed by Bowlby.

Stage	Name of Stage	Age	Attachment Behaviors
1			
2			
3			
4			

2. Classify each separation/reunion behavior pattern below according to Ainsworth's category of attachment that it represents.

_____(1) upset at separation but not comforted by mother's return

_____(2) easily separates and greets mother positively upon return

_____(3) not upset at separation; avoids mother at reunion

_____(4) inconsistent pattern of behavior at separation and reunion

CRITICAL THINKING

3. Look back at the discussion of synchrony at the beginning of this section. How do you think it is manifested in adult relationships, and in what way do you think synchrony, or the lack thereof, influences those relationships?

Personality, Temperament, and Self-Concept

personality a pattern of responding to people and objects in the environment

temperament inborn predispositions, such as activity level, that form the foundations of personality

Psychologists typically use the word **personality** to describe patterns in the way children and adults relate to the people and objects in the world around them. Individual differences in personality appear to develop throughout childhood and adolescence, based on a basic set of behavioral and emotional predispositions present at birth (McCrae & Costa, 2013). These predispositions are usually referred to as **temperament** (Rothbart, 2012).

Dimensions of Temperament

LO 6.9   On which dimensions of temperament do most developmentalists agree?

Psychologists who study infant temperament have yet to agree on a basic set of temperament dimensions. One influential early theory, proposed by Alexander Thomas (1913–2003) and his wife Stella Chess (1914–2007), the research team that authored one of the best-known longitudinal studies in developmental science, the New York Longitudinal Study, proposed that three temperament classifications apply to about 75% of infants (Thomas & Chess, 1977). The remaining 25% of infants exhibit combinations of two or three of the main types of temperament.

- *Easy children (40% of infants).* These children approach new events positively, display predictable sleeping and eating cycles, are generally happy, and adjust easily to change.
- *Difficult children (10% of infants).* Patterns that include irregular sleeping and eating cycles, emotional negativity and irritability, and resistance to change characterize children in this category.
- *Slow-to-warm-up children (15% of infants).* Children in this group display few intense reactions, either positive or negative, and appear nonresponsive to unfamiliar people.

Other researchers have examined temperament from a trait perspective rather than a categorical perspective. They view an individual infant's temperament as a function of how much or how little of various characteristics she possesses. For example, an infant in whom a high level of physical activity was combined with emotional irritability would have a different temperamental profile than an infant in whom high activity was combined with a more easygoing nature.

Temperament researchers are still struggling to define the key dimensions of temperament and have not reached a clear agreement (Thompson, Winer, & Goodvin, 2011). However, over the past decade or so, a consensus has emerged that is reflected in the writings of leading researchers in the field (Caspi & Shiner, 2006; Kagan & Herschkowitz, 2005; Rothbart, 2012). Many theorists are now emphasizing the following five key dimensions of temperament:

Even in the early years of life, differences in personality are evident.

- *Activity level.* A tendency to move often and vigorously rather than to remain passive or immobile.
- *Approach/positive emotionality/sociability.* A tendency to move toward rather than away from new people, situations, or objects, usually accompanied by positive emotion.
- *Inhibition and anxiety.* The flip side of approach/positive emotionality/sociability is a tendency to respond with fear or to withdraw from new people, situations, or objects.
- *Negative emotionality/irritability/anger/emotionality.* A tendency to respond with anger, fussiness, loudness, or irritability; a low threshold of frustration. This dimension appears to be what Thomas and Chess (1977) are tapping with their concept of the "difficult" child.
- *Effortful control/task persistence.* An ability to stay focused, to manage attention and effort.

Origins and Stability of Temperament

LO 6.10   What are the roles of heredity, neurological processes, and environment in the formation of temperament?

Because temperamental differences appear early in life, even during the prenatal period (see Chapter 3), it may seem that genes are entirely responsible for them. However, research suggests that both nature and nurture contribute to individual differences in temperament.

HEREDITY Studies of twins in many countries show that identical twins are more alike in their temperament than are fraternal twins (Lemery-Chalfant et al., 2013; Stilberg et al., 2005). For example, in one classic twin study, researchers tested 100 pairs of identical twins and 100 pairs of fraternal twins at both 14 and 20 months. At each age, the children's temperaments were rated by their mothers, and each child's level of behavioral inhibition was measured by observing how the child reacted to strange toys and a strange adult in a special laboratory playroom. Did the child approach the novel toys quickly and eagerly or hang back or seem fearful? Did the child approach the strange adult or remain close to the mother? The correlations between temperament scores on all four of these dimensions were consistently higher for identical than for fraternal twins, indicating a strong genetic effect (Emde et al., 1992; Plomin et al., 1993).

LONG-TERM STABILITY Research shows that some aspects of temperament are stable across infancy and into children's later years (Thompson et al., 2011). For example, there is growing evidence of consistency in temperamental ratings over rather long periods of infancy and childhood (Kagan & Herschkowitz, 2005). Longitudinal studies also suggest that temperamental differences are stable from the preschool years into adulthood (Caspi & Shiner, 2006).

Researchers have also found considerable consistency at various ages in inhibition. For example, in developmental psychologist Jerome Kagan's classic longitudinal study, half of the children who had shown high levels of crying and motor activity in response to a novel situation when they were 4 months old were still classified as highly inhibited at age 8, and three-fourths of those rated as uninhibited at 4 months remained in that category 8 years later (Kagan, Snidman, & Arcus, 1993). Subsequent studies showed that these trends continued into the children's teen and early adulthood years (Kagan & Herschkowitz, 2005).

NEUROLOGICAL PROCESSES Many temperament theorists take the heredity argument a step further and trace the basic differences in behavior to variations in underlying physiological patterns (Caspi & Shiner, 2006). For example, studies examining the genes that control the functions of two important neurotransmitters, *dopamine* and *serotonin*, support this hypothesis (Davies, Cicchetti, Hentges, & Sturge-Apple, 2013; Lakatos et al., 2003). These neurotransmitters regulate the brain's responses to new information and unusual situations—precisely the kinds of stimuli that appear to overstimulate shy children in most studies.

Another important neurological variable that has been found to be associated with shyness is *frontal lobe asymmetry* (LoBue, Coan, Thrasher, & DeLoache, 2011). In most people, the left and right hemispheres of the frontal lobes respond similarly to new stimuli; in other words, they exhibit *symmetry*. In shy infants, however, the two hemispheres respond differently—that is, *asymmetrically*—to such stimuli. Specifically, these children exhibit higher levels of arousal in the right hemisphere than in the left (Fox, Henderson, Rubin, Calkins, & Schmidt, 2001; Henderson, Marshall, Fox, & Rubin, 2004). Such findings make it tempting to conclude that temperamental differences are based in neurological processes. Research, however, suggests that it is difficult to say whether neurological differences are a cause or an effect of temperament. Developmentalists have found that shy infants whose temperaments change over the first 4 years of life—that is, those who become more outgoing—also become less likely to exhibit the asymmetrical pattern of arousal (Fox et al., 2001).

ENVIRONMENT Critics of neurological studies point out that it is impossible to know whether such findings are causes or effects (Johnson, 2003). They argue that behavior shapes the brain. Thus, shy children may exhibit different neurological patterns than outgoing children because their exhibition of shy behavior contributes to the neural networks that developmental processes in the brain, such as pruning, allow to develop and those that are shut down due to lack of use.

Consistent with these critics' claims, researchers have found that temperament-environment interactions tend to strengthen built-in qualities. For one thing, people of all ages choose their experiences, a process Sandra Scarr refers to as **niche picking** (Scarr & McCartney, 1983). Our choices reflect our temperaments. For example, highly sociable children seek out contact with others; children low on the activity dimension are more likely to choose sedentary pursuits, such as puzzles or board games, than active ones such as baseball.

niche picking the process of selecting experiences on the basis of temperament

Gender Differences in Temperament

What kinds of temperamental differences come to mind when you think about boys and girls? In some studies, researchers have found that boys are more physically active and impulsive than girls and that girls are generally more sociable (Gagne, Miller, & Goldsmith, 2013; Pérez-Edgar, Schmidt, Henderson, Schulkin, & Fox, 2008). Nevertheless, temperamental differences between boys and girls are much smaller than the differences *perceived* by parents and other adults (Olino, Durbin, Klein, Hayden, & Dyson, 2013). In one classic study, researchers found that adults viewing a videotape of an infant interpreted the baby's behavior differently depending on the gender label experimenters provided. Participants who were told the baby was a girl interpreted a particular behavior as expressing "fear." Amazingly, participants who believed the infant was a boy labeled the same behavior "anger" (Condry & Condry, 1976).

Temperamental stereotyping may affect the quality of the parent–infant relationship. For example, parents of a calm, quiet girl may respond positively to her because they perceive her behavior to be consistent with their concept of "girlness." In contrast, parents of a physically active girl may develop a rejecting, disapproving attitude because they view her behavior as excessively masculine. These differences in parental responses may affect all aspects of parent–child relationships such that parents display higher levels of affection for a girl whom they perceive to be "feminine" than for one whom they view as "masculine."

You should recognize these issues as yet another example of the nature–nurture debate. The findings of behavioral geneticists seem to argue strongly that these differences are inborn. Yet it is also clear that parents treat boys and girls differently beginning very early in infancy.

Thus, as children get older, gender differences in temperament are likely to be the result of both their inborn characteristics and the gender-based expectations and response patterns exhibited by their parents.

CRITICAL ANALYSIS

1. *In what ways might stereotypes influence the methods that researchers use to study gender differences in temperament?*

2. *How do differences between men and women, which have evolved over many years, contribute to expectations about how male and female infants differ in temperament? In other words, in your view, do adults engage in what might be called "backward generalization" from adults to infants with regard to their opinions about the existence of gender differences early in life?*

---

goodness-of-fit the degree to which an infant's temperament is adaptable to his or her environment and vice versa

Parents may also be able to either increase or decrease the effects of an infant's inborn temperamental tendencies. In one longitudinal study, researchers videotaped play sessions in which Chinese parents interacted with their 4-year-old children (Hou, Chen, & Chen, 2005). When the children were 7 years old, the researchers found that parent behavior at age 4 predicted behavioral inhibition (shyness) at age 7. Specifically, the more controlling parents were during the play sessions, the more likely their children were to be rated as more behaviorally inhibited at age 7 than they had been at age 4. Such findings suggest that, perhaps contrary to what you might expect, parents who accept an inhibited child's temperament may contribute more to the child's ability to overcome shyness later in life than parents who try to force a child to be more outgoing. Some experts suggest that parental influences may be greatest for children who are at the extremes of a given temperamental continuum. That is, children who are extremely inhibited may be more subject to parental influence than those who are moderately so (Buss & Plomin, 1984).

Developmentalists argue that the **goodness-of-fit** between children's temperaments and their environments influences how inborn temperamental characteristics are manifested later in life (Thomas & Chess, 1977). For example, if the parents of an irritable baby boy are good at tolerating his irritability and persist in establishing a synchronous relationship with him, then his irritability doesn't lead to the development of an insecure attachment. An infant's gender may also influence how the environment responds to his temperament, as discussed in *Research Report* above.

Research that has examined babies' ability to recognize themselves suggests that self-awareness develops in the middle of the second year.

Self-Concept

LO 6.11 How do the subjective self, the objective self, and the emotional self develop during the first 2 years?

During the same months when a baby is creating an internal model of attachment and expressing her own unique temperament, she is also developing an internal model of self. Freud suggested that the infant needed to develop a sense of separateness from her mother before she could form a sense of self. Piaget emphasized that the infant's understanding of the basic concept of object permanence was a necessary precursor for the child's attaining self-permanence. Both of these aspects of early self-development reappear in more recent descriptions of the emergence of the sense of self (Lewis, 1990, 1991).

THE SUBJECTIVE SELF The child's first task is to figure out that he is separate from others and that this separate self endures over time and space. Developmentalists call this aspect of the self-concept the **subjective self**, or sometimes the *existential self*, because the key awareness seems to be "I exist." The roots of this understanding lie in the myriad everyday interactions the baby has with the objects and people in his world that lead him to understand, during the first 2 to 3 months of life, that he can have effects on things (Thompson et al., 2011). For example, when the child touches a mobile, it moves; when he cries, someone responds. Predictably, the *social smile*, a facial expression that is directed at another person in order to elicit a response, appears about this time, although the frequency and duration of social smiles vary greatly from one baby to another (Levine, 2011). Through this process, the baby separates self from everything else and a sense of "I" begins to emerge.

By the time the infant has constructed a fairly complete understanding of object permanence, at about 8–12 months, the subjective self has fully emerged. Just as he is figuring out that Mom and Dad continue to exist when they are out of sight, he is figuring out—at least in some preliminary way—that he exists separately and has some permanence.

THE OBJECTIVE SELF The second major task is for the toddler to come to understand that she is also an object in the world (Thompson et al., 2011). Just as a ball has properties—roundness, the ability to roll, a certain feel in the hand—so the "self" has qualities or properties, such as gender, size, a name, shyness or boldness, coordination or clumsiness. This self-awareness is the hallmark of the second aspect of identity, the **objective self**, sometimes called the categorical self, because once the child achieves self-awareness, the process of defining the self involves placing oneself in a number of categories.

It has not been easy to determine just when a child has developed the initial self-awareness that delineates the formation of the objective self. The most commonly used procedure involves a mirror. First, the baby is placed in front of a mirror, just to see how she behaves. Most infants between about 9 and 12 months old will look at their own image, make faces, or try to interact with the baby in the mirror in some way. After allowing this free exploration for a time, the experimenter, while pretending to wipe the baby's face with a cloth, puts a spot of rouge on the baby's nose, and then lets the baby look in the mirror again. The crucial test of self-recognition, and thus of awareness of the self, is whether the baby reaches for the spot on her own nose rather than the nose on the face in the mirror (see Figure 6.2). Very few 9- to 12-month-olds touch their own nose, but three-quarters of the children aged 21 months do so, a developmental milestone that has been confirmed in a variety of research studies, including studies in Europe (Asendorpf, Warkentin, & Baudonnière, 1996; Lewis & Brooks, 1978). Neuroimaging studies suggest that maturity of the region in the brain where the temporal and parietal lobes meet underlies the appearance of self-recognition (Lewis & Carmody, 2008).

Figure 6.2 The Rouge Test

Mirror recognition and self-naming develop at almost exactly the same time.

As self-awareness develops, toddlers begin to show a newly proprietary attitude ("Mine!") toward toys or other treasured objects. They also begin to refer to themselves by name and, near the end of the second year, to label themselves as boys or girls. In addition, infants recognize that they belong to the "child" category. They also use categorical terms such as "good" and "big" to describe themselves. For example, a girl might say "good girl" when she obeys her parent or "big girl" when she is successful at a task like using the toilet (Stipek, Gralinski, & Kopp, 1990). **Watch** the **Video** *Self Awareness* in **MyPsychLab**.

THE EMOTIONAL SELF Development of the *emotional self* begins when babies learn to identify changes in emotion expressed in others' faces, at 2 to 3 months of age. Initially, they discriminate emotions best when they receive information on many channels simultaneously—such as when they see a particular facial expression and hear the same emotion expressed in the adult's voice (Walker-Andrews, 1997). Moreover, in these early weeks, infants are much better at discerning the emotional expressions of a familiar face than those of an unfamiliar face (Kahana-Kalman & Walker-Andrews, 2001). By 5 to 7 months, babies can begin to "read" one channel at a time, responding to facial expression alone or vocal expression alone, even when

subjective self an infant's awareness that she or he is a separate person who endures through time and space and can act on the environment

objective (categorical) self a toddler's understanding that she or he is defined by various categories such as gender or qualities such as shyness

the emotions are displayed by a stranger rather than Mom or Dad (Balaban, 1995). They also respond to a much wider variety of emotions than younger infants do and can distinguish among happy, surprised, angry, fearful, interested, and sad faces (Soken & Pick, 1999; Walker-Andrews & Lennon, 1991).

Near the end of the first year, infants' perceptions of others' emotions help them anticipate others' actions and guide their own behavior (Phillips, Wellman, & Spelke, 2002). For instance, they react to another infant's neutral facial expression by actively trying to elicit an emotional expression from that child (Striano & Rochat, 1999). Just as adults often work at getting a baby to smile at them, babies seem to be following the same sort of script by 8 to 10 months of age.

As an infant's understanding of others' emotions advances, it is matched by parallel progression in expression of emotions. At birth, infants have different facial expressions for interest, pain, and disgust, and an expression that conveys enjoyment develops very quickly. By the time a baby is 2 to 3 months old, adult observers can also distinguish expressions of anger and sadness, with expressions of fear appearing by 6 or 7 months (Izard et al., 1995; Izard & Harris, 1995). At about the same time, infants begin to smile more to human faces than to a doll's face or another inanimate object, suggesting that at this early stage the baby is already responding to the added social signals available in the human face (Ellsworth, Muir, & Hains, 1993; Legerstee, Pomerleau, Malcuit, & Feider, 1987).

Over the next several months, the infant's emotional expressions, and the behaviors that arise from them, become more sophisticated. For example, as you learned earlier in the chapter, infants who have formed an attachment to a caregiver (typically in the last few months of the first year) use the caregiver's emotions to guide their own feelings. Moreover, by this age, babies have learned to calm themselves when their caregivers behave in expected ways (Cole et al., 2004). For example, a baby who is frustrated by hunger will calm down when she sees her caregiver preparing to nurse her or to provide her with some other kind of nourishment. Finally, near the middle of the second year, at about the same time that a child shows self-recognition in the mirror, such self-conscious emotional expressions as embarrassment, pride, and shame emerge (Lewis, Allesandri, & Sullivan, 1992; Lewis, Sullivan, Stanger, & Weiss, 1989; Mascolo & Fischer, 1995).

test yourself before going on Study and Review in MyPsychLab

Answers to these questions can be found in the back of the book.

1. Classify each infant behavior pattern as consistent with (A) easy temperament, (B) difficult temperament, (C) slow-to-warm-up temperament
   _____ **(1)** irregular eating and sleeping
   _____ **(2)** regular eating and sleeping
   _____ **(3)** lack of responsiveness to unfamiliar people
   _____ **(4)** positive responses to new experiences
   _____ **(5)** irritability
   _____ **(6)** few intense emotions

2. What behaviors are associated with the development of each component of the self during infancy?

Component of Self	Behaviors
Subjective/existential	
Objective/categorical	
Emotional	

CRITICAL THINKING

3. How do you think your genes and environment interacted to produce the temperamental characteristics and self-concept that you have today?

Effects of Nonparental Care

Since the late 1970s, women in virtually every industrialized country in the world have been entering the workforce in great numbers. In the United States, the change has been particularly rapid and massive: In 1970, only 18% of U.S. married women with children under age 6 were in the labor force; today, 65% of such women (and more than half of women with children under age 1) were working outside the home at least part time (U.S. Bureau of Labor Statistics,

2013). The younger children are, the less likely they are to receive nonparental care. However, even among U.S. infants under the age of 2 years, half are cared for by someone other than a parent at least part time (FIFCFS, 2010). The key question for psychologists is, "What effect does such nonparental care have on infants and young children?" 👁 **Watch** the **Video** *Day Care* in **MyPsychLab**.

Difficulties in Studying Nonparental Care

LO 6.12 Why is it difficult to study the effects of nonparental care on development?

It might seem that the effect on infant development of the trend toward nonparental care could easily be determined by comparing babies receiving nonparental care to those cared for by their parents. However, both "nonparental care" and "parental care" are really complex interactions among numerous variables rather than single factors whose effects can be studied independently. Thus, interpretation of research on nonparental care has to take into account a variety of issues.

To begin with, in many studies, an enormous range of different care arrangements are all lumped under the general title of "nonparental care" (see Figure 6.3). Infants who are cared for by grandparents in their own homes, as well as those who are enrolled in day-care centers, receive nonparental care. In addition, infants enter these care arrangements at different ages and remain in them for varying lengths of time. Some have the same nonparental caregiver over many years; others shift often from one care setting to another. Moreover, nonparental care varies widely in quality (Corapci, 2010).

Research on nonparental care is complicated by the fact that families who place their children in nonparental care are different in a whole host of ways from those who care for their children primarily at home. How can researchers be sure that effects attributed to nonparental care are not instead the result of these other family differences? Mothers also differ widely in their attitudes toward the care arrangements they have made (Rose & Elicker, 2010). Yet studies of the effects of nonparental care rarely offer any information about the mother's level of satisfaction with her situation.

Most of the research on nonparental versus parental care has not taken these complexities into account. Researchers have frequently compared children "in day care" with those "reared at home" and assumed that any differences between the two groups were attributable to the day-care experience. Thus, clear answers to even the most basic questions about the impact of nonparental care on children's development are still not available. Nonetheless, because the issue is so critical, you need to be aware of what is and is not yet known.

Half of all infants in the United States now experience at least some nonparental care.

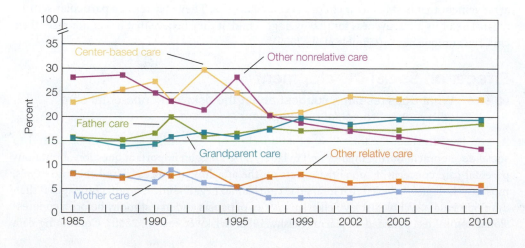

Figure 6.3 Nonparental Care Arrangements for Children under 6 in the United States

Children younger than 6 years whose mothers are employed are cared for in a variety of different settings in the United States.

(*Source:* Federal Interagency Forum on Child and Family Statistics, 2012.)

Effects on Physical and Cognitive Development

LO 6.13 What might be the effects of nonparental care on physical and cognitive development?

Child-care centers, with their attractive playgrounds and specially designed play equipment for infants, might seem to be ideal settings in which to encourage children to be physically fit from the earliest days of life. However, researchers have discovered that infants and young children in all types of nonparental care arrangements are more likely to be overweight both early in life and when they reach school age than children who are cared for exclusively by their parents (Geoffroy et al., 2013). The cause could lie in practices in nonparental care settings or in factors that vary across parental-care and nonparental-care families. Developmentalists are concerned about these findings because studies show that infants and young children who are overweight attain motor milestones more slowly and are less physically active than their peers, a pattern that continues into the middle childhood years and contributes to lifelong weight problems (Cawley & Spiess, 2008; Ridgway et al., 2009; Slining, Adair, Goldman, Borja, & Bentley, 2010). Thus, it is important to determine the reason for the association so that regulatory agencies can effect changes in the practices of nonparental caregivers or involve them in efforts to educate parents about the importance of proper nutrition and exercise for infants and young children (Kaphingst & Story, 2009).

Surveys show that school readiness is the primary goal of parents who choose nonparental care for toddlers and preschoolers (Gamble, Ewing, & Wilhelm, 2009). There is some evidence that high-quality day care has beneficial effects on many children's overall cognitive development (Vandell, Adair, Goldman, Borja, & Bentley, 2010). Some studies suggest that this effect is particularly strong for children from poor families, who show significant and lasting gains in IQ and later school performance after attending highly enriched day care throughout infancy and early childhood (Loeb, Fuller, Kagan, & Carrol, 2004; Love et al., 2003; Pungello et al., 2010).

However, the picture is not entirely rosy. Several studies in the United States point to possible negative effects of day-care experience on cognitive development. For instance, one study found that children who were first enrolled in nonparental care in the year before they entered school obtained lower scores on reading and math achievement tests at the end of kindergarten than peers who were cared for at home (Herbst & Tekin, 2008).

How can these conflicting findings be reconciled? One fairly straightforward possibility is that the crucial issue is the discrepancy between the level of stimulation the child would receive at home and the quality of the child care. When a particular day-care setting for a given child provides more enrichment than the child would have received at home, day-care attendance has some beneficial cognitive effects; when day care is less stimulating than full-time home care would be for that child, day care has negative effects. However, there are not yet enough well-designed, large studies to make developmentalists confident that this is the right way to conceptualize the process. Consequently, the most that can be said about the effects of nonparental care on cognitive development is that it seems to be beneficial for some children but not others. Parents appear to be keenly aware of the need to find the nonparental care arrangement that best fits their children's characteristics. They may reject a particular setting, regardless of its attractiveness for the "average" child, if they believe that it will not meet their children's unique needs (Gamble et al., 2009).

Effects on Social Development

LO 6.14 What does research suggest about the risks of nonparental care with respect to social development?

As you have learned, the formation of an attachment relationship appears to be central to social development during infancy and in later years. Thus, an important question about nonparental care concerns its potential effects on the attachment process. Until the mid-1980s, most psychologists believed that infant day care had no negative effect on attachment. But then developmental psychologist Jay Belsky, in a series of papers and in testimony before a congressional committee, sounded an alarm (Belsky, 1985; Belsky & Fearon, 2008). Combining data from several studies, he concluded that there was a heightened risk of an insecure attachment for infants who entered day care before their first birthday.

Since that time, other studies have supported Belsky's conclusions (e.g., Sagi, Korin-Karie, Gini, Ziv, & Joels, 2002). Moreover, a number of researchers have analyzed the combined results of large numbers of studies and confirmed Belsky's original conclusion. For example, a summary of the findings of 13 different studies involving 897 infants revealed that 35% of infants who had experienced at least 5 hours per week of nonparental care were insecurely attached, compared to 29% of infants with exclusively maternal care (Lamb, Sternberg, & Prodromidis, 1992).

Another study, involving more than 1,000 infants, demonstrated that infants whose parents exhibit behaviors associated with insecure attachment, such as poor sensitivity to the child's needs, are more likely to be negatively affected by nonparental care. When all of the infants were considered together, researchers found no differences in attachment quality between those who were in nonparental care and those who were cared for at home, regardless of the age at which they entered outside care or how many hours per week they were cared for there (NICHD Early Child Care Research Network, 1998). However, when researchers looked at only those babies whose parents displayed behaviors associated with insecure attachment, such as insensitivity to the child's needs, they found that children who were home-reared were more likely to be securely attached to their caregivers than those who were enrolled in nonparental care.

How does nonparental care affect other social relationships? Belsky argues that, when children reach school age, those who entered nonparental care during the early months of life and who have spent 20 or more hours per week in such care throughout early childhood are at greater risk for social problems than children who have spent less time in nonparental care (Belsky, 2001, 2002). A number of other studies support Belsky's view (Kim, 1997; NICHD, 2006). In fact, some research indicates that Belsky's hypothesis may have been overly optimistic with regard to the amount of nonparental care that may be harmful. One study showed that school-aged children who had spent as little as 10 hours per week in nonparental care during infancy and early childhood were more likely to display aggressiveness toward peers and disobedience toward teachers than peers who were entirely home-reared (NICHD, 2006). However, other studies suggest that the negative effects of nonparental care are no longer evident in children over the age of 7 (van Beijsterveldt, Hudziak, & Boomsma, 2005).

Interpreting Research on Nonparental Care

LO 6.15 What variables should be taken into account in interpretations of research on nonparental care?

What is it about nonparental care that predisposes infants to become aggressive, disobedient kindergartners? Studies of infants' neurobiological responses to nonparental care may hold a clue. Researchers have found that levels of the stress hormone *cortisol* increase from morning to afternoon in infants who are enrolled in center-based care, especially in children under the age of 3 years (Berry et al., 2014; Gunnar, Kryzer, Van Ryzin, & Phillips, 2010; Vermeer & van IJzendoorn, 2006; Sumner, Bernard, & Dozier, 2010). By contrast, cortisol levels decrease over the course of the day in home-reared infants. Interestingly, cortisol levels of home-reared and center-care infants are identical on weekends and holidays. For these reasons, some developmentalists argue that the higher levels of cortisol experienced by center-care infants affect their rapidly developing brains in ways that lead to problem behaviors. Research showing associations between individual differences in cortisol responses and problem behaviors in infancy and early childhood supports this view (Bagner, Scheinkopf, Vohr, & Lester, 2010; Berry et al., 2013). However, studies also suggest that stress hormones have both positive and negative effects on young brains (Gunnar et al., 2010; Lyons, Parker, & Schatzberg, 2010). Thus, although research has established that nonparental care increases cortisol levels in infants and young children, developmentalists do not yet have a definitive answer as to how this association affects the developing brain.

Some developmentalists argue that nonparental care arrangements probably vary in the degree to which they induce stress in infants and young children. In other words, they say, quality of care may be just as important as quantity of care (Maccoby & Lewis, 2003; Vandell et al., 2010). For example, some researchers have found that, when infants are cared for in high-quality centers, the amount of time they spend in such care is unrelated to social behavior (Love et al., 2003). Thus, developmentalists urge parents, especially those who must leave their infants in center-based care for extended periods of time, to make every effort to ensure that the arrangement they choose has the characteristics discussed in the *Developmental Science at Home* discussion above.

Another point to keep in mind is that individual and gender differences have been found to interact with nonparental care. For example, infants who are behaviorally inhibited, in Jerome Kagan's terms, may be more sensitive to the stresses associated with center-based care but may also benefit more from increased opportunities to interact with other children (Bohlin & Hagekull, 2009; Watamura et al., 2003). Moreover, boys in nonparental care are more likely than girls in similar care settings to be insecurely attached to their caregivers (Crockenberg, 2003). For these reasons, more research that takes into account temperament, gender, and other individual differences is needed before we can say for certain that nonparental care has uniformly negative effects on children's social development (Pluess & Belsky, 2009).

Finally, it is important to understand that, on average, the differences between children in nonparental care and their home-reared peers, both positive and negative, are very small (NICHD, 2006). Moreover, studies in several cultures that have attempted to examine all of the complex variables associated with parental and nonparental care, such as parents' level of education, have shown that family variables are more important than the type of day-care arrangements a family chooses (Anme et al., 2010; Belsky et al., 2007; Nomaguchi, 2006). Developmental psychologist Sandra Scarr, a leading day-care researcher, has suggested that the kind of day care parents choose is an extension of their own characteristics and parenting styles (Scarr, 1997). For example, poorly educated parents may choose day-care arrangements that do not emphasize infant learning. Similarly, parents whose focus is on intellectual development may not place a high priority on the emotional aspects of a particular day-care arrangement. Thus, Scarr claims, day-care effects are likely to be parenting effects in disguise.

Answers to these questions can be found in the back of the book.

1. Classify each statement as true or false.

_____(1) Research results on the effects of nonparental care on cognitive development are mixed.

_____(2) Infants in nonparental care are less likely to be overweight than infants who are cared for by their parents.

_____(3) Infants whose parents exhibit behaviors associated with insecure attachment, such as poor sensitivity to the child's needs, are more likely to be negatively affected by nonparental care.

_____(4) The levels of the stress hormone cortisol decrease from morning to afternoon in infants who are enrolled in center-based care.

_____(5) Family variables are more important than the type of day-care arrangements a family chooses.

CRITICAL THINKING

2. An experimental study could answer cause-and-effect questions about the effects of nonparental care, but why would such a study be unethical?

SUMMARY

Theories of Social and Personality Development (pp. 128–130)

LO 6.1 How do Freud's and Erikson's views of personality development in the first 2 years differ?

- Freud suggested that individual differences in personality originate in the nursing and weaning practices of infants' mothers. Erikson emphasized the roles of both mothers and fathers, as well as other adults in the infant's environment, in providing for all the infant's needs, thereby instilling a sense of trust concerning the social world.

LO 6.2 What are the main ideas of attachment theory?

- Ethologists hypothesize that early emotional bonds are the foundation of later personality and social development. They further suggest that the first 2 years of life are a sensitive, or critical, period for the development of attachment.

Attachment (pp. 130–137)

LO 6.3 How does synchrony affect parent–infant relations?

- For parents to form a strong attachment relationship with an infant, what is most crucial is the development of synchrony, a set of mutually reinforcing and interlocking behaviors that characterize most interactions between parent and infant. Fathers as well as mothers form strong bonds with their infants, but fathers show more physically playful behaviors with their children than do mothers.

LO 6.4 What are the four phases of attachment and the behaviors associated with them?

- Bowlby proposed that a child's attachment to a caregiver develops in four phases: (1) indiscriminate aiming of attachment behaviors toward anyone within reach; (2) focus on one or more figures; (3) "secure base behavior" at about 6 months of age, signaling the presence of a clear attachment; and (4) an internal model of attachment that influences current and future close relationships.

LO 6.5 What are the four attachment patterns that Ainsworth discovered?

- Using a procedure called the Strange Situation, Ainsworth identified four patterns of attachment distinguished by infants' responses to separations from and reunions with their mothers. *Securely attached* infants separate easily and greet mothers positively when they return. Infants with *insecure/avoidant attachments* avoid contact with mothers especially at reunion. Infants with *insecure/ambivalent attachments* are upset at separation but do not greet mothers positively at reunion. Infants with *insecure/disorganized attachment* display confused, contradictory patterns such as moving toward the mother while looking elsewhere. Attachment patterns remain stable as long as an infant's circumstances remain so. Most children with autism spectrum disorders are attached to their caregivers but lack the ability to form relationships with others.

LO 6.6 What variables might affect a parent's ability to establish an attachment relationship with an infant?

- Caregiver characteristics such as marital status, age, education level, and income can affect infants' attachment quality. Also, infants whose parents have psychiatric illnesses are more likely to form insecure attachments than babies whose parents do not have these disorders.

LO 6.7 What are the long-term consequences of attachment quality?

- The security of the initial attachment is reasonably stable; later in childhood, securely attached children appear to be more socially skillful, more curious and persistent in approaching new tasks, and more mature. The internal model of attachment that individuals develop in infancy affects how they parent their own babies.

LO 6.8 In what ways do patterns of attachment vary across cultures?

- Studies in many countries suggest that secure attachment is the most common pattern everywhere, but cultures differ in the frequency of different types of insecure attachment.

Personality, Temperament, and Self-Concept (pp. 138–142)

LO 6.9 On which dimensions of temperament do most developmentalists agree?

- Temperament theorists generally agree on the following basic temperament dimensions: activity level, approach/positive emotionality, inhibition, negative emotionality, and effortful control/task persistence.

LO 6.10 What are the roles of heredity, neurological processes, and environment in the formation of temperament?

- There is strong evidence that temperamental differences have a genetic component and that they are at least somewhat stable throughout infancy and childhood. However, temperament is not totally determined by heredity or neurological processes. The "fit" between children's temperaments and their environments may be more important than temperament itself.

LO 6.11 How do the subjective self, the objective self, and the emotional self develop during the first 2 years?

- The infant begins to develop a sense of self, including the awareness of a separate self and the understanding of self-permanence (which may be collectively called the subjective self) and awareness of herself as an object in the world (the objective self) during the middle of the second year. An emotional self develops in the first year. The range of emotions infants experience—as well as their ability to make use of information about emotions, such as facial expressions—increases dramatically over the first year.

Effects of Nonparental Care (pp. 142–147)

LO 6.12 Why is it difficult to study the effects of nonparental care on development?

- Comparing parental to nonparental care is difficult because there are many types of nonparental care arrangements. Families that choose nonparental care also differ from families that care for their children at home.

LO 6.13 What might be the effects of nonparental care on physical and cognitive development?

- Infants in nonparental care are more likely to be overweight than those who are cared for exclusively by parents. Research on the effects of nonparental care on cognitive developmental variables such as intelligence test scores and academic achievement have produced inconsistent results. Some studies show positive effects, but others do not. When a child receives more intellectual stimulation in nonparental care than he would at home, there are likely to be positive effects on cognitive development. But when the reverse is true, nonparental care may have neutral or negative effects on cognitive development.

LO 6.14 What does research suggest about the risks of nonparental care with respect to social development?

- The impact of day care on children's social development is unclear. Some studies show a small difference in security of attachment between children in day care and those reared at home; others suggest that home-care and day-care children do not differ with respect to attachment. Some studies show children who spend more time in day care to be more aggressive; others show them to be more socially skillful.

LO 6.15 What variables should be taken into account in interpretations of research on nonparental care?

- Infants' physiological responses to the stresses associated with nonparental care may underlie its association with developmental outcomes. The quality of nonparental care a child receives may be as important as the quantity of nonparental care. Individual differences and gender may interact with the quality of a care arrangement, the quantity of outside-the-home care a child receives, or both. Average differences between children who receive nonparental care and those who are cared for entirely in their own home are small.

KEY TERMS

attachment (p. 130)

attachment theory (p. 129)

autism spectrum disorders (ASD) (p. 134)

goodness-of-fit (p. 140)

insecure/ambivalent attachment (p. 133)

insecure/avoidant attachment (p. 133)

insecure/disorganized attachment (p. 133)

niche picking (p. 139)

objective (categorical) self (p. 141)

personality (p. 138)

secure attachment (p. 133)

separation anxiety (p. 132)

social referencing (p. 132)

stranger anxiety (p. 132)

subjective self (p. 141)

synchrony (p. 130)

temperament (p. 138)

CHAPTER TEST ✓ Study and Review in MyPsychLab

Answers to all the Chapter Test questions can be found in the back of the book.

1. Which of the following is a self-conscious emotion?
   a. anger
   b. shame
   c. sadness
   d. happiness

2. The term *niche picking* refers to _____.
   a. the process of selecting experiences on the basis of temperament
   b. the dimensions of infant temperament
   c. Erikson's trust-versus-mistrust stage
   d. the influence of heredity on temperament

3. Which statement about cross-cultural research on attachment is true?
   a. European countries value independence, fostering insecure attachment.
   b. Avoidant children are most common in Israel and Japan.
   c. Insecure attachment is most common in western cultures.
   d. Secure attachment is the most common pattern.

4. According to Freud, what is the basis of infant–caregiver attachment?
   a. infant–caregiver physical contact
   b. nursing followed by balanced weaning
   c. the mother's unconscious drives
   d. caregiver responses to infants' needs

5. Which of these statements is one of the difficulties involved in studying the effects of nonparental care?
   a. Most children experience several different kinds of nonparental care.
   b. Most parents who enroll their children in nonparental care have similar goals and expectations.
   c. There are no appropriate control groups.
   d. Few children are cared for by relatives, making it difficult to study that particular type of nonparental care.

6. Which of the following statements best fits the ethological perspective?
   a. The relationship between a mother and infant is symbiotic.
   b. Responsive caregiving helps infants develop a sense of trust.
   c. Physical contact is required for the development of an attachment bond.
   d. Infants are biologically predisposed to form attachment relationships with caregivers.

7. Bowlby proposed that infants develop _____ that shape future social relationships.
   a. positive reinforcers
   b. internal models
   c. behavioral fixations
   d. symbiotic relationships

8. Nonparental care is associated with increases in _____ in an infant's body.
   a. dopamine
   b. adrenaline
   c. cortisol
   d. serotonin

9. Activity level, inhibition, and sociability are _____.
   a. traits that vary little from one infant to another
   b. dimensions of temperament
   c. factors that increase the likelihood of insecure attachment
   d. parental characteristics that contribute to attachment

10. Which of the following terms refers to an infant's tendency to respond with fear to new people and situations?
    a. symbiosis
    b. niche picking
    c. social asymmetry
    d. inhibition

11. Which aspect of the self is on display when infants understand that they can cause things to happen in the world around them?
    a. subjective self
    b. emotional self
    c. psychosocial self
    d. objective self

12. At what age do infants display facial expressions that are associated with underlying emotions?
    a. birth
    b. 1 month
    c. 2 months
    d. 3 months

13. The more time an infant spends in nonparental care, _____.
    a. the better her social skills in preschool
    b. the lower her IQ
    c. the more likely she is to develop an insecure attachment relationship with her parent
    d. the less likely she is to require special education services in elementary school

14. According to this text, what is the cause of the relationship between nonparental care and overweight in infancy?
    a. Feeding practices and other factors by nonparental caregivers
    b. Feeding practices and other factors in the homes of infants receiving nonparental care
    c. Both A and B are correct.
    d. There is not yet enough research to justify a hypothesis to explain the relationship

15. According to this chapter, the most common nonparental care arrangement for children under age 2 is _____.
    a. enrollment in a child-care center
    b. care by a relative in the relative's or the child's home
    c. care by a nonrelative in the nonrelative's or the child's home
    d. none of the above

16. According to this chapter, a study found that kindergarteners who spent 10 or more hours per week in nonparental care when they were infants, on average, _____.
    a. were 1 year ahead of their peers in academic achievement
    b. had better social skills than their peers
    c. were more responsive to teachers than their peers
    d. were more aggressive than their peers

17. According to the text, most studies of father–infant relationships _____.
    a. include only families from North America or Europe
    b. take cultural context into account
    c. suggest that fathers behave pretty much the same way all over the world
    d. show that mothers and fathers interact with infants in identical ways in Western cultures

18. C. J. gains comfort through eating and drinking. She also cries to gain attention from her parents or to express discomfort. Freud would say that C. J. is in which stage of development?
    a. symbiotic
    b. oral
    c. dependency
    d. trust

19. Which of the following Piagetian milestones is associated with the development of the subjective self in infancy?
    a. deferred imitation
    b. object permanence
    c. A-not-B error
    d. means–end behavior

20. A researcher places a spot of lipstick on an infant's nose and puts him in front of a mirror. The researcher is testing the infant's _____.
    a. progression from symbiotic dependence to ontogenetic independence
    b. capacity for social referencing
    c. sense of self-awareness
    d. emotional self

21. Freud claimed that an infant _____.
    a. does not understand that he is a separate being from his mother
    b. desires physical contact with a caregiver more than food
    c. needs to develop a sense of trust in the first year of life
    d. is biologically predisposed to form attachments with as many caregivers as possible

22. Chad cries, and his mother responds immediately. When he coos at his mother, she smiles and cuddles him. Developmentalists would say that this is an example of which of the following?
    a. synchrony
    b. maternal instinct
    c. symbiosis
    d. ethological adaptation

23. Which of these infants would be classified as difficult, according to the categories proposed by Thomas and Chess?
    a. Brock approaches new events positively and displays regular eating and sleeping patterns.
    b. Samir displays irregular eating and sleeping patterns and is very irritable.
    c. Lucinda is unresponsive to unfamiliar people.
    d. Avi prefers to be cared for by his father rather than his mother.

24. According to this chapter, _____ is an indication that an infant has formed an attachment relationship with a caregiver.
    a. separation anxiety
    b. stranger anxiety
    c. social referencing
    d. all of the above

25. Eight-month-old Naveen squeals with delight when his mother returns home from work every day. According to Ainsworth, Naveen probably has developed a(n) _____.
    a. secure attachment.
    b. insecure attachment.
    c. avoidant attachment.
    d. disorganized attachment.

To 👁 **Watch** ✳ **Explore** ◉ **Simulate** ✓ **Study** and **Review**
and experience MyVirtualLife go to MyPsychLab.com

chapter 7

Physical and Cognitive Development in Early Childhood

Watch a group of 2- to 6-year-olds on a playground, and you are likely to be amazed by the pure joy they get from moving their bodies. They climb things, throw things, run, leap, and build elaborate forts out of blocks, a pattern of behavior you may have seen in the "child" you are raising in *MyVirtualLife*. When a child first masters any one of these skills, the utter delight and pride on the child's face is a wonder to behold. When a child is working hard on some physical skill—trying to string beads or

LEARNING OBJECTIVES

PHYSICAL CHANGES

7.1 What are the major milestones of growth and motor development between 2 and 6?

7.2 What important changes happen in the brain during these years?

7.3 What are the nutritional and health-care needs of young children?

7.4 What factors contribute to abuse and neglect, and how do these traumas affect children's development?

COGNITIVE CHANGES

7.5 What are the characteristics of children's thought during Piaget's preoperational stage?

7.6 How has recent research challenged Piaget's view of this period?

7.7 What is a theory of mind, and how does it develop?

7.8 How do information-processing and sociocultural theorists explain changes in young children's thinking?

CHANGES IN LANGUAGE

7.9 How does fast-mapping help children learn new words?

7.10 What happens during the grammar explosion?

7.11 What is phonological awareness, and why is it important?

DIFFERENCES IN INTELLIGENCE

7.12 What are the strengths and weaknesses of IQ tests?

7.13 What kinds of evidence support the nature and nurture explanations for individual differences in IQ?

7.14 What theories and evidence have been offered in support of genetic and cultural explanations of group differences in IQ scores?

MyVirtualLife

What decisions would you make while raising a child? What would the consequences of those decisions be?

Find out by accessing MyVirtualLife at www .MyPsychLab.com to raise a virtual child and live your own virtual life.

to build a castle out of blocks—she is likely to have a look of intense concentration. And even when children this age are clearly exhausted, they usually refuse to stop playing.

The young child's growth and mastery of these and other physical skills is the first topic we address in this chapter. Next we turn to the health needs of young children and some of the health hazards they face during this period. Finally, we consider two atypical developmental pathways that are usually diagnosed during early childhood.

Physical Changes

Chapter 4 chronicled the many rapid changes in an infant's body. The physical changes between ages 2 and 6 are less dramatic. Subtle though they may be, the physical changes of the early childhood period provide children with a foundation for the cognitive and social leaps that lie ahead of them.

Growth and Motor Development

LO 7.1   What are the major milestones of growth and motor development between 2 and 6?

Changes in height and weight happen far more slowly in the preschool years than in infancy. Each year, the child adds about 2 to 3 inches in height and about 6 pounds in weight. At the same time, the young child makes steady progress in motor development. The changes are not as dramatic as the beginning of walking, but they enable the child to acquire skills that markedly increase his independence and exploratory ability. ◉ **Watch** the **Video** *Early Childhood: The Growing Child* in **MyPsychLab**.

Table 7.1 lists the major motor skills that emerge in these preschool years. Most striking are the impressive gains the child makes in large-muscle skills. By age 5 or 6, children are running, jumping, hopping, galloping, climbing, and skipping. They can ride a tricycle; some can ride a two-wheeled bike. The degree of confidence with which a 5-year-old uses her body for these movements is impressive, particularly in contrast to the somewhat unsteady movements of an 18-month-old.

Fine-motor skills also improve in these years, but not to the same level of confidence. Three-year-olds can indeed pick up Cheerios, and 5-year-olds can thread beads on a string. But even at age 5 or 6, children are not highly skilled at such fine-motor tasks as using a pencil

TABLE 7.1   Milestones of Motor Development from Age 2 to Age 6

Age	Gross Motor Skills	Fine-Motor Skills
18–24 months	Runs awkwardly; climbs stairs with both feet on each step; pushes and pulls boxes or wheeled toys	Shows clear hand preference; stacks four to six blocks; turns pages one at a time; picks up things without overbalancing; unscrews lid on a jar
2–3 years	Runs easily; climbs on furniture unaided; hauls and shoves big toys around obstacles	Picks up small objects; throws small ball while standing
3–4 years	Walks up stairs one foot per step; skips on two feet; walks on tiptoe; pedals and steers tricycle; walks in any direction pulling large toys	Catches large ball between outstretched arms; cuts paper with scissors; holds pencil between thumb and fingers
4–5 years	Walks up and down stairs one foot per step; stands, runs, and walks on tiptoe	Strikes ball with bat; kicks and catches ball; threads beads on a string; grasps pencil properly
5–6 years	Skips on alternate feet; walks on a line; slides, swings	Plays ball games well; threads needle and sews large stitches.

(*Sources:* Connolly & Dalgleish, 1989; Diagram Group, 1977; Fagard & Jacquet, 1989; Mathew & Cook, 1990; Thomas, 1990.)

or crayon or cutting accurately with scissors. When a young child uses a crayon or a pencil, he uses his whole body—the tongue is moving and the whole arm and back are involved in the writing or drawing motion.

These are important facts for teachers of young children to understand. It is a rare kindergartener who is really skilled at such fine-motor tasks as writing letters. Younger preschoolers, of course, are even less skilled at these tasks. However, a "wait and see" strategy isn't the best approach to helping children learn to write letters and draw simple forms. Researchers have found that early training, beginning at about age 2½, can accelerate the rate at which young children acquire school-related fine-motor skills such as writing letters (Callaghan & Rankin, 2002; Callaghan, Rochat, & Corbit, 2012).

Training effects are evident in studies of children's drawing as well (Callaghan & Rankin, 2002). Nevertheless, drawing appears to follow the developmental sequence shown in Figure 7.1, even when accelerated by training (Toomela, 1999). Moreover, the effectiveness of training seems to depend on how well young children understand the figures that experimenters attempt to teach them how to draw. That is, a child who has some grasp of what letters are will be more responsive to training in letter writing (Callaghan, 1999). Thus, older preschoolers—those beyond age 3—benefit more from training than younger children. Moreover, learning to write letters appears to help children more fully understand them (Callaghan & Rankin, 2002). Thus, research examining young children's writing demonstrates that, in some cases, physical and cognitive development are interactive processes.

By three, most children can ride a tricycle.

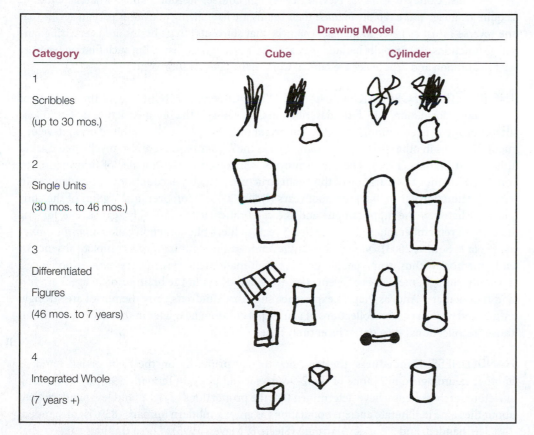

| | Drawing Model | |
Category	Cube	Cylinder
1 Scribbles (up to 30 mos.)		
2 Single Units (30 mos. to 46 mos.)		
3 Differentiated Figures (46 mos. to 7 years)		
4 Integrated Whole (7 years +)		

Figure 7.1 Stages in Children's Drawing

Examples of drawings in each category of two object forms.

(*Source:* From A. Toomela, "Drawing development: Stages in the representation of a cube and a cylinder," *Child Development,* Vol. 70, No. 5 (Sept/Oct 1999), p. 1141. Reprinted by permission.)

The Brain and Nervous System

LO 7.2   What important changes happen in the brain during these years?

Brain growth, synapse formation, and myelination continue in early childhood, although at a slower pace than in infancy (Stiles & Jernigan, 2010). However, the slower rate of growth should not be taken to mean that brain development is nearly complete. Indeed, a number of important neurological milestones are reached between the ages of 2 and 6. It is likely that these milestones represent the neurological underpinnings of the remarkable advances in thinking and language that occur during this period.

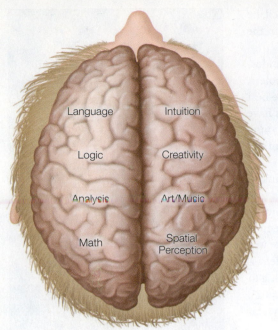

Figure 7.2 Lateralization of Brain Functions

Brain functions are lateralized as shown in the figure. Neurologists think that the basic outline of lateralization is genetically determined, whereas the specific timing of the lateralization of each function is determined by an interaction of genes and experiences.

Figure labels: Language, Intuition, Logic, Creativity, Analysis, Art/Music, Math, Spatial Perception

LATERALIZATION The **corpus callosum**, the brain structure through which the left and right sides of the cerebral cortex communicate, grows and matures more during the early childhood years than in any other period of life. The growth of this structure accompanies the functional specialization of the left and right hemispheres of the cerebral cortex. This process is called **lateralization**. Figure 7.2 shows how brain functions are lateralized in most people.

Neuroscientists suspect that our genes dictate which functions will be lateralized and which will not be. However, experience shapes the pace at which lateralization occurs. For example, in 95% of humans, language functions that enable us to understand the meanings of words and the structure of sentences are carried out in the left hemisphere. Studies of fetal responses to different kinds of sounds (i.e., language and music) show that this pattern is evident even before we are born (de Lacoste, Horvath, & Woodward, 1991). The fact that left-side processing of language appears so early in life suggests that lateralization of these functions is dictated by our genes.

Nevertheless, language functions are not as fully lateralized in fetuses as they are in children and adults. Moreover, research indicates that the degree to which these language functions are relegated to the left side of the brain is linked to individual differences in a number of cognitive functions (Prichard, Propper, & Christman, 2013). For example, Preschoolers who display the most advanced language skills in their everyday speech, as well as on standardized tests, show the highest levels of left-side lateralization of these functions (Mills, Coffey-Corina, & Neville, 1994). Of course, we don't know whether children acquire language more rapidly *because* their brains are lateralizing at a faster pace. It seems that the reverse is just as likely to be true—namely, that some children's brains are lateralizing language functions more rapidly because they are learning language faster. But such findings suggest that maturation and experience are both at work in the lateralization process.

THE RETICULAR FORMATION AND THE HIPPOCAMPUS Myelination of the neurons of the reticular formation, which (as described in Chapter 4) is the brain structure that regulates attention and concentration, is another important milestone of early childhood brain development. Neurons in other parts of the brain, such as the *hippocampus*, are also myelinated during this period (Tanner, 1990). The **hippocampus** is involved in the transfer of information to long-term memory. Maturation of this brain structure probably accounts for improvements in memory function across the preschool years (Rolls, 2000). Moreover, maturation of the connections between the hippocampus and the cerebral cortex is probably responsible for our inability to remember much about the first 3 years of life, a phenomenon called *infantile amnesia* (Zola & Squire, 2003). Note that infantile amnesia does not involve a complete absence of early memories; thus, some people do have legitimate memories of very early experiences. Typically, though, memories of events that were laid down in the brain prior to age 3 are few and fragmentary. And, as Piaget's experience suggests, children's early memories are strongly influenced by the verbal recollections of adults that children hear later in their lives, even when those "recollections" turn out to be entirely false.

HANDEDNESS **Handedness**, the tendency to rely primarily on the right or left hand, is another neurological milestone of the 2- to 6-year-old period (Tanner, 1990). By examining skeletons, archaeologists have determined that the proportions of right- and left-handers were about the same in illiterate ancient populations as among modern humans (83% right-handed, 14% left-handed, and 3% ambidextrous) (Steele & Mayes, 1995). These findings suggest that the prevalence of right-handedness is likely to be a result of genetic inheritance (Forrester et al., 2013). However, the genetic basis of handedness is quite complicated. Several years ago, geneticists at the National Cancer Institute (NCI) identified a dominant gene for right-handedness, which they believe to be so common in the human population that most people receive a copy of it from both parents (Klar, 2003). Moreover, another gene determines the degree to which a right-handed individual is dependent on the dominant hand (Arning et al., 2013). To further complicate the picture, an international team of researchers discovered yet another gene that predisposes children to be left-handed only when they receive it from their fathers (Francks et al., 2007).

corpus callosum the membrane that connects the right and left hemispheres of the cerebral cortex

lateralization the process through which brain functions are divided between the two hemispheres of the cerebral cortex

hippocampus a brain structure that is important in learning

handedness a strong preference for using one hand or the other that develops between 3 and 5 years of age

Persuasive evidence for the genetic hypothesis can be found in studies demonstrating that handedness appears very early in life—often before the first birthday—although it doesn't become well established until the preschool years (Stroganova, Posikera, Pushina, & Orek-hova, 2003). Research comparing children's right-hand and left-hand performance on manual tasks, such as moving pegs from one place to another on a pegboard, also supports the genetic hypothesis. Most of these studies show that older children are better at accomplishing fine-motor tasks with the nondominant hand than younger children are (Dellatolas et al., 2003; Roy, Bryden, & Cavill, 2003). Findings from studies comparing nondominant hand use in children and adults follow the same pattern (Annett, 2003; Cavill & Bryden, 2003). Thus, expe-rience in using the hands appears to moderate, rather than strengthen, the advantage of the dominant over the nondominant hand.

Health and Wellness

LO 7.3   **What are the nutritional and health-care needs of young children?**

Young children continue to require periodic medical check-ups as well as a variety of immunizations. Just as they do with infants, doctors monitor preschoolers' growth and motor development. At the same time, doctors and nurses often serve as parents' first source of help with children who have sensory or developmental disabilities that were not diagnosed in infancy (Levine, 2011). Further, health-care professionals can help parents deal with everyday issues, such as the kinds of sleep problems discussed in the *Developmental Science at Home* feature.

EATING PATTERNS Because children grow more slowly during the early child-hood years, they may seem to eat less than when they were babies. Moreover, food aversions often develop during the preschool years. For example, a child who loved carrots as an infant may refuse to eat them at age 2 or 3. Consequently, con-flicts between young children and their parents often focus on eating behavior (Wong, 1993).

Immunizing young children against a variety of diseases is an important goal of routine health care for this age group.

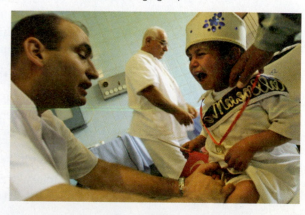

Nutritionists point out that it is important that parents not become so concerned about the quantity of food a child consumes that they cater to his preferences for sweets and other high-calorie or high-fat foods (Wong, 1993). Many children acquire eating habits during these years that lead to later weight problems. Surveys show that 16% of children aged 2 to 5 are overweight and another 16% are at risk of becoming so by the time they reach school age (Pediatric Nutrition Surveillance, 2012). Thus, nutritionists recommend keeping a variety of nutritious foods on hand and allowing a child's appetite to be a good guide to how much food he should eat. Of course, this approach works only if young children's access to sweets and other attractive, but nonnutritious, foods is limited.

Parents should also keep in mind that young children eat only about half as much food as adults, and, unlike adults, many don't consume the majority of their daily calories at regular meals (Wong, 1993). Nutritionists suggest that concerned parents keep a daily record of what their children are actually eating for a week. In most cases, parents will find that children are consuming plenty of food.

ILLNESSES AND ACCIDENTS In the United States, the average preschooler has six to seven colds each year, along with one or two episodes of gastrointestinal illness (Smith, 2011). Children who are experiencing high levels of stress or family upheaval are most likely to become ill. For example, a large nationwide study in the United States showed that children living in single-parent homes have more asthma, more headaches, and a generally higher vulnerability to illnesses of many types than do those living with both biological parents (Dawson, 1991; Weitoft, Hjern, Haglund, & Rosén, 2003).

Another danger for children is accidents. In any given year, about one-quarter of all children under 5 in the United States have at least one accident that requires some kind of medical attention, and accidents are the major cause of death in preschool and school-age children (Borse & Sleet, 2009). At every age, accidents are more common among boys than among girls, presumably because of their more active and daring styles of play. The majority of accidents among children in the preschool years—falls, cuts, accidental poisonings, and the like—occur at home. Drowning is the leading cause of accidental death in 1- to 4-year-olds; beyond age 5, motor vehicle accidents are the most frequent cause of death among children (Borse & Sleet, 2009). Experts point out that, while parents obviously can't keep preschoolers entirely free from injuries, many are preventable. Children can wear protective gear while riding tricycles and bicycles, and the proper use of car seats and restraint systems greatly reduces death rates that are due to auto accidents. Moreover, barriers that prevent children from getting into swimming pools, lakes, and the like can prevent drowning.

Abuse and Neglect

LO 7.4 What factors contribute to abuse and neglect, and how do these traumas affect children's development?

Legally, *child abuse* is defined as physical or psychological injury that results from an adult's intentional exposure of a child to potentially harmful physical stimuli, sexual acts, or neglect (Graff, 2013). *Neglect* is failure of caregivers to provide emotional and physical support for a child. However, it is fairly difficult to define child abuse and neglect in a practical sense. For example, if a parent allows a 2-year-old to play outdoors alone and the child falls and breaks her arm, has the injury resulted from an accident or from neglect? Such are the dilemmas confronting medical professionals, who are bound by law to report suspected cases of abuse and neglect to authorities. Doctors and nurses are reluctant to accuse parents of abuse in such situations, but they are also concerned about protecting children from further injury (Christian & Bloom, 2011). In addition, cultural values concerning acceptable and unacceptable treatment of children make it extremely difficult to define abuse so that child maltreatment can be studied cross-culturally. What is abusive in one culture may not be so regarded in another.

PREVALENCE In the United States, most cases of abuse and neglect that result in serious injury or death involve children under age 4 (U.S. Department of Health & Human Services, 2010). Because of the inherent difficulties in defining abuse, it is difficult to say just how many children suffer abuse. However, research suggests that 1–2% of U.S. infants and young children are treated each year by medical professionals for injuries resulting from abuse (U.S. Department of Health & Human Services, 2010). Moreover, physicians estimate that abuse and/or neglect are responsible for about 10% of emergency room visits involving children under age 5 (Sulkes, 1998). Sadly, more than 1,500 infants and children die as a result of abuse and/or neglect each year in the United States, and 80% of them are under the age of 4 years (U.S. Department of Health & Human Services, 2012).

The majority of child abuse cases involve physical injuries (Christian & Bloom, 2011). Others involve sexual abuse or neglect, such as underfeeding an infant. Other kinds of abuse include failure to obtain medical attention for an illness or injury, providing inadequate supervision, and drugging or poisoning children.

RISK FACTORS One useful model for explaining abuse classifies its causes into four broad categories: sociocultural factors, characteristics of the child, characteristics of the abuser, and family stresses (Bittner & Newberger, 1981). The main idea of this model is that episodes of abuse are typically precipitated by everyday interactions between parents and children—for example, when a parent reprimands a young child for spilling a glass of milk. At the time of the episode, several causal factors work together to produce abusive responses in parents. Thus, what differentiates abusive from nonabusive parents, according to this model, is the presence of a number of risk factors that shape how they respond to the ordinary stresses of parenting.

Sociocultural factors include personal or cultural values that regard physical abuse of children as morally acceptable. Parents are more likely to be abusive if they believe that there are few, if any, moral limits on what they can do to their children physically. Sociologists suggest that such beliefs stem from cultural traditions that regard children as property rather than human beings with individual rights (Mooney, Knox, & Schacht, 2000). Moreover, parents who live in communities where others share and act on these beliefs are more likely to be abusive.

Several characteristics of children or parents may set the stage for child abuse. For one thing, the younger children are, the more likely they are to be abused. As a result, about half of all abuse and neglect cases in the United States involve victims under the age of 5 years (U.S. Department of Human Services, 2012). Moreover, children with physical or mental disabilities or those who have difficult temperaments are more likely to be abused than others (U.S. Department of Health & Human Services, 2012). Parents who are depressed, lack parenting skills and knowledge, have a history of abuse themselves, or are substance abusers are more likely to abuse or neglect their children (Christian & Bloom, 2011; Eiden, Foote, & Schuetze, 2007). Keep in mind that no single factor produces abuse, but the presence of several of these variables in a particular family significantly increases the chances that the children will experience abuse.

CONSEQUENCES OF ABUSE Some children who are frequently or severely abused develop *posttraumatic stress disorder* (PTSD) (Giardino, Harris, & Giardino, 2009). This disorder involves extreme levels of anxiety, flashback memories of episodes of abuse, nightmares, and other sleep disturbances. Abused children are also more likely than nonabused peers to exhibit delays in all domains of development (Christian & Bloom, 2011; Cicchetti, Rogosch, Maughan, Toth, & Bruce, 2003).

On the positive side, children who are physically neglected typically recover rapidly once the abuse stops. In studies involving abused and/or neglected children who were placed in foster care, developmentalists have found that differences between abused and nonabused children in physical, cognitive, and social development disappear within 1 year (Oliván, 2003). As you might suspect, though, these studies suggest that the critical factor in the catching-up process is the quality of the post-abuse environment.

PREVENTION Preventing abuse begins with education. Informing parents about the potential consequences of some physical acts, such as the link between shaking an infant and brain damage, may help. In addition, parents need to know that injuring children is a crime, even if the intention is to discipline them. Parenting classes, perhaps as a required part of high school curricula, can help inform parents or future parents about principles of child development and appropriate methods of discipline (Mooney et al., 2000). 👁 **Watch** the **Video** *Child Abuse Mandatory Reporting* in **MyPsychLab**.

Another approach to prevention of abuse involves identification of families at risk. Physicians, nurses, and other professionals who routinely interact with parents of infants and young children have a particularly important role to play in this kind of prevention (Christian & Bloom, 2011). Parents who seem to have problems attaching to their children can sometimes be identified during medical office visits. These parents can be referred to parenting classes or to social workers for help. Similarly, parents may ask doctors or nurses how to discipline their children. Such questions provide professionals with opportunities to discuss which practices are appropriate and which are not.

Finally, children who are abused must be protected from further injury. This can be accomplished through vigorous enforcement of existing child abuse laws. As noted, health professionals must report suspected abuse. However, in most states, ordinary citizens are also legally required to report suspected abuse. And reporting is only part of the picture. Once abuse is reported, steps must be taken to protect injured children from suspected abusers.

test yourself before going on ✔️ **Study** and **Review** in **MyPsychLab**

Answers to these questions can be found in the back of the book.

1. At the end of the early childhood, children's (gross, fine) motor skills are developed to a higher level of confidence than their (gross, fine) motor skills are.

2. Match each term with its definition.

   _____(1) lateralization
   _____(2) reticular formation
   _____(3) hippocampus
   _____(4) handedness

   (a) the part of the brain involved in transferring information to long-term memory
   (b) the division of brain functions between the two hemispheres of the cerebral cortex
   (c) a strong preference for using one hand or another that develops between 2 and 6 years
   (d) the part of the brain that regulates attention and concentration

3. Preschoolers (consume, do not consume) the majority of their calories at regular meals.

4. What are the four broad categories of risk factors for abuse?

CRITICAL THINKING

5. Ask your friends and fellow students to estimate the age at which brain development is complete. How do you think people's assumptions about the completeness of brain development affect their attitudes and behavior toward children?

Cognitive Changes

If you were to visit a preschool and go from classroom to classroom, observing children in free play, what kind of activities do you think you would see? If you visited the classrooms in "chronological" order, you would see a progression of activities ranging from simple forms of constructive and pretend play among the 2-year-olds to sophisticated role-play and debates about the rules of board games among the 5- and 6-year-olds (see *Research Report*). Forms of play change over the early childhood years because children's thinking changes. At the beginning of the period, children are just beginning to learn how to accomplish goals. By the time they reach age 5 or 6, they are proficient at manipulating symbols and can make accurate judgments about others' thoughts, feelings, and behavior.

Piaget's Preoperational Stage

LO 7.5   What are the characteristics of children's thought during Piaget's preoperational stage?

semiotic (symbolic) function the understanding that one object or behavior can represent another

According to Piaget, children acquire the **semiotic (symbolic) function** between the ages of 18 and 24 months. The semiotic function is the understanding that one object or behavior can represent another—a picture of a chair represents a real chair, a child's pretending to feed a doll

RESEARCH REPORT

Children's Play and Cognitive Development

Careful observation of young children's play behaviors can give preschool teachers and parents useful information about cognitive development, because the forms of play change in very obvious ways during the years from 1 to 6, following a sequence that closely matches Piaget's stages (Rubin, Fein, & Vandenberg, 1983).

Constructive Play. By age 2 or so, children use objects to build or construct things, as the child in the accompanying photo is doing. Piaget hypothesized that this kind of play is the foundation of children's understanding of the rules that govern physical reality. For example, through block play, they come to understand that a tower that is broad at the top and narrow at the bottom will be unstable.

First Pretend Play. Piaget believed that pretend play was an important indicator of a child's capacity to use symbols. The first instances of such pretending are usually simple, like pretending to drink from a toy cup. Most children exhibit some pretending at around 12 months. Between 15 and

21 months, the recipient of the pretend action becomes another person or a doll. This change signals a significant movement away from sensorimotor and toward true symbolic thinking.

Substitute Pretend Play. Between 2 and 3 years of age, children begin to use objects to stand for something altogether different. For example, the 30-month-old boy in the photo above is using a carrot as an imaginary violin and a stick as a bow. Children this age may use a broom as a horse or make "trucks" out of blocks.

Sociodramatic Play. In the preschool years, children engage in mutual pretense. For example, in playing doctor, as the children in the photo are doing, participants fill roles such as "doctor," "nurse," and "patient." At first, children simply take up these roles; later, they name the various roles and may give each other explicit instructions about the right way to pretend a particular role. By age 4, virtually all children

engage in some play of this type (Howes & Matheson, 1992).

Rule-Governed Play. By age 5 or 6, children prefer rule-governed pretending and formal games. For example, children of this age use rules such as "Whoever is smallest has to be the baby" when playing "house" and play simple games such as "Red Rover" and "Red Light, Green Light." Younger children play these games as well, but 5- and 6-year-olds better understand their rules and will follow them for longer periods of time. Piaget suggested that older preschoolers' preference for rule-governed play indicates that they are about to make the transition to the next stage of cognitive development, *concrete operations*, in which they will acquire an understanding of rules (Piaget & Inhelder, 1969).

CRITICAL ANALYSIS

1. *Which of the research methods discussed in Chapter 1 is best suited to the study of age-related changes in children's play activities?*

2. *Many children have imaginary friends (a phenomenon that child psychologists consider to be entirely normal). In which of the stages of play would you expect to first see children inventing imaginary playmates?*

---

stands for a parent's feeding a baby, and so on. Once this understanding has been achieved, children are in Piaget's **preoperational stage**.

During the preoperational stage, children become proficient at using symbols for thinking and communicating but still have difficulty thinking logically. At age 2 or 3, children begin to pretend in their play (Walker-Andrews & Kahana-Kalman, 1999). A broom may become a horse, or a block may become a train. Cross-cultural research suggests that this kind of object use by 2- to 3-year-olds in pretend play is universal (Barthélémy-Musso, Tartas, & Guidetti, 2013; Haight et al., 1999). Young children also show signs of increasing proficiency at symbol use in their growing ability to understand models, maps, and graphic symbols such as letters (Callaghan, 1999; DeLoache, 1995).

Although young children are remarkably good at using symbols, their reasoning about the world is often flawed. For example, Piaget described the preoperational child's tendency to look at things entirely from her own point of view, a characteristic Piaget called **egocentrism**

preoperational stage Piaget's second stage of cognitive development, during which children become proficient in the use of symbols in thinking and communicating but still have difficulty thinking logically

egocentrism a young child's belief that everyone sees and experiences the world the way she does

Figure 7.3 Piaget's Three Mountains Task

The experimental situation shown here is similar to one Piaget used to study egocentrism in children. The child is asked to pick out a picture that shows how the mountains look to her, and then to pick out a picture that shows how the mountains look to the doll.

(Piaget, 1954). This term does not suggest that the young child is a self-centered egomaniac. It simply means that she assumes that everyone sees the world as she does. For example, while riding in the back seat of a car, a 3- or 4-year-old may suddenly call out "Look at that, Mom!"—not realizing that Mom can't see the object she's talking about. Moreover, the child doesn't realize that the car's motion prevents Mom from ever seeing the object in question. As a result, the youngster may become frustrated in her attempts to communicate with her mother about what she saw. ⊙ **Watch** the **Video** *The Preschool Years: Egocentrism* in **MyPsychLab**.

Figure 7.3 illustrates a classic experiment in which most young children demonstrate this kind of egocentrism. The child is shown a three-dimensional scene with mountains of different sizes and colors. From a set of drawings, she picks out the one that shows the scene the way she sees it. Most preschoolers can do this without much difficulty. Then the examiner asks the child to pick out the drawing that shows how someone else sees the scene, such as a doll or the examiner. At this point, most preschoolers choose the drawing that shows their own view of the mountains (Flavell, Everett, Croft, & Flavell, 1981; Gzesh & Surber, 1985).

Piaget also pointed out that a preschool-aged child's thinking is guided by the appearance of objects—a theme that still dominates the research on children of this age. Children may believe, for example, that any moving object is an animal of some kind. This kind of thinking reflects a child's tendency to think of the world in terms of one variable at a time, a type of thought Piaget called **centration**. Because of centration, a child progresses through a series of false conclusions to conclude that all moving objects are animals. The basis for these conclusions is the observation in everyday interactions with the world that all animals move—or, as scientists put it, have the capacity for *locomotion* (self-movement). But the preoperational thinker isn't capable of thinking of objects in terms of both their motion and their capacity for self-movement. Thus, movement, without regard to any other relevant characteristic of objects, becomes the sole criterion for distinguishing between living and nonliving objects. As a result, a child may fear a leaf that blows across the playground because he believes that the leaf is trying to follow him. Piaget used the term *animism* to refer to this particular product of preoperational logic.

As you learned in the *Research Report* in Chapter 2, some of Piaget's most famous experiments deal with a cognitive process called **conservation**, the understanding that matter can change in appearance without changing in quantity. Because of centration and irreversibility, children rarely show any kind of conservation before age 5. When they do begin to understand this concept, they demonstrate their understanding with arguments based on three characteristics of appearance-only transformations of matter. The first of these is *identity*, the knowledge that quantities are constant unless matter is added to or subtracted from them. The second is *compensation*, the understanding that all relevant characteristics of the appearance of a given quantity of matter must be taken into account before reaching a conclusion about whether the quantity has changed. The third is *reversibility*, the capacity to mentally compare the transformed appearance of a given quantity of matter to its original appearance. Some of the conservation tasks Piaget used, along with children's typical responses to them, are shown in Figure 7.4. As you can see, assessing a child's stage of cognitive development involves finding out how she arrived at her answer to a question, not just evaluating the answer as right or wrong. ⊙ **Watch** the **Video** *Conservation of Liquids* in **MyPsychLab**.

Challenges to Piaget's View

LO 7.6 How has recent research challenged Piaget's view of this period?

Studies of conservation have generally confirmed Piaget's observations (e.g., Baucal, Arcidiacono, & Budjevac, 2013; Ciancio et al., 1999; Desrochers, 2008; Gelman, 1972; Sophian, 1995; Wellman, 1982). Although younger children can demonstrate some understanding of conservation if the task is made very simple, most children cannot consistently solve conservation

centration a young child's tendency to think of the world in terms of one variable at a time

conservation the understanding that matter can change in appearance without changing in quantity

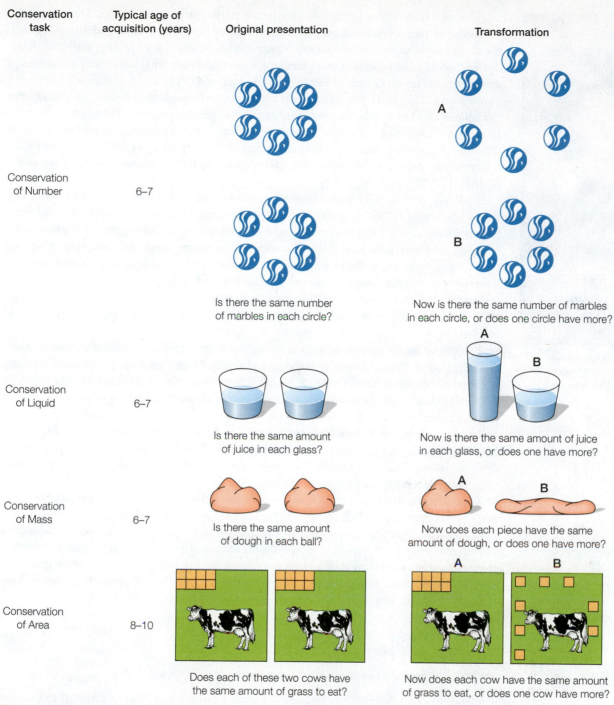

Conservation task	Typical age of acquisition (years)	Original presentation	Transformation

Conservation of Number — 6–7

Is there the same number of marbles in each circle?

Now is there the same number of marbles in each circle, or does one circle have more?

Conservation of Liquid — 6–7

Is there the same amount of juice in each glass?

Now is there the same amount of juice in each glass, or does one have more?

Conservation of Mass — 6–7

Is there the same amount of dough in each ball?

Now does each piece have the same amount of dough, or does one have more?

Conservation of Area — 8–10

Does each of these two cows have the same amount of grass to eat?

Now does each cow have the same amount of grass to eat, or does one cow have more?

Figure 7.4 Piaget's Conservation Tasks

Piaget's research involved several kinds of conservation tasks. He classified children's thinking as concrete operational with respect to a particular task if they could correctly solve the problem and provide a concrete operational reason for their answer. For example, if a child said, "The two circles of marbles are the same because you didn't add any or take any away when you moved them," the response was judged to be concrete operational. Conversely, if a child said, "The two circles are the same, but I don't know why," the response was not classified as concrete operational.

and other kinds of logical problems until at least age 5. However, evidence suggests that preschoolers are a great deal more cognitively sophisticated than Piaget thought.

Despite their egocentrism, children as young as 2 and 3 appear to have at least some ability to understand that another person sees things or experiences things differently than they do. For example, children this age adapt their speech or their play to the demands of a companion. They play differently with older and younger playmates and talk differently to a younger child (Brownell, 1990; Guralnik & Paul-Brown, 1984).

This young child is able to adapt his speech to the needs of his younger sibling, one of many indications that preschoolers are less egocentric than Piaget thought.

However, such understanding is clearly not perfect at this young age. Developmental psychologist John Flavell has proposed two levels of perspective-taking ability. At level 1, the child knows that other people experience things differently. At level 2, the child develops a whole series of complex rules for figuring out precisely what the other person sees or experiences (Flavell, Green, & Flavell, 1990). At 2 and 3 years old, children have level 1 knowledge but not level 2; level 2 knowledge begins to be evident in 4- and 5-year-olds. For example, a child of 4 or 5 understands that another person feels sad if she fails or happy if she succeeds. A preschool child also begins to figure out that unpleasant emotions occur in situations in which there is a gap between desire and reality. Sadness, for example, normally occurs when someone loses something that is valued or fails to acquire some desired object (Harris, 1989).

Studies of preschoolers' understanding of emotion have also challenged Piaget's description of the young child's egocentrism. For example, between 2 and 6, children learn to regulate or modulate their expressions of emotion to conform to others' expectations (Dunn, 1994). In addition, preschool children use emotional expressions such as crying or smiling to get things they want. These behaviors are obviously based at least in part on a growing awareness that other people judge your feelings by what they see you expressing. These behaviors wouldn't occur if children were completely incapable of looking at their own behavior from another person's perspective, as Piaget's assertions about egocentrism would suggest.

The young child's movement away from egocentrism seems to be part of a much broader change in her understanding of appearance and reality. Flavell has studied this understanding in a variety of ways (Flavell, Green, & Flavell, 1989; Flavell, Green, Wahl, & Flavell, 1987). In the most famous Flavell procedure, the experimenter shows the child a sponge that has been painted to look like a rock. Three-year-olds will say either that the object looks like a sponge and is a sponge or that it looks like a rock and is a rock. But 4- and 5-year-olds can distinguish between appearance and reality; they realize that the item looks like a rock but is a sponge (Flavell, 1986). Thus, the older children understand that the same object can be represented differently, depending on one's point of view.

Finally, some developmentalists have pointed out that the task of adopting another person's perspective can be challenging even for adults (Kesselring & Müller, 2010). For instance, a preschooler's egocentrism may impair his ability to communicate with a person who does not share his physical perspective. Similarly, the author of a cell phone user's manual may fail to provide users with clear instructions because of her difficulties in adopting the cognitive perspective of those who are unfamiliar with the device. Thus, egocentrism may be best thought of as a lifelong theme of cognitive development that is manifested differently in each of Piaget's stages.

Theories of Mind

LO 7.7   What is a theory of mind, and how does it develop?

Evidence like that described in the previous section has led a number of theorists to propose that the 4- or 5-year-old has developed a new and quite sophisticated **theory of mind**, or a set of ideas that explains other people's ideas, beliefs, desires, and behavior (Flavell, 1999).

UNDERSTANDING THOUGHTS, DESIRES, AND BELIEFS The theory of mind does not spring forth full-blown at age 4. Toddlers as young as 18 months have some beginning understanding of the fact that people (but not inanimate objects) operate with goals and intentions (Meltzoff, 1995). By age 3, children understand some aspects of the link between people's thinking or feeling and their behavior. For example, they know that a person who wants something will try to get it. They also know that a person may still want something even if she can't have it (Lillard & Flavell, 1992). But they do not yet understand the basic principle that each person's actions are based on her or his own representation of reality, which may differ from what is "really" there. It is this new aspect of the theory of mind that clearly emerges between 3 and 5.

theory of mind a set of ideas constructed by a child or an adult to explain other people's ideas, beliefs, desires, and behavior

Studies that examine the **false-belief principle** illustrate 3-year-olds' shortcomings in this area (Flavell, 1999). In one such study, children were presented with a box on which there were pictures of different kinds of candy. The experimenter shook the box to demonstrate that there was something inside and then asked 3- and 4-year-olds to guess what they would find if they opened it. Regardless of age, the children guessed that the box contained candy. Upon opening the box, though, the children discovered that it actually contained crayons. The experimenter then asked the children to predict what another child who saw the closed box would believe was in it. Three-year-olds thought that the child would believe that the box contained crayons, but the 4-year-olds realized that the pictures of candy on the box would lead the child to have a false belief that the box contained candy.

false-belief principle an understanding that enables a child to look at a situation from another person's point of view and determine what kind of information will cause that person to have a false belief

Still, there is much that a 4- or 5-year-old doesn't yet grasp about other people's thinking. A child of this age understands that other people think but does not yet understand that other people can think about him. A 4-year-old understands "I know that you know." But he does not yet fully understand that this process is reciprocal—namely, "You know that I know."

Understanding of the reciprocal nature of thought seems to develop between age 5 and age 7 for most children. This would seem to be a particularly important understanding, because it is probably necessary for the creation of genuinely reciprocal friendships, which begin to emerge in the elementary school years (Sullivan, Zaitchik, & Tager-Flusberg, 1994). In fact, the rate at which an individual preschooler develops a theory of mind is a good predictor of her social skills both later in early childhood and during the school years (Moore, Barresi, & Thompson, 1998; Watson, Nixon, Wilson, & Capage, 1999).

Furthermore, it is not until about age 6 that most children realize that knowledge can be derived through inference. For example, researchers in one study showed 4- and 6-year-olds two toys of different colors (Pillow, 1999). Next, they placed the toys in separate opaque containers. They then opened one of the containers and showed the toy to a puppet. When asked whether the puppet now knew which color toy was in each container, only the 6-year-olds said yes.

INFLUENCES ON THE DEVELOPMENT OF A THEORY OF MIND Developmentalists have found that a child's theory of mind is correlated with cognitive development. Performance on Piaget's tasks, as well as on more recently developed problems designed to assess egocentrism and appearance/reality, predict performance on theory-of-mind tasks (Melot & Houde, 1998; Yirmiya & Shulman, 1996). Pretend play also seems to contribute to theory-of-mind development. Shared pretense with other children, in particular, is strongly related to theory of mind (Lillard et al., 2013). In addition, researchers have discovered links between working memory development and theory of mind (Benson & Sabbagh, 2010).

Language skills are also related to theory-of-mind development (Tomasuolo, Valeri, Di Renzo, Pasqualetti, & Volterra, 2013). Indeed, some level of language facility may be a necessary condition for the development of a theory of mind. Developmentalists have found that children in this age range simply do not succeed at false-belief tasks until they have reached a certain threshold of general language skill (Astington & Jenkins, 1999; Jenkins & Astington, 1996; Watson et al., 1999). Further support for the same point comes from the finding that children with disabilities that affect language development, such as congenital deafness or intellectual disability, develop a theory of mind more slowly than others (Kendall & Comer, 2010; Losh, Martin, Klusek, Hogan-Brown, & Sideris, 2012).

THEORY OF MIND ACROSS CULTURES Cross-cultural psychologists claim that theory-of-mind research in the United States and Europe may not apply to children in other cultures and have produced some preliminary evidence to support this contention (Lillard, 2006). However, research also suggests that certain aspects of theory-of-mind development may be universal. For example, similar sequences of theory-of-mind development have been found in the United States, China, Japan, Europe, Indonesia, and India (Flavell, Zhang, Zou, Dong, & Qi, 1983; Jin et al., 2002; Joshi & MacLean, 1994; Kuntoro, Saraswati, Peterson, & Slaughter, 2013; Tardif & Wellman, 2000; Tardif, So, & Kaciroti, 2007; Wellman,

short-term storage space (STSS) neo-Piagetian theorist Robbie Case's term for the working memory

operational efficiency a neo-Piagetian term that refers to the maximum number of schemes that can be processed in working memory at one time

Cross, & Watson, 2001). Moreover, participation in shared pretending has been shown to contribute to theory-of-mind development cross-culturally (Tan-Niam, Wood, & O'Malley, 1998). Critics, however, argue that most of the societies where these results have been found are industrialized and that very different findings might emerge in studies of nonindustrialized societies. 👁 **Watch** the **Video** *Early Childhood: Theory of Mind across Cultures* in **MyPsychLab**.

In response to this argument, developmentalists presented false-belief tasks to a group called the Baka, who live in Cameroon (Avis & Harris, 1991). The Baka are hunter-gatherers who live together in camps. Each child was tested in his or her own hut, using materials with which the child was completely familiar. The child watched one adult, named Mopfana (a member of the Baka), put some mango kernels into a bowl with a lid. Mopfana then left the hut, and a second adult (also a group member) told the child they were going to play a game with Mopfana: They were going to hide the kernels in a cooking pot. Then he asked the child what Mopfana was going to do when he came back. Would he look for the kernels in the bowl or in the pot? Children between 2 and 4 years old were likely to say that Mopfana would look for the kernels in the pot; 4- and 5-year-olds were nearly always right. Even in very different cultures, then, something similar seems to be occurring between age 3 and age 5. In these years, all children seem to develop a theory of mind.

Alternative Theories of Early Childhood Thinking

LO 7.8 How do information-processing and sociocultural theorists explain changes in young children's thinking?

In recent years, a number of interesting theoretical approaches have attempted to explain both Piaget's original results and the more recent findings that contradict them.

Figure 7.5 Neo-Piagetian Matrix Task

Neo-Piagetians have used Piaget's matrix classification task in strategy-training studies with young children. Before training, most preschoolers say that a blue triangle or red circle belongs in the box with the question mark. After learning a two-step strategy in which they are taught to classify each object first by shape and then by color, children understand that a red triangle is the figure that is needed to complete the matrix.

NEO-PIAGETIAN THEORIES One set of alternative proposals is based on the idea that children's performance on Piaget's tasks can be explained in terms of working-memory limitations (Case, 1985, 1992). For example, Robbie Case (1944–2000), one of the best known neo-Piagetian theorists, used the term **short-term storage space (STSS)** to refer to the child's working memory. According to Case, there is a limit on the maximum number of schemes that can be attended to in STSS. He refers to this limit as **operational efficiency**. Improvements in operational efficiency occur through both practice (doing tasks that require memory use, such as learning the alphabet) and brain maturation as the child gets older. Thus, a 7-year-old is better able to handle the processing demands of conservation tasks than is a 4-year-old because of improvements in operational efficiency of the STSS.

A good example of the function of STSS may be found by examining *matrix classification*, a task Piaget often used with both young and school-aged children (see Figure 7.5). Matrix classification requires the child to place a given stimulus in two categories at the same time. Young children fail such tasks, according to neo-Piagetian theory, because they begin by processing the stimulus according to one dimension (either shape or color) and then either fail to realize that it is necessary to reprocess it along the second dimension or else forget to do so.

However, researchers have trained young children to perform correctly on such problems by using a two-step strategy. The children are taught to think of a red triangle, for example, in terms of shape first and color second. Typically, instruction involves a number of training tasks in which researchers remind children repeatedly to remember to reclassify stimuli with respect to the second variable. According to Case, both the children's failure prior to instruction and the type of strategy training to which they respond illustrate the constraints imposed on problem solving by the limited operational efficiency of the younger child's STSS. There is only room for one scheme at a time in the child's STS—either shape or color. The training studies show that younger children *can* learn to perform correctly, but their approach is qualitatively different from that of older children. The older child's more efficient STSS allows her to think about shape and color at the same time and, therefore, perform successfully without any training.

INFORMATION-PROCESSING THEORIES Information-processing theorists also maintain that children's ability to make efficient use of their memory system influences their performance on problem-solving tasks. For instance, *scripts*, cognitive structures that underlie behaviors that are often repeated, emerge during early childhood. They are especially useful for managing the memory demands of tasks that involve sequential steps. For example, to brush his teeth, a preschooler must first get his toothbrush. Next, he must apply toothpaste to the brush, and so on. Establishment of a tooth-brushing script frees up the preschooler's information-processing resources so that he can focus on the quality of his brushing rather than the procedure itself.

Information-processing theorists emphasize the importance of metamemory and metacognition. **Metamemory** is knowledge about and control of memory processes. For example, young children know that it takes longer to memorize a list of ten words than a list of five words, but they still aren't very good at coming up with strategies to apply to more difficult memory tasks (Kail, 1990). **Metacognition** is knowledge about and control of thought processes. For example, a child listening to a story may realize he has forgotten the main character's name and ask the reader what it is. Both knowing that the character's name has been forgotten and knowing that the character's name will make the story easier to understand are forms of metacognition.

Children's metamemory and metacognition improve during the early childhood period (Schneider, 2010). Between age 3 and age 5, for example, children figure out that in order to tell whether a sponge painted like a rock is really a sponge or a rock, a person needs to touch or hold it. Just looking at it doesn't give someone enough information (Flavell, 1993; O'Neill, Astington, & Flavell, 1992). Thus, by about age 4 or 5, children seem to have some beginning grasp of these processes, but they still have a long way to go. As a result, their ability to solve complex problems such as those Piaget used is limited compared to that of older children.

VYGOTSKY'S SOCIOCULTURAL THEORY In Chapter 2 you learned that psychologists' interest in Russian psychologist Lev Vygotsky's views on development has grown recently. Vygotsky's theory differs from both Piagetian and information-processing theory in its emphasis on the role of social factors in cognitive development. For example, two preschoolers working on a puzzle together discuss where the pieces belong. After a number of such dialogues, the participants internalize the discussion. It then becomes a model for an internal conversation the child uses to guide himself through the puzzle-solving process. In this way, Vygotsky suggested, solutions to problems are socially generated and learned. Vygotsky did not deny that individual learning takes place. Rather, he suggested that group learning processes are central to cognitive development. Consequently, from Vygotsky's perspective, social interaction is required for cognitive development (Crain, 2011).

Chapter 2 described two important general principles of Vygotsky's theory: *the zone of proximal development* and *scaffolding*. Vygotsky also proposed specific stages of cognitive development from birth to age 7. Each stage represents a step toward the child's internalization of the ways of thinking used by the adults around him.

In the first period, called the *primitive stage*, the infant possesses mental processes similar to those of lower animals. He learns primarily through conditioning, until language begins to develop in the second year. At that point, he enters the *naive psychology stage*, in which he learns to use language to communicate but still does not understand its symbolic character. For example, he doesn't realize that any collection of sounds could stand for the object "chair" as long as everyone agreed—that is, if all English speakers agreed to substitute the word *blek* for *chair*, we could do so because we would all understand what *blek* meant.

Once the child begins to appreciate the symbolic function of language, near the end of the third year of life, he enters the *private speech stage*. In this stage, he uses language as a guide to solving problems. In effect, he tells himself how to do things. For example, a 3-year-old walking down a flight of stairs might say "Be careful" to himself. Such a statement would be a result of his internalization of statements made to him by adults and older children.

Piaget recognized the existence and importance of private speech. However, he believed that such speech disappeared as the child approached the end of the preoperational stage. In contrast, Vygotsky claimed that private speech becomes completely internalized at age 6 or 7,

metamemory knowledge about how memory works and the ability to control and reflect on one's own memory function

metacognition knowledge about how the mind thinks and the ability to control and reflect on one's own thought processes

when children enter the final period of cognitive development, the *ingrowth stage*. Thus, he suggested that the logical thinking Piaget ascribed to older children results from their internalization of speech routines they acquire from older children and adults in the social world rather than from schemes the children construct for themselves through interaction with the physical world.

At present, there is insufficient evidence to either support or contradict most of Vygotsky's ideas (Thomas, 2005). However, studies have shown that young children whose parents provide them with more cognitive scaffolding during the preschool years exhibit higher levels of achievement in the early elementary grades than peers whose parents provide less support of this kind (Neitzel & Stright, 2003). In addition, researchers have found that private speech helps children solve problems (Montero & De Dios, 2006; Villegas, Castellanos, & Gutiérrez, 2009). Some intriguing research on children's construction of theory of mind during social interactions also lends weight to Vygotsky's major propositions. It seems that children in pairs and groups do produce more sophisticated ideas than individual children who work on problems alone. However, the sophistication of a group's ideas appears to depend on the presence of at least one fairly advanced individual child in the group (Tan-Niam et al., 1998).

test yourself before going on

☑ **Study** and **Review** in **MyPsychLab**

Answers to these questions can be found in the back of the book.

1. Match each term with its definition.
   _____(1) semiotic function
   _____(2) egocentrism
   _____(3) centration
   _____(4) conservation
   (a) thinking that focuses on one variable at a time
   (b) the belief that matter can change in appearance without changing in quantity
   (c) the understanding that one thing can stand for another
   (d) the belief that everyone experiences the world the same way that the self does

2. Some studies show that young children are less _____ than Piaget proposed.

3. The false-belief principle is one component of a child's _____ _____ _____ .

4. Match each alternative theory of cognitive development with its main emphasis.
   _____(1) Neo-Piagetian theory
   _____(2) information-processing theory
   _____(3) Vygotsky's sociocultural theory
   (a) social factors
   (b) working memory limitations
   (c) metamemory and metacognition

CRITICAL THINKING

5. Overcoming the egocentrism of early childhood is the foundation of many cognitive tasks later in life. For example, students who are writing research papers have to be able to look at their work from their professor's point of view in order to determine whether what they have written is understandable and in line with the requirements of the assignment. What other situations or tasks can you think of that require taking another person's perspective?

Changes in Language

To his credit, Piaget recognized that the overriding theme of cognitive development in the early childhood years is language acquisition. Of course, the process begins much earlier, as you learned in Chapter 5. Amazingly, though, children enter this period producing only a limited number of words and simple sentences but leave it as accomplished, fluent speakers of at least one language.

Fast-Mapping

LO 7.9   How does fast-mapping help children learn new words?

The average 2½-year-old's vocabulary of about 600 words is fairly impressive when we compare it to the dozen or so words most 1-year-olds know (Bates et al., 1994). This amounts to one or two new words every day between the ages of 12 and 24 months. Impressive though this feat is, it pales in comparison to the rate of vocabulary growth among preschoolers. By the time a child goes to school at age 5 or 6, total vocabulary has risen to perhaps 15,000 words—an astonishing increase of 10 words a day (Anglin, 1995; Pinker, 1994). Moreover, word learning appears to be the engine that drives the whole process of language development. That is, the more words a child knows, the more advanced she is with regard to grammar and other aspects of language (McGregor, Sheng, & Smith, 2005). What is the impetus behind word learning?

Researchers have found that around age 3, a momentous shift occurs in the way children approach new words. Children begin to pay attention to words in whole groups, such as words that name objects in a single class (e.g., types of dinosaurs or kinds of fruit) or words with similar meanings. In a sense, understanding of the categorical nature of words helps children develop what we might think of as mental "slots" for new words. Once the slots are in place, children seem to automatically organize the linguistic input they receive from parents, teachers, peers, books, television programs, advertisements, and every other source of language, extracting new words and filling the slots as quickly as possible.

Psychologists use the term **fast-mapping** to refer to this ability to categorically link new words to real-world objects or events (Carey & Bartlett, 1978). At the core of fast-mapping, say researchers, is a rapidly formed hypothesis about a new word's meaning (MacWhinney, 2011). The hypothesis is based on information derived from children's prior knowledge of words and word categories and from the context in which the word is used. Once formed, the hypothesis is tested through use of the word in the child's own speech, often immediately after learning it. The feedback children receive in response to use of the word helps them judge the accuracy of the hypothesis and the appropriateness of the category to which they have assumed that the word belongs. Perhaps this helps explain why preschoolers do so much talking and why they are so persistent at getting their listeners to actively respond to them.

The Grammar Explosion

LO 7.10 What happens during the grammar explosion?

In Chapter 5, you learned that the vocabulary explosion of the toddler period begins slowly. Similarly, the **grammar explosion**, the period during when the grammatical features of children's speech become more similar to those of adult speech, of the 2- to 6-year-old period starts with several months of simple sentences such as "Mommy sock." These utterances lack *inflections*—additions such as *'s* that would convey that the child is trying to say that the sock belongs to Mommy. Within each language community, children seem to add inflections and more complex word orders in fairly predictable sequences (Legendre, 2006). In a classic early study, Roger Brown found that the earliest inflection used among children learning English is typically *-ing* added to a verb, as in "I playing" or "Doggie running," expressions that are common in the speech of 2½- to 3-year-olds (Brown, 1973). Over the next year or so come (in order) prepositions such as "on" and "in," the plural *-s* on nouns, irregular past tenses (such as "broke" or "ran"), possessives, articles ("a" and "the" in English), the *-s* added to third-person verbs (such as "He wants"), regular past tenses (such as "played" and "wanted"), and various forms of auxiliary verbs, as in "I *am* going."

There are also predictable sequences in a child's developing use of questions and negatives. In each case, a child seems to go through periods when he creates types of sentences that he has not heard adults use but that are consistent with the particular set of rules he is using. For example, in the development of questions, there is a point at which a child can put a *wh-* word ("who," "what," "when," "where," "why") at the front end of a sentence but doesn't yet put the auxiliary verb in the right place, as in "Where you are going now?" Similarly, in the development of negatives, children go through a stage in which they put in *not* or *n't* or *no* but omit the auxiliary verb, as in "I not crying."

Another intriguing phenomenon, noted in Chapter 5, is **overregularization**, or overgeneralization. No language is perfectly regular; every language includes some irregularly conjugated verbs or

fast-mapping the ability to categorically link new words to real-world referents

grammar explosion the period during when the grammatical features of children's speech become more similar to those of adult speech

overregularization attachment of regular inflections to irregular words, such as the substitution of "goed" for "went"

These 2- to 3-year-olds probably speak to each other in short sentences that include uninflected nouns and verbs.

phonological awareness children's understanding of the sound patterns of the language they are acquiring

invented spelling a strategy young children with good phonological awareness skills use when they write

unusual forms of plurals. What 3- to 4-year-olds do is apply the basic rule to all these irregular instances, thus making the language more regular than it really is (Maratsos, 2000). In English, this is especially clear in children's creation of past tenses such as "wented," "blowed," and "sitted" or plurals such as "teeths" and "blockses" (Fenson et al., 1994).

After children have figured out inflections and the basic sentence forms using negatives and questions, they soon begin to create remarkably complex sentences, using a conjunction such as "and" or "but" to combine two ideas or using embedded clauses. Here are some examples that you might hear in the speech of 3- to 4-year-olds (de Villiers & de Villiers, 1992):

● Sal doesn't want to play with me, but Martin does!

● How many days did you say it is until my birthday? Those are just like the ones on TV, aren't they?

When you remember that only about 18 months earlier these children were using sentences little more complex than "See doggie," you can appreciate how far they have come in a short time.

Phonological Awareness

LO 7.11   What is phonological awareness, and why is it important?

Certain aspects of early childhood language development, such as rate of vocabulary growth, predict how easily a child will learn to read and write when she enters school (Wood & Terrell, 1998). However, one specific component, phonological awareness, seems to be especially important. **Phonological awareness** is a child's sensitivity to the sound patterns that are specific to the language being acquired. It also includes the child's knowledge of that particular language's system for representing sounds with letters. Researchers measure English-speaking children's phonological awareness with questions like these: "What would *bat* be if you took away the *b*? What would *bat* be if you took away the *b* and put *r* there instead?"

A child doesn't have to acquire phonological awareness in early childhood. It can be learned in elementary school through formal instruction (Bus & van IJzendoorn, 1999; Petrill et al., 2010). However, numerous studies have shown that the greater a child's phonological awareness *before* he enters school, the faster he learns to read (Melby-Lervåg, Lyster, & Hulme, 2012; National Institute for Literacy, 2008). In addition, phonological awareness in the early childhood years is related to rate of literacy learning in languages as varied as Korean, English, Punjabi, and Chinese (Cheung et al., 2010; Chiappe, Glaeser, & Ferko, 2007; Chiappe & Siegel, 1999; McBride-Chang & Ho, 2000).

Phonological awareness appears to develop primarily through word play. For example, among English-speaking children, learning and reciting nursery rhymes contributes to phonological awareness (Bryant, MacLean, & Bradley, 1990; Bryant, MacLean, Bradley, & Crossland, 1990; Layton, Deeny, Tall, & Upton, 1996). For Japanese children, a game called *shiritori*, in which one person says a word and another comes up with a word that begins with its ending sound, helps children develop these skills (Norboru, 1997; Serpell & Hatano, 1997). Educators have also found that using such games to teach phonological awareness skills to preschoolers is just as effective as more formal methods such as flash cards and worksheets (Brennan & Ireson, 1997).

Preschoolers with good phonological awareness skills—those who have learned a few basic sound–letter connections informally, from their parents or from educational TV programs or videos—often use a strategy called **invented spelling** when they attempt to write (see Figure 7.6). In spite of the many errors children make, researchers have found that invented spelling coupled with corrective feedback from parents and preschool teachers helps children learn their language's system for representing speech sounds with letters (Ouellette & Sénéchal, 2008). Thus, the evidence suggests that one of the best ways parents and preschool teachers can help young children prepare for formal instruction in reading is to engage them in activities that encourage word play and invented spelling.

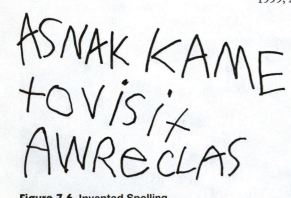

Figure 7.6 Invented Spelling

Translation: *A snake came to visit our class.* A 5-year-old used a strategy called invented spelling to write this sentence about a snake's visit (accompanied by an animal handler, we hope!) to her kindergarten class. Invented spelling requires a high level of phonological awareness. Research suggests that children who have well-developed phonological awareness skills by the time they reach kindergarten learn to read more quickly.

(*Source:* Courtesy of Jerry and Denise Boyd. Used with permission.)

Answers to these questions can be found in the back of the book.

1. _____ _____ is children's ability to rapidly form hypotheses about the meanings of new words.

2. During the grammar explosion, _____ appear in children's speech.

3. Mark "Y" by each example of phonological awareness and "N" by each non-example:
   _____(1)   a child recites the alphabet
   _____(2)   a child says *cat* when asked to suggest a word that rhymes with *hat*
   _____(3)   a child recognizes her written name
   _____(4)   a child writes *brn* and states that she has written the word *barn*

CRITICAL THINKING

4. Suppose you knew a parent who was thrilled that her 5-year-old was beginning to write words but was concerned about the little girl's spelling errors. How would you explain the errors to the mother, and what would you advise her to do about them?

Differences in Intelligence

Thanks to advances in language skills, intelligence testing is far more reliable among preschoolers than among infants. Psychologists can devise tests of intelligence for preschoolers to measure their vocabulary, reasoning skills, and other cognitive processes that depend on language. Consequently, a large number of standardized tests have been developed for use with young children. However, widespread use of these tests has led to an ongoing debate about the origins of score differences and the degree to which scores can be modified.

Measuring Intelligence

LO 7.12   What are the strengths and weaknesses of IQ tests?

An important assumption in studying differences in intelligence is that these differences can be measured. Thus, it's important to understand something about the tests psychologists use to measure intelligence, as well as the meaning and stability of the scores the tests generate.

THE FIRST TESTS The first modern intelligence test was published in 1905 by two Frenchmen, Alfred Binet and Theodore Simon (Binet & Simon, 1905). From the beginning, the test had a practical purpose—to identify children who might have difficulty in school. For this reason, the tasks Binet and Simon devised for the test were very much like some school tasks, including measures of vocabulary, comprehension of facts and relationships, and mathematical and verbal reasoning. For example, could the child describe the difference between wood and glass? Could the young child identify his nose, his ear, his head? Could he tell which of two weights was heavier?

Lewis Terman and his associates at Stanford University modified and extended many of Binet's original tasks when they translated and revised the test for use in the United States (Terman, 1916; Terman & Merrill, 1937). The Stanford-Binet, the name by which the test is still known, initially described a child's performance in terms of a score called an **intelligence quotient**, later shortened to IQ. This score was computed by comparing the child's chronological age (in years and months) with his mental age, defined as the level of questions he could answer correctly (Hegarty, 2007). For example, a child who could solve the problems for a 6-year-old but not those for a 7-year-old would have a mental age of 6. The formula used to calculate the IQ was

$$\text{mental age/chronological age} \times 100 = \text{IQ}$$

This formula results in an IQ above 100 for children whose mental age is higher than their chronological age and an IQ below 100 for children whose mental age is below their chronological age. ⊙ **Watch** the **Video** *Robert Stenberg on Intelligence* in **MyPsychLab**.

This system for calculating IQ is no longer used. Instead, IQ scores for the Stanford-Binet and all other intelligence tests are now based on a direct comparison of a child's performance

intelligence quotient (IQ) the ratio of mental age to chronological age; also, a general term for any kind of score derived from an intelligence test

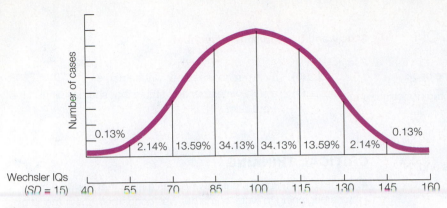

Figure 7.7 The Normal Curve

IQ scores form what mathematicians call a normal distribution—the famous "bell curve" you may have heard about. The two sides of a normal distribution curve are mirror images of each other. Thus, 34% of children score between 85 and 100 and another 34% score between 100 and 115. Likewise, 13% score between 70 and 85 and another 13% between 115 and 130. A few other human characteristics, such as height, are normally distributed as well.

with the average performance of a large group of other children of the same age. But the scoring is arranged so that an IQ of 100 is still average.

As you can see in Figure 7.7, about two-thirds of all children achieve scores between 85 and 115; roughly 96% of scores fall between 70 and 130. Children who score above 130 are often called *gifted*; those who score below 70 may be diagnosed with an intellectual disability, although this label should not be applied unless the child also has problems with "adaptive behavior," such as an inability to dress or feed himself, a problem getting along with others, or a significant problem adapting to the demands of a regular school classroom. Some children with IQ scores in this low range are able to function in a regular schoolroom.

MODERN INTELLIGENCE TESTS The tests psychologists use most frequently today were developed by David Wechsler. On all the Wechsler tests, the child is tested with several different types of problems, each ranging from very easy to very hard, that are divided into subgroups. *Verbal scales* include tasks measuring vocabulary, understanding of similarities between objects, and general knowledge about the world. *Performance scales* involve nonverbal tasks such as arranging pictures in an order that tells a story or copying a pattern using a set of colored blocks. *Working-memory scales* provide psychologists with information about a child's short-term memory capacity, and *processing-speed scales* provide them with insight into how efficiently a child processes information. Many psychologists find the Wechsler approach helpful because significant differences in a child's skills across scales may indicate particular kinds of learning problems.

STABILITY AND PREDICTIVE VALUE OF IQ SCORES The correlation between a child's IQ test score and her scores on tests that measure pre-academic skills such as letter knowledge is about .70 (Wechsler, 2002). The correlation with her current future grades in school is about .50–.60 (Brody, 1992; Neisser et al., 1996). This is a strong, but by no means perfect, correlation. It indicates that on the whole, children with high IQ scores will be among the high achievers in school, and those who score low will be among the low achievers. But success in school also depends on many factors other than IQ, including motivation, interest, and persistence. For this reason, some children with high IQ scores don't excel in school, while some lower-IQ children do.

The relationship between school performance and IQ scores holds within each social class and racial group in the United States, as well as in other countries and cultures. Among both the poor and the middle class, and among African Americans and Hispanic Americans as well as Whites, children with higher IQs are more likely to get good grades, complete high school, and go on to college (Brody, 1992; Konold & Canivez, 2010). Such findings have led a number of theorists to argue that intelligence adds to the child's resilience—a concept mentioned in Chapter 1. Numerous studies show that poor children—whether they are White, Hispanic, African American, or from another minority group—are far more likely to develop the kind of self-confidence and personal competence it takes to move out of poverty if they have higher IQs (Luthar & Zigler, 1992; Masten & Coatsworth, 1998; Werner & Smith, 1992).

IQ scores are also quite stable. If two tests are given a few months or a few years apart, the scores are likely to be very similar. The correlations between IQ scores from adjacent years in middle childhood, for example, are typically in the range of .80 (Wechsler, 2002). Yet this high level of predictability masks an interesting fact: Many children show quite wide fluctuations in their scores. In fact, about half of all children show noticeable changes from one testing to another and over time (McCall, 1993). Some show steadily rising scores, and some have declining ones; some show a peak in middle childhood and then a decline in adolescence. In rare cases, the shifts may cover a range as large as 40 points.

Such wide fluctuations are more common in young children. The general rule of thumb is that the older the child, the more stable the IQ score—although even in older children, scores may still fluctuate in response to major stresses such as parental divorce, a change of schools, or the birth of a sibling.

LIMITATIONS OF IQ TESTS Before moving on to the question of the possible origins of differences in IQ, we need to emphasize a few key limitations of IQ tests and the scores derived from them. IQ tests do not measure underlying competence. An IQ score cannot tell you (or a teacher or anyone else) that your child has some specific, fixed, underlying capacity. Traditional IQ tests also do not measure a whole host of skills that are likely to be highly significant for getting along in the world. Originally, IQ tests were designed to measure only the specific range of skills that are needed for success in school. This they do quite well. What they do *not* do is indicate anything about a particular person's creativity, insight, street smarts, ability to read social cues, or understanding of spatial relationships (Baron, 2003; Gardner, 2003). 👁 **Watch** the **Video** *Demographics and Intelligence Testing* in **MyPsychLab**.

Origins of Individual Differences in Intelligence

LO 7.13 What kinds of evidence support the nature and nurture explanations for individual differences in IQ?

If a couple whom you perceive to be smart conceives a child, what would you predict about their offspring's IQ scores? Most people know that differences in intelligence run in families. But why do related people seem to be alike in this regard? Is it nature or nurture that is responsible?

EVIDENCE FOR HEREDITY Both twin studies and studies of adopted children show strong hereditary influences on IQ, as you already know from the *Research Report* in Chapter 3. Identical twins are more like each other in IQ than are fraternal twins, and the IQs of adopted children are better predicted from the IQs of their natural parents than from those of their adoptive parents (Rizzi & Posthuma, 2013). These are precisely the findings researchers would expect if a strong genetic element were at work.

EVIDENCE FOR FAMILY INFLUENCES Adoption studies also provide some strong support for an environmental influence on IQ scores because the IQ scores of adopted children are clearly affected by the environment in which they have grown up. The clearest evidence for this comes from a classic study of 38 French children, all adopted in infancy (Capron & Duyme, 1989). Roughly half the children had been born to better-educated parents from a higher social class, while the other half had been born to working-class or poverty-level parents. Some of the children in each group had then been adopted by parents in a higher social class, while the others grew up in poorer families. The effect of rearing conditions was evident in that the children reared in upper-class homes had IQs 15–16 points higher than those reared in lower-class families, regardless of the social class level or education of the birth parents. A genetic effect was evident in that the children born to upper-class parents had higher IQs than those from lower-class families, no matter what kind of environment they were reared in.

When developmentalists observe how individual families interact with their infants or young children and then follow the children over time to see which ones later have high or low IQs, they begin to get some sense of the kinds of specific family interactions that foster higher scores. For one thing, parents of higher-IQ children provide them with an interesting and complex physical environment, including play materials that are appropriate for the child's age and developmental level (Bradley et al., 1989; Pianta & Egeland, 1994). They also respond warmly and appropriately to the child's behavior, smiling when the child smiles, answering the child's questions, and in myriad ways reacting to the child's cues (Barnard et al., 1989; Lewis, 1993). These kinds of parental behaviors may even help to limit the effects of poverty and other sources of family stress on children's intellectual development (Robinson, Lanzi, Weinberg, Ramey, & Ramey, 2002).

Parents of higher-IQ children also talk to them often, using language that is descriptively rich and accurate (Hart & Risley, 1995; Sigman et al., 1988). And when they play with or interact with their children, they operate in what Vygotsky referred to as the *zone of proximal development* (described in Chapter 2), aiming their conversation, their questions, and their assistance at a level that is just above the level the children could manage on their own, thus helping the children to master new skills (Landry, Garner, Swank, & Baldwin, 1996).

Nevertheless, developmentalists can't be sure that these environmental characteristics are causally important because parents provide both the genes and the environment. Perhaps these are simply the environmental features provided by brighter parents, and it is the genes and not the environment that cause the higher IQs in their children. However, the research on adopted children's IQs cited earlier suggests that these aspects of environment have a very real impact on children's intellectual development beyond whatever hereditary influences may affect them.

EVIDENCE FOR PRESCHOOL INFLUENCES Home environments and family interactions are not the only sources of environmental influence. Children's experiences in formal educational programs are also associated with IQ scores. As a result, many government programs for economically disadvantaged children (such as Head Start) are based on the assumption that a family's economic resources can limit their ability to provide their children with such experiences and that such experiences are vital to supporting children's intellectual development. Typically, these programs provide children with the same kinds of intellectual stimulation that are common in the private preschools attended by most middle-class children. Children are encouraged to acquire new vocabulary, new knowledge about the world, and skills that are vital to reading, such as phonological awareness. The goal behind such programs is to enable all children to enter school with an equal chance of success. Children in these programs normally show a gain of about 10 IQ points while enrolled in them, but this IQ gain typically fades and then disappears within the first few years of school (Zigler & Styfco, 1993).

However, on other kinds of measures, a residual effect of enriched preschool experiences can clearly be seen some years later. Children who go through Head Start or another quality preschool experience are less likely to be placed in special education classes, less likely to repeat a grade, and more likely to graduate from high school (Barnett, 1995; Darlington, 1991). They also have better health, better immunization rates, and better school adjustment than their peers (Zigler & Styfco, 1993). One very long-term longitudinal study even suggested that the impact of enriched programs may last well into adulthood. This study found that young adults who had attended a particularly good experimental preschool program, the Perry Preschool Project in Milwaukee, had higher rates of high school graduation, lower rates of criminal behavior, lower rates of unemployment, and a lower probability of being on welfare than did their peers who had not attended such a preschool (Barnett, 1993).

When the enrichment program is begun in infancy rather than at age 3 or 4, the positive effects persist into adulthood (Campbell et al., 2012). One very well designed and meticulously reported infancy intervention was called the Abecedarian project (Campbell & Ramey, 1994; Ramey, 1993; Ramey & Campbell, 1987). Infants from poverty-level families whose mothers had low IQs were randomly assigned either to a special day-care program or to a control group that received nutritional supplements and medical care but no special enriched day care. The special day-care program began when the infants were 6–12 weeks old and lasted until they started kindergarten.

Figure 7.8 graphs the average IQ scores of the children in each of these two groups from age 2 to age 12. You can see that the IQs of the children who had been enrolled in the special program were higher at every age. Fully 44% of the control group children had IQ scores classified as borderline or intellectual disabilities (scores below 85), compared with only 12.8% of the children who had been in the special program. In addition, the enriched day-care group had significantly higher scores on both reading and mathematics tests at age 12 and were only half as likely to have repeated a grade (Ramey, 1993).

Children who attend enrichment programs like this Head Start program typically do not show lasting gains in IQ, but they are more likely to succeed in school.

COMBINING THE INFORMATION Virtually all psychologists would agree that heredity is a highly important influence on IQ scores. Studies around the world consistently yield estimates that roughly 40% the variation in IQ within a given population of children is due to heredity (Rizzi & Posthuma, 2013). The remaining variation is clearly due to environment or to interactions between environment and heredity.

One useful way to think about this interaction is to use the concept of **reaction range**, a range between some upper and lower boundary of functioning established by one's genetic heritage; exactly where a child will fall within those boundaries is determined by environment. Some developmental psychologists estimate that the reaction range for IQ is about 20–25 points (Weinberg, 1989). That is, given a specific genetic heritage, a child's actual IQ test performance may vary by as much as 20 or 25 points, depending on the richness or poverty of the environment in which he grows up. When the child's environment is changed for the better, the child moves closer to the upper end of his reaction range. When the environment becomes worse, he falls toward the lower end. Thus, even though intelligence as measured on an IQ test is highly heritable and falls within the reaction range, the absolute IQ score is determined by environment.

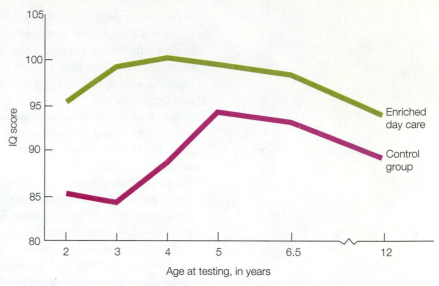

Figure 7.8 Early Education and IQ Scores

In Ramey's study, children from poverty-level families were randomly assigned in infancy to an experimental group that received special day care or to a control group, with the intervention lasting until age 5. At kindergarten, both groups entered public school. The difference in IQ between the experimental and control groups remained statistically significant even 7 years after the intervention had ended, when the children were age 12.

(*Source:* Ramey & Campbell, 1987, Fig. 3, p. 135, with additional data from Ramey, 1993, Fig. 2, p. 29.)

Group Differences in Intelligence-Test Scores

LO 7.14 What theories and evidence have been offered in support of genetic and cultural explanations of group differences in IQ scores?

There appear to be a number of consistent group differences in IQ test scores and other measures of intellectual performance. For instance, Chinese and Japanese children consistently demonstrate higher performance on achievement tests—particularly math and science tests (Gonzales, Guzman, et al., 2004). But the finding that has been most troublesome for researchers and theorists is that in the United States, African American children consistently score lower than White children on measures of IQ. Some theorists have suggested that this difference can be traced to anatomical and physiological variations across groups (Mackintosh, 2007; Rushton & Rushton, 2003). However, this difference, which is on the order of 6 to 15 IQ points, is not found on infant tests of intelligence or on measures of infant habituation rate; it becomes apparent by the time children are 2 or 3 years old and persists through adolescence and adulthood (Brody, 1992; Dombrowski, Noonan, & Martin, 2007; Fagan & Singer, 1983; Peoples, Fagan, & Drotar, 1995; Rowe, 2002; Rushton, Skuy, & Fridjhon, 2003). There is some indication that the size of the difference between African American and White children has been declining for several decades, but a noticeable difference persists (Neisser et al., 1996; Rushton & Jensen, 2006).

While granting that IQ is highly heritable, many developmentalists point out that the difference between average African American and White IQ scores falls well within the presumed reaction range of IQ. They emphasize that the environments in which African American and White children are typically reared differ sufficiently to account for the average difference in scores (Brody, 1992). Specifically, African American children in the United States are more likely to be undernourished and to have high blood levels of lead. Studies showing that African American and White adults who differ in IQ do not differ in performance on new verbal learning tasks support this view (Fagan & Holland, 2002). Moreover, one study found a strong association between low birth weight and IQ among African American 7-year-olds (Dombrowski et al., 2007). Children who weighed less than 4.5 pounds at birth averaged 86, while those with

reaction range a range, established by one's genes, between upper and lower boundaries for traits such as intelligence; one's environment determines where, within those limits, one will be

normal birth weight averaged 94, a score that is within the average range of 90–110. Recall from Chapter 4 that the prevalence of low birth weight is higher among African Americans than among other ethnic groups. Thus, studies that compare African American children's IQ test scores to those of children in other groups without taking into account the higher prevalence of low birth weight among African American children may overstate the size of group differences in average scores.

Some of the most convincing research supporting such an environmental explanation comes from mixed-race adoption studies (Scarr & Weinberg, 1983; Weinberg, Scarr, & Waldman, 1992). For example, researchers have found that African American children adopted at an early age into White middle-class families scored only slightly lower on IQ tests than did White children adopted into the same families. Similarly, regardless of race, the more education parents have, the higher their children's IQs (Sellers, Burns, & Guyrke, 2002). Thus, IQ differences in African American and White children may reflect their parents' differing amounts of experience with formal education.

Another recent entry into the debate on group differences in IQ scores is the finding that, during the 19th and 20th centuries, average IQ scores increased in every racial group throughout the industrialized world. This phenomenon, discovered by psychologist James Flynn (Flynn, 1999, 2003; Must, te Njienhuis, Must, & van Vianen, 2009), is known as the *Flynn effect*. Flynn's analyses of IQ data over several generations suggest that individuals of average IQ born in the late 19th century would have below-average IQs by today's standards (Williams, 2013). If IQ is largely genetic, Flynn argues, there should be a great deal of stability in any group's average score. Because IQ scores have changed so much in a relatively short period, Flynn suggests that cultural changes explain the effect that bears his name. Flynn suggests, similarly, that his cross-generational studies demonstrate that cultural factors are a likely explanation for cross-group differences as well. He points out that theorists from a variety of fields—from anthropology to medicine—have posited causes for cross-generational gains in IQ such as improved nutrition, greater access to media, and universal literacy. Flynn suggests that all of these factors vary across racial as well as generational groups.

Flynn further points out that many theorists have neglected to consider cultural beliefs in their search for a hereditary basis for intelligence. For example, some psychologists have argued that the differences between Asian and American children in performance on mathematics achievement tests result not from genetic differences in capacity but from differences in cultural beliefs (Stevenson & Lee, 1990). Specifically, Asian societies place little or no value on inborn talent. Instead, they believe that hard work can modify whatever talents a person was born with. Consequently, Asian parents and teachers require students to expend a great deal of effort trying to improve themselves intellectually and do not resort to ability-based explanations of failure. This means that an individual child does not simply accept academic failure as a sign of intellectual deficit but is encouraged by adults to keep on trying. As a result, Asian children spend more time on homework and other academic activities than do children in other cultures.

In contrast, U.S. schools emphasize ability through the routine use of IQ tests to place students in high-, average-, or low-ability classes. This approach reflects American society's greater acceptance of the idea that people are limited by the amount of ability they possess and that it is unfair to ask them to do more than tests suggest they are capable of. It is likely that these complex cultural variables affect children's environments in ways that lead to differences in IQ- and achievement-test scores (Chang & Murray, 1995; Schneider, Hieshima, Lee, & Plank, 1994; Stevenson & Lee, 1990; Stigler, Lee, & Stevenson, 1987).

Of course, the fact that group differences in IQ- or achievement-test performance may be explained by appealing to the concept of reaction range and to cultural beliefs does not make the differences disappear, nor does it make them trivial. Moreover, it's important to remember that there is the same amount of variation in IQ scores in all groups; there are many highly gifted African American children, just as there are many White children with intellectual disability. Finally, the benefits of having a high IQ, as well as the risks associated with low IQ, are the same in every racial group (see *No Easy Answers* on page 175).

To Test or Not to Test?

One of the questions that students often ask at this point is "Given all the factors that can affect a test score, is it worth bothering with IQ tests at all?" The answer is "yes." As long as the tests are used properly, intelligence testing can be very beneficial to children.

IQ tests are important tools for identifying children who have special educational needs, such as those who have intellectual disabilities. There are other methods for selecting children for special programs, such as teacher recommendations, but none is as reliable or as valid as an IQ test for measuring that set of cognitive abilities that are demanded by school. This is important because effective educational interventions are based on understanding how an individual's disability has affected the capacity to learn. Thus, IQ tests are a critical tool in the development of individualized educational plans for children with disabilities.

More controversial is routine testing of young children who have no disabilities. Most testing experts agree that using IQ tests to classify normal young children is of little value because their test scores tend to be far less reliable than those of older children. Moreover, labels based on IQ testing at an early age may be detrimental to young children's future development. Test-based labels may lead teachers and parents to make inappropriate assumptions about children's ability to learn. For example, parents of a high-IQ preschooler may expect her to act like a miniature adult, while the family of a young child whose IQ score is average may limit her opportunities to learn because they are afraid she will fail.

In summary, comprehensive intelligence testing with individual tests can be beneficial to any child who is known to have or is suspected of having a disability of any kind. However, labeling young children on the basis of IQ scores should be avoided.

YOU DECIDE

Decide which of these two statements you most agree with and think about how you would defend your position:

1. *School children should not be given IQ tests unless there is some reason to suspect that they have a disability.*
2. *Using IQ tests to screen all school children for potential learning problems is a good practice.*

---

test yourself before going on ☑ Study and Review in MyPsychLab

Answers to these questions can be found in the back of the book.

1. _____ coined the term "IQ."

2. Write "yes" for each factor that contributes to IQ scores in early childhood.

    _____ (1) heredity

    _____ (2) family environment

    _____ (3) preschool programs

3. The _____ _____ is the finding that increases in standards of living have increased IQ scores among all groups since the late 19th century.

CRITICAL THINKING

4. In which of Bronfenbrenner's contexts (see Chapter 2, p. 40) would you find cultural beliefs about ability? How might these beliefs be manifested in each of the other contexts, and how might they ultimately influence individual development?

SUMMARY

Physical Changes (pp. 152–158)

LO 7.1   What are the major milestones of growth and motor development between 2 and 6?

- Physical development is slower from age 2 to age 6 than it is in infancy, but it nevertheless progresses steadily. Motor skills continue to improve gradually, with marked improvement in gross motor skills (running, jumping, galloping) and slower advances in fine-motor skills.

LO 7.2   What important changes happen in the brain during these years?

- Significant changes in brain lateralization occur in early childhood. Handedness is another neurological milestone of this period.

LO 7.3   What are the nutritional and health-care needs of young children?

- Slower rates of growth contribute to declines in appetite. Stress is a factor in early childhood illnesses such as colds and flu.

LO 7.4   What factors contribute to abuse and neglect, and how do these traumas affect children's development?

- Children between the ages of 2 and 9 are more likely to be abused or neglected than are infants and older children. Certain characteristics of both children and parents increase the risk of abuse. Long-term consequences of abuse have been found across all domains of development.

Cognitive Changes (pp. 158–166)

LO 7.5   What are the characteristics of children's thought during Piaget's preoperational stage?

- Piaget marked the beginning of the preoperational period at about 18–24 months, at the point when the child begins to use mental symbols. Despite this advance, the preschool child still lacks many sophisticated cognitive skills. In Piaget's view, such children are still egocentric, lack understanding of conservation, and are often fooled by appearances.

LO 7.6 How has recent research challenged Piaget's view of this period?

- Research challenging Piaget's findings makes it clear that young children are less egocentric than Piaget thought. By age 4, they can distinguish between appearance and reality in a variety of tasks.

LO 7.7 What is a theory of mind and how does it develop?

- By the end of early childhood, children have a well-developed theory of mind. They understand that other people's actions are based on their thoughts and beliefs. The theory of mind includes the false-belief principle, an understanding of the factors that cause another person to believe something that isn't true.

LO 7.8 How do information-processing and sociocultural theorists explain changes in young children's thinking?

- Neo-Piagetian and information-processing theories explain early childhood cognitive development in terms of limitations on young children's memory systems. Vygotsky's sociocultural theory asserts that children's thinking is shaped by social interaction through the medium of language.

Changes in Language (pp. 166–169)

LO 7.9 How does fast-mapping help children learn new words?

- Fast-mapping, the use of categories to learn new words, enables young children to acquire new words rapidly. It involves the rapid formation of hypotheses about the meanings of new words based on the contexts in which they occur.

LO 7.10 What happens during the grammar explosion?

- During the grammar explosion, children make large advances in grammatical fluency. Inflections, complex word orders, negatives, and questions appear in their speech.

LO 7.11 What is phonological awareness, and why is it important?

- Development of an awareness of the sound patterns of a particular language during early childhood is important in learning to read during the school years. Children seem to acquire this skill through word play.

Differences in Intelligence (pp. 169–175)

LO 7.12 What are the strengths and weaknesses of IQ tests?

- Scores on early childhood intelligence tests are predictive of later school performance and are at least moderately consistent over time. However, there are many factors that influence school performance and other outcomes that are not measured by IQ tests. In addition, IQ tests reveal nothing about a child's creativity, insight, "street smarts," or social skills.

LO 7.13 What kinds of evidence support the nature and nurture explanations for individual differences in IQ?

- Differences in IQ have been attributed to both heredity and environment. Twin and adoption studies make it clear that at least half the variation in IQ scores is due to genetic differences, the remainder to environment and the interaction of heredity and environment. Family variables and preschool experiences also contribute to variation in IQ scores.

LO 7.14 What theories and evidence have been offered in support of genetic and cultural explanations of group differences in IQ scores?

- Genetic explanations of group differences are based on twin studies showing that individual differences in IQ are highly heritable and on the long-term stability of cross-group differences in average IQ scores. Cultural explanations are supported by research showing that groups with lower average IQ scores experience greater levels of exposure to risk factors such as poverty, poor nutrition, and toxic substances. The Flynn effect also demonstrates the power of cultural and historical forces in shaping IQ scores.

KEY TERMS

centration (p. 160)

conservation (p. 160)

corpus callosum (p. 154)

egocentrism (p. 159)

false-belief principle (p. 163)

fast-mapping (p. 167)

grammar explosion (p. 167)

handedness (p. 154)

hippocampus (p. 154)

intelligence quotient (IQ) (p. 169)

invented spelling (p. 168)

lateralization (p. 154)

metacognition (p. 165)

metamemory (p. 165)

operational efficiency (p. 164)

overregularization (p. 167)

phonological awareness (p. 168)

preoperational stage (p. 159)

reaction range (p. 173)

semiotic (symbolic) function (p. 158)

short-term storage space (STSS) (p. 164)

theory of mind (p. 162)

CHAPTER TEST   ✅ Study and Review in MyPsychLab

Answers to all the Chapter Test questions can be found in the back of the book.

1. A researcher presented four children with a baby doll. Which statement describes the behavior of the child whose response to the doll indicated she had moved into Piaget's preoperational stage?
   a. Shoshanna rocked the doll and pretended to feed it.
   b. Maria chewed on the doll's fingers.
   c. Lucy ignored the doll.
   d. Rolanda handed the doll back to the researcher.

2. Preschoolers grow _____.
   a. more rapidly than infants do
   b. at a fairly steady rate from one year to the next
   c. very little between the ages of 2 and 6
   d. to half their adult height by the age of 4 years

3. According to Piaget, at about age 2, the key cognitive tool that children acquire in the preoperational stage is the ability to use _____.
   a. abstractions   c. symbols
   b. comparisons   d. logic

4. Lateralization of functions in the brain during early childhood accompanies which of the following?
   a. growth of the corpus callosum
   b. massive pruning of the synapses in the left hemisphere
   c. maturation of the connections between the hippocampus and the cerebral cortex
   d. massive pruning of the synapses in the right hemisphere

5. Children whose IQ scores are below _____ may be diagnosed with _____ _____.
   a. 100; intellectual disabilities
   b. 100; Flynn effects
   c. 70; Flynn effects
   d. 70; intellectual disabilities

6. When a 3-year-old says "I eated my lunch" instead of "I ate my lunch," she is exhibiting _____.
   a. generalization
   b. overextension
   c. telegraphic speech
   d. overregularization

7. A 3-year-old child who uses language as a guide to solving problems, such as saying "This piece goes here" to himself as he assembles a puzzle, is using which of the following?
   a. scaffolding
   b. private speech
   c. social speech
   d. the zone of proximal development

8. Which formula corresponds to the way that Terman calculated IQ scores?
   a. CA/MA × 100   c. CA/MA × 1
   b. MA/CA × 100%   d. MA/CA × 100

9. According to Piaget, preschoolers' thinking is limited by _____.
   a. centration
   b. irreversibility
   c. thinking that is guided by the appearance of objects
   d. all of the above

10. Most people report that their earliest memory occurred when they were about 3 years old. Why?
    a. Links between the hippocampus and the cerebral cortex develop around age 3.
    b. Symbolic thought first develops around age 3.
    c. Preoperational thought is required before permanent memories can be formed.
    d. Vocabulary development limits memory function in the first 3 years of life.

11. Which of the following is a behavior seen in the parents of children with high IQs?
    a. Buying educational toys for children
    b. Talking to children often
    c. Encouraging children to acquire academic skills such as recitation of the alphabet
    d. Using computer games as part of their teaching repertoire

12. According to Case, preschoolers do not perform well on Piaget's tasks because of inefficiencies in _____.
    a. midrange memory   c. metalinguistic operations
    b. working schemes   d. short-term storage space

13. Which of the following is correct regarding the correlation between children's IQ test scores in early childhood and their later grades in school?
    a. The correlation between the two applies only to White and Asian American children.
    b. There is a positive correlation between the two variables.
    c. The correlation between the two applies only to African American children.
    d. There is no correlation between the two variables.

14. Which of the following is true about group differences in cognitive-test scores in the United States?
    a. Chinese and Japanese children get higher scores on achievement tests than do children in other groups.
    b. White children get higher scores on cognitive tests than do children in all other groups.
    c. Heredity explains group differences in cognitive-test scores.
    d. The difference in average IQ scores between African American and White children is increasing.

15. In which of the following families does a child have the highest risk of child abuse?
    a. a family in which the mother works full time
    b. a family in which one parent has a psychiatric disorder
    c. a family with only one child
    d. a family in which a grandparent lives in the home

16. Daniel is pretending that one of his blocks is a car. Daniel is exhibiting the _____ function.
    a. semiotic
    b. preoperational
    c. abstraction
    d. overextension

17. Marina complains that she has too many peas to eat. In response, her mother transfers the peas to a larger plate and says, "Now you don't have as many peas. Eat up!" Marina responds by rapidly and happily polishing off the peas. Marina responds positively to her mother's ploy because she lacks _____.
    a. centration
    b. symbolic thought
    c. conservation
    d. animism

18. Research on preschool interventions shows that _____.
    a. IQ is strongly influenced by heredity
    b. family variables are more important than education in determining children's IQ scores
    c. educational interventions can raise test scores
    d. adopted children benefit most from educational interventions

19. When Mickey was 5, he gave his younger sister a rock for her birthday. Mickey didn't understand why his sister didn't like her gift because he thought the rock was cool. This represents what type of thinking?
    a. arbitrary
    b. abstract
    c. polygenic
    d. egocentric

20. Simon is 3 years old and can recite several nursery rhymes from memory. Research indicates that Simon is likely to have an easier time learning to _____ than children who are unfamiliar with nursery rhymes.
    a. count
    b. read
    c. sing
    d. dance

21. Which of the following is a possible consequence of having been abused as a child?
    a. intellectual disabilities
    b. reduced likelihood of growing up to be an abusive parent
    c. depression
    d. posttraumatic stress disorder

22. Four-year-old Lisa refuses to eat anything other than peanut butter sandwiches because she says that all other foods are "yucky." According to the text, Lisa's behavior is _____.
    a. a sign that Lisa may have a psychiatric disorder
    b. in need of punishment
    c. typical among preschoolers
    d. a sign that Lisa may develop an eating disorder later in life

23. Which of the following activities would a 5-year-old be more likely to be able to do than a 3-year-old?
    a. thread beads on a string
    b. make a block tower
    c. pull a wheeled toy while walking
    d. ride a tricycle

24. Which of the following is *true* with regard to child abuse in the United States?
    a. Children with disabilities are less likely to be abused than those without disabilities.
    b. The risk of child abuse increases as children get older.
    c. Boys are more likely to be abused than girls are.
    d. Health-care professionals are required to keep suspicions regarding child abuse confidential.

25. What is the leading cause of accidental death among children over the age of 5 years in the United States?
    a. child abuse
    b. malnutrition
    c. motor vehicle accidents
    d. drowning

To 👁 **Watch** ✳ **Explore** ◉ **Simulate** ✔ **Study** and **Review** and experience **MyVirtualLife** go to **MyPsychLab.com**

chapter 8

Social and Personality Development in Early Childhood

If you asked a random sample of adults to tell you the most important characteristics of children between the ages of 2 and 6, the first thing on the list would probably be their rapidly changing social abilities during these years. Nay-saying, oppositional toddlers who spend most of their play time alone become skilled, cooperative playmates by age 5 or 6. Thus, the most obvious characteristic of 6-year-olds is how socially "grown up" they seem compared to 2-year-olds. Moreover, the blossoming physical,

LEARNING OBJECTIVES

THEORIES OF SOCIAL AND PERSONALITY DEVELOPMENT

8.1 What major themes of development did the psychoanalytic theorists propose for the early childhood period?

8.2 What are the findings of social-cognitive theorists with respect to young children's understanding of the social world?

PERSONALITY AND SELF-CONCEPT

8.3 How does temperament change in early childhood?

8.4 What changes take place in a young child's categorical, emotional, and social selves during the preschool years?

GENDER DEVELOPMENT

8.5 How do the major theoretical orientations explain gender development?

8.6 What are the characteristics of young children's sex-role knowledge?

8.7 How is the behavior of young children sex-typed?

FAMILY RELATIONSHIPS AND STRUCTURE

8.8 How does attachment change during the early childhood years?

8.9 How do parenting styles affect children's development?

8.10 How are ethnicity and socioeconomic status related to parenting style?

8.11 How is family structure related to children's development?

8.12 How does divorce affect children's behavior in early childhood and in later years?

8.13 What are some possible reasons for the relationship between family structure and development?

PEER RELATIONSHIPS

8.14 What are the various kinds of play exhibited by preschoolers?

8.15 What types of aggression do children display during early childhood?

8.16 How do prosocial behavior and friendship patterns change during early childhood?

cognitive, and language skills that you have probably observed in the child you are raising in *MyVirtualLife* lead to changes in how preschoolers view themselves and relate to their families. Most have also broadened their social networks to include peers.

In this chapter, we will discuss all these changes and the major theoretical explanations for them. We begin by reviewing the ideas proposed by the psychoanalytic theorists. Next, you will read about the very different explanations of the social-cognitive theorists. From there, we turn to the topics of personality and gender role development. Finally, we will address young children's relationships with others.

Theories of Social and Personality Development

What is the period of early childhood all about? One way to describe it would be to call it the "stepping out" phase, because that's precisely what 2- to 6-year-olds do. They "step out" from the safety of the strong emotional bonds that they share with their parents into the risky world of relationships with others. How do they do it? The psychoanalysts outlined the broad themes of this foundational time of life, and the work of more recent theorists has provided us with a few details about the skills that children develop in the process of stepping out. Before we get into the details, let's look at the themes.

Psychoanalytic Perspectives

LO 8.1 What major themes of development did the psychoanalytic theorists propose for the early childhood period?

You may remember that Freud described two stages during these preschool years. The developmental task of the *anal stage* (1 to 3 years) is toilet training. That of the *phallic stage*, you may remember, is to establish a foundation for later gender and moral development by identifying with the same-sex parent. We might sum up Freud's view of the early childhood period as the time in life when young children, first, gain control of their bodily functions and, second, renegotiate their relationships with their parents to prepare for stepping out into the world of peers.

Erikson agreed with Freud's views on bodily control and parental relationships during the preschool years, but he placed the emphasis somewhat differently. Both of the stages he identified in the preschool period (see Table 2.2, page 27) are triggered by children's growing physical, cognitive, and social skills. The stage Erikson called *autonomy versus shame and doubt*, for example, is centered around the toddler's new mobility and the accompanying desire for autonomy. The stage of *initiative versus guilt* is ushered in by new cognitive skills, particularly the preschooler's ability to plan, which accentuates his wish to take the initiative. However, his developing conscience dictates the boundaries within which this initiative may be exercised (Evans & Erikson, 1967). For example, think about a situation in which one child wants to play with another child's toy. His sense of initiative might motivate him to simply take it, but his conscience will likely prompt him to find a more socially acceptable way to gain the toy. If he fails to achieve the kind of self-control that is required to maintain conformity to his conscience, the child is likely to be hampered by excessive guilt and defensiveness in future psychosocial crises.

The key to healthy development during this period, according to Erikson, is striking a balance between the child's emerging skills and desire for autonomy and the parents' need to protect the child and control the child's behavior. Thus, the parents' task changes rather dramatically after infancy. In the early months of life, the parents' primary task is to provide enough warmth,

"Stepping out" is the major theme of social and personality development in early childhood. Maintaining strong bonds of affection with parents helps them feel secure enough to do so.

predictability, and responsiveness to foster a secure attachment and to support basic physiological needs. But once the child becomes physically, linguistically, and cognitively more independent, the need to control becomes a central aspect of the parents' task. Too much control, and the child will not have sufficient opportunity to explore; too little control, and the child will become unmanageable and fail to learn the social skills she will need to get along with peers as well as adults.

Social-Cognitive Perspectives

LO 8.2 What are the findings of social-cognitive theorists with respect to young children's understanding of the social world?

In contrast to the psychoanalytic tradition, **social-cognitive theory** assumes that social and emotional changes in the child are the result of—or at least are facilitated by—the enormous growth in cognitive abilities that happens during the preschool years, especially in the domain of theory of mind (Macrae & Bodenhausen, 2000; Smetana, Jambon, Conry-Murray, & Sturge-Apple, 2012). Over the past three decades, psychologists have devoted a great deal of theoretical and empirical attention to determining how the two domains are connected.

PERSON PERCEPTION Have you ever heard a child describe a peer as "nice" or "not nice"? Preschoolers' emerging capacity for applying categories to people is called **person perception**, or the ability to classify others. For example, by age 5 or so, children are capable of using trait labels such as "nice" and "not nice" to describe others (Heyman, 2009). Moreover, children of this age make judgments very similar to those of adults when asked to identify the most intelligent child in their class or play group (Droege & Stipek, 1993). Moreover, they describe their peers in terms of traits such as "grumpy" and "mean" (Yuill, 1997). They also make statements about other people's patterns of behavior—"Grandma always lets me pick the cereal at the grocery store." They use these observations to classify others into groups such as "people I like" and "people I don't like."

However, young children's observations and categorizations of people are far less consistent than those of older children. A playmate they judge to be "nice" one day may be referred to as "mean" the next. Developmentalists have found that young children's judgments about others are inconsistent because they tend to base them on their most recent interactions with those individuals (Ruble & Dweck, 1995). In other words, a 4-year-old girl describes one of her playmates as "nice" on Monday because she shares a cookie but as "mean" on Tuesday because she refuses to share a candy bar. Or the child declares, "I don't like Grandma anymore because she made me go to bed early."

Preschoolers also categorize others on the basis of observable characteristics such as race, age, and gender (Heyman, 2009). For example, the *cross-race effect*, a phenomenon in which individuals are more likely to remember the faces of people of their own race than those of people of a different race, is established by age 5 (Pezdek, Blandon-Gitlin, & Moore, 2003). Similarly, they talk about "big kids" (school-age children) and "little kids" (their agemates), and they seem to know that they fit in best with the latter. Self-segregation by gender—a topic you'll read more about later in the chapter—begins as early as age 2. Likewise, young children sometimes segregate themselves according to race (see *Research Report*).

UNDERSTANDING RULE CATEGORIES If you attended a formal dinner at which the forks were on the right side of the plates rather than on the left, would you be upset? Probably not because *social conventions*, such as customs that govern where to place flatware, are rules that have nothing to do with our fundamental sense of right and wrong. Consequently, most of us are not troubled when they are violated and take a dim view of people who are bothered by such trifles. By contrast, we have little tolerance for the breaking of rules that we view as having a basis in morality, such as laws that forbid stealing and unwritten rules like the one that prohibits you from flirting with your best friend's romantic partner (or with your romantic partner's best friend!). When and how did we learn to make such distinctions?

Social-cognitive theorists have found that children begin to respond differently to violations of different kinds of rules between 2 and 3 (Smetana, Schlagman, & Adams, 1993). For example, they view taking another child's toy without permission as a more serious violation of rules than forgetting to say "Thank you." They also say, just as adults would in response to

social-cognitive theory a theoretical perspective which asserts that social and personality development in early childhood is related to improvements in the cognitive domain

person perception the ability to classify others according to categories such as age, gender, and race

Racism in the Preschool Classroom

A preschool classroom or day-care center is often the only setting in which children of different races come together. Consequently, these classrooms are likely to be important to the development of racial attitudes. Preschool teachers, then, need to be aware of how such attitudes are formed.

Research suggests that, once young children form race schemas, they use them to make judgments about others (Macrae & Quadflieg, 2010). These early judgments probably reflect young children's egocentric thinking. Essentially, children view those like themselves as desirable companions and those who are unlike them—in gender, race, and other categorical variables—as undesirable (Doyle & Aboud, 1995). Thus, like the understanding of race itself, race-based playmate preferences probably result from immature cognitive structures rather than true racism.

Of course, cognitive development doesn't happen in a social vacuum, and by age 5, most White children in English-speaking countries have acquired an understanding of their culture's racial stereotypes and prejudices (Davis, Leman, & Barrett, 2007; Leman & Lam, 2008). Likewise, African American, Hispanic American, and Native American children become sensitive very early in life to the fact that people of their race are viewed negatively by many Whites. Moreover, White preschool teachers may not notice race-based behavior in their classrooms, but research suggests that minority children report a significant number of such events to their parents (Bernhard, Lefebvre, Kilbride, Chud, & Lange, 1998).

The key to preventing racial awareness from developing into racism, psychologists say, is for preschool teachers to discuss race openly and to make conscious efforts to help children acquire nonprejudiced attitudes (Cushner, McClelland, & Safford, 1993). Teachers can also assign children of different races to do projects together. In addition, they can make children aware of each other's strengths as individuals, since both children and adults seem to perceive individual differences only within their own racial group (Ostrom, Carpenter, Sedikides, & Li, 1993).

Ideally, all children should learn to evaluate their own and others' behavior according to individual criteria rather than group membership. Preschool teachers are in a position to provide young children with a significant push toward these important goals.

CRITICAL ANALYSIS

1. *How would you explain White preschool teachers' failure to notice race-based behaviors in their classrooms?*

2. *How would information-processing theory explain the influence of historical knowledge regarding slavery, discrimination, and the civil rights movement on the development of preschoolers' ideas about race?*

---

similar questions, that stealing and physical violence are wrong, even if their particular family or preschool has no explicit rule against them. This kind of understanding seems to develop both as a consequence of preschoolers' increasing capacity for classification and as a result of adults' tendency to emphasize transgressions that have moral overtones more than violations of customs and other arbitrary rules when punishing children (Smetana, 2006).

UNDERSTANDING OTHERS' INTENTIONS Would you feel differently about a person who deliberately smashed your car's windshield with a baseball bat than you would about someone else who accidentally broke it while washing your car for you? Chances are you would be far more forgiving of the person who unintentionally broke your windshield, because we tend to base our judgments of others' behavior and our responses to them on what we perceive to be their intentions. Working from his assumptions about young children's egocentrism, Piaget suggested that young children were incapable of such discriminations.

However, more recent research has demonstrated that young children do understand intentions to some degree (Zhang & Yu, 2002). For one thing, it's quite common for preschoolers to say "It was an accident. . . . I didn't mean to do it" when they are punished. Such protests suggest that children understand that intentional wrongdoing is punished more severely than unintentional transgressions of the rules.

Several studies suggest that children can make judgments about actors' intentions both when faced with abstract problems and when personally motivated by a desire to avoid punishment (Thompson, 2009). For example, in a classic study, 3-year-olds listened to stories about children playing ball (Nelson, 1980). Pictures were used to convey information about intentions (see Figure 8.1 on page 183). The children were more likely to label as "bad" or "naughty" the child who intended to harm a playmate than the child who accidentally hit another child in the head with the ball. However, the children's judgments were also influenced by outcomes. In other words, they were more likely to say a child who wanted to hurt his playmate was "good" if he failed to hit the child with the ball. These results suggest that children know more about intentions than Piaget thought, but, compared to older children, they are still limited in their ability to base judgments entirely on intentions (Jambon & Smetana, 2014).

Figure 8.1 A Test of Children's Understanding of Intentionality

Pictures like these have been used to assess young children's understanding of an actor's intentions.

test yourself before going on ✓ **Study** and **Review** in **MyPsychLab**

Answers to these questions can be found in the back of the book.

1. Classify each developmental milestone as associated with (a) Freud's theory, (b) Erikson's theory, or (c) social-cognitive theory.

_____(1) resolving the initiative-versus-guilt crisis

_____(2) toilet training

_____(3) distinguishing between social conventions and moral rules

_____(4) identifying with the same-sex parent

_____(5) understanding others' intentions

_____(6) resolving the autonomy-versus-shame-and-doubt crisis

_____(7) categorizing others

CRITICAL THINKING

2. How might the psychoanalytic and social-cognitive perspectives on early childhood development be integrated into a comprehensive explanation of age-related changes during this period?

Personality and Self-Concept

As young children gain more understanding of the social environment, their distinctive personalities begin to emerge. At the same time, their self-concepts become more complex, allowing them to exercise greater control over their own behavior.

From Temperament to Personality

LO 8.3   How does temperament change in early childhood?

Are you familiar with the children's game "Duck, Duck, Goose"? Here's how it goes. A child who has been assigned the role of "it" walks around the outside of a circle of children who are seated on the floor. As "it" passes by, he touches the head of each child and calls out "duck" until he comes to the child that he chooses to be the "goose." The "goose" then has to chase "it" around the circle and try to prevent him from taking goose's seat. If "goose" fails to beat "it," then she becomes "it" for the next round of the game. The difficult part of the game for many young children is waiting to be chosen to be the "goose."

Activities such as "Duck, Duck, Goose" may seem frivolous, but they contribute to the process through which temperament becomes modified into personality during the early childhood years. A child whose temperament includes a low ranking on the dimension of effortful

emotional regulation the ability to control emotional states and emotion-related behavior

control, for instance, may not be able to tolerate waiting for his turn in a game of "Duck, Duck, Goose" (Li-Grining, 2007). If he obeys his impulse to chase "it" and jumps up from his seat before he is declared the "goose," he will undoubtedly be scolded by his playmates. If his frustration leads him to withdraw from the game with the protest "I *never* get to be the goose!" he will miss out on the fun of participating. Either way, he will learn that controlling his impulses is more beneficial to him than submitting to them. A few such experiences will teach him to moderate the effects of his lack of effortful control on his social behavior. As a result, his lack of effortful control will become less prominent in the profile of characteristics that constitute his personality and will change how his peers respond to him. Their approval of his modified profile will encourage him to keep his impulses in check.

Similarly, children with difficult temperaments learn that the behaviors associated with difficultness, such as complaining, often result in peer rejection. As a result, many of them change their behavior to gain social acceptance. Similarly, some shy toddlers are encouraged by their parents to be more sociable, while the timidity of others is amplified by parental overprotectiveness (Kiel & Buss, 2012; Rubin, Burgess, & Hastings, 2002). Thus, personality represents the combination of the temperament with which children are probably born and the knowledge they gain about temperament-related behavior during childhood (Karreman, de Haas, Van Tuijl, van Aken, & Dekovic, 2010; McCrae, Costa, Ostendord, & Angleitner, 2000). Thus, infant temperament doesn't necessarily dictate the kind of personality a child will develop. Instead, it is one factor among many that contribute to an individual child's personality.

Self-Concept

LO 8.4   What changes take place in a young child's categorical, emotional, and social selves during the preschool years?

Ask a preschooler to describe herself, and you are likely to get an answer such as "I'm a girl." Pressed for more information, the child will add her hair color or some other physical characteristic, tell you who her friends are, or reveal who her favorite cartoon character is. These answers show that the categorical self, which first emerged during infancy, is becoming more mature. Likewise, the emotional self grows by leaps and bounds during these years, and a new component of self-concept, the *social self* emerges.

THE EMOTIONAL SELF   In recent years, research examining development of the emotional self during the early childhood years has focused on the acquisition of **emotional regulation**, or the ability to control emotional states and emotion-related behavior (Eisenberg & Sulik, 2012). For example, children exhibit emotional regulation when they find a way to cheer themselves up when they are feeling sad or when they divert their attention to a different activity when they get frustrated with something. Some studies have revealed relationships between the development of emotional regulation in early childhood and a variety of social variables. One study showed that level of emotional regulation at age 2 predicted level of aggressive behavior at age 4 in both boys and girls (Rubin, Burgess, Dwyer, & Hastings, 2003). Predictably, preschoolers who display high levels of emotional regulation are more popular with their peers than those who are less able to regulate their emotional behavior (Denham et al., 2003; Fantuzzo, Sekino, & Cohen, 2004). Emotional regulation skills appear to be particularly important for children whose temperaments include high levels of anger proneness (Diener & Kim, 2004). Further, longitudinal research has demonstrated that emotional regulation in early childhood is related to children's development of emotional problems and their ability to think about right and wrong during the school years (Kim-Spoon, Cicchetti, & Rogosch, 2013; Kochanska, Murray, & Coy, 1997).

The process of acquiring emotional regulation is one in which control shifts slowly from the parents to the child across the early childhood years (Brophy-Herb, Zajicek-Farber, Bocknek, McKelvey, & Stansbury, 2013; Houck & Lecuyer-Maus, 2004). Here again, the child's temperament is a factor. For example, preschoolers who have consistently exhibited difficult behavior since infancy are more likely to have self-control problems in early childhood (Schmitz et al., 1999). Similarly, preschoolers who were born prematurely or who were delayed in language development in the second year of life experience more difficulties with self-control during early childhood (Carson, Klee, & Perry, 1998; Schothorst & van Engeland, 1996).

All children get upset from time to time, but they vary widely in how they manage distressing feelings.

Difficult temperament and developmental delays are two important risk factors for *disruptive mood dysregulation disorder (DMDD)* (American Psychiatric Association, 2013; Bitter, Mills, Adler, Strakowski, & DelBello, 2011; West, Schenkel, & Pavuluri, 2008). Two to three times per week, preschoolers with DMDD exhibit tantrums characterized by intense rage and, often, aggressive and destructive behavior. Parents and teachers of children with DMDD typically require the assistance of a mental health professional to implement behavior management strategies that can help these children develop the capacity to regulate their emotions (West & Weinstein, 2012).

empathy the ability to identify with another person's emotional state

Another aspect of the emotional self involves **empathy**, the ability to identify with another person's emotional state. Empathy has two aspects: apprehending another person's emotional state or condition and then matching that emotional state oneself. An empathizing person experiences either the same feeling he imagines the other person to feel or a highly similar feeling. Empathy is negatively associated with aggression in the early childhood years; the more advanced preschoolers' capacity for empathy is, the less aggression they display (Findlay, Girardi, & Coplan, 2006; Hatakeyama & Katakeyama, 2012). Moreover, the development of empathy in early childhood appears to provide the foundation on which a more sophisticated emotion, *sympathy* (a general feeling of sorrow or concern for another person), is built in later childhood and adolescence (Sallquist Eisenberg, Spinrad, Reiser, et al., 2009). The most thorough analysis of the development of empathy and sympathy has been offered by Martin Hoffman (1982, 1988), who describes four broad stages, summarized in Table 8.1.

In addition to empathy, young children's emotional selves include an awareness of emotional states that are linked to their culture's definitions of right and wrong (Thompson & Newton, 2010). These feelings, which are sometimes called the *moral emotions*, include guilt, shame, and pride (Eisenberg, 2000). Guilt is usually thought of as the emotional state induced when a child breaks a rule. Consequently, a child who takes a forbidden cookie will experience guilt. Feelings of shame arise when she fails to live up to expectations. For instance, most parents and teachers urge young children to share their toys. Thus, when a child behaves selfishly and is reminded about the sharing rule, it is likely that he feels shame. By contrast, children feel pride when they succeed at meeting expectations. 👁 **Watch** the **Video** *Understanding Self and Others* in **MyPsychLab**.

Research suggests that the interplay among these three emotions, and young children's awareness of them, influence the development of behavior that children's cultures regard as morally acceptable (Eisenberg, 2000). Thus, they form the foundation of later moral

TABLE 8.1   Stages in Development of Empathy Proposed by Hoffman

Stage	Description
Stage 1: Global empathy	Observed during the first year. If the infant is around someone expressing a strong emotion, he may match that emotion—for example, by beginning to cry when he hears another infant crying.
Stage 2: Egocentric empathy	Beginning at about 12 to 18 months of age, when children have developed a fairly clear sense of their separate selves, they respond to another's distress with some distress of their own, but they may attempt to "cure" the other person's problem by offering what they themselves would find most comforting. They may, for example, show sadness when they see another child hurt, and go get their own mother to help.
Stage 3: Empathy for another's feelings	Beginning as young as age 2 or 3 and continuing through elementary school, children note others' feelings, partially match those feelings, and respond to the other's distress in nonegocentric ways. Over these years, children become able to distinguish a wider (and more subtle) range of emotions.
Stage 4: Empathy for another's life condition	In late childhood or adolescence, some children develop a more generalized notion of others' feelings and respond not just to the immediate situation but to the other individual's general situation or plight. Thus, a young person at this level may become more distressed by another person's sadness if she knows that the sadness is chronic or that the person's general situation is particularly tragic than if she sees it as a momentary problem.

Sources: Hoffman, 1982, 1988.

development. Studies suggest that these feelings evolve in the context of parent–child relationships. Young children who do not have warm, trusting relationships with their parents are at risk of failing to develop moral emotions or of developing feelings of guilt, shame, and pride that are too weak to influence their behavior (Koenig, Cicchetti, & Rogosch, 2004).

THE SOCIAL SELF Another facet of a child's emerging sense of self is an increasing awareness of herself as a player in the social game. By age 2, a toddler has already learned a variety of social "scripts"—routines of play or interaction with others. The toddler now begins to develop some implicit understanding of her own roles in these scripts (Case, 1991). So she may begin to think of herself as a "helper" in some situations or as "the boss" when she is telling some other child what to do.

You can see this clearly in children's sociodramatic play, as they begin to take explicit roles: "I'll be the daddy and you be the mommy" or "I'm the boss." As part of the same process, the young child also gradually comes to understand her place in the network of family roles. She has sisters, brothers, father, mother, and so forth.

Moreover, role scripts help young children become more independent. For example, assuming the "student" role provides a preschooler with a prescription for appropriate behavior in the school situation. Students listen when the teacher speaks to the class, get out materials and put them away at certain times, help their classmates in various ways, and so on. Once a preschooler is familiar with and adopts the student role, he can follow the role script and is no longer dependent on the teacher to tell him what to do every minute of the day.

test yourself before going on ✔ **Study** and **Review** in **MyPsychLab**

Answers to these questions can be found in the back of the book.

1. Interactions with _____ and _____ modify children's temperaments.

2. Research on the development of young children's emotional self has focused on _____ _____.

3. The ability to identify with another person's emotional state is _____.

4. Guilt, shame, and pride are _____ emotions that develop during early childhood.

CRITICAL THINKING

5. If parents received a description of their child's temperament at birth (sort of like the owner's manual you get with a new appliance), do you think it would help them to be better parents? Conversely, do you think it would cause them to be overly tolerant of temperamental characteristics that might need to be modified for the child's own benefit, such as irritability?

Gender Development

We noted earlier that preschoolers who are asked to describe themselves are likely to begin by stating whether they are boys or girls. In psychologists' terms, their tendency to do so suggests that "boy-ness" and "girl-ness" are *salient*, or important, categories for young children. Thus, one fascinating developmental process of the preschool period involves children's evolving sense of **gender**, the psychological and social associates and implications of biological sex.

Explaining Gender Development

LO 8.5 How do the major theoretical orientations explain gender development?

Developmentalists have proposed several explanations of gender development.

PSYCHOANALYTIC EXPLANATIONS As you remember from Chapter 2, Freud suggested that 3- to 6-year-olds overcome the anxiety they feel about their desires for the opposite-sex parent (the Oedipus or Electra conflict) through identification with the same-sex parent. In order to identify with the parent, the child must learn and conform to his or her sex-role concepts. Thus, according to Freud, children acquire gender through the process of identification.

gender the psychological and social associates and implications of biological sex

The difficulty with Freud's theory is that toddlers seem to understand far more about gender than the theory would predict. For example, many 18-month-olds accurately label themselves and others as boys or girls. Likewise, clearly sex-typed behavior appears long before age 4 or 5, when psychoanalytic theories claim identification occurs.

SOCIAL-LEARNING EXPLANATIONS Social-learning theorists have emphasized the role of parents in shaping children's gender development (Bandura, 1977b; Mischel, 1966, 1970). This notion has been far better supported by research than have Freud's ideas. Parents do seem to reinforce sex-typed activities in children as young as 18 months, not only by buying different kinds of toys for boys and girls but also by responding more positively when their sons play with blocks or trucks or when their daughters play with dolls (Fagot & Hagan, 1991; Lytton & Romney, 1991). Such differential reinforcement is particularly clear with boys, especially from fathers (Siegal, 1987).

Still, helpful as it is, a social-learning explanation is probably not sufficient. In particular, parents differentially reinforce boys' and girls' behavior less than you'd expect, and probably not enough to account for the very early and robust discrimination children seem to make on the basis of gender. Even young children whose parents seem to treat their sons and daughters in highly similar ways nonetheless learn gender labels and prefer same-sex playmates.

THE COGNITIVE-DEVELOPMENTAL EXPLANATION A third alternative, Kohlberg's cognitive-developmental theory, suggests that children's understanding of gender develops in stages (Kohlberg, 1966; Kohlberg & Ullian, 1974). First comes **gender identity**, which is simply a child's ability to label his or her own sex correctly and to identify other people as men or women, boys or girls. By age 2, most children correctly label themselves as boys or girls, and within 6–12 months, most can correctly label others as well. The second step is **gender stability**, which is the understanding that people stay the same gender throughout life. Researchers have measured this by asking children such questions as "When you were a little baby, were you a little girl or a little boy?" or "When you grow up, will you be a mommy or a daddy?" Most children understand the stability of gender by about age 4 (Slaby & Frey, 1975) (see Figure 8.2). The final step is the development of true **gender constancy**, the recognition that someone stays the same gender even though he may appear to change by wearing different clothes or changing his hair length. For example, boys don't change into girls by wearing dresses.

Numerous studies, including studies of children growing up in other cultures such as Kenya, Nepal, Belize, and Samoa, show that children go through this sequence (Martin & Ruble, 2004; Munroe, Shimmin, & Munroe, 1984). Moreover, progression through the sequence is related to general cognitive development (Trautner, Gervai, & Nemeth, 2003). Consequently, Kohlberg asserted that gender constancy is the organizing principle that children use to acquire knowledge of gender and to bring their own behavior into conformity with cultural standards. However, critics point out that Kohlberg's theory fails to explain why children show clearly different behavior, such as toy preferences, long before they achieve gender constancy.

THE INFORMATION-PROCESSING APPROACH Information-processing theorists use the term *schema* to refer to mental frameworks, such as categories, that help humans organize processes such as thinking and remembering. **Gender schema theory** assumes that the development of such a framework for gender underlies gender development. According to this perspective, the gender schema begins to develop as soon as the child notices the differences between male and female, knows his own gender, and can label the two groups with some consistency—all of which happens by age 2 or 3 (Bem, 1981; Martin & Ruble, 2002). Perhaps because gender is clearly an either/or category, children seem to understand very early that this is a key distinction, so the category serves as a kind of magnet for new information. Once the child has established even a primitive gender schema, a great many experiences can be assimilated to it. Thus, as soon as this schema begins to be formed, children may begin to show preference for same-sex playmates or for gender-stereotyped activities (Martin & Little, 1990).

Preschoolers first learn some broad distinctions about what kinds of activities or behavior "go with" each gender, both by observing other children and through the reinforcements they receive from parents. They also learn a few gender *scripts*—whole sequences of events that are normally

Figure 8.2 Gender Stereotyping in a Child's Drawing

In describing this self-portrait, the 5-year-old artist said, "This is how I will look when I get married to a boy. I am under a rainbow, so beautiful with a bride hat, a belt, and a purse." The girl knows she will always be female and associates gender with externals such as clothing (gender stability). She is also already quite knowledgeable about gender role expectations. (*Source:* Courtesy of Jerry and Denise Boyd. Used with permission.)

gender identity the ability to correctly label oneself and others as male or female

gender stability the understanding that gender is a stable, lifelong characteristic

gender constancy the understanding that gender is a component of the self that is not altered by external appearance

gender schema theory an information-processing approach to gender concept development, asserting that people use a schema for each gender to process information about themselves and others associated with a given gender, such as "fixing dinner" or "building with tools"—just as they learn other social scripts at about this age (Levy & Fivush, 1993). Then, between age 4 and age 6, the child learns a more subtle and complex set of associations for his own gender—what children of his own gender like and don't like, how they play, how they talk, and what kinds of people they associate with, along with cultural beliefs about the relative value or males and females (Halim, Ruble, & Tamis-LeMonda, 2013). Only between the ages of 8 and 10 does the child develop an equivalently complex view of the opposite gender (Martin, Wood, & Little, 1990).

The key difference between this theory and Kohlberg's gender constancy theory is that gender schema theory asserts that children need not understand that gender is permanent to form an initial gender schema. When they do begin to understand gender constancy, at about 5 or 6, children develop a more elaborate rule, or schema, of "what people who are like me do" and treat this rule the same way they treat other rules—as an absolute. Later, the child's application of the gender rule becomes more flexible. She knows, for example, that most boys don't play with dolls, but that they can do so if they like.

BIOLOGICAL APPROACHES For a long time, developmentalists dismissed the idea that biological differences between males and females were responsible for psychological differences between them. Today, though, they are taking another look at decades-old experimental studies with animals showing that prenatal exposure to male hormones such as *testosterone* powerfully influences behavior after birth (Lippa, 2005). Female animals exposed to testosterone behave more like male animals; for instance, they are more aggressive than females who do not experience prenatal exposure to testosterone. Similarly, when experimenters block the release of testosterone during prenatal development of male animal embryos, the animals exhibit behavior that is more typical of the females of their species.

Hormonal influences have been proposed to explain the outcomes of cases involving boys who carry a genetic defect that causes them to develop deformed genitalia. Decades ago, a few such boys were subjected to plastic surgery to give them female-appearing genitals and were raised as girls. At that time, however, doctors did not realize that the genetic defect in question interferes only with testosterone's effects on the sex organs; the brains of these fetuses were exposed to normal amounts of testosterone throughout prenatal development (Rosenthal & Gitelman, 2002). Follow-up studies found that many of these children, when they learned of their status, sought surgery to masculinize their bodies. Moreover, even those who elected to retain the feminine identities they had been given in infancy possessed many attributes and behaviors that are more typical of males than of females (Reiner & Gearhart, 2004). Such findings support the view that hormones play some role in gender development.

Sex-Role Knowledge

LO 8.6 What are the characteristics of young children's sex-role knowledge?

Figuring out your gender and understanding that it stays constant are only part of the story. Learning what goes with being a boy or a girl in a given culture is also a vital task for a child. Researchers have studied this in two ways—by asking children what boys and girls (or men and women) like to do and what they are like (which is an inquiry about gender stereotypes) and by asking children if it is okay for boys to play with dolls or girls to climb trees or do equivalent cross-sex things (an inquiry about roles).

In every culture, adults have clear gender stereotypes. Indeed, the content of those stereotypes is remarkably similar in cultures around the world. Psychologists who have studied gender stereotypes in many different countries, including non-Western countries such as Thailand, Pakistan, and Nigeria, find that the most clearly stereotyped traits are weakness, gentleness, appreciativeness, and soft-heartedness for women, and aggression, strength, cruelty, and coarseness for men (Eagly, Eaton, Rose, Riger, & McHugh, 2012; Williams & Best, 1990). In most cultures, men are also seen as competent, skillful, assertive, and able to get things done, while women are seen as warm and expressive, tactful, quiet, gentle, aware of others' feelings, and lacking in competence, independence, and logic.

Studies of children show that these stereotyped ideas develop early. It would not be uncommon to hear a 3-year-old in the United States say "Mommies use the stove, and Daddies use the grill." A 4-year-old might define gender roles in terms of competencies: "Daddies are better at fixing things, but Mommies are better at tying bows and decorating." Even 2-year-olds in the United States already associate certain tasks and possessions with men and women, such as vacuum cleaners and kitchen utensils food with women and cars and tools with men. By age 3 or 4, children can assign stereotypic occupations, toys, and activities to each gender. By age 5, children begin to associate certain personality traits, such as assertiveness and nurturance, with males or females (Parmley & Cunningham, 2008).

Studies of children's ideas about how men and women (or boys and girls) ought to behave add an interesting further element. For example, in an early study, a psychologist told a story to children aged 4–9 about a little boy named George who liked to play with dolls (Damon, 1977). George's parents told him that only little girls play with dolls; little boys shouldn't. The children were then asked questions about the story, such as "Why do people tell George not to play with dolls?" or "Is there a rule that boys shouldn't play with dolls?"

Four-year-olds in this study thought it was okay for George to play with dolls. There was no rule against it, and he should do it if he wanted to. Six-year-olds, in contrast, thought it was wrong for George to play with dolls. By about age 9, children had differentiated between what boys and girls usually do and what is "wrong." One boy said, for example, that breaking windows was wrong and bad but that playing with dolls was not bad in the same way. He described playing with dolls as something that boys usually do as opposed to breaking windows is wrong in and of itself.

Interestingly, more recent studies show that 21st-century children express ideas about gender-typed behavior that are quite similar to those of their 1970s counterparts (Gee & Heyman, 2007; Gelman, Taylor, Nguyen, Leaper, & Bigler, 2004). These studies suggest that a 5- to 6-year-old has figured out that gender is permanent and is searching for an all-or-none, totally reliable rule about how boys and girls behave (Martin & Ruble, 2004). The child picks up information from watching adults, from television, and from listening to the labels that are attached to different activities (e.g., "Boys don't cry"). Initially, children treat these as absolute, moral rules. Later, they understand that these are social conventions; at this point, gender concepts become more flexible and stereotyping declines somewhat (Martin & Ruble, 2004).

Sex-Typed Behavior

LO 8.7   How is the behavior of young children sex-typed?

The final element in the development of gender is the actual behavior children show with those of the same and the opposite sex. An unexpected finding is that **sex-typed behavior**, or different patterns of behavior among girls and boys, develops earlier than ideas about gender (Campbell, Shirley, & Candy, 2004). By 18–24 months, children begin to show some preference for sex-stereotyped toys, such as dolls for girls or trucks or building blocks for boys, which is some months before they can consistently identify their own gender (Thommessen & Todd, 2010). By age 3, children begin to show a preference for same-sex friends and are much more sociable with playmates of the same sex—at a time when they do not yet have a concept of gender stability (Corsaro, Molinari, Hadley, & Sugioka, 2003; Maccoby, 1988, 1990; Maccoby & Jacklin, 1987) (see Figure 8.3). 🌸 **Explore** the **Concept** *Adults' Perceptions of Boys and Girls* in **MyPsychLab**.

Not only are preschoolers' friendships and peer interactions increasingly sex-segregated; it is also clear that boy–boy interactions and girl–girl interactions differ in quality, even in these early years. One important part of same-sex interactions seems to involve instruction in and modeling of sex-appropriate behavior. In other words, older boys teach younger boys how to be "masculine," and older girls teach younger girls how to be "feminine" (Danby & Baker, 1998).

However, these "lessons" in sex-typed behavior are fairly subtle. Eleanor Maccoby, one of the leading theorists in this area, describes the girls' pattern as an *enabling style* (Maccoby,

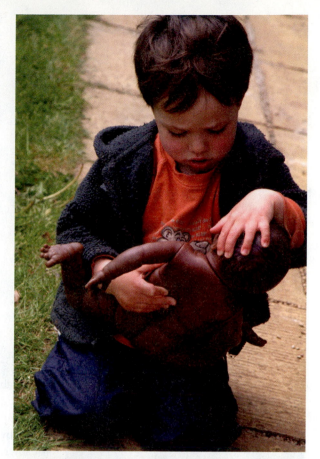

As gender develops, children change their views about whether it is acceptable for boys to play with dolls or for girls to play sports such as baseball.

sex-typed behavior different patterns of behavior exhibited by boys and girls

Figure 8.3 Gender and Playmate Preferences

In one classic study of playmate preferences, researchers counted how often preschool children played with same-sex and opposite-sex playmates. Children as young as 2½ already showed at least some preference for same-sex playmates.

(*Source:* Adapted from P. La Freniere, F. Strayer, & R. Gauthier, *Child Development*, Fig. 1, p. 1961, 1984. Reprinted by permission of Society for Research in Child Development.)

cross-gender behavior behavior that is atypical for one's own sex but typical for the opposite sex

Play may provide children with opportunities to learn about gender expectations.

1990). Enabling includes such behaviors as supporting the friend, expressing agreement, and making suggestions. All these behaviors tend to foster a greater equality and intimacy in the relationship and keep the interaction going. In contrast, boys are more likely to show what Maccoby calls a *constricting, or restrictive, style.* "A restrictive style is one that tends to derail the interaction—to inhibit the partner or cause the partner to withdraw, thus shortening the interaction or bringing it to an end" (1990, p. 517). Contradicting, interrupting, boasting, and other forms of self-display are all aspects of this style. Rough-and-tumble play and play fighting are other manifestations of boys' restrictive interaction style.

These two patterns begin to be visible in the preschool years. For example, beginning as early as age 3, boys and girls use quite different strategies in their attempts to influence each other's behavior (Maccoby, 1990). Girls generally ask questions or make requests; boys are much more likely to make demands or phrase things using imperatives ("Give me that!"). The really intriguing finding is that even at this early age, boys simply don't respond to the girls' enabling style. Thus, playing with boys yields little positive reinforcement for girls, and they begin to avoid such interactions and band together.

Another kind of learning opportunity happens when children exhibit **cross-gender behavior**—behavior that is atypical in their culture for their gender. For example, *tomboyishness*, girls' preference for activities that are more typical for boys, is a kind of cross-gender behavior. Generally, tomboyishness is tolerated by adults and peers (Sandnabba & Ahlberg, 1999). Not surprisingly, then, cross-gender behavior is far more common among girls than boys (Etaugh & Liss, 1992). Tomboyishness does not appear to interfere with the development of a "feminine" personality in adulthood, and it may allow girls to acquire positive characteristics such as assertiveness (Hilgenkamp & Livingston, 2002). In contrast, peers actively discourage boys from engaging in cross-gender behavior. Specifically, boys who play with dolls or behave in an effeminate manner are likely to elicit expressions of disapproval—or even ridicule—from other children (Martin, 1991). However, it cannot be assumed that the prevalence of sex-typed play among boys is strictly the result of adult and peer influence. For one thing, sex-typed play preferences appear earlier and are more consistent in boys, which suggests that these preferences begin to develop before environmental forces have had much chance to influence them (Blakemore, LaRue, & Olejnik, 1979; Fabes, Martin, & Hanish, 2003). Further, by age 3, boys are likely to show an actual aversion to girls' activities—for example, by saying "yuck" when experimenters offer them toys like dolls (Bussey & Bandura, 1992).

Individual differences in sex-typed behavior are highly stable across early and middle childhood—that is, among both boys and girls, those who exhibit the greatest amount of sex-typed behavior at age 2 continue to do so in the middle elementary school years (Golombok et al., 2008). In addition, cross-gender behavior in early childhood predicts subjective feelings of differentness from peers in adolescence (Golombok, Rust, Zervoulis, Golding, & Hines, 2012). These findings suggest that sex-typed behavior is part of a complex process of identity development and not just the result of cultural modeling and reinforcement.

test yourself before going on ✓ Study and Review in MyPsychLab

Answers to these questions can be found in the back of the book.

1. Match each theory with its main idea.

_____(1) psychoanalytic theory
_____(2) social-learning theory
_____(3) cognitive-developmental theory
_____(4) gender schema theory
_____(5) biological approaches

    (a) gender concept develops in stages
    (b) gender develops as children identify with the same-sex parent
    (c) children use a mental framework to organize ideas about gender
    (d) gender development is attributable to parental influences
    (e) hormones shape gender development

2. Classify each item in the list as (A) sex-role knowledge or (B) sex-typed behavior

_____(1) enabling style
_____(2) belief that boys shouldn't play with dolls
_____(3) girls' preference for "feminine" toys
_____(4) restrictive style
_____(5) associating women with domestic tasks such as cooking and cleaning

CRITICAL THINKING

3. To what degree do you think the enabling and constrictive interaction styles are exhibited in adults' social interactions?

Family Relationships and Structure

Psychologists agree that family relationships constitute one of the most, if not *the* most, influential factors in early childhood development. These relationships reflect both continuity and change. The preschooler is no less attached to her family than the infant but, at the same time, is struggling to establish independence.

Attachment

LO 8.8 How does attachment change during the early childhood years?

You'll remember from Chapter 6 that by 12 months of age, a baby has normally established a clear attachment to at least one caregiver. By age 2 or 3, the attachment is just as strong, but many attachment behaviors have become less visible. Three-year-olds still want to sit on Mom's or Dad's lap; they are still likely to seek some closeness when Mom returns from an absence. But when she is not afraid or under stress, the 3-year-old is able to wander farther and farther from her safe base without apparent distress. She can also deal with her potential anxiety due to separation by creating shared plans with the parents. For example, a parent might say "I'll be home after your naptime," to which the child may respond "Can we watch a movie then?" (Crittenden, 1992).

Attachment quality also predicts behavior during the preschool years. Children who are securely attached to parents experience fewer behavior problems. Specifically, those who are insecurely attached display more anger and aggression toward both peers and adults in social settings such as day care and preschool (DeMulder, Denham, Schmidt, & Mitchell, 2000; Schmidt, DeMulder, & Denham, 2002). Interestingly, insecurely attached preschoolers are also more likely than their securely attached peers to develop negative, critical attitudes toward themselves (Madigan, Atkinson, Laurin, & Benoit, 2013).

For most children, the attachment relationship, whether secure or not, seems to change at about age 4. Bowlby (1969) described this new stage, or level, as a *goal-corrected partnership*.

Off he goes, into greater independence. A child this age, especially one with secure attachment, is far more confident about being at a distance from his safe base.

Just as the first attachment probably requires the baby to understand that his mother will continue to exist when she isn't there, so the preschooler grasps that the *relationship* continues to exist even when the partners are apart. Also at about age 4, the child's internal model of attachment appears to generalize. Bowlby argued that the child's model becomes less a specific property of an individual relationship and more a general property of all the child's social relationships. Thus, it's not surprising that 4- and 5-year-olds who are securely attached to their parents are more likely than their insecurely attached peers to have positive relationships with their preschool teachers (DeMulder et al., 2000).

At the same time, advances in the internal working model lead to new conflicts. In contrast to infants, 2-year-olds realize that they are independent contributors to the parent-child relationship. This heightened sense of autonomy brings them into more and more situations in which parents want one thing and children another. However, contrary to popular stereotypes, 2-year-olds actually comply with parents' requests more often than not. They are more likely to comply with safety requests ("Don't touch that, it's hot!") or with prohibitions about care of objects ("Don't tear up the book") than they are with requests to delay ("I can't talk to you now, I'm on the phone") or with instructions about self-care ("Please wash your hands now"). On the whole, however, children of this age comply fairly readily (Gralinski & Kopp, 1993). When they resist, it is most likely to be passive resistance—simply not doing what is asked rather than saying "no."

Parenting Styles

LO 8.9 How do parenting styles affect children's development?

Earlier we discussed the fact that differences in temperament lead children to respond differently to situations. Parents differ in temperament themselves, so, just like their children, they vary in how they respond to situations. Consider, for example, the situation in which a child resists going to bed. One parent takes the nightly going-to-bed battle in stride and calmly insists that the child go to bed even when she throws a temper tantrum. Another parent responds to the child's emotional escalation by increasing the emotional intensity of his demands, leading to all-out warfare in which the parent assures his own victory by exploiting the physical, social, and emotional control he has over the child. Yet another parent may respond permissively and allow the child to go to bed whenever she wants to. Researchers call these differences **parenting styles**, or the characteristic strategies that parents use to manage children's behavior.

Of course, families vary in their responses to preschoolers' increasing demands for independence. Psychologists have struggled over the years to identify the best ways of defining parenting style. At present, the most fruitful conceptualization is one offered by developmentalist Diana Baumrind, who focuses on four aspects of family functioning: (1) warmth or nurturance; (2) clarity and consistency of rules; (3) level of expectations, which she describes in terms of "maturity demands"; and (4) communication between parent and child (Baumrind, 1972; 2013).

Each of these four dimensions has been independently shown to be related to various child behaviors. Children with nurturing and warm parents are more securely attached in the first 2 years of life than those with more rejecting parents; they also have higher self-esteem and are more empathetic, more altruistic, and more responsive to others' pain or distress; they have higher IQs, are more compliant in preschool and elementary school, do better in school, and are less likely to show delinquent behavior in adolescence or criminal behavior in adulthood (Keown, 2012; Maccoby, 1980; Maughan, Pickles, & Quinton, 1995; Simons, Robertson, & Downs, 1989; Stormshak et al., 2000).

High levels of affection can even buffer a child against the negative effects of otherwise disadvantageous environments. Several studies of children and teens growing up in poor, tough neighborhoods show that parental warmth is associated with both social and academic competence (Masten & Coatsworth, 1998; Odgers et al., 2012). In contrast, parental hostility is linked to declining school performance and higher risk of delinquency among poor children and adolescents (Melby & Conger, 1996).

The degree and clarity of the parents' control over the child are also significant. Parents with clear rules, consistently applied, have children who are much less likely to be defiant or noncompliant. Such children are also more competent and sure of themselves and less aggressive (Kurdek & Fine, 1994; Patterson, 1980).

parenting styles the characteristic strategies that parents use to manage children's behavior

Equally important is the form of control the parents use (Barber & Xia, 2013). The most optimal outcomes for a child occur when the parents are not overly restrictive, explain things to the child, and avoid the use of physical punishments. Children whose parents have high expectations (high "maturity demands," in Baumrind's language) also fare better. Such children have higher self-esteem and show more generosity and altruism toward others.

Finally, open and regular communication between parent and child has been linked to more positive outcomes. Listening to a child is as important as talking to him. Ideally, parents need to convey to a child that what the child has to say is worth listening to, that his ideas are important and should be considered in family decisions. Children of such parents have been found to be more emotionally and socially mature (Baumrind, 1971, 2013; Bell & Bell, 1982).

While each of these characteristics of families may be significant individually, they do not occur in isolation but in combinations and patterns. In her early research, Baumrind identified three patterns, or styles, of parenting (Baumrind, 1967, 2013). The **permissive parenting style** is high in nurturance but low in maturity demands, control, and communication. The **authoritarian parenting style** is high in control and maturity demands but low in nurturance and communication. The **authoritative parenting style** is high in all four dimensions.

Eleanor Maccoby and John Martin proposed a variation of Baumrind's category system (Maccoby & Martin, 1983). They categorize families on two dimensions: the degree of demand or control and the amount of acceptance versus rejection. The intersection of these two dimensions creates four types, three of which correspond to Baumrind's authoritarian, authoritative, and permissive types. Maccoby and Martin's conceptualization adds a fourth type, the **uninvolved parenting style**. 👁 **Watch** the **Video** *Parenting Styles* in **MyPsychLab**.

THE AUTHORITARIAN TYPE A parent who responds to a child's refusal to go to bed by asserting physical, social, and emotional control over the child is exhibiting the authoritarian style. Children growing up in authoritarian families—with high levels of demand and control but relatively low levels of warmth and communication—do less well in school, have lower self-esteem, and are typically less skilled with peers than are children from other types of families. Some of these children appear subdued; others may show high aggressiveness or other indications of being out of control. These effects are not restricted to preschool-aged children. In a series of large studies of high school students, including longitudinal studies of more than 6,000 teens, developmentalists found that teenagers from authoritarian families had poorer grades in school and more negative self-concepts than did teenagers from authoritative families, a finding that has been replicated in more recent cohorts of teens (Steinberg, Blatt-Eisengart, & Cauffman, 2006; Steinberg, Fletcher, & Darling, 1994).

THE PERMISSIVE TYPE The permissive type of parent responds to a child's refusal to go to bed by allowing the child to go to bed whenever she wants to. Children growing up with indulgent or permissive parents also show some negative outcomes. Researchers have found that these children do slightly worse in school during adolescence and are likely to be both more aggressive (particularly if the parents are specifically permissive toward aggressiveness) and somewhat immature in their behavior with peers and in school. They are less likely to take responsibility and are less independent.

THE AUTHORITATIVE TYPE Authoritative parents respond to undesirable behaviors such as a child's refusal to go to bed by firmly sticking to their demands without resorting to asserting their power over the child. The most consistently positive outcomes have been associated with an authoritative pattern in which the parents are high in both control and acceptance—setting clear limits but also responding to the child's individual needs. Children reared in such families typically show higher self-esteem and are more independent, and they are also more likely to comply with parental requests and may show more altruistic behavior as well. They are self-confident and achievement oriented in school and get better grades than do children

permissive parenting style a style of parenting that is high in nurturance and low in maturity demands, control, and communication

authoritarian parenting style a style of parenting that is low in nurturance and communication, but high in control and maturity demands

authoritative parenting style a style of parenting that is high in nurturance, maturity demands, control, and communication

uninvolved parenting style a style of parenting that is low in nurturance, maturity demands, control, and communication

inductive discipline a discipline strategy in which parents explain to children why a punished behavior is wrong

whose parents have other parenting styles (Crockenberg & Litman, 1990; Dornbusch, Ritter, Liederman, Roberts, & Fraleigh, 1987; Steinberg, Elmen, & Mounts, 1989).

THE UNINVOLVED TYPE Uninvolved parents do not bother to set bedtimes for children or even to tell them to go to bed. They appear to be totally indifferent to children's behavior and to the responsibilities of parenting. The most consistently negative outcomes are associated with the fourth pattern—the uninvolved, or neglecting, parenting style. You may remember from the discussion of secure and insecure attachments in Chapter 6 that a family characteristic often found in infants rated as insecure/avoidant is the "psychological unavailability" of the mother. The mother may be depressed or may be overwhelmed by other problems in her life and may simply not have made any deep emotional connection with the child. Likewise, a parent may be distracted from parenting by more attractive activities. Whatever the reason, such children continue to show disturbances in their social relationships for many years. In adolescence, for example, youngsters from neglecting families are more impulsive and antisocial, less competent with their peers, and much less achievement oriented in school (Block, 1971; Lamborn, Mounts, Steinberg, & Dornbusch, 1991; Pulkkinen, 1982).

EFFECTS OF PARENTING STYLES As we mentioned earlier, children of authoritative parents tend to get higher grades than children who are being raised by parents who exhibit other styles (Steinberg et al., 1994). Moreover, in a longitudinal analysis, researchers found that students who described their parents as most authoritative at the beginning of the study showed more improvement in academic competence and self-reliance and the smallest increases in psychological symptoms and delinquent behavior over the succeeding 2 years (Steinberg et al., 1994). So these effects persist.

The effects of the family system, however, are more complex than the figure shows. For example, authoritative parents are much more likely to be involved with their child's school, attending school functions and talking to teachers, and this involvement seems to play a crucial role in their children's better school performance. When an authoritative parent is not involved with the school, the academic outcome for the student is not so clearly positive. Similarly, a teenager whose parent is highly involved with the school but is not authoritative shows a less optimal outcome. It is the combination of authoritativeness and school involvement that is associated with the best results (Steinberg, Lamborn, Dornbusch, & Darling, 1992).

Another set of complexities is evident in the interaction between parenting style and child temperament (Eisenberg, Chang, Ma, & Huang, 2009). For example, authoritative parents often use **inductive discipline**, a discipline strategy in which parents explain to children why a punished behavior is wrong and typically refrain from physical punishment (Choe, Olson, & Sameroff, 2013; Hoffman, 1970). Inductive discipline helps most preschoolers gain control of their behavior and learn to look at situations from perspectives other than their own. Likewise, the majority of preschool-aged children of parents who respond to demonstrations of poor self-control, such as temper tantrums, by asserting their social and physical power—as often happens when parents physically punish children—have poorer self-control than preschoolers whose parents use inductive discipline (Houck & Lecuyer-Maus, 2004; Kochanska, 1997b; Kochanska, Murray, Jacques, Koenig, & Vandegeest, 1996). For this and other reasons, most developmentalists are opposed to physical punishment, as discussed in the *Developmental Science at Home* feature on page 195.

However, research on inductive discipline suggests that it is not equally effective for all children. Those who have difficult temperaments or who are physically active and who seem to enjoy risk taking—such as children who like to climb on top of furniture and jump off—seem to have a greater need for firm discipline and to benefit less from inductive discipline than do their peers whose temperamental makeup is different (Kochanska, 1997a). In fact, assumptions about the superiority of inductive discipline, as well as authoritative parenting in general, have been criticized by developmentalists who claim that correlations between discipline strategy and child behavior may arise simply because parents adapt their techniques to their children's behavior. Thus, parents of poorly behaved children may be more

To Spank or Not to Spank?

Marie is at her wits' end as to what to do about her 4-year-old daughter's whining. "What that child needs is a good spanking," Marie's grandmother declared one afternoon while the three were out shopping. Before she had children, Marie thought that she would never consider spanking them, but she now finds herself wondering whether her grandmother is right. Is Marie right to be reluctant to spank her daughter?

In the short term, spanking usually does get the child to stop an undesirable behavior and temporarily reduces the likelihood that the child will repeat it (Gershoff, 2002). In the long term, however, the effects of spanking are clearly negative, although modestly so (Ferguson, 2013). Research indicates that spanking (1) models infliction of pain as a means of getting someone to do what you want them to do, (2) associates the parent who spanks with the child's experience of physical pain, (3) leads to a family climate that is characterized by emotional rejection, and (4) is associated with higher levels of aggression among children who are spanked than among those who are not. Moreover, some

children appear to be especially vulnerable to these effects. For example, spanking combines with genetic factors such as a difficult temperament to significantly increase a child's risk of developing disruptive behavior disorders (Barnes, Boutwell, Beaver, & Gibson, 2013).

For these reasons, developmentalists recommend that spanking, if it is used at all, be reserved for behaviors that are potentially harmful to the child or others (Namka, 2002). In addition, spanking, like other forms of punishment, should always be accompanied by an explanation of why the child was punished and an assurance that she is loved. Finally, experts agree that physical punishment should never under any circumstances be used to discipline children younger than 2 years of age (DYG Inc., 2004).

Thinking back to the question we posed at the outset of this discussion, we must conclude that Marie's reservations about spanking her daughter are on target. Moreover, although Marie's grandmother recommended spanking, she probably told her own children, "If you don't

stop whining, I won't let you watch TV" before she started searching for a paddle. Unbeknown to her, Marie's grandmother, like generations of parents before her, was using an everyday variation of a behavior management technique that psychologists call the Premack principle, named after researcher David Premack, who demonstrated its effectiveness in a classic series of studies with primates and children (Premack, 1959). Thus, parents who employ the Premack principle instead of resorting to spanking can be assured of the support of grandmothers and psychologists alike.

REFLECTION

1. *Look back at the operant-conditioning principle of extinction in Chapter 1. How might it be used to diminish Marie's daughter's whining?*

2. *In what ways does having been spanked as a child influence an adult's views about the acceptability of spanking as a form of discipline?*

punitive or authoritarian because they have discovered that this is the kind of parenting their children need.

Ethnicity, Socioeconomic Status, and Parenting Styles

LO 8.10 How are ethnicity and socioeconomic status related to parenting styles?

Ethnicity and socioeconomic variables interact with parenting styles, although authoritative parenting is associated with positive developmental outcomes across all groups (Sorkhabi & Mandara, 2013). In a classic, large-scale, cross-sectional study involving roughly 10,000 9th-through 12th-grade students representing four ethnic groups (White, African American, Hispanic, and Asian), students answered questions about the acceptance, control, and autonomy they received from their parents (Steinberg, Mounts, Lamborn, & Dornbusch, 1991). When an adolescent described his family as above the average on all three dimensions, the family was classed as authoritative.

The authoritative pattern was most common among White families and least common among Asian Americans, but in each ethnic group, authoritative parenting was more common among middle class and two-parent families than among single-parent or step-parent families. Furthermore, these researchers found relationships between authoritative parenting and positive outcomes in all ethnic groups. In all four groups, for example, teenagers from authoritative families showed more self-reliance and less delinquency than did those from nonauthoritative families. However, this study also found links between authoritarian style and variables such as school performance and social competence.

Studies in which children provide information about their parents' style as well as those in which researchers conduct direct observation of parents have consistently found that, in general, Asian American parents display a more authoritarian style than those in other ethnic groups (Chao, 1994; Wang & Phinney, 1998). The finding that Asian American children score higher than their White counterparts on almost all measures of cognitive competence argues against the assumption that authoritative parenting is best. In fact, developmentalists have found a link between Asian American children's achievement and authoritarian parenting—that is, parents who have the most authoritarian parenting style have the highest-scoring children (Wang & Phinney, 1998). Likewise, longitudinal research suggests that authoritarian parenting reduces the risk of child abuse in African American single-parent families (Valentino, Nuttall, Comas, Borkowski, & Akai 2012). Similarly, authoritarian parenting has been shown to reduce the likelihood of substance abuse in both White and African American children (Broman, Reckase, & Freedman-Doan, 2006).

However, the key variable in these findings may not be ethnicity. Many studies have shown that parenting styles are grounded in parenting goals (e.g., Cheay & Rubin, 2004). Parenting goals are influenced by cultural values and by the immediate context in which parents are raising children (Choi, Kim, Kim, & Park, 2013; Valentino et al., 2012). Consequently, it's important to know that many Asian American participants in studies comparing their parenting behaviors to those of European Americans have been recent immigrants to the United States. Thus, Asian American parents may be authoritarian in response to living in an environment that is different from the one in which they grew up, not because they are Asian. Authoritarian parenting may help them achieve two important goals: to help their children succeed economically and to enable them to maintain a sense of ethnic identity. Evidence supporting this interpretation also comes from studies of families who have emigrated to Israel, Canada, France, and Norway (Camilleri & Malewska-Peyre, 1997; Chuang & Su, 2009; Javo, Ronning, Heyerdahl, & Rudmin, 2004; Roer-Strier & Rivlis, 1998).

The same link between parenting goals and parenting style may help explain the greater incidence of authoritarian behavior on the part of African American parents. Specifically, African American parents are keenly aware of the degree to which social forces such as racism may impede their children's achievement of educational, economic, and social success. Consequently, they may adopt an authoritarian style because they believe it will enhance their children's potential for success. In fact, the correlation between authoritarian parenting and variables such as self-control among African American children suggests that they may be right (Baumrind, 1980; Broman et al., 2006).

Another reason that authoritarian parenting may be more common in African American families is that they are more likely to be poor. As we noted earlier, authoritative parenting is generally less common among poor parents than among middle-class parents in all four major U.S. ethnic groups. It seems likely that the reason for this pattern is similar to the one mentioned above for African Americans—that is, poor parents believe authoritarian parenting will help their children attain important goals.

Family Structure

LO 8.11 How is family structure related to children's development?

Despite increases in the number of single-parent households, the two-parent family continues to be the dominant structure in the United States. In 1970, almost 95% of children lived in such families. By contrast, in 2010, only 70% of children were living in two-parent homes (U.S. Census Bureau, 2012). Moreover, the proportion of single-parent families in the United States far exceeds that in other industrialized countries, as you can see in Figure 8.4 on page 197 (Organisation for Economic Co-operation and Development, 2010).

DIVERSITY IN TWO-PARENT AND SINGLE-PARENT FAMILIES The two-parent family, though still the most common living arrangement for children in the United States, is far more diverse than in the past (Kreider, 2008). Just over 60% of all children in the United States live with both their biological or adoptive parents who are married. Another 3% live with their cohabiting biological or adoptive parents. About 7% live in two-parent households

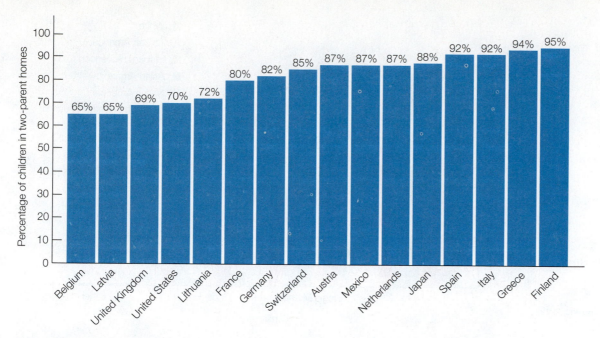

Figure 8.4 Two-Parent Families around the World

Children in the United States are less likely than children in many other industrialized nations to live in two-parent homes.

(*Source:* Organisation for Economic Co-operation and Development, 2010.)

that were created when a divorced, never-married, or widowed single biological or adoptive parent married another single parent or a nonparent. Thus, many children in two-parent households have experienced single-parenting at one time or another while growing up.

However, it's important to keep in mind that any set of statistics is like a snapshot of a single moment in time; it fails to capture the number of changes in family structure many children experience across their early years. For example, about 2% of children live in homes in which the "parents" are actually the child's grandparents (Kreider, 2008). In most cases, custodial grandparents are caring for the children of an adult child who has some kind of significant problem such as criminal behavior or substance abuse (Smith & Palmieri, 2007). These children are likely to have experienced a variety of living arrangements before coming to live with their grandparents.

Single-parent households are diverse as well. In contrast to stereotypes, some single parents are very financially secure. Surveys show that, while poverty rates are higher among single-parent families, about 8% of single-parent households in the United States have incomes in excess of $100,000 (U.S. Census Bureau, 2010a). Moreover, unmarried teenaged parents are likely to live with their own parents (Bowden & Greenberg, 2010). Consequently, single-parent households are no more alike than are two-parent households.

FAMILY STRUCTURE AND ETHNICITY Looking at family structure across ethnic groups further illustrates family diversity in the United States. You can get some feeling for the degree of variation from Figure 8.5. The figure graphs estimates of the percentages of three family types among White, African American, Asian American, Native American, and Hispanic American children in the United States.

Some "two-parent" households in the United States are actually those in which a child is being raised by her grandparents.

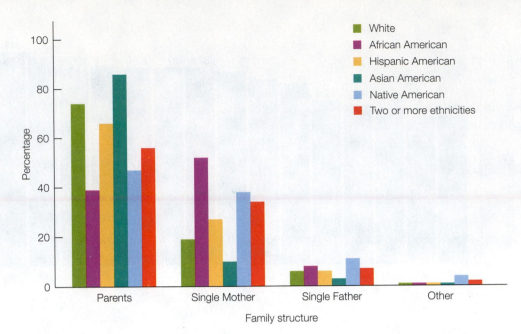

Figure 8.5 Ethnicity and Family Structure

Household types for U.S. children under 18 years of age.

(*Source:* Aud & Fox, 2010; U.S. Census Bureau, 2012.)

You can see that single-parent families are far more common among African Americans and Native Americans than among other groups (see Figure 8.6). A difference in the proportion of births to unmarried women is one contributing factor. Births to single women have increased rather dramatically across all racial and ethnic groups in the United States in the past few decades. However, the rates of such births are much higher among African American and Native American women than in other groups. (By the way, in all groups, more than three-quarters of single women giving birth are over the age of 20. Thus, teenage pregnancy contributes very little to the statistics on single motherhood.)

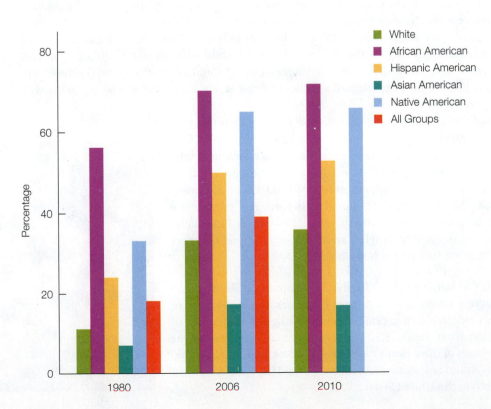

Figure 8.6 Ethnicity and Births to Unmarried Women

Percentage of births to unmarried women across racial/ethnic groups in the United States. The rate of births to unmarried women has increased across all groups in the United States over recent decades. These statistics are one reason for the growing number of school-aged and teenaged children who live in single-parent homes.

(*Source:* National Center for Health Statistics [NCHS], 2010; Martin et al., 2012.)

A second factor is that, although many African American and Native American single mothers eventually marry, adults in these groups—whether parents or not—are less likely to marry (Goodwin & Mosher, 2010; U.S. Census Bureau, 2007). For instance, among middle-aged adults (40–44 years of age), 12% of Asian Americans, 14% of Whites, and 16% of Hispanic Americans have never married (Goodwin & Mosher, 2010). By contrast, 30% of African American 40- to 44-year-olds have never married. Comparable statistics are not available for middle-aged Native Americans. However, surveys of adults from 15 to 44 years of age show that, within this very broad age range, 24% of Whites, 26% of Asian Americans, and 32% of Hispanic Americans have never married, compared to 41% and 35% of African Americans and Native Americans, respectively (Goodwin & Mosher, 2010; U.S. Census Bureau, 2007).

Most gay and lesbian parents are raising children who were conceived in prior heterosexual relationships. However, a growing number of couples are choosing to be parents through artificial insemination or adoption. Research suggests that the variables that contribute to effective parenting and positive developmental outcomes for children are the same, regardless of the sexual orientation of a child's parents.

Of course, statistics can't explain why African American and Native American families are more likely than families of other groups to be headed by single parents. Sociologists speculate that, in the case of African Americans, lack of economic opportunities for men renders them less able to take on family responsibilities (Cherlin, 1992). Others add that grandparents and other relatives in both groups traditionally help support single mothers. For instance, among Native Americans, a traditional cultural value sociologists call *kin orientation* views parenting as the responsibility of a child's entire family, including grandparents and aunts and uncles. As a result, Native American single parents, especially those who live in predominantly Native American communities, receive more material and emotional support than do single parents in other groups and may feel less pressure to marry (Ambert, 2001).

OTHER TYPES OF FAMILY STRUCTURES In contrast to the amount of research comparing two-parent and single-parent families, there are relatively few studies of the effects of other kinds of family structures. For example, research on custodial grandparenting tends to focus on the effects of the parenting experience on aging adults. Consequently, researchers know that grandparents' responses to children's problems are quite similar to those of parents (Daly & Glenwick, 2000). However, the stresses of parenting combined with the physical effects of aging are likely to cause older adults to feel more anxious and depressed than younger adults in similar situations (Burton, 1992; Jendrek, 1993). Some have suggested that rates of behavior problems are higher among children who are living with custodial grandparents. However, researchers point out that such children are often in the care of their grandparents due to a series of traumatic events that have disrupted their own families (Smith & Palmieri, 2007). These events can include abuse of the children. Thus, developmentalists know very little about how children raised by grandparents fare in the absence of such confounding factors.

Similarly, concerns about children's sex-role identity and sexual orientation have dominated research on gay and lesbian parenting. Studies have generally shown that children raised by gay and lesbian parents develop sex-role identities and sexual orientations in the same way as children of heterosexual parents (Golombok & Tasker, 1996). However, some studies suggest that they may be less sure about their future sexual orientation than children in families headed by heterosexual couples (e.g., Bos & Sandfort, 2010).

More comprehensive studies have attempted to answer general questions about cognitive and social development among the adopted children of gay and lesbian parents. Others have focused on developmental outcomes of children that gay and lesbian parents conceived in heterosexual relationships or through assisted reproductive technologies. In general, such studies have found that children raised by gay and lesbian parents do not differ from those raised by heterosexual parents (Chan, Raboy, & Patterson, 1998; Fitzgerald, 1999; Gartrell & Bos, 2010; Goldberg & Smith, 2013; Patterson, 2006).

Divorce

LO 8.12 How does divorce affect children's behavior in early childhood and in later years?

There can be little doubt that divorce is traumatic for children. It's important to note, however, that some of the negative effects of divorce are due to factors that were present *before* the divorce, such as difficult temperament in the child or excessive marital conflict between the parents (Cherlin, Chase-Lansdale, & McRae, 1998). It's also important to keep in mind that divorce is not a single variable; children are probably affected by a multitude of divorce-related factors—parental conflict, poverty, disruptions of daily routine, involvement of the noncustodial parent, and so on (Bailey & Zvonkovic, 2003; Wallerstein, Lewis, & Packer Rosenthal, 2013).

In the first few years after a divorce, children typically exhibit declines in school performance and show more aggressive, defiant, negative, or depressed behavior (Greene, Krcmar, Rubin, Walters, & Hale, 2002). By adolescence, the children of divorced parents are more likely than their peers to engage in criminal behavior (Price & Kunz, 2003; Wallerstein et al., 2013). Children living in step-parent families also have higher rates of delinquency, more behavior problems in school, and lower grades than do those in intact families (Jeynes, 2006).

The negative effects of divorce seem to persist for many years (Wallerstein et al., 2013). For example, children whose parents divorce have a higher risk of mental health problems in adulthood (Chase-Lansdale, Cherlin, & Kiernan, 1995; Cherlin et al., 1998; Wallerstein & Lewis, 1998). Many young adults whose parents are divorced lack the financial resources and emotional support necessary to succeed in college, and a majority report that they struggle with fears of intimacy in relationships (Cartwright, 2006). Not surprisingly, adults whose parents divorced are themselves more likely to divorce.

As a general rule, these negative effects are more pronounced for boys than for girls. However, some researchers have found that the effects are delayed in girls, making it more difficult to associate the effects with the divorce. Consequently, longitudinal studies often find that girls show equal or even greater negative effects (Amato, 1993; Hetherington, 1991a, 1991b). Age differences in the severity of the reaction have been found in some studies but not others. For example, one longitudinal study found that the effects of divorce were most severe in a group of 12-year-olds who experienced parental divorce in early childhood rather than during their school years (Pagani, Boulerice, Tremblay, & Vitaro, 1997).

Ethnicity, incidentally, does not appear to be a causal factor here. Yes, a larger percentage of African American children grow up in single-parent families. But the same negative outcomes occur in White single-parent families, and the same positive outcomes are found in two-parent non-white families. For example, the school dropout rate for White children from single-parent

Many single parents manage to overcome substantial obstacles to give their children the support and supervision they need.

families is higher than the dropout rate for Hispanic or African American children reared in two-parent families (McLanahan & Sandefur, 1994).

Understanding the Effects of Family Structure and Divorce

LO 8.13 What are some possible reasons for the relationship between family structure and development?

The broadest statement psychologists can make about the effects of family structure is that, at least in the United States, research suggests that the optimum situation for children appears to be one that includes two natural parents (Lamb & Lewis, 2010). Never-married mothers, divorced mothers or fathers who have not remarried, and step-parents are frequently linked to less positive outcomes. Factors associated with single-parenthood, such as poverty, may help explain its negative effects on development. Still, the differences between children who never experience single-parenting and those who do are too large to be completely explained by other variables. This means that at least part of the difference is connected to the family structure itself. Thus, it's important to know just what the differences are.

Children growing up in single-parent families are about twice as likely to drop out of high school, twice as likely to have a child before age 20, and less likely to have a steady job in their late teens or early 20s (Child Trends Data Bank, 2013). Children of adolescent mothers are particularly at risk. Differences between children of teenagers and those whose mothers are older are evident in early childhood. Preschoolers whose mothers are single teenagers display less advanced cognitive and social development than their peers (Coley & Chase-Lansdale, 1998).

How are we to understand these various findings? First, single parenthood or divorce reduces the financial and emotional resources available to support the child. With only one parent, the household typically has only one income and only one adult to respond to the child's emotional

---

NO EASY ANSWERS

When Divorce Is Unavoidable

Most parents know that divorce is traumatic for children and do their best to avoid it. However, as we all know, in some situations there is no alternative. In such cases, parents often turn to counselors and psychologists for advice on how to prevent the negative effects of divorce. As with so many other important challenges, in helping a child overcome the trauma of divorce, there is not a simple—or even complex—formula parents can follow.

It's important for divorcing parents to realize that they cannot eliminate all the short-term disruptive effects of this event on children. However, there are some specific things they can do to soften or lessen the effects:

- Try to keep the number of separate changes the child has to cope with to a minimum. If at all possible, keep the children in the same school or day-care setting and in the same house or apartment.
- If the children are teenagers, consider having each child live with the parent of the same gender. The data are not totally consistent, but it looks as if this may be a less stressful arrangement (Pickhardt, 2009).

- The custodial parent should help children stay in touch with the noncustodial parent. Likewise, the noncustodial parent should maintain as much contact as possible with the children, calling and seeing them regularly, attending school functions, and so on.
- Keep the open conflict to a minimum. Most of all, try not to fight in front of the children. Open conflict has negative effects on children, whether the parents are divorced or not (Boyan & Termini, 2005). Thus, divorce is not the only culprit; divorce combined with open conflict between the adults has worse effects.
- Do not use the children as go-betweens or talk disparagingly about the ex-spouse to them. Children who feel caught in the middle between the two parents are more likely to show various kinds of negative symptoms, such as depression or behavior problems (Buchanan, Maccoby, & Dornbusch, 1991).
- Do not expect the children to provide emotional support. Parents should maintain their own network of support and use that network liberally. They should stay in touch with

friends, seek out others in the same situation, and join a support group.

In the midst of the emotional upheaval that accompanies divorce, these prescriptions are not easy to follow. However, if divorcing parents are able to do so, their children will probably suffer less.

YOU DECIDE

Decide which of these two statements you most agree with and think about how you would defend your position:

1. *Given that divorce is traumatic for children, courts should require parents with children who want to divorce to go through counseling aimed at determining whether reconciliation is possible.*

2. *Courts should not require parents with children who want to divorce to go through counseling aimed at determining whether reconciliation is possible, because a conflict-ridden marriage may be just as harmful to children as divorce is.*

extended family a social network of grandparents, aunts, uncles, cousins, and so on

needs. Data from the United States indicate that a woman's income drops an average of 40–50% after a divorce (Bradbury & Katz, 2002; Smock, 1993).

Second, any family transition involves upheaval. Both adults and children adapt slowly and with difficulty to subtraction from or addition of new adults to the family system (Hetherington & Stanley-Hagan, 1995). The period of maximum disruption appears to last several years, during which the parents often find it difficult to monitor their children and maintain control over them.

Perhaps most importantly, single-parenthood, divorce, and step-parenthood all increase the likelihood that the family climate or style will shift away from authoritative parenting (Wallerstein et al., 2013). This shift is not uncommon in the first few years after a divorce, when the custodial parent (usually the mother) is distracted or depressed and less able to manage warm control; it occurs in step-families as well, where rates of authoritative parenting are lower than in intact families.

Remember, authoritarian or neglecting parenting is linked to poor outcomes whether it is triggered by a divorce, a stressful remarriage, the father's loss of a job, or any other stress (Goldberg, 1990). Ultimately, it is the parenting style, rather than any particular type of disruption, that is significant for the child (see *No Easy Answers*). Many families also construct a social network called an **extended family**, a family structure that includes parents, grandparents, aunts, uncles, cousins, and so on. Extended families seem to serve a protective function for children who are growing up in single-parent homes (Wilson, 1995). Grandmothers, for example, appear to be important sources of emotional warmth for the children of teenaged mothers (Coley & Chase-Lansdale, 1998). And, as mentioned earlier, extended family members often help single and divorced mothers with financial and emotional support as well as with child care. In the United States, such networks are more common among minorities than among Whites (Harrison, Wilson, Pine, Chan, & Buriel, 1990).

test yourself before going on ☑ **Study** and **Review** in **MyPsychLab**

Answers to these questions can be found in the back of the book.

1. List the changes in attachment relationships that the text associates with each age in the table below:

Age	Change in Attachment Relationship
2–3	
4	

2. Define each parenting style and summarize its effects on development:

Style	Definition	Effects on Development
Authoritarian		
Permissive		
Authoritative		
Uninvolved		

3. Among what groups is authoritarian parenting associated with positive effects on children's development?

4. There are few studies of children raised by _____ and _____ _____.

5. Divorce increases the likelihood that the family climate will shift away from _____ _____.

6. The _____ _____ serves a protective function for children growing up in single-parent homes.

CRITICAL THINKING

7. In what ways do you think parenting styles and family structure interact to affect development? For instance, might there be differences in how authoritarian parenting influences children in two-parent versus single-parent families?

Peer Relationships

What is the first thought that springs to mind when you think about 2- to 6-year-olds? Perhaps it is the phenomenon of play. Certainly, people of all ages enjoy playing, although they obviously define it differently, but in the early childhood period, playing is the predominant form of behavior. In the context of play, children learn the skills they need to relate to others, and they learn that relationships have both negative and positive aspects.

Relating to Peers through Play

LO 8.14 What are the various kinds of play exhibited by preschoolers?

social skills a set of behaviors that usually lead to being accepted as a play partner or friend by peers

In Chapter 7, you learned about the cognitive aspects of play. But what about the social features of children's play activities? The social dimensions of play were outlined in a classic observational study conducted by Mildred Parten (1932). If you observe young children who are engaged in free play, you will see that Parten's stages of play continue to be useful today.

At every age, children are likely to spend at least some of their time playing alone—a pattern known as *solitary play*. They may also exhibit *onlooker play*, a pattern in which they watch another child playing. However, children first begin to show some positive interest in playing with others as early as 6 months of age. If you place two babies that age on the floor facing each other, they will look at each other, touch, pull each other's hair, imitate each other's actions, and smile at each other. ⊙ **Watch** the **Video** *Play in Early Childhood* in **MyPsychLab**.

By 14–18 months, two or more children play together with toys—sometimes cooperating, but more often simply playing side by side with different toys. Developmentalists refer to this as *parallel play*. Toddlers this age express interest in one another and gaze at or make noises at one another. However, it isn't until around 18 months that children engage in *associative play*. In associative play, toddlers pursue their own activities but also engage in spontaneous, though short-lived, social interactions. For example, one toddler may put down a toy to spend a few minutes chasing another, or one may imitate another's action with a toy.

By 3 or 4, children begin to engage in *cooperative play*, a pattern in which several children work together to accomplish a goal. Cooperative play can be either constructive or symbolic. A group of children may cooperate to build a city out of blocks, or they may assign roles such as "mommy," "daddy," and "baby" to one another to play house.

As you learned in Chapter 7, play is related to cognitive development. Play is also related to the development of **social skills**, a set of behaviors that usually lead to being accepted as a play partner or friend by others. For example, many researchers have focused on the social skill of *group entry*. Children who are skilled in group entry spend time observing others to find out what they're doing and then try to become a part of it. Children who have poor group-entry skills try to gain acceptance through aggressive behavior or by interrupting the group. Developmentalists have found that children with poor group-entry skills are often rejected by peers (Fantuzzo, Coolahan, & Mendez, 1998). Peer rejection, in turn, is an important factor in future social development.

Because of the risks associated with poor social skills, developmentalists have turned their attention to social-skills training as a preventive measure. One important finding is that social skills training improves children's ability to regulate emotions (Calkins & Mackler, 2011). Thus, interventions that help children better manage their feelings and understand those of their peers may improve their social skills. Improving children's communication skills can also help. In one intervention study, socially withdrawn 4- and 5-year-olds were taught specific verbal phrases to use when trying to gain acceptance by a group of peers (Doctoroff, 1997). In addition, their socially accepted peers were taught to remind the trained children to use their new skills. For the most part, social-skills interventions like this one lead to immediate gains in social acceptance. However, the degree to which early childhood social-skills training can prevent later social difficulties is unknown at present.

Aggression

LO 8.15 What types of aggression do children display during early childhood?

Suppose you were the parent of two boys, a 4-year-old and a 6-year-old, and saw them laughing with delight while they were wrestling. What do you think might happen? You might remember a sequence of events like this one from your own childhood: First, one child "accidentally" punches the other too hard. Next, the victim's nascent sense of justice dictates that he respond in kind. Soon what started out as fun escalates into a full-blown fight.

Developmentalists distinguish between true aggression (intentional harm) and the accidental injuries that often occur during normal rough-and-tumble play.

TABLE 8.2 Changes in the Form and Frequency of Aggression from Age 2 to Age 8

	2- to 4-Year-Olds	4- to 8-Year-Olds
Physical aggression	At its peak	Declines
Verbal aggression	Relatively rare at 2; increases as child's verbal skills improve	Dominant form of aggression
Goal of aggression	Mostly instrumental	Mostly hostile
Occasion for aggression	Most often after conflicts with parents	Most often after conflicts with peers

(*Sources:* Cummings, Hollenbeck, Iannotti, Radke-Yarrow, & Zahn-Waxler, 1986; Goodenough, 1931; Hartup, 1974.)

Interactions of this kind are common in the early childhood period and even into the early adolescent years. **Aggression** is defined as behavior that is intended to injure another person or damage an object. The emphasis on intentionality helps separate true aggression from rough-and-tumble play in which children sometimes accidentally hurt one another. Every young child shows at least some aggressive behavior, but the form and frequency of aggression change over the preschool years, as you can see in the summary in Table 8.2. ◉ **Watch** the **Video** *Rough and Tumble Play* in **MyPsychLab**.

When 2- or 3-year-old children are upset or frustrated, they are most likely to throw things or hit each other. As their verbal skills improve, however, they shift away from such overt physical aggression toward greater use of verbal aggression, such as taunting or name calling, just as their defiance of their parents shifts from physical to verbal strategies.

The decline in physical aggression over these years also undoubtedly reflects the preschooler's declining egocentrism and increasing understanding of other children's thoughts and feelings. Yet another factor in the decline of physical aggression is the emergence of *dominance hierarchies*. As early as age 3 or 4, groups of children arrange themselves in well-understood *pecking orders* of leaders and followers (Strayer, 1980). They know who will win a fight and who will lose one, which children they dare attack and which ones they must submit to—knowledge that serves to reduce the actual amount of physical aggression.

A second change in the quality of aggression during the preschool years is a shift from *instrumental aggression* to *hostile aggression*. **Instrumental aggression** is aimed at gaining or damaging some object; the purpose of **hostile aggression** is to hurt another person or gain an advantage. Thus, when 3-year-old Sarah pushes aside her playmate Lucetta in the sandbox and grabs Lucetta's bucket, she is showing instrumental aggression. When Lucetta in turn gets angry at Sarah and calls her a dummy, she is displaying hostile aggression.

Psychologists have suggested several key factors in aggressive behavior. For example, one early group of American psychologists argued that aggression was always preceded by frustration, and that frustration was always followed by aggression (Dollard, Doob, Miller, Mowrer, & Sears, 1939). The frustration-aggression hypothesis turned out to be too broadly stated; not all frustration leads to aggression, but frustration does make aggression more likely. Toddlers and preschoolers are often frustrated—because they cannot always do what they want and because they cannot express their needs clearly—and they often express that frustration through aggression. As a child acquires greater ability to communicate, plan, and organize her activities, her frustration level declines, and overt aggression drops.

Other developmentalists argue that reinforcement and modeling are important. For instance, when Sarah pushes Lucetta away and grabs her toy, Sarah is reinforced for her aggression because she gets the toy. This straightforward effect of reinforcement clearly plays a vital role in children's development of aggressive patterns of behavior. Moreover, when parents give in to their young child's tantrums or aggression, they are reinforcing the very behavior they deplore, and they thereby help to establish a long-lasting pattern of aggression and defiance.

Modeling, too, plays a key role in children's learning of aggressive behaviors. In a classic series of studies, psychologist Albert Bandura found that children learn specific forms of aggression, such as hitting, by watching other people perform them (Bandura, Ross, & Ross, 1961, 1963). Clearly, entertainment media offer children many opportunities to observe aggressive behavior, but real-life

aggression behavior intended to harm another person or an object

instrumental aggression aggression used to gain or damage an object

hostile aggression aggression used to hurt another person or gain an advantage

aggressive models may be more influential. For example, children learn that aggression is an acceptable way of solving problems by watching their parents, siblings, and others behave aggressively. Indeed, parents who consistently use physical punishment have children who are more aggressive than those of parents who do not model aggression in this way (Stacks, Oshio, Gerard, & Roe, 2009). It should not be surprising that when children have many different aggressive models, especially if those aggressive models appear to be rewarded for their aggression, they learn aggressive behavior.

Whatever the cause, most children become less aggressive during the preschool years. There are a few children, however, whose aggressive behavior pattern in early childhood becomes quite literally a way of life, a finding that has been supported by cross-cultural research (Hart, Olsen, Robinson, & Mandleco, 1997; Henry, Caspi, Moffitt, & Silva, 1996; Newman, Caspi, Moffitt, & Silva, 1997; Röll, Koglin, & Petermann, 2012). Researchers have searched for causes of this kind of aggression, which some psychologists refer to as *trait aggression*, to distinguish it from developmentally normal forms of aggression.

Psychologists looking for a genetic basis for trait aggression have produced some supportive data (Hudziak et al., 2003; van Beijsterveldt, Bartels, Hudziak, & Boomsma, 2003; Yaman, Mesman, van IJzendoorn, & Bakermans-Kranenburg, 2010). Others suggest that trait aggression is associated with being raised in an aggressive environment, such as an abusive family (Dodge, 1993). Family factors other than abuse, such as lack of affection and the use of coercive discipline techniques, also appear to be related to trait aggression, especially in boys (Campbell, Spieker, Vandergrift, Belsky, & Burchinal, 2010; Chang, Schwartz, Dodge, & McBride-Chang, 2003). Young children's capacity for regulating their emotions also predicts aggressive behavior later in childhood (Röll, et al., 2012).

Still other developmentalists have discovered evidence that aggressive children may shape their environments in order to gain continuing reinforcement for their behavior. For example, aggressive boys as young as 4 years old tend to prefer other aggressive boys as playmates and to form stable peer groups. Boys in these groups develop their own patterns of interaction and reward each other with social approval for aggressive acts (Farver, 1996). This pattern of association among aggressive boys continues through middle childhood and adolescence.

Finally, social-cognitivists have produced a large body of research suggesting that highly aggressive children lag behind their peers in understanding others' intentions (Crick & Dodge, 1994; Meece & Mize, 2010). Research demonstrating that teaching aggressive children how to think about others' intentions reduces aggressive behavior also supports this conclusion (Crick & Dodge, 1996; Webster-Stratton & Reid, 2003). Specifically, these studies suggest that aggressive school-aged children seem to reason more like 2- to 3-year-olds about intentions. For example, they are likely to perceive a playground incident (say, one child accidentally tripping another during a soccer game) as an intentional act that requires retaliation. Training, which also includes anger-management techniques, helps aggressive school-aged children acquire an understanding of others' intentions that most children learn between the ages of 3 and 5.

Similar results have been obtained in studies examining aggressive children's ability to engage in other kinds of social reasoning (Harvey, Fletcher, & French, 2001). However, developmentalists have found that, like their reasoning about intentions, aggressive children's social reasoning can be improved with training. In one study, for example, researchers successfully used videotapes of children engaging in rough-and-tumble play to teach aggressive children how to recognize the difference between "play fighting" and aggressive acts that can cause physical pain (Smith, Smees, & Pellegrini, 2004). Thus, trait aggression may originate in some kind of deviation from the typical social-cognitive developmental path during the early childhood period, and it may be reduced with interventions aimed at returning children to that path.

Prosocial Behavior and Friendships

LO 8.16 How do prosocial behavior and friendship patterns change during early childhood?

At the other end of the spectrum of peer relationships is a set of behaviors psychologists call **prosocial behavior**. Like aggression, prosocial behavior is intentional and voluntary, but its purpose is to help another person in some way (Eisenberg, 1992). In everyday

prosocial behavior behavior intended to help another person language, such behavior is called *altruism*, and it changes with age, as do other aspects of peer behavior.

DEVELOPMENT OF PROSOCIAL BEHAVIOR Altruistic behaviors first become evident in children of about 2 or 3—at about the same time as real interest in playing with other children arises. They will offer to help another child who is hurt, share a toy, or try to comfort another person (Tomasello, 2009). As you read in Chapter 7, children this young are only beginning to understand that others feel differently than they do—but they obviously understand enough about the emotions of others to respond in supportive and sympathetic ways when they see other children or adults hurt or sad.

Beyond these early years, changes in prosocial behavior show a mixed pattern. Some kinds of prosocial behavior, such as taking turns, seem to increase with age. If you give children an opportunity to donate some treat to another child who is described as needy, older children donate more than younger children do. Helpfulness, too, seems to increase with age, through adolescence. But not all prosocial behaviors show this pattern. Comforting another child, for example, seems to be more common among preschoolers and children in early elementary grades than among older children (Eisenberg, 2004).

Children vary a lot in the amount of altruistic behavior they show, and young children who show relatively more empathy and altruism are also those who regulate their own emotions well. They show positive emotions readily and negative emotions less often and are also more popular with peers (Eisenberg, Fabes, & Spinrad 2006). These variations among childrens' levels of empathy or altruism seem to be related to specific kinds of child-rearing. In addition, longitudinal studies indicate that children who display higher levels of prosocial behavior in the preschool years continue to demonstrate higher levels of such behavior in adulthood (Eisenberg et al., 2014).

Prosocial behaviors, such as sharing, are influenced by cognitive development and by the deliberate efforts of parents and teachers to teach children to behave in such ways.

PARENTAL AND CULTURAL INFLUENCES ON PROSOCIAL BEHAVIOR Research suggests that parental behavior contributes to the development of prosocial behavior (Eisenberg, 2004). Specifically, parents of altruistic children create a loving and warm family climate. If such warmth is combined with clear explanations and rules about what to do as well as what not to do, the children are even more likely to behave altruistically. Such parents also often explain the consequences of the child's action in terms of its effects on others—for example, "If you hit Susan, it will hurt her." Stating rules or guidelines positively rather than negatively also appears to be important; for example, "It's always good to be helpful to other people" is more effective guidance than "Don't be so selfish!"

Providing prosocial *attributions*—positive statements about the underlying cause for helpful behavior—also helps. For example, a parent might praise a child by saying "You're such a helpful child!" or "You certainly do a lot of nice things for other people." Having heard such statements often during early childhood helps children incorporate them into their self-concepts later in childhood. In this way, parents may help create a generalized, internalized pattern of altruistic behavior in the child.

Parents of altruistic children also look for opportunities for them to do helpful things. For example, they allow children to help cook, take care of pets, make toys to give away, teach younger siblings, and so forth. Finally, parental modeling of thoughtful and generous behavior—that is, parents demonstrating consistency between what they say and what they do—is another contributing factor.

FRIENDSHIPS Beginning at about 18 months, a few toddlers show early hints of playmate preferences or individual friendships (Howes, 1983, 1987). However, by age 3, about 20% of children have a stable playmate. By 4, more than half spend 30% or more of their time with one other child

(Hinde, Titmus, Easton, & Tamplin, 1985). Thus, one important change in social behavior during early childhood is the formation of stable friendships (Hay, Payne, & Chadwick, 2004).

To be sure, these early peer interactions are still quite primitive. However, it is noteworthy that preschool friend pairs nonetheless show more mutual liking, more reciprocity, more extended interactions, more positive and less negative behavior, and more supportiveness in a novel situation than do nonfriend pairs at this same age—all signs that these relationships are more than merely passing fancies. Moreover, having had a friend in early childhood is related to social competence (Rubin, Coplan Chen, Bowker, & McDonald, 2011; Sebanc, 2003).

test yourself before going on ☑ Study and Review in MyPsychLab

Answers to these questions can be found in the back of the book.

1. Two children are building separate block structures without interacting. They are engaging in _____ play.

2. Which type of aggression is more common between the ages of 2 and 4—instrumental or hostile—and in what ways do preschoolers display it?

3. Define *prosocial behavior* and explain how it changes in early childhood.

4. At what age does each of these milestones in the development of friendship happen?
   _____(1) More than half of children spend 30% of their time with one peer.
   _____(2) Most children show hints of playmate preferences.
   _____(3) About 20% of children have a stable playmate.

CRITICAL THINKING

5. Do you think that peer relationships are necessary to social development in early childhood? That is, do you think that young children who have no exposure to children other than their own siblings are just as likely to emerge from early childhood with adequate social skills as those who have opportunities to interact with peers?

SUMMARY

Theories of Social and Personality Development (pp. 180–183)

LO 8.1 What major themes of development did the psychoanalytic theorists propose for the early childhood period?

- Freud and Erikson each described two stages of personality development during the preschool years: the anal and phallic stages in Freud's theory and the stages in which autonomy and initiative are developed in Erikson's theory. Both theories, but especially Freud's, place primary importance on the parent–child relationship. More recent psychoanalytic approaches emphasize the importance of relationships with peers and siblings.

LO 8.2 What are the findings of social-cognitive theorists with respect to young children's understanding of the social world?

- Social-cognitive theorists assert that advances in social and personality development are associated with cognitive development. Three topics of interest to such theorists are person perception, understanding of others' intentions, and understanding of different kinds of rules.

Personality and Self-Concept (pp. 183–186)

LO 8.3 How does temperament change in early childhood?

- During early childhood, children's temperaments are modified by social experiences both within and outside the family to form their personalities.

LO 8.4 What changes take place in a young child's categorical, emotional, and social selves during the preschool years?

- The preschooler continues to define himself along a series of objective dimensions but does not yet have a global sense of self. Children make major strides in self-control and in their understanding of their own social roles in the preschool years, as parents gradually turn over the job of control to the child.

Gender Development (pp. 186–191)

LO 8.5 How do the major theoretical orientations explain gender development?

- Freud's explanation of gender development has not received much support from researchers. Social-learning explanations are more persuasive but ignore the role of cognitive development.

Cognitive-developmental theory claims that gender development depends on children's understanding of the gender concept and that the latter develops in three stages. Between ages 2 and 6, most children move through a series of steps in their understanding of gender constancy: first labeling their own and others' gender, then understanding the stability of gender, and finally comprehending the constancy of gender at about age 5 or 6. Gender schema theory claims that children organize ideas about gender using a mental framework (schema) that they construct as soon as they can reliably label themselves and others as male and female.

LO 8.6   What are the characteristics of young children's sex-role knowledge?

- At about age 2, children begin to learn what is appropriate behavior for their gender. By age 5 or 6, most children have developed fairly rigid rules about what boys or girls are supposed to do and be.

LO 8.7   How is the behavior of young children sex-typed?

- Children display sex-typed behavior as early as 18–24 months of age. Some theorists think children play in gender-segregated groups because same-sex peers help them learn about sex-appropriate behavior.

Family Relationships and Structure (pp. 191–202)

LO 8.8   How does attachment change during the early childhood years?

- The young child's attachment to the parent(s) remains strong, but except in stressful situations, attachment behaviors become less visible as the child gets older. Preschoolers refuse or defy parental influence attempts more than infants do. Outright defiance, however, declines from age 2 to age 6. Both these changes are clearly linked to the child's language and cognitive gains.

LO 8.9   How do parenting styles affect children's development?

- Authoritative parenting, which combines warmth, clear rules, and communication with high maturity demands, is associated with the most positive outcomes for children. Authoritarian parenting has some negative effects on development. However, permissive and uninvolved parenting seem to be the least positive styles.

LO 8.10   How are ethnicity and socioeconomic status related to parenting style?

- Ethnicity and socioeconomic class are linked to parenting style. Asian American and African American parents are more authoritarian than those in other ethnic groups, and poor parents in all ethnic groups tend to be authoritarian. Studies of parenting style and developmental outcomes in ethnic groups suggest that, in some situations, authoritative parenting may not be the best style.

LO 8.11   How is family structure related to children's development?

- Family structure affects early childhood social and personality development. Data from U.S. studies suggest that any family structure other than one that includes two biological parents is linked to more negative outcomes.

LO 8.12   How does divorce affect children's behavior in early childhood and in later years?

- Following a divorce, children typically show disrupted behavior for several years. Parenting styles also change, becoming less authoritative. However, many effects of divorce on children are associated with problems that existed before the marriage ended.

LO 8.13   What are some possible reasons for the relationship between family structure and development?

- To understand the influence of family structure on development, a number of variables, such as poverty, associated with differences in family structure must be taken into account. However, these variables alone are insufficient to explain differences in children that are correlated with variations in family makeup.

Peer Relationships (pp. 202–207)

LO 8.14   What are the various kinds of play exhibited by preschoolers?

- Play with peers is evident before age 2 and becomes increasingly important through the preschool years. At every age, children spend some time in solitary play and may exhibit onlooker play, a pattern in which they watch another child play. By 14–18 months, children engage in parallel play, playing alongside each other but not interacting. At 18 months, associative play—play that includes some interaction—is apparent. By 3 or 4, children begin to engage in cooperative play, in which they work together to accomplish a goal.

LO 8.15   What types of aggression do children display during early childhood?

- Physical aggression toward peers increases and then declines during these years, while verbal aggression increases among older preschoolers. A shift from instrumental aggression, which is goal oriented, to hostile aggression, which aims to hurt others or gain an advantage over them, is also apparent. Some children display trait aggression, a pattern of aggressive behavior that continues to cause problems for them throughout childhood and adolescence.

LO 8.16   How do prosocial behavior and friendship patterns change during early childhood?

- Children as young as 2 show prosocial behavior toward others, and this behavior seems to become more common as the child's ability to take another's perspective increases. Stable friendships develop between children in this age range.

KEY TERMS

aggression (p. 204)

authoritarian parenting style (p. 193)

authoritative parenting style (p. 193)

cross-gender behavior (p. 190)

emotional regulation (p. 184)

empathy (p. 185)

extended family (p. 202)

gender (p. 186)

gender constancy (p. 187)

gender identity (p. 187)

gender schema theory (p. 187)

gender stability (p. 187)

hostile aggression (p. 204)

inductive discipline (p. 194)

instrumental aggression (p. 204)

parenting styles (p. 192)

permissive parenting style (p. 193)

person perception (p. 181)

prosocial behavior (p. 205)

sex-typed behavior (p. 189)

social-cognitive theory (p. 181)

social skills (p. 203)

uninvolved parenting style (p. 193)

CHAPTER TEST   ✅ Study and Review in MyPsychLab

Answers to all the Chapter Test questions can be found in the back of the book.

1. In a study of how ethnicity and socioeconomic status interact with parenting styles, researchers found that which parenting style was linked to positive outcomes for most adolescents?
   a. uninvolved
   b. authoritative
   c. authoritarian
   d. permissive

2. If Leila is in Kohlberg's gender stability stage, which of the following will she likely *not* understand?
   a. categorization of children as "boys" and "girls"
   b. that she will still be a girl even if she wears boys' clothing
   c. that she will grow up to be a woman
   d. categorization of toys and activities as "for girls" or "for boys"

3. According to Eleanor Maccoby, girls use a(n) _____ communication style that usually involves giving suggestions, expressing support, and seeking agreement with others?
   a. sex-typed
   b. enabling
   c. facilitating
   d. constricting

4. Six-year-old Bettina asks her mother if she can stay up until 9 p.m. on Friday night to watch a special educational TV program. Her mother says, "Your bedtime is 8:00, and rules are rules. Get ready for bed immediately or you'll have to be grounded to your room all day tomorrow." What is Bettina's mother's parenting style?
   a. authoritarian
   b. authoritative
   c. punishing
   d. neglectful

5. Which of the following is an example of a social convention?
   a. laws against murder
   b. faithfulness to marriage vows
   c. walking on the right side of a crowded hallway
   d. refraining from using the Internet for personal reasons at work

6. Which of the following does the text cite as a possible reason that immigrant families use an authoritarian parenting style with their children?
   a. They believe that authoritarian parenting will help children succeed and attain important goals.
   b. They value children less than non-immigrant families do.
   c. Authoritarian parenting is consistent with most immigrants' cultural beliefs.
   d. Immigrant families do not want their children to assimilate to the majority culture.

7. The parenting style that is high in nurturance and high in maturity demands, control, and communication is the _____ style.
   a. permissive
   b. authoritarian
   c. authoritative
   d. uninvolved

8. According to the text, preschoolers who are securely attached to their parents _____.
   a. do not develop an emotional self until age 5 or 6
   b. are less likely to develop gender stereotypes than children who are insecurely attached
   c. have little interest in playing with peers
   d. have positive relationships with teachers

9. According to the text, impulse control develops as a result of _____.
   a. attainment of Kohlberg's gender-constancy stage
   b. advances in cognitive development
   c. social interactions
   d. allowing children to express their individuality

10. Which of the following is *not* a descriptive characteristic of highly aggressive preschoolers?
    a. They prefer nonaggressive playmates whom they can bully.
    b. They are less able to understand others' intentions than nonaggressive children are.
    c. Most form stable peer groups.
    d. They develop social reasoning skills more slowly than their peers do.

11. Authoritarian and authoritative parents would vary most widely on which of the following dimensions of parenting?
    a. control and demands
    b. commitment to parenting goals
    c. attachment security
    d. acceptance

12. Which of the following is a central theme of Erikson's view of development during the preschool period?
   a. Families must balance their children's emerging skills and desire for autonomy with their parental need to protect and control their children.
   b. Language, cognition, and motor skills are developmentally intertwined, and one aspect of development supports other aspects of development.
   c. Children's sexual development is triggered by social and emotional interactions with peers.
   d. The basis for children's social and personality development is their cognitive development.

13. When 4-year-old Deidra acts in a way that is harmful to others, her parents attempt to get her to look at her actions from the other person's point of view in addition to punishing her. Deidra's parents use _____.
   a. a permissive parenting style
   b. inductive discipline
   c. positive reinforcement
   d. Freud's approach to understanding young children

14. Erikson asserted that young children must develop which of the following traits?
   a. impulse control and gender roles that are consistent with biological sex
   b. control of elimination and identification with same-sex parent
   c. an enabling communication style with parents and a restrictive style with peers
   d. autonomy and initiative

15. According to Freud, a preschool child's development is centered on _____.
   a. renegotiation of parental relationships
   b. increased autonomy
   c. the desire for peer acceptance
   d. improved social skills

16. Cross-cultural studies have found similar gender stereotypes across cultures. Which of the following is *not* a common gender stereotype for men?
   a. coarseness   c. warmth
   b. strength   d. assertiveness

17. Your text compares the concept of gender constancy to which of the following?
   a. Vygotsky's principle of scaffolding
   b. Erikson's principle of identity
   c. Freud's principle of egocentrism
   d. Piaget's principle of conservation

18. The children of gay and lesbian parents _____.
   a. have not been studied as much as children of heterosexual parents have
   b. do not develop sex-typed behavior
   c. are more cognitively advanced than their peers
   d. are likely to be homosexual in adulthood

19. Which of these variables is *not* associated with parenting style?
   a. ethnicity
   b. socioeconomic status
   c. immigration status
   d. sexual orientation

20. Which parenting style is associated with poor impulse control in children?
   a. permissive   c. authoritative
   b. authoritarian   d. uninvolved

21. Which statement about young children's preference for same-sex playmates is true?
   a. Boys' preference for male playmates can be changed through modeling and reinforcement.
   b. Girls express a stronger preference for same-sex playmates than boys do.
   c. The preference for same-sex companions appears very early in life.
   d. Children of parents who encourage cross-gender play are unlikely to prefer same-sex playmates.

22. Which of the following is *not* a component of a 4-year-old girl's negotiation of Erikson's initiative versus guilt crisis?
   a. newly emerging cognitive skills
   b. saying "no" to parental requests and commands
   c. concern for socially acceptable ways of accomplishing goals
   d. balancing her desires with the demands of her conscience

23. Professor Mbatu is studying 5-year-old children's ability to remember faces. According to the text, the children in his study are likely to remember _____.
   a. angry faces more frequently than happy ones
   b. faces of people in their own ethnic groups more frequently than those in other groups
   c. female faces more frequently than male faces
   d. children's faces more frequently than adults' faces

24. Will's mother and father think that making sure that children know they are loved is the most important goal of parenting. Their way of ensuring that this happens is to give Will pretty much whatever he asks for and constantly tell him that they love him. If Will gets in trouble at preschool, which happens often, his parents characterize the incident as a "personality conflict" with the teacher. They do not discuss it with Will or punish him in any way. Which parenting style would you say best describes Will's parents?
   a. permissive   c. authoritarian
   b. authoritative   d. uninvolved

25. Which theory of gender role development is based on information-processing theory?
   a. cognitive-developmental theory
   b. observational learning theory
   c. psychosexual theory
   d. gender schema theory

To 👁 **Watch** ❇ **Explore** ⊙→ **Simulate** ✓ **Study** and **Review** and experience MyVirtualLife go to MyPsychLab.com

chapter 9

Physical and Cognitive Development in Middle Childhood

The first day of school is viewed as one of the most important transition points in a child's life. In the United States, parents mark the occasion in a variety of ways—with new clothes, fresh school supplies, and carefully selected backpacks and lunch boxes. Some families take pictures of their children's first ride on the school bus or first classroom. All of these ways of recognizing this important milestone say to children that this day is unique, and they begin to think of themselves as "big kids" who are engaged in the serious

LEARNING OBJECTIVES

PHYSICAL CHANGES

9.1 What kinds of physical changes occur during middle childhood?

9.2 In what ways does the brain change during these years?

9.3 What are the three most important health hazards for 6- to 12-year-olds?

COGNITIVE CHANGES

9.4 How do vocabulary and other aspects of language change during middle childhood?

9.5 What cognitive advantages do children gain as they move through Piaget's concrete operational stage?

9.6 What is *horizontal decalage*, and how does Siegler explain concrete operational thinking?

9.7 How do children's information-processing skills improve during middle childhood?

SCHOOLING

9.8 What should be included in an effective literacy curriculum?

9.9 How do bilingual and ESL approaches to second-language instruction differ?

9.10 Why do schools administer achievement tests, and what kinds of items do they include?

9.11 What kinds of group differences in achievement have educational researchers found?

CHILDREN WITH SPECIAL NEEDS

9.12 Why is the term *learning disability* controversial?

9.13 How does attention-deficit/hyperactivity disorder affect a child's development?

business of going to school rather than "little kids" who spend most of their time playing.

Throughout the industrialized world, as well as in most developing areas, the years between 6 and 12 are devoted to formal education. This universal practice is shaped by the everyday observation that the physical and intellectual skills that formal learning requires begin to blossom around age 6 or 7, a characteristic that you probably notice in the "child" you are raising in *MyVirtualLife*. Furthermore, formal instruction provides children with learning experiences that both build on and expand their physical and cognitive abilities.

Physical Changes

Imagine a foot race between a 6-year-old and a 12-year-old. Although there certainly could be exceptions to this generalization, the odds definitely favor the older child. In all likelihood, the 12-year-old will not only surpass the 6-year-old in speed but also display greater strength, agility, and endurance. Such differences arise from a host of hidden, qualitative changes that take place in the major systems of children's bodies between the ages of 6 and 12. Likewise, cognitive contests that involve children at either age of this age range, such as a game of checkers, also bear witness to the qualitative changes in the brain that occur across these years. As you will see, these changes underlie improvements in both motor and cognitive skills.

Growth and Motor Development

LO 9.1   What kinds of physical changes occur during middle childhood?

Each year between ages 6 and 12, children grow 2 to 3 inches and add about 6 pounds. Large-muscle coordination continues to improve, and children become increasingly adept at skills like bike riding; both strength and speed also increase. Hand–eye coordination improves as well (Gabbard, 2012). As a result, school-aged children perform more skillfully in activities requiring coordination of vision with body movements, such as shooting a basketball or playing a musical instrument. ◉ **Watch** the **Video** *Physical Fitness in the Grade School Years* in **MyPsychLab**.

Perhaps even more significant is the school-aged child's improving fine-motor coordination. Improvements in fine-motor coordination enable writing as well as playing most musical instruments, drawing, cutting, and many other tasks and activities. Such accomplished uses of the hands are made possible by maturation of the wrist, which occurs more rapidly in girls than in boys (Tanner, 1990).

Girls in this age range are ahead of boys in their overall rate of growth as well. By 12, girls have attained about 94% of their adult height, while boys have reached only 84% of theirs (Tanner, 1990). Girls also have slightly more body fat and slightly less muscle tissue than boys. Sex differences in skeletal and muscular maturation cause girls to be better coordinated but slower and somewhat weaker than boys. Thus, girls outperform boys in activities requiring coordinated movement, and boys do better when strength and speed are advantages. Still, the overall sex differences in joint maturation, strength, and speed are small at this age.

The Brain and Nervous System

LO 9.2   In what ways does the brain change during these years?

Two major growth spurts happen in the brain during middle childhood (Spreen, Risser, & Edgell, 1995). In most healthy children, the first takes place between ages 6 and 8 and the second between ages 10 and 12. Both spurts involve development of new synapses as well as increases in the thickness of the cerebral cortex.

When school-aged boys and girls participate in co-ed sports, boys' superior speed and strength are offset by girls' advantage in coordination.

The primary sites of brain growth during the first spurt are the sensory and motor areas. Growth in these areas may be linked to the striking improvements in fine-motor skills and eye–hand coordination that usually occur between 6 and 8. During the second spurt of brain growth, the frontal lobes of the cerebral cortex become the focus of developmental processes (van der Molen & Molenaar, 1994). Predictably, the areas of the brain that govern logic and planning, two cognitive functions that improve dramatically during this period, are located primarily in the frontal lobes.

Myelination, which you learned about in Chapter 2, also continues through middle childhood. Of particular importance is the continued myelination of the frontal lobes, the reticular formation, and the nerves that link the reticular formation to the frontal lobes (Sowell et al., 2003). These connections are essential if the child is to be able to take full advantage of improvements in frontal lobe functions because, as you may recall, the reticular formation controls attention. It is well documented that the ability to control attention increases significantly during middle childhood (Wetzel, Widman, Berti, & Schröger, 2006).

Maturation of both the frontal lobes and the reticular formation work together so that 6- to 12-year-olds are able to develop a particular kind of concentration called *selective attention* (Aharon-Peretz & Tomer, 2007). **Selective attention** is the ability to focus cognitive activity on the important elements of a problem or situation. As you can probably guess, the development of selective attention is important to children's performance in school (Campos, Almeida, Ferreira, Martinez, & Ramalho, 2013). For example, suppose your psychology instructor, who usually copies tests on white paper, gives you a test printed on blue paper. You won't spend a lot of time thinking about why the test is blue instead of white; this is an irrelevant detail. Instead, your selective attention skills will prompt you to ignore the color of the paper and focus on the test questions. In contrast, some younger elementary school children might be so distracted by the unusual color of the test paper that their test performance would be affected. As the nerves connecting the reticular formation and the frontal lobes become more fully myelinated between ages 6 and 12, children begin to function more like adults in the presence of such distractions.

The neurons of the **association areas**—parts of the brain where sensory, motor, and intellectual functions are linked—are myelinated to some degree by the time children enter middle childhood. From 6 to 12, however, the nerve cells in these areas achieve nearly complete myelination. Neuroscientists believe that this advance contributes to increases in information-processing speed (Dockstader, Gaetz, Rockel, & Mabbott, 2012). For example, suppose you were to ask a 6-year-old and a 12-year-old to identify pictures of common items—a bicycle, an apple, a desk, a dog—as rapidly as possible. Both children would know the items' names, but the 12-year-old would be able to produce the names much more rapidly than the 6-year-old. Such increases in processing speed probably contribute to improvements in memory function, which you'll read about later in the chapter (Kail, 1990, 2008; Li, Lindenberger, Aschersleben, Prinz, & Baltes, 2004).

Another important advance in middle childhood occurs in the right cerebral hemisphere, with the lateralization of **spatial perception,** the ability to identify and act on relationships between objects in space. For example, when you imagine how a room would look with a different arrangement of furniture, you are using spatial perception. Perception of objects such as faces actually lateralizes before age 6. However, complex spatial perception, such as map reading, isn't strongly lateralized until about age 8.

A behavioral test of the lateralization of spatial perception often used by neuroscientists involves **relative right–left orientation,** the ability to identify right and left from multiple perspectives. Such a test usually shows that most children younger than 8 know the difference between their own right and left. Typically, though, only children older than 8 understand the difference between statements like "It's on *your* right" and "It's on *my* right." Lateralization of spatial perception may also be related to the increased efficiency with which older children learn math concepts and problem-solving strategies. In addition, it is somewhat correlated to performance on Piaget's conservation tasks (van der Molen & Molenaar, 1994).

However, the development of spatial perception is more than just a physiological process. Developmentalists know this, because this function lateralizes much more slowly in children who are blind. Thus, it appears that visual experience plays an important role in this aspect of brain development.

selective attention the ability to focus cognitive activity on the important elements of a problem or situation

association areas parts of the brain where sensory, motor, and intellectual functions are linked

spatial perception the ability to identify and act on relationships between objects in space

relative right–left orientation the ability to identify right and left from multiple perspectives

Myelination - process of forming a myelin sheath around a nerve to allow nerve impulses to move more quickly

spatial cognition the ability to infer rules from and make predictions about the movement of objects in space

traumatic brain injury (TBI) an injury to the head that results in diminished brain function such as a loss of consciousness, confusion, or drowsiness

asthma a chronic lung disease, characterized by sudden, potentially fatal attacks of breathing difficulty

excessive weight gain a pattern in which children gain more weight in a year than is appropriate for their age and height

Furthermore, some researchers propose that differences in visual experiences explain sex differences in spatial perception and the related function of **spatial cognition**, the ability to infer rules from and make predictions about the movement of objects in space. For example, when you are driving on a two-lane road and you make a judgment about whether you have enough room to pass a car ahead of you, you are using spatial cognition. From an early age, boys score much higher than girls, on average, on such spatial tasks (Casey, 2013). Some researchers suggest that boys' play preferences, such as their greater interest in constructive activities like building with blocks, help them develop more acute spatial perception and cognition.

Health and Wellness

LO 9.3   What are the three most important health hazards for 6- to 12-year-olds?

Generally speaking, most school-aged children are very healthy. However, they continue to benefit from regular medical care, and there are a few serious health concerns for this age group.

INJURIES As children become more active, participate in sports, and venture farther from home during middle childhood, their rates of various types of accidental injuries change. For instance, injuries due to falls are more common among 5- to 9-year-olds than they are among 10- to 14-year-olds. By contrast, 10- to 14-year-olds visit hospital emergency rooms seeking treatment for activity-related overexertion and for injuries resulting from bicycle accidents more frequently than those in the 5- to 9-year-old group do (Borse et al., 2008).

Bicycle accidents account for about a quarter of all cases of **traumatic brain injury (TBI)**, an injury to the head that results in diminished brain function such as a loss of consciousness, confusion, or drowsiness, among school-aged children (Dawodu, 2013). Most children who experience TBI recover fully (Lewis, 2011). Still, health professionals have been active over the past several years in informing the public about the effectiveness of helmets in preventing bicycle-related TBI and TBI-related death in children (Wesson et al., 2008). As a result, many jurisdictions have enacted laws requiring that children wear helmets when bicycling. Research indicates that such laws reduce death rates due to bicycle accidents by 50% or more among children (Wesson et al., 2008).

ASTHMA The most frequent cause of school absence for 6- to 12-year-olds is **asthma**, a chronic lung disease in which individuals experience sudden, potentially fatal attacks of breathing difficulty. According to health officials, about 9% of school-aged children and teens in the United States have been diagnosed with asthma (Lasley & Hetherington, 2011). The disease typically appears between ages 5 and 7 and is believed to be caused by hypersensitivity to allergens and environmental irritants such as dust, animal hair, and tobacco smoke. When a child who has asthma encounters these irritants, her bronchial tube linings become inflamed. In response, large amounts of mucus are produced, the airways become blocked, and the child has to gasp for air.

Doctors use a "step" approach to treating asthma, in which education and reduction of allergens and irritants in children's environments are the first lines of defense against the disease (Lasley & Hetherington, 2011). If these measures fail to control asthma symptoms, physicians move the child to the next step, which involves daily medication. However, the medicines used can have detrimental effects on children's cognitive development (Naude & Pretorius, 2003). For this reason, most health professionals who treat asthma try to avoid using daily medication (Lasley & Hetherington, 2011); they want to be certain that parents and children have fully complied with lower-level treatment before moving to more intense approaches.

As children grow and their lung capacity increases, asthma attacks decrease in both intensity and frequency (Overby, 2002). However, about half of children with asthma continue to experience symptoms throughout their lives.

EXCESSIVE WEIGHT GAIN In recent years, parents, health-care professionals, and others who are concerned about children's development have become increasingly aware of the fact that **excessive weight gain is the** most serious long-term health risk of the middle childhood period. Excessive weight gain is a pattern in which children gain more weight in a year than is appropriate for their height, age, and sex. If a child gains excessive amounts of weight over a number of years, she is at risk of having weight problems and a number of serious health problems in adulthood.

To simplify the process of determining whether an individual child's weight gain is appropriate, health-care professionals use a measure called **BMI-for-age**, a variation on the *body mass index* (*BMI*) that applies to adults (which we will discuss in Chapter 15). The BMI estimates a person's proportion of body fat (NCHS, 2000). A child's BMI-for-age is determined by calculating her BMI and comparing it to others her age. Age-based comparisons are needed because, in healthy children, the BMI itself naturally increases with age as the ratios of fat and muscle change. Moreover, different standards are needed for boys and girls, because their BMIs do not increase at the same rate. Children whose BMIs fall at the 95th percentile (the top 5%) on the Centers for Disease Control and Prevention (CDC) BMI-for-age growth charts are considered **obese**. Those whose BMIs are above the 99th percentile are classified as **severely obese**. Children with BMIs between the 85th and 95th percentiles are classified as **overweight**. However, because of growth spurts and the inherent instability of physical variables in childhood, multiple assessments are required before any of these classifications is applied to an individual child. Nevertheless, experts on childhood obesity warn against delaying diagnosis of obesity due to the serious risks it carries for children's development (Krebs & Primak, 2011). Consequently, researchers suggest that additional education about the physical, psychosocial, and cognitive risks associated with childhood obesity is needed for both the general public and health-care professionals (see Table 9.1).

As you can see in Figure 9.1, the prevalence of obesity among children in the United States has grown at an alarming rate over the past five decades, although the trend may be leveling off. Currently, almost 1 in 5 children between the ages of 6 and 11 is obese (Fryar, Carroll, & Ogden, 2012). Among children and teens with obesity, about 4% are severely obese, a rate that has tripled since the 1970s and that has increased by 70% since the 1990s (Skelton, Cook, Auinger, Klein, & Barlow, 2009). Similar increases have been documented in every country in the world that tracks the prevalence of overweight among children (Wang & Lobstein, 2006).

The older a child gets without stopping the pattern of excessive weight gain, the more likely the child is to be obese into the adult years (Krebs & Primak, 2011). Research shows that a child who is still obese at the end of the middle childhood period is twice as likely to be obese in adulthood as a child who is obese at the beginning of this period (Krebs & Primak, 2011). In addition, more than half of children with obesity have one or more risk factors, such as elevated levels of cholesterol or high blood pressure, that predispose them to heart disease later in life (Reinehr & Toschke, 2009).

As you might suspect, overeating or eating too much of the wrong foods causes excessive weight gain in children, just as it does in adults (Krebs & Primak, 2011). However, both twin and adoption studies suggest that obesity probably results from an interaction between a genetic predisposition for obesity and environmental factors that promote overeating or low levels of activity (Stunkard, Harris, Pedersen, & McClearn, 1990). Whatever the genetic contribution might be, research suggests that a cultural pattern of decreases in physical activity and increases in the consumption of high-calorie convenience foods has led to the current epidemic of overweight children and adults (Arluk, Swain, & Dowling, 2003; Hood & Ellison, 2003; Taveras, Gillman, Kleinman, Rich-Edwards, & Rifas-Shiman, 2010; Vandewater, Shim, & Caplovitz, 2004).

BMI-for-age comparison of an individual child's BMI against established norms for his or her age group and sex

obese a child whose BMI-for-age is at or above the 95th percentile

severely obese a child whose BMI-for-age is at or above the 99th percentile

overweight a child whose BMI-for-age is between the 85th and 95th percentiles

TABLE 9.1   Risks Associated with Childhood Obesity

Domain	Complication
Physical	Early puberty, sleep disorders, cardiovascular damage, joint problems, diabetes
Social/Personality	Peer discrimination, teasing, social isolation
Cognitive	Reduced rates of college attendance

(*Source:* Krebs & Primak, 2011.)

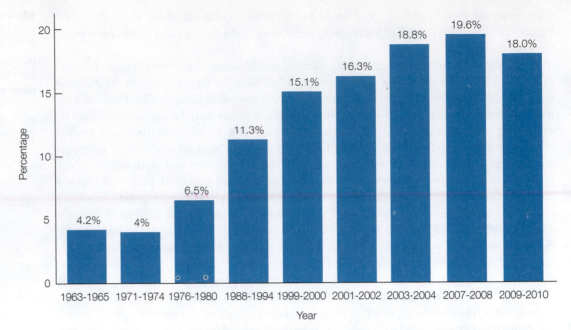

Figure 9.1 Prevalence of Obesity among 6- to 11-Year-Olds in the United States

The prevalence of obesity (BMI > 95th percentile) has increased dramatically in the United States over the past 50 years.

(*Source:* NCHS, 2007; Fryar, Carroll, & Ogden, 2012.)

It's important to keep in mind, though, that weight-loss diets for children can be fairly risky. Because children are still growing, the nutritional needs of overweight and obese children differ from those of adults with weight problems (Krebs & Primak, 2011). Consequently, children with obesity require special diets developed and supervised by nutritional experts (Krebs & Primak, 2011). Moreover, increasing the amount of exercise children get is just as important as changing their eating habits. Experts on weight management in childhood recommend that parents of overweight and at-risk children take the following steps (CDC, 2007c):

- Provide plenty of vegetables, fruits, and whole-grain products
- Include low-fat or nonfat milk or other dairy products
- Choose lean meats, poultry, fish, lentils, and beans for protein
- Serve reasonably sized portions
- Encourage everyone in the family to drink lots of water
- Limit sugar-sweetened vegetables
- Limit consumption of sugar and saturated fat
- Limit children's TV, video game, and computer time
- Involve the whole family in physical activities such as walking and bicycling

Media messages can help to raise public awareness about childhood obesity. Programs such as *Jamie Oliver's Food Revolution* educate children about good nutrition.

Answers to these questions can be found in the back of the book.

1. List four attention and perceptual skills that are associated with brain maturation during middle childhood.

   (a) _____

   (b) _____

   (c) _____

   (d) _____

2. In what order would a physician take these three steps in treating a child with asthma?

   _____ (a) Prescribe medication

   _____ (b) Identify and control environmental allergens and irritants

   _____ (c) Educate children and parents about the condition

3. A child whose BMI-for-age is above the 95th percentile is classified as _____.

CRITICAL THINKING

4. How do you think changes in children's frontal lobes during middle childhood affect their ability to manage health issues such as injuries, asthma, and overweight? What do these changes suggest about the need for parental monitoring with regard to these concerns?

Cognitive Changes

Along with impressive gains in physical development, children acquire some of the important hallmarks of mature thinking between ages 6 and 12.

Language

LO 9.4   How do vocabulary and other aspects of language change during middle childhood?

By age 5 or 6, virtually all children have mastered the basic grammar and pronunciation of their first language, but they still have a fair distance to go before reaching adult levels of fluency. During middle childhood, children become skilled at managing the finer points of grammar (Prat-Sala, Shillcock, & Sorace, 2000; Ragnarsdottir, Simonsen, & Plunkett, 1999). For example, by the end of middle childhood, most children understand various ways of saying something about the past, such as "I went," "I was going," "I have gone," "I had gone," "I had been going," and so on. Moreover, they correctly use such tenses in their own speech. Across the middle childhood years, children also learn how to maintain the topic of conversation, how to create unambiguous sentences, and how to speak politely or persuasively (Anglin, 1993). All of these improvements contribute to the school-aged child's emerging mastery of conversation. By the age of 9 years, most children are fully capable of engaging in fluent conversation with speakers of any age, and their speech rates approach those of adults (Sturm & Seery, 2007).

Between 6 and 12, children also continue to add new vocabulary at a fairly astonishing rate of from 5,000 to 10,000 words per year. This estimate comes from several careful studies by developmental psychologist Jeremy Anglin, who estimates children's total vocabularies by testing them on a sample of words drawn at random from a large dictionary (Anglin, 1993, 1995; Skwarchuk & Anglin, 2002). Anglin argues that at age 8 or 9, the child shifts to a new level of understanding of the structure of language, figuring out relationships between whole categories of words, such as between adjectives and adverbs ("happy" and "happily," "sad" and "sadly") and between adjectives and nouns ("happy" and "happiness"). Once he grasps these relationships, the child can understand and create a whole class of new words, and his vocabulary thereafter increases rapidly.

Piaget's Concrete Operational Stage

LO 9.5   What cognitive advantages do children gain as they move through Piaget's concrete operational stage?

Have you ever watched a group of children being entertained by a magician? If so, then you may have noticed that younger children, preoperational thinkers in Piaget's terms, don't find magic tricks to be all that interesting. Why? Because, as you'll recall from Chapter 7,

[handwritten note: children gain the abilities of conservation (number, area, volume, orientation) reversibility, seriation, transivity & class inclusion However, although children can solve problems in a logical fashion, they are typically not able to think abstractly or hypothetically ← simply Psychology]

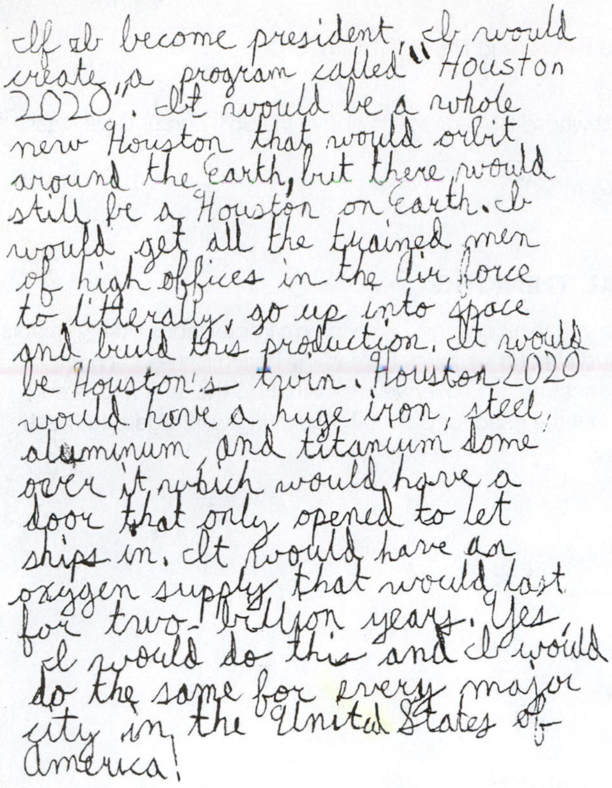

If I become president, I would create a program called "Houston 2020". It would be a whole new Houston that would orbit around the Earth, but there would still be a Houston on earth. I would get all the trained men of high offices in the Air force to litterally, go up into space and build this production. It would be Houston's twin. Houston 2020 would have a huge iron, steel, aluminum, and titanium dome over it which would have a door that only opened to let ships in. It would have an oxygen supply that would last for two-trillion years. Yes I would do this and I would do the same for every major city in the United States of America!

Figure 9.2 An Example of Concrete Operational Thinking

This fifth-grader's composition illustrates the difficulty school-aged children have with deductive logic. His response to a hypothetical premise is to reinvent the world as he knows it through his own experiences or through stories about real people, places, and things. True deductive logic goes beyond what is already known.

(*Source:* Courtesy of Jerry and Denise Boyd. Used with permission.)

concrete operational stage Piaget's third stage of cognitive development, during which children construct schemes that enable them to think logically about objects and events in the real world

decentration thinking that takes multiple variables into account

reversibility the understanding that both physical actions and mental operations can be reversed

inductive logic a type of reasoning in which general principles are inferred from specific experiences

deductive logic a type of reasoning, based on hypothetical premises, that requires predicting a specific outcome from a general principle

preoperational thinkers don't really understand the rules that govern physical reality. In middle childhood, children overcome this limitation and, as a result, they know that rabbits cannot be hidden in hats, and birds don't hide in the sleeves of a magician's jacket and fly out on cue. Knowing that the magician is appearing to do something that is physically impossible is what makes his performance interesting. Like adults, a school-aged child wonders "What's the trick?"

There is no better device for demonstrating a school-aged child's capacity for distinguishing between appearance and reality than Piaget's classic conservation tasks (see Figure 7.4 on page 161). By age 6, most children have begun to show some signs of the **concrete operational stage** and can quickly figure out that a lump of clay has the same mass no matter how its appearance is changed. Thus, this stage is devoted to the construction of schemes that enable children to think logically about objects and events in the real world.

The stage takes its name from a set of immensely powerful schemes Piaget called *concrete operations*. These operations include mental processes such as *decentration*. You learned about its opposite, *centration* (thinking in terms of single variables), in the discussion of preoperational thinking in Chapter 7. **Decentration** is thinking that takes multiple variables into account. As a result, a school-aged child can see that a clay ball rolled into a sausage shape is wider than it was before, but it is also shorter. Decentration leads him to conclude that the reduced height of the sausage shape compensates for its increased width and that it still has the same amount of clay.

As was mentioned in Chapter 7, preoperational children exhibit *irreversibility*, which is the inability to think of some transformed object as it was prior to the transformation. In contrast, concrete operational thinkers display its opposite, **reversibility**—the ability to mentally undo some kind of physical or mental transformation. Piaget thought that reversibility was the most critical of all the concrete operations. The clay sausage in a conservation experiment can be made back into a ball; the water can be poured back into the shorter, wider glass. Understanding of the basic reversibility of actions lies behind many of the gains made during the middle childhood period. For example, if a child has mastered reversibility, then knowing that A is larger than B also tells him that B is smaller than A. The ability to understand hierarchies of classes (such as Fido, spaniel, dog, and animal) also rests on this ability to move both ways in thinking about relationships.

Piaget also proposed that during this stage the child develops the ability to use **inductive logic**. She can go from her own experience to a general principle. For example, she can move from the observation "when a toy is added to a set of toys, it has one more than it did before" to the general principle "adding always makes more."

Elementary school children are fairly good observational scientists, and they enjoy cataloging, counting species of trees or birds, or figuring out the nesting habits of guinea pigs. But they are not yet good at **deductive logic** based on hypothetical premises, which requires starting with a general principle and then predicting some outcome or observation—like going from a theory to a hypothesis. For example, in the composition in Figure 9.2, a fifth-grader responded to the question "What would you do if you were president of the United States?" Responding to such a question requires deductive, not inductive, logic; this kind of task is difficult for 6- to 12-year-olds because they must imagine things they have not experienced. The concrete operations child is good at dealing with things she can see and manipulate or can imagine seeing or manipulating—that is, she is good with *concrete* things; she does not do well with manipulating ideas or possibilities. Thus, as the composition illustrates, children respond to deductive problems by generating ideas that are essentially copies of the things they know about in the concrete world.

Direct Tests of Piaget's View

LO 9.6 What is *horizontal decalage*, and how does Siegler explain concrete operational thinking?

class inclusion the understanding that subordinate classes are included in larger, superordinate classes

Piaget understood that it took children some years to apply their new cognitive skills to all kinds of problems, a phenomenon he called *horizontal decalage* (Feldman, 2004). (The French word *decalage* means "a shift.") However, other developmentalists have explained both consistencies and inconsistencies in school-aged children's reasoning as a result of their ability to use rules to solve problems.

HORIZONTAL DECALAGE Researchers have generally found that Piaget was right in his assertion that concrete operational schemes are acquired gradually across the 6- to 12-year-old period. Studies of conservation, for example, consistently show that children grasp conservation of mass or substance by about age 7. That is, they understand that the amount of clay is the same whether it is in a pancake or a ball or some other shape. They generally understand conservation of weight at about age 8, but they don't understand conservation of volume until age 11 (Tomlinson-Keasey, Eisert, Kahle, Hardy-Brown, & Keasey, 1979).

Studies of classification skills show that at about age 7 or 8, the child first grasps the principle of **class inclusion**, the understanding that subordinate classes are included in larger, superordinate classes. Bananas are included in the class of fruit, fruit is included in the class of food, and so forth. Preschool children understand that bananas are also fruit, but they do not yet fully understand the relationship between the classes.

A good illustration of all these changes comes from an early longitudinal study of concrete operational tasks conducted by Carol Tomlinson-Keasey and her colleagues (Tomlinson-Keasey et al., 1979). They followed a group of 38 children from kindergarten through third grade, testing them with five traditional concrete operational tasks each year: conservation of mass, conservation of weight, conservation of volume, class inclusion, and hierarchical classification. (As you recall from Chapter 7, *conservation* is the understanding that matter can change in appearance without changing in quantity.) You can see from Figure 9.3 that the children got better at all five tasks over the 3-year period, with a spurt between the end of kindergarten and the beginning of first grade (at about the age Piaget thought that concrete operations really arose) and another spurt during second grade.

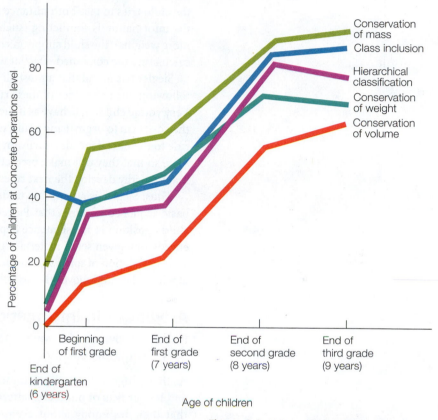

Figure 9.3 Within-Stage Development in Concrete Operations

In this classic longitudinal study, children were given the same set of concrete operational tasks five times, beginning in kindergarten and ending in third grade.

(*Source*: Tomlinson-Keasey et al., 1979, adapted from Table 2, p. 1158.)

CONCRETE OPERATIONS AS RULES FOR PROBLEM SOLVING Other psychologists have conceptualized performance on concrete operational tasks in terms of rules for problem solving. For example, Robert Siegler's approach is a kind of cross between Piagetian theory and information-processing theory. He argues that cognitive development consists of acquiring a set of basic rules that are then applied to a broader and broader range of problems on the basis of experience (Siegler & Lin, 2010). There are no stages, only sequences. Siegler proposes that problem-solving rules emerge from experience—from repeated trial and error and experimentation (Siegler, 1994).

Some of Siegler's own work on the development of rules illustrates how they may be acquired (Siegler & Chen, 2002). In one test, Siegler used a balance scale with a series of pegs on each side of the center, like the one in Figure 9.4. The child is asked to predict which way

Figure 9.4 Siegler's Balance Task

This balance scale is similar to what Siegler used in his experiments.

the balance will fall, depending on the location and number of disk-shaped weights placed on the pegs. A complete solution requires the child to take into account both the number of disks on each side and the specific location of the disks.

Children do not develop such a complete solution immediately. Instead, Siegler suggests that they develop four rules, in this order: Rule I is basically a preoperational rule, taking into account only one dimension, the number of weights. Children using this rule will predict that the side with more disks will go down, no matter which peg they are placed on. Rule II is a transitional rule. The child still judges on the basis of number, except when the same number of weights appears on each side; in that case, the child takes distance from the fulcrum (the point where the scale balances) into account. Rule III is basically a concrete operational rule; the child tries to take both distance and weight into account simultaneously, except that when the information is conflicting (such as when the side with weights closer to the fulcrum has more weights), the child simply guesses. Rule IV involves understanding the actual formula for calculating the combined effect of weight and distance for each side of the balance.

Siegler has found that almost all children perform on this and similar tasks as if they were following one or another of these rules and that the rules seem to develop in the given order. Very young children behave as if they don't have a rule (they guess or behave randomly); when they do seem to begin using a rule, it is always Rule I that comes first. But progression from one rule to the next depends heavily on experience. If children are given practice with the balance scale so that they can make predictions and then check which way the balance actually falls, many rapidly develop the next rules in the sequence.

Thus, Siegler is attempting to describe a logical sequence children follow, not unlike the basic sequence of stages that Piaget described. But Siegler's research shows that a particular child's position in the sequence depends not so much on age as on the child's specific experience with a given set of materials. In Piaget's terminology, this is rather like saying that when accommodation of some scheme occurs, it always occurs in a particular sequence, but the rate at which the child moves through that sequence depends on experience.

Advances in Information-Processing Skills

LO 9.7 How do children's information-processing skills improve during middle childhood?

As they progress through the middle childhood years, children are able to remember longer and longer lists of numbers, letters, or words. In fact, children's memories function so well that their testimony about events they have witnessed is usually accurate enough to be regarded as reliable in judicial proceedings. Moreover, school-aged children's rapidly improving memory skills enable them to acquire new information and skills at a far faster rate, and with greater understanding, than was possible in the early childhood years (Swanson & Alloway, 2012).

PROCESSING EFFICIENCY **Processing efficiency**, the ability to make efficient use of short-term memory capacity, increases steadily with age, a change that most developmentalists now see as the basis for cognitive development (e.g., Borst, Poirel, Pineau, Cassotti, & Houdé, 2013). The best evidence that cognitive processing becomes more efficient is that it gets steadily faster with age. Robert Kail has found virtually the same exponential increase in processing speed with age for a wide variety of tasks, including perceptual-motor tasks such as tapping in response to a stimulus (for example, pressing a button when you hear a buzzer) and cognitive tasks such as mental addition (Kail, 1991, 2008; Kail & Hall, 1994). He has found virtually identical patterns of speed increases in studies in Korea and in the United States, which adds cross-cultural validity to the argument.

AUTOMATICITY An important way in which processing efficiency grows in middle childhood is through the acquisition of **automaticity**, or the ability to recall information from long-term memory without using short-term memory capacity. For example, when children can respond "49" to the question "How much is 7 times 7?" without thinking about it, they have achieved automaticity with respect to that particular piece of information.

processing efficiency the ability to make efficient use of short-term memory capacity

automaticity the ability to recall information from long-term memory without using short-term memory capacity

Automaticity is critical to efficient information processing because it frees up short-term memory space for more complex processing. Thus, the child who knows "7 times 7" automatically can use that fact in a complex multiplication or division problem without giving up any of the short-term memory space he is using to solve the problem. As a result, he is better able to concentrate on the "big picture" instead of expending effort trying to recall a simple multiplication fact. Not surprisingly, researchers have found that elementary school children who have *automatized* basic math facts in this way learn complex computational skills more rapidly (Ashkenazi, Rubenstein, & Henik, 2009).

Automaticity is achieved primarily through practice. For instance, when children are first learning to read, they have to devote all their mental effort to linking letters to speech sounds, written words to spoken words, and so on. Once these tasks become automatic, children can devote more attention to the meaning of what they are reading. Likewise, college students who have achieved automaticity with regard to spelling produce higher-quality lecture notes than do classmates who are less proficient spellers (Peverly et al., 2007). Thus, automaticity is important to information processing throughout the lifespan. It is in middle childhood, however, that children begin automatizing large quantities of academic information and skills at a fairly rapid rate.

EXECUTIVE AND STRATEGIC PROCESSES If you wanted to recall a list of everyday items (chair, pencil, spaghetti, tree, . . .), you might consciously consider the various alternative strategies for remembering and then select the best one. You could also explain some things about how your mind works, such as which kinds of mental tasks you find most difficult. These are examples of *metacognition*—knowing about knowing or thinking about thinking—a set of skills first mentioned in Chapter 7. Metacognition is part of a large group of skills known as **executive processes**—information-processing skills that allow a person to devise and carry out alternative strategies for remembering and solving problems. Executive processes are based on a basic understanding of how the mind works. Such skills emerge around age 5 and improve a great deal during middle childhood (Blaye & Jacques, 2009). For example, 10-year-olds are more likely than 8-year-olds to understand that attending to a story requires effort (Parault & Schwanenflugel, 2000).

One of the advantages of having good metacognitive and executive processing skills is that they help the individual devise methods for remembering information, or **memory strategies**. Although many people possess their own unique methods for remembering, Table 9.2 lists a few common memory strategies. For the most part, these memory techniques first appear between the ages of 6 and 12 (Tam, Jarrold, Baddeley, & Sabatos-DeVito, 2010).

executive processes information-processing skills that involve devising and carrying out strategies for remembering and solving problems

memory strategies learned methods for remembering information

TABLE 9.2   Some Common Information-Processing Strategies Used in Remembering

Strategy	Description
Rehearsal	Either mental or vocal repetition; may occur in children as young as 2 years under some conditions and is common in older children and adults
Organization	Grouping ideas, objects, or words into clusters to help in remembering them, such as "all animals," "the ingredients in the lasagna recipe," or "the chess pieces involved in the move called *castling*." This strategy is more easily applied to something a person has experience with or particular knowledge about. Two-year-olds use primitive clustering strategies.
Elaboration	Finding shared meaning or a common referent for two or more things that need to be remembered
Mnemonic	A device to assist memory; the phrase for the notes of the lines on the musical staff ("Every Good Boy Does Fine") is a mnemonic
Systematic Searching	"Scanning" one's memory for the whole domain in which a piece of information might be found. Three- and 4-year-old children can begin to do this when they search for actual objects in the real world, but they are not good at doing this in memory. So, search strategies may first be learned in the external world and then applied to inner searches.

(*Source:* Flavell, 1985.)

Unless they are rank novices, these school-aged chess players will remember a series of chess moves or an arrangement of chess pieces far better than adults who don't play chess.

EXPERTISE A great deal of research shows that the amount of knowledge a person possesses makes a huge difference in how efficiently her information-processing system works. Children and adults who know a lot about a topic (dinosaurs, baseball cards, mathematics, or whatever it may be) categorize information about that topic in highly complex and hierarchical ways (Posner & Rothbart, 2007; Waters & Waters, 2010). They are also better at remembering and logically analyzing new information on that topic (Ni, 1998). In addition, children's capacity for creativity appears to greatly depend on how much knowledge they have about a topic (Sak & Maker, 2006).

Even typical age differences in strategy use or memory ability disappear when the younger group has more expertise than the older group. For example, psychologist Michelene Chi, in her now-classic early study, showed that expert chess players could remember the placement of chess pieces on a board much more quickly and accurately than novice chess players, even when the expert chess players were children and the novices were adults (Chi, 1978).

However, using advanced information-processing skills in their areas of expertise doesn't seem to help children's general memory and reasoning abilities (Ericsson & Crutcher, 1990). For this reason, many information-processing psychologists now believe that an individual's information-processing skills may depend entirely on the quantity and quality of relevant information stored in long-term memory. Thus, they say, to be able to learn scientific reasoning skills, for example, children must first acquire a body of knowledge about scientific topics (Zimmerman, 2000). To paraphrase developmental psychologist John Flavell, expertise makes any of us, including children, look very smart; lack of expertise makes us look very dumb (Flavell, 1985).

test yourself before going on

✅ **Study** and **Review** in **MyPsychLab**

Answers to these questions can be found in the back of the book.

1. Between 6 and 12, children add _____ to _____ new words to their vocabularies every year.

2. Two distinctive features of concrete operational thinking are _____, thinking that takes multiple variables into account, and _____, the understanding that physical and mental actions can be reversed.

3. In the table below, note the benefits of each advance in information-processing skills:

Advances	Benefits
Greater processing efficiency	
Automaticity	
Executive processes	
Memory strategies	
Expertise	

CRITICAL THINKING

4. In what ways do advances in language, reasoning, and information-processing skills help children succeed in school? How do you think schooling influences these skills?

Schooling

For children all over the world, formal education is well under way by the time they reach the age of 6 or 7. Every society endeavors to find effective ways of teaching children the skills they will need in adulthood. In general, studies show that teachers who display a teaching style similar to the approach that authoritative parents take to raising children—an approach that combines clear goals, good control, good communication, and high nurturance—are the most effective (Kiuru et al., 2012). In addition, at least in the United States, there is evidence that elementary schools with smaller classes, fewer than 20 pupils or so, are more effective than those with larger classes (Ecalle, Magnan, & Gibert, 2007). Still, quality considerations aside, because of its academic focus and the amount of time that children spend in school, formal education is one of the most important influences on the cognitive development of 6- to 12-year-olds.

Literacy

LO 9.8   What should be included in an effective literacy curriculum?

In the industrialized world, *literacy*, the ability to read and write, is the focus of education in the 6- to 12-year-old period. As you learned in Chapter 7, the skills children bring to school from their early childhood experiences may influence early reading as much as formal instruction (Crone & Whitehurst, 1999). Especially significant among these skills is the set known as *phonological awareness* (Pearson & Cervetti, 2013). Across the early elementary years, phonological awareness skills continue to increase and serve as the foundation for later-developing skills such as *oral reading fluency*, the ability to read aloud with emotional expressiveness and minimal effort, that strongly predict reading comprehension skills in the later elementary grades (Kim, Petscher, Schatschneider, & Foorman, 2010). Thus, children who lack such expertise at the start of school are likely to fall behind unless some systematic effort is made by teachers to provide them with a base of phonological knowledge (Houston, Al Otaiba, & Torgesen, 2006).

Research indicates that, to be effective, a beginning reading program must include a type of instruction called **systematic and explicit phonics** (Shanahan, 2006). *Systematic* means that instruction must follow a plan that begins with simple, one-letter/one-sound correspondences (e.g., the letter *b* for the sound /b/) and moves to those that involve two or more letters. The plan must be carefully developed so that instruction corresponds in meaningful ways to the spelling system of the language being learned. *Explicit* means that letter–sound correspondences are taught intentionally. Effective phonics curricula also provide beginning readers with ample opportunities for daily practice in using their knowledge of sound–symbol correspondences so that they can develop automaticity. Phonics researchers argue that children cannot easily comprehend written language until they can decode it automatically and fluently (Rego, 2006).

Nevertheless, advocates of the **balanced approach** to reading instruction point out that teachers must move beyond basic phonics. In *guided reading* sessions, for instance, teachers work with small groups of children on reading books that are somewhat challenging for them (recall Vygotsky's zone of proximal development) (Phillips, 2013). When a child makes an error, the teacher uses the opportunity to explain a reading strategy or one of the many idiosyncrasies of written English to all of the children in the group. Proponents of the balanced approach also point to studies showing that, in the later elementary grades, attainment of reading fluency requires that children learn about meaningful word parts, such as prefixes and suffixes (Adams & Henry, 1997; Berninger, Abbott, Nagy, & Carlisle, 2010). At the same time, instruction in comprehension strategies, such as identifying the main idea and purpose of a particular text, also helps (Johnston, Barnes & Desrochers, 2008; Van den Broek, Lynch, Naslund, Ievers-Landis, & Verduin, 2004). Of course, all along the way, children need to be exposed to good literature, both in their own reading and in what teachers and parents read to them.

Some of the strategies used to teach reading also help children learn writing, the other component of literacy. For example, instruction in sound–symbol connections helps children learn to spell as well as to read. Of course, good writing is far more than just spelling; it requires instruction and practice, just as reading does. Specifically, children need explicit instruction in language mechanics, such as how to construct simple, compound, and complex sentences, to become good writers (Saddler, 2007). They also need to learn to organize writing tasks into phases such as planning, drafting, editing, and revising (Graham & Harris, 2007).

Children's experiences in school are similar the world over. The similarities help explain why cognitive-developmental research involving 6- to 12-year-olds yields pretty much the same results in all cultures where children attend school.

systematic and explicit phonics planned, specific instruction in sound–letter correspondences

balanced approach reading instruction that combines explicit phonics instruction with other strategies for helping children acquire literacy

Despite educators' best efforts, many children fall behind their classmates in literacy during the early school years. In general, reading researchers have found that poor readers have problems with sound-letter combinations (Gersten et al., 2008). Thus, many children who have reading difficulties benefit from highly specific phonics approaches that provide a great deal of practice in translating letters into sounds and vice versa (Koppenhaver, Hendrix & Williams, 2007).

However, curriculum flexibility is also important in programs for poor readers. Some do not improve when exposed to phonics approaches. In fact, programs that combine sound–letter and comprehension training have proven to be highly successful in helping poor readers catch up, especially when the programs are implemented in the early elementary years (Gersten et al., 2008). Consequently, teachers need to be able to assess the effectiveness of whatever approach they are using and change it to fit the needs of individual students.

Second-Language Learners

LO 9.9   How do bilingual and ESL approaches to second-language instruction differ?

Worldwide patterns of population growth and movement have led to tremendous increases in the number of children attending school in the United States, Canada, Great Britain, and Australia whose first language is not English. About two-thirds of these children speak English well enough to function in school, but the rest essentially do not speak English. Educators in English-speaking countries use the term *English language learner* (*ELL*) to refer to non–English-speaking children—either immigrant children or native-born children.

The number of school-aged children who speak a language other than English at home increased from 2.5 million in 1991 to just over 11 million in 2009 (National Center for Education Statistics [NCES], 2013). Nearly 5 million of such children are enrolled in formal English instructional programs in public schools. These children represent about 10% of public school enrollment in the United States. However, there are wide differences in ELL enrollment across the country. For example, about 30% of school children in California are classified as ELL, while less than 1% of students in West Virginia are so classified. Most ELL students live in large cities. **Watch** the **Video** *Teaching in a Bilingual Classroom* in **MyPsychLab**.

Some ELL children, mostly those whose first language is Spanish, participate in **bilingual education**, in which instruction is given in two languages. Such programs have been developed for Spanish-speaking children because they constitute by far the largest group of ELL students in U.S. schools. Other English-speaking countries offer bilingual education to children from large non–English-speaking groups as well. For example, schools in Canada have provided both English- and French-speaking students in Quebec, a province whose residents primarily speak French, with bilingual education for decades.

However, bilingual education is logistically impossible for most school districts that include ELL children. For one thing, if a school system has only a handful of students who speak a particular language, it is not financially feasible to establish a separate curriculum for them. In addition, it may be impossible to find bilingual teachers for children whose language is spoken by very few people outside of their country of origin. For these reasons, about most ELL 6- to 12-year-olds in the United States are enrolled in **English-as-a-second-language (ESL) programs** (NCES, 2010). In ESL programs, children spend part of the day in classes to learn English and part in academic classes that are conducted entirely in English.

Research has shown that no particular approach to second-language learning is more successful than any other (Mohanty & Perregaux, 1997). There is some indication that programs that include a home-based component, such as those that encourage parents to learn the new language along with their children, may be especially effective (Koskinen et al., 2000). But it seems that any structured program, whether bilingual education or ESL, fosters higher achievement among non–English-speaking children than simply integrating them into English-only classes, an approach called *submersion*. Although most children in submersion programs eventually catch up to their English-speaking peers, many educators believe that instruction that supports children's home language and culture as well as their English-language skills enhances their overall development (Cushner, McClelland, & Safford, 2009).

bilingual education an approach to second-language education in which children receive instruction in two different languages

English-as-a-second-language (ESL) program an approach to second-language education in which children attend English classes for part of the day and receive most of their academic instruction in English

An ELL student does not have an increased risk of academic failure as long as the school provides some kind of transition to English-only instruction and school officials take care to administer all standardized tests in the language with which the child is most familiar (Cushner et al., 2009). Providing a transition to English-only instruction is necessary to optimize the ELL child's potential for achievement. Testing children in their native languages ensures that non–English-speaking children will not be misclassified as having intellectual disabilities or learning disabilities because of their limited English skills. Beyond these requirements, ELL students represent no particular burden to U.S. schools. Moreover, in all likelihood, their presence enriches the educational experience of children whose first language is English.

achievement test a test designed to assess specific information learned in school

Achievement and Intelligence Tests

LO 9.10 Why do schools administer achievement tests, and what kinds of items do they include?

Perhaps you remember taking standardized tests during your elementary school years. The term *standardized* simply means that each individual's performance is determined by comparing his or her score to the average score attained by a large sample of similar individuals. For instance, an achievement test for first-graders compares each child's score to the average achieved by a large group of first-graders who took the test prior to its publication. Most school systems in the United States administer standardized tests to students many times during their educational careers. The tests are generally of two types: *achievement tests* and *intelligence tests*.

TYPES OF TESTS **Achievement tests** are designed to assess specific information learned in school. Scores are based on comparison of an individual child's performance to those of other children in the same grade across the country. Critics of achievement tests point out that, although educators and parents may think of achievement tests as indicators of what children learn in school, they are actually very similar to IQ tests. For example, suppose an achievement test contains the math problem "4 × 4." A bright child who hasn't yet learned multiplication may reason his way to the correct answer of 16. Another child may give the correct answer because she has learned it in school. Still another may know the answer because he learned to multiply from his parents. Thus, critics suggest that comprehensive portfolios of children's school work may be better indicators of actual school learning than standardized achievement tests (Neill, 1998).

Most U.S. schools also require students to take intelligence tests at various points in their educational careers. These tests are usually paper-and-pencil multiple-choice tests that can be given to large numbers of children at the same time. Some critics of routine IQ testing say that such tests aren't as accurate as the individual tests you read about in Chapter 7. Others object to the use of IQ tests because they often result in misclassification of children in minority groups (see *No Easy Answers*). Nevertheless, IQ tests are often used to group children for instruction because they are strongly correlated with achievement-test scores.

THEORIES OF INTELLIGENCE Some developmentalists say that the problem with relying on IQ tests to predict achievement is that they fail to provide a complete picture of mental abilities. For example, psychologist Howard Gardner proposed a theory of *multiple intelligences* (Gardner, 1983). This theory claims there are eight types of intelligence:

- *Linguistic*—the ability to use language effectively
- *Logical/mathematical*—facility with numbers and logical problem solving
- *Musical*—the ability to appreciate and produce music
- *Spatial*—the ability to appreciate spatial relationships
- *Bodily kinesthetic*—the ability to move in a coordinated way, combined with a sense of one's body in space
- *Naturalist*—the ability to make fine discriminations among the plants and animals of the natural world or the patterns and designs of human artifacts
- *Interpersonal*—sensitivity to the behavior, moods, and needs of others
- *Intrapersonal*—the ability to understand oneself

IQ Testing in the Schools

Although IQ tests are frequently used in U.S. schools, they are very controversial. Everyone agrees that these tests have legitimate uses. For example, if a child is having difficulty learning to read, an IQ test can help determine the source of the problem. The arguments about IQ tests center on whether they ought to be used routinely to group elementary school children for instruction. Several strong reasons are usually given against such use.

First, as you may remember from earlier discussions, IQ tests do not measure all the facets of a child's functioning that may be relevant. For example, clinicians have found that some children with IQs below 70, who would be diagnosed with an intellectual disability if the score alone were used for classification, nonetheless have sufficient social skills to enable them to function well in classrooms with children who do not have intellectual disabilities. Second, there is the problem of the self-fulfilling prophecy that an IQ test score may establish. Because many parents and teachers still believe that IQ scores are a permanent feature of a child, once a child is labeled as "having" a particular IQ, that label tends to be difficult to remove. Psychologist Robert Rosenthal, in a series of famous studies, has shown that a teacher's belief about a given student's ability and potential has a small but significant effect on her behavior toward that student and on the student's eventual achievement (Rosenthal, 1994).

Another negative argument is that tests are biased in such a way that some groups of children are more likely to score high or low, even though their underlying ability is the same. For example, the tests may contain items that are not equally familiar to Whites and nonwhites. Researchers have devised *culturally reduced tests*, also called *culture-fair tests*, that minimize the impact of verbal knowledge, presumably the most culture-laden aspect of intelligence testing, on children's scores (Sattler, 2001). However, these tests do not correlate well with academic achievement, so they are not useful in the diagnosis of learning problems.

There is no quick or easy solution to this dilemma. On the one hand, IQ testing helps some children qualify for much-needed special classes. Yet it is also true that placing a child in a special class may create a self-fulfilling prophecy. However, to offer no special help to children who come to school lacking the skills needed to succeed seems equally unacceptable to many observers. Likewise, some bright children may benefit from acceleration. Thus, many developmentalists have concluded that IQ tests are more reliable and valid for grouping children than other alternatives such as teacher rating scales (Alvidrez & Weinstein, 1999).

YOU DECIDE

Decide which of these two statements you most agree with and think about how you would defend your position:

1. *IQ testing should be considered only when a child has demonstrated some kind of difficulty with learning or appears to be exceptionally bright.*

2. *Using routine IQ testing as a means of screening children for possible learning problems and for identifying gifted children is a good idea and ought to be continued.*

Gardner's theory is based on observations of people with brain damage, intellectual disabilities, and other severe mental disabilities. He points out that brain damage usually causes disruption of functioning in very specific mental abilities rather than a general decline in intelligence. He also notes that many individuals with mental deficits have remarkable talents. For example, some are gifted in music, while others can perform complex mathematical computations without using a calculator or pencil and paper. However, critics claim that Gardner's view, although intuitively appealing, has little empirical support (White, 2006).

Robert Sternberg's *triarchic theory of intelligence* proposes three components of human intelligence (Sternberg, 1988). *Contextual intelligence* has to do with knowing the right behavior for a specific situation. For example, South American street vendors, most of whom are of elementary school age but are unschooled, are good at doing practical calculations but perform poorly on more abstract, written math problems. These children are highly "intelligent" in their daily context, but in the school context they appear to lack intellectual ability.

Experiential intelligence, according to Sternberg, involves learning to give specific responses without thinking about them. For example, you can probably respond without thinking to the question "How much is 7 times 7?" Experiential intelligence also enables you to come up with novel solutions to everyday problems that you haven't quite been able to solve and to recognize when a tried-and-true solution is appropriate for a new problem.

Componential intelligence is a person's ability to come up with effective strategies. To Sternberg, this is the most important component of intelligence. He claims that intelligence tests are limited in their ability to identify gifted children because they put more emphasis on "correctness" of answers than on the quality of the strategies people use to arrive at them (Sternberg, 2002).

In general, Sternberg says, IQ tests measure how familiar a child is with "school" culture. Thus, children whose cultural background does not include formal schooling perform poorly because they are unfamiliar with the context of the test. Unfortunately, their poor performance is often mistakenly interpreted to mean that they lack intelligence (Sternberg & Grigorenko, 2006). Sternberg believes that intelligence tests should measure all three components of intelligence, and he has produced some research evidence suggesting that testing procedures based on his theory yield better performance predictions than conventional IQ tests (Sternberg, Wagner, Williams, & Horvath, 1995).

EMOTIONAL INTELLIGENCE Both Gardner's and Sternberg's theories have become important in helping educators understand the weaknesses of IQ tests. Moreover, psychologists such as Daniel Goleman, Peter Salovey, and John Mayer argue that *emotional intelligence* contributes just as much to achievement as the skills measured by traditional intelligence tests do (Goleman, 1995; Salovey & Mayer, 1990). Most theories of emotional intelligence assert that it has several components, including awareness of one's own emotions, the ability to express one's emotions appropriately, and the capacity to channel emotions into the pursuit of worthwhile goals. Without emotional intelligence, Goleman claims, it is impossible to achieve one's intellectual potential. However, research has yet to provide support for Goleman's hypothesis (Humphrey, Curran, Morris, Farrell, & Woods, 2007). Still, research on the relationship between self-control (the third component of emotional intelligence) in early childhood and achievement in adolescence suggests that Goleman's view is correct. Children's ability to exercise control over their emotions in early childhood is strongly related to measures of academic achievement in high school (Denham, 2006).

Group Differences in Achievement

LO 9.11 What kinds of group differences in achievement have educational researchers found?

Although intelligence testing is a prominent feature of the educational environment, teachers and administrators are usually more concerned about what children actually learn than they are about children's abilities. For this reason, a good deal of educational research focuses on finding explanations for group differences in achievement. These differences have been found across gender, ethnic groups, and cultures.

SEX DIFFERENCES IN ACHIEVEMENT Comparisons of total IQ test scores for boys and girls do not reveal consistent differences. It is only when the total scores are broken down into several separate skills that some patterns of sex differences emerge. On average, studies in the United States show that girls do slightly better on verbal tasks and at arithmetic computation and boys do slightly better at numerical reasoning. For example, more boys than girls test as gifted in mathematics (Halpern et al., 2007). This difference is evident as soon as children become developmentally capable of responding verbally to traditional ability tests—that is, around the age of 3 years (Locuniak & Jordan, 2008). Moreover, this early sex difference predicts differences in math achievement among boys and girls later in childhood (Jordan, 2010).

Where might such differences come from? The explanatory options should be familiar by now. As you learned earlier in this chapter, brain processes that underlie spatial perception and cognition are often argued to be the cause of sex differences in math achievement. To date, however, neurological research has failed to find sex differences in brain function large enough to explain sex differences in math achievement (Spreen et al., 1995). Consequently, most developmentalists believe that sex differences result from an interaction between biological and experiential factors. ◉ **Watch** the **Video** *Boys in Crisis* in **MyPsychLab**.

One important experiential factor is that both teachers and parents seem to believe that boys have more math ability than girls (Jussim & Eccles, 1992; Tiedemann, 2000). Thus, they are more likely to attribute a girl's success in mathematics to effort or good teaching; poor performance by a girl is attributed to

Encouragement from teachers and parents that is equal to that given to boys may help girls narrow the mathematics achievement gap.

analytical style a tendency to focus on the details of a task

relational style a tendency to ignore the details of a task in order to focus on the "big picture"

lack of ability. In contrast, teachers and parents attribute a boy's success to ability and his failure to lack of application (Jussim & Eccles, 1992). Moreover, children appear to internalize these beliefs, which, in turn, influence their interest in taking math courses and their beliefs about their likelihood of achieving success in math (Eccles, Jacobs, & Harold, 1990). The cumulative effects of these differences in expectations and treatment show up in high school, when sex differences on standardized math tests usually become evident. In part, then, the sex differences in math achievement-test scores appear to be perpetuated by subtle family and school influences on children's attitudes.

ETHNIC DIFFERENCES IN ACHIEVEMENT In the United States, there are ethnic group differences in achievement-test scores similar to the differences in IQ-test scores you read about in Chapter 7. Most developmentalists believe that the same factors that contribute to IQ score differences—economic status, access to prenatal care, family stability, and so on—also produce ethnic differences in measures of school performance such as grades and achievement-test scores.

Some educators have proposed that group differences in learning styles help to explain variations in achievement (Cushner et al., 2009). Research indicates that children who use an **analytical style** define learning goals and follow a set of orderly steps to reach them. These children are well organized, are good at learning details, and think of information in terms of "right" and "wrong." Other children use a **relational style**. These children focus attention on "the big picture" instead of on individual bits of information.

For example, Ayana, who has an analytical style, and Richard, who uses a relational style, both listen carefully as their fourth-grade teacher gives instructions for a complicated project. Ayana lists every detail of the teacher's instructions and how many points each part is worth. In contrast, Richard writes down his general impression of each part of the project.

In working on the project, Ayana concentrates her effort on the parts that are worth the most points. Richard pays more attention to the aspects of the project he finds interesting. When it is finished, Ayana's project conforms more exactly to the teacher's instructions than Richard's does, and she receives a higher grade. Ayana's way of approaching school work—her cognitive style—better fits school expectations, giving her an advantage over Richard. In addition, Ayana's way of learning helps her get high scores on achievement tests, which require detailed knowledge of specific information and skills.

Ethnic groups in the United States differ in the percentages of children who use each style. A higher percentage of Asian American and European American students are analyticals. In contrast, a higher percentage of African American, Hispanic American, and Native American children are relationals. Thus, differences among these groups in achievement test scores and school grades may be due to the different percentages of analyticals and relationals (Serpell & Hatano, 1997).

Achievement differences may also be due to philosophical beliefs that characterize some racial and ethnic groups in the United States. For example, American culture tends to be *individualistic*. In other words, it emphasizes the achievements of individuals and encourages competition rather than cooperation. However, some U.S. subcultures place more emphasis on interdependence, an outlook that sociologists and anthropologists usually refer to as *collectivist* (Serpell & Hatano, 1997). In Hawaii, educators tried changing their curriculum and teaching methods to better fit with the collectivist emphasis of Native Hawaiian children and families. The new approach involved more group work and cooperation among students, and it apparently helped children learn more (Cushner et al., 2009). The success of such interventions suggests that educational practices in the United States may be well adapted to some groups but not others, thereby producing differences in achievement between groups for whom the educational system is a good cultural "fit" and those for whom it is not.

Feelings of hopelessness on the part of some disadvantaged students may also be a factor. For example, some African American students in the United States, discouraged by racism and lack of opportunity, believe that they won't be able to succeed economically no matter how much they learn in school (Baranchik, 2002; Ogbu, 1990). Some research suggests that these feelings influence minority children's scores on standardized tests, as discussed in the *Research Report*. Educators believe schools can affect these students' beliefs by making sure textbooks and other materials accurately reflect the contributions of African Americans to American culture (Cushner et al., 2009).

CROSS-CULTURAL DIFFERENCES IN ACHIEVEMENT Cross-cultural studies of achievement that cross international boundaries are far more difficult to carry out than cross-cultural studies involving ethnic groups within one country. The primary obstacle to international studies is the lack of achievement tests that are reliable and valid both within and across cultures (Oakland, 2009). Researchers have had an especially difficult time devising valid achievement tests for rural school systems in developing countries (Stemler et al., 2009). For example, researchers have found that conventional Western intelligence tests administered in the early childhood years predict school achievement for rural Zambian boys but not for girls (Serpell & Jere-Folotiya, 2008). Further research is needed before developmentalists will know for sure whether these results reflect a real gender difference or a problem with the validity of the intelligence and achievement measures themselves. Until such questions are resolved, studies comparing children's achievement in rural Zambia to that of children in the industrialized world, or even in urban areas of Zambia where Western notions of intelligence, achievement, and gender roles are more influential, are unlikely to yield meaningful results.

Because of these difficulties, comparisons of students in school systems that are very similar, at least with regard to educational objectives, predominate among international cross-cultural studies. For instance, comparisons of school children in North American, European, and Pacific Rim nations such as Japan are common. In fact, however, the surface characteristics of schools and the children themselves are quite similar across these nations. As a result, when researchers find achievement differences, the reasons for them are often difficult to identify. Nevertheless, studies that look for subtle variations beneath the surface have yielded important insights into the influence of educational practices on achievement.

As you are probably aware, differences in math and science achievement between Asian children and North American children have been the focus of much study and debate. Over a 30-year period, studies have repeatedly shown that U.S. school children are significantly behind their peers in other industrialized nations (Provasnik & Gonzales, 2009). Yet studies show that underlying cognitive developmental processes are very similar in Asian and North

RESEARCH REPORT

Stereotype Threat

Suppose that on the first day of class, your professor had said that women usually get higher grades than men in human-development courses. Do you think such a statement would cause male students to slack off? If so, you would be in agreement with the central hypothesis of *stereotype threat theory*.

Psychologists Claude Steele and Joshua Aronson (Steele & Aronson, 1995) define stereotype threat as a subtle sense of pressure members of a particular group feel when they are attempting to perform well in an area in which their group is characterized by a negative stereotype. According to Steele and Aronson, African American students experience stereotype threat whenever they are faced with an important cognitive test, such as a college entrance exam or an IQ test, because of the general cultural stereotype that African Americans are less intellectually able than members of other groups. In order to avoid confirming the stereotype, says the theory, African Americans avoid putting forth their best effort because to fail after having put forth one's best effort would mean that the stereotype is true.

Numerous studies have confirmed the existence of stereotype threat among both children and adults (Appel & Kronberger, 2012; Nussbaum & Steele, 2007; Rydell, Shiffrin, Boucher, Van Loo, & Rydell, 2010; Steele & Aronson, 2004; Suzuki & Aronson, 2005). However, stereotype threat appears to have a smaller effect on children's test performance than on that of adults. Consequently, while the power of stereotype threat to influence adults' performance on cognitive tests has been well established by researchers, the jury is still out with regard to its importance in explaining group differences among children.

In addition, psychologist Paul Sackett points out that removing stereotype threat does not cause groups who are unequal to perform equally (Sackett, Hardison, & Cullen, 2004a, 2005). Sackett has also raised concerns about the degree to which the importance of stereotype threat has been misinterpreted in the popular press and about the dangers involved in generalizing laboratory studies to real-world testing situations (Ryan & Sackett, 2013; Sackett,

Hardison, & Cullen, 2004b). Often, they say, Steele and Aronson's findings are presented in ways that cause naive individuals to believe that ethnic group differences would disappear if stereotype threat could be eliminated somehow. In some cases, the inference has been drawn that scientists should refrain from publishing or even discussing racial group differences so as not to engender feelings of stereotype threat among members of minority groups. By contrast, they argue that continued discussion of these differences serves to accentuate the need for more research on the topic.

CRITICAL ANALYSIS

1. *If discussion of group differences in intelligence-test scores contributes to racial prejudice, do you think society would be better off if researchers stopped trying to discover the causes for them? Why or why not?*

2. *How might parents and teachers moderate the effects of stereotype threat on children's test performance?*

American children (Zhou & Boehm, 2004). Developmentalists speculate that the differences result from variations in both cultural beliefs and teaching methods.

With respect to cultural beliefs, developmentalists have found that North American parents and teachers emphasize innate ability, which they assume to be unchangeable, more than effort. For Asians, the emphasis is just the opposite: They believe that people can become smarter by working harder (Hatano, 2004; Shi, 2004). Because of these differences in beliefs, this theory claims, Asian parents and teachers have higher expectations for children and are better at finding ways to motivate them to do school work. Presumably for these same reasons, Asian families spend more time teaching their children specific academic skills than North American parents do (Sijuwade, 2003).

However, teaching methods in the two cultures also vary. For example, in a pioneering set of studies, educational psychologists James Stigler and Harold Stevenson observed teaching strategies in 120 classrooms in Japan, Taiwan, and the United States and became convinced that Asian teachers had devised particularly effective modes of teaching mathematics and science (Stevenson, 1994; Stigler & Stevenson, 1991). Their observations suggested that Japanese and Chinese teachers approached mathematics and science by crafting a series of "master lessons," each organized around a single theme or idea and each involving specific forms of student participation. These lessons were like good stories, with a beginning, a middle, and an end. In U.S. classrooms, by contrast, Stigler and Stevenson found that teachers rarely spent 30 or 60 minutes on a single coherent math or science lesson. Instead, teachers shifted topics often during a single math or science "lesson." Stigler and Stevenson also found striking differences in the amount of time teachers spent actually leading instruction for the whole class. In the U.S. classrooms, teachers spent 49% of their time instructing the entire class. In Japan and Taiwan, by contrast, group instruction occurred 74% and 90% of the time, respectively.

Although Stigler and Stevenson initiated their studies decades ago, their findings continue to inform developmentalists' understanding of cross-cultural differences in achievement, owing to the breadth and depth of the data they collected. Nevertheless, more recent work has expanded researchers' knowledge about the factors that contribute to cross-cultural differences in achievement, particularly in math and science. For example, many studies have shown that Asian and North American math instruction differs in the emphasis on *computational fluency*, the degree to which an individual can automatically produce solutions to simple calculation problems. Research has demonstrated that computational fluency in the elementary school years is related to concurrent and future calculation skills, achievement in advanced math classes such as algebra, *number sense*, an intuitive grasp of mathematics, and facility in solving word problems (Geary et al., 1999; Kail & Hall, 1999; Tolar, Lederberg, & Fletcher, 2009). Moreover, calculators are not commonly used in Asian schools. Many math educators suggest that, by the time they get to high school, U.S. students have learned to depend on calculators and, as a result, have a more difficult time learning algebra than their Asian counterparts do (Judson & Nishimori, 2005). These differences in algebra learning carry over into more advanced classes such as geometry and calculus. As a result, U.S. teens are often found to perform equally as well as their Asian peers with regard to mathematics concepts but fall short of them in problem solving.

The high levels of achievement that are attained by Asian students may be best explained by the fact that Asian teachers and parents regard instruction in computational skills as a parental responsibility and instruction in conceptual understanding as the responsibility of the school (Zhou et al., 2006). Thus, by the time children enter school, they have already spent a good deal of time rehearsing basic computational facts and are ready to think more deeply about mathematical concepts. Many are taught to use an *abacus*, the ancient Chinese calculating device. Others begin studying mathematics in the internationally popular *Kumon* and *Singapore Math* programs at the age of 3 years. The home-based approach

Across all cultures, parent involvement is associated with high achievement.

to mathematics education that is common in Asian societies is effective because the amount of time that is needed to master computational skills varies widely from one child to another. Parents and individualized programs such as Kumon can more easily adapt their curricula to each child's unique pace of learning than can schools.

Another difference between U.S. and Asian schools, especially at the elementary level, involves the use of rewards. Because of the influence of Skinner's operant conditioning theory on education in the United States, teachers commonly use material rewards, such as stickers, to motivate children. Such rewards are effective only when they are tied to high standards, yet teachers in the United States often use them to reward students for less-than-optimal performance (Deci, Koestner, & Ryan, 1999; Eisenberger, Pierce, & Cameron, 1999).

In response to these criticisms, many educators say that achievement differences between North American and Asian students have been exaggerated to make U.S. schools look worse than they actually are (Berliner & Biddle, 1997). Moreover, more than 70% of American parents give grades of A or B to the nation's public schools (ABC News, 2000). Educators and parents alike often claim that Asian schools teach students to value conformity, while American schools place more emphasis on creativity. Indeed, some Asian educators agree that their schools have sacrificed creativity in order to attain high achievement-test scores (Hatano, 1990).

test yourself before going on

✓ **Study** and **Review** in **MyPsychLab**

Answers to these questions can be found in the back of the book.

1. Research suggests that an effective literacy program must include _____ _____ _____ _____ instruction.

2. Most ELL children in the United States are enrolled in (bilingual/ESL) classes.

3. Some psychologists claim that conventional achievement and intelligence tests ignore the importance of _____ intelligence.

4. A higher proportion of (boys/girls) score in the gifted range on math achievement tests.

5. Children who exhibit a(n) _____ learning style tend to focus on details.

6. List three factors that have been included in explanations of differences in North American and Asian children's math achievement:

   (a) _____

   (b) _____

   (c) _____

CRITICAL THINKING

7. How did your elementary school experiences shape the rest of your life?

Children with Special Needs

Some children are born with or develop differences that may significantly interfere with their education unless they receive some kind of special instruction (see Table 9.3). In the United States, 13.4% of all school children receive such services (NCES, 2010). The categories listed in Table 9.3 on page 232 are defined by law, and public schools are legally obligated to provide special education services for all children who qualify for them.

Learning Disabilities

LO 9.12 Why is the term *learning disability* controversial?

The largest group served by U.S. special educators has some kind of **learning disability**, or difficulty in mastering a specific academic skill—most often reading—despite possessing normal intelligence and no physical or sensory disabilities (Snider & Dillow, 2012). When reading is the problem skill, the term **dyslexia** is often used (even though *dyslexia* also denotes a total absence of reading). Most children with reading disabilities can read, but not as well as others their age. Moreover, their skill deficits are specific to reading—such as an inability to automatize

learning disability a disorder in which a child has difficulty mastering a specific academic skill, even though she possesses normal intelligence and no physical or sensory disabilities

dyslexia problems in reading or the inability to read

TABLE 9.3 Disabilities for Which U.S. Children Receive Special Education Services

Disability Category	Percentage of Special Education Students in the Category	Description of Disability
Learning disability	38%	Achievement 2 or more years behind expectations based on intelligence tests Example: A fourth-grader with an average IQ who is reading at a first-grade level
Communication disorder in speech or language	22%	A disorder of speech or language that affects a child's education; can be a problem with speech or an impairment in the comprehension or use of any aspect of language Example: A first-grader who makes errors in pronunciation like those of a 4-year-old and can't connect sounds and symbols
Other health impairments	11%	A health problem that interferes with a child's education Example: A child with severe asthma who misses several weeks of school each year. (Children with ADHD are included in this category.)
Intellectual disability	7%	IQ significantly below average intelligence, together with impairments in adaptive functions Example: A school-aged child with an IQ lower than 70 who is not fully toilet trained and who needs special instruction in both academic and self-care skills
Emotional disturbance	6%	An emotional or behavior disorder that interferes with a child's education Example: A child whose severe temper tantrums cause him to be removed from the classroom every day
Developmental delay	6	A significant delay in any domain of development that affects a 3- to 9-year-old child's performance in school
Autistic spectrum disorders	6%	A group of disorders in which children's language and social skills are impaired Example: A child with autism who needs special training to acquire the capacity for verbal communication
Multiple disabilities	2%	Need for special instruction and ongoing support in two or more areas to benefit from education Example: A child with cerebral palsy who is also deaf, thus requiring both physical and instructional adaptations
Hearing impairment	1%	A hearing problem that interferes with a child's education Example: A child who needs a sign-language interpreter in the classroom
Orthopedic impairment	1%	An orthopedic disability that requires special adaptations Example: A child in a wheelchair who needs a special physical education class
Visual impairment	.4%	Impaired visual acuity or a limited field of vision that interferes with education Example: A blind child who needs training in the use of Braille to read and write
Traumatic brain injury	.4%	An acquired injury to the brain caused by an external physical force, resulting in total or partial functional disability or psychosocial impairment, or both, that adversely affects a child's educational performance. Example: A child with a history of traumatic brain injury who requires a learning environment with minimal distractions as well as extra time to complete assignments

(*Source:* Snider & Dillow, 2012.)

sound-letter correspondences—rather than the result of a general cognitive dysfunction (Wimmer, Mayringer, & Landerl, 1998). Current policy in the United States is that children must show a lack of response to interventions designed to remediate such skill deficits before they can be classified as having a learning disability (Reynolds & Shaywitz, 2009). ◉ **Watch** the **Video** *Dyslexia Doctor* in **MyPsychLab**.

What causes learning disabilities? One difficulty in answering this question is that children with learning disabilities rarely show any signs of major brain damage on any standard neurological tests. So, if a learning disability results from a neurological problem, the neurological problem must be a subtle one. Some researchers argue that there may not be any underlying neurological problem at all. Instead, children with learning disabilities (especially reading disabilities) may simply have a more general problem with understanding the sound and structure of language (Carroll & Snowling, 2004; Share & Leiken, 2004; Torgesen et al., 1999). There is also some evidence that learning disabilities, especially dyslexia, may have a genetic basis (Rosenberg, Pennington, Willcutt, & Olson, 2012).

There are also disagreements about learning disabilities at the practical level. Children are labeled as having learning disabilities and assigned to special classes, but a program that works well for one child may not work at all for another. Some parents of children with disabilities choose to homeschool (see *Developmental Science at Home* on page 234). One type of school intervention that shows promise is an approach called *reciprocal teaching*. In reciprocal teaching programs, children with learning disabilities work in pairs or groups. Each child takes a turn summarizing and explaining the material to be learned to the others in the group. A number of studies have found that, after participating in reciprocal teaching, children with learning disabilities improved in summarization skills and memory strategies (e.g., Menesses & Gresham, 2009).

School can be a discouraging and frustrating place for a child with a learning disability.

Current special education laws rest most centrally on the philosophical view that children with disabilities have a right to be educated in the same school environments as children without disabilities (e.g., Stainback & Stainback, 1985). Proponents have further argued that such **inclusive education** aids a child with disabilities by integrating him into the nondisabled world, thus facilitating the development of important social skills as well as providing more appropriate academic challenges than are often found in separate classrooms or special programs for the disabled (Siegel, 1996). Advocates of inclusion are convinced that children with mild intellectual disabilities and those with learning disabilities will show greater academic achievement if they are in classrooms with children who do not have disabilities.

Schools and school districts differ widely in the specific model of inclusion they use, although virtually all models involve a team of educators, including the classroom teacher, one or more special education teachers, classroom aides, and sometimes volunteers. Some schools follow a plan called a *pull-out program*, in which the student with the disability is placed in a classroom with children who do not have disabilities only part of each day, spending the remainder of the time working with a special education teacher in a special class or resource room. More common are full-inclusion systems in which the child spends the entire school day in a class with nondisabled children but receives help from volunteers, aides, or special education teachers who come to the classroom to work with the child there.

Attention-Deficit/Hyperactivity Disorder

LO 9.13 How does attention-deficit/hyperactivity disorder affect a child's development?

Some children experience learning difficulties that don't seem to fit the typical special education categories. For example, as many as 10% of U.S. school children have a mental disorder called **attention-deficit/hyperactivity disorder (ADHD)** (Gahagan, 2011). Children with ADHD are more physically active, impulsive, and/or less attentive than their peers (American Psychiatric Association, 2013). These characteristics often lead to both academic and behavioral problems in school.

inclusive education general term for education programs in which children with disabilities are taught in classrooms with nondisabled children.

attention-deficit/hyperactivity disorder (ADHD) a mental disorder that causes children to have difficulty attending to and completing tasks

Homeschooling

The Hannigan family is concerned about their son's progress in second grade. Although Michael struggled somewhat in first grade, he was eventually able to meet the minimum requirements for promotion to second grade. Now, however, he is beginning to fall seriously behind his classmates. Michael's teachers have suggested that he might benefit from special education services, but the Hannigans are exploring the possibility of homeschooling for Michael, an option that has been enthusiastically embraced by several of their neighbors. The Hannigans' neighbors have created a variety of opportunities for their children to interact so that they do not miss out on any of the social skills that children usually learn in school. But why would a parent want to take on the daunting task of educating a child at home?

Surveys of the families of the 2.4% of American children who are homeschooled can shed some light on this question (NCES, 2008; Snider & Dillow, 2012). The most frequent reasons parents cite for homeschooling are concern about the school environment (88%), a desire to include religious training in children's education (83%), and dissatisfaction with academic standards at public and private schools (72%) (NCES, 2008). About 21% of homeschool parents have children with special learning needs and another 16% have children with physical or mental challenges. The one-on-one teaching these children get at home often helps them achieve more than their peers with disabilities in public schools are able to (Duvall, Delquadri, & Ward, 2004). In addition, children with disabilities who are homeschooled don't have to deal with teasing from peers.

Research on homeschooling has been sparse until fairly recently. In one nationwide study of more than 11,000 homeschooled children, researchers found that these children scored in the top 20% across all academic subjects (Ray, 2010). Opponents of homeschooling, a group that includes most professional educators, claim that comparisons of homeschooling and public education are misleading. They point out that the characteristics of homeschool families vary widely from those whose children attend public schools. For example, 92% of the families that participated in the nationwide survey we discussed earlier were White (Ray, 2010).

Moreover, 98% were headed by married couples with an average of 3.5 children living at home. More than 60% of the parents possessed college or graduate degrees. Only 19% of mothers worked outside the home, and 99% of fathers were employed full time. Critics argue that public school children from demographically similar communities also get high scores on standardized achievement tests. Consequently, say critics, research on homeschooling reveals more about who homeschools than about the effects of homeschooling itself.

REFLECTION

1. *What factors would motivate you to consider homeschooling your child, and what are some reasons that might make you reluctant to do so?*

2. *If you were discussing homeschooling with a classmate who cited research showing that homeschoolers get higher achievement-test scores than children who are enrolled in public school, how would you explain the shortcomings of such research?*

Application of the special education classification to a child with ADHD depends on how the disorder has affected his education and how it is being treated. For example, a child whose ADHD has caused him to fall more than 2 years behind other children in his grade will be classified as having a learning disability. The point is that ADHD is not itself a legally recognized special education category in the United States. Rather, it is a psychological disorder that may cause a child to develop school problems so severe that he qualifies for services under one of the legally defined categories. ⊙ **Watch** the **Video** *Attention-Deficit/Hyperactivity Disorder (ADHD)* in **MyPsychLab**.

CAUSES OF ADHD The cause of ADHD is unknown. However, some developmentalists suggest that children with ADHD are neurologically different from their peers. Twin studies suggesting a genetic basis for the disorder support this hypothesis (Rosenberg et al., 2012). Some experts argue that serotonin function is impaired in children with ADHD (Kent et al., 2002). Other developmentalists hypothesize that children with ADHD require more sensory stimulation than their peers; thus, they move around more in order to get the stimulation they need (Antrop, Roeyers, Van Oost, & Buysse, 2000).

Cultural factors may also be important in ADHD, as some researchers claim that the disorder is rare outside of the United States (Faraone, Sergeant, Gillberg, & Biederman, 2003). Critics of using medication to control ADHD symptoms suggest that this cross-national difference is a result of overuse of the diagnosis in the United States. However, some developmentalists assert that educators and mental health professionals in other nations have failed to recognize the degree to which ADHD may be prevalent in their children (Ralston & Lorenzo, 2004). Others suggest that there is a real cross-cultural difference in the incidence of ADHD. For example, a study comparing African American and South African 6-year-olds who were similar in family structure and socioeconomic status found that a larger proportion of African American children, especially boys, scored higher on scales measuring hyperactivity (Barbarin, 1999).

Cross-national differences aside, psychologists are fairly sure that diet, environmental toxins, or brain damage is not the cause of ADHD, despite what some promoters of "cures" claim (Barkley, 2005). At present, most experts believe that each individual case of ADHD is caused by a complex interaction of factors unique to the specific child. These factors may include genetics, temperament, parenting styles, peer relations, the type and quality of the school a child attends, and stressors in the child's life such as poverty, family instability, and parental mental illness.

CHARACTERISTICS OF ADHD On many kinds of attention tasks, children with ADHD do not differ at all from normal children (Lawrence et al., 2004). They seem to vary from their peers who do not have ADHD in activity level, the ability to sustain attention (especially with boring and repetitive tasks), and the ability to control impulses. However, the degree of hyperactivity children with ADHD exhibit is unrelated to their performance on attention tasks. That is, a child can be very physically active and still be good at controlling his attention. Likewise, a child can be very calm yet have little ability to sustain attention

Most children with ADHD are successful in learning academic skills (Chadwick et al., 1999). However, their hyperactivity and/or inattentiveness often cause other kinds of problems. For one thing, children with both types of ADHD usually produce school work that is messy and filled with errors, causing them to get poor grades (Barkley, 2005). They may be disruptive in class and are often rejected by other children.

TREATING AND MANAGING ADHD By the time their children are diagnosed with ADHD, usually upon entering school, many parents have lost confidence in their ability to control them (Barkley, 2005). Some cope with their difficult child by being extremely permissive. Others respond by becoming excessively harsh and, out of frustration, sometimes treat the child abusively. Thus, parent training can be useful in helping parents cope with children who have ADHD.

The goal of such parenting programs is to help parents regain a sense of control (Barkley, 2005). For example, experts recommend that teachers provide parents with daily reports of their children's work in the various school subjects—language, math, social studies, and so on. Parents can then use the information to enforce a standing rule that the child must have completed all school work before watching television or doing other desired activities. Such approaches, when applied consistently, can help parents of children with ADHD manage their children's difficulties, as well as their own emotional reactions, more effectively.

Many children with ADHD take stimulant medications, such as methylphenidate (Ritalin). Most of these children are calmer and can concentrate better (Demb & Chang, 2004; Mehta, Goodyer, & Sahakian, 2004). However, some studies show that many children's "response to the medication" may actually be due to changes in expectations on the part of their teachers and parents—sort of a self-fulfilling prophecy (Spreen et al., 1995). In addition, studies suggest that the concentration skills of children with ADHD can be improved with training. For example, one study found that working-memory deficits and the inability to suppress impulses underlie many of the symptoms of ADHD. Moreover, providing children with training and practice in these two domains of cognitive functioning substantially reduces ADHD symptoms (Klingberg et al., 2005).

It's also important to note that medication doesn't always improve the grades of children with ADHD (Currie, Stabile, & Jones, 2013). For the most part, it seems that stimulant medications reduce such children's activity levels, help them control their impulses, and somewhat improve their social behavior. These effects usually result in improvements in classroom behavior and peer acceptance. Medications such as methylphenidate have the greatest effect on school grades among children whose ADHD symptoms are so severe that they interfere with actual learning (Spreen et al., 1995). For this reason, the use of stimulant medications for children who have mild or moderate ADHD symptoms is controversial. Studies also show that many of the newer drugs that are used to treat ADHD (e.g., Adderall) are associated with changes in thinking that may increase a child's risk of developing a more serious psychological disorder (Gardner, 2007). Moreover, many of these drugs, including methylphenidate, have been found to increase the risk of cardiovascular events such as strokes and heart attacks in adults.

Answers to these questions can be found in the back of the book.

1. Most children who receive special education services in the United States have some kind of _____ _____.

2. Children with ADHD are more _____, more _____, and less _____ than their peers.

CRITICAL THINKING

3. If you were the parent of a child with special needs, what reasons would you have for wanting your child to be placed in a special class, and what factors would motivate you to prefer that she be taught in a classroom with children who do not have disabilities? How would the nature of the child's disability affect your preference?

SUMMARY

Physical Changes (pp. 212–217)

LO 9.1 What kinds of physical changes occur during middle childhood?

- Physical development from age 6 to age 12 is steady and slow. Children gain 2 to 3 inches in height and about 6 pounds of weight each year. Sex differences in skeletal and muscular maturation may lead boys and girls to excel at different activities.

LO 9.2 In what ways does the brain change during these years?

- Major brain growth spurts occur in 6- to 8-year-olds and in 10- to 12-year-olds. Neurological development leads to improvements in selective attention, information-processing speed, and spatial perception.

LO 9.3 What are the three most important health hazards for 6- to 12-year-olds?

- School-aged children are healthy but benefit from regular medical care. Head injuries, asthma, and excessive weight gain are the most prevalent health problems of this age group.

Cognitive Changes (pp. 217–222)

LO 9.4 How do vocabulary and other aspects of language change during middle childhood?

- Language development continues in middle childhood with vocabulary growth, improvements in grammar, and understanding of the social uses of language.

LO 9.5 What cognitive advantages do children gain as they move through Piaget's concrete operational stage?

- Piaget proposed that a major change in a child's thinking occurs at about age 6, when the child begins to understand powerful operations such as reversibility and decentration. The child also learns to use inductive logic but does not yet use deductive logic.

LO 9.6 What is *horizontal decalage*, and how does Siegler explain concrete operational thinking?

- Children do not master all of Piaget's concrete operational tasks at the same time, a pattern he called horizontal decalage. Moreover, Siegler's research suggests that the "operations" he observed may actually be rules for solving specific types of problems.

LO 9.7 How do children's information-processing skills improve during middle childhood?

- Most information-processing theorists conclude that there are no age-related changes in children's information-processing capacity, but there are clearly improvements in speed and efficiency.

Schooling (pp. 222–231)

LO 9.8 What should be included in an effective literacy curriculum?

- To become literate, children need specific instruction in sound–symbol correspondences, word parts, and other aspects of written language. They also need to be exposed to good literature and to have lots of opportunities to practice their reading and writing skills.

LO 9.9 How do bilingual and ESL approaches to second-language instruction differ?

- Children who participate in bilingual education receive academic instruction in their first language until they develop sufficient English skills to be taught in English. Those in ESL classes attend language classes in which they learn English and are instructed in English in their academic classes.

LO 9.10 Why do schools administer achievement tests, and what kind of items do they include?

- Children's school progress is assessed with both IQ tests and achievement tests. Both types of tests may ignore important aspects of intellectual functioning.

LO 9.11 What kinds of group differences in achievement have educational researchers found?

- Boys typically do better on tests of advanced mathematical ability than girls. Girls do somewhat better than boys on verbal tasks. Although poverty and other social factors may play a role, ethnic differences in achievement may also result from differences in learning styles, philosophy, or attitudes toward school. Differences in both cultural beliefs and teaching practices are probably responsible for cross-cultural variations in math and science achievement.

Children with Special Needs (pp. 231–236)

LO 9.12 Why is the term *learning disability* controversial?

- There is considerable dispute about how to identify a genuine learning disability, and some children who are labeled as such have been misclassified. Practically speaking, "learning disability" serves as a catch-all term to describe children who, for unknown reasons, do not learn as quickly as their intelligence-test scores suggest they should.

LO 9.13 How does attention-deficit/hyperactivity disorder affect a child's development?

- Children with ADHD have problems with both academic learning and social relationships. Medication, parent training, and behavior modification are useful in helping children with ADHD overcome these difficulties.

KEY TERMS

achievement test (p. 225)

analytical style (p. 228)

association areas (p. 213)

asthma (p. 214)

attention-deficit/hyperactivity disorder (ADHD) (p. 233)

automaticity (p. 220)

balanced approach (p. 223)

bilingual education (p. 224)

BMI-for-age (p. 215)

class inclusion (p. 219)

concrete operational stage (p. 218)

decentration (p. 218)

deductive logic (p. 218)

dyslexia (p. 231)

English-as-a-second-language (ESL) program (p. 224)

excessive weight gain (p. 214)

executive processes (p. 221)

inclusive education (p. 233)

inductive logic (p. 218)

learning disability (p. 231)

memory strategies (p. 221)

obese (p. 215)

overweight (p. 215)

processing efficiency (p. 220)

relational style (p. 228)

relative right–left orientation (p. 213)

reversibility (p. 218)

selective attention (p. 213)

severely obese (p. 215)

spatial cognition (p. 214)

spatial perception (p. 213)

systematic and explicit phonics (p. 223)

traumatic brain injury (TBI) (p. 214)

CHAPTER TEST ✓ Study and Review in MyPsychLab

Answers to all the Chapter Test questions can be found in the back of the book.

1. Which of these children is demonstrating automaticity?
   a. Luc memorizes spelling words by repeating them over and over again.
   b. Shoshana can say "49" in response to "How much is 7 × 7?" without thinking about it.
   c. Seven-year-old Lida can process information more rapidly than her 3-year-old brother.
   d. Ten-year-old Dave knows everything there is to know about the New York Yankees.

2. Which of these children is demonstrating the rehearsal strategy?
   a. Luc memorizes spelling words by repeating them over and over again.
   b. Shoshana can say "49" in response to "How much is 7 × 7?" without thinking about it.
   c. Seven-year-old Lida can process information more rapidly than her 3-year-old brother.
   d. Ten-year-old Dave knows everything there is to know about the New York Yankees.

3. Which of the following describes one of the differences in math instruction in the United States and Asia?
   a. Many U.S. students are dependent on calculators rather than their own math skills.
   b. Asian families rely on the educational system to teach computational skills.
   c. Many Asian students are taught to use calculators as early as age 2.
   d. Asian teachers provide students with material rewards more often than American teachers do.

4. In Robert Siegler's research on problem solving, children who use Rule IV _____.
   a. can use a formula to systematically compare relevant factors
   b. calculate and estimate using multiple dimensions or characteristics
   c. take into account only one dimension of a problem
   d. require special cognitive training to move beyond this level

5. Mr. Henry uses the balanced approach to teach reading. Which of the teaching techniques below is he likely to use?
   a. Mr. Henry teaches students to write before he teaches them to read.
   b. Mr. Henry avoids directly teaching students about sound-letter connections.
   c. Mr. Henry does not encourage children to develop automaticity.
   d. When a student makes an error, Mr. Henry teaches him or her a new strategy.

6. According to Piaget, the concrete operational stage includes acquisition of the ability to _____.
   a. use language to communicate
   b. reason deductively
   c. reason inductively
   d. reason about hypothetical situations

7. Which of the following is an executive process?
   a. speaking a language fluently
   b. using memory strategies to process information
   c. knowing a great deal about a specific subject
   d. recalling information effortlessly

8. Some critics object to routine IQ testing in schools because such testing _____.
   a. can lead to misclassification of some children
   b. ignores the fact that there is no correlation between IQ scores and achievement
   c. takes time away from instruction
   d. cannot test large numbers of children in a timely manner

9. The last four digits of Chad's mother's work phone number are 0704. Chad remembers them by linking them to the date of Independence Day (July 4). Chad is using a memory strategy called _____.
   a. inductive reasoning
   b. elaboration
   c. mnemonics
   d. systematic searching

10. Between the ages of 6 and 12, children's vocabularies _____.
    a. are stable
    b. decrease as they develop habits of word usage (i.e., "use it or lose it")
    c. increase dramatically
    d. increase only if they read a large number of books

11. Concrete operations permit children to understand _____.
    a. the rules that govern the physical and social worlds
    b. how their memories work
    c. deductive reasoning
    d. others' emotions

12. Marisol has been diagnosed with a learning disability. Which of the following is likely to be true about Marisol?
    a. She is in third grade but reads on a first-grade level.
    b. She has a below-average IQ.
    c. She gets along well with her peers.
    d. She has a form of intellectual disability.

13. Metacognition is often described as _____.
    a. reasoning about abstract concepts
    b. an understanding of the elements of language
    c. thinking about thinking
    d. one of the cognitive strengths associated with Piaget's preoperational stage

14. The attention span of the average fourth-grader is much longer than that of the average first grader. Which of the following biological changes is primarily responsible for this?
    a. maturation of the reticular formation

    b. myelination of the neurons in the right side of the brain
    c. pruning of the synapses in the corpus callosum
    d. lateralization of spatial perception

15. On which of the following is children's capacity for creativity most dependent?
    a. their executive processing strategies
    b. their metacognitive skills
    c. their short-term memory abilities
    d. the amount of knowledge they have about a topic

16. Who is the theorist who proposed the triarchic theory of intelligence?
    a. Alfred Binet
    b. Howard Gardner
    c. David Wechsler
    d. Robert Sternberg

17. Which of the following is an essential component of concrete operational thinking?
    a. the ability to analyze one's memory functions
    b. reasoning based on hypothetical premises
    c. understanding that both physical actions and mental operations can be reversed
    d. the ability to understand abstract concepts such as justice and honor

18. _____ awareness is related to learning to read well in middle childhood.
    a. Literacy
    b. Phonological
    c. Elaborative
    d. Spatial

19. Children whose BMI-for-age is between the 85th and 95th percentiles are classified as _____, while those whose BMI-for-age is at or above the 95th percentile are classified as _____.
    a. obese, very severely obese
    b. overweight, obese
    c. obese, obese
    d. overweight, overweight

20. If Doreen understands class inclusion, which question of these researchers' questions can she answer correctly?
    a. If I pour your juice in a smaller glass, will you have more?
    b. Which is worth more, a quarter or a dime?
    c. What would your room look like if you were hanging upside down from the ceiling?
    d. If you have seven dogs and three cats, do you have more dogs or more animals?

21. Why would a group of concrete-operational children find magic tricks interesting?
    a. Because they understand that the tricks are fake.
    b. Because they are attracted to activities that include movement.
    c. Because they do not have the cognitive ability to make sense of the tricks.
    d. Because they don't understand natural laws.

22. Ms. Carver asked her third-graders to write a paragraph describing how their lives would be different if they were the opposite gender. She did not understand why the children were confused by the task. Piaget would say that Ms. Carver's assignment was difficult for her students because they lack the ability to _____.
    a. think about people of the opposite gender
    b. reason inductively
    c. see others' points of view
    d. reason deductively

23. Which of these brain-development processes underlies improvements in spatial perception in the middle childhood years?
    a. synaptogenesis
    b. lateralization

c. thinning of the cerebral cortex
d. myelination of links between the reticular formation and the frontal lobes

24. According to Howard Gardner's theory of multiple intelligences, which of the following represents the ability to understand others?
    a. natural
    b. bodily kinesthetic
    c. interpersonal
    d. intrapersonal

25. Which of the following is the most frequent cause of school absence in middle childhood?
    a. obesity
    b. traumatic brain injury
    c. asthma
    d. accidents

To 👁 **Watch** ✳ **Explore** ⊚ **Simulate** ✅ **Study** and **Review** and experience MyVirtualLife go to MyPsychLab.com

chapter 10

Social and Personality Development in Middle Childhood

Every culture in the world has a society of child-hood, in which children make up their own social rules that differ from those of adult society. For example, in most U.S. school lunchrooms, food trading is common. A child who refuses to trade may be seen as "stuck-up." But adults who try to talk co-workers into trading lunches are likely to be thought of as pushy or somewhat odd. Such comparisons show that children practice social competence by making up their own social rules rather than simply copying those that exist

LEARNING OBJECTIVES

THEORIES OF SOCIAL AND PERSONALITY DEVELOPMENT

10.1 How did the psychoanalytic theorists characterize the middle childhood years?

10.2 What are the main ideas of the trait and social-cognitive theorists?

SELF-CONCEPT

10.3 What are the features of the psychological self?

10.4 How does self-esteem develop?

ADVANCES IN SOCIAL COGNITION

10.5 How does children's understanding of others change in middle childhood?

10.6 How do children in Piaget's moral realism and moral relativism stages reason about right and wrong?

THE SOCIAL WORLD OF THE SCHOOL-AGED CHILD

10.7 How does self-regulation affect school-aged children's relationships with their parents?

10.8 What changes occur in children's understanding of friendships during this period?

10.9 In what ways do boys and girls interact during the middle childhood years?

10.10 What types of aggression are most common among school-aged children?

10.11 How do popular, rejected, and neglected children differ?

INFLUENCES BEYOND FAMILY AND PEERS

10.12 What factors contribute to resilience and vulnerability among poor children?

10.13 How do television, computers, and video games affect children's development?

in the adult world. Creating and enforcing such rules helps children learn to look at things from other people's points of view and to cooperate.

Clearly, cognitive development provides the intellectual foundation required to engage in rule-governed activities. But what makes each child's experiences unique within the context of such universal interactions are the emotional and behavioral responses that their distinctive personalities, self-concepts, and relationship histories contribute to the developmental equation. This is one reason each student's experience with raising a "child" in *MyVirtualLife* is unique. As in real life, there are common challenges that all developing individuals face, but we bring different approaches to them, based on our personalities and backgrounds. These differences are the topics of the present chapter. We begin with a consideration of the major themes of development that uniquely mark social and personality development in the middle childhood years and the different ways in which developmentalists have explained them.

MyVirtualLife
What decisions would you make while raising a child? What would the consequences of those decisions be?

Find out by accessing MyVirtualLife at www.MyPsychLab.com to raise a virtual child and live your own virtual life.

Theories of Social and Personality Development

Development of self-perceived competence is the overarching theme of social and personality development in the middle childhood years. How do children develop this critical attribute? Developmentalists representing different theoretical perspectives emphasize different sets of factors in their explanations.

Psychoanalytic Perspectives

LO 10.1   How did the psychoanalytic theorists characterize the middle childhood years?

When you think back to your middle childhood years, what kinds of experiences stand out? Most likely, you remember interacting with your peers and siblings. If Freud were called upon to explain how your feelings about your own competence developed, he would appeal to the emotional qualities of these interactions. According to the psychoanalytic perspective, and in line with our everyday experiences with children, children vary greatly in the ways that they respond to such situations. Some become angry and lash out at those who reject them. Others withdraw and develop a general fear of social interactions. Parents contribute to these responses. However, Freud thought that the challenge of the middle childhood years was to form emotional bonds with peers and to move beyond those that were developed with parents in earlier years. Thus, much of the modern-day research on peer rejection and other emotional features of middle childhood finds its roots in Freud's psychoanalytic approach.

Erik Erikson accepted Freud's view of the central role of peer relationships and the emotions that accompany them in middle childhood. He went beyond Freud's perspective, though, when he further characterized middle childhood as the period during which children experience the crisis of *industry versus inferiority*. During this stage, Erikson said, children develop a sense of their own competence through the achievement of culturally defined learning goals (see Table 2.2 on page 27). The psychosocial task of a 6- to 12-year-old is development of industry, or the willingness to work to accomplish goals. To develop industry, the child must be able to achieve the goals her culture sets for all children her age. In most countries, 6- to 12-year-olds must learn to read and write. If they fail to do so, Erikson's view claims, they will enter adolescence and adulthood with feelings of inferiority. These feelings of inferiority constitute an emotional mindset that can hamper an individual's ability to achieve for the rest of her life.

Contemporary studies that stress the child's need to feel competent are in tune with Erikson's views. Many of them suggest that he was right about the link between school experiences and an emerging sense of competence. It seems that most 6- to 12-year-olds gradually develop a view of their own competence as they succeed or fail at academic tasks such as reading and

trait a stable pattern of responding to situations

arithmetic (Harter, 2012). Thus, their self-assessments and actual achievements are strongly correlated; that is, those who are most successful judge themselves to be competent, while those who have difficulty perceive themselves as less so. However, individual differences in children's responses to success and failure moderate the effects of the experiences themselves. Some of these differences are found in the emotional realm, as suggested earlier.

Erikson also argued that children who lack success in school can develop it by participating in culturally valued pursuits outside academic settings. A child who is a mediocre student, for instance, may channel his need to develop self-perceived competence into athletics. Another child who gets poor grades may do so because she spends most of her time reading books that she finds to be more interesting than her school work. Outsiders may worry about her sense of competence, but, internally, she has no doubts about her abilities.

The Trait and Social-Cognitive Perspectives

LO 10.2 What are the main ideas of the trait and social-cognitive theorists?

Psychoanalytic theorists have given us some compelling ideas about how individual differences in emotional responses to childhood experiences shape development and self-perceived competence. However, they tell us little about the origins of those differences. The primary goal of *trait theories*, by contrast, is to do just that. A **trait** is a stable pattern of responding to situations. This definition should remind you of our discussions of temperament in earlier chapters because the study of infant and early childhood temperament is grounded in trait theory. By middle childhood, trait theorists argue, the various dimensions of temperament have evolved into the five dimensions of personality (the *Big Five personality traits*), shown in Table 10.1.

Research suggests that trait theorists are right about the emergence of stable traits in middle childhood. Moreover, these traits are known to contribute to the development of feelings of competence. For instance, a child who is reasonably *extraverted*, or outgoing, responds to peer rejection by becoming more determined to be accepted by the group. One who is *introverted*, or shy, would likely be so emotionally distraught by the taunts of her playmates that she would actively avoid social situations in the future. Still, trait theory leaves us wondering why extraversion doesn't always lead to social competence and why some people overcome their tendency toward introversion to become competent in the social arena.

From the social-cognitive perspective, both the psychoanalytic theorists and the trait perspective focus on only one set of factors that shape the development of self-perceived competence in middle childhood. Albert Bandura, for instance, proposed that the emotions described by psychoanalytic theorists and the stable patterns of responding that have been identified by trait theorists, together with cognitive factors, constitute one of three interactive components that influence social and personality development (see Figure 10.1). Bandura used the term *person component* to refer to this emotional/cognitive component. The other components of his model were the developing person's *behavior* and the responses of the *environment*.

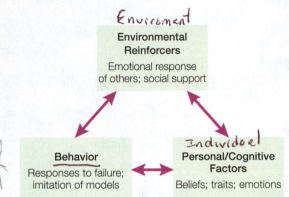

Figure 10.1 Bandura's Reciprocal Determinism

Bandura takes a social-cognitive view of personality. He suggests that three components—the external environment, individual behaviors, and cognitive factors, such as beliefs, expectancies, and personal dispositions—are all influenced by each other and play reciprocal roles in determining personality.

TABLE 10.1   The Big Five Personality Traits

Trait	Qualities of Individuals Who Show the Trait	Possible Temperament Components
Extraversion	Active, assertive, enthusiastic, outgoing	High activity level; sociability; positive emotionality; talkativeness
Agreeableness	Affectionate, forgiving, generous, kind, sympathetic, trusting	Perhaps high approach/positive emotionality; perhaps effortful control
Conscientiousness	Efficient, organized, prudent, reliable, responsible	Effortful control/task persistence
Neuroticism (also called emotional instability)	Anxious, self-pitying, tense, touchy, unstable, worrying	Negative emotionality; irritability
Openness/intellect	Artistic, curious, imaginative, insightful, original, wide interests	Sociability; low inhibition

(*Sources:* Ahadi & Rothbart, 1994; John, Caspi, Robins, Moffitt, & Stouthamer-Loeber, 1994, Table 1, p. 161; McCrae & Costa, 1990.)

Bandura proposed that the personal, behavioral, and environmental components interact in a pattern he termed **reciprocal determinism**. Each of the three components influences, and is influenced by, the other two. For example, when a child with a difficult temperament (personal component) throws a tantrum, the parents may ignore him (environmental component), leading him to become enraged and to misbehave even more (behavioral component). But if parents respond to an easygoing child's tantrum with inattention, the child may respond by stopping the tantrum to regain his parents' attention.

By organizing the various interactive influences in the way that it does, Bandura's model provides a more comprehensive explanation than either the psychoanalytic or the trait theorists do of how school-aged children develop ideas about their degrees of competence. Thus, Bandura's social-cognitive approach provides us with a way of taking into account the valuable insights of the psychoanalytic theorists relative to children's emotions along with those of the trait theorists. And by integrating both into the three-part model that Bandura proposed, we gain a more comprehensive understanding of the mechanisms that drive the development of self-perceived competence in the middle childhood years.

reciprocal determinism Bandura's model in which personal, behavioral, and environmental factors interact to influence personality development

psychological self an understanding of one's stable, internal traits

test yourself before going on ✓ Study and Review in MyPsychLab

Answers to these questions can be found in the back of the book. 495

1. In the table below, summarize what Erikson believed to be the factors that influence the outcome of the industry-versus-inferiority stage and the consequences that flow from each outcome.

Industry	Inferiority
Influences *accomplashing goals* *learning culturally valued skills, reading, making things*	*failure to learn skills, inability to accomplish goals*
Consequences *good foundation for future Psychosocial dev. Willingness to take on challenging tests*	*poor foundation for future Psysocial dev. reluctant to work hard*

2. Classify each behavior according to the Big Five personality trait that it represents:
   _A_ (1) talkativeness
   _B_ (2) courteousness ✗
   _D_ (3) irritability ✗
   _E_ (4) curiosity
   _C_ (5) responsibility
   (a) extraversion
   (b) neuroticism
   (c) conscientiousness
   (d) agreeableness
   (e) openness

3. Classify each variable according to the three components of Bandura's reciprocal determinism model of personality development: (A) person, (B) environment, (C) behavior
   _B_ (1) parents' responses to children's actions
   _A_ (2) temperament
   _C_ (3) children's actions

CRITICAL THINKING

4. How might you use Bandura's three-part model to create an explanation of how an event in your childhood influenced your development in the domain of personality development? What role did your emotional responses and personality traits play in the event?

Self-Concept

How much insight does a school-aged child really have into her own personality? The answer depends on whether we look at the child at the beginning of this period or near the end of it. Across the years from 6 to 12, children's understanding of themselves improves quite a bit. By the end of the middle childhood period, children's self-concepts include two new components: a *psychological self* and a *valued self*.

The Psychological Self

LO 10.3 What are the features of the psychological self?

The **psychological self** is a person's understanding of his or her enduring psychological characteristics. It first appears during the transition from early to middle childhood and becomes increasingly complex as the child approaches adolescence. It includes both basic information about the child's unique characteristics and self-judgments of competency.

self-efficacy belief in one's capacity to cause an intended event to occur or to perform a task

social comparisons conclusions drawn about the self based on comparisons to others

Your belief in your ability to solve a problem, reach a goal, complete a task & achieve what you set out to do

PERSONALITY TRAITS Children don't use the same terminology as the trait theories that you read about earlier in the chapter, but they do describe their own personalities with increasing degrees of precision across the middle childhood years. For example a 6-year-old might use simple psychological self-descriptors such as "smart" or "dumb." By 10, a child is more likely to use comparisons in self-descriptions: "I'm smarter than most other kids" or "I'm not as talented in art as my friend" (Harter, 2012).

This developmental trend was illustrated in the results of a classic study of the self-concepts of 9- to 18-year-olds (Montemayor & Eisen, 1977). Children who participated were asked to give 20 answers to the question, "Who am I?" The researchers found that the younger children were still using mostly surface qualities to describe themselves, as in this description by a 9-year-old:

> My name is Bruce C. I have brown eyes. I have brown hair. I have brown eyebrows. I am nine years old. I LOVE Sports! I have seven people in my family. I have great eye site! I have lots of friends! I live on 1923 Pinecrest Dr. I am going on 10 in September. I'm a boy. I have a uncle that is almost 7 feet tall. My school is Pinecrest. My teacher is Mrs. V. I play Hockey! I'm almost the smartest boy in the class. I LOVE food! I love fresh air. I LOVE school. (Montemayor & Eisen, 1977, p. 317)

In contrast, consider the self-description of this 11-year-old girl in sixth grade:

> My name is A. I'm a human being. I'm a girl. I'm a truthful person. I'm not very pretty. I do so-so in my studies. I'm a very good cellist. I'm a very good pianist. I'm a little bit tall for my age. I like several boys. I like several girls. I'm old-fashioned. I play tennis. I am a very good swimmer. I try to be helpful. I'm always ready to be friends with anybody. Mostly I'm good, but I lose my temper. I'm not well-liked by some girls and boys. I don't know if I'm liked by boys or not. (Montemayor & Eisen, 1977, pp. 317–318)

This girl, like the other 11-year-olds in the study, describes her external qualities, but she also emphasizes psychological factors such as personality traits.

Interestingly, too, the cultural context in which a child is growing up may influence his social self. For example, researchers have found that young children's inclusion of role terms (e.g., "daughter," "grandchild") in their self-descriptions varies across cultural groups. Pre-schoolers in Asian American families are more likely to include such descriptors than their European American counterparts are (Wang, 2006a). These differences may emerge from differences in the ways that parents from these two groups guide the formation of children's self-understanding through discussions of important events in their lives (Wang, 2006b).

Thus, as a child moves through the concrete operational period, her psychological self becomes more complex, more comparative, less tied to external features, and more centered on feelings and ideas.

SELF-EFFICACY As we noted earlier, middle childhood is the time when children develop perceptions of the degree to which they are competent. Albert Bandura has greatly advanced developmentalists' understanding of this crucial aspect of the psychological self. He defines **self-efficacy** as an individual's belief in her capacity to cause an intended event to occur (Bandura, 1997). How does it develop?

Bandura proposed that peer models are a primary source of self-efficacy beliefs (Bandura, 1997). However, **social comparisons**, conclusions drawn about the self based on comparisons to others, play an integral role in the degree to which children gain insight into their own self-efficacy from observing peers (Thompson, Winer, & Goodvin, 2011). Thus, simply watching other children model success at a task is insufficient for the development of self-efficacy in a child whom outsiders see as similar to the models. The child herself must perceive that similarity in order to be influenced by the models. Encouragement from sources of information that children value, such as teachers and parents, also contributes to self-efficacy.

The Valued Self

LO 10.4   How does self-esteem develop?

A child can have an accurate view of her personality traits, and even have a solid sense of self-efficacy, but still fail to value herself as an individual. To find out why, developmentalists have studied another aspect of self-concept development in middle childhood, the emergence of the *valued self*.

THE NATURE OF SELF-ESTEEM A child's evaluative judgments have several interesting features. First of all, over the years of elementary school and high school, children's evaluations of their own abilities become increasingly differentiated, with quite separate judgments about various *domains* of competence. These domains include academic skills, athletic skills, physical appearance, social acceptance, friendships, romantic appeal, and relationships with parents (Harter, 1990; Marsh, Craven, & Debus, 1999). Paradoxically, however, it is when they reach school age—around age 7—that children first develop a global self-evaluation. Seven- and 8-year-olds (but not younger children) readily answer questions about how well they like themselves as people, how happy they are, or how well they like the way they are leading their lives. It is this global evaluation of one's own worth that is usually referred to as **self-esteem**, and it is not merely the sum of all the separate assessments a child makes about his skills in different areas. How stable are self-esteem judgments? A number of longitudinal studies of elementary school–aged children and teenagers show that self-esteem is quite stable in the short term but somewhat less so over periods of several years. The correlation between two self-esteem scores obtained a few months apart is generally about .60. Over several years, the correlation drops to about .40 (Alsaker & Kroger, 2006). So, a child with high self-esteem at age 8 or 9 is likely to have high self-esteem at age 10 or 11. But it is also true that self-esteem is subject to a good deal of variation. To some degree, self-esteem is more stable in girls than in boys (Harter, 2006; Heinonen, Raikkonen, & Keltikangas-Jarvinen, 2003).

HOW SELF-ESTEEM DEVELOPS Developmental psychologist Susan Harter (1990, 2006, 2012) has studied the development of self-esteem extensively. She has found that self-esteem is strongly influenced by mental comparisons of children's ideal selves and their actual experiences. For example, social self-esteem, the assessment of one's own social skills, is higher in popular children than in those who are rejected by their peers (Jackson & Bracken, 1998). However, different children value each component of self-esteem differently. Thus, a child who perceives herself to have poor social skills because she is unpopular may not necessarily have low self-esteem. The degree to which her social self-assessment affects her self-esteem is influenced by how much she values social skills and popularity. In addition, she may see herself as very competent in another area—such as academic skills—that balances her lack of social skills.

The key to self-esteem, then, is the amount of discrepancy between what the child desires and what he thinks he has achieved. Thus, a child who values sports prowess but who isn't big enough or coordinated enough to be good at sports will have lower self-esteem than will an equally small or uncoordinated child who does not value sports skill so highly. Similarly, being good at something, such as singing or playing chess, won't raise a child's self-esteem unless the child values that particular skill.

The second major influence on a child's self-esteem is the overall support the child feels she is receiving from the important people around her, particularly parents and peers (Franco & Levitt, 1998). Apparently, to develop high self-esteem, children must first acquire the sense that they are liked and accepted in their families, by both parents and siblings. Next, they need to be able to find friends with whom they can develop stable relationships. Since childhood friendships begin with shared interests and activities, children need to be in an environment in which they can find others who like the same things they do and are similarly skilled. Athletic children need other athletic children to associate with, those who are musically inclined need to meet peers who are also musical, and so on.

The criteria by which children learn to evaluate themselves vary considerably from one society to another (Miller, Wang, Sandel, & Cho, 2002; Wang & Ollendick, 2001). In individualistic cultures, like that of the United States, parents focus on helping children develop a sense of self-esteem that is based in the children's own interests and abilities. In cultures that focus on interdependency, such as China's, children are taught to value themselves based on cultural ideals about what a "good" person is. Moreover, individuals raised in interdependent cultures experience more anxiety when they perceive large differences between their ideal and actual selves (Levinson & Rodebaugh, 2013). As a result, children growing up in such cultures may work harder to bring their real selves into conformity with an ideal self that is strongly influenced by cultural standards than their peers in individualist societies do.

Hitting a home run will raise this girl's self-esteem only if she places a high value on being good at sports or at baseball specifically.

self-esteem a global evaluation of one's own worth

From all these sources, a child fashions her ideas (her internal model) about what she should be and what she is. Like the internal model of attachment, self-esteem is not fixed in stone. It is responsive to changes in others' judgments as well as to changes in the child's own experience of success or failure. But once created, the model does tend to persist, both because the child tends to choose experiences that will confirm and support it and because the social environment—including the parents' evaluations of the child—tends to be at least moderately consistent.

test yourself before going on ☑ **Study** and **Review** in **MyPsychLab**

Answers to these questions can be found in the back of the book.

1. Write *Y* by the statement more likely to have been made by a 6- to 12-year-old and *N* by the one likely to have been made by a younger child.
   ___N___(a) I am a boy, and I like to play with trucks.
   ___Y___(b) I am a nice girl with brown hair, and I like school

2. Match each of the following terms with its definition.
   (1) an individual's belief in her capacity to cause an intended event to occur

(2) an individual's overall sense of his value
   ___1___(a) self-efficacy
   ___2___(b) self-esteem

CRITICAL THINKING

3. How might Bandura's reciprocal determinism model be applied to explaining how a child could have a good understanding of her personality and strong self-efficacy and yet still have low self-esteem?

Advances in Social Cognition

Children's ability to understand motivation is enhanced by the development of a theory of mind in early childhood. But by the end of the middle childhood period, children have developed a much broader understanding of others than they possessed at its beginning. Moreover, they are beginning to understand the moral aspects of social relationships.

The Child as Psychologist

LO 10.5 How does children's understanding of others change in middle childhood?

A number of early ground-breaking social-cognitive studies demonstrated that a child of this age looks beyond appearances and searches for deeper consistencies that will help him to interpret both his own and other people's behavior. Thus, like their understanding of the physical world, 6- to 12-year-olds' descriptions of other people move from the concrete to the abstract. If you ask a 6- or 7-year-old to describe others, he will focus almost exclusively on external features—what the person looks like, where he lives, what he does. This description by a 7-year-old boy, taken from a classic study of social-cognitive development, is typical:

> He is very tall. He has dark brown hair, he goes to our school. I don't think he has any brothers or sisters. He is in our class. Today he has a dark orange [sweater] and gray trousers and brown shoes. (Livesley & Bromley, 1973, p. 213)

When young children do use internal or evaluative terms to describe people, they are likely to use global terms, such as "nice" or "mean," "good" or "bad." Further, young children do not seem to see these qualities as lasting or general traits of the individual, applicable in all situations or over time (Rholes & Ruble, 1984). In other words, a 6- or 7-year-old has not yet developed a concept that might be called "conservation of personality."

Beginning at about age 7 or 8, a rather dramatic shift occurs in children's descriptions of others. The child begins to focus more on the inner traits or qualities of another person and to assume that those traits will be visible in many situations (Gnepp & Chilamkurti, 1988). Children this age still describe others' physical features, but their descriptions are now used as examples of more general points about internal qualities. You can see the change when you compare the 7-year-old's description given above with this description by a child nearly 10 years old:

> He smells very much and is very nasty. He has no sense of humour and is very dull. He is always fighting and he is cruel. He does silly things and is very stupid. He has brown hair and cruel eyes. He is sulky and 11 years old and has lots of sisters. I think he is the most horrible boy in the class. He has a croaky voice and always chews his pencil and picks his teeth and I think he is disgusting. (Livesley & Bromley, 1973, p. 217)

This description still includes many external physical features but goes beyond such concrete surface qualities to the level of personality traits, such as cruelty and lack of humor.

The movement from externals to internals in descriptions of others is well documented by research. For example, in one important early study, researchers asked 6-, 8-, and 10-year-olds to describe three other children; a year later, they asked them to do the same thing again (Barenboim, 1981). The researchers found that behavioral comparisons peaked at around age 8, but psychological comparisons increased steadily throughout middle childhood. A *behavioral comparison* involves comparing a child's behaviors or physical features with those of another child or with a norm—for example, "Billy runs a lot faster than Jason" or "She draws the best in our whole class." A statement that involves an internal personality trait—such as "Sarah is so kind" or "He's a real stubborn idiot!"—refers to a *psychological construct*. Thus, a child who is making a psychological comparison contrasts peers in terms of one or more psychological constructs. (e.g., "Billy is nicer than George.")

School-aged children also understand family roles and relationships much better than younger children do. For example, by about age 9, children who live in two-parent homes understand that their parents' roles as parents are distinct from their roles as partners or spouses (Jenkins & Buccioni, 2000). Thus, a 9-year-old is better able than a 5-year-old to understand when divorcing parents say that their love for the child hasn't changed, even though their relationship with each other has ended. Emotionally, the divorce experience may be just as difficult, but school-aged children are more capable of understanding it cognitively.

Moral Reasoning

LO 10.6   How do children in Piaget's moral realism and moral relativism stages reason about right and wrong?

Children's growing understanding of the internal experiences of other people helps them develop a better understanding of how they and others think about actions that have moral implications. *Moral reasoning* is the process of making judgments about the rightness or wrongness of specific acts. As you learned in Chapter 8, children learn to discriminate between intentional and unintentional acts between age 2 and age 6. However, using this understanding to make moral judgments is another matter. Piaget claimed that the ability to use reasoning about intentions to make judgments about the moral dimensions of behavior appears to emerge along with concrete operational reasoning.

PIAGET'S MORAL REALISM AND MORAL RELATIVISM   Piaget studied moral development by observing children playing games. He noticed that younger children seemed to have less understanding of the games' rules. Following up on these observations, Piaget questioned children of different ages about rules. Their answers led him to propose a two-stage theory of moral development (Piaget, 1932).

At the beginning of the middle childhood period, children are in what Piaget termed the **moral realism stage**. They believe that the rules of games can't be changed because they come from authorities, such as parents, government officials, or religious figures. For example, one 6-year-old told Piaget that the game of marbles was invented on Noah's ark. He went on to

Piaget suggested that there is a connection between children's understanding of the rules by which games are played and their reasoning about moral issues.

Encouraging Moral Reasoning

Much to the surprise of her mother, Andrea, 8-year-old Marisol was caught stealing a package of candy from a convenience store that she passed every day when she walked home from school. The manager called Marisol's mother to report what the girl had done, and by the time Andrea arrived, the little girl was crying and pledging never to steal again. "You still have to be punished," Andrea explained and told Marisol that she was taking away all of the girl's privileges for 2 weeks. However, like most other parents, Andrea wanted to be sure that Marisol understood why what she did was wrong. How can parents help children learn to reason about issues of right and wrong?

In his book *Raising Good Children*, developmental psychologist Thomas Lickona reminds readers that the development of mature moral reasoning takes many years (Lickona, 1994). At the same time, he offers parents and teachers several suggestions that will help them help their 6- to 12-year-olds prepare for movement to more mature levels. Following are some of his suggestions:

- Require kids to give reasons for what they want.
- Play developmentally appropriate games with them.
- Praise them for observing social conventions such as saying "please" and "thank you."
- When punishment is necessary, provide them with an explanation, advice on how to avoid punishment in the future, and a way of repairing any damage their misbehavior has caused.
- Teach them about reciprocity: "We do nice things for you, so you should be willing to help us."
- Give them meaningful chores so they will think of themselves as important family and community members.
- Help and encourage them to base obedience on love and respect rather than fear.
- Teach them religious and philosophical values, including the idea that some actions are right and others are wrong, regardless of circumstances.
- Challenge their egocentrism by asking questions such as, "How would you feel if someone did that to you?" when they violate others' rights.
- Include them in charitable projects, such as food drives, to extend the idea of love and caring beyond their own families.

REFLECTION

1. Which of Lickona's suggestions are most relevant to the situation in which Marisol's mother found herself?

2. Do you agree with Andrea that it was necessary to punish the girl? If so, what additional steps do you think Andrea should take to help Marisol learn the importance of respecting others' property?

---

moral relativism stage the second of Piaget's stages of moral development, in which children understand that many rules can be changed through social agreement

explain that the rules can't be changed because the "big ones," meaning adults and older children, wouldn't like it (Piaget, 1965, p. 60).

Moral realists also believe that all rule violations eventually result in punishment. For example, Piaget told children a story about a child who fell into a stream when he tried to use a rotten piece of wood as a bridge. Children younger than 8 told him that the child was being punished for something "naughty" he had done in the past.

After age 8, Piaget proposed, children move into the **moral relativism stage**, in which they learn that people can agree to change rules if they want to. They realize that the important thing about a game is that all the players follow the same rules, regardless of what those are. For example, 8- to 12-year-olds know that a group of children playing baseball can decide to give each batter four strikes rather than three. They understand that their agreement doesn't change the game of baseball and that it doesn't apply to other people who play the game. At the same time, children of this age get better at following the rules of games.

Eight- to 12-year-olds also know that you don't get punished for rule violations unless you get caught. As a result, they view events like the one in which the child fell into the stream as accidents. They understand that accidents are not caused by "naughty" behavior. Children older than 8 also understand the relationship between punishment and intentions. For example, Piaget's research suggests that children over 8 can distinguish between a child who unintentionally left a store without paying for a candy bar and another who deliberately took one. Older children are likely to say that both children should return or pay for the candy, but only the one who intentionally stole it should be punished.

Research supports Piaget's claim that school-aged children give more weight to intentions than consequences when making moral judgments (Killen, Mulvey, Richardson, Jampol, & Woodward, 2011; Zelazo, Helwig, & Lau, 1996). However, although their thinking is more mature than that of preschoolers, 6- to 12-year-olds' moral reasoning is still highly egocentric. For example, every parent has heard the exclamation "It's not fair!" when a child fails to receive the same treat or privilege as a sibling. It is rare, if not completely unknown, for a 6- to 12-year-old to protest the fairness of receiving something that a sibling didn't. Thus, school-aged children still have a long way to go with respect to mature moral reasoning, and we will return to this topic in the chapters on adolescent development (see the *Developmental Science at Home* box above).

Answers to these questions can be found in the back of the book.

1. Circle each characteristic that is not likely to appear in a description of a peer given by a child younger than 6.

   thin   brown   hair   (smart)   (happy)   (mean)   tall

2. Piaget claimed that the ability to use reasoning about intentions to make judgments about the moral dimensions of behavior appears to emerge along with ___concrete___ ___operational___ ___reasoning___ - Kids at this age become more logical about concrete & specific things, but they still struggle with abstract ideas,

CRITICAL THINKING

3. Children's understanding of others' traits and behaviors and their understanding of moral dilemmas advances dramatically after age 8. How does each of these important domains of development support the other?

The Social World of the School-Aged Child

School-aged children's growing ability to understand others changes their social relationships in important ways. Children continue to be attached to parents, but they are becoming more independent. Relationships with peers become more stable, and many ripen into long-term friendships. In fact, the quality of 6- to 12-year-olds' peer relationships shapes their futures in many important ways.

Relationships with Parents

LO 10.7   How does self-regulation affect school-aged children's relationships with their parents?

Middle childhood is a period of increasing independence of child from family. Yet attachments to parents continue to be important (Bokhorst, Sumter, & Westenberg, 2010). Children who have close, warm relationships with their parents tend to be socially competent with peers (Rispoli, McGoey, Koziol, & Schreiber, 2014). Relationships with siblings add another dimension to the social worlds of 6- to 12-year-olds who have them (see *Research Report*). What does change, though, is the agenda of issues between parent and child. Parents of 6- to 12-year-olds recognize their children's growing capacity for **self-regulation**, the ability to conform to parental standards of behavior without direct supervision. As a result, as children get older, parents are more likely to allow them to engage in activities such as bicycle riding and skateboarding without supervision (Soori & Bhopal, 2002). However, cultures vary to some degree in the specific age at which they expect this to occur. For example, White and Hispanic parents in the United States differ in their beliefs about the average age at which school-aged children can carry out specific tasks on their own (Savage & Gauvain, 1998). It appears that Hispanic American parents have less confidence in the self-regulatory abilities of younger school-aged children than White parents do. In general, though, most cultures expect 6- to 12-year-olds to be able to supervise their own behavior at least part of the time.

Some studies suggest that there are sex differences in parents' expectations with respect to self-regulatory behavior. For example, mothers make different kinds of demands on boys and girls. They appear to provide both with the same types of guidance but are likely to give boys more autonomy over their own behavior than they give girls. Nevertheless, they are likely to hold daughters to a higher standard of accountability for failure than they do sons (Pomerantz & Ruble, 1998). Developmentalists speculate that this difference may lead to stronger standards of behavior for girls in later developmental periods. ◉ **Watch** the **Video** *Sibling Rivalry* in **MyPsychLab**.

Researchers have learned that several parenting variables contribute to the development of self-regulation (Vazsony & Huang, 2010). First, the parents' own ability to self-regulate is important, perhaps because they are providing the child with models of good or poor self-regulation (Sanders & Mazzucchelli, 2013). Also, the degree of self-regulation expected by parents influences the child's self-regulatory behavior. Higher expectations,

self-regulation children's ability to conform to parental standards of behavior without direct supervision

Research suggests that only children are just as well adjusted as those who have siblings.

Only Children, Birth Order, and Children's Development

People often speculate that only children—those without siblings—are deprived of an important developmental experience and may be "spoiled" by their parents. Most research shows that only children grow up to be just as well adjusted as those who have brothers and sisters (Wang et al., 2000). Moreover, some studies have shown that only children may actually have an advantage over those who have siblings, at least with regard to cognitive development and academic achievement (Doh & Falbo, 1999; Falbo, 1992). Other studies suggest that the cognitive advantage enjoyed by only children may actually be due to birth order. First-borns, or the oldest surviving child in a family in which a first-born died in infancy, get higher scores, on average, on cognitive tests than later-borns do (Holmgren, Molander, & Nilsson, 2006; Kristensen & Bjerkedal, 2007). The *resource dilution* hypothesis explains these findings as resulting from the progressive "watering down" of the parents' material and psychological resources with each additional birth (Downey,

2001). Thus, from this perspective, parents have the greatest influence on the oldest child, an advantage that is shared by only children and the oldest child in a multichild family.

Critics of the resource dilution hypothesis point out that it places too much emphasis on what later-borns take away from the family and ignores the relationship-building opportunities that these children contribute to their older siblings' development (Gillies & Lucey, 2006). In support of their argument, critics cite research which suggests that later-borns have an advantage over their older siblings with regard to a variety of social skills, including the ability to negotiate solutions to interpersonal conflicts (Ross, Ross, Stein, & Trabasso, 2006). Likewise, first-borns who have siblings outperform only children on measures of social negotiation. First-borns with younger siblings also appear to gain self-reliance skills from serving as surrogate parents for younger siblings and report that they feel closer to their siblings than they do to their friends (Brody, Kim, Murry, & Brown, 2003;

Pollett & Nettle, 2009). Regardless of birth order, too, affectionate sibling relationships moderate the effects of stressful life events such as parental divorce, and they enable children to advance more rapidly than only children do with regard to understanding others' mental states and behaviors (Gass, Jenkins, & Dunn, 2007; McAlister & Peterson, 2006). Thus, only and first-born children may get more of the kind of attention from parents that is critical to cognitive development, but sibling relationships appear to make positive contributions to children's social and emotional development.

CRITICAL ANALYSIS

1. *What kinds of sibling relationships would harm rather than help a child's social and emotional development?*

2. *In what kinds of situations might you expect only children to show social skills that are superior to those of children who have siblings?*

together with parental monitoring to make certain the expectations are met, are associated with greater self-regulatory competence (Rodrigo, Janssens, & Ceballos, 1999).

You should recall that such parental behaviors are associated with the authoritative style of parenting. Longitudinal research has demonstrated that school-aged children whose parents have been consistently authoritative since they were toddlers are the most socially competent (Baumrind, 1991). Children rated "competent" were seen as both assertive and responsible in their relationships; those rated "partially competent" typically lacked one of these skills; those rated "incompetent" showed neither. In Baumrind's (1991) study, the majority of children from authoritative families were rated as fully competent, while most of those from neglecting families were rated as incompetent.

Friendships

LO 10.8 What changes occur in children's understanding of friendships during this period?

The biggest shift in relationships during middle childhood is the increasing importance of peers. One frequent manifestation of this trend is the appearance of "best-friend" relationships. Cross-cultural studies show that best-friend relationships, and the belief that having a best friend is important, are universal features of school-aged children's social development (Schraf & Hertz-Lazarowitz, 2003). Consequently, it isn't surprising that half to three-quarters of school-aged children tell researchers that they have at least one best friend and that best friendships in this age group persist for months or even years (McChristian, Ray, Tidwell, & LoBello, 2012). Moreover, best friendships are an important indicator of a child's overall social development and competence. That is, children who have a best friend are more likely than those without a best friend to have positive relationships with most of the children they know and to have larger social networks (McChristian et al., 2012). Additional evidence supporting the view that best friendships are developmentally important in middle childhood comes from studies showing that even children who are shy and socially withdrawn report having at least one best friend (Rubin, Wojslawowica, Rose-Krasnor, Booth-LaForce, & Burgess, 2006).

The emphasis on best friendships in middle childhood probably arises from children's increasing understanding of the nature of friendship. Social-cognitive researcher Robert Selman was one of the first to study children's understanding of friendships. He found that if you ask preschoolers and young school-aged children how people make friends, the answer is usually that they "play together" or spend time physically near each other (Damon, 1977, 1983; Selman, 1980).

In the later years of middle childhood, at around age 10, this view of friendship gives way to one in which the key concept seems to be reciprocal trust (Chen, 1997). Older children see friends as special people who possess desired qualities other than mere proximity, who are generous with each other, who help and trust each other, and so on. Figure 10.2 is a 10-year-old boy's definition of a friend. His characterization of a friend—as someone "you can trust," who "will always be there for you when you are feeling down in the dumps," and "always sits by you at lunch"—illustrates the older child's understanding of dimensions of friendships such as trust, emotional support, and loyalty. Thus, as children move through the middle childhood period, they use judgments of peers' trustworthiness to choose their friends (Rotenberg et al., 2004). ◉ **Watch** the **Video** *Child and Adolescent Friendships: Brett Laursen* in **MyPsychLab**.

Researchers have examined the relationship between children's understanding of friendship and the quantity and quality of their friendships. In one such study, researchers Amanda Rose and Steven Asher (2004) presented fifth-graders with hypothetical situations in which one friend might have an opportunity to help another. For instance, in one scenario, the researchers described a child who was teased by her classmates. Rose and Asher found that children who expressed the view that children should not help others in such situations, in order to avoid putting themselves at risk of being treated similarly by peers, had fewer friends than did children who expressed the view that friends should place their relationships above concerns about how their helping behavior would affect their own social status.

Evidence of the centrality of friends to social development in middle childhood also comes from studies of children's behavior within friendships. Children are more open and more supportive when with their chums, smiling at, looking at, laughing with, and touching one another more than they do when they are with nonfriends; they talk more with friends and cooperate and help one another more. Pairs of friends are also more successful than nonfriends are in solving problems or performing some task together. Yet school-aged children are also more critical of friends and have more conflicts with them; they are more polite with strangers (Hartup, 1996). At the same time, when conflicts with friends occur, children are more concerned about resolving them than they are about settling disagreements with nonfriends. Thus, friendship seems to represent an arena in which children can learn how to manage conflicts (Newcomb & Bagwell, 1995).

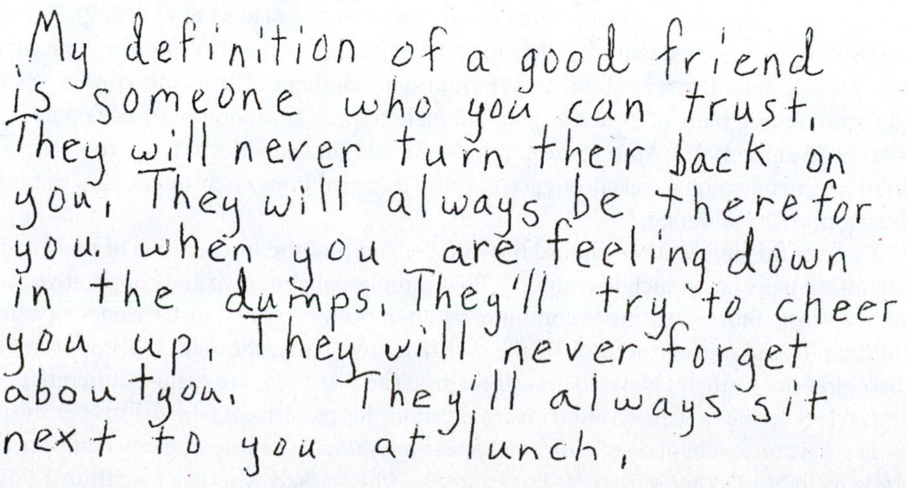

My definition of a good friend is someone who you can trust, They will never turn their back on you, They will always be there for you. when you are feeling down in the dumps, They'll try to cheer you up, They will never forget about you. They'll always sit next to you at lunch,

Figure 10.2 A 10-Year-Old's Explanation of Friendship

This description of friendship written by a 10-year-old illustrates the way older school-aged children think about friends.

(*Source:* Courtesy of Denise Boyd. Used with permission.)

Gender Self-Segregation

LO 10.9 In what ways do boys and girls interact during the middle childhood years?

In middle childhood, boys play with boys and girls play with girls. In fact, children's play groups are more sex-segregated at this age than at any other.

Possibly the most striking thing about peer group interactions in the elementary school years is how gender-segregated they are (self-segregation, not the kind of segregation that was once forced on children by external authorities). This pattern seems to occur in every culture in the world and is frequently visible in children as young as 3 or 4. Boys play with boys and girls play with girls, each in their own areas and at their own kinds of games (Cairns & Cairns, 1994; Harkness & Super, 1985). This pattern of preference for same-sex companions appears throughout the lifespan, by the way, although it is far less rigid among adults than among children (Martin & Ruble, 2010; Mehta & Strough, 2009). In fact, gender seems to be more important than age, race, or any other categorical variable in 6- to 12-year-olds' selection of friends; in addition, the strength of children's preference for same-sex associates increases substantially across middle childhood (Graham, Cohen, Zbikowski, & Secrist, 1998). Moreover, gender segregation is unrelated to sex differences in parenting or differences in preferred play activities, suggesting that it is a feature of 6- to 12-year-olds' social relationships that they construct for reasons of their own (Martin et al., 2013; McHale, Crouter, & Tucker, 1999).

However, there are some ritualized "boundary violations" between boys' and girls' groups, such as chasing games. For example, in one universal series of interactions, a girl taunts a boy with a statement like "You can't catch me, nyah nyah." Next, a boy chases and catches her, to the delight of both of their fully supportive same-sex peer groups (Thorne, 1986). As soon as the brief cross-gender encounter ends, both girl and boy return to their respective groups. On the whole, however, girls and boys between the ages of 6 and 12 actively avoid interacting with one another and show strong favoritism toward their own gender and negative stereotyping of the opposite gender (Powlishta, 1995).

Girls' and boys' friendships also differ in quality in intriguing ways. Boys' friendship groups are larger and more accepting of newcomers than are girls'. Boys play more outdoors and roam over a larger area in their play. Girls are more likely to play in pairs or in small, fairly exclusive groups, and they spend more playtime indoors or near home or school (Benenson, 1994; Gottman, 1986).

Sex differences also characterize the interaction between a pair of friends. Boys' friendships appear to be focused more on competition and dominance than are girls' friendships (Maccoby, 1995; Ricciardelli & Mellor, 2012). In fact, among school-aged boys, researchers see higher levels of competition between pairs of friends than between strangers—the opposite of what is observed among girls. Friendships between girls include more agreement, more compliance, and more self-disclosure than is true between boys (Rose et al., 2012). For example, "controlling" speech—a category that includes rejecting comments, ordering, manipulating, challenging, defiance, refutation, and resistance of another's attempts to control—is twice as common among pairs of 7- and 8-year-old male friends as among pairs of female friends of that age (Leaper, 1991). Among the 4- and 5-year-olds in Leaper's study, there were no sex differences in controlling speech, suggesting that these differences in interaction patterns arise during middle childhood.

None of this information should obscure the fact that the interactions of male and female friendship pairs have much in common. For example, collaborative and cooperative exchanges are the most common forms of communication in both boys' and girls' friendships in middle childhood. And it is not necessarily the case that boys' friendships are less important to them than girls' are to them. Nevertheless, it seems clear that there are gender differences in form and style that may well have enduring implications for patterns of friendship over the lifespan.

Furthermore, school-aged children appear to evaluate the role of gender in peer relationships in light of other variables. For example, when asked whether a fictitious boy would prefer to play with a boy who is a stranger or with a girl who has been his friend for a while, most school-aged children say the boy would prefer to play with the friend (Halle, 1999). Such results suggest that, even though gender is clearly important in school-aged children's peer relationships, they are beginning to understand that other factors may be more important. This is yet another example of how children's growing cognitive abilities—specifically, their ability to think about more than one variable at a time—influence their ideas about the social world.

Patterns of Aggression

LO 10.10 What types of aggression are most common among school-aged children?

You may remember from Chapter 8 that physical aggression declines over the preschool years, while verbal aggression increases. In middle childhood, physical aggression becomes even less common as children learn the cultural rules about when it is acceptable to display anger or aggression and how much of a display is acceptable. In most cultures, this means that anger is increasingly disguised and aggression is increasingly controlled as children get older (Underwood, Coie, & Herbsman, 1992).

Why do you think competition is such a strong feature of friendship interactions among boys? Do you think this is true in every culture?

One interesting exception to this general pattern is that in all-boy pairs or groups, in the United States and elsewhere, physical aggression seems to remain both relatively high and constant over the childhood years (Kawabata, Tseng, Murray-Close, & Crick, 2013). Indeed, at every age, boys show more physical aggression and more assertiveness than girls do, both within friendship pairs and in general (Fabes, Knight, & Higgins, 1995). Furthermore, school-aged boys often express approval for the aggressive behavior of peers (Rodkin, Farmer, Pearl, & Van Acker, 2000).

Results like these have been so clear and so consistent that most psychologists have concluded that boys are simply "more aggressive." But that conclusion may turn out to be wrong. Instead, it begins to look as if girls simply express their aggressiveness in a different way, using what has recently been labeled *relational aggression* instead of physical aggression. Physical aggression hurts others physically or poses a threat of such damage; **relational aggression** is aimed at damaging the other person's self-esteem or peer relationships, such as by ostracism or threats of ostracism ("I won't invite you to my birthday party if you do that"), cruel gossip, or facial expressions of disdain. Children are genuinely hurt by such indirect aggression, and they are likely to express dislike for others who use this form of aggression a lot (Cillessen & Mayeux, 2004).

Girls are more likely than boys to use relational aggression, especially toward other girls, a difference that begins as early as the preschool years and becomes very marked by fourth or fifth grade (Kawabata et al., 2013). For example, in one early study of nearly 500 children in third through sixth grades, researchers found that 17.4% of the girls but only 2% of the boys were rated high in relational aggression—almost precisely the reverse of what is observed for physical aggression (Crick & Grotpeter, 1995). More recent studies in Taiwan, Colombia, and the United States have found a similar pattern of sex differences in physical and relational aggression (Crapanzano, Frick, & Terranova, 2010; Kawabata et al., 2013; Velásquez, Santo, Saldarriaga, Lopez, & Bukowski, 2010). Some developmentalists suspect that this difference in form of aggression has some hormonal/biological basis (Rhee & Waldman, 2011). Research showing higher rates of physical aggression in males in every human society and in all varieties of primates support this hypothesis. And scientists know that some link exists between rates of physical aggression and testosterone levels (e.g., Mehta & Beer, 2010). However, cognitive variables contribute to both physical and relational aggression, and the association holds for both boys and girls. Such cognitive variables include the tendency to misjudge others' intentions among children who exhibit more physical and relational aggression than their peers do (Godleski & Ostrov, 2010). ◉ **Watch** the **Video** *Relational Aggression* in **MyPsychLab**.

relational aggression aggression aimed at damaging another person's self-esteem or peer relationships, such as by ostracism or threats of ostracism, cruel gossip, or facial expressions of disdain

retaliatory aggression aggression to get back at someone who has hurt you

bullying a complex form of aggression in which a bully routinely aggresses against one or more habitual victims

social status an individual child's classification as popular, rejected, or neglected

conduct disorder a psychological disorder in which children's social and/or academic functioning is impaired by patterns of antisocial behavior that include bullying, destruction of property, theft, deceitfulness, and/or violations of social rules

Adults' goals for children's socialization usually include teaching them how to manage conflicts without resorting to aggression.

Retaliatory aggression—aggression to get back at someone who has hurt you—increases among both boys and girls during the 6- to 12-year-old period (Astor, 1994). Anger over perceived threats, physical aggression, verbal insults, and the like plays a key role in retaliatory aggression (Hubbard, Romano, McAuliff, & Morrow, 2010). Its development is related to children's growing understanding of the difference between intentional and accidental actions. For example, if a child drops his pencil in the path of another child who is walking by and that child happens to kick the pencil across the floor, most 8-year-olds can identify this as an accident. Consequently, the child whose pencil was kicked feels no need to get back at the child who did the kicking. However, children over 8 view intentional harm differently. For example, let's say that one child intentionally takes another's pencil off her desk and throws it across the room. Most children over 8 will try to find a way to get back at a child who does something like this.

Peers may approve of retaliatory aggression, but most parents and teachers strive to teach children that, like other forms of intentional harm, such behavior is unacceptable. Research suggests that children can learn nonaggressive techniques for managing the kinds of situations that lead to retaliatory aggression. In one program, called PeaceBuilders, psychologists have attempted to change individual behavior by changing a school's overall emotional climate. In this approach, both children and teachers learn to use positive social strategies (Flannery et al., 2000). For example, both are urged to try to praise others more often than they criticize them. Research suggests that when such programs are integrated into students' classes every day for an entire school year or longer, aggression decreases and prosocial behavior increases. Thus, aggressive interactions between elementary school children may be common, but they do not appear to be an inevitable aspect of development.

Bullying is a complex form of aggression in which one child, the *bully*, routinely aggresses against one or more habitual *victims*. Bullies exhibit physical, verbal, and/or relational aggression toward their victims. As is the case with nonbullying aggression, male bullies are more likely to be physically and verbally aggressive toward their victims, but female bullies are more likely to engage relational aggression (Von Marées & Petermann, 2010).

When bullying is particularly severe and is accompanied by other antisocial behaviors such as destruction of property, theft, deceitfulness, and repetitive violations of family and school rules, a child may be diagnosed with **conduct disorder** (American Psychiatric Association, 2013). Children with conduct disorder do not appear to have any regard for the rights of others or the rules of society, a pattern of behavior that often persists into adulthood. You will learn more about conduct disorder in Chapter 12.

Bullies are more likely than nonbullies to see other people and environmental factors as the causes of their behavior (Georgiou & Stavrinides, 2008). Thus, they often do not accept responsibility for their behavior and view peers' and adults' negative responses to them as unjust. Researchers have also found that the families of children who bully and of habitual victims are more likely to exhibit maladaptive forms of interaction than are the families of nonbullies and nonvictims (Curtner-Smith, Smith, & Portner, 2010). Variables in the peer context, especially social rejection, contribute to bullying as well (Rubin, Coplan, Chen, Bowker, & McDonald, 2011). However, bullies are often popular and socially dominant, especially among children who have a tendency to be somewhat aggressive themselves (Reijntjes et al., 2013). Moreover, male bullies who victimize only unpopular boys are often popular with peers (Rodkin & Berger, 2008). Consequently, peers can serve as a source of either discouragement or encouragement for bullies. Such findings help to illustrate the complex and context-dependent nature of bullying (see *No Easy Answers*).

Social Status

LO 10.11 How do popular, rejected, and neglected children differ?

Developmentalists measure popularity and rejection by asking children to list peers they would not like to play with or by observing which children are sought out or avoided on the playground. These techniques allow researchers to group children according to the degree to

Bullies and Victims

Research shows that, across the middle childhood years, aggressive interactions become increasingly complex (Veenstra, Lindenberg, Munniksma, & Dijkstra, 2010). As children get older, they tend to take on consistent roles—perpetrator, victim, assistant to the perpetrator, reinforcing onlooker, nonparticipant onlooker, defender of the victim, and so on (Andreou & Metallidou, 2004). The occupant of each of these roles plays a part in maintaining a particular aggressive incident and in determining whether another aggressive interaction involving the same perpetrator and victim will occur in the future.

Until fairly recently, both research on and interventions aimed at reducing aggression focused on the habitual perpetrators, or bullies. However, most developmentalists now believe that changing the behavior of children who occupy other roles in aggressive interactions, especially those who are habitual victims of aggression, may be just as important as intervening with aggressive children themselves

(Green, 2001). Victims have certain characteristics in common, including anxiety, passivity, sensitivity, low self-esteem or self-confidence, lack of humor, and comparative lack of friends (Egan & Perry, 1998; Hodges, Malone, & Perry, 1997; Olweus, 1995). Cross-cultural studies show that these characteristics are found among habitual victims across a wide variety of cultural settings (Eslea et al., 2004). Among boys, victims are also often physically smaller or weaker than their peers.

Teaching victims to be more assertive might seem to be a good way to reduce the prevalence of bullying among school-aged children. However, critics of such programs argue that they send the message that the victim deserves to be bullied. Moreover, by identifying habitual victims and including them in counseling sessions and the like, the adults who are responsible for victim-training programs subject these children to further stigmatization. Thus, critics argue that programs aimed at reducing bullying should focus primarily on the bullies' behavior

and should include the clear message that bullying is wrong, regardless of their victims' behavior (Temko, 2005).

YOU DECIDE

Decide which of these two statements you most agree with and think about how you would defend your position:

1. *Programs that seek to reduce bullying among school-aged children should include a component that teaches victims to be more assertive because the skills that children will learn are more important than the risk of stigmatizing or of appearing to justify bullying.*

2. *Programs that seek to reduce bullying among school-aged children should focus on changing the bully's behavior and helping him or her to understand how hurtful bullying is to its victims and to the emotional climate of the social setting in which it occurs.*

which they are accepted by peers—a variable often called **social status**. Typically, researchers find three groups: *popular*, *rejected*, and *neglected*.

Some of the characteristics that differentiate popular children from those in the other two groups are things outside a child's control. In particular, attractive children and physically larger children are more likely to be popular. Conversely, being very different from her peers may cause a child to be neglected or rejected. For example, shy children usually have few friends (Fordham & Stevenson-Hinde, 1999). Similarly, highly creative children are often rejected, as are those who have difficulty controlling their emotions (Aranha, 1997; Maszk, Eisenberg, & Guthrie, 1999).

However, children's social behavior seems to be more important than looks or temperament (Rodkin, Ryan, Jamison, & Wilson, 2013). Most studies show that popular children behave in positive, supporting, nonpunitive, and nonaggressive ways toward most other children. They explain things, take their playmates' wishes into consideration, take turns in conversation, and are able to regulate the expression of their strong emotions. In addition, popular children are usually good at accurately assessing others' feelings and at regulating their own emotions (Sallquist et al., 2009; Underwood, 1997). Most are good at looking at situations from others' perspectives as well (Fitzgerald & White, 2003).

There are two types of rejected children. *Withdrawn/rejected* children realize that they are disliked by peers (Harrist, Zaia, Bates, Dodge, & Pettit, 1997). After repeated attempts to gain peer acceptance, these children eventually give up and become socially withdrawn. As a result, they often experience feelings of loneliness. *Aggressive/rejected* children are often disruptive, uncooperative, bossy, and usually believe that their peers like them (Lansford et al., 2006; Zakriski & Coie, 1996). Many appear to be unable to control the expression of strong feelings (Sallquist et al., 2009). They interrupt their play partners more often and fail to take turns in a systematic way.

Aggression, disruptive behavior, and a limited ability to assess how one's own behavior is perceived by others are often linked to rejection and unpopularity among Chinese children, just as they are among American children (Jie, Qinmei, & Jueyu, 2007; Yi-Bing & Ming-Gui, 2005; Yu & Liu, 2007). As you learned in Chapter 8, aggressive behavior persists into adulthood in some individuals. However, research suggests that aggression is most likely to become a stable characteristic among children who are *both* aggressive and rejected by peers.

Of course, not all aggressive children are rejected. Among girls, aggression, whether physical or relational, seems to lead to peer rejection consistently. Among boys, however, aggression may result in either popularity or rejection (Rodkin et al., 2000; Xie, Cairns, & Cairns, 1999). ◉ **Watch** the **Video** *Measuring Popularity in Young Children* in **MyPsychLab**.

Interestingly, too, aggressive boys and girls, although they are typically disliked by peers, are often perceived by them as having high social status, perhaps because of their ability to manipulate others and to control social situations (Cillessen & Mayeux, 2004; Rodkin et al., 2013). This association holds for both physical and relational aggression. However, as children enter adolescence, the link between physical aggression and social status becomes weaker, while the association between relational aggression and perceived status increases in strength. This may happen because, by age 11 or 12, children regard relational aggression as a more mature form of social manipulation than physical aggression. Consequently, they may admire peers who are skilled in the use of relational aggression, even though they don't like them and prefer not to associate with them.

Neglect seems to be much less stable over time than rejection. Neglected children show no differences in sociability or other traits compared to their popular peers (Nelson, Robinson, Hart, Albano, & Marshall, 2010). Their status seems to be a function of the situational factors that are part of a particular context. For example, a "new girl" may be neglected simply because of the cohesion of preexisting social relationships in a group she has recently joined. Consequently, neglected children sometimes move to the popular category when they become part of a new peer group. However, children who experience prolonged neglect are more prone to depression and loneliness than are popular children (Cillessen, van IJzendoorn, van Lieshout, & Hartup, 1992; Rubin, Hymel, Mills, & Rose-Krasnor, 1991; Wentzel & Asher, 1995). The association between peer neglect and depression may be explained by brain-imaging studies showing that, among school-aged children, social exclusion stimulates the same area of the brain as physical pain does (Eisenberger, 2003). In addition, this tendency toward depression among neglected children may be fostered by unrealistic expectations about adults' ability to "fix" the social situation—"Why doesn't the teacher make them be my friends?" (Galanaki, 2004).

test yourself before going on ☑ Study and Review in MyPsychLab

Answers to these questions can be found in the back of the book.

1. Briefly describe how each factor in the table contributes to self-regulation.

Factor	Contribution to Self-regulation
Culture	
Gender	
Parenting style	

2. Classify each social behavior as more typical of (A) girls or (B) boys.
   _____ (1) rough-and-tumble play
   _____ (2) sharing secrets
   _____ (3) interacting in groups rather than in pairs
   _____ (4) welcoming newcomers into friendship groups
   _____ (5) interacting in pairs or small groups more often than in large groups

3. Which of the following is a boundary violation of children's informal gender segregation rules?
   (a) A teacher creates mixed-gender groups for a science lesson.
   (b) A boy takes a girl's Barbie lunch box, runs away with it to make her chase him, and then gives it back to her.
   (c) Girls play together because they tend to enjoy the same activities.

CRITICAL THINKING

4. If you had to explain an important developmental outcome, such as variations in optimism among adults, as a function of childhood social experiences, what percentage of influence would you assign to each of these factors: relationships with parents, friendships, experiences with gender segregation, experiences with aggression, and social status?

Influences Beyond Family and Peers

The daily life of a school-aged child is shaped by more than the hours he spends with his family and peers. The circumstances in which a child lives also affect him. That is, a child is affected by his family's economic circumstances, the neighborhood he lives in, and the media to which he is exposed.

Poverty

LO 10.12 What factors contribute to resilience and vulnerability among poor children?

As you can see in Figure 10.3, the child poverty rate in the United States declined from 28% in 1959 to 22% in 2011 (U.S. Census Bureau, 2012). However, the child poverty rate continues to be higher in the United States than in many other industrialized countries in the world. By way of contrast, the poverty rate for children is roughly 9% in Denmark and less than 12% in Poland (Zero Poverty, 2010). Child poverty is also unequally distributed across ages, ethnic groups, and family structures. With respect to age, children under 6 are more likely to live in poverty than those who are older (McLoyd, 1998). In addition, the proportions of African American, Native American, and Hispanic American children living in poverty are two to three times the overall child poverty rate (Nichols, 2006). Likewise, children reared by single mothers are far more likely than others to be living in poverty (Evans, 2004).

THE EFFECTS OF POVERTY ON FAMILIES AND CHILDREN Overall, poor families live in more chaotic environments, are more highly stressed, and have fewer psychological and social resources than those who are more economically secure (Ackerman, Brown, & Izard, 2004; Huston & Bentley, 2010). As a result, parents living in poverty tend to treat their children differently than do working-class or middle-class parents. They talk to them less, provide fewer age-appropriate toys, spend less time with them in intellectually stimulating activities, explain things less often and less fully, are less warm, and are stricter and more physical in their discipline (Dodge, Pettit, & Bates, 1994; Evans, 2004; Sampson & Laub, 1994). Some of this pattern of parental behavior is undoubtedly a response to the extraordinary stresses and special demands of living in poverty. To some extent, the stricter discipline and emphasis on obedience of poor parents may be thought of as a logical response to the realities of life in the neighborhoods in which they live.

Not surprisingly, children in low-income families differ from their better-off peers across all developmental domains (Huston & Bentley, 2010). The physical effects of poverty are evident very early in life. Infants born into low-income homes have higher rates of birth defects

Poverty is associated with stresses that lead some children to develop post-traumatic stress disorder.

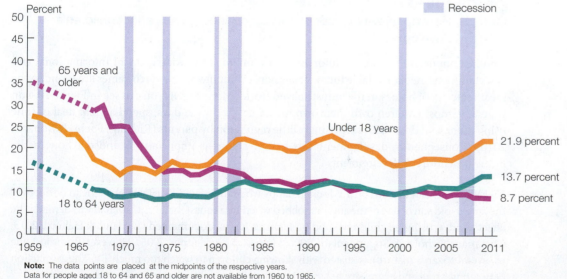

Note: The data points are placed at the midpoints of the respective years.
Data for people aged 18 to 64 and 65 and older are not available from 1960 to 1965.

Figure 10.3 Poverty and Age

The graph shows the percentage of people in the United States living in poverty from 1959 to 2011, including children under 18. For families with at least one child, poverty is defined as annual income of less than $15,825 (in 20011 dollars).

(*Source:* U. S. Census Bureau, 2012.)

and early disabilities. As they grow older, poor children are also more often ill and more likely to be undernourished. With regard to intellectual development, low-income children have lower average IQ scores, move through Piaget's stages of cognitive development more slowly, and perform more poorly in school (Brooks-Gunn, 1995). Social development varies with income as well. Children from low-income homes exhibit more behavior problems in school than do peers whose families have more economic resources (Hurd, Stoddard, & Zimmerman, 2013; Qi & Kaiser, 2003).

The negative effects of poverty are exacerbated for children growing up in neighborhoods where they are exposed to street gangs and street violence, to drug pushers, to overcrowded homes, and to abuse. Surveys indicate that nearly half of inner-city elementary and high school students have witnessed at least one violent crime in the past year (Osofsky, 1995). Predictably, children who are victimized by or who witness such crimes are more likely to suffer from emotional problems than are peers who are spared these experiences (Purugganan, Stein, Johnson Silver, & Benenson, 2003).

Many children living in such neighborhoods show all the symptoms of posttraumatic stress disorder, including sleep disturbances, irritability, inability to concentrate, and angry outbursts (Garbarino, Dubrow, Kostelny, & Pardo, 1992; Owen, 1998). Many experience flashbacks or intrusive memories of traumatic events. For some, these symptoms persist into adulthood (Koenen, Moffitt, Poulton, Martin, & Caspi, 2007).

PROTECTIVE FACTORS Of course, most poor children develop along the same lines as their more economically secure peers. For developmentalists, *resilient children* are those whose development is comparable to that of children who are not poor, and *vulnerable children* are those who develop problems as a result of living in poverty. To help sort out differences between poor children who do well and those who do not, developmentalists think of poverty in terms of accumulated stresses (Huston & Bentley, 2010). For example, parental alcoholism added to family poverty results in a greater risk of negative developmental outcomes for a child (Malo & Tramblay, 1997). Studies of resilient and vulnerable children suggest that certain characteristics or circumstances may help protect some children from the detrimental effects of the cumulative stressors associated with poverty. Among the key protective factors are high IQ in the child and the presence of intellectually stimulating toys and activities in the home (Huston & Bentley, 2010; Koenen et al., 2007). Another important protective factor is parental supervision and monitoring of children's activities (Eamon & Mulder, 2005). Thus, the effects of poverty depend on the combined effects of the number of stressors the child must cope with and the range of competencies or advantages the child brings to the situation. Poverty does not guarantee bad outcomes, but it stacks the deck against many children. Moreover, the same kinds of factors interact to affect development in other stressful contexts, such as neighborhoods in countries torn by war.

Media Influences

LO 10.13 How do television, computers, and video games affect children's development?

Another important feature of children's environment is the wide array of informational and entertainment media available today. Televisions, computers, and video games are found in the great majority of homes in the industrialized world. Moreover, as you can see in Figure 10.4 on page 259, most children own their own media devices these days, spend a great deal of time using them, and do so with surprisingly little regulation by parents (Rideout, Foehr, & Roberts, 2010). Consequently, developmentalists believe that it is important to find out how media influence children's development.

TELEVISION "But the kids on TV look so happy when they eat it! Don't you want me to be happy?" the 7-year-old son of one of the authors sobbed when his request for a sugary cereal was denied. The effect of advertising on children's food preferences is well documented (Boyland & Halford, 2013; Chapman, Nicholas, & Supramaniam, 2006; Livingstone & Helsper, 2006). However, this is just one of several hazards that are associated with allowing children to watch too much TV. The association between viewing and aggressive behavior is perhaps of greatest concern.

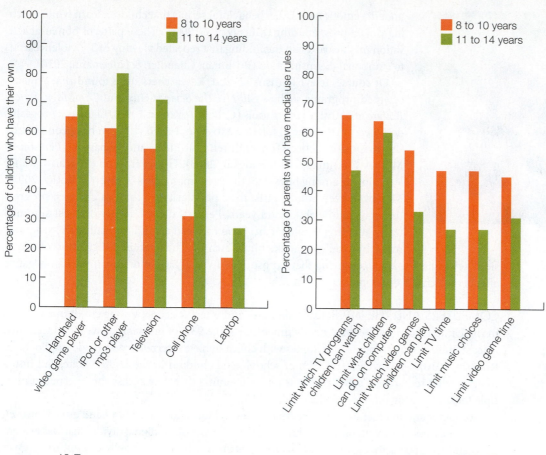

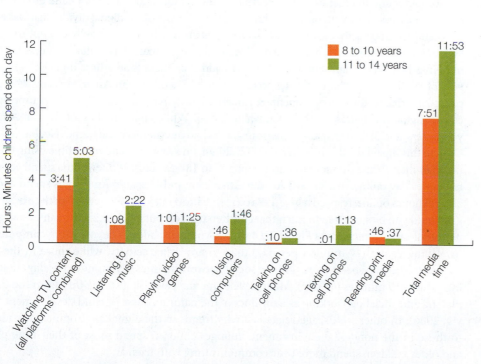

Figure 10.4 Age Trends in Children's Media Device Ownership, Parents' Rules for Media Use, and Time Spent Using Media

As children get older, a higher percentage of them own their own media devices, and parents become less likely to regulate children's use of media. In addition, older children spend more time using electronic media and less time reading print media than younger children do.

(*Source:* Rideout, Foehr, & Roberts, 2010.)

Albert Bandura demonstrated the effects of televised violence on children's behavior in his classic "Bobo doll" studies (Bandura, Ross, & Ross, 1961, Bandura & Ross, 1963). In these experiments, children were found to imitate adults' violent treatment of an inflatable clown that was depicted on film. Recent research suggests that such effects persist into the adult years. Psychologist L. Rowell Huesmann and his colleagues have studied the effects of television violence for several decades (e.g., Huesmann, Dubow, & Yang 2013). In one study, Huesmann and others (2003) found that individuals who watched the greatest number of violent television programs in childhood were the most likely to engage in actual acts of violence as young adults. Brain-imaging studies suggest that these long-term effects may be the result of patterns of neural activation that

In the United States, children between 6 and 12 spend more time consuming television content than they do playing.

underlie emotionally laden behavioral scripts that children learn while watching violent programming (Murray et al., 2006). These patterns of neural activation may also explain the finding that repeated viewing of TV violence leads to emotional desensitization (Bushman, Chandler, & Huesmann, 2010).

Of course, television isn't all bad. Researchers have found that science-oriented programs such as *Bill Nye the Science Guy* and *The Magic School Bus* are effective teaching tools (Calvert & Kotler, 2003). Likewise, programs designed to teach racial tolerance to school-aged children have consistently shown positive effects on children's attitudes and behavior (Persson & Musher-Eizenman, 2003; Shochat, 2003). However, such programs are far less popular among boys than they are among girls (Calvert & Kotler, 2003). Moreover, even among girls, their popularity declines as children progress through middle childhood years. Perhaps these findings are best summed up by adapting an old cliché: "You can lead a child to quality TV programming, but you can't make him watch it." Thus parental regulation of television viewing is the key to ensuring that exposure to TV will have more positive than negative effects on a child's development.

COMPUTERS AND THE INTERNET Computer and internet access among children and teens in the United States has become nearly universal. Some 93% of households with children own at least one computer, and 84% of homes with children have internet access (Rideout, Foehr, & Roberts, 2010). Moreover, about 25% of school-aged children in the United States fall into a category that researchers call *high connectivity*, meaning that they access the internet in multiple locations using multiple devices (File, 2013).

Computer and internet use rates are nearly identical for school-aged boys and girls. However, computer access varies with parental education, although the deep "digital divide" that was evident as recently as 2004 across low-, middle-, and high-income homes is rapidly disappearing. Over 90% of families with children that are headed by college graduates have internet access, as do 74% of homes headed by high school graduates. In addition, there is an ethnic digital divide. Nearly 90% of White children have internet access, but just 78% of African Americans and 74% of Hispanic Americans do (Rideout, Foehr, & Roberts, 2010). Yet just a relatively short time ago, the ethnic digital divide was much larger, when 77% of White children, 43% of African American youngsters, and 37% of Hispanic American youths had internet access at home (Neuburger, 2001). Despite this digital divide, minority-group children, on average, spend more time using the internet than their White counterparts do. Among 8- to 18-year-olds, White youths spend about 1.25 hours per day online. In contrast, African Americans and Hispanic Americans spend about 1.5 and 1.8 hours online, respectively. ◉ **Watch** the **Video** *Internet Kids* in **MyPsychLab**.

Would you be surprised to learn that children use computers in much the same ways as they use other environments? As Figure 10.4 shows, younger children devote more computer time to playing games (17 minutes per day) than to any other activity, while those in the 11- to 14-year-old group spend more on time social networking sites (29 minutes per day) than playing games (19 minutes per day). Many developmental psychologists see this age trend in game playing and social networking as a product of the natural course of child development (Sandvig, 2006). In other words, age-related activity trends in the digital environment are identical to those in the nondigital environment: Younger children spend most of their time playing, and older children spend more time communicating with friends.

VIDEO GAMES Figure 10.4 indicates that playing video games is a popular activity among both 8- to 10-year-olds and 11- to 14-year-olds. Thus, developmentalists have looked at how these games affect children's cognitive and social/emotional development. Some studies suggest that video game playing enhances children's spatial-cognitive skills and may even eliminate the well-documented gender difference in this domain (Feng, Spence, & Pratt, 2007; Ferguson, 2010; Greenfield, Brannon, & Lohr, 1994). Similarly, children who perform poorly in school may gain a sense of competence from mastering video games, especially those that are complex and require sophisticated strategies, that helps to offset the deterioration of self-esteem that may be brought on by school failure (Przbyiski, Rigby, & Ryan, 2010).

Nevertheless, research suggests that even short-term exposure to violent video games in laboratory settings increases research participants' general level of emotional hostility (Anderson & Dill, 2000; Bushman & Huesmann, 2006). Apparently, increases in emotional hostility and decreases in the capacity to empathize with others, which are engendered by violent video games, are the motivating forces behind the increases in aggressive behavior that often result from playing such games for extended periods of time (Funk, Buchman, Jenks, & Bechtoldt, 2003; Gentile, Lynch, Linder, & Walsh, 2004).  **Watch** the **Video** *Violence and Video Games: Douglas Gentile* in **MyPsychLab**.

Critics of video game research point out that many such studies are methodologically flawed and, as a result, exaggerate the potential negative effects of violent games (Ferguson & Kilburn, 2010; Ferguson, Garza, Jerabeck, Ramos, & Galindo, 2013). These researchers point out that the effect of a particular game often depends on who is playing it. For example, violent video games appear to be part of an overall pattern linking preferences for violent stimuli to aggressive behavior. The more violent television programs children watch, the more violent video games they prefer, and the more aggressively they behave toward peers (Mediascope, 1999). This finding holds for both boys and girls. Most girls aren't interested in violent games and respond negatively to the hypersexualized female characters that most such games include (Behm-Morowitz & Mastro, 2009; Ferguson & Olson, 2013). However, like boys, the minority of girls who enjoy playing violent video games tend to be more physically aggressive than average. Consequently, parents who notice that aggressive and violent themes characterize most of their children's leisure-time interests as well as their interactions with peers should worry about their children playing video games (Funk, Buchman, Myers, & Jenks, 2000).

test yourself before going on ✓ Study and Review in MyPsychLab

Answers to these questions can be found in the back of the book.

1. List four negative developmental outcomes that are correlated with self-care:

   (a) _____

   (b) _____

   (c) _____

   (d) _____

2. Which effect below is associated with (A) television, (B) the internet, and (C) video games? (Each effect can be associated with more than one medium.)

   _____ (1) girls respond negatively to hypersexualized female characters

   _____ (2) positive effects on learning

   _____ (3) viewing aggressive behavior may increase aggressiveness

CRITICAL THINKING

3. You have learned about some of the factors that determine a child's vulnerability or resilience to poverty. How do you think after-school care arrangements and media influences contribute to vulnerability and resilience among children from low-income families?

SUMMARY

Theories of Social and Personality Development (pp. 241–243)

LO 10.1 How did the psychoanalytic theorists characterize the middle childhood years?

- Freud claimed that the libido is dormant between ages 6 and 12, a period he called the *latency* stage. Erikson theorized that 6- to 12-year-olds acquire a sense of industry by achieving educational goals determined by their cultures.

LO 10.2 What are the main ideas of the trait and social-cognitive theorists?

- Trait theories propose that people possess stable characteristics that emerge during middle childhood as experiences modify the dimensions of temperament. Social-cognitive theories, such as Bandura's reciprocal determinism, argue that traits, and the emotional aspects of personality that were emphasized by psychoanalytic theories, represent one of three interaction sets of factors that shape personality: person factors, environmental factors, and behavioral factors.

Self-Concept (pp. 243–246)

LO 10.3 What are the features of the psychological self?

- Between 6 and 12, children construct a psychological self. As a result, their self-descriptions begin to include personality traits, such as intelligence and friendliness, along with physical characteristics.

LO 10.4 How does self-esteem develop?

- Self-esteem appears to be shaped by two factors: the degree of discrepancy a child experiences between goals and achievements and the degree of perceived social support from peers and parents.

Advances in Social Cognition (pp. 246–249)

LO 10.5 How does children's understanding of others change in middle childhood?

- Between ages 6 and 12, children's understanding of others' stable, internal traits improves.

LO 10.6 How do children in Piaget's moral realism and moral relativism stages reason about right and wrong?

- Piaget claimed that moral reasoning develops in sequential stages that are correlated with his cognitive-developmental stages. Children in the moral realism stage believe that authority figures establish rules that must be followed, under threat of punishment. Children in the moral relativism stage understand that rules can be changed through social agreement. Their moral judgment is colored more by intentions than by consequences.

The Social World of the School-Aged Child (pp. 249–256)

LO 10.7 How does self-regulation affect school-aged children's relationships with their parents?

- Relationships with parents become less overtly affectionate, with fewer attachment behaviors, in middle childhood. The strength of the attachment, however, appears to persist.

LO 10.8 What changes occur in children's understanding of friendships during this period?

- Friendships become stable in middle childhood. Children's selection of friends depends on variables such as trustworthiness as well as overt characteristics such as play preferences and gender.

LO 10.9 In what ways do boys and girls interact during the middle childhood years?

- Gender segregation of peer groups is at its peak in middle childhood and appears in every culture. Individual friendships also become more common and more enduring; boys' and girls' friendships appear to differ in specific ways.

LO 10.10 What types of aggression are most common among school-aged children?

- Physical aggression declines during middle childhood, although verbal aggression increases. Boys show markedly higher levels of physical and direct verbal aggression than girls, while girls show higher rates of relational aggression than boys. Children whose bullying is accompanied by destruction of property, theft, deceitfulness, and/or violations of social rules may be diagnosed with conduct disorder.

LO 10.11 How do popular, rejected, and neglected children differ?

- Rejected children are most strongly characterized by high levels of aggression or bullying and low levels of agreeableness and helpfulness, but some aggressive children are very popular. Neglected children may suffer depression.

Influences beyond Family and Peers (pp. 256–261)

LO 10.12 What factors contribute to resilience and vulnerability among poor children?

- Children in low-income families are markedly disadvantaged in many ways. They do worse in school and move through the stages of cognitive development more slowly. Protective factors, including a secure attachment, relatively high IQ, authoritative parenting, and effective schools, can counterbalance poverty effects for some children.

LO 10.13 How do television, computers, and video games affect children's development?

- Experts agree that watching violence on television and playing violent video games increase the level of personal aggression or violence shown by a child.

KEY TERMS

bullying (p. 254)

conduct disorder (p. 254)

moral realism stage (p. 247)

moral relativism stage (p. 248)

psychological self (p. 243)

reciprocal determinism (p. 243)

relational aggression (p. 254)

retaliatory aggression (p. 254)

self-efficacy (p. 244)

self-esteem (p. 245)

self-regulation (p. 249)

social comparisons (p. 244)

social status (p. 254)

trait (p. 242)

✓ **Study** and **Review** in **MyPsychLab**

Answers to all the Chapter Test questions can be found in the back of the book.

1. How has the percentage of children living in poverty changed from the 1950s to now?
   a. It is impossible to know because of the number of homeless families in the United States.
   b. It has declined.
   c. It has remained the same.
   d. It has increased.

2. Which of the following behaviors is seen in children diagnosed with conduct disorder?
   a. aggression
   b. destruction of property
   c. theft
   d. all of the above

3. Which of the following is a major influence in a child's self-esteem?
   a. The general support the child feels from her parents, peers and others
   b. The child's perceived popularity by others
   c. The evaluations of teachers and whether they match the child's self-evaluation
   d. Internal characteristics transmitted genetically from the parents

4. According to Erikson, children resolve the psychosocial task of middle childhood through their _____.
   a. friendships
   b. learning and demonstrating culturally valued skills
   c. relationships with parents and siblings
   d. choosing a future career

5. According to the text, which of the following is linked to popularity among children?
   a. the ability to control social situations
   b. shyness
   c. average appearance, neither more nor less attractive than others
   d. the capacity to look at situations from others' perspectives

6. Bandura's model of personality development emphasizes _____.
   a. conditioning
   b. interactions among personal, behavioral, and environmental variables
   c. hereditary traits
   d. unconscious drives

7. What was the goal of Bandura's "Bobo doll" studies?
   a. to demonstrate the contribution of self-efficacy to social development
   b. to examine how observations of aggressive behavior affect children's own behavior
   c. to study the development of fear in school-aged children
   d. to find out how children go about resolving conflicts

8. Which of the following refers to children's global self-evaluation, which includes factors such as how well they like themselves and how happy they are?
   a. self-construct
   b. self-esteem
   c. intrapersonal perception
   d. introspection

9. Which statement describes the progression of children in low-income homes through Piaget's stages of cognitive development?
   a. They progress through the stages more slowly.
   b. IQ is unrelated to cognitive development among poor children.
   c. Parents respond to children's cognitive needs in ways that negate the potentially effects of poverty on cognitive development.
   d. As long as they live in safe neighborhoods, children in low-income homes do not differ in cognitive development from peers in middle- and high-income homes.

10. Psychologists have begun to believe that girls may not be less aggressive than boys but rather may express themselves by using which form of aggression?
    a. covert hostility
    b. verbal hostility
    c. relational aggression
    d. parallel aggression

11. Which of the following seems to be the most important factor in selection of friends among 6- to 12-year-olds?
    a. socioeconomic similarity
    b. race
    c. age
    d. gender

12. Monica is an only child. Which of the following statements is *not* likely to be true regarding Monica?
    a. Her family is less likely to suffer from resource dilution.
    b. Research indicates that she will be as well adjusted as children who have siblings.
    c. She will likely get as much of her parents' attention as a first-born child.
    d. She will have difficulty making friends when she starts school.

13. Which of the following is the child's ability to conform to parental standards of behavior without direct supervision?
    a. interdependence
    b. self-evaluation
    c. independence
    d. self-regulation

14. This chapter suggests a reason why parents living in poverty are more likely to be stricter and place more emphasis on obedience. What is that reason?
    a. They place greater emphasis on punishment.
    b. It is a logical response to the neighborhoods they are likely to be living in.
    c. Lack of education causes parents to overreact and overemphasize control.
    d. They are more likely to have many children, requiring discipline to minimize a chaotic household environment.

15. A researcher told 9-year-olds a story about two children who damaged their father's car, one intentionally and the other accidentally. If the children are in Piaget's autonomous stage of moral development, which child will they say deserves to be punished?
    a. The one who damaged the car accidentally deserves to be punished.
    b. The one who damaged the car intentionally deserves to be punished.
    c. The question is too complex for nine-year-olds. They won't be able to answer.
    d. Their answers will depend on how advanced their vocabularies are.

16. Which of the following best defines self-efficacy?
    a. the belief that one is responsible for one's own internal behaviors
    b. the belief that the environment influences one's internal thoughts
    c. the belief in one's ability to cause an intended event to happen
    d. the belief in one's influence over events which have nothing to do with them

17. Many children who grow up in neighborhoods with street violence, gang activity, and overcrowded homes suffer from which of the following?
    a. posttraumatic stress disorder
    b. attention-deficit/hyperactivity disorder
    c. obsessive-compulsive disorder
    d. panic disorder

18. According to Susan Harter's research, children's self-esteem is based on _____.
    a. encouragement from parents
    b. perceived discrepancies between their ideal and actual selves
    c. performance in school
    d. success experiences

19. Which of the following children would be likely to be rejected or neglected by peers in middle childhood?
    a. Larry, who is taller than his peers and considered handsome
    b. Abraham, who is very shy
    c. Elizabeth, who throws temper tantrums and cries easily
    d. Juan, who loves to write and perform various types of music

20. According to Piaget's ideas about children's moral development, a child who believes that the rules of games cannot be changed is demonstrating moral development at which stage?
    a. moral realism
    b. ego ideal
    c. preconventional
    d. moral relativism

21. Penny broke her brother's baseball trophy after he used her favorite doll to play tug-of-war with their dog. Which type of aggression is Penny demonstrating?
    a. relational aggression
    b. hostile aggression
    c. instrumental aggression
    d. retaliatory aggression

22. How do violent video games affect male players' behavior?
    a. They become more emotionally hostile.
    b. They become more socially outgoing.
    c. They become quickly bored with the repetitive nature of such games.
    d. They respond negatively to the hypersexualized female characters in such games.

23. Which of the following seems to be the most important element in a child's acceptance by her peers?
    a. social behavior
    b. physical appearance
    c. socioeconomic status
    d. intelligence

24. In what way might only children have an advantage over children who have siblings?
    a. They are likely to show higher cognitive development and higher levels of academic achievement.
    b. They are more likely to go to college than children with siblings.
    c. They are likely to suffer from resource dilution.
    d. They are less likely to engage in gender-stereotypical behaviors.

25. Rudolf is struggling with his math and reading skills but excels at soccer. What would Erikson say about Rudolf's sense of competence?
    a. Since soccer is a European sport, Rudolf will not develop a sense of confidence.
    b. Since his teachers are likely to treat Rudolf badly, he will disregard the sense of competence that he feels at soccer.
    c. Rudolf will successfully resolve the conflict of this stage through his competence at soccer.
    d. Rudolf will not successfully resolve this stage because his peers are likely to make fun of him.

To 👁 **Watch** ✳ **Explore** ⊚ **Simulate** ✅ **Study** and **Review** and experience MyVirtualLife go to MyPsychLab.com

chapter 11

Physical and Cognitive Development in Adolescence

How do the experiences of the teenaged "child" you are raising in *MyVirtualLife* compare to yours? For instance, do you remember making elaborate plans when you were an adolescent, plans that usually didn't work out quite the way you thought they would? Perhaps you planned to go to an out-of-town concert with friends, only to find out that the parents of the one licensed driver in your group wouldn't allow him or her to go. Or you may have mapped out a cross-country motorcycle trip with your best friend, even though neither

LEARNING OBJECTIVES

PHYSICAL CHANGES

11.1 How do the brains and other body systems of adolescents differ from those of younger children?

11.2 What are the major milestones of puberty?

11.3 What are the consequences of early, "on time," and late puberty for boys and girls?

ADOLESCENT SEXUALITY

11.4 What are the patterns of adolescent sexual behavior in the United States?

11.5 Which teenaged girls are most likely to get pregnant?

11.6 What are some causes that have been proposed to explain homosexuality?

ADOLESCENT HEALTH

11.7 How does sensation seeking affect risky behavior in adolescents?

11.8 What patterns of drug, alcohol, and tobacco use have been found among adolescents in the United States?

11.9 What are the characteristics and causes of eating disorders?

11.10 Which adolescents are at greatest risk of depression and suicide?

CHANGES IN THINKING AND MEMORY

11.11 What are the characteristics of thought in Piaget's formal operational stage?

11.12 What are some major research findings regarding the formal operational stage?

11.13 What kinds of advances in information-processing capabilities occur during adolescence?

SCHOOLING

11.14 How do changes in students' goals contribute to the transition to secondary school?

11.15 What gender and ethnic differences in science and math achievement have researchers found?

11.16 What variables predict the likelihood of dropping out of high school?

of you owned or knew how to operate a motorcycle. Perhaps one of your friends and his or her romantic partner planned to marry immediately after graduation, with little thought about how they would support themselves.

Such actions arise from a new form of thinking that is characteristic of **adolescence**, the transitional period between childhood and adulthood. The powerful intellectual tools that emerge in the early teens allow adolescents to make plans and to mentally project themselves into those plans as a way of testing them. The process is somewhat akin to that of a scientist who formulates a hypothesis and devises an experiment to test it. Armed with this new way of thinking, young adolescents embark upon a period of development characterized by risks and opportunities that compete for their attention. Some of their choices are good ones, but others reflect poor judgment. Most of teenagers' poor choices turn out to have little long-term effect, but others can significantly alter the developmental trajectory of an adolescent's life. How these risks and opportunities are manifested in the physical and cognitive domains is the topic of this chapter.

Physical Changes

When we think of the physical changes of adolescence, we usually give the greatest amount of attention to the reproductive system. Reproductive changes are important, as the text will point out. But momentous changes occur in other systems, and we will discuss those as well.

Brain Development and Physical Growth

LO 11.1   How do the brains and other body systems of adolescents differ from those of younger children?

Although puberty and sexual behavior may first come to mind when we think about how teens differ from younger children, the advances in cognition and the changes in the brain that facilitate them are equally striking (Ernst & Hardin, 2010; Giedd, 2004). For instance, have you noticed that you are much better able to make realistic plans now than you could when you were 13 or 14? If so, then you have first-hand knowledge of the changes in the brain during adolescence that facilitate planning and logic. Likewise, you were probably better coordinated and had more physical endurance at 18 than you did at 13, thanks to changes in the body's other organ systems during the teen years.

THE BRAIN   There are two major brain growth spurts in the teenaged years. The first occurs between ages 13 and 15 (Spreen et al., 1995). During this spurt, the cerebral cortex becomes thicker, and the neuronal pathways become more efficient. In addition, more energy is produced and consumed by the brain during this spurt than in the years that precede and follow it (Fischer & Rose, 1994). For the most part, these growth and energy spurts take place in parts of the brain that control spatial perception and motor functions. Consequently, by the mid-teens, adolescents' abilities in these areas far exceed those of school-aged children.

Neuropsychologists Kurt Fischer and Samuel Rose believe that a qualitatively different neural network emerges during the brain growth spurt that occurs between ages 13 and 15, which enables teens to think abstractly and to reflect on their cognitive processes (Fischer & Rose, 1994). As evidence, these researchers cite numerous neurological and psychological studies revealing that major changes in brain organization show up between ages 13 and 15 and that qualitative shifts in cognitive functioning appear after age 15. They claim that the consistency of these research findings is too compelling to ignore.

The 13-to-15 spurt is also associated with profound changes in the **prefrontal cortex (PFC)** (Gogtay et al., 2004; Kanemura, Aihara, Aoke, Araki, & Nakazawa, 2004). The PFC is the part

adolescence the transitional period between childhood and adulthood

prefrontal cortex (PFC) the part of the frontal lobe that is just behind the forehead and is responsible for executive processing

of the frontal lobe that is just behind the forehead (see Figure 11.1). It is responsible for *executive processing*, a set of information-processing skills that we mentioned in Chapter 9. These skills enable us to consciously control and organize our thought processes. Just prior to puberty, the neurons in the PFC rapidly form new synapses with those in other parts of the brain. Over the first few years of adolescence, the brain prunes away many of the least efficient of these synapses, a process that continues into the mid-20s (Giedd, Blumenthal, & Jeffries, 1999; Kolb et al., 2012). As a result, by mid-adolescence, teenagers' executive processing skills far exceed those of middle childhood. Moreover, studies of patients with damage to the PFC suggest that maturation of this part of the brain contributes to advances in social perception, particularly those that involve the interpretation of nonverbal information such as facial expressions (Mah, Arnold, & Grafman, 2005).

The second adolescent brain growth spurt begins around age 17 and continues into early adulthood (van der Molen & Molenaar, 1994). This time, the frontal lobes of the cerebral cortex are the focus of development (Davies & Rose, 1999). You may recall that this area of the brain controls logic and planning. Thus, it is not surprising that older teens differ from younger teens in terms of how they deal with problems that require these cognitive functions.

OTHER BODY SYSTEMS An adolescent may grow 3 to 6 inches a year for several years. After the growth spurt, teenagers add height and weight slowly until they reach their adult size. Girls attain most of their height by age 16, while boys continue to grow until they are 18–20 years old (Tanner, 1990).

The shape and proportions of an adolescent's body also go through a series of changes. During the growth spurt, the normal cephalocaudal and proximodistal patterns (introduced in Chapter 3) are reversed. Thus, a teenager's hands and feet are the first body parts to grow to full adult size, followed by the arms and legs; the trunk is usually the slowest-growing part. In fact, a good signal for a parent that a child is entering puberty is a rapid increase in the child's shoe size. Because of this asymmetry in the body parts, adolescents are often stereotyped as awkward or uncoordinated. Although they may look awkward, they are better coordinated than school-aged children (Gabbard, 2012).

Joint development enables adolescents to achieve levels of coordination that are close to those of adults. As they do at younger ages, boys continue to lag behind girls. You may remember from earlier chapters that boys' fine-motor skills are poorer than girls' because their wrists develop more slowly. In early adolescence, this sex difference is very large; girls achieve complete development of the wrist by their mid-teens (Tanner, 1990). A similar pattern of sex differences is evident in other joints as well, enabling early-adolescent girls to outperform boys of the same age on a variety of athletic skills that require coordination, such as pitching a softball. However, by age 17 or 18, boys finally catch up with girls in joint development and, on average, gain superiority over them in coordinated movement.

Muscle fibers become thicker and denser, and adolescents become quite a lot stronger in just a few years. Both boys and girls show this increase in strength, but it is much greater in boys (Buchanan & Vardaxis, 2003). This difference in strength reflects the underlying sex difference in muscle tissue that is accentuated at adolescence: Among adult men, about 40% of total body mass is muscle, compared to only about 24% in adult women. This sex difference in muscle mass (and accompanying strength) seems to be largely a result of hormone differences. But sex differences in exercise patterns or activities may also be involved.

During the teenaged years, the heart and lungs increase considerably in size, and the heart rate drops. Both of these changes are more marked in boys than in girls—another factor that makes boys' capacity for sustained physical effort greater than that of girls. Before about age 12, boys and girls have similar endurance limits, although even at these earlier ages, when there is a difference, it is usually boys who have greater endurance because of their lower levels of body fat. After puberty, boys have a clear advantage in endurance, as well as in size, strength, and speed (Klomsten, Skaalvik, & Espnes, 2004).

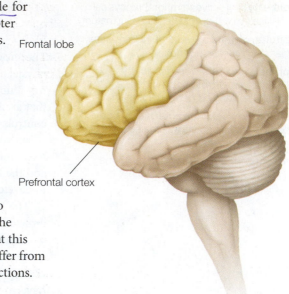

Frontal lobe

Prefrontal cortex

Figure 11.1 The Prefrontal Cortex

The prefrontal cortex matures rapidly during adolescence and contributes to advances in executive processing.

Adolescent girls reach adult height sooner than boys do because their bones grow and their joints develop more rapidly.

Milestones of Puberty

LO 11.2 What are the major milestones of puberty?

The growth and development of teenagers' brains and bodies is remarkable. However, the physical change that most people associate with adolescence is the attainment of sexual maturity. **Puberty** is a collective term that encompasses all of the changes, both seen and unseen, that are needed for reproductive maturity. It begins when the **pituitary gland**, the gland that controls all of the body's other glands, signals a child's adrenal gland to step up its production of androgen (see Table 11.1). This milestone, called *adrenarche*, occurs around age 7 or 8. Next, the pituitary begins secreting hormones that stimulate the growth of the ovaries in girls and the testes in boys. As they grow, these glands secrete hormones that cause the sex organs to develop—testosterone in boys and a form of estrogen called *estradiol* in girls.

The pituitary also secretes two other hormones, *thyroid stimulating hormone* and *general growth hormone*; these, along with adrenal androgen, interact with the specific sex hormones and affect growth. Adrenal androgen, which is chemically very similar to testosterone, plays a particularly important role for girls, triggering the growth spurt and affecting development of pubic hair. For boys, adrenal androgen is less significant, presumably because boys already have so much male hormone in the form of testosterone in their bloodstreams. These hormonal changes trigger two sets of body changes: development of the sex organs and a much broader set of changes in the brain, bones, muscles, and other body organs.

The most obvious changes of puberty are those associated with sexual maturity. Changes in **primary sex characteristics** include growth of the testes and penis in the male and of the ovaries, uterus, and vagina in the female. Changes in **secondary sex characteristics** include breast development in girls, changing voice pitch and beard growth in boys, and the growth of body hair in both sexes. These physical developments occur in a defined sequence that is customarily divided into five stages, following a system originally suggested by J. M. Tanner (Tanner, 1990), examples from which are shown in Table 11.2 on page 269.

SEXUAL DEVELOPMENT IN GIRLS Studies of preteens and teens in both Europe and North America show that the various sequential changes are interlocked in a particular pattern in girls. The first steps are the early changes in breasts and pubic hair, closely followed by the peak of the growth spurt and by the development of breasts and pubic hair. First menstruation, an event called **menarche** (pronounced men-ARE-kee), typically occurs 2 to 3 years after the beginning of other visible changes and is succeeded only by the final stages of breast and pubic hair development, typically between the ages of 10 and 15 (Blake & Davis, 2011; Kaplowitz, 2013). Among girls in the United States today, about 10% experience menarche earlier than age 11, and more than 90% have reached menarche by age 14 (Chumlea et al., 2003).

puberty collective term for the physical changes which culminate in sexual maturity

pituitary gland gland that triggers other glands to release hormones

primary sex characteristics the sex organs: ovaries, uterus, and vagina in the female; testes and penis in the male

secondary sex characteristics body parts such as breasts in females and pubic hair in both sexes

menarche the beginning of menstrual cycles

TABLE 11.1 Major Hormones That Contribute to Physical Growth and Development

Gland	Hormone(s)	Aspects of Growth Influenced
Thyroid gland	Thyroxine	Normal brain development and overall rate of growth
Adrenal gland	Adrenal androgen	Some changes at puberty, particularly the development of secondary sex characteristics in girls
Testes (boys)	Testosterone	Crucial in the formation of male genitals prenatally; also triggers the sequence of changes in primary and secondary sex characteristics at puberty in males
Ovaries (girls)	Estrogen (estradiol)	Development of the menstrual cycle and breasts in girls; has less to do with other secondary sex characteristics than testosterone does for boys
Pituitary gland	General growth hormone, thyroid stimulating hormone, and other activating hormones	Rate of physical maturation; signals other glands to secrete

TABLE 11.2 Examples of Tanner's Stages of Pubertal Development

Stage	Female Breast Development	Male Genital Development
1	No change except for some elevation of the nipple.	Testes, scrotum, and penis are all about the same size and shape as in early childhood.
2	Breast bud stage: elevation of breast and the nipple as a small mound. Areolar diameter increases compared to stage 1.	Scrotum and testes are slightly enlarged. Skin of the scrotum reddens and changes texture, but little or no enlargement of the penis.
3	Breast and areola both enlarged and elevated more than in stage 2, but no separation of their contours.	Penis slightly enlarged, at first mainly in length. Testes and scrotum are further enlarged. First ejaculation.
4	Areola and nipple form a secondary mound projecting above the contour of the breast.	Penis further enlarged, with growth in breadth and development of glans. Testes and scrotum further enlarged, and scrotum skin still darker.
5	Mature stage. Only the nipple projects, with the areola recessed to the general contour of the breast.	Genitalia achieve adult size and shape.

(*Source:* Marshall & Tanner, 1986.)

It is possible to become pregnant shortly after menarche, but irregular menstrual cycles are the norm for some time. In as many as three-quarters of the cycles in the first year after menarche, and half of the cycles in the second and third years, the girl's body produces no ovum (Adelman & Ellen, 2002). Full adult fertility thus develops over a period of years. Such irregularity no doubt contributes to the widespread (but false) assumption among younger teenaged girls that they cannot get pregnant.

THE SECULAR TREND Interestingly, the timing of menarche changed rather dramatically between the mid-19th and the mid-20th centuries. In 1840, the average age of menarche in Western industrialized countries was roughly 17; the average dropped steadily from that time until the 1950s at a rate of about 4 months per decade among European populations, an example of what psychologists call a **secular trend** (Roche, 1979). The change was most likely caused by significant changes in lifestyle and diet, particularly increases in protein and fat intake, that resulted in an increase in the proportion of body fat in females.

Data collected over much shorter periods of time in developing countries support the nutritional explanation of the secular trend. In one study, researchers found that the average age of menarche was 16 among North Korean girls who lived in squalid refugee camps (Ku et al., 2006). By contrast, studies involving impoverished groups in which food supplies suddenly increase reveal that the age of menarche can plummet from 16 to 13 within just a few years after improvements in nutrition are experienced (Khanna & Kapoor, 2004). Consequently, any change in eating patterns that affects girls' body fat, which must reach a critical value of 17% before menarche can occur, is likely to lead to a change in the age of menarche (Adelman & Ellen, 2002). But is there a lower limit on how early menarche can occur?

Exaggerated media accounts of the secular trend would have us believe that girls may some day attain sexual maturity during infancy (Viner, 2002). However, there is strong evidence for a genetic limit on the age range within which menarche may occur. For one thing, studies involving hundreds of thousands of girls indicate that the average age of menarche for White girls in the United States ranges from 12.6 to 12.9 years, depending on the study involved, and that it has not changed since the mid-1940s (Blake & Davis, 2011; Kaplowitz & Oberfield, 1999; Rosenfield, Lipton, & Drum, 2009; Viner, 2002). Moreover, the average age at menarche stands at 12.1 among African American girls and 12.3 among Hispanic American girls, both of which represent a drop of about 2 months since the mid-1960s (Kaplowitz & Oberfield, 1999; Rosenfield et al., 2009; Wu, Mendola, & Buck, 2002). Thus, the average age at menarche for the whole population of girls in the United States was stable from 1945 to 1965 and declined about 2.5 months between 1965 and 1995 before it became stable once again (Kaplowitz & Oberfield, 1999).

In contrast to the stability of menarche, the average ages at which girls show secondary sex characteristics, such as the appearance of breast buds and pubic hair, have dropped significantly in recent decades (Rosenfield et al., 2009). On average, girls today show these signs

secular trend a change that occurs in developing nations when nutrition and health improve—for example, the decline in average age of menarche and the increase in average height for both children and adults that happened between the mid-18th and mid-19th centuries in Western countries

somewhat earlier than their mothers and grandmothers did, resulting in a lengthening of the average time between the appearance of secondary sex characteristics and menarche (Parent et al., 2003). Researchers have found that this trend is attributable to the increased prevalence of obesity among children that you read about in Chapter 9 (Jasik & Lustig, 2008; Rosenfield et al., 2009). Nevertheless, the appearance of breasts or pubic hair in girls younger than 7 years continues to be atypical. Thus, a girl younger than 7 who exhibits these signs may be diagnosed with *precocious puberty*, a diagnosis that requires follow-up to determine whether a tumor, hormonal disorder, or other condition or disease is responsible (Kaplowitz, 2013).

Obesity is both a cause and a consequence of development of early secondary sex characteristics, because the hormonal changes that trigger the appearance of these characteristics also signal the body's weight regulation mechanisms to increase fat stores (Pierce & Leon, 2005; Jasik & Lustig, 2008). Little is known about how these early hormonal shifts affect girls' later health. Several studies are underway to determine whether obese girls who exhibit early secondary-sex-characteristic development are at increased risk for breast cancer (National Cancer Institute, 2006). To date these studies have produced mixed results, so researchers are still unsure whether a long-term health risk is entailed (Kaplowitz, 2010).

SEXUAL DEVELOPMENT IN BOYS In boys, as in girls, the peak of the growth spurt typically comes fairly late in the sequence of physical development. Studies suggest that, on average, a boy completes stages 2, 3, and 4 of genital development and stages 2 and 3 of pubic hair development before reaching the peak of the growth spurt (Blake & Davis, 2011). His first ejaculation, or *spermarche*, occurs between 13 and 14 years of age, but the production of viable sperm production does not happen until a few months after the first ejaculation. Most boys do not attain adult levels of sperm production until stage 5 of genital development. The development of facial hair and the lowering of the voice occur near the end of the sequence. Precisely when in this sequence the boy begins to produce viable sperm is very difficult to determine, although current evidence places this event sometime between ages 12 and 14, usually before the boy has reached the peak of the growth spurt (Adelman & Ellen, 2002).

Interestingly, the secular trend in pubertal development has been far less dramatic among boys than among girls (Aksglaede, Olsen, Sørensen, & Juul, 2008; Kaplowitz, 2013). Moreover, research findings on the link between obesity and pubertal development in boys have been inconsistent. Some studies suggest that obesity delays male puberty (e.g., Wang, 2002). Other research indicates that obesity speeds up pubertal development in boys just as it does in girls (e.g., Rosenfield et al., 2009). As developmentalists often say, "more research is needed."

Timing of Puberty

LO 11.3 What are the consequences of early, "on time," and late puberty for boys and girls?

Although the order of physical developments in adolescence seems to be highly consistent, there is quite a lot of individual variability. In any random sample of 12- and 13-year-olds, you will find some who are already at stage 5 and others still at stage 1 in sexual maturation. We have already discussed the contribution of diet, exercise, and body fat to the timing of puberty. Researchers think that hereditary and behavioral factors also contribute to hormonal secretions in the bodies of individual teenagers, thereby controlling the timing of puberty (Dorn, Susman, & Ponirakis, 2003). Discrepancies between an adolescent's expectation and what actually happens determine the psychological effect of puberty. Those whose development occurs outside the desired or expected range are likely to think less well of themselves, to be less happy with their bodies and with the process of puberty. They may also display other signs of psychological distress.

Research in the United States indicates that early-developing girls (who experience major body changes before age 10 or 11) possess consistently more negative body images, such as thinking of themselves as too fat (Kaplowitz, 2013; Sweeting & West, 2002). Such girls are also more likely to get into trouble in school and at home, more likely to become sexually active and be depressed than are girls who are average or late developers (Kaltiala-Heino, Kosunen, Rimpela, 2003). Among boys, both very early and very late puberty are associated with depression (Kaltiala-Heino et al., 2003). However, researchers have also consistently found that boys who are slightly ahead of their peers in pubertal development exhibit more prosocial behavior (Carlo, Crockett, Wolff, & Beal, 2012). In addition, they often occupy leadership roles and are more academically and economically successful in adulthood (Taga, Markey, & Friedman, 2006). In addition, substance use is associated with early puberty in both girls and boys, perhaps because, based on their appearance, early maturers are often invited to join groups of older teens among whom substance use is an important social activity (Costello, Sun, Worthman, & Angold, 2007).

Girls who develop early report much less positive adolescent experiences and more depression than girls who develop "on time" or later.

Research also indicates that pubertal timing interacts with a number of other variables to produce both positive and negative effects on adolescents' development. For instance, personality traits contribute to the effects of pubertal timing (Markey, Markey, & Tinsley, 2003). It appears that girls who experience early puberty and who are high in the Big Five trait of openness to experience are more likely to be sexually active at an early age than are girls who are early but who do not possess this trait. Parenting also moderates the effects of pubertal timing such that both early-maturing boys and girls are more likely to become involved in sexual activity and substance abuse if their parents are permissive (Costello et al., 2007).

Moreover, longitudinal research suggests that children who live in low-risk households are less likely than peers in high-risk households to exhibit negative effects of early puberty such as substance abuse (Hummel, Shelton, Heron, Moore, & van den Bree, 2013; Lynne-Landsman, Graber, & Andrews, 2010). Low-risk households are those in which parents have adequate material resources and stable intimate relationships, are not involved in substance abuse, and have good relationships with children. Likewise, maternal depression and family stresses, such as parental job loss, increase depression rates among early-maturing girls (Rudolph & Troop-Gordon, 2010). Thus, the family context in which early puberty occurs can either diminish or intensify its effects on adolescents.

Peer contexts also affect how pubertal timing affects adolescents. Consider the case of girls who are involved in activities that, by their nature, inhibit development of the proportion of body fat required to initiate puberty, such as ballet and gymnastics. In these contexts, girls who are late by general cultural standards are on time for the reference group with which they spend most of their time. Thus, early puberty may cause them to believe they can no longer be successful in their chosen pursuit and may devastate their self-esteem, whereas late puberty may enhance their self-confidence and self-esteem (Brooks-Gunn, 1987; Graber, Nichols, & Brooks-Gunn, 2010).

test yourself before going on ✓ Study and Review in MyPsychLab

Answers to these questions can be found in the back of the book.

1. Changes in the _____ are responsible for improvements in executive processing skills in early adolescence.

2. In what order do these milestones of puberty occur in girls?
   _____ (a) menarche
   _____ (b) breast development
   _____ (c) peak of the growth spurt

3. In what order do these milestones of puberty occur in boys?
   _____ (a) production of viable sperm
   _____ (b) genitals increase in size
   _____ (c) peak of the growth spurt

4. What negative effect of early puberty is found in both boys and girls?

CRITICAL THINKING

5. Suppose you were asked to give a talk to parents about young teenagers' need for sex education and for adult guidance with regard to romantic relationships. How would you integrate the information on brain development with the discussion of the stages of puberty in your presentation?

Adolescent Sexuality

Puberty brings with it the hormonal changes that underlie both sexual attraction and sexual behavior. Still, these important domains of experience are not entirely controlled by hormones. Each has psychological and social components, as you will see.

Sexual Behavior

LO 11.4 What are the patterns of adolescent sexual behavior in the United States?

Television programs aimed at adolescent audiences often portray teens in sexual situations, such as these two from the popular show *Pretty Little Liars*.

Do you remember your first sexual experience? Today, most people have their first sexual encounter in the mid- to late teens (Fryar et al., 2007). However, teens vary widely in how often they have sex and in how many partners they have.

PREVALENCE OF SEXUAL BEHAVIOR Figure 11.2 graphs findings from a 2011 national survey of high school students in the United States (Eaton et al., 2013). As you can see, boys were found to be more sexually active than girls. Furthermore, the proportion of sexually experienced teens increased across grades 9 to 12. However, rates of sexual activity have declined substantially over the past three decades. In 1988, 60% of male and 51% of female 15- to 19-year-olds reported having had sex at least once in their lives. In 2008, the rates were 43% and 42%, respectively (Abma, Martinez, & Cohen, 2010).

According to national surveys, sexual activity varies somewhat across racial and ethnic groups in the United States (Eaton et al., 2013). Among female highs school students, 45% of Whites, 44% of Hispanics, and 54% of African Americans are sexually experienced. Among males, 44% of Whites, 53% of Hispanics, and 67% of African Americans tell researchers that they have had sex at least once. African American teens were also more likely than Hispanic American and White teens to have had their first sexual encounter before age 13 (14% versus 7% and 4%, respectively) (Eaton et al., 2013). There are also age differences among students who are currently sexually active—defined as having had sex at least once within 3 months of responding to a survey. For example, in one national survey, 19% of 9th-grade females and 51% of twelfth-grade females reported sexual activity within the past 3 months, compared to 24% and 44% of males in the two ages groups, respectively (Eaton et al., 2013).

Although sexual activity among boys is somewhat correlated with the amount of testosterone in the blood, social factors are much better predictors than hormones of teenagers' sexual activity (Halpern, Udry, Campbell, & Suchindran, 1993; Udry & Campbell, 1994). In fact, cross-cultural evidence suggests that the same factors are related to sexual behavior even in societies with very low rates of teenaged sexual activity, such as Taiwan (Wang & Chou, 1999). Those who begin sexual activity early are more likely to live in poor neighborhoods in which young people are not well monitored by adults. They come from poorer families or from families in which sexual activity is condoned and dating rules are lax. They are more likely to use alcohol. Many were abused and/or neglected in early childhood (Herrenkohl, Herrenkohl, Egolf, & Russo, 1998).

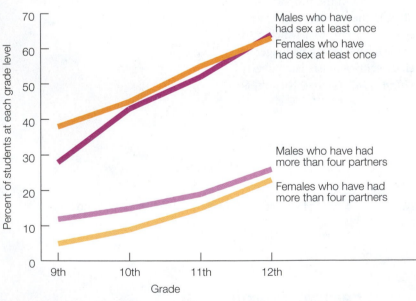

Figure 11.2 Sexual Activity among High School Students

The graph illustrates the data from a representative sample of more than 15,000 high school students interviewed in 2011.

(*Source:* Eaton et al., 2013.)

Among girls, those who are sexually active are also more likely to have experienced early menarche, to have problems in school, to have had their first date at a relatively early age, and to have a history of sexual abuse (Buzi, Roberts, Ross, Addy, & Markham, 2003; Ompad et al., 2006). The greater the number of risk factors present in the life of an individual teenager, the greater the likelihood that he or she will be sexually active. However, adolescents' moral beliefs and the activities in which they participate also predict their sexual activity. For example, teenagers who believe that premarital sex is morally wrong and who attend religious services frequently are less likely than their peers to become sexually active before reaching adulthood (Abma et al., 2010). Rates of sexual activity are also lower among teens who are involved in sports or other after-school pursuits than among their peers who do not participate in such activities (Savage & Holcomb, 1999). Moreover, alcohol use is associated with 22% of adolescent sexual encounters; thus, teens who do not use alcohol are less likely to be sexually active than are their peers who drink (Eaton et al., 2010).

Teens who date in early adolescence, as these middle-schoolers may be doing, are more likely to become sexually active while still in school than peers who begin dating later.

CONTRACEPTIVE USE Nearly 90% of sexually active high school students report having used some form of contraception the last time they had intercourse (Eaton et al., 2013). Moreover, rates of condom use have increased among teens. In 1988, only 31% of sexually experienced females and 53% of sexually experienced males reported having used a condom (Abma et al., 2010). By 2011, rates of condom use rose to 54% of female and 67% of male teens. However, teens today are less likely to use birth control pills than their counterparts in earlier decades. Just over 23% of sexually active high school females in 2011 reported being on the pill, compared to 42% of this age group in 1988. Thus, many developmentalists and public health advocates say that more effective sex education programs are needed. Most suggest that programs that include training in social and decision-making skills, as well as information about STDs and pregnancy, are more likely than information-only approaches to reduce the prevalence of sexual activity and to increase the number of teens who protect themselves against disease and pregnancy when they do have sex. Programs that involve parents also appear to be more successful than those that target only teenagers themselves (Lederman & Mian, 2003; Wilson & Donenberg, 2004). However, no clear consensus about the effectiveness of various approaches to sex education has emerged, and some studies show that even carefully designed sex education programs have little or no long-term effect on adolescents' sexual behavior (Henderson et al., 2007).

Many adults object to sex education because they believe it will cause teenagers who are not sexually active to become so. Research suggests that such fears are unfounded (Berne & Huberman, 1996). There are also debates over the degree to which sex education programs should emphasize abstaining from sex or using contraceptives (Santelli et al., 2006). Studies examining several types of programs indicate that abstinence-based sex education is most likely to result in delay of first sexual intercourse when it is initiated with younger students—seventh- or eighth-graders—who are not yet sexually active (Borawski, Trapl, Lovegreen, Colabianchi, & Block, 2005). Moreover, students who participate in multisession programs are more likely to remain abstinent than those who are exposed to single-session presentations about abstinence (Postrado & Nicholson, 1992).

Sex education advocates suggest that abstinence and contraceptive education should not be thought of in either/or terms (Borawski et al., 2005). They point to research suggesting that programs that both encourage abstinence *and* provide basic information about reproduction and contraception appear to influence teen participants both to delay sexual intercourse and to use contraception when they do decide to become sexually active (St. Pierre, Mark, Kaltreider, & Aiken, 1995). Indeed, finding a way to encourage teens to avoid becoming sexually active too early may be critical to influencing contraceptive use. The older teenagers are when they become sexually active, the more likely it is that they will be cognitively capable of weighing the various options and consequences associated with intercourse.

Adolescent Pregnancy

LO 11.5 Which teenaged girls are most likely to get pregnant?

The rate of pregnancy among adolescents is higher in the United States than in many other industrialized countries (Abma et al., 2010). For example, the overall annual rate is about 40 pregnancies per 1,000 teens in the United States; it is only 27 pregnancies per 1,000 in the

United Kingdom, 10 per 1,000 in Germany, and 5 per 1,000 in Japan (Abma et al., 2010). Ethnic differences exist within the United States as well (Martin et al., 2012). Births to teenagers represent 16% of all births to Native American women, 15% to African American women, and 13% to Hispanic American women. By contrast, among Whites and Asian Americans, teen mothers account for 9% and 2% of all births, respectively.

However, teen pregnancy statistics can be confusing because they usually refer to all pregnancies among women under age 20. To clarify the extent of the teen pregnancy problem, it is useful to break down the statistics by adolescent subgroups. For example, in the United States, the annual pregnancy rate is less than 1% for girls younger than 15; 4% among girls aged 15 to 17; and 11% among 18- to 19-year-olds (Ventura, Curtin, & Abma, 2012). Looking at the numbers this way shows that teen pregnancy is far more frequent among older adolescents and, in fact, is most likely to happen after a girl leaves high school.

The age at which an adolescent becomes a parent is only one aspect of the teen pregnancy issue. Birth rates among teenagers have actually dropped in the entire U.S. population since the 1960s, including among 15- to 19-year-olds. However, the rate of births to unmarried teens has increased. During the 1960s, more than 80% of teens who gave birth were married. By contrast, in 2003, only 14% of teenaged mothers were married (Martin et al., 2010).

The proportion of teenaged mothers who eventually marry the baby's father has also declined in recent years, and, again, there are ethnic differences. Less than 5% of African American teen mothers marry the baby's father, compared to 26% of Hispanics and 41% of whites (Population Resource Center, 2004). Moreover, across ethnic groups, only 17% of teen mothers maintain romantic relationships with their babies' fathers beyond the first few months after birth (Gee & Rhodes, 1999, 2003).

Whether a girl becomes pregnant during her teenaged years depends on many of the same factors that predict sexual activity in general (Miller, Benson, & Galbraith, 2001). The younger a girl is when she becomes sexually active, the more likely she is to become pregnant. Among teenaged girls who are from poor families, single-parent families, or families with relatively uneducated parents, or whose mothers gave birth to them before age 20, pregnancy rates are higher (Martin et al., 2010). ◉ **Watch** the **Video** *Today I Found Out: A Girl Discusses Her Best Friend's Teenage Pregnancy* in **MyPsychLab**.

In contrast, the likelihood of pregnancy is lower among teenaged girls who do well in school and have strong educational aspirations. Such girls are both less likely to be sexually active at an early age and more likely to use contraception if they are sexually active. Girls who have good communication about sex and contraception with their mothers are also less likely to get pregnant.

When teenaged girls become pregnant, in most cases, they face the most momentous set of decisions they have encountered in their young lives (see the *Developmental Science in the Clinic* box). About one-third of teen pregnancies across all ethnic groups end in abortion, and about 14% result in miscarriages (Alan Guttmacher Institute, 2004). Among Whites, 7% of teens carry the baby to term and place it for adoption, but only 1% of African American teens relinquish their babies to adoptive families.

The children of teenaged mothers are more likely than children born to older mothers to grow up in poverty, with all the accompanying negative consequences for the child's optimum development (Burgess, 2005). For instance, they tend to achieve developmental milestones more slowly than infants of older mothers (Pomerleau, Scuccimarri, & Malcuit, 2003). However, the children of teenaged mothers whose own parents help with child care, finances, and parenting skills are less likely to suffer such negative effects (Birch, 1998; Uno, Florsheim, & Uchino, 1998). Moreover, social programs that provide teenaged mothers with child care and the support they need to remain in school positively affect both these mothers and their babies. Such programs also improve outcomes for teenaged fathers (Kost, 1997).

Sexual Minority Youth

LO 11.6 What are some causes that have been proposed to explain homosexuality?

The emergence of a physical attraction to members of the opposite sex, or *heterosexuality*, is one of the defining features of adolescence for the great majority of teenagers. For some,

Crisis Intervention for the Pregnant Teen

Brianna was a high school junior who had recently become sexually active. She feared that she was pregnant, but she didn't know where to turn for help. Finally, after a great deal of agonizing over her situation, Brianna visited the clinic at her school, pretending to be suffering from a stomach ache. In her conversation with the nurse, Brianna casually asked about whether a girl who thought she was pregnant could talk to the school nurse about it without fearing that the nurse would tell her parents. The nurse recognized that Brianna was actually talking about herself. After some initial awkwardness, the nurse succeeded in establishing a trusting relationship with the girl through which she was able to use her crisis intervention skills to help Brianna deal with her situation.

A crisis intervention model proposed nearly half a century ago continues to be helpful to health professionals, teachers, and parents in understanding and helping teens in crisis (Caplan, 1964). The first stage in a crisis, called the *initial phase*, is characterized by anxiety and confusion. Thus, the first step in crisis intervention in many teenaged pregnancies often happens when a significant adult in the teenager's life recognizes a change in behavior and questions the girl about it. However, mental health professionals recommend gentle confrontation during this phase (Blau, 1996). For example, a pregnant

teenager might be reminded that it isn't possible to keep a pregnancy secret for very long, but this is clearly not the time to bombard them with questions such as "How are you going to support a baby? What about school? Are you going to go to college?"

The second stage of a crisis, the *escalation phase*, happens as the teenager begins to try to confront the crisis. In many cases, adolescents in this phase feel too overwhelmed to maintain daily functions such as getting to school and keeping track of homework. Teens in this phase may be responsive to helpers who simplify their decision making by directly telling them what to do. For example, a pregnant teen's mother may make a doctor's appointment for her and see that she keeps it instead of nagging her to do it herself.

The third stage of a crisis is called the *redefinition phase*. Those who are providing emotional support for the pregnant teen in this stage can help by guiding her through the process of breaking the problem down into small pieces. For a teen who wants to raise her baby, counselors or parents can divide the decisions to be made into financial and educational categories. They can help the teen identify short-term and long-term goals in each category and assist her in finding the answers to important questions. For example, in the financial category, the girl

must find out how much financial support she can expect to receive from the baby's father. With respect to continuing her education, she must determine the available day-care options.

Teens who leave the redefinition phase with a realistic plan of action are typically no longer in a crisis mode. However, teens who fail to redefine their problem appropriately enter the fourth crisis stage, the *dysfunctional phase*. In this stage, either the pregnant adolescent gives up hope or she goes into denial. The goal of crisis intervention is to prevent either of the stage-four outcomes. Yet the entire process probably depends on whether a pregnant teen has a sensitive adult in her life who will recognize the signs of the initial phase—just one more reason why teenagers, who may seem very grown up, still need warm, authoritative parenting.

REFLECTION

1. *In which crisis phase was Brianna when she visited the school clinic?*

2. *Think about how the crisis phases might be manifested in a different kind of crisis. For instance, what phase-related behaviors might be shown by a teenager who has been arrested for under-age drinking?*

though, adolescence is the time when they discover, or confirm a long-standing suspicion, that they are attracted to people of the same sex (*homosexuality*) or to both sexes (*bisexuality*). Still others become increasingly convinced that their psychological gender is inconsistent with their biological sex (*transgenderism*).

GAY, LESBIAN, AND BISEXUAL ADOLESCENTS Surveys involving thousands of teens in the United States have found that about 96% identify themselves as exclusively heterosexual in *sexual orientation*, a person's tendency to be attracted to same- or opposite-sex partners (Kann et al., 2011). About 1.4% of teens report that they are still unsure of their sexual orientation, a status that many researchers call *questioning*. Just under 1% classify themselves as exclusively gay or lesbian, and 3.5% identify as bisexual. By adulthood, 94% report being exclusively heterosexual, and just over 5% describe themselves as gay, lesbian, or bisexual, leaving only a very small proportion who are still questioning (Langer, Arnedt, & Sussman, 2004).

Lay people and researchers alike have wondered what causes some people to develop a gay, lesbian, or bisexual orientation. Several twin studies show that when one identical twin is homosexual, the probability that the other twin will also be homosexual is 50–60%, whereas the concordance rate is only about 20% for fraternal twins and only about 11% for pairs of biologically unrelated boys adopted into the same family (Dawood, Pillard, Horvath, Revelle, & Bailey, 2000; Kendler, Thornton, Gilman, & Kessler, 2000). Family studies also suggest that male homosexuality runs in families—that is, the families of most gay men have a higher proportion of homosexual males than do the families of heterosexual men (Bailey et al., 1999). Such findings strengthen the hypothesis that homosexuality has a biological basis (Dawood et al., 2000). Such evidence does not mean that environment plays no role in homosexuality.

For example, when one identical twin is homosexual, the other twin does *not* share that sexual orientation 40–50% of the time. Something beyond biology must be at work, although developmentalists do not yet know what environmental factors may be involved.

Research involving the *Kinsey Scale*, a scale that describes an individual's variation between exclusive heterosexuality (a score of 0) and exclusive homosexuality (a score of 6) on specific behaviors such as attraction and fantasizing, provides some clues as to the possible hormonal origins of homosexuality. For example, in a classic study, researchers found that more women whose mothers took the drug diethylstilbestrol (DES, a synthetic estrogen) during pregnancy scored between 2 and 6 on the Kinsey Scale with regard to a number of sexual behaviors than non-DES exposed women did (Meyer-Bahlburg et al., 1995). For example, 23% of women with DES exposure scored between 2 and 6 on sexual fantasizing compared to 3% of a non-DES-exposed control group. However, self-identification as heterosexual, homosexual, or bisexual did not vary with DES exposure. Nevertheless, such studies are consistent with the hypothesis that biological factors contribute to sexual orientation.

Whatever the cause of variations in sexual orientation, the process through which an individual comes to realize that he or she is homosexual appears to be gradual. Some researchers think that the process begins in middle childhood as a feeling of doubt about one's heterosexuality (Carver, Egan, & Perry, 2004; Wallien & Cohen-Kettenis, 2008). Retrospective studies have found that many gay men and lesbians recall having had homosexual fantasies during their teen years, but few fully accepted their homosexuality while still in adolescence (Wong & Tang, 2004). Instead, the final steps toward full self-awareness and acceptance of one's homosexuality appear to take place in early adulthood.

As homosexual teens grapple with questions about their sexual orientation, many report feeling isolated from and unaccepted by their peers (Martin & D'Augelli, 2003). Homosexual and questioning teens are also more likely to report being bullied by peers than heterosexual adolescents are (Berlan, Corliss, Field, Goodman, & Austin, 2010). These findings may help explain why rates of depression, attempted suicide, and substance abuse are higher among homosexual and questioning teens than among heterosexual teens (Corliss et al., 2010; Kann et al., 2011; Zhao, Montoro, Igartua, & Thombs, 2010). Many mental health professionals suggest that, to respond to these adolescents' needs, school officials provide emotional and social support for homosexual teens (Rostosky, Owens, Zimmerman, & Riggle, 2003; van Wormer & McKinney, 2003).

TRANSGENDERED TEENS **Transgendered** teens and adults are those whose psychological gender is the opposite of their biological sex. Some studies suggest that transgendered individuals may have been exposed to atypical amounts of androgens in the womb (Lippa, 2005). However, most do not have such histories, so the cause of transgenderism remains a mystery. Nevertheless, transgendered adolescents usually report that, since early childhood, they have been more interested in activities that are associated with the opposite sex than in those that are typical for their own (Lippa, 2005). However, most children who are attracted to cross-gender activities, and even those who express a desire to be the opposite gender, do not exhibit transgenderism after puberty (Wallien & Cohen-Kettenis, 2008). Thus, such behaviors on the part of children are not considered to be predictive of the development of transgenderism in adolescence ⊙ **Watch** the **Video** *Gender Roles: Charlotte Anjelica, Transsexual* in **MyPsychLab**.

Out of fear of being stigmatized, most teens who suspect that they are transgendered keep their feelings to themselves. The denial and anger that is often expressed by family members when transgendered adolescents do venture to "come out" amplifies these teens' distress (Zamboni, 2006). As a result, like gay, lesbian, and bisexual teens, transgendered teens are more likely to suffer from depression and are at higher risk of suicide than heterosexual adolescents are (Rosenberg, 2003).

Once individuals accept their transgendered status, some choose to live as the opposite gender on a full-time basis, a pattern called *transsexualism*. Most transsexuals are content with their lives, but others are so anguished by the conflict between their sex and their psychological gender that they seek *sex reassignment*—a process involving hormonal treatment, reconstructive surgery, and psychological counseling—in order to achieve a match between the two. Typically, sex reassignment is reserved for adults, but some sex reassignment specialists accept

transgendered a person whose psychological gender is the opposite of his or her biological sex

teenaged patients (Smith, van Goozen, Kuiper, & Cohen-Kettenis, 2005). Regardless of the age at which sex reassignment is sought, at least half of those who explore this option, with the help of skilled counselors, ultimately reject it in favor of less drastic ways of coping with their dilemma. Among those who do actually go through the procedure, most are happy with the results and experience relief from their preoperative emotional distress.

test yourself before going on ☑ Study and Review in MyPsychLab

Answers to these questions can be found in the back of the book.

1. In the United States, (more than half/fewer than half) of 15- to 19-year-olds are sexually experienced.

2. List three factors that increase the risk of adolescent pregnancy.

   (1) _____

   (2) _____

   (3) _____

3. When is full acceptance of a homosexual orientation most likely to occur?

CRITICAL THINKING

4. Look back at Bronfenbrenner's ecological model of development in Chapter 2 (pages xx–xx). Think of sexually developing adolescents as being in the innermost circle, or the biological context, and explain how the microsystem, exosystem, and macrosystem affect sexually active teens, pregnant adolescents, and sexual minority youth.

Adolescent Health

For most individuals, adolescence is one of the healthiest periods of life. However, as adolescents gain independence, they encounter numerous health risks.

Sensation Seeking

LO 11.7 How does sensation seeking affect risky behavior in adolescents?

Teenagers appear to have what many developmentalists describe as a heightened level of *sensation seeking*, or a desire to experience increased levels of arousal such as those that accompany fast driving or the "highs" associated with drugs. Sensation seeking leads to recklessness, which, in turn, leads to markedly increased rates of accidents and injuries in this age range. For example, adolescents drive faster and use seat belts less often than adults do (Centers for Disease Control and Prevention [CDC], 2009c). To reduce the number of accidents among teenaged drivers, many states in the United States have enacted laws establishing "graduated" driver's licenses (Cobb, 2000). Sixteen-year-olds can drive in most such states, but they must remain accident- and ticket-free for a certain period of time before they can have privileges such as driving at night.

Risky behaviors may be more common in adolescence than other periods because they help teenagers gain peer acceptance and establish autonomy with respect to parents and other authority figures (Donenberg, Emerson, Bryant, & King, 2006; Horvath Lewis, & Watson, 2012). Permissive parenting contributes as well (Tanski, Cin, Stoolmiller, & Sargent, 2010). In addition, adolescents who are not involved in extracurricular activities at school or to whom popularity is important are more likely than their peers who value popularity less to engage in risky behavior (Latimer & Zur, 2010; Melnick et al., 2010). Some developmental scientists view lack of maturity in the prefrontal cortex and other brain structures as the reason that teens exhibit higher levels of sensation seeking than adults do (Breyer & Winters, 2005).

The messages conveyed in the popular media about sex, violence, and drug and alcohol use may influence teens' risky behavior (Stoolmiller, Gerrard, Sargent, Worth, & Gibbons, 2010). These media messages interact with individual differences in sensation seeking (Greene, Krcmar, Rubin, Walters, & Hale, 2002). Thus, teens who are highest in sensation seeking are those who are most strongly influenced by media portrayals of risky behavior.

Drugs, Alcohol, and Tobacco

LO 11.8   What patterns of drug, alcohol, and tobacco use have been found among adolescents in the United States?

You probably remember some of the poor decisions you made in your teenage years. Most such decisions turn out to have little impact on teens' later lives. However, the choices that teenagers make about substance use can have lifelong consequences.

As you can see in Figure 11.3, illicit drug use is far less common among recent than in past cohorts of teenagers (Johnston, O'Malley, Bachman, & Schulenberg, 2013). Researchers attribute this trend to declining approval of drug use among adolescents and to contemporary teens' better understanding of the negative consequences of taking drugs. Still, experts agree that drug use among teens continues to be a significant problem because of the risks to which teens expose themselves, such as drunk driving and the possibility of lifelong addiction, when they use these substances.

Alcohol is the substance that teens use most often. In fact, more than a quarter of twelfth-graders reported having been drunk in the month prior to the survey. However, a surprising number of teenagers are using prescription drugs such as Ritalin, Adderall, OxyContin, and Vicodin. Similar percentages of teens use over-the-counter drugs such as cough medicines. (*Note:* Inclusion of such drugs in this discussion refers only to their use for purposes other than those for which they have been medically approved.)

What makes a teenager want to use alcohol or drugs? Those who express the most interest in sensation seeking are most likely to use drugs and consume alcohol (Wu, Liu, & Fan, 2010). Indeed, researchers have found that individual levels of sensation seeking predict peer associations—that is, teens who are high sensation-seekers choose friends who are similar. Once such groups are formed, sensation seeking becomes a central feature of their activities. So, for example, if one member tries marijuana or alcohol, others do so as well. However, teens who spend a lot of time alone may also be vulnerable to substance abuse. Researchers have found that shy adolescents, particularly those who are high in neuroticism, are more likely to use alcohol and drugs than are peers who are more outgoing (Kirkcaldy, Siefen, Surall, & Bischoff, 2004). ◉ **Watch** the **Video** *Teen Alcoholism* in **MyPsychLab**.

Sensation seeking also interacts with parenting style to increase the likelihood of drug use. Authoritative parenting seems to protect high sensation-seeking teenagers against their reckless tendencies (Wu et al., 2010). In fact, for African American adolescents, authoritative parenting may entirely negate the potential influence of drug-using peers. Moreover, parents who have realistic perceptions of the prevalence of teenaged drinking are also less likely to have teenaged children who are drinkers. These parents, who are aware of the prevalence of alcohol use among adolescents, try to prevent their children from getting into situations, such as attending unsupervised social events, where drinking is likely to happen (Bogenschneider, Wu, Raffaelli, & Tsay, 1998).

Sensation seeking seems to be less important in tobacco use. Surveys suggest that 25% of U.S. high school seniors are regular smokers, and 55% have tried smoking (Eaton et al., 2013). Smoking rates have dropped somewhat since the mid-1970s, when about 30% of older teenagers were regular smokers. Researchers argue that, thanks to public education campaigns and the inclusion of antismoking information in school curricula, more teenagers are aware of the health consequences of smoking than earlier cohorts. Moreover, many teens report that

Figure 11.3 Illicit Drug Use Trends among Teenagers
This figure shows the percentage of teens who admitted to using illicit drugs in the previous 12 months. As you can see, drug use rates have declined since the 1970s.

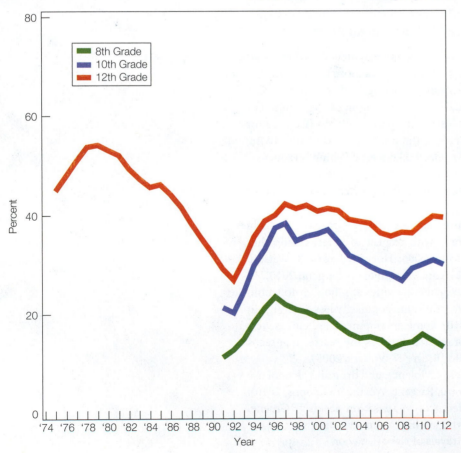

they oppose smoking because of its potential effect on their attractiveness to potential romantic partners.

Peer influence plays an important role in teen smoking. A nonsmoking teenager who begins associating with a cohesive group of adolescents among whom smoking is a prominent behavior and a sign of group membership is likely to take up the habit, too. In fact, some developmentalists advise parents that if their teenaged child's friends smoke, especially close friends and romantic partners with whom the child spends a lot of time, parents should probably assume that their child smokes as well (Holliday, Rothwell, & Moore, 2010). Moreover, the period between ages 15 and 17 seems to be the time during which a teenager is most susceptible to peer influences with regard to smoking (West et al., 1999). Clearly, then, by monitoring the friends of their 15- to 17-year-olds and discouraging them from associating with smokers, parents may help prevent their teens from smoking (Mott, Crowe, Richardson, & Flay, 1999).

Eating Disorders

LO 11.9 What are the characteristics and causes of eating disorders?

Have you ever tried to lose weight? If so, you have a lot of company. Surveys show that 68% of women and 37% of men in the United States have been on a weight-loss diet at some point in their adult lives (Rasmussen Reports, 2010). Thus, it isn't surprising that 52% of adolescent females and 28% of teenaged males diet regularly, and 5% of them use extreme measures such as taking diet pills (Eaton et al., 2010). However, dieting is quite different from an *eating disorder*, which is a category of mental disorders in which eating behaviors go far beyond most people's everyday experience with trying to lose weight (American Psychiatric Association, 2013). Most importantly, individuals with an eating disorder have a distorted body image that, in extreme cases, causes them to believe that they are overweight when they are actually on the verge of starvation. These disorders, which can be fatal, tend to make their first appearance in individuals' lives during the mid to late teens. They are more common among girls than boys, but gay, lesbian, and questioning youth are also at higher risk than their heterosexual peers of developing eating disorders (Austin et al., 2004; Austin et al., 2008). Surveys suggest that 25% of teenaged girls have at least one symptom of an eating disorder. These symptoms include vomiting, exercising more than once a day, and binge eating one or more times per week.

ANOREXIA NERVOSA Teenagers who suffer from **anorexia nervosa** usually have a more distorted body image than those who have bulimia. This eating disorder is characterized by extreme dieting, intense fear of gaining weight, and obsessive exercising. In girls or women (who are by far the most common sufferers), the weight loss eventually produces a variety of physical symptoms associated with starvation: sleep disturbance, cessation of menstruation, insensitivity to pain, loss of hair on the head, low blood pressure, a variety of cardiovascular problems, and reduced body temperature. Anorexia can be fatal, with suicide being the most common cause of death followed by physical complications of self-starvation such as damage to the heart (Cushing, 2013). ● **Watch** the **Video** *Anorexia Nervosa* in **MyPsychLab**.

BULIMIA NERVOSA **Bulimia nervosa** involves an intense concern about weight combined with twice-weekly or more frequent cycles of binge eating followed by purging, through self-induced vomiting, excessive use of laxatives, or excessive exercising (Yager, 2013). Teens with bulimia are ordinarily not exceptionally thin, but they are obsessed with their weight, feel intense shame about their abnormal behavior, and often experience significant depression. The physical consequences of bulimia include marked tooth decay (from repeated vomiting), stomach irritation, lowered body temperature, disturbances of body chemistry, and loss of hair (Yager, 2013). Current estimates are that 1.5% of adolescent girls and young adult women in the United States show the full syndrome of bulimia (Yager, 2013).

RISK FACTORS Some theorists have proposed biological causes for eating disorders such as some kind of brain dysfunction. Researchers have also determined that heredity contributes to the development of eating disorders (Bernstein, 2010; Cushing, 2013; Yager, 2013). Others, however, argue for a psychoanalytic explanation, such as a fear of growing up. But the most

anorexia nervosa an eating disorder characterized by self-starvation

bulimia nervosa an eating disorder characterized by binge eating and purging

When this 15-year-old with anorexia looks at herself in the mirror, chances are she sees herself as "too fat," despite being obviously emaciated.

promising explanation may lie in the discrepancy between the young person's internal image of a desirable body and her (or his) perception of her (or his) own body.

Some developmentalists suggest that an emphasis on thinness as a characteristic of attractive women, which is common in Western cultures, contributes to the prevalence of eating disorders (Pelletier, Dion, & Levesque, 2004). In one approach to testing this hypothesis, 6- to 12-year-old girls' responses to images of thin, sexy women were compared to boys' reactions to images of muscular, hyper-masculine men in order to find out how early children become aware of cultural stereotypes about ideal male and female body types (Murnen, Smolak, Mills, & Good, 2003). Researchers found that even the youngest children in this age group express admiration for the appearance of the models depicted in such images and that children are most interested in idealized images of adults of their own gender. However, girls are more likely than boys to compare their own appearance to that of the models. Moreover, among girls, those who are happiest with their own physical appearance are the least likely to compare their own bodies to media images of attractive women (Murnen et al., 2003; Rabasca, 1999).

These findings support the assertion of many developmentalists that girls internalize images representing what might be called the "thin ideal" during the middle childhood years and use them as standards against which to compare the changes in their bodies that happen during puberty (Hermes & Keel, 2003). In fact, research shows that, by age 11, girls are significantly more dissatisfied with their bodies than boys are with theirs, and the gender gap in body satisfaction increases across the teen years (Sweeting & West, 2002). As you might expect, given these results, researchers have also found that the tendency of girls to compare themselves to the thin ideal increases as they advance through puberty (Hermes & Keel, 2003).

Recent thinking, however, has placed more emphasis on the preexisting psychological health of people who develop eating disorders than on cultural influences (Cushing, 2013). Some researchers assert that the body images of individuals who have eating disorders are the result of a general tendency toward distorted thinking (Dyl, Kittler, Phillips, & Hunt, 2006). In other words, these researchers say that people who have eating disorders tend to think in distorted ways about many things, not just their bodies. From this perspective, internalized images of the "perfect" body fuel the sales of diet products among psychologically healthy people, but they trigger a far more serious outcome, a true eating disorder, in individuals who have a mentally unhealthy tendency toward thought distortion. Longitudinal evidence seems to support this view. In one such study, young women who had anorexia in adolescence (94% of whom had recovered from their eating disorders) were found to be far more likely than the general population to suffer from a variety of mental disorders (Nilsson, Gillberg, Gillberg, & Rastam, 1999). *Obsessive-compulsive personality disorder*, a condition characterized by an excessive need for control of the environment, seemed to be especially prevalent in this group. The study's authors further stated that the young women's mental difficulties did not appear to be the result of having previously suffered from an eating disorder. Instead, both the adolescent eating disorders and the women's problems in adulthood seem to have been produced by a consistent tendency toward distorted perceptions.

Depression and Suicide

LO 11.10 Which adolescents are at greatest risk of depression and suicide?

Epidemiological studies reveal that, at any given time, about 5% of adolescents are in the midst of an enduring depression (Benton, 2010). Moreover, 11% of males and 22% of females report having experienced bouts of depression at some time during the teen years (Benton, 2010). This sex difference persists throughout adolescence and into adulthood. It has been found in a number of industrialized countries and across ethnic groups in the United States (Nolen-Hoeksema & Girgus, 1994; Petersen et al., 1993; Roberts & Sobhan, 1992).

Neuroimaging studies suggest that adolescent depression may be associated with some kind of dysfunction in the pituitary gland (MacMaster & Kusumakar, 2004). But what causes the pituitary to function inappropriately in the first place? Genetic factors may be involved, as children growing up with parents diagnosed with depression are much more likely to develop depression than are those growing up with parents who do not have depression (Eley et al., 2004; Merikangas & Angst, 1995). The genetic hypothesis has also received support from at least a few studies of twins and adopted children (Petersen et al., 1993). However, the link between parental and child depression may also be explained in terms of the parenting behaviors of parents with depression, which you read about in earlier chapters. Furthermore, the contributions of a variety of family stressors to adolescent depression are just as clear among children whose parents are not depressed. Any combination of stresses—such as the parents' divorce, the death of a parent or another loved person, parental job loss, a move, a change of schools, or lack of sleep—increases the likelihood of depression or other kinds of emotional distress in the adolescent (Compas, Ey, & Grant, 1993; D'Imperio, Dubow, & Ippolito, 2000; Fredriksen, Rhodes, Reddy, & Way, 2004). Personality traits in the adolescent herself also contribute to depression. For instance, longitudinal studies indicate that children who have difficulty regulating their emotions and low self-efficacy for self-control are at increased risk of depression in the teen years (Caprara, Gerbino, Paciello, Di Giunta, & Pastorelli, 2010).

Depression can hinder academic achievement because it interferes with memory. For example, adolescents with depression are more likely to remember negative information than positive information (Neshat-Doost, Taghavi, Moradi, Yule, & Dalgleish, 1998). If a teacher says to an adolescent with depression, "You're going to fail algebra unless you start handing in your homework on time," the teenager is likely to remember the part about failing algebra and forget that the teacher also provided a remedy—getting homework done on time. Further, adolescents with depression seem to be less able than their peers who do not have depression to store and retrieve verbal information (Horan, Pogge, Borgaro, & Stokes, 1997). Consequently, therapeutic interventions, such as antidepressant medications, may improve the academic performance and emotional state of a teenager with depression. Most such treatments have been shown to be as effective for adolescents as they are for adults with depression (Findling, Feeny, Stansbrey, Delporto-Bedoya, & Demeter, 2004). ⊙ **Watch** the **Video** *Depression, Reward Regions, and the Brain: Erika Forbes* in **MyPsychLab**.

In some teenagers, sadly, the suicidal thoughts that often accompany depression lead to action. Surveys suggest that 16% of high school students in the United States have thought seriously about taking their own lives, and 8% have actually attempted suicide (Eaton et al., 2013). A very small number of teens, about 1 in 10,000, actually succeed in killing themselves (Xu, Kochanek, Murphy, & Tejada-Vera, 2010). However, public health experts point out that many teenaged deaths, such as those that result from single-car crashes, may be counted as accidents when they are actually suicides (NCIPC, 2000).

Although depression is more common among girls, the likelihood of dying as a result of a suicide attempt is almost four times as high for adolescent boys as for adolescent girls (CDC, 2007b). In contrast, suicide attempts are estimated to be twice as common among girls as among boys (Eaton et al., 2013). Girls, more often than boys, use methods that are less likely to succeed, such as self-poisoning. Contributing factors to completed suicides include:

- *Some triggering stressful event.* Studies of suicides suggest that this triggering event is often a disciplinary crisis with the parents or some rejection or humiliation, such as breaking up with a girlfriend or boyfriend or failing in a valued activity.

- *An altered mental state.* Such a state might be a sense of hopelessness, reduced inhibitions from alcohol consumption, or rage.

- *An opportunity.* A loaded gun in the house or a bottle of sleeping pills in the parents' medicine cabinet creates an opportunity for a teenager to carry out suicidal plans.

Because suicide is far more common among adults than it is among teenagers, we will have much more to say on this topic in later chapters. However, the risk factors for suicide are the same throughout the lifespan. For instance, breaking up with a romantic partner may be a triggering event for an adolescent, while loss of a spouse may be the triggering event for an adult. Thus, regardless of age, disruptions in a person's most significant social relationships increase the risk of suicide. Likewise, hopelessness and access to a gun or other means of committing suicide contribute to a person's decision to end his or her life across all ages. Fortunately, mental health professionals possess a number of effective strategies for intervening in the lives of individuals who are considering suicide. If you know someone who may be thinking about suicide, talk to a mental health professional to find out what you can do to increase the person's chances of seeking professional help.

Answers to these questions can be found in the back of the book.

1. List the four factors that contribute to adolescent sensation seeking.

   (1) _____

   (2) _____

   (3) _____

   (4) _____

2. Drug use among teens in the United States has (increased/decreased) since the 1970s.

3. Classify each symptom as characteristic of (A) anorexia nervosa, (B) bulimia nervosa, or (C) both anorexia and bulimia.

_____(1) distorted body image

_____(2) self-starvation

_____(3) binging and purging

_____(4) increased risk of another psychological disorder

4. Adolescent depression may be associated with dysfunction of the _____ gland.

CRITICAL THINKING

5. If you had the power to change U.S. culture in ways that you think would reduce the prevalence of the problems discussed in this section, what changes would you make?

Changes in Thinking and Memory

At the outset of the chapter, we asked you to recall some of the elaborate plans you made during your own teen years. The kind of thinking that adolescents use to formulate such plans was discovered by Piaget near the beginning of the 20th century. Such thinking enables adolescents to create an imaginary reality in their minds and project themselves into it (see *Research Report* on page 283). By the end of adolescence, teenagers' capacity to engage in this kind of thinking, which is similar to that of scientists, has dramatically improved.

Piaget's Formal Operational Stage

LO 11.11 What are the characteristics of thought in Piaget's formal operational stage?

Piaget carried out a number of studies suggesting that an entirely new form of thought emerges between about age 12 and age 16. He called the stage associated with this kind of thought the **formal operational stage**. Typically, this stage is defined as the period during which adolescents learn to reason logically about abstract concepts. Formal operational thinking has a number of key elements.

SYSTEMATIC PROBLEM SOLVING One important feature of formal operations is **systematic problem solving**—the ability to search methodically for the answer to a problem. To study this, Piaget and his colleague Barbel Inhelder (Inhelder & Piaget, 1958) presented adolescents with complex tasks, mostly drawn from the physical sciences. In one of these tasks, subjects were given varying lengths of string and a set of objects of various weights that could be tied to the strings to make a swinging pendulum. They were shown how to start the pendulum different ways—by pushing the weight with differing amounts of force and by holding the weight at different heights. The subject's task was to figure out which factor or combination of factors—length of string, weight of object, force of push, or height of push—determines the "period" of the pendulum (that is, the amount of time for one swing). (In case you have forgotten your high school physics, the answer is that only the length of the string affects the period of the pendulum.)

If you give this task to a concrete operational child, she will usually try out many different combinations of length, weight, force, and height in an inefficient way. She might try a heavy weight on a long string and then a light weight on a short string. Because she has changed both string length and weight in these two trials, there is no way she can draw a clear conclusion about either factor. In contrast, an adolescent using formal operations is likely to be more organized, attempting to vary just one of the four factors at a time. She may try a heavy object with a short string, then with a medium string, then with a long one. After that, she might try a light object with the three lengths of string. Of course not all adolescents (or all adults, for

formal operational stage the fourth of Piaget's stages, during which adolescents learn to reason logically about abstract concepts

systematic problem solving the process of finding a solution to a problem by testing single factors

Formal Operational Thinking and Everyday Problem Solving

Developmentalists have attempted to learn why adolescents fail to use formal operational thinking to solve everyday problems. In her classic study, Catherine Lewis (1981) found that younger teenagers were more likely than those who were older to base solutions on incomplete formulations of problems. For instance, Lewis asked eighth-, tenth-, and twelfth-grade students to respond to a set of dilemmas that involved a person facing a difficult decision, such as whether to have an operation to repair a facial disfigurement (Lewis, 1981). Forty-two percent of the twelfth-graders, but only 11% of the eighth-graders, mentioned future possibilities in their comments on these dilemmas.

What accounts for this pattern of findings? Perhaps younger teens fail to use formal operational thinking effectively because the parts of the brain needed to connect it to everyday problems may not be sufficiently developed until the late teens. Neuroimaging studies comparing the

brain activity of children, teens, and adults while they were engaged in a gambling task provide support for this hypothesis (Crone & van der Molen, 2004; Smith, Xiao, & Bechara, 2012). However, Piaget would probably argue that young teens aren't good at applying their formal operational schemes to everyday problems because they haven't had much practice using them—a hypothesis that might also explain these neuroimaging results.

Recall Piaget's hypothesis that, when we apply a scheme to a problem, we are engaging in assimilation. According to his view, when teens assimilate problems to immature formal operational schemes, their failures trigger equilibration, the process that kicks in when our schemes don't faithfully represent reality. Equilibration leads to accommodations, or changes in the schemes, that are put to work the next time an appropriate problem comes around. Applying the accommodated scheme to a new problem initiates a new

cycle of assimilation, equilibration, and accommodation. Through this back-and-forth process, teenagers' formal operational schemes become more reliable. Thus, young teens have to experiment with their formal operational schemes in the real world before they can be expected to be able to be proficient at using them.

CRITICAL ANALYSIS

1. *How do the characteristics of adolescent thinking come into play when teenagers have to come up with ways of coping with teachers whom they don't like or of raising a failing grade?*

2. *To what extent does teens' limited ability to use formal operational thinking in everyday contexts explain findings about the ineffectiveness of sex education programs that you read about earlier in the chapter?*

---

that matter) are quite this methodical in their approach. Still, there is a very dramatic difference in the overall strategies used by 10-year-olds and 15-year-olds that marks the shift from concrete to formal operations.

LOGIC Another facet of this shift is the appearance in the adolescent's repertoire of skills of what Piaget called **hypothetico-deductive reasoning**, or the ability to derive conclusions from hypothetical premises. You may remember from Chapter 9 Piaget's suggestion that a concrete operational child can use inductive reasoning, which involves arriving at a conclusion or a rule based on a lot of individual experiences, but will perform poorly when asked to reason deductively. Recall that deductive reasoning involves considering hypotheses or hypothetical premises and then deriving logical outcomes. For example, the statement "If all people are equal, then you and I must be equal" involves logic of this type. Although children as young as 4 or 5 can understand some deductive relationships if the premises given are factually true, both cross-sectional and longitudinal studies support Piaget's assertion that only at adolescence are young people able to understand and use the basic logical relationships (Ward & Overton, 1990; Mueller, Overton, & Reene, 2001).

Piaget suggested that hypothetico-deductive thinking underlies many ideas and behaviors that are common to adolescents. For instance, hypothetico-deductive thinking leads to an outlook he called *naive idealism* in many adolescents (Piaget & Inhelder, 1969). Naive idealism is manifested when adolescents use formal operational thinking to mentally construct an ideal world and then compare the real world to it. Not surprisingly, the real world often falls short. As a result, some teenagers become so dissatisfied with the world that they resolve to change it. For many, the changes they propose are personal. So a teen whose parents have been divorced for years may suddenly decide she wants to live with the noncustodial parent because she expects that her life will be better. Another may express naive idealism by becoming involved in a political or religious organization.

ADOLESCENT EGOCENTRISM Psychologist David Elkind hypothesized that another common manifestation of hypothetico-deductive reasoning is a type of thought he called *adolescent egocentrism*—the belief that one's thoughts, beliefs, and feelings are unique. One component of adolescent egocentrism, Elkind said, is the **personal fable**, the belief that the

High school science classes may be one of the first places where adolescents are required to use deductive logic—a skill Piaget did not think was developed until the period of formal operations.

hypothetico-deductive reasoning the ability to derive conclusions from hypothetical premises

personal fable the belief that the events of one's life are controlled by a mentally constructed autobiography

imaginary audience an internalized set of behavioral standards usually derived from a teenager's peer group

events of one's life are controlled by a mentally constructed autobiography (Elkind, 1967). For example, a sexually active teenage girl might be drawing upon such a personal fable when she says, "I just don't see myself getting pregnant" in response to suggestions that she use contraception. In contrast to this inappropriately rosy view of the future, a teen who is involved in a violent street gang may say, "I'll probably get shot before I make 18" when advised to leave the gang and focus on acquiring the academic skills needed to graduate from high school.

Elkind also proposed that adolescent egocentrism drives teenagers to try out various attitudes, behaviors, and even clothing choices in front of an **imaginary audience**—an internalized set of behavioral standards usually derived from a teenager's peer group. Consider a teenaged girl who is habitually late for school because she changes clothes two or three times every day before leaving home. Each time the girl puts on a different outfit, she imagines how her peers at school will respond to it. If the imaginary audience criticizes the outfit, the girl feels she must change clothes in order to elicit a more favorable response. 👁 **Watch** the **Video** *Imaginary Audience* in **MyPsychLab**.

Many developmentalists have found Elkind's personal fable and imaginary audience to be helpful in explaining a variety of adolescents' everyday behaviors. However, research examining these constructs has produced mixed results (Bell & Bromnick, 2003; Galanaki, 2012). While it is true that adolescents use idealized mental models to make all kinds of decisions about their own and others' behavior, researchers have found that school-aged children sometimes exhibit similar forms of thought (Vartanian, 2001). Furthermore, studies suggest that older adolescents think in these ways far more often than Elkind originally hypothesized (Schwartz, Maynard, & Uzelac, 2008). Nevertheless, developmentalists agree that the tendency to exaggerate others' reactions to one's own behavior and to base decisions on unrealistic ideas about the future are two characteristics that distinguish adolescents from younger children (Alberts, Elkind, & Ginsberg, 2007).

Direct Tests of Piaget's View

LO 11.12 What are some major research findings regarding the formal operational stage?

In an early cross-sectional study, researchers tested 20 girls in each of four grades (sixth, eighth, tenth, and twelfth) on 10 different tasks that required one or more of what Piaget called formal operational skills (Martorano, 1977). Indeed, many of the tasks the researchers used were those Piaget himself had devised. Results of performance on two of these tasks are graphed in Figure 11.4. The pendulum problem is the one described earlier in this section; the balance problem requires a youngster to predict whether two different weights, hung at varying distances on each side of a scale, will balance—a task similar to the balance-scale problem Siegler used (recall Figure 9.5 on page xx). To solve this problem using formal operations, the teenager must consider both weight and distance simultaneously. You can see from Figure 11.4 that older students generally did better, with the biggest improvement in scores between eighth and tenth grades (between ages 13 and 15).

Formal operational reasoning also seems to enable adolescents to understand figurative language, such as metaphors, to a greater degree. For example, one early study found that teenagers were much better than younger children at interpreting proverbs (Saltz, 1979). Statements such as "People who live in glass houses shouldn't throw stones" are usually interpreted literally by 6- to 11-year-olds. By 12 or 13, most adolescents can easily understand them, even though it isn't until much later that teenagers actually use such expressions in their everyday speech (Gibbs & Beitel, 1995).

Take another look at Figure 11.4: Only about 50–60% of twelfth-graders solved the two formal operations problems, and only 2 of the 20 twelfth-grade participants used formal operational logic on all 10 problems. Further, studies have found rates of formal operational thinking in high school students that are very similar to those found in studies conducted in the 1960s, 1970s, and 1980s (Bradmetz, 1999). The consistency of such findings over several cohorts of adolescents suggests that Piaget's predictions about adolescents' thinking abilities were overly optimistic—in contrast to his overly pessimistic estimates of young children's abilities, which you read about in earlier chapters.

Figure 11.4 Within-Stage Development in Formal Operations

These are the results from 2 of the 10 different formal operational tasks used in Martorano's cross-sectional study.

(*Source:* Martorano, 1977, p. 670. Copyright by the American Psychological Association.)

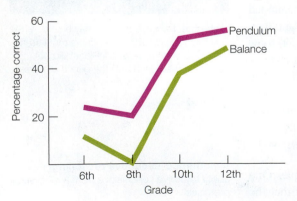

In adulthood, rates of formal operational thinking increase with education. Generally, the better educated the adult participants in a study of formal operational thinking, the greater the percentage who display this kind of reasoning (Mwamwenda, 1999). Piaget's belief in the universality of formal operations may have resulted from his failure to appreciate the role of education in the development of advanced forms of thought. The current consensus among developmentalists is that all teenagers and adults without intellectual disabilities have the capacity for formal operational thinking, but they actually acquire it in response to specific demands, such as those imposed by higher levels of education. Thus, people whose life situations or cultures do not require formal operational thinking do not develop it.

Advances in Information Processing

LO 11.13 What kinds of advances in information-processing capabilities occur during adolescence?

Adolescents process information faster, use processing resources more efficiently, understand their own memory processes better, and have more knowledge than do elementary school children (Kail, 1990, 1997). As a result, their working memories function more efficiently and they outperform school-aged children even on such simple memory tasks as recognizing faces (Gathercole, Pickering, Ambridge, & Wearing, 2004; Itier & Taylor, 2004). Moreover, they are much better at using strategies to help themselves remember things and can more easily understand and remember complex information, such as that presented in a textbook.

METACOGNITION, METAMEMORY, AND STRATEGY USE By age 13 or 14, the metacognitive and metamemory skills of adolescents far exceed those of younger children, and these skills continue to improve throughout adolescence (and into the adult years, by the way) (Weil et al., 2013). For example, in one classic study, 10- and 14-year-olds were instructed to do a particular activity for exactly 30 minutes (Ceci & Bronfenbrenner, 1985). Experimenters provided them with a clock and instructed them to use it to determine when they should stop. Few of the 10-year-olds periodically checked the time to see if 30 minutes had elapsed, but most of the 14-year-olds did. As a result, less than half of the younger participants succeeded in stopping on time, but more than three-quarters of the teenagers did so.

Another early study of metamemory involved offering fifth-graders, eighth-graders, and college students the opportunity to earn money for remembering words (Cuvo, 1974). Researchers designated the words to be recalled as being worth either 1 cent or 10 cents. Fifth-graders rehearsed 1-cent and 10-cent words equally. In contrast, eighth-graders and college students put more effort into rehearsing the 10-cent words. At the end of the rehearsal period, fifth-graders recalled equal numbers of 1- and 10-cent words, while older participants remembered more 10-cent words. Further, college students outperformed eighth-graders in both rehearsal and recall. This finding suggests that the capacity to apply memory strategies selectively, based on the characteristics of a memory task, appears early in the teenaged years and continues to improve throughout adolescence.

Training studies, in which children and adolescents are taught to use a particular memory strategy, also suggest that metacognitive abilities enable teenagers to benefit more from training than younger children do. For example, researchers taught elementary school students and high school students a strategy for memorizing the manufacturing products associated with different cities (for example, Detroit–automobiles) (Pressley & Dennis-Rounds, 1980). Once participants had learned the strategy and were convinced of its effectiveness, researchers presented them with a similar task, memorizing Latin words and their English translations. Experimenters found that only the high school students made an effort to use the strategy they had just learned to accomplish the new memory task. The elementary school children used the new strategy only when researchers told them to and demonstrated how it could be applied to the new task. High school students' success seemed to be due to their superior ability to recognize the similarity between the two tasks—an aspect of metamemory.

TEXT LEARNING Differences between younger children's and adolescents' processing of and memory for text are even more dramatic. In a classic study of text processing, experimenters asked 10-, 13-, 15-, and 18-year-olds to read and summarize a 500-word passage. The researchers hypothesized that participants would use four rules in writing summaries (Brown & Day, 1983). First, they would delete trivial information. Second, their summaries would show categorical organization—that is, they would use terms such as "animals" rather than specific names of animals mentioned in the text. Third, the summaries would use topic sentences from the text. Finally, the participants would invent topic sentences for paragraphs that didn't have them.

The results of the study suggested that participants of all ages used the first rule because all the summaries included more general than detailed or trivial information about the passage. However, the 10-year-olds and 13-year-olds used the other rules far less frequently than did the 15- and 18-year-olds. There were also interesting differences between the two older groups. Fifteen-year-olds used categories about as frequently as 18-year-olds did, but the oldest group used topic sentences far more effectively. This pattern of age differences suggests that the ability to summarize a text improves gradually during the second half of adolescence.

Studies of text outlining reveal a similar pattern (Drum, 1985). Both elementary and high school students know that an outline should include the main ideas of a passage along with supporting details. However, research suggests that 17-year-olds generate much more complete outlines than 14-year-olds do. Moreover, 11-year-olds' outlines usually include only a few of the main ideas of a passage and provide little or no supporting details for those main ideas.

test yourself before going on ✓ **Study** and **Review** in **MyPsychLab**

Answers to these questions can be found in the back of the book.

1. The ability to reason from premises that are not necessarily factually true is called _____ _____.

2. Research indicates that formal operational thinking develops (earlier/later) than Piaget hypothesized.

3. List three ways in which teens' information-processing skills differ from those of children.

   (1) _____

   (2) _____

   (3) _____

CRITICAL THINKING

4. How could some of the cognitive advances that emerge during adolescence be used in an essay countering negative stereotypes of teenagers in the media?

Schooling

Do you remember your first day of secondary school (middle school, junior high school, and high school)? How many times did you get lost looking for a classroom? Did you carry all your books with you to avoid having to go to your locker between periods? Perhaps you forgot the combination to your locker. Such are the experiences of children who must transition from the relative simplicity of elementary school to the intimidating complexity of secondary school. Eventually, most students adjust to the new setting. Yet, as you will see, both benefits and costs are associated with such transitions.

Transition to Secondary School

LO 11.14 How do changes in students' goals contribute to the transition to secondary school?

In many places in the world, including some in North America, children attend a lower school for 8 years before moving on to a high school for 4 years. Such an arrangement is known as an *8–4 system*. Students typically show achievement declines after entering high school, and these declines predict persistence in the first two years of college (Smith, 2006). Consequently, educators have developed two models that include a transitional school—a junior high school or middle school—between elementary and high school. The junior high system typically includes 6 years of elementary school followed by 3 years of junior high and 3 years of high school. The middle school model includes 5 years of elementary school, 3 years of middle school, and 4 years of high school.

Neither the junior high nor the middle school approach seems to have solved the transition problem. Students show losses in achievement and in self-esteem, along with increases in depression, across both transition points in the 6–3–3 and 5–3–4 systems (Bélanger & Marcotte, 2013). Further, students in both of these systems show greater losses during the transition to high school than do those in 8-4 systems (Alspaugh, 1998; Anderman, 1998; Linnenbrink, 2010; Offenburg, 2001). As a result, educators and developmentalists are currently searching for explanations and practical remedies.

Some developmentalists argue that the transition to middle school or junior high school is difficult for many young adolescents because they are not developmentally ready for the secondary-school model. Children who attend middle and junior high schools where close relationships between teachers and students are encouraged, as they are in elementary school, show smaller declines in achievement and self-esteem.

MIDDLE SCHOOL One potential explanation for transition-related achievement declines associated with the transition to middle school is that students' academic goals change once they leave elementary school. These changes in goals influence behaviors such as the amount of time that students devote to school work (Hamm et al., 2013). Researchers group academic goals into two very broad categories: *task goals* and *ability goals*. **Task goals** are based on personal standards and a desire to become more competent at something. For example, a runner who wants to improve her time in the 100-meter dash has a task goal. An **ability goal** defines success in competitive terms—being better than another person at something. For example, a runner who wants to be the fastest person on her team has an ability goal. Longitudinal research shows that most fifth-graders have task goals, but by the time they have been in sixth grade a few months, most children have shifted to ability goals (Anderman & Anderman, 1999; Anderman & Midgley, 1997).

A student's goal influences his behavior in important ways. Task goals are associated with a greater sense of personal control and more positive attitudes about school (Anderman, 1999; Gutman, 2006). A student who takes a task-goal approach to school work tends to set increasingly higher standards for his performance and attributes success and failure to his own efforts. For example, a task-goal–oriented student is likely to say he received an A in a class because he worked hard or because he wanted to improve his performance.

In contrast, students with ability goals adopt relative standards—that is, they view performance on a given academic task as good as long as it is better than someone else's. Consequently, such students are more strongly influenced by the group with which they identify than by internal standards that define good and bad academic performance. Ability-goal–oriented students are also more likely than others to attribute success and failure to forces outside themselves. For example, such a student might say he got an A in a class because it was easy or because the teacher liked him. Moreover, such students are likely to have a negative view of school (Anderman, 1999).

Because middle schools emphasize ability grouping and performance on standardized tests more than elementary schools do, it is likely that many middle school students change their beliefs about their own abilities during these years (Anderman & Anderman, 2009; Anderman, Maehr, & Midgley, 1999). Thus, high-achieving elementary students who maintain their levels of achievement across the sixth-grade transition gain confidence in their abilities (Pajares & Graham, 1999). In contrast, the changes in self-concept experienced by high achievers who fail to meet expectations in middle school as well as average and low-achieving students do probably lead to self-esteem losses for many of them. Once an ability-goal–oriented student adopts the belief that her academic ability is less than adequate, she is likely to stop putting effort into school work. In addition, such students are likely to use ineffective cognitive strategies when attempting to learn academic material (Young, 1997). Consequently, achievement suffers along with self-esteem. Fortunately, however, teachers and administrators can increase the chances that middle school students will adopt task goals by making it clear to students that learning is more important than outperforming peers on standardized tests or report card grades (Anderman & Anderman, 2009).

task goals goals based on a desire for self-improvement

ability goals goals based on a desire to be superior to others

Another factor that influences young adolescents' adjustment to secondary school is their perception of the school's climate. One factor that positively influences school climate and student achievement is the degree to which teachers focus on task goals, sometimes called a *mastery approach* to instruction (Upadyaya & Salmela-Aro, 2013). With regard to the emotional aspects of school climate, however, researchers have found that many middle school students perceive their schools to be impersonal and unsupportive (Barber & Olsen, 2004). To address this perception, some schools provide students with an adult mentor, either a teacher or a volunteer from the community, to whom they are assigned for a transitional period or throughout the middle school years. In practice, the characteristics of mentoring programs vary widely (Galassi, Gulledge, & Cox, 1997). Some consist simply of giving sixth-graders the name of a teacher they can consult if they encounter any problems. At the other end of the spectrum, some mentoring programs assign each student to a teacher, who is supposed to monitor several students' daily assignment sheets, homework completion, grades, and even school supplies. The homeroom teacher also maintains communication with each child's parents regarding these factors. If a student isn't doing his math homework or doesn't have any pencils, it is the homeroom teacher's responsibility to tell his parents about the problem. The parents are then responsible for follow-up.

Research suggests that programs of this level of intensity are highly successful in improving middle school students' grades (Callahan, Rademacher, & Hildreth, 1998; Hanlon, Simon, O'Grady, Carswell, & Callaman, 2009; Rosenblatt & Ellis, 2008). Their success probably lies in the fact that the homeroom teacher functions very much like an elementary school teacher. This is significant because, despite cultural expectations to the contrary, a sixth-grader is developmentally a child, whether she is in an elementary school or a middle school. Consequently, it isn't surprising that a strategy that makes a middle school more like an elementary school—a school designed for children, not adolescents—is successful. In fact, some observers think that middle schools have failed to meet their goal of easing the transition to high school because they have simply duplicated high school organization and imposed it on students who are not developmentally ready, rather than providing them with a real transition.

One approach aimed at making middle schools truly transitional involves organizing students and teachers into teams. For example, in some schools, sixth, seventh, and eighth grades are physically separated in different wings of the school building. In such schools, each grade is a sort of school-within-a-school. Teachers in each grade-level team work together to balance the demands of different subject-area classes, assess problems of individual students, and devise parent involvement strategies. Preliminary research suggests that the team approach helps to minimize the negative effects of the middle school transition. As a result, it has become the recommended approach of the National Middle School Association in the United States (NMSA, 2004).

HIGH SCHOOL Regardless of the type of school they attended previously, the early days of high school set a general pattern of success or failure for teenagers that continues into their adult years. For example, teenagers who fail one or more courses in the first year of high school are far less likely than their peers to graduate (Neild, 2009; Neild & Balfanz, 2006; Roderick & Camburn, 1999). It appears that minority students have a particularly difficult time recovering from early failure.

However, some psychologists emphasize the positive aspects of transition to high school, claiming that participation in activities that are usually offered only in high school allows students opportunities to develop psychological attributes that can't be acquired elsewhere. To demonstrate the point, a number of research studies had high school students use pagers to signal researchers whenever they were experiencing high levels of intrinsic motivation along with intense mental effort (Larson, 2000). The results showed that students experienced both states in elective classes and during extracurricular activities far more often than in academic classes (Larson & Brown, 2007). In other words, a student engaged in an art project or sports practice is more likely to experience this particular combination of states than one who is in a history class. Consequently, educators may be able to ease the transition to high school for many students by offering a wide variety of elective and extracurricular activities and encouraging students to participate.

Gender, Ethnicity, and Achievement in Science and Math

LO 11.15 What gender and ethnic differences in science and math achievement have researchers found?

Girls seem to be at particular risk for achievement losses after the transition to high school. For example, eighth-grade boys outscore girls in science achievement, and the gap widens substantially by the time adolescents reach tenth grade (Burkham, Lee, & Smerdon, 1997). Moreover, research suggests that the gender gap is widest among the most intellectually talented students. Nevertheless, girls possess characteristics that educators can build upon to improve their achievement in science classes. For one thing, associating with same-sex peers who are interested in and perform well in science classes influences girls' achievement in this domain (Riegle-Crumb, Farkas, & Muller, 2006). Thus, offering girls the opportunity to participate in science clubs and *learning communities*—small groups of students who take courses together—may be an effective means of increasing their science achievement (Reid & Roberts, 2006). Furthermore, girls' choices in course-taking during middle school are more influenced by parental encouragement than are those of boys (Simpkins, Davis-Kean, & Eccles, 2006). Thus, parental involvement may be the key to enhancing middle-school girls' interest in science and motivating them to take more advanced science courses in high school.

Like their scientifically talented peers, mathematically gifted high school girls have considerably less confidence in their abilities than their male counterparts do, even though the girls typically get better grades (Guzzetti & Williams, 1996; Marsh & Yeung, 1998). Research demonstrates that girls' beliefs about their abilities shape their interest in taking higher-level high school and college math courses (Simpkins et al., 2006). Furthermore, as we noted with regard to science, girls whose same-sex friends are interested in math have more confidence in their math ability and are more open to taking advanced coursework in mathematics. Studies have shown that enrolling mathematically talented middle-school girls in single-sex, math-focused extracurricular activities increases their interest in the subject and their math-related confidence (Reid & Roberts, 2006).

As striking as the gender differences in math are, they pale in comparison to ethnic variations (Davenport et al., 1998). For example, 42% of Asian American students and 18% of Whites take calculus in high school, but only 6% of African Americans, 3% of Native Americans, and 9% of Hispanic Americans do so (NCES, 2010, 2013). One reason for these ethnic differences is that Asian American and White students are more likely to enter ninth grade with the skills they need to take their first algebra class. More than half of African American and Hispanic American teens are required to take remedial courses before beginning algebra, compared to about one-third of Asian American and White students (Davenport et al., 1998). Observers point out that about the same proportion of high school students across all ethnicities expect to go to college. However, it appears that Asian American and White students are much more likely to enter high school prepared to pursue college-preparatory courses (Thompson & Joshua-Shearer, 2002). Many researchers conclude that rigorous transitional classes in eighth and ninth grade might enable greater numbers of African American and Hispanic American students to complete college-preparatory math classes in high school (Gamoran, Porter, Smithson, & White, 1997).

Evidence for this position is drawn from studies involving mathematically talented students. There are large ethnic differences in high school course choices among highly able students—those who score in the top 25% of standardized math achievement tests. One study found that 100% of Asian American and 88% of White high school students scoring at this level were enrolled in advanced mathematics courses. In contrast, only 40% of mathematically talented African American and Hispanic American students were enrolled in such classes (Education Trust, 1996). It may be that high school counselors more often encourage Asian American and White students to take advanced math classes (Davenport, 1992).

Ethnic group variations in parental expectations may explain why students entering high school in some groups are better prepared to take on college preparatory courses than their peers in other groups.

Dropping Out of High School

LO 11.16 What variables predict the likelihood of dropping out of high school?

Dropping out of high school, like academic success, results from a complex interaction of academic and social variables (Garnier, Stein, & Jacobs, 1997). The proportion of U.S. students who drop out has steadily declined over the past few decades. Over 90% of high school students in the United States receive a diploma (NCES, 2013). Hispanic Americans have the highest dropout rate at 14%, compared with 7% for African Americans and 5% for Whites (NCES, 2013). Just under 2% of Asian Americans leave high school, and about 15% of Native American students do so (U.S. Census Bureau, 2010b).

Despite ethnic differences in dropout rates, social class is a better predictor of school completion than is ethnicity. Children growing up in low-income families are considerably more likely to drop out of high school than are those from more economically advantaged families. For instance, in 2008, the dropout rate for students whose families were in the lowest income quartile in the United States was 16%, while that of students whose household income placed them in the top quartile was only 2% (NCES, 2010). Because Hispanic, African American, and Native American teenagers in the United States are so much more likely to come from poor families, they are also more likely to drop out of school. The key factors linking income to high school completion appear to be the level of parental education, parental aspirations for children's education attainment, and children's own expectations for the future (Freeman & Fox, 2005). Thus, effective interventions for dropouts must address students' beliefs about the importance of education to economic well-being (see *No Easy Answers* on page xx).

It is important to remember, however, that the majority of students across all ethnic and income groups stay in school. Those who don't, again regardless of group, share several risk factors. Longitudinal studies show that students who have a history of academic failure, a pattern of aggressive behavior, and poor decisions about risky behavior are most likely to drop out (Darney, Reinke, Herman, Stormont, & Ialongo, 2013; Farmer et al., 2003). With respect to risky behavior, decisions about sexual intercourse seem to be especially critical. For girls, giving birth and getting married are strongly linked to dropping out. Another risky behavior, adolescent drug use, is also a strong predictor of dropping out (Garnier et al., 1997). Peer influence may also be a factor. Teens who quit school are likely to have friends who have dropped out or who are contemplating

---

NO EASY ANSWERS

Reaching High School Dropouts

One of the greatest challenges facing educators is how to motivate teenagers who have dropped out of high school to return. To address the problem, educators have developed programs for teenagers who have left school. A national network of such programs, YouthBuild USA, is a good example. The goal of YouthBuild USA is to provide dropouts with marketable skills that are tailored to the needs of the communities in which individual program units are located. For example, YouthBuild/Boston offers low-income dropouts an opportunity to achieve three goals. First, students learn marketable construction-related job skills such as carpentry, safety management, and computer-aided drafting. Second, they work toward either a GED or a high school diploma. Third, students work on construction projects that help provide poor families in the Boston area with affordable housing. The program includes counseling, help with goal setting, and leadership skill development. Students

also get help with material needs such as child care and income assistance through a network of social service providers, to which they are referred by school counselors.

YouthBuild USA programs attract large numbers of applicants. Due to funding limitations, however, many youths are turned away or put on waiting lists. Consequently, YouthBuild staff, students, graduates, and supporters must devote some of their time to fund-raising. In pursuit of program funds, advocates inform government officials, charitable foundations, and potential donors about studies demonstrating the program's effectiveness. For instance, research shows that the program has an impressive record of success with one especially vulnerable group: youths who have been incarcerated (Abrazaldo et al., 2009). While only 9% of such participants enter the program with a high school diploma, 33% receive one shortly after admission (Abrazaldo et al., 2009). Two-thirds obtain

employment after graduation, and three-fourths have no subsequent incarcerations. However, many students drop out of YouthBuild programs. As a result, each local program has developed strategies for screening applicants to identify those that have the greatest chances of success.

YOU DECIDE

Decide which of these two statements you most agree with and think about how you would defend your position:

1. Since a large proportion of students drop out of them, programs such as YouthBuild USA appear to be a waste of taxpayers' money.

2. The public should support programs such as YouthBuild USA because they may save money in the long run by preventing high school dropouts from ending up on the welfare rolls.

---

leaving school (Ellenbogen & Chamberland, 1997). Family variables are also linked to dropping out. For example, children whose families move a lot when they are in elementary or middle school are at increased risk for dropping out of high school (Worrell, 1997).

Perhaps the most critical factor in a teenager's decision to leave school is engagement in academic subject matter (Upadyaya & Salmela-Aro, 2013). In one important large-scale survey, young adults (16- to 25-year-olds) across all ethnic and income groups who dropped out of high school reported that their primary reason for doing so was that their classes were uninteresting (Bridgeland, DiIulio, & Morison, 2006). Dropouts also said that the feeling that they had fallen behind and could not catch up contributed to their decision to leave school. They also reported that peers who were also planning to drop out influenced them and that lack of parental monitoring also played a role. Nearly three-quarters said that they regretted the decision to quit school.

One group of researchers has explored the possibility that, by taking into consideration several relevant factors, a general profile of high school students who are potential dropouts can be identified. Their research has led to identification of the type of high school student who is likely to drop out: one who is quiet, disengaged, low-achieving, and poorly adjusted (Janosz, Le Blanc, Boulerice, & Tremblay, 2000). Many such students display a pattern of chronic class-cutting prior to dropping out (Fallis & Opotow, 2003). Thus, students who exhibit this pattern may be targeted for dropout prevention programs.

test yourself before going on ✓ Study and Review in MyPsychLab

Answers to these questions can be found in the back of the book.

1. _____ goals are motivated by a desire to outperform others.

2. In which ethnic group are teens most likely to take calculus in high school?

3. In a survey of young adults who had dropped out of high school, most said that they did so because their classes were (uninteresting/too difficult).

CRITICAL THINKING

4. What kind of mentoring programs would you propose for helping children transition to secondary school, increasing math and science achievement among girls and minorities, and preventing high school students from dropping out?

SUMMARY

Physical Changes (pp. 266–271)

LO 11.1   How do the brains and other body systems of adolescents differ from those of younger children?

- The brain continues to develop in adolescence. There are two major brain growth spurts: the first between ages 13 and 15 and the second between ages 17 and 19. Puberty is accompanied by a rapid growth spurt in height and an increase in muscle mass and in fat. Boys add more muscle, and girls add more fat.

LO 11.2   What are the major milestones of puberty?

- Puberty is triggered by a complex set of hormonal changes, beginning at about age 7 or 8. Very large increases in gonadotrophic hormones are central to the process. In girls, mature sexuality is achieved as early as 12 or 13. Sexual maturity is achieved later in boys, with the growth spurt occurring a year or more after the start of genital changes.

LO 11.3   What are the consequences of early, "on time," and late puberty for boys and girls?

- Variations in the rate of pubertal development have some psychological effects. In general, children whose physical development occurs markedly earlier or later than they expect or desire show more negative effects than do those whose development is "on time."

Adolescent Sexuality (pp. 272–277)

LO 11.4   What are the patterns of adolescent sexual behavior in the United States?

- Sexual activity among teenagers has increased in recent decades in the United States. Roughly half of all U.S. teens have had sexual intercourse by the time they reach their last year of high school.

LO 11.5   Which teenaged girls are most likely to get pregnant?

- Factors that predispose girls to teen pregnancy include early sexual activity, being raised by a single parent, having parents with a low level of education, low socioeconomic status, and having a parent who gave birth to a child in adolescence. Factors that protect against teen pregnancy include academic achievement, high aspirations for future education and career, and good communication about sex and contraception with parents.

LO 11.6 What are some causes that have been proposed to explain homosexuality?

- Hormonal, genetic, and environmental factors have been proposed to explain homosexuality. The process of realizing one's sexual orientation is a gradual one that often isn't completed until early adulthood.

Adolescent Health (pp. 277–282)

LO 11.7 How does sensation seeking affect risky behavior in adolescents?

- Sensation seeking, a desire to experience heightened levels of arousal, is associated with higher rates of various kinds of risky behavior, including unprotected sex, drug use, and fast driving. Lack of maturity in the prefrontal cortex may explain the link between sensation seeking and risky behavior, but environmental factors also play a role. These factors include permissive parenting, a desire for peer approval and independence from parents, media influences, and lack of involvement in school-related activities.

LO 11.8 What patterns of drug, alcohol, and tobacco use have been found among adolescents in the United States?

- Alcohol and drug use among U.S. teenagers, after declining for several decades, is now on the rise. Those most likely to use or abuse drugs are those who also show other forms of deviant or problem behavior, including poor school achievement.

LO 11.9 What are the characteristics and causes of eating disorders?

- Eating disorders such as bulimia nervosa and anorexia nervosa are more common among teenaged girls than among teenaged boys. Some theorists hypothesize that media images of thin models and celebrities cause the body-image distortions that underlie eating disorders. Others have proposed biological and socioeconomic causes. Still others emphasize the tendency of individuals with eating disorders to exhibit other kinds of distorted thoughts and be diagnosed with other psychological disorders.

LO 11.10 Which adolescents are at greatest risk of depression and suicide?

- Depression and suicide are mental health problems that are common during adolescence. Both are more common among girls, although boys are more likely to succeed with a suicide attempt.

Changes in Thinking and Memory (pp. 282–286)

LO 11.11 What are the characteristics of thought in Piaget's formal operational stage?

- Piaget proposed a fourth stage of cognitive development in adolescence. The formal operational stage is characterized by the ability to apply basic cognitive operations to ideas and possibilities, in addition to actual objects.

LO 11.12 What are some major research findings regarding the formal operational stage?

- Researchers have found clear evidence of such advanced forms of thinking in at least some adolescents. But formal operational thinking is not universal, nor is it consistently used by those who are able to do it.

LO 11.13 What kinds of advances in information-processing capabilities occur during adolescence?

- Memory function improves in adolescence as teens become more proficient in metacognition, metamemory, and strategy use.

Schooling (pp. 286–291)

LO 11.14 How do changes in students' goals contribute to the transition to secondary school?

- The transition to middle school may be accompanied by changes in children's goal orientation that result in declines in achievement and self-esteem. The high school transition offers many teens more opportunities to pursue special interests and extracurricular activities.

LO 11.15 What gender and ethnic differences in science and math achievement have researchers found?

- Female, African American, and Hispanic American high school students score lower on science and math achievement tests and choose to take courses in these disciplines less often than do White and Asian American males. Girls may view success in science and math as unacceptable for women. African American and Hispanic American students may not be getting the preparation they need in middle school for advanced high school math courses.

LO 11.16 What variables predict the likelihood of dropping out of high school?

- Those who succeed academically in high school are typically from authoritative families. Those who drop out are more likely to be from low-income families or to be doing poorly in school.

KEY TERMS

ability goals (p. 287)

adolescence (p. 266)

anorexia nervosa (p. 279)

bulimia nervosa (p. 279)

formal operational stage
  (p. 282)

hypothetico-deductive
  reasoning (p. 283)

imaginary audience (p. 284)

menarche (p. 268)

personal fable (p. 284)

pituitary gland (p. 268)

prefrontal cortex (PFC) (p. 266)

primary sex characteristics
  (p. 268)

puberty (p. 268)

secondary sex characteristics
  (p. 268)

secular trend (p. 269)

systematic problem solving
  (p. 282)

task goals (p. 287)

transgendered (p. 276)

CHAPTER TEST

☑ **Study** and **Review** in **MyPsychLab**

Answers to all the Chapter Test questions can be found in the back of the book.

1. According to this chapter, over the past several decades, the secular trend has caused the *greatest* change in the average age at which _____.
   a. menarche occurs
   b. secondary sex characteristics develop
   c. the ovaries contain eggs
   d. ovulatory cycles appear

2. Which of the following statements about gender differences is *true*?
   a. More girls than boys take calculus in high school.
   b. Boys get higher grades in math classes than girls do.
   c. More boys than girls take advanced classes other than calculus and AP calculus in high school.
   d. Mathematically gifted girls have less confidence in their abilities than equally gifted boys do.

3. Which of the following statements best summarizes the research as to the causes of homosexuality?
   a. Genetics plays a strong role in the development of sexual orientation.
   b. Homosexual behaviors are a matter of choice.
   c. The majority of teens who identify as homosexual report having been sexually abused as children.
   d. The research does not clearly point to either genetics or environment, but rather indicates that sexual orientation is a result of both genetic and environmental factors.

4. Which of the following is *not* a change in primary sex characteristics which takes place during puberty?
   a. growth of breasts   c. growth of the penis
   b. formation of a uterus   d. growth of the testes

5. Which of the following terms applies to a person whose psychological gender does not match their physical sex?
   a. gender dysfunctional   c. transgendered
   b. homosexual   d. cross-typed

6. Which of the following is a component of adolescent egocentrism according to Elkind?
   a. concrete thinking
   b. the imaginary audience
   c. hypothetical-inductive reasoning
   d. self-biography

7. Which of the following is true of spermarche?
   a. It typically occurs between 13 and 14 years of age, but the production of viable sperm does not happen until a few months later.
   b. It typically occurs between 15 and 16 years of age.
   c. Its onset varies considerably between different ethnic groups.
   d. Viable sperm production usually occurs a few months prior to the first ejaculation.

8. Among teenagers, what is the most commonly used drug?
   a. diet pills   c. alcohol
   b. marijuana   d. cocaine

9. Which statement about adolescent pregnancy is true?
   a. Eighteen- and 19-year-olds are less likely to get pregnant than younger teens.
   b. More teen mothers are unmarried today than in the past.
   c. The teen pregnancy rate is higher among girls under 15 than among 15- to 17-year-olds.
   d. Girls whose mothers were pregnant as teens are less likely than others to get pregnant.

10. Which of the following best defines menarche?
    a. growth of the uterus during puberty
    b. the onset of menstruation at puberty
    c. the beginning of puberty marked by the development of breast buds
    d. increase in body fat at puberty

11. Which of the following is associated with adolescent depression?
    a. growing up in a low-socioeconomic-status family
    b. growing up with a depressed parent
    c. having many siblings
    d. growing up in a religion that emphasizes traditional gender roles

12. Which of the following statements about teen sexuality is true?
    a. Most teens have had four or more sexual partners by twelfth grade.
    b. Surveys indicate that a minority of teens are currently sexually active (sex in the 4 weeks prior to the survey).
    c. More teens use birth control pills than condoms to prevent pregnancy.
    d. Hispanic American adolescents are more likely to have had sex at least once than African American teens.

13. Shelly is a high school sophomore who got pregnant in her freshman year. Even though she is sexually active, she doesn't use any form of contraception because she says, "I just can't see myself getting pregnant twice." Shelly's thinking reflects _____.
    a. Elkind's personal fable
    b. Piaget's naive idealism
    c. a good understanding of human reproduction
    d. the effective application of formal operational thinking to a practical decision

14. The changes in the patterns of physical growth and development that are known as the secular trend are most likely caused by which of the following?
    a. changes in nutrition and health care
    b. cultural values that favor a thin, angular body image
    c. an increasingly sexualized society
    d. increased levels of demand and stress placed upon children and adolescents

15. Which of the following is the best example of a child who has task goals for academic achievement?
    a. Darren wants to do another biology project on fruit flies because he learned so much on his first project.
    b. Cindy hopes to score higher on her college entrance exam than any of her brothers and sisters.

c. Eduardo hopes to do well in school to please his parents.

d. Julia has an intense fear of failure, so she studies more than is actually necessary.

16. During the adolescent growth spurt, which is (are) likely to grow first?
    a. the torso
    b. the brain
    c. hands and feet
    d. arms and legs

17. Which of the follow is *not* a typical characteristic of anorexia nervosa?
    a. significant weight loss
    b. episodes of binge eating that are followed by purging activities
    c. obsessive dieting that results in death by starvation
    d. presence of another psychological disorder

18. Thomas is 15 and has been transgendered for as long as he can remember. His parents took him to a psychiatrist to learn about sex reassignment surgery. What advice is the psychiatrist most likely to give to Thomas and his parents?
    a. It is unethical for surgeons to perform sex reassignment surgery on individuals younger than 18.
    b. Begin the transition process as soon as possible to avoid further distress.
    c. Explore other options as well because half of transgendered people find less drastic ways of dealing with their dilemma.
    d. Sex reassignment surgery is more appropriate for adolescent girls than for boys.

19. Which of the following teens is most likely to have had sex at least once?
    a. an African American male
    b. an Asian American female
    c. a White male
    d. a Hispanic American female

20. When teens mentally construct a perfect world, compare the real world to it, and express frustration over the disparity

between the two, they are exhibiting a characteristic of adolescent thought that Piaget called _____.
    a. adolescent egocentrism
    b. naive idealism
    c. systematic problem solving
    d. egocentric worldview

21. Which of the following is an example of changes in primary sex characteristics during puberty?
    a. lowering of the voice in boys
    b. growth of the breasts
    c. growth of the ovaries and testes
    d. growth spurt

22. Girls in whom secondary sex characteristics appear before the age of 7 _____.
    a. may be diagnosed with precocious puberty
    b. are unlikely to be obese
    c. are within the normal range
    d. are likely to have been sexually abused

23. Which of the following best defines adolescence?
    a. It is the transitional period between childhood and adulthood.
    b. It is synonymous with puberty.
    c. It begins when children enter secondary school.
    d. It ends at age eighteen when the brain achieves full maturity.

24. Which of the following is a defining feature of Piaget's formal operational stage?
    a. logical thinking about real-world events and objects
    b. fluency in the use of symbols
    c. hypethetico-deductive thinking
    d. the use of sound reasoning to make practical decisions

25. Which of the following groups is more likely to occupy leadership roles, but also be at increased risk for depression?
    a. late-maturing boys
    b. late-maturing girls
    c. early-maturing girls
    d. early-maturing boys

To 👁 **Watch** ❇ **Explore** ⊙ **Simulate** ✓ **Study** and **Review**
and experience MyVirtualLife go to MyPsychLab.com

chapter 12

Social and Personality Development in Adolescence

Has the teenaged "child" you are raising in *MyVirtualLife* started dating yet? If so, he or she is participating in an activity that informally marks the transition from childhood to adolescence. Some societies mark this transition in more formal ways, a practice that some developmentalists argue helps to explain cross-cultural differences in adolescence. Taking their cue from the pioneering work of psychoanalytic theorist Erik Erikson (1963), these developmentalists believe that the absence of formal *rites of passage*—ceremonies

LEARNING OBJECTIVES

In rites-of-passage programs, African American girls learn about the traditional styles of dress among African women.

identity an understanding of one's unique characteristics and how they have been, are, and will be manifested across ages, situations, and social roles

identity versus role confusion in Erikson's theory, the stage during which adolescents attain a sense of who they are

that mark the transition from childhood to adulthood—in industrialized societies makes adolescents more vulnerable to risky behaviors such as alcohol use, unprotected sex, and aggression. Teens who become involved in these activities, say some observers, are attempting to invent their own rites of passage. How adolescents accomplish this goal depends on the peer group with which they identify. For one teenager, the rite may involve preparing for a standardized test such as the PSAT that may earn her a college scholarship. For another adolescent, it may involve joining a street gang.

Consideration of rites of passage brings to mind Vygotsky's concept of scaffolding. Adolescents are conscious of the need to transition to adulthood, and they take many steps toward this goal on their own. But they need adults to lead the way and to support them when their steps toward maturity turn out to be missteps, whether that support occurs in the context of formal rites of passage or in more informal ways. This chapter begins with an examination of the aspects of the transition to adulthood that occur within adolescents themselves followed by a discussion of how the social world supports them.

Theories of Social and Personality Development

Thirteen-year-old Brendon took a deep breath to steady his nerves and punched in Melissa's cell phone number. He continued to breathe deeply as he waited for her to answer. Over the past few minutes, he had attempted to call her three times. However, the fear of rejection had overcome him each time, and he had hung up before she could answer. This time he was determined to at least say, "Hi."

Such dramas are played out every day in the world of young adolescents, and there is no denying the fact that the emergence of romantic interests is a prominent feature of this period of development. For Freud, these interests were the central theme of adolescence. Erikson and other theorists proposed models of adolescent development that are much broader in scope.

Psychoanalytic Perspectives

LO 12.1 What happens during Erikson's identity-versus-role-confusion stage?

According to Freud, the postpubertal years constitute the last stage of personality development; so both adolescents and adults are in what Freud called the *genital stage*, the period during which psychosexual maturity is reached. Freud believed that puberty awakens the sexual drive that has lain dormant during the latency stage. Thus, for Freud, the primary developmental task of adolescence is to channel the libido into a healthy sexual relationship.

Erikson, though not denying the importance of achieving sexual maturity, proposed that achievement of a sense of personal *identity* is a far more important developmental task faced by adolescents. He described *identity* as a sense of self-continuity (Erikson, 1963). More recent theorists, elaborating on his idea, define **identity** as an understanding of one's unique characteristics and how they are manifested across ages, situations, and social roles. Thus, in Erikson's model, the central crisis of adolescence is **identity versus role confusion**.

Erikson argued that the child's early sense of identity comes partly "unglued" in early adolescence because of the combination of rapid body growth and the sexual changes of puberty. Erikson claimed that during this period, the adolescent's mind is in a kind of moratorium between childhood and adulthood. The old identity will no longer suffice; a new identity must be forged, one that will equip the young person for the myriad roles of adult life—occupational roles, sexual roles, religious roles, and others.

Confusion about all these role choices is inevitable and leads to a pivotal transition Erikson called the *identity crisis*. The **identity crisis** is a period during which an adolescent is troubled by his lack of an identity. Erikson believed that adolescents' tendency to identify with peer groups was a defense against the emotional turmoil engendered by the identity crisis. In a sense, he claimed, teens protect themselves against the unpleasant emotions of the identity crisis by merging their individual identities with that of a group (Erikson, 1980a). The teen-aged group thus forms a base of security from which the young person can move toward a unique solution of the identity crisis. Ultimately, however, each teenager must achieve an inte-grated view of himself, including his own pattern of beliefs, occupational goals, and relation-ships. ◉ **Watch** the **Video** *Adolescence Identity and Role Development* in **MyPsychLab**.

Marcia's Theory of Identity Achievement

LO 12.2 How does Marcia explain identity development?

Nearly all the current work on the formation of adolescent identity has been based on James Marcia's descriptions of *identity statuses*, which are rooted in Erikson's general conceptions of the adolescent identity process (Marcia, 1966, 1980). Following one of Erikson's ideas, Marcia argues that adolescent identity formation has two key parts: a crisis and a commitment. By *crisis*, Marcia means a period of decision making when old values and old choices are reexamined. This may occur as a sort of upheaval—the classic notion of a crisis—or it may occur gradually. The out-come of the reevaluation is a *commitment* to some specific role, value, goal, or ideology.

If you put these two elements together, as shown in Figure 12.1, you can see that four different *identity statuses* are possible.

- **Identity achievement**: The person has been through a crisis and has reached a commitment to ideological, occupational, or other goals.

- **Moratorium**: A crisis is in progress, but no commitment has yet been made.

- **Foreclosure**: The person has made a commitment without having gone through a crisis. No reassessment of old positions has been made. Instead, the young person has simply accepted a parentally or culturally defined commitment.

- **Identity diffusion**: The young person is not in the midst of a crisis (although there may have been one in the past) and has not made a com-mitment. Diffusion may thus represent either an early stage in the process (before a crisis) or a failure to reach a commitment after a crisis.

The whole process of identity formation may occur later than Erikson and Marcia thought, perhaps because cognitive development is more strongly related to identity formation than either believed. Research suggests that teens who are most advanced in the development of logical thinking and other information-processing skills are also the most likely to have attained Marcia's status of identity achievement (Klaczynski, Fauth, & Swanger, 1998). In addition, identity statuses fluctuate during the teen years (Klimstra et al., 2010). That is, a teen who reaches Marcia's identity-achievement status doesn't necessarily retain that status over time.

There is also evidence that the quest for personal identity continues throughout the lifes-pan, with alternating periods of instability and stability (Marcia, 2010). For example, a person's sense of being "young" or "old" and her integration of that idea into a sense of belonging to a particular generation appear to change several times over the course of the adolescent and adult years (Sato, Shimonska, Nakazato, & Kawaai, 1997). Consequently, adolescence may be only one among several periods of identity formation.

Some research suggests that individuals who have attained Marcia's identity-achievement status sometimes regress to other categories (Kroger, Martinussen, & Marcia, 2010). This may happen because the achievement status may not be the most adaptive one in every situation. For example, teenagers facing extreme stressors, such as life-threatening illnesses, seem to be most optimally adjusted when they adopt the status of foreclosure (Madan-Swain et al., 2000). Accept-ing others' goals for them, at least temporarily, seems to protect these teens against some of the negative emotional effects of the difficulties they must face. In fact, one of the important func-tions of traditional rites of passage such as the Jewish *bar mitzvah* and *bat mitzvah*, as well as the rituals in which teenaged boys in traditional African societies participate, is to emphasize the degree to which teens are expected to conform to cultural expectations regarding adult roles.

identity crisis Erikson's term for the psychological state of emotional turmoil that arises when an adolescent's sense of self becomes "unglued" so that a new, more mature sense of self can be achieved

identity achievement in Marcia's theory, the identity status achieved by a person who has been through a crisis and reached a commitment to ideological or occupational goals

moratorium in Marcia's theory, the identity status of a person who is in a crisis but has made no commitment

foreclosure in Marcia's theory, the identity status of a person who has made a commitment without having gone through a crisis; the person has simply accepted a parentally or culturally defined commitment

identity diffusion in Marcia's theory, the identity status of a person who is not in the midst of a crisis and who has made no commitment

		Commitment	
		Present	**Absent**
CRISIS/EXPLORATION	PRESENT	**Identity achievement** "I want to help people and am good at science, so I decided to be a nurse."	**Moratorium** "I like psychology and am taking a variety of courses to determine whether I want to major in it or not."
	ABSENT	**Identity foreclosure** "I am going into the military, because that's what everyone in my family does when they finish high school."	**Identity diffusion** "I haven't given the future a lot of thought. I'm sure something will come along to push me in one direction or another."

Figure 12.1 Marcia's Identity Statuses

The four identity statuses proposed by Marcia, based on Erikson's theory. For a fully achieved identity, the young person must have both examined her values or goals and reached a firm commitment.

(*Source:* Based on Marcia, 1980.)

In the Jewish ceremony called bar mitzvah (for boys) or bat mitzvah (for girls), 13-year-olds read from the Torah in Hebrew and are admitted to full adult status in the congregation. The Tanzanian boy has had his face painted with white clay as part of an adolescent rite of passage.

Thus, the idea that progression to identity achievement is the most psychologically healthy response to the identity crisis clearly doesn't apply to some adolescents.

As you might suspect, ideas about adolescent identity development and the kinds of experiences that drive it are firmly rooted in cultural assumptions. For example, in the United States, both parents and teenagers tend to believe that paid employment during adolescence helps adolescents sort out the career-selection aspects of identity development (Greenberger & Steinberg, 1986; Runyan, Vladutiu, Schulman, & Rauscher, 2011). Predictably, cross-cultural studies show that teens in the United States spend a great deal more time working than do their peers in other industrialized nations (Larson & Verma, 1999; Österbacka & Zick, 2009) (see *Research Report*). Such cultural beliefs and the experiences that flow from them are likely to affect the process of identity development.

Clearly, too, the concept of an adolescent identity crisis has been strongly influenced by current cultural assumptions in Western societies, in which full adult status is postponed for almost a decade after puberty. In such cultures, young people do not normally or necessarily adopt the same roles or occupations as their parents. Indeed, they are encouraged to choose for themselves. These adolescents are faced with what may be a bewildering array of options, a pattern that might well foster the sort of identity crisis Erikson described. In less industrialized cultures, there may well be a shift in identity from that of child to that of adult, but without a crisis of any kind. Further, adolescents' search for identity in other cultures may be better supported by cultural initiation rites that clearly, at least in a symbolic sense, separate childhood from adulthood.

RESEARCH REPORT

The Effects of Teenaged Employment

In the United States, surveys of teenagers suggest that deciding on a career is one of the central themes of adolescent identity development (Mortimer, Zimmer-Gembeck, Holmes, & Shanahan, 2002). Moreover, many teens believe that engaging in part-time work during high school will help them with this aspect of identity achievement. Parents, too, often encourage their adolescent children to obtain part-time employment on the grounds that it "builds character" and teaches young people about "real life" (Runyan et al., 2011).

Are American teens and parents right about such beneficial effects of work? Research across the past two decades suggests that the more hours teenagers work during high school, the more likely they are to become sexually active, use drugs (alcohol, cigarettes, marijuana, cocaine), display aggression toward peers, argue with parents, get inadequate sleep, and be dissatisfied with life (Bachman & Schulenberg, 1993; Bachman, Safron, Sy, & Schulenberg, 2003; Bozick, 2006; Kaestner, Sasso, Callison, & Yarnoff, 2013).

Moreover, individuals who work while in high school are less likely than peers who do not work to go to college. Thus working may actually decrease teens' chances for successful careers during adulthood, which is precisely the opposite of what many adolescents and parents believe.

A quite different answer to the question of the impact of teenaged employment comes from studies that take into consideration the kind of work teenagers do (Mortimer & Finch, 1996; Mortimer, Finch, Dennehy, Lee, & Beebe, 1995; Mortimer & Harley, 2002). These findings indicate that unskilled work is much more likely to be associated with poor outcomes than is complex, skilled work. They also suggest that adolescents who have skill-based work experiences develop increased feelings of competence. In addition, those students who see themselves as gaining useful skills through their work also seem to develop confidence in their ability to achieve economic success in adulthood (Grabowski, Call, & Mortimer, 2001).

It is not clear how we should add up the results of these studies. At the very least, this mixture of results should make parents think twice before encouraging teenagers to work. However, parents need to consider the quality of work a teen will do before assuming that a job will negatively affect his or her development.

CRITICAL ANALYSIS

1. *Teen employment may be correlated with developmental outcomes because teens who work differ from those who do not in ways that are also related to such outcomes. What variables do you think might distinguish teens who choose to work from their peers who don't have jobs?*

2. *Are there developmental outcomes that have not been addressed by the research described in this discussion that you think might be positively affected by teen employment?*

Answers to these questions can be found in the back of the book.

1. According to Erikson, a teen who fails to successfully resolve the identity crisis risks developing a sense of _____ _____.

2. Classify each of these behaviors as indicative of (A) identity achievement, (B) moratorium, (C) foreclosure, or (D) identity diffusion.

_____(1)   Lucy has decided on a premed major because her mother and grandmother are physicians.

_____(2)   Carl is taking a few college courses in different disciplines to figure out what he wants to major in.

_____(3)   After considering several different options, Rosa has decided to join the Marines after graduation.

_____(4)   Sean dropped out of high school at 16 and since then has moved from one minimum-wage job to another. He gives little thought to his future.

CRITICAL THINKING

3. The implication in Marcia's formulation is that foreclosure is a less developmentally mature status—that one must go through a crisis in order to achieve a mature identity. Does this make sense to you? What is your current identity status? Has it changed much over the past few years?

Self-Concept

In Chapter 11, you read that thinking becomes more abstract in adolescence. Thus, you shouldn't be surprised to find that teenagers' self-concepts are a lot more complex than those of younger children.

Self-Understanding

LO 12.3   In what way does self-understanding in adolescence differ from that in childhood?

Through the elementary school years, the child's self-concept becomes more focused on enduring internal characteristics—the psychological self. This trend continues in adolescence, with self-definition becoming more abstract. Advances in self-understanding among adolescents are both facilitated by and contribute to the increasing stability of the Big Five personality traits during this period. As a result, enduring traits such as shyness—or *introversion* in Big Five terminology—show up in adolescents' self-descriptions far more often than they do in those of younger children. This change was evident in the replies of a 9-year-old and an 11-year-old to the question "Who am I?" that you may recall from Chapter 10. Internal traits are even more pronounced in this 17-year-old's answer to the same question:

> I am a human being. I am a girl. I am an individual. I don't know who I am. I am a Pisces. I am a moody person. I am an indecisive person. I am an ambitious person. I am a very curious person. I am not an individual. I am a loner. I am an American (God help me). I am a Democrat. I am a liberal person. I am a radical. I am a conservative. I am a pseudoliberal. I am an atheist. I am not a classifiable person (i.e., I don't want to be). (Montemayor & Eisen, 1977, p. 318)

Clearly, this girl's self-concept is even less tied to her physical characteristics or even her abilities than are those of younger children. She is describing abstract traits or ideology.

You can see the change very graphically in Figure 12.2, which is based on the answers of all 262 participants in Montemayor and Eisen's classic study. Each of the answers to the "Who am I?" question was categorized as a reference either to physical properties ("I am tall," "I have blue eyes") or to ideology ("I am a Democrat," "I believe in God"). As you can see, appearance was a highly prominent dimension in the preteen and early teen years but became less dominant in late adolescence, a time when ideology and belief became more important. By late adolescence, most teenagers think of themselves in terms of enduring traits, beliefs, personal philosophy, and moral standards (Damon & Hart, 1988).

Figure 12.2 Changes in Teens' Self-Descriptions

As they get older, children and adolescents define themselves less and less by what they look like and more and more by what they believe or feel.

(*Source:* Montemayor & Eisen, 1977, from Table 1, p. 316.)

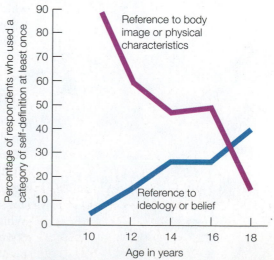

At the same time, the adolescent's self-concept becomes more differentiated, as she comes to see herself somewhat differently in each of several roles: as a student, with friends, with parents, and in romantic relationships (Harter, 2012). Once these self-concepts are formed, they begin to influence adolescents' behavior. For example, teens who get high scores on measures of athletic self-concept are more likely to exercise than those who get lower scores (Anderson, Masse, Zhang, Coleman, & Chang, 2009). Similarly, teens whose academic self-concepts are strong take more difficult courses in high school than do teens who believe themselves to be less academically able. Further, they tend to select courses in disciplines in which they believe they have the greatest ability and to avoid courses in perceived areas of weakness (Marsh & Yeung, 1997). In addition, teens' academic self-concepts influence their decisions about behaviors such as completing homework. For example, those who view themselves as competent in math and who believe that doing well in math is important are more likely to complete homework and get good grades in math classes (Bouchey & Harter, 2005).

Adolescents' academic self-concepts seem to come both from internal comparisons of their performance to a self-generated ideal and from external comparisons to peer performance (Harter, 2012). It also appears that perceived competency in one domain affects how a teenager feels about his ability in other areas. For example, if a high school student fails a math course, it is likely to affect his self-concept in other disciplines as well as in math. This suggests that teens' self-concepts are hierarchical in nature: Perceived competencies in various domains serve as building blocks for creating a global academic self-concept (Cheng, Xiaoyan, Dajun, 2006; Yeung, Chui, & Lau, 1999).

Social self-concepts also predict behavior. For example, a teenager's family self-concept reflects his beliefs about the likelihood of attaining and/or maintaining satisfactory relationships with family members. Developmentalists have found that adolescents who are estranged from their families, such as runaways, perceive themselves to be less competent in the give-and-take of family relations than teens who are close to parents and siblings (Swaim & Bracken, 1997). Indeed, the perceived lack of competency in family relations appears to be distinct from other components of self-concept.

Girls and boys also appear to construct the various components of self-concept somewhat differently (Harter, 2012). For example, a study of teens' evaluations of their own writing abilities found that boys and girls rated themselves as equally capable writers (Pajares & Valiante, 1999). However, the girls scored higher on objective tests of writing ability. In addition, the girls were more likely to describe themselves as being better writers than their peers of both genders. The boys, by contrast, seemed to perceive few ability differences in their peers. In other words, the boys believed they were good writers, but they also thought that their classmates were as good as they were.

Such findings are predictable, given the information in the previous section about girls being influenced by both internal and external comparisons while boys attend more to internal, self-defined standards. The findings also raise interesting questions about the degree to which self-concept development is influenced by cultural ideas about sex roles. Perhaps girls pay more attention to their own and others' writing skills because they know that girls are supposed to be better at language skills than boys.

Self-Esteem

LO 12.4 How does self-esteem change across the teenage years?

Self-esteem shows some interesting shifts during the teenaged years. The overall trend is a steady rise in self-esteem through the years of adolescence. The average 19- or 20-year-old has a considerably more positive sense of her global self-worth than she did at age 8 or 11 (Harter, 2012). However, the rise to higher self-esteem during adolescence is not continuous. At the beginning of adolescence, self-esteem very often drops rather abruptly. In one classic study, developmentalists followed a group of nearly 600 Hispanic American, African American, and White youngsters over the 2 years from sixth to seventh grade (Seidman, Allen, Aber, Mitchell, & Feinman, 1994). Researchers found a significant average drop in self-esteem over that period, a decline that occurred in each of the three ethnic groups.

To study the relationship of self-esteem to important developmental outcomes, such as school achievement, researchers often divide teens into four groups based on the stability of their self-esteem ratings across adolescence (Diehl, Vicary, & Deike, 1997; Zimmerman, Copeland, Shope, & Dielman, 1997). The largest group, about half in most studies, displays consistently high self-esteem throughout adolescence. The self-esteem of those in the second group steadily increases, and that of those in the third group is consistently low. Teens in the fourth group enjoy moderate to high self-esteem at the beginning of the period, but it declines steadily as adolescence progresses. One finding of concern is that girls outnumber boys in the third and fourth groups (Zimmerman et al., 1997). In addition, several studies have found that high self-esteem is correlated with positive developmental outcomes. For example, teens with high self-esteem are better able to resist peer pressure, get higher grades in school, and are less likely to be depressed (Moksnes, Moljord, Espnes, & Byrne, 2010; Repetto, Caldwell, & Zimmerman, 2004). You may also remember from Chapter 11 that such teens are less likely to become involved in substance abuse or early sexual intercourse.

Gender Roles

LO 12.5 What are the gender role concepts of adolescents?

Developmentalists use the term **gender role identity** to refer to gender-related aspects of the psychological self. In contrast to younger children, adolescents understand that gender roles are social conventions, and their attitudes toward them are more flexible (Katz & Ksansnak, 1994). Parental attitudes and parental behavior become increasingly important in shaping teens' ideas about gender and sex roles (Cox, Mezulis, & Hyde, 2010; Raffaelli & Ontai, 2004; Ridolfo, Chepp, & Milkie, 2013). In addition, concepts that were largely separate earlier in development, such as beliefs about gender roles and sexuality, seem to become integrated into a conceptual framework that teens use to formulate ideas about the significance of gender in personal identity and social relationships (Mallet, Apostolidis, & Paty, 1997).

In the early days of research on gender role identity, psychologists conceived of masculinity and femininity as polar opposites. A person could be masculine or feminine but couldn't be both. However, theories first advanced in the 1970s by Sandra Bem and others have resulted in a large body of research in support of the notion that masculinity and femininity are separate dimensions and each may be found in varying quantities in the personalities of both men and women (Bem, 1974; Spence & Helmreich, 1978). A male or a female can be high or low on masculinity, femininity, or both. Indeed, if people are categorized as high or low on each of these two dimensions, based on their self-descriptions, four basic gender role types emerge: *masculine, feminine, androgynous,* and *undifferentiated* (see Figure 12.3).

The masculine and feminine types are the traditional categories; a person in either of these categories sees himself or herself as high in one and low in the other. A "masculine" teenager or adult, according to this view, is thus one who perceives himself (or herself) as having many traditional masculine qualities and few traditional feminine qualities. A feminine teenager or adult shows the reverse pattern. In contrast, androgynous individuals see themselves as having both masculine and feminine traits; undifferentiated individuals describe themselves as lacking both.

Interestingly, research suggests that either an androgynous or a masculine gender role identity is associated with higher self-esteem among both boys and girls (Gurňáková & Kusá, 2004; Huang, Zhu, Zheng, Zhang, & Shiomi, 2012; Woo & Oei, 2006). Similarly, girls with a feminine gender identity are more prone to *rumination*, a thought process that focuses on anxiety-inducing stimuli (e.g., peer judgments of physical attractiveness) and can lead to depression (Cox et al., 2010). These findings make sense in light of the existence of a "masculine bias" in American and other Western societies, which causes both men and women to value traditionally masculine qualities such as independence and competitiveness more than many traditionally female qualities.

Cross-cultural research suggests, however, that adoption of an androgynous or masculine orientation by a girl can lead to lower self-esteem. For example, one study of Israeli girls found that preteens who thought of themselves as tomboys and who rated themselves high on masculine personality

gender role identity the gender-related aspects of the psychological self

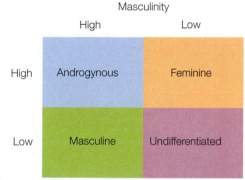

Figure 12.3 Bem's Gender Role Categories

Figure 12.3 Bem's Gender Role Categories

This diagram illustrates how the dimensions of masculinity and femininity interact to produce four types of sex-role orientation.

Teenaged boys like these may have an easier time achieving high self-esteem than girls of the same age because both boys and girls seem to place a higher value on certain traditionally "masculine" qualities than on traditionally "feminine" qualities.

ethnic identity a sense of belonging to an ethnic group

traits were less popular and had lower self-esteem than their more feminine peers (Lobel, Slone, & Winch, 1997). Consequently, when considering gender roles and gender role identity, it is important to remember that both are very strongly tied to culture. A particular society may value the masculine role more highly but also actively discourage girls from adopting it. Thus, it may not be universally true that teens who adopt the more highly valued gender role identity gain self-esteem.

Ethnic Identity

LO 12.6 How do minority, biracial, and immigrant teens develop a sense of ethnic identity?

Minority teenagers, especially those of color in a predominantly White culture, face the task of creating two identities in adolescence. Like other teens, they must develop a sense of individual identity that they believe sets them apart from others. In addition, they must develop an **ethnic identity** that includes self-identification as a member of their specific group, commitment to that group and its values and attitudes, and some attitudes (positive or negative) about the group to which they belong. Many minority families support children's ethnic identity development by providing them with specific teaching about how their group differs from the dominant one. Similarly, some families who speak a language different from that of the dominant group support children's ethnic identity development by teaching them the language of their home country. Researchers have found that minority teenagers whose families engage in such practices are likely to develop a strong sense of ethnic identity (Davey, Fish, Askew, & Robila, 2003; Oh & Fuligni, 2010).

Psychologist Jean Phinney has proposed that, in adolescence, the development of a complete ethnic identity moves through three stages (Phinney, 1990; Phinney & Rosenthal, 1992). The first stage is an *unexamined ethnic identity*. For some subgroups in U.S. society, such as African Americans and Native Americans, this unexamined identity typically includes the negative images and stereotypes common in the wider culture (see *Developmental Science in the Classroom*). Indeed, it may be especially at adolescence, with the advent of the cognitive ability to reflect and interpret, that a young person becomes keenly aware of how his own group is perceived by the majority.

DEVELOPMENTAL SCIENCE IN THE CLASSROOM

Role Models in Life and in the Media

Like many other youngsters, Chérie idolizes professional athletes. Her current heroine is professional tennis star Serena Williams. Like her idol, Chérie is African American, and she is inspired not only by Williams's dynamic style of play but also by the fact that Williams has become a star in what was once an all-White sport. Interestingly, Chérie's uncle is a professor of English literature at an ethnically diverse private college. He, too, has achieved success in a profession that was at one time closed to minorities. So, why does Chérie idolize Serena Williams and other professional athletes rather than her own uncle and others like him?

A good illustration of the complex nature of the influence of models comes from a survey in which 4,500 African American boys aged 10 to 18 were asked to name an important role model outside their own families (Assibey-Mensah, 1997). A large majority of the boys named a professional athlete. Not a single boy named a teacher as an important personal role model, despite that fact that the boys in the study, no doubt, interact with teachers every day.

Findings such as these have raised concerns about the ways in which media portrayals of various occupational roles influence children's career aspirations. For example, news reports about public education often characterize schools with large proportions of minority students as failures. The implication is that teachers in such schools are ineffective. In contrast, stories about athletes are dominated by themes of fame, wealth, popularity, and record-breaking achievements. Considering the contrast between the two, it isn't surprising that African American boys prefer athletes as role models rather than teachers, even though they know many teachers and most likely have themselves no personal interactions with professional athletes.

The need to better inform African American youths about the various avenues to career success that are available to them has been the impetus behind publication of books such as *Real Role Models* (Spearman & Harrison, 2010). The book profiles 23 successful African Americans, most of whom grew up in disadvantaged circumstances. The authors' goal is to acquaint minority youths with individuals from backgrounds that are similar to theirs who have achieved success in business, politics, education, and other fields.

REFLECTION

1. *How might frequent interaction make it less likely that a child will view someone as a role model?*

2. *In your opinion, to what extent are the concerns developmentalists have expressed about African American children's responses to celebrity and everyday role models applicable to children of other ethnicities?*

Phinney's second stage is the *ethnic identity search*. This search is typically triggered by some experience that makes ethnicity relevant—perhaps an example of blatant prejudice or merely the widening experience of high school. At this point, the young person begins to compare his own ethnic group with others, to try to arrive at his own judgments.

This exploration stage is eventually followed by the *ethnic identity achievement* stage, in which adolescents develop strategies for solving conflicts between the competing demands of the dominant culture and those of the ethnic group with which they identify. Most deal with such conflicts by creating two identities, displaying one in the presence of members of the dominant group and another with members of their own group.

In both cross-sectional and longitudinal studies, Phinney has found that African American teens and young adults do indeed move through these steps or stages toward a clear ethnic identity. The "bicultural" orientation of the last stage has been found to be a consistent characteristic of adolescents and adults who have high self-esteem and enjoy good relations with members of both the dominant culture and their own ethnic group (Berry & Sabatier, 2010; Chen et al., 2013; Phinney, 2008; Yamada & Singelis, 1999).

BIRACIAL ADOLESCENTS Biracial adolescents experience a unique pathway to ethnic identity, one that highlights the difference between the biological aspects of race and the psychosocial nature of ethnic identity. Studies showing that biracial siblings often develop different ethnic identities highlight this distinction. To explain these surprising findings, psychologist Maria Root, who has studied identity development in biracial teens for two decades, has proposed a theoretical model that includes four sets of factors that interact with a biracial adolescent's personality to shape the development of her ethnic identity (Root, 2004).

Hazing and the emotional trauma that it engenders represent one factor. Often, Root says, biracial teens are challenged to prove their "authenticity" by the racial group of one parent. Such challenges force them to adopt new music and clothing preferences, change their speech patterns, and reject peers who represent their other parent's group. This kind of hazing, says Root, leads biracial teens to reject the group by whom they are hazed, even if, for the sake of social survival, they outwardly appear to have conformed to it.

Family and neighborhood variables constitute the second and third factors. If a biracial teen is abused or rejected by a parent, she tends to reject the ethnicity of that parent. Moreover, if a biracial adolescent grows up in a neighborhood in which the ethnic group of one of her parents is highly dominant, she is likely to adopt the ethnicity of that dominant group.

The fourth factor that influences ethnic identity development in biracial teens is the presence of other salient identities. For example, for teens growing up in military families, the identity of "Army brat" or "Air Force brat" supersedes ethnic identity.

IMMIGRANT TEENS Adolescents in immigrant families often feel caught between the culture of their parents and that of their new homes. For example, cultures that emphasize the community rather than the individual view teens' acceptance of family responsibilities as a sign of maturity. A question such as whether a teen should get a job is decided in terms of family needs. If the family needs money, the adolescent might be encouraged to work. However, if the family needs the teenager to care for younger siblings while the parents work, then a part-time job is likely to be forbidden. By contrast, most American parents think that part-time jobs help teens mature and allow their children to work even if their doing so inconveniences the parents in some way. As a result, the immigrant teen feels that his parents are preventing him from fitting in with his American peers.

Young people of color often develop two identities: a psychological sense of self and an ethnic identity. Those who succeed at both tasks often think of themselves as "bicultural" and have an easier time relating to peers of the same and other ethnicities.

Research involving Asian American teenagers helps to illustrate this point. Psychologists have found that first-generation Asian American teens often feel guilty about responding to the individualistic pressures of North American culture. Their feelings of guilt appear to be based on their parents' cultural norms, which hold that the most mature adolescents are those who take a greater role in the family rather than trying to separate from it (Chen, 1999). Moreover, differences between parents and teens about the degree to which "Americanized" adolescent behavior is acceptable is a source of conflict in immigrant families (Kim, Chen, Wang, Shen, & Orozco-Lapray, 2013). Thus, for many Asian American adolescents, achievement of personal and ethnic identity involves balancing the individualistic demands of North American culture against the familial obligations of their parents' cultures. Consequently, many teens in immigrant families develop a bicultural identity (Chen et al., 2013; Farver, Bradha, & Narang, 2002; Kim et al., 2013).

test yourself before going on ✔ **Study** and **Review** in **MyPsychLab**

Answers to these questions can be found in the back of the book.

1. Which of the following characteristics are likely to be included in a teenager's self-description but not in a school-aged child's self-description (T), and which might be included in both (B)?
   _____(1) happy
   _____(2) honest
   _____(3) tall
   _____(4) friendly
   _____(5) environmentalist

2. Self-esteem is (higher/lower) in early adolescence than in the later teen years.

3. Classify each description as indicative of one of the following gender role identities: (A) androgynous, (B) masculine, (C), feminine, or (D) undifferentiated sex role.
   _____(1) Luis views assertiveness as the defining characteristic of his personality.
   _____(2) Sandra's ability to offer compassionate and caring responses to her friends' problems is the trait she feels best defines her personality.
   _____(3) Montel prides himself on responding according to the demands of different situations. If a problem calls for assertiveness, he can tackle it head on. If a problem calls for empathy or patience, he feels that he can handle that as well.
   _____(4) Keisha has a poorly developed sense of self and has trouble describing her identity in terms of personality traits.

4. In the table below, briefly summarize Phinney's stages of ethnic identity development.

Stage	Summary
Unexamined	
Search	
Achievement	

CRITICAL THINKING

5. Which of Bem's gender role identity categories best describes you? (Look back at Figure 12.3.) Do you think your gender role identity has changed since you were a teenager?

Moral Development

As you learned in Chapter 10, theorists representing various orientations think differently about moral development. The theorist whose work has had the most powerful impact has been psychologist Lawrence Kohlberg (Bergman, 2002; Colby, Kohlberg, Gibbs, & Lieberman, 1983; Kohlberg, 1976, 1981). Theories of moral reasoning have also been important in explanations of adolescent antisocial behavior. ◎ **Simulate** the **Experiment** *Kohlberg's Stages of Moral Reasoning* in **MyPsychLab**.

Kohlberg's Theory of Moral Reasoning

LO 12.7 What are the features of moral reasoning at each of Kohlberg's stages?

You may recall from Chapter 10 that Piaget proposed two stages in the development of moral reasoning. Working from Piaget's basic assumptions, Kohlberg devised a way of measuring moral reasoning based on research participants' responses to moral dilemmas such as the following:

In Europe, a woman was near death from a special kind of cancer. There was one drug that the doctors thought might save her. It was a form of radium that a druggist in the same town had recently discovered. The drug was expensive to make, but the druggist was charging ten times what the drug cost him to make. He paid $200 for the radium and charged $2000 for a small dose of the drug. The sick woman's husband, Heinz, went to everyone he knew to borrow the money, but he could only get together about $1000. . . . He told the druggist that his wife was dying, and asked him to sell it cheaper or let him pay later. But the druggist said, "No, I discovered the drug and I'm going to make money from it." So Heinz got desperate and broke into the man's store to steal the drug for his wife. (Kohlberg & Elfenbein, 1975, p. 621)

Kohlberg analyzed participants' answers to questions about such dilemmas (for example, "Should Heinz have stolen the drug? Why?") and concluded that there were three levels of moral development, each made up of two substages, as summarized in Table 12.1. It is important to understand that what determines the stage or level of a person's moral judgment is not any specific moral choice but the form of reasoning used to justify that choice. For example, either response to Kohlberg's dilemma—that Heinz should steal the drug or that he should not—could be justified with logic at any given stage.

AGE AND MORAL REASONING The stages are correlated somewhat loosely with age. Very few children reason beyond stage 1 or 2, and stage 2 and stage 3 reasoning are the types most commonly found among adolescents (Walker, de Vries, & Trevethan, 1987). Among adults, stages 3 and 4 are the most common (Gibson, 1990). Two research examples illustrate these overall age trends. The first, shown in Figure 12.4, comes from Kohlberg's own longitudinal study of 58 boys, first interviewed when they were 10 and then followed for more than 20 years (Colby et al., 1983). Figure 12.5 (page 306) shows cross-sectional data from a study by Lawrence Walker and his colleagues (1987). They studied 10 boys and 10 girls at

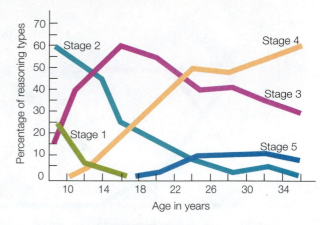

Figure 12.4 Colby and Kohlberg's Longitudinal Study of Moral Reasoning

These findings are from Colby and Kohlberg's long-term longitudinal study of a group of boys who were asked about Kohlberg's moral dilemmas every few years from age 10 through early adulthood. As they got older, the stage or level of their answers changed, with conventional reasoning appearing fairly widely at high school age. Postconventional, or principled, reasoning was not very common at any age.

(*Source:* A. Colby et al., "A longitudinal study of moral judgment," *Monographs of the Society for Research in Child Development*, Vol. 48, Nos. 1 and 2, Fig. 1, p. 46, © 1983 The Society for Research in Child Development. Reprinted by permission.)

TABLE 12.1 Kohlberg's Stages of Moral Development

Level	Stages	Description
Level I: Preconventional	Stage 1: Punishment and obedience orientation	The child or teenager decides what is wrong on the basis of what is punished. Obedience is valued for its own sake, but the child obeys because the adults have superior power.
	Stage 2: Individualism, instrumental purpose, and exchange	Children and teens follow rules when it is in their immediate interest. What is good is what brings pleasant results.
Level II: Conventional	Stage 3: Mutual interpersonal expectations, relationships, and interpersonal conformity	Moral actions are those that live up to the expectations of the family or other significant group. "Being good" becomes important for its own sake.
	Stage 4: Social system and conscience (law and order)	Moral actions are those so defined by larger social groups or the society as a whole. One should fulfill duties one has agreed to and uphold laws, except in extreme cases.
Level III: Postconventional	Stage 5: Social contract or utility and individual rights	This stage involves acting so as to achieve the "greatest good for the greatest number." The teenager or adult is aware that most values are relative and laws are changeable, although rules should be upheld in order to preserve the social order. Still, there are some basic absolute values, such as the importance of each person's life and liberty.
	Stage 6: Universal ethical principles	The small number of adults who reason at stage 6 develop and follow self-chosen ethical principles in determining what is right. These ethical principles are part of an articulated, integrated, carefully thought out, and consistently followed system of values and principles.

(*Sources:* Kohlberg, 1976; Lickona, 1978.)

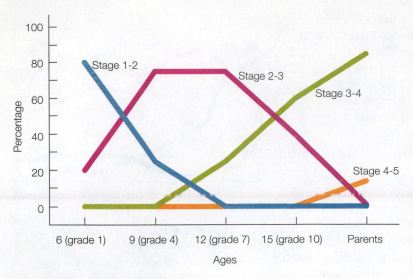

Figure 12.5 Percentages of Children and Parents Who Show Moral Reasoning at Each of Kohlberg's Stages

(*Source:* L. J. Walker et al., "Moral stages and moral orientations in real-life and hypothetical dilemmas," *Child Development*, Vol. 60 (1987), pp. 842–858, Table 1, p. 849.)

each of four ages, and they interviewed the parents of each child as well. The results of these two studies, although not identical, point to remarkably similar conclusions about the order of emergence of the various stages and about the approximate ages at which they predominate. In both studies, stage 2 reasoning dominates at around age 10, and stage 3 reasoning is most common at about age 16.

PRECONVENTIONAL REASONING At level I, **preconventional morality**, the child's judgments are based on sources of authority who are close by and physically superior—usually the parents. Just as descriptions of others are largely external at this level, so the standards the child uses to judge rightness or wrongness are external rather than internal. In particular, it is the outcome or consequence of an action that determines the rightness or wrongness of the action.

In stage 1 of this level—*punishment and obedience orientation*—the child relies on the physical consequences of some action to decide whether it is right or wrong. If he is punished, the behavior was wrong; if he is not punished, it was right. He is obedient to adults because they are bigger and stronger.

In stage 2—*individualism, instrumental purpose, and exchange*—the child or adolescent operates on the principle that you should do things that are rewarded and avoid things that are punished. For this reason, the stage is sometimes called *naive hedonism*. If it feels good or brings pleasant results, it is good. Some beginning of concern for other people is apparent during this stage, but only if that concern can be expressed as something that benefits the child or teenager himself as well. So he can enter into agreements such as "If you help me, I'll help you."

To illustrate, here are some responses to variations of the Heinz dilemma, drawn from studies of children and teenagers in a number of different cultures, all of whom were at stage 2:

> He should steal the [drug] for his wife because if she dies he'll have to pay for the funeral, and that costs a lot. [Taiwan]

> [He should steal the drug because] he should protect the life of his wife so he doesn't have to stay alone in life. [Puerto Rico] (Snarey, 1985, p. 221)

CONVENTIONAL REASONING At the next major level, that of **conventional morality**, rules or norms of a group to which the individual belongs become the basis of moral judgments, whether that group is the family, the peer group, a church, or the nation. What the chosen reference group defines as right or good is right or good in the individual's view. Again, very few children exhibit conventional thinking, but many adolescents are capable of this kind of moral reasoning.

Stage 3 (the first stage of level II) is that of *mutual interpersonal expectations, relationships, and interpersonal conformity* (sometimes also called the *good boy/nice girl stage*). Regardless of age, individuals who reason at this stage believe that good behavior is what pleases other people. They value trust, loyalty, respect, gratitude, and maintenance of mutual relationships.

Another mark of this third stage is that the individual makes judgments based on intentions as well as on outward behavior. If someone "didn't mean to do it," the wrongdoing is seen as less serious than if the person did it "on purpose."

Stage 4, the second stage of the conventional morality level, incorporates the norms of a larger reference group into moral judgments. Kohlberg labeled this the stage of social system and conscience. It is also sometimes called the *law-and-order orientation*. People reasoning at this stage focus on doing their duty, respecting authority, following rules and laws. The emphasis is less on what is pleasing to particular people (as in stage 3) and more on adhering to a complex set of regulations. However, the regulations themselves are not questioned, and morality and legality are assumed to be equivalent. Therefore, for a person at stage 4, something that is legal is right, whereas something that is illegal is wrong. Consequently, changes in law can effect changes in the moral views of individuals who reason at stage 4.

preconventional morality in Kohlberg's theory, the level of moral reasoning in which judgments are based on authorities outside the self

conventional morality in Kohlberg's theory, the level of moral reasoning in which judgments are based on rules or norms of a group to which the person belongs

POSTCONVENTIONAL REASONING The transition to level III, **postconventional morality**, is marked by several changes, the most important of which is a shift in the source of authority. Individuals who reason at level I see authority as totally outside of themselves; at level II, the judgments or rules of external authorities are internalized, but they are not questioned or analyzed; at level III, a new kind of personal authority emerges, in which an individual makes choices and judgments based on self-chosen principles or on principles that are assumed to transcend the needs and concerns of any individual or group. Postconventional thinkers represent only a minority of adults and an even smaller minority of adolescents.

In stage 5 at this level, which Kohlberg called the *social contract orientation*, such self-chosen principles begin to be evident. Rules, laws, and regulations are not seen as irrelevant; they are important ways of ensuring fairness. But people operating at this level also acknowledge that there are times when the rules, laws, and regulations need to be ignored or changed.

The American civil rights movement of the 1950s and 1960s is a good example of stage 5 reasoning in action. *Civil disobedience*—deliberately breaking laws that were believed to be immoral—arose as a way of protesting racial segregation. For example, in restaurants, African Americans intentionally took seats that were reserved for Whites. It is important to note that the practice of civil disobedience does not usually involve avoiding the penalties that accompany criminal behavior. Indeed, some of the most effective and poignant images from that period of U.S. history are photographs of individuals who surrendered and were jailed for breaking segregation laws. This behavior illustrates the stage 5 view that, as a general principle, upholding the law is important, even though a specific law that is deemed to be immoral can—or even should—be broken when breaking it will serve to promote the common good.

In his original writing about moral development, Kohlberg also included a sixth stage, *the universal ethical principles orientation*. Stage 6 reasoning involves balancing equally valid, but conflicting, moral principles against one another in order to determine which should be given precedence with respect to a specific moral issue. For example, in arguing against capital punishment, some people say that an individual's right to life is more important than society's right to exact justice from those who are convicted of heinous crimes. Such a claim might or might not be an example of stage 6 reasoning. Remember, the key to assessing an individual's stage of moral development is to fully probe the reasoning behind his or her answer to a question about a moral dilemma. Sometimes this kind of probing reveals that arguments that, on first glance, appear to represent stage 6 thinking are actually based on the authority of a religious tradition or a highly respected individual, in which case the reasoning is conventional rather than postconventional. Occasionally, though, the individual making such an argument is able to explain it in terms of a universal ethical principle that must always be adhered to regardless of any other considerations. In the case of opposition to the death penalty, the universal ethical principle would be the idea that the maintenance of human life is the highest of all moral principles. Note, however, that a person reasoning at stage 6 would not argue that society has no right to punish criminals. Instead, he or she would say that, in situations where upholding such rights involves termination of a human life, the right to life of the person whose life would be ended takes precedence.

Kohlberg argued that this sequence of reasoning is both universal and hierarchically organized. That is, each stage grows out of the preceding one. Kohlberg did not suggest that all individuals eventually progress through all six stages—or even that each stage is tied to specific ages. But he insisted that the order is invariant and universal. He also believed that the social environment determines how slowly or rapidly individuals move through the stages.

The evidence seems fairly strong that the stages follow one another in the sequence Kohlberg proposed. Long-term longitudinal studies of teenagers and young adults in the United States, Israel, and Turkey show that changes in participants' reasoning nearly always occur in the hypothesized order (Colby et al., 1983; Nisan & Kohlberg, 1982; Snarey, Reimer, & Kohlberg,

Civil disobedience involves intentionally breaking laws one believes to be immoral. For example, in the early years of the U.S. civil rights movement, African Americans broke laws that excluded them from certain sections of restaurants by "sitting in" at Whites-only lunch counters. Practitioners of civil disobedience do not try to evade the consequences of their actions, because they believe in upholding the law as a general principle even though they may view some specific laws as immoral. Thus, the thinking that underlies acts of civil disobedience represents Kohlberg's postconventional level of moral reasoning.

postconventional morality in Kohlberg's theory, the level of moral reasoning in which judgments are based on an integration of individual rights and the needs of society

1985; Walker, 1989). People do not skip stages, and movement down the sequence rather than up occurs only about 5–7% of the time.

Variations of Kohlberg's dilemmas have been used with children in a wide range of countries, including both Western and non-Western, industrialized and nonindustrialized (Snarey, 1985). In every culture, researchers find higher stages of reasoning among older children, but cultures differ in the highest level of reasoning observed. In urban cultures (both Western and non-Western), stage 5 is typically the highest stage observed; in agricultural societies and those in which there is little opportunity for formal education, stage 4 is typically the highest. Collectively, this evidence seems to provide quite strong support for the universality of Kohlberg's stage sequence, although emergence of the higher stages is strongly influenced by formal education (Myyry, Juujärvi, & Pesso, 2013).

Causes and Consequences of Moral Development

LO 12.8   What are some important causes and effects in the development of moral reasoning?

The most obvious reason for the general correlations between Kohlberg's stages and chronological age is cognitive development. Specifically, it appears that children must have a firm grasp of concrete operational thinking before they can develop or use conventional moral reasoning. Likewise, formal operational thinking appears to be necessary for advancement to the postconventional level.

To be more specific, Kohlberg and many other theorists suggest that the decline of egocentrism that occurs as an individual moves through Piaget's concrete and formal operational stages is the cognitive-developmental variable that matters most in moral reasoning. The idea is that the greater a child's or adolescent's ability to look at a situation from another person's perspective, the more advanced she is likely to be in moral reasoning. Psychologists use the term **role-taking** to refer to this ability (Selman, 1980). Research has provided strong support for the hypothesized link between role-taking and moral development (Kuhn, Kohlberg, Languer, & Haan, 1977; Walker, 1980).

Nevertheless, cognitive development isn't enough. Kohlberg thought that the development of moral reasoning also required support from the social environment. Specifically, he claimed that in order to foster mature moral reasoning, a child's or teenager's social environment must provide him with opportunities for meaningful, reciprocal dialogue about moral issues.

Longitudinal research relating parenting styles and family climate to levels of moral reasoning suggests that Kohlberg was right (Pratt, Arnold, & Pratt, 1999). Parents' ability to identify, understand, and respond to children's and adolescents' less mature forms of moral reasoning seems to be particularly important to the development of moral reasoning. This ability is important because people of all ages have difficulty understanding and remembering moral arguments that are at a more advanced level than their own (Narvaez, 1998). Thus, a parent who can express her own moral views in words that reflect her child's level of understanding is more likely to be able to influence the child's moral development.

As an individual's capacity for moral reasoning grows, so does her ability to think logically about issues in other domains. For example, the complexity of an individual's political reasoning is very similar to the complexity of her moral reasoning (Raaijmakers, Verbogt, & Vollebergh, 1998). Further, attitudes toward the acceptability of violence also vary with levels of moral reasoning. Individuals at lower levels are more tolerant of violence (Sotelo & Sangrador, 1999).

Perhaps most importantly, teenagers' level of moral reasoning appears to be positively correlated with prosocial behavior and negatively related to antisocial behavior (Ma, 2012; Schonert-Reichl, 1999). In other words, the highest levels of prosocial behavior are found among teens at the highest levels of moral reasoning (compared to their peers). Alternatively, the highest levels of antisocial behavior are found among adolescents at the lowest levels of moral reasoning.

Criticisms of Kohlberg's Theory

LO 12.9   How has Kohlberg's theory been criticized?

role-taking the ability to look at a situation from another person's perspective

Criticisms of Kohlberg's theory have come from theorists representing different perspectives.

CULTURE AND MORAL REASONING Cross-cultural research provides strong support for the universality of Kohlberg's stage sequence (Snarey, 1985, 1995). Nevertheless, cross-cultural researchers have argued that his approach is too narrow to be considered truly universal. These critics point out that many aspects of moral reasoning found in non-Western cultures do not fit in well with Kohlberg's approach (Branco, 2012; Eckensberger & Zimba, 1997). The root of the problem, they say, is that Kohlberg's theory is strongly tied to the idea that justice is an overriding moral principle. To be sure, say critics, justice is an important moral concept throughout the world, and thus it isn't surprising that Kohlberg's stage sequence has been so strongly supported in cross-cultural research. These critics argue, however, that the notion that justice supersedes all other moral considerations is what distinguishes Western from non-Western cultures. These criticisms would predict, and research has shown, that the responses of individuals in non-Western cultures to Kohlberg's classic dilemmas often include ideas that are not found in his scoring system (Baek, 2002).

For example, in many cultures, respect for one's elders is an important moral principle that often overrides other concerns (Eckensberger & Zimba, 1997). Thus, if researchers alter the Heinz dilemma such that the sick woman is Heinz's mother rather than his wife, Western and non-Western research participants are likely to respond quite differently. Such differences are difficult to explain from the justice-based, stage-oriented perspective of Kohlberg's theory. Advocates for the theory have argued that respect for elders as the basis of moral reasoning represents Kohlberg's conventional level. Critics, by contrast, say that this classification underestimates the true moral reasoning level of individuals from non-Western cultures.

MORAL REASONING AND EMOTIONS Researchers studying the link between moral emotions and moral reasoning have also criticized the narrowness of Kohlberg's justice-based approach (Keller, 2012). Psychologist Nancy Eisenberg, for example, suggests that *empathy*, the ability to identify with others' emotions, is both a cause and a consequence of moral development (Eisenberg, 2000; Eisenberg, Eggum, & Edwards, 2010). Similarly, Eisenberg suggests that a complete explanation of moral development should include age-related and individual variations in the ability to regulate emotions (such as anger) that can motivate antisocial behavior.

Likewise, Carol Gilligan claims that an ethic based on caring for others and on maintaining social relationships may be as important to moral reasoning as are ideas about justice. Gilligan's theory argues that there are at least two distinct "moral orientations": justice and care (Gilligan, 1982; Gilligan & Wiggins, 1987). Each has its own central injunction—not to treat others unfairly (justice) and not to turn away from someone in need (caring). Research suggests that adolescents do exhibit a moral orientation based on care and that care-based reasoning about hypothetical moral dilemmas is related to reasoning about real-life dilemmas (Skoe et al., 1999). In response, Kohlberg acknowledged in his later writings that his theory deals specifically with development of reasoning about justice and does not claim to be a comprehensive account of moral development (Kohlberg, Levine, & Hewer, 1983). Thus, some developmentalists view Gilligan's ideas about moral development as an expansion of Kohlberg's theory rather than a rejection of it (Jorgensen, 2006).

Possible sex differences in moral reasoning are another focus of Gilligan's theory. According to Gilligan, boys and girls learn both justice and care orientations, but girls are more likely to operate from the care orientation and boys from a justice orientation. Because of these differences, girls and boys tend to perceive moral dilemmas quite differently.

Given the emerging evidence on sex differences in styles of interaction and in friendship patterns, Gilligan's hypothesis makes some sense. Perhaps girls, focused more on intimacy in their relationships, judge moral dilemmas by different criteria. But, in fact, research on moral dilemmas has not consistently shown that boys are more likely to use justice reasoning or that girls to use care reasoning. Several studies of adults do show such a pattern (e.g., Wark & Krebs, 1996). However, studies of children and teenagers generally have not (e.g., Jadack, Hyde, Moore, & Keller, 1995).

MORAL REASONING AND BEHAVIOR Finally, critics have questioned the degree to which moral reasoning predicts moral behavior (Krebs & Denton, 2006). Researchers have found a correlation, but the relationship is far from perfect. To explain inconsistencies between reasoning and behavior, learning theorists suggest that moral reasoning is situational rather than developmental (van IJzendoorn, Bakermans-Kranenburg, Pannebakker, & Out, 2010). They point to a variety of studies to support this assertion.

First, neither adolescents nor adults reason at the same level in response to every hypothetical dilemma (Rique & Camino, 1997). An individual research participant might reason at the conventional level in response to one dilemma and at the postconventional level with respect to another. Second, the types of characters in moral dilemmas strongly influence research participants' responses, especially when the participants are adolescents. For example, hypothetical dilemmas involving celebrities as characters elicit much lower levels of moral reasoning from teenagers than those involving fictional characters such as Heinz (Einerson, 1998).

In addition, research participants show disparities in levels of moral reasoning invoked in response to hypothetical dilemmas and real-life moral issues. For example, Israeli Jewish, Israeli Bedouin, and Palestinian youths living in Israel demonstrate different levels of moral reasoning when responding to hypothetical stories such as the Heinz dilemma than they exhibit in discussing the moral dimensions of the long-standing conflicts among their ethnic groups (Elbedour, Baker, & Charlesworth, 1997). In addition, situational variables such as perceived anonymity strongly influence decisions about moral behavior (Zhong, Bohns, & Gino, 2010). Thus, for decisions about actual moral behavior—as learning theorists predict—contextual factors may be more important variables than the level of moral reasoning exhibited in response to hypothetical dilemmas.

Moral Development and Antisocial Behavior

LO 12.10 What are the moral reasoning abilities and other characteristics of delinquents?

The consistent finding of low levels of moral reasoning among adolescents who engage in serious forms of antisocial behavior has been of particular interest to developmentalists (e.g., Ashkar & Kenny, 2007; Brugman, 2010; Ma, 2003, 2012). Likewise, teens who are aggressive typically lack empathy and are especially vulnerable to situational factors that contribute to poor moral decision making. These factors are prominent in research that has examined why some adolescents engage in **cyberbullying**, a form of aggression in which electronic communications are used to intentionally inflict harm on others (Ang & Goh, 2010). In fact, two-thirds of cyberbullies exhibit aggressive behavior in other contexts as well (Twyman, Saylor, Taylor, & Comeaux, 2010). Because they lack empathy, cyberbullies typically have little sensitivity to the speed with which electronic communications of an aggressive nature, such as digitally altered or embarrassing photos, can spread throughout a peer context such as a school or neighborhood (Renati, Berrone, & Zanetti, 2012; Smith & Slonje, 2010). They may even regard the spreading of such information as a measure of cyberbullying success and display little concern about how such experiences affect their victims. Being able to act aggressively with relative degrees of anonymity and in a way that distances the perpetrator from the victim's immediate responses may also contribute to cyberbullying.

Delinquency is distinguished from other forms of antisocial behavior, such as cyberbullying, on the basis of actual law-breaking. Thus, the term **delinquency** applies specifically to adolescent behavior that violates the law. Serious forms of delinquency, such as rape and murder, have increased dramatically in the United States in recent years. Nevertheless, there is a distinction between teens whose delinquent acts are isolated incidents and those for whom delinquency is one feature of a pattern that includes other antisocial behaviors such as cyberbullying.

In Chapter 10 you learned that school-aged children who display a consistent pattern of antisocial behavior may be diagnosed with *conduct disorder* (American Psychiatric Association, 2013). Teens who exhibit such patterns may be diagnosed with the disorder as well. Children and adolescents with conduct disorder appear to be behind their peers in moral reasoning because of deficits in role-taking skills (Barnett & Mann, 2013). For example, researchers have found that teenagers who can look at actions they are contemplating from their parents' perspective are less likely to engage in antisocial behavior than adolescents who cannot do so (Wyatt & Carlo, 2002). Most youths with conduct disorder also seem to be unable to look at their offenses or to assess hypothetical offenses from the victim's perspective. Thus, programs aimed at helping youths with conduct disorder develop more mature levels of moral reasoning usually focus on heightening their awareness of the victim's point of view. However, few such

cyberbullying a form of aggression in which electronic communications are used to intentionally inflict harm on others

delinquency antisocial behavior that includes law-breaking

programs have been successful (Armstrong, 2003; Barnett & Mann, 2013). Consequently, psychologists believe that there is far more to delinquency than just a lack of role-taking and moral reasoning skills.

One important factor in conduct disorder is the age at which a child or teenager's antisocial behavior begins (American Psychiatric Association, 2013). The symptoms of individuals with *childhood-onset conduct disorder*, those whose pattern of antisocial behavior appears before puberty, are more serious and are more likely to persist into adulthood than those of individuals whose problems began after puberty. The antisocial behaviors of teens with *adolescent-onset conduct disorder* are typically milder and more transitory, apparently more a reflection of peer-group processes or a testing of the limits of authority than a deeply ingrained behavior problem.

The developmental pathway for childhood-onset conduct disorder seems to be directed by factors inside the child, such as temperament and personality. In early life, these children tend to be hyperactive, throw tantrums, and defy parents; they may also develop insecure attachments (Greenberg, Speltz, & DeKlyen, 1993; Klein et al., 2012). Once the defiance appears, if the parents are not successful at controlling the child, his behavior worsens. He may begin to display overt aggression toward others, who then reject him, which aggravates the problem. The seriously aggressive child is pushed in the direction of other children with similar problems, who then become the child's only supportive peer group (Powers & Bierman, 2013; Shaw, Kennan, & Vondra, 1994).

By adolescence, youngsters with childhood-onset conduct disorder may exhibit serious disturbances in thinking (Aleixo & Norris, 2000; Savina, 2009). Most have friends drawn almost exclusively from among other antisocial teens (Lansford et al., 2009). Teens with childhood-onset conduct disorder are also highly likely to display a cluster of other problem behaviors, including drug and alcohol use, truancy or dropping out of school, and early and risky sexual behavior, including having multiple sexual partners (Dishion, French, & Patterson, 1995; Mason & Spoth, 2012) (see *No Easy Answers*).

Adolescents who commit crimes are less advanced than their peers in moral reasoning because they lack the ability to look at situations from others' points of view.

NO EASY ANSWERS

Interventions for Aggressive Teens

Unfortunately, many teens do not feel safe at school (NCES, 2007). Most adolescents' fears involve being targeted by an aggressive peer. About 7% of high school students report having been threatened with a weapon by another student at school, and 33% report having been in a physical fight within the last year (Eaton et al., 2013). Thus, school officials have turned to psychologists for help in designing programs to change the behavior of violent teens.

A number of psychologists have contributed to the development and evaluation of a promising program called the Fast Track Project, which involves several hundred aggressive elementary school children in four different U.S. cities (Conduct Problems Research Group, 2004). The children are divided into experimental and control groups. In special class sessions, children in the experimental group learn how to recognize others' emotions. They also learn strategies for controlling their own feelings, managing aggressive impulses, and resolving conflicts with peers.

Teachers in the program use a series of signals to help children maintain control. For example, a red card or a picture of a red traffic light might be used to indicate unacceptable behavior. A yellow card would mean something like "Calm down. You're about to lose control." Parenting classes and support groups help parents learn effective ways of teaching children acceptable behavior, rather than just punishing unacceptable behavior. In addition, parents are encouraged to maintain communication with their children's teachers. These strategies decrease the frequency of aggressive behavior among participants and enable them to manage their emotions more effectively and to get along better with their peers (Conduct Problems Research Group, 2004).

Clearly, such interventions require a considerable commitment of time and resources. Furthermore, they aren't effective for every teen. However, they are the best options developmentalists have to offer at this point. When

balanced against the suffering of the half million or so victims of youth violence each year in the United States or against the personal consequences of violent behavior for the young perpetrators of these crimes, the costs don't seem quite so extreme.

YOU DECIDE

Decide which of these two statements you most agree with and think about how you would defend your position:

1. *When adolescents behave aggressively, they should be referred to programs such as the Fast Track Project rather than punished.*

2. *Programs such as the Fast Track Project should not take the place of punishment; both punishment and emotional management skills are important in helping violent teenagers learn to behave less aggressively.*

For young people whose pattern of antisocial behavior appears first in adolescence, the pathway is different. They, too, have friends who frequently exhibit antisocial behavior. However, associating with such peers worsens the behavior of teens whose antisocial behavior did not appear until after puberty, while the behavior of those with childhood-onset conduct disorder remains essentially the same, whether they have antisocial friends or are "loners" (Vitaro, Tremblay, Kerr, Pagani, & Bukowski, 1997). Moreover, the antisocial behavior patterns of teens with adolescent-onset conduct disorder often change as their relationships change (Laird, Pettit, Dodge, & Bates, 1999). Consequently, peer influence seems to be the most important factor in the development of adolescent-onset conduct disorder.

Apart from peer influence, several personal factors contribute to adolescent-onset conduct disorder. Personality is one important factor. Teens who are low in the Big Five trait of agreeableness, low in self-efficacy for emotional regulation, and high in neuroticism are more likely to exhibit antisocial behavior than peers with different trait profiles (Caprara, Alessandri, Di Giunta, Panerai, & Eisenberg, 2010; Savina, 2009). *Narcissism*, the tendency to exaggerate one's importance, is also associated with conduct disorder (Fossati, Borroni, Eisenberg, & Maffei, 2010; Muris, Meesters, & Timmermans, 2013).

Social variables contribute to conduct disorder as well. Most teens with the disorder have parents who do not monitor them sufficiently. At the same time, their individual friendships are not very supportive or intimate, and they are drawn to peer groups that include some teens who are experimenting with drugs or mild law-breaking (Lansord et al., 2009). However, when parents do provide good monitoring and emotional support, their adolescent child is unlikely to get involved in delinquent acts or drug use, even if she hangs around with a tough crowd or has a close friend who engages in such behavior (Brown & Huang, 1995; Mounts & Steinberg, 1995).

test yourself before going on ✅ Study and Review in MyPsychLab

Answers to these questions can be found in the back of the book.

1. List the factors that influence progression through Kohlberg's stages.
   (a) _____
   (b) _____
   (c) _____
   (d) _____

2. A person's ability to look at a situation from another's perspective is called _____.

3. Learning theorists argue that moral decision making is more influenced by _____ factors than by stages of moral reasoning.

4. Conduct disorders that emerge during (childhood/adolescence) are generally more serious than those that develop during (childhood/adolescence).

CRITICAL THINKING

5. How might Kohlberg's views and those of his critics be integrated to explain variations in moral behavior among adolescents?

Social Relationships

Fifteen-year-old Sheronnah's mother told her long ago that she would not be able to go out on a date until she was 16. Recently, however, a boy at school has begun to pursue Sheronnah, and she has spent untold hours debating the issue with her mother. However, her mother has refused to relent and, as a result, Sheronnah is giving her mother the "silent treatment." Sheronnah's predicament illustrates the growing importance of peer relationships in adolescence

Relationships with Parents

LO 12.11 **What are the features of adolescents' relationships with their parents?**

Teenagers have two, apparently contradictory, tasks in their relationships with their parents: to establish autonomy from them and to maintain a sense of relatedness with them. As a result, the frequency of parent-child conflicts increases. This trend has been documented by a number of researchers (e.g., Flannery, Montemayor, & Eberly, 1994; Laursen, 1995). In the great majority of families, these conflicts center around everyday issues such as chores or personal rights—for example, whether the adolescent should be allowed to wear a bizarre hairstyle or whether and when the teen should be required to do chores. Teenagers and their parents also often disagree about the age at which certain privileges—such as dating—ought to be granted and about the amount of parental supervision teenagers need (Cunningham, Swanson, Spencer, & Dupree, 2003; Laird, Marrero, Melching, & Kuhn, 2013).

Despite these conflicts, teenagers' underlying emotional attachment to their parents remains strong on average. Virtually all the researchers who have explored this question find that a teenager's sense of well-being or happiness is more strongly correlated with the quality of her attachment to her parents than with the quality of her relationships with peers (e.g., Nichikawa, Hägglöf, & Sundbom, 2010; Raja, McGee, & Stanton, 1992). Moreover, research findings regarding the centrality of parent–teen relationships have been consistent across a variety of cultures (Claes, 1998; Okamoto & Uechi, 1999).

While it is true that the physical changes of puberty are often followed by an increase in the number of conflicts, it is a myth that conflict is the main feature of the parent–adolescent relationship.

Research in several countries has also found that teens who remain closely attached to their parents have less difficulty resolving conflicts with them (García-Ruiz et al., 2013). They are also the more likely to be academically successful and to enjoy good peer relations than peers who are less securely attached (Mayseless & Scharf, 2007; Turnage, 2004; Weimer, Kerns, & Oldenburg, 2004; Zimmermann, 2004). They are also less likely to engage in antisocial behavior (Ma, Shek, Cheung, & Oi Bun Lam, 2000). Further, the quality of attachment in early adolescence predicts drug use in later adolescence and early adulthood (Brook, Whiteman, Finch, & Cohen, 2000). Teens who are close to their parents are less likely to use drugs than peers whose bonds with parents are weaker. Thus, even while teenagers are becoming more autonomous, they need their parents to provide a psychological safe base.

Friendships

LO 12.12 What are the characteristics of adolescents' friendships?

Despite the importance of family relationships to adolescents, it is clear that peer relationships become far more significant in adolescence than they have been at any earlier period. For many adolescents, electronic communications platforms of various types serve as hubs around which their social networks revolve. Surveys indicate that 69% of 11- to 14-year-olds and 85% of 15- to 18-year-olds have their own cell phones (Rideout, Foehr, & Roberts, 2010). Teens in both age groups spend an average of about 2 hours a day talking with and texting peers on their cell phones. They devote an additional 45 minutes or so each day to communicating with friends via instant messaging and social networking websites. Moreover, many teenagers have one group of friends with whom they communicate by phone, another with whom they exchange online instant messages and e-mail, and yet another with which they associate through social networking (Foehr, 2006). As a result, teenagers have a wider range of acquaintances than their parents did in adolescence. However, they do not necessarily have more close friends.

Cross-sectional studies suggest children's belief in the importance of popularity and peer acceptance strengthens slowly over the elementary school years and peaks during early adolescence (LaFontana & Cillessen, 2010). During these years—age 12 to 15 or so—teens place more emphasis on popularity and peer acceptance than on any other dimension of peer relations. As adolescents get older, the quality of peer relationships becomes more important to them than popularity. Consequently, as they approach adulthood, their friendships become increasingly intimate, in the sense that adolescent friends share more and more of their inner feelings and secrets and are more knowledgeable about each other's feelings. Loyalty and faithfulness become more valued characteristics of friendship. However, the ability to display intimacy, loyalty, and faithfulness in the context of a friendship doesn't come automatically with age. In fact, teens vary considerably in these interpersonal skills. The variation may be the result of individual differences in temperament and personality or of teens' experiences with family relationships (Updegraff & Obeidallah, 1999).

Adolescent friendships are also more stable than those of younger children (Bowker, 2004). In one longitudinal study, researchers found that only about 20% of friendships among fourth-graders lasted as long as a year, whereas about 40% of friendships formed by these same youngsters when they were tenth-graders were long-lasting (Cairns & Cairns, 1994). Friendship stability probably increases in adolescence because older teens work harder than younger teens and elementary school children at maintaining positive relationships with friends through negotiation of conflicts (Nagamine, 1999).

Adolescents tend to choose friends who share their social status (Dijkstra, Cillessen, & Borch, 2013). That is, popular teens are most likely to be friends with others who are popular, and rejected teens are likely to associate with others who have been rejected. In addition, teens often choose friends who are committed to the same activities they are. For example, many teens, especially boys, report that peer companionship is their primary motive for playing computer and video games (Chou & Tsai, 2007; Colwell & Kato, 2005). Some studies suggest that shared video game–playing experiences promote the development of a masculine gender role among male teens (Sanford & Madill, 2006). Some developmentalists also argue that playing these games in group settings helps male adolescents learn to channel aggressive and competitive impulses into socially acceptable ways of expressing them (Jansz & Martens, 2005). ◉ **Watch** the **Video** *Intimacy in Adolescent Friendships* in **MyPsychLab**.

Finally, adolescents' reasons for ending friendships reflect the influence of individual differences in rate of development of social skills. For example, a change in identity status from a less mature to a more mature level often leads to acquisition of new friends (Akers, Jones, & Coyl, 1998). Likewise, girls seem to prefer friendships with other girls whose romantic status is the same as their own—that is, girls who have boyfriends prefer female friends who also have boyfriends. In fact, a girl who gets a boyfriend is likely to spend less time with female peers and to end long-standing friendships with girls who haven't yet acquired a romantic partner (Benenson & Benarroch, 1998; Zimmer-Gembeck, 1999). For boys, differences in athletic achievements can lead to the end of previously important friendships. Both boys and girls tend to end relationships with peers who show a propensity for socially victimizing others by means such as spreading rumors (Sijtsema, Rambaran, & Ojanen, 2013).

Peer Groups

LO 12.13 How do peer groups change over the teen years?

Like friendships, peer groups become relatively stable in adolescence. Although peer influences are often thought of as primarily negative in nature, social networks have both positive and negative influences on teenagers' development (Eccles & Roeser, 2011; Ulmer, Desmond, Jang, & Johnson, 2012). For one thing, adolescents typically choose to associate with a group that shares their values, attitudes, behaviors, and identity status (Berger & Rodkin, 2012; Mackey & La Greca, 2007). When the values that drive peer associations are those that lead to adaptive developmental outcomes, such as graduating from high school, peers become an important source of reinforcement that keeps teens on developmentally positive pathways. Moreover, researchers have found that if the discrepancy between their own ideas and those of their friends becomes too great, teens are more likely to switch to a more compatible group of friends than to be persuaded to adopt the first group's values or behaviors (Verkooijen, de Vries, & Nielsen, 2007).

Peer-group structures change over the years of adolescence. The classic, widely quoted early study is that of Dunphy (1963) on the formation, dissolution, and interaction of teenaged groups in a high school in Sydney, Australia, between 1958 and 1960. Dunphy identified two important subvarieties of groups. The first type, which he called a **clique**, is made up of four to six young people who appear to be strongly attached to one another. Cliques have strong cohesiveness and high levels of intimate sharing. However, most cliques also feature a considerable amount of within-group aggression aimed at maintaining the groups' status hierarchies (Closson, 2010). Typically, aggressive acts within cliques are perpetrated by dominant members against lower-status members (Closson, 2010). Furthermore, research suggests that cliques that nonmembers perceive as highly popular tolerate higher levels of within-group aggression than less popular cliques do. Thus, even though teens may enhance their popularity by associating with popular cliques, being accepted by these groups may require adolescents to endure being targeted by the groups' high-status members. ◉ **Watch** the **Video** *Adolescent Cliques* in **MyPsychLab**.

clique four to six young people who appear to be strongly attached to one another

In the early years of adolescence, cliques are almost entirely same-sex groups—a holdover from the preadolescent pattern. Gradually, however, the cliques combine into larger sets that Dunphy called **crowds**, which include both males and females. Finally, the crowd breaks down again into mixed-gender cliques and then into loose associations of couples. In Dunphy's study, the period during which adolescents socialized in crowds was roughly between 13 and 15—the very years when they display the greatest conformity to peer pressure.

More recent researchers on adolescence have changed Dunphy's labels somewhat (Brown, 1990; Brown, Mory, & Kinney, 1994). They use the word *crowd* to refer to the *reputation-based group* with which a young person is identified, either by choice or by peer designation. In U.S. schools, these groups have labels such as "jocks," "brains," "nerds," "dweebs," "punks," "druggies," "toughs," "normals," "populars," "preppies," and "loners." Studies in American secondary schools make it clear that teenagers can readily identify each of the major crowds in their school and have quite stereotypical—even caricatured—descriptions of them (e.g., "The partyers goof off a lot more than the jocks do, but they don't come to school stoned like the burnouts do") (Brown et al., 1994, p. 133). Each of these descriptions serves as what Brown calls an *identity prototype*. Labeling others and oneself as belonging to one or more of these groups helps to create or reinforce the adolescent's own identity (Brown et al., 1994). Such labeling also helps the adolescent identify potential friends or foes.

Through the years of secondary education, the social system of crowds becomes increasingly differentiated, with more and more distinct groups. For example, in one midwestern school system, researchers found that junior high students labeled only two major crowds: one small high-status group, called "trendies" in this school, and the great mass of lower-status students, called "dweebs" (Kinney, 1993). A few years later, the same students named five distinct crowds: three with comparatively high social status and two low-status groups ("grits" and "punkers"). By late high school, these students identified seven or eight crowds, but the crowds now appeared to be less significant in the social organization of the peer group. These observations support other research that finds that mutual friendships and dating pairs are more central to social interactions in later adolescence than are cliques or crowds (Urberg, Degirmencioglu, Tolson, & Halliday-Scher, 1995).

In the early teen years, same-sex peer groups predominate.

Romantic Relationships

LO 12.14 How does interest in romantic relationships emerge among heterosexual and homosexual teens?

Heterosexual and homosexual teens follow somewhat different pathways. For both, the ups and downs that are associated with early romances are an important theme of development during adolescence.

HETEROSEXUAL TEENS Most teens display a gradual progression from same-sex friendships to heterosexual relationships. The change happens gradually, but it seems to proceed at a somewhat more rapid pace in girls than in boys. At the beginning of adolescence, teens are still fairly rigid about their preferences for same-sex friends (Bukowski, Sippola, & Hoza, 1999). Over the next year or two, they become more open to opposite-sex friendships (Harton & Latane, 1997; Kuttler, LaGreca, & Prinstein, 1999). The skills they gain in relating to opposite-sex peers in such friendships and in mixed-gender groups as well as interactions with opposite-sex parents prepare them for romantic relationships which begin to become common among teens at around age 15 or so (Bucx, & Seiffge-Krenke, 2010; Feiring, 1999; Seiffge-Krenke & Connolly, 2010). Thus, although adults often assume that sexual desires are the basis of emergent romantic relationships, it appears that social factors are just as important (Rauer, Pettit, Lansford, Bates, & Dodge, 2013).

crowd a combination of cliques, which includes both males and females

Interpretations of research on couple formation must take into account the general finding that the development of romantic relationships in adolescence varies across cultures (Seiffge-Krenke & Connolly, 2010). In one study that compared Chinese and Canadian 16- and 17-year-olds, researchers found that far fewer Chinese than Canadian teens were involved in or desired to be involved in romantic relationships (Li, Connolly, Jiang, Pepler, & Craig, 2010). Analyses of these findings suggested that the underlying variable was cross-cultural variation in the centrality of peer and parental relationships. Chinese teens, on average, felt emotionally closest to their parents, while their Canadian counterparts reported greater emotional closeness to friends. However, among Chinese teens who reported being emotionally closer to friends than to parents, romantic relationships were more frequent than among peers who felt closer to their parents. Thus, these findings suggest that, across cultures, peer associations in early adolescence are foundational to the development of romantic relationships later in the teen years.

By 12 or 13, most adolescents have a basic conception of what it means to be "in love," and the sense of being in love is an important factor in adolescent dating patterns (Montgomery & Sorell, 1998). Thus, many teenagers prefer to date those with whom they believe they are in love, and they view falling out of love as a reason for ending a dating relationship. However, other teens form romantic attachments that are based on a desire for companionship rather than romantic love (Bucx & Seiffge-Krenke, 2010). In addition, for girls (but not for boys), romantic relationships are seen as a context for self-disclosure. Put another way, girls seem to want more psychological intimacy from these early relationships than their partners do (Feiring, 1999).

Early dating and early sexual activity are more common among the poor of every ethnic group and among those who experience relatively early puberty. Religious teachings and individual attitudes about the appropriate age for dating and sexual behavior also make a difference, as does family structure. Girls with parents who are divorced or remarried, for example, report earlier dating and higher levels of sexual experience than do girls from intact families, and those with a strong religious identity report later dating and lower levels of sexuality (Bingham, Miller, & Adams, 1990; Ivanova, Mills, & Veenstra, 2011; Miller & Moore, 1990). But for every group, these are years of experimentation with romantic relationships. 👁 **Watch** the **Video** *Dating in Adolescence* in **MyPsychLab**.

HOMOSEXUAL TEENS Romantic relationships emerge somewhat differently in the lives of homosexual teens than in those of heterosexual teens. Researchers have found that homosexual teenagers are more comfortable about revealing their sexual orientation to their parents and to their peers than was true in past cohorts (Riley, 2010). Nevertheless, a comprehensive review of research on the coming-out process found that it varies across ethnic groups (Heatherington & Lavner, 2008). White teens appear to be most comfortable with and most likely to reveal their sexual orientations to parents and peers, while Asian Americans are least comfortable and least likely to disclose. Hispanic and African American adolescents fall between these two groups. Fear of disclosure is associated with concerns about parents' and peers' negative responses and, especially among Asian teens, a desire to respect traditional cultural values.

Like their heterosexual peers, homosexual teenagers become aware of same-sex attraction at around age 11 or 12 (Rosario, Scrimshaw, & Hunter, 2004). In contrast to heterosexual teens, boys notice and act on same-sex attraction at somewhat earlier ages than girls do (Grov, Bimbi, Nanin, & Parsons, 2006). However, girls who ultimately commit to a homosexual orientation express more certainty about their sexual identity than boys do (Rosario, Scrimshaw, Hunter, & Braun, 2006).

Many boys and girls, however, experience some degree of attraction to both sexes prior to self-identifying as gay or lesbian. Thus, many homosexual teens go through a period of sexual discovery that begins with experimentation with heterosexual relationships. Shortly thereafter, these teenagers begin to experiment with same-sex relationships. By age 15 or so, most have classified themselves as primarily heterosexual or committed to a gay, lesbian, or bisexual orientation (Rosario et al., 2004). Many of those who are gay, lesbian, or bisexual participate in clubs and extracurricular activities that are designed to help sexual minority youth form social connections. In the company of these like-minded peers, gay, lesbian, and bisexual teens meet potential romantic partners and find important sources of social support (Rosario et al., 2004). 👁 **Watch** the **Video** *Being Gay in High School* in **MyPsychLab**.

test yourself before going on ✓ Study and Review in MyPsychLab

Answers to these questions can be found in the back of the book.

1. Most parent–teen conflicts involve _____ issues.
2. Today's teens have more _____ than their parents did but not necessarily more close friends.
3. Status hierarchies within cliques are maintained through within-group _____.
4. Both heterosexual and homosexual adolescents become aware of sexual attraction at around the age of _____.

CRITICAL THINKING

5. Think back to your own high school years and draw a diagram or map to describe the organization of crowds and cliques. Were those crowds or cliques more or less important in the last few years of high school than they had been earlier? In what ways did the formation of romantic relationships disrupt or reinforce crowds and cliques?

SUMMARY

Theories of Social and Personality Development (pp. 296–299)

LO 12.1   What happens during Erikson's identity-versus-role-confusion stage?

- According to Freud, adolescents are in the genital stage, a period during which sexual maturity is reached. Erikson viewed adolescence as a period when a person faces a crisis of identity versus role confusion, out of which the teenager must develop a sense of who he is and where he belongs in his culture.

LO 12.2   How does Marcia explain identity development?

- Building on Erikson's notion of an adolescent identity crisis, Marcia identified four identity statuses: identity achievement, moratorium, foreclosure, and identity diffusion. Research suggests that the process of identity formation may take place somewhat later than either Erikson or Marcia believed. Moreover, it continues throughout the lifespan.

Self-Concept (pp. 299–304)

LO 12.3   In what way does self-understanding in adolescence differ from that in childhood?

- Self-definitions become increasingly abstract at adolescence, with more emphasis on enduring internal qualities and ideology.

LO 12.4   How does self-esteem change across the teenage years?

- Self-esteem drops somewhat at the beginning of adolescence and then rises steadily throughout the teenaged years.

LO 12.5   What are the gender role concepts of adolescents?

- Teenagers increasingly define themselves in terms that include both masculine and feminine traits. When high levels of both masculinity and femininity are present, the individual is described as androgynous. Androgyny is associated with higher self-esteem in both male and female adolescents.

LO 12.6   How do minority, biracial, and immigrant teens develop a sense of ethnic identity?

- Young people in clearly identifiable minority groups, biracial teens, and teens in immigrant families have the additional task in adolescence of forming an ethnic identity. Phinney proposed a series of ethnic identity stages that are similar to those in Marcia's model of general identity development. Phinney's stages are unexamined ethnic identity, ethnic identity search, and ethnic identity achievement. Biracial teens may be challenged to prove their ethnic authenticity by one parent's group. For immigrant teens, the process of identity development includes reconciling differences in their own and their parents' views of the cultural values of their new and former homes.

Moral Development (pp. 304–312)

LO 12.7   What are the features of moral reasoning at each of Kohlberg's stages?

- Kohlberg proposed six stages of moral reasoning, organized into three levels. Preconventional moral reasoning includes reliance on external authority: What is punished is bad, and what feels good is good. Conventional morality is based on rules and norms provided by outside groups, such as the family, church, or society. Postconventional morality is based on self-chosen principles. Research evidence suggests that these levels and stages are loosely correlated with age, develop in a specified order, and appear in this same sequence in all cultures studied so far.

LO 12.8   What are some important causes and effects in the development of moral reasoning?

- The acquisition of cognitive role-taking skills is important to moral development, but the social environment is important as well. Specifically, to foster moral reasoning, adults must provide children with opportunities for discussion of moral issues. Moral reasoning and moral behavior are correlated, though the relationship is far from perfect.

LO 12.9   How has Kohlberg's theory been criticized?

- Kohlberg's theory has been criticized by theorists who place more emphasis on learning moral behavior and others who believe that moral reasoning may be based more on emotional factors than on ideas about justice and fairness.

LO 12.10   What are the moral reasoning abilities and other characteristics of delinquents?

- Delinquent teens are usually found to be far behind their peers in both role-taking and moral reasoning. However, other factors, such as parenting style, may be equally important in delinquency.

Social Relationships (pp. 312–317)

LO 12.11   What are the features of adolescents' relationships with their parents?

- Adolescent–parent interactions typically become somewhat more conflicted in early adolescence, an effect possibly linked to the physical changes of puberty. Strong attachments to parents remain so and are predictive of good peer relations.

LO 12.12   What are the characteristics of adolescents' friendships?

- Thanks to electronic communications, teens today have more acquaintances than their parents did. Over the teen years, friendships become increasingly intimate and stable. Adolescents value loyalty, intimacy, and faithfulness in their friends and typically form friendships with peers who share their interests and are their equals with regard to social skill development.

LO 12.13   How do peer groups change over the teen years?

- In the early years of adolescence, cliques are almost entirely same-sex cliques. Between ages 13 and 15, cliques combine into crowds that include both males and females. This is the time when teens are most susceptible to peer influences. Crowds break down into mixed-gender cliques and then into small groups of couples.

LO 12.14   How does interest in romantic relationships emerge among heterosexual and homosexual teens?

- Heterosexual teens gradually move from same-sex peer groups to heterosexual couples. The feeling of being "in love" is important to the formation of couple relationships. Many homosexual teens experiment with heterosexual and homosexual relationships before committing to a gay, lesbian, or bisexual orientation in mid-adolescence.

KEY TERMS

clique (p. 314)
conventional morality (p. 306)
crowd (p. 315)
cyberbullying (p. 310)
delinquency (p. 310)

ethnic identity (p. 302)
foreclosure (p. 297)
gender role identity (p. 301)
identity (p. 296)
identity achievement (p. 297)

identity crisis (p. 297)
identity diffusion (p. 297)
identity versus role confusion (p. 296)
moratorium (p. 297)

postconventional morality (p. 307)
preconventional morality (p. 306)
role-taking (p. 308)

CHAPTER TEST   ✅ Study and Review in MyPsychLab

Answers to all the Chapter Test questions can be found in the back of the book.

1. Marcia's theory of adolescent identity achievement suggests that adolescent identity formation involves _____ and _____.
   a. crisis; commitment
   b. confusion; resolution
   c. extrusion; inclusion
   d. identity; confusion

2. Which of the following did Kohlberg propose as the foundation of moral reasoning?
   a. role reversal
   b. perspective assumptions
   c. role-taking
   d. egocentrism

3. Chris is about to graduate from high school. He has given no thought to whether to attend college or seek full-time employment. When asked what he has planned for his future, he just shrugs his shoulders. Whenever he is asked for an opinion about the current presidential elections, his response is, "I don't really care." According to Marcia, Chris's attitudes demonstrate which identity status?
   a. identity foreclosure
   b. identity achievement
   c. identity diffusion
   d. identity moratorium

4. Which of the following is *not* one of the four basic sex-role types identified by researchers?
   a. incomplete
   b. masculine
   c. androgynous
   d. undifferentiated

5. Which of the following best defines the term *antisocial* as psychologists use it to refer to adolescents' behavior?
   a. having a moral stance that disregards the norms of society
   b. choosing to live away from other people
   c. deciding for oneself what is right and wrong
   d. going against the rules of one's peer group

6. In contrast to other forms of antisocial behavior, delinquency includes _____.
   a. egocentrism
   c. law-breaking
   b. role-taking
   d. bullying

7. The second stage of Phinney's theory of ethnic identity is _____.
   a. an unexamined ethnic identity
   b. a role-oriented ethnic identity
   c. the exploration stage
   d. ethnic identity search

8. Among adolescents, peer group pressures usually involve _____.
   a. positive activities such as school involvement
   b. both positive and negative activities
   c. misconduct such as vandalism or delinquency
   d. behaviors consistent with parents' standards for teen behavior

9. Which of the following might be an advantage of cultures that have clearly identified rites of passage into adulthood?
   a. Teenagers are able to establish a clear transition from childhood to adulthood.
   b. Teenagers are encouraged to make career decisions for themselves.
   c. Teenagers are able to take on careers earlier.
   d. Teenagers can more easily resolve the crisis of identity confusion.

10. If you believe that there are distinct differences in the way that boys and girls perceive moral dilemmas, which theorist would you most likely support?
    a. Nancy Eisenberg
    c. Carol Gilligan
    b. Lawrence Kohlberg
    d. Samuel Elkind

11. Which of the following is likely to be true of social interactions in early adolescence?
    a. Adolescents who don't belong to a clique or a crowd tend to date more frequently.
    b. Mutual friendships and dating pairs become more important than cliques or crowds.
    c. Young teens prefer same-sex friends.
    d. Belonging to a clique of high status becomes more important.

12. Which of the following terms would be applied to someone who is high in both masculinity and femininity?
    a. androgynous
    c. undifferentiated
    b. animistic
    d. transgendered

13. Which of the following explains cultural differences in heterosexual couple formation?
    a. comparing notes with their friends of the same sex
    b. discussions with parents
    c. sex education courses
    d. emotional closeness of parent and peer relationships

14. Which of the following is believed by Kohlberg and others to strongly influence moral reasoning?
    a. a person's stage of cognitive development
    b. situational factors
    c. models who have high moral standards
    d. an ethic of caring

15. In what period does the importance of popularity peak?
    a. middle childhood
    c. middle adolescence
    b. early adolescence
    d. late adolescence

16. Eighteen-year-old Roderick has decided to become an accountant because his father is a CPA and has plans for Roderick to take over his practice at some time in the future. Marcia would describe Roderick's identity status as _____.
    a. achieved
    c. in moratorium
    b. foreclosed
    d. diffused

17. According to James Marcia, the identity status of a person who wants to take a few different courses before deciding on a career path is probably _____.
    a. diffusion
    b. achievement
    c. foreclosure
    d. moratorium

18. Which of the following is *not* true of homosexual teens?
    a. Some who don't disclose their sexual orientations are motivated by a desire to respect traditional cultural values.
    b. Many experience some degree of opposite-sex attraction even if they later identify as homosexual.
    c. Their willingness to come out to parents and peers varies across ethnic groups.
    d. Girls who express a homosexual orientation express less certainty about it than homosexual boys do.

19. Researchers who have studied Marcia's model of identity development have found that identity development _____.
    a. may occur later than he proposed
    b. fluctuates across the teen years
    c. continues throughout the lifespan
    d. all of the above

20. Which of the following statements is true regarding adolescent self-esteem?
    a. White teens in the United States are more likely to experience a steady level of self-esteem as they transition through adolescence.
    b. Teens of all ethnicities in the United States are likely to experience a brief increase in self-esteem as they transition into early adolescence.
    c. Teens of all ethnicities in the United States are likely to experience a drop in self-esteem as they transition from childhood to early adolescence.
    d. Teens in ethnic minorities are likely to experience a drop in self-esteem as they transition from childhood to early adolescence.

21. Theorists such as Nancy Eisenberg focus on moral _____.
    a. behavior
    b. emotions
    c. reasoning
    d. problem solving

22. More recent theorists have elaborated on Erikson's definition to include which of the following?
    a. the addition of morals and values to one's identity
    b. understanding the importance of birth order to understand individual identity
    c. understanding of one's unique characteristics and how they are manifested across ages, situations, and social roles
    d. the application of social roles as they are manifest in one's personality

23. Cyberbullying _____.
    a. is similar to other types of bullying
    b. is usually exhibited by teens who have more concern for their victims' feelings than conventional bullies do
    c. involves acts that are usually known only by the cyberbully and his or her victim
    d. none of the above

24. Compared to teens in other industrialized nations, adolescents in the United States are _____.
    a. less likely to be employed
    b. more likely to prefer studying to other leisure-time activities
    c. more likely to be employed
    d. less likely to be involved in romantic relationships

25. Carol Gilligan argues that there are two distinct moral orientations. What are they?
    a. judgment and nurture
    b. fairness and ethics
    c. justice and care
    d. intimacy and legality

To 👁 **Watch** ✳ **Explore** ◉ **Simulate** ✔ **Study** and **Review** **and experience MyVirtualLife go to MyPsychLab.com**

chapter 13

Physical and Cognitive Development in Early Adulthood

Have you kept up with your high school friends via Facebook or some other social networking platform? If you have, then you are very aware of how divergent developmental pathways become in early adulthood, something you will learn by simulating important life decisions in *MyVirtualLife*. When you were 10 years old, everyone you knew was in school, and the schools they attended were very similar to one another. The same was true when you were 14. Now, however, you're in college, but some of your high school friends

LEARNING OBJECTIVES

PHYSICAL FUNCTIONING

13.1 What is the difference between primary and secondary aging?

13.2 What changes in the brain take place in early adulthood?

13.3 How do other body systems change during early adulthood?

HEALTH AND WELLNESS

13.4 What habits and personal factors are associated with good health?

13.5 What are some of the viral and bacterial STDs that afflict young adults?

13.6 What are the causes and effects of intimate partner abuse?

13.7 Which mental disorders occur most frequently in young adulthood?

13.8 What is the difference between physical and psychological substance dependence?

COGNITIVE CHANGES

13.9 What types of postformal thought have developmentalists proposed?

13.10 How do the concepts of crystallized and fluid intelligence help to explain age-related changes in IQ scores?

POSTSECONDARY EDUCATION

13.11 What are some of the ways in which college attendance affects individual development?

13.12 What is the impact of gender, ethnicity, and disability on the college experience?

have taken their lives in other directions. Some may be parents already, and some may be serving in the military. Don't be surprised if your friends' lives become even more diverse over the next few years. ● **Watch** the **Video** *Early Adulthood: Social Networking* in **MyPsychLab**.

Despite the variations in adult developmental pathways, most developmental scientists agree that it is still useful to divide the adult years into three roughly equal parts: early adulthood, from 20 to 40; middle adulthood, from 40 to about 65; and late adulthood, from 65 until death. This way of dividing adulthood reflects the fact that optimum physical and cognitive functioning, achieved in the 20s and 30s, begins to wane in some noticeable and measurable ways in the 40s and 50s. We will follow this way of dividing the adult years and define early adulthood as the period from age 20 to 40. In this chapter, you will read about the changes that occur during these years, along with a number of variables that are associated with variation from the "typical" pathway.

Physical Functioning

Do you see yourself continuing to play your favorite recreational sport—basketball, skiing, tennis, golf, softball, or flag football—through your 20s and into your 30s? If so, then you should be prepared for the fact that "weekend" athletes suffer more injuries and take longer to heal than their professional counterparts do (Stroud, 2004). Sports-related injuries trend upward in the 20s and 30s because most people reach their physical peak in their late teens or very early 20s and begin declining almost immediately. Of course, factors such as diet and exercise slow down these declines, but many of them are inevitable.

Primary and Secondary Aging

LO 13.1   What is the difference between primary and secondary aging?

Researchers distinguish between two types of aging. The basic, underlying, inevitable aging process is called **primary aging** (sometimes called senescence), by most developmentalists. Gray hair, wrinkles, and changes in visual acuity, for example, are attributable to primary aging.

Secondary aging, in contrast, is the product of environmental influences, health habits, or disease, and it is neither inevitable nor experienced by all adults. Research on age differences in health and death rates reveals the expected pattern. For example, 18- to 40-year-olds rarely die from disease (Murphy, Xu, & Kochanek, 2013). However, researchers have found that age interacts with other variables to influence health, a pattern suggesting the influence of secondary aging. ● **Watch** the **Video** *Early Adulthood: Happiness and Attitude toward Aging* in **MyPsychLab**.

For example, age interacts with social class such that differences among young adults across social class groups are fairly small. However, with increasing age, the differences become much larger. Such social class differences in adult health have been found in all of the industrialized nations of the world, and they occur within ethnic groups in the United States as well as in the overall population (Kelleher, Friel, Gabhainn, & Tay, 2003; Mercado, Havemann, Sami, & Ueda, 2007; Mladovsky et al., 2009; National Center for Health Statistics [NCHS], 2013; Torpy, 2007).

Social class differences in health may be due to group variations in patterns of primary aging. However, most developmentalists believe that they represent secondary aging (Koster et al., 2006). In other words, the health differences result from income-related variations in both social environments and individual behavior. For example, people who live in crime-ridden neighborhoods are unlikely to feel safe enough to go walking, biking, or jogging as their counterparts in neighborhoods with lower crime rates often do. This is the kind of variation that shows up in surveys as a difference in individual exercise rates but is actually attributable to differences across social environments that are related to income. Nevertheless, the effect of

primary aging (senescence) age-related physical changes that have a biological basis and are universally shared and inevitable

secondary aging age-related changes that are due to environmental influences, poor health habits, or disease

TABLE 13.1 Benefits of Lifestyle Changes

Lifestyle Change	Benefits
If overweight, lose just 10% of your body weight.	Reduction in triglyceride levels; decrease in total cholesterol; increase in HDL ("good" cholesterol); significant reduction in blood pressure; decreased risk of diabetes, sleep apnea, and osteoarthritis (Fransen, 2004; Wee, Hamel, Dans, & Phillips, 2004).
Add 20 to 30 grams of fiber to your diet each day.	Improved bowel function; reduced risk of colon cancer and other digestive-system diseases; decrease in total cholesterol; reduced blood pressure; improved insulin function in both diabetics and nondiabetics (Mayo Clinic, 2005).
Engage in moderate physical activity every day (e.g., walk up and down stairs for 15 minutes; spend 30 minutes washing a car).	Reduced feelings of anxiety and sadness; increased bone density; reduced risk of diabetes, heart disease, high blood pressure, and many other life-shortening diseases (Centers for Disease Control and Prevention [CDC], 2007a).
Stop smoking at any age, after any number of years of smoking.	*Immediate:* Improved circulation; reduced blood level of carbon monoxide; stabilization of pulse rate and blood pressure; improved sense of smell and taste; improved lung function and endurance; reduced risk of lung infections such as pneumonia and bronchitis. *Long-term:* Reduced risk of lung cancer (declines substantially with each year of abstinence); decreased risk of other smoking-related illnesses such as emphysema and heart disease; decreased risk of cancer recurrence in those who have been treated for some form of cancer (National Cancer Institute, 2000).
Get recommended annual or 5-year screenings beginning at these ages.	*Women:* (21) Chlamydia, cervical cancer, screenings if sexually active; (35) cholesterol test; (50) mammogram, colorectal exam; (65) vision, hearing tests *Men:* (30) EKG, cholesterol test; (40) PSA test for prostate cancer; (50) colorectal exam; (65) vision, hearing tests

this social difference is seen at the individual level—that is, the less a person exercises, the greater her risk of developing cardiovascular disease and other chronic conditions.

The emotions underlying individuals' perceptions of their social class may be even more important than their actual economic status. Some researchers have found that people who are unhappy with their economic situation are more likely to be sick than those who are relatively satisfied, regardless of income level (Operario, Adler, & Williams, 2004). Thus, as you can see, the link between social class and secondary aging is fairly complex. Research also suggests that, regardless of income level, changes in behavior such as those listed in Table 13.1 may prevent or even reverse the effects of aging.

The Brain and Nervous System

LO 13.2 What changes in the brain take place in early adulthood?

No matter what age or gender an individual is, new synapses are forming, myelination is occurring, and old connections are dying off. (See the *Research Report* on page 324.) Further, there is recent evidence that, contrary to what neurologists have believed for a long time, some parts of the brain produce new neurons to replace those that die, even in the brains of older adults (Gould, Reeves, Graziano, & Gross, 1999; Leuner & Gould, 2010). Interestingly, too, animal research suggests that production of these new neurons is stimulated by an enriched environment, as well as by physical exercise (Cao et al., 2004; Rhodes et al., 2003). Thus, just as is true in childhood and adolescence, in adulthood, a challenging environment probably supports brain development. At some point in development, though, usually in the late teens, developmental processes reach a balance and the brain attains a stable size and weight. Similarly, by early adulthood, most functions have become localized in specific areas of the brain (Gaillard et al., 2000).

Neurologists have found two spurts in brain growth in early adulthood, like those you have read about in earlier chapters. As you may remember from Chapter 11, a major spurt in the growth of the frontal lobes—the area of the brain devoted to logic, planning, and emotional control—begins around age 17. This spurt continues until age 21 or 22 (Crone, Wendelken, Donohue, van Leijenhorst, & Bunge, 2006; Gogtay et al., 2004). Many neuropsychologists

Gender Differences in the Brain

As you should remember from earlier chapters, the brains of males and females differ to some extent at every age. However, sex differences are even more striking in the adult brain. For example, the brain contains two types of tissue: *gray matter* and *white matter*. Gray matter is made up of cell bodies and axon terminals (look back at Figure 3.3 on page 62); white matter contains myelinated axons that connect one neuron to another. Men have a higher proportion of white matter than women do (Gur et al., 1999; Haier, 2007). In addition, the distributions of gray and white matter differ in the brains of men and women. Men have a lower proportion of white matter in the left brain than in the right brain. In contrast, the proportions of gray matter and white matter in the two hemispheres are equal in

women's brains. Such findings have led some neuropsychologists to speculate that men's overall superior spatial perception is associated with sex differences in the distribution of gray and white matter.

However, neuroscientists are discovering that white matter/gray matter differences in men's and women's brains are more subtle than was once believed. For example, when dealing with an emotion-provoking stimulus, women more often than men respond with *reappraisal*, a strategy in which a cognitive interpretation of such a stimulus moderates its effects on a person's emotions (Zuurbier, Nikolova, Ahs, & Hariri, 2013). Neuroimaging studies suggest that this difference may be attributable to the greater number of myelinated neurons that connect the

brain's emotional center, the *amygdala*, to the thinking part of the brain, the cortex. However, there isn't yet enough consistency across studies of this type to allow neuroscientists to draw definitive conclusions about sex differences in brain function. Moreover, these scientists are still a long way from finding direct links between neurological and behavioral sex differences.

CRITICAL ANALYSIS

1. *In what ways might the experiences of men and women contribute to gender differences in the brain?*
2. *How might the research on gender differences in the brain be distorted and misused to justify discrimination against women?*

It's hard to draw a clear line between "early adulthood" and "middle adulthood" because the physical and mental changes are so gradual; even at 30, adults may find that it takes a bit more work to get into or stay in shape than it did at 20.

believe that this spurt is strongly connected to the increases in the capacity for formal operational thinking and other kinds of abstract reasoning that occur in late adolescence.

In addition to this brain growth spurt between 17 and 21, some neuropsychologists hypothesize that another peak in brain development happens in the mid- to late 20s (Fischer & Rose, 1994). They claim that the cognitive skills that emerge in the middle of the early adulthood period seem to depend on changes in the brain. For example, when you take a multiple-choice test, you need to be able to keep yourself from responding too quickly to the options in order to carefully weigh them all. Neuropsychologists suggest that this kind of *response inhibition* may depend on the ability of the frontal lobes of the brain to regulate the **limbic system**, or the emotional part of the brain. Many scientists believe that the capacity to integrate various brain functions in this way does not become fully developed until early adulthood (Spreen et al., 1995).

Still, the brain begins to lose volume in the early adulthood period (Mann et al., 2011; Raz et al., 2006). Moreover, the gradual loss of speed in virtually every aspect of bodily function appears to be the result of very gradual changes at the neuronal level, particularly the loss of dendrites and a slowing of the "firing rate" of nerves (Birren & Fisher, 1995; Earles & Salthouse, 1995; Salthouse, 1993). As you get older, it takes longer to warm up after you have been very cold or to cool off after you have been hot. Your reaction time to sudden events slows; you don't respond quite as quickly to a swerving car, for example.

Other Body Systems

LO 13.3 How do other body systems change during early adulthood?

Young adults perform better than do the middle-aged or old on virtually every physical measure. Compared to older adults, adults in their 20s and 30s have more muscle tissue; maximum bone calcium; more brain mass; better eyesight, hearing, and sense of smell; greater oxygen capacity; and a more efficient immune system. A young adult is stronger, faster, and better able to recover from exercise or to adapt to changing conditions, such as alterations in temperature or light levels.

limbic system the part of the brain that regulates emotional responses

maximum oxygen uptake (VO₂ max) a measure of the body's ability to take in and transport oxygen to various body organs

DECLINES IN PHYSICAL FUNCTIONING There is a gradual decline on almost every measure of physical functioning through the years of adulthood. Table 13.2 summarizes these changes. Most

TABLE 13.2   A Summary of Age Changes in Physical Functioning

Body Function	Age at Which Change Begins to Be Clear or Measurable	Nature of Change
Vision	Mid-40s	Lens of eye thickens and loses accommodative power, resulting in poorer near vision and more sensitivity to glare
Hearing	50 or 60	Loss of ability to hear very high and very low tones
Smell	About 40	Decline in ability to detect and discriminate among different smells
Taste	None	No apparent loss in taste discrimination ability
Muscles	About 50	Loss of muscle tissue, particularly in "fast twitch" fibers used for bursts of strength or speed
Bones	Mid-30s (women)	Loss of calcium in the bones, called osteoporosis; also wear and tear on bone in joints, called osteoarthritis, more marked after about 60
Heart and lungs	35 or 40	Most functions (such as aerobic capacity or cardiac output) do not show age changes at rest but do show age changes during work or exercise
Nervous system	Probably gradual throughout adulthood	Some loss (but not clear how much) of neurons in the brain; gradual reduction in density of dendrites; gradual decline in total brain volume and weight
Immune system	Adolescence	Loss in size of thymus; reduction in number and maturity of T cells; not clear how much of this change is due to stress and how much is primary aging
Reproductive system	Mid-30s (women)	Increased reproductive risk and lowered fertility
	Early 40s (men)	Gradual decline in viable sperm beginning at about age 40; very gradual decline in testosterone from early adulthood
Cellular elasticity	Gradual	Gradual loss of elasticity in most cells, including skin, muscle, tendon, and blood vessel cells; faster deterioration in cells exposed to sunlight
Height	40	Compression of disks in the spine, with resulting loss of height of 1 to 2 inches by age 80
Weight	Nonlinear	In U.S. studies, weight reaches a maximum in middle adulthood and then gradually declines in old age
Skin	40	Increase in wrinkles, as a result of loss of elasticity; oil-secreting glands become less efficient.
Hair	Variable	Hair becomes thinner and may gray

(*Sources:* Bartoshuk & Weiffenbach, 1990; Blatter et al., 1995; Braveman, 1987; Briggs, Raz, & Marks, 1999; Brock, Guralnik, & Brody, 1990; Doty et al., 1984; Fiatarone & Evans, 1993; Fozard, 1990; Fozard, Metter, & Brant, 1990; Gray, Berlin, McKinlay, & Longcope, 1991; Hallfrisch, Muller, Drinkwater, Tobin, & Adres, 1990; Hayflick, 1994; Ivy, MacLeod, Petit, & Marcus, 1992; Kallman, Plato, & Tobin, 1990; Kline & Scialfa, 1996; Kozma, Stones, & Hannah, 1991; Lakatta, 1990; Lim, Zipursky, Watts, & Pfefferbaum, 1992; McFalls, 1990; Miller, 1990; Mundy, 1994; Scheibel, 1992, 1996; Shock et al., 1984; Weisse, 1992.)

of the summary statements in the table are based on both longitudinal and cross-sectional data; many are based on studies in which both experimental and control groups consisted of participants in good health. So developmentalists can be reasonably confident that most of the age changes listed reflect primary aging and not secondary aging. The center column of the table lists the approximate age at which the loss or decline reaches the point where it becomes fairly readily apparent. Virtually all these changes begin in early adulthood. But the early losses or declines are not typically noticeable in everyday physical functioning during these years.

Another way to think of these changes is in terms of a balance between physical demand and physical capacity (Welford, 1993). In early adulthood, almost all of us have ample physical capacity to meet the physical demands we encounter in everyday life. We can read the fine print in the telephone book without bifocals; we can carry heavy boxes or furniture when we move to a new home; our immune systems are strong enough to fight off most illnesses, and we recover quickly from sickness. As we move into middle adulthood, the balance sheet changes: We find more and more arenas in which our physical capacities no longer quite meet the demands.

HEART AND LUNGS The most common measure of overall aerobic fitness is **maximum oxygen uptake (VO$_2$ max)**, which reflects the ability of the body to take in and transport oxygen to various body organs. When VO$_2$ max is measured in a person at rest, scientists find only minimal decrements associated with age. But when they measure VO$_2$ max during exercise (such as during a treadmill test), it shows a systematic decline with age of about 1% per year, beginning between ages 35 and 40 (Goldberg, Dengel, & Hagberg, 1996).

VO$_2$ max during exercise declines more with age than does VO$_2$ max at rest for a variety of reasons. Primary aging effects have been demonstrated in studies showing that, even in healthy individuals who exercise regularly, age is associated with a loss of arterial elasticity and with calcification of the valves that regulate the flow of blood to and from the heart (Cheitlin, 2003). As a result, an older adult's heart responds less efficiently to the demands of exercise than does a younger adult's. In addition, the ability of muscle tissue to utilize oxygen declines with age (Betik & Hepple, 2008). Research has also revealed, however, that aerobic exercise can improve VO$_2$ max in both younger and older adults (Wilmore et al., 2001). Thus, age-related declines in this variable may reflect the cumulative effects of a *sedentary lifestyle*, a lifestyle that does not include regular physical activity.

STRENGTH AND SPEED The collective effect of changes in muscles and cardiovascular fitness is a general loss of strength and speed with age—not just in top athletes, but in all of us. For example, grip strength peaks from the 20s through the early 30s and then declines steadily (Kallman, Plato, & Tobin, 1990). Once again, though, such a difference might be a result of the fact that younger adults are more physically active or more likely to be engaged in activities or jobs that demand strength. Arguing against this conclusion, however, are studies of physically active older adults, who also show loss of muscle strength (e.g., Phillips, Bruce, Newton, & Woledge, 1992).

REPRODUCTIVE CAPACITY In Chapter 3, you read that the risk of miscarriage and other complications of pregnancy is higher in a woman's 30s than in her 20s. An equivalent change occurs in fertility—the ability to conceive—which begins to decline in the early 30s and drops dramatically in the late 30s (Korula & Kamath, 2005). Men's reproductive capacity declines as well, but not until the late 30s or early 40s (Matorras, Matorras, Exposito, Martinez, & Crisol, 2010). Moreover, older men have a diminished sperm count, but, as long as their reproductive organs remain disease free, men retain the ability to father children throughout their lives. Why does this pattern of reproductive aging exist?

Genetic studies in mice suggest that a single protein is responsible for the regulation of reproductive aging in both sexes (Baker et al., 2004). However, the end point of the reproductive aging process is different for men and women. Men's capacity diminishes, as stated earlier, but remains intact. By contrast, the end point of reproductive aging for women involves a total loss of the capacity for reproduction. Because of this difference, fertility problems in men (e.g., low sperm count) are almost always the result of some kind of disease, abnormal developmental process, or exposure to environmental agents that are known to reduce sperm counts (e.g., some pesticides) (Joensen, Skakkebaek, & Jørgensen, 2008). By contrast, fertility problems in women are more often a by-product of the normal aging process.

As you will learn in Chapter 15, in preparation for menopause, ovulation becomes sporadic and unpredictable in many women, sometimes as soon as the early 30s. Consequently, the natural process of reproductive aging leads many women to experience periods of time during which conception is impossible. However, because menstrual cycles continue to occur, many women who are ovulating intermittently are unaware of the problem. Thus, to achieve conception, many women in their 30s turn to specialists in reproductive medicine who can help them identify the times when they are fertile or can prescribe drugs that stimulate the ovaries to produce more eggs, as discussed in *No Easy Answers*.

IMMUNE SYSTEM FUNCTIONING The two key organs in the immune system are the thymus gland and the bone marrow. Between them, they create two types of cells, B cells and T cells, each of which plays a distinct role. B cells fight against external threats by producing antibodies against such disease organisms as viruses or bacteria; T cells defend against essentially

Assisted Reproductive Technology

As you have learned, reproductive capacity declines with age. Thus, as the age at which couples begin attempting to conceive has risen in recent years, so has the proportion who are treated for *infertility* (failing to conceive after twelve months of attempting to do so) (Macaluso et al., 2008). These days, about 12% of women in the United States have difficulty conceiving and seek infertility treatment (CDC, 2009d). As a result, researchers are making amazing advances in developmentalists' understanding of the earliest hours of life almost every day. These advances have led to the development of *assisted reproductive techniques* (*ART*) for helping couples who have difficulty conceiving. The most common of these techniques is *in vitro fertilization* (*IVF*; *in vitro* is Latin for *glass*), popularly known as the "test-tube baby" method. In IVF treatment, eggs are extracted from a woman's ovaries and combined with sperm in a laboratory dish. If conception takes place, one or more embryos—ideally at the six- to eight-cell stage of development—are transferred to the woman's uterus. The eggs used in IVF can come from the woman who will carry the child or from a donor. Likewise, the sperm can be from the woman's partner or a donor.

The type of IVF treatments with the highest success rate involves *nondonor fresh eggs*. In the first stage of such treatment, the woman takes drugs that stimulate her ovaries to produce eggs. If her ovaries respond, treatment advances to the *egg retrieval* stage, in which eggs are extracted from her body and quickly transported to the laboratory and exposed to sperm while still fresh. If fertilization occurs, the *transfer* phase is initiated in which one or more

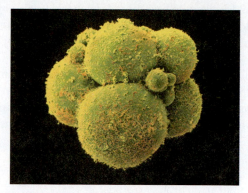

An eight-celled embryo is ideal for an IVF transfer. Pictured here is an embryo on the day of transfer into a woman's uterus.

embryos are injected into the woman's uterus or fallopian tubes. If one or more embryos implant into the lining of the uterus, a pregnancy is achieved that may progress to a live birth. Overall, only 30% of nondonor fresh egg treatments that are initiated result in live birth (CDC, 2012a). However, once pregnancy has been achieved, IVF treatment with nondonor fresh eggs has an 82% success rate (CDC, 2012a). By contrast, only 17% of IVF treatments involving *nondonor frozen eggs* result in live births. Treatment failure is most often due to inadequate egg production.

The older a woman is, the lower the probability that she will be able to have a successful IVF pregnancy using nondonor fresh eggs. Among women over 40, only 18% of such IVF procedures are successful (CDC, 2012a). Consequently, among older woman, treatment with *donor eggs* is recommended by fertility specialists.

Successful IVF carries a different set of risks. Multiple birth is more frequent among IVF patients, primarily because doctors often transfer several embryos at once in order to increase the likelihood of at least one live birth (CDC, 2012a). Consequently, 29% of IVF pregnancies result in the birth of twins and 1.5% in triplets (CDC, 2012a). As you learned in Chapter 3, multiple pregnancies are associated with premature birth, low birth weight, and birth defects.

Researchers have also found that, even when only one embryo is transferred, IVF is still associated with a higher rate of multiple births than is natural conception (CDC, 2012a). For reasons that are not yet understood, implanted zygotes conceived through IVF are more likely to spontaneously divide into two embryos than are naturally conceived zygotes (Blickstine, Jones, & Keith, 2003). This finding suggests that multiple pregnancy must always be considered as a possible outcome when infertile couples are advised of the risks associated with IVF.

YOU DECIDE

Decide which of these two statements you most agree with and think about how you would defend your position:

1. **The benefits of ART outweigh its risks. If I were faced with fertility problems, I would look into ART.**

2. **The risks of ART outweigh its benefits. If I were faced with fertility problems, I would prefer to adopt a child rather than to seek help from an ART specialist.**

---

internal threats, such as transplanted tissue, cancer cells, and viruses that live within the body's cells (Kiecolt-Glaser & Glaser, 1995). It is T cells that decline most in number and efficiency with age (Nikolich-Žugich, 2005).

Changes in the thymus gland appear to be central to the aging process (Cohen, 2006). This gland is largest in adolescence and declines dramatically thereafter in both size and mass. By age 45 or 50, the hormone-producing cells of the thymus in many adults are no longer capable of maintaining optimum immune-system functioning (Yang et al., 2009). This smaller, less functional thymus is less able to turn the immature T cells produced by the bone marrow into fully "adult" cells. As a result, both of the basic protective mechanisms work less efficiently. Adults produce fewer antibodies than do children or teenagers. And T cells partially lose the ability to "recognize" a foreign cell, so that the body may fail to fight off some disease cells (cancer cells, for example). Thus, one of the key physical changes over the years of adulthood is an increasing susceptibility to disease.

But it is not entirely clear whether this susceptibility is due to primary or secondary aging. These changes in the immune system are found in healthy adults, which makes them look like part of primary aging. But there also is growing evidence that the functioning of the immune system is impaired by chronic conditions such as diabetes to which lifestyle factors contribute (Nikolich-Žugich, 2005). The system is also highly responsive to psychological stress and depression (Hawkley & Cacioppo, 2004). College students, for example, show lower levels of one variety of T cells ("natural killer" T cells) during exam periods than at other times (Glaser et al., 1992). And adults who have recently been widowed show a sharp drop in immune-system functioning (Irwin & Pike, 1993). Chronic stress, too, has an effect on the immune system, stimulating an initial increase in immune efficiency, followed by a drop (Hawkley & Cacioppo, 2004).

Collectively, this research points to the possibility that life experiences that demand high levels of change or adaptation will affect immune system functioning. Over a period of years and many stresses, the immune system may become less and less efficient. It may well be that the immune system changes with age in basic ways regardless of the level of stress. But it is also possible that what is thought of as normal aging of the immune system is a response to cumulative stress.

test yourself before going on ✔ Study and Review in MyPsychLab

Answers to these questions can be found in the back of the book.

1. Label each age-related change as (P) primary aging, (S) secondary aging, or (P + S) influenced by both.
   _____(1) decline in ability to detect and discriminate among various smells
   _____(2) reduction in the density of dendrites
   _____(3) lowered fertility of women
   _____(4) obesity
   _____(5) thinning of hair

2. Response inhibition is linked to maturation of the _____ _____, the emotional part of the brain.

3. Measured in a person at rest, VO_2 begins to decline between the ages of _____ and _____.

CRITICAL THINKING

4. Elite swimmers reach their peak in their early 20s, while the best amateur and professional golfers are at their best in their 30s. How do the physical changes that you have learned about in this section explain this difference?

Health and Wellness

Early adulthood is a relatively healthy period of life, but risky behaviors—having multiple sex partners or engaging in substance use, for example—along with generally poor health habits can be problematic.

Health Habits and Personal Factors

LO 13.4 What habits and personal factors are associated with good health?

Do you remember Ponce de Leon, the 16th-century Spanish explorer who traveled to the New World in search of the "fountain of youth"? Although de Leon was responsible for providing his fellow European mariners with their first chart of the Gulf Stream, he never succeeded in finding a source of everlasting youth. Like de Leon, many adults today are searching for a vitamin or a special diet that can keep them young forever. The truth is, though, that maintaining optimum health results from the development of health-enhancing habits and the cultivation of personal factors that can stave off some of the effects of primary aging. 👁 **Watch** the **Video** *Early Adulthood: Portraits of Early Adult Physical Health* in **MyPsychLab**.

HEALTH HABITS The best evidence for the long-term effects of various health habits comes from the Alameda County Study, a major longitudinal epidemiological study conducted in a county in California (Housman & Dorman, 2005). The study began in 1965, when a random sample of all residents of the county, a total of 6,928 people, completed an extensive questionnaire about many aspects of their lives, including their health habits and their health and disability. These participants were contacted again in 1974 and in 1983, when they again described their health and disability. The researchers also monitored death records and were able to specify the date of death of each of the participants who died between 1965 and 1983. They could then link health practices reported in 1965 to later death, disease, or disability. The researchers initially identified seven good health habits that they thought might be critical: getting physical exercise; not smoking, drinking, over- or undereating, or snacking; eating breakfast; and getting regular sleep.

Data from the first 9 years of the Alameda study show that five of these seven practices were independently related to the risk of death. Only snacking and eating breakfast were unrelated to mortality. When the five strong predictors were combined in the 1974 data, researchers found that, in every age group, those with poorer health habits had a higher risk of mortality. Not surprisingly, poor health habits were also related to disease and disability rates over the 18 years of the study. Those who described poorer health habits in 1965 were more likely to report disability or disease symptoms in 1974 and in 1983 (Breslow & Breslow, 1993; Guralnik & Kaplan, 1989; Strawbridge, Camacho, Cohen, & Kaplan, 1993). Moreover, the study showed that a sedentary lifestyle in early adulthood predisposes people to develop life-threatening illnesses such as diabetes in later years (Hu, Li, Colditz, Willet, & Manson, 2003).

Sexually transmitted diseases are a significant health risk of young adulthood. Casual sexual encounters with multiple partners carry with them a higher risk of contracting such diseases than do more careful relationship choices.

The Alameda study is not the only one to show these connections between health habits and mortality. For example, an 8-year study of older Taiwanese adults found that those who exercised least were the most likely to die (Chen, Fox, Ku, Sun, & Chou, 2012). Similarly, a 20-year longitudinal study in Sweden produced similar results (Lissner, Bengtsson, Bjorkelund, & Wedel, 1996). In addition, the Nurses' Health Study, a longitudinal investigation that examined the health behaviors of more than 115,000 nurses in the United States for almost 2 decades, found that the lower a woman's initial body mass index (BMI; a measure of weight relative to height), the lower her likelihood of death (Manson et al., 1995).

These longitudinal studies suggest that the lifestyle choices of early adulthood have cumulative effects. For example, the effect of a high-cholesterol diet appears to add up over time. However, reducing levels of saturated fats in the diet may reverse the process of cholesterol build-up in the blood vessels (Citkowitz, 2012). Similarly, the effects of smoking begin to reverse themselves shortly after a person quits (see *Developmental Science in the Clinic*). Thus, the long-term effects of lifestyle choices made in early adulthood may be either negative or positive. So there is likely to be a payoff for changing your health habits.

SOCIAL SUPPORT Abundant research shows that adults with adequate *social support* have lower risk of disease, death, and depression than do adults with weaker social networks or less supportive relationships (Baker, 2005). The link between social support and health was revealed in some of the findings from the Alameda study. In this study, the *social network index* reflected an objective measurement: number of contacts with friends and relatives, marital status, and church and group membership. Even using this less-than-perfect measure of support, the relationship is vividly clear: Among both men and women in three different age groups (30–49, 50–59, and 60–69), those with the fewest social connections had higher death rates than those with more social connections. Since similar patterns have been found in other countries, including Sweden and Japan, this link between social contact and physical hardiness is not restricted to the United States or to Western cultures (Orth-Gomér, Rosengren, & Wilhelmsen, 1993; Sugisawa, Liang, & Liu, 1994).

How does social support contribute to health? One reason may be that the size and perceived adequacy of a person's social network is correlated with the functioning of her immune system (Bouhuys, Flentge, Oldehinkel, & van den Berg, 2004). Likewise, adults who have adequate social support are less likely than their peers to be depressed, a factor that indirectly affects the immune system (Symister & Friend, 2003).

A SENSE OF CONTROL Another personal characteristic that affects health is an individual's level of *self-efficacy*, the belief in one's ability to perform some action or to control one's behavior or environment, to reach some goal or to make something happen (Bandura, 1977a, 1982,

locus of control a set of beliefs about the causes of events

1986). As you learned in Chapter 10, this aspect of the psychological self first appears in middle childhood. In adulthood, it is linked to many health outcomes. For instance, individuals who are high in self-efficacy are more likely than those who are low to follow medical advice with regard to health issues such as cardiac rehabilitation following a heart attack (Rodgers, Murray, Selzler, & Norman, 2013).

A similar variable, **locus of control**, which is an individual's set of beliefs about the causes of events, also contributes to health. A person who has an *internal* locus of control sees herself as capable of exerting some control over what happens to her (Rotter, 1990). One who has an *external* locus of control believes that other people or uncontrollable forces such as luck determine the future.

To understand how locus of control influences health, think about what would happen if you had an ear infection for which a doctor prescribed an antibiotic that you took for only half as long

Research shows that social support, as exhibited between these two women, lowers the risk of disease, death, and depression in adults.

as directed. If your ear infection failed to go away, how would you explain it? If you have an internal locus of control, you would have no difficulty acknowledging the fact that your failure to take the medicine as directed was responsible for your still aching ear. However, if you have an external locus of control, you might respond to the pain in your ear with a remark such as, "Just my luck! Nothing ever goes my way."

Research suggests that the tendency to make realistic attributions is what counts when it comes to health (Frick, Fegg, Tyroller, Fischer, & Bumeder, 2007). Patients experience the best outcomes when they are able to accurately determine which aspects of their conditions are controllable and which are not. For instance, with regard to our ear-infection example, a person who is able to balance attributions in this way would realize that taking medicine is under her control and would take responsibility for that aspect of her treatment. However, she would understand that the physician is responsible for determining which antibiotic to prescribe. Balancing her thinking about the reasons for her recovery or her failure to recover helps her cope with the stress of being ill.

Both self-efficacy and locus of control are related to yet another control-related psychological characteristic, the continuum that ranges from *optimism* to *pessimism* (Seligman, 2006). The pessimist, who feels helpless, believes that misfortune will last a long time, will undermine everything, and is his own fault. The optimist believes that setbacks are temporary and usually caused by circumstances. He is convinced that there is always some solution and that he will be able to work things out. Confronted by defeat, the optimist sees it as a challenge and tries harder, whereas the pessimist gives up. Not surprisingly, optimism affects health in many ways, including enhancing the effects of medication (Geers, Kosbab, Helfer, Weiland, & Wellman, 2007). That is, optimists show larger benefits from medication than pessimists do. These results are in line with other studies showing that optimism has positive effects on the immune system (Low, Bower, Moskowitz, & Epel, 2011). In addition, it fits with the results of a classic longitudinal study which found that pessimism at age 25 was correlated with poor health in middle and late adulthood (Peterson, Seligman, & Vaillant, 1988).

Sexually Transmitted Diseases

LO 13.5 What are some of the viral and bacterial STDs that afflict young adults?

In contrast to other types of disease, most sexually transmitted diseases (STD)—including gonorrhea, syphilis, genital herpes, and HIV—are more common among 15- to 24-year-olds than in any other age group (CDC, 2012b). In Chapter 3, you learned about how these diseases affect prenatal development in pregnant women. Now, we will consider how a few such diseases affect those who carry them.

BACTERIAL STDS Bacterial STDs are caused by microorganisms that can be eradicated through the use of antibiotic medications. The most prevalent of the bacterial STDs is *chlamydia*, a bacterial infection that can be transmitted through many kinds of physical contact involving the genitals, as well as actual intercourse (CDC, 2012b). Women are about three times as likely as men to suffer from chlamydia. Community studies show that as many as one-third of young women who are screened at family planning clinics are infected with chlamydia. Many of these women are symptom free because the disease can remain hidden for several years. Unfortunately, undiagnosed chlamydia can lead to **pelvic inflammatory disease**, an infection of the female reproductive tract that can cause infertility. ◉ **Watch** the **Video** *Common Misconceptions about STDs: Michael Bailey* in **MyPsychLab**.

Another bacterial STD is *gonorrhea*. Because of educational programs about the disease and increased use of condoms, the prevalence of gonorrhea has declined considerably in recent years (CDC, 2012b). However, the strains that infect today's gonorrhea sufferers are far more resistant to antibiotics than those that existed decades ago (CDC, 2012b). As a result, in some cases the disease is extremely difficult to cure and causes long-term damage to the reproductive systems of those who suffer from it. Men and women experience roughly equivalent rates of gonorrhea, but women's bodies are more susceptible to long-term damage from this infection.

Another bacterial STD is *syphilis*, a disease that can lead to serious mental disorders and death if not treated in the early stages. Fortunately, widespread screening for the disease has led to significant declines in its prevalence. Only about 7,000 cases were reported to the Centers for Disease Control and Prevention in 2002 (CDC, 2003b). However, syphilis rates have increased dramatically since then. In 2011, more than 13,000 cases were reported. The increase in syphilis infection is largely confined to men, because the number of cases among homosexual males who live in highly populated urban areas continues to rise each year at an alarming rate (CDC, 2012b).

VIRAL STDS Unlike STDs caused by bacteria, STDs caused by viruses cannot be treated with antibiotics. In fact, these diseases are considered to be incurable. One such disease is *genital herpes*. This disease can be acquired through either intercourse or oral sex. Researchers at the Centers for Disease Control and Prevention report that 19% of the adult population in the United

pelvic inflammatory disease an infection of the female reproductive tract that may result from a sexually transmitted disease and can lead to infertility

States is infected with herpes (CDC, 2012b). Attacks of the disease, which include the development of painful blisters on the genitals, occur periodically in most people who carry the virus.

A more serious viral STD is *genital warts* caused by the *human papillomavirus* (*HPV*). The primary symptom of the disease, the presence of growths on the genitals, is not its most serious effect. The general prevalence of HPV is unknown. However, among women who experience reproductive-tract symptoms such as inflammation of the cervix, HPV infection rates are very high. Studies indicate that, in the United States, 35% of 14- to 19-year-olds with such symptoms, 29% of those in their 20s, and 13% of women in their 30s are infected with HPV (CDC, 2012b). Moreover, the virus is strongly associated with cervical cancer, accounting for more than 80% of all cases (CDC, 2006a).

In 2006, the Food and Drug Administration approved a vaccine that officials believe will protect young men and women against four types of HPV (CDC, 2012b). However, researchers do not yet know how long its protective effects will last. Moreover, officials point out that there are other forms of HPV against which the vaccine offers no protection. For these reasons, public health officials state that women who get the vaccine should continue to be vigilant about safe sex practices and routine medical screening.

HIV/AIDS The most feared STD is the *human immunodeficiency virus* (*HIV*), the virus that causes *acquired immune deficiency syndrome* (*AIDS*). Becoming better informed about HIV/AIDS can help allay fear of the diseases (see Table 13.3). Since HIV was discovered in the early 1980s, more than 1 million cases have been documented in the United States (Merson, 2006). By contrast, more than 20 million people in sub-Saharan Africa are HIV positive (Joint United Nations Programme on HIV/AIDS, 2010). HIV is transmitted through an exchange of bodily fluids. Such exchanges can happen during sexual intercourse, when intravenous drug users share needles, or as a result of a blood transfusion or other kinds of invasive medical treatment. Male homosexuals have higher rates of HIV than other groups primarily because of the tendency to engage in anal intercourse, during which bodily fluids are more likely to be exchanged than in other kinds of sexual encounters (CDC, 2013). ⊙ Watch the Video *Nightmare on AIDS Street: Taking an HIV Test* in **MyPsychLab**.

PREVENTION Older teens and young adults have higher rates of STDs than older people primarily because they are more likely to engage in sexually risky behavior (CDC, 2013). For instance, about a quarter of college students report having had intercourse with four or more

TABLE 13.3 AIDS Quiz

Answer these questions True or False

1. AIDS is a single disease.
2. AIDS symptoms vary widely from country to country and even from risk group to risk group.
3. Those at greatest risk for getting AIDS are people who have sex without using condoms, drug users who share needles, and infants born to AIDS-infected mothers.
4. AIDS is one of the most highly contagious diseases.
5. One way to avoid contracting AIDS is to use an oil-based lubricant with a condom.

Answers:

1. False: AIDS is not a single disease. Rather, a severely impaired immune system leaves a person with AIDS highly susceptible to a whole host of infections and diseases.
2. True: In the United States and Europe, AIDS sufferers may develop Kaposi's sarcoma (a rare form of skin cancer), pneumonia, and tuberculosis. In Africa, people with AIDS usually waste away with fever, diarrhea, and symptoms caused by tuberculosis.
3. True: These groups are at greatest risk. Screening of blood donors and testing of donated blood have greatly reduced the risk of contracting AIDS through blood transfusions. Today, women make up the fastest-growing group of infected people worldwide, as AIDS spreads among heterosexuals, especially in Africa.
4. False: AIDS is not among the most highly infectious diseases. You cannot get AIDS from kissing, shaking hands, or using objects handled by people who have AIDS.
5. False: Do not use oil-based lubricants, which can eat through condoms. Latex condoms with an effective spermicide are safer. Learn the sexual history of any potential partner, including HIV test results. Don't have sex with prostitutes.

partners in the previous 12 months (American College Health Association, 2009). While fewer than 20% of young adults report being hesitant to discuss STD prevention with a new partner, only about half actually use condoms consistently (American College Health Association, 2009; Martinez, Chandra, Abma, Jones, & Mosher, 2006). Thus, reducing the rates of such risky behaviors could reduce the rates of STDs and prevent many young adults from experiencing the adverse health consequences associated with them.

intimate partner abuse physical acts or other behavior intended to intimidate or harm an intimate partner

Intimate Partner Abuse

LO 13.6 What are the causes and effects of intimate partner abuse?

Researchers define **intimate partner abuse** as physical acts or other behavior intended to intimidate or harm an intimate partner. Intimate partners are couples who are dating, cohabiting, engaged, or married or who were formerly partners. The more common term, *domestic abuse*, refers only to incidents involving individuals who live in the same household.

PREVALENCE When intimate partners get into a physical altercation, men and women are about equally likely to push, slap, or kick their partners. However, analyses of medical records show that, throughout the world, women are more likely than men to be injured during physical confrontations between intimate partners (McHugh, 2005). Moreover, rates of abuse among women vary significantly around the world, as Figure 13.1 reveals (World Health Organization [WHO], 2000, 2013).

In the United States, surveys suggest that 6 of every 1,000 women are injured by a partner each year, compared to 1 per 1,000 men (Catalano, 2012). The rate of abuse has declined substantially since the early 1990s, when 16 of every 1,000 women were abused annually. Nevertheless, intimate partner abuse varies across ethnic groups within the United States. Rates are highest among African American women (8 per 1,000) and lowest among Hispanic women (4 per 1,000), with the rate of White women between the two (6 per 1,000). Careful analyses of these findings show that social factors rather than ethnicity underlie these differences (Catalano, 2012). Specifically,

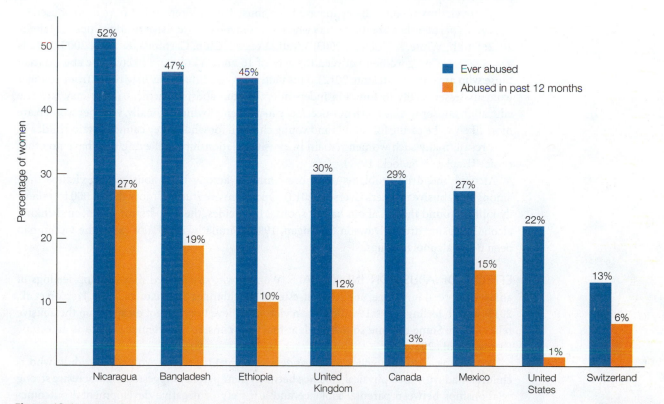

Figure 13.1 Rates of Physical Abuse among Women around the World

These data on physical abuse are based on a World Health Organization international survey of medical records.
(*Source:* WHO, 2000.)

Criminologists point out that intimate partner abuse happens most often in the context of arguments over long-standing disagreements that take place when partners are home from work in the evening, on holidays, or on weekends and/or have been drinking or using drugs.

among single women who head households with children, the rate of intimate partner abuse is 32 per 1,000, and such women are disproportionately African American.

Researchers estimate that gay men and lesbians are about as likely to be abused by a partner as are women in heterosexual relationships (Freedberg, 2006). However, the exact prevalence rate of abuse in same-sex relationships is difficult to ascertain because homosexuals are less likely than heterosexuals to seek medical attention for their injuries due to fear of discrimination. When gays and lesbians do seek help, researchers have found that health-care professionals tend to overlook intimate partner abuse as a possible source of their injuries. As a result, emergency medical personnel may fail to question gays and lesbians about intimate partner abuse as they would heterosexuals.

CAUSES OF PARTNER ABUSE Cultural attitudes contribute to rates of abuse (McHugh, 2005). Specifically, in many societies, women are regarded as property, and a man's "right" to beat his partner may be protected by law (Dabby, 2007). In fact, there was a time when, based on English common law traditions, this was true in the United States. This factor may help explain why nearly three-quarters of male victims report the incident to police, compared to only half of female victims (Catalano, Rand, Smith, & Snyder, 2009).

In addition to cultural beliefs, a number of characteristics of abusers and their victims are associated with intimate partner abuse. For example, the same cluster of personality traits in abusers contributes to abuse in both heterosexual and homosexual couples (Burke & Follingstad, 1999). The cluster includes a tendency toward irrational jealousy, a need for the partner's dependency and for control in a relationship, sudden mood swings, and a quick temper (Landolt & Dutton, 1997). Men who are generally aggressive are also more likely than less aggressive men to abuse their partners (Kane, Staiger, & Ricciardelli, 2000). In addition, men who are high school dropouts or who are frequently unemployed abuse their partners more often than other men (Kyriacou et al., 1999).

Abuse victims are more likely to have been abused as children and to have been abused by a previous partner than are their peers who are not involved in abusive relationships (Catalano, 2012; Smith, White, & Holland, 2003; Wyatt, Axelrod, Chin, Carmona, & Loeb, 2000). Age is also a factor. Young women between the ages of 16 and 24 are more likely to be abused than those who are older (Catalano, 2012). This pattern of age differences may result from younger women's lesser ability to function independently from abusive partners. They may lack the education and/or work experience necessary to gain employment. Finally, younger women are more likely to be caring for infants and young children for whom they cannot obtain childcare. As a result, many such women remain in abusive relationships, believing they have no other choice (Kaplan & Sadock, 1991).

Alcohol and drug problems are more common among both abusers and victims than among nonabusive partners (Iverson, 2013). One extensive study of more than 8,000 intrafamily killings found that, in about half of spousal homicides, the perpetrator had been drinking alcohol or using drugs (Dawson & Langan, 1994). Similarly, in 50% of cases, the victim had been using alcohol or drugs.

EFFECTS OF ABUSE ON INDIVIDUALS Women who are abused may develop feelings of anxiety, depression, shame, and low self-esteem (Buchbinder & Eisikovits, 2003; Iverson et al., 2013;). Such feelings are intensified when victims believe they cannot escape from the abusive relationship. Some become so despondent that they consider or attempt suicide as an escape (Iverson et al., 2013).

Witnessing abuse influences children's development. One study involving 420 adults who as children had witnessed physical violence between their parents suggested that there are strong relationships between parental violence and a variety of negative developmental outcomes (McNeal & Amato, 1998). For one thing, many of these adults were found to have poor relationships with their own partners and children. Moreover, many had become perpetrators or victims of partner abuse themselves.

PREVENTION Vigorous law enforcement is one approach to prevention (Dugan, Nagin, & Rosenfeld, 2003). Advocates of this approach suggest that the stigma of arrest may force abusers to face the reality that they have a serious problem. Training programs for law-enforcement officials and hospital emergency-room personnel that teach them to recognize signs of abuse are also essential (Hamberger & Minsky, 2000). Many experts also recommend training physicians and nurses to recognize and question patients about signs of abuse during routine medical exams (Scholle et al., 2003). As a result of such training, advocates claim, perpetrators may be identified and prosecuted even when victims do not voluntarily report abusive incidents.

A different approach—one that aims to stop intimate partner abuse before it occurs—is to provide victims with problem-solving skills and temporary shelters that may prevent their revictimization (Dutton, 2012). Further, communitywide and school-based approaches to prevention seek to educate the public about intimate partner abuse and to change attitudes about the acceptability of violence in intimate relationships, so that abuse will not happen in the first place.

SEXUAL VIOLENCE **Sexual violence** is the term applied to episodes of partner abuse in which one individual uses force to coerce the other into engaging in sexual acts. Many such episodes involve strangers; however, more than half of sexually violent incidents in the United States occur in the context of some kind of intimate relationship (Black et al., 2011). Surveys indicate that 18% of heterosexual women have been victims of sexual violence, while fewer than 1% of heterosexual men report such experiences (Black et al., 2011). Among lesbians and bisexual women, 12% and 43%, respectively, report having been sexually victimized by a man (Walters, Chen, & Breiding, 2013). By contrast, sexual victimization occurs even less frequently among gay and bisexual men than it does among heterosexual men (Walters et al., 2013).

The psychological effects of being a victim of sexual violence include the development of sexual dysfunctions and posttraumatic stress disorder, as well as the possibility of physical trauma and pregnancy (Elliott, Mok, & Briere, 2004). Men who are raped by other men also sometimes experience doubts about their sexual orientation (Kaplan & Sadock, 1991). Moreover, the psychological effects of sexual violence have been found to persist more than a decade in many victims (Elliott et al., 2004). Thus, being victimized by sexual violence can, overall, be one of the most traumatic episodes in a young adult's life.

One particularly troubling type of sexual violence among young adults is *date rape*, or rape that occurs in the context of a date. Many cases of date rape are premeditated and involve the use of alcohol and drugs to loosen the inhibitions of the victim. Research indicates that such episodes may be more traumatic than rapes perpetrated by strangers because victims of date rape believe they should have been able to prevent the assault. Victims who were coerced with drugs and/or alcohol also frequently have incomplete memories of the event, a factor that increases their vulnerability to long-term negative emotional consequences (Gauntlett-Gilbert, Keegan, & Petrak, 2004).

Prevention of sexual violence often involves training potential victims to avoid situations in which such episodes are likely to occur (Kalmuss, 2004). Training in self-defense techniques, both verbal and physical, can also help women learn how to deal effectively with the initial phases of a threatened sexual assault (Hollander, 2004).

Mental Health Problems

LO 13.7 What mental disorders occur most frequently in young adulthood?

Studies in a number of industrialized countries show that the risk of virtually every kind of emotional disturbance is higher in early adulthood than in middle age (Kessler et al., 2005). In fact, survey research suggests that as many as 10% of younger adults, those aged 18 to 24, have seriously considered committing suicide (Brener, Hassan, & Barrios, 1999).

CAUSES AND CONSEQUENCES OF MENTAL DISORDERS The most plausible explanation for the differing rates of mental illness between young adults and middle-aged adults is that early adulthood is the period in which adults have both the highest expectations and the

sexual violence the use of physical coercion to force a person to engage in a sexual act against his or her will

phobia an irrational fear of an object, a person, a place, or a situation

highest levels of role conflict and role strain. These are the years when each of us must learn a series of major new roles (spouse, parent, worker). If we fall short of our expectations, emotional difficulties such as anxiety and depression become more likely.

Some people respond very effectively to the challenges of young adulthood, while others do not. For example, the personal factors you read about in an earlier section are important to mental health as well as physical health. However, with respect to mental illness, researchers' attention is becoming more focused on biological causes.

First, mental illnesses tend to run in families, suggesting a genetic factor. In fact, the number of close relatives a person has who suffer from depression or other mood disorders is the best predictor of the likelihood that the individual will develop a mood disorder (Kendler et al., 1995). In addition, an increasing number of studies demonstrate links between mental illnesses and disturbances in specific brain functions (Drevets et al., 1997; Monarch, Saykin, & Flashman, 2004). Consequently, the current view of most psychologists is that mental disorders result from an interaction of biological and environmental factors.

When a young adult develops a mental health problem, its long-term impact depends on the degree to which it diverts her from an adaptive developmental pathway. For instance, if a college student develops one of these problems, she may have to leave school. Thus, many mental health professionals believe that once an effective treatment has been identified, educational and vocational rehabilitation services are critical to the young adult's full recovery. Longitudinal studies involving young adults with mental illnesses who have participated in educational/vocational rehabilitation programs support this view (Ellison, Danley, Bromberg, & Palmer-Erbs, 1999; Gralinski-Bakker et al., 2005).

ANXIETY AND DEPRESSION The most common mental disorders are those that are associated with fear and anxiety (Kessler et al., 1994). For example, *phobias* are fairly common. A **phobia** is an irrational fear of an object, a person, a place, or a situation. Most phobias are learned through association of the experience of being in a state of fear with a specific stimulus. For example, a college student who was injured in a car crash may avoid the intersection where the crash occurred, even though doing so adds time and distance to his daily trip from home to campus. ◉ **Watch** the **Video** *Phobias* in **MyPsychLab**.

Since phobias are usually learned, therapeutic interventions usually involve some process of *un*learning the association. The most common way of accomplishing this is to expose a person to the stimulus that she is afraid of in some systematic way (Hirsch, 2012). In fact many people "cure" their own phobias simply by exposing themselves to the fear-producing stimulus until it no longer induces anxiety. Thus, the student with a phobia about a particular intersection may tell himself that he is being silly and force himself to drive through it repeatedly until the phobic reaction no longer occurs.

After anxiety disorders, problems associated with moods are the most common type of mental difficulty (Kessler et al., 2005). Depression is the most frequent of these disorders. About 10% of 18- to 24-year-olds report having experienced a serious episode of depression in the past year (Substance Abuse and Mental Health Services Administration, 2006). Among those who experienced depression, 53% thought seriously about committing suicide. Suicidal thoughts can also lead to substance abuse. For example, more than 60% of young adults who consider suicide also engage in binge drinking (usually defined as consuming five or more drinks on one occasion). Thus, paradoxically, the time of life in which people experience their peak of physical and intellectual functioning is also the time when they may be most prone to feelings of despair. Depression rates may be higher in early adulthood because these are the years when people must create new attachment relationships while at the same time separating from parents (Erikson's task of *intimacy*). Consequently, feelings of loneliness and social failure may lead to depression (Jaremka et al., 2013).

Researchers have found that about 40% of those who are diagnosed with depression display no signs of the disorder one year later (American Psychiatric Association [APA], 2013). Another 20% have slight depression, but not sufficiently so to warrant a formal diagnosis of depression. Despite this rosy outlook, depression is a recurrent problem for many young adults (NCIPC, 2007). Antidepressant drugs help some people with depression recover, but some studies suggest that psychotherapy can be just as effective (Hollon, Thaw, & Markowitz, 2002).

For some young adults, periods of depression are offset by *manic episodes*, periods of euphoria, hyperactivity, grandiose ideas, and impulsive behavior. Individuals who experience emotional shifts of this kind may be diagnosed with *bipolar disorder*, a condition marked by extreme highs and lows that occur in cycles. Bipolar disorder is far less common than depression, affecting just under 2% of adults in the United States (American Psychiatric Association, 2013). For most adults, bipolar disorder interferes with social, occupational, and academic functioning. The disorder also increases suicide risk. Thankfully, with the aid of medication and psychotherapy, most adults who are diagnosed with the disorder can successfully manage its symptoms. However, a number of factors influence the degree to which an adult with bipolar disorder recovers. Those who are married, well educated, and receive the diagnosis fairly early in the course of the disorder are more likely to be restored to full functionality than those who do not enjoy these protective factors.

PERSONALITY DISORDERS In a few cases, the stresses of young adulthood, presumably in combination with some biological factor, lead to serious disturbances in cognitive, emotional, and social functioning that are not easily treated. For example, a **personality disorder** is an inflexible pattern of behavior that leads to difficulties in social, educational, and occupational functioning. In many cases, the problems associated with these disorders appear early in life. However, the behavior pattern is usually not diagnosed as a mental disorder until late adolescence or early adulthood (APA, 2013). Five common types of personality disorders are listed in Table 13.4.

Some young adults may exhibit behavior that suggests a personality disorder because of stressors such as the break-up of a long-term relationship. For this reason, mental health professionals have to assess an individual's long-term and current levels of functioning in order to diagnose personality disorders. Ethnic and cultural standards of behavior also have to be taken into account, and physical illnesses that can cause abnormal behavior, such as disturbances in the endocrine system, have to be ruled out. Clinicians also have to keep in mind that some of these disorders are closely related, such as the narcissistic and histrionic disorders, and that some individuals have more than one.

Generally, to be diagnosed with any of the disorders in Table 13.4, a young adult has to have been exhibiting the associated behavior since mid- or late adolescence. In addition, the person should demonstrate the behavior consistently, across all kinds of situations. For example, a person who steals from an employer but generally respects the property rights of others outside the work environment would probably not be diagnosed with antisocial personality disorder. The individual's functioning at work, at school, or in social relationships also must be impaired to some degree. Psychological tests can be helpful in distinguishing whether an individual simply has a troublesome personality trait, such as suspiciousness, or a genuine mental illness, such as paranoid personality disorder.

Some personality disorders, such as antisocial and borderline disorders, improve on their own as adults gain maturity (APA, 2013). However, most of these disorders remain problematic throughout adult life. In addition, they are not easily treated. In most cases, they do not respond to psychotherapy, because those who have them seem to believe their problems result from others' behavior rather than their own.

personality disorder an inflexible pattern of behavior that leads to difficulty in social, educational, and occupational functioning

schizophrenia a serious mental disorder characterized by disturbances of thought such as delusions and hallucinations

TABLE 13.4 Personality Disorders

Disorder Type	Characteristics
Antisocial	Difficulty forming emotional attachments; lack of empathy; little regard for the rights of others; self-centered; willing to violate the law or social rules to achieve a desired objective
Paranoid	Suspicious of others' behavior and motives; emotionally guarded and highly sensitive to minor violations of personal space or perceived rights
Histrionic	Irrational, attention-seeking behavior; inappropriate emotional responses; sexually seductive behavior and clothing
Narcissistic	Exaggerated sense of self-importance; craves attention and approval; exploits others; lack of empathy
Borderline	Unstable moods, relationships; fear of abandonment; tendency to self-injury; highly dependent on others; impulsive and reckless behavior

(*Source:* APA, 2013.)

SCHIZOPHRENIA Another type of serious mental illness that is often first diagnosed in early adulthood is **schizophrenia**, a mental disorder characterized by false beliefs known as *delusions* and false sensory experiences called *hallucinations*. For example, a first-year biology student who breaks into a laboratory on his college campus to work on a cure for cancer he has just thought of may suffer from a *delusion of grandeur*. Likewise, a young woman who hears voices that guide her behavior is likely to be experiencing hallucinations. Some people with schizophrenia have difficulties with feeling and expressing emotion as well.

For most people with schizophrenia, these disturbances of thought become so severe that they can no longer function at work, at school, or in social relationships. In fact, many engage in behavior that endangers themselves or others. For example, a person with schizophrenia may believe that he can fly and jump out of an upper-story window. Consequently, people with schizophrenia are frequently hospitalized. Fortunately, powerful antipsychotic medications can help most people with schizophrenia regain some degree of normal functioning (Lauriello, McEvoy, Rodriguez, Bossie, & Lasser, 2005). Yet many continue to experience recurring episodes of disturbed thinking even when medication helps them to gain control over their behavior.

Substance Use and Abuse

LO 13.8 What is the difference between physical and psychological substance dependence?

Alcoholism and significant drug addiction also peak between ages 18 and 40, after which they decline gradually. The rates of addiction are higher for men than for women, but the age pattern is very similar in both genders (Thompson & Lande, 2007). Binge drinking is also particularly common among 18- to 25-year-olds in the United States. Although most binge drinkers do not think of themselves as having a problem with alcohol, they clearly display a variety of problem behaviors, including substantially higher rates of unprotected sex, physical injury, driving while intoxicated, and trouble with the police (CDC, 2010). Thus, alarmed by surveys showing that as many as 25% of 18- to 25-year-olds engage in binge drinking, a growing number of colleges and universities are strictly enforcing rules against on-campus substance use (National Institute on Alcohol Abuse and Alcoholism, 2006). Many also provide students with treatment for alcohol- and substance-abuse problems. Binge drinking is one of several substance use behaviors that can lead to **substance abuse**, a pattern of behavior in which a person continues to use a substance even though doing so interferes with psychological, occupational, educational, and social functioning. The journey from first use of a drug to abuse may be long or short. Four factors influence the addictive potential of a drug:

- How fast the effects of the drug are felt
- How pleasurable the drug's effects are in producing euphoria or in extinguishing pain
- How long the pleasurable effects last
- How much discomfort is experienced when the drug is discontinued

Some drugs create a physical or chemical dependence; others create a psychological dependence. *Physical drug dependence* comes about as a result of the body's natural ability to protect itself against harmful substances by developing a *drug tolerance*. This means that the user becomes progressively less affected by the drug and must take larger and larger doses to get the same effect or high (APA, 2013). Tolerance occurs because the brain adapts to the presence of the drug by responding less intensely to it. In addition, the liver produces more enzymes to break down the drug. The various bodily processes adjust in order to continue to function with the drug present in the system.

Once drug tolerance is established, a person cannot function normally without the drug. If the drug is taken away, the user begins to suffer withdrawal symptoms. The *withdrawal symptoms*, both physical and psychological, are usually the exact opposite of the effects produced by the drug. For example, withdrawal from stimulants leaves a person exhausted and depressed; withdrawal from tranquilizers leaves a person nervous and agitated. Since taking the drug is the only way to escape these unpleasant symptoms, withdrawal can lead to relapse into addiction.

Simulate the **Experiment** *General Model of Drug Addiction* in **MyPsychLab**.

Psychological drug dependence is a craving or irresistible urge for the drug's pleasurable effects, and it is more difficult to combat than physical dependence (O'Brien, 1996). Some experts believe that drug cravings are controlled by a neural network that operates independently from and competes with a different network that controls deliberative decision making (Bechara, 2005). The drug-craving network acts on impulse that is largely influenced by the desire for immediate gratification. By contrast, the decision-making network identifies the consequences of potential actions and makes conscious decisions to engage in constructive behaviors and to avoid those that are destructive. This model of competing neural networks may explain why individuals who suffer from addiction often relapse despite their knowledge of the painful consequences that may occur as a result of doing so. Continued use of drugs to which an individual is physically addicted is influenced by the psychological component of the habit. There are also drugs that are probably not physically addictive but may create psychological dependence. Learning processes are important in the development and maintenance of psychological dependence. For example, drug-taking cues—the people, places, and things associated with using—can produce a strong craving for the abused substance (Hillebrand, 2000).

Alcohol is but one of many potentially addictive substances. However, it is the most commonly used of all of those that are listed in Table 13.5. As a result of the widespread availability of alcohol, and the social acceptability of drinking, rates of abuse are much higher for alcohol than they are for other substances. Experts estimate that more than 30% of adults in the United States have abused alcohol at some time in their lives (Hasin, Stinson, Ogburn, & Grant, 2007). Moreover, many individuals who abuse alcohol use other substances as well, and only one in four ever seek treatment for their drinking problems.

TABLE 13.5 Substances Often Abused

Drug	Effects	Withdrawal Symptoms
Stimulants		
Caffeine	Produces wakefulness and alertness; increases metabolism but slows reaction time	Headache, depression, fatigue
Nicotine (tobacco)	Effects range from alertness to calmness; lowers appetite for carbohydrates; increases pulse rate and other metabolic processes	Irritability, anxiety, restlessness, increased appetite
Amphetamines	Increase metabolism and alertness; elevate mood, cause wakefulness, suppress appetite	Fatigue, increased appetite, depression, long periods of sleep, irritability, anxiety
Cocaine	Brings on euphoric mood, energy boost, feeling of excitement, suppresses appetite	Depression, fatigue, increased appetite, long periods of sleep, irritability
Depressants		
Alcohol	First few drinks stimulate and enliven while lowering anxiety and inhibitions; higher doses have a sedative effect, slowing reaction time; impairing motor control and perceptual ability	Tremors, nausea, sweating, depression, weakness, irritability, and in some cases hallucinations
Barbiturates	Promote sleep, have calming and sedative effect, decrease muscular tension, impair coordination and reflexes	Sleeplessness, anxiety, sudden withdrawal can cause seizures, cardiovascular collapse, and death
Tranquilizers (e.g., Valium, Xanax)	Lower anxiety, have calming and sedative effect, decrease muscular tension	Restlessness, anxiety, irritability, muscle tension, difficulty sleeping
Narcotics	Relieve pain; produce paralysis of intestines	Nausea, diarrhea, cramps, insomnia
Hallucinogens		
Marijuana	Generally produces euphoria	Anxiety, difficulty sleeping, decreased appetite, hyperactivity
LSD	Produces excited exhilaration	None known
MDMA (Ecstasy)	Typically produces euphoria and feelings of understanding others and accepting them; lowers inhibitions; often causes overheating	Depression, fatigue, and in some cases a "crash," during which the person may be sad, scared, or annoyed

Answers to these questions can be found in the back of the book.

1. The _____ _____ _____ was a longitudinal study that discovered the association between health habits and aging.

2. Antibiotics can cure _____ STDs but not _____ STDs.

3. List four factors that increase the risk of intimate partner abuse:
   (a) _____
   (b) _____
   (c) _____
   (d) _____

4. _____ is a serious mental disorder that usually first appears in early adulthood.

5. _____ drug dependence includes craving for the drug's pleasurable effects.

CRITICAL THINKING

6. How would you rate your own health habits and personal factors, and how vulnerable do you think you are to sexually transmitted diseases, intimate partner abuse, mental health problems, and substance abuse? What behavioral changes might you make to reduce your risk?

Cognitive Changes

Like most aspects of physical functioning, intellectual processes are at their peak in early adulthood. Indeed, it now seems clear that the intellectual peak lasts longer than many early researchers had thought and that the rate of decline is quite slow. Current research also makes clear that the rate and pattern of cognitive decline vary widely—differences that appear to be caused by a variety of environmental and lifestyle factors, as well as by heredity.

Formal Operations and Beyond

LO 13.9 What types of postformal thought have developmentalists proposed?

As you should recall from Chapter 11, Piaget's formal operational stage emerges in mid- to late adolescence, but some theorists dispute Piaget's hypothesis that the formal operations stage is the last stage of cognitive development (Labouvie-Vief, 2006). These theorists hypothesize that a fifth stage emerges in early adulthood, typically in the early 20s, in response to the kinds of problems that are unique to adult life. The term **postformal thought** is collectively applied to the types of thinking that these theorists propose to be characteristic of the fifth stage of cognitive development.

The work of postformal theorists owes its origins to the ideas of Lawrence Kohlberg, whose theory of moral development you read about in Chapter 12, and William Perry (Labouvie-Vief, 2006). Kohlberg and Perry emphasized the shift toward **relativism**, the idea that some propositions cannot be adequately described as either true or false, that occurs in early adulthood (Kohlberg & Kramer, 1969; Perry, 1968). Perry studied undergraduates at Harvard University in the 1960s and concluded that they began their studies with the view that knowledge is comprised of truthful statements and that the purpose of education is to accumulate an increasing number of such propositions. As young adults progress through college, Perry's work suggested, conflicts among the many ideas to which they are exposed push them toward a relativistic approach that enables them to evaluate propositions in terms of their underlying assumptions and the contexts in which they occur.

For example, in the United States, most high school history students learn that slavery was the main cause of the Civil War (1861–1865). According to Perry's view, a student who is presented with a different idea about the main cause of the war is likely to dismiss it as "false" rather than to analyze it with regard to the supporting evidence that is cited by the person who advocates it. Perry argued that college classes reframe the "facts" that students acquired in earlier years in just this way and, in the process, help students develop a postformal approach to such complex issues. As Kohlberg and Perry would predict, researchers have found correlations between tests of postformal thought and adults' perception of ambiguity and their understanding of irony and metaphor (Blouin & McKelvie, 2012).

postformal thought types of thinking that are associated with a hypothesized fifth stage of cognitive development

relativism the idea that some propositions cannot be adequately described as either true or false

Another theorist, Michael Basseches, points out that many young adults turn away from a purely logical, analytic approach toward a more open, perhaps deeper, mode of understanding that accepts paradox and uncertainty. He calls this new adult type of thinking **dialectical thought** (Basseches, 1984, 1989). According to this view, adults do not give up their ability to use formal reasoning. Instead, they acquire a new ability to deal with the fuzzier problems that make up the majority of the problems of adulthood—problems that do not have a single solution or in which some critical pieces of information may be missing. Choosing what type of refrigerator to buy might be a decision aided by formal operational thought. But such forms of logical thought may not be helpful in making a decision about whether to adopt a child or whether to place an aging parent in a nursing home. Basseches argues that such problems demand a different kind of thinking—not a "higher" kind of thinking, but a different one.

What kind of thinking might this young couple be using to make a budget decision?

Psychologists Patricia King and Karen Kitchener (2004) have proposed that **reflective judgment**, the capacity to identify the underlying assumptions of differing perspectives on controversial issues, is an important feature of postformal thought. For example, reflective thinkers can ascertain that a person who argues that the key to reducing drug use is to educate people about the adverse effects of drugs is assuming that those who use drugs do so because they lack such knowledge. According to the studies that King and Kitchener have carried out, the capacity to analyze arguments in this way develops in a series of seven stages across childhood, adolescence, and adulthood (King & Kitchener, 2004). Like Kohlberg's stages of moral judgment, these stages are loosely tied to age and are influenced by an individual's level of education.

Many of these new theories of adult cognition are intriguing, but they remain highly speculative, with little empirical evidence to back them up. More generally, psychologists do not yet agree on whether these new types of thinking represent "higher" forms of thought, built on the stages Piaget described, or whether it is more appropriate simply to describe them as different forms of thinking that may or may not emerge in adulthood. What may be most important about such theories is their emphasizing that the normal problems of adult life, with their inconsistencies and complexities, cannot always be addressed fruitfully using formal operational logic. It seems entirely plausible that adults are pushed toward more pragmatic, relativistic forms of thinking and use formal operational thinking only occasionally, if at all. Postformal theorists agree that this change should not be thought of as a loss or a deterioration, but rather as a reasonable adaptation to a different set of cognitive tasks.

Intelligence

LO 13.10 How do the concepts of crystallized and fluid intelligence help to explain age-related changes in IQ scores?

Examination of intelligence in early adulthood suggests that both continuity and change characterize this component of cognitive functioning (Schroeder & Salthouse, 2004). IQ scores remain quite stable across middle childhood, adolescence, and early adulthood. For example, a classic study of Canadian army veterans, tested first when they were in their early 20s and then again in their early 60s, yielded similar results; there was a correlation of .78 between verbal IQ scores achieved at the two ages (Gold et al., 1995). Over shorter intervals, the correlations were even higher.

The best single source of evidence on the stability of IQ in adulthood is a remarkable 50-year study by Werner Schaie, referred to as the Seattle Longitudinal Study (Schaie, 2013). Schaie's study has provided developmentalists with a number of important insights into how intellectual functioning changes across adulthood. One is the finding that longitudinal and cross-sectional data yield somewhat different pictures of these changes, a phenomenon first reported by Schaie in 1983 (Schaie, 2009; Schaie & Hertzog, 1983). He began in 1956 with a set of cross-sectional samples; the participants in different samples were 7 years apart in age and ranged in age from 25 to 67. All participants took an IQ test at the outset of the study; a subset of the participants in each age group was then followed over 35 years and retested every 7 years. In 1963, another set of cross-sectional samples, covering the same age ranges, was tested, and a subset of these was retested 7, 14, 21, and 28 years later. Further samples were added in 1970, 1977, 1984, and 1991. This remarkable data-collection process enabled

dialectical thought a form of thought involving recognition and acceptance of paradox and uncertainty

reflective judgment the ability to identify the underlying assumptions of differing perspectives on controversial issues

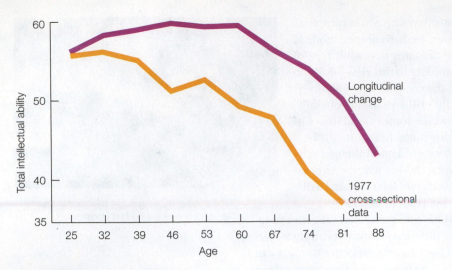

Figure 13.2 Cross-Sectional and Longitudinal Data on IQ Scores

These results from the Seattle Longitudinal Study show both cross-sectional and longitudinal data for a measure of overall intellectual skill (average score = 50).

(*Source:* Schale, 1983.)

crystallized intelligence knowledge and judgment acquired through education and experience

fluid intelligence the aspect of intelligence that reflects fundamental biological processes and does not depend on specific experiences

Schaie to look at IQ changes over 7-, 14-, 21-, and 28-year intervals for several sets of participants, each from a slightly different cohort. Figure 13.2 graphs one set of cross-sectional comparisons made in 1977, as well as 14-year longitudinal results smoothed over the whole age range. The test involved in this case is a measure of global intelligence on which the average score is set at 50 points (equivalent to an IQ of 100 on most other tests).

You can see that the cross-sectional comparisons show a steady drop in IQ. But the longitudinal evidence suggests that overall intelligence-test scores actually rise in early adulthood and then remain quite constant until perhaps age 60, when they begin to decline. Since this pattern has also been found by other researchers (e.g., Sands, Terry, & Meredith, 1989; Siegler, 1983), there is good support for the temptingly optimistic view that intellectual ability remains essentially stable through most of adulthood.

Looking at different components of intellectual ability gives a clearer picture of change and stability across the adult years. **Crystallized intelligence** depends heavily on education and experience (Horn, 1982). It consists of the set of skills and bits of knowledge that every adult learns as part of growing up in any given culture, such as vocabulary, the ability to read and understand the newspaper, and the ability to evaluate experience. Technical skills you may learn for your job or your life—balancing a checkbook, using a computer, making change, finding the mayonnaise in the grocery store—also represent crystallized intelligence. **Watch** the **Video** *Early Adulthood: Robert Sternberg: Culture Influences* in **MyPsychLab**.

Fluid intelligence, in contrast, involves more "basic" abilities—it is the aspect of intelligence that depends more on the efficient functioning of the central nervous system and less on specific experience (Horn, 1982). A common measure of fluid intelligence is a "letter series test," in which a participant is given a series of letters (e.g., A C F J O) and must figure out what letter should go next. This problem demands abstract reasoning rather than reasoning about known or everyday events. Most tests of memory also measure fluid intelligence, as do many tests measuring response speed and those measuring higher-level or abstract mathematical skills. Schaie's results suggest that adults maintain crystallized intelligence throughout early and middle adulthood but that fluid intelligence declines fairly steadily over adulthood, beginning at perhaps age 35 or 40 (Schaie, 2013). **Watch** the **Video** *Developing a Wiser Population: Robert Sternberg* in **MyPsychLab**.

So where does this leave us in answering the question about intellectual maintenance or decline over adulthood? It seems safe to conclude, at least tentatively, that intellectual abilities show essentially no decline in early adulthood except at the very top levels of intellectual demand. In middle adulthood, though, declines on fluid-intelligence abilities—those tasks that are thought to represent the efficiency of the basic physiological process—become evident (Schaie, 2013).

test yourself before going on   ✔ **Study** and **Review** in **MyPsychLab**

Answers to these questions can be found in the back of the book.

1. Some researchers have proposed that a new stage of cognitive development called _____ _____ emerges in early adulthood.

2. Research indicates that (crystallized/fluid) intelligence increases in adulthood, but (crystallized/fluid) intelligence declines.

CRITICAL THINKING

3. Earlier in the chapter you learned that most people reach their physical peak during early adulthood. What would you conclude about the development of a cognitive peak? When is it likely to occur, and in what ways is the process similar to and different from the development of one's physical peak?

Postsecondary Education

postsecondary education any kind of formal educational experience that follows high school

In today's high-tech, global economy, **postsecondary education**—any kind of formal educational experience that follows high school—has become a necessity for virtually everyone. For some, postsecondary education may be a 1-year course of study that culminates in a certificate attesting to a marketable set of job skills, such as training in medical office management. For others, it takes the form of enrollment in a 2- or 4-year college. At some point in their academic careers, most college students wonder whether all the hassles they experience are really worth the effort, as perhaps you may have. It should be somewhat heartening, then, to learn that college attendance is associated with a number of positive developmental outcomes.

Developmental Impact

LO 13.11 What are some of the ways in which college attendance affects individual development?

There is no doubt about the economic value of postsecondary education. College graduates earn more than nongraduates for a variety of reasons (Aud et al., 2013; Baum & Ma, 2007). First, graduates get more promotions and are far less likely than nongraduates to be unemployed for prolonged periods of time (Dohm & Wyatt, 2002). Second, many high-paying fields, such as engineering, are closed to individuals who do not have at least a bachelor's degree. Even in careers that do not require a degree, college graduates are more likely than nongraduates to get high-status managerial and technical positions, and they are viewed by those who make hiring decisions as more desirable employees than are nongraduates. This finding raises the question of whether college graduates are really different from nongraduates or are simply perceived to be. However, longitudinal evidence suggests that the longer a person remains in college, the better her performance on Piaget's formal operational tasks and other measures of abstract reasoning (Lehman & Nisbett, 1990; Pascarella, 1999).

There is also evidence that, during their years of college enrollment, students' academic and vocational aspirations rise (Sax & Bryant, 2006). For example, a young woman may enter college with the goal of becoming a biology teacher but graduate with the intention of going on to medical school. What seems critical to such decisions is that college-level classes allow students to make realistic assessments—for better or worse—of their academic abilities. Thus, another student may intend to be a doctor when he is a freshman but soon conclude that becoming a biology teacher is a more realistic, attainable goal, given his performance in college-level classes. Further, college attendance enhances students' internal locus of control and, as a result, helps them to understand how the daily behavioral choices they make shape their future lives (Wolfle & List, 2004).

In addition to having cognitive and motivational benefits, going to college provides students with new socialization opportunities. Many students encounter people from racial or ethnic groups other than their own for the first time in college. Advances in moral and social reasoning, as well as increases in the capacity to empathize with others' feelings, are also linked to college attendance (Chickering & Reisser, 1993; Pascarella & Terenzi, 1991). However, the relationships among authoritative parenting, academic performance, and social adjustment you have read about so often in earlier chapters hold true for college students as well (Wintre & Yaffe, 2000). Thus, students' social experiences prior to entering postsecondary education seem to be critical to their ability to benefit fully from the college experience.

College attendance is associated with developmental advances in both the cognitive and social domains.

Gender, Ethnicity, and Disability and the College Experience

LO 13.12 What is the impact of gender, ethnicity, and disability on the college experience?

The advantages associated with post-secondary education are relevant to all groups. However, the experience of attending a post-secondary institution varies across males and females as well as across ethnic groups. Post-secondary students with disabilities also face unique challenges.

GENDER More than half of college students are female, and women have slightly higher graduation rates than men at all degree levels (Aud et al., 2013). Women's higher graduation rates may be due to their tendency to spend almost twice as much time studying as men do, while men spend about 50% more time partying than women do (Sax, Lindholm, Astin, Korn, & Mahoney, 2002). **Watch** the **Video** *Women and the Field of Psychology: Florence Denmark* in **MyPsychLab**.

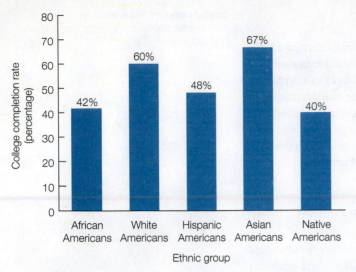

Figure 13.3 Degree Completion Rates in the United States

College completion rates vary considerably from one racial group to another. These figures represent the percentage of students who complete a degree within 6 years of taking their first course as a degree-seeking student.

(*Source:* NCES, 2010.)

Gender differences in major choices also contribute to differences in graduation rates (Conger & Long, 2010). One such difference is that women seem to be more proficient than men at choosing majors appropriate for their academic abilities and interests. In addition, because of the majors women tend to choose, such as English, they take more courses with flexible grading standards than men do. For example, women outnumber men in writing-course enrollment, but men outnumber women in math courses. Thus, females' higher grades and college completion rates are likely to be at least partially attributable to gender differences in patterns of major selection and course taking.

Outside the classroom, male and female students differ in behavior in ways that also contribute to gender differences in college performance. For example, binge drinking is more prevalent among college men than women (Keller, Maddock, Laforge, Velicer, & Basler, 2007). Some researchers hypothesize that gender differences in such behaviors arise from male students' desire to assert a masculine identity that is clearly distinct from that of women in settings in which women are in the majority (Harris & Edwards, 2010). In such contexts, which include most college campuses these days, masculine identity assertion is manifested as disengagement from academic pursuits and heightened interest in risky behaviors. However, a great deal more research is needed before developmentalists will know what, if any, influence students' gender identity priorities have on their performance in college.

ETHNICITY As you can see in Figure 13.3, graduation rates vary across ethnic groups in the United States. Note, however, that these data refer to degree completion within a 6-year time frame. Economic pressures often force students from disadvantaged groups to leave college temporarily or to reduce the number of credit hours they take each semester. As a result, these students may be less likely to finish college in 6 years than more economically advantaged Asian and White students (Seidman, 2005).

Of course, economic reasons alone cannot fully explain race differences in college completion. As we discussed in Chapter 11, many minority high school graduates lack the necessary academic preparation for college. Moreover, minority students who attend colleges that offer supportive programs whose aim is to prevent them from dropping out have higher graduation rates than their peers who do not attend such institutions (Gary, Kling, & Dodd, 2004; Perkins, Malone, & Barabino, 2013).

The success of supportive programs for minority students may derive from their capacity for helping such students develop a sense of belonging to the college community. Research examining the relationship between student success and the ethnic composition of a college's student population support this view (Seidman, 2005). Studies have shown that Hispanic Americans, for example, exhibit higher levels of academic success when they attend colleges at which their ethnic group is in the majority and is also well represented among the faculty (Flores & Park, 2013). Similarly, studies indicate that African American students who attend historically Black institutions show more gains in both cognitive and social competence than their peers who attend predominantly White colleges (Flowers, 2002; Flowers & Pascarella, 1999). In addition, attending historically Black colleges may help African American students achieve a stronger sense of ethnic identity, a factor that is correlated with persistence in college (Albritton, 2012).

Since 1972, the tribal college movement led by Native American educators has been working to provide the same type of culturally sensitive learning environment for reservation-dwelling Native Americans that historically Black colleges provide for African American students (American Indian Higher Education Council, 2013). Studies show that tribal colleges are helping many young Native Americans gain access to and experience success in postsecondary education (American Indian College Fund, 2006). ◉ **Watch** the **Video** *Emerging Adulthood: Postsecondary Education across Cultures* in **MyPsychLab**.

STUDENTS WITH DISABILITIES Students with disabilities now make up about 11% of the college population in the United States (NCES, 2006c). Although it is still too early to draw firm conclusions from research on college students with disabilities, recent studies contain some hints about how such students fare. For example, one reason for recent increases in college enrollment among students with disabilities is their belief that the required instructional modifications make it possible for them to compete academically with other students. The most common modification for such students is extended time for taking tests (Ofiesh, Hughes, & Scott, 2004). Research suggests that, with extended time, students with disabilities are able to approach or meet the same standards of academic performance required of other students in college classes (Alster, 1997). In addition, tutoring that helps them learn reading strategies that are particularly helpful for reading college-level textbooks increase these students' chances for success (Gajria, Jitendra, Sood, & Sacks, 2007). 👁 **Watch** the **Video** *Coping with Disability* in **MyPsychLab**.

test yourself before going on ✅ Study and Review in MyPsychLab

Answers to these questions can be found in the back of the book.

1. Classify each statement about gender differences in college students as characteristic of (F) females or (M) males:
   _____(1) take more math courses
   _____(2) engage in more risky behavior
   _____(3) use more effective study strategies
   _____(4) adapt more easily to the demands of new learning situations

2. The _____ _____ _____ seeks to provide a culturally sensitive learning environment for Native American students.

3. The most common modification for students with disabilities is _____ _____ for taking tests.

CRITICAL THINKING

4. Review Erikson's stage of industry versus inferiority, discussed in Chapter 10. What would his theory predict about the link between experiences in elementary school and obtaining a college degree?

SUMMARY

Physical Functioning (pp. 322–328)

LO 13.1   What is the difference between primary and secondary aging?

- It is important to distinguish between the unavoidable effects of primary aging and the preventable consequences of secondary aging. Primary aging is a result of biological factors that are largely uncontrollable. Secondary aging can be influenced by lifestyle changes.

LO 13.2   What changes in the brain take place in early adulthood?

- The brain reaches a stable size and weight in early adulthood. There is strong evidence that at least one spurt in brain development occurs between ages 17 and 21. Neuropsychologists hypothesize that a second spurt occurs in the mid- to late 20s. Sex differences are apparent in the adult brain, although their significance has yet to be established.

LO 13.3   How do other body systems change during early adulthood?

- It is clear that adults are at their peak both physically and cognitively between ages 20 and 40. In these years, a person has more muscle tissue, more calcium in the bones, better sensory acuity, greater aerobic capacity, and a more efficient immune system.

Health and Wellness (pp. 328–340)

LO 13.4   What habits and personal factors are associated with good health?

- Several longitudinal studies have shown that habits and personal factors influence good health. Lifestyle factors include avoiding smoking, drinking, overeating, undereating, and a sedentary lifestyle; exercise; regular sleep; and low BMI. Personal factors include social support, self-efficacy, an internal locus of control, and optimism.

LO 13.5   What are some of the viral and bacterial STDs that afflict young adults?

- In contrast to other diseases, sexually transmitted diseases are more common among young adults than among older adults. Bacterial STDs can be treated with antibiotics and include chlamydia, gonorrhea, and syphilis. Viral STDs are incurable and include herpes, HPV, and HIV/AIDS. A vaccine is now available for HPV.

LO 13.6   What are the causes and effects of intimate partner abuse?

- Intimate partner abuse is a significant global health problem. Causal factors include cultural beliefs about gender roles, as well as personal variables such as alcohol and drug use. Women who are abused develop feelings of anxiety, shame, and low self-esteem. Witnessing abuse negatively affects children's development.

LO 13.7 Which mental disorders occur most frequently in young adulthood?

- Rates of mental illness are higher in early adulthood than in middle adulthood; young adults are more likely to have depression or anxiety or to be lonely than are middle-aged adults. Early adulthood is the period during which personality disorders and schizophrenia are usually diagnosed.

LO 13.8 What is the difference between physical and psychological substance dependence?

- Physical dependence occurs when changes in the brain make it necessary to take a drug in order to avoid withdrawal symptoms. Psychological dependence is the craving that some substance abusers have for the effects of the drugs on which they are dependent.

Cognitive Changes (pp. 340–342)

LO 13.9 What types of postformal thought have developmentalists proposed?

- There may be a change in cognitive structure in adult life, and theorists have suggested that cognitive development goes beyond Piaget's formal operational stage. Postformal thought, a proposed fifth stage of cognitive development, includes various types of thinking. These types of thinking are relativism, dialectical thought, and reflective judgment.

LO 13.10 How do the concepts of crystallized and fluid intelligence help to explain age-related changes in IQ scores?

- Some studies of measures of intelligence show a decline with age, but the decline occurs quite late for well-exercised abilities (crystallized abilities) such as vocabulary. A measurable decline occurs earlier for so-called fluid abilities.

Postsecondary Education (pp. 343–345)

LO 13.11 What are some of the ways in which college attendance affects individual development?

- Postsecondary education has beneficial effects on both cognitive and social development in addition to being associated with higher income.

LO 13.12 What is the impact of gender, ethnicity, and disability on the college experience?

- Female students seem to have a number of important advantages over male students, including a higher graduation rate. However, many women lack confidence in their academic abilities and are reluctant to enter traditionally male occupations. African American students are less likely to complete postsecondary programs than other groups, perhaps because they perceive White-dominated educational environments as hostile. Modifications such as extended time for taking exams help college students with disabilities attain their academic goals.

KEY TERMS

crystallized intelligence (p. 342)
dialectical thought (p. 341)
fluid intelligence (p. 342)
intimate partner abuse (p. 333)
limbic system (p. 324)
locus of control (p. 330)

maximum oxygen uptake (VO$_2$ max) (p. 324)
pelvic inflammatory disease (p. 331)
personality disorder (p. 337)
phobia (p. 336)

postformal thought (p. 340)
postsecondary education (p. 343)
primary aging (senescence) (p. 322)
reflective judgment (p. 341)

relativism (p. 340)
schizophrenia (p. 337)
secondary aging (p. 322)
sexual violence (p. 335)
substance abuse (p. 338)

CHAPTER TEST ✓ **Study** and **Review** in **MyPsychLab**

Answers to all the Chapter Test questions can be found in the back of the book.

1. According to the World Health Organization, which of these countries has the lowest rate of physical abuse among women?
   a. Switzerland
   b. The United States
   c. Nicaragua
   d. Bangladesh

2. Which of the following best describes changes in reproductive functioning as men age?
   a. Reproductive ability ends around age 70.
   b. Lower sperm counts in men are almost always related to some kind of disease or adverse condition.
   c. Men produce more sperm as they get older.
   d. The quality of sperm does not change as men get older.

3. Pregnancies that result from *in vitro* fertilization _____.
   a. are less likely to end in a live birth than natural pregnancies
   b. usually result in the delivery of infants with disabilities
   c. are more likely to end in a live birth than natural pregnancies
   d. none of the above

4. Which of the following is the most common measure of overall aerobic fitness of the heart and lungs?
   a. VO$_2$ max
   b. carbon dioxide production
   c. heart rate
   d. systolic blood pressure

5. Which of the following is a category of mental disorders characterized by an inflexible pattern of behavior that eventually leads to difficulty in several areas of functioning, such as social or vocational?
   a. mood disorder
   b. mood disorder with mixed emotional features
   c. anxiety disorder
   d. personality disorder

6. Which category of psychological disorders occurs most frequently in early adulthood?
   a. mood disorders
   b. schizophrenia
   c. anxiety disorders
   d. personality disorders

7. According to developmentalists, which of the following most strongly influences health among adults?
   a. health-related behaviors such as smoking
   b. optimism
   c. genetics
   d. social support

8. Among college students, binge drinking is most common among
   a. African Americans
   b. Hispanic Americans
   c. females
   d. males

9. Which mental disorder is characterized by disturbances of thought, such as delusions and hallucinations?
   a. schizophrenia
   b. narcissistic personality disorder
   c. anxiety disorder
   d. mood disorder

10. Marcus gets a flat tire on the way to work. He curses and says, "This always happens to me! I have worse luck than anybody I know." Marcus has known for several months that he needed to buy new tires for his car. This is an example of _____.
    a. self-denial
    b. an external locus of control
    c. self-efficacy
    d. an internal locus of control

11. Which statement about aging and the immune system is true?
    a. The immune system's functioning improves with age.
    b. The thymus gland's ability to maintain immune functioning declines.
    c. The body produces more B and T cells than it needs as adults get older.
    d. Research has shown that declines in immune functioning are entirely due to secondary aging.

12. One reason for the finding that females get higher grades than males in college is that _____.
    a. getting good grades is part of a feminine gender identity
    b. women are more likely than men to engage in binge drinking

    c. female students are more likely than male students to select majors that match their abilities and interests
    d. men get lower scores on college entrance exams

13. Which of the following drugs does *not* belong in the same category as the others?
    a. barbiturates
    b. cocaine
    c. alcohol
    d. tranquilizers

14. In the Alameda study, which of the following was *not* defined as part of the social network index?
    a. ethnicity
    b. group membership
    c. number of contacts with friends and relatives
    d. marital status

15. A young adult who is deciding whether to rent or purchase a home would probably use which of these types of thinking?
    a. concrete operational thought
    b. psychosocial investment balancing
    c. reflective judgment
    d. dialectical thought

16. Most of the sexual violence in the United States takes place in which of the following contexts?
    a. stalking of the victim by an unknown person
    b. social or romantic relationships
    c. a nonpremeditated attack by a stranger
    d. the workplace

17. Which of the following is linked to depression and suicidal thoughts?
    a. poor grades in college
    b. binge drinking
    c. driving while intoxicated
    d. unprotected sex

18. The ability to identify the underlying assumptions of differing perspectives on issues is called _____.
    a. postformal thought
    b. dialectical thought
    c. formal operational thinking
    d. reflective judgment

19. Which of the following is an episode of partner abuse that involves the use of physical coercion to force a person to engage in a sexual act against his or her will?
    a. sexual violence
    b. battery
    c. sexual harassment
    d. intimate partner abuse

20. Which of the following best summarizes the differences between men's and women's brains in young adulthood?
    a. The corpus callosum develops faster in young men than in young women.
    b. The amount, distribution, and ratio of gray matter to white matter differs between men and women in young adulthood.
    c. The distribution of glial cells is markedly different between young men and young women.
    d. The sex differences that were seen in childhood and adolescence become less pronounced in young adulthood.

21. What is the name of the "fifth stage of cognitive development," which many theorists believe applies to young adulthood?
    a. formal operational thought
    b. postrelative thinking
    c. postcognitive thought
    d. postformal thought

22. Walter Schaie's research showed that _____.
    a. cross-sectional studies overestimate age-related declines in cognitive functioning
    b. longitudinal studies overestimate age-related declines in cognitive functioning
    c. age-related declines in cognitive functioning begin at age 30
    d. cognitive functioning is stable across the adult years

23. Georgia has a serious visual impairment. Which statement best describes the effects of her disability on her college experience?
    a. She will be restricted to taking courses that do not require good vision.
    b. She is more likely to graduate than students who don't have disabilities.
    c. Appropriate modifications will increase her chances for college success.
    d. She will be doubtful about her ability to compete with students who do not have disabilities.

24. Which of the following best describes the years between 18 and 40?
    a. They represent a dramatic shift from postformal thought.
    b. They are the beginning of rapid physical and cognitive decline.
    c. They are a time of peak physical and cognitive functioning, but also a time of decline in both domains.
    d. They are a time when neither physical nor cognitive functioning have reached peak levels.

25. Which group is most likely to complete a degree within 6 years of starting college?
    a. Whites
    b. African Americans
    c. Native Americans
    d. Asian Americans

To 👁 **Watch** ❋ **Explore** ◉ **Simulate** ✅ **Study** and **Review**
and experience MyVirtualLife, go to MyPsychLab.com.

chapter 14

Social and Personality Development in Early Adulthood

One of the advantages of a simulation such as *MyVirtualLife* is that students are able to try out roles that they have yet to assume in real life. But if you stop and think about it, you already occupy several social roles. At the very least, you're a son or daughter. Perhaps you're also a boyfriend, girlfriend, fiancé, or even a spouse or a parent. And what about your nonfamily roles? You're a student, but you may also be a roommate, an employee, or a volunteer. What's clear about early adulthood is that it is the time in

LEARNING OBJECTIVES

THEORIES OF SOCIAL AND PERSONALITY DEVELOPMENT

14.1 What did Erikson mean when he described early adulthood as a crisis of intimacy versus isolation?

14.2 What is a life structure, and how does it change?

14.3 What are the characteristics of emerging adulthood?

INTIMATE RELATIONSHIPS

14.4 What factors do evolutionary and social role theorists emphasize in their theories of mate selection?

14.5 How do marriage and divorce affect the lives of young adults?

14.6 What factors contribute to the relationship between premarital cohabitation and divorce?

14.7 In what ways are gay and lesbian couples similar to and different from heterosexual couples?

14.8 How do singles accomplish Erikson's psychosocial developmental task of intimacy?

PARENTHOOD AND OTHER RELATIONSHIPS

14.9 What happens during the transition to parenthood?

14.10 How are family and friends important to young adults?

THE ROLE OF WORKER

14.11 What factors influence an individual's occupational choices?

14.12 How do career goals and job satisfaction change over time?

14.13 What are some of the innovations that are associated with the quality of work–life movement?

14.14 In what way do women's work patterns differ from those of men?

people's lives when the number of roles in which they must function effectively grows by leaps and bounds. As you will learn in this chapter, even under the best of circumstances, the role transitions of early adulthood can be stressful. Part of the stress comes from the fact that so many transitions occur in such a relatively short time. Still, each transition brings with it new opportunities for personal growth.

Theories of Social and Personality Development

Psychoanalytic theories view adult development, like development at younger ages, as a result of a struggle between a person's inner thoughts, feelings, and motives and society's demands. Other perspectives provide different views of this period. Integrating ideas from all of them allows us to better understand early adult development.

Erikson's Stage of Intimacy versus Isolation

LO 14.1   What did Erikson mean when he described early adulthood as a crisis of intimacy versus isolation?

For Erikson, the central crisis of early adulthood is **intimacy versus isolation**. The young adult must find a life partner, someone outside his own family with whom she can share his life, or face the prospect of being isolated from society. More specifically, **intimacy** is the capacity to engage in a supportive, affectionate relationship without losing one's own sense of self. Intimate partners can share their views and feelings with each other without fearing that the relationship will end. They can also allow each other some degree of independence without feeling threatened. ⊙ **Watch** the **Video** *Early Adulthood: Early Adulthood Relationships* in **MyPsychLab**.

As you might suspect, researchers have found that a successful resolution of the intimacy-versus-isolation stage depends on a good resolution of the identity-versus-role-confusion crisis you read about in Chapter 12 (Beyers & Seiffge-Krenke, 2010). Erikson predicted that individuals who reached early adulthood without having established a sense of identity would be incapable of intimacy. That is, such young adults would be, in a sense, predestined to social isolation.

intimacy versus isolation   Erikson's early adulthood stage, in which an individual must find a life partner or supportive friends in order to avoid social isolation

intimacy   the capacity to engage in a supportive, affectionate relationship without losing one's own sense of self

Social scientists have not done very well at devising theories to explain lovely romantic moments like these.

Still, a poor sense of identity is only one barrier to intimacy. Misunderstandings stemming from sex differences in styles of interaction can also get in the way. To women, intimacy is bound up with self-disclosure. Thus, women who are involved with a partner who does not reveal much that is personal perceive the relationship as lacking in intimacy. However, most men don't see self-disclosure as essential to intimacy. Consequently, many men are satisfied with relationships that their female partners see as inadequate.

Though many people involved in intimate relationships wish their relationships were better, most adults succeed in establishing some kind of close relationship. Not everyone marries, of course, but many adults develop affectionate, long-lasting friendships that are significant sources of support for them and may, in some cases, serve the same functions as having an intimate life partner.

Levinson's Life Structures

LO 14.2 What is a life structure, and how does it change?

Daniel Levinson's concept of *life structure* represents a different approach to adult development (Levinson, 1978, 1990). A **life structure** includes all the roles an individual occupies, all of his or her relationships, and the conflicts and balance that exist among them. Figure 14.1 illustrates how life structures change over the course of adulthood.

Like Erikson, Levinson theorized that each of these periods presents adults with new developmental tasks and conflicts. He believed that individuals respond psychologically to these tasks and conflicts by creating new life structures. Consequently, adults cycle through periods of stability and instability.

As adults enter a period in which a new life structure is required, there is a period of adjustment, which Levinson called the *novice* phase. In the *mid-era* phase, adults become more competent at meeting the new challenges through reassessment and reorganization of the life structure they created during the novice phase. Stability returns in the *culmination* phase, when adults have succeeded in creating a life structure that allows them to manage the demands of the new developmental challenges with more confidence and less distress. 👁 **Watch** the **Video** *Early Adulthood: Stress about the Future: Gary* in **MyPsychLab**. 👁 **Watch** the **Video** *Early Adulthood: Stress about the Future: Amanda* in **MyPsychLab**.

For example, marriage requires a new life structure. Even if the newlyweds have known each other for a very long time or have been living together, they have not known each other in the roles of husband and wife. Moreover, they have never had in-laws. So, young adults who

life structure in Levinson's theory, the underlying pattern or design of a person's life at a given time, which includes roles, relationships, and behavior patterns

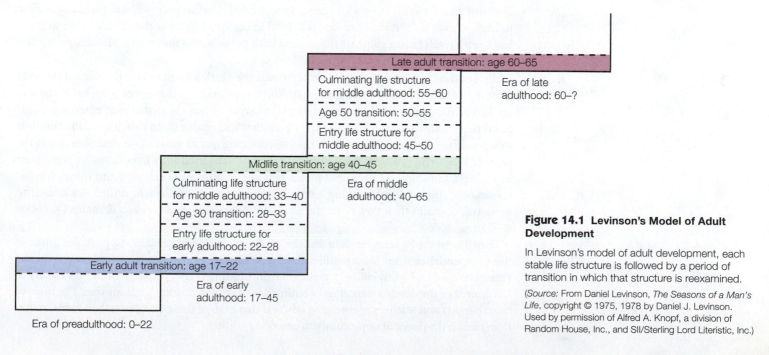

Figure 14.1 Levinson's Model of Adult Development

In Levinson's model of adult development, each stable life structure is followed by a period of transition in which that structure is reexamined.

(*Source:* From Daniel Levinson, *The Seasons of a Man's Life*, copyright © 1975, 1978 by Daniel J. Levinson. Used by permission of Alfred A. Knopf, a division of Random House, Inc., and SII/Sterling Lord Literistic, Inc.)

marry acquire a new set of relationships. At the same time, they face many new day-to-day, practical issues such as how finances will be managed, how housekeeping chores will be done, and whose family they will visit on which holidays. As Levinson's theory predicts, newlyweds usually go through a period of adjustment, during which they experience more conflict than before the wedding, and after which things are much calmer. The calm comes, as Levinson would put it, when each spouse has achieved a new life structure that is adapted to the demands of marriage.

Emerging Adulthood

LO 14.3 What are the characteristics of emerging adulthood?

Like Levinson, a growing number of developmentalists view the period between 17 and 22 as a transitional one. Psychologist Jeffrey Arnett has proposed that the educational, social, and economic demands that modern cultures make in individuals in this age range have given rise to a new developmental period he calls **emerging adulthood**. Arnett defines this phase as the period from the late teens to the early 20s when individuals experiment with options prior to taking on adult roles (Arnett, 2000). He argues that emerging adulthood is not necessarily a universal phase of development. Instead, it arises in cultures where individuals in their late teens face a wide array of choices about the occupational and social roles they will occupy in adulthood (Jensen & Arnett, 2012). Research examining the self-concepts of men and women in this age group support Arnett's view. His own studies and those of other researchers indicate that, at least in the United States, young people do not tend to think of themselves as having fully attained adulthood until the age of 25 or so (Galambos, Turner, & Tilton-Weaver, 2005; Kins & Beyers, 2010).

Neuroimaging studies have provided some support for the notion that emerging adulthood is a unique period of life. These studies suggest that the parts of the brain that underlie rational decision making, impulse control, and self-regulation mature during these years (Crone, Wendelken, Donohue, van Leijenhorst, & Bunge, 2006; Gogtay et al., 2004). As a result, early on in this phase of life, individuals make poorer decisions about matters such as risky behaviors (e.g., unprotected sex) than they do when these brain areas reach full maturity in the early to mid-20s.

The neurological changes of the emerging adult period combine with cultural demands to shape the psychosocial features of this period of development. Researcher Glenn Roisman and his colleagues have hypothesized that emerging adults must address developmental tasks in five domains: academic, friendship, conduct, work, and romantic (Roisman, Masten, Coatsworth, & Tellegen, 2004). Roisman's research suggests that skills within the first three of these domains transfer easily from adolescence to adulthood. Useful study skills (academic) acquired in high school, for instance, are just as helpful in college. Likewise, the skills needed to make and keep friends (friendship) are the same in both periods, and the process of adapting to rules (conduct) is highly similar as well.

By contrast, emerging adults must approach the work and romantic domains differently than they did as adolescents, according to Roisman. Certainly, many teenagers have jobs and are involved in romances. However, the cultural expectations associated with emerging adulthood require them to commit to a career path that will enable them to achieve full economic independence from their families. Likewise, emerging adults must make decisions about the place of long-term romantic relationships in their present and future lives as well as participate in such relationships. As predicted by his hypothesis, Roisman's findings and those of other researchers suggest that emerging adults experience more adjustment difficulties related to these two domains than they do in the academic, friendship, and conduct domains (Korobov & Thorne, 2006).

Finally, psychologists speculate that the tendency of emerging adults to push the limits of the independence from their families that most acquire in the late teens contributes to the remarkable neurological changes that occur during this phase. Thus, the road that leads to fulfillment of the developmental tasks outlined by Roisman is often a bumpy one. The hope of most parents and teachers of emerging adults is that each of these bumps further opens, rather than closes, the doors of opportunity to emerging adults.

Answers to these questions can be found in the back of the book.

1. According to Erikson, an adult who fails to establish an intimate relationship risks _____ from society.

2. In what order do these periods of adjustment occur in Levinson's theory of life structures?

   _____ **(a)** culmination phase

   _____ **(b)** mid-era phase

   _____ **(c)** novice phase

3. Emerging adults face developmental tasks in the domains of _____, _____, _____, _____, and _____.

CRITICAL THINKING

4. What are the similarities and differences among Erikson's, Levinson's, and Arnett's approach to early adulthood?

Intimate Relationships

Was Erikson correct about the importance of intimate relationships in early adulthood? Statistics on household composition in the United States suggest that he was (see Figure 14.2). Households are about evenly divided between those headed by a married couple and those involving other kinds of relationships (Lofquist, Lugalla, O'Connell, & Feliz, 2012). However, a broader interpretation of the data suggests that "coupled" households continue to be more common among adults than those that are headed by singles (55% versus 42%). Furthermore, many individuals in the single-person-household and single-parent-household groups were previously married or partnered, and many of them have partners who also live in single-person households. Thus, partnering, or as Erikson would put it, the search for intimacy, continues to be an important facet of adult life in the United States.

Theories of Mate Selection

LO 14.4 What factors do evolutionary and social role theorists emphasize in their theories of mate selection?

What characteristics do men and women look for in an intimate partner? Some theorists claim that males and females answer this question differently because of evolutionary pressures. Others argue that the roles that men and women occupy in the cultures in which they live shape their ideas about what kind of person would be an ideal mate. ◉ **Watch** the **Video** *Dating and Finding a Mate* in **MyPsychLab**.

EVOLUTIONARY THEORIES As you should remember from Chapter 2, evolutionary explanations of behavior focus on survival value. Heterosexual relationships ensure the survival of the species, of course, because they are the context in which conception takes place. However, when choosing a mate, heterosexuals don't simply look for someone of the opposite sex. Instead, mating is a selective process, and evolutionary theorists often cite research on sex differences in mate preferences and mating behavior in support of their views. Cross-cultural studies conducted over a period of several decades suggest that men prefer physically attractive, younger women, while women look for men whose socioeconomic status is higher than their own, who offer earning potential and stability (Buss, 1999; Schmidt, Shackelford, & Buss, 2001).

The reasons behind men's and women's divergent mating goals are explained by **parental investment theory** (Trivers, 1972). This theory proposes that men value health and availability in their mates and are less selective because their minimum

parental investment theory the theory that sex differences in mate preferences and mating behavior are based on the different amounts of time and effort men and women must invest in child rearing

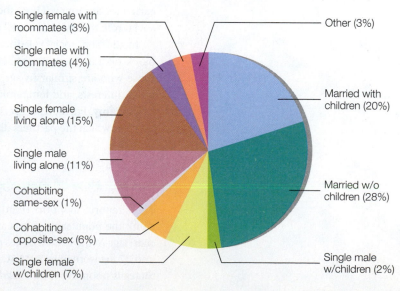

Figure 14.2 Household Composition in the United States

(*Source:* Lofquist et al., 2012.)

Single female with roommates (3%)
Single male with roommates (4%)
Single female living alone (15%)
Single male living alone (11%)
Cohabiting same-sex (1%)
Cohabiting opposite-sex (6%)
Single female w/children (7%)
Other (3%)
Married with children (20%)
Married w/o children (28%)
Single male w/children (2%)

investment in parenting offspring—a single act of sexual intercourse—requires only a few minutes. In contrast, women's minimum investment in childbearing involves nurturing an unborn child in their own body for 9 months as well as enduring the potentially physically traumatic experience of giving birth. Given their minimum investments, men seek to maximize the likelihood of survival of the species by maximizing the number of their offspring; women seek to minimize the number of their offspring because their investment is so much greater.

Further, evolutionary theorists argue that both men and women realize that a truly adaptive approach to child rearing requires much more than a minimum investment (Buss, 1999). Human offspring cannot raise themselves. Therefore, men value health and youth in their mates not only because these traits suggest fertility but also because a young, healthy woman is likely to live long enough to raise the children. Similarly, women realize that to be able to nurture children to adulthood, they must have an economic provider so that they will be able to invest the time needed to raise offspring. Consequently, they look for men who seem to be capable of fulfilling these requirements.

As mentioned above, consistent sex differences in mate preferences and mating behavior have been found across many cultures, and evolutionary theorists suggest that this cross-cultural consistency is strong evidence for a genetic basis for the behavior (Frederick, Reynolds, & Fisher, 2013). However, these claims take us back to the basic nature-versus-nurture arguments we have examined so often before (Eagly & Wood, 2013). Certainly, these sex differences are consistent, but they could be the result of variations in gender roles that are passed on within cultures.

SOCIAL ROLE THEORY **Social role theory** provides a different perspective on sex differences in mating (Eagly & Wood, 2012). According to this view, such differences are adaptations to gender roles that result from present-day social realities rather than from natural-selection pressures that arose in a bygone evolutionary era. To test this hypothesis, social role theorists reanalyzed a very large set of cross-cultural data produced and interpreted by evolutionary psychologist David Buss in support of parental investment theory (Buss et al., 1990). In their reanalysis, advocates of social role theory found that both men's and women's mate preferences changed as women gained economic power (Wood & Eagly, 2007). Women's emphasis on potential mates' earning power declined, and men's focus on potential mates' domestics skills decreased.

Researchers have also found that college-educated women with high earning potential prefer to date and marry men whose income potential is higher than their own (Wiederman & Allgeier, 1992). In fact, the more a woman expects to earn herself, the higher are her income requirements in a prospective mate. This study was widely cited by evolutionary theorists as supporting their view that such preferences are genetic and are not influenced by cultural conditions. However, a different perspective on the same study, proposed by social role theorists, led to a different conclusion (Wood & Eagly, 2007). These theorists suggest that many of today's high-income women desire to take time off to have and raise children. To be able to do so without lowering their standard of living substantially, these women require a mate who can earn a lot of money. Thus, social role theorists say, such research findings can be explained by social role theory just as well as by evolutionary theory.

In addition, social role theorists point out that high-income women desire high-income husbands because members of both sexes prefer mates who are like themselves. People are drawn to those who are similar in age, education, social class, ethnic-group membership, religion, attitudes, interests, and temperament. Sociologists refer to this tendency as **assortative mating**, or **homogamy**. Further, partnerships based on homogamy are much more likely to endure than are those in which the partners differ markedly (Smith, Maas, & van Tubergen, 2012).

Marriage

LO 14.5 How do marriage and divorce affect the lives of young adults?

News reports about the trend toward later marriage in the United States today might make you think the popularity of this ancient institution is on the wane. Indeed, the average age at first marriage in the United States rose from about 21 for both men and women in 1970 to 29 for men and 27 for women in 2011 (U.S. Census Bureau, 2013). Still, the wedding industry in the United States is booming (*The Wedding Report*, Inc. 2012). Marketing surveys show that more than 2 million weddings take place every year, with an average of 138 guests in attendance. June is still the favored month for marrying, and brides overwhelmingly choose to adorn their bridesmaids in blues, pinks, and purples (*Wedding Report*, 2013). Couples spend over $50 billion on engagement jewelry, engagement and wedding social gatherings (e.g., engagement parties, showers), wedding books and magazines, wedding apparel, wedding accessories (e.g., flowers), catering, bride's and groom's cakes, disc jockeys and bands, photographers and videographers, honeymoons, and other wedding-related items (*The Wedding Report*, Inc. 2012). What has changed in recent years is that couples are more likely to pay for their own weddings these days than in the past, when they relied on parents to fund nuptial ceremonies. In addition, wedding apparel, locations, and other features vary widely from one couple to another. In fact, the largest proportion of weddings, some 37%, are classified by wedding planners as "fun" weddings with themes such as the couple's favorite sport, movie, or band (*The Wedding Report*, Inc. 2012). Clearly, the institution of marriage is alive and well (see *No Easy Answers*).

NO EASY ANSWERS

Wedding Stress Management

Did you know that getting married is one of life's most stressful events? It would probably be so even without the added stress of planning a wedding. Thus, it's no wonder that a quick internet search using the key words "wedding stress management" will pull up dozens of links to websites that offer tips for avoiding the frenzy that often surrounds the process of planning and successfully staging a wedding. Moreover, there are dozens of books devoted to advice on how to reduce wedding-related stress.

Marriage rituals, of course, have been an integral part of societies all over the world for thousands of years. The difference between the modern-day version and those that were common in earlier days is one of degree. The *average*

wedding in the United States now costs about $26,000, but the price tag varies widely from one part of the country to another (*The Wedding Report, Inc., 2012*). In some cities, the average wedding costs $50,000 or more. At www.costofwedding.com, you can enter your zip code and find out the average for your area.

With so much money at stake and with the potential for hurt feelings on the part of acquaintances who aren't invited to the reception or cousins who aren't asked to be members of the wedding party, wedding stress can significantly diminish an individual's quality of life. Thus, learning to manage wedding stress can increase the chances that an event that ought to be one of the most joyous in life will actually be so. Psychological research says that the best approach to managing wedding-related stress is one that balances *problem-focused coping* and *emotion-focused coping* (Folkman & Lazarus, 1980). Problem-focused coping involves managing the actual source of stress. When couples set firm budget guidelines for themselves and research ways to limit spending in order to conform to them, they are engaging in this kind of coping. Emotion-focused coping has to do with managing emotional responses to current or potential stressors. Couples who treat themselves to a massage in the midst of the wedding-planning frenzy are using emotion-focused coping.

Finally, most couples today enroll in wedding-gift registries so that those who want to give them gifts will know what kinds of dishes, sheets, and other household items they want. However, the best gift for a couple to request might be a package of postwedding counseling sessions that help couples cope with the transition to marriage. In fact, if you peruse the websites of marriage and family therapists in your area, you'll probably find that many of them advertise postwedding counseling packages for just this

purpose. Such a gift may help future spouses remember that a beautiful wedding doesn't ensure a happy marriage.

YOU DECIDE

Decide which of these two statements you most agree with and think about how you would defend your position:

1. *A wedding marks one of the most important events in a person's life; thus it is worth whatever it costs both financially and psychologically.*

2. *It is foolish to spend thousands of dollars on an event that usually lasts only a few hours, and such spending takes funds away from the couple's financial goals such as buying their first home.*

Sex Differences in the Impact of Marriage

As you have learned, married adults appear to be healthier and happier than their single counterparts. Why? One possible explanation is that married adults have better health practices. Moreover, researchers have found that partners support each other's efforts to make changes such as quitting smoking and often jointly decide to establish new patterns of health-related behavior as a couple (Lewis et al., 2006; Reczek, 2012).

However, an important finding in this body of research is that, at least in the United States, men generally benefit more from marriage than do women on measures of physical and mental health. That is, married men are generally the healthiest and live the longest, while unmarried men are collectively the worst off. The two groups of women fall in between, with married women at a slight advantage over unmarried women. But unmarried women are considerably healthier and happier than are unmarried men. Why should this difference exist?

An interesting two-phase study of marital quality and health looked for a possible correlation between levels of a stress-related hormone called *cortisol* and marriage quality (Kiecolt-Glaser, 2000). Researchers focused on cortisol because it is known to increase when individuals experience negative emotions, and it is one of many stress hormones that are thought to impair immune-system functioning. Thus, it may be an important mechanism through which relationship quality affects health.

Investigators measured newlyweds' cortisol levels after they had discussed issues involving conflict, such as in-law relationships and finances. As expected, both husbands' and wives' cortisol levels were somewhat elevated after these discussions. Next, researchers asked couples to tell the story of how they met. As expected, in the majority of both husbands and wives, cortisol levels dropped as they discussed the emotionally neutral topic of relationship history. However, cortisol levels dropped least in those participants who were the most emotionally negative (as measured by number of negative words used) in describing their relationships. This component of the study demonstrated a direct link between stress hormones and marital negativity.

In addition, an important sex difference emerged. When couples described negative events in their relationships, wives' cortisol levels increased, while husbands' levels remained constant. This finding suggests that women may be more physiologically sensitive to relationship negativity than men. These results may help explain why marriage is a more consistent protective factor for men than for women.

Sex differences were also apparent in the study's second phase, during which researchers surveyed participants 8 to 12 years later to find out whether they were still married. Remarkably, they found that the higher the wife's cortisol response to emotional negativity in the first phase, the more likely the couple was to be divorced. Consequently, researchers hypothesized that women's physiological responses to marital quality are an important determinant of relationship stability.

CRITICAL ANALYSIS

1. *In your view, what is it about marriage that causes spouses to follow better health practices than their single counterparts?*

2. *Aside from women's sensitivity to relationship negativity, what are some possible reasons for the finding that the psychological benefits of marriage are greater among men than they are among women?* 👁 **Watch** the **Video** *Early Adulthood: Marriage and Love Relationships across Cultures* in **MyPsychLab**.

Moreover, most marriages endure. The often-quoted statistic of a 50% divorce rate represents a cohort effect in that it is based on marriages that occurred during the 1970s, a period of upheaval in family life that sociologists and researchers in other fields still don't fully understand (Stevenson & Wolfers, 2007). Longitudinal studies of marital duration that include marriages that took place from the 1980s through the early 2000s suggest that only one-third of first marriages end in divorce before the tenth anniversary (Goodwin, Mosher, & Chandra, 2010).

On average, married adults are happier and healthier, live longer, and have lower rates of a variety of psychiatric problems and other behavioral patterns that threaten their well-being than do adults without committed partners—findings that are discussed further in *Research Report* (Doherty & Ensminger, 2013; Williams, Frech, & Carlson, 2010). Clearly, though, not all marriages are happy ones. What factors contribute to marital satisfaction?

RELATIONSHIP QUALITY While we often discuss differences across ethnic groups, you can see in Figure 14.3 on page 357 that there is a remarkable amount of agreement across groups about what makes a marriage work (Taylor, Funk, & Clark, 2007). Importantly, a large majority of adults in all groups believe that intimacy issues—that is, faithfulness and a satisfactory sexual relationship—are more important than the material aspects of marriage, such as how labor is divided and having an adequate income. Thus, relationship quality appears to be what most people look for to judge whether their marriages are satisfactory.

Many powerful influences on marital success are in place long before a marriage even begins. Each partner brings to the relationship certain skills, resources, and traits that affect the emerging partnership system. The personality characteristics of the partners seem especially important. For example, shyness in one or both spouses is associated with low levels of marital satisfaction, presumably because of the link between shyness and effective communication skills

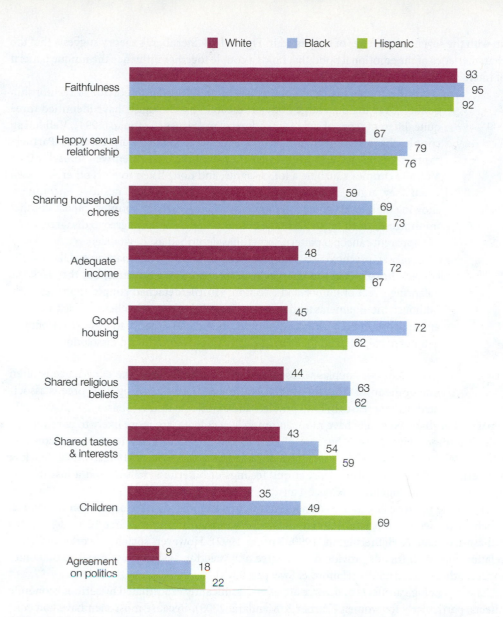

Figure 14.3 Rating Components of Marital Success, by Race and Ethnicity

Percentage saying each component is very important for a successful marriage.
Note: Whites include only non-Hispanic Whites. Blacks include only non-Hispanic Blacks. Hispanics are of any race.

(*Source:* From *Generation Gap in Values, Behaviors as Marriage and Parenthood Drift Apart, Public Is Concerned about Social Impact*, © 2007, Pew Research Center, Social and Demographic Trends project. http://pewresearch.org/assets/social/pdf/Marriage.pdf)

(Baker & McNulty, 2010). In addition, neuroticism and personality-disorder symptoms in one or both partners usually leads to dissatisfaction and instability in the relationship (Stroud, Durbin, Saigal, & Knobloch-Fedders, 2010).

Another important factor appears to be the security of each partner's attachment to his or her family of origin. Longitudinal research suggests that the parental attachment relationship contributes to the construction of an internal model of intimate relationships that children bring with them into adulthood and into their marriages (Fraley, Roisman, Booth-LaForce, Owen, & Holland, 2013; Mikulincer & Shaver, 2011). Research supports this hypothesis to some degree (Simpson, Collins, Tran, & Haydon, 2008). However, the relationship between attachment security early in life and intimate relationships in adulthood is not a simple, direct one (Dinero, Conger, Shaver, Widaman, & Larsen-Rife, 2008). Research suggests that attachment security is one of several variables that work together to influence relationship satisfaction later in life. These variables include the quality of partners' peer relationships, life stresses such as unemployment, and patterns of interaction between partners that develop over the duration of the relationship (Dinero et al., 2008; Neff & Karney, 2009).

Emotional affection contributes to relationship quality as well. The most compelling theory of romantic love comes from Robert Sternberg, who argues that love has three key components: (1) *intimacy*, which includes feelings that promote closeness and connectedness; (2) *passion*, which includes a feeling of intense longing for union with the other person, including sexual union; and (3) *commitment to a particular other*, often over a long period of time (Sternberg, 1987). When these three components are combined in all possible ways, you end

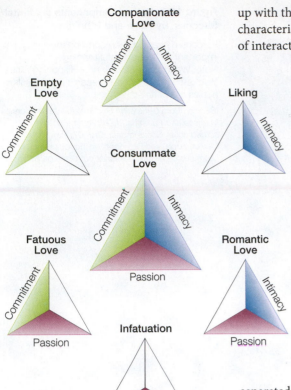

Figure 14.4 Sternberg's Theory of Love
Sternberg's theory postulates three components of love: passion, intimacy, and commitment. Relationships can be classified according to which of the three components is present.

up with the seven subvarieties of love listed in Figure 14.4. Sternberg's theory suggests that the characteristics of the emotional bond that holds a couple together influence the unique pattern of interaction that develops in each intimate relationship.

How a couple manages conflict is also an important predictor of relationship quality. Drawing on a large body of research, psychologists have identified three quite different types of stable, or enduring, marriages (Gottman, 1994). **Validating couples** have disagreements, but the disagreements rarely escalate. Partners express mutual respect, even when they disagree, and listen well to each other. **Volatile couples** squabble a lot, disagree, and don't listen to each other very well when they argue. But they still have more positive than negative encounters, showing high levels of laughter and affection. **Avoidant couples**, called "conflict minimizers," don't try to persuade each other; they simply agree to disagree, without apparent rancor, a pattern sometimes described as "devitalized."

Similarly, psychologists find two types of unsuccessful marriages. Like volatile couples, **hostile/engaged couples** have frequent hot arguments, but they lack the balancing effect of humor and affection. **Hostile/detached couples** fight regularly (although the arguments tend to be brief), rarely look at each other, and lack affection and support. In both unsuccessful types, the ratio of negative to positive encounters gets out of balance, and the marriage spirals downward toward dissolution.

DIVORCE For couples whose marriages end in divorce, the experience is often one of the most stressful of their entire lives. Not surprisingly, divorce is associated with increases in both physical and emotional illness (Sbarra, 2012). Recently separated or divorced adults have more automobile accidents, are more likely to commit suicide, lose more days at work because of illness, and are more likely to become depressed (Bloom, White, & Asher, 1979; Menaghan & Lieberman, 1986; Stack, 1992a, 1992b; Stack & Wasserman, 1993). They also report strong feelings of bitterness, failure, and a loss of self-esteem, as well as loneliness (Chase-Lansdale & Hetherington, 1990; Hahlweg & Baucom, 2011). These negative effects are strongest in the first months after the separation or divorce, much as we see the most substantial effects for children during the first 12 to 24 months (Chase-Lansdale & Hetherington, 1990; Kitson, 1992). However, social networks and close relationships with friends provide some degree of protection against these negative outcomes for recently divorced adults (Halford & Sweeper, 2013).

The psychological effects of divorce are often significantly exacerbated by serious economic effects, particularly for women (Varner & Mandara, 2009). Because most men have had continuous work histories, they commonly leave a marriage with far greater earning power than do women. Not only do women typically lack high earning capacity, they also usually retain custody of any children, with attendant costs.

Cohabiting Heterosexual Couples

LO 14.6 What factors contribute to the relationship between premarital cohabitation and divorce?

About half of young adults in the United States have lived with a romantic partner of the opposite sex at some time in their lives (Goodwin et al., 2010). Most such couples plan to marry. However, research has shown that those who cohabit before marriage are less satisfied with their marriages and more likely to divorce than are those who marry without cohabiting (Godwin et al., 2010; Tach & Halpern-Meekin, 2012). Research has also shown that this relationship exists across historical cohorts. That is, couples who cohabited prior to marriage during the period of the 1980s to the early 2000s display the same rates of marital dissatisfaction and divorce as those who cohabited in the 1960s and 1970s (Dush, Cohan, & Amato, 2003; Goodwin et al., 2010).

Several theories have been proposed to explain the relationship between premarital cohabitation and divorce. First, couples who cohabit are less *homogamous* (similar) than those who do not. That is, cohabitating couples are more dissimilar in ethnicity, educational attainment, and socioeconomic status than married couples are (Mäenpää & Jalovaara, 2013; Morgan,

validating couples partners who express mutual respect, even in disagreements, and are good listeners

volatile couples partners who argue a lot and don't listen well but still have more positive than negative interactions

avoidant couples partners who agree to disagree and who minimize conflict by avoiding each other

hostile/engaged couples partners who have frequent arguments and lack the balancing effect of humor and affection

hostile/detached couples partners who fight regularly, rarely look at each other, and lack affection and support

2012; Schwartz, 2010). Cohabiting couples also differ more often in religious beliefs (Blackwell & Lichter, 2000). Homogamy contributes to relationship stability. Thus, the difference in marital stability between premarital cohabitants and noncohabitants may be a matter of self-selection, not a result of some causal process attributable to cohabitation itself.

Other developmentalists believe that these findings result from the tendency of researchers to lump all kinds of cohabiting couples into a single category. This kind of aggregation, they say, may distort a study's findings because it ignores that there are two rather distinct types of heterosexual cohabitation (Kline, Stanley, Markman, & Olmos-Gallo, 2004). One type involves couples who are fully committed to a future marriage. In most cases, these couples have firm wedding plans and choose to live together for convenience or for economic reasons. In the second type of cohabitation, the relationship between the two partners is more ambiguous. Many such couples regard future marriage as a possibility but also believe that the relationship may be temporary.

Sociologist Jay Teachman points out that one important difference between these two types of couples is previous cohabitation and premarital sexual experience (Teachman, 2003). His findings are derived from the National Survey of Family Growth, a longitudinal study that focuses on women's family transitions. Teachman's analyses of these data show that married women whose premarital cohabitation and sexual experience was limited to their future husband are no more likely to divorce than women who did not cohabit prior to marriage. Thus, says Teachman, the critical variable at work in the cohabitation–divorce relationship is the fact that a large proportion of cohabitants have been in prior cohabiting or sexual relationships.

Researchers have also identified interaction differences between cohabitants with firm intentions to marry and those whose future plans are less clear (Guzzo, 2009). For instance, cohabiting men who intend to marry their partner do more housework than men who are not so committed (Ciabittari, 2004). This difference may be the result of communication patterns that distinguish cohabiting women of the two types. In other words, cohabiting women who intend to marry their partner may do a better job of communicating their expectations about a fair division of labor. Another important finding is that cohabiting couples who are clear about their intentions to marry are happier during the period of cohabitation than couples whose future plans are more ambiguous (Brown, 2003; Goodwin et al., 2010). Thus, looking at the kinds of interaction patterns that exist among cohabitants who intend to marry helps us understand why, after marriage, they differ little in satisfaction and stability from those who do not cohabit until after marriage (Brown, 2003; Brown & Booth, 1996; Goodwin et al., 2010; Kline et al., 2004; Teachman, 2003).

Gay and Lesbian Couples

LO 14.7 In what ways are gay and lesbian couples similar to and different from heterosexual couples?

More than 600,000 households in the United States are headed by partners of the same sex (Lofquist et al., 2012). Further, there is a growing international movement to legalize same-sex marriage. As a result, in recent years, developmentalists have become interested in whether the same factors that predict satisfaction and stability in heterosexual partnerships also relate to these variables in same-sex partnerships (Cherlin, 2013).

RELATIONSHIP SATISFACTION One factor that appears to be just as important to same-sex unions as it is to opposite-sex relationships is attachment security (Elizur & Mintzer, 2003). Moreover, as is true for heterosexual couples, neuroticism in one or both partners is related to relationship quality and length (Kurdek, 1997, 2000). Homosexual couples argue about the same things as heterosexual couples, and, like heterosexual marriages, gay and lesbian relationships are of higher quality if the two partners share similar backgrounds and are equally committed to the relationship (Krueger-Lebus & Rauchfleisch, 1999; Kurdek, 1997; Peplau, 1991; Solomon, Rothblum, & Balsam, 2004).

Despite these similarities, there are important differences between the two kinds of relationships. For one, gay and lesbian partners are often more dependent on each other for social support than are men and women in heterosexual partnerships. This happens because many homosexuals are isolated from their families of origin, primarily because of their family members' disapproving attitudes towards homosexuality (Hill, 1999). Thus, many gays and lesbians build what researchers often call *families of choice* for themselves. These social networks typically consist of a stable partner and a circle of close friends. They provide for gay and lesbian couples the kind of social support that most heterosexual adults receive from their families of origin (Kurdek, 2003; Weeks, 2004).

Another difference is in the nature of the power relationship between the partners. Homosexual couples seem to be more egalitarian than heterosexual couples, with less specific role prescriptions. For example, one study of gay, lesbian, and heterosexual couples who had recently adopted a child found that the homosexual couples were more likely to share parental responsibilities equally (Goldberg, Smith, & Perry-Jenkins, 2012). Homosexual and heterosexual partners appear to differ with regard to expectations for monogamy. Both men and women in heterosexual relationships overwhelmingly state that they expect their partners to be sexually faithful to them. Similarly, lesbian partners often insist on sexual exclusivity. However, gay men, even those who are married or in long-term partnerships, do not necessarily regard sexual fidelity as essential to their relationships (Parsons, Starks, Garnarel, & Grov, 2012). Couples therapists report that monogamy is important to gay men, but it is an issue that is considered to be negotiable by most (Bonello & Cross, 2010; Garza-Mercer, Christenson, & Doss, 2006). What is the cause of this difference?

Some evolutionary psychologists suggest that the openness of gay relationships is an adaptation to the finding that males, both heterosexual and homosexual, desire sex more frequently than females do (Buss, 1999). Thus, sexual contact with individuals outside the partnership is less likely to lead to termination of relationships among gay couples than among heterosexuals or lesbians (Bonello & Cross, 2010).

SAME-SEX MARRIAGE Because legal recognition of same-sex relationships is a fairly new phenomenon, there has yet to be a sufficient number of studies to draw firm conclusions about its effects on gay and lesbian relationships and individuals. However, a few studies have examined whether the health benefits associated with traditional marriage are evident in legally recognized unions of same-sex couples (Cherlin, 2013). These studies generally show that gays and lesbians in legally recognized partnerships experience less emotional distress and have a greater sense of personal well-being than do those in other types of partnerships (Riggle, Rostosky, & Horne, 2010). 👁 **Watch** the **Video** *A Family with Two Fathers* in **MyPsychLab**.

Singlehood

LO 14.8 How do singles accomplish Erikson's psychosocial developmental task of intimacy?

For the most part, the same factors contribute to relationship satisfaction among heterosexual and homosexual couples.

In the United States, about 52% of adults between the ages of 18 and 34 have never been married (Lofquist et al., 2012). Surveys show that about two-thirds of them will have married at least once by the time they reach their mid-40s. In general, large-scale surveys suggest that single adults are less healthy and satisfied with their lives than their peers who are married are (Robards, Evandrou, Falkingham, & Vlachantoni, 2013). However, at the individual level, the impact of singlehood on their lives depends on the reason for their relationship status. For instance, *continuous singlehood* is associated with greater individual autonomy and capacity for personal growth than is a life path that has included divorce or loss of a spouse (Marks & Lamberg, 1998). Another important point to keep in mind is that many single adults participate in intimate relationships that do not involve either cohabitation or marriage. These people show up in surveys and census reports as "single" but might be better described as "partnered." Even among singles who have an intimate partner, though, close relationships with their families of origin are more likely to be an important source of psychological and emotional intimacy than they are for individuals who are married or cohabiting (Allen & Pickett, 1987; Campbell, Connidis, & Davies, 1999). Further, close friends are likely to play a more prominent role in the social networks of singles than among people who are married or cohabiting.

The number of years an individual has been single appears to be an important factor in the influence of singlehood on his or her development. Developmentalists have found that there is a transition during which long-term singles move from thinking of themselves as people who will be married or partnered in the future to viewing themselves as single by choice (Davies, 2003). Afterward, singlehood becomes an important, positive component of the individual's identity. This kind of self-affirmation may protect singles from some of the negative health consequences associated with singlehood that you read about earlier.

Close friends play an important role in the social networks of singles.

test yourself before going on ☑ Study and Review in MyPsychLab

Answers to these questions can be found in the back of the book.

1. Write "E" beside each factor in mate selection that evolutionary theory emphasizes and "S" beside those factors that social role theory emphasizes.

   _____(1) women's physical attractiveness
   _____(2) homogamy
   _____(3) economic opportunities for women
   _____(4) men's financial resources
   _____(5) parental investment

2. List three factors that contribute to marital success and satisfaction:
   (a) _____
   (b) _____
   (c) _____

3. Researchers have identified two types of cohabiting couples based on partners' commitment to future _____.

4. Gays and lesbians often form social networks researchers refer to as _____ when they are isolated from their families of origin._____ _____ _____.

5. Which group of singles experiences the most positive adult life path, on average—continuous singles, divorced singles, or widowed singles?

CRITICAL THINKING

6. A statement widely attributed to anthropologist Margaret Mead is, "One of the oldest human needs is having someone to wonder where you are when you don't come home at night." In what way does the research in this section suggest that Mead made a profoundly accurate statement about human nature?

Parenthood and Other Relationships

Referring to couples who do not have children, comedian Bill Cosby once said, "Why shouldn't you be miserable like the rest of us?" Yet, despite all the trials and tribulations of parenting, 85% of parents cite relationships with their children as the most fulfilling aspect of their lives (Taylor et al., 2007). However, the transition to parenthood is stressful, and to make matters more complicated, it usually happens at a time when most other social relationships are in transition as well.

Parenthood

LO 14.9 What happens during the transition to parenthood?

Most parents would agree that parenthood is a remarkably mixed emotional experience. On one hand, the desire to become a parent is, for many adults, extremely strong. Thus, fulfilling that desire is an emotional high point for most. On the other hand, parenthood results in a number of stressful changes.

For most couples in long-term relationships, especially those who are married, having a child is an important goal.

BECOMING A PARENT A large majority of young adults who do not have children say that they would like to become parents (Riskind & Patterson, 2010; Virtala, Kunttu, Huttunen, & Virjo, 2006). Despite the opportunistic attitude toward mating that evolutionary theory ascribes to men, the percentage of men who feel strongly that they want to become parents and who view parenting as a life-enriching experience is actually greater than the percentage of women who feel this way (Horowitz, McLaughlin, & White, 1998; Muzi, 2000). Furthermore, most expectant fathers become emotionally attached to their unborn children during the third trimester of pregnancy and eagerly anticipate the birth (White, Wilson, Elander, & Persson, 1999).

As we noted in Chapter 3, in 1970, the average age at which a woman delivered her first child was 21.4 years in the United States. By contrast, in 2010, the average was 25 years (Martin et al., 2012). One reason that contemporary cohorts delay parenthood is that more of them are enrolled in postsecondary education than were their parents and grandparents in their own early adulthood years. Moreover, the majority of young adults in the United States believe that the best environment for raising a child is a household headed by a married couple (Taylor et al., 2007). Thus, the *social clock*—the ages at which adults are expected to achieve specific milestones—underlies all these trends. Although it doesn't include specific ages for the milestones of adulthood, the social clock in the United States today does include the idea that people ought to become socially and economically established before they bring children into the world.

THE TRANSITION EXPERIENCE The transition to parenthood can be very stressful. New parents may argue about child-rearing philosophy, as well as how, when, where, and by whom child-care chores should be done (Reichle & Gefke, 1998). Both parents are usually also physically exhausted, perhaps even seriously sleep deprived, because their newborn keeps them up for much of the night. Predictably, new parents report that they have much less time for each other—less time for conversation, for sex, for simple affection, or even for doing routine chores together (Belsky, Lang, & Rovine, 1985). However, the quality of new parents' relationship helps to moderate the stresses associated with caring for a newborn. The more secure and committed the relationship is, the more resilient the parents and their relationship are (Bouchard, 2014). ⊙ **Watch** the **Video** *Transition to Parenthood* in **MyPsychLab**.

Some cultures have developed ritualized rites of passage for this important transition, which can help new parents manage stress. For example, in Hispanic cultures, *la cuarenta* is a period of 40 days following the birth of a child, during which fathers are expected to take on typically feminine tasks such as housework. Extended-family members are also expected to help out. Researchers have found that Hispanic couples who observe *la cuarenta* adjust to parenthood more easily than those who do not (Niska, Snyder, & Lia-Hoagberg, 1998).

POSTPARTUM DEPRESSION Between 10% and 15% of new mothers experience a severe mood disturbance called *postpartum depression* (PPD)—a disorder that has been found across a diverse range of nations, including Australia, Canada, China, India, Japan, Sweden, Scotland, and the United States (Joy, 2012). Women who develop PPD suffer from feelings of sadness for several weeks after the baby's birth. Most cases of PPD persist only a few weeks, but 1–2% of women experience symptoms for a year or more. Moreover, more than 90% of women who have PPD after their first pregnancy experience the disorder again following subsequent deliveries (Joy, 2012).

The presence of major life stressors during pregnancy or immediately after the baby's birth—such as a move to a new home, the death of someone close, or job loss—increases the risk of PPD (Swendsen & Mazure, 2000). Fatigue and difficult temperament in the infant can also contribute to PPD (Fisher, Feekery, & Rowe-Murray, 2002). However, the best predictor of postpartum depression is depression during pregnancy (Da Costa, Larouche, Dritsa, & Brender, 2000; Martinez-Schallmoser, Telleen, & MacMullen, 2003). Thus, many cases of PPD can probably be prevented by training health professionals to recognize depression in pregnant women. Similarly, family members of women with absent or unsupportive partners can help them locate agencies that provide material and social support.

DEVELOPMENTAL IMPACT OF PARENTHOOD Despite its inherent stressfulness, the transition to parenthood is associated with positive behavior change: Sensation seeking and risky behaviors decline considerably when young adults become parents (Arnett, 1998). However, marital satisfaction tends to decline after the birth of a child. The general pattern is that such satisfaction is at its peak before the birth of the first child, after which it drops and remains at a lower level until the last child leaves home (Rollins & Feldman, 1970). The best-documented portion of this curvilinear pattern is the drop in marital satisfaction after the birth of the first child, for which there is both longitudinal and cross-sectional evidence. Other studies suggest that the decline in marital satisfaction is characteristic of contemporary cohorts of new parents as well, and researchers have found a pattern of marital satisfaction similar to that reported by Rollins and Feldman across a variety of cultures (Bouchard, 2014; Hirschberger, Srivastava, Marsh, Cowan, & Cowan, 2009; Twenge, Campbell, & Foster, 2003). Nevertheless, studies that examine the relationship between marital satisfaction and parenthood in a more complex fashion suggest that it is neither universal nor inevitable. Longitudinal studies show that the length of time that a couple have been together before having their first child, the amount of education they have, and the number of children that they have are all positively related to marital satisfaction (Jose & Alfons, 2007).

The link between marital satisfaction and parenthood probably results from one or more underlying factors. One such factor is the division of labor. The more a partner feels that he or she is carrying an unfair proportion of the economic, household, or child-care workload, the greater his or her loss of satisfaction (Wicki, 1999). Support from extended-family members is another variable that predicts maintenance or loss of satisfaction (Lee & Keith, 1999). Moreover, couples who have established effective conflict-resolution strategies before the birth of a child experience less loss of satisfaction (Bouchard, 2014; Cox, Paley, Burchinal, & Payne, 1999; Lindahl, Clements, & Markman, 1997). ◉ **Watch** the **Video** *Middle Adulthood: Portraits of Marriage and Parenthood* in **MyPsychLab**.

It's important to keep in mind, too, that new parents who are married or cohabiting experience a much smaller decline in overall life satisfaction than new single parents, whose lives are far more complicated and stressful (Copeland & Harbaugh, 2010; Lee, Law, & Tam, 1999). Likewise, single mothers are less likely to advance to management positions at work, perhaps because they are viewed less positively than single fathers or married parents of both genders (DeJean, McGeorge, & Carlson, 2012; Tharenou, 1999). Instead of focusing on declines in relationship satisfaction, some developmentalists suggest that more attention be paid to the consistent finding that having a parenting partner—especially one to whom one is married—is a significant protective factor in managing the stressful transition to parenthood.

CHILDLESSNESS Like parenthood, childlessness affects the shape of an adult's life, both within marriages and in work patterns. Without the presence of children, marital satisfaction fluctuates less over time. Like all other couples, those who do not have children are likely to experience some drop in satisfaction in the first months and years of marriage. But over the range of adult life, their curve of marital satisfaction is much flatter than the one shown in Figure 14.5 (Houseknecht, 1987; Keizer & Schenk, 2012; Somers, 1993). Childless couples in their 20s and 30s consistently report higher cohesion in their marriages than do couples with children.

Childlessness also affects the role of worker, especially for women. Childless married women, like unmarried women, are much more likely to have full-time continuous careers (Abma & Martinez, 2006). However, a survey involving more than 2,000 participants found that single, childless women had no higher rates of managerial advancement than mothers (Tharenou, 1999). Thus, one disadvantage associated with childlessness may be that it is always socially a bit risky to be seen as "different" from others in any important way (Mueller & Yoder, 1999). Tharenou's survey's finding that married fathers whose wives were not employed were more likely to advance than workers of any other marital or parental status supports this conclusion.

Social Networks

LO 14.10 How are family and friends important to young adults?

Creating a partnership may be the most central task of the process of achieving intimacy, but it is certainly not the only reflection of that basic process. In early adult life, each of us creates a social network made up of family and friends as well as our life partner.

FAMILY If you ask children and adults, "Who is the person you don't like to be away from?" or "Who is the person you know will always be there for you?" children and teenagers most often list their parents, while adults most often name their spouse or partner and almost never mention their parents (Hazan, Hutt, Sturgeon, & Bricker, 1991). However, most adults feel emotionally close to their parents and see or talk to them regularly (Belsky, Jaffee, Caspi, Moffitt, & Silva, 2003; Campbell et al., 1999; Lawton, Silverstein, & Bengtson, 1994).

Not surprisingly, the amount and kind of contact an adult has with kin are strongly influenced by proximity. Adults who live within 2 hours of their parents and siblings see them far more often than those who live farther away. But distance does not prevent a parent or sibling from being part of an individual adult's social network. These relationships can provide support in times of need, even if physical contact is infrequent.

There are also important cultural differences in young adults' involvement with their families. For example, one study compared the development of social independence among Australian, Canadian, and Japanese children and adults (Takata, 1999). In all three cultures, the sense of being independent from parents and family increased with age. However, Australian and Canadian participants appeared to develop self-perceptions of independence earlier in life. Consequently, Japanese young adults reported a greater sense of connectedness to their families of origin than either Australian or Canadian young adults.

Although patterns of interaction with family members are similar across U.S. ethnic groups, Hispanic Americans perceive family ties to be more important than young adults of other races or ethnicities (Schweizer, Schnegg, & Berzborn, 1998). Given a choice, many non-Hispanics de-emphasize kin networks in early adulthood, whereas Hispanic Americans embrace them enthusiastically (Vega, 1990). In the Hispanic American culture, extensive kin networks are the rule rather than the exception, with frequent visiting and exchanges not only between parents, children, and siblings, but with grandparents, cousins, aunts, and uncles (Keefe, 1984). These frequent contacts facilitate the development of mentoring relationships between young adults and the older members of their extended families (Sánchez, Reyes, & Singh, 2006).

African American young adults also tend to value family connections highly, although the reasons are somewhat different. For one thing, African American young adults are less likely to marry than are young adults in other groups (Johnson & Dye, 2005). Consequently, more African American young adults live in multigenerational households and report higher levels of intimacy and warmth in relationships with parents than do Whites (Brent, 2006; Kane, 1998). Frequent kin contact is also a significant part of the daily life of most African American adults who do not live in extended-family households (Hatchett & Jackson, 1993).

FRIENDS Friends, too, are important members of a social network, even those with whom young adults interact exclusively online (Sherman, Lansford, & Volling, 2006). We choose our friends, as we choose our partners, from among those who are similar to us in education, social class, interests, family background, or family life-cycle stage. Cross-sex friendships are more common among adults than they are among 10-year-olds, but they are still outnumbered by same-sex friendships. Young adults' friends are also overwhelmingly drawn from their own age group. Beyond this basic requirement of similarity, close friendship seems to rest on mutual openness and personal disclosure.

Because of the centrality of the task of intimacy in early adulthood, most researchers and theorists assume that young adults have more friends than do middle-aged or older adults. Research has offered some hints of support for this idea, but it has been a difficult assumption to test properly. Developmentalists lack longitudinal data and do not agree on definitions of friendship, which makes combining data across studies very difficult.

SEX DIFFERENCES IN RELATIONSHIP STYLES As in childhood, there are very striking sex differences in both the number and the quality of friendships in the social network of young adults (Radmacher & Azmitia, 2006). Women have more close friends, and their friendships are more intimate, with more self-disclosure and more exchange of emotional support. Young men's friendships, like those of boys and older men, are more competitive. Male friends are less likely to agree with each other or to ask for or provide emotional support to one another (Dindia & Allen, 1992; Maccoby, 1990). Adult women friends talk to one another; adult men friends do things together.

Another facet of this difference is that women most often fill the role of **kin keeper** (Merrill, 2011; Saslari & Zhang, 2006). They write the letters, make the phone calls, arrange the gatherings of family and friends. (In later stages of adult life, it is also the women who are likely to take on the role of caring for aging parents—a pattern you'll learn more about in Chapter 16.)

Taken together, all this means that women have a much larger "relationship role" than men do. In virtually all cultures, it is part of the female role to be responsible for maintaining the emotional aspects of relationships—with a spouse, with friends, with family members, and, of course, with children.

kin keeper a family role, usually occupied by a woman, which includes responsibility for maintaining family and friendship relationships

---

test yourself before going on   ✓ **Study** and **Review** in **MyPsychLab**

Answers to these questions can be found in the back of the book.

1. List three factors that influence the impact of having a child on a couple's levels of relationship satisfaction:

   (a) _____

   (b) _____

   (c) _____

2. In addition to a romantic partner, the social networks of most young adults include _____ and _____.

CRITICAL THINKING

3. Having children often means that a couple's social networks change such that the parents of their children's playmates take the place of other adults with whom they have associated in the past. What are the long-term advantages and disadvantages of this trend for parents' future post-child-rearing lives?

The Role of Worker

In addition to the roles of spouse or partner and parent, a large percentage of young adults are simultaneously filling yet another major and relatively new role: that of worker. Most young people need to take on this role to support themselves economically. But that is not the only reason for its centrality. Satisfying work also seems to be an important ingredient in mental health and life satisfaction for both men and women (Leong, Hartung, & Pearce, 2014). Before looking at what developmentalists know about career steps and sequences in early adulthood, let's examine how young people choose an occupation.

Choosing an Occupation

LO 14.11 What factors influence an individual's occupational choices?

As you might imagine, a multitude of factors influence a young person's choice of job or career. For instance, some young adults base their choices on the financial rewards associated with various careers, while others are more concerned about factors such as community service (Schlosser, Safran, & Sabaratta, 2010). Other contributing variables include family background and values, intelligence, education, gender, personality, ethnicity, self-concept, and school performance. **Watch** the **Video** *Workforce* in **MyPsychLab**.

Young adults who enter military service differ from peers who go to college or who go into civilian careers. Their parents are less likely to have gone to college and more likely to be poor than parents of young adults who do not go into military service. However, some families encourage their young adult children to join the military in order to have access to educational opportunities that they cannot afford to provide but that often accompany military service.

FAMILY AND EDUCATIONAL INFLUENCES Typically, young people choose occupations at the same general social class level as those of their parents—although this is less true today than it was a decade or two ago (Biblarz, Bengtson, & Bucur, 1996; Leeman, 2002). In part, this effect operates through the medium of education. For example, researchers have found that young adults whose parents are college graduates are less likely to enlist in the military than those whose parents have less education (Bachman, Segal, Freedman-Doan, & O'Malley, 2000). Such findings suggest that parents who have higher-than-average levels of education themselves are more likely to encourage their children to go on to post-secondary education. Such added education, in turn, makes it more likely that the young person will qualify for middle-class jobs, for which a college education is frequently a required credential.

Families also influence job choices through their value systems (Jacobs, Chin, & Bleeker, 2006). In particular, parents who value academic and professional achievement are far more likely to have children who attend college and choose professional-level jobs (Flouri & Hawkes, 2008). This effect is not just social-class difference in disguise. Among working-class families, it is the children of those who place the strongest emphasis on achievement who are most likely to move up into middle-class jobs (Gustafson & Magnusson, 1991). Further, families whose career aspirations for their children are high tend to produce young adults who are more intrinsically motivated as employees (Cotton, Bynum, & Madhere, 1997). ◉ **Watch** the **Video** *Early Adulthood: Perspectives on Choosing a Career* in **MyPsychLab**.

GENDER Specific job choice is also strongly affected by gender. Despite the women's movement and despite the vast increase in the proportion of women working, it is still true that sex-role definitions designate some jobs as "women's jobs" and some as "men's jobs" (Reskin, 1993; Zhou, Dawson, Herr, & Stukas, 2004). Stereotypically male jobs are more varied, more technical, and higher in both status and income (e.g., business executive, carpenter). Stereotypically female jobs are concentrated in service occupations and are typically lower in status and lower paid (e.g., teacher, nurse, secretary). One study found that gender differences in career choice are rooted in gender differences in risk aversion; that is, the income security associated with a particular career influences its appeal to women (Sapienza, Zingales, & Mae-stripieri, 2009).

Children learn these cultural definitions of "appropriate" jobs for men and women in their early years, just as they learn all the other aspects of sex roles. So it is not surprising that most young women and men choose jobs that fit these sex-role designations. Nonstereotypical job choices are much more common among young people who see themselves as androgynous or whose parents have unconventional occupations. For instance, young women who choose traditionally masculine careers are more likely to have a mother who has had a long-term career and are more likely to define themselves either as androgynous or as masculine (Betz & Fitzgerald, 1987; Fitzpatrick & Silverman, 1989).

PERSONALITY Another influence on job choice is the young adult's personality. John Holland, whose work has been the most influential in this area, proposes six basic personality types, summarized in Table 14.1 on page 367 (Holland, 1973, 1992). Holland's basic hypothesis is that each of us tends to choose, and be most successful at, an occupation that matches our personality.

Research in non-Western as well as Western cultures, and with African Americans, Hispanic Americans, and Native Americans as well as Whites in the United States, has generally supported Holland's proposal (Joeng, Turner, & Lee, 2013; Spokane & Cruza-Guet, 2005). Ministers, for example, generally score highest on Holland's social scale, engineers highest on the investigative scale, car salespeople on the enterprising scale, and career army officers on the realistic scale.

TABLE 14.1 Holland's Personality Types and Work Preferences

Personality Type	Work Preferences
Realistic	Aggressive, masculine, physically strong, often with low verbal or interpersonal skills; prefer mechanical activities and tool use, choosing jobs such as mechanic, electrician, or surveyor
Investigative	Oriented toward thinking (particularly abstract thinking), organizing, and planning; prefer ambiguous, challenging tasks, but are low in social skills; are often scientists or engineers
Artistic	Asocial; prefer unstructured, highly individual activity; are often artists
Social	Extraverts; people oriented and sociable and need attention; avoid intellectual activity and dislike highly ordered activity; prefer to work with people and choose service jobs like nursing and education
Enterprising	Highly verbal and dominating; enjoy organizing and directing others; are persuasive and strong leaders, often choosing careers in sales
Conventional	Prefer structured activities and subordinate roles; like clear guidelines and see themselves as accurate and precise; may choose occupations such as bookkeeping or filing

(*Source:* Holland, 1973, 1992.)

People whose personalities match their jobs are also more likely to be satisfied with their work. Moreover, obtaining a personality assessment prior to making an occupational choice is associated with greater feelings of confidence about the decision (Francis-Smythe & Smith, 1997).

career development the process of adapting to the workplace, managing career transitions, and pursuing goals through employment

Career Development

LO 14.12 How do career goals and job satisfaction change over time?

Once the job or career has been chosen, what kinds of experiences do young adults have in their work life? **Career development** is the process of adapting to the workplace, managing career transitions, and pursuing personal goals through employment. Psychologists who study career development focus on issues such as the phases of workplace adaptation, job satisfaction, and the ways in which individuals integrate work with other aspects of their lives.

SUPER'S STAGE OF CAREER DEVELOPMENT Psychologist Donald Super claims that the roots of the career development process are found in infancy. Between birth and age 14, Super says, we are in the *growth stage*, a period during which we learn about our abilities and interests. Next comes the *exploratory stage*, roughly from 15 to 24. In this stage, the young person must decide on a job or career, and he searches for a fit between his interests and personality and the jobs available. The whole process involves a good deal of trial and error as well as luck or chance. Perhaps because many of the jobs available to those in this age range are not terribly challenging and because many young adults have not yet found the right fit, job changes are at their peak during this period.

Next comes the *establishment stage* (also called the *stabilization stage*), roughly from age 25 to age 45. Having chosen an occupation, the young person must learn the ropes and begin to move through the early steps in some career ladder as he masters the needed skills, perhaps with a mentor's help. In this period, the worker also focuses on fulfilling whatever aspirations or goals he may have set for himself. In Levinson's terms, he tries to fulfill his dream. The young scientist pushes himself to make an important discovery; the young attorney strives to become a partner; the young business executive tries to move as far up the ladder as he can; the young blue-collar worker may aim for job stability or promotion to foreman. It is in these years that most promotions occur.

Which of Holland's personality types best suits a young adult for working in a setting such as this?

Assistance with child care is one of many quality of work–life (QWL) policies that some organizations have implemented in recent years.

The final phase of career development in Super's model is the *maintenance stage*. It begins around age 45 and ends at retirement. The primary goals of the maintenance stage are to protect and maintain the gains that were made during the establishment stage. To accomplish these goals, older workers must keep up with new developments in their fields. They must also acquire new skills in order to avoid becoming obsolete. Moreover, individuals in the maintenance phase must make preparations for retirement.

Super's model is useful for describing the challenges that individuals face in the various phases of their careers. However, to be validly applied in today's rapidly changing economy, Super's stages must be thought of independently from the ages to which he originally linked them (Super, 1990). This is necessary because of the frequency with which adults change careers or move from one workplace to another. Thus, regardless of age, a person who makes a major career change probably exhibits the characteristics of Super's exploratory stage prior to doing so and experiences some of the features of his establishment and maintenance phases in the years following the change.

JOB SATISFACTION Early studies of job satisfaction found that it was at its lowest in early adulthood and rose steadily until retirement (Glenn & Weaver, 1985). More recently, however, researchers have found that satisfaction is lowest at mid-career, usually toward the end of the early adulthood period (Fullerton & Wallace, 2007; Larson, 2012). This trend is attributable to changes in workers' perceptions of job security. In the past, security increased with time on the job. Today, job security is elusive because of the speed with which job requirements and employers' priorities shift. Thus, workers who have been on the job for some time are no longer assured of having greater security, higher incomes, or higher-status positions than beginning workers.

Research also suggests that a number of important variables contribute to job satisfaction in young adults. As with almost every life situation, individual personality traits such as optimism and neuroticism affect job satisfaction (Judge, Bono, & Locke, 2000; Wright & Bonett, 2007). Moreover, the degree to which a worker perceives his career as consistent with his personality predicts his level of job satisfaction (Harzer & Ruch, 2013). In addition, young adults engaged in careers for which they prepared in high school or college have higher levels of satisfaction (Blustein, Phillips, Jobin-Davis, & Finkelberg, 1997).

The Quality of Work–Life Movement

LO 14.13 What are some of the innovations that are associated with the quality of work–life movement?

Workers who are happy have lower turnover rates, meaning that companies are spared the expense of searching for and training replacements for them (Castle, Engberg, & Anderson, 2007; Matz, Wells, Minor, & Angel, 2013; Wright & Bonett, 2007). This factor influences an organization's efficiency and profitability. Therefore, job satisfaction can be just as important to employers as it is to their employees.

In an effort to enhance job satisfaction among employees, employers have developed new policies that focus on a variable called **work–life balance**, the interactions among workers' work and nonwork roles. Research has shown that work–life issues affect not only workers' mental and physical health but also their job performance (Thompson, Brough, & Schmidt, 2006). Moreover, workers are more satisfied with their jobs when they believe that their supervisors share their views on work life. Thus, to address the work–life needs of today's employees, psychologists have developed the **quality of work–life (QWL) movement**. Advocates of the QWL movement emphasize job and workplace designs based on analyses of the quality of

work–life balance the interactive influences among employees' work and nonwork roles

quality of work–life (QWL) movement an approach to enhancing job satisfaction by basing job and workplace design on analyses of the quality of employee experiences in an organization

employees' experiences in an organization. The idea is that when people are happier at work, they will be more productive. For example, the on-site child-care center is an innovation that has come about because of concern for the quality of work life. Even though providing it can be expensive, QWL advocates argue that on-site child care will pay for itself in terms of reduced absences and lower stress levels among employees who are parents.

Another QWL innovation is *telecommuting*. Telecommuters work in their homes and are connected to their workplaces by computer, fax, and telephone. Some telecommuters work at home every day; others do so only 1 or 2 days each week. Such flexibility can increase job satisfaction (Wilde, 2000). Moreover, telecommuting helps employees balance work and family responsibilities. It can also be helpful to employees who have disabilities that make it difficult for them to get around. Government statistics in the United States show that 12% of employees now work at home at least part of the time (U.S. Bureau of Labor Statistics, 2009).

Flextime is another QWL innovation. Employees of organizations that offer flextime benefits are allowed to create their own work schedules. Most organizations that use flextime have certain times (usually called "core hours") when all employees must be present. At other times, though, employees are free to come and go, as long as their work is done and they put in the required number of hours. Many employees take advantage of the flextime option to reduce work–family conflicts (Shockley & Allen, 2012). Others use this option to enhance their job performance by coming to the workplace at times when they believe they can be most productive. Further, flextime workers report that they experience less transportation-related stress—that is, they don't worry as much about rush-hour traffic jams and late trains or buses as they would if working a conventional schedule (Lucas & Heady, 2002). Researchers have found that flextime helps to build employee loyalty, thereby reducing turnover (Roehling, Roehling, & Moen, 2001).

Women are working in larger and larger numbers, but fewer than a third work continuously during the early adult years.

Women's Work Patterns

LO 14.14 In what way do women's work patterns differ from those of men?

Some findings about work patterns hold true for both women and men. For example, women's work satisfaction goes up with age (and with job tenure), just as men's does. But women's work experience in early adulthood differs from men's in one strikingly important respect: The great majority of women move in and out of the workforce at least once, usually to have and raise children (Hofferth & Curtin, 2006; Yerkes, 2010). Most such women return to work and, as a result, the representation of mothers in the workplace has increased dramatically over the past three decades. In 1975, only 39% of women with children under the age of 6 were employed. Today, the proportion is 65% (U.S. Bureau of Labor Statistics, 2013). Although there was a slight decline in the percentage of mothers who worked outside the home in the early years of the 21st century, more than 71% of mothers of children under age 18 are employed at least part time.

Prior to actually having children, many women tell researchers that they intend to return to full-time work shortly after the birth of their first child. However, longitudinal research shows that many women change their plans after giving birth. In one study, researchers found that only 44% of female professionals followed through on their pre-pregnancy intention to return to full-time work shortly after giving birth (Abele, 2005). In contrast, very few of the male professionals that these researchers followed over the same period made any kind of change to their working conditions after becoming fathers.

Such findings often lead researchers to conclude that work–family conflict more strongly influences women's career decisions than those of men (see *Developmental Science at Home* box). Research showing that women are both more concerned about and more adept at integrating work and family roles than men are provides support for this view (Hoff, Grote, Dettmer, Hohner, & Olos, 2005; Kafetsios, 2007; Wharton & Blair-Loy, 2006). However, some researchers point out that it may be more useful to think of work–family conflict as qualitatively different for mothers and fathers rather than important to one but not the other (McElwain, Korabik, & Rosin, 2005). Because of the traditional division of labor, they say, most of women's concerns about work–family conflicts involve situations in which family demands override those of work. For instance, a woman may worry that her decision to take time off from work for

Strategies for Coping with Conflict between Work and Family Life

Ramona had just settled in at her office, ready for a full day's work, when her cell phone rang. Recognizing the number on the screen as that of the woman who cared for her 3-year-old son, she reluctantly answered. When told that the child had a fever, Ramona knew that she would have to miss yet another day of work. During her last evaluation, Ramona's supervisor had noted that she was an excellent employee, but her frequent absences were standing in the way of her advancement in the organization. Moreover, tensions were rising between Ramona and her husband, because she resented his failure to volunteer to miss part or all of a workday to take their son to the doctor.

The need to balance work and family roles is one of the major themes of young adults' lives these days. But can a person really balance the demands of these roles? While there is no magic formula for creating such a balance and eliminating

conflict and distress, there are some strategies that can help.

The most helpful strategy overall is something psychologists call *cognitive restructuring*—recasting or reframing the situation for yourself in a way that identifies the positive elements. Cognitive restructuring might include reminding yourself that you had good reasons for choosing to have both a job and a family and recalling other times when you have coped successfully with similar problems (Liossis, Shochet, Millear, & Biggs, 2009).

A related kind of restructuring involves redefining family roles. A couple could begin the process by making a list of household chores, child-care responsibilities, and other tasks and noting which person does each chore. If the responsibilities were unbalanced, then the couple could work toward finding a more equitable distribution of labor. If economic

resources were sufficient, the couple could also hire help.

Finally, a stressed-out Supermom or Superdad might find it helpful to take a class in time management. Research reveals that good planning can, in fact, reduce the sense of strain you feel (Paden & Buehler, 1995). You have probably already heard lots of advice about how to organize things better. Easier said than done! But there are techniques that can help, and many of them are taught in workshops and classes in most cities. What does not help is simply trying harder to do it all yourself.

REFLECTION

1. *How do you think Ramona should approach her husband about sharing responsibility for taking care of their son when he is ill?*

2. *What are some ways that young adults can cope with the pressure to "do it all"?*

teacher–parent conferences will reduce her chances of advancing to a higher position. Among men, the pattern is the opposite; their work–family stress is more likely to involve prioritizing work over family than vice versa. For example, a father may regret that a business trip caused him to miss his daughter's dance recital.

Supporting this view are surveys showing that the division of work and family responsibilities among couples has changed very little in the last few decades despite the growing participation of mothers in the workforce (Crompton, Brockman, & Lyonnette, 2005; Goldberg et al., 2012). For instance, fathers are seldom thought of as having a choice between working and staying home to rear children (Daly & Palkovitz, 2004). Like their fathers and grandfathers before them, they are expected to provide material support to their families even when their wives are pursuing their own lucrative careers. However, it is also important to note that most men and women willingly adapt their work lives to the demands of raising children simply because that is what they believe is best for their families rather than out of a sense of duty to culturally prescribed roles or the fear that they will be blamed if their children develop problems.

test yourself before going on ✓ Study and Review in MyPsychLab

Answers to these questions can be found in the back of the book.

1. List three influences on career choice:

   (a) _____
   (b) _____
   (c) _____

2. According to Super, the career-development process begins between the ages of _____ and _____.

3. What is the goal of the quality of work–life movement?

4. _____ _____ more strongly influences women's career decisions than those of men.

CRITICAL THINKING

5. What are your own plans for achieving a satisfactory work–life balance after graduating from college? Based on the research in this section, how realistic do you think your goals are?

SUMMARY

Theories of Social and Personality Development (pp. 350–353)

LO 14.1 What did Erikson mean when he described early adulthood as a crisis of intimacy versus isolation?

- Erikson proposed that young adults who fail to establish a stable relationship with an intimate partner or a network of friends become socially isolated.

LO 14.2 What is a life structure, and how does it change?

- Levinson's concept of the life structure includes all the roles that a person occupies, all of his or her relationships, and the conflicts and balance that exist among them. He hypothesized that adult development involves alternating periods of stability and instability, through which adults construct and refine life structures.

LO 14.3 What are the characteristics of emerging adulthood?

- The parts of the brain involved in decision making and self-control mature between the late teens and early 20s. Emerging adults use skills they acquired earlier in life to accomplish developmental tasks in the academic, conduct, and friendship domains. New skills are required for tasks in the work and romantic domains.

Intimate Relationships (pp. 353–361)

LO 14.4 What factors do evolutionary and social role theorists emphasize in their theories of mate selection?

- Evolutionary theories of mate selection suggest that sex differences in mate preferences and mating behavior are the result of natural selection. Social role theory emphasizes factors such as gender roles, similarity, and economic exchange in explaining sex differences in mating.

LO 14.5 How do marriage and divorce affect the lives of young adults?

- Personality characteristics, as well as attachment and love, contribute to marital success. In general, married adults are happier, healthier, live longer, and have lower rates of psychological disorders than singles do. Divorce tends to increase young adults' risk of depression, suicide, and adverse outcomes such as accidents, absenteeism from work, illness, loss of self-esteem, feelings of failure, and loneliness.

LO 14.6 What factors contribute to the relationship between premarital cohabitation and divorce?

- People who cohabit prior to marriage are more likely to divorce than those who don't. However, research has shown that among cohabiting couples in which the intention to marry is firm and the woman has had no prior cohabitation experience, divorce or dissatisfaction with the relationship is no more likely than among couples who do not live together before marriage.

LO 14.7 In what ways are gay and lesbian couples similar to and different from heterosexual couples?

- The factors that contribute to relationship satisfaction are similar across homosexual and heterosexual couples. However, the two types of couples often differ in the power relation within the partnership. Further, monogamy is not as important to gay male couples as it is to lesbian or heterosexual partners.

LO 14.8 How do singles accomplish Erikson's psychosocial developmental task of intimacy?

- People who do not have intimate partners rely on family members and friends for intimacy. After many years of singlehood, unpartnered adults tend to incorporate "singleness" into their sense of personal identity. Continuous singles are more likely to experience a positive adult developmental path than divorced or widowed singles.

Parenthood and Other Relationships (pp. 361–365)

LO 14.9 What happens during the transition to parenthood?

- Most men and women want to become parents because they view raising children as a life-enriching experience. The transition to parenthood is stressful and leads to a decline in relationship satisfaction. Factors such as the division of labor between mother and father, individual personality traits, and the availability of help from extended-family members contribute to relationship satisfaction.

LO 14.10 How are family and friends important to young adults?

- Young adults' relationships with their parents tend to be steady and supportive, even if they are less central than they were at earlier ages. The quality of attachment to parents continues to predict a number of important variables in early adulthood. Each young adult creates a network of relationships with friends as well as with a partner and family members.

The Role of Worker (pp. 365–370)

LO 14.11 What factors influence an individual's occupational choices?

- The specific job or career a young adult chooses is affected by his or her education, intelligence, family background and resources, family values, personality, and gender. The majority of adults choose jobs that fit the cultural norms for their social class and gender. More intelligent young people, and those with more education, are more upwardly mobile.

LO 14.12 How do career goals and job satisfaction change over time?

- Job satisfaction rises steadily throughout early adulthood, in part because the jobs typically available to young adults are less well paid, more repetitive, and less creative and allow the worker very little power or influence.

LO 14.13 What are some of the innovations that are associated with the quality of work–life movement?

- The QWL movement includes on-site child care, telecommuting, flextime, and job sharing. These innovations help employees achieve a balance between work and nonwork roles.

LO 14.14 In what way do women's work patterns differ from those of men?

- For most women, the work role includes an additional in-and-out stage, in which periods of focusing on family responsibilities alternate with periods of employment. The more continuous a woman's work history, the more successful she is likely to be at her job.

KEY TERMS

assortative mating (homogamy) (p. 354)

avoidant couples (p. 358)

career development (p. 367)

emerging adulthood (p. 352)

hostile/detached couples (p. 358)

hostile/engaged couples (p. 358)

intimacy (p. 350)

intimacy versus isolation (p. 350)

kin keeper (p. 365)

life structure (p. 351)

parental investment theory (p. 353)

quality of work–life (QWL) movement (p. 368)

social role theory (p. 354)

validating couples (p. 358)

volatile couples (p. 358)

work–life balance (p. 368)

CHAPTER TEST ✓ Study and Review in MyPsychLab

Answers to all the Chapter Test questions can be found in the back of the book.

1. What do statistics say about the household composition of families in the United States?
   a. Single heads of household are becoming less common.
   b. Coupled households are disproportionately headed by men.
   c. The majority of households are made up of single persons living alone.
   d. Coupled (married and cohabiting) households are more common among adults than those headed by singles.

2. Which of the following statements about the impact of childlessness in adulthood is *false*?
   a. Couples who do not have children do not experience the drop in marital satisfaction that typically occurs across the first year of marriage.
   b. Young adult childless couples report higher marital cohesion than do couples with children.
   c. Without the presence of children, marital satisfaction fluctuates less across time.
   d. Childless married women are more likely to have full-time continuous careers.

3. Marvin is 27 years old. Which of Erikson's adult crises is he in the process of resolving?
   a. generativity versus stagnation
   b. ego integrity versus despair
   c. intimacy versus isolation
   d. identity versus role confusion

4. Andre's company uses flextime. Employees are allowed to create their own work schedules, but at certain times all employees must be present. Andre's working conditions are part of a trend called _____.
   a. come-and-go hours
   b. the family first initiative
   c. innovative scheduling
   d. the quality of work–life movement

5. Quang and Nguyen are a married couple. They argue frequently, and neither of them listens very well. Still, most of the time they get along well, and neither has any thoughts of getting divorced. What term would John Gottman use to describe Quang and Nguyen?
   a. disengaged couple
   b. fatuous couple
   c. volatile couple
   d. validating couple

6. Which of the following theories ascribes to the view that sex differences in relationships are adaptations to gender roles that result from external realities such as interactions with others?
   a. gender selection theory
   b. homogamy theory
   c. social role theory
   d. evolutionary role theory

7. Brian is very creative. If he goes a week without seeing another person, he doesn't even notice. He likes to garden and is currently redesigning the entire landscape around his property. According to Holland's theory, what type of person is Brian?
   a. realistic
   b. investigative
   c. enterprising
   d. artistic

8. Greg is the "strong silent type" who prefers work that does not require him to interact with other people. He is very skilled with hand and power tools and enjoys his job as a furniture craftsman. According to Holland, what is Greg's personality type?
   a. investigative
   b. artistic
   c. realistic
   d. conventional

9. All of the following are elements of evolutionary theories of mate selection, *except* _____.
   a. men prefer mates who are younger and physically attractive, and women prefer mates who have financial resources
   b. women invest more than men in childbearing and parenting
   c. women choose mates more slowly and carefully than men
   d. both women and men are likely to select mates who are opposite themselves in key characteristics such as ethnicity, religion, and age

10. When comparing women's jobs with men's jobs, which of the following statements is most accurate?
    a. Men's jobs tend be less varied but higher in both status and income.
    b. Women's jobs are concentrated in service occupations that are typically lower in status and lower paid.
    c. Seventy-five percent of all working women hold clerical jobs.
    d. The job stereotypes of the past have pretty much been eliminated.

11. Which of the following is *false* regarding women's work lives?
    a. Very few women with children younger than 6 years of age are employed.
    b. Women's work patterns tend to be less continuous than those of men.
    c. Women are more likely to choose service-oriented occupations than men are.
    d. Most women intend to return to work after having a child.

12. Which of the following terms did Levinson use to refer to the underlying pattern of an individual's life at a given time, including balances and conflicts among roles, relationships, and behavior patterns?
    a. life era
    b. cognitive structure
    c. life structure
    d. evolutionary plan

13. Which of the following is *false* with regard to marriage?
    a. In the United States, one-third of first marriages end before the tenth anniversary.
    b. Low levels of relationship satisfaction are often attributable to factors that were present before the marriage.
    c. Couples who cohabit before marriage are less likely to divorce.
    d. Relationship satisfaction declines after the birth of a child.

14. Which of the following ethnic groups is most likely to place a proportionately higher emphasis on the importance of children as a contributor to a successful marriage?
    a. Black
    b. Asian
    c. Hispanic
    d. White

15. What happens during the *la cuarenta* period in Hispanic cultures?
    a. The mother of a newborn child is expected to live with her parents for 40 days following the birth of the child.
    b. The parents of the newborn rely on the extended family to care for the child during the 40 days following the birth of the child.
    c. The father of the newborn is expected to celebrate and party for 40 days following the birth of the child.
    d. The father of a newborn is expected to take on typically feminine tasks such as housework for 40 days following the birth of the child.

16. Which of the following terms describes the capacity to engage in a supportive, affectionate relationship without losing one's own sense of self?
    a. generativity
    b. identity infusion
    c. attachment
    d. intimacy

17. Compared to peers who are married, single young adults more often derive social support from their _____.
    a. former romantic partners
    b. co-workers
    c. close friends
    d. neighbors

18. What is the most reliable predictor of PPD?
    a. difficulty during the pregnancy
    b. an unplanned pregnancy
    c. prenatal hormone deficiencies
    d. depression during pregnancy

19. Which of the following is *not* true of gay and lesbian relationships?
    a. Sexual fidelity is more important to gay couples than to lesbian couples.
    b. The same variables that predict relationship satisfaction among heterosexual couples predict satisfaction among gays and lesbians.
    c. Sexual fidelity is more important to lesbian couples than to gay couples.
    d. Gay and lesbian couples are more egalitarian than heterosexual couples are.

20. Which of the following is not one of the components of romantic love described by Sternberg's theory?
    a. passion
    b. commitment
    c. reliability
    d. intimacy

21. According to Erikson, in order to successfully resolve the intimacy-versus-isolation crisis, a young adult must _____.
    a. have the capacity for self-disclosure
    b. have experienced a successful resolution of the identity-versus-role-confusion crisis in adolescence
    c. be high in the Big Five personality trait of extraversion
    d. get married

22. In which domain can emerging adults *least* effectively apply skills acquired earlier in life?
    a. academic pursuits
    b. maintaining friendships
    c. finding a romantic partner
    d. learning to adapt to rules that adults must follow

23. Which of these statements about postpartum depression is true?
    a. It is found only in the United States.
    b. It is unknown in Asian countries.
    c. It occurs only in highly technical societies.
    d. It has been found in a wide variety of nations.

24. Jennifer and James say they feel close, connected, and committed to each other, but their relationship is no longer exactly what either would call passionate. How would Sternberg most likely describe their relationship?

a. permissive   c. companionate
b. fatuous   d. validating

25. Which of the following behaviors is exhibited by people who occupy the kin-keeper role in a family?
    a. settling family arguments
    b. arranging family gatherings
    c. setting up blind dates for unmarried young adults in the family
    d. providing financial assistance to family members who are struggling

To 👁 Watch ✳ Explore ◉ Simulate ✔ Study and Review and experience MyVirtualLife go to MyPsychLab.com

chapter 15

Physical and Cognitive Development in Middle Adulthood

Nearly every middle-aged person has a story about a peer who has died unexpectedly from an undiagnosed disease. The rates of such deaths remain fairly stable through the 20s and early 30s, and there is about 1 disease-related death for every 1,000 people between the ages of 20 to 35. Then the rates begin to double every 10 years, reaching 1 per 100 people by age 65 (National Vital Statistics System, 2006).

Clearly, middle age is the period when poor health habits begin to catch up with us—one of the realities of

LEARNING OBJECTIVES

PHYSICAL CHANGES

15.1 What do researchers know about brain function in middle age?

15.2 How does reproductive function change in men and women in middle age?

15.3 What is osteoporosis, and what factors are associated with it?

15.4 How do vision and hearing change in middle age?

HEALTH AND WELLNESS

15.5 How does cardiovascular disease develop?

15.6 What factors contribute to cancer?

15.7 What are some important differences in the health of middle-aged men and women?

15.8 How are socioeconomic status and ethnicity related to health in middle adulthood?

15.9 What are some of the consequences of alcoholism for middle-aged adults?

COGNITIVE FUNCTIONING

15.10 How do Denney's and the Balteses' models explain the relationship

between health and cognitive functioning in middle age?

15.11 What has research revealed about the link between health and cognitive functioning?

15.12 How do young and middle-aged adults differ in performance on memory tests?

15.13 What does research suggest about age-related changes in creativity?

aging that you may have encountered in *MyVirtualLife*—but physicians note that the advent of emergency treatments that can stop a heart attack in its tracks have made middle-aged adults complacent about their health-related behaviors (Eckel, 2006). While noting the value of these treatments, cardiologists point out that by changing their health habits, middle-aged adults can slow the progress of diseases that have already begun, prevent others from ever developing at all, and avoid ever having to rely on emergency treatment techniques (Eckel, 2006).

In this chapter you will learn that, with advancing age, the story of human development continues to become more of an account of differences than a description of universals. This happens because many factors—behavioral choices, poor health, and so on—determine the specific developmental pathway an adult follows. Most middle-aged adults are healthy, energetic, and intellectually productive, but others are in decline. Moreover, because developmental psychology has focused more on younger individuals, there simply isn't as much knowledge about universal changes in adulthood.

Physical Changes

What comes to mind when you think about middle age—graying hair, reading glasses, an expanding waistline? As you learned in Chapter 13, some of these characteristics, such as graying hair and the need for reading glasses, are the result of primary aging (look back at Table 13.2 on page 325 for a review). Others, such as an expanding waistline, are usually due to secondary aging. Nevertheless, the effects of primary aging, though subtle during the early adult years, become far more obvious after age 40. ◉ **Watch** the **Video** *Physical Changes in Middle Adulthood* in **MyPsychLab**.

The Brain and Nervous System

LO 15.1   **What do researchers know about brain function in middle age?**

Relatively little is known about the normal, undamaged brains of middle-aged adults. This is because research has focused on changes associated with trauma and disease rather than changes due to primary aging. However, in recent years, neuropsychologists have learned a great deal about the extent to which changes in cognitive functioning are attributable to age-related changes in the brain. To examine this question, researchers examine how the brains of young and middle-aged people respond to cognitive tasks. Such studies have produced a rather complex set of findings.

One bit of good news is that, when it comes to creating and processing mental images, the middle-aged brain is just as efficient as the young adult brain (Caçola, Roberson, & Gabbard, 2013). However, another fairly consistent finding is that middle-aged adults' brains respond more slowly to cognitive tasks than those of younger adults (Zysset, Schroeder, Neumann, & von Cramon, 2007). Another is that such tasks activate a larger area of brain tissue in middle-aged adults than they do in younger adults (Gunter, Jackson, & Mulder, 1998). Of course, neuropsychologists don't know why, but they speculate that cognitive processing is less selective in middle-aged adults than it is in younger adults. It's as if the middle-aged brain has a more difficult time finding just the right neurological tool to carry out a particular function, and so it activates more tools than are necessary. This lack of selectivity could account for differences between age groups in the speed at which cognitive tasks are carried out.

However, researchers have found evidence of declines in processing speed among middle-aged adults with chronic health problems such as diabetes (Tufvesson et al., 2013). Moreover, experimental studies show that training strongly affects older adults' performance on speeded memory tasks and that these training gains are still evident for several years after the experiments take place (Ball et al., 2002). Thus, declines in processing speed across the middle and later adult years may be a function of secondary rather than primary aging.

The brains of middle-aged and younger adults also respond differently to sensory stimuli (Cheng & Lin, 2012). For example, when participants are presented with a simple auditory stimulus such as a musical tone, patterns of brain waves in different areas vary across age groups (Yordanova, Kolev, & Basar, 1998). Research along this line has suggested that middle-aged adults may have less ability to control attention processes by inhibiting brain responses to irrelevant stimuli (Amenedo & Diaz, 1998, 1999). Their difficulty with attentional control could be another reason for the average difference in processing speed between young and middle-aged adults.

Such findings might lead you to conclude that, in everyday situations requiring intense concentration and rapid judgments, middle-aged adults would perform more poorly than their younger counterparts. Interestingly, though, researchers seldom find differences in everyday memory function that distinguish young from middle-aged adults (Salthouse, 2012). In fact, some studies show that middle-aged adults outperform those who are younger. For example, researchers have found that younger drivers exhibit more lapses in attention and driving errors than middle-aged drivers (Dobson, Brown, Ball, Powers, & McFadden, 1999). These lapses and errors, combined with younger drivers' greater likelihood of driving after drinking alcohol, help account for the different accident rates of young and middle-aged adults. Such findings, when considered with those on age differences in brain function, illustrate the difficulty researchers face in finding direct relationships between age-related brain differences and cross-age variations in behavior.

Another point to keep in mind about studies of the middle-aged brain is that the results of these studies are likely due to both primary and secondary aging. That is, part of the difference in brain function between young and middle-aged adults is due to natural aging processes. The remainder is attributable to the effects of health. Studies show, for example, that health-related changes in the circulatory system cause damage in the parts of the brain that are critical to processing speed, planning, and memory in middle age (Raz & Rodrigue, 2006; Raz, Rodrigue, Kennedy, & Acker, 2007). Consequently, healthy middle-aged adults exhibit both neurological and cognitive functioning that is more similar to that of young adults than their peers who have health conditions that affect the circulatory system. **Watch** the **Video** *Middle Adulthood: Happiness and Attitude toward Aging* in **MyPsychLab**.

The Reproductive System

LO 15.2 How does reproductive function change in men and women in middle age?

If you were asked to name a single significant physical change occurring in the years of middle adulthood, chances are you'd say *menopause*—especially if you're a woman. The more general term is the **climacteric**, which refers to the years of middle or late adulthood in both men and women during which reproductive capacity declines or is lost.

MALE CLIMACTERIC In men, the climacteric is extremely gradual, with a slow loss of reproductive capacity, although the rate of change varies widely from one man to the next, and there are documented cases of men in their 90s fathering children. On average, the quantity of viable sperm produced declines slightly, beginning perhaps at about age 40. The testes also shrink very gradually, and the volume of seminal fluid declines after about age 60.

The causal factor is most likely a very slow drop in testosterone levels, beginning in early adulthood and continuing well into old age. This decline in testosterone is implicated in the gradual loss of muscle tissue (and hence strength) that becomes evident in the middle and later years, as well as in the increased risk of heart disease in middle and old age. It also appears to affect sexual function. In particular, in the middle years, the incidence of *erectile dysfunction* (the inability to achieve or maintain an erection; also called *impotence*) begins to increase—although many things other than the slight decline in testosterone contribute to this change, including an increased incidence of poor health (especially heart disease), obesity, use of blood-pressure medication (and other medications), alcohol abuse, and smoking.

climacteric the term used to describe the adult period during which reproductive capacity declines or is lost

menopause the cessation of monthly menstrual cycles in middle-aged women

premenopausal phase the stage of menopause during which estrogen levels fall somewhat, menstrual periods are less regular, and anovulatory cycles begin to occur

perimenopausal phase the stage of menopause during which estrogen and progesterone levels are erratic, menstrual cycles may be very irregular, and women begin to experience symptoms such as hot flashes

During middle age, supportive partners help each other cope with the changes in sexual function that are brought about by the natural aging of the reproductive system.

Lifestyle changes can sometimes restore sexual function. In one study, researchers enrolled 35- to 55-year-old obese men with erectile dysfunction in a 2-year weight-loss program that required participants to make changes in their diets and exercise habits (Esposito et al., 2004). About one-third of the men experienced improvements in erectile dysfunction along with the reductions in body fat.

Among healthy middle-aged men, performance anxiety is a frequent cause of erectile dysfunction. The drugs *sildenafil* (Viagra), *tadalafil* (Cialis), and *vardenafil* (Levitra) have been found to be effective in treating this problem (Kim, 2013). However, physicians warn that men with erectile dysfunction should avoid so-called natural treatments such as food supplements because most of them have not been studied in placebo-controlled experiments (Rowland & Tai, 2003). Moreover, men who turn to supplements for symptom relief may delay seeking medical attention and, as a result, may continue to have a serious underlying condition without realizing it.

MENOPAUSE Declines in key sex hormones are also clearly implicated in the set of changes in women called **menopause**, which means literally the cessation of the menses. You'll remember from Chapter 11 that secretion of several forms of estrogen by the ovaries increases rapidly during puberty, triggering the onset of menstruation as well as stimulating the development of breasts and secondary sex characteristics. In the adult woman, estrogen levels are high during the first 14 days of the menstrual cycle, stimulating the release of an ovum and the preparation of the uterus for possible implantation. *Progesterone*, which is secreted by the ruptured ovarian follicle from which the ovum emerges, rises during the second half of the menstrual cycle and stimulates the sloughing off of accumulated material in the uterus each month if conception has not occurred.

The average age of menopause for both African American and White American women, and for women in other countries for which data are available, is roughly age 50; anything between ages 40 and 60 is considered within the normal range (Curran, 2009). Twin studies indicate that heredity contributes to the timing of menopause (Kok, van Asselt, van der Schouw, Peeters, & Wijmenga, 2005; Snieder, MacGregor, & Spector, 1998). In addition, early menopause is associated with smoking, a medical history that includes autoimmune diseases such as lupus, and chemotherapy treatment (Curran, 2009). Moreover, like puberty, menopause is not a single event but a series of changes that are strongly influenced by hormones. ⊙ **Watch** the **Video** *Menopause* in **MyPsychLab**.

MENOPAUSAL PHASES Menopause, like puberty, is often thought of as a single event. However, it actually occurs over several years, and researchers generally agree that it consists of three phases. First, during the **premenopausal phase**, estrogen levels begin to fluctuate and decline, typically in the late 30s or early 40s, producing irregular menstrual periods in many women. The ovaries are less sensitive to cyclical hormonal signals, and many women experience *anovulatory cycles*, in which no ovum is released. Even though no ovum is produced, estrogen levels are high enough in premenopausal women to produce periodic bleeding. However, the lack of ovulation results in a dramatic drop in progesterone. As a result, women are exposed to high levels of estrogen for prolonged periods of time during and after menopause. This is significant because estrogen exposure increases cancer risk (Coney, 2013).

During the **perimenopausal phase**, a period that can last up to 6 years before complete cessation of menstruation, estrogen levels decrease and women experience more extreme variations in the timing of their menstrual cycles (Coney, 2013). In addition, about 75% of perimenopausal women experience *hot flashes*—sudden sensations of feeling hot. It is hypothesized that fluctuating levels of estrogen and other hormones cause a woman's blood vessels to expand and contract erratically, thus producing hot flashes (see *No Easy Answers* on page 379).

During a hot flash, the temperature of the skin can rise as much as 1–7 degrees in some parts of the body, although the core body temperature actually drops (Kronenberg, 1994). Hot flashes last, on average, a few minutes and may recur as

The Pros and Cons of Hormone Therapy

Most of the physical symptoms and effects of menopause—including hot flashes, thinning of the vaginal wall, and loss of vaginal lubrication—can be reduced by taking estrogen and progesterone (*hormone therapy [HT]*). Moreover, in the 1990s, physicians thought that HT would protect women against heart disease and dementia. Thus, they commonly prescribed HT for women who complained of menopausal symptoms such as hot flashes.

Everything changed in 2002, with the publication of the results of the Women's Health Initiative (WHI), a longitudinal placebo-controlled study of HT (Writing Group for the Women's Health Initiative Investigators, 2002). These results included alarming evidence showing that long-term use of either estrogen alone or combined estrogen–progesterone hormone replacement therapy significantly increased the risk of both breast and ovarian cancers (Chlebowski et al., 2003; Lacey et al., 2002). Data from the Heart and Estrogen Replacement Study (HERS) also showed that HT provided women with no protection against cardiovascular disease and may even have increased the severity of the

disease among study participants who already had it (Grady et al., 2002; Hulley et al., 2002). The evidence suggesting that HT might seriously harm women's health was so strong that the WHI was immediately terminated; all of the study's participants who had been given HT were advised to stop taking it (Writing Group for the Women's Health Initiative Investigators, 2002). Consequently, the number of women who take HT declined dramatically soon after these results were published (Udell, Fischer, Brookhart, Solomon, & Choudhry, 2006).

To date, the accumulated evidence indicates that the only consistent benefits associated with hormone replacement therapy are the reduction of hot flashes and protection against osteoporosis (Kaur, 2012). As a result of the most recent findings, the American College of Obstetricians and Gynecologists recommends that women be extremely cautious about entering into any regimen involving HT (Szymanski & Bacon, 2008). First, they say that women should aim for the lowest dosage that provides symptom relief and avoid taking hormones for more than a year or two. Second, they suggest that hormone

treatment be symptom specific. For example, if a woman's main complaint is vaginal dryness, then the best treatment for her is a vaginal cream. Finally, doctors recommend that women undergoing any kind of treatment for menopausal symptoms see their doctors regularly and follow their instructions with regard to cancer screenings (e.g., mammograms) (Szymanski & Bacon, 2008).

YOU DECIDE

Decide which of these two statements you most agree with and think about how you would defend your position:

1. *Due to the risks involved, hormone therapy should be a last resort for menopausal women who have hot flashes and other symptoms.*

2. *No medical treatment is entirely free of risk, so women who want to take hormone therapy to relieve symptoms of menopause should do so.* ◉ **Watch** the **Video** *Middle Adulthood: Estrogen and Memory* in **MyPsychLab**.

---

seldom as daily or as often as three times per hour (Coney, 2013). Most women learn to manage these brief periods of discomfort if they occur during the day. However, hot flashes frequently disrupt women's sleep. When this happens, it sets in motion a series of changes that are actually due to sleep deprivation rather than menopause. For example, lack of sleep can lead to mental confusion, difficulty with everyday memory tasks, and emotional instability (Philip et al., 2012). Thus, perimenopausal women may have the subjective feeling that they are "going crazy" when the real problem is that hot flashes are preventing them from getting enough sleep. The general light-headedness and shakiness that accompany some women's hot flashes can add to this sensation.

Eventually, estrogen and progesterone drop to consistently low levels, and menstruation ceases altogether. Once a woman has ceased to menstruate for a year, she is in the **postmenopausal phase**. In postmenopausal women, estradiol and estrone, both types of estrogen, drop to about a quarter or less of their premenopausal levels. Progesterone decreases even more, as a result of the cessation of ovulation, although the adrenal glands continue to provide postmenopausal women with some progesterone.

The reduction in estrogen during the perimenopausal and postmenopausal phases also has effects on genital and other tissue. The breasts become less firm, the genitals and the uterus shrink somewhat, and the vagina becomes both shorter and smaller in diameter. The walls of the vagina also become somewhat thinner and less elastic and produce less lubrication during intercourse (Coney, 2013).

PSYCHOLOGICAL EFFECTS OF MENOPAUSE One other aspect of the climacteric in women deserves some mention. It has been part of folklore for a very long time that menopause involves major emotional upheaval as well as clear physical changes. However, research findings are mixed. Longitudinal studies show that depressive symptoms increase during menopause (Bromberger et al., 2010). Nevertheless, experts note that serious depression is no

postmenopausal phase the last stage of menopause, which begins when a woman has had no menstrual periods for a year or more

more frequent among menopausal women than among those who are nonmenopausal (Bromberger et al., 2007; Judd, Hickey, & Bryant, 2012).

A woman's overall negativity and number of life stressors before entering menopause contributes to her emotional state (Dennerstein, Lehert, & Guthrie, 2002). In other words, a woman's negativity may be attributed to menopause when, in reality, it may be a longstanding component of her personality. Alternatively, she may have a particularly stressful life, and menopausal symptoms are just one more source of difficulty.

In addition, the actual level of symptoms women experience makes a difference (Bromberger et al., 2010). It isn't surprising that women who are most uncomfortable because of hot flashes and other physical changes, and whose symptoms last the longest, experience the most depression and negative mood. Researchers have also found that menopausal women who experience sleep deprivation due to hot flashes at night or night sweats may be misdiagnosed with generalized anxiety disorder. Not only are the symptoms of the two conditions similar, but electroencephalographic studies reveal that the patterns of brain activity across the two conditions are quite similar, too (Terashima et al., 2004).

Women's attitudes toward menopause vary somewhat across ethnic groups. Interestingly, one study suggested that these views are linked to women's general feelings about getting older (Sommer et al., 1999). The researchers found that women who agreed with the statement "the older a woman is, the more valued she is" were likely to disagree with the statement "a woman is less attractive after menopause." African American participants expressed a more positive view of aging and a less negative view of menopause than did women in the other groups. Interestingly, however, African American women, on average, experience more menopause symptoms such as hot flashes than women in other groups (Gold et al., 2006). Thus, having a positive outlook on aging and menopause does not appear to protect women against its symptoms. Moreover, across all groups, menopausal status is only one of many aspects of midlife that women consider when they are asked to evaluate the quality of their lives (Beyene, Gillis, & Lee, 2007). Thus, some researchers argue that menopause should be studied within the whole context of a middle-aged woman's life rather than as the universal defining feature of this period of life.

SEXUAL ACTIVITY Despite changes in the reproductive system, the great majority of middle-aged adults remain sexually active, although the frequency of sex declines somewhat during these years (Association of Reproductive Health Professionals, 2000; Laumann, Gagnon, Michael, & Michaels, 1994; Michael, Gagnon, Laumann, & Kolata, 1994). It is unlikely that this decline during midlife is due wholly or even largely to drops in sex-hormone levels; women do not experience major estrogen declines until their late 40s, but the decline in sexual activity begins much sooner. And the drop in testosterone among men is so gradual and slight during these years that it cannot be the full explanation. An alternative explanation is that the demands

Menopause ends a woman's child-bearing years but, for many women, coincides with the beginning of a new phase of life that offers new opportunities for personal growth such as grandparenting.

of other roles are simply so pressing that middle-aged adults find it hard to find time for sex. Increasing rates of chronic diseases such as diabetes and arthritis may also explain the declines in the frequency of sexual activity among people in their 50s (Association of Reproductive Health Professionals, 2000).

The Skeletal System

LO 15.3 What is osteoporosis, and what factors are associated with it?

Another change that begins to be quite significant in middle adulthood is a loss of calcium from the bones, resulting in reduced bone mass and more brittle and porous bones. This process is called **osteoporosis**. Bone loss begins at about age 30 for both men and women, but in women the process is accelerated by menopause. The major consequence of this loss of bone density is a significantly increased risk of fractures, beginning as early as age 50 for women and much later for men. Among older women (and men), such fractures can be a major cause of disability and reduced activity, so osteoporosis is not a trivial change.

In women, it is clear that bone loss is linked quite directly to estrogen and progesterone levels. Researchers know that these hormones fall dramatically after menopause, and it is the timing of menopause rather than age that signals the increase in rate of bone loss (Jacobs-Kosmin, 2013). Researchers also know that the rate of bone loss drops to premenopausal levels among women who take hormones, all of which makes the link quite clear (Rossouw et al., 2002). While the overall pattern of bone loss seems to be a part of primary aging, the amount of such loss nonetheless varies quite a lot from one individual to another. Table 15.1 lists the known risk factors for osteoporosis.

Aside from taking hormones, women can help prevent osteoporosis with one or both of the following strategies. First, they can get enough calcium during early adulthood so that peak levels of bone mass are as robust as possible. Second, throughout adult life women can exercise regularly, particularly doing weight-bearing exercise such as walking or strength training (Tolomio, Ermolao, Lalli, & Zaccaria, 2010). In one study, a group of middle-aged or older women were randomly assigned to a strength-training program consisting of twice-weekly sessions for a year. They showed a gain in bone density over the year, whereas women in a control group without such weight training showed a loss (Nelson et al., 1994). Third, *bone mineral density* (*BMD*) tests can identify osteoporosis long before it causes serious damage to bones. Once BMD is diagnosed, women can take bone-building medications such as *alendronate sodium* (Fosamax). Studies show that the combination of BMD testing and medication use dramatically reduces the risk of fractures among women over the age of 50 (Jaglal et al., 2005).

Any weight-bearing exercise—even walking— will help prevent osteoporosis.

osteoporosis loss of bone mass with age, resulting in more brittle and porous bones

TABLE 15.1 Risk Factors for Osteoporosis

Risk Factor	Explanation
Race	Whites are at higher risk than other races.
Gender	Women have considerably higher risk than men.
Weight	Those who are underweight are at higher risk.
Timing of climacteric	Women who experience early menopause and those who have had their ovaries removed are at higher risk, presumably because their estrogen levels decline at earlier ages.
Family history	Those with a family history of osteoporosis are at higher risk.
Diet	A diet low in calcium during adolescence and early adulthood results in lower peak levels of bone mass and hence greater risk of falling below critical levels later. Whether there is any benefit in increasing intake of calcium postmenopausally remains in debate. Diets high in either caffeine (especially black coffee) or alcohol are also linked to higher risk.
Exercise	Those with a sedentary lifestyle are at higher risk. Prolonged immobility, such as bed rest, also increases the rate of bone loss. Exercise reduces the rate of bone loss.

(*Sources:* Duursma et al., 1991; Gambert, Schultz, & Hamdy, 1995; Goldberg & Hagberg, 1990; Gordon & Vaughan, 1986; Lindsay, 1985; Morrison et al., 1994; Smith, 1982.)

presbyopia normal loss of visual acuity with aging, especially the ability to focus the eyes on near objects

presbycusis normal loss of hearing with aging, especially of high-frequency tones

Vision and Hearing

LO 15.4   How do vision and hearing change in middle age?

One of the most noticeable physical changes occurring in the middle years is a loss of visual acuity. Two changes in the eyes, collectively called **presbyopia**, are involved. First, the lens of the eye thickens. In a process that begins in childhood but produces noticeable effects only in middle adulthood, layer after layer of slightly pigmented material accumulates on the lens. Because light coming into the eye must pass through this thickened, slightly yellowed material, the total amount of light reaching the retina decreases, which reduces a person's overall sensitivity to light waves, particularly short wavelengths that are perceived as blue, blue-green, and violet (Schachar, 2010).

Because of this thickening of the lens, it is also harder and harder for the muscles surrounding the eye to change the shape of the lens to adjust the focus. In a young eye, the shape of the lens readily adjusts for distance, so no matter how near or far away some object may be, the light rays passing through the eye converge where they should, on the retina in the back of the eye, giving a sharp image. But as the thickening increases, the elasticity of the lens declines, and it can no longer make these fine adjustments. Many images become blurry. In particular, the ability to focus clearly on near objects deteriorates rapidly in the 40s and early 50s. As a result, middle-aged adults often hold books and other items farther and farther away because only in that way can they get a clear image. Finally, of course, they cannot read print at the distance at which they can focus, and they are forced to wear reading glasses or bifocals. These same changes also affect the ability to adapt quickly to variations in levels of light or glare, such as from passing headlights when driving at night or in the rain. So driving may become more stressful. All in all, these changes in the eyes, which appear to be a genuine part of primary aging, require both physical and psychological adjustment.
✳ **Explore** the **Concept** *Normal Vision, Nearsightedness* in **MyPsychLab**.

The equivalent process in hearing is called **presbycusis**. The auditory nerves and the structures of the inner ear gradually degenerate as a result of basic wear and tear, resulting primarily in losses in the ability to hear sounds of high and very low frequencies. But these changes do not accumulate to the level of significant hearing loss until somewhat later in life than is typical for presbyopia. Hearing loss is quite slow until about age 50. After age 50 or 55, however, the rate of hearing loss accelerates. Some of this loss is due to conditions that are more common among older adults than among younger individuals, such as excessive ear wax, chronic fluid in the ear, or abnormal growth of the bones of the inner ear (National Institute on Aging, 2010). Most commonly, however, hearing loss in adulthood appears to be the result of lifelong exposure to excessive noise (Rabinowitz, 2000).

By age 45 or 50, nearly everyone needs glasses, especially for reading.

test yourself before going on   ✅ **Study** and **Review** in **MyPsychLab**

Answers to these questions can be found in the back of the book.

1. Middle-aged adults are most likely to perform more poorly than young adults on tasks involving _____.

2. The _____ is the time in middle or late adulthood when the reproductive capacity declines or is lost.

3. _____ _____ _____ tests identify osteoporosis before it seriously damages the bones.

4. Match each term with its definition.

_____(1)   presbycusis
_____(2)   presbyopia
   (a)   age-related vision decline of near vision
   (b)   age-related hearing loss

CRITICAL THINKING

5. Given the changes in the brain, reproductive system, bones, and sensory abilities that you have learned about in this section, how would you evaluate a statement such as "age is just a state of mind"?

Health and Wellness

How long do you expect to live? Most young and middle-aged people these days expect to live into their 80s. The reason for this optimistic prediction is that most adults are aware of the trend toward increased life expectancy shown in Figure 15.1. Still, many are concerned about the quality of their lives, and no single variable affects the quality of life in middle and late adulthood as much as health. A middle-aged person in good health often functions as well and has as much energy as much younger adults. ⊙ **Watch** the **Video** *Middle Adulthood: Portraits of Middle Adult Physical Health* in **MyPsychLab**.

cardiovascular disease (CVD) a set of disease processes in the heart and circulatory system

atherosclerosis narrowing of the arteries caused by deposits of a fatty substance called plaque

Cardiovascular Disease

LO 15.5 How does cardiovascular disease develop?

Cardiovascular disease (CVD), a group of disease processes in the heart and circulatory system, is responsible for about 27% of deaths each year in the United States (Heron & Tejada-Vera, 2009). As such, it is the leading cause of death in the nation. However, many people are unaware of the fact that they have heart disease. In middle age, a sudden heart attack, technically known as an *acute myocardial infarction*, is sometimes the first indication of a problem. Sudden heart attacks are often caused when an accumulation of *plaque* in the arteries that supply the muscles of the heart with oxygen that has developed gradually over many years (a disease process called **athersclerosis**) ruptures (Kalyanasundaram & Shirani, 2010). After the plaque fractures, fragments enter the bloodstream and block the arteries and/or valves of the heart. Although the risk of athersclerosis increases with age, it is important to keep in mind that it is a disease that is strongly associated with lifestyle factors such as smoking, diet, and exercise rather than a natural consequence of aging. Therefore, it is preventable. ⊙ **Watch** the **Video** *Death and Afterlife Beliefs: Coronary Heart Disease* in **MyPsychLab**.

GENERAL RISK FACTORS The best information about who is at risk for CVD comes from a number of long-term epidemiological studies, such as the Framingham study, the Nurses' Health Study, the Physicians' Health Study, and the Fragmin and/or Early Revascularization During Instability in Coronary Artery (FRISC)-II study in which the health and habits of large

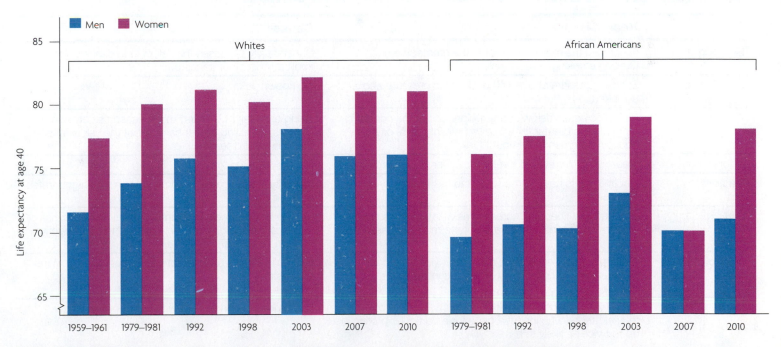

Figure 15.1 **Trends in Life Expectancy for White and African American Men and Women in the United States**

Life expectancy at age 40 in the United States from 1959 through 1998 for women and men, blacks and whites.

(*Sources:* Xu et al., 2010; CDC, 1998; U.S. Census Bureau, 1990, 1995; NCHS, 2013.)

numbers of individuals have been tracked over time (McPherson, 2010). In the Framingham study, 5,209 adults were first studied in 1948, when they were aged 30 to 59. Their health (and mortality) has since been assessed repeatedly, which makes it possible to identify characteristics that predict CVD (Anderson, Castelli, & Levy, 1987; Dawber, Kannel, & Lyell, 1963; Garrison, Gold, Wilson, & Kannel, 1993; Kannel & Gordon, 1980). The left side of Table 15.2 lists the well-established risk factors that emerged from the Framingham study and similar studies, along with a few other risk factors that are more speculative.

More recent studies continue to suggest the same risk factors but also offer hope for reversal of CVD (McPherson, 2010). One important recent development is the availability of laboratory tests that measure levels of *C-reactive protein* (*CRP*) in the bloodstream. Higher-than-normal levels of CRP indicate that an individual has an undiagnosed build-up of plaque in his or her cardiovascular system. In the Physicians' Health Study, CVD-related deaths fell 56% among participants who took low-dose aspirin after being advised to do so on the basis of CRP test results (McPherson, 2010). Likewise, administration of *statin drugs*, medications that reduce cholesterol levels and may reverse plaque build-up, reduced death rates by 54% in participants in the FRISC-II study whose cholesterol levels indicated they were at risk of having a heart attack.

As you can probably guess by looking over Table 15.2, the great majority of Americans have at least one of these risk factors (National Center for Health Statistics [NCHS], 2010). Moreover, it is important to understand that these risks are cumulative in the same way that the health habits investigated in the Alameda County study seem to be cumulative: The more high-risk behaviors or characteristics you have, the higher your risk of heart disease; the effect is not just additive. For example, high cholesterol is more serious for a person who has diabetes and high blood pressure than it is for adults who do not have these conditions (Cohen, Hailpern, & Alderman, 2004).

PERSONALITY AND HEALTH Personality may also contribute to heart disease. The *Type A personality* was first described by two cardiologists, Meyer Friedman and Ray Rosenman (1974; Rosenman & Friedman, 1983). They were struck by the apparently consistent presence among patients who had heart disease of several other characteristics, including competitive

TABLE 15.2 Risk Factors for Heart Disease and Cancer

Risk	Heart Disease	Cancer
Smoking	Major risk; the more you smoke, the greater the risk. Quitting smoking reduces risk.	Substantially increases the risk of lung cancer; also implicated in other cancers.
Blood pressure	Systolic pressure above 140 or diastolic pressure above 90 linked to higher risk.	No known risk.
Weight	Some increased risk with any weight above the normal range; risk is greater for those with weight 20% or more above recommended amount.	Being overweight is linked to increased risk of several cancers, including breast cancer, but the risk is smaller than for heart disease.
Cholesterol	Clear risk with elevated levels of low-density lipoproteins.	No known risk.
Inactivity	Inactive adults have about twice the risk of those who exercise.	Inactivity is associated in some studies with higher rates of colon cancer.
Diet	High-fat, low-fiber diet increases risk; antioxidants such as vitamin E, vitamin C, or beta-carotene may decrease risk.	Results are still unclear; a high-fat diet is linked to risk of some cancers; high-fiber diets appear to be protective for some cancers.
Alcohol	Moderate intake of alcohol, especially wine, linked to decreased CVD risk. Heavy drinking can weaken the heart muscle.	Heavy drinking is associated with cancers of the digestive system.
Heredity	Those with first-degree relatives with CVD have 7 to 10 times the risk; those who inherit a gene for a particular protein are up to twice as likely to have CVD.	Some genetic component with nearly every cancer.

(*Sources:* Centers for Disease Control and Prevention, 1994; Dwyer et al., 2004; Gaziano & Hennekens, 1995; Hunter et al., 1996; Lee, Manson, Hennekens, & Paffenbarger, 1993; Manson et al., 1995; Manson et al., 2002; Morris, Kritchevsky, & Davis, 1994; Rich-Edwards, Manson, Hennekens, & Buring, 1995; Risch, Jain, Marrett, & Howe, 1994; Rose, 1993; Stampfer et al., 1993; Trichopoulou, Costacou, Bamia, & Trichopoulou, 2003; Willett et al., 1992, 1995; Woodward & Tunstall-Pedoe, 1995.)

striving for achievement, a sense of time urgency, and hostility or aggressiveness. These people, whom Friedman and Rosenman categorized as Type A personalities, were perpetually comparing themselves to others, always wanting to win. They scheduled their lives tightly, timed themselves in routine activities, and often tried to do such tasks faster each time. They had frequent conflicts with their co-workers and family members. *Type B personality* people, in contrast, were thought to be less hurried, more laid back, less competitive, and less hostile.

Early research by Friedman and Rosenman suggested that Type A behavior was linked to higher levels of cholesterol and hence to increased risk of CVD, even among people who did not have observable heart disease. Contradictory results from more extensive studies since then, however, have forced some modifications in the original hypothesis (e.g., Miller, Turner, Tindale, Posavac, & Dugoni, 1991; O'Connor, Manson, O'Connor, & Buring, 1995). However, not all facets of the Type A personality, as originally described, seem to be equally significant for CVD. The most consistent link has been found between CVD and hostility (Mohan, 2006; Olson et al., 2005). Moreover, careful studies have shown that anger and hostility may be part of a larger complex of variables that includes anger, anxiety, cynicism, and other negative emotions (Kubzansky, Cole, Kawachi, Vokonas, & Sparrow, 2006; Olson et al., 2005).

The finding that negative emotions are correlated with CVD has led some researchers to propose a new classification, *Type D personality* (D for distress; Denollet, 1997). People with this profile exhibit a chronic pattern of emotional distress combined with a tendency to suppress negative emotions. In one study of men who were enrolled in a rehabilitative therapy program after having had a heart attack, those with the Type D profile were found to have four times the risk of death as other patients in the program (Sher, 2004).

Most people who have analyzed this research would now agree that there is some kind of connection between personality and CVD. What is less clear is just which aspects of personality are most strongly predictive. Some research suggests that measures of neuroticism or depression may be even better risk predictors than measures of hostility (e.g., Cramer, 1991).

Cancer

LO 15.6   What factors contribute to cancer?

The second leading cause of death among adults over the age of 45 is cancer (Xu, Kochanek, Murphy, & Tejada-Vera, 2010). In middle-aged men, the likelihood of dying of heart disease or cancer is about equal. Among middle-aged women, though, cancer is considerably more likely than heart disease to cause death.

Like heart disease, cancer does not strike in a totally random fashion. Indeed, as you can see in the right-hand column of Table 15.2, some of the same risk factors are implicated in both diseases. Most of these risk factors are at least partially under your own control. It helps to have established good health habits in early adulthood, but it is also clear from the research that improving your health habits in middle age can reduce your risks of both cancer and heart disease.

Television personality Katie Couric became an advocate for routine cancer screening after losing her husband to colon cancer in 1998 and her sister to pancreatic cancer in 2001.

The most controversial item listed in Table 15.2 is diet; in particular, scientists debate the role of dietary fat as a potential risk factor. However, there is some evidence that reducing consumption of red meat may decrease the risk of colorectal cancer (Kushi & Giovannucci, 2002).

While the debate over the role of diet continues, there is now little doubt that several types of cancers are caused by infectious agents (Ewald, 2000). For example, in Chapter 13 you learned about the link between the human papilloma virus (HPV) and cervical cancer (Castellsagué et al., 2002). This sexually transmitted disease is apparently also responsible for many cancers of the mouth, nose, and throat, presumably because of oral sex, and for some cases of anal cancer in gay men (Frisch et al., 1997; Mork et al., 2001).

Studies have shown that a virus called Epstein-Barr virus is also associated with cancers of the nose and throat, as well as one type of non-Hodgkin's lymphoma (Chien et al., 2001). Another virus, hepatitis B, is linked to liver cancer (Yang et al., 2002). Thus, screening people who do not yet have symptoms of these viral infections may help to identify cancers at very early stages of development, when they are most curable.

Correlations between bacterial infections and cancer have also been identified. For example, one bacterial infection called *Helicobacter pylori* has been implicated in many studies of stomach cancer and one type of non-Hodgkin's lymphoma (Uemura et al., 2001). This microorganism also causes stomach ulcers. Typically, antibiotic treatment clears up both the infection and the ulcers and, coincidentally, reduces the risk of stomach cancer. However, most people who carry *H. pylori* do not have ulcers or any other symptoms. Moreover, a fairly high proportion of people, especially those in developing nations with poor water-purification systems, carry the infection (Brown, 2000). Research indicates that antibiotic treatment of people with *H. pylori* infections who do not have symptoms may reduce rates of stomach cancer in these areas; however, more research is needed before investigators can be certain about the effectiveness of such treatments (Wong et al., 2004). ◉ **Watch** the **Video** *Prostate Cancer* in **MyPsychLab**.

Studies of the role of infection in the development of cancer provide yet another example of the importance of health-related choices. Specifically, safe sex practices can limit an individual's risk of contracting sexually transmitted diseases and the cancers in which they have been implicated. Moreover, vaccines against many viruses, including HPV and hepatitis B, are widely available. ◉ **Watch** the **Video** *Middle Adulthood: Health in Middle Adulthood across Cultures* in **MyPsychLab**.

Gender and Health

LO 15.7 What are some important differences in the health of middle-aged men and women?

Figure 15.1 makes clear that women's life expectancy is greater than men's. But what is not evident is an interesting paradox: Women live longer, but they have more diseases and disabilities. Women are more likely to describe their health as poor, to have chronic conditions such as arthritis, and to be limited in their daily activities. Such differences have been found in every country in which the pattern has been studied, including nonindustrialized countries (Rahman, Strauss, Gertler, Ashley, & Fox, 1994).

This difference is already present in early adulthood and grows larger with age. By old age, women are substantially more likely than men to be chronically ill (Guralnik et al., 1993; Kunkel & Applebaum, 1992). In early adulthood, this gender difference in disease rate can be largely attributed to health problems associated with childbearing. At later ages, the difference cannot be explained in this same way.

How is it possible that men die younger but are healthier while they are alive? Researchers suggest that the apparent paradox can be resolved by considering sex differences in potentially fatal conditions such as cardiovascular disease (Verbrugge, 1989). In the United States, 88 of every 100,000 men between the ages of 45 and 54 die of heart disease annually, compared with only 49 of every 100,000 women (NCHS, 2010). This difference in rates of heart disease diminishes once women are past menopause, although it does not disappear totally even in late old age.

It isn't just that men have higher rates of CVD; they also are more likely to die from the disease once it has been acquired. One reason may be that the heart muscles of women who have CVD seem to be better able to adapt to stresses such as physical exertion (van Doornen, Snieder, & Boomsma, 1998). In addition, once they have a heart attack, women recover to a higher level of physical functioning than men do (Bosworth et al., 2000). Sex differences in health habits also seem to contribute to women's greater ability to recover from CVD. For example, women are more likely to get regular checkups and to seek help early in an illness than men are (Addis & Mahalik, 2003; Verbrugge & Wingard, 1987).

By contrast, women are more likely than men to have nonfatal chronic ailments such as arthritis. Because chronic pain is characteristic of arthritis, the activities of women who have it are often limited. Understandably, too, living with chronic pain affects their general sense of well-being.

Socioeconomic Class, Ethnicity, and Health

LO 15.8 How are socioeconomic status and ethnicity related to health in middle adulthood?

hypertension elevated blood pressure

While emphasizing preventive actions such as exercise, developmentalists cannot ignore the importance for health and mental ability in middle adulthood of those familiar demographic variables social class and race. In Chapter 13 you learned that social class differences in secondary aging increase as adults get older. In middle adulthood, occupational level and education (both of which correlate strongly with socioeconomic class) interact to influence health (Volkers, Westert, & Schellevis, 2007). Research suggests that such findings help explain health disparities among Whites, Hispanic Americans, and African Americans (Chatters, 1991; James, Keenan, & Browning, 1992; Markides & Lee, 1991). However, one interesting deviation from this pattern occurs among men in high-status occupations, such as business owners and attorneys. Men in such occupations who also view seeking health care as "unmanly" are less likely to get check-ups and follow physicians' advice than men with similar beliefs in lower-status occupations (Springer, 2009). As a result, they are less healthy overall.

Ethnicity is also linked to overall health. For example, African Americans have shorter life expectancies than White Americans, as Figure 15.1 on page 383 shows (NCHS, 2013). There are also ethnic group differences in incidence of specific diseases (CDC, 2003a). In recent years, public health officials in the United States have begun to study and address these disparities. These efforts have focused on three diseases: cardiovascular disease, diabetes, and cancer.

CARDIOVASCULAR DISEASE Cardiovascular disease (heart attack and stroke) is the leading cause of death in all ethnic groups, and some surveys show lower rates of heart disease among minorities than among Whites (NCHS, 2013). However, heart disease is more often disabling and prematurely fatal to Native Americans, African Americans, and Hispanic Americans than it is to Whites and Asian Americans (Office of Minority Health, 2012b). Among minority women, the major factor seems to be obesity. For example, about 75% of Mexican American, 70% of Native American, and 80% of African American women are overweight, compared to 60% of White women (Office of Minority Health, 2012b). Among men, the key risk factor is high blood pressure, or **hypertension** (Office of Minority Health, 2012b). About 30% of White and Mexican American men have elevated blood pressure, compared to 39% of Native American men and 41% of African American men.

DIABETES The proportion of adults in the United States who have diabetes is growing in all ethnic groups, but minorities have significantly higher rates of the condition than Whites (NCHS, 2010). Public education about diabetes has become a major health goal in the United States because the disease can lead to severe complications such as cardiovascular disease, kidney failure, and blindness (Ligaray & Isley, 2010). Just as they are more likely than Whites to have the disease in the first place, minority adults who have been diagnosed with diabetes are more likely than their White counterparts to develop complications (Office of Minority Health, 2012a). Although diabetes itself kills few people, it is the underlying cause of many other potentially deadly diseases and conditions; death rates among adults who have diabetes are about twice as high at every age as those among individuals who do not have this disease (CDC, 1998a). ⊙ **Watch** the **Video** *Coping with Diabetes* in **MyPsychLab**.

Public health officials don't yet have an explanation for ethnic-group differences in diabetes rates. However, they hypothesize that complication rates vary because minorities tend to develop the disease earlier in life than Whites do (U.S. Department of Health and Human Services, 1998). Therefore, it affects all of their body systems for a longer period of time. Once diagnosed, minority adults often have less access to regular medical care than Whites. However, researchers have found that, even among diabetic Whites and African Americans who have the same health-insurance benefits and equal access to diabetes care services, African Americans are less likely to seek care for complications at a point when medical intervention can be most effective (U.S. Department of Health and Human Services, 1998).

CANCER African Americans have higher incidences of some types of cancer (Ries et al., 2007). For example, African Americans have the highest rates of prostate, colon, and lung cancer in the United States (Ries et al., 2007). Asian Americans have the highest rate of liver cancer, and Native Americans are more often diagnosed with cancer of the kidney than those in other groups.

The main cause for ethnic group variations in cancer rates, according to public health officials, is failure to receive routine cancer screenings. Minority men and women are less likely than Whites to obtain cancer screening tests such as PSA tests for prostate cancer in men, mammograms and pap smears for breast and cervical cancer in women, and colorectal examinations for intestinal tract cancers in both men and women. Thanks to recent improvements in public knowledge about and access to such screenings, the 5-year survival rates of adults who are diagnosed with cancer are highly similar across ethnic groups (Ries et al., 2007). Still, ensuring that screened adults have access to follow-up care is another public health goal.

Alcoholism

LO 15.9 What are some of the consequences of alcoholism for middle-aged adults?

There is a tendency today to use the term *addiction* to label any form of behavior that people engage in to excess (see *Research Report*). However, addiction, or substance abuse as psychologists call it, involves both psychological and physical dependence on a stimulus; simply spending a lot of time doing something doesn't mean that you are addicted to it. Moreover, substance abuse, especially when it occurs over a long period of time, causes a significant amount of damage to the body's organs.

As you learned in Chapter 13, alcohol is the most frequently abused substance in the United States. Between 14% and 24% of adults in the United States report having had a problem with alcohol abuse at some time in their lives (Thompson, Lande, & Kalapatapu, 2010). And, as you probably know, **alcoholism**, defined as psychological and physical dependence on alcohol, can develop at any age. However, during the middle adulthood years, as the toxic effects of heavy drinking combine with those of primary aging and other sources of secondary aging, alcoholism begins to take a heavy toll on the body (Thompson, 2013).

Long-term heavy drinking damages every organ in the body. It is especially harmful to the liver, and it weakens the heart muscle and the valves and walls of the blood vessels. Individuals with alcoholism are also more likely to smoke than those without the disorder (Thompson, 2013). Thus, rates of liver disease, cardiovascular disease, and cancers of the digestive and urinary systems are higher among alcoholics than they are among nonalcoholics (Thompson, 2013). Moreover, heavy alcohol use damages the brain, causing impairments in memory and language functions (Daurignac et al., 2005).

The result of this interaction between aging and alcohol abuse is that alcoholics face an increased risk of death (Thompson, 2013). A longitudinal study involving more than 40,000 males in Norway found that the rate of death prior to age 60 was significantly higher among alcoholics than among nonalcoholics (Rossow & Amundsen, 1997). Studies further indicate that the death rates of men with alcoholism who are in their 50s and early 60s are five to six times higher than those of nonalcoholics in the same age group (Kristenson, Österling, Nilsson, & Lindgärde, 2002). Thankfully, the effects of alcohol on the brain may be reversible if an alcoholic quits drinking (Kensinger, Clarke, & Corkin, 2003). Likewise, giving up alcohol is essential to stopping the progression of alcohol-induced liver damage. A drug called *acamprosate* can be prescribed to help recovering alcoholics deal with withdrawal symptoms and maintain abstinence from alcohol (Mason, Goodman, Chabac, & Lehert, 2006).

alcoholism physical and psychological dependence on alcohol

Internet Addiction Disorder

Recently, some mental health professionals have raised concerns about the amount of time some individuals spend online. Some claim to have discovered a new disorder they call *internet addiction disorder*, or *IAD* (Pies, 2009; Young, 1998). To be diagnosed with IAD, a person must demonstrate a pattern of internet use that interferes with normal educational, occupational, and social functioning.

Most mental health professionals view IAD as a disorder of impulse control, much like compulsive gambling, rather than the sort of addiction that results from craving for a substance-induced altered state of consciousness (Meerkerk, van den Ejinden, Franken, & Garretsen, 2010). In support of this perspective, experts cite studies showing that individuals who exhibit IAD also often have other types of disorders of impulse control. For example, people with IAD also tend to spend inordinate amounts of time watching television and playing video games. They are also more likely to be addicted to alcohol and other substances (Yellowlees & Marks, 2007).

Such findings suggest that the internet may simply provide people who are impulsive and have a tendency toward developing compulsive behavior patterns with an additional avenue through

which to express these traits (Fabi, 2004; Griffiths, 2003). Research examining compulsive use of internet pornography supports this hypothesis (Twohig, Crosby, & Cox, 2009). Researchers have found that the factors that predict compulsive use of pornographic materials such as videos and magazines are the same as those that predict compulsive use of online pornography. However, because of the accessibility, privacy, and realism associated with internet pornography, compulsive use is often more problematic for individuals who view online pornography than for those who are drawn to other media (Buzzell, 2005).

In some cases, IAD may be part of a set of symptoms that includes depression rather than a pattern of compulsive behavior (Morrison & Gore, 2010). For example, some people spend so much time online that they don't have time for interactions with family members and friends. Among such users, depression is more common than it is among people whose internet usage is of a more moderate nature. However, mental health experts point out that depressive symptoms drive some people to the internet rather than the other way around. Such people spend hours jumping from one internet site to another with no particular goal in mind and may

be doing so in an attempt to escape from their feelings of loneliness and despair.

A treatment approach called *Acceptance and Commitment Therapy (ACT)* has been found to be effective in helping people overcome IAD (Twohig & Crosby, 2010). With the help of a therapist, individuals with this problem learn to identify cues that trigger the impulse to go online. They next learn to accept the triggers rather than to struggle against them, equipped with the knowledge that if they refuse to act on an impulse, it will eventually subside. The power to refrain from responding to such impulses comes from a firm commitment to act in accordance with values that the person deems to be more important than his or her interest in spending time online.

CRITICAL ANALYSIS

1. *In your view, why is the internet a more attractive means of "escaping" from the stresses of everyday life than books, movies, and other forms of entertainment?*

2. *How can researchers determine whether depressive symptoms drive internet use or spending large amount of time online produces such symptoms?*

---

test yourself before going on ✓ Study and Review in MyPsychLab

Answers to these questions can be found in the back of the book.

1. Write "CVD" beside each risk factor for cardiovascular disease, "C" beside each risk factor for cancer, and "Both" beside each risk factor that applies to both.
   _____(1) low-fiber diet
   _____(2) smoking
   _____(3) high blood pressure
   _____(4) heavy drinking
   _____(5) heredity

2. Women are more likely than men to have _____ _____ ailments.

3. Which ethnic group has the highest rates of each of these cancers?

   _____(1) lung cancer
   _____(2) prostate cancer
   _____(3) breast cancer
   _____(4) liver cancer
   _____(5) kidney cancer

4. Which diseases are more common among alcoholics than nonalcoholics?

CRITICAL THINKING

5. Considering all the risk factors for the various health problems that were described in this section, what can you predict about your own health in middle age? Which factors can you change?

Cognitive Functioning

In the middle adult years, some cognitive abilities improve, while others slow down a bit. Still, many adults have acquired large bodies of knowledge and skill that help them compensate for losses and solve problems within their areas of expertise more efficiently than younger adults do.

Models of Physical and Cognitive Aging

LO 15.10 How do Denney's and the Balteses' models explain the relationship between health and cognitive functioning in middle age?

Many of the various bits and pieces of information you've encountered so far about physical and cognitive changes in adulthood can be combined in a single model, suggested by Nancy Denney and illustrated in Figure 15.2 (Denney 1982, 1984). Denney proposed that on nearly any measure of physical or cognitive functioning, age-related changes follow a typical curve, like those shown in the figure. But she also argued that the height of this curve varies, depending on the amount an individual exercises some ability or skill. Denney used the word *exercise* very broadly, to refer not only to physical exercise but also to mental exercise and to the extent to which some specific task has been performed before. Unexercised abilities generally have a lower peak level of performance; exercised abilities generally have a higher peak.

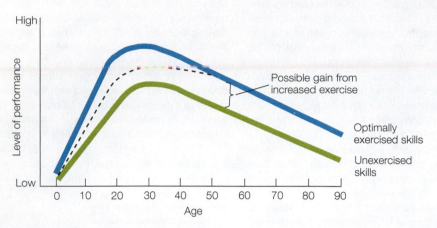

Figure 15.2 Denney's Model of Physical and Cognitive Aging

Denney's model suggests both a basic decay curve and a fairly large gap between actual level of performance on exercised and unexercised abilities.

(*Source:* Denney, 1982, 1984.)

Many laboratory tests of memory, for example, such as memorizing lists of names, tap unexercised abilities. Everyday memory tasks, such as recalling details from a newspaper column, tap much more exercised abilities. The distinction is somewhat similar to the distinction between crystallized and fluid abilities (see Chapter 13). Most crystallized abilities are at least moderately exercised, whereas many fluid abilities are relatively unexercised. But Denney was making a more general point: Whether abilities are crystallized or fluid, those that are more fully exercised will have a higher peak.

The gap between the curve for unexercised abilities and the curve for maximally exercised abilities represents the degree of improvement that would be possible for any given skill. Any skill that is not fully exercised can be improved if the individual begins to exercise that ability. There is clear evidence, for example, that aerobic capacity (VO_2 max) can be increased at any age if a person begins a program of physical exercise (e.g., Blumenthal et al., 1991; Buchner, Beresford, Larson, LaCroix, & Wagner, 1992; Cheitlin, 2003). Nonetheless, in Denney's model, the maximum level an adult will be able to achieve, even with optimum exercise, will decline with age, just as a top athlete's performance declines, even with optimum training regimens. One implication of this is that young adults are more likely to be able to get away with laziness or poor study habits and still perform well; as they age, this becomes less and less true, because they are fighting against the basic decay curve of aging.

Researchers Paul Baltes (1939–2006) and Margaret Baltes (1939–2000) took a somewhat different approach. In their view, the physical declines of middle age give rise to a strategy they call **selective optimization with compensation**, the process of balancing the gains and losses associated with aging (Baltes & Baltes, 1990). The idea is that, as the body ages, resources such as physical agility and working memory capacity decrease. In order to manage the demands of competing tasks, aging adults select one to which they devote most or all of these resources. Moreover, adults optimize the skills that they believe can be improved by exercising them as much as possible. At the same time, they use compensatory strategies to offset the effects of aging.

Selection occurs when a middle-aged adult reduces distractions in order to more efficiently carry out a cognitive task. For example, a middle-aged college student might be more likely than a younger student to turn off the television when she studies. Optimization is involved when middle-aged adults work to improve their physical fitness or to expand their knowledge. Compensation takes many forms, including the use of reading glasses to correct for presbyopia and the development of organizational strategies, such as being diligent about recording important events on a calendar, to offset declines in memory.

selective optimization with compensation the process of balancing the gains and losses associated with aging

Health and Cognitive Functioning

LO 15.11   What has research revealed about the link between health and cognitive functioning?

You should remember from Chapter 13 that it is often difficult to separate the effects of primary and secondary aging because they happen at the same time. Research examining correlations between health and cognition helps developmentalists understand the effects of secondary aging. Specifically, many of the same characteristics that are linked to increased or decreased risk of heart disease and cancer are also linked to the rate of change or the maintenance of intellectual skill in the middle years.

Research shows that middle-aged adults who are physically active have lower mortality rates over the next 20–30 years than their peers who are less active. Physical exercise during middle age is also positively correlated with scores on tests of intellectual functioning.

One illustration of this relationship comes from Warner Schaie's analysis of data from the Seattle Longitudinal Study (Schaie, 2013). He found that those research participants who had some kind of cardiovascular disease (either coronary heart disease or high blood pressure) showed earlier and larger declines on intellectual tests than did those who were disease free. Other researchers have found similar linkages. Even adults whose blood pressure is controlled by medication seem to show earlier declines (Sands & Meredith, 1992; Schultz, Elias, Robbins, Streeten, & Blakeman, 1986). Schaie cautions against taking these findings too far. The size of the effect is quite small, and it may operate indirectly rather than directly. For example, adults with cardiovascular disease may become physically less active as a response to their disease. The lower level of activity, in turn, may affect the rate of intellectual decline. This raises the possibility that exercise may be one of the critical factors in determining an individual person's overall physical health and cognitive performance during middle adulthood. A growing amount of information confirms such an effect.

One particularly large and well-designed study of the effects of exercise on physical health involved 17,321 Harvard alumni who had been students between 1916 and 1950. In 1962 or 1966, when the men were in their 30s, 40s, or 50s, each man provided detailed information about his daily levels of physical activity (Lee, Hsieh, & Paffenbarger, 1995). (The measures of physical activity were quite detailed. Each man reported how many blocks he normally walked each day, how often he climbed stairs, the amount of time per week he normally engaged in various sports, and so on. All the answers were then converted into estimates of calories expended per week. For example, walking 1 mile on level ground uses roughly 100 calories; climbing one flight of stairs uses about 17.) The researchers tracked all these men until 1988 to identify who had died and of what cause. They found that the more exercise a man reported, the lower his mortality risk.

Researchers were careful to exclude from the study any man who was known to have heart disease or other disease at the onset of the study, in the 1960s. Furthermore, the groups differed *only* in level of energy expenditure; they did not differ in age or whether they smoked, had high blood pressure, were overweight, or had a family history of early death—which makes the effect of exercise even clearer. To be sure, because the level of exercise was each man's own choice, there may have been other differences separating the various exercise groups that could account for the different death rates. But the pattern, which has been replicated in more recent cohorts of both men and women, is so substantial and striking that alternative explanations are hard to come by (e.g., Blair et al., 1995; Byberg et al., 2009; Lissner, Bengtsson, Björkelund, & Wedel, 1996). By far the most likely explanation is that there is a causal connection between longevity and level of physical activity.

Physical exercise also seems to help maintain cognitive abilities in the middle adult years, very likely because it helps to maintain cardiovascular fitness (Guiney & Machado, 2013; Rogers, Meyer, & Mortel, 1990). These effects are not restricted to those who participate in formal, structured exercise programs. Among physically healthy middle-aged and older adults, those who are more physically active—doing everyday activities such as gardening and heavy housework—score higher on tests of reasoning, reaction time, and short-term memory (Van Boxtel et al., 1997).

episodic memories recollections of personal events

semantic memories general knowledge

A different approach to studying exercise and cognitive functioning would involve randomly assigning some people to an exercise program and some to a nonexercise control group and then seeing whether the two groups differed in their cognitive functioning after a period of exercise. The results of the small number of studies of this type have been quite mixed. Every study finds that exercise increases measures of physical functioning, such as VO_2 max, even in very elderly adults. Some—but not all—such studies also show that exercise improves thinking (Hawkins, Kramer, & Capaldi, 1992; Hill, Storandt, & Malley, 1993; Winter et al., 2007). Other studies do not reach that conclusion (e.g., Buchner et al., 1992; Emery & Gatz, 1990). In most cases, the experimental exercise program lasts only a few months, and that may not be sufficient to make any difference in mental functioning. Still, because researchers already know that exercise is linked to lower levels of disease and greater longevity, prudence alone would argue for including it in your life.

Changes in Memory and Cognition

LO 15.12 How do young and middle-aged adults differ in performance on memory tests?

When developmentalists study changes in cognitive functioning in middle age, they find almost precisely what Denney's model and Schaie's longitudinal study suggest. That is, lack of mental exercise tends to be correlated with declines in memory and cognitive skills, but major deficits are not found until after age 60 to 65.

MEMORY FUNCTION Drawing conclusions about memory function in middle age is difficult because studies of age differences in adult memory rarely include middle-aged people. Typically, researchers compare very young adults, such as college students, to adults in their 60s and 70s. When the two groups are found to differ, psychologists often infer that middle-aged adults' performance falls somewhere between the two. In other words, they assume that memory function declines steadily, in linear fashion, across the adult years—but this assumption may not be true.

One thing developmentalists know about memory is that the subjective experience of forgetfulness clearly increases with age. The older we get, the more forgetful we think we are (Scheibner & Leathem, 2012). However, it may be that the memory demands of middle-aged adults' everyday lives are greater than those of young adults'. Remember, working memory is limited, and the more you try to remember at one time, the more you will forget.

Nevertheless, there seem to be some real differences in the memory performance of young and middle-aged adults. For example, performance on memory tasks such as remembering lists of words and passages of text declines with age, but usually not until after about age 55. In contrast, recognition of words and texts appears to remain stable throughout adulthood (Zelinski & Burnight, 1997). Such findings suggest that there are age differences in working memory. Research examining short-term memory capacity at various ages shows that it remains very stable throughout early, middle, and late adulthood. What changes, apparently, is the ability to make efficient use of available capacity (Lincourt, Rybash, & Hoyer, 1998).

Some declines in cognitive performance, such as increased reaction times, are evident even when middle-aged individuals are engaged in activities with which they have had many years of relevant experience. However, expertise is associated with the development of cognitive strategies that help to buffer the effects of aging (Morrow et al., 2003). Consequently, middle-aged adults are able to maintain high levels of performance on cognitively demanding tasks, such as flying a commercial airliner.

SEMANTIC AND EPISODIC MEMORIES Researchers can gain additional insight into age-related memory changes by studying how well young and middle-aged adults encode different kinds of memories. **Episodic memories** are recollections of personal events or episodes. **Semantic memories** represent general knowledge. For example, a person's memories of a vacation in Hawaii are episodic, and her knowledge that Hawaii was the 50th state is semantic.

Researchers find that young and middle-aged adults differ more with respect to new episodic memories than they do with respect to semantic memories (Gallo & Wheeler, 2013). For example, a middle-aged person attending a baseball game may forget where he parked his car (episodic memory). However, he is unlikely to forget the basic rules of the game (semantic memory).

Middle-aged adults are very proficient at overcoming episodic memory limitations by using reminders, or *cues*, to help themselves remember information. Thus, the middle-aged person who knows that she may forget where her car is parked makes a point of noting nearby landmarks that will help her remember its location. This may be because middle-aged adults, in contrast to those who are older, continue to have a high sense of self-efficacy with respect to memory (Lineweaver & Hertzog, 1998). In other words, they believe their efforts will make a difference, so they actively work to improve their memories.

USE IT OR LOSE IT? In general, adults maintain or even gain in skill on any task that they use often or that is based on specific learning. For example, verbal abilities increase in middle age (Giambra, Arenberg, Zonderman, Kawas, & Costa, 1995; Salthouse, 2004). It appears that vocabulary—or, more precisely, performance on vocabulary tests—doesn't begin to decline until about age 65. And the "use it or lose it" dictum seems to hold true for cognitive abilities. That is, adults who engage in intellectually challenging activities show fewer losses in cognitive skills than those who do not (Salthouse, 2004; Schaie, Nguyen, Willis, Dutta, & Yue, 2001).

Similarly, expertise in a particular field helps to compensate for age-related deficits in cognitive functioning (Colonia-Willner, 1999; Morrow et al., 2003; Tsang, 1998). For example, in one study, researchers examined 17- to 79-year-old participants' ability to recognize melodies performed at varying tempos (Andrews, Dowling, Bartlett, & Halpern, 1998). Some tunes were played very rapidly and then slowed until participants could recognize them. Both age and years of musical training predicted participants' ability to recognize melodies presented in this way, but the relationship between age and recognition was much weaker than the relationship between recognition and musical training. Other melodies were played too slowly to be recognized at the beginning and then speeded up. Interestingly, only musical training correlated with recognition of tunes played this way; there was no association with age whatsoever.

Due to the accumulated effects of many years of using some cognitive skills and the development of a large body of relevant information in long-term memory, middle-aged adults outperform those who are younger on tasks that involve comprehending and remembering reading material. For instance, researchers have found that middle-aged and younger adults take different approaches to learning from expository text (the kind of text you're reading right now!) (Matzen & Benjamin, 2013). Younger adults focus on creating a word-for-word representation of the text in their memories. By contrast, middle-aged adults pay more attention to overarching themes than to details. In memory, this difference might be reflected in a decline in memory for surface detail, accompanied by an increase in memory for themes and meanings.

A study in which researchers asked adults of various ages to read a story and then to recall it immediately afterward, in writing, yielded support for this hypothesis (Adams, 1991). Younger adults were more likely to report specific events or actions in the story, while middle-aged adults recalled more of the psychological motivations of the characters and offered more interpretations of the story in their recall. What this may mean is that, along with a shift in schematic processing, the encoding process changes as we get older. We may not attempt to encode as much detail but may store more summarizing information.

Creativity

LO 15.13 What does research suggest about age-related changes in creativity?

A somewhat different question about cognitive functioning in the middle years of adulthood has to do with **creativity**, the ability to produce original, appropriate, and valuable ideas and/or solutions to problems. One psychologist looked at the lifetime creativity of thousands of notable scientists from the 19th century and earlier (Simonton, 1991, 2000). Simonton identified the age at which these individuals (nearly all men) published their first significant work, their best work, and their last work. In every scientific discipline represented, the thinkers

creativity the ability to produce original, appropriate, and valuable ideas and/or solutions to problems

Maintaining the Creative "Edge" at Midlife and Beyond

The songwriting career of music legend Willie Nelson began when he started writing poetry at the age of 5. When his grandparents gave him a guitar, he figured out how to set his poems to music. Nearly 3,000 songs later, Nelson continues to be inspired more by lyrics than he is by melodies. And even though Nelson is in his late 70s, he doesn't seem to have lost his creative edge. What is the secret to maintaining one's creativity and productivity through middle age and into the later years?

In a fascinating set of interviews, a number of highly successful and creative older adults described how they viewed creativity ("The creators," 2000). Interestingly, all reported that they viewed themselves as more creative than they had been when they were younger. Their comments suggested that the creative process is a highly individualized intellectual activity. However, what was remarkable was that, by middle age, all had arrived at firm conclusions about what did and did not work for them. So, some part of the maintenance of creativity included acceptance of their own creative idiosyncrasies. Some, for example, expressed the need for external motivation, such as a deadline. Guitarist B. B. King, who was 74 at the time of the interview and is still performing in his late 80s, emphasized his need for a deadline. Others were more motivated by self-imposed standards than by externals. For example, writer Isabel Allende, 57 at the time of the interview, reported that she always begins a new work on January 8 because the date is a personally meaningful anniversary for her. Advertising writer Stan Freberg, who was in his early 70s when the article's authors interviewed him, claimed that when he needs an idea, he takes a shower because he often gets inspiration while in the shower.

A second theme pervaded these reports. Each creative person, in one way or another, recognized the value of accumulated knowledge and experience. These people also tended to acknowledge important sources of this knowledge, such as parents, spouses, and friends. Consequently, they saw their creative work not only as the product of their own abilities but also as a result of a complex network of influential individuals, life experiences, and their own capacity to reflect on their lives.

From these extraordinary individuals, we can learn two important things about maintaining creativity and productivity in the middle and late adult years. First, being consciously aware of one's own creative process—and accepting its boundaries—seems to be critical. Second, some degree of humility, a sense of indebtedness to those who have contributed to and supported one's creative development, appears to be associated with continuing productivity in the middle and late adult years.

REFLECTION

1. *To what extent can a young adult improve his or her own creativity and productivity by following the example of a successful middle-aged or older adult?*

2. *Why is humility important to maintaining creativity?*

produced their best work at about age 40, on average. But most of them were publishing significant, even outstanding, research through their 40s and into their 50s.

You might be wondering how the creative process actually works (see *Developmental Science in the Workplace*). Psychologists have been studying it for some time and still have much to learn. However, one useful approach describes creativity as a type of thought process called *divergent thinking* (Guilford, 1967). A person who uses divergent thinking can provide multiple solutions to problems that have no clear answer. Thus, divergent thinking is as vital to science as it is to art. For instance, when scientists were faced with the problem of identifying the cause of AIDS, they proposed and tested many hypotheses before it became clear that the disease was caused by a virus. Likewise, a novelist who wants to provide readers with insight into a character's motivations tries out several ways of communicating the information before she settles on the one that works best.

Creative solutions sometimes pop into the mind of a creative person fully formed, but most of the time they arise from bits and pieces of several solutions that she has been mulling over for a while. Psychologist Daniel Goleman describes this mulling-over process, when it is used to solve problems, as involving four stages (Goleman, Kaufman, & Ray, 1992). During *preparation*, relevant information is gathered. The next phase, *incubation*, involves digesting the information without actually trying to work on the problem. *Illumination* occurs when this digestive process produces an *aha!* moment in which the solution to the problem becomes clear. Finally, during *translation*, the solution is applied to the problem and adjustments are made, as needed. As you probably know from experience, it is the last step that is the most difficult and time-consuming because, in the real world, things don't often go as we imagine they will. As Thomas Edison put it, "Genius is 1% inspiration and 99% perspiration." Edison should know; after theoretically working out how to design a commercially viable electric light bulb, he spent over a year making prototypes before he finally found the design that worked. Thus, Edison believed that failure is essential to the creative process.

Answers to these questions can be found in the back of the book.

1. Would Denney agree or disagree with the following statement? "Through lifestyle changes, a middle-aged adult can regain the peak levels of fitness he or she enjoyed in early adulthood."

2. What was the main finding of the Harvard alumni study?

3. Write "Y" by memory functions that decline with age and "N" by those that do not.
   _____(1) episodic memory
   _____(2) semantic memory
   _____(3) performance on complex memory tasks
   _____(4) comprehending and remembering reading material
   _____(5) visual memory

4. Creativity often involves _____ thinking.

CRITICAL THINKING

5. Given what you have learned in this section, where would you place cognitive functioning in middle age on a 10-point scale ranging from "age and health have no effect on cognitive functioning" at the low end to "age and health cause inevitable declines in cognitive functioning" at the high end? What reasons would you give if you were asked to explain your assessment?

SUMMARY

Physical Changes (pp. 376–382)

LO 15.1   What do researchers know about brain function in middle age?

- Brain size diminishes a bit in the middle adult years. Some changes in brain function suggest that middle-aged adults are more subject to distraction. However, middle-aged adults often outperform younger adults on everyday tasks that require concentration and rapid judgments, such as driving.

LO 15.2   How does reproductive function change in men and women in middle age?

- The loss of reproductive capacity, called the climacteric in both men and women, occurs very gradually in men and more rapidly in women. Menopause is a three-phase process that results from a series of hormonal changes.

LO 15.3   What is osteoporosis, and what factors are associated with it?

- Bone mass declines significantly beginning at about age 30; accelerated declines in women at menopause are linked to decreased levels of estrogen and progesterone. Faster bone loss occurs in women who experience early menopause, who are underweight, who exercise little, or who have low-calcium diets.

LO 15.4   How do vision and hearing change in middle age?

- Thickening of the lens of the eye, with accompanying loss of elasticity, reduces visual acuity noticeably in the 40s or 50s. Hearing loss is more gradual.

Health and Wellness (pp. 383–389)

LO 15.5   How does cardiovascular disease develop?

- Cardiovascular disease is not a normal part of aging; it is a disease for which there are known risk factors, including smoking, high blood pressure, high blood cholesterol, obesity, and a high-fat diet.

LO 15.6   What factors contribute to cancer?

- Cancer has known risk factors, including smoking, obesity, and an inactive lifestyle. The role of a high-fat diet has been debated, but most evidence supports the hypothesis that such a diet contributes to the risk. Several cancers are caused by infectious agents (viral and bacterial).

LO 15.7   What are some important differences in the health of middle-aged men and women?

- Women tend to live longer than men but are more likely to have chronic illnesses. Women recover more readily from heart attacks because of gender differences in the heart itself and women's greater tendency to get follow-up care.

LO 15.8   How are socioeconomic status and ethnicity related to health in middle adulthood?

- Low-income adults have more chronic illnesses and a higher rate of death than those who are better off economically. African Americans, Hispanic Americans, and Native Americans are more likely to have cardiovascular disease, cancer, and diabetes than Whites.

LO 15.9   What are some of the consequences of alcoholism for middle-aged adults?

- Alcoholism can develop at any age, but its effects become evident in middle age, when it is associated with increased mortality.

Cognitive Functioning (pp. 389–395)

LO 15.10   How do Denney's and the Balteses' models explain the relationship between health and cognitive functioning in middle age?

- Denney's model of aging suggests that exercising either physical or cognitive abilities can improve performance at any age, but the upper limit on improvement declines with increasing age.

Paul and Margaret Baltes assert that middle-aged adults balance the gains and losses associated with aging by selecting tasks on which to focus limited resources, optimizing some skills through practice, and compensating for declines.

LO 15.11   What has research revealed about the link between health and cognitive functioning?

- Some studies suggest that differences in health contribute to variations in cognitive functioning among middle-aged adults. Exercise clearly affects the physical health of middle-aged adults, but research is less conclusive with regard to its effects on cognitive functioning.

LO 15.12   How do young and middle-aged adults differ in performance on memory tests?

- Verbal abilities continue to grow in middle age. Some loss of memory speed and skill occurs, but by most measures the loss is quite small until fairly late in the middle adult years. Expertise helps middle-aged adults compensate for losses in processing speed.

LO 15.13   What does research suggest about age-related changes in creativity?

- Creative productivity appears to remain high during middle adulthood, at least for adults in challenging jobs (the category of adults on whom most of this research has focused).

KEY TERMS

alcoholism (p. 388)
atherosclerosis (p. 383)
cardiovascular disease (CVD) (p. 383)
climacteric (p. 377)

creativity (p. 393)
episodic memories (p. 392)
hypertension (p. 387)
menopause (p. 378)
osteoporosis (p. 381)

perimenopausal phase (p. 378)
postmenopausal phase (p. 379)
premenopausal phase (p. 378)

presbycusis (p. 382)
presbyopia (p. 382)
selective optimization with compensation (p. 390)
semantic memories (p. 392)

CHAPTER TEST   ✓ Study and Review in MyPsychLab

Answers to all the Chapter Test questions can be found in the back of the book.

1. Which of the following is true of cognitive functioning and automobile accidents?
   a. Young adults are more likely to get into an accident because of larger synaptic gaps.
   b. Young adults are more likely to get into an accident because of lapses of judgment and a higher likelihood of drinking alcohol.
   c. Middle-aged adults are more likely to get into an accident because of the lapses in cognition and slower reaction times.
   d. There isn't a statistically significant difference between the accident rates of middle-aged adults and younger adults.

2. Which of the following is a reason middle-aged adults take longer to perform cognitive tasks than younger adults take?
   a. A larger area of the cortex is activated; therefore, it takes longer to process information.
   b. It is more difficult for the middle-aged brain to activate large areas of the cortex.
   c. The middle-aged brain does not react to perceptual stimuli as fast as the young adult brain.
   d. Decreased blood supply to the brain results from the build-up of plaque.

3. Why do women fare better after a heart attack than men?
   a. Women are more likely to have other chronic diseases that diminish the risk of a heart attack.

   b. Men's hearts are larger and therefore suffer more damage from a heart attack.
   c. Men are more likely to smoke than women.
   d. Women's heart muscle seems to be better able to adapt to stressors and physical exertion.

4. Jose and Isabella want to repaint their entire house and renovate some of the rooms as well. They look at many paint samples and magazine pictures, and they try out several different arrangements of furniture. This process represents what type of thinking?
   a. divergent   c. convergent
   b. optimized   d. selective

5. Which of the following statements is *false*?
   a. Asian Americans have the highest rates of liver cancer.
   b. Native Americans have higher rates of kidney cancer than other groups.
   c. White Americans have the highest rates of breast cancer.
   d. African Americans have the highest rates of prostate, colon, and lung cancer.

6. A researcher who is testing the cognitive functioning of middle-aged adults would find which of the following to be true of her subjects regarding well-rehearsed, familiar tasks?
   a. Their performance is impaired.
   b. They maintain or gain skills.
   c. They show gradual decrements.
   d. They have difficulty performing them.

7. Which of the following statements best summarizes the current research on hormone therapy (HT) for menopause?
   a. Natural supplements should be used whenever possible in place of synthetic forms of HT.
   b. The use of HT should be approached cautiously and should be symptom specific.
   c. The use of HT causes more risks than benefits, so most physicians are recommending that it not be used at all.
   d. HT has been in use since the early 20th century and has proven to be safe and reliable.

8. In middle adulthood, which of the following correlates of socioeconomic class interact to influence health?
   a. ethnicity and social networks
   b. occupational level and education
   c. overall health and income level
   d. educational level and ethnicity

9. Which of the following is *not* associated with osteoporosis?
   a. being female
   b. the timing of menopause
   c. obesity
   d. exercise

10. Which of the following is a risk factor for both heart disease and cancer?
    a. smoking
    b. high blood pressure
    c. moderate alcohol use
    d. high cholesterol

11. Alleena has noticed that, along with having hot flashes, she is becoming forgetful, she sometimes gets words mixed up, and her emotions seem to be "making her crazy." She is also very fatigued. What is the likely cause?
    a. The hot flashes and hormonal changes of perimenopause are probably disturbing her sleep, so she is sleep deprived.
    b. Alleena has just started going through menopause
    c. Alleena's menstrual flow has stopped, and she is probably concerned about being pregnant.
    d. These symptoms are usually associated with the cessation of ovulation.

12. Fifty-year-old Evan has begun to experience difficulty achieving and maintaining an erection. These changes might indicate that Evan is experiencing _____.
    a. the climacteric
    b. heart disease
    c. osteoporosis
    d. menopause

13. What is the average age for the onset of menopause in the United States?
    a. 40
    b. 45
    c. 50
    d. 60

14. Adella has never had anything but perfect vision, but shortly after her 40th birthday, she noticed it was getting more and more difficult to read the morning newspaper, as if her arms were not long enough to hold the paper far enough away to get it in focus. If Adella visits her ophthalmologist, she will likely be diagnosed with which of the following?
    a. glaucoma
    b. stereopsis
    c. presbycusis
    d. presbyopia

15. Which statement about aging and memory is true?
    a. By age 45, an individual would have more difficulty retrieving a semantic memory than an episodic memory.
    b. With advancing age, auditory memory declines rapidly, but visual memory is stable or improves.
    c. Memory ability declines with age, and by middle adulthood significant decline has occurred.
    d. With advancing age, individuals tend to remember fewer specific details of a story and more of the theme or meaning of the story.

16. What term do Baltes and Baltes use to refer to the process of balancing the gains and losses associated with aging?
    a. senescence
    b. judicial optimization of resources
    c. selective optimization with compensation
    d. selective remembering with mnemonic compensation

17. Which hormone rises during the second half of the menstrual cycle and stimulates the sloughing off of accumulated material in the uterus each month if conception has not occurred?
    a. progesterone
    b. serotonin
    c. testosterone
    d. estrogen

18. Age-related hearing loss is often due to _____.
    a. exposure to excessive noise
    b. build-up of plaque in the arteries that serve the ears
    c. deterioration of the auditory nerve
    d. a genetic disorder

19. Sudden heart attacks among middle-aged adults are often caused by _____.
    a. emotionally shocking events
    b. rupture of built-up plaque in the arteries
    c. low blood pressure
    d. excessive physical exercise

20. Which of the following factors contributes to the risk of osteoporosis?
    a. excessive alcohol consumption
    b. insufficient calcium intake in early adulthood
    c. excessive sugar consumption
    d. excessive caffeine consumption

21. Joe underwent a blood test for C-reactive protein (CRP). His doctor told him that his CRP levels were above normal. Which course of action is the doctor likely to recommend?
    a. He will tell Joe that he has to have heart surgery immediately.
    b. He will give Joe a prescription for statin drugs.
    c. He will advise Joe to take low-dose aspirin.
    d. He will advise Joe to get his financial affairs in order and prepare for imminent death.

22. Which of the following is *false* concerning the risk factors for cardiovascular disease?
    a. The more high-risk behaviors or characteristics a person has, the higher the person's risk of heart disease.
    b. Certain risk factors, such as high cholesterol, are enhanced if they coexist with other risk factors, such as smoking.

c. The primary risk factors have been well known for a long time.

d. There are no laboratory tests that can help doctors diagnose cardiovascular disease.

23. Which of the following is a condition of primary aging characterized by loss of bone mass and brittle, porous bones in both men and women?

   a. hypothyroidism   **c.** rickets
   b. Perthes' disease   **d.** osteoporosis

24. Which of the following individuals might be expected to experience earlier or larger intellectual declines?

   a. Mrs. Anderson, age 50, who is in the postmenopausal phase

   b. Mr. Jones, age 70, who has taken medication for high blood pressure for 20 years

   c. Mrs. Green, age 65, who has recently been diagnosed with breast cancer

   d. Mr. Brown, age 50, who has been warned by his physician to lose 25 pounds

25. How do the death rates of men with alcoholism in their 50s and early 60s compare with those of nonalcoholics?

   a. Alcoholics are more likely to die in later adulthood.
   b. Alcoholics are more likely to live to be 100 years old.
   c. Alcoholics are more likely to die in midlife.
   d. They are the same.

To ● **Watch** ✳ **Explore** ◉ **Simulate** ✓ **Study** and **Review** and experience MyVirtualLife go to MyPsychLab.com

chapter 16

Social and Personality Development in Middle Adulthood

Think about the social roles that are prominent in each phase of life. Peer and family relationships are of primary importance to the social lives of adolescents and young adults. Peers and families matter to middle-aged adults, too. However, the role of worker is typically the center of a middle-aged adult's social network. Despite the centrality of work in midlife, in order to understand the changes that happen during this phase of life, it's important to keep in mind that most middle-aged adults occupy several social roles throughout this

LEARNING OBJECTIVES

THEORIES OF SOCIAL AND PERSONALITY DEVELOPMENT

16.1 How do the views of Erikson and Vaillant differ with regard to generativity?

16.2 How do proponents of the midlife crisis and the life events perspective approach middle age differently?

CHANGES IN RELATIONSHIPS AND PERSONALITY

16.3 What contributes to the "mellowing" of partnerships in middle adulthood?

16.4 How do multigenerational caregiving and caregiver burden affect middle-aged adults' lives?

16.5 How does the grandparent role affect middle-aged adults?

16.6 How do social networks change during middle adulthood?

16.7 What is the evidence for continuity and change in personality throughout adulthood?

MIDLIFE CAREER ISSUES

16.8 What factors influence work satisfaction in middle adulthood?

16.9 What strategies do middle-aged workers use to maintain job performance at a satisfactory level?

16.10 What factors contribute to career transitions in midlife?

16.11 How do Baby Boomers differ from previous cohorts with respect to preparation for retirement?

period. And, as you may have learned in *MyVirtualLife*, middle-aged adults must often deal with conflicts among these roles. By the end of middle age, however, these roles have begun to shift dramatically. Children leave home, job promotions have usually reached their limit, and aging parents often make new demands on middle-aged adults' financial, psychological, and social resources. The prospect of preparing for the next phase of life also looms large as the middle adult years draw to a close. In this chapter, you will read about how adults between ages 40 and 65 progress through and adapt to all these changes.

Theories of Social and Personality Development

generativity a sense that one is making a valuable contribution to society by bringing up children or mentoring younger people in some way midlife

You should remember from Chapter 2 that Erik Erikson viewed middle age as a period when attention turns to creation of a legacy. Adults do this by influencing the lives of those in younger generations. Yet many have characterized middle age less positively, suggesting that it is a period of intense crisis.

Erikson's Generativity-versus-Stagnation Stage

LO 16.1 How do the views of Erikson and Vaillant differ with regard to generativity?

Middle-aged adults are in Erikson's *generativity-versus-stagnation stage*. Their developmental task is to acquire a sense of **generativity**, which involves an interest in establishing and guiding the next generation. Generativity is expressed not only in bearing or rearing one's own children but through teaching, serving as a mentor, or taking on leadership roles in various civic, religious, or charitable organizations. The optimum expression of generativity requires turning outward from a preoccupation with self, a kind of psychological expansion toward caring for others. Those who fail to develop generativity often suffer from a "pervading sense of stagnation and personal impoverishment [and indulge themselves] as if they were their own one and only child" (Erikson, 1963, p. 267).

Erikson proposed that passing on one's knowledge to younger individuals is the primary theme of psychosocial development in middle adulthood.

RESEARCH ON GENERATIVITY Research has produced hints of a developmental stage that involves generativity, but the findings are much less clear than data on changes in earlier years. One cross-sectional study of young, midlife, and older women found that generativity increased in middle age, as Erikson's theory suggests (Zucker, Ostrove, & Stewart, 2002). Contrary to what his theory would predict, however, the oldest group of participants, whose average age was 66, cited generative concerns as being important to them just as frequently as the middle-aged group did. These findings support Erikson's claim that generativity is more common in middle adulthood than in early adulthood, but they also indicate that generativity continues to be important in old age. Other research suggests that generativity is a more prominent theme in the lives of middle-aged women than in the lives of middle-aged men (Jones & McAdams, 2013).

Despite these inconsistencies, studies support Erikson's belief that generativity is related to mental health among middle-aged adults. For instance, researchers have found that generativity is positively related to satisfaction in life and work and to emotional well-being (Ackerman, Zuroff, & Moskowitz, 2000; Tomás, Sancho, Gutiérrez, & Galiana, 2013). Further, in a study that measured middle-aged women's sense of being burdened by caring for elderly parents, those who exhibited the highest levels of generativity felt the least burdened by elder care (Peterson, 2002).

Erikson's theory also raises questions about the impact of childlessness on adult development. One very interesting analysis comes from a 40-year longitudinal study of a group of inner-city, nondelinquent boys who had originally served as a comparison group in a study of delinquent boys (Snarey, Son, Kuehne, Hauser, & Vaillant,

1987). Of the 343 married men who were still part of this sample in their late 40s, 29 had fathered no children. Researchers found that the way a man had responded earlier to his childlessness was predictive of his psychological health at age 47. At that age, each man was rated on his degree of generativity. A man was considered to be "generative" if he had participated in some kind of mentoring or other teaching or supervising of children or younger adults. Among those with no children, those who were rated as most generative were likely to have responded to their childlessness by finding another child to nurture. They adopted a child, became Big Brothers, or helped with the rearing of someone else's child, such as a niece or nephew. Childless men rated as nongenerative were more likely to have chosen a pet as a child substitute.

VAILLANT'S REVISION OF ERIKSON'S THEORY Psychiatrist George Vaillant has spent several decades chronicling the development of several hundred adults through early, middle, and late adulthood. His research emphasizes resilience and has included measures of change in the physical, cognitive, personality, and social domains (Vaillant, 2012). His findings for the middle adulthood period prompted him to propose a modification of Erikson's theory of lifespan development (Vaillant, 2002).

Vaillant argued that there is a stage between intimacy and generativity called *career consolidation*. Like Erikson, Vaillant tended to define the domains of life fairly broadly, so "career" may mean a paid vocation, or it could involve a decision to be a stay-at-home mother or father. The outcome of this phase is the creation of a new social network for which the middle-aged adult's primary work serves as a hub. Involvement with this social network helps the individual meet the psychosocial needs of this substage. Such needs include contentment, compensation, competence, and commitment (Vaillant, 2002). Individuals need to be happy with the work-related choices they have made, to feel that they are adequately compensated, to view themselves as competent in their chosen field, and to be able to maintain a sense of commitment to their work.

Following generativity versus stagnation, Vaillant argued, is another stage called *keeper of the meaning*. In this phase, middle-aged adults focus on preserving the institutions and values of their culture that they believe will benefit future generations. For some, religious organizations become paramount. Others focus on the arts, educational institutions, historical preservation societies, or political organizations. The key is that participation in these institutions is motivated by the desire to ensure their survival rather than by a concern for how the institution can benefit the individual middle-aged adult. In other words, a well-adjusted adult in the *keeper of the meaning* stage wants to give something to the institution rather than to get something from it. Moreover, the social networks that are created through middle-aged adults' associations with institutions support their need to feel that the work they are doing will make a difference for future generations.

When civil rights icon Rosa Parks passed away in 2005, Oprah Winfrey spoke at her funeral and explained how Ms. Parks's defiance of an Alabama law that required African Americans to give up their seats to Whites on buses inspired her as a young girl growing up in the segregated South. According to Vaillant, such actions represent middle-aged adults' function as "keepers of the meaning" who serve as bridges between past and future generations.

Midlife Crisis: Fact or Fiction?

LO 16.2 How do proponents of the midlife crisis and the life events perspective approach middle age differently?

You may recall that the crisis concept is central to Erikson's theory, and a specific midlife crisis has been part of several other theories as well, including Levinson's (see Chapter 14). Levinson argued that each person must confront a constellation of difficult tasks at midlife: accepting one's own mortality, recognizing new physical limitations and health risks, and adapting to major changes in most roles. Dealing with all these tasks, according to Levinson, is highly likely to exceed an adult's ability to cope, thus creating a crisis.

When developmentalists look at the relevant research evidence, however, they often question this conclusion (Farrow, 2012). Just over a quarter of middle-aged and older adults report having had a crisis such as the one that Levinson's theory predicts (Lachman, 2004). However, these crises appear to have been triggered by specific events such as the loss of a job or the death of a close friend or relative. Thus, some developmentalists argue that a **life events approach** to explaining the unique stresses of the middle adulthood period is preferable to a theoretical perspective that proposes a universal crisis. The life events approach focuses on normative and nonnormative events and middle-aged adults' responses to them.

life events approach a theoretical perspective on middle adulthood that focuses on normative and nonnormative events and how adults in this age group respond to them

role conflict any situation in which two or more roles are at least partially incompatible, either because they call for different behaviors or because their separate demands add up to more hours than there are in the day

The physical changes of middle age that you learned about in Chapter 15 are the backdrop against which the major life events of this period are played out. Consequently, all middle-aged adults are dealing with new stressors with which they must develop new ways of coping, and research shows that concerns about the limitations imposed by these physical changes increase across the middle adulthood years (Cate & John, 2007). In addition, most middle-aged adults experience the loss of a parent or must cope with major declines in their parents' ability to care for themselves. Most also deal with work-related issues. At the same time, for those who have children, major shifts are occurring in the nature of parent–child relationships. Another important factor, one that adds another layer of complexity, is that many of these stressors last for some time. A middle-aged person can spend years, for example, caring for an incapacitated parent. With all these changes going on at the same time, it isn't surprising that middle-aged adults often feel stressed. Thus, some developmentalists argue that the best way to understand middle adulthood is to study how people in this age group manage to integrate all of these changes and their interpretations of them into the coherent stories of their own middle adulthood experiences (Farrow, 2012).

Finally, the stresses associated with the events of middle age are often complicated by **role conflict**—any situation in which two or more roles are at least partially incompatible, either because they call for different behaviors or because their separate demands add up to more hours than there are in the day. Role conflict happens, for example, when a middle-aged father must choose between helping his aging parents with financial or health problems and attending his teenaged son's football games. A person experiences *role strain* when her own qualities or skills do not measure up to the demands of some role. For example, a 40-year-old worker who is forced to return to college to acquire new skills after a job layoff and who feels anxious about her ability to succeed is experiencing role strain.

test yourself before going on ✅ **Study** and **Review** in **MyPsychLab**

Answers to these questions can be found in the back of the book.

1. Match each term with its major emphasis.
   _____(1) normative and nonnormative events and adults' responses to them
   _____(2) the need to make a valuable contribution to society
   _____(3) social networks for which an individual's work serves as the hub
   _____(4) preserving institutions and values for future generations
   _____(5) two or more roles that an adult occupies are incompatible

   (a) generativity
   (b) life events approach
   (c) role conflict
   (d) keeper of the meaning
   (e) career consolidation

CRITICAL THINKING

2. How could the stage models of Erikson and Vaillant be integrated with the life events approach to provide a more comprehensive description of middle adulthood than any of them could alone?

Changes in Relationships and Personality

As suggested previously, family roles are still an important part of life in middle age. However, these roles change significantly during this period of life. ◉ **Watch** the **Video** *Middle Adulthood: Family Relationships in Middle Adulthood across Cultures* in **MyPsychLab**.

Partnerships

LO 16.3 What contributes to the "mellowing" of partnerships in middle adulthood?

Several lines of evidence suggest that, on average, marital stability and satisfaction increase in midlife as conflicts over child rearing and other matters decline (Huber, Navarro, Wombie, & Mumme, 2010). In addition, as couples get older, the number of shared friends they have increases and the number of nonshared friends decreases (Kalmijn, 2003). As a result, the social network tends to get a bit tighter—and probably more supportive—in middle age. This may be one reason for age-related improvements in relationship satisfaction. So, despite considerable diversity among midlife marriages and partnerships, overall they are less conflicted than those of young adults.

Improvements in marital satisfaction may also derive from middle-aged adults' increased sense of control—a kind of marital self-efficacy (Lachman & Weaver, 1998). It is likely that middle-aged partners' identification of successful problem-solving strategies contributes to the sense that they have control over their relationship. Research has provided useful illustrations of this point. For example, researchers typically find that marital problem themes among middle-aged couples are remarkably similar to those of younger adults. Wives complain of an unjust division of labor; husbands express dissatisfaction with limits on their freedom. Yet relationship stability among middle-aged couples is maintained through the practice of what one researcher called "skilled diplomacy"—an approach to solving problems that involves confrontation of the spouse about an issue, followed by a period during which the confronting spouse works to restore harmony (Perho & Korhonen, 1999). Skilled diplomacy is practiced more often by wives than by husbands, but it appears to be an effective technique for marital problem solving no matter which spouse uses it.

Research suggests that middle-aged women are better able to cope with divorce then younger women (Marks & Lambert, 1998). Perhaps a "mellowing" of personality (which you will read about later in this chapter) renders the middle-aged woman more resilient in the face of such traumatic events. Moreover, some women remain in unsatisfactory marriages through their 20s and 30s because they think that divorce will be harmful to their children. Once the children are grown, such women feel free to move out of these relationships, and they report that the stress associated with divorce was less problematic than the emotional turmoil they experienced in the years prior to splitting from their husbands (Enright, 2004).

Once the children are grown and gone, many couples find it easier to spend time together—perhaps one of the reasons that marital satisfaction generally rises in middle age.

Research suggests that middle-aged women are more resilient than younger women in managing transitions such as divorce.

The Role of Caregiver

LO 16.4 How do multigenerational caregiving and caregiver burden affect middle-aged adults' lives?

The discussion of the relationship between young adults and their families in Chapter 14 focused almost entirely on connections *up* the chain of family generations—that is, relationships between the young adults and their own middle-aged parents. When looking at family relationships from the perspective of middle age, we have to look in both directions: down the generational chain to relationships with grown children (see *Research Report* on page 404) and up the chain to relationships with aging parents.

Each position in a family's generational chain has certain role prescriptions (Hagestad, 1986, 1990). In middle adulthood, the family role involves not only giving assistance in both directions in the generational chain but also shouldering the primary responsibility for maintaining attachment relationships. These responsibilities produce what is sometimes called the midlife "squeeze," and those being squeezed are called **multigenerational caregivers**, sometimes referred to as the *sandwich generation*.

Such a squeeze was illustrated in the results of a classic study of more than 13,000 adults in one frequently cited national survey. Among many other things, respondents were asked about the amount of help of various kinds—financial, child care, household assistance, and so forth—they gave to and received from both adult children and aging parents (Bumpass & Aquilino, 1995).

multigenerational caregivers middle-aged adults who provide assistance to their parents and adult children at the same time

The Empty Nest and the Revolving Door

Folklore in Western cultures argues that the role of mother is so central to women's lives that they suffer from "empty nest" syndrome—a pattern of symptoms characterized by anxiety and depression—when their grown children leave home. However, research suggests that most women are happy when they reach this milestone (Segatto & Di Filippo, 2003). But what happens when the children don't leave home?

In 1970 only 8% of 25-year-olds in the United States lived with their parents (Furedi, 2003). Today, about 20% of 25-year-olds do so (Taylor et al., 2010). As a result, in a survey of middle-aged adults in the United States, 38% reported that they had at least one child between the ages of 18 and 29 living in their homes (Painter, 2013). Moreover, the phenomenon of young adults living with parents is a global one. Some sources estimate up to 70% of Japanese young adults live with their parents (Furedi, 2003). In the United Kingdom, about 40% of male and 20% of female 25-year-olds reside with their parents (Berrington, Stone, & Falkingham, 2009). Such findings have been described as the *revolving door* pattern, in which children

leave home at the end of high school and return one or more times before becoming fully independent. What's behind this trend?

One explanation for the trend that some writers have called "Peter Pandemonium" is that many of today's young adults simply do not want to grow up (Furedi, 2003). Marketing studies which show that stay-at-home adult children spend a great deal of money on luxuries while their parents are footing the bill for their living expenses support this view. However, a psychosocial explanation would hypothesize that single young adults, like all human beings, enjoy and are nurtured by family life (Robbins, 2001). With today's singles marrying and having their own children at later ages, some observers argue that it is natural for unattached young adults to turn to the most reliable source of nurturance and social connectedness that they know—that is, to their family of origin (Taylor et al., 2010).

How do these "boomerang kids" affect the lives of their middle-aged parents? There is little doubt that dealing with an adult child who appears to be unwilling to leave home is a stressful experience, perhaps because it happens at the same

time as other stress-inducing events, such as the need to care for aging parents and to prepare for retirement (Lachman, 2004). It should be noted, however, that there are many middle-aged parents who welcome the opportunity to maintain warm relationships with their adult children that is afforded by having them remain at home (Painter, 2013). Thus, like so many other trends that involve changing family structures in today's world, this one should be viewed as a function of personal choice and, in most cases, representative of a living situation that is viewed as mutually beneficial by those who are involved in it.

CRITICAL ANALYSIS

1. *Aside from that which was cited in this discussion, what evidence would suggest that the economic explanation of the "revolving door" is the best one? What kinds of data would favor the psychosocial explanation?*

2. *The discussion mentioned some advantages enjoyed by single young adults who live with their parents. What are some of the disadvantages of such a living arrangement?*

The results, graphed in Figure 16.1, make clear that those between ages 40 and 65 give more help than they receive in both directions within the family—to adult children and to aging parents—a pattern confirmed in a variety of other studies (Gonyea, 2013).

Surveys in the United States and the United Kingdom indicate that about one-third of women in their 50s are multigenerational caregivers (Grundy & Henretta, 2006). These surveys also show that a strong sense of family solidarity motivates such women to help both their parents and adult children. Nevertheless, longitudinal studies show that multigenerational caregivers have poorer health habits than peers who do not have responsibility for both elders and young adult children, a behavior pattern that increases their risk of poor health in their own later adult years (Chassin, Macy, Seo, & Presson, 2010). In addition, the multigenerational caregiver's own situation contributes to the sense of feeling burdened (Andrén & Elmståhl, 2007). Those who lack sufficient income to care for their elders and whose own health is less than optimal feel more burdened by the responsibility of caring for an elderly parent. The social clock is also relevant because adult children who feel that their parents' need for care is "on time" feel less burdened than those whose parents' incapacity is perceived as "early." ◉ **Watch** the **Video** *Sandwich Generation: Amy, 42 Years Old* in **MyPsychLab**.

Even when middle-aged adults render assistance exclusively up the generational chain—that is, to their parents—caregiving can be a stressful experience (see *No Easy Answers*). The cumulative evidence indicates that middle-aged adults who serve as caregivers for their elderly parents experience more depression and have lower marital satisfaction than those in comparison groups of similar age and social class (Rezende, Coimbra, Costallat, & Coimbra, 2010; Wright et al., 2010). Some research also suggests that those who care

Contrary to popular belief, when this woman's daughter leaves the nest in a few years, it will be a joyful experience.

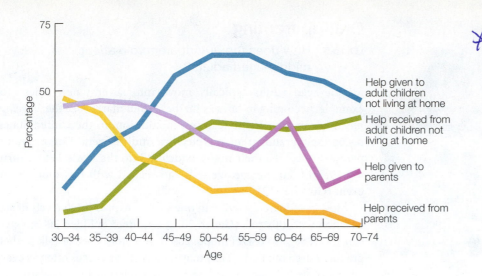

Figure 16.1 The Middle-Age "Squeeze"

The midlife "squeeze," or "sandwich genera-tion," is illustrated in this graph of data from a national survey of adults. Middle-aged adults give more help to both their adult children and their own parents than they receive.

(*Source:* Bumpass & Aquilino, 1995, data from Tables 11, 12, 25, and 26.)

for frail elders are more often ill themselves or have some reduced efficiency of immune-system function (Gallagher et al., 2008). Collectively, these effects are often termed **care-giver burden**.

The quality of a caregiver's social relationships moderates the effects of caregiver burden. Caregivers whose interactions with their spouses are generally positive and whose friends and relatives provide them with social support are the least likely to experience symptoms of depression (Braun, Mura, Peter-Wight, Hornung, & Scholz, 2010; Kaufman, Kosberg, Leeper, & Tang, 2010; Tang et al., 2013). Moreover, for the majority of midlife adults, the relationship with aging parents is mostly positive. Most give more assistance to their parents than they did before, but they also continue to see them regularly for ceremonial and cele-bratory occasions and to feel affection as well as filial responsibility (Stein et al., 1998). Par-ents are also symbolically important to middle-aged adults because as long as they are alive, they occupy the role of elder in the family lineage. When they are gone, each generation moves up a notch in the sequence: Those in the middle generation must come to terms with the fact that they have now become the elders and are confronted more directly with their own mortality.

caregiver burden a term for the cumulative negative effects of caring for an elderly or disabled person

---

NO EASY ANSWERS

Who Cares for Aging Parents?

One of the most difficult dilemmas of midlife arises when elderly parents become incapable of caring for themselves. Inevitably, the issue of who will care for them creates conflicts. Between 40 and 50% of middle-aged adults in the United States spend at least some of their time provid-ing care to an elder, typically a parent (U.S. Bureau of Labor Statistics, 2013). Moreover, 16% of those over the age of 65 provide care for an elderly parent. Within a group of siblings, the one most likely to take on the task of caregiving is the one who has no children still at home, is not working, is not married, and lives closest to the aging parent (Brody, Litvin, Albert, & Hoff-man, 1994; Stoller, Forster, & Duniho, 1992). Most of these factors combine to make a

daughter or daughter-in-law the most likely can-didate for the role of caregiver (U.S. Bureau of Labor Statistics, 2013).

Researchers have found that multidimen-sional interventions can ease the strain of the caregiver burden (Pinquart & Sorensen, 2006). These interventions should include education for the caregiver about the care recipient's condi-tion or illness. The educational component should include information on the availability of resources such as daycare and home health aides, both of which can provide the caregiver with a much-needed respite from the physical aspects of caring for an elderly parent. Similarly, counseling sessions and support groups can help with the emotional aspects of caregiving.

YOU DECIDE

Decide which of these two statements you most agree with and think about how you would defend your position:

1. *Caring for aging parents is a moral duty even if doing so interferes with a middle-aged adult's other family and professional responsibilities.*

2. *Caring for aging parents is a moral duty, but it must be balanced with a middle-aged adult's other family and professional respon-sibilities that sometimes must take prece-dence over caring for an elder.*

Daughters, far more than sons, are likely to take on the role of significant caregiver for a disabled parent or a parent with dementia, as this daughter has done now that her mother is suffering from Alzheimer's disease.

remote relationships relationships in which grandparents do not see their grandchildren often

companionate relationships relationships in which grandparents have frequent contact and warm interactions with grandchildren

involved relationships relationships in which grandparents are directly involved in the everyday care of grandchildren or have close emotional ties with them

Grandparenting

LO 16.5 How does the grandparent role affect middle-aged adults?

Middle-aged adults typically move into several new roles—for example, becoming in-laws as their children marry (see the *Developmental Science at Home* feature). In addition, in the United States, becoming a grandparent is typically a midlife event. Half of grandparents welcomed their first grandchild into the world before turning 50, with an average age of 47 associated with this momentous event (Goyer, 2012).

Most grandparents—92% in one study—express high levels of satisfaction with this role (Goyer, 2012; Kaufman & Elder, 2003; Peterson, 1999; Segatto & Di Filippo, 2003). A majority see or talk to their grandchildren regularly. They may write, call, or visit as often as every couple of weeks, and most describe their relationships as warm and loving. Likewise, many studies have demonstrated the positive impact of warm relationships with grandparents on children's development (Adkins, 1999). 👁 **Watch** the **Video** *Becoming a Grandparent* in **MyPsychLab**.

Fortunately, most parents welcome the involvement of their own parents in their children's lives, and surveys suggest that grandparents and grandchildren engage in many of the same activities—watching television, shopping, attending religious services—that parents and children share (Goyer, 2012). However, while parenthood clearly involves full-time responsibility, there are many degrees of being a grandparent.

Most behavioral scientists place grandparents in one of several categories, derived from a study in which researchers interviewed a nationally representative sample of more than 500 grandparents (Cherlin & Furstenberg, 1986). In one study, 29% of grandparents had **remote relationships**; they saw their grandchildren relatively infrequently and had little direct influence over their grandchildren's lives. The most common reason for this remoteness was physical distance.

By contrast, this statement by one of the grandmothers in the study illustrates a different kind of relationship, for which researchers used the term **companionate relationship**:

> When you have grandchildren, you have more love to spare. Because the discipline goes to the parents and whoever's in charge. But you just have extra love and you will tend to spoil them a little bit. And you know, you give. (Cherlin & Furstenberg, 1986, p. 55)

Just over half of the survey's participants exhibited such attitudes toward their grandchildren and responded that they had very warm, pleasurable relationships with them. Yet these grandparents also said that they were glad they no longer had the day-to-day responsibility. They could love the grandchildren and then send them home.

The third and least common (16%) type of relationship was exhibited by grandparents who had **involved relationships** with their grandchildren. These grandparents were everyday participants in the rearing of their grandchildren. Some of them lived in three-generation households with one or more children and grandchildren; some had nearly full-time care of the grandchildren. But involved relationships also occurred in some cases in which the grandparent had no daily responsibility for the grandchildren's care but created an unusually close link.

About 8% of children in the United States live with one or more of their grandparents (U.S. Census Bureau, 2009b). However, the incidence of custodial grandparenting has increased in all ethnic and socioeconomic groups in recent years (Goodman & Silverstein, 2002). Across groups, about 11% of grandparents have had full-time responsibility for a grandchild for 6 months or longer (Goyer, 2012). Full-time grandparent care is especially likely when the grandchild's mother is unmarried (U.S. Census Bureau, 2009b). In such cases, the grandmother frequently takes on child-care responsibilities so that her daughter can continue in school or hold down a job.

This girl seems delighted with her grandmother, with whom she seems to have what Cherlin and Furstenberg would call a "companionate" relationship.

Me, a Mother-in-Law?

Sophia was thrilled when her son announced that he was engaged and that the couple planned to have the kind of traditional wedding that Sophia knew her large Italian American family would enjoy. But as she sat watching her future daughter-in-law open gifts at yet another bridal shower, she was struck by the realization that she was about to acquire one of society's most maligned roles: that of mother-in-law. Mother-in-law jokes abound in films and TV shows, and relationships between mothers-in-law and their children's spouses are regularly characterized as full of tension and conflict. Typically, it is the relationship between the mother-in-law and the daughter-in-law that is depicted most negatively (Owens, 2009). Thus, it isn't surprising that most middle-aged women don't look forward to becoming mothers-in-law. But is the negative stereotyping of mothers-in-law justified?

Research in some societies (e.g., rural communities in Latin America, India, Jordan, China, and Korea) suggests that the stereotype is somewhat accurate. In these societies, newlyweds usually reside with the husband's parents, and the mother-in-law is responsible for socializing her daughter-in-law into the family. In such cultures, wives remain under the authority of their mothers-in-law for many years, usually until the older woman is no longer physically able to fulfill her role's requirements.

Despite the cultural reinforcement of the relationship between mother-in-law and daughter-in-law in traditional societies, these relationships are often high in conflict (Chiapin, DeAraujo, & Wagner, 1998). Most such conflicts involve the husband: The daughter-in-law thinks her husband is too loyal to his mother, or the mother-in-law thinks her son's wife is trying to undermine her relationship with him. Some mothers-in-law go so far as to physically abuse daughters-in-law, and abusive husbands sometimes receive praise from their mothers for keeping young wives in line (Gangoli & Rew, 2011; Oweis, Gharaibeh, & Alhourani, 2010).

Parallels exist in more industrialized societies (Merrill, 2007; Wu, Liu, & Fan, 2010). Mothers-in-law are perceived as interfering in the marital relationship; daughters-in-law are accused of trying to turn their husbands against their mothers. Conflicts arise over child rearing as well (Shih & Pyke, 2010). Consequently, family therapists have devised recommendations to help middle-aged women such as Sophia adjust to the mother-in-law role and to forestall conflict (Greider, 2000). Here are a few such recommendations:

- Don't give unsolicited advice or make unannounced visits.
- When asked for your advice, share your experience in a nonjudgmental way.
- Don't criticize your daughters- or sons-in-law behind their backs.
- Don't insist on being visited every weekend or holiday.
- Respect your children's wishes regarding how grandchildren are to be cared for.

REFLECTION

1. *How much of the conflict between mothers-in-law and their children's spouses is brought about by expectations based on cultural stereotypes?*

2. *What would you include in a list of tips that might help spouses avoid conflicts with their in-laws?*

Friends

LO 16.6   How do social networks change during middle adulthood?

The scant research on friendships in middle adulthood suggests that the total number of friendships is lower in these years than in young adulthood (Kalmijn, 2003). At the same time, other bits of research suggest that midlife friendships are as intimate and close as those at earlier ages. For example, researchers have analyzed information from the files of 50 participants in the now-familiar Berkeley/Oakland longitudinal study, who had been interviewed or tested repeatedly from adolescence through age 50 (Carstensen, 1992). These analyses revealed that the frequency of interaction with best friends dropped between age 17 and age 50 but that the best-friend relationships remained very close. These studies suggest that the social network of middle-aged adults is relatively small, although relationships are just as intimate as they were at earlier ages.

It may be that the social network shrinks as adults age because there is less need for it. Role conflict and role strain decline significantly in middle age, and the need for emotional support from a social network outside the family seems to decrease accordingly (Due, Holstein, Lund, Modvig, & Avlund, 1999). Yet because the relationships that do endure are close, the social network is available when needed. Friendship depends less on frequent contact than on a sense that friends are there to provide support as needed. Thus, the nature of friendship itself may be different in middle age.

Continuity and Change in Personality

LO 16.7 What is the evidence for continuity and change in personality throughout adulthood?

Can developmentalists tell what kind of person someone will be in middle adulthood, based on what is known about his childhood, adolescence, or early adult life? As you learned in Chapter 10, a stable set of personality traits that psychologists call the *Big Five* emerge during middle childhood. Notice in this brief review of the traits that they can be easily remembered with the acronym *OCEAN*:

- *Openness:* willingness to try new things
- *Conscientiousness:* need for order in the environment
- *Extraversion:* sociability
- *Agreeableness:* ease with which a person gets along with others
- *Neuroticism:* emotional negativity, pessimism, and irritability

Many studies show that the Big Five traits are relatively stable across the adult years (Hampson & Goldberg, 2006; Kandler et al., 2010). Such findings are consistent with the proposition that the five factors are determined very early in life and are stable throughout the lifespan (Shiner & Caspi, 2012). However, there are subtle age-related changes in the five factors across the years of adulthood (Terracciano et al., 2005). Longitudinal research indicates that openness, extraversion, and neuroticism decline as adults age. Agreeableness increases, as does conscientiousness, up until around age 70, when it begins to show declines. Thus, the best statement that we can make about the stability of the Big Five is that these traits follow a general pattern of stability in most people but that they are also subject to some degree of modification (Branje, Van Lieshout, & Gerris, 2007).

Studies of negative and positive emotionality suggest a similar pattern. Even though negative emotionality in early adulthood is moderately to strongly correlated with negative emotionality in middle adulthood, longitudinal studies show that many individuals, particularly women, become *less* negative over time (Kopala-Sibley, Mongrain, & Zuroff, 2013; Srivastava, John, Gosling, & Potter, 2003). Similarly, agreeableness appears to increase with age (Srivastava et al., 2003). At the same time, tolerance for risk taking and impulsivity decline with age (Deakin, Aitken, Robbins, & Sahakian, 2004). Apparently, then, when researchers consider large groups—which they must do to correlate variables such as personality factors—they find that personality is fairly stable over time. However, the correlations can mask a number of individual cases in which there is a great deal of change. Consequently, the best conclusion to draw is that stability is the general pattern, but the increased individual variability in personality that is typically found among middle-aged and older adults suggests that change is clearly possible and may even be common (Nelson & Dannefer, 1992).

Personality is an important contributor to middle-aged adults' capacity for managing stress. For example, in one study researchers found that adults who were higher in extraversion and conscientiousness were less likely to feel strained by work-related stressors (Grant & Langan-Fox, 2007). By contrast, those who were high in neuroticism were less able to cope with on-the-job problems. Other researchers have found that individuals who are high in neuroticism are more likely than peers to have stress-related conditions such as chronic fatigue syndrome (Poeschla, Strachan, Dansie, Buchwald, & Afari, 2013).

---

test yourself before going on ✓ Study and Review in MyPsychLab

Answers to these questions can be found in the back of the book.

1. Many middle-aged adults occupy four family roles. What are they?
   - (a) _____
   - (b) _____
   - (c) _____
   - (d) _____

2. Studies of negative and positive emotionality show that adults become (more, less) negative as they move through the middle adult years.

CRITICAL THINKING

3. In your view, how do the changes in social relationships that are described in this section contribute to maintaining some personality traits while modifying others in middle age?

Midlife Career Issues

burnout lack of energy, exhaustion, and pessimism that result from chronic stress

Work in midlife is characterized by two paradoxes: First, work satisfaction is at its peak in these years, even though most adults receive few work promotions in middle age. Second, the quality of work performance remains high, despite declines in some cognitive and physical skills. **Watch** the **Video** *Middle Adulthood: Perspectives on Work and Career Path* in **MyPsychLab**.

Work Satisfaction

LO 16.8 What factors influence work satisfaction in middle adulthood?

As we have noted before, many aspects of life improve with age. Interestingly, middle-aged workers are less likely than younger workers to experience work-related **burnout** (Freudenberger & Richelson, 1981). People with burnout lack energy, feel emotionally drained, and are pessimistic about the possibility of changing their situations. People who feel that their work is unappreciated are more subject to burnout than others. For example, one survey suggested that nearly half of the social workers in the United Kingdom suffer from burnout, and the sense of being unappreciated was the best predictor of the condition (Evans et al., 2006). Developmentalists suggest that middle-aged workers who have avoided burnout in high-stress professions are those who have learned to pace themselves and to rely less on external sources of job satisfaction (Randall, 2007).

In addition, despite the plateau in promotions that occurs for most adults in the middle years, job satisfaction is typically at its peak, as is a sense of power, or job clout. One reason may be that careers become more stable in middle age, with fewer interruptions caused by either voluntary or involuntary job changes (Boxall, Macky, & Rasmussen, 2003). However, patterns of work and work satisfaction vary between men and women in middle adulthood.

Some studies suggest that women and men use the same criteria to assess whether they are satisfied with their jobs. In one study, for example, researchers found that male and female workers across four different countries (China, Japan, Germany, and the United States) had similar preferences with regard to performance awards and management styles (Gunkel, Lusk, Wolff, & Li, 2007). However, research also suggests that men and women think differently about their work. For instance, one consistent finding is that women worry much more about the effects of having children on their career advancement (Hagan & Kay, 2007; Stewart & Ostrove, 1998).

Similarly, men and women may follow somewhat different pathways to job satisfaction (Perho & Korhonen, 1999). Men and women cite the same sources of work dissatisfaction in middle age: time pressure, difficult co-workers, boring tasks, and fear of losing one's job. However, they cope with these challenges differently. Men are more likely to negotiate with supervisors and co-workers directly to effect change. In contrast, women tend to withdraw and to engage in collective complaining with female co-workers. Still, women are better able than men to balance their dissatisfactions with areas of contentment. Consequently, a statement such as "I don't like the boss, but the hours fit my needs" is more likely to come from a woman than a man. Because of their different coping styles, men are more likely to improve their level of satisfaction in situations where change is possible. By contrast, women are probably better able to cope with work settings where they must adjust to dissatisfaction because the situation can't be changed.

Despite their differences, both men and women in midlife have a greater sense of control over their work lives than younger adults do (Lachman & Weaver, 1998). One reason may be that social-cognitive skills improve from early to middle adulthood (Blanchard-Fields, Chen, Schocke, & Hertzog, 1998; Hess, Bolstad, Woodburn, & Auman, 1999). Middle-aged adults are better than they were when younger at "sizing up" people, relationships, and situations. At the same time, by middle age, they have become proficient at directing their own behavior in ways that allow them to maintain levels of personal satisfaction even in unpleasant circumstances.

Studies show that men are more likely than women to use problem-focused strategies to cope with job stress. By contrast, women use emotion-focused coping more often than men. These differences help explain why middle-aged men and women differ in work satisfaction.

Job Performance

LO 16.9 What strategies do middle-aged workers use to maintain job performance at a satisfactory level?

Early studies suggested that job performance remained high throughout middle adulthood except in professions in which speed is a critical element (Sparrow & Davies, 1988). More recent cohorts of middle-aged adults in such professions, such as air traffic controllers, have been found to perform equally as well as their younger peers (Broach & Schroeder, 2006). Improvements in health that have led to increases in general life expectancy are also credited with producing this historical change. As a result, many governments around the world are examining regulations that force employees in these professions to retire at a certain age. Instead, research-based reform proposals argue that older occupants of these jobs should be tested individually to determine whether they can continue.

Researchers Paul and Margaret Baltes have argued, as you should recall from Chapter 15, that maintaining high job productivity or performance is possible because adults, faced with small but noticeable erosions of cognitive or physical skill, engage in a process the Balteses call "selective optimization with compensation" (Baltes & Baltes, 1990). Three subprocesses are involved:

- *Selection.* Workers narrow their range of activities—for example, by focusing on only the most central tasks, delegating more responsibilities to others, or giving up or reducing peripheral job activities.

- *Optimization.* Workers deliberately "exercise" crucial abilities—such as by taking added training or polishing rusty skills—so as to remain as close to maximum skill levels as possible.

- *Compensation.* Workers adopt pragmatic strategies for overcoming specific obstacles—for example, getting stronger glasses or hearing aids, making lists to reduce memory loads, or even carefully emphasizing strengths and minimizing weaknesses when talking to co-workers or bosses.

A growing body of evidence supports the Balteses' view (Baltes & Heydens-Gahir, 2003; Young, Baltes, & Pratt, 2007). Researchers have tested this model in a study of 224 working adults aged 40 to 69 (Abraham & Hansson, 1995). Measuring each of the three aspects of the proposed compensatory process as well as job competence, they found that the link between the use of selection, optimization, and compensation on the one hand and the quality of work performance on the other got stronger with increasing age. That is, the older the worker, the more it mattered whether she used helpful compensatory practices. In the older groups (primarily those in their 50s and early 60s), those who used the most selection, optimization, and compensation had the highest work performance. But among the younger workers in this sample (those in their early 40s), the same relationship did not hold. This is obviously only one study, but the results provide some support for the idea that job performance remains high during middle age at least in part because adults take deliberate compensatory actions.

Unemployment and Career Transitions

LO 16.10 What factors contribute to career transitions in midlife?

In today's rapidly changing job market, it is not unusual for men and women to change occupations. However, career transitions can be more difficult in middle age. For one thing, potential employers tend to believe that young adults are more capable of learning a new job than are middle-aged applicants, even though research suggests that this generalization is untrue (Wrenn & Maurer, 2004). Employers give middle-aged applicants higher ratings on variables such as dependability, but they tend to think that younger applicants will be able to acquire new skills (especially computer skills) more rapidly. Thus, midlife career changers must often overcome ageism in obtaining new employment.

Career counselors also point out that to understand midlife career changes, it is useful to categorize workers on the basis of their reasons for changing occupations (Zunker, 2006). They suggest that people change careers for either external or internal reasons and can thus be classified as either *involuntary* or *voluntary* career changers.

INVOLUNTARY CAREER CHANGERS Involuntary career changers are people who are in transition for external reasons: Their skills have become obsolete, their jobs have been eliminated through organizational restructuring, or they have been laid off because of shifting economic conditions. They experience heightened levels of anxiety and depression and higher risk of physical illness in the months after the job loss (Crowley, Hayslip, & Hobdy, 2003; He, Colantonio, & Marshall, 2003; Isakson, Johansson, Bellaagh, & Sjöberg, 2004). Such effects are not unique to workers in the United States. Similar results have been found in studies in Australia, England, Denmark, and other Western developed countries (e.g., Broom et al., 2007; Iversen & Sabroe, 1988; Warr, Jackson, & Banks, 1988). Interestingly, just as remarriage alleviates many of the stresses associated with divorce, reemployment seems to restore health, emotional stability, and a sense of well-being quite rapidly.

Involuntary career changers must confront a series of stressful situations, such as applying for unemployment benefits.

The effects of job loss include changes in family relationships and loss of self-esteem. Most strikingly, marital relationships deteriorate rapidly after one or the other spouse has been laid off. The number of hostile or negative interactions increases, and the number of warm and supportive interactions declines—which means that the crucial ratio of positive to negative interactions spirals downward. Separation and divorce become much more common as a result (Ahituv & Lehman, 2004).

Predictably, the Big Five personality dimensions, especially neuroticism and openness to experience, contribute to mental health during involuntary career transitions across all racial and ethnic groups (Heppner, Fuller, & Multon, 1998). Nevertheless, mental health professionals suggest that the impact of an involuntary career change on an individual's life may be more directly affected by his or her coping skills (Zunker, 2006). For example, the person must be able to assess the situation realistically. If new work skills are needed, then the person must be able to formulate and carry out a plan for obtaining such skills. Researchers have found that midlife career changers who have good coping skills and use them to manage involuntary transitions are less likely to experience depression (Cook & Heppner, 1997).

As with all other types of stress, the effects of unemployment can be partially buffered by having adequate social support (Vinokur & van Ryn, 1993). Further, involuntary career changers benefit from career counseling that addresses both their occupational needs and their psychosocial development (Schadt, 1997). Counselors can help people who are forced to change jobs learn to think of the transition as an opportunity to reexamine goals and priorities—to treat the crisis as an opportunity (Zunker, 2006).

VOLUNTARY CAREER CHANGERS Voluntary career changers leave one career to pursue another for a variety of internal reasons (Zunker, 2006). For example, they may believe that the new job will be more fulfilling. One pattern occurs when workers look at the next step on the career ladder and decide they don't want to pursue further advancement in their current occupation. For example, both male and female certified public accountants are more likely to leave their profession for this reason than for any other (Greenhaus, Collins, Singh, & Parasuraman, 1997).

Twin studies suggest that the tendency to change careers voluntarily in adulthood may have a genetic basis (McCall, Cavanaugh, Arvey, & Taubman, 1997). These findings further suggest that such transitions are a by-product of personality. Specifically, voluntary job changers appear to have a higher tolerance for risk taking than do people who generally do not actively seek to change jobs (Roth, 2003). Most also appear to be people who do not regard either working or job seeking as particularly stressful (Mao, 2003). However, voluntary job changers who exhibit the *honeymoon–hangover effect* seem to be chronically dissatisfied with their jobs. They experience high levels of satisfaction immediately after changing jobs (the "honeymoon"), closely followed by feelings of regret over having left behind the parts of their former jobs that they enjoyed (the "hangover"). This pattern increases the likelihood of frequent voluntary job changes (Boswell, Boudreau, & Tichy, 2005; Boswell, Shipp, Payne, & Culbertson, 2009).

Although voluntary career changers have a better sense of control over their situation than do people whose job changes are forced on them, the transition may still be stressful. Spouses and family members may not understand why the person wants to change careers. Moreover, changing careers can involve periods of unemployment and, often, a reduction in income. Thus, voluntary career changers manifest many of the same symptoms of anxiety and depression seen in involuntary career changers (Ahituv & Lehman, 2004). Consequently, they, too, benefit from social support and career counseling.

Preparing for Retirement

LO 16.11 How do Baby Boomers differ from previous cohorts with respect to preparation for retirement?

Studies done in the 1980s and 1990s suggested that many middle-aged adults begin to prepare for retirement as early as 15 years before their anticipated retirement date (e.g., Herzog, House, & Morgan, 1991). However, the notion of retirement is relatively new and tends to be exclusive to industrialized cultures, and the retirement preparations of the Baby Boom cohort—the large cohort of individuals who were born between 1946 and 1964—are quite different from those of their parents (Monroy, 2000; Phillipson, 2013). For one thing, among their parents, retirement planning was primarily a male responsibility. In contrast, Baby Boom women are also doing retirement planning, sometimes together with their husbands and sometimes independently (Dietz, Carrozza, & Ritchey, 2003; Glass & Kilpatrick, 1998). Further, instead of transitioning directly from a full-time career to full-time retirement, most Baby Boomers seek *bridge employment*, typically a job that is related to a retiree's career but is less demanding than the job from which he or she is retiring (Gobeski & Beehr, 2009).

A comprehensive survey done while the oldest Baby Boomers were still in their middle adulthood years found that most expected to die in their mid-80s or later but expected to retire fairly early, in their early 60s (Monroy, 2000). Follow-up surveys indicate that these Boomers changed their plans somewhat and planned to continue working longer than they thought they would a few years before (Anrig & Parekh, 2010). Nevertheless, the typical Boomer expects to be retired for 20 years or more, far longer than people of earlier generations. What do Boomers plan to do with all that time?

One difference between Baby Boomers and earlier cohorts is that among Baby Boomers, more women are involved in retirement planning.

In a survey involving more than 3,000 Boomers, gerontologist Ken Dychtwald found that virtually all of the respondents intended to continue working into retirement, but most intended to combine paid work with other pursuits (Mauldin, 2005). Dychtwald identified five distinct approaches to what those nonwork pursuits should be (Mauldin, 2005). *Wealth Builders* (31%) intend to spend their spare time finding new ways to make money and building upon the wealth that they have already accumulated. Predictably, this group plans to devote more hours to paid work than their peers in other groups do. *Anxious Idealists* (20%) would like to do volunteer work and give money to charity after they retire, but they recognize that their tendency toward impracticality has left them with insufficient economic resources to do either. *Empowered Trailblazers* (18%) expect to spend time traveling, taking classes, and doing volunteer work, and they believe that they are financially secure enough to meet these goals. *Stretched and Stressed* Boomers (18%) are in deep trouble financially, and they are well aware of it. Most are worried about how they will be able to pay for basic necessities such as food and health care. *Leisure Lifers* (13%) intend to spend most of their time engaging in recreational pursuits and are geared toward very early retirement in their early to mid-50s.

Clearly, Boomers have devoted a great deal of thought to what they would like to do during their retirement years. Few, however, have devoted as much energy to preparing for the financial aspects of retirement. Dychtwald's survey and others have found that fewer than half of all Boomers have actually saved enough money to be able to do what they say they wanted to do in retirement (Insured Retirement Institute, 2013; Mauldin, 2005). Consequently, many Boomers appear to be headed on a path toward disappointment when financial realities set in. ◉ **Watch** the **Video** *Transitioning to Retirement: Mary and George* in **MyPsychLab**.

Nevertheless, economic analysts predict that as a group Boomers are likely to enjoy levels of affluence in retirement that far exceed those of their parents (Brucker & Leppel, 2013). Further, Boomers are projected to be the healthiest, best-educated, and longest-living retirees in history. Thus, they are likely to substantially change ideas about both preparing for retirement and retirement itself.

test yourself before going on ✓ Study and Review in MyPsychLab

Answers to these questions can be found in the back of the book.

1. Write "M" by the work-related coping strategies that most men use, "W" by those that women tend to use, and "M W" by those that both use.
   _____(1) negotiate with supervisors
   _____(2) use well-developed skills at "sizing up" people, relationships, and situations
   _____(3) collectively complain
   _____(4) balance areas of dissatisfaction and contentment
   _____(5) confront challenges directly

2. Both voluntary and involuntary career changers experience symptoms of _____ and _____.

3. List two ways in which Baby Boomers differ from their parents' generation with regard to preparing for retirement.
   (a) _____
   (b) _____

CRITICAL THINKING

4. How do the retirement plans of Baby Boomers fit in with the stage and life events approaches to middle age that you learned about at the beginning of the chapter?

SUMMARY

Theories of Social and Personality Development (pp. 400–402)

LO 16.1 How do the views of Erikson and Vaillant differ with regard to generativity?

- Erikson proposed that the primary developmental task of middle adulthood is to acquire a sense of generativity through mentoring younger individuals. Vaillant proposed that the stage of career consolidation precedes Erikson's generativity stage, and that of keeper of the meaning follows it.

LO 16.2 How do proponents of the midlife crisis and the life events perspective approach middle age differently?

- Many different models of the "midlife crisis" in middle adulthood have been proposed, but none has been strongly supported by research. A life events approach to understanding the unique stresses of middle age is more useful.

Changes in Relationships and Personality (pp. 402–408)

LO 16.3 What contributes to the "mellowing" of partnerships in middle adulthood?

- Marital satisfaction is typically higher at midlife than it is earlier. This higher level of satisfaction appears to be due primarily to a decline in problems and conflicts.

LO 16.4 How do multigenerational caregiving and caregiver burden affect middle-aged adults' lives?

- Middle-aged adults have significant family interactions both up and down the generational chain. The two-way responsibilities of multigenerational caregiving can create a midlife "squeeze," or a "sandwich generation." Middle adults provide more assistance in both directions and attempt to influence both preceding and succeeding generations. Only a minority of middle-aged adults seem to take on the role of significant caregiver for an aging parent. Those who do report feeling a considerable burden and experience increased depression, particularly if the parent being cared for suffers from some form of dementia. Women are two to four times as likely as men to fulfill the role of caregiver to a frail elder.

LO 16.5 How does the grandparent role affect middle-aged adults?

- Most adults become grandparents in middle age. The majority have warm, affectionate relationships with their grandchildren, although there are also many remote relationships. A minority of grandparents are involved in day-to-day care of grandchildren.

LO 16.6 How do social networks change during middle adulthood?

- Friendships appear to be somewhat less numerous in middle adulthood than in younger adulthood, although they appear to be as intimate and central to the individual.

LO 16.7 What is the evidence for continuity and change in personality throughout adulthood?

- The Big Five personality traits and other aspects of personality are correlated across early and middle adulthood. There is evidence for personality change in middle age as well.

Midlife Career Issues (pp. 409–413)

LO 16.8 What factors influence work satisfaction in middle adulthood?

- Job satisfaction is at its peak in middle adulthood, and productivity remains high. But the centrality of the work role appears to wane somewhat, and job satisfaction is less clearly linked to overall life satisfaction than at earlier ages. Research suggests that patterns of work and satisfaction are different for men and women in middle age.

LO 16.9 What strategies do middle-aged workers use to maintain job performance at a satisfactory level?

- Levels of job performance in middle adulthood are consistent with those at earlier ages, with the exception of work that involves physical strength or reaction time.

LO 16.10 What factors contribute to career transitions in midlife?

- Involuntary career changes are associated with anxiety and depression. Even many middle-aged adults who make voluntary career transitions experience negative emotions.

LO 16.11 How do Baby Boomers differ from previous cohorts with respect to preparation for retirement?

- Middle-aged adults prepare for retirement in several ways, not only through specific planning but also by reducing the number of hours they work.

KEY TERMS

burnout (p. 409)

caregiver burden (p. 405)

companionate relationships (p. 406)

generativity (p. 400)

involved relationships (p. 406)

life events approach (p. 401)

multigenerational caregivers (p. 403)

remote relationships (p. 406)

role conflict (p. 402)

CHAPTER TEST ✅ Study and Review in MyPsychLab

Answers to all the Chapter Test questions can be found in the back of the book.

1. What are the cumulative negative effects to the caregiver that are associated with caregiving collectively termed?
   a. caregiver burden
   b. midlife squeeze
   c. gerontological expense
   d. generativity exhaustion

2. When I retire, I plan to continue teaching one class per semester and spend the rest of my time doing whatever I please. Dychtwald would classify me as which type of retiree?
   a. Wealth Builder
   b. Leisure Lifer
   c. Stretched and Stressed
   d. Anxious Idealist

3. Psychiatrist George Vaillant has identified a stage between intimacy and generativity. What is the name of this stage?
   a. career consolidation
   b. career generativity
   c. midlife transition
   d. job satisfaction

4. Which of the Big Five traits are likely to decline as adults age?
   a. extraversion, agreeableness, conscientiousness
   b. neuroticism, openness, agreeableness
   c. openness, extraversion, neuroticism
   d. conscientiousness, extraversion, neuroticism

5. Mrs. Jiminez has recently been promoted to administrator at the local nursing home, which means that she must be at work by 7:00 a.m. Mrs. Jiminez also believes that she should provide her children with breakfast and supervision before they get on the school bus at 7:30 each morning. What is Mrs. Jiminez experiencing?
   a. stasis
   b. social life stress
   c. role conflict
   d. role strain

6. Which life transition do half of women experience by their early 50s?
   a. loss of a parent
   b. becoming the family's keeper of the meaning
   c. grandparenthood
   d. primary caregiver for an aging parent

7. Which of the following reflects the findings of Ken Dychtwald in a survey of more than 3,000 Baby Boomers?
   a. Most plan to retire in their 50s.
   b. Baby Boomers have more anxiety about retirement than previous generations.
   c. Most plan to work into retirement but to combine paid work with other pursuits.
   d. Most are financially prepared for retirement.

8. According to research on grandparent–grandchildren relationships, what is the most common explanation for a remote relationship between grandparents and their grandchildren?
   a. physical distance
   b. interference by parents

c. disinterest on the part of either or both parties

d. absence of emotional bonds or affectional ties

9. At what age are parents most likely to receive financial or other help from their children who do not live at home?

   a. 70–74   **c.** 50–54

   b. 60–64   **d.** 80–84

10. Which of the following would be a typical response for a middle-aged man who is dissatisfied with his job?

   a. complain to his friends about it and do nothing

   b. negotiate with his boss to try to change the working situation to better fit his needs

   c. quit and find a new job

   d. resign himself to the fact that he has to change and adjust to the dissatisfaction

11. What does the term "Peter Pandemonium" refer to?

   a. adolescents who leave home

   b. children who leave home and then return

   c. young adults who don't want to grow up

   d. adults who are overanxious to get their grown children out of the house

12. For individuals who are involuntary career changers, which of the following is most closely linked to improved health, emotional stability, and sense of well-being?

   a. job training   **c.** unemployment benefits

   b. transferrable job skills   **d.** going to work at a new job

13. When a couple has learned which strategies work best when resolving disagreements, and therefore sense that they have control of the relationship, they have accomplished which of the following?

   a. marital stability

   b. marital self-efficacy

   c. marital satisfaction

   d. relationship confidence

14. Which of the following is *not* a characteristic of the involved grandparent relationship identified by behavioral scientists?

   a. They are especially likely when the grandchild's mother is unmarried.

   b. They are more common among middle- or upper-socioeconomic-status families than low-socioeconomic-status families.

   c. They often result in teenage mothers being able to complete more years of education.

   d. They are more common among African Americans than among Whites.

15. Lauren used to work as a customer service agent in the call center of a large corporation. Recently the company decided to go to an automated customer help system in which computers answer calls and refer callers to the company's website. Lauren was laid off, making her what this chapter would call _____.

   a. a career transitioner.

   b. an involuntary career changer.

   c. an employment liability.

   d. a volunteer career shifter.

16. Which of the following best describes the nature of friendship in middle adulthood?

   a. The need for a social network increases across midlife.

   b. The social circle is smaller, but the friendships are as intimate and close as at earlier ages.

   c. Adults have more friends in midlife than at any other point in adulthood.

   d. The increased role strain and role conflict of middle adulthood require additional emotional support from friends outside the family.

17. An increase in life expectancy has caused one aspect of family life to change. Which of the following best illustrates this change?

   a. Adults are likely to spend more years caring for both younger and older generations in their family.

   b. Adults spend fewer years in occupational roles and therefore have more time to spend with their family.

   c. Multigeneration families are much rarer than was true a generation ago.

   d. Parents have more children, and the average family size is larger than ever before in history.

18. Many potential employers believe that middle-aged workers are less able to learn new computer skills than their young-adult counterparts. This is an example of _____.

   a. selective optimization

   b. compensation

   c. reality

   d. ageism

19. The Fowler family lives in a duplex. Grandma Fowler lives in one half, and Mr. and Mrs. Fowler and their children live in the other half. Every day when the children get off of the school bus, grandma meets them and prepares their afternoon snack. She helps them with their homework until their parents get home from work. What kind of relationship does Grandma Fowler have with her grandchildren?

   a. custodial

   b. remote

   c. companionate

   d. involved

20. Which of the following persons is most likely to deal effectively with on-the-job stress?

   a. Melva, who is high in extraversion and conscientiousness

   b. Jonathan, who is low in conscientiousness and extraversion

   c. Jackson, who is high in agreeableness and neuroticism

   d. Mabel, who is low in openness and extraversion

21. Georgina is a middle-aged woman who volunteers as a tour guide at the local art museum and at the Museum of Asian Culture. She does this because she believes that the arts are an important part of culture and must be preserved and passed on to future generations. What term would Vaillant apply to Georgina?

   a. keeper of the meaning

   b. caregiver of future generations

   c. generatively enabled

   d. career committed

22. Orland, age 50, has always been the top seller in her real estate company. Nonetheless, she never rests on her laurels. Three times a year, she attends workshops on salesmanship, closing, and real estate law. Baltes & Baltes would suggest that Orland is using the _____ strategy.
    a. selection
    b. management
    c. optimization
    d. compensation

23. Which of the following is a common experience for voluntary career changers?
    a. Their families may not understand the path they have taken.
    b. They usually regret their decision to change careers.
    c. They have a low tolerance for risk taking.
    d. They usually make more money in their new careers.

24. Which of the following is *not* one of the types of grandparent relationships mentioned in this text?
    a. generative relationships
    b. remote relationships
    c. involved relationships
    d. companionate relationships

25. Paul drags himself to work every day. He no longer finds his work interesting or rewarding, but he doesn't believe he has any options other than to continue in his present position. Moreover, he thinks that his boss and co-workers do not appreciate the quality of his work. George seems to be experiencing _____.
    a. role conflict
    b. work-related strain
    c. burnout
    d. regressive generativity

To 👁 **Watch** ✳ **Explore** ⊙ **Simulate** ✓ **Study** and **Review** **and experience MyVirtualLife go to MyPsychLab.com**

Physical and Cognitive Development in Late Adulthood

How long do you expect to live? You may be one of the increasing number of people who live to be 100 years of age or more. Centenarians (people who live to the age of 100) are the fastest-growing segment of the population in developed countries.

Approximately 60,000 centenarians now live in the United States, and if current trends continue, there will be more than 700,000 by the year 2060 (Meyer, 2012; U.S. Census Bureau, 2012). An online quiz can help you determine your chances of living to 100 (http://calculator.livingto100.com/calculator).

LEARNING OBJECTIVES

VARIABILITY IN LATE ADULTHOOD

17.1 What factors contribute to life expectancy and longevity?

17.2 What variables contribute to individual differences in health among older adults?

PHYSICAL CHANGES

17.3 How does the brain change in late adulthood?

17.4 What types of sensory changes occur in late adulthood?

17.5 How do theories explain biological aging?

17.6 What are the behavioral effects of changes in the various body systems of older adults?

MENTAL HEALTH

17.7 What is Alzheimer's disease, and how does it differ from other dementias?

17.8 What does research suggest about depression among older adults?

COGNITIVE CHANGES

17.9 What kinds of memory differences distinguish older and younger adults?

17.10 What do theory and research on wisdom and creativity reveal about cognitive functioning in late adulthood?

Most people, when they think about the prospect of living 80, 90, or 100 years, worry about age-related declines in health, mobility, and cognitive functioning, the types of late-adulthood changes you may have experienced in *MyVirtualLife*. Certainly there are some very real physical declines as we age. But for many people, as you will learn in this chapter, even very old age is a time of continuing health and enthusiasm for life.

Variability in Late Adulthood

The scientific study of aging is known as **gerontology**. For many years, gerontologists thought about old age almost exclusively in terms of decline and loss. However, perspectives on the later years are rapidly changing, and late adulthood is now thought of as a period of tremendous individual variability rather than one of universal decline. 👁 **Watch** the **Video** *Late Adulthood: Portraits of Late Adult Health* in **MyPsychLab**.

Life Expectancy and Longevity

LO 17.1   What factors contribute to life expectancy and longevity?

Animal species vary widely in their expected lifespans. Fruit flies, for instance, live for only a few weeks, while giant Galapagos tortoises often live to be more than 100 years old. Among humans, cases such as that of Jeanne Calmet, a French woman who lived to be 122 years old, suggest that the maximum lifespan is about 120 years, but this estimate may change as more individuals pass the centenarian mark. Yet there is no denying that death rates increase dramatically when humans reach their 60s, and scientists are learning more about the variables that distinguish individuals who die in their 60s from those who live for 100 years or more. 👁 **Watch** the **Video** *Centenarian* in **MyPsychLab**.

TRENDS IN LIFE EXPECTANCY You have probably heard that life expectancy in the industrialized world these days is far greater than in the past. The average male infant who was born in the United States in 1930 lived to be 58, and his female counterpart survived to age 62 (Federal Interagency Forum on Aging-Related Statistics [FIFARS], 2012). By contrast, the average male born today is expected to live 76 years and the average female is expected to live to age 81 (FIFARS, 2012). However, such predictions are strongly influenced by the fact that the highest death rates in the entire human lifespan are found in the first few years of life. Thus, the increases in average life expectancy that have occurred over the past 7 to 8 decades result from improvements in nutrition, health care, and general living conditions for pregnant women, infants, and young children.

Improvements in these variables among the elderly themselves over the past several decades are responsible for changes in the expected lifespans of adults in their 60s and beyond. For example, in the United States, the average 65-year-old man lives to about age 83, but once a man reaches 85, he is likely to live to be 91 (FIFARS, 2012). Life expectancy among women is even longer. The average 65-year-old woman lives to the age of 85, and the average 85-year-old woman can expect to live to over 92. Because of this sex difference in life expectancy, there are more elderly women than men. Life expectancy varies by racial group as well. In general, 65- to 74-year-old White Americans have longer life expectancies than African Americans in this age group, perhaps because of different rates of cancer and the other diseases you learned about in Chapter 15. However, by age 75, the life expectancies of White American and African American elders are essentially equivalent (FIFARS, 2012).

SUBGROUPS Gerontologists divide older adults into subgroups of *young old* (aged 60–75), the *old old* (aged 75–85), and the *oldest old* (aged 85 and over). The oldest old are the fastest-growing segment of the population in the United States, which means that terms such as *octogenarian* (a person in his or her 80s) and *centenarian* (a person over 100 years of age) will be used far more often than in the past. From 1950 to 2010, the population of the United States

gerontology the scientific study of aging

The Coming Demographic Crisis

Every industrialized nation in the world will face a demographic crisis in the near future. The reason is that an extraordinarily large number of people were born in the years from 1946 until the early 1960s. (In the United States, this cohort is known as the Baby Boomers.) In 2008, just 2 years after the first wave of Boomers became eligible for early-retirement Social Security pensions (reduced payments for individuals who elect to retire at age 62), Social Security payments exceeded income from Social Security taxes for the first time since the country suffered a deep recession in 1983 ("Social Security: More going out than coming in," August 5, 2010). Consequently, the federal government may lack sufficient tax revenues to pay for the many benefits they have guaranteed to current and future senior citizens.

With respect to pension plans, such as the Social Security system in the United States, there are really only two options: decreasing benefits to recipients or increasing taxes on workers. Moreover, economic analysts report that neither option alone will solve the problem. Any workable solution must include both reducing the financial burden of elderly entitlements and generating additional revenues.

Unfortunately, polls suggest that the public is opposed to both options (Hogan, 2013). Voters in the United States overwhelmingly oppose reducing benefits for the current cohort of retired people and are only slightly less opposed to reducing benefits for future retirees (Public

Agenda, Inc., 2007). At the same time, most workers believe that their Social Security taxes are already too high but do not want the government to use other funds, such as those generated by income taxes, to pay for Social Security benefits. Moreover, U.S. workers blame the problem on government mismanagement rather than on the mathematical inevitabilities of the demographic crisis. Consequently, lawmakers face a dilemma: A solution must be found, or governments may go bankrupt trying to fulfill their obligations to future elderly citizens. However, any solution politicians impose on voters is likely to be unpopular.

For these reasons, policymakers are looking for ways to make elderly entitlement reform more palatable to voters. For example, one proposal involves workers taking responsibility for their own retirement income by directing how their Social Security taxes are to be invested. The appeal of this option is that it offers workers more autonomy. However, unlike the current system, it would not include a guaranteed retirement income. Those who invest wisely will enjoy a comfortable retirement; those who are less astute may be left with little or nothing.

Surveys suggest that the public wants both: autonomy over retirement investments and a guaranteed income (Public Agenda, Inc., 2007). People would like to be able to invest their own Social Security taxes and retain the present system. Clearly, U.S. voters are reluctant to acknowledge that it is impossible to create a system that offers benefits without costs. As a result, workers in the United States are likely to end up with a solution that is imposed on them by legislators rather than one that represents a public consensus.

YOU DECIDE

Decide which of these two statements you most agree with and think about how you would defend your position:

1. Having autonomy over how my Social Security taxes are invested is more important to me than having a guaranteed income when I reach retirement age.

2. Having a guaranteed income when I reach retirement age is more important to me than having autonomy over how my Social Security taxes are invested.

approximately doubled, from about 150 million persons to just over 300 million. By contrast, the over-65 population more than tripled, from 13 to 40 million, while the over-85 population increased nearly 12-fold, from one-half million to 6 million (FIFARS, 2012). Furthermore, every industrialized country in the world is experiencing this same kind of growth in the elderly population (FIFARS, 2012). (See *No Easy Answers.*)

Health

LO 17.2 What variables contribute to individual differences in health among older adults?

Stereotypes may lead you to think that most elders are in poor health. However, the majority of older adults do not have ailments that seriously impair their day-to-day functioning (FIFARS, 2012). Moreover, the inevitable physical declines that are associated with aging do not seem to decrease older adults' satisfaction with their lives. 👁 **Watch** the **Video** *Late Adulthood: Physical Health in Late Adulthood* in **MyPsychLab**.

SELF-RATED HEALTH As Figure 17.1 on page 420 indicates, a majority of older adults across all three age subgroups regard their health as good (FIFARS, 2012). These data contradict stereotypes of old age as a period of illness. However, the proportions of elderly with good health are a

Percentage of people age 65 and over with respondent-assessed good to excellent health status by age group and race and Hispanic origin, 2008–2010

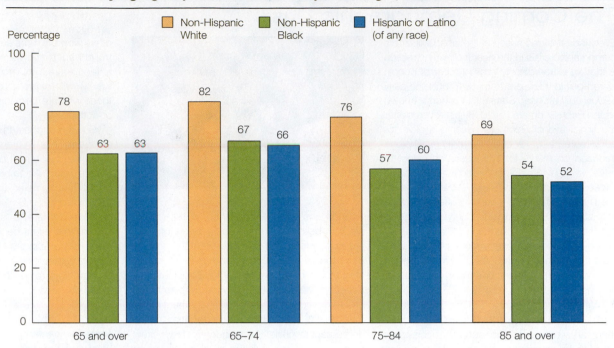

Figure 17.1 Self-Rated Health Status among Older Adults

Most elders rate their health positively.

(*Source:* FIFARS, 2012.)

great deal lower than the equivalent proportions for young and middle-aged adults. Thus, as you might suspect, health is the single largest factor determining the trajectory of an adult's physical or mental status over the years beyond age 65. As you read more about the prevalence of disability and disease among older adults, keep Figure 17.1 in mind. You will see that these data are a testimony to the emotional resilience of older adults, a majority of whom are able to maintain an optimistic view of themselves and their lives in the face of growing physical challenges.

Further, their optimistic view seems to help protect older adults against the long-term effects of serious health threats such as strokes. Researchers have found that elders who rate their health as good, regardless of how an objective observer might rate it, recover more physical and cognitive functions after a stroke than their peers who rate their health more poorly (Hillen, Davies, Rudd, Kieselbach, & Wolfe, 2003). Older adults who already have one or more chronic diseases at 65 show far more rapid declines than do those who begin late adulthood with no disease symptoms. In part, of course, this is an effect of the disease processes themselves. Cardiovascular disease results, among other things, in restricted blood flow to many organs, including the brain, with predictable effects on an adult's ability to learn or remember. Longitudinal studies show that adults with this disease show earlier declines in all mental abilities (Schaie & Willis, 2005). And, of course, those experiencing the early stages of Alzheimer's disease or another disease that causes dementia will experience far more rapid declines in mental abilities than will those who do not have such diseases.

LIMITATIONS ON ACTIVITIES Gerontologists generally define a *disability* as a limitation in an individual's ability to perform certain roles and tasks, particularly self-help tasks and other chores of daily living (Jette, 1996). Daily living tasks are grouped into two categories. **Activities of daily living**, or **ADLs**, include bathing, dressing, and using the toilet. **Instrumental activities of daily living**, or **IADLs**, include activities that are more intellectually demanding, such as managing money.

As you might expect, proportions of older adults with disabilities rise with age. Nearly half of those over 75 report at least some level of difficulty performing some basic daily life activities (FIFARS, 2010). But this means that half of these elders do *not* have such problems. To be sure, surveys generally exclude adults who are living in institutions, the vast majority of whom are severely disabled, according to the usual definition. Still, it is important to understand that among the oldest old who live outside nursing homes, the proportion who have some disability is nowhere near 100%. Even more encouraging is the finding that the rate of disability among the old old and the oldest old has been declining slowly but steadily in the past few decades in the United States, perhaps because of better health care or better health habits (FIFARS, 2012).

As you would probably predict, disability rates increase dramatically as elders get older. Among those over the age of 85, 60% have some kind of disability and more than half require help with at least one ADL (National Center for Health Statistics [NCHS], 2009). Consequently, the increase in their numbers means that the population of **frail elderly**, older adults who cannot care for themselves, is also likely to grow significantly. Demographers and economists have become concerned about the ability of young and middle-aged adults to support the growing number of elderly.

CHRONIC HEALTH CONDITIONS As Figure 17.2 shows, the prevalence of chronic health conditions increases with age. The most common of these conditions are *hypertension*, also known as high blood pressure, followed by *arthritis*, inflammation in the joints that causes pain and stiffness. Not everyone with these problems is disabled. But the risk of some kind of

activities of daily living (ADLs) self-help tasks such as bathing, dressing, and using the toilet

instrumental activities of daily living (IADLs) more intellectually demanding daily living tasks such as doing housework, cooking, and managing money

frail elderly older adults whose physical and/or mental impairments are so extensive that they cannot care for themselves

Percentage of people age 65 and over who reported having selected chronic health conditions, by sex, 2009–2010

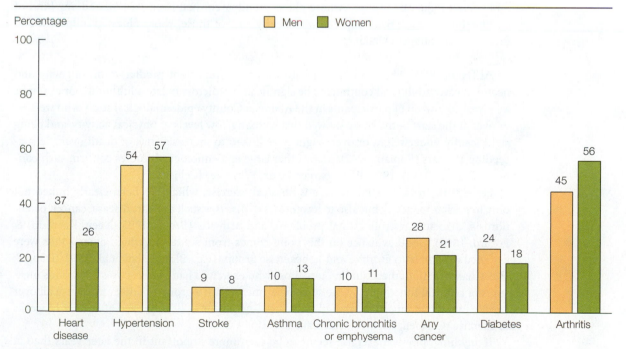

Figure 17.2 **Chronic Conditions among Older Adults**

Chronic conditions such as these often interfere with older adults' daily lives.

(*Source:* FIFARS, 2012.)

There are many ways to maintain physical fitness in old age. In China, elderly people often can be found practicing Tai Chi in the early morning.

functional disability is two to three times higher among elders who have these diseases than among those who do not (FIFARS, 2012).

You can also see from Figure 17.2 that women are considerably more likely than men to have arthritis, so they are also more often limited in their ability to carry out the various movements and tasks necessary for independent life (FIFARS, 2012). Since women are more likely to be widowed and thus to lack a partner who can assist with these daily living tasks, it is not surprising that more women than men live with their children or in nursing homes.

RACIAL AND ETHNIC DIFFERENCES Among ethnic minorities, as among White Americans, individual variability in old age is the rule rather than the exception. Certainly, averages for life expectancy and disabling conditions such as heart disease differ somewhat across groups. For example, the prevalence of arthritis among elderly White and African Americans is about 53%, whereas 44% of Hispanic Americans have this potentially disabling condition (FIFARS, 2012). Nevertheless, as Figure 17.1 showed, a majority of elders across these three ethnic groups rate their health as good to excellent.

Moreover, everything you have learned so far about the correlations between health habits and health status in adulthood is just as applicable to minorities as to Whites. Thus, improved diet, increased physical activity, and participation in treatment programs for debilitating chronic ailments can potentially benefit elders of any race or ethnic group.

HEREDITY Some general tendency to live a long life is clearly inherited (Heun & Bonsignore, 2004). Identical twins are more similar in length of life than are fraternal twins, and adults whose parents and grandparents were long lived are also likely to live longer (Plomin & McClearn, 1990). Twin studies in Sweden showed that identical twins have more similar illness rates than do fraternal twins (Pedersen & Harris, 1990). Similarly, for the Harvard men in the Grant study sample discussed in Chapter 1, there was a small but significant correlation between health and the longevity of each man's parents and grandparents (Vaillant, 1977). Only about a quarter of those whose oldest grandparent had lived past 90 had any kind of chronic illness at age 65, compared with nearly 70% of those whose oldest grandparent had died at 78 or younger (Vaillant, 1991).

HEALTH HABITS The same health habits that are important predictors of longevity and health in early adulthood continue to be significant predictors in late adulthood. For example, a 17-year follow-up of participants in the Alameda County epidemiological study who were 60 or over at the start of the study showed that smoking, low levels of physical activity, and being significantly underweight or overweight were linked to increased risk of death over the succeeding 17 years (Kaplan, 1992). Many other large epidemiological studies confirm such connections (e.g., Brody, 1996; Paffenbarger, Hyde, Wing, & Hsieh, 1987).

Perhaps the most crucial variable is physical exercise, which has been clearly linked not only to greater longevity but also to lower rates of diseases such as heart disease, cancer, osteoporosis, diabetes, gastrointestinal problems, and arthritis (Brody, 1995; Deeg, Kardaun, & Fozard, 1996). Good evidence on this point comes from studies in which older adults were assigned randomly to exercise and nonexercise groups (e.g., Blumenthal et al., 1991; Tsang & Hui-Chan, 2003). In these studies, too, those who exercised had better scores on various measures of physical functioning. One such experiment, with a group of adults who were all over age 80, found that muscular strength increased and motor skills improved after only 12 weeks of exercise (Carmeli, Reznick, Coleman, & Carmeli, 2000).

If anything, physical exercise seems to be even more important in the later years than at earlier ages. For example, one investigation used medical records and self-reports of exercise to examine the degree to which physical activity influenced height loss in the elderly (Sagiv, Vogelaere, Soudry, & Shrsam, 2000). Investigators found that study participants who had exercised regularly lost significantly less height over a 30-year period than those who had not exercised. Further, exercise after age 40 seemed to be especially important in preventing height loss. As public awareness of the importance of exercise has grown in recent years, rates of regular exercise have increased among older adults just as they have among those who are younger. In 1998, 9% of elders over the age of 85 reported engaging in daily exercise; by 2008, the rate had risen to 11% (FIFARS, 2010). 👁 **Watch** the **Video** *Active Seniors* in **MyPsychLab**.

---

test yourself before going on ✅ Study and Review in MyPsychLab

Answers to these questions can be found in the back of the book.

1. Glenn has just turned 60. He belongs to the _____ _____ subgroup of older adults, while his 88-year-old mother belongs to the _____ _____ subgroup.

2. Match each term with its definition.
_____(1) activities of daily living
_____(2) instrumental activities of daily living
_____(3) hypertension
_____(4) arthritis

(a) personal tasks such as bathing
(b) high blood pressure
(c) tasks such as paying bills
(d) inflammation of the joints

CRITICAL THINKING

3. How would you characterize your own chances for a long life based on the genes you have inherited and on your health habits?

Physical Changes

Despite variability in health among the elderly, there are several changes in physical functioning that characterize the late adult years for almost everyone.

The Brain and Nervous System

LO 17.3 How does the brain change in late adulthood?

If you look back at the discussion of aging in Chapter 13, you'll see four main changes in the brain during the adult years: a reduction of brain weight, a loss of gray matter, a decline in the density of dendrites, and slower synaptic speed. The most central of these changes is the loss of dendritic density (Wong, 2002). You'll remember from Chapter 4 that dendrites are "pruned" during the first few years after birth so that redundant or unused pathways are eliminated. The loss of dendrites in middle and late adulthood does not seem to be the same type of pruning. Rather, it appears to be a decrease in useful dendritic connections.

However, research suggests that experience as well as aging is involved in the loss of dendritic density. Neurologists have found that, across the years from 60 to 90, adults with higher levels of education show significantly less atrophy of the cerebral cortex than those who have fewer years of schooling (Coffey, Saxton, Ratcliff, Bryan, & Lucke, 1999; Farfel et al., 2013). Moreover, the brains of well-educated and poorly educated elderly adults do not differ in areas that are less involved in academic learning than the cerebral cortex is. This finding suggests that education itself is the cause of the reduced atrophying of the cerebral cortex rather than some general factor, such as socioeconomic status, that is coincidentally related to education.

Dendritic loss also results in a gradual slowing of synaptic speed, with a consequent increase in reaction time for many everyday tasks. Neural pathways are redundant enough that it is nearly always possible for a nerve impulse to move from neuron A to neuron B or from neuron A to some muscle cell. Neurologists usually refer to this redundancy as **synaptic plasticity**. But with the increasing loss of dendrites, the shortest route may be lost, so plasticity decreases and reaction time increases. 👁 **Watch** the **Video** *Late Adulthood: Happiness and Attitude toward Aging* in **MyPsychLab**.

synaptic plasticity the redundancy in the nervous system that ensures that it is nearly always possible for a nerve impulse to move from one neuron to another or from a neuron to another type of cell (e.g., a muscle cell)

tinnitus persistent ringing in the ears

The Senses

LO 17.4   What types of sensory changes occur in late adulthood?

In Chapter 15 you read about declines in sensory and other physical functions that occur in middle age. Such deficits become larger in late adulthood, and several more serious threats to the health of these systems arise.

VISION   In addition to presbyopia (farsightedness), late adulthood can bring other vision defects due to body changes. For example, blood flow to the eye decreases (perhaps as a side effect of atherosclerosis), which results in an enlarged "blind spot" on the retina and thus a reduced field of vision. The pupil does not widen or narrow as much or as quickly as it previously did, which means that the older adult has more difficulty seeing at night and responding to rapid changes in brightness (Kline & Scialfa, 1996).

In addition, many older adults have diseases of the eye that further diminish visual acuity and adaptability. For example, one of the leading causes of visual disability among older adults is *age-related macular degeneration* (*AMD*), a disease of the retina that diminishes vision for fine details. Individuals with AMD gradually lose their central vision and, with it, the ability to read and engage in other activities that require discrimination of fine details.

About 17% of adults over the age of 40 in the United States have been diagnosed with *cataracts*, a condition in which the lens inside the eye becomes clouded and obscures vision (Centers for Disease Control and Prevention [CDC], 2013). Fortunately, cataracts can be surgically corrected. In fact, cataract surgery is now the most frequently performed and most effective surgical procedure in the world (Tan, Wang, Rochtchina, & Mitchell, 2006). You might be surprised to learn that 5% of adults in the United States have had cataract surgery (CDC, 2013).

HEARING   You'll recall from Chapter 15 that wear and tear on the auditory system results in some hearing loss (*presbycusis*) beginning in middle adulthood, but these gradual losses don't typically add up to functionally significant loss until late adulthood. Auditory problems, unlike many other disabilities of old age, are more likely to be experienced by men than by women. Nearly half of men over the age of 65 report hearing difficulties, compared to just under a third of older women (FIFARS, 2012). This sex difference is normally attributed to differential exposure to noise: More men have worked in environments with high levels of noise (at least in current cohorts of older adults in developed countries).

Hearing difficulties in late adulthood have several components: First, there is the loss of ability to hear high-frequency sounds (Roland, 2012). Both cross-sectional and longitudinal studies suggest that, for the range of sounds used in normal human speech, the loss after age 60 is such that a given sound has to be about 1–2 decibels louder each year for the individual to report that he hears it (Fozard, 1990; Kline & Scialfa, 1996).

Second, most older adults develop difficulties with word discrimination (Roland, 2012). Even when the sound is loud enough, older adults have more difficulty identifying individual words they have just heard (Schieber, 1992). In addition, many adults over the age of 60 have problems hearing under noisy conditions. The loss of ability to discriminate individual words is even greater in such situations, so large gatherings become increasingly difficult for older adults.

Tinnitus, a persistent ringing in the ears, also increases in incidence with age, although this problem appears to be independent of the other changes just described. Between 12 and 14% of adults over 65 experience this problem (Asplund, 2003), which may be caused by exposure to noise, although that is not well established. 👁 **Watch** the **Video** *Ear Ringing* in **MyPsychLab**.

Even mild hearing loss can pose communication problems in some situations. Those with such problems may be perceived by others as disoriented or experiencing poor memory, especially if the person with the hearing loss is unwilling to admit the problem and ask for a comment or an instruction to be repeated. Nonetheless, an older adult with a hearing impairment is *not* necessarily socially isolated or unhappy. Mild and moderate hearing losses, even if uncorrected with a hearing aid, are simply not correlated with measures of general social, emotional, or psychological health among elderly adults.

Presbycusis and the other changes in hearing seem to result from gradual degeneration of virtually every part of the auditory system. Older adults secrete more ear wax, which may

Hearing aids improve the quality of life for many older adults.

block the ear canal; the bones of the middle ear become calcified and less elastic; the cochlear membranes of the inner ear become less flexible and less responsive; and the nerve pathways to the brain show some degeneration (Roland, 2012).

TASTE, SMELL, AND TOUCH The ability to taste the four basic flavors (salty, bitter, sweet, and sour) does not seem to decline over the years of adulthood. Taste receptor cells (taste buds) have short lives and are continually replaced (Bornstein, 1992). But other changes in the taste system affect older adults, such as the secretion of somewhat less saliva, producing a sensation of "wooly mouth" for some. Many elders also report that flavors seem blander than in earlier years, leading them to prefer more intense concentrations of flavors, particularly sweetness (de Graaf, Polet, & van Staveren, 1994). But it may well be that this perception of flavor blandness is due largely to a loss of the sense of smell.

The sense of smell clearly deteriorates in old age. The best information comes from a classic cross-sectional study in which researchers tested nearly 2,000 children and adults on their ability to identify 40 different smells—everything from pizza to gasoline (Doty et al., 1984). Young and middle-aged adults had equally good scores on this smell identification test, but scores declined rapidly after age 60. However, the loss of sensitivity to odors is far greater among elderly men than among elderly women (Morgan, Covington, Geisler, Polich, & Murphy, 1997).

Interestingly, like hearing loss, the loss of the sense of smell seems to have an environmental component. Specifically, both men and women who worked in factories (where, presumably, they were exposed to more pollutants) show much greater losses of sense of smell in old age than do those who worked in offices (Corwin, Loury, & Gilbert, 1995).

The skin of elderly adults is also less responsive to cold and heat (Kingma, Frijns, Saris, van Steenhoven, & van Marken Lichtenbelt, 2010). Research suggests that the loss of sensitivity occurs in a pattern that is a reversal of the proximodistal principle of growth you learned about in Chapter 3. In other words, the extremities, usually the feet, are the first body parts to decline in sensitivity. Consequently, elderly people are less able to benefit from the potential comforts associated with physical stimuli than are younger people. For example, for an elderly person to be able to feel a warm bath, the water temperature may have to be so high that it will burn the skin. Similarly, older adults have an increased risk of hypothermia because their skin doesn't signal the brain efficiently when it is exposed to low temperatures that make younger people quick to pull on a jacket or cover up with a blanket (Kingma et al., 2010).

Theories of Biological Aging

LO 17.5 How do theories explain biological aging?

What are the causes of physical aging? Current theorists agree that the most likely explanation lies in basic cellular processes, which appear to change with age in specific ways that reduce the efficiency of cellular functioning. A number of theoretical variations on this theme have been proposed.

THE HAYFLICK LIMIT As we pointed out earlier, species vary widely in how long, on average, individuals live. For humans, the maximum lifespan seems to be about 110 or 120 years. These differences have persuaded some biologists that there may be a universal genetic process that triggers age-related declines and limits the lifespan (e.g., Hayflick, 1977, 1987). For tortoises, the lifespan is far longer, and for chickens, far shorter.

Advocates of this view support their argument with research demonstrating that cells taken from the embryos of different species and placed in nutrient solution double only a fixed number of times, after which the cell colony degenerates. Human embryo cells double about 50 times; those from the Galapagos tortoise double roughly 100 times; chicken cells double only about 25 times. Furthermore, cells taken from human adults double only about 20 times, as if they had already "used up" some of their genetic capacity. The theoretical proposal that emerges from such observations is that each species is subject to a time limit, known as the **Hayflick limit** (because it was proposed by biologist Leonard Hayflick), beyond which cells simply lose their capacity to replicate themselves (Norwood, Smith, & Stein, 1990).

Hayflick limit the genetically programmed time limit to which each species is theoretically proposed to be subject, after which cells no longer have any capacity to replicate themselves accurately

telomere a string of repetitive DNA at the tip of each chromosome in the body that appears to serve as a kind of timekeeping mechanism

programmed senescence theory the view that age-related declines are the result of species-specific genes for aging

cross-linking the formation of undesirable bonds between proteins or fats

free radicals molecules or atoms that possess an unpaired electron

The genetic limits argument has been strengthened by the discovery that each chromosome in the human body (and presumably in other species, too) has, at its tip, a string of repetitive DNA called a **telomere** (Angier, 1992; Campisi, Dimri, & Hara, 1996). Among other functions, telomeres appear to serve as a kind of timekeeping mechanism for the organism. Researchers have found that the number of telomeres is reduced slightly each time a cell divides, so the number remaining in a 70-year-old is much lower than what is found in a child. This raises the possibility that there may be a crucial minimum number of telomeres; when the total falls below that number, disease or death comes fairly quickly. Some researchers have found a correlation between telomere loss and death, providing support for this hypothesis (Kimura et al., 2008).

GENETICALLY PROGRAMMED SENESCENCE *Senescence*, as you learned in Chapter 13, is the gradual deterioration of body systems that happens as organisms age. **Programmed senescence theory** suggests that age-related physical declines result from species-specific genes for aging. Evolutionary theorists argue that programmed senescence prevents older, presumably less fit, individuals from becoming parents at an age when they are unlikely to be able to raise offspring to maturity (Buss, 1999). The idea is that these aging genes are equipped with some kind of built-in clock that prevents the genes from having an effect when humans are in their reproductive years but switches them on once the reproductive peak has passed.

REPAIR OF GENETIC MATERIAL AND CROSS-LINKING Another theory of aging focuses on the cells' ability to repair breaks in DNA. Breaks in DNA strands are common events, resulting from unknown metabolic processes. Because the organism is apparently unable to repair all the damage, the theory proposes, the accumulation of unrepaired breaks results over time in a loss of cellular function, and the organism ages (Tice & Setlow, 1985).

A related theory focuses on another cellular process called cross-linking, which occurs more often in cell proteins of older adults than in those of younger adults. **Cross-linking** occurs when undesirable chemical bonds form between proteins or fats. In skin and connective tissue, for example, two proteins called *collagen* and *elastin* form cross-linkages, either between their molecules or within a given molecule. The resulting molecules cannot assume the correct shape for proper function, leading to effects such as wrinkling of the skin and arterial rigidity. (An equivalent process, by the way, occurs in old rubber, which explains why windshield wipers become stiffer over time.)

FREE RADICALS A third type of cellular process that may contribute to aging relates to the body's ability to deal with free radicals. **Free radicals**, which are molecules or atoms that possess an unpaired electron, are a normal by-product of body metabolism and also arise as a result of exposure to certain substances in foods, sunlight, x-rays, or air pollution. They may also occur more frequently in older than in younger people's bodies because of age-related deterioration of the mitochondria, the cell structures that convert food into energy (Nichols & Melov, 2004). These radicals, especially the subgroup called *oxygen free radicals*, enter into many potentially harmful chemical reactions, resulting in irreparable cellular damage that accumulates with age. For example, oxidation reactions caused by free radicals can damage cell membranes, thereby reducing the cell's protection against toxins and carcinogens.

Laboratory studies show that reducing free radicals can improve the condition of damaged brain tissue (Moldzio et al., 2013). In addition, research on diet variations points to the possibility that some foods, especially those high in fat and/or food additives such as preservatives, promote the formation of oxygen free radicals, whereas others, referred to as *antioxidants*, inhibit the formation of these radicals or promote chemical processes that help the body defend against them. Foods high in vitamins C and E and beta carotene (vitamin A) all belong in the latter group, as do tea, coffee, red wine, garlic, and a host of other food substances (International Food Information Council Foundation, 2009). Several large epidemiological studies show that people who eat diets high in antioxidants or who take regular supplements of vitamin E or beta-carotene live somewhat longer and have lower rates of heart disease (Willcox, Curb, & Rodriguez, 2008).

Such findings do not mean that age-related problems such as heart disease and vision loss are *caused* by antioxidant deficiencies. For one thing, experimental studies in which individuals with cardiovascular and other types of diseases are treated with antioxidant diets and/or supplements have produced mixed results (Willcox et al., 2008). In some studies, patients have improved, but in others they have not. Moreover, some studies suggest that antioxidant therapy increases the risk of some diseases, such as skin cancer (Hercberg et al., 2007). Nevertheless, animal and laboratory studies showing that antioxidants improve physiological functioning at the cellular level support the general notion that many of the effects of aging are modifiable and perhaps even preventable (Prasthani et al., 2010; Skulachev, 2009).

TERMINAL DECLINE Some theorists claim that physical and mental declines in old age are actually part of the dying process. For example, the **terminal decline hypothesis** asserts that all adults retain excellent physical and mental function until just a few years before death, at which time there are significant declines in all functions (Kleemeier, 1962). Longitudinal research provides some support for the terminal decline hypothesis. Researchers have found that declines occur more rapidly during the 7 to 8 years just prior to death than they did earlier in life (Muniz-Terrera, van den Hout, Piccinin, Matthews, & Hofer, 2013). However, the degree of change in the terminal period is moderated by gender, with women showing a more rapid rate of change than men. Moreover, the later death occurs in the lifespan, the slower the rate of change during the terminal period.

terminal decline hypothesis the hypothesis that mental and physical functioning decline drastically only in the few years immediately preceding death

Behavioral Effects of Physical Changes

LO 17.6 What are the behavioral effects of changes in the various body systems of older adults?

The great majority of older adults cope effectively with most everyday tasks—buying groceries, managing their finances, reading bus schedules, and so on—despite changes in vision, hearing, and other physical functions. Thus, in addition to knowing what these changes are and how they might be explained, it's important to know just how they affect older adults' daily lives.

GENERAL SLOWING The biggest single behavioral effect of age-related physical changes is a general slowing down. Dendritic loss at the neuronal level clearly contributes substantially to this general slowing, but other factors are also involved, including arthritic changes in the joints and loss of elasticity in the muscles. Everything takes longer—writing things down, tying one's shoes, and adapting to changes in temperature or changes in light conditions (Schaie & Willis, 2005). Even tasks that involve word skills, which tend to decline very little in accuracy with age, nonetheless are done more slowly (Cona, Arcara, Amodio, Schiff, & Bisiacchi, 2013; Spieler & Griffin, 2006).

Further, many developmentalists believe that the decline in the speed of nerve impulses is responsible for age-related difficulties in translating thoughts into action. For example, neurologists sometimes assess nervous-system functioning by having patients demonstrate a physical action involving a tool, such as hammering. Demonstrating an appropriate hand posture and moving the arm in an appropriate way are taken as indicators of neurological health. Developmentalists have found that healthy individuals in late adulthood make more initial errors than younger adults in trying to carry out such activities (Peigneux & van der Linden, 1999). However, they correct their errors just as quickly as those who are younger. Consequently, neuropsychologists think that general slowing of brain activity interferes with older adults' retrieval of the knowledge they need to accomplish the task and that they use behavioral feedback to compensate for mistakes.

Age-related general slowing affects complex motor activities such as driving. Young adults have more auto accidents than any other age group, primarily because they drive too fast. But adults over the age of 80 have more accidents per miles driven (Market Wire, 2003). Of course, other physical changes beyond general slowing contribute to driving problems in old age. Changes in the eyes mean that older adults have more trouble reading signs at night and adjusting to the glare of oncoming headlights. In addition, reduced range of motion in the neck, which often accompanies arthritis, may contribute to automobile accidents involving elderly drivers. And the general increase in reaction time affects elders' ability to

This older man has bought himself a very sporty car and doubtless thinks of himself as still being a skillful driver. Nonetheless, many of the physical changes associated with aging will make it harder for him to respond quickly, to see clearly in glare, and to adapt rapidly to changing driving conditions.

switch attention from one thing to the next or to react quickly and appropriately when a vehicle or obstacle appears unexpectedly. Unfortunately, researchers have found that older adults are typically unaware of the ways in which their driving skills have diminished since they were younger (Horswill, Sullivan, Lurie-Beck, & Smith, 2013). For many, the first indication that their driving skills are impaired is a serious accident.

SLEEPING AND EATING PATTERNS Another common effect of physical change is a shift in sleep patterns in old age, which occurs among both healthy and less healthy elders (Maglione & Ancoli-Israel, 2012). Adults older than 65 typically wake up more frequently in the night and show decreases in rapid eye movement (REM) sleep, the lighter sleep state in which dreaming occurs. Older adults are also more likely to wake early in the morning and go to bed early at night. They become "morning people" instead of "night people." And because their night sleep is more often interrupted, older adults also nap more during the day in order to accumulate the needed amount of sleep. These changes in sleep and activity patterns are presumed to be related to changes in nervous-system functioning.

The ability of the brain to regulate appetite also changes with advancing age. When you eat, your blood sugar rises, resulting in a chemical message to the brain that creates a sensation called **satiety**, the sense of being full. The feeling of satiety continues until your blood sugar drops, at which time another chemical message is sent to the brain that causes you to feel hunger. In older adults, the satiety part of the pattern seems to be impaired (Keene, Hope, Rogers, & Elliman, 1998). As a result, older adults may feel hungry all the time and may overeat. To compensate, they come to rely more on habits such as taking their meals at certain times and eating the same foods every day. Thus, they may seem to be unnecessarily rigid to those who are younger when, in reality, their adherence to a particular eating regime is simply a (perhaps unconscious) way of coping with a physiological change.

MOTOR FUNCTIONS The various physical changes associated with aging also combine to produce a reduction in stamina, dexterity, and balance. The loss of stamina clearly arises in large part from changes in the cardiovascular system, as well as from changes in muscles. Dexterity is lost primarily as a result of arthritic changes in the joints.

Another significant change, one with particularly clear practical ramifications, is a gradual loss of the sense of balance, which is at least partly attributable to the effects of aging on white matter in the parts of the brain that control balance and motor functions (Van Impe, Coxon, Goble, Doumas, & Swinnen, 2012). As a result, older adults, who may be quite mobile in their home environments, are likely to have greater difficulty handling an uneven sidewalk or adapting their bodies to a swaying bus. Such situations require the ability to adjust rapidly to changing body cues and the muscular strength to maintain body position, both of which decline in old age. So older adults fall more often. However, the kinds of activities in which older adults participate affect both the sense of balance and the frequency of falls. Older adults who practice Tai Chi or play golf regularly are better able to maintain their balance than those who do not engage in these activities (Tsang & Hui-Chan, 2004).

Older adults also have more problems with fine motor movements (Smith, Sharit, & Czaja, 1999). Such losses are small and gradual with respect to well-practiced skills such as handwriting. Moreover, fine motor skills with older adults' areas of expertise, such as playing a musical instrument, decline little and actually can continue to improve in old age with additional practice (Krampe, 2002; Liubicich, Magistro, Candela, Rabaglietti, & Ciairano, 2012). However, research suggests that some fine motor activities, especially those that require learning a new pattern of movement, may be extremely difficult for elderly people to acquire. For example, older adults take far longer than young and middle-aged adults do to learn complex computer mouse skills such as clicking and dragging objects across the screen (Smith et al., 1999; Voelcker-Rehage, Godde, & Staudinger, 2010).

SEXUAL ACTIVITY Another behavior affected by the cumulative physical changes of aging is sexual behavior. You read in Chapter 15 that the frequency of sexual activity declines gradually in middle adulthood. Both cross-sectional and longitudinal data suggest that this trend continues in late adulthood (Lindau et al., 2007).

The decline in the frequency of sexual activity in late adulthood doubtless has many causes (National Institute on Aging [NIA], 2000b). The continuing decline in testosterone levels among men clearly plays some role. The state of one's overall health plays an increasingly larger role with advancing age. For example, blood-pressure medication sometimes produces impotence as a side effect; chronic pain may also affect sexual desire. Stereotypes that portray old age as an essentially asexual period of life may also have some effect.

Despite declining frequency, though, more than 70% of elders in the young old subgroup and about half of adults in the old old subgroup continue to be sexually active in old age (Lindau et al., 2007). Moreover, the physiological capacity to respond to sexual stimulation, unlike other aspects of functioning, appears not to diminish with age. Indeed, some studies suggest that older adults, especially women, are more sexually adventurous; that is, they appear to be more willing to engage in sexual experimentation than young and middle-aged adults (Purnine & Carey, 1998).

test yourself before going on ✓ Study and Review in MyPsychLab

Answers to these questions can be found in the back of the book.

1. The brain loses interconnectivity as a result of decreases in
   _____.

2. An older adult is most likely to perform at the same levels as she did in earlier adulthood on tasks involving the sense of
   _____.

3. Match each term with its definition.
   _____ (1) cross-linking
   _____ (2) free radicals
   _____ (3) Hayflick limit
   _____ (4) programmed senescence theory
   _____ (5) terminal decline hypothesis
   _____ (6) satiety

(a) molecules that possess an unpaired electron

(b) the view that age-related declines are the result of species-specific genes for aging

(c) the view that mental and physical functioning decline drastically immediately before death

(d) feeling of fullness after eating

(e) formation of undesirable bonds between proteins or fats

(f) genetically programmed limit on the body's tissues capacity for self-repair

CRITICAL THINKING

4. In what ways do you think the behavioral effects of aging influence stereotypes about older adults?

Mental Health

The best-known mental health problems of old age are the **dementias**, a group of neurological disorders involving problems with memory and thinking that affect an individual's emotional, social, and physical functioning. Dementia is one of the leading causes of institutionalization of the elderly in the United States (FIFARS, 2012). However, depression is also a concern in the late adult years.

Alzheimer's Disease and Other Dementias

LO 17.7 What is Alzheimer's disease, and how does it differ from other dementias?

Alzheimer's disease (technically known as *neurocognitive disorder due to Alzheimer's Disease*) is a very severe form of dementia. The early stages of Alzheimer's disease usually become evident very slowly, beginning with subtle memory difficulties, repetitive conversation, and disorientation in unfamiliar settings. Then, memory for recent events begins to go. Memory for long-ago events or for well-rehearsed cognitive procedures, such as simple calculations, is often retained until late in the illness, presumably because these memories can be accessed through many alternative neural pathways (Anderson, 2013a). ◉ **Watch** the **Video** *Late Adulthood: Alzheimer's* in **MyPsychLab**.

Eventually, however, an individual with Alzheimer's disease may fail to recognize family members and may be unable to remember the names of common objects or how to perform such routine activities as brushing her teeth or dressing. Those with Alzheimer's disease experience

dementia a neurological disorder involving problems with memory and thinking that affect an individual's emotional, social, and physical functioning

Alzheimer's disease a very severe form of dementia, the cause of which is unknown

declines in the ability to communicate, as well as the ability to carry out daily self-care routines. The changes in appetite regulation you read about earlier in this chapter are particularly problematic for those with Alzheimer's because they can't rely on habit to regulate their eating behavior, as healthy older people do. Left to their own devices, people with Alzheimer's may consume as many as three or four complete meals at one sitting without realizing how much they have eaten. Consequently, their eating behavior must be closely supervised.

People with Alzheimer's also have difficulty processing information about others' emotions, such as facial expressions (Burnham & Hogervorst, 2004). Some have problems controlling their own emotions and display sudden bursts of anger or even rage. Others exhibit an increased level of dependency and clinginess toward family members or friends (Raskind & Peskind, 1992). Research suggests that the incidence of depression among elders with Alzheimer's disease may be as high as 40% (Harwood et al., 2000). ◉ **Watch** the **Video** *Alzheimer's and Dementia* in **MyPsychLab**.

DIAGNOSING AND TREATING ALZHEIMER'S DISEASE Alzheimer's disease can be definitively diagnosed only after a person has died. At autopsy, the brains of those with Alzheimer's are far more likely to contain extensive *neurofibrillary tangles* than are the brains of individuals with other kinds of dementia (Anderson, 2013a). Neurofibrillary tangles are stringy masses of tissue that appear to "clog" connections between neurons. They are typically surrounded by deposits of proteins and other substances called *plaques*.

The difficulty involved in diagnosing Alzheimer's disease is magnified by the fact that a great many elderly individuals complain of memory problems (Anderson, 2013a). As a result, researchers are currently looking for a set of predictors that may distinguish individuals who are in the process of developing Alzheimer's from those who are experiencing the effects of normal aging. A few indicators, such as the syndrome known as *mild cognitive impairment*, show promise (see *Research Report*). At present, though, a diagnosis of Alzheimer's disease represents a health professional's best educated guess about the source of an individual's cognitive difficulties.

A few drugs—such as *galantamine*, a drug that increases the amounts of some neurotransmitters in the brain—appear to slow down progress of Alzheimer's disease (Anderson, 2013a). Experimental studies have shown that training people with Alzheimer's to use specific strategies (e.g., making notes in a journal) can to some degree improve their performance of everyday memory tasks such as associating names with faces and remembering to take medication (Lowenstein, Acevedo, Czaja, & Duara, 2004).

HEREDITY AND ALZHEIMER'S DISEASE Genetic factors seem to be important in some, but not all, cases of Alzheimer's (Anderson, 2013a). Researchers have found a gene on chromosome 19 (apolipoprotein E, or ApoE) that controls production of a protein that is linked to Alzheimer's disease (Anderson, 2013a). When errors in the production of this protein occur, the dendrites and axons of neurons in the brain become tangled and, as a result, do not function as efficiently as they once did. However, this gene does not act alone. Many other genes combine with ApoE in ways that researchers don't yet fully understand to trigger the onset of the disease (Bertram, McQueen, Mullin, Blacker, & Tanzi, 2007; Reiman et al., 2007).

Even in families with very high prevalences of Alzheimer's disease, ages of onset are highly variable. In one family study, age of onset ranged from 44 to 67 years, and in another, onset ranged from the early 60s to the mid-80s (Axelman, Basum, & Lannfelt, 1998; Silverman, Ciresi, Smith, Marin, & Schnaider-Beeri, 2005). Moreover, there were wide variations in the severity of the behavioral effects of the disease and in the length of time the people lived once they developed Alzheimer's.

OTHER TYPES OF DEMENTIA Strictly speaking, dementia is a symptom and not a disease, and neurological research indicates that Alzheimer's and non-Alzheimer's dementias involve very different disease processes. For example, signs of dementia frequently appear after a person experiences multiple small strokes; in this case, the condition is called **vascular dementia** (Kannayiram, 2012). The brain damage caused by such strokes is irreversible. However, in contrast to the situation with most cases of Alzheimer's disease, various forms of therapy—occupational, recreational, and physical—can improve victims' functioning (see *Developmental Science in the Clinic* on page 431).

vascular dementia a form of dementia caused by one or more strokes

RESEARCH REPORT

Mild Cognitive Impairment and Alzheimer's Disease

When an elder seeks help for memory problems or difficulties with logical thinking but is clearly not experiencing any kind of dementia, health-care professionals usually try to determine whether he should be diagnosed with *mild cognitive impairment* (*MCI*) or with *age-associated cognitive decline* (*AACD*). Criteria for both diagnoses include a gradual decline in cognitive function along with low scores on standardized tests (compared to scores of others of the same age). Physicians must also rule out the possibility that the individual is experiencing a specific disorder that might account for his symptoms (e.g., brain tumor, stroke, depression). Of the two disorders, AACD is the more common, afflicting just under one-third of older adults (Hanninen et al., 1996). By contrast, MCI is found in about 10% of elders in their 70s and 25% of those in their 80s (Anderson, 2013b).

The procedures involved in determining which diagnosis is appropriate can take several weeks to complete and must usually be repeated a few months later. Although this process can be frustrating for elderly adults and their caregivers, getting the correct diagnosis is important because MCI is believed to be a precursor to Alzheimer's disease, while AACD is not (Bannon, Boswell, & Schneider, 2010). Thus, the prognosis for individuals with MCI is quite different from that for elders with AACD. Moreover, many researchers think that the progression to dementia in patients with MCI can be slowed or even prevented through the use of drugs that have shown to be effective against fully developed Alzheimer's (Amieva et al., 2004; Maruyama et al., 2003).

However, the idea that MCI is an early stage in the development of Alzheimer's disease is somewhat controversial. Some of the strongest evidence in favor of the stage hypothesis has involved brain-imaging and DNA studies. Generally, imaging studies show similar patterns of brain degeneration in individuals with MCI and Alzheimer's disease (Johnson, Vogt, Kim, Cotmam, & Head, 2004), and these patterns appear to be distinguishable from those associated with both normal aging and other kinds of dementia. Similarly, defects in the *apolipoprotein E* gene are strongly associated with both Alzheimer's disease and MCI (Tervo et al., 2004).

Additional support for the stage view comes from other kinds of physiological research. For example, individuals with either MCI or Alzheimer's disease differ from typically aging older adults in the degree to which free-radical-fighting substances such as vitamin C are present in their bloodstreams (Rinaldi et al., 2003). Further, studies examining substances in the cerebrospinal fluid of normal elderly adults, elders with MCI, and those with Alzheimer's indicate that both MCI and Alzheimer's are associated with rapid neuronal death (Maruyama et al., 2003).

Despite these compelling lines of evidence, it is abundantly clear that MCI does not inevitably lead to Alzheimer's disease. Longitudinal studies show that only one-third of adults aged 70 and over exhibit full-blown dementia within 2 years of receiving the diagnosis of MCI (Amieva et al., 2004). In addition, the cognitive functioning of many of those with MCI remains entirely stable for many years.

Scientists on both sides of the debate about the nature of the MCI–Alzheimer's link agree that continued research into the correlation between the two is important to discovering the disease process that underlies the symptoms of Alzheimer's disease. Such research could lead to preventive measures that spare many of those with MCI from this devastating disease.

CRITICAL ANALYSIS

1. *In what way is research on the links among AACD, MCI, and Alzheimer's disease related to the issues discussed in the No Easy Answers box on page 419?*

2. *In your opinion, to what degree might misdiagnosis of AACD as MCI contribute to the finding that only one-third of individuals who are diagnosed with MCI develop full-blown Alzheimer's disease?*

In addition, dementia can be caused by depression, cardiovascular disease, metabolic disturbances, drug intoxication, Parkinson's disease, hypothyroidism, multiple blows to the head (frequent among boxers), a single head trauma, some kinds of tumors, vitamin B12 deficiency, anemia, or alcohol abuse (Anthony & Aboraya, 1992; Butters et al., 2004; Suryadevara, Storey, Aronow, & Ahn, 2003). Clearly, many of these causes are treatable; indeed, roughly 10% of all those evaluated for dementia turn out to have some reversible problem. So, when an older person shows signs of dementia, it is critical to arrange for a careful diagnosis.

GROUP DIFFERENCES IN THE RATES OF DEMENTIA Evidence from research in nations across the globe shows that somewhere between 2 and 8% of all adults over age 60 exhibit significant symptoms of some kind of dementia (Prince et al., 2013). Experts also agree that the rates of all kinds of dementias, including Alzheimer's disease, rise rapidly among people in their 70s and 80s. For instance, studies in the United States suggest that 19% of 75- to 84-year-olds have Alzheimer's disease, while 42% of adults over the age of 85 have it (Alzheimer's Association, 2007).

Base rates of dementia vary despite the consistency of age trends across groups. For instance, Alzheimer's disease is less prevalent in Africa than it is in the United States. Yet African Americans exhibit higher rates of the disease than White Americans do (Hendrie, 2006). Studies show that such variations are associated with group differences in the frequencies of the genes that contribute to Alzheimer's disease, in experiential factors such as education, and in rates of vascular disease (Green et al., 2002).

Computers in Rehabilitation Programs

Although her children and grandchildren had been urging her for a long time to get a computer, at 75, Leta believed that she had little need for one. Then, when she had a mild stroke, Leta learned that computers have uses far beyond the e-mail tools and online information sources that her family had encouraged her to learn how to use. The rehabilitation specialists who helped Leta recover showed her how to use them to overcome the language deficits that had resulted from her stroke. Leta enjoyed the computer training sessions so much that she decided that her family was right about her need for a computer and about their insistence that she join the millions of other senior citizens who have embraced the information age.

Computers are becoming increasingly important in the treatment of neurological disorders affecting the elderly. For example, many stroke victims have problems with comprehending speech and/or speaking themselves. Researchers

have found that computerized speech-rehabilitation programs are highly effective at improving the language skills of such people (e.g., Propopenko et al., 2013). Virtual-reality programs also help people recover motor functions after a stroke (Teasell & Kalra, 2004).

People with dementia benefit from computerized rehabilitation as well (Cipriani, Bianchetti, & Trabucchi, 2005). For example, one program

trains those with Alzheimer's and other types of dementia to remember routes from one place to another by guiding them through a virtual apartment. Neuropsychologists report that practicing route-learning in the virtual environment improves these patients' ability to remember such routes in their own living environments (Schreiber, Lutz, Schweizer, Kalveram, & Jaencke, 1998; Schreiber, Schweizer, Lutz, Kalveram, & Jaencke, 1999).

REFLECTION

1. *If you worked in a rehabilitation facility and had to convince a technophobic older adult to participate in a computer-based program, what strategies would you use to persuade the patient to give the new technology a try?*

2. *How do you think computers might be useful to older adults who complain of everyday memory problems?*

Depression

LO 17.8 What does research suggest about depression among older adults?

The earliest studies of age differences in depression suggested that older adults were at higher risk for this disorder than any other age group, which contributed to a widespread cultural stereotype of the inevitably depressed elder. Certainly, suicide statistics suggest that depression increases in old age (see Figure 17.3). However, the full story on depression in late adulthood is complex. ⊙ **Watch** the **Video** *Depression in Later Life* in **MyPsychLab**.

PREVALENCE AND RISK FACTORS Rates of depression rise somewhat across the years of late adulthood. About 12% of 65- to 69-year-olds have the diagnosis, compared to about 18% of those over 85 (FIFARS, 2012). The risk factors for depression among the elderly include inadequate social support, inadequate income, emotional loss (such as following the death of spouse, family, or friends), and nagging health problems. However, the strongest predictor appears to be health status. Across all ethnic and socioeconomic groups, the more disabling conditions older adults have, the more depressive symptoms they have (Emptage, Sturm, & Robinson, 2005). Determining the direction of causation in the association between health status and depression is difficult because depression impairs an older adult's ability to respond to therapeutic interventions that might be helpful (Mast, Azar, MacNeil, & Lichtenberg, 2004). To put it differently, elders who have chronic health conditions such as arthritis are more likely to have depression than their peers who do not, but depression is a risk factor for a poor response to therapy. Thus, for many elderly adults, the link between health and depression becomes circular.

As is true of younger adults, in adults over the age of 65, depression rates are higher among women (16%) than among men (11%) (FIFARS, 2012). It's not easy, however, to sort out the causes of this difference. One possible explanation is that women are more willing to seek help for depression and, as a result, are more often diagnosed.

Figure 17.3 Gender Differences in Suicide Rates

The data on which this figure is based indicate that suicide rates increase substantially in old age among men but remain fairly stable among women.

(*Sources:* NCHS, 2009.)

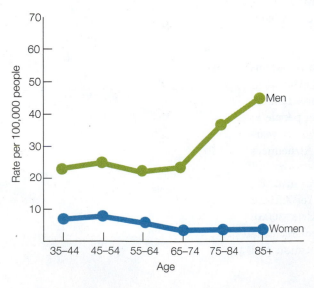

There is a fair amount of consistency in findings that elders living in poverty are at higher risk for depression than others (Areán et al., 2010). Education is also independently related to depression; that is, poorly educated older adults are more likely to have depression (Gallagher-Thompson, Tazeau, & Basilio, 1997; Miech & Shanahan, 2000). The association between education and depression exists among elderly adults at all levels of income and in all racial and ethnic groups.

African American elders may be less likely to be depressed than their peers in other ethnic groups because they may treat sad feelings as a spiritual issue rather than a mental health problem.

ETHNIC AND CULTURAL DIFFERENCES Poverty and education account for only some of the ethnic differences in depression among older adults. Other differences are explained by health status. That is, on average, minorities have poorer health than Whites in the United States; so, on average, most minority groups have higher rates of depression.

For example, some studies have found rates of depression as high as 37% among elderly Korean Americans (Kang, Basham, & Kim, 2013). Similarly, the rate of depression among Chinese American and Mexican American elders may be near 20% (Black et al., 1998; Lam et al., 1997). There is an association between health and depression in these groups, just as there is in others (Schneider, 2004). However, researchers point out that, in addition, many older Asian Americans and Mexican Americans are recent immigrants to the United States, have poor English skills, and report feeling distressed and anxious about the differences between their home cultures and that of the United States. These factors may help explain their higher incidence of depression (Kang et al., 2013). This means that the longer older Asian American and Mexican American immigrants have been in the United States, and the better integrated they are into the society, the less likely they are to have depression.

Depressive symptoms appear to occur much less often in African Americans (Akincigil et al., 2012). For example, a study of several thousand men admitted to veterans' hospitals revealed that African Americans were half as likely as Whites to be depressed (Kales, Blow, Bingham, Copeland, & Mellow, 2000). Furthermore, a study in which researchers reviewed the medical records of several hundred African American and White American patients produced similar findings (Leo et al., 1997). However, in both studies, researchers found that elderly African Americans were more likely than elderly White Americans to have schizophrenia. In addition, among those older African Americans who have depression, the tendency toward suicidal thoughts may be greater than it is among older White Americans with depression (Leo et al., 1997).

Researchers often attribute low rates of depression in African Americans to underdiagnosis. They hypothesize that African Americans' lack of access to mental health services, reluctance to seek help, and unwillingness to take antidepressant medications contribute to underdiagnosis (Blazer, Hybels, Simonsick, & Hanlon, 2000; Steffens, Artigues, Ornstein, & Krishnan, 1997). Importantly, too, research indicates that physicians are no more or less likely to diagnose depression in African Americans than in people in other ethnic groups, given the same symptom profiles (Kales et al., 2005).

Some developmentalists argue that cultural differences between African Americans and other groups are responsible for differences in depression rates. Specifically, African Americans are more likely to view feelings of sadness as a spiritual issue rather than a mental health problem. Research examining the association between depression and religious beliefs and activities has shown that the tendency to turn to faith and the church for support in times of emotional difficulty is much more prevalent among African Americans than among White Americans (Jang, Borenstein, Chiriboga, & Mortimer, 2005; Chatters, Taylor, Jackson, & Lincoln, 2008). In fact, research demonstrates that religious faith and practice are associated with lower incidences of long-term depression in most ethnic groups, no matter what religion is considered (Braam, Beekman, Deeg, Smit, & van Tilburg, 1997; Idler & Kasl, 1997a; Meisenhelder & Chandler, 2000; Musick, Koenig, Hays, & Cohen, 1998; Tapanya, Nicki, & Jarusawad, 1997). And, as you will learn in Chapter 18, these effects are a result of the way elders think about their lives in religious terms rather than being due to self-selection or the social support provided to elders by religious institutions.

Interacting with children may help prevent depression in late adulthood.

SUICIDE Despite higher rates of depression among women and some minority groups in the United States, elderly White men are more likely to commit suicide than any other group (NCHS, 2009). Thus, White males are largely responsible for the dramatic increase with age in male suicide illustrated in Figure 17.3. However, the overall age-related pattern of sex differences indicated by the figure exists among minority groups as well (NCHS, 2009).

The reasons for this dramatic sex difference are not entirely clear. The loss of economic status through retirement may be more troubling for men than for women in present cohorts of the elderly because traditional socialization patterns may have led men to equate earnings with self-worth (Mooney, Knox, & Schacht, 2000). Similarly, declining health may cause an elderly man to view himself as a burden on others. Finally, as is true of younger people, older women attempt suicide more often than older men do, but the men complete the act more often, mostly because they are more likely than women to choose violent methods such as using firearms.

THERAPY, MEDICATION, AND PREVENTION Therapies for depression are the same for older adults as for those who are younger. Psychotherapy is often recommended, especially interventions that help people with depression develop optimistic thought patterns (Leatherman & McCarty, 2005). However, as with younger adults, therapy appears to be most effective when combined with antidepressant medications (Leatherman & McCarthy, 2005).

Experts point out that appropriate use of antidepressant medications among the elderly is critical. For one thing, antidepressants may reduce the effectiveness of the life-sustaining drugs some older adults take (NIA, 2000a). In addition, antidepressants are linked to an increased incidence of falls among the institutionalized elderly. One study found a remarkable 80% increase in falls in a group of more than 2,000 nursing home residents who began taking antidepressants (Bender, 1999). However, studies have shown that elders taking antidepressants are at increased risk for falling only during the first few days after initiation of antidepressant therapy (Berry et al., 2011). Consequently, some experts argue that, with increased monitoring by facility staff, elders with depression who live in nursing homes can be safely and successfully treated with antidepressant medications.

Social involvement may be important in preventing depression in the elderly. For example, in one study, researchers in Mexico examined how participation in activities with children, such as attending children's plays or helping plan children's parties, might affect nursing home residents' emotions (Saavedra, Ramirez, & Contreras, 1997). Researchers found that such activities significantly improved participants' emotional states. So periodic involvement with children might be an effective way to prevent depression in institutionalized elders. Likewise, *pet therapy* or *animal-assisted therapy* has been shown to be effective at improving institutionalized elders' quality of life (Menna et al., 2012).

In addition, research on the connection between religion and depression suggests that caretakers can help elders avoid depression by supporting their spiritual needs. Many older adults need help getting to religious services; those who live in institutions may need to have services brought to them. Declines in vision may mean that an elderly person can no longer read religious books and may deeply appreciate having someone read to him or provide him with recordings. Helping elders maintain religious faith and practice in these ways may be an important key to reducing depression rates.

---

test yourself before going on   **Study** and **Review** in **MyPsychLab**

Answers to these questions can be found in the back of the book.

1. Declines in cognitive functioning that appear after a person has several small strokes are called _____ _____.

2. The entire cluster of depressive symptoms occurs less frequently among older _____ _____ than in their peers in other ethnic groups.

CRITICAL THINKING

3. Many of the techniques that mental health professionals use require them to empathize with and develop trusting relationships with the people whom they are trying to help. In what ways do the characteristics of Alzheimer's disease and depression interfere with mental health professionals' efforts to do so with people who have those characteristics?

Cognitive Changes

Among the young old (aged 65–75), cognitive changes are still fairly small, and these older adults show little or no average decline on a few measures, such as vocabulary knowledge. But the old old and the oldest old show average declines on virtually all measures of intellectual skill, with the largest declines evident on any measures that involve speed or unexercised abilities (Cunningham & Haman, 1992; Giambra et al., 1995). Such declines in cognitive functioning are distressing to elders and represent one of the most important threats to older adults' overall sense of well-being (Wilson et al., 2013).

Memory

LO 17.9   What kinds of memory differences distinguish older and younger adults?

As you learned in Chapter 15, and as Figure 17.4 shows, forgetfulness becomes more frequent with age (Ponds, Commissaris, & Jolles, 1997). However, it's important to remember that the same basic rules seem to apply to memory processes among both older and younger adults. For both groups, for example, recognition is easier than recall, tasks that require speed are more difficult, and metamemory skills are important to memory function (Olin & Zelinski, 1997). Further, in many studies, older adults achieve scores very similar to those of younger adults on tests of memory accuracy, although they typically take longer to complete memory tasks and make more errors (Babiloni et al., 2004). Nevertheless, training programs designed to increase elders' information-processing speed have demonstrated the role that experience plays in the speed with which individuals perform memory tasks (Edwards, Ruva, O'Brien, Haley, & Lister, 2013). Consequently, we should not assume that losses in speed of processing are entirely due to biological aging, nor are they necessarily inevitable or permanent.

SHORT-TERM MEMORY FUNCTION   One area in which researchers see significant changes in late adulthood is in short-term, or working, memory capacity (Hester, Kinsella, & Ong, 2004; Jenkins, Myerson, Hale, & Fry, 1999). You should remember from earlier chapters that there is a limitation on the number of items a person can retain in her memory at once. The more pieces of information she has to handle, the more she forgets, and the poorer her performance on memory and other kinds of cognitive tasks. Thus, the more any given cognitive task makes demands on working memory, the larger the decline with age.

Figure 17.4 Percentage of Older Adults with Moderate to Severe Memory Impairment

The prevalence of memory problems increases as older adults age.

(*Source:* FIFARS, 2006.)

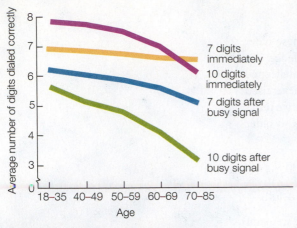

Figure 17.5 West and Crook's Classic Study of Memory across Adulthood

The graph shows the results from West and Crook's classic study of memory for telephone numbers. Notice that there is no loss of memory in middle adulthood for the most common condition: a 7-digit number dialed immediately. But if the number of digits increases or if you have to remember the number a bit longer, some decline in memory begins around age 50 or 60.

(*Source:* West & Crook, 1990, from Table 3, p. 524.)

Figure 17.6 Strategic Learning in Later Adulthood

These results from Kliegel's classic study show that older adults can learn complex information-processing skills and improve their performance after training, but they don't gain as much as younger adults do. However, this study also suggests that, given enough time, older adults can learn new strategies.

(*Source:* Adapted from R. Kliegel, J. Smith, and P. B. Baltes, "On the Locus and Process of Magnification of Age Differences during Mnemonic Training," *Developmental Psychology*, Vol. 26, Fig. 2, p. 899. Copyright © 1990 by the American Psychological Association. Adapted with permission.)

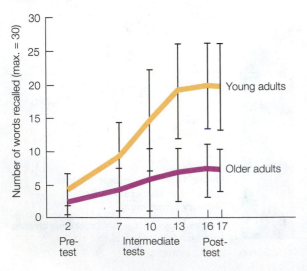

A good illustration comes from a study involving a familiar, everyday task—remembering telephone numbers (West & Crook, 1990). Participants were shown a series of 7-digit or 10-digit telephone numbers on a computer screen, one at a time. The participant said each number as it appeared; then the number disappeared from the screen, and the participant had to dial the number she had just seen on a pushbutton phone attached to the computer. On some trials, the participants got a busy signal when they first dialed and then had to dial the number over again. Figure 17.5 shows the relationship between age and the correct recall of the phone numbers under these four conditions.

Notice that there is essentially no decline with age in immediate recall of a normal 7-digit telephone number (the equivalent of what you do when you look up a number in the phone book, say it to yourself as you read it, and then dial it immediately). When the length of the number increases to the 10 digits used for long-distance numbers, however, a decline with age becomes evident, beginning at about age 60. And with even a brief delay between saying the number and dialing it, the decline occurs earlier.

However, patterns of age differences are not identical for all memory tasks. For example, older adults typically perform more poorly than younger adults on tasks involving *retrospective memory*, or recalling something in the past (Henry, MacLeod, Phillips, & Crawford, 2004). By contrast, older adults' performance on *prospective memory tasks* (which require individuals to remember to do something in the future) depends on the type of task involved. On laboratory prospective memory tasks that have little relevance to everyday life, young adults do somewhat better than elders. However, several naturalistic studies have shown that older adults outperform those who are younger on everyday memory tasks of this kind (Henry et al., 2004; Rendell & Thomson, 1999). Likewise, older adults often show superior recall on memory tasks that tap into general knowledge, such as remembering words in the context of complex sentences (Matzen & Benjamin, 2013).

STRATEGY LEARNING   A classic study of older adults in Germany provides a good example of research findings on strategy learning and memory in older adults (Baltes & Kliegl, 1992; Kliegl, Smith, & Baltes, 1990). Researchers tested 18 college students and 19 older, but physically healthy, adults who ranged in age from 65 to 80, with an average age of 71.7 years. Participants were shown sets of pictures of 30 familiar buildings in Berlin and asked to use the pictures to create associations that would help them remember a list of 30 words. For example, a castle might be paired with the word "bicycle." A typical association would be to imagine someone riding a bicycle in front of a castle. The pictures in each set were displayed for different amounts of time, ranging from 20 seconds each to 1 second each. After participants attempted to learn each list of words, the experimenters asked what images they had used and suggested possible improvements. Training sessions were interspersed with test sessions to check on the participants' progress.

Figure 17.6 shows the results for pictures and words presented at 5-second intervals. You can see that the older adults showed improvement after training, but their performance was poorer than that of younger adults. These findings suggest that the learning process simply takes longer for older adults—more time is needed to create the mental image and to link that image up with the word in the list. However, when older adults were allowed more time to associate each picture and word, their performance was more like that of younger participants. 👁 **Watch** the **Video** *Memory and Exercise* in **MyPsychLab**.

EVERYDAY MEMORY   One common argument from those who take an optimistic view of the effects of aging on cognitive functioning is that older adults may be able to remember just as well as younger adults but may simply be less motivated to memorize lists of unrelated words given to them by researchers in a laboratory. However, on virtually all everyday tasks—remembering the main points of a story or a newspaper article; recalling movies, conversations, grocery lists, or recipes; recalling the information from a medicine label; remembering whether they did something ("Did I turn off the stove before I left the house?"); or remembering where they heard something (called *source memory*)— older adults perform less well than younger adults (Dixon, Rust, Feltmate, & See, 2007). These results have been found in longitudinal as well as cross-sectional studies (Craik, 2002). However, researchers have found that many older adults are quite skilled at using strategies such as written reminders that help them compensate for some of these losses (Delprado, Kinsella, Ong, & Pike, 2013).

Moreover, task-specific knowledge seems to make a difference among the elderly. For example, older adults who have larger vocabularies outperform peers who know fewer words on tasks involving rapid recognition of words (Kitzan, Ferraro, Petros, & Ludorf, 1999). Researchers know that prior knowledge is the critical factor in such findings because elders with large vocabularies perform just as poorly as their less knowledgeable peers on tasks involving nonsense words.

Older adults' memories function most proficiently when they are engaged in activities in which they have a great deal of prior experience, but they are still capable of learning new skills and strategies.

PRELIMINARY EXPLANATIONS How do researchers account for these changes in memory? Neuroimaging studies show that age-related memory decline is associated with changes in the ratio of gray to white matter in the brain (Kramer et al., 2007). In addition, a reduction in the volume of the hippocampus is associated with memory deficits among the elderly.

Functionally speaking, forgetfulness among the elderly may result from the kind of general slowing that you read about earlier in the chapter. Older adults take longer to register some new piece of information, encode it, and retrieve it. Some of the clearest evidence of the important role of speed in memory decline in old age comes from an extensive series of studies by Timothy Salthouse (e.g., Salthouse, 2004, 2011).

Salthouse has tested both basic reaction speed and memory or other cognitive skills in adults of various ages. According to Salthouse, a very large portion of the age decline in memory can be attributed to the slower reaction times in older adults. He is convinced that the loss of speed occurs at the level of the central nervous system and not in the peripheral nerves. So physiological changes in neurons and the accompanying loss of nerve conductance speed may be the root causes of these changes in memory.

Virtually all experts now agree with Salthouse that loss of speed is a key aspect of the process of memory decline, and studies have shown that quantitative losses in speed of information processing very strongly predict qualitative changes in memory function (Verhaegen, 2013). But most also believe that speed is not the entire explanation. There appear to be other factors as well, such as changes in attention strategies that lead to less effective processing of information.

wisdom a cognitive characteristic that includes accumulated knowledge and the ability to apply that knowledge to practical problems of living, popularly thought to be more commonly found in older adults

Wisdom and Creativity

LO 17.10 What do theory and research on wisdom and creativity reveal about cognitive functioning in late adulthood?

Theorists who study cognition in older adults have begun to ask whether elders might have some advantages over the young because of their accumulation of knowledge and skills. In other words, older adults might be more wise. Researchers have not yet agreed on a common definition of wisdom, but most authors emphasize that it goes beyond mere accumulations of facts. **Wisdom** reflects understanding of "universal truths" or basic laws or patterns; it is knowledge that is blended with values and meaning systems; it is knowledge based on the understanding that clarity is not always possible, that unpredictability and uncertainty are part of life (Baltes & Kunzmann, 2004).

You may be wondering how researchers measure wisdom. The leading researcher in this field, Paul Baltes (1939–2006), devised a useful technique (Baltes & Staudinger, 2000). He presented research participants with stories about fictional characters who were trying to

Seeking advice from an elder who is presumed to be wise is one way younger individuals act on the belief that those who are older have accumulated knowledge and information that can benefit them.

make some major life decision. For example, one dilemma Baltes used involved a 15-year-old girl who wanted to get married. Participants' responses to the stories were judged according to five criteria Baltes hypothesized to be central to wisdom as it relates to solving practical life problems:

- Factual knowledge
- Procedural knowledge
- Understanding of the relevance of context
- Understanding of the relevance of values
- Recognition that it is impossible to know in advance how any decision will ultimately affect one's life

A person would be judged to be low in wisdom if her response were something like the following: "A 15-year-old getting married? That's stupid. I would tell the girl to forget about it until she's older." The answer of a person judged to be high in wisdom would be more complex. A wise person might point out, "There are circumstances when marriage at such a young age might be a good decision. Is she motivated by a desire to make a home for a child she is expecting? Also, the girl might come from a culture where marriage at 15 is quite common. You have to consider people's motivations and their backgrounds to understand their decisions. You also have to know how the person involved views the situation to be able to give advice."

Virtually all theorists who have written about wisdom assume that it is more likely to be found in the middle-aged and the elderly than in the young. However, Baltes has found that younger adults perform as well as older adults in response to the fictional dilemma task. In fact, Baltes has found that, rather than age, intelligence and professional experience are correlated with responses to the dilemma task. So, Baltes's research seems to suggest that the popular notion that age and wisdom are associated is probably not true. Wisdom does not appear to be a characteristic of the elderly that distinguishes them from other subgroups of adults.

Critics have suggested that Baltes is simply measuring general cognitive ability rather than what is usually thought of as wisdom. Nevertheless, Baltes's research has produced an important finding about wisdom and old age: In contrast to performance on information-processing tasks such as memorizing nonsense words, performance on wisdom tasks does not decline with age (Baltes & Staudinger, 2000). Moreover, the speed of accessing wisdom-related knowledge remains constant across adulthood, unlike the speed of information processing in other domains.

Enhanced creativity may also be an element of cognition in older adults. As you learned in Chapter 15, some highly creative individuals, especially composers and artists, reach their peak in late adulthood. To describe the potential for creative work in the later years, a leading gerontologist, Gene Cohen, has developed a four-stage theory of mid- to late-life creativity (Cohen, 2000). Cohen's theory has been the basis of successful art therapy programs for elderly adults with a variety of psychological problems (Malchiodi, 2012).

Cohen believes that these phases apply to ordinary people who are more creative than others in their everyday lives as well as to "professional creators" such as composers and artists. Cohen proposes that at around age 50, creative individuals enter a *reevaluation phase*, during which they reflect on past accomplishments and formulate new goals. The reevaluation process, along with an increasing sense of time limitations, leads to an intensification of the desire to create and produce. During the next stage, the *liberation phase*, individuals in their 60s become freer to create because most have retired from everyday work. Most are also more tolerant of their own failures and thus are willing to take risks they would not have taken when younger. In the *summing-up phase*, creative people in their 70s have a desire to knit their accomplishments together into a cohesive, meaningful story. They begin to view their early accomplishments in terms of how they prefigured later achievements. Finally, in the *encore phase*, during the 80s and beyond, there is a desire to complete unfinished works or to fulfill desires that have been put aside in the past.

Answers to these questions can be found in the back of the book.

1. What two factors were found by West and Crook's study of older adults' ability to recall digits?
2. According to Baltes, what are the five elements of wisdom?

CRITICAL THINKING

3. Make a list of the people you think of as wise. How old are they? Is old age necessary for wisdom? If not, how do you think wisdom is acquired?

SUMMARY

Variability in Late Adulthood (pp. 418–423)

LO 17.1 **What factors contribute to life expectancy and longevity?**

- Developmentalists group the elderly into three subgroups: the young old (60–75), the old old (75–85), and the oldest old (85 and older). The oldest old are the fastest-growing group of the elderly in the United States. Heredity, overall health, current and prior health habits (particularly exercise), and availability of adequate social support influence longevity.

LO 17.2 **What variables contribute to individual differences in health among older adults?**

- Most elders view their health status positively. With increasing age, the proportion of elders whose health interferes with activities of living rises. Chronic diseases such as arthritis and hypertension afflict many older adults.

Physical Changes (pp. 423–429)

LO 17.3 **How does the brain change in late adulthood?**

- Changes in the brain associated with aging include, most centrally, a loss of dendritic density of neurons, which has the effect of slowing reaction time for almost all tasks.

LO 17.4 **What types of sensory changes occur in late adulthood?**

- Older adults have more difficulty adapting to darkness and light than do younger adults. Loss of hearing is more common and more noticeable after 65 than at earlier ages. Taste discrimination remains largely unchanged with age, but ability to discriminate smells declines substantially in late adulthood.

LO 17.5 **How do theories explain biological aging?**

- Theories of biological aging emphasize the possible existence of genetic limiting mechanisms and/or the cumulative effects of malfunctions within cells. One proposal involves the Hayflick limit, a genetic mechanism that imposes time limits on the capacity of the body's cells to reproduce. Other proposals claim that programmed senescence, cross-linking, free radicals, and terminal decline strongly influence the aging process.

LO 17.6 **What are the behavioral effects of changes in the various body systems of older adults?**

- General slowing alters behavior in old age and makes tasks such as driving more dangerous. Older adults also change their sleeping and eating patterns. Motor abilities decline, causing more accidents due to falls. Sexual activity also decreases in frequency, although most older adults continue to be sexually active.

Mental Health (pp. 429–434)

LO 17.7 **What is Alzheimer's disease, and how does it differ from other dementias?**

- Dementia is rare before late adulthood, and it becomes steadily more common with advancing age. The most common cause of dementia is Alzheimer's disease. It is difficult to diagnose definitively, and its causes are not fully understood. Neurofibrillary tangles are far more likely to be present in the brains of individuals with Alzheimer's disease than in those of people with other types of dementia.

LO 17.8 **What does research suggest about depression among older adults?**

- Mild or moderate depression appears to rise in frequency after age 70 or 75. Serious clinical depression, however, does not appear to become more common in old age. Ethnic groups vary in rates of depression, with older African Americans being the least likely to be depressed.

Cognitive Changes (pp. 435–439)

LO 17.9 **What kinds of memory differences distinguish older and younger adults?**

- The elderly experience difficulties in a variety of mental processes, which appear to reflect a general slowing of the nervous system and perhaps a loss of working-memory capacity.

LO 17.10 **What do theory and research on wisdom and creativity reveal about cognitive functioning in late adulthood?**

- Wisdom and creativity may be important aspects of cognitive functioning in old age. According to Baltes, decision making that is characterized by wisdom includes factual knowledge, procedural knowledge, an understanding of the relevance of context, an understanding of the relevance of values, and recognition that it is impossible to know in advance how a decision will affect one's life. Cohen proposed that creative individuals over the age of 50 pass through a series of stages in which they evaluate and reshape their lives.

KEY TERMS

activities of daily living (ADLs) (p. 421)
Alzheimer's disease (p. 429)
cross-linking (p. 426)
dementia (p. 429)
frail elderly (p. 421)

free radicals (p. 426)
gerontology (p. 418)
Hayflick limit (p. 425)
instrumental activities of daily living (IADLs) (p. 421)

programmed senescence theory (p. 426)
satiety (p. 428)
synaptic plasticity (p. 424)
telomere (p. 426)

terminal decline hypothesis (p. 427)
tinnitus (p. 424)
vascular dementia (p. 430)
wisdom (p. 437)

CHAPTER TEST   ✓ Study and Review in MyPsychLab

Answers to all the Chapter Test questions can be found in the back of the book.

1. Some researchers suggest that African Americans have lower rates of depression than White Americans because they are especially likely to utilize _____ when dealing with emotional difficulties.
   a. their religious faith and their church
   b. physical exercise
   c. antidepressant medications and mental health services
   d. a social support network of friends

2. Which of these factors was identified as an important contributor to health status among participants in the Alameda County study?
   a. physical activity
   b. socialization
   c. calorie restriction
   d. familial support

3. Which of the following is the name of the theory which says that aging is a result of species-specific genes?
   a. the Hayflick limit
   b. telomeric theory
   c. race-specific DNA theory
   d. programmed senescence theory

4. Which of the following is definitively diagnostic of Alzheimer's disease?
   a. the presence of neurofibrillatory tangles in the brain
   b. the presence of plaque in the arteries of the brain
   c. changes seen on an MRI scan as the person is showing cognitive declines
   d. the presence of chronic mild dementia

5. Mr. Garrett often overeats, complaining that he feels hungry all the time. His doctor has suggested that this problem is due to a malfunction in the sensation associated with blood-sugar levels known as _____.
   a. deprivation
   b. satiety
   c. diabetes
   d. insulin

6. Which of the following is true regarding the risk factors for depression among the elderly?
   a. Elders who live in poverty are at a higher risk for depression than others.
   b. The strongest predictor of depression and dysthymia among older persons is marital status.

   c. Among the elderly, depressed men outnumber depressed women two to one.
   d. Well-educated older adults are more likely to be depressed.

7. Which of the following does research indicate to be the strongest predictor of depression among older adults?
   a. loss of a spouse
   b. poor health
   c. other forms of mental illness
   d. loss of income

8. Which of the following is likely to be true of older adults who are experiencing hearing loss?
   a. They are likely to be women.
   b. They are likely to be socially isolated and unhappy.
   c. They may be perceived as disoriented or forgetful.
   d. They may be clinically depressed.

9. Which of the following is true regarding the life expectancies of African and White Americans by age 75?
   a. There is not enough data on this age group to know.
   b. White Americans have longer life expectancies than African Americans.
   c. African Americans have longer life expectancies than White Americans.
   d. Their life expectancies will be essentially equivalent.

10. Which statement about mild cognitive impairment (MCI) and Alzheimer's disease is true?
    a. Almost all seniors who develop MCI eventually develop dementia.
    b. MCI is not necessarily a sign that an older adult is developing Alzheimer's disease.
    c. MCI is more difficult to diagnose than Alzheimer's disease.
    d. Some older adults with an Alzheimer's diagnosis may actually have MCI instead.

11. Which of the following is *not* likely to affect sexual activity in older age?
    a. lack of interest
    b. declining testosterone levels
    c. overall health
    d. medications

12. Which of the following terms applies to intellectually demanding tasks such as managing finances and paying bills?
    a. instrumental personal tasks
    b. instrumental activities of daily living
    c. daily tasks
    d. activities of daily living

13. Which of the following changes in vision is associated with aging?
    a. increased capacity to adapt to changes in vision
    b. declining risk of glaucoma
    c. decrease in serious diseases of the retina
    d. deterioration of night vision

14. Which of the following suggests that all adults retain excellent function until their physical and mental functioning plummets in the few years before death?
    a. the spiral hypothesis
    b. the terminal decline hypothesis
    c. the downward trajectory hypothesis
    d. the final rest hypothesis

15. This chapter suggests that burns are more common in late adulthood than earlier. Why?
    a. Impaired ability to concentrate or focus on complex tasks leads to an increased incidence of various injuries, including burns.
    b. An older person's skin is more heat responsive and less able to withstand a level of temperature that would have been tolerated earlier.
    c. Loss of sensitivity to heat and a slower reaction time lead to increases in accidental burns.
    d. Older persons cook for themselves more often and thus have more opportunity to be injured.

16. What is the single largest factor that determines the trajectory of an adult's physical or mental status beyond age 65?
    a. social support system   c. health
    b. socioeconomic status   d. marital status

17. Which of the following is the *best* definition of Alzheimer's disease?
    a. the mental deterioration that strikes the oldest old and the frail elderly
    b. a more severe variation of Wernicke's syndrome
    c. a severe form of dementia for which the cause is unknown
    d. the late stage of alcohol-induced dementia

18. Which of the following senses is least likely to change because of physical deterioration in old age?
    a. hearing   c. taste
    b. vision   d. smell

19. Which of the following is *not* a benefit of foods that are high in antioxidants?
    a. somewhat increased longevity
    b. improvements in vision for patients with retinal degeneration
    c. lower rates of heart disease
    d. decreased terminal decline period

20. How are the length of time spent in the United States and depression correlated among elderly Chinese and Hispanic immigrants?
    a. They are positively correlated.
    b. There is a positive correlation among Hispanic immigrants and a negative correlation among Chinese immigrants.
    c. They are not correlated.
    d. They are negatively correlated.

21. Which of the following is *not* one of the diseases of vision found in later adulthood?
    a. glaucoma
    b. retinal pigmentosis
    c. macular degeneration
    d. cataracts

22. What have researchers learned about calorie restriction in late adulthood?
    a. It decreases life expectancy.
    b. It interferes with metabolic functioning.
    c. It improves biological markers of aging.
    d. It damages the cardiovascular system.

23. Ninety-year-old Mrs. Gonzalez is no longer able to manage tasks such as bathing or using the toilet by herself but can still manage activities such as paying her bills on her own. A gerontologist most likely would determine that Mrs. Gonzalez needs help with _____.
    a. independence skills
    b. activities of daily living
    c. both activities of daily living and her instrumental activities of daily living
    d. instrumental activities of daily living

24. Which of the following terms refers to the redundancy in the nervous system that enables neural pathways to move from one set of neurons to another?
    a. neural redundancy   c. neural transporting
    b. synaptic plasticity   d. synaptic pruning

25. In the United States, which of these is the fastest-growing subgroup of older adults?
    a. young old   c. oldest old
    b. old old   d. centenarians

To 👁 **Watch** ✳ **Explore** 💿 **Simulate** ✅ **Study** and **Review** and experience MyVirtualLife go to MyPsychLab.com

chapter 18

Social and Personality Development in Late Adulthood

Now that you have reached your "golden" years in *MyVirtualLife*, what do you think about the decisions you made earlier in life about long-term relationships? There is little doubt that long-term social relationships, especially those in which partners are bound by deep bonds of affection, enhance our quality of life in late adulthood. But can you imagine being married for 80 years? Thanks to increases in longevity and the relatively young ages at which couples married in times past, an increasing number of elderly couples are

LEARNING OBJECTIVES

THEORIES OF SOCIAL AND PERSONALITY DEVELOPMENT

18.1 What does research say about Erikson's stage of ego integrity versus despair?

18.2 What are the main ideas of activity, disengagement, and continuity theory?

INDIVIDUAL DIFFERENCES

18.3 How is successful aging manifested in the lives of older adults?

18.4 How does religious coping influence physical and mental health in late adulthood?

SOCIAL RELATIONSHIPS

18.5 What are the living arrangements of most elderly people in the United States and in other industrialized countries?

18.6 How do intimate partnerships contribute to development in late adulthood?

18.7 What is the significance of family relationships and friendships for older adults?

18.8 What are some gender and ethnic differences in older adults' social networks?

CAREER ISSUES IN LATE LIFE

18.9 What factors contribute to the decision to retire?

18.10 How does retirement affect the lives of older adults?

celebrating their 60th, 70th, and even 80th anniversaries. According to the *Guinness Book of World Records*, Herbert and Zelmyra Fisher of Craven County, North Carolina, achieved the distinction of having the longest marriage in history when they celebrated their 85th anniversary in May 2010. Their marriage endured until Mr. Fisher passed away in 2011. Zelmyra followed in 2013.

No matter how long an older couple has been together, the emotional support that most elders derive from an intimate partnership helps them cope with the loudly ticking biological clock that reminds them every day that they aren't as young as they used to be. As you will learn in this chapter, changes in roles and relationships are perhaps just as significant as physical ones. And for many older adults, these changes are perceived not as losses but as opportunities to create new roles and to make old age a time of personal and social gains.

MyVirtualLife

What decisions would you make while living your life? What would the consequences of those decisions be?

Find out by accessing MyVirtualLife at www.MyPsychLab.com to live your own virtual life.

Theories of Social and Personality Development

If the social and personality changes of young adulthood can be described as "individuation" and those of middle adulthood can be described (more tentatively) as "mellowing," how might the changes of late adulthood be described? Several theorists have hypothesized specific forms of change, but there is little agreement among them and very little information supporting any of their theories.

Erikson's Stage of Ego Integrity versus Despair

LO 18.1 What does research say about Erikson's stage of ego integrity versus despair?

Erikson termed the last of his eight life crises the *ego-integrity-versus-despair stage*. He thought that the task of achieving **ego integrity**, the sense that one has lived a useful life, began in middle adulthood but was most central in late adulthood. To achieve ego integrity, the older adult must come to terms with who she is and has been, how her life has been lived, the choices she has made, and the opportunities gained and lost. The process also involves coming to terms with death and accepting its imminence. Erikson hypothesized that failure to achieve ego integrity in late adulthood would result in feelings of hopelessness and despair because there would be too little time to make changes before death.

Developmentalists have essentially no longitudinal or even cross-sectional data to suggest whether older adults are more likely than younger or middle-aged adults to achieve such self-acceptance. What they have instead are a few bits of information suggesting that adults become more reflective and somewhat more philosophical in orientation as they move through the late adulthood years (Prager, 1998). Moreover, those who use their growing capacity for philosophical reflection to achieve a degree of self-satisfaction are less fearful of death. There is also some evidence that older adults are more likely than young and middle-aged adults to respond to thwarted personal goals with feelings of sadness—a hint that the kind of despair Erikson talked about may be more common in old age than earlier in life (Levine & Bluck, 1997).

One aspect of Erikson's theory that has received much attention from researchers is the notion that the process of **reminiscence**—thinking about the past—is a necessary and healthy part of achieving ego integrity and thus an important aspect of old age and preparation for death. However, few developmentalists today would say that the only—or even the most important—purpose of these processes is to help an individual prepare for death. Instead, research has examined the link between reminiscence and health. Most studies focus on group therapies that provide participants with structured opportunities for reminiscence. Studies in a variety of cultures—Iran, China, the United States, Japan, and Portugal—have demonstrated that participating in a reminiscence group reduces elders' risk of depression and increases subjective quality-of-life ratings (Afonso, Bueno, Loureiro, & Pereira, 2011; Fukase & Okamoto, 2012; Majzoobi, Momeni,

ego integrity the feeling that one's life has been worthwhile

reminiscence reflecting on past experience

life review an evaluative process in which elders make judgments about past behavior

activity theory the idea that it is normal and healthy for older adults to try to remain as active as possible for as long as possible

disengagement theory the theory that it is normal and healthy for older adults to scale down their social lives and to separate themselves from others to a certain degree

Amani, & Khah, 2013; Zhou et al., 2012). There is also some evidence that reminiscence therapy improves cognitive functioning in individuals with dementia (Cotelli, Maneti, & Zanetti, 2012). Furthermore, researchers have found that structured reminiscence interviews involving college students and older adults are beneficial to both students and elders (Gallagher & Carey, 2012). Students' stereotypes about the elderly are challenged, and elders appreciate having had an opportunity to pass on their experiences to a young adult.

Among older adults, reminiscence is also the foundation for the process of **life review**, an evaluative process in which elders make judgments about their past behavior (Butler, 1963, 2002). Consistent with Erikson's view of the ego integrity/despair crisis, life review results in both positive and negative emotional outcomes, and the overall balance of positive and negative emotions that results from the life review process is correlated with elders' mental health. Researchers have found that elders whose life reviews produce more regrets over past mistakes and missed opportunities than satisfaction with how they handled problems earlier in life are more prone to depression than those who have generally positive feelings about their lives.

Other Theories of Late-Life Psychosocial Functioning

LO 18.2 What are the main ideas of activity, disengagement, and continuity theory?

As you learned in Chapter 16, the ideas of Paul and Margaret Baltes about selection, optimization, and compensation have been important in the study of middle-aged adults' psychosocial functioning. They are often applied to the study of older adults as well. Recall the Balteses' proposal that, as adults get older, they maintain high levels of performance by focusing on their strengths. In this way, they compensate for weaknesses.

Another theoretical perspective on old age focuses on whether it is normal, necessary, or healthy for older adults to remain active as long as possible, or whether the more typical and healthy pattern is some kind of gradual turning inward. The perspective typically referred to as **activity theory** argues that the psychologically and physically healthiest response to old age is to maintain the greatest possible level of activity and involvement in the greatest possible number of roles.

Activity theorists often cite research demonstrating that the most active older adults report slightly greater satisfaction with themselves or their lives, are healthiest, and have the highest morale (McIntosh & Danigelis, 1995; Park, 2009). The effect is not large, but its direction is consistently positive: Social involvement is linked to positive outcomes such as optimism and self-ratings of health (e.g., Maniecka-Bryla, Gajewska, Burzynska, & Bryla, 2013). Yet it is also true that every in-depth study of lifestyles of older adults identifies at least a few who lead socially isolated lives but remain contented, sometimes because they are engaged in an all-consuming hobby (e.g., Maas & Kuypers, 1974; Rubinstein, 1986).

Some older adults are quite content with solitary lives, but disengagement from social contacts is neither a typical nor an optimal choice for most elders.

An alternative theory on social and personality development in old age is disengagement theory, first proposed as a formulation of the central psychological process for older adults (Cumming, 1975; Cumming & Henry, 1961). **Disengagement theory** proposes that aging has three aspects:

- *Shrinkage of life space.* As people age, they interact with fewer and fewer others and fill fewer and fewer roles.

- *Increased individuality.* In the roles and relationships that remain, the older individual is much less governed by strict rules or expectations.

- *Acceptance of these changes.* The healthy older adult actively disengages from roles and relationships, turning increasingly inward and away from interactions with others.

The first two of these aspects seem largely beyond dispute. What has been controversial about disengagement theory is the third aspect.

Advocates argue that the normal and healthy response to the shrinkage of roles and relationships is for the older adult to step back still further, to stop seeking new roles, to spend more time alone, to turn inward. In essence, they propose a kind of personality change, not just a decline in involvement.

Although it is possible to choose a highly disengaged lifestyle in late adulthood and to find satisfaction in it, such disengagement is neither normal for the majority of older adults nor necessary for overall mental health in the later years. For most elders, some level of social involvement is a sign—and probably a cause—of higher morale and lower levels of depression and other psychiatric symptoms (Zunzunegui, Alvarado, Del Ser, & Otero, 2003).

Finally, **continuity theory** argues that the primary means by which elders adjust to aging is by engaging in the same kinds of activities that interested and challenged them in their earlier years (Atchley, 1989). For instance, an older woman who was an avid gardener during early and middle adulthood, but whose physical condition renders continuation of this hobby impossible, may adjust to her body's decline by limiting her passion for gardening to a small selection of potted plants. Research supports continuity theorists' assertions that aging adults work to maintain consistency of this kind and that achieving such consistency is essential to older adults' maintenance of a positive outlook on the aging process (Agahi, Ahacic, & Parker, 2006; Greenfield & Marks, 2007; Tatzer, van Nes, & Jonsson, 2012). Therefore, they argue, providing ways in which elders can meet these continuity goals should be integral to their care.

continuity theory the idea that older adults adapt lifelong interests and activities to the limitations imposed upon them by physical aging

successful aging the term gerontologists use to describe maintaining one's physical health, mental abilities, social competence, and overall satisfaction with one's life as one ages

test yourself before going on ✓ Study and Review in MyPsychLab

Answers to these questions can be found in the back of the book.

1. Match each term with its definition.
   _____(1) ego integrity
   _____(2) reminiscence
   _____(3) life review
   (a) reflecting on past experience
   (b) the feeling that one's life has been worthwhile
   (c) judgments about past behavior

2. The main idea of _____ theory is that elders adjust to aging by engaging in the same kinds of activities that interested them in their earlier years.

CRITICAL THINKING

3. Think about the oldest person you know. How are the themes of ego integrity, reminiscence, life review, activity, disengagement, and continuity manifested in his or her life?

Individual Differences

Individual differences continue to make substantial contributions to the experiences of older men and women. In fact, research suggests that differences in a variety of behaviors are related to overall quality of life as well as to longevity. Similarly, individual differences in reliance on religious beliefs and institutions as sources of support are also correlated with well-being in late adulthood.

The Successful Aging Paradigm

LO 18.3 How is successful aging manifested in the lives of older adults?

In recent years, a dominant theme in gerontology literature has been the concept of successful aging. As defined by authors John Rowe and Robert Kahn, **successful aging** has three components: good physical health, retention of cognitive abilities, and continuing engagement in social and productive activities (Rowe & Kahn, 1998). An additional aspect of successful aging is an individual's subjective sense of life satisfaction. (Table 18.1 describes these components.) The concept of successful aging is referred to as a *paradigm* because it presents patterns for or examples of such aging. Rather than state a theory of development, the paradigm of successful aging offers a way of thinking about late adulthood and about how earlier decisions and patterns of behavior contribute to quality of life at later ages.

TABLE 18.1 The Components of Successful Aging

Health	Good health must be maintained through middle and late adulthood.
Mental activity	Engaging in cognitively stimulating activities and hobbies helps older adults retain mental abilities.
Social engagement	Remaining socially active is critical; social contacts that involve helping others are especially important.
Productivity	Volunteer activities can help by engaging retired adults in productive pursuits.
Life satisfaction	Older adults must learn how to adjust expectations such that life satisfaction remains high.

STAYING HEALTHY AND ABLE By now, you should be familiar with the factors that predict health and physical functioning across the lifespan: diet, exercise, avoidance of tobacco, and so on. In a sense, older people reap the consequences of the behavioral choices they made when younger. Thus, it isn't surprising that making wise choices in this domain during early and middle adulthood, especially with regard to the factors that influence cardiovascular health, is essential to successful aging later in life (Hughes & Hayman, 2007). However, there are also aspects to staying healthy and able that most of us never face until old age.

For example, when an older adult suffers a heart attack, his willingness to engage in the sometimes painful process of rehabilitation significantly affects his degree of recovery. Researchers have found that older adults vary considerably in their willingness to comply with physicians and therapists who supervise their rehabilitation after such events. Predictably, patients who participate in all recommended rehabilitation activities are healthier at follow-up than those who do not participate (Leung et al., 2011). Thus, lifelong health habits contribute to successful aging, but individuals' responses to the health crises of old age also matter.

RETAINING COGNITIVE ABILITIES The degree to which elders maintain cognitive functioning is a crucial component of successful aging (Fiocco & Yaffe, 2010). As you learned in Chapter 17, those who are the best educated show the least cognitive decline.

In addition to education, the complexity of the cognitive challenges older adults are willing to take on influences their cognitive functioning. Psychologists suggest that self-stereotyping contributes to this reluctance; older people may believe that they can't learn as well as younger people can, and so they stick to established routines and disengage from new challenges (Ennis, Hess, & Smith, 2013). However, neuropsychologists suggest that such avoidance of learning may actually contribute to cognitive decline (Volz, 2000). New learning, these scientists hypothesize, helps to establish new connections between neurons, connections that may protect the aging brain against deterioration (Calero & Navarro, 2007). Thus, what might be called *cognitive adventurousness*, a willingness to learn new things, appears to be a key component of successful aging.

SOCIAL ENGAGEMENT Social connectedness and participation in productive activities are clearly important to successful aging (Huxhold, Fiori, & Windsor, 2013). For example, nursing home residents report greater satisfaction with their lives when they have frequent contact with family and friends (Guse & Masesar, 1999). Similarly, among elders with disabilities, frequency of contact with family and friends is associated with reduced feelings of loneliness (Liu & Richardson, 2012).

Social engagement contributes to successful aging because it provides opportunities for older adults to give support as well as to receive it. Researchers studying Japanese elders, for example, found that a majority of them say that helping others contributes to their own health and personal sense of well-being (Krause, Ingersoll-Dayton, Liang, & Sugisawa, 1999). In addition, researchers who have asked U.S. nursing home residents to rate various quality-of-life factors have found that they often give high ratings to "opportunities to help others" (Guse & Masesar, 1999). Thus, even when elderly adults have significant disabilities, many are still oriented toward helping others and feel more satisfied with their lives when they can do so.

PRODUCTIVITY Contributing to a social network may be one important way of remaining productive, especially for older adults who are retired. **Volunteerism**, or performing unpaid work for altruistic reasons, has been linked to successful aging. Remarkably, a California study involving nearly 2,000 older adults found that mortality rates were 60% lower among volunteers than among nonvolunteers (Oman, Thoresen, & McMahon, 1999). Another found that elders who volunteered 200 hours or more per year were less likely to develop hypertension than nonvolunteers (Sneed & Cohen, 2013).

For some elders, remaining productive means venturing into new hobbies such as painting, sculpting, or other artistic pursuits.

Some older adults remain productive by venturing into new pursuits, such as taking music lessons, attending college classes, or learning to paint or sculpt (Malchiodi, 2012; Sherrod, 2012). Researchers conducting a study of 36 artists over age 60 asked them to explain how artistic productivity contributed to their successful aging (Fisher & Specht, 1999). Their responses contained several themes: Producing art gave them a purpose in life, opportunities to interact with like-minded peers, and a sense of competence. The older artists also claimed that creating art helped them stay healthy. Thus, creative productivity may help older adults maintain an optimistic outlook, which, as you have learned, contributes to physical and mental health (Flood, 2007).

LIFE SATISFACTION *Life satisfaction*, or a sense of personal well-being, is also an important component of successful aging. What is critical to life satisfaction in almost all cases is an individual's perception of her own situation, which seems to be more important than objective measures (Gana, Alphilippe, & Bailly, 2004). Perceived adequacy of social support and perceived adequacy of income are critical. Moreover, self-ratings of health, rather than objective measures of health, may be the most significant predictors of life satisfaction and morale (Draper, Gething, Fethney, & Winfield, 1999).

Research also suggests that social comparisons—how well an older adult thinks he is doing compared to others his age—are just as important to these perceptions as the older adult's awareness of the changes he has undergone since his younger years (Robinson-Whelen & Kiecolt-Glaser, 1997). A majority of older adults, no matter what their personal circumstances, believe that most others their age are worse off than they are (Heckhausen & Brim, 1997). Developmentalists speculate that the tendency to see others as having more problems is an important self-protective psychological device employed by those who are aging successfully (Frieswijk, Buunk, Steverink, & Slaets, 2004).

CRITICISMS OF THE SUCCESSFUL AGING PARADIGM Critics of the successful aging paradigm suggest that the concept can be misleading. For one thing, they say, the paradigm has the potential to become a new kind of ageist stereotype, one that portrays older adults who have disabilities as incompetent (Dillaway & Byrnes, 2009; Minkler & Fadem, 2012). Such critics point out that, for many elderly adults, no amount of optimism, willingness to rehabilitate, social support, or involvement in intellectually demanding activities can moderate their physical limitations. For example, studies comparing the performance of university professors over age 70 and graduate students on reading comprehension tests show that some degree of age-based cognitive decline can be expected, even among very bright, highly experienced, and productive adults (Christensen, Henderson, Griffiths, & Levings, 1997). Thus, these critics claim, the danger of the successful aging paradigm is that it can give the erroneous impression that all the effects of aging are under one's control (Holstein & Minkler, 2003).

Nevertheless, critics concede that the successful aging paradigm has broadened gerontologists' approaches to studying old age. Thus, they agree that its influence has been largely positive. Still, keeping their criticisms in mind can help balance the optimism of the successful aging paradigm against the realities of life in late adulthood and the need to continue to encourage researchers to search for treatments for age-related diseases such as Alzheimer's.

volunteerism performance of unpaid work for altruistic motives

religious coping the tendency to turn to religious beliefs and institutions for support in times of difficulty

Religious Coping

LO 18.4 How does religious coping influence physical and mental health in late adulthood?

Religion appears to be one factor contributing to individual differences in life satisfaction among the elderly (Sørensen, Lien, Holmen, & Danbolt, 2012). Psychologists use the term **religious coping** to refer to the tendency to turn to religious beliefs and institutions in times of stress or trouble. People of all ages use religious coping. However, many developmentalists suggest that religious coping may be particularly important in the later years because of the high number of life stressors—including deaths of loved ones, chronic illnesses, and declining sensory abilities. And elders themselves often cite religious coping as their primary means of managing stress (Barusch, 1999). 🔘 **Watch** the **Video** *Late Adulthood: Religion and Spirituality* in **MyPsychLab**.

RACIAL AND SEX DIFFERENCES As you learned in Chapter 17, the tendency to turn to religion for comfort is stronger among African Americans than among other racial or ethnic groups. For example, research suggests that participation in church social activities is linked to high reported levels of well-being among older African Americans more than among older White Americans (Mattis & Grayman-Simpson, 2013). Further, the negative correlation between church involvement and depressive feelings is stronger for elderly African Americans with cancer than for their White counterparts (Musick, Koenig, Hays, & Cohen, 1998).

In addition, some studies suggest that women make more use of religious coping than men do (e.g., Coke, 1992). Most developmentalists attribute this finding to sex differences in social behavior that are observed across the lifespan. It's important to keep in mind, however, that even though the frequency with which religious coping is used may differ according to race and gender, its effects seem to be similar in all racial and ethnic groups and for both women and men. These effects can be best examined by separating the psychological and social components of religious coping.

RELIGIOUS BELIEFS The psychological component of religious coping involves people's beliefs and attitudes. A number of investigators have examined links between religious beliefs and various measures of well-being among the elderly. For example, elders who place a great deal of emphasis on religious faith worry much less than those who do not (Tapanya, Nicki, & Jarusawad, 1997). Moreover, associations between religious faith and physical and mental health have been found among older adults of diverse faiths—Christians, Buddhists, Muslims, Hindus, Taoists, and Sikhs—and from a variety of cultures and ethnic groups (Krause et al., 1999; Meisenhelder & Chandler, 2000; Park & Roh, 2013; Tapanya et al., 1997; Zhou, Yao, & Xu, 2002). Thus, the positive effects of religious faith may have more to do with a general attitude of *spirituality*, a tendency to focus on the aspects of life that transcend one's physical existence, than on any particular set of doctrines or teachings. 👁 **Watch** the **Video** *Religion and Longevity* in **MyPsychLab**.

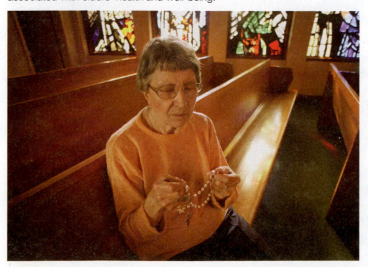

Strong religious beliefs appear to be positively associated with elders' health and well-being.

The positive effects of religious coping seem to arise from its influence on what people believe about the meaning of their lives (Park, Edmondson, & Mills, 2010). For example, older adults who rate their religious beliefs as highly important to them are more likely than others to think that their lives serve an important purpose (Gerwood, LeBlanc, & Piazza, 1998). In addition, religious faith seems to provide older adults with a theme that integrates the various periods of their lives. As a result, religious elders are more likely than their nonreligious peers to view old age as a chapter in an ongoing story rather than as primarily a period of loss of capacities. Further, among low-income elders, divine power is viewed as a resource on which those who have little social power in the material world can rely (Williams, Keigher, & Williams, 2012).

ATTENDANCE AT RELIGIOUS SERVICES The social aspect of religious coping most often examined by researchers is attendance at religious services. Research suggests that adults who regularly attend such services are physically and emotionally healthier than their nonattending peers (Bosworth, Park, McQuoid, Hays, & Steffens, 2003; Koenig, 2007). Healthy lifestyle choices appear to be an important connection between religious attendance and health. For example, African American elders with hypertension who attend church regularly are more likely than those who attend intermittently to comply with medical advice regarding blood pressure medication; also, the average blood pressure readings of the regular attendees are lower (Koenig et al., 1998). Researchers don't know why, but one explanation might be that church attendance provides opportunities for interaction with peers who have the same disorder. In the context of such interactions, African American elders may receive encouragement to persevere in dealing with such chronic ailments as hypertension by complying with medical advice.

Elders themselves cite a number of reasons for the benefits of religious involvement. For example, many say that religious institutions provide them with opportunities to help others (Krause et al., 1999; la Cour, Avlund, & Schultz-Larsen, 2006). Intergenerational involvement is another aspect of religious participation often mentioned by older adults. For many, religious institutions provide a structure within which they can pass on their knowledge and beliefs to younger individuals.

ALTERNATIVE EXPLANATIONS When examining links between variables such as religious coping and health, researchers must always consider selection effects. There are other possible confounding factors as well. For example, religious and nonreligious elders may differ in personality traits. It seems likely that those with higher levels of extraversion would be the most comfortable in religious social environments—and scientists know that extraversion is correlated with successful aging. Thus, the connection between religious coping and health in old age may be a manifestation of personality rather than an independent effect of religion.

In addition, research on the association between religious faith and health focuses on the personal relevance of spirituality rather than on intellectual acceptance of a set of doctrines. So it may be the intensity and the personal nature of these beliefs, rather than their religious focus, that are responsible for the correlations. In addition, in most research studies, the participants have had longstanding belief and attendance patterns. Thus, these elders may persist in religious faith and involvement, even when they are ill or disabled, because it helps them achieve a sense of continuity of identity. That is, religious involvement may allow an older adult to feel that, despite physical losses, she is still the same person. So it may be that the sense of personal integration that religion provides is responsible for the correlations. Whatever the reasons, the research evidence suggests that supporting the spiritual needs of the elderly may be just as important to maintaining their health and functioning as meeting their physical and material needs.

test yourself before going on ☑ **Study** and **Review** in **MyPsychLab**

Answers to these questions can be found in the back of the book.

1. According to critics, the successful aging paradigm is a new kind of _____ _____ that portrays elders with disabilities as incompetent.

2. The psychological component of religious coping is _____, and the social aspect is _____.

CRITICAL THINKING

3. How do the concepts of successful aging and religious coping apply to people who have not yet reached late adulthood?

Social Relationships

The social roles older adults occupy are usually different from those they held when younger. Nevertheless, most elderly adults cite meaningful social roles as essential to life satisfaction (Bowling et al., 2003). Moreover, there is no doubt that social relationships contribute to older adults' sense of well-being. Both consistency and change characterize social relationships during this period. **Watch** the **Video** *Late Adulthood: Late Adulthood Relationships* in **MyPsychLab**.

aging in place living in a noninstitutional environment, to which modifications have been made to accommodate an older adult's needs

Living Arrangements

LO 18.5 What are the living arrangements of most elderly people in the United States and in other industrialized countries?

Most older adults prefer to live in private homes. However, the physical changes associated with aging mean that some kind of change in living arrangements generally must be made at some point in an individual's later years.

AGING IN PLACE Elders' preference for living in a private home environment has led to a pattern known as **aging in place**. Aging in place involves making modifications to a private residence in response to the changing needs of older adults, such as making doorways wider to accommodate a wheelchair. It may also include hiring a *home health aide* to provide assistance with ADLs when necessary. At the core of the aging-in-place concept is the idea that, as much as possible, changing a normal living environment to meet an elder's needs is preferable to moving the elder to an institutional environment. Aging in place can involve the services of a wide range of health-care professionals, including physical therapists and mental health counselors. Researchers have found that comprehensive home-based care of this kind has strong positive effects on elders' physical and mental health (Gill et al., 2002). Thus, compared to institutional care, aging in place is believed by many to be both more supportive of elders' psychosocial needs and less costly.

For more than 90% of men and 80% of women over the age of 65 in the United States, aging in place means living in their own homes either alone or with a spouse. However, as you can see in Figure 18.1, the percentage who live alone varies across ethnic groups

Living arrangements of the population age 65 and over, by sex and race and Hispanic origin, 2010

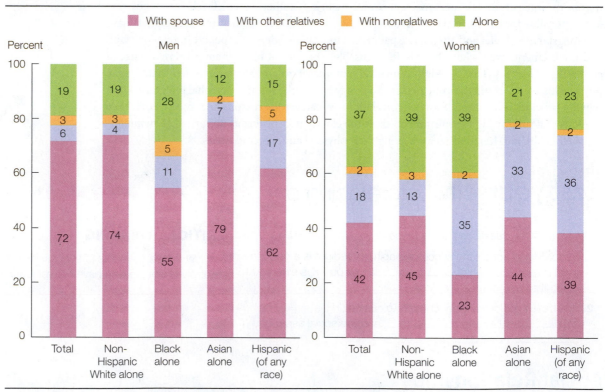

Figure 18.1 Older Adults' Living Arrangements

In the United States, most older adults live with a spouse or alone, but living arrangements vary to some degree across ethnic groups.

(*Source:* FIFARS, 2012.)

(see *Research Report* on page 452) (Federal Interagency Forum on Aging Statistics [FIFARS], 2012). Another variation on the aging-in-place theme arises when an older adult moves into the home of a relative, usually one of his own children. In many such cases, modifications must be made to the caretaker's home in order to meet the elder's needs, and a home health aide may be hired to help with ADLs. In the United States, 6% of men and 18% of women over 65 live in the homes of relatives, usually their adult children (FIFARS, 2012). Four factors influence an older adult's decision to live with an adult child:

- **Health.** Elders who need help with ADLs because of health problems are more likely to live in the homes of family members than are those who can manage the physical demands of living independently (Choi, 2003).

- **Income.** Those with lower incomes are more likely to live with family members (Choi, 1991).

- **Adult children's characteristics.** Elders with several daughters are more likely than those with few daughters to live with grown children (Soldo, Wolf, & Agree, 1990). Married adults are more likely than those who are single to take in their aging parents (Choi, 2003).

- **Ethnicity.** Hispanic American, African American, and Asian American elders are more likely to live with relatives than Whites are (FIFARS, 2012).

Adapting living spaces to the physical needs of elderly adults helps them achieve the goal of aging in place.

RESIDENTIAL OPTIONS FOR OLDER ADULTS Older adults who are no longer able to live independently or who don't want to deal with the demands of caring for a home often turn to one of several residential options. An *independent living community* is an apartment complex or housing development in which all the residents are over a certain age, typically 55 or 60. In most such communities, residents join together for a variety of social activities and outings. Thus, independent living communities offer older adults the opportunity to remain socially active without having to travel far from home. However, these communities typically do not provide residents with any kind of health-care assistance.

When older adults need more help than is available in an independent living community, an *assisted living facility* is another option. Surveys suggest that about 4% of older adults in the United States live in these facilities (FIFARS, 2012). The average age of assisted living residents is 80, and most require help with one or two activities of daily living (toileting, bathing, and so on). In most assisted living facilities, residents live in small apartments and get help with housework and meal preparation along with ADL assistance. Nurses are on site around the clock and can be called upon in emergencies, but residents are generally responsible for routine health care such as taking medications. Still, just in knowing that help is close by if they need it, elders who move from their own homes to an assisted living facility have less stress and an enhanced sense of well-being (Cutchin, Owen, & Chang, 2003; Fonda, Clipp, & Maddox, 2002). Assisted living facilities also provide senior citizens with organized social activities. Researchers have found that activity options and choices are important to the overall life satisfaction and mental health of elders in assisted living facilities (Kelley-Gillespie, 2012; Zimmerman et al., 2003).

When older adults need more help with ADLs than is available in an assisted living facility, many turn to nursing homes, or *skilled nursing facilities*. Between 3% and 4% of the elderly adults in the United States live in nursing homes (FIFARS, 2012). About 14% of those over the age of 85 live in such facilities. The typical nursing home resident is a female in her late 70s or early 80s (Jones, Dwyer, Bercovitz, & Strahan, 2009). Most require help with three to four ADLs. About half of nursing home residents have dementia. Of course, the decision to admit an elderly adult to a skilled nursing facility can be difficult (see *No Easy Answers*). However, for older adults who require 24-hour supervision, particularly those with dementia, nursing homes often represent the best residential option.

RESEARCH REPORT

Filial Piety

In the United States and in other Western nations, most elderly people live on their own, but in Asian societies, allowing one's elders to live alone has traditionally been viewed as a violation of a set of cultural beliefs called *filial piety* (Chen & Chen, 2012; Maeda, 2004). Central to this set of beliefs is the notion that children have a duty to care for their elderly parents. As a result, few elders in such societies live on their own. In Japan, for example, only 10% of older men and 25% of older women live alone (Fukue, 2010). The majority live with their children.

The concept of filial piety exists in Western cultures as well. However, among Westerners, filial piety is more often based on affection and attachment than on a sense of duty (Datta, Poortinga, & Marcoen, 2003; Klaus, 2009). Spiritual and religious values also often motivate families to provide care for their elders (Klaus, 2009; Pierce, 2001). Further, individualistic values motivate elderly adults in Western cultures to take into account their children's own financial and social resources, as well as their need for independence, when making judgments about whether their children have met their filial piety obligations (Lecovich & Lankri, 2002). Thus, unlike elders in Asian cultures, adults in Western societies who must depend on their children for financial help, especially men, often experience emotional distress (Nagumey, Reich, & Newsom, 2004). Moreover, Western nations have developed large networks of publicly and privately supported

In Asian countries, most elderly adults live with their adult children.

pension and health-care programs for older adults in response to their desire to live as independently as possible.

The spread of Western ideas to non-Western societies via mass media and other means appears to be changing the concept of filial piety in Asian countries. Researchers have found that the concept of filial piety held by both middle-aged and elderly adults in highly Westernized areas, such as Hong Kong and Japan, is much more like that of North Americans and Europeans than that of traditional Asian culture (Maeda, 2004; Ng, Ying, Phillips, & Lee, 2002). For example, filial piety is viewed as a societal as well as an individual responsibility in Japan, a factor that underlies the nation's government-sponsored support programs for the elderly (Maeda, 2004). By contrast, many Asian countries, such as

China, have minimal pension programs that cover only a small proportion of elderly citizens (Wee, 2012). At the same time, as a result of the population-control policies that have been in place in China since the 1980s, most elders in that country have only one child to rely on for assistance (French, 2007). Moreover, with economic globalization, China and other Asian nations have become more individualistic, a shift that has caused more elders to desire to live on their own and their children to view parents' financial needs as burdensome.

Taken together, all of these social factors have had a number of adverse consequences for elderly Asians. In some locales, older adults must work several part-time jobs after retirement to make ends meet (French, 2007). Consequently, governments in many of these countries are beginning to recognize that a shift toward Western values will necessitate adoption of Western-style government programs for the elderly (French, 2007; Fukue, 2010; McDonald, 2004).

CRITICAL ANALYSIS

1. *In what ways do Western families display filial piety other than by having elders live in their homes?*

2. *Beyond the influence of Western media, what kinds of internal social changes in Asian societies might have contributed to declines in filial piety?*

Finally, *continuing-care retirement communities* (*CCRCs*) offer a continuum of care ranging from independent living to skilled nursing care. Residents can move from one level of care to another on an as-needed basis while remaining within the same community. For example, an elder who lives in the independent living part of the facility can temporarily move to the skilled nursing sector for a few days or weeks while she recovers from surgery or an accident. Similarly, a resident who is in the process of developing dementia may start out in independent living and move to assisted living before finally being admitted to skilled nursing care.

Only a tiny fraction of older adults in the United States currently live in this new kind of community, but interest in CCRCs is growing. Like assisted living facilities, they are most popular with seniors who pay for their own care. The flexibility and social continuity provided by CCRCs are the keys to their appeal.

Partnerships

LO 18.6 How do intimate partnerships contribute to development in late adulthood?

Because women live longer than men, a man can normally expect to have a spouse or intimate partner until he dies. The normal expectation for a woman is that she will eventually be without such a partner, often for many years. Clearly this helps explain why there are more women

Deciding on Nursing Home Care

A relatively small number of elderly adults in the United States lives in nursing homes. Even among the oldest old, only 14% reside in such institutions (FIFARS, 2012). Furthermore, most people would prefer to take care of their older loved ones at home. However, when elders require assistance with several activities of daily living (e.g., bathing, cooking, taking medication) or when they require medical procedures that are difficult to manage at home (e.g., tube feeding), many families decide that moving the older adult into a long-term care facility is the best available option. How do families choose such a facility?

The pathway toward finding the best long-term placement for an older adult begins with an assessment of his or her needs and resources. Elders who are still able to function somewhat independently may be best served by an assisted living facility. However, assisted living facilities are not covered by government insurance programs such as Medicare and Medicaid. Moreover, skilled nursing care is not covered by either government or private insurance unless it is medically necessary. Thus, cost is often a barrier that prevents an older adult from receiving the kind of care that best suits his or her needs. For this reason, a growing number of young and middle-aged adults are opting to buy long-term care insurance. Long-term care insurance enables elders and their families to make decisions about their needs with less regard for cost than is required for those who do not have such coverage.

Beyond cost considerations, agencies that serve older adults have suggested several criteria for evaluating a long-term care facility (U.S. Department of Health and human Services, 2007). Here are a few.

- Be certain that the facility has the staff and equipment required to meet your elder's physical needs.
- Check with authorities to see whether any complaints have been filed and how they were resolved; avoid facilities with many outstanding complaints.
- Research the results of state and local inspections and the extent to which any deficiencies were corrected; do not admit your elder to a facility that has any current deficiencies.
- Visit at different times such as during meals, recreation periods, early morning, late evening, and so on to note how residents are cared for in different situations.
- Talk to family members of other residents if possible.
- Ask about the facility's policies regarding medical emergencies.

Of course, a facility can receive high marks on these criteria and still not be the best one for an older adult. Thus, once a facility has satisfied these basic criteria, families must determine whether it can meet their older loved one's cognitive, social, and spiritual needs. Moreover, once an elder has been admitted, family members should closely monitor their care and be prepared to make a change if needed.

YOU DECIDE

Decide which of these two statements you most agree with and think about how you would defend your position:

1. *In some cases, an older adult is probably better off living in a long-term care facility than with a family member.*
2. *Living with a family member is always preferable to placement in a long-term care facility.*

than men in nursing homes and among the victims of elder abuse (see *Developmental Science at Home*). But what are the marital relationships of older adults like?

Cross-sectional comparisons show that marital satisfaction is higher in the late adult years than when children are still at home. But this high marital satisfaction may have a somewhat different basis than that of the early years of marriage. In late adulthood, marriages tend to be based less on passion and mutual disclosure and more on loyalty, familiarity, mutual investment in the relationship, and companionship (Bengtson et al., 1990; Fouquereau & Baudoin, 2002). In Sternberg's terms (look back at Figure 14.4, page 358), late adult marriages are more likely to reflect companionate love than romantic or even consummate love.

Of course, this does not mean that the marriages of older adults are necessarily passionless. That may well be true of some marriages, but there is evidence to the contrary for many. You'll recall from Chapter 17 that the majority of older adult couples are still sexually active and may be somewhat more sexually adventurous than younger adults. In addition, older couples spend more time with each other than with other family members or friends, and although much of this time is spent in passive or basic maintenance activities—watching TV, doing housework, running errands—it is also true that those married elders who spend more time with their spouses report high levels of happiness (Larson, Mannell, & Zuzanek, 1986). Relationship satisfaction is linked to overall life satisfaction and to health. Elders in satisfying, long-term relationships are more satisfied with life and generally healthier than peers who are not in such relationships (Landis, Peter-Wight, Martin, & Bodenmann, 2013; Proulx, & Snyder-Rivas, 2013).

Further evidence of the deep bond that continues to exist in late-life marriages is the remarkable degree of care and assistance older spouses give each other when one or the other is disabled. For married elders with some kind of disability, by far the greatest source of assistance is the spouse, not children or friends. Many husbands and wives care for spouses who are ill or who have dementia for very long periods of time. And even when both spouses have

Elder Abuse

Fred is a 43-year-old unemployed cocaine addict. When Fred's father died, his mother received a $50,000 life-insurance payment. Since she had almost no savings, Fred's mother put the money into a savings account and restricts her living expenses to the amount of her monthly Social Security check. Having the money has helped her worry less about the future. However, shortly after his father's death, Fred began nagging his mother about his new "life plan." His plan is to move in with her and to use her insurance money to finance his enrollment in a drug rehabilitation program. As soon as he is off cocaine and finds a job, Fred has vowed, he will pay her back. Fred's siblings say that he is "abusing" their mother by manipulating her emotions in order to get financial support from her.

Little is known about the prevalence of elder abuse or the factors that contribute to it (FIFARS,

2012). Moreover, many experts believe that only 20% of elder-abuse cases are reported, perhaps because health-care providers do not get enough training in recognizing its effects (National Center on Elder Abuse [NCEA], 2005; Thobaben & Duncan, 2003). The few studies that have been done suggest that between 2% and 10% of U.S. elders are abused by family members or by workers in elder-care facilities (NCEA, 2005). Psychological abuse is more subtle and difficult for observers outside an older adult's immediate social network to identify. This kind of abuse includes financial exploitation or failure to provide needed aid.

Researchers have identified several risk factors for elder abuse, including mental illness or alcoholism in the abuser, financial dependency of the abuser on the victim, social isolation, and external stresses (Pillemer & Suitor, 1990, 1992).

A likely victim of abuse is an elderly widow sharing her household with a dependent son who has a mental disorder or a drug or alcohol problem; the mother is typically too dependent on her son to kick him out and too ashamed of the abuse to tell others about it (Bengtson, Rosenthal, & Burton, 1996). Abuse is also more likely when the elder with dementia is physically violent and when a husband has physically abused his wife throughout their adult lives and simply continues to do so in old age.

REFLECTION

1. *What arguments could be made for and against the claim that Fred's behavior toward his mother is abusive?*

2. *If you were one of Fred's siblings, how would you handle the situation?*

---

significant disabilities, they nonetheless continue to care for each other "until death do us part." Marriages may thus be less romantic or less emotionally intense in late adulthood than they were in earlier years, but they are typically satisfying and highly committed.

Researchers have found similar characteristics and effects in long-term gay and lesbian relationships (Grossman, Daugelli, & Hershberger, 2000). Like heterosexuals, elderly homosexuals who have a long-term partner typically identify the partner as their most important source of emotional support. In addition, those who live with a partner report less loneliness and better physical and mental health. 👁 Watch the Video *Love Again* in **MyPsychLab**.

Married older adults, like married adults of any other age, have certain distinct advantages: They have higher life satisfaction, better health, and lower rates of institutionalization (Iwashyna & Christakis, 2003; Waldinger & Schulz, 2010). Such differential advantages are generally greater for married older men than for married older women (Again, this is also true among younger adults.) This difference might be interpreted as indicating that marriage affords more benefits to men than to women or that men rely more on their marriage relationship for social support and are thus more affected by its loss. Whatever the explanation, it seems clear that, for older women, marital status is less strongly connected to health or life satisfaction, but still strongly connected to financial security.

Affection between married partners and pleasure in each other's company clearly do not disappear in old age.

The protective nature of marriage for older adults is supported by research showing that single adults over the age of 65 have higher mortality rates, even when factors such as poverty are controlled (Manzoli, Villari, Pironec, & Boccia, 2007). Moreover, these rates are consistent across gender and culture. Interestingly, though, elders whose single status is the result of divorce have higher mortality rates than either those who have been widowed or peers who have never married. In addition, divorced older adults have higher rates of alcohol abuse, depression, and suicide (Hahn, Yang, Yang, Shih, & Lo, 2004; Lorant, Kunst, Huisman, Bopp, & Mackenbach, 2005; Onen et al., 2005). This may be the case because divorced elders, especially men, are more likely to be disconnected from their families than their never-married or widowed peers are (Tomassini et al., 2004). However, participation in religious activities and other forms of social engagement appear to moderate the associations among single status, substance abuse, depression, poor health, and mortality risk (Hahn et al., 2004). Thus, the key advantage of intimate partnerships for older adults is that they provide them with readily available sources of support (Landis et al., 2013). For single elders, more effort is required to identify and connect with sources of support, and physical disabilities are more likely to interfere with maintaining them than is the case for partnered elders who share the same household.

Family Relationships and Friendships

LO 18.7   What is the significance of family relationships and friendships for older adults?

Elderly newlyweds report higher levels of personal happiness than either long-married or single peers.

Folklore and descriptions of late adulthood in the popular press suggest that family, particularly children and grandchildren, forms the core of the social life of older adults, perhaps especially those who are widowed. Older adults do describe intergenerational bonds as strong and important; most report a significant sense of family solidarity and support (Bengtson et al., 1996). These bonds are reflected in, among other things, regular contact between elders and family members. Moreover, researchers have found that family relationships become more harmonious as adults get older (Akiyama, Antonucci, Takahashi, & Langfahl, 2003). Thus, they represent an important component of most elders' overall life satisfaction.

CONTACTS WITH ADULT CHILDREN In one national sample of more than 3,000 adults aged 65 and older, 86% reported that they saw at least one of their children once a week or more often (Taylor, Funk, Craighill, & Kennedy, 2006). Regular contact is made easier by the fact that even in the highly mobile U.S. society, 65% of elders live within an hour's travel of at least one of their children. Very similar figures are reported by researchers in other developed countries such as those in the European Union, so this pattern is not unique to the United States (Hank, 2007). Moreover, about a quarter of older adults in the United States use social networking sites such as Facebook to communicate with adult children, grandchildren, and other family members (Madden, 2010).

Part of the regular contact between elders and their adult children, of course, involves giving aid to or receiving it from the elder person—a pattern you learned about in Chapter 16. Most of the time, when older adults need help that cannot be provided by a spouse, it is provided by other family members, principally children. However, relationships between older parents and their adult children cannot be reduced simply to the exchange of aid. A great deal of the interaction is social as well as functional, and the great majority of older adults describe their relationships with their adult children in positive terms. Most see their children not only out of a sense of obligation or duty but because they take pleasure in such contact, and a very large percentage describe at least one child as a confidant (Taylor et al., 2006).

EFFECTS OF RELATIONSHIPS WITH ADULT CHILDREN Some studies indicate that when relationships between elders and adult children are warm and close, they are more important to elders' sense of well-being than any other kind of social relationship (Pinquart & Soerensen, 2000). By contrast, other researchers have found that elders who see their children more often or report more positive interactions with their children do not describe themselves as happier or healthier overall than do those who have less frequent contact or less positive relationships with their children (e.g., Mullins & Mushel, 1992). Moreover, such results have been obtained in very different cultural settings, such as in India and among Mexican Americans (Lawrence, Bennett, & Markides, 1992; Venkatraman, 1995). In all these studies, the older adults reported regular contact with their children and said that they enjoyed it, but these relationships did not seem to enhance happiness or health. Moreover, research has shown that childless elders are just as happy and well adjusted as those who have children (Taylor et al., 2006). Many developmentalists have concluded that good relationships and regular contact with adult children can add to an elderly adult's quality of life, but are not necessary for it.

Most elders enjoy maintaining relationships with younger family members. However, research suggests that such connections are not essential to life satisfaction in old age.

One possible explanation for this inconsistency in findings is that the relationship with one's children is still governed by role prescriptions, even in old age. It may be friendly, but it is not chosen in the same way that a relationship with a friend is. With your friend, you feel free to be yourself and feel accepted as who you are. With your children, you may feel the need to live up to their demands and expectations. This hypothesis may explain why elders' levels of distress increase whenever their adult children experience problems with their careers or intimate relationships (Milkie, Bierman, & Scheiman, 2008). That is, threats to adult children's independence such as job loss and divorce may cause elders to become anxious about being thrust back into an active parenting role.

GRANDCHILDREN AND SIBLINGS As you learned in Chapter 16, interactions between grandchildren and middle-aged grandparents are beneficial to both. However, in late adulthood, contact between grandchildren and grandparents declines as the grandchildren become adults themselves (Barer, 2001; Silverstein & Long, 1998). Thus, grandchildren are rarely part of an elderly adult's close family network.

Interestingly, though, it appears that relationships with siblings may become more important in late adulthood (Taylor et al., 2006). Siblings seldom provide much practical assistance to one another in old age, but they can and often do serve two other important functions. First, siblings can provide a unique kind of emotional support for one another, based on shared reminiscences and companionship. Once parents are gone, no one else knows all the old stories, all the family jokes, and the names and history of former friends and neighbors. Second, many elders see their siblings as a kind of "insurance policy" in old age, a source of support of last resort (Connidis, 1994).

FRIENDSHIPS Mounting evidence suggests that contact with friends has a significant impact on overall life satisfaction, on self-esteem, and on the amount of loneliness reported by older adults (Antonucci, 1990; Antonucci, Lansford, & Akiyama, 2001; Jerrome, 1990). Moreover, for those elders whose families are unavailable, friendships seem to provide an equally effective support network (Takahashi, Tamura, & Tokoro, 1997). This is particularly true of unmarried elders, but is at least somewhat true of married ones as well.

Friends meet different kinds of needs for older adults than do family members. For one thing, relationships with friends are likely to be more reciprocal or equitable, and developmentalists know that equitable relationships are more valued and less stressful. Friends provide companionship, opportunities for laughter, and shared activities. In one Canadian study, for example, friends were second only to spouses as sources of companionship among those over 65 (Connidis & Davies, 1992). Friends may also provide assistance with daily tasks, such as shopping or housework, although they typically provide less help of this kind than do family members.

Gender and Ethnic Differences in Social Networks

LO 18.8 What are some gender and ethnic differences in older adults' social networks?

As at earlier ages, women and men in late adulthood appear to form different kinds of social networks, with men's friendships involving less disclosure and less intimacy than women's. In addition, older women's networks tend to be larger and closer than those of older men. Developmentalists attribute these findings to a continuation of a pattern evident across most of the lifespan (Taylor et al., 2006). If you think back on what you learned about sex differences in the chapters on childhood, adolescence, early adulthood,

Friends seem to play an important role in late adulthood, perhaps because they share the same background and memories—like favorite old tunes and dances.

and middle adulthood, sex differences in late adulthood social networks should not be surprising.

However, it would be a mistake to assume that, because men have smaller social networks, their relationships are unimportant to them. Some developmentalists suggest that research on social networks may be biased in such a way that women will always be found to have stronger networks. This bias, critics say, originates in the fact that research emphasizes shared activities and frequency of contact more than the quality of the relationships. Indeed, when quality of relationships is considered, research shows that men's social networks are just as important to them and provide them with the same kinds of emotional support as women's networks, even though men's networks tend to be smaller (Riggs, 1997).

African Americans tend to have warmer relationships with their siblings and to live with their children more often than White Americans do. In addition, they show another distinctive pattern in their social networks. They create strong relationships with *fictive kin*. In African American groups, friends often acquire the status of a close sibling, aunt, uncle, or grandparent. Such fictive kin may be important sources of both emotional and instrumental support among elders of all ethnic groups, but the pattern is particularly prevalent among African Americans (Johnson & Barer, 1990; MacRae, 1992).

Other ethnic groups, including Hispanic Americans and Asian Americans, are also often found to have more extensive social networks than White Americans. However, the correlations between social networks and various measures of well-being seem to be similar across these groups (Barker, Morrow, & Mitteness, 1998; Baxter et al., 1998; Takahashi et al., 1997). Moreover, most studies suggest that the quality of the social network, not just its size, is important. Thus, as the earlier discussion of successful aging suggested, the number of contacts with family and friends and the quality of interactions with them are important predictors of elders' well-being.

test yourself before going on ✓ Study and Review in MyPsychLab

Answers to these questions can be found in the back of the book.

1. What two living arrangements are most common among older adults live in the United States?

2. A married older adult with a significant disability or dementia is most likely to be cared for by a(n) _____.

3. For most elders, friends provide (more, less) help than family members.

4. Older men have (larger, smaller) social networks than older women do.

CRITICAL THINKING

5. What kinds of physical and social barriers are there to creating new social relationships in late adulthood?

Career Issues in Late Life

A remarkable capacity for adaptation marks the transition from work to retirement. Although this transition certainly brings the loss of a major role, virtually all the folklore about the negative effects of this particular role loss turns out to be incorrect. As you will see, for many older adults, retirement brings with it unique opportunities for personal growth. ◉ Watch the Video *Late Adulthood: Work and Retirement across Cultures* in **MyPsychLab**.

Timing of and Reasons for Retirement

LO 18.9 What factors contribute to the decision to retire?

One inaccurate bit of folklore is that 65 is the normal age of retirement. As recently as 1970, 65 was indeed the most common age of retirement for workers in the United States. However, retirement has become a life event whose timing varies widely across individuals.

DELAYED RETIREMENT Those in challenging and interesting jobs or who are self-employed are likely to postpone retirement or reject entirely the idea of leaving paid work unless they are pushed into such a decision by ill health or attracted by some extra financial inducement (Sloan Center on Aging & Work at Boston College, 2009). Consequently, nearly 40% of older adults with salaried jobs and 57% of those who are self-employed plan to continue working past the typical retirement age (Sloan Center on Aging & Work at Boston College, 2009). 👁 Watch the **Video** *Seniors Say No to Retirement* in **MyPsychLab**.

Moreover, retirement has become more of a multiphase process than a single life event (Feldman & Beehr, 2011). As you learned in Chapter 16, many retirees hold *bridge jobs* that allow them to transition from full-time work to full-time retirement, and they can do so for many years before withdrawing entirely from the workforce (Adams & Rau, 2004). Researchers have found correlations between post-retirement employment and life satisfaction (Bhatia, Sharma, & Sharma, 2013). Thus, the desire to enhance one's quality of life is probably the primary reason many senior citizens choose to work after retirement. Not surprisingly, the phased-retirement trend has led to changes in the economic circumstances of older adults. The percentage of older adults' income derived from employment was only 10% in 1967; today it is about 30% (FIFARS, 2012). Moreover, 45% of the income of the top 20% of earners over the age of 65 comes from work.

Family composition is another factor that contributes to the decision to delay retirement. Elders who are still supporting minor or college-aged children retire later than their peers whose children are economically independent. Furthermore, due to increases in life expectancy, it isn't unusual today for people in their 60s to have living parents in their 80s or 90s, many of whom require financial assistance. Consequently, the concept of the sandwich generation that you read about in Chapter 16 is relevant to many older adults and influences their decisions about retirement.

OLDER WORKERS The greatest obstacle facing older adults who wish to continue working is that many potential employers express concerns about older adults' ability to learn new job skills (Forte & Hansvick, 1999). However, research shows that, with appropriately designed training, older adults can acquire new work-related skills. Pacing is an important element of instructional design because older adults learn more efficiently when smaller chunks of information are presented than is typical in many job-training programs (Foos & Goolkasian, 2010). In addition, designers of computer-based training must take into account the increased prevalence of visual difficulties among older trainees by creating visual interfaces that include high contrast and larger text than is typically used with younger workers (Rivera-Novar & Pomales-García, 2010).

About 37% of 65- to 69-year-old men and 15% of those over 70 are employed (FIFARS, 2012). Among 65- to 69-year-old women, 27% work at least part time, while less than 10% of women over 70 are employed (FIFARS, 2012). Further, a fairly high proportion of middle-aged people say they plan to work at least part time after retirement. Consequently, employers are eager to learn how to best train older workers.

With respect to aspects of job functioning other than learning of new skills, supervisors typically give older adults higher ratings than they give younger adults (Forte & Hansvick, 1999). For example, they view older employees as more reliable. In addition, managers typically report that although younger workers produce a greater quantity of work, the quality of older employees' work is better (Rao & Rao, 1997). Consequently, many employers view older adults as desirable employees.

EARLY RETIREMENT At the other end of the spectrum, there are many older adults who choose to retire before the traditional age of 65. Poor health provides a particularly strong push toward early retirement (Sloan Center on Aging & Work at Boston College, 2009). Poor health lowers the average age of retirement by 1–3 years, an effect seen among Hispanic Americans and African Americans as well as among White Americans, and in countries other than the United States (Hayward, Friedman, & Chen, 1996; Stanford, Happersett, Morton, Molgaard, & Peddecord, 1991).

GENDER DIFFERENCES Women retire at about the same age as men do, on average, but retirement benefits, health, or job characteristics do not predict just when they will retire. One factor that tends to keep older professional women in the labor force is that many encounter the best opportunities for advanced and leadership roles that they have ever experienced at just about the time they reach traditional retirement age (Lips & Hastings, 2012). Others keep working in order to maintain sufficient earnings to augment future Social Security benefits—a factor that may be especially important for women who took several years off from full-time work in order to raise children. However, financial experts point out that even if retirement-aged women have as many years of full-time employment as men do, they are still likely to receive less money from pensions and Social Security because, on average, their earnings are lower (Powell, 2006).

The factors that lead to positive views of retirement are very similar for men and women. For example, one study found that health was the most important predictor of quality of life in retirement for both sexes (Quick & Moen, 1998). However, extensive retirement planning seemed to be more important for men. Almost all of the study's male participants had worked continuously until retirement. Although some of the retired women had worked continuously, others had spent a significant number of years in the home or in part-time employment. The researchers found that those who had worked continuously expressed more satisfaction with the quality of their retirement.

Effects of Retirement

LO 18.10 How does retirement affect the lives of older adults?

A number of shifts take place at retirement, some positive and some negative. Overall, retirement seems to have positive effects on the lives of older adults.

INCOME One potentially significant change at retirement is a change in income. In the United States, retired adults have five potential sources of income: government pensions, such as Social Security; other pensions, such as those offered through an employer or the military; earnings from continued work; income from savings or other assets; and, for those living below the poverty line, public assistance, including food stamps and Supplemental Security Income. For most elderly people in the United States, Social Security is the largest source of income (FIFARS, 2012).

In the United States, as in many other developed countries, many retired adults own their own homes and thus have no mortgage payments, and their children are self-reliant. Furthermore, retirees are eligible for Medicare as well as for many special senior citizen benefits. When these factors are taken into consideration, retired adults in the United States, Australia, and most European countries have, on average, higher net worth (assets such as stocks, homes, minus liabilities such as loans) and greater disposable income than most younger adults (FIFARS, 2012).

POVERTY It used to be that postretirement income losses resulted in high poverty rates among the elderly. However, over the past several decades, poverty rates among the elderly have declined substantially. In 1959, 35% of adults over 65 in the United States were living below the poverty line. In 2010, 9% were at that low economic level (FIFARS, 2012).

A variety of factors are responsible for declining poverty rates among the elderly. For one thing, significant improvements in Social Security benefits in the United States (and equivalent improvements in many other countries), including regular cost-of-living increases, have meant that the relative financial position of the elderly has improved more than that of any other age group in the population. Moreover, more elderly adults than ever before are high school or college graduates. In 1950, only 18% of adults over 65 were high school graduates, compared to 80% of the over-65 population in 2010 (FIFARS, 2012). Thus, most elderly adults today had better jobs and earned a great deal more money before retirement than did members of previous cohorts. As a result, today's elders have more savings and better retirement benefits.

However, low rates of poverty in the total elderly population obscure much higher rates in various subgroups. Figure 18.2 shows poverty rates of men and women in the major ethnic groups in the United States in 2010 (FIFARS, 2012). Clearly, large disparities across groups remain. Moreover, poverty is strongly associated with disability among the elderly across all ethnic groups. Thus, low-income older adults are more highly represented among elders with disabilities than they are in the general population. Some studies show that even relatively young elders, those between 55 and 65 years of age, who live below the poverty level, are six times as likely to need assistance with at least one activity of daily living as their peers who are better off (Minkler, Fuller-Thomson, & Guralnik, 2006). Such disparities diminish with age, but income-related differences in disability rates are found even among elders who are in their 80s.

Ethnic-group differences in poverty are, no doubt, related to differences in educational attainment. Among older adults in the United States today, 84% of Whites and 74% of Asian Americans are high school graduates (FIFARS, 2012). So it is perhaps not surprising that these two groups have the lowest poverty rates. By contrast, 64% of African Americans and 47% of Hispanic Americans graduated from high school (FIFARS, 2012). Consequently, the employment histories of these groups are different, leading to income disparities in retirement. However, in future cohorts of retirees, these disparities are likely to diminish because of greatly increased rates of high school graduation and college attendance among younger minorities (FIFARS, 2012).

Similarly, single older adults continue to be more likely to be poor than their married peers, and among older singles, women are more likely to be poor than men (12% versus 7%, respectively) (O'Brien, Wu, & Baer, 2010). Different poverty rates for single men and women in old

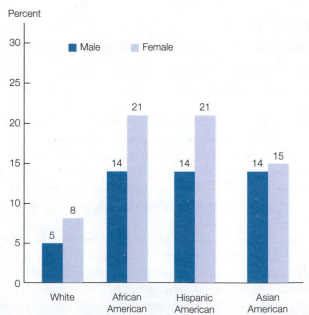

Figure 18.2   Ethnicity and Poverty among the Elderly in the United States

These data show the percentages of White, African American, Hispanic American, and Asian American males and females over the age of 65 who were classified as poor in 2011.

(*Source:* FIFARS, 2012.)

age arise from a number of differences in adult life experiences. Current cohorts of older women are much less likely than their male peers to have had paid employment, are less likely to have earned retirement benefits even if they did work, and generally worked for lower wages (Powell, 2006). As a result, many older widows rely entirely on Social Security income. Women in younger cohorts are more likely to have been employed and to have participated in a retirement plan, but, as you learned in earlier chapters, gender differences in work patterns still exist. Moreover, many more retirement-age women today are divorced than in past cohorts. The combination of income inequality and the increased prevalence of divorce are likely to lead to a dramatic rise in the number of women who live in poverty after retirement (Powell, 2006).

HEALTH, ATTITUDES, AND EMOTIONS Longitudinal studies indicate quite clearly that health does not change, for better or worse, simply because of retirement (van Solinge, 2007). When ill health accompanies retirement, the causal sequence is nearly always that the individual retired because of poor health. Nevertheless, for some individuals, retirement is accompanied by changes in behaviors that increase the risk of cardiovascular disease and other chronic conditions. For example, many people's BMIs increase after retirement as they increase caloric intake and reduce physical activity (Behncke, 2012). Such individuals' risk of disease rises accordingly. Consequently, changes in health after retirement are not inevitable but are influenced by the lifestyle choices you read about in Chapters 13 and 15—good nutrition, exercise, regular health screenings, and so on.

Interestingly, too, despite stereotypes to the contrary, older adults do not find retirement to be particularly stressful. One set of data that makes this point particularly clearly comes from a classic study of a group of more than 1,500 men over a period of years (Bossé, Aldwin, Levenson, & Workman-Daniels, 1991). In the most recent interviews, participants were asked to indicate which of 31 possibly stressful life events they had experienced in the past year and to rate the overall stressfulness of each of these events. Retirement was ranked 30th out of 31 in overall stressfulness, below even such items as "move to a less desirable residence" and "decrease in responsibilities or hours at work or where you volunteer." Of those who had retired in the previous year, 7 out of 10 said that they found retirement either not stressful at all or only a little stressful. Among the 30% of retired men in this study who did list some problems with retirement, poor health and poor family finances were the most likely causes. Those with marital problems were also likely to report more daily hassles in their retired lives.

Other evidence suggests that those who respond least well to retirement are those who had the least control over the decision (Smith & Moen, 2004). For example, those who go into retirement because of a late-career job loss show declines in physical and mental health (Halleröd, Örestig, & Stattin, 2013). Similarly, those who are forced to retire by poor health typically adjust more poorly to retirement (Hardy & Quadagno, 1995). Even workers who accept special early-retirement offers from their employers are likely to report lower satisfaction and higher levels of stress than do those who feel they had more control over the retirement decision (Herzog, House, & Morgan, 1991). But for those for whom retirement is anticipated, planned, and in tune with the individual's definition of "on-time" retirement, this role loss is not stressful.

It appears that what predicts life satisfaction in late adulthood is not whether a person has retired but whether he was satisfied with life in earlier adulthood. We take ourselves with us through the years: Grumpy, negative young people tend to be grumpy, negative old people, and satisfied young adults find satisfaction in retirement as well. The consistency of this finding is quite striking and provides very good support for continuity theories of adulthood. Work does shape daily life for 40 years or more of adulthood, but a person's happiness or unhappiness with life, her growth or stagnation, seems less a function of the specifics of the work experience than a function of the attitudes and qualities she brings to the process.

MOBILITY For many adults, retirement brings an increase in choices about where to live. When your job or your spouse's job no longer ties you to a specific place, you can choose to move to sunnier climes or to live nearer one of your children. Surprisingly, however, most retirees stay fairly close to the place they have called home for many years (Brown, 2004).

Elders who have moved to resort communities specifically designed for retired people have made what social scientists call an amenity move.

Charles Longino (1938–2008), who was one of the most diligent investigators of residential moves among the elderly, suggested that elderly adults make three types of moves (Longino, 2003). The first type, which he called an *amenity move*, is the one most of us probably think of when we think of older adults changing residences. If an older adult makes such a move, it is almost always right around the time of retirement. Most typically, an **amenity move** is in a direction away from the older person's children, frequently to a warmer climate. Florida, California, and Arizona are the most popular destinations for amenity moves in the United States. In Canada, amenity moves are most often westward, particularly to British Columbia; in Britain, the equivalent move is to the seaside.

Those who make amenity moves are likely to be still married and relatively healthy and to have adequate or good retirement income (Cress, 2007). Often the relocating couple has vacationed in the new location; many couples have planned such a move carefully over a number of years (Longino, Bradley, Stoller, & Haas, 2008). Most report higher levels of life satisfaction or morale after such a move, although some move back to where they came from because they find themselves too isolated from family and friends.

Another pattern of amenity move is to move seasonally rather than make a permanent move to a new location. Some elders, often called "snowbirds," spend the winter months in sunnier areas and the summer months at home, closer to their families. One survey of older retired residents of Minnesota found that 9% followed such a pattern (Hogan & Steinnes, 1994). Likewise, snowbirding is popular among European retirees. Millions of older French men and women, for example, spend the summer on the Moroccan coast (Viallon, 2012). Researchers have found that seasonal relocation enhances most snowbirds' life satisfaction (Bjelde & Sanders, 2009).

The second type of move, which Longino calls **compensatory (kinship) migration**, occurs when the older adult—most often a widow living alone—develops such a level of chronic disability that she has serious difficulty managing an independent household. When a move of this type occurs, it is nearly always a shift to be closer to a daughter, son, or some other relative who can provide regular assistance. In some cases, this means moving in with that daughter or son, but often the move is to an apartment or a house nearby or into a retirement community in which the individual can live independently but has supportive services available. The final type of move in late adulthood is what Longino calls **institutional migration**, to nursing home care.

Of course, very few older adults actually move three times. Longino's point is that these are three very different kinds of moves, made by quite different subsets of the population of elderly and at different times in the late adult years. Amenity moves usually occur early, kinship or compensatory migration is likely to occur in middle to late old age, and institutional migration clearly occurs late in life. Only amenity moves reflect the increase in options that may result from retirement.

amenity move a postretirement move away from kin to a location that has some desirable feature, such as year-round warm weather

compensatory (kinship) migration a move to a location near family or friends that happens when an elder requires frequent help because of a disability or disease

institutional migration a move to an institution such as a nursing home that is necessitated by a disability

---

test yourself before going on ✓ **Study** and **Review** in **MyPsychLab**

Answers to these questions can be found in the back of the book.

1. _____ is the most important predictor of quality of life in retirement.

2. An older adult who moves in order to be closer to an adult child had made a type of move that Longino calls a(n) _____.

3. Why is pacing important in job-training programs for older adults?

CRITICAL THINKING

4. In what ways do the educational and career decisions that people make in their 20s and 30s shape the decisions they make about retirement in late adulthood?

SUMMARY

Theories of Social and Personality Development (pp. 443–445)

LO18.1 What does research say about Erikson's stage of ego integrity versus despair?

- Erikson's concept of ego integrity has been influential, but research does not indicate that the development of ego integrity is necessary to adjustment in old age. The notions of reminiscence and life review have been helpful in researchers' attempts to understand development in late adulthood.

LO18.2 What are the main ideas of activity, disengagement, and continuity theory?

- Activity theory proposes that it is both normal and healthy for older adults to try to stay as active as possible. Disengagement theory asserts that it is normal for older adults to separate themselves from others. In addition, the theory argues that aging has three components: shrinkage of life space, increased individuality, and acceptance of age-related changes. Continuity theory views later adulthood as a time when elders cope with age-related changes by continuing to engage in activities that interested and challenged them earlier in life.

Individual Differences (pp. 445–449)

LO18.3 How is successful aging manifested in the lives of older adults?

- Successful aging is defined as maintenance of health along with cognitive and social functioning. Productivity and life satisfaction are also elements of successful aging.

LO18.4 How does religious coping influence physical and mental health in late adulthood?

- Religious coping has psychological and social components. It is associated with a lower mortality rate as well as with better physical and mental health. Researchers find that African Americans use religious coping more often than individuals in other groups.

Social Relationships (pp. 449–457)

LO18.5 What are the living arrangements of most elderly people in the United States and in other industrialized countries?

- Among unmarried elders in the United States, living alone is the most common living arrangement. However, a number of residential options are available for seniors who do not want to care for a home or who have become physically disabled.

LO18.6 How do intimate partnerships contribute to development in late adulthood?

- Marriages in late adulthood are, on average, highly satisfying for both spouses, who exhibit strong loyalty and mutual affection. In addition, marriage is associated with better physical and mental health, higher levels of life satisfaction, and lower rates of institutionalizations. Spouses are typically the primary caregivers to married elders who have disabilities.

LO18.7 What is the significance of family relationships and friendships for older adults?

- The majority of elders see their children regularly. There is some indication that relationships with siblings may become more significant in late adulthood than at earlier ages. Degree of contact with friends is correlated with overall life satisfaction among older adults.

LO18.8 What are some gender and ethnic differences in older adults' social networks?

- Women in this age group continue to have larger social networks than men do, and African Americans tend to have larger social networks than White Americans.

Career Issues in Late Life (pp. 457–462)

LO18.9 What factors contribute to the decision to retire?

- Many elders who choose not to retire do so for economic reasons. Those who are self-employed or have particularly strong commitments to work are also less likely to retire than their peers. Research indicates that older adults can learn new job skills, but training programs are most effective when they take into consideration age-related changes in physical and cognitive functioning. Time of retirement is affected by health, family responsibilities, adequacy of anticipated pension income, general economic conditions, and satisfaction with one's job.

LO18.10 How does retirement affect the lives of older adults?

- Income typically decreases with retirement. Poverty rates are lower for older adults than for younger ones. Among elders, women and minorities are most likely to live in poverty. Retirement has little effect on elders' health, and most do not view the transition from work to retirement as stressful. The minority of older adults who find retirement stressful are likely to be those who feel they have least control over the decision to retire. Many older adults move at some time during retirement. Types of moves include amenity moves, compensatory migrations, and institutional migrations.

KEY TERMS

activity theory (p. 444)

aging in place (p. 450)

amenity move (p. 462)

compensatory (kinship)
migration (p. 462)

continuity theory (p. 445)

disengagement theory (p. 444)

ego integrity (p. 443)

institutional migration (p. 462)

life review (p. 444)

religious coping (p. 448)

reminiscence (p. 443)

successful aging (p. 445)

volunteerism (p. 447)

CHAPTER TEST ☑ Study and Review in MyPsychLab

Answers to all the Chapter Test questions can be found in the back of the book.

1. What effect is retirement likely to have on health?
   a. The health of men declines rapidly after retirement.
   b. Retirement has little or no effect on health.
   c. It is likely to affect men but not women.
   d. The health of women is more likely to be affected by retirement.

2. An important factor in determining when a woman will retire is _____.
   a. whether or not her spouse has retired
   b. the likelihood that her Social Security income will decrease if she keeps working
   c. pressure from her children to retire
   d. he possibility of higher earnings that will augment her retirement income

3. Nick and Kathy love to play golf and swim. They recently moved to an apartment complex in Florida where everyone is about their age or perhaps a little older. They live autonomously but share common interests with their many neighbors and enjoy socializing on an almost daily basis. Nick and Kathy are probably living in which of the following?
   a. an assisted living center
   b. a CCRC
   c. a skilled nursing facility
   d. an independent living community

4. At 83 years old, Claudette happily recalls life when she was younger. She also enjoys spending time with her grandchildren and their children. According to Erikson, what has Claudette achieved?
   a. autonomy
   b. life competency
   c. ego integrity
   d. closure

5. Which of the following is *false* regarding the role of reminiscence in human development?
   a. Young adults use reminiscence for problem solving.
   b. Young adults reminisce more often than middle-aged or older adults.
   c. Structured reminiscence increases life satisfaction and can have therapeutic value.
   d. The most important function of reminiscence is preparation for death.

6. Professor Smith is 70 years old. She is considering retirement but has decided to move to Hawaii and teach one online class per semester. This is an example of which of the following?
   a. practical retirement
   b. social retirement
   c. a transitional job
   d. a bridge job

7. What term do gerontologists use to describe maintaining one's physical health, mental abilities, social competence, and general satisfaction with life?
   a. nonresistant aging
   b. successful aging
   c. elderpeace
   d. aging gracefully

8. Frank worked as a professional cabinet maker most of his adult life. He very much enjoyed this work, but now his physical ability to handle large pieces of carpentry is somewhat limited. Frank currently builds smaller pieces of furniture, such as coffee tables. Which of the following explains Frank's behavior?
   a. shrinkage of life space
   b. continuity theory
   c. disengagement theory
   d. acceptance of changes

9. Which of the following is the normal expectation for a woman in late adulthood in the United States?
   a. that she will live with her spouse or intimate partner until she dies
   b. that she will live with her spouse until she has difficulty performing activities of daily living, at which time she will move to a nursing home
   c. that she will live with her spouse until she begins to experience health problems, at which time she will move in with a child or family member
   d. that she will live alone, even if she experiences health problems or mild to moderate disability

10. When you contact a retired neighbor to ask if she is interested in participating in a charity fundraiser, she tells you that she is no longer interested in activities such as this, and she is content to do as little as possible since she retired. Your neighbor's perspective is most consistent with which of the following views on aging?
    a. adaptation
    b. social reticence
    c. discontinuity theory
    d. disengagement

11. Which of the following is the best example of an institutional migration after retirement, as described by Charles Longino?
    a. When Mr. and Mrs. Polanski retired, they wanted year-round opportunities to hike and bird-watch, so they moved to a retirement community in Arizona.
    b. When Mrs. Short became disabled by arthritis and could no longer live independently in her home, she decided to move into an apartment in the town where her daughter lived.
    c. After Mr. Brown was released from the hospital, he entered a nursing home where he was cared for until he died.
    d. After Mr. and Mrs. Garcia retired, they assumed custody of their grandchildren and moved to a larger house.

12. Which of the following is true regarding the positive effects of marriage on physical and psychological functioning of older adults?
    a. They occur among both women and men but are generally greater for men than women.
    b. They are greater for women than for men.
    c. They exist for men, but there are no benefits for older women.
    d. Those that were seen in early and middle adulthood have largely disappeared by late adulthood.

13. Bertie is pretty spry, and she likes her independence, which is considerable for a 94-year-old. Still, she is no longer able to

cook for herself, and she has some difficulty with certain activities of daily living. Miss Bertie might be a good candidate for living in _____.

    a. a nursing home   **c.** an assisted living facility

    b. a home-health facility   **d.** a skilled nursing center

14. Which of the following describes a common belief in Asian cultures that children have the responsibility to care for their aging parents?

    a. paternal devotion   **c.** collectivism

    b. familial cohesion   **d.** filial piety

15. According to research, what is the most common effect of activity on later life?

    a. fatigue and depression from overwhelming roles and responsibilities

    b. more rewarding relationships with members of the social support network

    c. greater life satisfaction and morale

    d. increased mortality because the effects of disabling conditions such as diabetes may be magnified

16. What is the largest source of income for most elderly adults in the United States?

    a. income from savings or other assets

    b. public assistance

    c. Social Security

    d. pension funds

17. Which of the following best represents poverty trends among the elderly in the United States over the past 50 years?

    a. Poverty levels have not changed.

    b. Poverty rates have risen.

    c. Poverty rates have declined.

    d. No clear trend has been found in research examining poverty among the elderly.

18. Which of the following is *not* a characteristic that is known to predict life satisfaction among older adults?

    a. an extroverted personality

    b. favorable comparisons to others of the same age

    c. self-ratings of health

    d. perceptions that important aspects of life, such as income or social support, are adequate

19. Which of the following individuals is likely to retire earliest?

    a. an individual who will rely solely on Social Security for support during retirement

    b. an individual who still has young children at home

    c. an individual in poor health

    d. an individual in good health

20. Which of the following individuals is most likely to turn to religion for comfort in times of stress?

    a. Mai Ling, an Asian American woman who is 76 years old.

    b. Albert DeNida, a 72-year-old Italian American.

    c. Della Reed, an African American who is 83 years old.

    d. Michael Smith, a White American who is 63 years old.

21. Which of the following is the best definition of *spirituality*?

    a. belonging to a mainstream religious group

    b. a general tendency to focus on aspects of life which transcend one's physical existence

    c. the adherence to a strictly defined set of beliefs

    d. a tendency to focus on the philosophical aspects of one's physical existence

22. Which statement most accurately describes the relationships of older adults and their children?

    a. Most contacts between older adults and their children occur in order to fulfill obligations and a sense of duty.

    b. Good relationships and regular contact between older adults and their children are beneficial but not essential for happiness or life satisfaction in old age.

    c. Older adults who need aid or assistance that cannot be provided by a spouse typically rely on friends, neighbors, and community agencies for the services they need.

    d. Very few adults over age 65 have regular contact or spend time with their children.

23. Which of the following is a component of successful aging?

    a. retaining cognitive abilities

    b. continuing to work beyond typical retirement age

    c. an interesting and enjoyable hobby

    d. staying in contact with co-workers after retirement

24. Which of the following is *false* regarding the nature of marital status and living arrangements in late adulthood in the United States?

    a. The normal expectation for a woman is that she will eventually be without an intimate partner or spouse.

    b. Most elders with mild to moderate disability or health problems do not live with relatives.

    c. In the United States, living alone is the most common and the most preferred living arrangement among unmarried elders.

    d. Older men are more likely to live alone than older women.

25. Associations between religious coping and health among older adults may be explained by

    a. selection effects

    b. social support available from fellow members of a religious institutions

    c. effects on older adults' thinking

    d. all of the above

To 👁 **Watch** ❄ **Explore** ◉ **Simulate** ✓ **Study** and **Review** and experience MyVirtualLife go to MyPsychLab.com

chapter 19

Death, Dying, and Bereavement

Every story has an ending. For the human lifespan, that ending is death. Even though every individual's life story ends with the same event, there is a great deal of variation from one person to another in how that event manifests itself. These variations contribute to how the dying and the bereaved cope with the emotional turmoil and sense of loss that typically accompany death. In this chapter you will learn about variations in the events surrounding death and in the strategies that individuals use to cope with death's inevitability.

LEARNING OBJECTIVES

THE EXPERIENCE OF DEATH

19.1 What are the characteristics of clinical death, brain death, and social death?

19.2 How do hospice and hospital care differ with respect to their effects on terminally ill patients?

THE MEANING OF DEATH ACROSS THE LIFESPAN

19.3 What are the characteristics of children's and adolescents' ideas about death?

19.4 How do young, middle-aged, and older adults think about death?

19.5 What factors are related to fear of death in adults?

19.6 How do adults prepare for death?

THE PROCESS OF DYING

19.7 How did Kübler-Ross explain the process of dying?

19.8 What are some other views of the process of dying?

19.9 How do people vary in the ways they adapt to impending death?

THEORETICAL PERSPECTIVES ON GRIEVING

19.10 How does Freud's psychoanalytic theory view grief?

19.11 What are the theories of Bowlby and Sanders regarding grief?

19.12 What theories of grief have been proposed by critics of psychoanalytic and attachment theories?

THE EXPERIENCE OF GRIEVING

19.13 How do funerals and ceremonies help survivors cope with grief?

19.14 What factors influence the grieving process?

19.15 How does grief affect the physical and mental health of widows and widowers?

The Experience of Death

Most of us use the word *death* as if it described a simple phenomenon. You are either alive or dead. But, in fact, death is a process as well as a state, and physicians have different labels for different aspects of this process. Moreover, for both the deceased and the bereaved, the experience of death is shaped by the circumstances surrounding the end of life.

Death Itself

LO 19.1   What are the characteristics of clinical death, brain death, and social death?

The term **clinical death** refers to the few minutes after the heart has stopped pumping, when breathing has stopped and there is no evident brain function, but during which resuscitation is still possible. Heart-attack patients are sometimes brought back from clinical death; presumably those who report near-death experiences were in a state of clinical death.

Brain death describes a state in which the person no longer has reflexes or any response to vigorous external stimuli and no electrical activity in the brain. When the cortex, but not the brain stem, is affected, the person may still be able to breathe without assistance and may survive for long periods in a vegetative state or on life-support systems. When the brain stem is also dead, no body functioning can occur independently, and the individual is said to be legally dead (Detchant, 1995). Brain death most often occurs after a period of 8–10 minutes of clinical death, but there are cases in which brain death has occurred because of brain injury, as in an auto accident, and other body functions can still be maintained artificially. In such cases, other body organs, such as the heart and kidneys, can be used for organ donation, as long as they are removed without delay.

Social death occurs at the point when other people treat the deceased person like a corpse. For instance, someone may close the eyes or sign a death certificate. Once social death has been acknowledged, family and friends must begin to deal with the loss.

Where Death Occurs

LO 19.2   How do hospice and hospital care differ with respect to their effects on terminally ill patients?

Until recently, the great majority of adults died in hospitals. As a result of rising health-care costs and changing views about the process of dying, just over 40% of deaths in the United States occur in hospitals these days, as you can see in Figure 19.1, while just a decade ago over half of all deaths took place in hospitals (NCHS, 2013). The decline in hospital deaths is largely attributable to changing beliefs about what constitutes a "good death." One outcome of these changing beliefs is **hospice care**, an approach to caring for the dying that emphasizes individual and family control of the process.

Hospice care emerged in England in the late 1960s and in the United States in the early 1970s (Mor, 1987). By 1982, the idea had gained so much support in the United States that Congress was persuaded to add hospice care to the list of benefits Medicare pays for. There are now more than 5,000 hospice programs in the United States, serving more than a million terminally ill patients and their families (National Hospice and Palliative Care Organization [NHPCO], 2012). In the United States, roughly 45% of individuals with terminal illnesses receive some kind of hospice care.

The philosophy that underlies this alternative approach to the dying patient has several aspects (Bass, 1985):

- Death should be viewed as normal, not to be avoided but to be faced and accepted.

- The patient and family should be encouraged to prepare for the death by examining their feelings, planning for after the death, and talking openly about the death.

clinical death   a period during which vital signs are absent but resuscitation is still possible

brain death   the point at which vital signs, including brain activity, are absent and resuscitation is no longer possible

social death   the point at which family members and medical personnel treat the deceased person as a corpse

hospice care   an approach to care for the terminally ill that emphasizes individual and family control of the process of dying

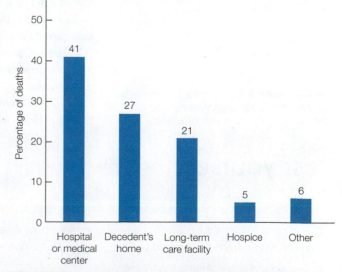

Figure 19.1   Where Death Occurs in the United States

(*Source:* NCHS, 2013.)

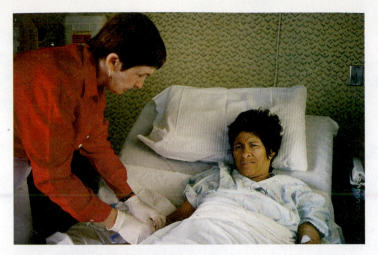

This woman, who is dying of cancer, has chosen to stay at home during her last months, supported by regular visits from hospice nurses.

- The family should be involved in the patient's care as much as is physically possible, not only because this gives the patient the emotional support of loved ones but also because it allows each family member to come to some resolution of her or his relationship with the dying person.

- Control over the patient's care should be in the hands of the patient and the family. They decide what types of medical treatment they will ask for or accept; they decide whether the patient will remain at home or be hospitalized.

- Medical care should be primarily **palliative care** rather than curative treatment. The emphasis of palliative care is on controlling pain and maximizing comfort, not on invasive or life-prolonging measures.

Three somewhat different types of hospice programs have been developed following these general guidelines. The most common hospice programs are residence based, in which one family caregiver—most frequently, the dying person's spouse—provides constant care for the dying person, with the support and assistance of specially trained nurses or other staff who visit regularly, provide medication, and help the family deal psychologically with the impending death. The patient's residence is most often a private home, but many patients are also served in nursing homes. Two-thirds of hospice patients receive residence-based services (NHPCO, 2012). A second type of program is a special hospice center, where about one-quarter of patients in the last stages of a terminal disease are cared for in a homelike setting. Finally, hospital-based hospice programs serve 11% of terminally ill patients (NHPCO, 2012). These programs provide palliative care according to the basic hospice philosophy, with daily involvement of family members and hospital staff in the patient's care (NHPCO, 2012). ● Watch the Video Hospice in MyPsychLab.

Terminally ill patients who are cared for at home through hospice arrangements are admitted to the hospital less often in the last several months of life than those who do not receive home-based care, even though they tend to survive longer (Connor, Pyenson, Fitch, Spence, & Kosuke, 2007; Gozalo & Miller, 2007; NHPCO, 2012). Thus, the economic costs of death are reduced by hospice care (Stevenson & Bramson, 2009). At the same time, both studies make clear that home-based hospice care is a considerable burden, especially on the central caregiver, who may spend as many as 19 hours a day in physical care.

Despite widespread use of hospice services, both patients and caregivers express concerns about hospice care. For example, both sometimes have more faith in hospital personnel when it comes to providing pain relief. Consequently, patients and their caregivers want assurances that the medical care they will receive in a hospice arrangement will be equivalent in quality to that of a hospital (Vachon, 1998).

In addition, hospice care providers must recognize that caregivers have needs as well. In fact, caring for a dying loved one, particularly someone with dementia, induces a grief response (Lindgren, Connelly, & Gaspar, 1999; Rudd, Viney, & Preston, 1999). Consequently, another important element of hospice care is grief support for the primary caregiver, including both psychosocial and educational components (NHPCO, 2012). Similarly, hospice care providers themselves also often require support services because of the emotional strain involved in caring for patients who are terminally ill.

palliative care a form of care for terminally ill people that focuses on relieving patients' pain rather than curing their diseases

---

test yourself before going on   ✓ Study and Review in MyPsychLab

Answers to these questions can be found in the back of the book.

1. A person who has survived on a life-support system for several years has probably experienced _____ death.

2. A growing number of families are turning to _____ care for their dying loved ones, a form of care that emphasizes the normative nature of death.

CRITICAL THINKING

3. What are the advantages and disadvantages of hospice care, and how would you balance them in making a decision about this option for yourself or a loved one?

The Meaning of Death across the Lifespan

As an adult, you understand that death is irreversible, that it comes to everyone, and that it means a cessation of all function. But do children and teenagers understand these aspects of death? And what does death mean to adults of different ages?

Children's and Adolescents' Understanding of Death

LO 19.3 What are the characteristics of children's and adolescents' ideas about death?

Results from a variety of studies suggest that preschool-aged children typically understand none of these aspects of death. They believe that death can be reversed through, for instance, prayer, magic, or wishful thinking; they believe that dead persons can still feel or breathe. Research shows that young children's ideas about death are rooted in their lack of understanding of life (Slaughter & Lyons, 2003). This link between understanding life and understanding death has been illustrated in a series of studies showing that teaching young children about the nature of biological life helps them understand what causes death and why it is irreversible.

By the time they start school, just about the time Piaget described as the beginning of concrete operations, most children seem to understand both the permanence and the universality of death. Children 6 to 7 years of age comprehend death as a biological event in which the heart ceases to beat, the lungs no longer take in air, and brain activity stops (Barrett & Behne, 2005; Slaughter, 2005).

As is true of so many other milestones of this age range, a child's specific experience seems to make a good deal of difference. Young children who have had direct experience with the death of a family member are more likely to understand the permanence of death than are those who have had no such personal experience (Bonoti, Leondari, & Mastora, 2013). Experiences in which children discover a dead animal, lose a pet, or are exposed to a story in which a character dies (e.g., *Bambi, The Lion King*) can also speed up somewhat the process of developing an understanding of death (Cox, Garrett, & Graham, 2004–2005). Such experiences influence children's understanding of death because they serve as a catalyst for discussions of death with children's parents. Such discussions, when they focus on the concrete, biological aspects of death, provide children with the scaffolding they need to achieve a cognitive understanding of death (Moore & Moore, 2010). Linking death to broader values with which children are familiar helps them grasp the social aspects of death.

Adolescents understand the finality of death better than children do. Moreover, in an abstract sense, they understand that death is inevitable. Nevertheless, adolescents tend to overestimate their own chances of death (Fischoff, de Bruin, Parker, Millstein, & Halpern-Felsher, 2010). This phenomenon is most pronounced among teens who have personal experience with death, particularly those who live in high-crime neighborhoods.

Unrealistic beliefs about personal death also appear to contribute to adolescent suicide. Typically, teens who attempt suicide claim to understand that death is final, but many tell researchers and counselors that the purpose of their suicidal behavior was to achieve a temporary escape from a stressful personal problem (Blau, 1996). (See *Developmental Science in the Classroom* on page 470.) Further, researchers have found that some teenagers who attempt suicide believe that death is a pleasurable experience for most people who die (Gothelf et al., 1998). Certainly, such distorted beliefs may result from the powerful emotions that lead teens to attempt suicide rather than from adolescent thinking. However, suicidal adults typically think of death, even when it is desired, as painful and unpleasant. So there may be a developmental difference between suicidal adolescents' and suicidal adults' understanding of death.

Like those of children, adolescents' ideas about death are affected by their personal experiences. Experiencing the death of a family member or friend, especially someone who is near the teenager's own age, tends to shake an adolescent's confidence in her own immortality.

These children being comforted by an adult at a loved one's grave are likely to have far more mature concepts of death than others their age who have not encountered death firsthand.

Copycat Suicide and the Internet

From the outside looking in, Brent, a popular senior at Pine Ridge High School, seemed happy and carefree. Consequently, Brent's teachers were shocked when his body was discovered late one night on a hiking path near his home, and it was immediately apparent that he had died of a self-inflicted gunshot wound to the head. Subsequent investigation showed that Brent had posted a suicide note on his social networking page a few days before his death and that a few students at the school were aware of his plans. Although Mr. Jones, Pine Ridge's principal, was just as saddened as everyone else about Brent's passing, the well-being of other students at the school was also of great concern to him. He knew that, thanks to social networking and text messaging, the news of Brent's suicide would travel rapidly through the student grapevine at Pine Ridge. Mr. Jones's greatest fear was that Brent's suicide would inspire other students to commit so-called "copycat" suicides. As a result, he advised teachers to avoid discussing Brent's death or the issue of suicide in general. Was Mr. Jones right to be concerned about the potential impact of Brent's death on students at Pine Ridge High School?

The events surrounding a series of suicides in which several teens in the small Welsh community of Bridgend hanged themselves suggest that Mr. Jones's concerns are well founded (Salkeld & Koster, 2008). Several of the teens knew each other personally, but others were connected to the group only through online relationships. Many of them openly discussed their suicide plans on social networking sites, even going so far as to post messages about the dates on which they planned to kill themselves. None of the teachers or parents of these teens were aware that their children had been discussing suicide online, but many of their peers were.

Investigations of the Bridgend case and others like it have revealed that teens' near-universal access to the Internet and facility with the skills needed to create online videos and sophisticated websites have given those who want to gain celebrity status through committing suicide a means of doing so (Birbal et al., 2009; Naito, 2007; Nicolis, 2007). In addition, numerous online prosuicide forums and websites that provide information about reliable methods of committing suicide have appeared in recent years (Scott & Temporini, 2010). Researchers have found that, in many cases, teenaged suicide victims consult such sites prior to killing themselves.

Research suggests that training parents and teachers to recognize signs of depression and substance abuse can help prevent suicide in individual teens (Galaif, Sussman, Newcomb, & Locke, 2007). However, copycat suicides that involve teenagers who use social media to publicize their intentions may be driven by a desire for fame rather than the psychological factors that mental health professional typically associate with suicide. Consequently, mental health professionals acknowledge that much more research needs to be done before they will be able to provide school officials in Mr. Jones's situation with advice on the way to prevent copycat suicides (Naito, 2007).

REFLECTION

1. *Do you agree with Mr. Jones's decision to discourage students from discussing Brent's death? Why or why not?*

2. *In your opinion, what steps should governments, school officials, and/or parents take to address the issue of dissemination of information about suicide methods to adolescents on the Internet?*

In fact, research suggests that the loss of someone close, such as a sibling, may lead an adolescent to critically reexamine her ideas about death—both as a general concept and as something that is inevitable for herself (Batten & Oltjenbruns, 1999).

The Meaning of Death for Adults

LO 19.4 How do young, middle-aged, and older adults think about death?

Adults' ideas about death vary with age. Death seems remote to most young adults. The notion of personal mortality is a more common focus of thought in middle age, and by the later years, the idea of death becomes very personally relevant for most adults.

EARLY ADULTHOOD In recent years, research examining young adults' views on death has been guided by a theoretical concept similar to the personal fable. Psychologists point out that young adults have a sense of **unique invulnerability**—a belief that bad things, including death, happen to others but not to themselves. Although young adults are more realistic about personal mortality than adolescents are, researchers find that many believe they possess unique personal characteristics that somehow protect them against death. Some studies suggest that many young adults engage in high-risk activities such as rock-climbing because succeeding at them reinforces invulnerability beliefs (Popham, Kennison, & Bradley, 2011).

However, the loss of a loved one appears to shake a young adult's belief in unique invulnerability and, as a result, is often more traumatic for younger than for older adults (Liu & Aaker, 2007). In fact, such losses frequently lead to suicidal thoughts in young adults. Young adults who have recently lost a loved one in an accident or to a homicide or suicide are about five

unique invulnerability the belief that bad things, including death, happen only to others

times as likely to formulate a suicide plan as young adults who have not had such a loss, although most never follow through with their plans (Prigerson et al., 1999).

Analyses of public reactions to the deaths of relatively young celebrities, such as Princess Diana, crocodile hunter Steve Irwin, actor Heath Ledger, and Corey Monteith, provide additional insight into young adults' ideas about death. As you may have noticed, public interest in the events surrounding celebrities' deaths, as evidenced by the frequency of tabloid headline stories devoted to them, continues for many years afterward (Brown, Basil, & Bocarnea, 2003). Likewise, purchases of products that are associated with a celebrity who dies in early adulthood typically rise dramatically immediately after his or her death (Radford & Bloch, 2013). Psychologists hypothesize that such early deaths challenge young people's beliefs in unique invulnerability and, therefore, provoke defensive reactions that cause them to place those who die young in a special category. In other words, to maintain belief in their own unique invulnerability, young people must come up with reasons why death came early to a young celebrity but will not happen to them. As a result, they elevate such figures to near-sainthood.

MIDDLE AND LATE ADULTHOOD In middle and late adulthood, an understanding of death goes well beyond the simple acceptance of finality, inevitability, and universality. A death changes the roles and relationships of everyone else in a family. For example, when an elder dies, everyone else in that particular lineage "moves up" in the generational system. As you learned in Chapter 16, the death of a parent can be particularly unsettling for a middle-aged adult if he does not consider himself ready to assume the elder role.

An individual's death also affects the roles of people beyond the family, such as younger adults in a business organization, who then take on new and perhaps more significant roles. Retirement serves the same function, as an older adult steps aside for a younger one. But death brings many permanent changes in families and social systems. At an individual level, the prospect of death may shape one's view of time (Kalish, 1985). In middle age, most people exhibit a shift in their thinking about time, thinking less about "time since birth" and being more aware of "time till death."

Such an "awareness of finitude" is not a part of every middle-aged or older adult's view of death (Marshall, 1975). One study of a group of adults aged 72 and older found that only about half thought in terms of "time remaining" (Keith, 1981/1982). Interestingly, those who did think of death in these terms had less fear of death than did those who thought of their lives as "time lived." Other research confirms this: Middle-aged and older adults who continue to be preoccupied with the past are more likely to be fearful and anxious about death (Pollack, 1979/1980).

After the death of pop legend Michael Jackson, members of the public left thousands of flowers and gifts in front of his Neverland Ranch home in California in a spontaneous gesture of grief. Based on analyses of such responses to the deaths of public figures, some developmentalists believe that young adults idealize celebrities who die earlier in life than is typical in order to avoid confronting their own mortality.

DEATH AS LOSS The most pervasive meaning of death for adults of all ages is loss. Which of the many potential losses is feared or dreaded the most seems to change with age. Young adults are more concerned about loss of opportunity to experience things and about the loss of family relationships; older adults worry more about the loss of time to complete inner work. Such differences are evident in the results of a classic study in which researchers interviewed roughly 400 adults, equally divided into four ethnic groups: African American, Japanese American, Mexican American, and White American (Kalish & Reynolds, 1976). Among many other questions, researchers asked, "If you were told that you had a terminal disease and 6 months to live, how would you want to spend your time until you died?" (Think about this question for a moment yourself before reading on.) The only sizable ethnic difference that the researchers found was that Mexican Americans were the most likely to say that they would increase the time they spent with family or other loved ones. Age differences were more substantial. Younger adults were more likely to say that they would seek out new experiences; older adults were considerably more likely to say that they would turn inward—an interesting piece of support for disengagement theory. **◉ Watch** the **Video** *Death, Grief, and Mourning* in **MyPsychLab**.

Fear of Death

LO 19.5   What factors are related to fear of death in adults?

Survey questions such as "Do you fear death?" are far too simplistic to capture how people really feel about an issue as momentous as their own death. Thus, psychologists who study people's death-related fears have tried a number of ways to elicit more thoughtful responses than are typically generated by surveys. One such approach is to ask participants to indicate, on a five-point scale, how disturbed or anxious they feel when thinking about various aspects of death or dying, such as "the shortness of life" or "never thinking or experiencing anything again" or "your lack of control over the process of dying" (Lester, 1990). Another approach asks participants to respond to statements such as "I fear dying a painful death" or "Coffins make me anxious" or "I am worried about what happens to us after we die" (Thorson & Powell, 1992).

FEAR OF DEATH ACROSS ADULTHOOD Although you might think that those closest to death would fear it the most, research suggests that middle-aged adults are most fearful of death (Kumabe, 2006). For young adults, the sense of unique invulnerability probably prevents intense fears of death. In middle age, though, belief in one's own immortality begins to break down, resulting in increasing anxiety about the end of life. However, by late life, the inevitability of death has been accepted, and anxieties are focused on how death will actually come about.

However, older adults do not become less preoccupied with death, and most would prefer to extend their lives as long as possible (Cicirelli, 2011). Nevertheless, to an older person, particularly one who has a strong sense of having lived for some higher purpose, death is highly important, but it is apparently not as frightening as it was at midlife (Cicirelli, 2006). Older adults are more likely to fear the period of uncertainty before death than they are to fear death itself (Sullivan, Ormel, Kempen, & Tymstra, 1998). They are anxious about where they may die, who will care for them until they do, and whether they will be able to cope with the pain and loss of control and independence that may be part of the last months or years of life (Marshall & Levy, 1990).

RELIGIOUS BELIEFS Researchers typically find that adults who are religious are less afraid of death than are those who describe themselves as less religious (Ardelt, 2003; Landes & Ardelt, 2011; Lin, 2003). In some instances, however, researchers have found that both those who are deeply religious and those who are totally irreligious report less fear of death (Landes & Ardelt, 2011). Thus, the most fearful may be those who are uncertain about or dissatisfied with their spiritual beliefs.

Religious beliefs may moderate fears of death because religious people tend to view death as a transition from one form of life to another, from physical life to some kind of immortality. In the United States, roughly 74% of the population believes in some kind of life after death (Pew Research Center, 2010). Such a belief is more common among women than among men, and it is more common among Catholics and Protestants than among Jews, but there is no age difference. Twenty-year-olds are just as likely to report such a belief as are those over 60.

In addition to framing death as a transition rather than an end, religious beliefs provide adults with death stories that help them cope with both their own deaths and those of loved ones (Winter, 1999). For example, Jewish scriptures, the Christian Bible, and the Muslim Quran all contain many stories that convey the idea that death comes when one's purpose in life has been fulfilled. Many such stories also teach that each individual life is part of a larger, multigenerational story. In this larger context, death is portrayed as a necessary part of the transfer of responsibility from one generation to another. This kind of philosophical approach to death leads believers to focus on the contributions to family and community that they have made during their lives rather than on the losses they will experience at their deaths.

PERSONAL WORTH   Feelings about death are also linked to one's sense of personal worth or competence (Tam, 2013). Adults who feel that they have achieved the goals they set out to achieve or who believe that they have become the person they wanted to be are less anxious about death than are those who are disappointed in themselves (Ardelt & Koenig, 2006). Adults who believe that their lives have had some purpose or meaning also appear to be less fearful of death, as do those who have some sense of personal competence (Durlak, 1972; Pollack, 1979/1980).

Such findings suggest the possibility that adults who have successfully completed the major tasks of adult life, who have adequately fulfilled the demands of the roles they occupied, and who have developed inwardly are able to face death with greater equanimity. Adults who have not been able to resolve the various tasks and dilemmas of adulthood face their late adult years more anxiously, even with what Erikson described as despair. Fear of death may be merely one facet of such despair.

Preparation for Death

LO 19.6   How do adults prepare for death?

Preparation for death occurs on a number of levels (see *No Easy Answers* on page 474). At a practical level, regardless of age, most adults agree that it is important to make preparations for death (Steinhauser et al., 2001). Such preparations typically include purchasing life insurance, making a will, and preparing written instructions regarding end-of-life care, often called an *advance directive*. Individuals can use advance directives to make clear to health-care professionals and to their families that they either do or do not wish to have their lives prolonged with feeding tubes and other devices. Similarly, a *health-care power of attorney* specifies who can make decisions for an individual in the event that he or she becomes unable to do so. Moreover, most people agree that advance funeral planning can help bereaved family members deal with the many decisions they must make in the hours and days following the death of a loved one. However, researchers have found that older adults are far more likely than younger adults to have actually made such preparations (Moorman & Inoue, 2013).

At a somewhat deeper level, adults may prepare for death through some process of reminiscence. Deeper still, there may be unconscious changes that occur in the years just before death, which might be thought of as a type of preparation. You read in Chapter 17 about the physical and mental changes associated with terminal decline. Research has pointed to the possibility that there may be terminal psychological changes as well.

For example, in a still influential study, researchers studied a group of older adults longitudinally, interviewing and testing each participant regularly over a period of 3 years (Lieberman, 1965; Lieberman & Coplan, 1970). After the testing, investigators kept track of the participants and noted when they died. They were able to identify one group of 40 participants who had all died within 1 year of the end of the interviewing and to compare them with another group of 40, matched to the first group by age, sex, and marital status, who had survived at least 3 years after the end of the testing. By comparing the psychological test scores obtained by those in these two groups during the course of the 3 years of testing, researchers could detect changes that occurred near death.

Saying Goodbye

The Kaliai, a small Melanesian society in Papua New Guinea, believe that all deaths are caused by a person or spirit whom the dying person has offended in some way (Counts, 1976/1977). Any person who feels that he is near death moves from his house into a temporary shelter, where he attempts to appease whichever person or spirit he thinks he may have offended. He also attempts to thwart death through the use of various medicines and cures. When death becomes imminent, family members and friends return items borrowed from the dying person and pay debts they owe him. Likewise, the dying person returns borrowed items and repays debts owed to family members and friends. The Kaliai believe that this process of bringing relationships into balance prepares the dying person for an afterlife in which he will become a powerful superhuman being.

But how do you say goodbye to a dying loved one, or how does a dying person say goodbye to loved ones, in a culture where discussions of death are largely taboo?

A classic study in Australia gives a glimpse of the variety of goodbyes devised by the dying (Kellehear & Lewin, 1988/1989). Researchers interviewed 90 terminally ill cancer patients, all of whom expected to die within a year. Most had known of their cancer diagnosis for at least a year prior to the interview but had only recently been given a short-term prognosis. As part of the interview, these 90 people were asked if they had already said farewell to anyone and to describe any plans they had for future farewells. To whom did they want to say goodbye, and how would they say it?

About a fifth of these people planned no farewells. Another three-fifths thought it was important to say goodbye but wanted to put it off until very near the end so as to distress family and friends as little as possible. They hoped that there would then be time for a few final words with spouses, children, and close friends. The remaining fifth began their farewells much earlier and used many different avenues. In a particularly touching farewell gesture, one woman who had two grown daughters but no grandchildren knitted a set of baby clothes for each daughter, for the grandchildren she would never see.

Kellehear and Lewin make the important point that such farewells are a kind of gift. They signal that the dying person feels that someone is worthy of a last goodbye. Such farewells may also represent a balancing of the relationship slate just as important as the balancing of material possessions is among the Kaliai.

Farewells also may allow the dying person to disengage more readily when death comes closer and to warn others that death is indeed approaching. Hearing someone say farewell may thus help the living to begin a kind of anticipatory grieving and, in this way, prepare better for the loss.

YOU DECIDE

Decide which of these two statements you most agree with and think about how you would defend your position:

1. **Neither a person who is ill nor her loved ones should ever give up on life. They should always be thinking in terms of how to help the sick person survive rather than focusing on saying goodbye.**

2. **Acknowledging the reality of approaching death is the best way to help a person who is ill and those who are close to her cope with the stress of losing a loved one.**

The study's results revealed that those nearer death not only showed terminal decline on tests of memory and learning but also became less emotional, introspective, and aggressive or assertive and more conventional, docile, dependent, and warm. In those near death, all these characteristics increased over the 3 years of interviewing, a pattern that did not occur among those of the same age who were further from death. Thus, conventional, docile, dependent, and nonintrospective adults did not die sooner; rather, these qualities became accentuated in those who were close to death.

This is only a single study. As always in such cases, it's important to be careful about drawing sweeping conclusions from limited evidence. But the results are intriguing and suggestive. They paint a picture of a kind of psychological preparation for death—conscious or unconscious—in which an individual "gives up the fight," becoming less active physically and psychologically. Thus, near death, individuals do not necessarily become less involved with other people, but they do seem to show some kind of disengagement.

test yourself before going on ☑ Study and Review in MyPsychLab

Answers to these questions can be found in the back of the book.

1. Children begin to understand that death is a biological event at about age _____.

2. Young adults' thinking about death is often influenced by a set of beliefs called _____ _____.

3. Which age group, middle-aged or elderly, fears death the most?

4. As a result of the terminal psychological changes that occur in the 3 years prior to death, individuals become more _____, _____, _____, and _____.

CRITICAL THINKING

5. What role do age and fear of death play in people's decisions about death preparations such as living wills and prepaid funeral arrangements?

The Process of Dying

Elisabeth Kübler-Ross (1926–2004) was a Swiss-American psychiatrist who studied the experiences of the dying and their loved ones. In the 1960s she formulated a model asserting that those who are dying go through a series of psychological stages. This model of dying, formulated on the basis of interviews with approximately 200 adults who were dying of cancer, continues to be highly influential, although it has many critics. In addition, research suggests that individual differences affect the process of dying in important ways.

Kübler-Ross's Stages of Dying

LO 19.7   How did Kübler-Ross explain the process of dying?

In Kübler-Ross's early writings, she proposed that those who know they are dying move through a series of steps, or stages, arriving finally at the stage she called *acceptance* (see Table 19.1). Kübler-Ross's ideas and her terminology are still widely used (Roos, 2013). In fact, surveys of death education programs suggest that Kübler-Ross's model is the only systematic approach to the dying process to which health professionals-in-training are exposed (Downe-Wamboldt & Tamlyn, 1997). Thus, you should at least be familiar with the stages she proposed.

Kübler-Ross's model predicts that most people who are confronted with a terminal diagnosis react with some variant of "Not me," "It must be a mistake," "I'll get another opinion," or "I don't feel sick." All of these are forms of *denial*, a psychological defense that may be highly useful in the early hours and days after such a diagnosis. Denial of this kind may be helpful in insulating a person's emotions from the trauma of hearing such news. Keeping emotions in check in this way may help an individual formulate a rational plan of action based on "What if it's true?" Having a plan of action may help moderate the effects of acknowledging the reality of the diagnosis. Kübler-Ross thought that these extreme forms of denial would fade within a few days, to be replaced by *anger*.

The model further suggests that anger among the dying expresses itself in thoughts like "It's not fair!" but a dying person may also express anger toward God, the doctor who made the diagnosis, nurses, or family members. The anger seems to be a response not only to the diagnosis but also to the sense of loss of control and helplessness that many patients feel in impersonal medical settings.

Bargaining follows anger in the Kübler-Ross model. This is a form of defense in which the patient tries to make "deals" with doctors, nurses, family, or God: "If I do everything you tell me, then I'll live until spring." Kübler-Ross gave a particularly compelling example of this defense reaction: A patient with terminal cancer wanted to live long enough to attend the wedding of her eldest son. The hospital staff, to help her try to reach this goal, taught her self-hypnosis to deal with her pain, and she was able to attend the wedding. Kübler-Ross reported, "I will never forget the moment when she returned to the hospital. She looked tired and somewhat exhausted and—before I could say hello—said, 'Now don't forget, I have another son!'" (1969, p. 83).

TABLE 19.1 Stages of Dying Proposed by Kübler-Ross

Denial	People's first reaction to news of a terminal diagnosis is disbelief.
Anger	Once the diagnosis is accepted as real, individuals become angry.
Bargaining	Anger and stress are managed by thinking of the situation in terms of exchanges (e.g., If I take my medicine, I will live longer; if I pray hard enough, God will heal me).
Depression	Feelings of despair follow when the disease advances despite the individual's compliance with medical and other advice.
Acceptance	Grieving for the losses associated with one's death results in acceptance.

Children use some of the same defenses as adults to deal with impending death. Young cancer patients may deny or bargain—for instance, "If I take my medicine, I'll be able to go back to school in the fall."

Bargaining may be successful as a defense for a while, but the model predicts that, eventually, bargaining breaks down in the face of signs of declining health. At this point, Kübler-Ross's theory predicts, the patient enters the stage of *depression*. According to Kübler-Ross, depression, or despair, is a necessary preparation for the final stage of *acceptance*. In order to reach acceptance, the dying person must grieve for all that will be lost with death.

Criticisms and Alternative Views

LO 19.8 What are some other views of the process of dying?

Kübler-Ross's model has provided a common language for those who work with dying patients, and her highly compassionate descriptions have, without doubt, sensitized health-care workers and families to the complexities of the process of dying. At some moments, what the patient needs is cheering up; at other moments, he simply needs someone to listen to him. There are times to hold his hand quietly and times to provide encouragement or hope. Many new programs for terminally ill patients are clearly outgrowths of this greater sensitivity to the dying process.

These are all worthwhile changes. But Kübler-Ross's basic thesis—that the dying process necessarily involves these specific five stages, in this specific order—has been widely criticized (Roos, 2013). Kübler-Ross responded to critics by pointing out that she had not meant the stages she proposed to be interpreted as rigidly as some researchers and practitioners suggested they should be. Nevertheless, criticisms of her model go beyond concerns about its stages.

METHODOLOGICAL PROBLEMS Kübler-Ross's hypothesized sequence was initially based on clinical observation of 200 patients, and she did not provide information about how frequently she talked to them or over how long a period she continued to assess them. She also did not report the ages of the patients she studied, although it is clear that many were middle-aged or young adults, for whom a terminal illness was obviously "off time." Nearly all were apparently cancer patients. Would the same processes be evident in those dying of other diseases, for which it is much less common to have a specific diagnosis or a short-term prognosis? In other words, Kübler-Ross's observations might be correct, but only for a small subset of dying individuals.

CULTURAL SPECIFICITY A related question has to do with whether reactions to dying are culture specific or universal. Kübler-Ross wrote as if the five stages of dying were universal human processes. However, cross-cultural studies suggest that cultures vary considerably in what they believe to be a "good death" (Westerhof, Katzko, Dittman-Kohli, & Hayslip, 2001). For individuals in Western societies, such as the United States, maintenance of individual autonomy over the dying process is of paramount importance. The idea that a dying person

In Mexican culture, the Day of the Dead is an important feast day on which the lives of the dead are remembered and honored.

should have the right to take his or her own life is more widely accepted in individualistic than in collectivist cultures (Kemmelmeier, Wieczorkowska, Erb, & Burnstein, 2002). Thus, certain aspects of Kübler-Ross's theory, such as the concepts associated with the bargaining stage, may be less important to people in collectivist cultures than they were to the people who participated in her initial studies.

Similarly, in some Native American cultures, death is to be faced and accepted with composure. Because it is part of nature's cycle, it is not to be feared or fought (DeSpelder & Strickland, 1983). And, in Mexican culture, death is seen as a mirror of the person's life. Thus, your way of dying tells much about what kind of person you have been. Furthermore, in Mexican culture, death is discussed frequently, even celebrated in a national feast day, the Day of the Dead (DeSpelder & Strickland, 1983). Would it be reasonable to expect denial, anger, bargaining, and so on, in the context of such cultural expectations?

Finally, you have already read about the influence of religious beliefs on adults' ideas about death. The belief that death is a transition to immortality implies that one should face death with a sense of joy. Exhibitions of denial, anger, and bargaining may seem to indicate a lack of faith and, as a result, may be actively avoided by dying people who are religious. Thus, Kübler-Ross's model may fail to predict reactions to impending death by the religious.

THE STAGE CONCEPT   The most potent criticism of Kübler-Ross's model, however, centers on the issue of stages. Many clinicians and researchers who have attempted to study the process systematically have found that not all dying patients exhibit these five emotions, let alone in a specific order. Of the five, only depression seems to be common among Western patients. Edwin Shneidman (1980, 1983), a major theorist and clinician in the field of **thanatology** (the scientific study of death and dying), argues that people who are dying display a wide range of emotional responses and do not all have the same needs. Instead of stages, Shneidman suggests that the dying process has many "themes" that can appear, disappear, and reappear in any one patient in the process of dealing with death. These themes include terror, pervasive uncertainty, fantasies of being rescued, incredulity, feelings of unfairness, a concern with reputation after death, and fear of pain.

Another alternative to Kübler-Ross's model is a "task-based" approach suggested by Charles Corr (1991/1992). In his view, coping with dying is like coping with any other problem or dilemma: You need to take care of certain specific tasks. He suggests four such tasks for the dying person:

- Satisfying bodily needs and minimizing physical stress
- Maximizing psychological security, autonomy, and richness of life
- Sustaining and enhancing significant interpersonal attachments
- Identifying, developing, or reaffirming sources of spiritual energy, and thereby fostering hope

Corr does not deny the importance of the various emotional themes described by Shneidman. Rather, he argues that for health professionals who deal with dying individuals, it is more helpful to think in terms of the patient's tasks because the dying person may need help in performing some or all of them.

Whichever model one uses, what is clear is that there are no common patterns that typify most or all reactions to impending death. Common themes exist, but they are blended together in quite different patterns by each person who faces this last task.

Responses to Impending Death

LO 19.9   How do people vary in the ways they adapt to impending death?

Individual variations in responding to imminent death have themselves been the subject of a good deal of research interest in recent decades. In one study involving 26 terminally ill men, researchers found that many of the men believed that they could avoid entering into the process of actively dying by continuing to engage in their favorite hobbies (Vig & Pearlman, 2003). Such findings raise questions about whether attitudes and behavioral choices can influence the course of a terminal disease.

Some of the most influential research along these lines has been the work of Steven Greer and his colleagues (Greer, 1991, 1999; Greer, Morris, & Pettingale, 1979; Pettingale, Morris, Greer, & Haybittle, 1985). In Greer's initial study in the 1970s, he followed a group of 62 women diagnosed in the early stages of breast cancer. Three months after the original diagnosis, each woman was interviewed at some length, and her reaction to the diagnosis and to her treatment was classed in one of five groups:

- **Denial (positive avoidance).** Person rejects evidence about diagnosis; insists that surgery was just precautionary.
- **Fighting spirit.** Person maintains an optimistic attitude and searches for more information about the disease. These patients often see their disease as a challenge and plan to fight it with every method available.

thanatology   the scientific study of death and dying

- **Stoic acceptance (fatalism).** Person acknowledges the diagnosis but makes no effort to seek any further information, or person ignores the diagnosis and carries on normal life as much as possible.

- **Helplessness/hopelessness.** Person acts overwhelmed by diagnosis; sees herself as dying or gravely ill and as devoid of hope.

- **Anxious preoccupation.** Women in this category had originally been included in the helplessness group, but they were separated out later. The category includes those whose response to the diagnosis is strong and persistent anxiety. If they seek information, they interpret it pessimistically; they monitor their body sensations carefully, interpreting each ache or pain as a possible recurrence.

Greer then checked on the survival rates of these five groups after 5, 10, and 15 years. Only 35% of those whose initial reaction had been either denial or fighting spirit had died of cancer 15 years later, compared with 76% of those whose initial reaction had been stoic acceptance, anxious preoccupation, or helplessness/hopelessness. Because those in the five groups did not differ initially in the stage of their disease or in their treatment, these results support the hypothesis that psychological responses contribute to disease progress—just as coping strategies more generally affect the likelihood of disease in the first place. However, in a subsequent study in the 1990s, Greer reported that the link between the fighting spirit and cancer survival was likely to have been due to an absence of an anxious or hopeless approach to the disease (Greer, 1999). That is, having a fighting spirit does not necessarily increase a cancer patient's chances of survival, but an anxious or hopeless attitude reduces it. As a result, Greer has been a strong advocate for psychotherapeutic interventions that help patients with anxiety or hopelessness develop a more positive outlook (Greer, 2008).

Similar results have emerged from studies of patients with melanoma (a form of skin cancer), as well as other cancers, and from several studies of AIDS patients (Juan et al., 2003; Penedo et al., 2005). And at least one study of coronary bypass patients showed that men who had a more optimistic attitude before the surgery recovered more quickly in the 6 months after surgery and returned more fully to their presurgery pattern of life (Scheier et al., 1989). In general, individuals who report less hostility, who express more stoic acceptance and more helplessness, and who fail to express negative feelings die sooner (O'Leary, 1990). Those who struggle the most, who fight the hardest, who express their anger and hostility openly, and who also find some sources of joy in their lives live longer.

Furthermore, a few studies have linked optimism to immune-system functioning (Low, Bower, Moskowitz, & Epel, 2011). A particular subset of immune cells called NK cells, thought to form an important defense against cancer, have been found in higher numbers among patients who are optimistic and openly express their anger about being ill (Penedo et al., 2005). And one study of AIDS patients showed that T-cell counts declined more rapidly among those who responded to their disease with repression (similar to the stoic acceptance and helplessness groups in the Greer study), while those who showed a fighting spirit had slower loss of T cells (Solano et al., 1993).

Despite the consistency of these results, two important cautions are in order before you leap to the conclusion that a fighting spirit is the optimum response to any disease. First, some careful studies find no link between depression, stoic acceptance, or helplessness and more rapid death from cancer (e.g., Cassileth, Walsh, & Lusk, 1988; Kung et al., 2006; Richardson, Zarnegar, Bisno, & Levine, 1990). Second, it is not clear that the same psychological response is necessarily appropriate for every disease. Consider heart disease, for example. There is a certain irony in the fact that many of the responses to cancer that appear to be optimum could be considered as reflections of a type A personality. Because having a type A personality constitutes a risk factor for heart disease, a "fighting spirit" response to a diagnosis of advanced heart disease might not be the most desirable. The growing body of research on responses to diseases does confirm, though, that there are connections between psychological defenses or ways of coping and physical functioning, even in the last stages of life.

Another important ingredient in an individual's response to imminent death is the amount of social support he has. Those with positive and supportive relationships describe lower levels of pain and less depression during their final months of illness (Carey, 1974; Hinton, 1975). Such well-supported patients also live longer. For example, both African American and White American heart-attack patients who live alone are more likely to have a second heart attack than are those who live with someone else. Similarly, those with significant levels of atherosclerosis live longer if they have a confidant than if they do not (Case, Moss, Case, McDermott, & Eberly, 1992; Williams, 1992). This link between social support and length of survival has also been found in experimental studies in which patients with equivalent diagnoses and equivalent medical care have been randomly assigned either to an experimental group in which they participate in regular support group sessions or to a control group in which they have no such support system. In one study of a group of 86 women with metastatic breast cancer (that is, cancer that had spread beyond the original site), researchers found that the average length of survival was 36.6 months for those who had access to the support group compared with 18.9 months for those in the control group (Spiegel, Bloom, Kraemer, & Gottheil, 1989). Thus, just as social support helps to buffer children and adults from some of the negative effects of many kinds of nonlethal stress, so it seems to perform a similar function for those facing death.

test yourself before going on ✓ Study and Review in MyPsychLab

Answers to these questions can be found in the back of the book.

1. Number Kübler-Ross's stages of dying in the order in which they occur.

_____ (a) acceptance

_____ (b) denial

_____ (c) bargaining

_____ (d) anger

_____ (e) depression

2. The scientific study of death is called _____.

3. Some studies have linked optimism to _____ _____ _____ among individuals with terminal diagnoses.

CRITICAL THINKING

4. In what ways is Kübler-Ross's model helpful to health-care professionals who work with terminal patients, and in what ways might the model interfere with their responses to the needs of patients?

Theoretical Perspectives on Grieving

There are a number of ways of looking at the emotion of grief, but the two that have had the greatest influence on the way psychologists think about grief are Freud's psychoanalytic theory and Bowlby's attachment theory (Granek, 2010).

Freud's Psychoanalytic Theory

LO 19.10 How does Freud's psychoanalytic theory view grief?

From the psychoanalytic perspective, the death of a loved one is an emotional trauma. As with any other trauma, the ego, or mind, tries to insulate itself from the unpleasant emotions such losses induce through the use of defense mechanisms, including denial and repression. However, Freud believed that defense mechanisms were only temporary devices for dealing with negative emotions. Eventually, he thought, the individual must examine the emotions and their source directly. Otherwise, such emotions lead to the development of physical symptoms and, perhaps, mental illnesses.

Freud's view has been very influential in grief counseling and in popular notions about the necessity of "working through" grief in order to avoid its long-term negative effects. It is generally accepted that bereaved individuals need to talk openly about their loss. Thus, grief counselors often recommend that friends of a bereaved person encourage the person to cry or express grief in other ways.

Psychoanalytically based grief therapy for children often emphasizes the use of defense mechanisms other than denial and repression to cope with grief. Following this approach, therapists sometimes encourage children to express their feelings through art. The idea is that this kind of defense mechanism, known as *sublimation*, will lead to better health outcomes than avoidance of emotions through more negative defense mechanisms (Glazer, 1998). Similarly, some therapists advocate encouraging children to use another defense mechanism, *identification*, to manage their grief. This goal can be accomplished by having the child watch popular films depicting children's grief, such as *The Lion King*; discuss the young characters' feelings; and compare the characters' emotions to their own (Sedney, 1999).

In addition, the psychoanalytic perspective has shaped grief research by characterizing the loss of a loved one as a trauma. An important concept in such research is that the more traumatic the death, the more likely it is to be followed by physical or mental problems. In fact, researchers have found that people who lose loved ones in sudden, tragic ways, such as to a drunk-driving accident or a murder, are more likely to display symptoms of posttraumatic stress disorder (Murphy et al., 1999; Sprang & McNeil, 1998).

Bowlby's Attachment Theory

LO 19.11 What are the theories of Bowlby and Sanders regarding grief?

John Bowlby and other attachment theorists argue that intense grief reactions are likely to occur at the loss of any person to whom one is attached, whether a partner, a parent, or a child (Bowlby, 1980; Sanders, 1989; Stroebe, 2002). Moreover, their theories predict that the quality of attachment to the loved one should be related in some way to the experience of grief. Research seems to confirm this aspect of their view. The stronger the attachment between a mourner and a lost loved one, the deeper and more prolonged the grief response (van Doorn, Kasl, Beery, Jacobs, & Prigerson, 1998; Waskowic & Chartier, 2003). By contrast, the death of someone who is part of one's social network but not an intimate confidant or an attachment figure is less likely to trigger an intense emotional reaction (Murrell & Himmelfarb, 1989). ◉ **Watch** the **Video** *Death and Afterlife Beliefs: Grieving Part 1* in **MyPsychLab**.

Bowlby proposed four stages of grief, and Catherine Sanders, another attachment theorist, proposed five stages, but as you can see in Table 19.2 on page 481, the two systems overlap a great deal. In the first period, that of shock or numbness, people say things that reveal their state of mind:

> "I feel so vague. I can't keep my mind on anything for very long." (Bowlby, 1980, p. 47)

> "I'm afraid I'm losing my mind. I can't seem to think clearly." (Bowlby, 1980, p. 48)

> "It was so strange. I was putting on my makeup, combing my hair, and all the time it was as if I were standing by the door watching myself go through these motions." (Sanders, 1989, p. 56).

In the stage of awareness of loss, or yearning, when anger is a common ingredient, people say things such as "His boss should have known better than to ask him to work so hard." Bowlby suggested that this is equivalent to the behavior observed in young children when they're temporarily separated from their closest attachment figures; they go from room to room in search of this favored person. Adults who are widowed do some of the same searching—sometimes physically, sometimes mentally.

In the stage of disorganization and despair, the restlessness of the previous period disappears and is replaced by a great lethargy. One 45-year-old whose child had just died described her feelings:

> I can't understand the way I feel. Up to now, I had been feeling restless. I couldn't sleep. I paced and ranted. Now, I have an opposite reaction. I sleep a lot. I feel fatigued and worn out. I don't even want to see the friends who have kept me going. I sit and stare, too exhausted to move. . . . Just when I thought I should be feeling better, I am feeling worse. (Sanders, 1989, p. 73)

TABLE 19.2 Stages of Grief

Stage	Bowlby's Label	Sanders's Label	General Description
1	Numbness	Shock	Characteristic of the first few days after the death of the loved one and occasionally longer; mourner experiences disbelief, confusion, restlessness, feelings of unreality, a sense of helplessness.
2	Yearning	Awareness	The bereaved person tries to recover the lost person; may actively search or wander as if searching; may report that he sees the dead person; mourner feels full of anger, anxiety, guilt, fear, frustration; may sleep poorly and weep often.
3	Disorganization and despair	Conservation/withdrawal	Searching ceases and the loss is accepted, but acceptance of loss brings depression and despair or a sense of helplessness; this stage is often accompanied by great fatigue and a desire to sleep all the time.
4	Reorganization	Healing and renewal	Sanders views this as two periods, Bowlby as only one. Both see this as the period when the individual takes control again. Some forgetting occurs and some sense of hope emerges, along with increased energy, better health, better sleep patterns, and reduced depression.

(*Sources:* Bowlby, 1980; Sanders, 1989.)

Finally, the resolution of the grieving process comes in Bowlby's stage of reorganization. Sanders hypothesized that this stage comprises two separate periods: healing and renewal. The outcome, from both Bowlby's and Sanders's perspectives, is that the grieving person begins to be able to maintain control. Sleep patterns return to normal, and a more optimistic outlook is typical.

These descriptions of the grieving process are highly evocative and can be useful in counseling grieving individuals. Discussion of the stages helps those who are grieving communicate with therapists about how they are feeling and describe the kinds of symptoms they are experiencing. Stage approaches also help survivors realize that their emotions and physical symptoms are normal and that the grieving process is complex.

However, as with the concept of stages of dying, there are two important questions about these proposed stages of grieving:

1. Do they really occur in fixed stages?

2. Does everyone feel all these feelings, in whatever sequence?

The answer to both questions, as you'll see, seems to be "no."

Alternative Perspectives

LO 19.12 What theories of grief have been proposed by critics of psychoanalytic and attachment theories?

A growing set of "revisionist" views of grieving gives a rather different picture from that of either Freud or the attachment theorists. First, research suggests that, contrary to psychoanalytic hypotheses, avoiding expressions of grief neither prolongs the experience of grief nor leads inevitably to physical or mental health problems (García, Landa, Grandes, Pombo, & Mauriz, 2013). In fact, at least one study suggests that bereaved individuals who avoid talking about the deceased or their feelings of loss actually experience milder grief and are less likely to suffer long-term effects (Bonanno, Znoj, Siddique, & Horowitz, 1999).

Second, many researchers and theorists find that grieving simply does not occur in fixed stages, with everyone following the same pattern (Wortman & Boerner, 2007; Wortman & Silver, 1990). There may be common themes, such as anger, guilt, depression, and restlessness, but these do not seem to appear in a fixed order.

Psychologists Camille Wortman and Roxane Silver have amassed an impressive amount of evidence to support such a view (Silver & Wortman, 2007; Wortman & Silver, 1989, 1990, 1992; Wortman, Silver, & Kessler, 1993). They dispute the traditional view of grieving expressed in both Freud's and Bowlby's theories. First, Wortman and Silver do not agree that distress is an inevitable response to loss. Second, their research challenges the notion that failure to experience distress is a sign that the individual has not grieved "properly."

Based on their findings, Wortman and Silver conclude that there are at least four distinct patterns of grieving (Wortman & Silver, 1990):

- *Normal.* The person feels great distress immediately following the loss, with relatively rapid recovery.

- *Chronic.* The person's distress continues at a high level over several years.

- *Delayed.* The grieving person feels little distress in the first few months but high levels of distress some months or years later.

- *Absent.* The person feels no notable level of distress either immediately or at any later time.

Contrary to the predictions of stage theories of grief, it turns out that the pattern of absent grief is remarkably common. In Wortman and Silver's first study, 26% of bereaved participants showed essentially no distress, either immediately after the death or several years later, a pattern confirmed in other research (Levy, Martinkowski, & Derby, 1994; Wortman & Silver, 1990). The least common pattern is delayed grief. Only 1–5% of adults appear to show such a response to loss, while as many as a third show chronic grief. Thus, Wortman and Silver find little support for either aspect of the traditional view: High levels of distress are neither an inevitable nor a necessary aspect of the grieving process. Many adults seem to handle the death of a spouse, a child, or a parent without significant psychological dislocation—although it remains true that, on average, bereaved persons have more depression, less life satisfaction, and a greater risk of illness than the nonbereaved.

The *dual-process model* takes a different approach to grief (Stroebe & Schut, 1999). Psychologists Margaret Stroebe and Henk Schut, developers of the model, propose that bereaved individuals alternate between an emotional state in which they confront their loss and actively grieve (confrontation) and another in which they focus on moving forward with their lives (restoration). In a sense, the restoration phase provides the bereaved with a respite from the emotional turmoil that is characteristic of the confrontation phase. Like Bowlby's model, the dual-process approach suggests that the attachment relationship between the bereaved and the deceased influences the grieving process (Stroebe, Schut, & Stroebe, 2005). But the model also emphasizes the loss of a loved one as analogous to other forms of stress (Stroebe, Folkman, Hansson, & Schut, 2006).

Finally, it's important not to lose sight of the fact that loss can lead to growth. Indeed, the majority of widows say not only that they changed as a result of their husbands' deaths but that the change was toward greater independence and greater skill (Wortman & Silver, 1990). Like all other crises and all other major life changes, bereavement can be an opportunity as well as—or instead of—a disabling experience. Which way a person responds is likely to depend very heavily on the patterns established from early childhood: in temperament or personality, in internal working models of attachment and self, in intellectual skills, and in social networks. Ultimately, we respond to death—our own or someone else's—as we have responded to life.

test yourself before going on ☑ **Study** and **Review** in **MyPsychLab**

Answers to these questions can be found in the back of the book.

1. Freud's approach to grieving emphasizes the use of _____ _____ to cope with the trauma of losing a loved one.

2. Sanders revised _____ description of the stages of grieving.

3. The proposal that, at any given time, a bereaved person may experience many different feelings is part of a model of grieving proposed by _____.

CRITICAL THINKING

4. How can the theories discussed in this section be integrated into a comprehensive explanation of the process of grieving?

The Experience of Grieving

In virtually every culture, the immediate response to a death is some kind of funeral ritual. However, a death ritual is only the first step in the process of **grieving**—the emotional response to a death—which may take months or years to complete.

Psychosocial Functions of Death Rituals

LO 19.13 How do funerals and ceremonies help survivors cope with grief?

Funerals, wakes, and other death rituals help family members and friends manage their grief by giving them a specific set of roles to play. Like all other roles, these include both expected behaviors and prohibited or discouraged behaviors. The content of these roles differs markedly from one culture to another, but their clarity in most cases gives a shape to the days or weeks immediately following the death of a loved person. Among Tibetan Buddhists, for instance, dead persons are believed to be unaware of their state for the first 4 days after their deaths. Mourners are expected to pray that they will realize that they are dead soon enough to avoid having to be reborn as another human or in another life form. In American culture, the rituals prescribe what one should wear, who should be called, who should be fed, what demeanor one should show, and far more. Depending on one's ethnic or religious background, one may gather family and friends for a wake or to "sit shiva," a traditional Jewish 7-day period of mourning during which family members stay in the same home and formally mourn a deceased loved one. One may be expected to respond stoically or to wail and tear one's hair. Friends and acquaintances, too, have guiding rules, at least for those first few days. They may bring food, write letters of condolence, offer help, and attend wakes and funerals. 👁 **Watch** the **Video** *Death and Afterlife Beliefs: Remembering and Honoring the Dead across Cultures* in **MyPsychLab**.

Death rituals also bring family members together as no other occasion does (with the possible exception of weddings). Frequently, cousins and other distant relatives see one another for the first time in many years at funerals. Such occasions typically inspire shared reminiscences and renew family relationships that have been inactive for a long time. In this way, death rituals can strengthen family ties, clarify the new lines of influence or authority within a family, and "pass the torch" in some way to the next generation. Likewise, funerals help establish deaths as shared milestones for family members—"that was before Grandpa died" or "the last time I saw her was at Grandpa's funeral." A death can become an important organizer of experience that separates the past from the present. Dividing time in this way seems to help survivors cope with grief (Katz & Bartone, 1998).

The emotional tone of death rituals varies across cultures. African Americans in the city of New Orleans have a tradition of celebrating the passing of their loved ones with a parade that features upbeat music that reminds mourners that the departed has gone on to a better place.

grieving the emotional response to a death or other type of loss

Each culture has its own death rituals. The customarily quiet graveside service in the United States would seem strange to people in many other societies.

Death rituals are also designed to help the survivors understand the meaning of death itself, in part by emphasizing the meaning of the life of the person who has died. It is not accidental that most death rituals include testimonials, biographies, and witnessing. By telling the story of a person's life and describing that life's value and meaning, others can more readily accept the person's death. 👁 **Watch** the **Video** *Buddhist and Christian Funeral Rituals* in **MyPsychLab**.

Finally, death rituals may give some transcendent meaning to death itself by placing it in a philosophical or religious context (Pang & Lam, 2002). In this way, they provide comfort to the bereaved by offering answers to that inevitable question: "Why?"

The Process of Grieving

LO 19.14   What factors influence the grieving process?

The ritual of a funeral, in whatever form it occurs, can provide structure and comfort in the days immediately following a death. But what happens when that structure is gone? How do people handle the sense of loss? Answering that question requires a look at a number of factors associated with grief.

AGE OF THE BEREAVED Children express feelings of grief very much the same way teens and adults do (Auman, 2007). Like adults, children demonstrate grief through sad facial expressions, crying, loss of appetite, and age-appropriate displays of anger such as temper tantrums (Oatley & Jenkins, 1996). Funerals seem to serve the same adaptive function for children as for adults, and most children resolve their feelings of grief within the first year after the loss. In addition, knowing that a loved one or even a pet is ill and in danger of death helps children cope with the loss in advance, just as it does for those who are older (Jarolmen, 1998).

Although the behavioral aspects of adolescents' grief responses vary little from those of adults, teens may be more likely than children or adults to experience prolonged grief. One study found that more than 20% of a group of high school students who had a friend killed in an accident continued to experience intense feelings of grief 9 months after the death (Dyregrov, Gjestad, Bie Wikander, & Vigerust, 1999). Adolescents may also grieve longer than children or adults for lost siblings; in some cases, teens continue to have problems with grief-related behaviors, such as intrusive thoughts about the deceased, for as long as 2 years after the death of a sibling (Lohan & Murphy, 2001/2002). Other research suggests that adolescent girls whose mothers have died run a particularly high risk of developing long-term grief-related problems (Lenhardt & McCourt, 2000). Teenagers may also be more likely than adults to experience grief responses to the deaths of celebrities or to idealize peers' suicides.

Adolescents' grief responses are probably related to their general cognitive characteristics. You should remember from Chapters 11 and 12 that adolescents often judge the real world based on idealized images. Consequently, a teenager may become caught up in fantasizing about how the world would be different if a friend or loved one had not died. In addition, prolonged grieving among adolescents may be rooted in their tendency to engage in "what if" thinking. This kind of thinking may lead teens to believe that they could have prevented the death and, thus, cause them to develop irrational guilt feelings (Cunningham, 1996).

MODE OF DEATH How an individual dies contributes to the grief process of those who are in mourning. For example, widows who have cared for spouses during a period of illness prior to death are less likely to become depressed after the death than those whose spouses die suddenly (Carnelley, Wortman, & Kessler, 1999; Schaan, 2013). Grief-related depression seems to emerge during the spouse's illness rather than after the death. The spouse's death is thought of as an escape from suffering for the one who dies and a release from grieving for the caregiver. Similarly, a death that has intrinsic meaning, such as that of a young soldier who dies defending his country, is not necessarily easier to cope with but does provide the bereaved with a sense that the death has not been without purpose (Malkinson & Bar-Tur, 1999). Consequently, mourners have a built-in cognitive coping device—a rational explanation for the death—that allows them to grieve but also protects them from long-term depression.

However, sudden and violent deaths, especially those that involve suicide, evoke more intense grief responses (Brent, Melhelm, Donohoe, & Walker, 2009; Lichtenthal, Neimeyer,

Currier, Roberts, & Jordan, 2013). One study found that 36% of widows and widowers whose spouses had died in accidents or by suicide were suffering from symptoms of posttraumatic stress disorder (e.g., nightmares) 2 months after the death, compared to only 10% of widows and widowers whose spouses had died of natural causes (Zisook, Chentsova-Dutton, & Shuchter, 1998). Moreover, almost all of those whose spouses had died unnaturally and who had PTSD symptoms also had depression.

Death in the context of a natural disaster is also associated with prolonged grieving and development of symptoms of PTSD (Kilic & Ulusoy, 2003; Rajkumar, Mohan, & Tharyan, 2013). Such events bring to mind the inescapable reality of the fragility of human life. Public memorial services in which the common experiences of survivors are recognized and the differences between controllable and uncontrollable aspects of life are emphasized can help survivors cope with this kind of grief.

Public memorials can also be helpful to survivors whose loved ones have died as a result of what might be called "politically motivated" mass murders—such as the 1995 bombing of a federal government office building in Oklahoma City and the terrorist attacks of September 11, 2001 (Shapiro, 2002). Moreover, political activism on the part of survivors aimed at preventing future events of this kind may be helpful to policymakers and also may serve as a coping mechanism for those who engage in it (Shapiro, 2002; Stein, 2007).

By contrast, the most frustrating aspect of the grieving process for people who have lost a loved one through a violent crime is the inability to find meaning in the event (Currier, Holland, & Neimeyer, 2006; Lichtenthal et al., 2013). In the initial phases of the grief process, survivors protect themselves against such frustration through cognitive defenses such as denial and by focusing on tasks that are immediately necessary (Goodrum, 2005). Next, survivors often channel their grief and anger into the criminal justice process through which they hope that the perpetrator of the crime will be justly punished. Ultimately, many survivors become involved in organizations that support crime victims and survivors of murdered loved ones or those that seek to prevent violence (Stetson, 2002).

Suicide is associated with a unique pattern of responses among survivors (Bailley, Kral, & Dunham, 1999). In general, family members and close friends of someone who commits suicide experience feelings of rejection and anger. Moreover, their grief over the loss of the loved one is complicated by the feeling that they could or should have done something to prevent the suicide. They are less likely to discuss the loss with other family members or with friends because of their sense that a suicide in the family is a source of shame. For these reasons, suicide survivors may be more likely than others who have lost loved ones to experience long-term negative effects.

Widowhood

LO 19.15 How does grief affect the physical and mental health of widows and widowers?

Some September 11 survivors have become involved in political activism aimed at preventing future terrorist attacks.

The relationship between the deceased and those who are in mourning affects the grieving process. For example, children who lose a sibling sometimes worry that thoughts produced by sibling rivalry, such as wishing a brother or sister would die, caused the death (Crehan, 2004). As a general rule, though, the most difficult death to recover from is that of a spouse (Kaslow, 2004) (see *Research Report*). **Watch** the **Video** *Death of a Spouse* in **MyPsychLab**.

WIDOWHOOD AND PHYSICAL HEALTH The experience of widowhood appears to have both immediate and longer-term effects on the immune system (Jones, Bartrop, Forcier, & Penny, 2010; Utz, Caserta, & Lund, 2012). (The term *widowhood* applies to both men and women; *widow* refers to women and *widower* to men.) In one Norwegian study, researchers measured immune functioning in widows twice, shortly after their husbands' deaths and 1 year later (Lindstrom, 1997). Investigators found that the widows' immune systems were suppressed somewhat immediately after the death but in most cases had returned to normal a year later.

Ethnicity and the Widowhood Effect

In celebration of their 50th wedding anniversary, British couple Brian and Betty Eckersley took their children and grandchildren on a vacation to Spain. The day before the family was scheduled to return home, Betty suffered a brain hemorrhage that doctors said was fatal. Her family faced the agonizing decision to discontinue artificial means of maintaining her life. Shortly thereafter, Brian suffered a heart attack. Within hours, both of the Eckersleys had passed away.

Brian Eckersley's heart attack is an extreme example of the *widowhood effect*, a phenomenon in which the death of one spouse is soon followed by the other. It is thought to result from the immune system's response to emotional trauma. However, the widowhood effect varies considerably across ethnic groups in the United States, and the reasons for it are poorly understood (Moon, Kondo, Glymour, & Subramanian, 2011).

Researchers were astonished at the results of a study of the widowhood effect in which the medical records of nearly half a million widows and widowers were examined (Elwert & Christakis, 2006). Consistent with earlier research, the risk of death was elevated by 50% to 60% among White widows and widowers during the first year of bereavement. For their African American counterparts, though, there was no increase in mortality whatsoever among individuals who had lost a spouse. Mortality rates among interracial couples were even more startling. African American widows of White men and White widowers of African American women showed no increase in mortality. By contrast, White widows of African American men and African American widowers of White women were at increased risk of death. Interestingly, too, studies involving Hispanic Americans suggest that the widowhood effect occurs only among Hispanic men (Stimpson, Kuo, Ray, Raji, & Peek, 2006).

Researchers hypothesize that a protective factor exists in African American culture that moderates the effects of spousal death on the immune system (Elwert & Christakis, 2006). However, the benefits associated with this factor appear to extend to the White husbands of African American women but not to the White wives of African American men. Thus, some theorists suggest that the factor operates through African American women's traditional kin-keeper role. A similar factor may also protect Hispanic women from the widowhood effect. Ethnic-group differences in family support, social networks, religious coping, and other factors among widows and widowers are currently being studied in an effort to find an explanation for this puzzling phenomenon.

CRITICAL ANALYSIS

1. *In Chapter 18, you learned that African American and Hispanic American elders are more likely to share a household with relatives than their White peers. In your view, how does the ethnic-group difference in living arrangements contribute to the findings on the widowhood effect?*

2. *You have also learned that African American and Hispanic American men have shorter average life expectancies than White men do. How might this difference contribute to the absence of the widowhood effect among African American and Hispanic American women?*

Similarly, a study comparing widows to married women in the Netherlands found that widows' immune responses continued to differ from those of married participants 7 months after the spouses' deaths, even though psychological differences (such as feelings of sadness) between the two groups had disappeared (Beem et al., 1999). Thus, the bereaved may continue to suffer at a biochemical level even after obvious signs of grieving have subsided (O'Connor et al., 2013). Moreover, the association between death of a spouse and ensuing illness in the surviving partner may result from the effects of grief on the body's defenses against disease agents such as viruses and bacteria.

WIDOWHOOD AND MENTAL HEALTH   In the year following bereavement, the incidence of depression among widows and widowers rises substantially, though rates of death and disease rise only slightly (Onrust & Cuijpers, 2006; Schaan, 2013). In one important longitudinal study, researchers repeatedly interviewed a sample of 3,000 adults, all age 55 or older at the beginning of the study (Norris & Murrell, 1990). Forty-eight of these adults were widowed during the 2½ years of the study, which allowed investigators to look at depression and health status before and immediately after bereavement. They found no differences in physical health between widowed and nonwidowed participants, but they did note a rise in depression among the widowed immediately following the loss and then a decline within a year after bereavement.

However, other researchers have found that older adults whose spouses have died differ in mental health for several years following the death from peers whose spouses are still alive (Bennett, 1997). So it appears that declines in physical and mental health follow bereavement fairly consistently, but how long such effects last may be highly variable. Several factors contribute to this variability.

One such factor is mental health history. Older adults who enter widowhood with a history of depression or poor health are more likely to experience depression after the death of their spouse (Utz et al., 2012; Zisook, Paulus, Shuchter, & Judd 1997). Lack of social support, both actual and perceived, also contributes to variability in depression among widows and widowers (Reed, 1998; Tomita et al., 1997). Moreover, the quality of the relationship of the widow or widower with the deceased spouse is related to depressive symptoms. Widows who report high levels of marital satisfaction are more likely than less satisfied widows to experience depression (Schaan, 2013). Economic changes accompany the loss of a spouse and add to the overall stress involved in the transition to widowhood. Women typically suffer greater economic losses after the death of a spouse than men do, usually because they lose their husbands' income or pension (Zick & Holden, 2000). Thus, the degree to which an individual's economic status changes as a result of a spouse's death is probably another factor that contributes to individual differences in the long-term effects of bereavement.

COMPLICATED GRIEF   Some psychologists argue that **complicated grief**—depressionlike symptoms following the death of a loved one—should be thought of as a separate disorder from depression (Stroebe et al., 2000). They suggest that individuals who continue to experience grief symptoms, such as loss of appetite, more than 2 months following loss of a loved one may be developing complicated grief. Stress hormones that increase bereaved individuals' levels of anxiety appear to be a key factor in the development of complicated grief (O'Connor et al., 2013). 👁 Watch the **Video** *Death and Afterlife Beliefs: Grieving Part 2* in **MyPsychLab**.

Diagnosis and treatment of complicated grief may be important for preventing problems in both mental and physical health among widows and widowers. Researchers have found that survivors whose grief symptoms continue for 6 months or longer are more likely to suffer long-term depression, as well as physical ailments such as cancer and heart disease (Prigerson et al., 1997). Moreover, they continue to show important differences in physical and mental functioning for up to 2 years after their spouse's death.

However, it's important to keep in mind that many aspects of grief are culturally determined. Beliefs about how long mourning should last and how the bereaved should behave vary widely from one culture to another (Braun & Nichols, 1997; Rubin & Schechter, 1997). For example, Orthodox Jewish men traditionally do not shave or trim their beards for 30 days after the death of a family member. Furthermore, mourning traditions among Orthodox Jews require abstaining from entertainment such as attending the theater or seeing movies for an entire year after the death of someone close (Bial, 1971).

Since inattention to grooming and lack of interest in social activities are also sometimes signs of depression, observers who are unfamiliar with Orthodox Jewish mourning practices might conclude that those who follow them are exhibiting complicated rather than normal grieving. Thus, mental health professionals are advised to learn about an individual's cultural beliefs before forming conclusions about grief-related behavior. Likewise, friends, neighbors, and co-workers of someone who is mourning the death of a spouse or other close family member should be careful to interpret any grief-related behaviors within the context of the person's cultural background. Moreover, it is not unusual for nondepressed widows and widowers to express feelings of grief even decades after their spouses have died (Carnelley, Wortman, Bolger, & Burke, 2006).

PREVENTING LONG-TERM PROBLEMS   Some research suggests that the "talk it out" approach to managing grief can be helpful in preventing grief-related depression, especially when feelings are shared with others who have had similar experiences, in the context of a support group (Francis, 1997; Schneider, 2006). Research also indicates that developing a coherent personal narrative of the events surrounding the spouse's death helps widows and widowers manage grief (Haase & Johnston, 2012; Neimeyer, Prigerson, & Davies, 2002; van den Hoonaard, 1999). Participating in support groups—or even jointly recalling relevant events with close family members—can facilitate the formation of such stories.

Clearly, this kind of psychosocial management of grief requires time. Mental health professionals advise employers that providing bereaved employees (especially those whose spouses have died) with sufficient time off to grieve may be critical to their physical and mental health. In the long run, illness and depression among bereaved workers who return to their jobs too soon may be more costly to employers than providing additional time off (Eyetsemitan, 1998).

complicated grief symptoms of depression brought on by the death of a loved one

test yourself before going on ✓ Study and Review in MyPsychLab

Answers to these questions can be found in the back of the book.

1. How do funerals help grieving individuals manage grief?

2. Write "Y" beside each factor that increases a bereaved person's risk of prolonged grief and "N" by each factor that does not increase it.

_____ (a) the bereaved is a middle-aged adult

_____ (b) the deceased died after a long illness

_____ (c) the bereaved is a teenager

_____ (d) the deceased committed suicide

_____ (e) the deceased died in a natural disaster

3. Depression-like symptoms that follow the death of a loved one are called _____ _____.

CRITICAL THINKING

4. Given what you have learned in this section, what kinds of factors would lead you to make different predictions about how long a person who has lost a loved one will grieve?

SUMMARY

The Experience of Death (pp. 467–468)

LO 19.1 What are the characteristics of clinical death, brain death, and social death?

- *Death* is a somewhat nonspecific term. Medical personnel refer to *clinical death* and *brain death*; *social death* occurs when the people treat the deceased person like a corpse.

LO 19.2 How do hospice and hospital care differ with respect to their effects on terminally ill patients?

- About half of adults in industrialized countries die in hospitals. Hospice care emphasizes patient and family control of the dying process and palliative care rather than curative treatment. Some studies suggest that patients and families are slightly more satisfied with hospice care than hospital care, but hospice care is also highly burdensome for the caregiver.

The Meaning of Death across the Lifespan (pp. 469–474)

LO 19.3 What are the characteristics of children's and adolescents' ideas about death?

- Until about age 6 or 7, children do not understand that death is permanent and inevitable and involves loss of function. Teens understand the physical aspects of death much better than children do, but they sometimes have distorted ideas about it, especially their own mortality.

LO 19.4 How do young, middle-aged, and older adults think about death?

- Many young adults believe they possess unique characteristics that protect them from death. For middle-aged and older adults, death has many possible meanings: a signal of changes in family roles, a transition to another state (such as a life after death), and a loss of opportunity and relationships. Awareness of death may help a person organize her remaining time.

LO 19.5 What factors are related to fear of death in adults?

- Fear of death appears to peak in midlife, after which it drops rather sharply. Older adults talk more about death but are less afraid of it. Deeply religious adults are typically less afraid of death.

LO 19.6 How do adults prepare for death?

- Many adults prepare for death in practical ways, such as by buying life insurance, writing a will, and making a living will. Reminiscence may also serve as preparation. There are some signs of deeper personality changes immediately before death, including more dependence and docility and less emotionality and assertiveness.

The Process of Dying (pp. 475–479)

LO 19.7 How did Kübler-Ross explain the process of dying?

- Kübler-Ross suggested five stages of dying: denial, anger, bargaining, depression, and acceptance. Research fails to support the hypothesis that all dying adults go through all five stages or that the stages necessarily occur in this order. The emotion most commonly observed is depression.

LO 19.8 What are some other views of the process of dying?

- Critics of Kübler-Ross suggest that her findings may be culture specific. They also argue that the process of dying is less stagelike than her theory claims.

LO 19.9 How do people vary in the ways they adapt to impending death?

- Research with cancer and AIDS patients suggests that those who are most pessimistic and docile in response to diagnosis and treatment have shorter life expectancies. Those who fight hardest, and even display anger, live longer. Dying adults who have better

Theoretical Perspectives on Grieving (pp. 479–482)

LO 19.10   How does Freud's psychoanalytic theory view grief?

- Freud's psychoanalytic theory emphasizes loss as an emotional trauma, the effects of defense mechanisms, and the need to work through feelings of grief.

LO 19.11   What are the theories of Bowlby and Sanders regarding grief?

- Bowlby's attachment theory views grief as a natural response to the loss of an attachment figure. Attachment theorists suggest that the grief process involves several stages.

LO 19.12   What theories of grief have been proposed by critics of psychoanalytic and attachment theories?

- Alternative views suggest that neither Freud's nor Bowlby's theory accurately characterizes the grief experience. Responses are more individual than either theory might suggest. The dual-process model suggests that bereaved individuals alternate between confrontation and restoration phases.

The Experience of Grieving (pp. 483–488)

LO 19.13   How do funerals and ceremonies help survivors cope with grief?

- Funerals and other rituals after death serve important functions, including defining roles for the bereaved, bringing family together, and giving meaning to the deceased's life and death.

LO 19.14   What factors influence the grieving process?

- Grief responses depend on a number of variables. The age of the bereaved and the mode of death shape the grief process.

LO 19.15   How does grief affect the physical and mental health of widows and widowers?

- In general, the death of a spouse evokes the most intense and long-lasting grief. Widows and widowers show high levels of illness and death in the months immediately after the death of a spouse, perhaps as a result of the effects of grief on the immune system. Widowers appear to have a more difficult time than widows do in managing grief.

KEY TERMS

brain death (p. 467)

clinical death (p. 467)

complicated grief (p. 487)

grieving (p. 483)

hospice care (p. 467)

palliative care (p. 468)

social death (p. 467)

thanatology (p. 477)

unique invulnerability (p. 470)

CHAPTER TEST   ✓ Study and Review in MyPsychLab

Answers to all the Chapter Test questions can be found in the back of the book.

1. Britt knows that he is dying. "I will donate a large sum of money to cancer research if I can just live long enough to see my grandchild born," he pleads. Britt is most likely in which stage of dying, according to Kübler-Ross?
   a. accommodation
   b. bargaining
   c. acceptance
   d. denial

2. Which of the following is an approach to caring for the terminally ill that focuses on individual and family control over the process of dying?
   a. DNR
   b. skilled nursing
   c. home-based care
   d. hospice care

3. What would be the most likely age of a child who said, "My cat died, but if I get her some medicine, she will feel better tomorrow"?
   a. 4 years
   b. 7 years
   c. 10 years
   d. 13 years

4. What circumstances constitute clinical death?
   a. when resuscitation is possible even though there is no evidence of brain function or respiration and the heart has stopped
   b. when there is no electrical activity in the brain and the person no longer has reflexes or responds to vigorous external stimuli
   c. when a physician pronounces the person to be dead
   d. when the brain stem is dead and there is no independent body functioning

5. Which of the following is true regarding Wortman and Silver's proposed absent pattern of grief, in which an individual expresses no notable distress either immediately or at a later time following the death of a loved one?
   a. This pattern of grief is very unhealthy and typically has severe negative consequences.
   b. This pattern is associated with increased mortality of survivors.

c. This pattern is the healthiest form of grief because it indicates rapid and complete psychological adjustment to the loss.

d. The person feels little or no notable distress at any time following a death.

6. While Bowlby suggests that the first stage of grief is numbness, Sanders suggests that it is _____.
a. shock
b. anger
c. anxiety
d. denial

7. Which of the following are two major criticisms of Kübler-Ross's theory of dying?
a. her methodology and her claim that these processes are culturally universal
b. her claim that these processes are universal and gender specific
c. her claim that religiosity is tied to the five stages and that persons of non-Christian religions will react differently
d. her methodology and her claim that people of all ages react the same

8. Which of these responses is typical of bereaved individuals whose loved one has committed suicide?
a. anger
b. denial
c. indifference
d. none of the above

9. According to research, who would be least afraid to die?
a. 17-year-old Susan
b. 25-year-old Mr. James
c. 50-year-old Mrs. Washington
d. 75-year-old Mr. Jackson

10. Which of the following age groups is *least* likely to make a change in lifestyle in response to a hypothetical impending death?
a. 16–20
b. 20–39
c. 40–59
d. 60+

11. Following the loss of his life partner, Joel has decided to move to Florida and pursue a graduate degree. According to the dual-process model, in which emotional state is Joel?
a. restoration
b. denial
c. confrontation
d. absent

12. The hospice movement emphasizes _____.
a. the normative nature of dying
b. palliative care
c. greater control of the dying person and his or her family over the process of dying
d. all of the above

13. Some grief therapists encourage bereaved children to express their feelings through art. In doing so, they are helping children develop a defense mechanism called _____.
a. identification
b. reaction formation
c. sublimation
d. denial

14. Which of these bereaved individuals is most likely to fantasize about how her life would have been different if her loved one hadn't died?
a. 15-year-old Jeanine
b. 70-year-old Lucille
c. 45-year-old Kamitra
d. 27-year-old Jennifer

15. Charles has recently learned that he is terminally ill. He has since begun to lash out at his family and at the medical personnel involved in his care. Kübler-Ross would suggest that Charles is going through the _____ stage of the dying process.
a. denial
b. anger
c. bargaining
d. depression

16. Which type of care focuses on relieving a terminally ill patient's pain rather than curing the illness?
a. euthanasia
b. palliative
c. merciful
d. hospital

17. Jerilyn is in the early stages of an inoperable cancer. She has prepared a signed and witnessed written document directing her family not to allow any artificial or heroic steps to be taken in the event that she is unable to make her wishes known at the appropriate time. What is this document called?
a. power of attorney
b. advance directive
c. living trust
d. executive trust

18. Which age group is at greatest risk of prolonged grieving?
a. children
b. adolescents
c. young adults
d. middle-aged adults

19. In which type of hospice programs are family caregivers supported by specially trained health-care workers?
a. hospital based
b. filial oriented
c. assisted living facility based
d. home based

20. A dying person who says "There must have been some kind of mistake" is in which stage of psychological preparation for death, according to Elizabeth Kübler-Ross?
a. denial
b. anger
c. rejection
d. depression

21. Which of the following is *not* an accurate statement about sex differences in widowhood?
a. Suicidal thoughts are more common in widowers than in widows.
b. In the early months of widowhood, men are more likely than women to die from either natural causes or suicide.
c. Women have a more difficult time than men do in returning to the level of emotional functioning they exhibited prior to their spouse's death.
d. Research reveals that widowers withdraw from social activities to a greater degree than widows do in the early months of bereavement.

22. Which statement about copycat suicides and the media among teens is *false*?
a. Exposure to media reports about suicide victims does not increase teens' risk of suicide.
b. Some teens who kill themselves use the Internet to learn about suicide methods.
c. Journalists often report details regarding suicides even though ethical guidelines discourage them from doing so.
d. Social networking plays a role in some teen suicides.

23. Kathy has breast cancer. She has kept a positive attitude and has been doing research to learn more about her type of cancer. She readily tells her doctors that she is going to fight with everything she has to beat her cancer. Greer and other researchers would suggest that Kathy has _____.
   a. a fighting spirit
   b. a realistic attitude
   c. helplessness/hopelessness
   d. stoic acceptance (fatalism)

24. Which group is *least* likely to make any changes if they thought they were going to die?
   a. Mexican Americans
   b. White Americans
   c. Japanese Americans
   d. African Americans

25. Which of the following is *not* an accurate statement about the fear of death?
   a. Old age is the time when death is most feared.
   b. Researchers have found that adults who are deeply religious and adults who are totally irreligious may fear death less than those who are ambivalent about a religious or philosophical tradition.
   c. Adults who believe their lives have had purpose or meaning appear to be less fearful of death.
   d. Older adults fear the period of uncertainty before death, such as whether they will be able to cope with the loss of control and independence.

To 👁 **Watch** ✳ **Explore** ↻ **Simulate** ✔ **Study** and **Review** and experience MyVirtualLife go to MyPsychLab.com

Answer Key

Chapter 1

An Introduction to Human Development (p. 2)

1. (1) Augustine, (2) John Locke, (3) Jean-Jacques Rousseau
2. (1) kept baby biographies, (2) first scientific study of children, (3) established norms for physical maturation
3. lifespan perspective
4.

Domain	Example
Physical	Puberty
Cognitive	Memory
Social	Individual differences in personality

5.

Period	Beginning Milestone	Ending Milestone
Prenatal	Conception	Birth
Infancy	Birth	Language
Early childhood	Language	School entrance
Middle childhood	School entrance	Puberty
Adolescence	Puberty	18 years
Early adulthood	18 years	40 years
Middle adulthood	40 years	60 years
Late adulthood	60 years	Death

Key Issues in the Study of Human Development (p. 6)

1. inborn bias
2. qualitative
3.

Type of Change	Example
Normative age-graded	Infants crawling, walking
Normative history-graded	Older adults who grew up during the Great Depression
Nonnormative	Genetic influences

4. Critical
5. A vulnerable child in a poor environment

Research Methods and Designs (p. 11)

1. describe, explain, predict, influence
2. (1) c (2) d (3) b (4) e (5) a
3.

Method	Advantages	Disadvantages
Cross-sectional	Quick access to data	Ignores individual differences; cohort effects
Longitudinal	Tracking of changes in individuals over time	Time-consuming; finding may apply only to group studied
Sequential	Cross-sectional and longitudinal data relevant to same hypotheses	Time-consuming; attrition rates differ across groups

4. (1) identify universal changes
   (2) identify variables that influence development
5.

Issue	What Researchers Must Do
Protection from harm	Avoid research that may cause harm; provide remediation for any possible temporary harmful effects
Informed consent	Obtain permission from institutions (e.g., schools), parents, and children themselves; allow participants to withdraw
Confidentiality	Keep identities of participants confidential
Knowledge of results	Provide participants, parents, and institutions with research results
Deception	Provide debriefing if deception is involved

Chapter 2

Psychoanalytic Theories (p. 24)

1. emotions; internal drives
2. (1) E (2) F (3) F (4) E (5) F (6) F (7) E (8) F (9) F (10) E

Learning Theories (p. 29)

1. classical; operant
2. reinforcement; punishment
3. attention; memory; physical ability to imitate the behavior, motivation to perform the behavior
4. self-efficacy

Cognitive Theories (p. 33)

1. schemes
2. (1) c (2) a (3) b
3. zone of proximal development
4. expand on

Biological and Ecological Theories (p. 38)

1. (1) b (2) c (3) a
2. macrosystem, exosystem, microsystem

Comparing Theories (p. 41)

1. (1) P (2) P (3) A (4) A (5) A (6) A (7) P (8) P
2. heuristic
3. It provides a comprehensive explanation of development.

Chapter 3

Conception and Genetics (p. 49)

1. (1) b (2) i (3) h (4) g (5) a (6) c (7) d (8) e (9) f (10) j

2.

Inheritance	Definition and Examples
Dominant/recessive	Single pairs of genes; trait occurs if one dominant or two recessive genes present; eye color, blood type, sickle-cell, Huntington's disease
Polygenic	Many genes; genes from some polygenic traits include dominant/recessive pattern, others do not; skin tone, eye color, height
Multifactorial	Genes and environmental variables interact; psychological traits

Genetic and Chromosomal Disorders (p. 54)

1. childhood; adulthood
2. sex-linked

Pregnancy and Prenatal Development (p. 57)

1. (1) A (2) C (3) B (4) A (5) C (6) B
2. (1) fetal (2) embryo (3) embryo (4) fetal
3. sex hormones
4. Norms can help health-care professionals better assess fetal health and predict postnatal problems.

Problems in Prenatal Development (p. 64)

1. embryonic
2.

Drug	Effect
Heroin	Miscarriage; premature labor; early death; postnatal addiction and withdrawal symptoms
Cocaine	Difficult to determine due to influence of multiple co-occurring factors such as poor maternal health, poverty, lack of prenatal care, postnatal neglect
Marijuana	Tremors; sleep problem; postnatal lethargy; short stature
Tobacco	Low birth weight; higher risk of learning problems and antisocial behavior
Alcohol	Fetal alcohol syndrome; short stature

3. (1) a, d, f (2) b (3) a, e, f (4) a, c, e (5) e, f, g
4. CVS; amniocentesis

Birth and the Neonate (p. 72)

1. All drugs enter the fetus's bloodstream.
2. (a) 6 (b) 2 (c) 3 (d) 1 (e) 4 (f) 5
3. Apgar scale
4. 1,500 grams; small-for-date

Chapter 4

Physical Changes (p. 83)

1. (1) b (2) e (3) c (4) d (5) a
2. (a) inborn genetic factors; (b) environmental variables such as the availability of adequate nutrition

Health and Wellness (p. 89)

1. Women who take drugs, either illegal drugs or prescription drugs that are needed for a health condition, should not breastfeed. In addition, preterm infants sometimes need special formulas due to their immature digestive systems. Mothers who are vegetarians whose diets are deficient may not be able to produce breast milk that meets babies' nutritional needs.
2. (1) B (2) D (3) C (4) A
3. Infants need well baby check-ups to keep track of their growth and development. They also need immunizations.

Infant Mortality (p. 91)

1. (1) Y (2) Y (3) N (4) Y (5) Y (6) N (7) N
2. (1) 5 (2) 3 (3) 2 (4) 6 (5) 1 (6) 4

Sensory Skills (p. 95)

1. Auditory, visual
2. Infants' preferences for umami and sweet tastes may explain their attraction to breast milk.

Perceptual Skills (p. 97)

1. Franz
2. more
3. The visual cliff experiment showed that 6-month-olds have depth perception.
4. one
5. (1) A (2) B (3) B (4) A

Chapter 5

Cognitive Changes (p. 106)

1. (a) 3 (b) 1 (c) 4 (d) 2
2. motor skill
3. Spelke

Learning, Categorizing, and Remembering (p. 112)

1. successful
2. schematic
3. context

The Beginnings of Language (p. 114)

1. Behaviorists
2. infant-directed speech
3. (a) 6 (b) 1 (c) 2 (d) 3 (e) 4 (f) 5
4. The order of nouns and verbs in telegraphic speech varies according to the rules of the languages that children are learning. Turkish children do not exhibit telegraphic speech.

Measuring Intelligence in Infancy (p. 122)

1. sensory and motor skills
2. underestimate

Chapter 6

Theories of Social and Personality Development (p. 128)

1. (1) A (2) B (3) B (4) A (5) C (6) B (7) C

Attachment (p. 130)

1.

Stage	Name of Stage	Age	Attachment Behaviors
1	Nonfocused orienting and signaling	0–3 months	Crying, smiling, making eye contact to draw the attention of anyone with whom infants come in contact
2	Focus on one or more figures	3–6 months	Direct "come here" signals to fewer people, those with whom they spend the most time; less responsive to unfamiliar people
3	Secure base behavior	6–24 months	True attachment to primary caregiver; proximity seeking such as following and clinging to caregivers when anxious, injured, or in need
4	Internal model	24+ months	Anticipate how actions will affect socioemotional bonds with caregivers and others

2. (1) ambivalent (2) secure (3) avoidant (4) disorganized

Personality, Temperament, and Self-Concept (p. 138)

1. (1) B (2) A (3) C (4) A (5) B (6) C
2.

Component of Self	Behaviors
Subjective/existential	Awareness of existence; effects on objects and people enable baby to separate self from the outside world; object permanence enables him/her to understand that the self is stable and permanent
Objective/categorical	Awareness of properties of the self and responses to objects and other people in the environment; mirror test suggests objective self-awareness emerges around 20 months along with words *I* and *me* and *mine*
Emotional	Awareness of own and others' emotions; babies respond to others' facial expression in first few months; by 5 to 7 months respond to both facial and vocal expressions of emotion; by end of first year try to elicit positive emotional expressions from others; social referencing and ability to deliberately alter his/her emotional estate emerges around baby's first birthday; self-conscious emotions (e.g., embarrassment) appear at same time as self-recognition

Effects of Nonparental Care (p. 142)

1. (1) T (2) F (3) T (4) F (5) T

Chapter 7

Physical Changes (p. 152)

1. gross; fine
2. (1) b (2) d (3) a (4) c
3. do not consume
4. sociocultural factors, characteristics of the child, characteristics of the abuser, family stresses

Cognitive Changes (p. 158)

1. (1) c (2) d (3) a (4) b
2. egocentric
3. theory of mind
4. (1) b (2) c (3) a

Changes in Language (p. 166)

1. fast-mapping
2. inflections
3. (1) N (2) Y (3) N (4) Y

Differences in Intelligence (p. 169)

1. Terman
2. (1) Yes (2) Yes (3) Yes
3. Flynn effect

Chapter 8

Theories of Social and Personality Development (p. 180)

1. (1) b (2) a (3) c (4) a (5) c (6) b (7) c

Personality and Self-Concept (p. 183)

1. peers, parents
2. emotion regulation
3. empathy
4. moral

Gender Development (p. 186)

1. (1) b (2) d (3) a (4) c (5) e
2. (1) B (2) A (3) B (4) B (5) A

Family Relationships and Structure (p. 191)

1.

Age	Change in Attachment Relationship
2–3	Attachment behaviors such as proximity seeking become less visible.
4	Internal models of attachment influence other relationships.

2.

Style	Definition	Effects on Development
Authoritarian	High control; low nurturance, communication	Lower achievement, self-esteem, social skills than authoritative
Permissive	High nurturance; low maturity demands, control, communication	Lower achievement; higher aggressiveness
Authoritative	High nurturance, maturity demands, control, communication	Most consistently associated with positive outcomes
Uninvolved	Low nurturance, maturity demands, control, and communication	Poorest outcomes; disturbances in social relationships, poor achievement

3. immigrants, African Americans

4. grandparents, homosexual couples
5. authoritative parenting
6. extended family

Peer Relationships (p. 202)

1. parallel
2. Instrumental aggression is more common between 2 and 4. When frustrated, children this age express themselves by throwing things or hitting other children. Taunting and name-calling become more common as children's language skills improve.
3. Prosocial behavior is intended to help another person. These behaviors become more common as children develop more interest in playing with others, around 2 or 3. Turn-taking increases with age, but comforting others declines.
4. (a) 4 (b) 18 months (c) 3

Chapter 9

Physical Changes (p. 212)

1. (a) selective attention, (b) spatial perception, (c) right–left orientation, (d) spatial cognition
2. (a) 3 (b) 2 (c) 1
3. obese

Cognitive Changes (p. 217)

1. 5,000, 10,000
2. decentration, reversibility
3.

Advances	Benefits
Greater processing efficiency	More efficient use of working memory; faster processing of information
Automaticity	Frees up space in working memory to manage complex problems
Executive processes	Ability to devise and carry out alternative ways of processing information
Memory strategies	Improved capacity for remembering information
Expertise	Improved IP system efficiency, memory, categorization, creativity

Schooling (p. 222)

1. systematic and explicit phonics
2. ESL
3. emotional
4. boys
5. analytical
6. (a) beliefs about innate ability, (b) teaching methods, (c) emphasis on computational fluency

Children with Special Needs (p. 231)

1. learning disability
2. active, impulsive, attentive

Chapter 10

Theories of Social and Personality Development (p. 241)

1.

	Industry	Inferiority
Influences	Learning culturally valued skills, such as reading; making things; accomplishing goals	Failing to learn skills; inability to accomplish goals
Consequences	Good foundation for future psychosocial development; willingness to take on challenging tasks	Poor foundation for future psychosocial development; reluctance to work hard to accomplish desired goals

2. (1) a (2) b (3) d (4) e (5) c
3. (1) B (2) A (3) C

Self-Concept (p. 243)

1. (a) N (b) Y
2. (1) a (2) b

Advances in Social Cognition (p. 246)

1. smart, happy, mean
2. concrete operational reasoning

The Social World of the School-Aged Child (p. 249)

1.

Factor	Contribution to Self-Regulation
Culture	Groups vary in the ages at which they expect children to be able to regulate their own behavior
Gender	Parents have higher expectations for girls' self-regulation
Parenting style	Authoritative parents encourage self-regulation

2. (1) B (2) A (3) B (4) A (5) B
3. (b)

Influences beyond Family and Peers (p. 256)

1. (a) increased birth defects (b) more illnesses (c) more children are undernourished (d) more behavior problems in school
2. (1) C (2) A, B, C (3) A, C

Chapter 11

Physical Changes (p. 266)

1. prefrontal cortex
2. (a) 3 (b) 1 (c) 2
3. (a) 2 (b) 1 (c) 3
4. increased risk of substance use

Adolescent Sexuality (p. 272)

1. fewer than half
2. (1) having a mother who became pregnant in adolescence (2) poverty (3) younger age at first sexual intercourse
3. in early adulthood

1. (1) lack of maturity in the prefrontal cortex; (2) the desire to be accepted by peers; (3) the need to establish autonomy from parents; (4) permissive parenting
2. decreased
3. (1) C (2) A (3) B (4) C
4. pituitary

Changes in Thinking and Memory (p. 282)

1. hypothetico-deductive reasoning
2. later
3. (1) teens process information faster; (2) teens understand their memory systems better; (3) teens use processing resources more efficiently

Schooling (p. 286)

1. ability
2. Asian American
3. uninteresting

Chapter 12

Theories of Social and Personality Development (p. 296)

1. role confusion
2. (1) C (2) B (3) A (4) D

Self-Concept (p. 299)

1. (1) B (2) T (3) B (4) T (5) T
2. higher
3. (1) B (2) C (3) A (4) D
4.

Stage	Summary
Unexamined	Integration of society's negative stereotypes into one's sense of identity
Search	Comparisons of one's own group with others; may be triggered by an episode in which attention is drawn to the teen's ethnicity, such as an incidence of blatant racism
Achievement	Teens develop strategies for solving conflicts between the demands of the dominant culture and those of their own ethnic group

Moral Development (p. 304)

1. (a) cognitive development (b) role-taking skills (c) social support in the form of reciprocal dialogue about moral issues (d) parents' ability to express their own moral views in ways that make them understandable to children and teenagers
2. role-taking
3. situational
4. childhood, adolescence

Social Relationships (p. 312)

1. everyday
2. acquaintances
3. aggression
4. 11 or 12

Chapter 13

Physical Functioning (p. 322)

1. (1) P (2) P + S (3) P (4) S (5) P
2. limbic system
3. 35, 40

Health and Wellness (p. 328)

1. Alameda County Study
2. bacterial, viral
3. (a) cultural beliefs (b) substance abuse (c) personality traits (d) history of child abuse
4. schizophrenia
5. psychological

Cognitive Changes (p. 340)

1. postformal thought
2. crystallized, fluid

Postsecondary Education (p. 343)

1. (1) M (2) F (3) M (4) F (5) F
2. tribal college movement
3. extended time

Chapter 14

Theories of Social and Personality Development (p. 350)

1. isolation
2. (a) 3 (b) 2 (c) 1
3. academic, friendship, conduct, work, romantic

Intimate Relationships (p. 353)

1. (1) E (2) S (3) S (4) E (5) E
2. (a) personality (b) attitudes toward divorce (c) attachment security
3. marriage
4. families of choice
5. continuous singles

Parenthood and Other Relationships (p. 361)

1. (a) how long a couple has been together before the birth (b) education (c) number of children; other acceptable answers are division of labor, support from extended family, effective conflict-resolution strategies.
2. parents, friends

The Role of Worker (p. 365)

1. (a) family/education (b) gender (c) personality
2. 15, 24
3. to enhance job satisfaction by analyzing the quality of employees' work lives
4. Work–family conflict

Chapter 15

Physical Changes (p. 376)

1. speed
2. climacteric
3. Bone mineral density
4. (1) b (2) a

Health and Wellness (p. 383)

1. (1) both (2) both (3) CVD (4) both (5) both
2. nonfatal chronic
3. (1) African Americans (2) African Americans (3) African Americans (4) Asian Americans (5) Native Americans
4. liver disease, CVD, cancers of the digestive and urinary systems

Cognitive Functioning (p. 389)

1. disagree
2. exercise is negatively correlated with mortality
3. (1) Y (2) N (3) Y (4) N (5) Y
4. divergent

Chapter 16

Theories of Social and Personality Development (p. 400)

1. (1) b (2) a (3) e (4) d (5) c

Changes in Relationships and Personality (p. 402)

1. (a) partner (b) parent (c) child (d) grandparent
2. less

Midlife Career Issues (p. 409)

1. (1) M (2) M W (3) W (4) W (5) M
2. anxiety, depression
3. (a) women are involved in retirement planning (b) expect to be retired for 20 years or more

Chapter 17

Variability in Late Adulthood (p. 418)

1. young old, oldest old
2. (1) a (2) c (3) b (4) d

Physical Changes (p. 423)

1. dendrites
2. taste
3. (1) e (2) a (3) f (4) b (5) c (6) d

Mental Health (p. 429)

1. multi-infarct dementia
2. African Americans

Cognitive Changes (p. 435)

1. number of digits, delayed versus immediate recall
2. factual knowledge, procedural knowledge, understanding of context, understanding of values, recognition that it is impossible to know in advance how any decision will ultimately affect one's life

Chapter 18

Theories of Social and Personality Development (p. 443)

1. (1) b (2) a (3) c
2. continuity

Individual Differences (p. 445)

1. ageist stereotype
2. religious beliefs, attendance at religious services

Social Relationships (p. 449)

1. living with a spouse or alone
2. spouse
3. less
4. smaller

Career Issues in Late Life (p. 457)

1. health
2. compensatory (or kinship) migration
3. Pacing is important because older adults may require more time to learn new skills than younger adults do.

Chapter 19

The Experience of Death (p. 467)

1. brain
2. hospice

The Meaning of Death Across the Lifespan (p. 469)

1. 6 or 7
2. unique invulnerability
3. middle-aged
4. conventional, docile, dependent, warm

The Process of Dying (p. 475)

1. (a) 5 (b) 1 (c) 3 (d) 2 (e) 4
2. thanatology
3. immune system functioning

Theoretical Perspectives on Grieving (p. 479)

1. defense mechanisms
2. Bowlby's
3. Jacobs

The Experience of Grieving (p. 483)

1. by providing them with roles to play
2. (a) N (b) N (c) Y (d) Y (e) Y
3. complicated grief

Chapter Test Answer Key

Chapter 1

1. d
2. a
3. b
4. a
5. c
6. b
7. c
8. c
9. b
10. a
11. b
12. a
13. c
14. b
15. d
16. d
17. b
18. d
19. b
20. d
21. b
22. d
23. d
24. d
25. c

Chapter 2

1. b
2. c
3. c
4. d
5. b
6. d
7. c
8. a
9. b
10. a
11. b
12. a
13. a
14. b
15. b
16. a
17. b
18. c
19. a
20. d

21. c
22. c
23. c
24. c
25. a

Chapter 3

1. c
2. c
3. d
4. c
5. a
6. c
7. a
8. c
9. d
10. b
11. c
12. d
13. d
14. a
15. c
16. a
17. a
18. a
19. b
20. c
21. a
22. d
23. d
24. b
25. a

Chapter 4

1. c
2. b
3. a
4. c
5. b
6. a
7. d
8. d
9. b
10. c
11. a
12. d
13. b
14. a

15. d
16. b
17. a
18. b
19. a
20. b
21. a
22. a
23. d
24. d
25. a

Chapter 5

1. d
2. b
3. c
4. d
5. a
6. d
7. c
8. c
9. a
10. a
11. b
12. b
13. c
14. c
15. a
16. a
17. d
18. d
19. b
20. b
21. c
22. c
23. c
24. a
25. b

Chapter 6

1. b
2. a
3. d
4. b
5. a
6. d
7. b
8. c
9. b

10. d
11. a
12. a
13. c
14. c
15. b
16. d
17. a
18. b
19. b
20. c
21. a
22. a
23. b
24. d
25. a

Chapter 7

1. a
2. b
3. c
4. a
5. d
6. d
7. b
8. d
9. d
10. a
11. b
12. d
13. b
14. a
15. b
16. a
17. c
18. c
19. d
20. b
21. d
22. c
23. a
24. c
25. c

Chapter 8

1. b
2. b
3. b

4. a
5. c
6. a
7. c
8. d
9. b
10. a
11. d
12. a
13. b
14. d
15. a
16. c
17. d
18. d
19. d
20. a
21. c
22. b
23. b
24. a
25. d

Chapter 9

1. b
2. a
3. a
4. a
5. d
6. c
7. b
8. a
9. b
10. c
11. a
12. a
13. c
14. a
15. d
16. d
17. c
18. b
19. b
20. d
21. a
22. b
23. b
24. c
25. c

Chapter 10

1. b
2. d
3. a
4. b
5. d
6. b
7. b
8. b
9. a
10. c
11. d
12. b
13. d
14. b
15. b
16. c
17. a
18. b
19. c
20. a
21. d
22. a
23. a
24. a
25. c

Chapter 11

1. b
2. d
3. d
4. a
5. c
6. b
7. a
8. c
9. b
10. b
11. b
12. b
13. a
14. a
15. a
16. c
17. b
18. c
19. a
20. b

21. c
22. a
23. a
24. c
25. d

Chapter 12

1. a
2. c
3. c
4. a
5. a
6. c
7. d
8. b
9. a
10. c
11. a
12. b
13. d
14. a
15. b
16. b
17. d
18. d
19. d
20. c
21. b
22. c
23. a
24. c
25. c

Chapter 13

1. a
2. b
3. a
4. a
5. d
6. c
7. a
8. d
9. a
10. b
11. b
12. c
13. b
14. a
15. d
16. b
17. b
18. d
19. a
20. b
21. d
22. a
23. b
24. c
25. d

Chapter 14

1. d
2. a
3. c
4. d
5. c
6. c
7. d
8. c
9. d
10. b
11. a
12. c
13. c
14. c
15. b
16. d
17. c
18. d
19. a
20. c
21. b
22. c
23. d
24. c
25. b

Chapter 15

1. b
2. a
3. d
4. a
5. c
6. b
7. b
8. b
9. c
10. a
11. a
12. a
13. c
14. d
15. d
16. c
17. d
18. a
19. b
20. b
21. c
22. d
23. d
24. b
25. c

Chapter 16

1. a
2. b
3. a
4. c
5. c
6. c
7. c
8. a
9. a
10. b
11. c
12. d
13. b
14. b
15. b
16. b
17. a
18. d
19. d
20. a
21. a
22. c
23. a
24. a
25. c

Chapter 17

1. a
2. a
3. d
4. a
5. b
6. a
7. b
8. c
9. d
10. b
11. a
12. b
13. d
14. b
15. c
16. c
17. c
18. c
19. d
20. d
21. b
22. c
23. b
24. b
25. c

Chapter 18

1. b
2. a
3. d
4. c
5. d
6. d
7. b
8. b
9. d
10. d
11. c
12. a
13. c
14. d
15. c
16. c
17. c
18. a
19. c
20. c
21. b
22. b
23. a
24. d
25. d

Chapter 19

1. b
2. d
3. a
4. a
5. d
6. a
7. a
8. a
9. d
10. d
11. a
12. a
13. c
14. a
15. b
16. b
17. b
18. b
19. d
20. a
21. c
22. c
23. a
24. a
25. a

Glossary

ability goals goals based on a desire to be superior to others

accommodation a change to a scheme as a result of some new information

achievement test a test designed to assess specific information learned in school

activities of daily living (ADLs) self-help tasks such as bathing, dressing, and using the toilet

activity theory the idea that it is normal and healthy for older adults to try to remain as active as possible for as long as possible

adaptive reflexes reflexes, such as sucking, that help newborns survive

adolescence the transitional period between childhood and adulthood

ageism prejudicial attitudes about older adults that characterize them in negative ways

aggression behavior intended to harm another person or an object

aging in place living in a noninstitutional environment to which modifications have been made to accommodate an older adult's needs

alcoholism physical and psychological dependence on alcohol

Alzheimer's disease a very severe form of dementia, the cause of which is unknown

amenity move a postretirement move away from kin to a location that has some desirable feature, such as year-round warm weather

amnion a fluid-filled sac in which a fetus floats until just before it is born

analytical style a tendency to focus on the details of a task

anorexia nervosa an eating disorder characterized by self-starvation

A-not-B error substage 4 infants' tendency to look for an object in the place where it was last seen (position A) rather than in the place to which they have seen a researcher move it (position B)

anoxia oxygen deprivation experienced by a fetus during labor and/or delivery

assimilation the process of using a scheme to make sense of an event or experience

association areas parts of the brain where sensory, motor, and intellectual functions are linked

assortative mating (homogamy) sociologists' term for the tendency to mate with someone who has traits similar to one's own

asthma a chronic lung disease, characterized by sudden, potentially fatal attacks of breathing difficulty

atherosclerosis narrowing of the arteries caused by deposits of a fatty substance called plaque

attachment the emotional tie to a parent experienced by an infant, from which the child derives security

attachment theory the view that infants are biologically predisposed to form emotional bonds with caregivers and that the characteristics of those bonds shape later social and personality development

attention-deficit/hyperactivity disorder (ADHD) a mental disorder that causes children to have difficulty attending to and completing tasks

atypical development development that deviates from the typical developmental pathway in a direction that is harmful to the individual

auditory acuity how well one can hear

authoritarian parenting style a style of parenting that is low in nurturance and communication and high in control and maturity demands

authoritative parenting style a style of parenting that is high in nurturance, maturity demands, control, and communication

autism spectrum disorders (ASD) a group of disorders that impair an individual's ability to understand and engage in the give-and-take of social relationships

automaticity the ability to recall information from long-term memory without using short-term memory capacity

avoidant couples partners who agree to disagree and who minimize conflict by avoiding each other

axons taillike extensions of neurons

babbling the repetitive vocalizing of consonant–vowel combinations by an infant

balanced approach reading instruction that combines explicit phonics instruction with other strategies for helping children acquire literacy

Bayley Scales of Infant Development the best-known and most widely used test of infant "intelligence"

behavior genetics the study of the role of heredity in individual differences

behaviorism the view that defines development in terms of behavior changes caused by environmental influences

bilingual education an approach to second-language education in which children receive instruction in two different languages

bioecological theory Bronfenbrenner's theory that explains development in terms of relationships between individuals and their environments, or interconnected contexts

BMI-for-age comparison of an individual child's BMI against established norms for his or her age group and sex

brain death the point at which vital signs, including brain activity, are absent and resuscitation is no longer possible

bulimia nervosa an eating disorder characterized by binge eating and purging

bullying a complex form of aggression in which a bully routinely aggresses against one or more habitual victims

burnout lack of energy, exhaustion, and pessimism that result from chronic stress

cardiovascular disease (CVD) a set of disease processes in the heart and circulatory system

career development the process of adapting to the workplace, managing career transitions, and pursuing goals through employment

caregiver burden a term for the cumulative negative effects of caring for an elderly or disabled person

case study an in-depth examination of a single individual

cell body the part of a neuron that contains the nucleus and is the site of vital cell functions

centration a young child's tendency to think of the world in terms of one variable at a time

cephalocaudal pattern growth that proceeds from the head downward

cesarean section (c-section) delivery of an infant through incisions in the abdominal and uterine walls

chromosomes strings of genetic material in the nuclei of cells

class inclusion the understanding that subordinate classes are included in larger, superordinate classes

classical conditioning learning that results from the association of stimuli

climacteric the term used to describe the adult period during which reproductive capacity declines or is lost

clinical death a period during which vital signs are absent but resuscitation is still possible

clique four to six young people who appear to be strongly attached to one another

cognitive domain changes in thinking, memory, problem solving, and other intellectual skills

cognitive theories theories that emphasize mental processes in development, such as logic and memory

cohort effects findings that result from historical factors to which one age group in a cross-sectional study has been exposed

colic an infant behavior pattern involving intense daily bouts of crying totaling 3 or more hours a day

companionate relationships relationships in which grandparents have frequent contact and warm interactions with grandchildren

compensatory (kinship) migration a move to a location near family or friends that happens when an elder requires frequent help because of a disability or disease

complicated grief symptoms of depression brought on by the death of a loved one

concrete operational stage Piaget's third stage of cognitive development, during which children construct schemes that enable them to think logically about objects and events in the real world

conduct disorder a psychological disorder in which children's social and/or academic functioning is impaired by patterns of antisocial behavior that include bullying, destruction of property, theft, deceitfulness, and/or violations of social rules

conservation the understanding that matter can change in appearance without changing in quantity

continuity theory the idea that older adults adapt lifelong interests and activities to the limitations imposed upon them by physical aging

control group the group in an experiment that receives either no special treatment or a neutral treatment

conventional morality in Kohlberg's theory, the level of moral reasoning in which judgments are based on rules or norms of a group to which the person belongs

cooing making repetitive vowel sounds, particularly the *uuu* sound

corpus callosum the membrane that connects the right and left hemispheres of the cerebral cortex

correlation a relationship between two variables that can be expressed as a number ranging from −1.00 to +1.00

creativity the ability to produce original, appropriate, and valuable ideas and/or solutions to problems

critical period a specific period in development when an organism is especially sensitive to the presence (or absence) of some particular kind of experience

cross-gender behavior behavior that is atypical for one's own sex but typical for the opposite sex

cross-linking the formation of undesirable bonds between proteins or fats

cross-sectional design a research design in which groups of people of different ages are compared

crowd a combination of cliques, which includes both males and females

crystallized intelligence knowledge and judgment acquired through education and experience

cyberbullying a form of aggression in which electronic communications are used to intentionally inflict harm on others

decentration thinking that takes multiple variables into account

deductive logic a type of reasoning, based on hypothetical premises, that requires predicting a specific outcome from a general principle

deferred imitation imitation that occurs in the absence of the model who first demonstrated it

delinquency antisocial behavior that includes law breaking

dementia a neurological disorder involving problems with memory and thinking that affect an individual's emotional, social, and physical functioning

dendrites branchlike protrusions from the cell bodies of neurons

deoxyribonucleic acid (DNA) chemical material that makes up chromosomes and genes

dependent variable the characteristic or behavior that is expected to be affected by the independent variable

dialectical thought a form of thought involving recognition and acceptance of paradox and uncertainty

disengagement theory the theory that it is normal and healthy for older adults to scale down their social lives and to separate themselves from others to a certain degree

dishabituation responding to a somewhat familiar stimulus as if it were new

dominant–recessive pattern a pattern of inheritance in which a single dominant gene influences a person's phenotype but two recessive genes are necessary to produce an associated trait

dynamic systems theory the view that several factors interact to influence development

dyslexia problems in reading or the inability to read

eclecticism the use of multiple theoretical perspectives to explain and study human development

ego according to Freud, the thinking element of personality

ego integrity the feeling that one's life has been worthwhile

egocentrism a young child's belief that everyone sees and experiences the world the way she does

embryonic stage the second stage of prenatal development, from week 2 through week 8, during which the embryo's organ systems form

emerging adulthood the period from the late teens to early 20s when individuals explore options prior to committing to adult roles

emotional regulation the ability to control emotional states and emotion-related behavior

empathy the ability to identify with another person's emotional state

empiricists theorists who argue that perceptual abilities are learned

English-as-a-second-language (ESL) program an approach to second-language education in which children attend English classes for part of the day and receive most of their academic instruction in English

episodic memories recollections of personal events

equilibration the process of balancing assimilation and accommodation to create schemes that fit the environment

ethnic identity a sense of belonging to an ethnic group

ethnography a detailed description of a single culture or context

ethology a perspective on development that emphasizes genetically determined survival behaviors presumed to have evolved through natural selection

excessive weight gain a pattern in which children gain more weight in a year than is appropriate for their age and height

executive processes information-processing skills that involve devising and carrying out strategies for remembering and solving problems

experiment a study that tests a causal hypothesis

experimental group the group in an experiment that receives the treatment the experimenter thinks will produce a particular effect

expressive language the ability to use sounds, signs, or symbols to communicate meaning

extended family a social network of grandparents, aunts, uncles, cousins, and so on

extinction the gradual elimination of a behavior through repeated nonreinforcement

false-belief principle an understanding that enables a child to look at a situation from another person's point of view and determine what kind of information will cause that person to have a false belief

fast-mapping the ability to categorically link new words to real-world referents

fetal stage the third stage of prenatal development, from week 9 to birth, during which growth and organ refinement take place

fluid intelligence the aspect of intelligence that reflects fundamental biological processes and does not depend on specific experiences

foreclosure in Marcia's theory, the identity status of a person who has made a commitment without having gone through a crisis; the person has simply accepted a parentally or culturally defined commitment

formal operational stage the fourth of Piaget's stages, during which adolescents learn to reason logically about abstract concepts

frail elderly older adults whose physical and/or mental impairments are so extensive that they cannot care for themselves

free radical a molecule or an atom that possesses an unpaired electron

gametes cells that unite at conception (ova in females; sperm in males)

gender the psychological and social associates and implications of biological sex

gender constancy the understanding that gender is a component of the self that is not altered by external appearance

gender identity the ability to correctly label oneself and others as male or female

gender role identity the gender-related aspects of the psychological self

gender schema theory an information-processing approach to gender concept development which asserts that people use a schema for each gender to process information about themselves and others

gender stability the understanding that gender is a stable, lifelong characteristic

generativity a sense that one is making a valuable contribution to society by bringing up children or mentoring younger people in some way

genes pieces of genetic material that control or influence traits

genotype the unique genetic blueprint of each individual

germinal stage the first stage of prenatal development, beginning at conception and ending at implantation (approximately 2 weeks)

gerontology the scientific study of aging

glial cells the "glue" that holds neurons together to give form to the structures of the nervous system

gonads sex glands (ovaries in females; testes in males)

goodness-of-fit the degree to which an infant's temperament is adaptable to his or her environment and vice versa

grammar explosion the period during when the grammatical features of children's speech become more similar to those of adult speech

grieving the emotional response to a death or other type of loss

habituation a decline in attention that occurs because a stimulus has become familiar

handedness a strong preference for using one hand or the other that develops between 3 and 5 years of age

Hayflick limit the genetically programmed time limit to which each species is theoretically proposed to be subject, after which cells no longer have any capacity to replicate themselves accurately

hippocampus a brain structure that is important in learning

holophrases combinations of gestures and single words that convey more meaning than just a word alone

hospice care an approach to care for the terminally ill that emphasizes individual and family control of the process of dying

hostile aggression aggression used to hurt another person or gain an advantage

hostile/detached couples partners who fight regularly, rarely look at each other, and lack affection and support

hostile/engaged couples partners who have frequent arguments and lack the balancing effect of humor and affection

human development the scientific study of age-related changes in behavior, thinking, emotion, and personality

hypertension elevated blood pressure

hypothetico-deductive reasoning the ability to derive conclusions from hypothetical premises

id in Freud's theory, the part of the personality that comprises a person's basic sexual and aggressive impulses; it contains the libido and motivates a person to seek pleasure and avoid pain

identity an understanding of one's unique characteristics and how they have been, are, and will be manifested across ages, situations, and social roles

identity achievement in Marcia's theory, the identity status achieved by a person who has been through a crisis and reached a commitment to ideological or occupational goals

identity crisis Erikson's term for the psychological state of emotional turmoil that arises when an adolescent's sense of self becomes "unglued" so that a new, more mature sense of self can be achieved

identity diffusion in Marcia's theory, the identity status of a person who is not in the midst of a crisis and who has made no commitment

identity versus role confusion in Erikson's theory, the stage during which adolescents attain a sense of who they are

imaginary audience an internalized set of behavioral standards usually derived from a teenager's peer group

implantation attachment of a blastocyst to the uterine wall

inclusive education general term for education programs in which children with disabilities are taught in classrooms with nondisabled children.

independent variable the presumed causal element in an experiment

inductive discipline a discipline strategy in which parents explain to children why a punished behavior is wrong

inductive logic a type of reasoning in which general principles are inferred from specific experiences

infant mortality death within the first year of life

infant-directed speech (IDS) the simplified, higher-pitched speech that adults use with infants and young children

inflections additions to words that change their meaning (e.g., the *s* in *toys*, the *ed* in *waited*)

information-processing theory a theoretical perspective that uses the computer as a model to explain how the mind manages information

insecure/ambivalent attachment a pattern of attachment in which the infant shows little exploratory behavior, is greatly upset when separated from the mother, and is not reassured by her return or efforts to comfort him

insecure/avoidant attachment a pattern of attachment in which an infant avoids contact with the parent and shows no preference for the parent over other people

insecure/disorganized attachment a pattern of attachment in which an infant seems confused or apprehensive and shows contradictory behavior, such as moving toward the mother while looking away from her

institutional migration a move to an institution such as a nursing home that is necessitated by a disability

instrumental activities of daily living (IADLs) more intellectually demanding daily living tasks such as doing housework, cooking, and managing money

instrumental aggression aggression used to gain or damage an object

intelligence the ability to take in information and use it to adapt to the environment

intelligence quotient (IQ) the ratio of mental age to chronological age; also, a general term for any kind of score derived from an intelligence test

interactionists theorists who argue that language development is a subprocess of general cognitive development and is influenced by both internal and external factors

intermodal perception formation of a single perception of a stimulus that is based on information from two or more senses

intimacy the capacity to engage in a supportive, affectionate relationship without losing one's own sense of self

intimacy versus isolation Erikson's early adulthood stage, in which an individual must find a life partner or supportive friends in order to avoid social isolation

intimate partner abuse physical acts or other behavior intended to intimidate or harm an intimate partner

invented spelling a strategy young children with good phonological awareness skills use when they write

involved relationships relationships in which grandparents are directly involved in the everyday care of grandchildren or have close emotional ties with them

kin keeper a family role, usually occupied by a woman, which includes responsibility for maintaining family and friendship relationships

laboratory observation observation of behavior under controlled conditions

language acquisition device (LAD) an innate language processor, theorized by Chomsky, that contains the basic grammatical structure of all human language

lateralization the process through which brain functions are divided between the two hemispheres of the cerebral cortex

learning disability a disorder in which a child has difficulty mastering a specific academic skill, even though she possesses normal intelligence and no physical or sensory disabilities

learning theories theories asserting that development results from an accumulation of experiences

life events approach a theoretical perspective on middle adulthood that focuses on normative and nonnormative events and how adults in this age group respond to them

life review an evaluative process in which elders make judgments about past behavior

life structure in Levinson's theory, the underlying pattern or design of a person's life at a given time, which includes roles, relationships, and behavior patterns

lifespan perspective the current view of developmentalists that important changes occur throughout the entire human lifespan and that these changes must be interpreted in terms of the culture and context in which they occur; thus, interdisciplinary research is critical to understanding human development

limbic system the part of the brain that regulates emotional responses

locus of control a set of beliefs about the causes of events

longitudinal design a research design in which people in a single group are studied at different times in their lives

low birth weight (LBW) newborn weight below 5.5 pounds

maturation the gradual unfolding of a genetically programmed sequential pattern of change

maximum oxygen uptake (VO$_2$ max) a measure of the body's ability to take in and transport oxygen to various body organs

means–end behavior purposeful behavior carried out in pursuit of a specific goal

memory strategies learned methods for remembering information

menarche the beginning of menstrual cycles

menopause the cessation of monthly menstrual cycles in middle-aged women

metacognition knowledge about how the mind thinks and the ability to control and reflect on one's own thought processes

metamemory knowledge about how memory works and the ability to control and reflect on one's own memory function

moral realism stage the first of Piaget's stages of moral development, in which children believe rules are inflexible

moral relativism stage the second of Piaget's stages of moral development, in which children understand that many rules can be changed through social agreement

moratorium in Marcia's theory, the identity status of a person who is in a crisis but has made no commitment

multifactorial inheritance inheritance affected by both genes and the environment

multigenerational caregivers middle-aged adults who provide assistance to their parents and adult children at the same time

myelinization (myelination) a process in neuronal development in which sheaths made of a substance called myelin gradually cover individual axons and electrically insulate them from one another to improve the conductivity of the nerve

naming explosion the period when toddlers experience rapid vocabulary growth, typically beginning between 16 and 24 months

nativists theorists who claim that perceptual abilities are inborn

naturalistic observation the process of studying people in their normal environments

nature–nurture debate the debate about the relative contributions of biological processes and experiential factors to development

neonate term for babies between birth and 1 month of age

neo-Piagetian theory an approach that uses information-processing principles to explain the developmental stages identified by Piaget

neurons specialized cells of the nervous system

niche picking the process of selecting experiences on the basis of temperament

nonnormative changes changes that result from unique, unshared events

normative age-graded changes changes that are common to every member of a species

normative history-graded changes changes that occur in most members of a cohort as a result of factors at work during a specific, well-defined historical period

norm-referenced tests standardized tests that compare an individual child's score to the average score of others her age

norms average ages at which developmental milestones are reached

obese a child whose BMI-for-age is at or above the 95th percentile

object concept an infant's understanding of the nature of objects and how they behave

object permanence the understanding that objects continue to exist when they can't be seen

objective (categorical) self a toddler's understanding that she or he is defined by various categories such as gender or qualities such as shyness

observational learning (modeling) learning that results from seeing a model reinforced or punished for a behavior

operant conditioning learning to repeat or stop behaviors because of their consequences

operational efficiency a neo-Piagetian term that refers to the maximum number of schemes that can be processed in working memory at one time

organogenesis the process of organ development

osteoporosis loss of bone mass with age, resulting in more brittle and porous bones

overregularization attachment of regular inflections to irregular words, such as the substitution of "goed" for "went"

overweight a child whose BMI-for-age is between the 85th and 95th percentiles

palliative care a form of care for terminally ill people that focuses on relieving patients' pain rather than curing their diseases

parental investment theory the theory that sex differences in mate preferences and mating behavior are based on the different amounts of time and effort men and women must invest in child rearing

parenting styles the characteristic strategies that parents use to manage children's behavior

pelvic inflammatory disease an infection of the female reproductive tract that may result from a sexually transmitted disease and can lead to infertility

perimenopausal phase the stage of menopause during which estrogen and progesterone levels are erratic, menstrual cycles may be very irregular, and women begin to experience symptoms such as hot flashes

permissive parenting style a style of parenting that is high in nurturance and low in maturity demands, control, and communication

person perception the ability to classify others according to categories such as age, gender, and race

personal fable the belief that the events of one's life are controlled by a mentally constructed autobiography

personality a pattern of responding to people and objects in the environment

personality disorder an inflexible pattern of behavior that leads to difficulty in social, educational, and occupational functioning

phenotype an individual's particular set of observed characteristics

phobia an irrational fear of an object, a person, a place, or a situation

phonological awareness children's understanding of the sound patterns of the language they are acquiring

physical domain changes in the size, shape, and characteristics of the body

pituitary gland a gland that triggers other glands to release hormones

placenta a specialized organ that allows substances to be transferred from mother to embryo and from embryo to mother, without their blood mixing

plasticity the ability of the brain to change in response to experience

polygenic inheritance a pattern of inheritance in which many genes influence a trait

population the entire group that is of interest to a researcher

postconventional morality in Kohlberg's theory, the level of moral reasoning in which judgments are based on an integration of individual rights and the needs of society

postformal thought types of thinking that are associated with a hypothesized fifth stage of cognitive development

postmenopausal phase the last stage of menopause, which begins when a woman has had no menstrual periods for a year or more

postsecondary education any kind of formal educational experience that follows high school

preconventional morality in Kohlberg's theory, the level of moral reasoning in which judgments are based on authorities outside the self

preference technique a research method in which a researcher keeps track of how long a baby looks at each of two objects shown

prefrontal cortex (PFC) the part of the frontal lobe that is just behind the forehead and is responsible for executive processing

premenopausal phase the stage of menopause during which estrogen levels fall somewhat, menstrual periods are less regular, and anovulatory cycles begin to occur

preoperational stage Piaget's second stage of cognitive development, during which children become proficient in the use of symbols in thinking and communicating but still have difficulty thinking logically

presbycusis normal loss of hearing with aging, especially of high-frequency tones

presbyopia normal loss of visual acuity with aging, especially the ability to focus the eyes on near objects

primary aging (senescence) age-related physical changes that have a biological basis and are universally shared and inevitable

primary circular reactions Piaget's phrase to describe a baby's simple repetitive actions in substage 2 of the sensorimotor stage, organized around the baby's own body

primary sex characteristics the sex organs: ovaries, uterus, and vagina in the female; testes and penis in the male

primitive reflexes reflexes, controlled by "primitive" parts of the brain, that disappear during the first year of life

processing efficiency the ability to make efficient use of short-term memory capacity

programmed senescence theory the view that age-related declines are the result of species-specific genes for aging

prosocial behavior behavior intended to help another person

proximodistal pattern growth that proceeds from the middle of the body outward

pruning the process of eliminating unused synapses

psychoanalytic theories theories proposing that developmental change happens because of the influence of internal drives and emotions on behavior

psychological self an understanding of one's stable, internal traits

psychosexual stages Freud's five stages of personality development through which children move in a fixed sequence determined by maturation; the libido is centered in a different body part in each stage

psychosocial stages Erikson's eight stages, or crises, of personality development in which inner instincts interact with outer cultural and social demands to shape personality

puberty collective term for the physical changes that culminate in sexual maturity

punishment anything that follows a behavior and causes it to stop

qualitative change a change in kind or type

quality of work–life (QWL) movement an approach to enhancing job satisfaction by basing job and workplace design on analyses of the quality of employee experiences in an organization

quantitative change a change in amount

reaction range a range, established by one's genes, between upper and lower boundaries for traits such as intelligence; one's environment determines where, within those limits, one will be

receptive language comprehension of spoken language

reciprocal determinism Bandura's model in which personal, behavioral, and environmental factors interact to influence personality development

reflective judgment the ability to identify the underlying assumptions of differing perspectives on controversial issues

reinforcement anything that follows a behavior and causes it to be repeated

relational aggression aggression aimed at damaging another person's self-esteem or peer relationships, such as by ostracism or threats of ostracism, cruel gossip, or facial expressions of disdain

relational style a tendency to ignore the details of a task in order to focus on the "big picture"

relative right–left orientation the ability to identify right and left from multiple perspectives

relativism the idea that some propositions cannot be adequately described as either true or false

religious coping the tendency to turn to religious beliefs and institutions for support in times of difficulty

reminiscence reflection on past experience

remote relationships relationships in which grandparents do not see their grandchildren often

representative sample a sample that has the same characteristics as the population to which a study's findings apply

research ethics the guidelines researchers follow to protect the rights of animals used in research and humans who participate in studies

retaliatory aggression aggression to get back at someone who has hurt you

reticular formation the part of the brain that regulates attention

reversibility the understanding that both physical actions and mental operations can be reversed

role conflict any situation in which two or more roles are at least partially incompatible, either because they call for different behaviors or because their separate demands add up to more hours than there are in the day

role-taking the ability to look at a situation from another person's perspective

sample a subset of a group that is of interest to a researcher who participates in a study

satiety the feeling of fullness that follows a meal

schematic learning organization of experiences into expectancies, called schemas, that enable infants to distinguish between familiar and unfamiliar stimuli

scheme in Piaget's theory, an internal cognitive structure that provides an individual with a procedure to use in a specific circumstance

schizophrenia a serious mental disorder characterized by disturbances of thought such as delusions and hallucinations

secondary aging age-related changes that are due to environmental influences, poor health habits, or disease

secondary circular reactions repetitive actions in substage 3 of the sensorimotor period, oriented around external objects

secondary sex characteristics body parts such as breasts in females and pubic hair in both sexes

secular trend a change that occurs in developing nations when nutrition and health improve—for example, the decline in average age of menarche and the increase in average height for both children and adults that happened between the mid-18th and mid-19th centuries in Western countries

secure attachment a pattern of attachment in which an infant readily separates from the parent, seeks proximity when stressed, and uses the parent as a safe base for exploration

selective attention the ability to focus cognitive activity on the important elements of a problem or situation

selective optimization with compensation the process of balancing the gains and losses associated with aging

self-efficacy belief in one's capacity to cause an intended event to occur or to perform a task

self-esteem a global evaluation of one's own worth

self-regulation children's ability to conform to parental standards of behavior without direct supervision

semantic memories general knowledge

semiotic (symbolic) function the understanding that one object or behavior can represent another

sensitive period a span of months or years during which a child may be particularly responsive to specific forms of experience or particularly influenced by their absence

sensorimotor stage Piaget's first stage of development, in which infants use information from their senses and motor actions to learn about the world

separation anxiety expressions of discomfort, such as crying, when separated from an attachment figure

sequential design a research design that combines cross-sectional and longitudinal examinations of development

severely obese a child whose BMI-for-age is at or above the 99th percentile

sex-typed behavior different patterns of behavior exhibited by boys and girls

sexual violence the use of physical coercion to force a person to engage in a sexual act against his or her will

short-term storage space (STSS) neo-Piagetian theorist Robbie Case's term for the working memory

social clock a set of age norms defining a sequence of life experiences that is considered normal in a given culture and that all individuals in that culture are expected to follow

social comparisons conclusions drawn about the self based on comparisons to others

social death the point at which family members and medical personnel treat the deceased person as a corpse

social domain changes in variables that are associated with the relationship of an individual to others

social referencing an infant's use of others' facial expressions as a guide to his or her own emotions

social role theory the idea that sex differences in mate preferences and mating behavior are adaptations to gender roles

social skills a set of behaviors that usually lead to being accepted as a play partner or friend by peers

social status an individual child's classification as popular, rejected, or neglected

social-cognitive theory a theoretical perspective which asserts that social and personality development in early childhood is related to improvements in the cognitive domain

sociobiology the study of society using the methods and concepts of biology; when used by developmentalists, an approach that emphasizes genes that aid group survival

sociocultural theory Vygotsky's view that complex forms of thinking have their origins in social interactions rather than in an individual's private explorations

spatial cognition the ability to infer rules from and make predictions about the movement of objects in space

spatial perception the ability to identify and act on relationships between objects in space

stages qualitatively distinct periods of development

stranger anxiety expressions of discomfort, such as clinging to the mother, in the presence of strangers

subjective self an infant's awareness that she or he is a separate person who endures through time and space and can act on the environment

substance abuse a pattern of behavior in which a person continues to use a substance even though it interferes with psychological, occupational, educational, and social functioning

successful aging the term gerontologists use to describe maintaining one's physical health, mental abilities, social competence, and overall satisfaction with one's life as one ages

sudden infant death syndrome (SIDS) a phenomenon in which an apparently healthy infant dies suddenly and unexpectedly

superego Freud's term for the part of personality that is the moral judge

survey a data-collection method in which participants respond to questions

synapses connections between neurons. They are tiny spaces across which neural impulses flow from one neuron to the next

synaptic plasticity the redundancy in the nervous system which ensures that it is nearly always possible for a nerve impulse to move from one neuron to another or from a neuron to another type of cell (e.g., a muscle cell)

synaptogenesis the process of synapse development

synchrony a mutual, interlocking pattern of attachment behaviors shared by a parent and child

systematic and explicit phonics planned, specific instruction in sound–letter correspondences

systematic problem solving the process of finding a solution to a problem by testing single factors

task goals goals based on a desire for self-improvement

telegraphic speech simple two-word sentences that usually include a noun and a verb

telomere a string of repetitive DNA at the tip of each chromosome in the body that appears to serve as a kind of timekeeping mechanism

temperament inborn predispositions, such as activity level, that form the foundations of personality

teratogens substances, such as viruses and drugs, that can cause birth defects

terminal decline hypothesis the hypothesis that mental and physical functioning decline drastically only in the few years immediately preceding death

tertiary circular reactions the deliberate experimentation with variations of previous actions that occurs in substage 5 of the sensorimotor period

thanatology the scientific study of death and dying

theory of mind a set of ideas constructed by a child or an adult to explain other people's ideas, beliefs, desires, and behavior

tinnitus persistent ringing in the ears

tracking the smooth movements of the eye to follow the track of a moving object

trait a stable pattern of responding to situations

transgendered a person whose psychological gender is the opposite of his or her biological sex

traumatic brain injury (TBI) an injury to the head that results in diminished brain function such as a loss of consciousness, confusion, or drowsiness

umbilical cord an organ that connects the embryo to the placenta

uninvolved parenting style a style of parenting that is low in nurturance, maturity demands, control, and communication

unique invulnerability the belief that bad things, including death, happen only to others

validating couples partners who express mutual respect, even in disagreements, and are good listeners

vascular dementia a form of dementia caused by one or more strokes

viability the ability of the fetus to survive outside the womb

violation-of-expectations method a research strategy in which researchers move an object in one way after having taught an infant to expect it to move in another

visual acuity how well one can see details at a distance

volatile couples partners who argue a lot and don't listen well but still have more positive than negative interactions

volunteerism performance of unpaid work for altruistic motives

wisdom a cognitive characteristic that includes accumulated knowledge and the ability to apply that knowledge to practical problems of living, popularly thought to be more commonly found in older adults

work–life balance the interactive influences among employees' work and nonwork roles

zygote a single cell created when sperm and ovum unite

References

Aarnoudse-Moens, C., Duivenvoorden, H., Weisglas-Kuperus, N., van Goudoever, J., & Oosterlaan, J. (2012). The profile of executive function in very preterm children at 4 to 12 years. *Developmental Medicine & Child Neurology, 54*, 247–253.

ABC News. (2000, August 22). *Poll: Americans like public school.* Retrieved August 23, 2000, from http://www.abcnews.com.

Abele, A. (2005). Goals, gender-related self-concept, and work-life balance in long-term life pursuit: Findings from the Erlangen longitudinal study BELA-E. *Zeitschrift für Arbeits und Organisationspsychologie, 49*, 176–186.

Abma, J., & Martinez, G. (2006). *Childlessness among older women in the United States: Trends and profiles.* Journal of Marriage and Family, 68, 1045–1056.

Abma, J., Martinez, G., & Copen, C. (2010). *Teenagers in the United States: Sexual activity, contraceptive use, and childbearing.* Vital Health Statistics, 23, 1–86.

Abraham, J. D., & Hansson, R. O. (1995). Successful aging at work: An applied study of selection, optimization, and compensation through impression management. *Journals of Gerontology: Psychological Sciences, 50B*, P94–P103.

Abrazaldo, W., Adefuin, J., Henderson-Frakes, J., Lea, C., Leufgen, J., Lewis-Charp, H., Soukamneuth, S., & Wiegand, A. (2009). *Evaluation of the YouthBuild youth offender grants.* Retrieved July 14, 2013, from http://wdr.doleta.gov/research/FullText_Documents/Evaluation%20of%20the%20YouthBuild%20Youth%20Offender%20Grants%20-%20Final%20Report.pdf.

Accardo, P., Tomazic, T., Fete, T., Heaney, M., Lindsay, R., & Whitman, B. (1997). Maternally reported fetal activity levels and developmental diagnoses. *Clinical Pediatrics, 36*, 279–283.

Ackerman, B., Brown, E., & Izard, C. (2004). The relations between contextual risk, earned income, and the school adjustment of children from economically disadvantaged families. *Developmental Psychology, 40*, 204–216.

Ackerman, S., Zuroff, D., & Moskowitz, D. (2000). Generativity in midlife and young adults: Links to agency, communion and subjective well-being. *Aging and Human Development, 50*, 17–41.

Adams, C. (1991). Qualitative age differences in memory for text: A life-span developmental perspective. *Psychology & Aging, 6*, 323–336.

Adams, G., & Rau, B. (2004). Job seeking among retirees seeking bridge employment. *Personnel Psychology, 57*, 719–744.

Adams, M., & Henry, M. (1997). Myths and realities about words and literacy. *School Psychology Review, 26*, 425–436.

Addis, M., & Mahalik, J. (2003). Men, masculinity, and the contexts of help seeking. *American Psychologist, 58*, 5–14.

Adelman, W., & Ellen, J. (2002). Adolescence. In A. Rudolph, R. Kamei, & K. Overby (Eds.), *Rudolph's fundamentals of pediatrics* (3rd ed., pp. 70–109). New York: McGraw-Hill.

Adkins, V. (1999). Grandparents as a national asset: A brief note. *Activities, Adaptation, & Aging, 24*, 13–18.

Adolph, E., & Berger, S. (2011). Physical and motor development. In M. Bornstein & M. Lamb (Eds.), *Developmental science: An advanced textbook* (6th ed., pp. 241–302). New York: Psychology Press.

Afonso, R., Bueno, B., Loureiro, M., & Pereira, H. (2011). Reminiscence, psychological well-being, and ego integrity in Portuguese elderly people. *Educational Gerontology, 37*, 1063–1080.

Agahi, N., Ahacic, K., & Parker, M. (2006). Continuity of leisure participation from middle age to old age. *The Journals of Gerontology Series B: Psychological Sciences and Social Sciences, 61*, S340–S346.

Ahadi, S. A., & Rothbart, M. K. (1994). Temperament, development, and the big five. In C. F. Halverson, Jr., G. A. Kohnstamm, & R. P. Martin (Eds.), *The developing structure of temperament and personality from infancy to adulthood* (pp. 189–207). Hillsdale, NJ: Erlbaum.

Aharon-Peretz, J., & Tomer, R. (2007). Traumatic brain injury. In B. Miller & J. Cummings (Eds.), *The human frontal lobes: Functions and disorders* (2nd ed.) (pp. 540–551). New York: Guilford Press.

Ahituv, A., & Lehman, R. (2004). *Job turnover, wage rates, and marital stability.* Retrieved July 7, 2007 from http://www.urban.org/UploadedPDF/411148_job_turnover.pdf.

Ainsworth, M. D. S., Blehar, M., Waters, E., & Wall, S. (1978). *Patterns of attachment.* Hillsdale, NJ: Erlbaum.

Akers, J., Jones, R., & Coyl, D. (1998). Adolescent friendship pairs: Similarities in identity status development, behaviors, attitudes, and interests. *Journal of Adolescent Research, 13*, 178–201.

Akincigil, A., Olfson, M., Siegel, M., Zurlo, K., Walkup, J., & Crystal, S. (2012). Racial and ethnic disparities in depression care in community-dwelling elderly in the United States. *American Journal of Public Health, 102*, 319–328.

Akiyama, H., Antonucci, T., Takahashi, K., & Langfahl, E. (2003). Negative interactions in close relationships across the life span. *Journals of Gerontology, Series B: Psychological Sciences & Social Sciences, 58B*, P70–P79.

Aksglaede, L., Olsen, L., Sørensen, T., & Juul, A. (2008). Forty years trends in timing of pubertal growth spurt in 157,000 Danish school children. *Public Library of Science ONE, 3*, e2728.

Aksu-Koc, A. A., & Slobin, D. I. (1985). The acquisition of Turkish. In D. I. Slobin (Ed.), *The crosslinguistic study of language acquisition: Vol. 1: The data* (pp. 839–878). Hillsdale, NJ: Erlbaum.

Alan Guttmacher Institute. (2004). *U.S. teenage pregnancy statistics with comparative statistics for women aged 20–24.* Retrieved July 9, 2004, from http://www.guttmacher.org/pubs/teen_stats.html.

Alberg, A., Patnaik, J., May, J., Hoffman, S., Gitchelle, J., Comstock, G., & Helzlsouer, K. (2005). Nicotine replacement therapy use among a cohort of smokers. *Journal of Addictive Diseases, 24*, 101–113.

Alberts, A., Elkind, D., & Ginsberg, S. (2007). The personal fable and risk-taking in early adolescence. *Journal of Youth and Adolescence, 36*, 71–76.

Albritton, T. (2012). Educating our own: The historical legacy of HBCUs and their relevance for educating a new generation of leaders. *Urban Review, 44*, 311–331.

Aleixo, P., & Norris, C. (2000). Personality and moral reasoning in young offenders. *Personality and Individual Differences, 28*, 609–623.

Allen, K. R., & Pickett, R. S. (1987). Forgotten streams in the family life course: Utilization of qualitative retrospective interviews in the analysis of lifelong single women's family careers. *Journal of Marriage & the Family, 49*, 517–526.

Alsaker, F., & Kroger, J. (2006). Self-concept, self-esteem, and identity. In S. Jackson, S., & L. Goossens, L. (Eds.), *Handbook of adolescent development* (pp. 90–113). New York, NY, USA: Psychology Press.

Alspaugh, J. (1998). Achievement loss associated with the transition to middle school and high school. *Journal of Educational Research, 92*, 20–25.

Alster, E. (1997). The effects of extended time on algebra test scores for college students with and without learning disabilities. *Journal of Learning Disabilities, 30*, 222–227.

Alvidrez, J., & Weinstein, R. (1999). Early teacher perceptions and later student academic achievement. *Journal of Educational Psychology, 91*, 731–746.

Alzheimer's Association. (2007). *Alzheimer's disease facts and figures.* Retrieved July 31, 2007 from www.alz.org/national/documents/Report_2007FactsAndFigures.pdf.

Amato, P. R. (1993). Children's adjustment to divorce: Theories, hypotheses, and empirical support. *Journal of Marriage & the Family, 55*, 23–38.

Ambert, A. (2001). *Families in the new millennium.* Boston: Allyn & Bacon.

Amenedo, E., & Diaz, F. (1998). Aging-related changes in processing of nontarget and target stimuli during an auditory oddball task. *Biological Psychology, 48*, 235–267.

Amenedo, E., & Diaz, F. (1999). Aging-related changes in the processing of attended and unattended standard stimuli. *Neuroreport: For Rapid Communication of Neuroscience Research, 10*, 2383–2388.

American Association of Colleges and Universities. (2006). Student debt burden. *Policy Matters, 3(8).* Retrieved June 30, 2007 from www.aascu.org/policy_matters/v3_8/default.htm.

American College Health Association. (2009). *National college health assessment II.* Retrieved August 24, 2010 from http://www.achancha.org/docs/ACHA-NCHA_Reference_Group_Report_Fall2009.pdf

American College of Obstetrics and Gynecology. (2002, November 29). *Rubella vaccination recommendation changes for pregnant women.* Retrieved April 2, 2004, from http://www.acog.org.

American Indian College Fund. (2006). *Championing success: A report on the progress of tribal college and university alumni.* Retrieved July 18, 2013, from http://www.collegefund.org/userfiles/file/FINALIHEP-rpt-TribalAlumni-4-10.pdf.

American Indian Higher Education Consortium (AIHEC). (2013). *AIHEC's history and mission*. Retrieved July 18, 2013, from http://www.aihec.org/about/historyMission.cfm.

American Psychiatric Association (APA). (2013). *Diagnostic and statistical manual of mental disorders, fifth edition (DSM-5)*. Washington, DC, USA: Author.

American Psychiatric Association. (2000). *Diagnostic and statistical manual of mental disorders* (4th ed., Text Revision). Washington, DC: Author.

American Psychiatric Association. (2013). *DSM-5*. Arlington, VA, USA: American Psychiatric Association.

Amieva, H., Lentenneur, L., Dartigues, J., Rouch-Leroyer, I., Sourgen, C., D'Alchée-Birée, F., Dib, M., Barberger-Gateau, P., Orgogozo, J., & Fabrigoule, C. (2004). Annual rate and predictors of conversion to dementia in subjects presenting mild cognitive impairment criteria defined according to a population-based study. *Dementia & Geriatric Cognitive Disorders, 18*, 87–93.

Anderman, E. (1998). The middle school experience: Effects on the math and science achievement of adolescents with LD. *Journal of Learning Disabilities, 31*, 128–138.

Anderman, E., & Midgley, C. (1997). Changes in achievement goal orientations, perceived academic competence, and grades across the transition to middle-level schools. *Contemporary Educational Psychology, 22*, 269–298.

Anderman, E., Maehr, M., & Midgley, C. (1999). Declining motivation after the transition to middle school: Schools can make a difference. *Journal of Research & Development in Education, 32*, 131–147.

Anderman, L. (1999). Classroom goal orientation, school belonging and social goals as predictors of students' positive and negative affect following the transition to middle school. *Journal of Research & Development in Education, 32*, 89–103.

Anderman, L., & Anderman, E. (1999). Social predictors of changes in students' achievement goal orientations. *Contemporary Educational Psychology, 24*, 21–37.

Anderman, L., & Anderman, E. (2009). Oriented towards mastery: Promoting positive motivational goals for students. In Gilman, R., Huebner, E., & Furlong, M. (Eds.) *Handbook of positive psychology in schools* (pp. 161–173). New York, NY: Routledge/Taylor & Francis Group.

Anderson, C., & Dill, K. (2000). Video games and aggressive thoughts, feelings, and behavior in the laboratory and in life. *Journal of Personality & Social Psychology, 78*, 772–790.

Anderson, C., Masse, L., Zhang, H., Coleman, K., & Chang, S. (2009). Contribution of athletic identity to child and adolescent physical activity. *American Journal of Preventive Medicine, 37*, 220–226.

Anderson, H. (2013a). *Alzheimer disease*. Retrieved July 16, 2013, from http://emedicine.medscape.com/article/1134817-overview.

Anderson, H. (2013b). *Mild cognitive impairment*. Retrieved July 21, 2013, from http://emedicine.medscape.com/article/1136393-overview#aw2aab6b6.

Anderson, K. M., Castelli, W. P., & Levy, D. (1987). Cholesterol and mortality: 30 years of follow–up from the Framingham study. *Journal of the American Medical Association, 257*, 2176–2180.

Anderson, R. (1998). Examining language loss in bilingual children. *Electronic Multicultural Journal of Communication Disorders, 1*.

Andrén, S., & Elmstahl, S. (2007). Relationships between income, subjective health, and caregiver burden in caregivers of people with dementia in group living care: A cross-sectional community-based study. *International Journal of Nursing Studies, 44*, 435–446.

Andreou, E., & Metallidou, P. (2004). The relationship of academic and social cognition to behaviour in bullying situations among Greek primary school children. *Educational Psychology, 24*, 27–41.

Andrews, M., Dowling, W., Bartlett, J., & Halpern, A. (1998). Identification of speeded and slowed familiar melodies by younger, middle-aged, and older musicians and nonmusicians. *Psychology & Aging, 13*, 462–471.

Ang, R., & Goh, D. (2010). Cyberbullying among adolescents: The role of affective and cognitive empathy, and gender. *Child Psychiatry and Human Development, 41*, 387–397.

Angier, N. (June 9, 1992). Clue to longevity found at chromosome tip. *New York Times*, pp. B5, B9.

Anglin, J. M. (1993). Vocabulary development: A morphological analysis. *Monographs of the Society for Research in Child Development, 58* (Serial No. 238).

Anglin, J. M. (1995, March). *Word learning and the growth of potentially knowable vocabulary*. Paper presented at the biennial meetings of the Society for Research in Child Development, Indianapolis, IN.

Anisfeld, M. (2005). No compelling evidence to dispute Piaget's timetable of the development of representational imitation in infancy. In S. Hurley & N. Chater (Eds.), *Perspectives on imitation: From neuroscience to social science: Volume 2: Imitation, human development, and culture* (pp. 107–131). Cambridge, MA: MIT Press.

Anme, T., Tanaka, H., Shinohara, R., Sugisawa, Y., Tanaka, E., Tong, L., Watanabe, T., Onda, Y., Kawashima, Y., Tomisaki, E., Mochizuki, H., Hirano, M., Morita, K., Gan-Yadam, A., & Segal, U. (2010). Effectiveness of Japan's extended/night child care: A five-year follow up. *Procedia: Social and Behavioral Sciences, 2*, 5573–5580.

Annett, M. (2003). Do the French and the English differ for hand skill asymmetry? Handedness subgroups in the sample of Doyen and Carlier (2002) and in English schools and universities. *Laterality: Asymmetries of Body, Brain & Cognition, 8*, 233–245.

Anrig, G., & Parekh, M. (2010). *The Century Foundation issue brief: The impact of housing and investment market declines on the wealth of baby boomers*. Retrieved August 29, 2010 from http://www.tcf.org/publications/economic-sinequality/parekh_brief.pdf.

Anthony, J. C., & Aboraya, A. (1992). The epidemiology of selected mental disorders in later life. In J. E. Birren, R. B. Sloane, & G. D. Cohen (Eds.), *Handbook of mental health and aging* (2nd ed., pp. 28–73). San Diego, CA: Academic Press.

Antonucci, T. C. (1990). Social supports and social relationships. In R. H. Binstock & L. K. George (Eds.), *Handbook of aging and the social sciences* (3rd ed., pp. 205–226). San Diego, CA: Academic Press.

Antonucci, T., Lansford, J., & Akiyama, H. (2001). Impact of positive and negative aspects of marital relationships and friendships on well-being of older adults. *Applied Developmental Science, 5*, 68–75.

Antrop, I., Roeyers, H., Van Oost, P., & Buysse, A. (2000). Stimulation seeking and hyperactivity in children with ADHD. *Journal of Child Psychology, Psychiatry & Allied Disciplines, 41*, 225–231.

Apgar, V. A. (1953). A proposal for a new method of evaluation of the newborn infant. *Current Research in Anesthesia and Analgesia, 32*, 260–267.

Appel, M., & Kronberger, N. (2012). Stereotypes and the achievement gap: Stereotype threat prior to test taking. *Educational Psychology Review, 24*, 609–634.

Arabin, B. (2009). Development of the senses. In Levene, M., & Chervenak, F. (Eds), *Fetal and neonatal neurology and neurosurgery*, (4th ed., pp. 111–127). Philadelphia, PA, USA: Churchill Livingstone Elsevier.

Aranha, M. (1997). Creativity in students and its relation to intelligence and peer perception. *Revista Interamericana de Psicologia, 31*, 309–313.

Archibald, L., & Joanisse, M. (2013). Domain-specific and domain-general constraints on word and sequence learning. *Memory & Cognition, 41*, 268–280.

Ardelt, M. (2003). Effects of religion and purpose in life on elders' subjective well-being and attitudes toward death. *Journal of Religious Gerontology, 14*, 55–77.

Ardelt, M., & Koenig, C. (2006). The role of religion for hospice patients and relatively healthy older adults. *Research on Aging, 28*, 184–215.

Areán, P., Mackin, S., Vargas-Dwyer, E., Raue, P., Sirey, J., Kanellopoulos, D., & Alexopoulos, G. (2013). Treating depression in disabled, low-income elderly: A conceptual model and recommendations for care. *International Journal of Geriatric Psychiatry, 25*, 765–769.

Arluk, S., Swain, D., & Dowling, E. (2003). Childhood obesity's relationship to time spent in sedentary behavior. *Military Medicine, 168*, 583–586.

Armstrong, T. (2003). Effect of moral reconation therapy on the recidivism of youthful offenders: A randomized experiment. *Criminal Justice & Behavior, 30*, 668–687.

Arnett, J. (1998). Risk behavior and family role transitions during the twenties. *Journal of Youth & Adolescence, 27*, 301–320.

Arnett, J. (2000). Emerging adulthood: A theory of development from the late teens through the twenties. *American Psychologist, 57*, 774–783.

Arning, L., Ocklenburg, S., Schulz, S., Ness, V., Gerding, W., Hengstler, J., Falkenstein, M., Epplen, J., Gunturkun, O., & Beste, C. (2013). PCSK6 VNTR polymorphism is associated with degree of handedness but not direction of handedness. *Public Library of Science One, 8*, e67251.

Asendorpf, J. B., Warkentin, V., & Baudonnière, P. (1996). Self-awareness and other-awareness. II: Mirror self-recognition, social contingency awareness, and synchronic imitation. *Developmental Psychology, 32*, 313–321.

Ashkar, P., & Kenny, D. (2007). Moral reasoning of adolescent male offender: Comparison of sexual and nonsexual offenders. *Criminal Justice and Behavior, 34*, 108–118.

Ashkenazi, S., Rubinsten, O., & Henik, A. (2009). Attention, automaticity, and developmental dyscalculia. *Neuropsychology, 23*, 535–540.

Aslin, R. (1987). Motor aspects of visual development in infancy. In N. P. Salapatek & L. Cohen (Eds.), *Handbook of infant perception, Vol. 1: From sensation to perception* (pp. 43–113). Orlando, FL: Academic Press.

Aslin, R., Saffran, J., & Newport, E. (1998). Computation of conditional probability statistics by 8-month-old infants. *Psychological Science, 9*, 321–324.

Asplund, R. (2003). Sleepiness and sleep in elderly persons with tinnitus. *Archives of Gerontology and Geriatrics, 37*, 139–145.

Assibey-Mensah, G. (1997). Role models and youth development: Evidence and lessons from the perceptions of African-American male youth. *Western Journal of Black Studies, 21*, 242–252.

Association of Reproductive Health Professionals (ARHP). (2000). *Mature sex.* Retrieved August 26, 2004, from http://www.ahrp.org/maturesex.

Astington, J., & Jenkins, J. (1999). A longitudinal study of the relation between language and theory-of-mind development. *Developmental Psychology, 35*, 1311–1320.

Astor, R. (1994). Children's moral reasoning about family and peer violence: The role of provocation and retribution. *Child Development, 65*, 1054–1067.

Atchley, R. (1989). A continuity theory of normal aging. *The Gerontologist, 29*, 183–190.

Atzil, S., Hendler, T., Zagoory-Sharon, O., Winetraub, Y, & Feldman, R. (2012). Synchrony and specificity in the maternal and paternal brain: Relations to oxytocin and vasopressin. *Journal of the American Academy of Child & Adolescent Psychiatry, 51*, 798–811.

Aud, S., & Fox, M. (2010). *Status and trends in the education of racial and ethnic groups.* Retrieved July 27, 2010 from http://nces.ed.gov/pubs2010/2010015.pdf.

Aud, S., Wilkinson-Flicker, S., Kristapovich, P., Rathbun, A., Wang, X., & Zhang, J. (2013). *The condition of education 2013* (NCES 2013-037). U.S. Department of Education, National Center for Education Statistics. Washington, DC. Retrieved [July 18, 2013] from http://nces.ed.gov/pubsearch.

Auman, M. (2007). Bereavement support for children. *The Journal of School Nursing, 23*, 34–39.

Austin, S., Ziyadeh, N., Farman, S., Prokop, L., Keliher, A., & Jacobs, D. (2008). Screening high school students for eating disorders: Results of a national initiative. *Prevention of Chronic Disease, 5*, 1–10.

Austin, S., Ziyadeh, N., Kahn, J., Camargo, C., Colditz, G., & Field, A. (2004). Sexual orientation, weight concerns, and eating-disordered behaviors in adolescent girls and boys. *Journal of the American Academy of Child & Adolescent Psychiatry, 43*, 1115–1123.

Auyeung, B., Lombardo, M., & Baron-Cohen, S. (2013). Prenatal and postnatal hormone effects on the human brain and cognition. *Pflugers Archives, 465*, 557–571.

Avis, J., & Harris, P. L. (1991). Belief-desire reasoning among Baka children: Evidence for a universal conception of mind. *Child Development, 62*, 460–467.

Axelman, K., Basun, H., & Lannfelt, L. (1998). Wide range of disease onset in a family with Alzheimer disease and a His163Tyr mutation in the presenilin-I gene. *Archives of Neurology, 55*, 698–702.

Babiloni, C., Babiloni, F., Carducci, F., Cappa, S., Cincotti, F., Del Percio, C., Miniussi, C., Moretti, D., Rossi, S., Sosta, K., & Rossini, P. (2004). Human cortical rhythms during visual delayed choice reaction time tasks: A high-resolution EEG study on normal aging. *Behavioural Brain Research, 153*, 261–271.

Bachman, J. G., & Schulenberg, J. (1993). How part-time work intensity relates to drug use, problem behavior, time use, and satisfaction among high school seniors: Are these consequences or merely correlates? *Developmental Psychology, 29*, 220–235.

Bachman, J., Safron, D., Sy, S., & Schulenberg, J. (2003). Wishing to work: New perspectives on how adolescents' part-time work intensity is linked to educational disengagement, substance use, and other problem behaviours. *International Journal of Behavioral Development, 27*, 301–315.

Bachman, J., Segal, D., Freedman-Doan, P., & O'Malley, P. (2000). Who chooses military service? Correlates of propensity and enlistment in the U.S. Armed Forces. *Military Psychology, 12*, 1–30.

Baddeley, A. (1998). *Human memory: Theory and practice.* Boston, MA: Allyn & Bacon.

Baek, H. (2002). A comparative study of moral development of Korean and British children. *Journal of Moral Education, 31*, 373–391.

Bagner, D., Sheinkopf, S., Vohr, B., & Lester, B. (2010). A preliminary study of cortisol reactivity and behavior problems in young children born premature. *Developmental Psychobiology, 52*, 574–582.

Bahrick, L., & Lickliter, R. (2000). Intersensory redundancy guides attentional selectivity and perceptual learning in infancy. *Developmental Psychology, 36*, 190–201.

Bailey, J. M., & Pillard, R. C. (1991). A genetic study of male sexual orientation. *Archives of General Psychiatry, 48*, 1089–1096.

Bailey, J., Pillard, R., Dawood, K., Miller, M., Farrer, L., Trivedi, S., & Murphy, R. (1999). A family history study of male sexual orientation using three independent samples. *Behavior Genetics, 29*, 79–86.

Bailey, S., & Zvonkovic, A. (2003). Parenting after divorce: Nonresidential parents' perceptions of social and institutional support. *Journal of Divorce & Remarriage, 39*, 59–80.

Baillargeon, R. (1994). How do infants learn about the physical world? *Current Directions in Psychological Science, 3*, 133–140.

Baillargeon, R. (2004). Infants' reasoning about hidden objects: Evidence for event-general and event-specific expectations. *Developmental Science, 7*, 391–424.

Baillargeon, R., Li, J., Ng, W., & Yuan, S. (2009). An account of infants' physical reasoning. In A. Woodward & A. Needham (Eds.), *Learning and the infant mind.* (pp. 66–116). New York: Oxford University Press.

Bailley, S., Kral, M., & Dunham, K. (1999). Survivors of suicide do grieve differently: Empirical support for a common sense proposition. *Suicide & Life-Threatening Behavior, 29*, 256–271.

Baker, D., Jeganathan, K., Cameron, D., Thompson, M., Juneja, S., Kopecka, A., Kumar, R., Jenkins, R., de Groen, P., Roche, P., & van Deursen, J. (2004). BubR1 insufficiency causes early onset of aging-associated phenotypes and infertility in mice. *Nature Genetics, 36*, 744–749.

Baker, E. (2005). Social support and physical health: Understanding the health consequences of relationships. *American Journal of Epidemiology, 161*, 297–298.

Baker, L., & McNulty, J. (2010). Shyness and marriage: Does shyness shape even established relationships? *Personality and Social Psychology Bulletin, 36*, 665–676.

Balaban, M. (1995). Affective influences on startle in five-month-old infants: Reactions to facial expressions of emotion. *Child Development, 66*, 28–36.

Ball, K., Berch, D., Helmers, K., Jobe, J., Leveck, M., Marsiske, M., Morris, J., Rebok, G., Smith, D., Tennstedt, S., Unversagt, F., & Willis, S. (2002). Effects of cognitive training interventions with older adults: A randomized controlled trial. *Journal of the American Medical Association, 288*, 18.

Baltes, B., & Heydens-Gahir, H. (2003). Reduction of work-family conflict through the use of selection, optimization, and compensation behaviors. *Journal of Applied Psychology, 88*, 1005–1018.

Baltes, P. B., & Baltes, M. M. (1990). Psychological perspectives on successful aging: The model of selective optimization with compensation. In P. B. Baltes & M. M. Baltes (Eds.), *Successful aging* (pp. 1–34). Cambridge, UK: Cambridge University Press.

Baltes, P., & Klegl, R. (1992). Further testing of limits of cognitive plasticity: Negative age differences in a mnemonic skill are robust. *Developmental Psychology, 28*, 121–125.

Baltes, P., & Kunzmann, U. (2004). The two faces of wisdom: Wisdom as a general theory of knowledge and judgment about excellence in mind and virtue vs. wisdom as everyday realization in people and products. *Human Development, 47*, 290–299.

Baltes, P., & Staudinger, U. (2000). Wisdom: A metaheuristic (pragmatic) to orchestrate mind and virtue toward excellence. *American Psychologist, 55*, 122–136.

Baltes, P., Staudinger, U., & Lindenberger, U. (1999). Lifespan psychology: Theory and application to intellectual functioning. *Annual Review of Psychology, 50*, 471–507.

Bandura, A. (1977a). *Social learning theory.* Englewood Cliffs, NJ: Prentice-Hall.

Bandura, A. (1977b). Self-efficacy: Toward a unifying theory of behavioral change. *Psychological Review, 84*, 91–125.

Bandura, A. (1982). The psychology of chance encounters and life paths. *American Psychologist, 37*, 747–755.

Bandura, A. (1986). *Social foundations of thought and action: A social cognitive theory.* Englewood Cliffs, NJ: Prentice-Hall.

Bandura, A. (1989). Social cognitive theory. *Annals of Child Development, 6*, 1–60.

Bandura, A. (1997). *Self-efficacy: The exercise of control.* New York: Freeman.

Bandura, A., Ross, D., & Ross, S. (1963). Initiation of film-mediated aggressive models. *The Journal of Abnormal and Social Psychology, 66*, 3–11.

Bandura, A., Ross, D., & Ross, S. A. (1961). Transmission of aggression through imitation of aggressive models. *Journal of Abnormal & Social Psychology, 63*, 575–582.

Bandura, A., Ross, D., Ross, S. A. (1963). Imitation of film-mediated aggressive models. *Journal of Abnormal and Social Psychology* 66 (1): 3–11. doi:10.1037/h0048687.

Bannon, G., Boswell, L., & Schneider, R. (2010). *Alzheimer disease.* Retrieved August 31, 2010 from http://emedicine.medscape.com/article/295558-overview.

Baranchik, A. (2002). Identifying gaps in mathematics preparation that contribute to ethnic, gender, and American/foreign differences in precalculus performance. *Journal of Negro Education, 71*, 253–268.

Barbarin, O. (1999). Social risks and psychological adjustment: A comparison of African American and South African children. *Child Development, 70*, 1348–1359.

Barber, B., & Xia, M. (2013). The centrality of control to parenting and its effects. In Larzelere, R., Morris, A., & Harrist, A. (Eds.). *Authoritative parenting: Synthesizing nurturance and discipline for optimal child development* (pp. 61–87). Washington, DC, USA: American Psychological Association.

Barenboim, C. (1981). The development of person perception in childhood and adolescence: From behavioral comparisons to psychological constructs to psychological comparisons. *Child Development, 52*, 129–144.

Barer, B. (2001). The "grands and greats" of very old black grandmothers. *Journal of Aging Studies, 15*, 1–11.

Barker, J., Morrow, J., & Mitteness, L. (1998). Gender, informal social support networks, and elderly urban African Americans. *Journal of Aging Studies, 12*, 199–222.

Barkley, R. (2005). *Attention-deficit hyperactivity disorder: A handbook for diagnosis and treatment* (3rd ed.). New York: Guilford Press.

Barnard, K. E., Hammond, M. A., Booth, C. L., Bee, H. L., Mitchell, S. K., & Spieker, S. J. (1989). Measurement and meaning of parent-child interaction. In J. J. Morrison, C. Lord, & D. P. Keating (Eds.), *Applied developmental psychology, Vol. 3* (pp. 40–81). San Diego, CA: Academic Press.

Barnes, J., Boutwell, B., Beaver, K., & Gibson, C. (2013). Analyzing the origins of childhood externalizing behavioral problems. *Developmental Psychology 49*, 2272–2284.

Barnett, G., & Mann, R. (2013). Empathy deficits and sexual offending: A model of obstacles to empathy. *Aggression and Violent Behavior, 18*, 228–239.

Barnett, W. S. (1993). Benefit-cost analysis of preschool education: Findings from a 25-year follow-up. *American Journal of Orthopsychiatry, 63*, 500–508.

Barnett, W. S. (1995). Long-term effects of early childhood programs on cognitive and school outcomes. *The Future of Children, 5* (3), 25–50.

Baron, I. (2003). *Neuropsychological evaluation of the child.* New York: Oxford University Press.

Barr, R., Marrott, H., & Rovee-Collier, C. (2003). The role of sensory preconditioning in memory retrieval by preverbal infants. *Learning & Behavior, 31*, 111–123.

Barrett, H., & Behne, T. (2005). Children's understanding of death as the cessation of agency: A test using sleep versus death. *Cognition, 96*, 93–108.

Barsh, G. (2003). What controls variation in human skin color? *Public Library of Science: Biology, 1*, e27.

Barthélémy-Musso, Tartas, V., & Guidetti, M. (2013). Taking objects' uses seriously: Developmental approach of children's co-construction of semiotic convention. *Psychologie Française, 58*, 67–88.

Bartoshuk, L.M. and Weiffenbach, J. M. Taste and Aging. In E.L. Schneider and J.W. Rowe (Eds.), *Handbook of the biology of aging,* New York: Academic Press, 1990, pp. 429–443.

Barusch, A. (1999). Religion, adversity and age: Religious experiences of low-income elderly women. *Journal of Sociology & Social Welfare, 26*, 125–142.

Bass, D. (1985). The hospice ideology and success of hospice care. *Research on Aging, 7*, 307–328.

Basseches, M. (1984). *Dialectical thinking and adult development.* Norwood, NJ: Ablex.

Basseches, M. (1989). Dialectical thinking as an organized whole: Comments on Irwin and Kramer. In M. L. Commons, J. D. Sinnott, F. A. Richards, & C. Armon (Eds.), *Adult development: Vol. 1. Comparisons and applications of developmental models* (pp. 161–178). New York: Praeger.

Bates, E., Marchman, V., Thal, D., Fenson, L., Dale, P., Reznick, J. S., Reilly, J., & Hartung, J. (1994). Developmental and stylistic variation in the composition of early vocabulary. *Journal of Child Language, 21*, 85–123.

Bates, E., O'Connell, B., & Shore, C. (1987). Language and communication in infancy. In J. D. Osofsky (Ed.), *Handbook of infant development* (2nd ed., pp. 149–203). New York: Wiley.

Batten, M., & Oltjenbruns, K. (1999). Adolescent sibling bereavement as a catalyst for spiritual development: A model for understanding. *Death Studies, 23*, 529–546.

Baucal, A., Arcidiacono, F., & Budjevac, N. (2013). "Is there an equal amount of juice?" Exploring the repeated question effect in conservation through conversation. *European Journal of Psychology of Education, 28*, 475–495.

Bauer, P., Schwade, J., Wewerka, S., & Delaney, K. (1999). Planning ahead: Goal-directed problem solving by 2-year-olds. *Developmental Psychology, 35*, 1321–1337.

Baum, S., & Ma, J. (2007). *Education pays: The benefits of higher education for individuals and society.* Retrieved August 24, 2010 from http://www.collegeboard.com/prod_downloads/about/news_info/trends/ed_pays_2007.pdf

Baumrind, D. (1967). Child care practices anteceding three patterns of preschool behavior. *Genetic Psychology Monographs, 75*, 43–88.

Baumrind, D. (1971). Current patterns of parental authority. *Developmental Psychology Monograph, 4*(1, Part 2).

Baumrind, D. (1972). Socialization and instrumental competence in young children. In W. W. Hartup (Ed.), *The young child: Reviews of research, Vol. 2* (pp. 202–224). Washington, DC: National Association for the Education of Young Children.

Baumrind, D. (1980). New directions in socialization research. *American Psychologist, 35*, 639–652.

Baumrind, D. (1991). Effective parenting during the early adolescent transition. In P. A. Cowan & M. Hetherington (Eds.), *Family transitions* (pp. 111–163). Hillsdale, NJ: Erlbaum.

Baumrind, D. (2013). Authoritative parenting revisited: History and current status. In Larzelere, R., Morris, A., & Harrist, A. (Eds.). *Authoritative parenting: Synthesizing nurturance and discipline for optimal child development* (pp. 11–34). Washington, DC, USA: American Psychological Association.

Baxter, J., Shetterly, S., Eby, C., Mason, L., Cortese, C., & Hamman, R. (1998). Social network factors associated with perceived quality of life: The San Luis Valley Health and Aging Study. *Journal of Aging & Health, 10*, 287–310.

Bayley, N. (1969). *Bayley scales of infant development.* New York: Psychological Corporation.

Bayley, N. (1993). *Bayley scales of infant development: Birth to two years.* San Antonio, TX: Psychological Corporation.

Bayley, N. (2006). *Bayley scales of infant and toddler development-Third Edition.* San Antonio, TX: Harcourt Assessment, Inc.

Bayley, N. (2006). *Bayley scales of infant and toddler development* 3rd ed. San Antonio, TX, USA: The Psychological Corporation.

Béanger, M., & Marcotte, D. (2013). Longitudinal study of the link between the changes experienced during the primary-secondary transition and depressive symptoms in adolescents. *Canadian Journal of Behavioural Science, 45*, 159–172.

Bearce, K., & Rovee-Collier, C. (2006). Repeated priming increases memory accessibility in infants. *Journal of Experimental Child Psychology, 93*, 357–376.

Bearss, K., Johnson, C., Handen, B., Smith, T., & Scahill, L. (2013). A pilot study of parent training in young children with autism spectrum disorders and disruptive behavior. *Journal of Autism and Developmental Disorders, 43*, 829–840.

Bechara, A. (2005). Decision making, impulse control and loss of willpower to resist drugs: A neurocognitive perspective. *Nature Neuroscience, 18*, 1458–1463.

Bee, H. L., Barnard, K. E., Eyres, S. J., Gray, C. A., Hammond, M. A., Spietz, A. L., Snyder, C., & Clark, B. (1982). Prediction of IQ and language skill from perinatal status, child performance, family characteristics, and mother-infant interaction. *Child Development, 53*, 1135–1156.

Beem, E., Hooijkaas, H., Cleriren, M., Schut, H., Garssen, B., Croon, M., Jabaaij, L., Goodkin, K., Wind, H., & de Vries, M. (1999). The immunological and psychological effects of bereavement: Does grief counseling really make a difference? A pilot study. *Psychiatry Research, 85*, 81–93.

Behm-Morawitz, E., & Mastro, D. (2009). The effects of the sexualization of female video game characters on gender stereotyping and female self-concept. *Sex Roles, 61*, 808–823.

Behncke, S. (2012). Does retirement trigger ill health? *Health Economics, 21*, 282–300.

Bell, J., & Bromnick, R. (2003). The social reality of the imaginary audience: A ground theory approach. *Adolescence, 38*, 205–219.

Bell, L. G., & Bell, D. C. (1982). Family climate and the role of the female adolescent: Determinants of adolescent functioning. *Family Relations, 31*, 519–527.

Belsky, J. (1985). Prepared statement on the effects of day care. In Select Committee on Children, Youth, and Families, House of Representatives, 98th Congress, Second Session, *Improving child care services: What can be done?* Washington, DC: U.S. Government Printing Office.

Belsky, J., & Fearon, R. (2008). Precursors of attachment security. In D. Cassidy, D., & P. Shaver, P. (Eds.), *Handbook of attachment: Theory, research, and clinical applications* (2nd ed.) (pp. 295–316). New York, NY, USA: Guilford Press.

Belsky, J., Jaffee, S., Caspi, A., Moffitt, T., & Silva, P. (2003). Intergenerational relationships in young adulthood and their life course, mental health, and personality correlates. *Journal of Family Psychology, 17*, 460–471.

Belsky, J., Lang, M. E., & Rovine, M. (1985). Stability and change in marriage across the transition to parenthood: A second study. *Journal of Marriage & the Family, 47*, 855–865.

Belsky, J., Vandell, D., Burchinal, M., Clarke-Stewart, A., McCartney, K., Owen, M, & the NICHD Early Child Car Research Network. (2007). Are there long-term effects of early child care? *Child Development, 78*, 681–701.

Bem, S. (1981). Gender schema theory: A cognitive account of sex-typing. *Psychological Review, 88*, 354–364.

Bem, S. L. (1974). The measurement of psychological androgyny. *Journal of Consulting & Clinical Psychology, 42*, 155–162.

Bender, K. (1999). Assessing antidepressant safety in the elderly. *Psychiatric Times, 16*. Retrieved February 7, 2001, from http://www.mhsource.com/pt/p990151.html.

Benenson, J. F. (1994). Ages four to six years: Changes in the structures of play networks of girls and boys. *Merrill-Palmer Quarterly, 40*, 478–487.

Benenson, J., & Benarroch, D. (1998). Gender differences in responses to friends' hypothetical greater success. *Journal of Early Adolescence, 18*, 192–208.

Bengston, V., Cuellar, J., & Ragan, P. (1977). Stratum contrasts and similiarities in attitudes toward death. *Journal of Gerontology, 32*, 76–88.

Bengtson, V., Rosenthal, C., & Burton, L. (1996). Paradoxes of families and aging. In R. H. Binstock & L. K. George (Eds.), *Handbook of aging and the social sciences* (4th ed., pp. 253–282). San Diego, CA: Academic Press.

Bennett, M. (1997). A longitudinal study of wellbeing in widowed women. *International Journal of Geriatric Psychiatry, 12*, 61–66.

Benson, J., & Sabbagh, M. (2010). Theory of mind and executive functioning: A developmental neuropsychological approach. In P. Zelazo, M. Chandler, & E. Crone (Eds.), *Developmental social cognitive neuroscience*. New York: Psychology Press.

Benton, T. (2010). *Depression*. Retrieved August 16, 2010 from http://emedicine.medscape.com/article/914192-overview.

Bergeman, C. S., Chipuer, H. M., Plomin, R., Pedersen, N. L., McClearn, G. E., Nesselroade, J. R., Costa, P. T., & McCrae, R. R. (1993). Genetic and environmental effects on openness to experience, agreeableness, and conscientiousness: An adoption/twin study. *Journal of Personality, 61*, 159–179.

Berger, C., & Rodkin, P. (2012). Group influences on individual aggression and prosociality: Early adolescents who change peer affiliations. *Social Development, 21*, 396–413.

Bergeson, T., & Trehub, S. (1999). Mothers' singing to infants and preschool children. *Infant Behavior & Development, 22*, 53–64.

Bergman, R. (2002). Why be moral? A conceptual model from developmental psychology. *Human Development, 45*, 104–124.

Berlan, E., Corliss, H., Field, A., Goodman, E., & Austin, S. (2010). Sexual orientation and bullying among adolescents in the growing up today study. *Journal of Adolescent Health, 46*, 366–371.

Berliner, D., & Biddle, B. (1997). *The manufactured crisis: Myths, fraud, and the attack on America's public schools*. New York: Addison-Wesley.

Berne, L., & Huberman, B. (1996, February). Sexuality education works: Here's proof. *Education Digest*, 25–29.

Bernhard, J., Lefebvre, M., Kilbride, K., Chud, G., & Lange, R. (1998). Troubled relationships in early childhood education: Parent-teacher interactions in ethnoculturally diverse child care settings. *Early Education & Development, 9*, 5–28.

Berninger, V., Abbott, R., Nagy, W., & Carlisle, J. (2010). Growth in phonological, orthographic. and morphological awareness in grades 1 to 6. *Journal of Psycholinguistic Research, 39*, 141–163.

Bernstein, B. (2010). *Eating disorder, anorexia*. Retrieved August 16, 2010 from http://emedicine.medscape.com/article/805152-overview.

Berrrington, Stone, & Falkingham. (2009). The changing living arrangements of young adults in the UK. *Population Trends, 138*, 27–37.

Berry, D., Blair, C., Ursache, A., Willoughby, M., Garrett-Peters, P., Vernon-Feagans, L., Bratsch-Hines, M., Mills-Koonce, W., & Granger, D. (2014). Child care and cortisol across early childhood: Context matters. *Developmental Psychology* [in press].

Berry, J., & Sabatier, C. (2010). Acculturation, discrimination, and adaptation among second generation immigrant youth in Montreal and Paris. *International Journal of Intercultural Relations, 34*, 191–207.

Berry, J., Poortinga, Y., Poortinga, M., & Dasen, P. (2002). *Cross-cultural psychology: Research and applications*. Cambridge, UK: Cambridge University Press.

Berry, S., Zhang, Y., Lipsitz, L., Mittleman, M., Solomon, D., & Kiel, D. (2011). Antidepressant prescriptions: An acute window for falls in the nursing home. *Journal of Gerontology A: Biological Scientific Medical Science, 66A*, 1124–1130.

Berthier, N., DeBlois, S., Poirier, C., Novak, M., & Clifton, R. (2000). Where's the ball? Two- and three-year-olds reason about unseen events. *Developmental Psychology, 36*, 394–401.

Bertram, L., McQueen, M., Mullin, K., Blacker, D., & Tanzi, R. (2007). Systematic meta-analyses of Alzheimer disease genetic association studies: The AlzGene database. *Nature Genetics, 39*, 17–23.

Best, R., & Gregg, A. (2009). *Patau syndrome*. Retrieved June 27, 2010 from http://emedicine.medscape.com/article/947706-overview.

Betancourt, H., & Lopez, S. R. (1993). The study of culture, ethnicity, and race in American psychology. *American Psychologist, 48*, 629–637.

Bethus, I., Lemaire, V., Lhomme, M., & Goodall, G. (2005). Does prenatal stress effect latent inhibition? It depends on the gender. *Behavioural Brain Research, 158*, 331–338.

Betik, A., & Hepple, R. (2008). Determinants of VO2 max decline with aging: An integrated perspective. *Applied Physiology, Nutrition, and Metabolism, 33*, 130–140.

Betz, N. E., & Fitzgerald, L. F. (1987). *The career psychology of women*. Orlando, FL: Academic Press.

Beukens, P., Curtis, S., & Alayon, S. (2003). Demographic and health surveys: Caesarean section rates in sub-Saharan Africa. *British Medical Journal, 326*, 136.

Beyene, Y., Gilliss, C., & Lee, K. (2007). "I take the good with the bad, and I moisturize": Defying middle age in the new millennium. *Menopause, 14*, 734–741.

Beyers, W., & Seiffge-Krenke, I. (2010). Does identity precede intimacy? Testing Erikson's theory on romantic development in emerging adults of the 21st century. *Journal of Adolescent Research, 25*, 387–415.

Bhatia, H., Sharma, D., & Sharma, P. (2012). *Impact of post retirement working on psychological well being and perceived physical health*. Paper presented at the 2nd Indian Psychological Science Congress, October 5—6, Chandigarh, India.

Bial, M. (1971). *Liberal Judaism at home*. New York: Union of American Hebrew Congregations.

Bialystok, E. (2007). Acquisition of literacy in bilingual children: A framework for research. *Language Learning, 57*, 45–77.

Bialystok, E., Majumder, S., & Martin, M. (2003). Developing phonological awareness: Is there a bilingual advantage? *Applied Linguistics, 24*, 27–44.

Bialystok, E., Shenfield, T., & Codd, J. (2000). Languages, scripts, and the environment: Factors in developing concepts of print. *Developmental Psychology, 36*, 66–76.

Biblarz, T. J., Bengtson, V. L., & Bucur, A. (1996). Social mobility across three generations. *Journal of Marriage & the Family, 58*, 188–200.

Bielde, K., & Sanders, G. (2009). Snowbird intergenerational family relationships. *Activities, Adaptation & Aging, 33*, 81–95.

Binet, A., & Simon, T. (1905). Méthodes nouvelles pour le diagnostic du niveau intellectuel des anormaux [New methods for diagnosing the intellectual level of the abnormal]. *L'Anée Psychologique, 11*, 191–244.

Bingham, C. R., Miller, B. C., & Adams, G. R. (1990). Correlates of age at first sexual intercourse in a national sample of young women. *Journal of Adolescent Research, 5*, 18–33.

Birbal, R., Maharaih, H., Birbal, R., Clapperton, M., Jarvis, J., Ragoonath, A., & Uppalapati, K. (2009). Cybersuicide and the adolescent population: Challenges of the future. *International Journal of Adolescent Medicine and Health, 21*, 151–159.

Birch, D. (1998). The adolescent parent: A fifteen-year longitudinal study of school-age mothers and their children. *International Journal of Adolescent Medicine & Health, 19*, 141–153.

Biringen, A. (2000). Emotional availability: Conceptualization and research findings. *American Journal of Orthopsychiatry, 70*, 104–114.

Birney, D., & Sternberg, R. (2011). The development of cognitive abilities. In M. Bornstein & M. Lamb (Eds.), *Developmental science: An advanced textbook* (6th ed., pp. 353–388). New York: Psychology Press.

Birren, J. E., & Fisher, L. M. (1995). Aging and speed of behavior: Possible consequences for psychological functioning. *Annual Review of Psychology, 56,* 329–353.

Biswas, M. K., & Craigo, S. D. (1994). The course and conduct of normal labor and delivery. In A. H. DeCherney & M. L. Pernoll (Eds.), *Current obstetric and gynecologic diagnosis and treatment* (pp. 202–227). Norwalk, CT: Appleton & Lange.

Bitter, S., Mills, N., Adler, C., Strakowski, S., & DelBello, M. (2011). Progression of amygdala volumetric abnormalities in adolescents after their first manic episode. *Journal of the American Academy of Child & Adolescent Psychiatry, 50,* 1017–1026.

Bittner, S., & Newberger, E. (1981). Pediatric understanding of child abuse and neglect. *Pediatric Review, 2,* 198.

Bjelde, K., & Sanders, G. (2009). Snowbird intergenerational family relationships. *Activities, Adaptation & Aging, 33,* 81–95.

Black, K., Markides, K., & Miller, T. (1998). Correlates of depressive symptomatology among older community-dwelling Mexican Americans: The Hispanic EPESE. *Journals of Gerontology, Series B, 53B,* S198–S208.

Black, M., Basile, K., Breiding, M., Smith, S., Walters M., Merrick, M., Chen, J., & Stevens, M. (2011). *The National Intimate Partner and Sexual Violence Survey (NISVS): 2010 summary report.* Retrieved July 18, 2013, from http://www.cdc.gov/violenceprevention/pdf/nisvs_report2010-a.pdf.

Blackwell, D., & Lichter, D. (2000). Mate selection among married and cohabiting couples. *Journal of Family Issues, 21,* 275–302.

Blair, S. N., Kohl, H. W., III, Barlow, C. E., Paffenbarger, R. S., Gibbons, L. W., & Macera, C. A. (1995). Changes in physical fitness and all-cause mortality. *Journal of the American Medical Association, 273,* 1093–1098.

Blake, K., & Davis, V. (2011). Adolescent medicine. In K. Marcdante, R. Kliegman, H. Jensen, & R. Behrman (Eds.), *Nelson's essential of pediatrics* (6th ed., pp. 265–284). New York: Elsevier Health Publishers.

Blakemore, J., LaRue, A., Olejnik, A. (1979). Sex-appropriate toy preference and the ability to conceptualize toys as sex-role related. *Developmental Psychology, 15,* 339–340.

Blanchard-Fields, F., Chen, Y., Schocke, M., & Hertzog, C. (1998). Evidence for content-specificity of causal attributions across the adult life span. *Aging, Neuropsychology, & Cognition, 5,* 241–263.

Blatter, D., Bigler, E., Gale, S., Johnson, S., Anderson, C., Burnett, B., Parner, N, Kurth, S., & Horn, S. (1995). Quantitative volumetric analysis of brain MR: Normative database spanning 5 decades of life. *American Journal of Neuroradiology, 16,* 241–251.

Blau, G. (1996). Adolescent depression and suicide. In G. Blau & T. Gullotta (Eds.), *Adolescent dysfunctional behavior: Causes, interventions, and prevention* (pp. 187–205). Newbury Park, CA: Sage.

Blaye, A., & Jacques, S. (2009). Categorical flexibility in preschoolers: Contributions of conceptual knowledge and executive control. *Developmental Science, 12,* 863–873.

Blazer, D., Hybels, C., Simonsick, E., & Hanlon, J. (2000). Marked differences in antidepressant use by race in an elderly community sample: 1986–1996. *American Journal of Psychiatry, 157,* 1089–1094.

Blehar, M., Lieberman, A., & Ainsworth, M. (1977). Early face-to-face interaction and its relation to later infant—mother attachment. *Child Development, 48,* 182–194.

Blickstine, I., Jones, C., & Keith, L. (2003). Zygotic-splitting rates after single-embryo transfers in in vitro fertilization. *New England Journal of Medicine, 348,* 2366–2367.

Block, J. (1971). *Lives through time.* Berkeley, CA: Bancroft.

Bloom, B. L., White, S. W., & Asher, S. J. (1979). Marital disruption as a stressful life event. In C. Levinger & O. C. Moles (Eds.), *Divorce and separation: Context, causes, and consequences* (pp. 184–200). New York: Basic Books.

Bloom, D. (2004) Children think before they speak. *Nature, 430,* 410–411.

Bloom, L. (1973). *One word at a time.* The Hague: Mouton.

Bloom, L. (1997, April). *The child's action drives the interaction.* Paper presented at the biennial meetings of the Society for Research in Child Development, Washington, DC.

Blouin, P., & McKelvie, S. (2012). Postformal thinking as a predictor of creativity and of the identification and appreciation of irony and metaphor. *North American Journal of Psychology, 14,* 39–50.

Blumenthal, J. A., Emery, C. F., Madden, D. J., Schniebolk, S., Walsh-Riddle, M., George, L. K., McKee, D. C., Higginbotham, M. B., Cobb, R. R., & Coleman, R.

E. (1991). Long-term effects of exercise on physiological functioning in older men and women. *Journals of Gerontology: Psychological Sciences, 46,* P352–361.

Blustein, D., Phillips, S., Jobin-Davis, K., & Finkelberg, S. (1997). A theory-building investigation of the school-to-work transition. *Counseling Psychology, 25,* 364–402.

Bogenschneider, K., Wu, M., Raffaelli, M., & Tsay, J. (1998). Parent influences on adolescent peer orientation and substance use: The interface of parenting-practices and values. *Child Development, 69,* 1672–1688.

Bohlin, G., & Hagekull, B. (2009). Socio-emotional development: From infancy to young adulthood. *Scandinavian Journal of Psychology, 50,* 592–601.

Bokhorst, C., Sumter, S., & Westenberg, P. (2010). Social support from parents, friends, classmates, and teachers in children and adolescents aged 9 to 18 years: Who is perceived as most supportive? *Social Development, 19,* 417–426.

Bonanno, G., Znoi, H., Siddique, H., & Horowitz, M. (1999). Verbal-autonomic dissociation and adaptation to midlife conjugal loss: A follow-up at 25 months. *Cognitive Therapy & Research, 23,* 605–624.

Bonello, K., & Cross, M. (2010). Gay monogamy: I love you but I can't have sex with only you. *Journal of Homosexuality, 57,* 117–139.

Bonoti, F., Leondari, A., & Mastora, A. (2013). Exploring children's understanding of death: Through drawings and the Death Concept Questionnaire. *Death Studies, 37,* 47–60.

Borawski, E., Trapl, E., Lovegreen, L., Colabianchi, N., & Block, T. (2005). Effectiveness of abstinence-only intervention in middle school teens. *American Journal of Health Behavior, 29,* 423–434.

Borkowski, M., Hunter, K., & Johnson, C. (2001). White noise and scheduled bedtime routines to reduce infant and childhood sleep disturbances. *Behavior Therapist, 24,* 29–37.

Bornstein, M. H. (1992). Perception across the life span. In M. H. Bornstein & M. E. Lamb (Eds.), *Developmental psychology: An advanced textbook* (3rd ed., pp. 155–210). Hillsdale, NJ: Erlbaum.

Bornstein, M., Arterberry, M., & Mash, C. (2011). Perceptual development. In M. Bornstein & M. Lamb (Eds.), *Developmental science: An advanced textbook* (6th ed., 303–352). New York: Psychology Press.

Borse, N., & Sleet, D. (2009). CDC childhood injury report: Patterns of unintentional injuries among 0–19 year olds in the United States, 2000–2006. *Family & Community Health, 32,* 189.

Borst, G., Poirel, N., Pineau, A., Cassotti, M., & Houdé, O. (2013). Inhibitory control efficiency in a Piaget-like class inclusion task in school-age children and adults: A developmental negative priming study. *Developmental Psychology, 49,* 1366–1374.

Bos, H., & Sandfort, T. (2010). Children's gender identify in lesbian and heterosexual two-parent families. *Sex Roles, 62,* 114–126.

Bossé, R., Aldwin, C. M., Levenson, M. R., & Workman-Daniels, K. (1991). How stressful is retirement? Findings from the normative aging study. *Journals of Gerontology: Psychological Sciences, 46,* P9–14.

Boswell, W., Boudreau, J., & Tichy, J. (2005). The relationship between employee job change and job satisfaction: The honeymoon-hangover effect. *Journal of Applied Psychology, 90,* 882–892.

Boswell, W., Shipp, A., Payne, S., & Culbertson, S. (2009). Changes in newcomer job satisfaction over time: Examining the pattern of honeymoons and hangover. *Journal of Applied Psychology, 94,* 844–858.

Bosworth, H., Park, K., McQuoid, D., Hays, J., & Steffens, D. (2003). The impact of religious practice and religious coping on geriatric depression. *International Journal of Geriatric Psychiatry, 18,* 905–914.

Bosworth, H., Siegler, I., Brummett, B., Barefoot, J., Williams, R., Clapp-Channing, N., & Mark, D. (2000, August). *Health-related quality of life in a coronary artery sample.* Paper presented at the annual meeting of the American Psychological Association. Washington, DC.

Bouchard, G. (2013). The quality of the parenting alliance during the transition to parenthood. *Canadian Journal of Behavioural Science* [in press].

Bouchey, H., & Harter, S. (2005). Reflected appraisals, academic self-perceptions, and math/science performance during early adolescence. *Journal of Educational Psychology, 97,* 673–686.

Bouhuys, A., Flentge, F., Oldehinkel, A., & van den Berg, M. (2004). Potential psychosocial mechanisms linking depression to immune function in elderly subjects. *Psychiatry Research, 127,* 237–245.

Bowden, V., & Greenberg, C. (2010). *Children and their families: The continuum of care* (2nd ed.). New York: Lippincott, Williams, & Wilkins.

Bowen, J., Gibson, F., & Hand, P. (2002). Educational outcome at 8 years for children who were born extremely prematurely: A controlled study. *Journal of Pediatrics & Child Health, 38*, 438–444.

Bowerman, M. (1985). Beyond communicative adequacy: From piecemeal knowledge to an integrated system in the child's acquisition of language. In K. E. Nelson (Ed.), *Children's language, Vol. 5* (pp. 369–398). Hillsdale, NJ: Erlbaum.

Bowlby, J. (1969). *Attachment and loss, Vol. 1: Attachment*. New York: Basic Books.

Bowlby, J. (1980). *Attachment and loss, Vol. 3: Loss, sadness, and depression*. New York: Basic Books.

Bowling, A., Fleissig, A., Gabriel, Z., Banister, D., Dyjes, J., Dowding, L., Sutton, S., & Evans, O. (2003). Let's ask them: A national survey of definitions of quality of life and its enhancement among people aged 65 and over. *International Journal of Aging & Human Development, 56*, 269–306.

Bowman, P. (2013). A strengths-based social psychological approach to resiliency: Cultural diversity, ecological, and life span issues. In Prince-Embury, S., & Saklofske, D. (Eds.), *Resilience in children, adolescents, and adults: Translating research into practice* (pp. 299–324). New York, NY, USA: Springer Science + Business Media.

Boxall, P., Macky, K., & Rasmussen, E. (2003). Labour turnover and retention in New Zealand: The causes and consequences of leaving and staying with employers. *Asia Pacific Journal of Human Resources, 41*, 195–214.

Boyan, S., & Termini, A. (2005). *The psychotherapist as parent coordinator in high-conflict divorce: Strategies and techniques*. Binghamton, NY: Haworth Clinical Practice Press.

Boyland, E., & Halford, J. (2013). Television advertising and branding. Effects on eating behavior and food preferences in children. *Appetite, 62*, 236–241

Bozick, R. (2006). Precocious behaviors in early adolescence: Employment and the transition to first sexual intercourse. *The Journal of Early Adolescence, 26*, 60–86.

Braam, A., Beekman, A., Deeg, D., Smit, J., & van Tilburg, W. (1997). Religiosity as a protective or prognostic factor of depression in later life: Results from a community survey in the Netherlands. *Longitudinal Aging Study, 96*, 199–205.

Bradbury, K., & Katz, J. (2002). Women's labor market involvement and family income mobility when marriages end. *New England Economic Review, Q4*, 41–74.

Bradley, R. H., Caldwell, B. M., Rock, S. L., Barnard, K. E., Gray, C., Hammond, M. A., Mitchell, S., Siegel, L., Ramey, C. D., Gottfried, A. W., & Johnson, D. L. (1989). Home environment and cognitive development in the first 3 years of life: A collaborative study involving six sites and three ethnic groups in North America. *Developmental Psychology, 25*, 217–235.

Bradmetz, J. (1999). Precursors of formal thought: A longitudinal study. *British Journal of Developmental Psychology, 17*, 61–81.

Branco, A. (2012). Values and socio-cultural practices: Pathways to moral development. In J. Valsiner, J. (Ed.), *The Oxford handbook of culture and psychology* (pp. 749–766). New York, NY, USA: Oxford University Press.

Branje, S., Van Lieshout, C., & Gerris, J. (2007). Big Five personality development in adolescence and adulthood. *European Journal of Personality, 21*, 45–62.

Braun, K., & Nichols, R. (1997). Death and dying in four Asian American cultures: A descriptive study. *Death Studies, 21*, 327–359.

Braun, M., Mura, K., Peter-Wight, M., Hornung, R., & Scholz, U. (2010). Toward a better understanding of psychological well-being in dementia caregivers: The link between marital communication and depression. *Family Process, 49*, 185–203.

Braveman, N. S. (1987). Immunity and aging immunologic and behavioral perspectives. In M. W. Riley, J. D. Matarazzo, & A. Baum (Eds.), *Perspectives in behavioral medicine: The aging dimension* (pp. 94–124). Hillsdale, NJ: Erlbaum.

Brazelton, T. B. (1984). *Neonatal Behavioral Assessment Scale*. Philadelphia: Lippincott.

Bremner, J. (2002). The nature of imitation by infants. *Infant Behavior & Development, 25*, 65–67.

Brener, N., Hassan, S., & Barrios, L. (1999). Suicidal ideation among college students in the United States. *Journal of Consulting & Clinical Psychology, 67*, 1004–1008.

Brennan, F., & Ireson, J. (1997). Training phonological awareness: A study to evaluate the effects of a program of metalinguistic games in kindergarten. *Reading & Writing, 9*, 241–263.

Brent, B. (2006). What accounts for race and ethnic differences in parental financial transfers to adult children in the United States. *Journal of Family Issues, 27*, 1583–1604.

Brent, D., Melhem, N., Donohoe, M., & Walker, M. (2009). The incidence and course of depression in bereaved youth 21 months after the loss of a parent to suicide, accident, or sudden natural death. *The American Journal of Psychiatry, 166*, 786–794.

Breslow, L., & Breslow, N. (1993). Health practices and disability: Some evidence from Alameda County. *Preventive Medicine, 22*, 86–95.

Breyer, J., & Winters, K. (2005). *Adolescent brain development: Implications for drug use prevention*. Retrieved April 15, 2008 from http://www.mentorfoundation.org/pdfs/prevention_perspectives/19.pdf

Bridgeland, J., DiIulio, J., & Morison, K. (2006). The silent epidemic: Perspectives of high school dropouts. Retrieved August 17, 2010 from http://www.civicenterprises.net/pdfs/thesilentepidemic3-06.pdf.

Briggs, S., Raz, N., & Marks, W. (1999). Age-related deficits in generation and manipulation of mental images: I. The role of sensorimotor speed and working memory. *Psychology and Aging, 14*, 427–435.

Broach, D., & Schroeder, D. (2006). Air traffic control specialist age and en route operational errors. *International Journal of Aviation Psychology, 16*, 363–373.

Brock, D., Guralnik, J., & Brody, J. (1990). Demography and epidemiology of aging in the United States. In Schneider, E., & Rowe, J. (Eds.). *The handbook of the biology of aging*, 3rd ed. (pp. 3–23). San Diego, CA: Academic Press.

Brockington, I. (1996). *Motherhood and mental health*. Oxford, England: Oxford University Press.

Brody, E. M., Litvin, S. J., Albert, S. M., & Hoffman, C. J. (1994). Marital status of daughters and patterns of parent care. *Journals of Gerontology: Social Sciences, 49*, S95–103.

Brody, G., Kim, S., Murry, V., & Brown, A. (2003). Longitudinal direct and indirect pathways linking older sibling competence to the development of younger sibling competence. *Developmental Psychology, 39*, 618–628.

Brody, J. E. (1995, October 4). Personal health. *New York Times*, p. B7.

Brody, J. E. (1996, February 28). Good habits outweigh genes as key to a healthy old age. *New York Times*, p. B9.

Brody, N. (1992). *Intelligence* (2nd ed.). San Diego, CA: Academic Press.

Broman, C., Reckase, M., & Freedman-Doan, C. (2006). The role of parenting in drug use among Black, Latino and White adolescents. *Journal of Ethnicity in Substance Abuse, 5*, 39–50.

Bromberger, J., Matthews, K., Schott, L., Brockwell, S., Avis, N., Kravitz, H., Everson-Rose, S., Gold, E., Sowers, M., & Randolph, J. (2007). Depressive symptoms during the menopausal transition: The Study of Women's Health Across the Nation (SWAN). *Journal of Affective Disorders, 103*, 267–272.

Bromberger, J., Schott, L., Kravitz, H., Sowers, M., Avis, N., Gold, E., Randolph, J., & Matthews, K. (2010). Longitudinal change in reproductive hormones and depressive symptoms across the menopausal transition: Results from the Women's Health across the Nation (SWAN). *Archives of General Psychiatry, 67*, 598–607.

Bronfenbrenner, U. (1979). *The ecology of human development*. Cambridge, MA: Harvard University Press.

Bronfenbrenner, U. (1993). The ecology of cognitive development: Research models and fugitive findings. In R. H. Wozniak and K. W. Fischer (Eds.), *Development in context: Acting and thinking in specific environments*. Hillsdale, NJ: Erlbaum.

Brook, J., Whiteman, M., Finch, S., & Cohen, P. (2000). Longitudinally foretelling drug use in the late twenties: Adolescent personality and social-environmental antecedents. *Journal of Genetic Psychology, 161*, 37–51.

Brooks-Gunn, J. (1987). Pubertal processes and girls' psychological adaptation. In R. M. Lerner & T. T. Foch (Eds.), *Biological-psychosocial interactions in early adolescence* (pp. 123–154). Hillsdale, NJ: Erlbaum.

Brooks-Gunn, J. (1995). Children in families in communities: Risk and intervention in the Bronfenbrenner tradition. In P. Moen, G. H. Elder Jr., & K. Lüscher (Eds.), *Examining lives in context: Perspectives on the ecology of human development* (pp. 467–519). Washington, DC: American Psychological Association.

Broom, D., D'Souza, R., Rennie, M., Strazdins, L., Butterworth, P., Parslow, R., & Rodgers, B. (2007). The lesser evil: Bad jobs or unemployment? A survey of mid-aged Australians. *Social Science & Medicine, 63*, 575–586.

Brophy-Herb, H., Zajicek-Farber, M., Bocknek, E., McKelvey, L., & Stnansbury, K. (2013). Longitudinal connections of maternal supportiveness and early emotion regulation to children's school readiness in low-income families. *Journal of the Society for Social Work and Research, 4*, 2–19.

Brown, A., & Day, J. (1983). Macrorules for summarizing text: The development of expertise. *Journal of Verbal Learning & Verbal Behavior, 22*, 1–14.

Brown, B. (2004). *Homes for a booming market.* Retrieved August 2, 2007 from www .aarp.org/bulletin/yourlife/a2004-08-11-boomingmarket.html.

Brown, B. B. (1990). Peer groups and peer cultures. In S. S. Feldman & G. R. Elliott (Eds.), *At the threshold: The developing adolescent* (pp. 171–196). Cambridge, MA: Harvard University Press.

Brown, B. B., & Huang, B. (1995). Examining parenting practices in different peer contexts: Implications for adolescent trajectories. In L. J. Crockett & A. C. Crouter (Eds.), *Pathways through adolescence* (pp. 151–174). Mahwah, NJ: Erlbaum.

Brown, B. B., Mory, M. S., & Kinney, D. (1994). Casting adolescent crowds in a relational perspective: Caricature, channel, and context. In R. Montemayor, G. R. Adams, & T. P. Gullotta (Eds.), *Personal relationships during adolescence* (pp. 123–167). Thousand Oaks, CA: Sage.

Brown, L. (2000). *Helicobacter pylori*: Epidemiology and routes of transmission. *Epidemiology Review, 22,* 283–297.

Brown, R. (1973). *A first language: The early stages.* Cambridge, MA: Harvard University Press.

Brown, R., & Bellugi, U. (1964). Three processes in the acquisition of syntax. *Harvard Educational Review, 334,* 133–151.

Brown, S. (2003). Relationship quality dynamics of cohabiting unions. *Journal of Family Issues, 24,* 583–601.

Brown, S., & Booth, A. (1996). Cohabitation versus marriage: A comparison of relationship quality. *Journal of Marriage & the Family, 58,* 668–678.

Brown, S., Estroff, J., & Barnewolf, C. (2004). Fetal MRI. *Applied Radiology, 33,* 9–25.

Brownell, C. A. (1990). Peer social skills in toddlers: Competencies and constraints illustrated by same-age and mixed-age interaction. *Child Development, 61,* 836–848.

Brucker, E., & Leppel, K. (2013). Retirement plans: Planners and nonplanners. *Educational Gerontology, 39,* 1–11.

Bruer, J. (1999). *The myth of the first three years.* New York: Free Press.

Brugman, D. (2010). Moral reasoning competence and the moral judgment-action discrepancy in young adolescents. In W. Koops, D. Brugman, T. Ferguson, & A. Sanders (Eds.), *The development and structure of conscience* (pp. 119–133). New York: Psychology Press.

Brumariu, L., & Kerns, K. (2010). Parent-child attachment and internalizing symptoms in childhood and adolescence: A review of empirical findings and future directions. *Development and Psychopathology, 22,* 177–203.

Bryant, P. E., MacLean, M., Bradley, L. L., & Crossland, J. (1990). Rhyme and alliteration, phoneme detection, and learning to read. *Developmental Psychology, 26,* 429–438.

Bryant, P., MacLean, M., & Bradley, L. (1990). Rhyme, language, and children's reading. *Applied Psycholinguistics, 11,* 237–252.

Buchanan, C. M., Maccoby, E. E., & Dornbusch, S. M. (1991). Caught between parents: Adolescents' experience in divorced homes. *Child Development, 62,* 1008–1029.

Buchanan, P., & Vardaxis, V. (2003). Sex-related and age-related differences in knee strength of basketball players ages 11–17 years. *Journal of Athletic Training, 38,* 231–237.

Buchbinder, E., & Eisikovits, Z. (2003). Battered women's entrapment in shame: A phenomenological study. *American Journal of Orthopsychiatry, 73,* 355–366.

Buchner, D. M., Beresford, S. A. A., Larson, E. B., LaCroix, A. Z., & Wagner, E. H. (1992). Effects of physical activity on health status in older adults II: Intervention studies. *Annual Review of Public Health, 13,* 469–488.

Bucx, F., & Seiffge-Krenke, I. (2010). Romantic relationships in intra-ethnic and inter-ethnic adolescent couples in Germany: The role of attachment to parents, self-esteem, and conflict resolution skills. *International Journal of Behavioral Development, 34,* 128–135.

Bugental, D., & Happaney, K. (2004). Predicting infant maltreatment in low-income families: The interactive effects of maternal attributions and child status at birth. *Developmental Psychology, 40,* 234–243.

Bukowski, W., Sippola, L., & Hoza, B. (1999). Same and other: Interdependency between participation in same- and other-sex friendships. *Journal of Youth & Adolescence, 28,* 439–459.

Bumpass, L. L., & Aquilino, W. S. (1995). *A social map of midlife: Family and work over the middle life course.* Report of the MacArthur Foundation research network on successful midlife development, Vero Beach, FL.

Bureau of Labor Statistics. (2013). *American time use survey summary.* Retrieved July 21, 2013 from http://www.bls.gov/news.release/atus.nr0.htm.

Bureau of Labor Statistics. (2013). *Employment characteristics of families summary.* Retrieved June 20, 2013 from http://www.bls.gov/news.release/famee.nr0.htm.

Burgess, S. (2005). The preschool home literacy environment provided by teenage mothers. *Early Child Development & Care, 175,* 249–258.

Burke, L., & Follingstad, D. (1999). Violence in lesbian and gay relationships: Theory, prevalence, and correlational factors. *Clinical Psychology Review, 19,* 487–512.

Burkham, D., Lee, V., & Smerdon, B. (1997). Gender and science learning early in high school: Subject matter and laboratory experiences. *American Educational Research Journal, 34,* 297–332.

Burnham, H., & Hogervorst, E. (2004). Recognition of facial expressions of emotion by patients with dementia of the Alzheimer type. *Dementia & Geriatric Cognitive Disorders, 18,* 75–79.

Burton, L. (1992). Black grandparents rearing children of drug-addicted parents: Stressors, outcomes, and social service needs. *Gerontologist, 31,* 744–751.

Bus, A., & van IJzendoorn, M. (1999). Phonological awareness and early reading: A meta-analysis of experimental training studies. *Journal of Educational Psychology, 91,* 403–414.

Bushman, B., & Huesmann, R. (2006). Short-term and long-term effects of violent media on aggression in children and adults. *Archives of Pediatric Adolescent Medicine, 160,* 348–352.

Bushman, B., Chandler, J., & Huesmann, L. (2010). Do violent media numb our consciences? In Koops, Willem, Brugman, Daniel, Ferguson, Tamara J., Sanders, Andries F. (Eds.), (2010). *The development and structure of conscience.,* (pp. 237–251). New York, NY, US: Psychology Press, xii, 364.

Buss, A. H., & Plomin, R. (1984). *Temperament: Early developing personality traits.* Hillsdale, NJ: Erlbaum.

Buss, D. (1999). *Evolutionary psychology.* Boston: Allyn & Bacon.

Buss, D., Abbott, M., Algleitner, A., Ahserian, A., Biaggio, A., et al. (1990). International preferences in selecting mates: A study of 37 cultures. *Journal of Cross-Cultural Psychology, 21,* 5–47.

Bussey, K., & Bandura, A. (1992). Self-regulation mechanisms governing gender development. *Child Development, 63,* 1236–1250.

Butler, R. (1963). The life review: An interpretation of reminiscence in the aged. *Psychiatry: Interpersonal & Biological Processes, 26,* 65–76.

Butler, R. (2002). The life review. *Journal of Geriatric Psychiatry, 35,* 7–10.

Butters, M., Whyte, E., Nebes, R., Begley, A., Dew, M., Mulsant, B., Zmuda, M., Bhalla, R., Meltzer, C., Pollock, B., Reynolds, C., & Becker, J. (2004). Nature and determinants of neuropsychological functioning in late-life depression. *Archives of General Psychiatry, 61,* 587–595.

Buzi, R., Roberts, R., Ross, M., Addy, R., & Markham, C. (2003). The impact of a history of sexual abuse on high-risk sexual behaviors among females attending alternative schools. *Adolescence, 38,* 595–605.

Buzzell, T. (2005). Demographic characteristics of persons using pornography in three technological contexts. *Sexuality & Culture: An Interdisciplinary Quarterly, 9,* 28–48.

Byberg, L., Melhus, H., Gedeborg, R., Sundstrom, J., Ahlbom, A., Zethelius, B., Berglund, L., Wolk, A., & Michaelsson, K. (2009). Total mortality after changes in leisure time physical activity in 50 year old men: 35 year follow up of population based cohort. *British Journal of Medicine, 338,* b688.

Caçola, P., Roberson, J., & Gabbard, C. (2013). Aging in movement representations for sequential finger movements: A comparison between young-, middle-aged, and older adults. *Brain and Cognition, 82,* 1–5.

Cairns, R. B., & Cairns, B. D. (1994). *Lifelines and risks: Pathways of youth in our time.* Cambridge, UK: Cambridge University Press.

Calero, M., & Navarro, E. (2007). Cognitive plasticity as a modulating variable on the effects of memory training in elderly persons. *Archives of Clinical Neuropsychology, 22,* 63–72.

Calkins, S., & Mackler, J. (2011). Temperament, emotion regulation, and social development. In Underwood, M., & Rosen, L. (#Eds.), *Social development: Relationships in infancy, childhood, and adolescence* (pp. 44–70). New York, NY, USA: Guilford Press.

Callaghan, T. (1999). Early understanding and production of graphic symbols. *Child Development, 70,* 1314–1324.

Callaghan, T., & Rankin, M. (2002). Emergence of graphic symbol functioning and the question of domain specificity: A longitudinal training study. *Child Development, 73,* 359–376.

Callaghan, T., Rochat, P., & Corbit, J. (2012). Young children's knowledge of the representational function of pictorial symbols: Development across the preschool years in three cultures. *Journal of Cognition and Development, 13,* 320–353.

Callahan, K., Rademacher, J., Hildreth, B., & Hildreth, B. (1998). The effect of parent participation in strategies to improve the homework performance of students who are at risk. *Remedial & Special Education, 19*, 131–141.

Calvert, S., & Kotler, J. (2003). Lessons from children's television: The impact of the Children's Television Act on children's learning. *Applied Developmental Psychology, 24*, 275–335.

Camilleri, C., & Malewska-Peyre, H. (1997). Socialization and identity strategies. In J. Berry, P. Dasen, & T. Saraswathi (Eds.), *Handbook of cross-cultural psychology, Vol. 2: Basic processes and human development.* Boston: Allyn & Bacon.

Campbell, A., Shirley, L., & Candy, J. (2004). A longitudinal study of gender-related cognition and behavior. *Developmental Science, 7*, 1–9.

Campbell, F. A., & Ramey, C. T. (1994). Effects of early intervention on intellectual and academic achievement: A follow-up study of children from low-income families. *Child Development, 65*, 684–698.

Campbell, F., Pungello, E., Burchinal, M. Kainz, K., Pan, Y., Wasik, B., Barbarin, O., Sparling, J., & Ramey, C. (2012). Adult outcomes as a function of an early childhood educational program: An Abcedarian Project follow-up. *Developmental Psychology, 48*, 1033–1043.

Campbell, L., Connidis, I., & Davies, L. (1999). Sibling ties in later life: A social network analysis. *Journal of Family Issues, 20*, 114–148.

Campbell, S., Spieker, S., Vandergrift, N., Belsky, J., & Burchinal, M. (2010). Predictors and sequelae of trajectories of physical aggression in school-age boys and girls. *Development and Psychopathology, 22*, 133–150.

Campisi, J., Dimri, G., & Hara, E. (1996). Control of replicative senescence. In E. L. Schneider & J. W. Rowe (Eds.), *Handbook of the biology of aging* (4th ed., pp. 121–149). San Diego, CA: Academic Press.

Campos, I., Almeida, L., Ferreira, A., Martinez, L., & Ramalho, G. (2013). Cognitive processes and math performance: A study with children at third grade of basic education. *European Journal of Psychology of Education, 28*, 421–436.

Cao, L., Jiao, X., Zuzga, D., Liu, Y., Fong, D., Young, D., & During, M. (2004). VEGF links hippocampal activity with neurogenesis, learning and memory. *Nature Genetics, 36*, 827–835.

Caplan, G. (1964). *Principles of preventive psychiatry.* New York: Basic Books.

Caprara, G., Alessandri, G., Di Giunta, L., Panerai, L., & Eisenberg, N. (2010). The contribution of agreeableness and self-efficacy beliefs to prosociality. *European Journal of Personality, 24*, 36–55.

Capron, C., & Duyme, M. (1989). Assessment of effects of socio-economic status on IQ in a full cross-fostering study. *Nature, 340*, 552–554.

Capute, A. J., Palmer, F. B., Shapiro, B. K., Wachtel, R. C., Ross, A., & Accardo, P. J. (1984). Primitive reflex profile: A quantification of primitive reflexes in infancy. *Developmental Medicine & Child Neurology, 26*, 375–383.

Carey, R. G. (1974). Living until death: A program of service and research for the terminally ill. *Hospital Progress.* (Reprinted in E. Kübler-Ross [Ed.], *Death. The final stage of growth.* Englewood Cliffs, NJ: Prentice-Hall, 1975.)

Carey, S., & Bartlett, E. (1978). Acquiring a single new word. *Papers & Reports on Child Language Development, 15*, 17–29.

Carlo, G., Crockett, L., Wolff, J., & Beal, S. (2012). The role of emotional reactivity, self-regulation, and puberty in adolescents' prosocial behaviors. *Social Development, 21*, 667–685.

Carlson, E. A., & Sroufe, L. A. (1995). Contribution of attachment theory to developmental psychopathology. In D. Cicchetti & D. J. Conen (Eds.), *Developmental psychopathology, Vol. 1: Theory and methods* (pp. 581–617). New York: Wiley.

Carlson, E., Sroufe, A., & Egeland, B. (2004). The construction of experience: A longitudinal study of representation and behavior. *Child Development, 75*, 66–83.

Carmeli, E., Reznick, A., Coleman, R., & Carmeli, V. (2000). Muscle strength and mass of lower extremities in relation to functional abilities in elderly adults. *Gerontology, 46*, 249–257.

Carnelley, K., Wortman, C., & Kessler, R. (1999). The impact of widowhood on depression: Findings from a prospective survey. *Psychological Medicine, 29*, 1111–1123.

Carnelley, K., Wortman, C., Bolger, N., & Burke, C. (2006). The time course of grief reactions to spousal loss: Evidence from a national probability sample. *Journal of Personality and Social Psychology, 91*, 476–492.

Carroll, J., & Snowling, M. (2004). Language and phonological skills in children at high risk of reading difficulties. *Journal of Child Psychology & Psychiatry, 45*, 631–640.

Carson, D., Klee, T., & Perry, C. (1998). Comparisons of children with delayed and normal language at 24 months of age on measures of behavioral difficulties, social and cognitive development. *Infant Mental Health, 19*, 59–75.

Carstensen, L. L. (1992). Social and emotional patterns in adulthood: Support for socioemotional selectivity theory. *Psychology & Aging, 7*, 331–338.

Cartwright, C. (2006). You want to know how it affected me? Young adults' perceptions of the impact of parental divorce. *Journal of Divorce & Remarriage, 44*, 125–143.

Carver, L., & Cornew, L. (2009). The development of social information gathering in infancy: A model of neural substrates and developmental mechanisms. In M. de Haan, M., & M. Gunnar, M. (Eds.) *Handbook of developmental social neuroscience.* (pp. 122–141). New York,, NY, USA: Guilford Press.

Carver, P., Egan, S., & Perry, D. (2004). Children who question their heterosexuality. *Developmental Psychology, 40*, 43–53.

Casasola, M., & Cohen, L. (2000). Infants' association of linguistic labels with causal actions. *Developmental Psychology, 36*, 155–168.

Case, R. (1985). *Intellectual development: Birth to adulthood.* New York: Academic Press.

Case, R. (1991). Stages in the development of the young child's first sense of self. *Developmental Review, 11*, 210–230.

Case, R. (1992). *The mind's staircase: Exploring thought and knowledge.* Hillsdale, NJ: Erlbaum.

Case, R. (1997). The development of conceptual structures. In B. Damon (General Ed.) and D. Kuhn & R. S. Siegler (Series Eds.), *Handbook of child psychology, Vol. 2: Cognitive, language, and perceptual development.* New York: Wiley.

Case, R. B., Moss, A. J., Case, N., McDermott, M., & Eberly, S. (1992). Living alone after myocardial infarction: Impact on prognosis. *Journal of the American Medical Association, 267*, 515–519.

Casey, B. (2013). Individual and group differences in spatial ability. In Waller, D., & Hadel, L. (Eds.), *Handbook of spatial cognition* (pp. 117–134). Washington, DC, USA: American Psychological Association.

Cashon, C., & Cohen, L. (2000). Eight-month-old infants' perceptions of possible and impossible events. *Infancy, 1*, 429–446.

Cashon, C., & Cohen, L. (2000). Eight-month-old infants' perceptions of possible and impossible events. *Infancy, 1*, 429–446.

Caspi, A., & Shiner, R. (2006). Personality development. In W. Damon & R. Lerner (Eds.), *Handbook of child psychology, Volume 3: Social, emotional, and personality development* (6th ed.) (pp. 300–365). New York: John Wiley Publishers.

Cassibba, R., van IJzendoorn, M., & Coppola, G. (2012). Emotional availability and attachment across generations: Variations in patterns associated with infant health risk status. *Child: Care, Health and Development, 38*, 538–544.

Cassidy, J., & Berlin, L. J. (1994). The insecure/ambivalent pattern of attachment: Theory and research. *Child Development, 65*, 971–991.

Cassileth, B. R., Walsh, W. P., & Lusk, E. J. (1988). Psychosocial correlates of cancer survival: A subsequent report 3 to 8 years after cancer diagnosis. *Journal of Clinical Oncology, 6*, 1753–1759.

Castellsagué, X., Bosch, X., Muñoz, N., Meijer, C., Shah, K., Sanjosé, S., Eluf-Neto, J., Ngelangel, C., Chicareon, S., Smith, J., Herrero, R., Moreno, V., & Franceschi, F. (2002). Male circumcision, penile human papillomavirus infection, and cervical cancer in female partners. *New England Journal of Medicine, 346*, 1105–1112.

Castle, N., Engberg, J., & Anderson, R. (2007). Job satisfaction of nursing home administrators and turnover. *Medical Care Research and Review, 64*, 191–211.

Catalano, S. (2012). *Intimate partner violence, 1993—2010.* Retrieved July 18, 2013, from http://www.bjs.gov/content/pub/pdf/ipv9310.pdf.

Catalano, S., Smith, E., Snyder, H., & Rand, M. (2009). *Female victims of violence.* Retrieved August 24, 2010 from http://bjs.ojp.usdoj.gov/content/pub/pdf/fvv.pdf.

Cate, R., & John, O. (2007). Testing models of the structure and development of future time perspective: Maintaining a focus on opportunities in middle age. *Psychology and Aging, 22*, 186–201.

Cavanaugh, J., & Whitbourne, S. (1999). *Gerontology: An interdisciplinary perspective.* New York: Oxford University Press.

Cavill, S., & Bryden, P. (2003). Development of handedness: Comparison of questionnaire and performance-based measures of preference. *Brain & Cognition, 53*, 149–151.

Cawley, J., & Spiess, C. (2008). *Obesity and skill attachment in early childhood.* National Bureau for Economic Researche. Retrieved July 18, 2010 from http://www.nber.org/papers/w13997.

Ceci, S. J., & Bruck, M. (1993). Suggestibility of the child witness: A historical review and synthesis. *Psychological Bulletin, 113*, 403–439.

Ceci, S., & Bronfenbrenner, U. (1985). "Don't forget to take the cupcakes out of the oven": Prospective memory, strategic time-monitoring, and context. *Child Development, 56,* 152–164.

Celia, S. (2004). Interventions with infants and families at risk: Context and culture. *Infant Mental Health Journal, 25,* 502–507.

Centers for Disease Control (CDC). (2005). *Birth defects: Frequently asked questions.* Retrieved June 7, 2007 from www.cdc.gov/ncbddd/bd/facts.htm.

Centers for Disease Control (CDC). (2007b). *Suicide: Fact sheet.* Retrieved June 22, 2007 from http://www.cdc.gov/ncipc/factsheets/suifacts.htm.

Centers for Disease Control and Prevention (2009c). *Sexually transmitted disease surveillance, 2008.* Retrieved August 23, 2010 from http://www.cdc.gov/std/stats08/surv2008-Complete.pdf.

Centers for Disease Control and Prevention (CDC). (2007a). *Tips for parents: Ideas and tips to help prevent child overweight.* Retrieved June 19, 2007 from www.cdc.gov/nccdphp/dnpa/obesity/childhood/tips_for_parents.htm

Centers for Disease Control and Prevention (CDC). (2007c). *The importance of physical activity.* Retrieved July 4, 2007 from www.cdc.gov/nccdphp/dnpa/physical/importance/index.htm.

Centers for Disease Control and Prevention (CDC). (2013). *Common eye disorders.* Retrieved July 16, 2013, from http://www.cc.gov/visionhealth/basic_information/eye-disorders.htm.

Centers for Disease Control and Prevention, American Society for Reproductive Medicine, Society for Assisted Reproductive Technology. (2009d). *2007 assisted reproductive technology success rates: National summary and fertility clinic reports.* Retrieved August 22, 2010 from http://www.cdc.gov/art/ART2007/PDF/COMPLETE_2007_ART.pdf.

Centers for Disease Control and Prevention. (1994). Prevalence of adults with no known major risk factors for coronary heart disease—behavioral risk factor surveillance system, 1992. *Morbidity & Mortality Weekly Report, 43,* 61–69.

Centers for Disease Control and Prevention. (2003b). *About minority health.* Retrieved August 26, 2004, from http://www.cdc.gov/omy/AMH/AMH.htm.

Centers for Disease Control and Prevention. (2010). *Behavioral risk factor surveillance system, prevalence and trends data.* Retrieved August 24, 2010 from http://www.cdc.gov/brfss/.

Centers for Disease Control and Prevention. (2012a). *Assisted reproductive technology: 2010 national summary report.* Retrieved July 21, 2013, from http://www.cdc.gov/art/ART2010/PDFs/ART_2010_National_Summary_Report.pdf.

Centers for Disease Control and Prevention. (2012b). *Sexually transmitted disease surveillance 2011.* Retrieved January 8, 2013, from http://www.cdc.gov/std/stats11/Surv2011.pdf.

Centers for Disease Control and Prevention. (2013). *HIV surveillance report, Volume 23, 2011.* Retrieved July 18, 2013, from http://www.cdc.gov/hiv/pdf/statistics_2011_HIV_Surveillance_Report_vol_23.pdf.

Centers for Disease Control. (1998a). *National diabetes fact sheet.* Retrieved October 11, 2000, from http://www.cdc.gov.

Centers for Disease Control. (1998b). Single-year U.S. mortality rates. *National Vital Statistics Reports, 47,* 10, Table 3.

Centers for Disease Control. (CDC). (2006a). *Sudden Infant Death Syndrome (SIDS): Risk factors.* Retrieved June 8, 2007 from www.cdc.gov/SIDS/riskfactors.htm.

Central Intelligence Agency (CIA). (2013). *CIA world factbook: Military service age and obligation.* Retrieved June 6, 2013 from https://www.cia.gov/library/publications/the-world-factbook/fields/2024.html.

Cernoch, J. M., & Porter, R. H. (1985). Recognition of maternal axillary odors by infants. *Child Development, 56,* 1593–1598.

Cevasco, A., & Grant, R. (2005). Effects of the Pacifier Activity Lullaby (PAL) on weight gain in premature infants. *Journal of Music Therapy, 42,* 123–139.

Chadwick, O., Taylor, E., Taylor, A., Heptinstall, E. et al., (1999). Hyper-activity and reading disability: A longitudinal study of the nature of the association. *Journal of Child Psychology & Psychiatry, 40,* 1039–1050.

Chaillet, N., Dube, E., Dugas, M., Francoeur, D., Dube, J., Gagnon, S., Poitras, L., & Dumont, A (2007). Identifying barriers and facilitators towards implementing guidelines to reduce caesarean section rates in Quebec. *Bulletin of the World Health Organization, 85,* 733–820.

Chan, R., Raboy, B., & Patterson, C. (1998). Psychosocial adjustment among children conceived via donor insemination by lesbian and heterosexual mothers. *Child Development, 69,* 443–457.

Chang, L., & Murray, A. (1995, March). *Math performance of 5- and 6-year-olds in Taiwan and the U.S.: Maternal beliefs, expectations, and tutorial assistance.* Paper presented at the biennial meetings of the Society for Research in Child Development, Indianapolis, IN.

Chang, L., Schwartz, D., Dodge, K., & McBride-Chang, C. (2003). Harsh parenting in relation to child emotion regulation and aggression. *Journal of Family Psychology, 17,* 598–606.

Chao, R. (1994). Beyond parental control and authoritarian parenting style: Understanding Chinese parenting through the cultural notion of training. *Child Development, 65,* 1111–1119.

Chapman, K., Nicholas, P., & Supramaniam, R. (2006). How much food advertising is there on Australian television? *Health Promotion International, 21,* 172–180.

Chase-Lansdale, P. L., & Hetherington, E. M. (1990). The impact of divorce on life-span development: Short and long term effects. In P. B. Baltes, D. L. Featherman, & R. M. Lerner (Eds.), *Life-span development and behavior, Vol. 10* (pp. 107–151). Hillsdale, NJ: Erlbaum.

Chase-Lansdale, P. L., Cherlin, A. J., & Kiernan, K. E. (1995). The long-term effects of parental divorce on the mental health of young adults: A developmental perspective. *Child Development, 66,* 1614–1634.

Chassin, L., Macy, J., Seo, D., & Presson, C. (2010). The association between membership in the sandwich generation and health behaviors: A longitudinal study. *Journal of Applied Developmental Psychology, 31,* 38–46.

Chatters, L. M. (1991). Physical health. In J. S. Jackson (Ed.), *Life in black America* (pp. 199–220). Newbury Park, CA: Sage.

Chatters, L., Taylor, R., Jackson, J., & Lincoln, K. (2008). Religious coping among African Americans, Caribbean Blacks, and non-Hispanic Whites. *Journal of Community Psychology, 36,* 371–386.

Cheay, C., & Rubin, K. (2004). European American and mainland Chinese mothers' responses to aggression and social withdrawal in preschoolers. *International Journal of Behavioral Development, 28,* 83–94.

Cheitlin, M. (2003). Cardiovascular physiology: Changes with aging. *American Journal of Geriatric Cardiology, 12,* 9–13.

Chen, H. (2009). *Trisomy 18.* Retrieved June 27, 2010 from http://emedicine.medscape.com/article/943463-overview

Chen, H. (2010). *Down syndrome.* Retrieved June 27, 2010 from http://emedicine.medscape.com/article/943216-overview

Chen, L., Fox, K., Ku, P., Sun, W., & Chou, P. (2012). Prospective associations between household-, work-, and leisure-based physical activity and all-cause mortality among older Taiwanese adults. *Asia-Pacific Journal of Public Health, 24,* 795–805.

Chen, S. (1997). Child's understanding of secret and friendship development. *Psychological Science (China), 20,* 545.

Chen, S., Benet-Martinez, V., Wu, W., Lam, B., & Bond, M. (2013). The role of dialectical self and bicultural identity integration in psychological adjustment. *Journal of Personality, 81,* 61–75.

Chen, X., Wen, S., Fleming, N., Demissie, K., Rhoads, G., & Walker, M. (2007). Teenage pregnancy and adverse birth outcomes: A large population based retrospective cohort study. *International Journal of Epidemiology, 36,* 368–373.

Chen, Y., & Chen, C. (2012). Living arrangement preferences of elderly people in Taiwan as affected by family resources and social participation. *Journal of Family History, 37,* 381–394.

Chen, Z. (1999). Ethnic similarities and differences in the association of emotional autonomy and adolescent outcomes: Comparing Euro-American and Asian-American adolescents. *Psychological Reports, 84,* 501–516.

Cheng, C., & Lin, Y. (2012). The effects of aging on lifetime of auditory sensory memory in humans. *Biological Psychology, 89,* 307–312.

Cheng, G., Xiaoyan, H., & Dajun, Z. (2006). A review of academic self-concept and its relationship with academic achievement. *Psychological Science (China), 29,* 133–136.

Cherlin, A. (1992). *Marriage, divorce, remarriage,* Cambridge, MA: Harvard University Press.

Cherlin, A. (2013). Health, marriage, and same-sex partnerships. *Journal of Health and Social Behavior, 54,* 64–66.

Cherlin, A., & Furstenberg, F. F. (1986). *The new American grandparent.* New York: Basic Books.

Cherlin, A., Chase-Lansdale, P., & McRae, C. (1998). Effects of parental divorce on mental health throughout the life course. *American Sociological Review, 63,* 239–249.

Cheung, H., Chung, K., Wong, S., McBride-Chang, C., Penney, T., & Ho, C. (2010). Speech perception, metalinguistic awareness, reading, and vocabulary in Chinese-English bilingual children. *Journal of Educational Psychology, 102,* 367–380.

Chi, M. T. (1978). Knowledge structure and memory development. In R. S. Siegler (Ed.), *Children's thinking: What develops?* (pp. 73–96). Hillsdale, NJ: Erlbaum.

Chiapin, G., DeAraujo, G., & Wagner, A. (1998). Mother-in-law and daughter-in-law: How is the relationship between these two women? *Psicologia: Reflexao e Critica, 11,* 541–550.

Chiappe, P., & Siegel, L. (1999). Phonological awareness and reading acquisition in English- and Punjabi-speaking Canadian children. *Journal of Educational Psychology, 91,* 20–28.

Chiappe, P., Glaeser, B., & Ferko, D. (2007). Speech perception, vocabulary, and the development of reading skills in English among Korean- and English-speaking children. *Journal of Educational Psychology, 99,* 154–166.

Chickering, A., & Reisser, L. (1993). *Education and identity* (2nd ed.). San Francisco: Jossey-Bass.

Chien, Y., Cheng, J., Liu, M., Yang, H., Hsu, M., Chen, C., & Yang, C. (2001). Serologic markers of Epstein-Barr virus infection and nasopharyngeal carcinoma in Taiwanese men. *New England Journal of Medicine, 345,* 1877–1882.

"Chincotta, D., & Underwood, G. (1997). Estimates, language of schooling and bilingual digit span. *European Journal of Cognitive Psychology, 9,* 325–348.

Child Trends Data Bank. (2012). *Low and very low birthweight infants: Indicators on children and youth.* Retrieved June 11, 2013, from http://www.childtrends.org/wp-content/uploads/2012/11/57_Low_Birth_Weight.pdf.

Child Trends Data Bank. (2013). *Family structure.* Retrieved July 9, 2013, from http://www.childtrends.org/wp-content/uploads/2011/12/59_Family_Structure.pdf.

Chlebowski, R., Hendrix, S., Langer, R., Stefanick, M., Gass, M., Lane, D., Rodabough, R., Gilligan, M., Cyr, M., Thomson, C., Khandekar, J., Petrovitch, H., & McTiernan, A. (2003). Influence of estrogen plus progestin on breast cancer and mammography in healthy postmenopausal women: The Women's Health Initiative randomized trial. *Journal of the American Medical Association, 289,* 3243–3253.

Choe, D., Olson, S., & Sameroff, A. (2013). The interplay of externalizing problems and physical and inductive discipline during childhood. *Developmental Psychology 49,* 2245–2256.

Choi, N. (2003). Nonmarried aging parents' and their adult children's characteristics associated with transitions into and out of intergenerational coresidence. *Journal of Gerontological Social Work, 40,* 7–29.

Choi, N. G. (1991). Racial differences in the determinants of living arrangements of widowed and divorced elderly women. *The Gerontologist, 31,* 496–504.

Choi, Y., Kim, Y., Kim, S., & Park, I. (2013). Is Asian American parenting controlling and harsh? Empirical testing of relationships between Korean American and Western parenting measures. *American Journal of Psychology, 4,* 19–29.

Chomsky, N. (1959). Review of Skinner's *Verbal Behavior. Language, 35,* 26–58.

Chou, C., & Tsai, M. (2007). Gender differences in Taiwan high school students' computer game playing. *Computers in Human Behavior, 23,* 812–824.

Christakis, D., Zimmerman, F., DiGiuseppe, D., & McCarty, C. (2004). Early television exposure and subsequent attentional problems in children. *Pediatrics, 113,* 708–713.

Christensen, H., Henderson, A., Griffiths, K., & Levings, C. (1997). Does aging inevitably lead to declines in cognitive performance? A longitudinal study of elite academics. *Personality & Individual Differences, 23,* 67–78.

Christian, C., & Bloom, N. (2011). In K. Marcdante, R. Kliegman, H. Jensen, & R. Behrman (Eds.), *Nelson's essentials of pediatrics* (pp. 81–103). New York: Elsevier Health Publishers.

Christian, P., & Stewart, C. (2010). Maternal micronutrient deficiency, fetal development, and risk of chronic disease. *The Journal of Nutrition, 140,* 437–445.

Chuang, S., & Su, Y. (2009). Do we see eye to eye? Chinese mothers' and fathers' parenting beliefs and values for toddlers in Canada and China. *Journal of Family Psychology, 23,* 331–341.

Chumlea, W., Schubert, C., Roche, A., Kulin, H., Lee, P., Himes, J., & Sun, S. (2003). Age at menarche and racial comparisons in US girls. *Pediatrics, 111,* 110–113.

Ciancio, D., Sadovsky, A., Malabonga, V., Trueblood, L., et al. (1999). Teaching classification and seriation to preschoolers. *Child Study Journal, 29,* 193–205.

Cicchetti, D., Rogosch, F., Maughan, A., Toth, S., & Bruce, J. (2003). False belief understanding in maltreated children. *Development & Psychopathology, 15,* 1067–1091.

Cicirelli, V. (2006). Fear of death in mid-old age. *Journals of Gerontology: Series B: Psychological Sciences and Social Sciences, 61B,* P75–P81.

Cicirelli, V. (2011). Elders' attitudes toward extending the healthy life span. *Journal of Aging Studies, 25,* 84–93.

Cillessen, A. H. N., van IJzendoorn, H. W., van Lieshout, C. F. M., & Hartup, W. W. (1992). Heterogeneity among peer-rejected boys: Subtypes and stabilities. *Child Development, 63,* 893–905.

Cillessen, A., & Mayeux, L. (2004). From censure to reinforcement: Developmental changes in the association between aggression and social status. *Child Development, 75,* 147–163.

Cipriani, G., Bianchetti, A., & Trabucchi, M. (2005). Outcomes of a computer-based cognitive rehabilitation program on Alzheimer's disease patients compared with those on patients affected by mild cognitive impairment. *Archives of Gerontology and Geriatrics, 43,* 327–335.

Citkowitz, E. (2012). *Polygenic hypercholesterolemia.* Retrieved July 18, 2013, from http://emedicine.medscape.com/article/121424-overview.

Claes, M. (1998). Adolescents' closeness with parents, siblings, and friends in three countries: Canada, Belgium, and Italy. *Journal of Youth and Adolescence, 217,* 165–184.

Clarke-Stewart, A. (1992). Consequences of child care for children's development. In Booth, A. (Ed.) *Child care in the 1990s: Trends and consequences.* (pp. 63–82). Hillsdale, NJ, USA: Lawrence Erlbaum Associates, Inc.

Closson, R. (2010). Critical race theory and adult education. *Adult Education Quarterly, 60,* 261–283.

Cobb, K. (2000, September 3). Breaking in drivers: Texas could join states restricting teens in effort to lower rate of fatal accidents. *Houston Chronicle,* pp. A1, A20.

Coffey, C., Saxton, J., Ratcliff, G., Bryan, R., & Lucke, J. (1999). Relation of education to brain size in normal aging: Implications for the reserve hypothesis. *Neurology, 53,* 189–196.

Cohen, G. (2000). *The creative age: Awakening human potential in the second half of life.* New York: Avon Books.

Cohen, H., & Amerine-Dickens, M., & Smith, T. (2006). Early intensive behavioral treatment: Replication of the UCLA model in a community setting. *Journal of Developmental & Behavioral Pediatrics, 27,* S145–S155.

Cohen, H., Hailpern, S., & Alderman, M. (2004). Glucose-cholesterol interaction magnifies coronary disease risk for hypertensive patients. *Hypertension, 43,* 983.

Cohen, S. (2006). Aging changes in immunity. *Medline: Medical encyclopedia.* Retrieved www.nlm.nih.gov/medlineplus/ency/article/004008.htm.

Cohen-Bendahan, C., van de Beek, C., & Berenbaum, S. (2004). Prenatal sex hormone effects on child and adult sex-typed behavior: Methods and findings. *Neuroscience and Behavioral Reviews, 29,* 353–384.

Coke, M. (1992). Correlates of life satisfaction among elderly African Americans. *Journals of Gerontology, 47,* P316–P320.

Colby, A., Kohlberg, L., Gibbs, J., & Lieberman, M. (1983). A longitudinal study of moral judgment. *Monographs of the Society for Research in Child Development, 48* (1–2, Serial No. 200).

Cole, M. (1992). Culture in development. In M. H. Bornstein & M. E. Lamb (Eds.), *Developmental psychology: An advanced textbook* (pp. 731–789). Hillsdale, NJ: Erlbaum.

Cole, M., & Packer, M. (2011). Culture and development. In M. Bornstein & M. Lamb (Eds.), *Developmental science: An advanced textbook* (6th ed., pp. 51–108). New York: Psychology Press.

Cole, P., Martin, S., & Dennis, T. (2004). Emotion regulation as a scientific construct: Methodological challenges and directions for child development research. *Child Development, 75,* 317–333.

Coley, R., & Chase-Lansdale, L. (1998). Adolescent pregnancy and parenthood: Recent evidence and future directions. *American Psychologist, 53,* 152–166.

Colombo, J. (1993). *Infant cognition: Predicting later intellectual functioning.* Newbury Park, CA: Sage.

Colonia-Willner, R. (1999). Investing in practical intelligence: Ageing and cognitive efficiency among executives. *International Journal of Behavioral Development, 23,* 591–614.

Compas, B. E., Ey, S., & Grant, K. E. (1993). Taxonomy, assessment, and diagnosis of depression during adolescence. *Psychological Bulletin, 114,* 323–344.

Cona, G., Arcara, G., Amodio, P., Schiff, S., & Bisiacchi, P. (2013). Does executive control really play a crucial role in explaining age-related cognitive and neural differences? *Neuropsychology, 27,* 378–389.

Condry, J., & Condry, S. (1976). Sex differences: A study in the eye of the beholder. *Child Development, 47,* 812–819.

Conduct Problems Research Group. (2004). The Fast Track experiment: Translating the developmental model into a prevention design. In J. Kupersmidt & K. Dodge (Eds.), *Children's peer relations: From development to intervention.* (pp. 181–208). Washington, DC: American Psychological Association.

Coney, P. (2013). *Menopause.* Retrieved July 17, 2013, from http://emedicine.medscape.com/article/264088-overview#aw2aab6b2.

Conger, D., & Long, M. (2010). Why are men falling behind? Gender gaps in college performance and persistence. *Annals of the American Academy of Political and Social Science, 627,* 184–214.

Connidis, I. A. (1994). Sibling support in older age. *Journals of Gerontology: Social Sciences, 49*, S309–317.

Connidis, I. A., & Davies, L. (1992). Confidants and companions: Choices in later life. *Journals of Gerontology: Social Sciences, 47*, S115–122.

Connolly, K., & Dalgleish, M. (1989). The emergence of a tool-using skill in infancy. *Developmental Psychology, 25*, 894–912.

Connor, S., Pyenson, B., Fitch, K., Spence, C., & Kosuke, I. (2007). Comparing hospice and nonhospice patient survival among patients who die within a three-year window. *Journal of Pain and Symptom Management, 33*, 238–246.

Cook, S., & Heppner, P. (1997). Coping control, problem-solving appraisal, and depressive symptoms during a farm crisis. *Journal of Mental Health Counseling, 19*, 64–77.

Cooper, R. P., & Aslin, R. N. (1994). Developmental differences in infant attention to the spectral properties of infant-directed speech. *Child Development, 65*, 1663–1677.

Copeland, D., & Harbaugh, B. (2010). Psychosocial differences related to parenting infants among single and married mothers. *Issues in Comprehensive Pediatric Nursing, 33*, 129–148.

Corapci, F. (2010). Child-care chaos and child development. In G. Evens & T. Wachs (Eds.), *Chaos and its influence on children's development: An ecological perspective* (pp. 67–82). Washington, DC: American Psychological Association.

Corliss, H., Rosario, M., Wypij, D., Wylie, S., Frazier, A., & Austin, S. (2010). Sexual orientation and drug use in a longitudinal study of U.S. adolescents. *Addictive Behaviors, 35*, 517–521.

Cornelius, M., Goldschmidt, L., Day, N., & Larkby, C. (2002). Alcohol, tobacco and marijuana use among pregnant teenagers: 6-year follow-up of offspring growth effects. *Neurotoxicology & Teratology, 24*, 703–710.

Corsaro, W., Molinari, L., Hadley, K., & Sugioka, H. (2003). Keeping and making friends: Italian children's transition from preschool to elementary school. *Social Psychology Quarterly, 66*, 272–292.

Corwin, J., Loury, M., & Gilbert, A. N. (1995). Workplace, age, and sex as mediators of olfactory function: Data from the National Geographic smell survey. *Journals of Gerontology: Psychological Sciences, 50B*, P179–186.

Costello, E., Sung, M., Worthman, C., & Angold, A. (2007). Pubertal maturation and the development of alcohol use and abuse. *Drug and Alcohol Dependence, 88*, S50–S59.

Cotelli, M., Manenti, R., & Zanetti, O. (2012). Reminiscence therapy in dementia: A review. *Maturitas, 72*, 203–205.

Cotton, L., Bynum, D., & Madhere, S. (1997). Socialization forces and the stability of work values from late adolescence to early adulthood. *Psychological Reports, 80*, 115–124.

Counts, D. R. (1976/1977). The good death in Kaliai: Preparation for death in western New Britain. *Omega, 7*, 367–372.

Courage, M., & Howe, M. (2002). From infant to child: The dynamics of cognitive change in the second year of life. *Psychological Bulletin, 128*, 250–277.

Coury, D. (2002). Developmental and behavioral pediatrics. In A. Rudolph, R. Kamei, & K. Overby (Eds.), *Rudolph's fundamentals of pediatrics* (3rd ed., pp. 110–124). New York: McGraw-Hill.

Cox, M., Garrett, E., & Graham, J. (2004–2005). Death in Disney films: Implications for children's understanding of death. *Omega: Journal of Death and Dying, 50*, 267–280.

Cox, M., Paley, B., Burchinal, M., & Payne, C. (1999). Marital perceptions and interactions across the transition to parenthood. *Journal of Marriage & the Family, 61*, 611–625.

Cox, S., Mezulis, A., & Hyde, J. (2010). The influence of child gender role and maternal feedback to child stress on the emergence of the gender difference in depressive rumination in adolescence. *Developmental Psychology, 46*, 842–852.

Craik, F. (2002). Human memory and aging. In L. Backman & C. von Hofsten (Eds.), *Psychology at the turn of the millennium, Volume 1: Cognitive, biological, and health perspectives* (pp. 261–280). Hove, UK: Psychology Press/Taylor & Francis (UK).

Crain, W. (2011). *Theories of development* (6th ed.). Upper Saddle River, NJ: Pearson Prentice Hall.

Crain, W. (2011). *Theories of development* 6th Ed. Upper Saddle River, NJ, USA: Pearson Prentice-Hall.

Crain, W. (2011). *Theories of development*, 6th Ed. Upper Saddle River, NJ, USA: Pearson Prentice-Hall.

Cramer, D. (1991). Type A behavior pattern, extraversion, neuroticism and psychological distress. *British Journal of Medical Psychology, 64*, 73–83.

Crapanzano, A., Frick, P., & Terranova, A. (2010). Patterns of physical and relational aggression in a school-based sample of boys and girls. *Journal of Abnormal Child Psychology, 38*, 433–445.

Creators, the. (2000, March/April). *Modern Maturity*, pp. 38–44.

Crehan, G. (2004). The surviving sibling: The effects of sibling death in childhood. *Psychoanalytic Psychotherapy, 18*, 202–219.

Cress, C. (2007). *Geriatric care management*. Sudbury, MA: Jones & Bartlett Learning.

Crick, N. R., & Grotpeter, J. K. (1995). Relational aggression, gender, and social-psychological adjustment. *Child Development, 66*, 710–722.

Crick, N., & Dodge, K. (1994). A review and reformulation of social information processing mechanisms in children's social adjustment. *Psychological Bulletin, 115*, 74–101.

Crick, N., & Dodge, K. (1996). Social information-processing mechanisms in reactive and proactive aggression. *Child Development, 67*, 993–1002.

Cristia, A. (2013). Input to language: The phonetics and perception of infant-directed speech. *Language and Linguistics Compass, 7*, 157–170.

Crittenden, P. M. (1992). Quality of attachment in the preschool years. *Development & Psychopathology, 4*, 209–241.

Crockenberg, S. (2003). Rescuing the baby from the bathwater: How gender and temperament (may) influence how child care affects child development. *Child Development, 74*, 1034–1038.

Crockenberg, S., & Litman, C. (1990). Autonomy as competence in 2-year-olds: Maternal correlates of child defiance, compliance, and self-assertion. *Developmental Psychology, 26*, 961–971.

Crockenberg, S., Leerkes, E., & Lekka, S. (2007). Pathways from marital aggression to infant emotion regulation: The development of withdrawal in infancy. *Infant Behavior & Development, 30*, 97–113.

Crompton, R., Brockmann, M., & Lyonette, C. (2005). Attitudes, women's employment and the domestic division of labour: A cross-national analysis in two waves. *Work, Employment, and Society, 19*, 213–233.

Crone, D., & Whitehurst, G. (1999). Age and schooling effects on emergent literacy and early reading skills. *Journal of Educational Psychology, 91*, 594–603.

Crone, E., van der Molen, M. (2004). Developmental changes in real life decision making: Performance on a gambling task previously shown to depend on the ventromedial prefrontal cortex. *Developmental Neuropsychology, 25*, 251–279.

Crone, E., Wendelken, C., Donohue, S., van Leijenhorst, L., & Bunge, S. (2006). Neurocognitive development of the ability to manipulate information in working memory. *Proceedings for the National Academy of Sciences, 103*, 9315–9320.

Crook, C. (1987). Taste and olfaction. In P. Salapatek & L. Cohen (Eds.), *Handbook of infant perception, Vol. 1: From sensation to perception* (pp. 237–264). Orlando, FL: Academic Press.

Crowley, B., Hayslip, B., & Hobdy, J. (2003). Psychological hardiness and adjustment to life events in adulthood. *Journal of Adult Development, 10*, 237–248.

Cumming, E. (1975). Engagement with an old theory. *International Journal of Aging & Human Development, 6*, 187–191.

Cumming, E., & Henry, W. E. (1961). *Growing old*. New York: Basic Books.

Cummings, E. M., Hollenbeck, B., Iannotti, R., Radke-Yarrow, M., & Zahn-Waxler, C. (1986). Early organization of altruism and aggression: Developmental patterns and individual differences. In C. Zahn-Waxler, E. M. Cummings, & R. Iannotti (Eds.), *Altruism and aggression* (pp. 165–188). Cambridge, UK: Cambridge University Press.

Cunningham, L. (1996). *Grief and the adolescent*. Newhall, CA: TeenAge Grief, Inc.

Cunningham, M., Swanson, D., Spencer, M., & Dupree, D. (2003). The association of physical maturation with family hassles among African American adolescent males. *Cultural Diversity and Ethnic Minority Psychology, 9*, 276–288.

Cunningham, W. R., & Haman, K. L. (1992). Intellectual functioning in relation to mental health. In J. E. Birren, R. B. Sloane, & G. D. Cohen (Eds.), *Handbook of mental health and aging* (2nd ed., pp. 340–355). San Diego, CA: Academic Press.

Curran, D. (2009). *Menopause*. Retrieved August 27, 2010 from http://emedicine.medscape.com/article/264088-overview.

Currie, J., Stabile, M., & Jones, L. (2013). *Do stimulant medications improve educational and behavioral outcomes for children with ADHD?* National Bureau of Economic Research Working Paper No. 19105.

Currier, J., Holland, J., & Neimeyer, R. (2006). Sense-making, grief, and the experience of violent loss: Toward a mediational model. *Death Studies, 30*, 403–428.

Curtner-Smith, M., Smith, P., & Porter, M. (2010). Family-level perspective on bullies and victims. In E. Vernberg & B. Biggs (Eds.), *Preventing and treating bullying and victimization* (pp. 75–106). New York: Oxford University Press.

Cushing, T. (2013). *Emergent management of anorexia nervosa.* Retrieved July 13, 2013, from http://emedicine.medscape.com/article/805152-overview#aw2aab6b2b5.

Cutchin, M., Owen, S., & Chang, P. (2003). Becoming "at home" in assisted living residences: Exploring place integration processes. *Journals of Gerontology, Series B: Psychological & Social Sciences, 58B,* S234–S243.

Cuvo, A. (1974). Incentive level influence on overt rehearsal and free recall as a function of age. *Journal of Experimental Child Psychology, 18,* 167–181.

D'Imperio, R., Dubow, E., & Ippolito, M. (2000). Resilient and stress-affected adolescents in an urban setting. *Journal of Clinical Child Psychology, 29,* 129–142.

Da Costa, D., Larouche, J., Dritsa, M., & Brender, W. (2000). Psychosocial correlates of prepartum and postpartum depressed mood. *Journal of Affective Disorders, 59,* 31–40.

Dabby, F. (2007). *Domestic violence against Asian and Pacific Islander women.* Retrieved August 24, 2010 from http://www.vaw.umn.edu/documents/dvagainstapi/dvagainstapi.pdf.

Daly, K., & Palkovitz, R. (2004). Guest editorial: Reworking work and family issues for fathers. *Fathering, 2,* 211–213.

Daly, S., & Glenwick, D. (2000). Personal adjustment and perceptions of grandchild behavior in custodial grandmothers. *Journal of Clinical Child Psychology, 29,* 108–118.

Dammeijer, P., Schlundt, B., Chenault, M., Manni, J., & Anteunis, l. (2002). Effects of early auditory deprivation and stimulation on auditory brainstem responses in the rat. *Acta Oto-Laryngologica, 122,* 703–708.

Damon, W. (1977). *The social world of the child.* San Francisco: Jossey-Bass.

Damon, W. (1983). The nature of social-cognitive change in the developing child. In W. F. Overton (Ed.), *The relationship between social and cognitive development* (pp. 103–142). Hillsdale, NJ: Erlbaum.

Damon, W., & Hart, D. (1988). *Self understanding in childhood and adolescence.* New York: Cambridge University Press.

Danby, S., & Baker, C. (1998). How to be masculine in the block area. *Childhood: A Global Journal of Child Research, 5,* 151–175.

Darlington, R. B. (1991). The long-term effects of model preschool programs. In L. Okagaki & R. J. Sternberg (Eds.), *Directors of development* (pp. 203–215). Hillsdale, NJ: Erlbaum.

Darney, D., Reinke, W., Herman, K., Stormont, M., & Ialongo, N. (2013). Children with co-occurring academic and behavior problems in first grade: Distal outcomes in twelfth grade. *Journal of School Psychology, 51,* 117–128.

Datta, P., Poortinga, Y., & Marcoen, A. (2003). Parent care by Indian and Belgian caregivers in their roles of daughter/daughter-in-law. *Journal of Cross-Cultural Psychology, 34,* 736–749.

Davenport, E. (1992). *The making of minority scientists and engineers.* Invited address presented at the annual meeting of the American Educational Research Association, San Francisco, CA.

Davenport, E., Davison, M., Kuang, H., Ding, S., Kim, S., & Kwak, N. (1998). High school mathematics course-taking by gender and ethnicity. *American Educational Research Journal, 35,* 497–514.

Davey, M., Fish, L., Askew, J., & Robila, M. (2003). Parenting practices and the transmission of ethnic identity. *Journal of Marital & Family Therapy, 29,* 195–208.

Davies, L. (2003). Singlehood: Transitions within a gendered world. *Canadian Journal on Aging, 22,* 343–352.

Davies, P., & Rose, J. (1999). Assessment of cognitive development in adolescents by means of neuropsychological tasks. *Developmental Neuropsychology, 15,* 227–248.

Davies, P., Cicchetti, D., Hentges, R., & Sturge-Apple, M. (2013). The genetic precursors and the advantageous and disadvantageous sequelae of inhibited temperament: An evolutionary perspective. *Developmental Psychology, 49,* 2285–2300.

Davis, S., Leman, P., & Barrett, M. (2007). Children's implicit and explicit ethnic group attitudes, ethnic group identification, and self-esteem. *International Journal of Behavioral Development, 31,* 514–525.

Dawber, T. R., Kannel, W. B., & Lyell, L. P. (1963). An approach to longitudinal studies in a community: The Framingham study. *Annals of the New York Academy of Science, 107,* 539–556.

Dawodu, S. (2013). *Traumatic brain injury (TBI): Definition, epidemiology, pathophysiology.* Retrieved July 10, 2013, from http://emedicine.medscape.com/article/326510-overview.

Dawood, K., Pillard, R., Horvath, C., Revelle, W., & Bailey, J. (2000). Familial aspects of male homosexuality. *Archives of Sexual Behavior, 29,* 155–163.

Dawson, D. A. (1991). Family structure and children's health and well-being: Data from the 1988 National Health Interview Survey on child health. *Journal of Marriage & the Family, 53,* 573–584.

Dawson, J., & Langan, P. (1994). *Murder in families.* Washington, DC: U.S. Department of Justice.

de Graaf, C., Polet, P., & van Staveren, W. A. (1994). Sensory perception and pleasantness of food flavors in elderly subjects. *Journals of Gerontology: Psychological Sciences, 49,* P93–99.

de Haan, M., Luciana, M., Maslone, S. M., Matheny, L. S., & Richards, M. L. M. (1994). Development, plasticity, and risk: Commentary on Huttenlocher, Pollit and Gorman, and Gottesman and Goldsmith. In C. A. Nelson (Ed.), *The Minnesota Symposia on Child Psychology, Vol. 27* (pp. 161–178). Hillsdale, NJ: Erlbaum.

de Lacoste, M., Horvath, D., & Woodward, J. (1991). Possible sex differences in the developing human fetal brain. *Journal of Clinical & Experimental Neuropsychology, 13,* 831.

de Villiers, P. A., & de Villiers, J. G. (1992). Language development. In M. H. Bornstein & M. E. Lamb (Eds.), *Developmental psychology: An advanced textbook* (3rd ed., pp. 337–418). Hillsdale, NJ: Erlbaum.

Deakin, J., Aitken, M., Robbins, T., & Sahakian, B. (2004). Risk taking during decision-making in normal volunteers changes with age. *Journal of the International Neuropscyhological Society, 10,* 590–598.

DeCasper, A. J., & Spence, M. J. (1986). Prenatal maternal speech influences newborns' perception of speech sounds. *Infant Behavior and Development, 9,* 133–150.

DeCasper, A. J., Lecaneut, J., Busnel, M., Granier-DeFerre, C., & Maugeais, R. (1994). Fetal reactions to recurrent maternal speech. *Infant Behavior & Development, 17,* 159–164.

DeCasper, A., & Fifer, W. (1980). Of human bonding: Newborns prefer their mothers' voices. *Science, 208,* 1174–1176.

Deci, E., Koestner, R., & Ryan, R. (1999). A meta-analytic review of experiments examining the effects of extrinsic rewards on intrinsic motivation. *Psychological Bulletin, 125,* 627–668.

Deeg, D. J. H., Kardaun, W. P. F., & Fozard, J. L. (1996). Health, behavior, and aging. In J. E. Birren & K. W. Schaie (Eds.), *Handbook of the psychology of aging* (4th ed., pp. 129–149). San Diego, CA: Academic Press.

DeJean, S., McGeorge, C., & Carlson, T. (2012). Attitudes toward never-married single mothers and fathers: Does gender matter? *Journal of Feminist Family Therapy: An International Forum, 24,* 121–138.

Dellatolas, G., de Agostini, M., Curt, F., Kremin, H., Letierce, A., Maccario, J., & Lellouch, J. (2003). Manual skill, hand skill asymmetry, and cognitive performances in young children. *Laterality: Asymmetries of Body, Brain & Cognition, 8,* 317–338.

DeLoache, J. S. (1995). Early understanding and use of symbols: The model model. *Current Directions in Psychological Science, 4,* 109–113.

Delprado, J., Kinsella, G., Ong, B., & Pike, K. (2013). Naturalistic measures of prospective memory in amnestic mild cognitive impairment. *Psychology and Aging, 28,* 322–332.

Demb, H., & Chang, C. (2004). The use of psychostimulants in children with disruptive behavior disorders and developmental disabilities in a community setting. *Mental Health Aspects of Developmental Disabilities, 7,* 26–36.

DeMulder, E., Denham, S., Schmidt, M., & Mitchell, J. (2000). Q-sort assessment of attachment security during the preschool years: Links from home to school. *Developmental Psychology, 36,* 274–282.

Den Ouden, L., Rijken, M., Brand, R., Verloove-Vanhorick, S. P., & Ruys, J. H. (1991). Is it correct to correct? Developmental milestones in 555 "normal" preterm infants compared with term infants. *Journal of Pediatrics, 118,* 399–404.

Denham, S. (2006). Social-emotional competence as support for school readiness: What is it and how do we assess it? *Early Education and Development, 17,* 57–89.

Denham, S., Blair, K., DeMulder, E., Levitas, J., Sawyer, K., Auerbach-Major, S., & Queenan, P. (2003). Preschool emotional competence: Pathway to social competence. *Child Development, 74,* 238–256.

Dennerstein, L., Dudley, E., & Guthrie, J. (2002). Empty nest or revolving door? A prospective study of women's quality of life in midlife during the phase of children leaving and re-entering the home. *Psychological Medicine, 32,* 545–550.

Dennerstein, L., Lehert, P., & Guthrie, J. (2002). The effects of the menopausal transition and biopsychosocial factors on well-being. *Archives of Women's Mental Health, 5,* 15–22.

Denney, N. W. (1982). Aging and cognitive changes. In B. B. Wolman (Ed.), *Handbook of developmental psychology* (pp. 807–827). Englewood Cliffs, NJ: Prentice-Hall.

Denney, N. W. (1984). Model of cognitive development across the life span. *Developmental Review, 4*, 171–191.

Denollet, J. (1997). Personality, emotional distress and coronary heart disease. *European Journal of Personality, 11*, 343–357.

DeRegnier, R., Wewerka, S., Georgieff, M., Mattia, F., & Nelson, C. (2002). Influences of postconceptional age and postnatal experience on the development of auditory recognition memory in the newborn infant. *Developmental Psychobiology, 41*, 215–225.

DeSpelder, L. A., & Strickland, A. L. (1983). *The last dance: Encountering death and dying.* Palo Alto, CA: Mayfield.

Desrochers, S. (2008). From Piaget to specific Genevan developmental models. *Child Development Perspectives, 2*, 7–12.

Detchant, Lord Walton. (1995). Dilemmas of life and death: Part one. *Journal of the Royal Society of Medicine, 88*, 311–315.

Dewsbury, D. (2009). Charles Darwin and psychology at the bicentennial and sesquicentennial: An introduction. *American Psychologist, 64*, 67–74.

Dezoete, J., MacArthur, B., & Tuck, B. (2003). Prediction of Bayley and Stanford-Binet scores with a group of very low birthweight children. *Child: Care, Health, & Development, 29*, 367–372.

Dharan, V., & Parviainen, E. (2009). *Psychosocial and environmental pregnancy risks.* Retrieved June 27, 2010 from http://emedicine.medscape.com/article/259346-overview.

Diagram Group (1977). *Child's body.* New York: Paddington.

Diehl, L., Vicary, J., & Deike, R. (1997). Longitudinal trajectories of self-esteem from early to middle adolescence and related psychosocial variables among rural adolescents. *Journal of Research on Adolescence, 7*, 393–411.

Diener, M., & Kim, D. (2004). Maternal and child predictors of preschool children's social competence. *Journal of Applied Developmental Psychology, 25*, 3–24.

Dieni, S., & Rees, S. (2003). Dendritic morphology is altered in hippocampal neurons following prenatal compromise, *55*, 41–52.

Diesendruck, G., & Shatz, M. (2001). Two-year-olds' recognition of hierarchies: Evidence from their interpretation of the semantic relation between object labels. *Cognitive Development, 16*, 577–594.

Dietz, B., Carrozza, M., & Ritchey, P. (2003). Does financial self-efficacy explain gender differences in retirement saving strategies? *Journal of Women & Aging, 15*, 83–96.

Dijkstra, J., Cillessen, A., & Borch, C. (2013). Popularity and adolescent friendship networks: Selection and influence dynamics. *Developmental Psychology, 49*, 1242–1252.

Dillaway, H., & Byrnes, M. (2009). Reconsidering successful aging: A call for renewed and expanded academic critiques and conceptualizations. Journal of Applied Gerontology, 28, 702–722. Chapter 18.

Dindia, K., & Allen, M. (1992). Sex differences in self-disclosure: A meta-analysis. *Psychological Bulletin, 112*, 106–124.

Dinera, R., Conger, R., Shaver, P., Widaman, K., & Larsen-Rife, D. (2008). Influence of family of origin and adult romantic partners on romantic attachment security. *Journal of Family Psychology, 22*, 622–632.

DiPietro, J. (2010). Psychological and psychophysiological considerations regarding the maternal-fetal relationship. *Infant and Child Development, 19*, 27–38.

DiPietro, J., Caulfield, L., Costigan, K., Merialdi, M., Nguyen, R., Zavaleta, N., & Gurewitsch, E. (2004). Fetal neurobehavioral development: A tale of two cities. *Developmental Psychology, 40*, 445–456.

DiPietro, J., Ghera, M., & Costigan, K. (2008). Prenatal origins of temperamental reactivity in early infancy. *Early Human Development, 84*, 569–575.

DiPietro, J., Hodgson, D., Costigan, K., & Johnson, T. (1996). Fetal antecedents of infant temperament. *Child Development, 67*, 2568–2583.

Dishion, T. J., French, D. C., & Patterson, G. R. (1995). The development and ecology of antisocial behavior. In D. Cicchetti & D. J. Cohen (Eds.), *Developmental psychopathology, Vol. 2: Risk, disorder, and adaptation* (pp. 421–471). New York: Wiley.

Dishion, T. J., Patterson, G. R., Stoolmiller, M., & Skinner, M. L. (1991). Family, school, and behavioral antecedents to early adolescent involvement with antisocial peers. *Developmental Psychology, 27*, 172–180.

Dixon, R., Rust, T., Feltmate, S., & See, S. (2007). Memory and aging: Selected research directions and application issues. *Canadian Psychology, 48*, 67–76.

Dobson, A., Brown, W., Ball, J., Powers, J., & McFadden, M. (1999). Women drivers' behaviour, socio-demographic characteristics and accidents. *Accident Analysis & Prevention, 31*, 525–535.

Dockstader, C., Gaetz, W., Rockel, C., & Mabbott, D. (2012). White matter maturation in visual and motor areas predicts the latency of visual activation in children. *Human Brain Mapping, 33*, 179–191.

Doctoroff, S. (1997). Sociodramatic script training and peer role prompting: Two tactics to promote and sociodramatic play and peer interaction. *Early Child Development & Care, 136*, 27–43.

Dodge, K. (1993). Social-cognitive mechanisms in the development of conduct disorder and depression. *Annual Review of Psychology, 44*, 559–584.

Dodge, K. A., Pettit, G. S., & Bates, J. E. (1994). Socialization mediators of the relation between socioeconomic status and child conduct problems. *Child Development, 65*, 649–665.

Doh, H. S., & Falbo, T. (1999). Social competence, maternal attentiveness and overprotectiveness: Only children in Korea. *International Journal of Behavioral Development, 23(1)*, 149–162.

Doherty, E., & Ensminger, M. (2013). Marriage and offending among a cohort of disadvantaged African Americans, *Journal of Research in Crime and Delinquency, 50*, 104–131.

Dohm, A., & Wyatt, I. (2002). College at work: Outlook and earnings for college graduates, 2000–10. *Occupational Outlook Quarterly, 46*, 1–15.

Dollard, J., Doob, L. W., Miller, N. E., Mowrer, O. H., & Sears, R. R. (1939). *Frustration and aggression.* New Haven, CT: Yale University Press.

Dombrowski, S., Noonan, K., & Martin, R. (2007). Low birth weight and cognitive outcomes: Evidence for a gradient relationship in an urban, poor, African American birth cohort. *Advances in Neonatal Care, 10, 4*, 188–193.

Donenberg, G., Emerson, E., Bryant, F., & King, S. (2006). Does substance use moderate the effects of parents and peers on risky sexual behavior? *AIDS Care, 18*, 194–200.

Dorn, L.D., Susman, E., & Ponirakis, A. (2003). Pubertal Timing and Adolescent Adjustment and Behavior: Conclusions Vary by Rater. *Journal of Youth and Adolescence, 32*, 157-167.

Dornbusch, S. M., Ritter, P. L., Liederman, P. H., Roberts, D. F., & Fraleigh, M. J. (1987). The relation of parenting style to adolescent school performance. *Child Development, 58*, 1244–1257.

Doty, R. L., Shaman, P., Appelbaum, S. L., Bigerson, R., Sikorski, L., & Rosenberg, L. (1984). Smell identification ability: Changes with age. *Science, 226*, 1441–1443.

Downe-Wamboldt, B., & Tamlyn, D. (1997). An international survey of death education trends in faculties of nursing and medicine. *Death Studies, 21*, 177–188.

Downey, D. (2001). Number of siblings and intellectual development: The resource dilution explanation. *American Psychologist, 56*, 497–504.

Doyle, A. B., & Aboud, F. E. (1995). A longitudinal study of white children's racial prejudice as a social-cognitive development. *Merrill-Palmer Quarterly, 41*, 209–228.

Draper, B., Gething, L., Fethney, J., & Winfield, S. (1999). The Senior Psychiatrist Survey III: Attitudes towards personal ageing, life experiences and psychiatric practice. *Australian & New Zealand Journal of Psychiatry, 33*, 717–722.

Drevets, W., Price, J., Simpson, J., Todd, R., Reich, T., Vannier, M., & Raichle, M. (1997). Subgenual prefrontal cortex abnormalities in mood disorders. *Nature, 386*, 824–827.

Droege, K., & Stipek, D. (1993). Children's use of dispositions to predict classmates' behavior. *Developmental Psychology, 29*, 646–654.

Drum, P. (1985). Retention of text information by grade, ability and study. *Discourse Processes, 8*, 21–52.

Due, P., Holstein, B., Lund, R., Modvig, J., & Avlund, K. (1999). Social relations: Network, support and relational strain. *Social Science & Medicine, 48*, 661–673.

Dugan, L., Nagin, D., & Rosenfeld, R. (2003). Do domestic violence services save lives? *National Institute of Justice Journal, 250*, 1–6.

Dunn, J. (1994). Experience and understanding of emotions, relationships, and membership in a particular culture. In P. Ekman & R. J. Davidson (Eds.), *The nature of emotion: Fundamental questions* (pp. 352–355). New York: Oxford University Press.

Durlak, J. A. (1972). Relationship between attitudes toward life and death among elderly women. *Developmental Psychology, 8*, 146.

Dush, C., Cohan, C., & Amato, P. (2003). The relationship between cohabitation and marital quality and stability: Change across cohorts? *Journal of Marriage & the Family, 65*, 539–549.

Dutton, D. (2012). The prevention of intimate partner violence. *Prevention Science, 13*, 395–397.

Duursma, S., Raymakers, J., Boereboom, F., & Scheven, B. (1991). Estrogen and bone metabolism. *Obsterical & Gynecological Survey, 47*, 38–44.

Duvall, S., Delquadri, J., & Ward, D. (2004). A preliminary investigation of the effectiveness of homeschool instructional environments for students with attention-deficit/hyperactivity disorder. *School Psychology Review, 33*, 140–158.

Dwyer, J., Allayee, H., Dwyer, K., Fan, J., Wu, H., Mark, R., Lusis, A., & Mehrabian, M. (2004). Arachidonate 5-lipoxygenase promoter genotype, dietary arachidonic acid, and atherosclerosis. *New England Journal of Medicine, 350,* 29–37.

DYG, Inc. (2004). *What grown-ups understand about children: A national benchmark survey.* Retrieved June 15, from www.zerotothree.org/site/DocServer/surveyexecutivesummary.pdf?docID=821&AddInterest=1153

Dyl, J., Kittler, J., Phillips, K., & Hunt, J. (2006). Body dysmorphic disorder and other clinically significant body image concerns in adolescent psychiatric inpatients: Prevalance and clinical characteristics. *Child Psychiatry and Human Development, 36,* 369–382.

Dyregrov, A., Gjestad, R., Bie Wikander, A., & Vigerust, S. (1999). Reactions following the sudden death of a classmate. *Scandinavian Journal of Psychology, 40,* 167–176.

Eagly, A., & Wood, W. (2012). Social role theory. In Van Lange, P. Kruglanski, A., & Higgins, E. (Eds.), *Handbook of theories of social psychology* (Vol. 2). (pp. 458–476). Thousand Oaks, CA: Sage Publications.

Eagly, A., Eaton, A., Rose, S., Riger, S., & McHugh, M. (2012). xxx. *American Psychologist, 67,* 211–230.

Eagtly, A., & Wood, W. (2013). The nature—nurture debates: 25 years of challenges in understanding the psychology of gender. *Perspectives on Psychological Science, 8,* 340–357.

Eamon, M., & Mulder, C. (2005). Predicting antisocial behavior among Latino young adolescents: An ecological systems analysis. *American Journal of Orthopsychiatry, 75,* 117–127.

Earles, J. L., & Salthouse, T. A. (1995). Interrelations of age, health, and speed. *Journals of Gerontology: Psychological Sciences, 50B,* P33–41.

Eaton, D., Kann, L., Kinchen, S., Shanklin, S., Flint, K., Hawkins, J., Harris, W., Lowry, R., McManus, T., Chyen, D., Whittle, L., Lim, C., & Wechsler, H. (2013). *Youth risk behavior surveillance: United States, 2011.* Retrieved July 13, 2013, from http://www.cdc.gov/mmwr/pdf/ss/ss6104.pdf.

Eaton, D., Kann, L., Kinchen, S., Shanklin, S., Flint, K., Hawkins, J., Harris, W., Lowry, R., McManus, T., Chyen, D., Whittle, L., Lim, C., & Wechsler, H. (2013). *Youth risk behavior surveillance: United States, 2011.* Retrieved July 13, 2013, from http://www.cdc.gov/mmwr/pdf/ss/ss6104.pdf.

Eaton, D., Kann, L., Kinchen, S., Shanklin, S., Ross, J., Hawkins, J., Harris, W., Lowry, R., McManus, T., Chyen, D., Lim, C., Whittle, L., Brener, N., & Wechsler, H. (2010). Youth risk behavior surveillance—United States, 2009. *Morbidity and Mortality Weekly Report, 59,* 1–148.

Eaton, L., Pitpitan, E., Kalichman, S., Sikkema, K., Skinner, D., Watt, M., Pieterse, D., & Cain, D. (2013). Food insecurity and alcohol use among pregnant women at alcohol-serving establishments in South Africa. *Preventive Science* [in press].

Ecalle, J., Magnan, A., & Gibert, F. (2006). Class size effects on literacy skills and literacy interest in first grade: A large-scale investigation. *Journal of School Psychology, 44,* 191–209.

Eccles, J., & Roeser, R. (2011). School and community influences on human development. In M. Bornstein & M. Lamb (Eds.), *Developmental science: An advanced textbook* (6th ed, pp. 571–644). New York: Psychology Press.

Eccles, J., Jacobs, J., & Harold, R. (1990). Gender role stereotypes, expectancy effects, and parents' socialization of gender differences. *Journal of Social Issues, 46,* 183–201.

Eckel, R. (2006). Preventive cardiology by lifestyle intervention: Opportunity and/or challenge? *Circulation, 113,* 2657–2661.

Eckensberger, E., & Zimba, R. (1997). The development of moral judgment. In J. Berry, P. Dasen, & T. Saraswathi (Eds.), *Handbook of cross-cultural psychology, Vol. 2.* (pp. 299–328). Boston: Allyn & Bacon.

Education Trust. (1996). *Education watch: The 1996 Education Trust state and national data book.* Washington, DC: Author.

Edwards, J., Ruva, C., O'Brien, J., Haley, C., & Lister, J. (2013). Naturalistic measures of prospective memory in amnestic mild cognitive impairment. *Psychology and Aging, 28,* 322–332.

Egan, S. K., & Perry, D. G. (1998). Does low self-regard invite victimization? *Developmental Psychology, 34,* 299–309.

Eichorn, D. H., Clausen, J. A., Haan, N., Honzik, M. P., & Mussen, P. H. (Eds.). (1981). *Present and past in middle life.* New York: Academic Press.

Eiden, R., Foote, A., & Schuetze, P. (2007). Maternal cocaine use and caregiving status: Group differences in caregiver and infant risk variables. *Addictive Behaviors, 32,* 465–476.

Einerson, M. (1998). Fame, fortune, and failure: Young girls' moral language surrounding popular culture. *Youth & Society, 30,* 241–257.

Eisenberg, N. (1992). *The caring child.* Cambridge, MA: Harvard University Press.

Eisenberg, N. (2000). Emotion, regulation, and moral development. *Annual Review of Psychology, 51,* 665–697.

Eisenberg, N. (2004). Prosocial and moral development in the family. In T. Thorkildsen & H. Walberg (Eds.), *Nurturing morality: Issues in children's and families' lives* (pp. 119–135). New York: Kluwer Academic/Plenum Publishers.

Eisenberg, N., & Sulik, M. (2012). Emotion-related self-regulation in children. *Teaching of Psychology, 39,* 77–83.

Eisenberg, N., Chang, L., Ma, Y., & Huang, X. (2009). Relations of parenting style to Chinese children's effortful control, ego resilience, and maladjustment. *Development and Psychopathology, 21,* 455–477.

Eisenberg, N., Eggum, N., & Edwards, A. (2010). Empathy-related responding and moral development. In W. Arsenio & E. Lemerise (Eds.), *Emotions, aggression, and morality in children: Bridging development and psychopathology* (pp. 115–135). Washington, DC: American Psychological Association.

Eisenberg, N., Fabes, R., & Spinrad, T. (2006). Prosocial development. In N. Eisenberg (Ed.), *Handbook of Child Psychology, Volume 3: Social, Emotional, and Personality Development* (6th ed.) (pp. 646–718). Hoboken, NJ: John Wiley & Sons.

Eisenberg, N., Hofer, C., Sulik, M., & Liew, J. (2014). The development of prosocial moral reasoning and a prosocial orientation in young adulthood: Concurrent and longitudinal correlates. *Developmental Psychology 50,* 58–70.

Eisenberger, N. (2003). Does rejection hurt? An fMRI study of social exclusion. *Science, 302,* 290–292.

Eisenberger, R., Pierce, W., & Cameron, J. (1999). Effects of reward on intrinsic motivation-negative, neutral, and positive: Comment on Deci, Koestner, and Ryan. *Psychological Bulletin, 125,* 677–691.

Elbedour, S., Baker, A., & Charlesworth, W. (1997). The impact of political violence on moral reasoning in children. *Child Abuse & Neglect, 21,* 1053–1066.

Elder, G. H., Jr. (1974). *Children of the Great Depression.* Chicago: University of Chicago Press.

Elder, G. H., Jr. (1978). Family history and the life course. In T. Hareven (Ed.), *Transitions: The family and the life course in historical perspective* (pp. 17–64). New York: Academic Press.

Elder, G. H., Jr., Liker, J. K., & Cross, C. E. (1984). Parent-child behavior in the Great Depression: Life course and intergenerational influences. In P. B. Baltes & O. G. Brim, Jr. (Eds.), *Life-span development and behavior, Vol. 6* (pp. 111–159). New York: Academic Press.

Eley, T., Liang, H., Plomin, R., Sham, P., Sterne, A., Williamson, R., & Purcell, S. (2004). Parental familial vulnerability, family environment, and their interactions as predictors of depressive symptoms in adolescents. *Journal of the American Academy of Child Psychiatry, 43,* 298–306.

Elizur, Y., & Mintzer, A. (2003). Gay males' intimate relationship quality: The roles of attachment security, gay identity, social support, and income. *Personal Relationships, 10,* 411–435.

Elkind, D. (1967). Egocentrism in adolescence. *Child Development, 38,* 1025–1033.

Ellenbogen, S., & Chamberland, C. (1997). The peer relations of dropouts: A comparative study of at-risk and not at-risk youths. *Journal of Adolescence, 20,* 355–367.

Elliott, D., Mok, D., & Briere, J. (2004). Adult sexual assault: Prevalence, symptomatology, and sex differences in the general population. *Journal of Traumatic Stress, 17,* 203–211.

Ellis, E., & Thal, D. (2008). Early language delay and risk for language impairment. *Perspectives on Language Learning and Education, 15,* 93–100.

Ellison, M., Danley, K., Bromberg, C., & Palmer-Erbs, V. (1999). Longitudinal outcome of young adults who participated in a psychiatric vocational rehabilitation program. *Psychiatric Rehabilitation Journal, 22,* 337–341.

Ellsworth, C. P., Muir, D. W., & Hains, S. M. J. (1993). Social competence and person-object differentiation: An analysis of the still-face effect. *Developmental Psychology, 29,* 63–73.

Elsner, B., Jeschonek, S., & Pauen, S. (2013). Event-related potentials for 7-month-olds' processing of animals and furniture items. *Developmental Cognitive Neuroscience, 3,* 53–60.

Elwert, F., & Christakis, N. (2006). Widowhood and race. *American Sociological Review, 71,* 16–41.

Emde, R. N., Plomin, R., Robinson, J., Corley, R., DeFries, J., Fulker, D. W., Reznick, J. S., Campos, J., Kagan, J., & Zahn-Waxler, C. (1992). Temperament, emotion, and cognition at fourteen months: The MacArthur longitudinal twin study. *Child Development, 63,* 1437–1455.

Emery, C. F., & Gatz, M. (1990). Psychological and cognitive effects of an exercise program for community-residing older adults. *The Gerontologist, 30,* 184–192.

Emptage, N., Sturm, R., & Robinson, R. (2005). Depression and comorbid pain as predictors of disability, employment, insurance status, and health care costs. *Psychiatric Services, 56,* 468–474.

Ennis, G., Hess, T., & Smith, B. (2013). The impact of age and motivation on cognitive effort: Implications for cognitive engagement in older adulthood. *Psychology and Aging, 28*, 495–504.

Enright, E. (2004). A house divided. *AARP Magazine.* Retrieved July 7, 2007 from www.aarpmagazine.org/family/Articles/a2004-05-26-mag-divorce.html.

Ericsson, K. A., & Crutcher, R. J. (1990). The nature of exceptional performance. In P. B. Baltes, D. L. Featherman, & R. M. Lerner (Eds.), *Life-span development and behavior, Vol. 10* (pp. 188–218). Hillsdale, NJ: Erlbaum.

Erikson, E. H. (1950). *Childhood and society.* New York: Norton.

Erikson, E. H. (1963). *Childhood and society* (2nd ed.). New York: Norton.

Erikson, E. H. (1980b). Themes of adulthood in the Freud-Jung correspondence. In N. J. Smelser & E. Erikson (Eds.), *Themes of work and love in adulthood* (pp. 43–76). Cambridge, MA: Harvard University Press.

Erikson, E. H. (1982). *The life cycle completed.* New York: Norton.

Erikson, E. H., Erikson, J. M., & Kivnick, H. Q. (1906). *Vital involvement in old age.* New York: Norton.

Erikson, E.H. (1980a). *Identity and the life cycle.* New York: Norton (originally published 1959).

Ernst, M., & Hardin, M. (2010). Neurodevelopment underlying adolescent behavior: A neurobiological model. In P. Zelazo, M. Chandler, & E. Crone (Eds.), *Developmental social cognitive neuroscience.* The Jean Piaget symposium series (pp. 165–189). New York: Psychology Press.

Eslea, M., Menesini, E., Morita, Y., O'Moore, M., Mora-Merchan, J., Pereira, B., & Smith, P. (2004). Friendship and loneliness among bullies and victims: Data from seven countries. *Aggressive Behavior, 30*, 71–83.

Esposito, K., Giugliano, F., Di Palo, C., Giugliano, G., Marfella, R., D'Andrea, F., D'Armiento, M., & Giugliano, D. (2004). Effect of lifestyle changes on erectile dysfunction in obese men: A randomized controlled trial. *Journal of the American Medical Association, 291*, 2978–2984.

Espy, K., Stalets, M., McDiarmid, M., Senn, T., Cwik, M., & Hamby, A. (2002). Executive functions in preschool children born preterm: Application of cognitive neuroscience paradigms. *Child Neuropsychology, 8*, 83–92.

Etaugh, C., & Liss, M. (1992). Home, school, and playroom: Training grounds for adult gender roles. *Sex Roles, 26*, 129–147.

EURO-PERISTAT Project. (2008). *European perinatal health report.* Retrieved July 4, 2010 from http://www.europeristat.com/bm.doc/european-perinatal-health-report.pdf.

Evans, G. (2004). The environment of childhood poverty. *American Psychologist, 59*, 77–92.

Evans, R. I. (1969). *Dialogue with Erik Erikson.* New York: Dutton.

Ewald, P. (2000). *Plague time.* New York: Free Press.

Eyetsemitan, F. (1998). Stifled grief in the workplace. *Death Studies, 22*, 469–479.

Fabes, R. A., Knight, G. P., & Higgins, D. A. (1995, March). *Gender differences in aggression: A meta-analytic reexamination of time and age effects.* Paper presented at the biennial meetings of the Society for Research in Child Development, Indianapolis, IN.

Fabes, R., Martin, C., & Hanish, L. (2003). Young children's play qualities in same-, other-, and mixed-sex peer groups. *Child Development, 74*, 921–932.

Fabi, M. (2004). Review of Cybersex: The dark side of the force. *International Journal of Applied Psychoanalytic Studies, 1*, 208–209.

Fagan, J. F., & Singer, L. T. (1983). Infant recognition memory as a measure of intelligence. In L. P. Lipsett (Ed.), *Advances in infancy research, Vol. 2* (pp. 31–78). Norwood, NJ: Ablex.

Fagan, J., & Holland, C. (2002). Equal opportunity and racial differences in IQ. *Intelligence, 30*, 361–387.

Fagard, J., & Jacquet, A. (1989). Onset of bimanual coordination and symmetry versus asymmetry of movement. *Infant Behavior & Development, 12*, 229–235.

Fagot, B. I., & Hagan, R. (1991). Observations of parent reactions to sex-stereotyped behaviors: Age and sex effects. *Child Development, 62*, 617–628.

Falbo, T. (1992). Social norms and the one-child family: Clinical and policy implications. In F. Boer & J. Dunn (Eds.), *Children's sibling relationships: Developmental and clinical issues* (pp. 71–82). Hillsdale, NJ: Erlbaum.

Fallis, R., & Opotow, S. (2003). Are students failing school or are schools failing students? Class cutting in high school. *Journal of Social Issues, 59*, 103–119.

Fantuzzo, J., Coolahan, K., & Mendez, J. (1998). Contextually relevant validation of peer play constructs with African American Head Start children: Penn Interactive Peer Play Scale. *Early Childhood Research Quarterly, 13*, 411–431.

Fantuzzo, J., Sekino, Y., & Cohen, H. (2004). An examination of the contributions of interactive peer play to salient classroom competencies for urban Head Start children. *Psychology in the Schools, 41*, 323–336.

Faraone, S., Sergeant, J., Gillberg, C., & Biederman, J. (2003). The worldwide prevalence of ADHD: Is it an American condition? *World Psychiatry, 2*, 104–113.

Farfel, J., Nitrini, R., Suemoto, C., Grinberg, l., Ferretti, R., Paraizo Leite, R., Tempellini, E., Lima, L., Farias, D., Neves, R., Rodriguez, R., Menezes, P., Fregni, F., Bennett, D., Pasqualucci, C., Filho, W., (2013). Very low levels of education and cognitive reserve: A clinicopathologic study. *Neurology, 81*, 650–657.

Farmer, T., Estell, D., Leung, M., Trott, H., Bishop, J., & Cairns, B. (2003). Individual characteristics, early adolescent peer affiliations, and school dropout: An examination of aggressive and popular group types. *Journal of School Psychology, 41*, 217–232.

Farrar, M. J. (1992). Negative evidence and grammatical morpheme acquisition. *Developmental Psychology, 28*, 90–98.

Farrow, J. (2012). The adult years. In O. Sahler, J. Carr, J. Frank, & J. Nunes, (Eds.), *The behavioral sciences and health care* (3rd ed. pp. 112–120). Cambridge, MA, USA: Hogrefe Publishing.

Farver, J. (1996). Aggressive behavior in preschoolers' social networks: Do birds of a feather flock together? *Early Childhood Research Quarterly, 11*, 333–350.

Farver, J., Bhadha, B., & Narang, S. (2002). Acculturation and psychological functioning in Asian Indian adolescents. *Social Development, 11*, 11–29.

Federal Interagency Forum on Aging Statistics (FIFARS). (2010). *Older Americans 2010: Key indicators of well-being.* Retrieved August 29, 2010 from http://www.agingstats.gov/agingstatsdotnet/Main_Site/Data/2010_Documents/Docs/OA_2010.pdf.

Federal Interagency Forum on Aging Statistics (FIFARS). (2012). *Older Americans: Key indicators of well-being.* Retrieved July 16, 2013, from http://www.aging-stats.gov/Main_Site/Data/2012_Documents/docs/EntireChartbook.pdf.

Federal Interagency Forum on Aging Statistics (FIFARS). (2012). *Older Americans: Key indicators of well-being.* Retrieved July 16, 2013, from http://www.aging-stats.gov/Main_Site/Data/2012_Documents/docs/EntireChartbook.pdf.

Federal Interagency Forum On Child And Family Statistics (FIFCFS). (2010). *America's children in brief: Key national indicators of well-being, 2010.* Retrieved July 18, 2010 from http://www.childstats.gov/americaschildren/index.asp.

Federal Interagency Forum on Child and Family Statistics. (2012). *America's children in brief: Key national indicators of well-being, 2012.* Retrieved June 18, 2013, from http://www.childstats.gov/americaschildren/index.asp.

Feiring, C. (1999). Other-sex friendship networks and the development of romantic relationships in adolescence. *Journal of Youth & Adolescence, 28*, 495–512.

Feldman, D. (2004). Piaget's stages: The unfinished symphony of cognitive development. *New Ideas in Psychology, 22*, 175–231.

Feldman, D., & Beehr, T. (2011). A three-phase model of retirement decision making. *American Psychologist, 66*, 193–203.

Feldman, R. (2003). Paternal socio-psychological factors and infant attachment: The mediating role of synchrony in father-infant interactions. *Infant Behavior and Development, 25*, 221–236.

Feldman, R., & Masalha, S. (2010). Parent-child and triadic antecedents of children's social competence: Cultural specificity, shared process. *Developmental Psychology, 46*, 455–467.

Feng, J., Spence, I., & Pratt, J. (2007). Playing an action video game reduces gender differences in spatial cognition. *Psychological Science, 18*, 850–855.

Fenson, L., Dale, P. S., Reznick, J. S., Bates, E., Thal, D. J., & Pethick, S. J. (1994). Variability in early communicative development. *Monographs of the Society for Research in Child Development, 59* (5, Serial No. 242).

Ferguson, C. (2010). Blazing angels or resident evil? Can violent video games be a force for good? *Review of General Psychology, 14*, 68-81.

Ferguson, C. (2013). Spanking, corporal punishment and negative long-term outcomes: A meta-analytic review of longitudinal studies. *Clinical Psychology Review, 33*, 196–208.

Ferguson, C., & Kilburn, J. (2010). Much ado about nothing: The misestimation and overinterpretation of violent video game effects in Eastern and Western nations: Comment on Anderson et al. (2010). *Psychological Bulletin, 136*, 174–178.

Ferguson, C., & Olson, C. (2013). Friends, fund, frustration and fantasy: Child motivations for video game play. *Motivation and Emotion, 37*, 154–164.

Ferguson, C., Garza, A., Jerabeck, J., Ramos, R., & Galindo, M. (2013). Not worth the fuss after all? Cross-sectional and prospective data on violent video game influences on aggression, visuospatial cognition and mathematics ability in a sample of youth. *Journal of Youth and Adolescence, 42*, 109–122.

Fiatarone, M., & Evans, W. (1993). The etiology and reversibility of muscle dysfunction in the elderly. *Journal of Gerontology, 48*, 77-83.

File, T. (2013). *Computer and internet use in the United States.* Retrieved July 11, 2013, from http://www.census.gov/prod/2013pubs/p20-569.pdf.

Findlay, L., Girardi, A., & Coplan, R. (2006). Links between empathy, social behavior, and social understanding. *Early Childhood Research Quarterly, 21*, 347–359.

Findling, R., Feeny, N., Stansbrey, R., Delporto-Bedoya, D., & Demeter, C. (2004). Special articles: Treatment of mood disorders in children and adolescents: Somatic treatment for depressive illnesses in children and adolescents. *Psychiatric Clinics of North America, 27*, 113–137.

fInternational Food Information Council Foundation. (2009). *Functional foods fact sheet: Antioxidants*. Retrieved August 31, 2010 from http://www.foodinsight.org/Resources/Detail.aspx?topic=Functional_Foods_Fact_Sheet_Antioxidants.

Fiocco, A., & Yaffe, K. (2010). Defining successful aging: The importance of including cognitive function over time. Archives of Neurology, 67, 876–880.

Fischer, K., & Rose, S. (1994). Dynamic development of coordination of components in brain and behavior: A framework for theory and research. In K. Fischer & G. Dawson (Eds.), *Human behavior and the developing brain* (pp. 3–66). New York: Guilford Press.

Fischoff, B., de Bruin, W., Parker, A., Millstein, S., & Halpern-Felsher, B. (2010). Adolescents' perceived risk of dying. *Journal of Adolescent Health, 46*, 265–259.

Fisher, B., & Specht, D. (1999). Successful aging and creativity in later life. *Journal of Aging Studies, 13*, 457–472.

Fisher, J., Feekery, C., & Rowe-Murray, H. (2002). Nature, severity and correlates of psychological distress in women admitted to a private mother-baby unit. *Journal of Paediatrics & Child Health, 38*, 140–145.

Fitzgerald, B. (1999). Children of lesbian and gay parents: A review of the literature. *Marriage & Family Review, 29*, 57–75.

Fitzgerald, D., & White, K. (2003). Linking children's social worlds: Perspective-taking in parent-child and peer contexts. *Social Behavior & Personality, 31*, 509–522.

Fitzpatrick, J. L., & Silverman, T. (1989). Women's selection of careers in engineering: Do traditional-nontraditional differences still exist? *Journal of Vocational Behavior, 34*, 266–278.

Flannery, D. J., Montemayor, R., & Eberly, M. B. (1994). The influence of parent negative emotional expression on adolescents' perceptions of their relationships with their parents. *Personal Relationships, 1*, 259–274.

Flannery, D., Vazsonyi, A., Embry, D., Powell, K., Atha, H., Vesterdal, W., & Shenyang, G. (2000, August). *Longitudinal effectiveness of the Peace-Builders' universal school-based violence prevention program*. Paper presented at the annual meeting of the American Psychological Association, Washington, DC.

Flavell, J. (1963). *The developmental psychology of Jean Piaget*. New York: D. Van Nostrand.

Flavell, J. (1999). Cognitive development: Children's knowledge about the mind. *Annual Review of Psychology, 50*, 21–45.

Flavell, J. H. (1985). *Cognitive development* (2nd ed.). Englewood Cliffs, NJ: Prentice-Hall.

Flavell, J. H. (1986). The development of children's knowledge about the appearance-reality distinction. *American Psychologist, 41*, 418–425.

Flavell, J. H. (1993). Young children's understanding of thinking and consciousness. *Current Directions in Psychological Science, 2*, 40–43.

Flavell, J. H., Everett, B. A., Croft, K., & Flavell, E. R. (1981). Young children's knowledge about visual perception: Further evidence for the Level 1–Level 2 distinction. *Developmental Psychology, 17*, 99–103.

Flavell, J. H., Green, F. L., & Flavell, E. R. (1989). Young children's ability to differentiate appearance-reality and level 2 perspectives in the tactile modality. *Child Development, 60*, 201–213.

Flavell, J. H., Green, F. L., & Flavell, E. R. (1990). Developmental changes in young children's knowledge about the mind. *Cognitive Development, 5*, 1–27.

Flavell, J. H., Green, F. L., Wahl, K. E., & Flavell, E. R. (1987). The effects of question clarification and memory aids on young children's performance on appearance-reality tasks. *Cognitive Development, 2*, 127–144.

Flavell, J. H., Zhang, X.-D., Zou, H., Dong, Q., & Qi, S. (1983). A comparison of the appearance-reality distinction in the People's Republic of China and the United States. *Cognitive Psychology, 15*, 459–466.

Flom, R., & Bahrick, L. (2007). The development of infant discrimination of affect in multimodal and unimodal stimulation: The role of intersensory redundancy. *Developmental Psychology, 43*, 238–252.

Flood, M. (2007). Exploring the relationship between creativity, depression, and successful aging. *Activities, Adaptation, & Aging, 31*, 55–71.

Flores, S., & Park, T. (2013). Race, ethnicity, and college success: Examining the continued significance of the minority-serving institution. *Educational Researcher, 42*, 115–128.

Flouri, E., & Hawkes, D. (2008). Ambitious mothers—successful daughters: Mothers' early expectations for children's education and children's earnings and sense of control in adult life. *British Journal of Educational Psychology, 78*, 411–433.

Flowers, L. (2002). The impact of college racial composition on African American students' academic and social gains: Additional evidence. *Journal of College Student Development, 43*, 403–410.

Flowers, L., & Pascarella, E. (1999). Cognitive effects of college racial composition on African American students after 3 years of college. *Journal of College Student Development, 40*, 669–677.

Flynn, J. (1999). Searching for justice: The discovery of IQ gains over time. *American Psychologist, 54*, 5–20.

Flynn, J. (2003). Movies about intelligence: The limitations of g. *Current Directions in Psychological Science, 12*, 95–99.

Foehr, T., & Roberts, D. (2010). *Generation M2: Media in the lives of 8- to 18-year-olds*. Retrieved October 8, 2013 from http://kaiserfamilyfoundation.files.wordpress.com/2013/01/8010.pdf.

Foehr, U. (2006). Media multitasking among American youth: Prevalence, predictors and pairings. Menlo Park, CA: Henry J. Kaiser Foundation. Retrieved June 26, 2007 from http://kff.org/entmedia/upload/7592.pdf

Folkman, S., & Lazarus, R. (1980). An analysis of coping in a middle-aged community sample. *Journal of Personality and Social Psychology, 70*, 336–348.

Folven, R. J., & Bonvillian, J. D. (1991). The transition from nonreferential to referential language in children acquiring American Sign Language. *Developmental Psychology, 27*, 806–816.

Fonda, S., Clipp, E., & Maddox, G. (2002). Patterns in functioning among residents of an affordable assisted living housing facility. *Gerontologist, 42*, 178–187.

Foos, P., & Goolkasian, P. (2010) Age differences and format effects in working memory. *Experimental Aging Research, 36*, 273–286.

Fordham, K., & Stevenson-Hinde, J. (1999). Shyness, friendship quality, and adjustment during middle childhood. *Journal of Child Psychology & Psychiatry & Allied Disciplines, 40*, 757–768.

Forrester, M., (2013). Human handedness: An inherited evolutionary trait. *Behavioural Brain Research, 237*, 200–206.

Forte, C., & Hansvick, C. (1999). Applicant age as a subjective employability factor: A study of workers over and under age fifty. *Journal of Employment Counseling, 36*, 24–34.

Fossati, A., Borroni, S., Eisenberg, N., & Maffei, C. (2010). Relations of proactive and reactive dimensions of aggression to overt and covert narcissism in nonclinical adolescents. *Aggressive Behavior, 36*, 21–27.

Foulder-Hughes, L., & Cooke, L. (2003a). Do mainstream schoolchildren who were born preterm have motor problems? *British Journal of Occupational Therapy, 66*, 9–16.

Fouquereau, E., & Baudoin, C. (2002). The Marital Satisfaction Questionnaire for Older Persons: Factor structure in a French sample. *Social Behavior & Personality, 30*, 95–104.

Fox, N., Henderson, H., Rubin, K., Calkins, S., & Schmidt, L. (2001). Continuity and discontinuity of behavioral inhibition and exuberance: Psychophysiological and behavioral influences across the first four years of life. *Child Development, 72*, 1–21.

Fozard, J. L. (1990). Vision and hearing in aging. In J. E. Birren & K. W. Schaie (Eds.), *Handbook of the psychology of aging* (3rd ed., pp. 150–171). San Diego, CA: Academic Press.

Fozard, J. L., Metter, E. J., & Brant, L. J. (1990). Next steps in describing aging and disease in longitudinal studies. *Journals of Gerontology: Psychological Sciences, 45*, P116–127.

Fozard, J. L., Metter, E. J., & Brant, L. J. (1990). Next steps in describing aging and disease in longitudinal studies. *Journals of Gerontology: Psychological Sciences, 45*, P116–127.

Fozard, J., (1990). Vision and hearing in aging. In Birren, J., & Schaie, K. (Eds.), *Handbook of the psychology of aging* (3rd ed.). (pp. 150–171). San Diego, CA: Academic Press.

Fraley, R., Roisman, G., Booth-LaForce, C., Owen, M., & Holland, A. (2013). Interpersonal and genetic origins of adult attachment styles: A longitudinal study from infancy to early adulthood. *Journal of Personality and Social Psychology, 104*, 817–838.

Fraley, R., Roisman, G., Booth-LaForce, C., Owen, M., & Holland, A. (2013). Interpersonal and genetic origins of adult attachment styles: A longitudinal study from infancy to early adulthood. *Journal of Personality and Social Psychology, 104*, 817–838.

Francis, L. (1997). Ideology and interpersonal emotion management: Redefining identity in two support groups. *Social Psychology Quarterly, 60*, 153–171.

Francis-Smythe, J., & Smith, P. (1997). The psychological impact of assessment in a development center. *Human Relations, 50*, 149–167.

Francks, C., Maegawa, S., Lauren, J., Abrahams, B., Velayos-Baeza, A., Medland, S., Colella, S., Groszer, M., McAuley, E., Caffrey, T., Timmusk, T., Pruunsild, P., Koppel, I., Lind, P., Natsummoto-Itaba, N., Nicok, J., Xiong, L., Joober, R., Enard, W., Krinsky, B., Nanba, E., Richardson, A., Riley, B., Martin, N., Strittmatter, S., Miller, H., Rejuescu, D., St. Clair, D., Muglia, P., Roos, J., Fisher, S., Wade-Martins, R., Rouleau, G., Stain, J., Karayiorgou, M., Geschwind, D., Ragoussis, J., Kendler, K., Airaksinen, M., Oshimura, M., DeLisi, L., & Monaco, A. (2007). LRRTM1 on chromosome 2p12 is a maternally suppressed gene that is associated paternally with handedness and schizophrenia. *Molecular Psychiatry, 12*, 1129–1139.

Franco, N., & Levitt, M. (1998). The social ecology of middle childhood: Family support, friendship quality, and self-esteem. *Family Relations: Interdisciplinary Journal of Applied Family Studies, 47*, 315–321.

Fransen, M. (2004). Dietary weight loss and exercise for obese adults with knee osteoarthritis: Modest weight loss targets, mild exercise, modest effects. *Arthritis and Rheumatology, 50*, 1366–1369.

Frederick, D., Reynolds, T., & Fisher, M. (2013). The importance of female choice: Evolutionary perspectives on constraints, expressions, and variations in female mating strategies. In Fisher, M., Garcia, J., & Sokol Chang, R. (Eds.), *Evolution's empress: Darwinian perspectives on the nature of women* (pp. 304–329). New York, NY, USA: Oxford University Press.

Fredriksen, K., Rhodes, J., Reddy, R., & Way, N. (2004). Sleepless in Chicago: Tracking the effects of adolescent sleep loss during the middle school years. *Child Development, 75*, 84–95.

Freedberg, P. (2006) Health care barriers and same-sex intimate partner violence: a review of the literature, *Journal of Forensic Nursing, 2*, 1, 15–41.

Freeman, C., & Fox, M. (2005). *Status and trends in the education of American Indians and Alaska Natives*. Retrieved June 27, 2008 from http://nces.ed.gov/pubs2005/2005108.pdf.

French, H. (2007). *Pension crisis looms large for China*. Retrieved September 1, 2010 from http://www.nytimes.com/2007/03/20/world/asia/20iht-china.4969919.html.

Freudenbeger, H., & Richelson, G. (1981). *Burnout: The high cost of high achievement*. New York, NY: Bantam Books.

Frick, E., Fegg, M., Tyroller, M., Fischer, N., & Bumeder, I. (2007). Patients' health beliefs and coping prior to autologous peripheral stem cell transplantation. *European Journal of Cancer Care, 16*, 156–163.

Friedman, M., & Rosenman, R. H. (1974). *Type A behavior and your heart*. New York: Knopf.

Frieswijk, N., Buunk, B., Steverink, N., & Slaets, J. (2004). The effect of social comparison information on the life satisfaction of frail older persons. *Psychology & Aging, 19*, 183–190.

Frisch, M., Glimelius, B., van den Brule, A., Wohlfahrt, J., Meijer, C., Walboomers, J., Goldman, S., Svensson, C., Hans-Olov, A., & Melbye, M. (1997). Sexually transmitted infection as a cause of anal cancer. *New England Journal of Medicine, 337*, 1350–1358.

Fryar, C., Carroll, M., & Ogden, C. (2012). *Prevalence of obesity among children and adolescents: United States, Trends 1963—1965 through 2009—2010*. Retrieved July 10, 2013, from http://www.cdc.gov/nchs/data/hestat/obesity_child_09_10/obesity_child_09_10.pdf.

Fryar, C., Hirsch, R., Porter, K., Kottiri, B., Brody, D., & Louis, T. (2007). Drug use and sexual behaviors reported by adults: 1999–2002. *Vital and Health Statistics, 384*, 1–15.

Fukase, Y., & Okamoto, Y. (2012). The process of mutual relationships with a maternal person based on reminiscences of elderly people. *Japanese Journal of Developmental Psychology, 23*, 55–65.

Fukue, N. (2010). *Elderly living alone increasingly dying the same way*. Retrieved September 1, 2010 from http://search.japantimes.co.jp/cgi-bin/nn20100721f1.html.

Fullerton, A., & Wallace, M. (2007). Traversing the flexible turn: US workers' perceptions of job security, 1977–2002. *Social Science Research, 36*, 201–221.

Funk, J., Buchman, D., Jenks, J., & Bechtoldt, H. (2003). Playing violent video games, desensitization, and moral evaluation in children. *Journal of Applied Developmental Psychology, 24*, 413–436.

Funk, J., Buchman, D., Myers, B., & Jenks, J. (2000, August). *Asking the right questions in research on violent electronic games*. Paper presented at the annual meeting of the American Psychological Association, Washington, DC.

Furedi, F. (2003). *Therapy culture: Cultivating vulnerability in an uncertain age*. London, UK: Routledge.

Gabbard, C. (2012). *Lifelong motor development* (6th ed.). San Francisco, CA, USA: Pearson Benjamin Cummings.

Gabbard, C. (2012). *Lifelong motor development*. San Francisco, CA, USA: Pearson Benjamin Cummings.

Gagne, J., Miller, M., & Goldsmith, H. (2013). Early—but modest—gender differences in focal aspects of childhood temperament. *Personality and Individual Differences, 55*, 95–100.

Gahagan, S. (2011). Behavioral disorders. In K. Marcdante, R. Kliegman, H. Jensen, & R. Behrman (Eds.), *Nelson's essentials of pediatrics* (6th ed., pp. 45–62). New York: Elsevier Health Publishers.

Gahagan, S. (2011). Behavioral disorders. In Marcdante, K., Kliegman, R., Jenson, H., & Behrman, R. (Eds). *Nelson essentials of pedatrics* 6th ed. (pp. 45–62). Philadelphia, PA, USA: Saunders Elsevier.

Gaillard, W., Hertz-Pannier, L., Mott, S., Barnett, A., LeBihan, D., & Theodore, W. (2000). Functional anatomy of cognitive development: fMRI of verbal fluency in children and adults. *Neurology, 54*, 180–185.

Gajria, M., Jitendra, A., Sood, S., & Sacks, G. (2007). Improving comprehension of expository text in students with LD: A research synthesis. *Journal of Learning Disabilities, 40*, 210–225.

Galaif, E., Sussman, S., Newcomb, M., & Locke, T. (2007). Suicidality, depression, and alcohol use among adolescents: A review of empirical findings. *International Journal of Adolescent Medicine and Health, 19*, 27–35.

Galambos, N., Turner, P., & Tilton-Weaver, L. (2005). Chronological and subjective age in emerging adulthood: The crossover effect. *Journal of Adolescent Research, 20*, 538–556.

Galanaki, E. (2004). Teachers and loneliness: The children's perspective. *School Psychology International, 25*, 92–105.

Galanaki, E. (2012). The imaginary audience and the personal fable: A test of Elkind's theory of adolescent egocentrism. *Psychology, 3*, 457–466.

Galassi, J., Gulledge, S., & Cox, N. (1997). Middle school advisories: Retrospect and prospect. *Review of Educational Research, 67*, 301–338.

Gallagher, P., & Carey, K. (2012). Connecting with the well-elderly through reminiscence: Analysis of lived experience. *EducaitonalEducational Gerontology, 38*, 576–582.

Gallagher, S., Phillips, A., Evans, P., Der, G., Hunt, K., & Carroll, D. (2008). *Brain, Behavior, and Immunity, 22*, 565–572.

Gallagher-Thompson, D., Tazeau, Y., & Basilio L. (1997). The relationships of dimensions of acculturation to self-reported depression in older Mexican-American women. *Journal of Clinical Geropsychology, 3*, 123–137.

Gallo, D., & Wheeler, M. (2013). Episodic memory. In D. Reisberg, D. (Ed.), *The Oxford handbook of cognitive psychology*. (pp. 189–205). New York, NY, USA: Oxford University Press.

Gambert, S., Schultz, B., & Handy, R. (1995). Osteoporosis: Clinical features, prevention, and treatment. *Endocrinology and Metabolism Clinics of North America, 24*, 317–371.

Gamble, W., Ewing, A., & Wilhelm, M. (2009). Parental perceptions of characteristics of non-parental child care: Belief dimensions, family and child correlates. *Journal of Child and Family Studies, 18*, 70–82.

Gamoran, A., Porter, A., Smithson, J,. & White, P. (1997). Upgrading high school mathematics instruction: Improving learning opportunities for low-achieving, low-income youth. *Educational Evaluation and Policy Analysis, 19*, 325–338.

Gana, K., Alaphilippe, D., & Bailly, N. (2004). Positive illusions and mental and physical health in later life. *Aging & Mental Health, 8*, 58–64.

Gangoli, G., & Rew, M. (2011). Mothers-in-law against daughters-in-law: Domestic violence and legal discourses around mother-in-law violence against daughters-in-law in India. *Women's Studies International Forum, 34*, 420–429.

Garbarino, J., Dubrow, N., Kostelny, K., & Pardo, C. (1992). *Children in danger: Coping with the consequences of community violence*. San Francisco: Jossey-Bass.

García, J., Landa, V., Grandes, G., Pombo, H., & Mauriz, A. (2013). Effectiveness of "primary bereavement care" for widows: A cluster randomized controlled trial involving family physicians. *Death Studies, 37*, 287–310.

Garcáa-Ruiz, M., Rodrigo, M., Hernández-Cabrera, J., Máiquez, M., & Deković, M. (2013). Resolution of parent-child conflicts in the adolescence. *European Journal of Psychology of Education, 28*, 173–188.

Gardner, A. (2007). *ADHD drugs need better warnings on heart, psychiatric risks: FDA*. Retrieved June 19, 2007 from www.healthfinder.org/news/newsstory.asp?docID=602115

Gardner, H. (1983). *Frames of mind: The theory of multiple intelligence.* New York: Basic Books.

Gardner, H. (2003). Three distinct meanings of intelligence. In Sternberg, R., Lautrey, J., & Lubart, T. (Eds.), *Models of intelligence: International perspectives.* (pp. 43–54). Washington, DC: American Psychological Association.

Gardner, J., Karmel, B., Freedland, R., Lennon, E., Flory, M., Miroschnichenko, I., Phan, H., Barone, A., & Harm, A. (2006). Arousal, attention, and neurobehavioral assessment in the neonatal period: Implications for intervention and policy. *Journal of Policy and Practice in Intellectual Disabilities, 3,* 22–32.

Garnier, H., Stein, J., & Jacobs, J. (1997). The process of dropping out of high school: A 19-year perspective. *American Educational Research Journal, 34,* 395–419.

Garrison, R. J., Gold, R. S., Wilson, P. W. F., & Kannel, W. B. (1993). Educational attainment and coronary heart disease risk: The Framingham offspring study. *Preventive Medicine, 22,* 54–64.

Gartrell, N., & Bos, H. (2010). U. S. National Longitudinal Lesbian Family Study: Psychological adjustment of 17-year-old adolescents. *Pediatrics, 126,* 1–9.

Gary, J., Kling, B., & Dodd, B. (2004). A program for counseling and campus support services for African American and Latino adult learners. *Journal of College Counseling, 7,* 18-23.

Garza-Mercer, F., Christensen, A., & Doss, B. (2006). Sex and affection in heterosexual and homosexual couples: An evolutionary perspective. *Electronic Journal of Human Sexuality, 9,* Retrieved August 26, 2010 from http://ejhs.org/volume9/Garza.htm.

Gass, K., Jenkins, J., & Dunn, J. (2007). Are sibling relationships protective? A longitudinal study. *Journal of Child Psychology and Psychiatry, 48,* 167–175.

Gathercole, S., Pickering, S., Ambridge, B., & Wearing, H. (2004). The structure of working memory from 4 to 15 years of age. *Developmental Psychology, 40,* 177–190.

Gauntlett-Gilbert, J., Keegan, A., & Petrak, J. (2004). Drug-facilitated sexual assault: Cognitive approaches to treating the trauma. *Behavioral & Cognitive Psychotherapy, 32,* 211.

Gaziano, J., & Hennekens, C. (1995). Dietary fat and risk of prostate cancer. *Journal of the National Cancer Institute, 87,* 1427–1428.

Geary, D., Lin, F., Chen, G., Saults, S., et al. (1999). Contributions of computational fluency to cross-national differences in arithmetical reasoning abilities. *Journal of Educational Psychology, 91,* 716–719.

Geber, M., & Dean, R. (1957). Gesell tests on African children. *Pediatrics, 20,* 1055–1065.

Gee, C., & Heyman, G. (2007). Children's evaluation of other people's self-descriptions. *Social Development, 16,* 800–818.

Gee, C., & Rhodes, J. (1999). Postpartum transitions in adolescent mothers' romantic and maternal relationships. *Merrill-Palmer Quarterly, 45,* 512–532.

Gee, C., & Rhodes, J. (2003). Adolescent mothers' relationship with their children's biological fathers: Social support, social strain and relationship continuity. *Journal of Family Psychology, 17,* 370–383.

Geers, A., Kosbab, K., Helfer, S., Weiland, P., & Wellman, J. (2007). Further evidence for individual differences in placebo responding: An interactionist perspective. *Journal of Psychosomatic Research, 62,* 563–570.

Gelman, R. (1972). Logical capacity of very young children: Number invariance rules. *Child Development, 43,* 75–90.

Gelman, S., Taylor, M., Nguyen, S., Leaper, C., & Bigler, R. (2004). Mother-child conversations about gender: Understanding the acquisition of essentialist beliefs. *Monographs of the Society for Research in Child Development, 69,* 1–127.

Gentile, D., Lynch, P., Linder, J., & Walsh, D. (2004). The effects of violent video game habits on adolescent hostility, aggressive behaviors, and school performance. *Journal of Adolescence, 27,* 5–22.

Geoffroy, M., Power, C., Touchette, E., Dubois, L., Boivin, M., Seguin, J., Tremblay, R., & Cote, S. (2013). Childcare and overweight or obesity over 10 years of follow-up. *Journal of Pediatrics, 162,* 753–758.

George, M., Cummings, E., & Davies, P. (2010). Positive aspects of fathering and mothering, and children's attachment in kindergarten. *Early Child Development and Care, 180,* 107–119.

Georgieff, M. K. (1994). Nutritional deficiencies as developmental risk factors: Commentary on Pollitt and Gorman. In C. A. Nelson (Ed.), *The Minnesota Symposia on Child Development, Vol. 27* (pp. 145–159). Hillsdale, NJ: Erlbaum.

Georgiou, S., & Stavrinides, P. (2008). Bullies, victims, and bully-victims: Psychosocial profiles and attribution styles. *School Psychology International, 29,* 574–589.

Gerken, L., & Aslin, R. (2005) Thirty years of research on infant speech perception: The legacy of Peter W. Jusczyk. *Language Learning and Development, 1,* 5–21.

Gershoff, E. (2002). Corporal punishment by parents and associated child behaviors and experiences: A meta-analytic and theoretical review. *Psychological Bulletin, 128,* 539–579.

Gersten, R., Compton, D., Connor, C., Dimino, J., Santoro, L., Linan-Thompson, S., & Tilly, W. (2008). Assisting students struggling with reading: Response to intervention and multi-tier intervention for reading in the primary grades. A practice guide. Retrieved August 10, 2010 from http://ies.ed.gov/ncee/wwc/pdf/practiceguides/rti_reading_pg_021809.pdf.

Gersten, R., Dimino, J., & Jayanthi, M. (2008). Reading comprehension and vocabulary instruction: Results of an observation study of first grade classrooms. Paper presented at the annual meeting of the Society for the Scientific Study of Reading, Asheville, NC, July 10–12, 2008.

Gerwood, J., LeBlanc, M., Piazza, N. (1998). The purpose-in-life test and religious denomination: Protestant and Catholic scores in an elderly population. *Journal of Clinical Psychology, 54,* 49–53.

Gesell, A. (1925). The mental growth of the preschool child. New York: Macmillan.

Giambra, L. M., Arenberg, D., Zonderman, A. B., Kawas, C., & Costa, P. T., Jr. (1995). Adult life span changes in immediate visual memory and verbal intelligence. *Psychology & Aging, 10,* 123–139.

Giardino, A., Harris, T., & Giardino, E. (2009). *Child abuse & neglect, posttraumatic stress disorder.* Retrieved July 21, 2010 from http://emedicine.medscape.com/article/916007-overview.

Gibbs, R., & Beitel, D. (1995). What proverb understanding reveals about how people think. *Psychological Bulletin, 118,* 133–154.

Gibson, D. R. (1990). Relation of socioeconomic status to logical and sociomoral judgment of middle-aged men. *Psychology and Aging, 5,* 510–513.

Gibson, E. J., & Walk, R. D. (1960). The "visual cliff." *Scientific American, 202,* 80–92.

Giedd J., Blumenthal, J., & Jeffries N. (1999). Brain development during childhood and adolescence: A longitudinal MRI study. *Nature Neuroscience, 2,* 861–3.

Giedd, J. (2004). Structural magnetic resonance imaging of the adolescent brain. *Annals of the New York Academy of Sciences, 1021,* 77–85.

Gill, T., Baker, D., Gottschalk, M., Peduzzi, P., Allore, H., & Byers, A. (2002). A program to prevent functional decline in physically frail, elderly persons who live at home. *Medical Care Research & Review, 60,* 223–247.

Gillies, V., & Lucey, H. (2006). "It's a connection you can't get away from": Brothers, sisters and social capital. *Journal of Youth Studies, 9,* 479–493.

Gilligan, C. (1982). *In a different voice: Psychological theory and women's development.* Cambridge, MA: Harvard University Press.

Gilligan, C., & Wiggins, G. (1987). The origins of morality in early childhood relationships. In J. Kagan & S. Lamb (Eds.), *The emergence of morality in young children* (pp. 277–307). Chicago: University of Chicago Press.

Glaser, R., Kiecolt-Glaser, J. K., Bonneau, R. H., Malarkey, W., Kennedy, S., & Hughes, J. (1992). Stress-induced modulation of the immune response to recombinant hepatitis B vaccine. *Psychosomatic Medicine, 54,* 22–29.

Glass, J., & Kilpatrick, B. (1998). Gender comparisons of baby boomers and financial preparation for retirement. *Educational Gerontology, 24,* 719–745.

Glazer, H. (1998). Expressions of children's grief: A qualitative study. *International Journal of Play Therapy, 7,* 51–65.

Gleitman, L. R., & Gleitman, H. (1992). A picture is worth a thousand words, but that's the problem: The role of syntax in vocabulary acquisition. *Current Directions in Psychological Science, 1,* 31–35.

Glenn, N., & Weaver, C. (1985). Age, cohort, and reported job satisfaction in the United States. In Blau, A. (Ed.). *Current perspectives on aging and the life cycle, A research annual, Vol. 1: Work, retirement and social policy* (pp. 89–110). Greenwich, CT: JAI Press.

Gnepp, J., & Chilamkurti, C. (1988). Children's use of personality attributions to predict other people's emotional and behavioral reactions. *Child Development, 50,* 743–754.

Gobeski, K., & Beehr, T. (2009). How retirees work: Predictors of different types of bridge employment. *Journal of Organizational Behavior, 30,* 401–425.

Godleski, S., & Ostrov, J. (2010). Relational aggression and hostile attribution biases: Testing multiple statistics methods and models. *Journal of Abnormal Child Psychology, 38,* 447–458.

Goertz, C., Lamm, B., Graf, F., Kolling, T., Knopf, M., & Keller, H. (2011). Deferred imitation in 6-month-old German and Cameroonian Nso infants. *Journal of Cognitive Education and Psychology, 10,* 44–55.

Gogtay, N., Giedd, J., Lusk, L., Hayashi, K., Greenstein, D., Vaituzis, A., Nugent, T., Herman, D., Clasen, L., Toga, A., Rapoport, J., & Thompson, P. (2004). Dynamic mapping of human cortical development during childhood through early adulthood. *Proceedings of the National Academy of Sciences, 17*, 17.

Gold, D. P., Andres, D., Etezadi, J., Arbuckle, T., Schwartzman, A., & Chaikelson, J. (1995). Structural equation model of intellectual change and continuity and predictors of intelligence in older men. *Psychology & Aging, 10*, 294–303.

Gold, E., Colvin, A., Avis, N., Bromberger, J., Greendale, G., Powell, L., Sternfeld, B., & Matthews, K. (2006). Longitudinal analysis of the association between vasomotor symptoms and race/ethnicity across the menopausal transition: Study of women's health across the nation. *American Journal of Public Health, 96*, 1225–1235.

Goldberg, A. P., Dengel, D. R., & Hagberg, J. M. (1996). Exercise physiology and aging. In E. L. Schneider & J. W. Rowe (Eds.), *Handbook of the biology of aging* (4th ed., pp. 331–354). San Diego, CA: Academic Press.

Goldberg, A., & Hagberg, J. (1990). Physical exercise in the elderly. In Schneider, E., & Rowe, J. (Eds.), *Handbook of the biology of aging* (3rd ed. pp. 407–428). San Diego, CA: Academic Press.

Goldberg, A., & Smith, J. (2013). Predictors of psychological adjustment in early placed adopted children with lesbian, gay, and heterosexual parents. *Journal of Family Psychology, 27*, 431–442.

Goldberg, A., Smith, J., & Perry-Jenkins, M. (2012). The division of labor in lesbian, gay, and heterosexual new adoptive parents. *Journal of Marriage and Family, 74*, 812–828.

Goldberg, W. A. (1990). Marital quality, parental personality, and spousal agreement about perceptions and expectations for children. *Merrill-Palmer Quarterly, 36*, 531–556.

Goldfield, B. A., & Reznick, J. S. (1990). Early lexical acquisition: Rate, content, and the vocabulary spurt. *Journal of Child Language, 17*, 171–183.

Goldin-Meadow, S. (2002). Constructing communication by hand. *Cognitive Development, 17*, 1385-1405.

Goldschmidt, L., Richardson, G., Willford, J., & Day, N. (2008). Prenatal marijuana exposure and intelligence test performance at age 6. *Journal of the American Academy of Child and Adolescent Psychiatry, 47*, 254–263.

Goleman, D. (1995). *Emotional intelligence.* New York: Bantam.

Goleman, D. D., Kaufman, P., & Ray, M. (1992). *The creative spirit.* New York: Dutton.

Golombok, S., & Tasker, F. (1996). Do parents influence the sexual orientation of their children? Findings from a longitudinal study of lesbian families. *Developmental Psychology, 32*, 3–11.

Golombok, S., Rust, J., Zervoulis, K., Croudace, T., Golding, J., & Hines, M. (2008). Developmental trajectories of sex-typed behavior in boys and girls: A longitudinal general population study of children aged 2.5–8 years. *Child Development, 79*, 1583–1593.

Golombok, S., Rust, J., Zervoulis, K., Golding, J., & Hines, M. (2012). Continuity in sex-typed behavior from preschool to adolescence: A longitudinal population study of boys and girls aged 3-13 years. *Archives of Sexual Behavior, 41*, 591–597.

Gonyea, J. (2012). Midlife, multigenerational bonds, and caregiving. In R. Talley, R., & R. Montgomery, R. (Eds.), *Caregiving across the lifespan: Research, practice, policy* (pp. 105–130). New York, NY, USA: Springer Science + Business Media.

Gonzales, P., Guzman, J., Partelow, L., Pahlke, E., Jocelyn, L., Kastberg, D., & Williams, T. (2004). *Highlights from the Trends in International Mathematics and Science Study: TIMSS 2003.* Retrieved June 17, 2008 from http://nces.ed.gov/pubsearch/pubsinfo.asp?pubid=2005005

Goodenough, F. L. (1931). *Anger in young children.* Minneapolis: University of Minnesota Press.

Goodman, C., & Silverstein, M. (2002). Grandmothers raising grandchildren: Family structure and well-being in culturally diverse families. *Gerontologist, 42*, 676–689.

Goodman, S., & Brand, S. (2009). Infants of depressed mothers: Vulnerabilities, risk factors, and protective factors for the later development of psychopathology. In C. Zeanah (Ed.), *Handbook of infant mental health* (3rd ed.) (pp. 153–170). New York: Guilford Press.

Goodrum, S. (2005). The interaction between thoughts and emotions following the news of a loved one's murder. *Omega: Journal of Death and Dying, 51*, 143–160.

Goodwin, P., & Mosher, C. (2010). *Marriage and cohabitation in the United States: A statistical portrait based on cycle 6 (2002) of the National Survey of Family Growth.* Retrieved July 27, 2010 from http://www.cdc.gov/nchs/data/series/sr_23/sr23_028.pdf.

Goodwin, P., Mosher, W., & Chandra, A. (2010). *Marriage and cohabitation in the United States: A statistical portrait based on Cycle 6 (2002) of the National Survey of Family Growth. Vital Health Statistics, 23*, 1–55.

Gordon, G., & Vaughan, C. (1986). Calcium and osteoporosis. *Journal of Nutrition, 116*, 319–322.

Gothelf, D., Apter, A., Brand-Gothelf, A., Offer, N., Ofek, H., Tyano, S., & Pfeffer, C. (1998). Death concepts in suicidal adolescents. *Journal of the American Academy of Child & Adolescent Psychiatry, 37*, 1279–1286.

Gottman, J. M. (1986). The world of coordinated play: Same- and cross-sex friendship in young children. In J. M. Gottman & J. G. Parker (Eds.), *Conversations of friends: Speculations on affective development* (pp. 139–191). Cambridge, UK: Cambridge University Press.

Gottman, J. M. (1994). *Why marriages succeed or fail.* New York: Simon & Schuster.

Gould E., Reeves A, J., Graziano M, S, A, & Gross, C, G. (1999). Neurogenesis in the neocortex of adult primates. *Science, 286*, 548-552.

Gowen, C. (2011). Fetal and neonatal medicine. In Marcdante, K., Kliegman, R., Jenson, H., & Behrman, R. (Eds.) *Nelson essentials of pediatrics* (6th ed., pp. 213–264). Philadelphia, PA, USA: Saunders Elsevier.

Goyer, A. (2012). *AARP survey: Grandparents providing more care, money, and advice.* Retrieved July 17, 2013 from http://blog.aarp.org/2012/03/28/grandparent-roles-survey-amy-goyer/

Gozalo, P., & Miller, S. (2007). Hospice enrollment and evaluation of its causal effect on hospitalization of dying nursing home patients. *Health Services Research, 42*, 587–610.

Graber, J., Nichols, T., & Brooks-Gunn, J. (2010). Putting pubertal timing in developmental context: Implications for prevention. *Developmental Psychobiology, 52*, 254–262.

Grabowski, L., Call, K., & Mortimer, J. (2001). Global and economic self-efficacy in the educational attainment process. *Social Psychology Quarterly, 64*, 164–197.

Grady, D., Herrington, D., Bittner, V., Blumenthal, R., Davidson, M., Hlatky, M., Hsia, J., Hulley, S., Herd, A., Khan, S., Newby, K., Waters, D., Vittinghoff, E., & Wenger, N. (2002). Cardiovascular disease outcomes during 6.8 years of hormone therapy: Heart and estrogen/progestin replacement study follow-up (HERS II). *Journal of the American Medical Association, 288*, 49–57.

Graff, N., (2013). Abuse, child. In Ferri, F. (Ed.). *Ferri's clinical advisor 2013* (pp. 16–18). Philadelphia, PA, USA: Elsevier Mosby.

Graham, J., Cohen, R., Zbikowski, S., & Secrist, M. (1998). A longitudinal investigation of race and sex as factors in children's classroom friendship choices. *Child Study Journal, 28*, 245–266.

Graham, S., & Harris, K. (2007). Best practices in teaching planning. In S. Graham, C. MacArthur, & J. Fitzgerald (Eds.), *Best practices in writing instruction* (pp. 119–140). New York: Guilford Press.

Gralinski, J. H., & Kopp, C. B. (1993). Everyday rules for behavior: Mothers' requests to young children. *Developmental Psychology, 29*, 573–584.

Gralinski-Bakker, J., Hauser, S., Billings, R., Allen, J., Lyons, P., & Melton, G. (2005). Transitioning to adulthood for young adults with mental health issues. *Network on Transitions to Adulthood Policy Brief, 21*, 1–3.

Granek, L. (2010). Grief as pathology: The evolution of grief theory in psychology from Freud to the present. *History of Psychology, 13*, 46–73.

Granic, I., & Patterson, G. (2006). Toward a comprehensive model of antisocial development: A dynamic systems approach. *Psychological Review, 113*, 101–131.

Grant, S., & Langan-Fox, J. (2007). Personality and the occupational stressor-strain relationship: The role of the Big Five. *Journal of Occupational Health Psychology, 112*, 20–33.

Gray A., Berlin J.A., McKinlay J.B., Longcope C. An examination of research design effects on the association of testosterone and male aging results of a meta-analysis. *J Clinic Epidemiol. 44*(7):671–84, 1991

Green, R., Cupples, A., Go, R., Benke, K., Edeki, T., Griffith, P., Williams, M., Hipps, Y., Graff-Radford, N., Bachman, D., & Farrer, L. (2002). Risk of dementia among white and African American relatives of patients with Alzheimer's disease. *Journal of the American Medical Association, 287*, 329–336.

Green, S. (2001). Systemic vs. individualistic approaches to bullying. *Journal of the American Medical Association, 286*, 787.

Greenberg, M., Speltz, M., & DeKlyen, M. (1993). The role of attachment in the early development of disruptive behavior problems. *Development and Psychopathology, 5*, 191–213.

Greenberger, E., & Steinberg, L. (1986). *When teenagers work: The psychological and social costs of adolescent employment.* New York: Basic Books.

Greene, K., Krcmar, M., Rubin, D., Walters, L., & Hale, J. (2002). Elaboration in processing adolescent health messages: The impact of egocentrism and sensation seeking on message processing. *Journal of Communication, 52*, 812–831.

Greenfield, E., & Marks, N. (2007). Continuous participation in voluntary groups as a protective factor for the psychological well-being of adults who develop functional limitations: Evidence from the National Survey of Families and Households. *The Journals of Gerontology Series B: Psychological Sciences and Social Sciences, 62*, S60–S68.

Greenfield, P., Brannon, C., & Lohr, D. (1994). Two-dimensional representation of movement through three-dimensional space: The role of video game expertise. *Journal of Applied Developmental Psychology, 15*, 87–104.

Greenhaus, J., Collins, K., Singh, R., & Parasuraman, S. (1997). Work and family influences on departure from public accounting. *Journal of Vocational Behavior, 50*, 249–270.

Greenough, W., Black, J., & Wallace, C. (1987). Experience and brain development. *Child Development, 58*, 539–559.

Greer, S. (1991). Psychological response to cancer and survival. *Psychological Medicine, 21*, 43–49.

Greer, S. (1999). Mind-body research in psychooncology. *Advances in Mind-Body Medicine, 15*, 236–244.

Greer, S. (2008). CBT for emotional distress of people with cancer: Some personal observations. *Psycho-Oncology, 17*, 170–173.

Greer, S., Morris, T., & Pettingale, K. W. (1979). Psychological response to breast cancer: Effect on outcome. *Lancet*, 785–787.

Greider, L. (2000, March/April). How not to be a monster-in-law. *Modern Maturity, 43*(2), 56–59, 81.

Griffiths, M. (2003). Internet gambling: Issues, concerns, and recommendations. *CyberPsychology & Behavior, 6*, 557–568.

Groome, L., Mooney, D., Holland, S., Smith, L., Atterbury, J., & Dykman, R. (1999). Behavioral state affects heart rate response to low-intensity sound in human fetuses. *Early Human Development, 54*, 39–54.

Grossman, A., Daugelli, A., & Hershberger, S. (2000). Social support networks of lesbian, gay, and bisexual adults 60 years of age and older. *Journals of Gerontology, Series B: Psychological Sciences & Social Sciences, 55B*, P171–P179.

Grov, C., Bimbi, D., Nanin, J., & Pasrons, J. (2006). Race, ethnicity, gender, and generational factors associated with the coming-out process among gay, lesbian, and bisexual individuals. *Journal of Sex Research, 43*, 115–121.

Grundy, E., & Henretta, J. (2006). Between elderly parents and adult children: A new look at the intergenerational care provided by the "sandwich generation." *Ageing & Society, 26*, 707–722.

Grusec, J. (1992). Social learning theory and developmental psychology: The legacies of Robert Sears and Albert Bandura. *Developmental Psychology, 28*, 776–786.

Guilford, J. P. (1967). Creativity: Yesterday, today, and tomorrow. Guilford.

Guiney, H., & Machado, L. (2013). Benefits of regular aerobic exercise for executive functioning in healthy populations. *Psychonomic Bulletin & Review, 20*, 73–86.

Gunkel, M., Lusk, E., Wolff, B., & Li, F. (2007). Gender-specific effects at work: An empirical study of four countries. *Gender, Work & Organization, 14*, 56–79.

Gunnar, M., Kryzer, E., Van Ryzin, M., & Phillips, D. (2010). The rise in cortisol in family day care: Association with aspects of care quality, child behavior, and child sex. *Child Development, 81*, 851–869.

Gunter, T., Jackson, J., & Mulder, G. (1998). Priming and aging: An electrophysiological investigation of N400 and recall. *Brain & Language, 65*, 333–355.

Gur, R. C., Turetsky, B., Matsui, M., Yan, M., Bilker, W., Hughett, P., & Gur, R. E. (1999). Sex differences in brain gray and white matter in healthy young adults: Correlations with cognitive performance. *Journal of Neuroscience, 19*, 4065–4072.

Guralnik, J. M., & Kaplan, G. A. (1989). Predictors of healthy aging: Prospective evidence from the Alameda County Study. *American Journal of Public Health, 79*, 703–708.

Guralnik, J. M., & Paul-Brown, D. (1984). Communicative adjustments during behavior-request episodes among children at different developmental levels. *Child Development, 55*, 911–919.

Guralnik, J. M., Land, K. C., Blazer, D., Fillenbaum, G. G., & Branch, L. G. (1993). Educational status and active life expectancy among older blacks and whites. *New England Journal of Medicine, 329*, 110–116.

Gurňáková, J., & Kusá, D. (2004). Gender self-concept in personal theories of reality. *Studia Psychologica, 46*, 49–61.

Guse, L., & Masesar, M. (1999). Quality of life and successful aging in long-term care: Perceptions of residents. *Issues in Mental Health Nursing, 20*, 527–539.

Gustafson, S. B., & Magnusson, D. (1991). *Female life careers: A pattern approach.* Hillsdale, NJ: Erlbaum.

Gutman, L. (2006). How student and parent goal orientations and classroom goal structures influence the math achievement of African Americans during the high school transition. *Contemporary Educational Psychology, 31*, 44–63.

Guzzetti, B., & Williams, W. (1996). Gender, text, and discussion: Examining intellectual safety in the science classroom. *Journal of Research in Science Teaching, 33*, 5–20.

Guzzo, K. (2009). Marital intentions and the stability of first cohabitations. *Journal of Family Issues, 30*, 179–205.

Gzesh, S. M., & Surber, C. F. (1985). Visual perspective-taking skills in children. *Child Development, 56*, 1204–1213.

Haase, T., & Johnston, N. (2012). Making meaning out of loss: A story and study of young widowhood. *Journal of Creativity in Mental Health, 7*, 204–221.

Hagan, J., & Kay, F. (2007). Even lawyers get the blues: Gender, depression, and job satisfaction in legal practice. *Law & Society Review, 41*, 51–78.

Hagestad, G. O. (1986). Dimensions of time and the family. *American Behavioral Scientist, 29*, 679–694.

Hagestad, G. O. (1990). Social perspectives on the life course. In R. H. Binstock & L. K. George (Eds.), *Handbook of aging and the social sciences* (3rd ed., pp. 151–168). San Diego, CA: Academic Press.

Hahlweg, K., & Baucom, D. (2011). Relationships and embitterment. In M. Linden, M., & A. Maercker, A. (Eds.), *Embitterment: Societal, psychological, and clinical perspectives* (pp. 119–128). New York, NY, USA: Springer-Verlag Publishing.

Hahn, C., Yang, M-S., Yang, M-J., Shih, C., & Lo, H. (2004). Religious attendance and depressive symptoms among community dwelling elderly in Taiwan. *International Journal of Geriatric Psychiatry, 19*, 1148–1154.

Haier, R. (2007). Brains, bias, and biology: Follow the data. In S. Ceci & W. Williams (Eds.),*Why aren't more women in science: Top researchers debate the evidence* (pp. 113–119).

Hakansson, G., Salameh, E., & Nettelbladt, U. (2003). Measuring language development in bilingual children: Swedish-Arabic children with and without language impairment. *Linguistics, 41*, 255–288.

Halford, W., & Sweeper, S. (2013). Trajectories of adjustment to couple relationship separation. *Family Process, 52*, 228-243.

Halim, M., Ruble, D., & Tamis-LeMonda, C. (2013). Four-year-olds' beliefs about how others regard males and females. *British Journal of Developmental Psychology, 31*, 128–135.

Halle, T. (1999). Implicit theories of social interactions: Children's reasoning about the relative importance of gender and friendship in social partner choices. *Merrill-Palmer Quarterly, 45*, 445–467.

Hallerod, B., Orestig, J., & Stattin, M. (2013). Leaving the labour market: The impact of exit routes from employment to retirement on health and wellbeing in old age. *European Journal of Ageing, 10*, 25–35.

Hallfrisch, J., Muller, D., Drinkwater, D., Tobin, J., & Andres, R. (1990). Continuing diet trands in men: The Baltimore Longitudinal Study of Aging (1961-1987). *Journal of Gerontology, 45*, M186-191.

Halpern, C. T., Udry, J. R., Campbell, B., & Suchindran, C. (1993). Testosterone and pubertal development as predictors of sexual activity: A panel analysis of adolescent males. *Psychosomatic Medicine, 55*, 436–447.

Halpern, D., Benbow, C., Geary, D., Gur, R., Hyde, J., & Gernsbache, M. (2007). The science of sex differences in science and mathematics. *Psychological Science in the Public Interest, 8*, 1–51.

Hamberger, K., & Minsky, D. (2000, August). *Evaluation of domestic violence training programs for health care professionals.* Paper presented at the annual meeting of the American Psychological Association. Washington, DC.

Hamilton, C. E. (1995, March). *Continuity and discontinuity of attachment from infancy through adolescence.* Paper presented at the biennial meetings of the Society for Research in Child Development, Indianapolis, IN.

Hamm, J., Stewart, T., Perry, R., Clifton, R., Chipperfield, J., & Heckhausen, J. (2013). *Basic and Applied Social Psychology, 36*, 286–297.

Hammond, M., Landry, S., Swank, P., & Smith, K. (2000). Relation of mothers' affective development history and parenting behavior: Effects on infant medical risk. *American Journal of Orthopsychiatry, 70*, 95–103.

Hampson, S., & Goldberg, L. (2006). A first large cohort study of personality trait stability over the 40 years between elementary school and midlife. *Journal of Personality and Social Psychology, 91*, 763–779.

Hank, K. (2007). Proximity and contacts between older parents and their children: A European comparison. *Journal of Marriage and Family, 69*, 157–173.

Hanley, G., Janssen, P., & Greyson, D. (2010). Regional variation in the cesarean delivery and assisted vaginal delivery rates. *Obstetrics & Gynecology, 115,* 1201–1208.

Hanlon, T., Simon, B., O'Grady, K., Carswell, S., & Callaman, J. (2009). The effectiveness of an after-school program targeting urban African American youth. *Education and Urban Society, 42,* 96–118.

Hanna, E., & Meltzoff, A. N. (1993). Peer imitation by toddlers in laboratory, home, and day-care contexts: Implications for social learning and memory. *Developmental Psychology, 29,* 701–710.

Hannigan, J., O'Leary-Moore, S., & Berman, R. (2007). Postnatal environmental or experiential amelioration of neurobehavioral effects of perinatal alcohol exposure in rats. *Neuroscience & Biobehavioral Reviews, 31,* 202–211.

Harkness, S. (1998). Time for families. *Anthropology Newsletter, 39,* 1, 4.

Harkness, S., & Super, C. M. (1985). The cultural context of gender segregation in children's peer groups. *Child Development, 56,* 219–224.

Harlow, H., & Zimmerman, R. (1959). Affectional responses in the infant monkey. *Science, 130,* 421–432.

Harris, F., & Edwards, K. (2010). College men's experiences as men: Findings and implications from two grounded theory studies. *Journal of Student Affairs Research and Practice, 47,* 43–62.

Harris, P. L. (1989). *Children and emotion: The development of psychological understanding.* Oxford: Blackwell.

Harrison, A., Wilson, M., Pine, C., Chan, S., & Buriel, R. (1990). Family ecologies of ethnic minority children. *Child Development, 61,* 347–362.

Harrist, A., Zaia, A., Bates, J., Dodge, K., & Pettit, G. (1997). Subtypes of social withdrawal in early childhood: Sociometric status and social-cognitive differences across four years. *Child Development, 68,* 278–294.

Hart, B., & Risley, T. R. (1995). *Meaningful differences in the everyday experience of young American children.* Baltimore, MD: Brookes.

Hart, C., Olsen, S., Robinson, C., & Mandleco, B. (1997). The development of social and communicative competence in childhood: Review and a model of personal, familial, and extrafamilial processes. *Communication Yearbook, 20,* 305–373.

Harter, S. (1990). Causes, correlates, and the functional role of global self-worth: A life-span perspective. In R. Sternberg, R. & J. Kolligian, J. (Eds.), *Competence considered* (pp. 67–97). New Haven, CT, USA: Yale University Press.

Harter, S. (1990). Processes underlying adolescent self-concept formation. In R. Montemayor, G. R. Adams, & T. P. Gullotta (Eds.), *From childhood to adolescence: A transitional period?* (pp. 205–239). Newbury Park, CA: Sage.

Harter, S. (2006). Developmental and individual difference perspectives on self-esteem. In D. Mroczek & T. Little (Eds.), *Handbook of personality development* (pp. 311–334). Mahwah, NJ: Lawrence Erlbaum Associates Publishers.

Harter, S. (2012). *The construction of the self: Developmental and sociocultural foundations* (2nd ed.). New York, NY, USA: Guilford Press.

Harter, S. (2012). *The construction of the self: Developmental and sociocultural foundations* (2nd ed.). New York, NY, USA: Guilford Press.

Harton, H., & Latane, B. (1997). Social influence and adolescent lifestyle attitudes. *Journal of Research on Adolescence, 7,* 197–220.

Hartup, W. W. (1974). Aggression in childhood: Developmental perspectives. *American Psychologist, 29,* 336–341.

Hartup, W. W. (1996). The company they keep: Friendships and their developmental significance. *Child Development, 67,* 1–13.

Harvey, R., Fletcher, J., & French, D. (2001). Social reasoning: A source of influence on aggression. *Clinical Psychology Review, 21,* 447–469.

Harwood, D., Barker, W., Ownby, R., Bravo, M., Aguero, H., & Duara, R. (2000). Depressive symptoms in Alzheimer's disease: An examination among community-dwelling Cuban American patients. *American Journal of Geriatric Psychiatry, 8,* 84–91.

Harzer, C., & Ruch, W. (2013). The application of signature character strengths and positive experiences. *Journal of Happiness Studies, 14,* 965-983.

Hasin, D., Stinson, F., Ogburn, M., & Grant, B. (2007). Prevalence, correlates, disability, and comorbidity of *DSM-IV* alcohol abuse and dependence in the United States. *Archives of General Psychiatry, 64,* 830–842.

Hatakeyama, M., & Hatakeyama, H. (2012). Developmental study of empathy, moral judgment, and social information processing in preschoolers with relational aggression. *Japanese Journal of Developmental Psychology, 23,* 1–11.

Hatano, G. (1990). Toward the cultural psychology of mathematical cognition: Commentary. In H. Stevenson & S. Lee (Eds.), *Contexts of achievement. Monographs of the Society for Research in Child Development, 55* (12, Serial No. 221), 108–115.

Hatano, G. (2004). The Japanese conception of and research on intelligence. In R. Sternberg (Ed.) *The international handbook of intelligence* (pp. 302–324). New York: Cambridge University Press.

Hatchett, S. J., & Jackson, J. S. (1993). African American extended kin systems: An assessment. In H. P. McAdoo (Ed.), *Family ethnicity: Strength in diversity* (pp. 90–108). Newbury Park, CA: Sage.

Hawkins, H. L., Kramer, A. F., & Capaldi, D. (1992). Aging, exercise, and attention. *Psychology & Aging, 7,* 643–653.

Hawkley, L., & Cacioppo, J. (2004). Stress and the aging immune system. *Brain, Behavior, and Immunity, 18,* 114–119.

Hay, D., Payne, A., & Chadwick, A. (2004). Peer relations in childhood. *Journal of Child Psychology and Psychiatry, 45,* 84–108.

Hayflick, L. (1977). The cellular basis for biological aging. In C. E. Finch & L. Hayflick (Eds.), *Handbook of the biology of aging* (pp. 159–186). New York: Van Nostrand Reinhold.

Hayflick, L. (1987). Origins of longevity. In H. R. Warner, R. N. Butler, R. L. Sprott, & E. L. Schneider (Eds.), *Aging, Vol. 31. Modern biological theories of aging* (pp. 21–34). New York: Raven Press.

Hayflick, L. (1994). *How and why we age.* New York, NY: Ballantine Books.

Hayward, M. D., Friedman, S., & Chen, H. (1996). Race inequities in men's retirement. *Journals of Gerontology: Social Sciences, 51B,* S1–10.

Hazan, C., Hutt, M., Sturgeon, J., & Bricker, T. (1991, April). *The process of relinquishing parents as attachment figures.* Paper presented at the biennial meetings of the Society for Research in Child Development, Seattle, WA.

He, Y., Colantonio, A., & Marshall, V. (2003). Later-life career disruption and self-rated health: An analysis of General Social Survey data. *Canadian Journal on Aging, 22,* 45–57.

Heatherington, L., & Lavner, J. (2008). Coming to terms with coming out: Review and recommendations for family systems-focused research. *Family Psychology, 22,* 329–343.

Heckhausen, J., & Brim, O. (1997). Perceived problems for self and others: Self-protection by social downgrading throughout adulthood. *Psychology & Aging, 12,* 610–619.

Hegarty, P. (2007). From genius inverts to gendered intelligence: Lewis Terman and the power of the norm. *History of Psychology, 10,* 132–155.

Heidelise, A., Duffy, F., McAnulty, G., Rivkin, M., Vajapeyam, S., Mulkern, R., Warfield, S., Huppi, P., Butler, S., Conneman, N., Fischer, C., & Eichenwald, E. (2004). Early experience alters brain function and structure. *Pediatrics, 113,* 846–857.

Heinonen, K., Raikkonen, K., & Keltikangas-Jarvinen, L. (2003). Maternal perceptions and adolescent self-esteem: A six-year longitudinal study. *Adolescence, 38,* 669–687.

Helson, R., Mitchell, V., & Moane, G. (1984). Personality and patterns of adherence and nonadherence to the social clock. *Journal of Personality & Social Psychology, 46,* 1079–1096.

Henderson, H., Marshall, P., Fox, N., & Rubin, K. (2004). Psychophysiological and behavioral evidence for varying forms and functions of nonsocial behavior in preschoolers. *Child Development, 75,* 236–250.

Henderson, M., Wight, D., Raab, G., Abraham, C., Parkes, A., Scott, S., & Hart, G. (2007). Impact of a theoretically based sex education programme (SHARE) delivered by teachers on NHS registered conceptions and terminations: Final results of cluster randomised trial. *BMJ: British Medical Journal, 334,* 7585.

Hendricks, P., Ditre, J., Drobes, D., & Brandon, T. (2006). The early time course of smoking withdrawal effects. *Psychopharmacology, 187,* 385–396.

Hendrie, H. (2006). Lessons learned from international comparative crosscultural studies on dementia. *American Journal of Geriatric Psychiatry, 14,* 480–488.

Henry, B., Caspi, A., Moffitt, T., & Silva, P. (1996). Temperamental and familial predictors of violent and nonviolent criminal convictions: Age 3 to age 18. *Developmental Psychology, 32,* 614–623.

Henry, J., MacLeod, M., Phillips, L., & Crawford, J. (2004). A meta-analytic review of prospective memory and aging. *Psychology & Aging, 19,* 27–39.

Heppner, M., Fuller, B., & Multon, K. (1998). Adults in involuntary career transition: An analysis of the relationship between the psychological and career domains. *Journal of Career Assessment, 6,* 329–346.

Herbert, J., Gross, J., & Hayne, H. (2006). Age-related changes in deferred imitation between 6 and 9 months of age. *Infant Behavior & Development, 29,* 136–139.

Herbst, C., & Tekin, E. (2008). *Child care subsidies and child development.* Institute for the study of labor. Retrieved July 18, 2010 from http://papers.ssrn.com/sol3/papers.cfm?abstract_id=1305820.

Hercberg, S., Ezzedine, K., Guinot, C., Preziosi, P., Galan, P., Bertrais, S., Estaquio, C., Briancon, S., Favier, A., Latreille, J., & Malvy, D. (2007). Antioxidant supplementation increases the risk of skin cancers in women but not in men. *Journal of Nutrition, 137*, 2098–2105.

Hermes, S., & Keel, P. (2003). The influence of puberty and ethnicity on awareness and internalization of the thin ideal. *International Journal of Eating Disorders, 33*, 465–467.

Heron, M., & Tejada-Vera, B. (2009). Deaths: Leading causes for 2001. *National Vital Statistics Reports, 58*, 1–98,

Herrenkohl, E., Herrenkohl, R., Egolf, B., & Russo, M. (1998). The relationship between early maltreatment and teenage parenthood. *Journal of Adolescence, 21*, 291–303.

Herzog, A. R., House, J. S., & Morgan, J. N. (1991). Relation of work and retirement to health and well-being in older age. *Psychology & Aging, 6*, 202–211.

Hespos, S., & Baillargeon, R. (2008). Young infants' actions reveal their developing knowledge of support variables: Converging evidence for violation-of-expectation findings. *Cognition, 107*, 304–316.

Hess, E. H. (1972). "Imprinting" in a natural laboratory. *Scientific American, 227*, 24–31.

Hess, T., Bolstad, C., Woodburn, S., & Auman, C. (1999). Trait diagnosticity versus behavioral consistency as determinants of impression change in adulthood. *Psychology & Aging, 14*, 77–89.

Hester, R., Kinsella, G., & Ong, B. (2004). Effect of age on forward and backward span tasks. *Journal of the International Neuropsychological Society, 10*, 475–481.

Hetherington, E. M. (1991a). Presidential address: Families, lies, and videotapes. *Journal of Research on Adolescence, 1*, 323–348.

Hetherington, E. M. (1991b). The role of individual differences and family relationships in children's coping with divorce and remarriage. In P. A. Cowen & M. Hetherington (Eds.), *Family transitions* (pp. 165–194). Hillsdale, NJ: Erlbaum.

Hetherington, E. M., & Stanley-Hagan, M. M. (1995). Parenting in divorced and remarried families. In M. H. Bornstein (Ed.), *Handbook of parenting, Vol. 3: Status and social conditions of parenting* (pp. 233–254). Mahwah, NJ: Erlbaum.

Heun, R., & Bonsignore, M. (2004). No evidence for a genetic relationship between Alzheimer's disease and longevity. *Dementia & Geriatric Cognitive Disorders, 18*, 1–5.

Heyman, G. (2009). Children's reasoning about traits. In P. Bauer (Ed.). *Advances in child development, Volume 37* (pp. 105–144). San Diego, CA: Academic Press.

Hilgenkamp, K., & Livingston, M. (2002). Tomboys, masculine characteristics, and self-ratings of confidence in career success. *Psychological Reports, 90*, 743–749.

Hill, C. (1999). Fusion and conflict in lesbian relationships. *Feminism & Psychology, 9*, 179–185.

Hill, J., Brooks–Gunn, J., & Waldfogel, J. (2003). Sustained effects of high participation in an early intervention for low-birth-weight premature infants. *Developmental Psychology, 39*, 730–744.

Hill, R. D., Storandt, M., & Malley, M. (1993). The impact of long-term exercise training on psychological function in older adults. *Journals of Gerontology: Psychological Sciences, 48*, P12–17.

Hillebrand, J. (2000). New perspectives on the manipulation of opiate urges and the assessment of cognitive effort associated with opiate urges. *Addictive Behaviors, 25*, 139–143.

Hillen, T., Davies, S., Rudd, A., Kieselbach, T., & Wolfe, C. (2003). Self ratings of health predict functional outcome and recurrence free survival after stroke. *Journal of Epidemiology & Community Health, 57*, 960–966.

Hinde, R. A., Titmus, G., Easton, D., & Tamplin, A. (1985). Incidence of "friendship" and behavior toward strong associates versus nonassociates in preschoolers. *Child Development, 56*, 234–245.

Hinton, J. (1975). The influence of previous personality on reactions to having terminal cancer. *Omega, 6*, 95–111.

Hirsch, J. (2012). Virtual reality exposure therapy and hypnosis for flying phobia in a treatment-resistant patient: A case report. *American Journal of Clinical Hypnosis, 55*, 168–173.

Hirsschberger, G., Srivastava, S., March, P., Cowan, C., & Dowan, P. (2009). Attachment, marital satisfaction, and divorce during the first fifteen years of parenthood. *Personal Relationships, 16*, 401–420.

Hochmann, J., Endress, A., & Mehler, J. (2010). Word frequency as a cue for identifying function words in infancy. *Cognition, 115*, 444–457.

Hodges, E. V. E., Malone, M. J., & Perry, D. G. (1997). Individual risk and social risk as interacting determinants of victimization in the peer group. *Developmental Psychology, 33*, 1032–1039.

Hoff, E., Grote, S., Dettmer, S., Hohner, H., & Olos, L. (2005). Work-life balance: Professional and private life arrangement forms of women and men in highly qualified professions. *Zeitscrift für Arbeits und Organisationspsychologie, 49*, 196–207.

Hofferth, S., & Curtin, S. (2006). Parental leave statutes and maternal return to work after childbirth in the United States. *Work and Occupations, 33*, 73–105.

Hoffman, M. (1970). Conscience, personality, and socialization techniques. *Human Development, 13*, 90–126.

Hoffman, M. (1988). Moral development. In M. Bornstein & M. Lamb (Eds.), *Developmental psychology: An advanced textbook* (2nd ed., pp. 497–548). Hillsdale, NJ: Erlbaum.

Hoffman, M. L. (1982). Development of prosocial motivation: Empathy and guilt. In N. Eisenberg (Ed.), *The development of prosocial behavior* (pp. 281–314). New York: Academic Press.

Hogan, B. (2013). *Older voters oppose switch to chained CPI.* Retrieved July 21, 2013, from http://www.aarp.org/politics-society/government-elections/info-04-2013/older-voters-oppose-switch-to-chained-cpi.html.

Hogan, T. D., & Steinnes, D. N. (1994). Toward an understanding of elderly seasonal migration using origin-based household data. *Research on Aging, 16*, 463–475.

Holland, J. L. (1973). *Making vocational choices: A theory of careers.* Englewood Cliffs, NJ: Prentice-Hall.

Holland, J. L. (1992). *Making vocational choices: A theory of vocational personalities and work environments* (2nd ed.). Odessa, FL: Psychological Assessment Resources.

Hollander, J. (2004). "I Can Take Care of Myself": The impact of self-defense training on women's lives. *Violence Against Women, 10*, 205–235.

Holliday, J., Rothwell, H., & Moore, L. (2010). The relative importance of different measures of peer smoking on adolescent smoking behavior: Cross-sectional and longitudinal analyses of a large British cohort. *Journal of Adolescent Health, 47*, 58–66.

Hollon, S., Thas, M., & Markowitz, J. (2002). Treatment and prevention of depression. *Psychological Science in the Public Interest, 3*, 39–77.

Holmgren, S., Molander, B., & Nilsson, L. (2006). Intelligence and executive functioning in adult age: Effects of sibship size and birth order. *European Journal of Cognitive Psychology, 18*, 138–158.

Holstein, M., & Minkler, M. (2003). Self, society, and the "new gerontology." *Gerontologist, 43*, 787–796.

Hood, M., & Ellison, R. (2003). Television viewing and change in body fat from preschool to early adolescence: The Framingham Children's Study. *International Journal of Obesity & Related Metabolic Disorders, 27*, 827–833.

Horan, W., Pogge, D., Borgaro, S., & Stokes, J. (1997). Learning and memory in adolescent psychiatric inpatients with major depression: A normative study of the California Verbal Learning Test. *Archives of Clinical Neuropsychology, 12*, 575–584.

Horn, J. (1982). The theory of fluid and crystallized intelligence in relation to concepts of cognitive psychology and aging in adulthood. In Craik, F., & Trehub, S. (Eds.). *Aging and cognitive processes* (pp. 237–278). New York, NY: Plenum.

Horowitz, A., McLaughlin, J., & White, H. (1998). How the negative and positive aspects of partner relationships affect the mental health of young married people. *Journal of Health & Social Behavior, 39*, 124–136.

Horowitz, F. D. (1990). Developmental models of individual differences. In J. Colombo & J. Fagen (Eds.), *Individual differences in infancy: Reliability, stability, prediction* (pp. 3–18). Hillsdale, NJ: Erlbaum.

Horswill, M., Sullivan, K., Luri-Beck, J., & Smith, S. (2013). How realistic are older drivers' ratings of their driving ability? *Accident Analysis and Prevention, 50*, 130–137.

Horton-Ikard, R., & Weismer, S. (2007). A preliminary examination of vocabulary and word learning in African American toddlers from middle and low socioeconomic status homes. *American Journal of Speech-Language Pathology, 16*, 381–392.

Horvath, C., Lewis, I., & Watson, B. (2012). The beliefs which motivate young male and female drivers to speed: A comparison of low and high intenders. *Accident Analysis and Prevention, 45*, 334–341.

Hou, J., Chen, H., & Chen, X. (2005). The relationship of parent-children interaction in the free play session and copy-modeling session with the development of children's behavioral inhibition in Chinese families. *Psychological Science (China), 28*, 820–825.

Houck, G., & Lecuyer-Maus, E. (2004). Maternal limit setting during toddlerhood, delay of gratification and behavior problems at age five. *Infant Mental Health Journal, 25*, 28–46.

Houseknecht, S. K. (1987). Voluntary childlessness. In M. B. Sussman & S. K. Steinmetz (Eds.), *Handbook of marriage and the family* (pp. 369–395). New York: Plenum.

Housman, J., & Dorman, S. (2005). The Alameda County Study: A systematic, chronological review. *American Journal of Health Education, 36*, 302–308.

Houston, D., Al Otaiba, S., & Torgesen, J. (2006). Learning to read: Phonics and fluency. In D. Browder, & F. Spooner (Eds.), *Teaching language arts, math & science to students with significant cognitive disabilities* (pp. 93–123). Baltimore, MD: Paul H. Brookes Publishing.

Howes, C. (1983). Patterns of friendship. *Child Development, 54*, 1041–1053.

Howes, C., & Matheson, C. C. (1992). Sequences in the development of competent play with peers: Social and pretend play. *Developmental Psychology, 28*, 961–974.

Howes, C., Phillips, D., & Whitebook, M. (1992). Thresholds of quality: Implications for the social development of children in center-based child care. *Child Development, 63*, 449–460.

Hu, F., Li, T., Colditz, G., Willet, W., & Manson, J. (2003). Television watching and other sedentary behavior in relation to risk of obesity and type 2 diabetes mellitus in women. *Journal of the American Medical Association, 289*, 1785–1791.

Huang, X., Zhu, X., Zheng, J., Zhang, L., & Shiomi, K. (2012). Relationships among androgyny, self-esteem, and trait coping style of Chinese university students. *Social Behavior and Personality, 40*, 1005–1014.

Hubbard, J., Romano, L., McAuliffe, M., & Morrow, M. 2010). In M. Potegal, G. Stemmler, & C. Spielberger (Eds.), *International handbook of anger: Constituent and concomitant biological, psychological, and social processes* (pp. 231–239). New York: Springer Science & Business Media.

Hubel, D. H., & Weisel, T. N. (1963). Receptive fields of cells in striate cortex of very young, visually inexperienced kittens. *Journal of Neurophysiology, 26*, 994–1002.

Huber, C., Navarro, R., Wombie, M., & Mumme, F. (2010). Family resilience and midlife marital satisfaction. *The Family Journal, 18*, 136–145.

Hudziak, J., van Beijsterveldt, C., Bartels, M., Rietveld, M., Rettew, D., Derks, E., & Boomsma, D. (2003). Individual differences in aggression: Genetic analyses by age, gender, and informant in 3-, 7-, and 10-year-old Dutch twins. *Behavior Genetics, 33*, 575–589.

Huesmann, L., Dubow, E., & Yang, G. (2013). Why it is hard to believe that media violence causes aggression. iIn E. Dill, E. (Ed.), *The Oxford handbook of media psychology* (pp. 159–171). New York, NY, USA: Oxford University Press.

Hughes, S., & Hayman, L. (2007). Cardiovascular risk reduction: The fountain of youth. *Journal of Cardiovascular Nursing, 22*, 84–85.

Hulley, S., Furberg, C., Barrett-Connor, E., Cauley, J., Grady, D., Haskell, W., Knopp, R., Lowery, M., Satterfield, S., Schrott, H., Vittinghoff, E., & Hunninghake, D. (2002). Noncardiovascular disease outcomes during 6.8 years of hormone therapy: Heart and estrogen/progestin replacement study follow-up (HERS II). *Journal of the American Medical Association, 288*, 58–64.

Hummel, A., Shelton, K., Heron, J., Moore, L., & van den Bree, M. (2013). A systematic review of the relationships between family functioning, pubertal timing and adolescent substance use. *Addiction, 108*, 487–496.

Humphrey, N., Curran, A., Morris, E., Farrell, P., & Woods, K. (2007). Emotional intelligence and education: A critical review. *Educational Psychology, 27*, 235–254.

Hunter, D., Spiegelman, D., Adami, H., Beeson, L., van den Brandt, P., Folsom, A., Fraswer, G., Goldbohm, A., Graham, S., Howe, G., Kushi, L., Marshall, J., McDermott, A., Miller, A., Speizer, F., Wolk, A., Yuan, S., & Willett, W. (1996). Cohort studies of fat intake and the risk of breast cancer-a pooled analysis. *New England Journal of Medicine, 334*, 356–361.

Hurd, N., Stoddard, S., & Zimmerman, M. (2013). Neighborhoods, social support, and African American adolescents mental health outcomes: A multilevel path analysis. *Child Development, 84*, 858–874.

Huston, A., & Bentley, A. (2010). Development in societal context. *Annual Review of Psychology, 61*, 411–438.

Huth-Bocks, A., Levendosky, A., Bogat, G., & von Eye, A. (2004). The impact of maternal characteristics and contextual variables on infant-mother attachment. *Child Development, 75*, 480–496.

Huxhold, O., Fiori, K., & Windsor, T. (2013). The dynamic interplay of social network characteristics, subjective well-being, and health: The costs and benefits of socio-emotional selectivity. *Psychology and Aging, 28*, 3–16.

Idler, E., & Kasl, S. (1997a). Religion among disabled and nondisabled persons I: Cross-sectional patterns in health practices, social activities, and well-being. *Journals of Gerontology, Series B: Psychological Sciences & Social Sciences, 52B*, S294–S305.

Ierardi-Curto, L. (2013). *Lipid storage disorders*. Retrieved July 5, 2013, from http://emedicine.medscape.com/article/945966-overview#a0199.

Inhelder, B., & Piaget, J. (1958). *The growth of logical thinking from childhood to adolescence*. New York: Basic Books.

Insured Retirement Institute. (2013). *The great divide: Financial comparison of early and late Boomers' retirement preparedness*. Retrieved July 17, 2013, from https://avectra.myirionline.org/eweb/uploads/2013%20JUNE%20Research%20-%20Early%20v%20Late%20Boomers.pdf.

Irwin, M., & Pike, J. (1993). Bereavement, depressive symptoms, and immune function. In M. S. Stroebe, W. Stroebe, & R. O. Hansson (Eds.), *Handbook of bereavement: Theory, research, and intervention* (pp. 160–171). Cambridge, UK: Cambridge University Press.

Isabella, R. A. (1995). The origins of infant-mother attachment: Maternal behavior and infant development. *Annals of Child Development, 10*, 57–81.

Isaksson, K., Johansson, G., Bellaagh, K., & Sjöberg, A. (2004). Work values among the unemployed: Changes over time and some gender differences. *Scandinavian Journal of Psychology, 45*, 207–214.

Itier, R., & Taylor, M. (2004). Face inversion and contrast-reversal effects across development: In contrast to the expertise theory. *Developmental Science, 7*, 246–260.

Ivanova, K., Mills, M., & Veenstra, R. (2011). The initiation of dating in adolescence: The effect of parental divorce. The TRAILS study. *Journal of Research on Adolescence, 21*, 769–775.

Iversen, L., & Sabroe, S. (1988). Psychological well-being among unemployed and employed people after a company closedown: A longitudinal study. *Journal of Social Issues, 44*, 141–152.

Iverson, K., Dick, A., McLaughlin, K., Smith, B., Bell, M., Gerber, M., Cook, N., & Mitchell, K. (2013). Exposure to interpersonal violence and its associations with psychiatric morbidity in a U. S. national sample: A gender comparison. *Psychology of Violence, 3*, 273–287.

Iverson, T., Larsen, L., & Solem, P. (2009). A conceptual analysis of ageism. *Nordic Psychology, 61*, 4–22.

Ivy, G. O., MacLeod, C. M., Petit, T. L., & Marcus, E. J. (1992). A physiological framework for perceptual and cognitive changes in aging. In F. I. M. Craik & T. A. Salthouse (Eds.), *The handbook of aging and cognition* (pp. 273–314). Hillsdale, NJ: Erlbaum.

Iwashyna, T., & Christakis, N. (2003). Marriage, widowhood, and health-care use. *Social Science & Medicine, 57*, 2137–2147.

Izard, C. E., & Harris, P. (1995). Emotional development and developmental psychopathology. In D. Cicchetti & D. J. Cohen (Eds.), *Developmental psychopathology, Vol. 1: Theory and methods* (pp. 467–503). New York: Wiley.

Izard, C. E., Fantauzzo, C. A., Castle, J. M., Haynes, O. M., Rayias, M. F., & Putnam, P. H. (1995). The ontogeny and significance of infants' facial expressions in the first 9 months of life. *Developmental Psychology, 31*, 997–1013.

Jackson, L., & Bracken, B. (1998). Relationship between students' social status and global and domain-specific self-concepts. *Journal of School Psychology, 36*, 233–246.

Jacobs, J., Chin, C., & Bleeker, M. (2006). Enduring links: Parents' expectations and their young adult children's gender-typed occupational choices. *Educational Research and Evaluation, 12*, 395–407.

Jacobs-Kosmin, D. (2013). *Osteoporosis*. Retrieved July 17, 2013, from http://emedicine.medscape.com/article/264088-overview#aw2aab6b2.

Jadack, R. A., Hyde, J. S., Moore, C. F., & Keller, M. L. (1995). Moral reasoning about sexually transmitted diseases. *Child Development, 66*, 167–177.

Jaglal, S., Weller, I., Mamdani, M., Hawker, G., Kreder, H., Jaakkimainen, L., & Adachi, J. (2005). Population trends in BMD testing, treatment, and hip and wrist fracture rates: Are the hip fracture projections wrong? *Journal of Bone and Mineral Research, 20*, 898–905.

Jambon, M., & Smetana, J. (2014). Moral complexity in middle childhood: Children's evaluations of necessary harm. *Developmental Psychology 50*, 22–33.

James, S. A., Keenan, N. L., & Browning, S. (1992). Socioeconomic status, health behaviors, and health status among blacks. In K. W. Schaie, D. Blazer, & J. M. House (Eds.), *Aging, health behaviors, and health outcomes* (pp. 39–57). Hillsdale, NJ: Erlbaum.

Jang, Y., Borenstein, A., Chiriboga, D., & Mortimer, J. (2005). Depressive symptoms among African American and White older adults. *The Journals of Gerontology: Series B, 60*, 313–319.

Janosz, M., Le Blanc, M., Boulerice, B., & Tremblay, R. (2000). Predicting different types of school dropouts: A typological approach with two longitudinal samples. *Journal of Educational Psychology, 92*, 171–190.

Jansz, J., & Martens, L. (2005). Gaming at a LAN event: The social context of playing video games. *New Media & Society, 7,* 333–355.

Jaremka, L., Fagundes, C., Glaser, R., Bennett, J., Malarkey, W., & Kiecolt-Glaser, J. (2013). Loneliness predicts pain, depression, and fatigue: Understanding the role of immune dysregulation. *Psychoneuroendocrinology, 38,* 1310–1317.

Jarolmen, J. (1998). A comparison of the grief reaction of children and adults: Focusing on pet loss and bereavement. *Omega, 37,* 133–150.

Jasik, C., & Lustig, R. (2008). Adolescent obesity and puberty: The "perfect storm." *Annals of the New York Academy of Sciences, 1135,* 265–279.

Javo, C., Ronning, J., Heyerdahl, S., & Rudmin, F. (2004). Parenting correlates of child behavior problems in a multiethnic community sample of preschool children in northern Norway. *European Child & Adolescent Psychiatry, 13,* 8–18.

Jendrek, M. (1993). Grandparents who parent their grandchildren: Effects on lifestyle. *Journal of Marriage and the Family, 55,* 609–621.

Jenkins, J. & Buccioni, J. (2000). Children's understanding of marital conflict and the marital relationship. *Journal of Child Psychology & Psychiatry & Allied Disciplines, 41,* 161–168.

Jenkins, J. M., & Astington, J. W. (1996). Cognitive factors and family structure associated with theory of mind development in young children. *Developmental Psychology, 32,* 70–78.

Jenkins, L., Myerson, J., Hale, S., & Fry, A. (1999). Individual and developmental differences in working memory across the life span. *Psychonomic Bulletin & Review, 6,* 28–40.

Jensen, L., & Arnett, J. (2012). Going global: New pathways for adolescents and emerging adults in a changing world. *Journal of Social Issues, 68,* 473–492.

Jerrome, D. (1990). Intimate relationships. In J. Bond & P. Coleman (Eds.), *Aging in society* (pp. 181–208). London: Sage.

Jette, A. M. (1996). Disability trends and transitions. In R. H. Binstock & L. K. George (Eds.), *Handbook of aging and the social sciences* (4th ed., pp. 94–116). San Diego, CA: Academic Press.

Jewell, J. (2009). *Fragile X syndrome.* Retrieved June 27, 2010 from http://emedicine.medscape.com/article/943776-overview.

Jeynes, W. (2006). The impact of parental remarriage on children: A meta-analysis. *Marriage & Family Review, 40,* 75–102.

Jie, H., Qinmei, X., & Jueyu, W. (2007). Preschoolers' acceptance of peers with angry or sad disposition. *Psychological Science (China), 30,* 1229–1232.

Jin, Y., Jing, J., Morinaga, R., Miki, K., Su, X., & Chen, X. (2002). A comparative study of theory of mind in Chinese and Japanese children. *Chinese Mental Health Journal, 16,* 446–448.

Jirtle, R., & Weidman, J. (2007). Imprinted and more equal. *American Scientist, 95,* 143–149.

Joeng, J., Turner, S., & Lee, K. (2013). South Korean college students' Holland types and career compromise processes. *The Career Development Quarterly, 61,* 64–73.

Joensen, U., Skakkebaek, N, & Jørgensen, N. (2008). Is there a problem with male reproduction? *Nature Clinical Practice Endocrinology & Metabolism, 5,* 144–145.

John, O. P., Caspi, A., Robins, R. W., Moffitt, T. E., & Stouthamer-Loeber, M. (1994). The "little five": Exploring the nomological network of the five-factor model of personality in adolescent boys. *Child Development, 65,* 160–178.

Johnson, C. L., & Barer, B. M. (1990). Families and networks among older inner-city blacks. *The Gerontologist, 30,* 726–733.

Johnson, H., Nusbaum, B., Bejarano, A., & Rosen, T. (1999). An ecological approach to development in children with prenatal drug exposure. *American Journal of Orthopsychiatry, 69,* 448–456.

Johnson, J., Vogt, B., Kim, R., Cotman, C., & Head, E. (2004). Isolated executive impairment and associated frontal neuropathology. *Dementia & Geriatric Cognitive Disorders, 17,* 360–367.

Johnson, L., O'Malley, P., Bachman, J., & Schulenberg, J. (2013). *Monitoring the future: National results on drug use: 2012 overview: Key findings on adolescent drug use.* Retrieved July 13, 2013, from http://www.monitoringthefuture.org/pubs/monographis/mtf-overview2012.pdf.

Johnson, M. (2003). Development of human brain functions. *Biological Psychiatry, 54,* 1312–1316.

Johnson, M. (2011). Developmental neuroscience, psychophysiology, and genetics. In M. Bornstein & M. Lamb (Eds.), *Developmental science: An advanced textbook* (6th ed., pp. 201–240). New York: Psychology Press.

Johnson, T., & Dye, J. (2005). *Indicators of marriage and fertility in the United States from the American Community Survey: 2000 to 2003.* Retrieved July 5, 2007 from www.census.gov/population/www/socdemo/fertility/mar-fert-slides.html.

Johnston, A., Barnes, M., & Desrochers, A. (2008). Reading comprehension: Developmental processes, individual differences, and interventions. *Candian Psychology, 49,* 125–132.

Johnston, L. D., O'Malley, P. M., Bachman, J. G., & Schulenberg, J. E. (2010). *Monitoring the Future: National results on adolescent drug use: Overview of key findings, 2009* (NIH Publication No. 10-7583). Bethesda, MD: National Institute on Drug Abuse, 77 pp.

Johnston, L., O'Malley, P., Bachman, J., & Schulenberg, J. (2013). *Monitoring the future: National results on drug use: 2012 overview: Key findings on Adolescent Drug use.* Retrieved July 13, 2013 from

Jones, A., Dwyer, L., Bercovitz, A., & Strahan, G. (2009). *The National Nursing Home Survey: 2004 overview.* Retrieved September 1, 2010 from http://www.cdc.gov/nchs/data/series/sr_13/sr13_167.pdf.

Jones, B., & McAdams, D. (2013). Becoming generative: Socializing influences recalled in life stories in late midlife. *Journal of Adult Development, 20,* 158–172.

Jones, M., Bartrop, R., Forcier, L., & Penny, R. (2010). The long-term impact of bereavement upon spouse health: A 10-year follow-up. *Acta Neuropsychiatrica, 22,* 212–217.

Jordan, N. (2010). Early predictors of mathematics achievement and mathematics learning difficulties. In R. Tremblay, R. Barr, R. Peters, & M. Boivin (Eds.), *Encyclopedia on early childhood development* [online]. Retrieved August 11, 2010 from http://www.child-encyclopedia.com/documents/JordanANGxp.pdf.

Jorgensen, G. (2006). Kohlberg and Gilligan: Duet or duel? *Journal of Moral Education, 35,* 179–196.

Jose, O., & Alfons, V. (2007). Do demographics affect marital satisfaction? *Journal of Sex & Marital Therapy, 33,* 73–85.

Joseph, R. (2000). Fetal brain behavior and cognitive development. *Developmental Review, 20,* 81–98.

Joshi, M. S., & MacLean, M. (1994). Indian and English children's understanding of the distinction between real and apparent emotion. *Child Development, 65,* 1372–1384.

Jospe, N., (2011). Endocrinology. In Marcdante, K., Kliegman, R., Jenson, H., & Behrman, R. (Eds.) *Nelson essentials of pedatrics* 6th ed. (pp. 625–670). Philadelphia, PA, USA: Saunders Elsevier.

Journal of Creative Behavior, 1, 3–14.

Joy, S. (2012). *Postpartum depression.* Retrieved July 19, 2013, from http://reference.medscape.com/article/271662-overview#a1http://reference.medscape.com/article/271662-overview#a1.

Juan, E., Blascao, T., Font, A., Doval, E., Sanz, A., Maroto, P., & Pallares, C. (2003). Perception of control and survival in patients with advanced lung cancer referred for palliative treatment. *Ansiedad y Estres, 9,* 1–5.

Judd, F., Hickey, M., & Bryant, C. (2012). Depression and midlife: Are we over-pathologising the menopause? *Journal of Affective Disorders, 136,* 199–211.

Judge, T., Bono, J., & Locke, E. (2000). Personality and job satisfaction: The mediating role of job characteristics. *Journal of Applied Psychology, 85,* 237–249.

Judson, T., & Nishimori, T. (2005). Concepts and skills in high school calculus: An examination of a special case in Japan and the United States. *Journal for Research in Mathematics, 36,* 24–43.

Juffer, F., & Rosenboom, L., (1997). Infant mother attachment of internationally adopted children in the Netherlands. *International Journal of Behavioral Development, 20,* 93–107.

Juffer, F., van IJzendoorn, M., & Bakermans-Kranenburg, (2008). Supporting adoptive families with video-feedback intervention. In F. Juffer, M. Bakermans-Kranenburg, & M. van IJzendoorn (Eds.), *Promoting positive parenting: An attachment-based intervention* (pp. 139–153). New York: Taylor & Francis Group/Lawrence Erlbaum Associates.

Juffer, F., Van IJzendoorn, M., & Palacios, J. (2011). Children's recovery after adoption. *Journal for the Study of Education and Development, 34,* 3–18.

Jussim, L., & Eccles, J. (1992). Teacher expectations II: Construction and reflection of student achievement. *Journal of Personality & Social Psychology, 63,* 947–961.

Kaestner, R., Sasso, A., Callison, K., & Yarnoff, B. (2013). Youth employment and substance use. *Social Science Research, 42,* 169–185.

Kafetsios, K. (2007). Work-family conflict and its relationship with job satisfaction and psychological distress: The role of affect at work and gender. *Hellenic Journal of Psychology, 4,* 15–35.

Kagan, J. (2008). In defense of qualitative changes in development. *Child Development, 79,* 1606–1624.

Kagan, J., & Herschkowitz, N. (2005). *A young mind in a growing brain.* Hillsdale, NJ: Erlbaum.

Kagan, J., Snidman, N., & Arcus, D. (1993). On the temperamental categories of inhibited and uninhibited children. In K. H. Rubin & J. B. Asendorpf (Eds.), *Social withdrawal, inhibition, and shyness in childhood* (pp. 19–28). Hillsdale, NJ: Erlbaum.

Kahana-Kalman, R., & Walker-Andrews, A. (2001). The role of person familiarity in young infants' perception of emotional expressions. *Child Development, 72,* 352–369.

Kail, R. (1990). *The development of memory in children* (3rd ed.). New York: Freeman.

Kail, R. (1991). Processing time declines exponentially during childhood and adolescence. *Developmental Psychology, 27,* 259–266.

Kail, R. (1997). Processing time, imagery, and spatial memory. *Journal of Experimental Child Psychology, 64,* 67–78.

Kail, R. (2008). Speed of processing in childhood and adolescence: Nature, consequences, and implications for understanding atypical development. In J. DeLuca & J. Kalmar (Eds.), *Studies on neuropsychology, neurology, and cognition* (pp. 101–123). Philadelphia: Taylor & Francis.

Kail, R., & Hall, L. (1999). Sources of developmental change in children's word-problem performance. *Journal of Educational Psychology, 91,* 660–668.

Kail, R., & Hall, L. K. (1994). Processing speed, naming speed, and reading. *Developmental Psychology, 30,* 949–954.

Kales, H., Blow, F., Bingham, R., Copeland, L. & Mellow, A. (2000, June). Race and inpatient psychiatric diagnoses among elderly veterans. *Psychiatric Services Journal, 51,* 795–800.

Kales, H., Neighbors, H., Blow, F., Taylor, K., Gillon, L., Welsh, D., Maixner, S., & Mellow, A. (2005). Race, gender, and psychiatrists' diagnosis and treatment of major depression among elderly patients. *Psychiatric Services, 56,* 721–728.

Kalish, R. A. (1985). The social context of death and dying. In R. H. Binstock & E. Shanas (Eds.), *Handbook of aging and the social sciences* (2nd ed., pp. 149–170). New York: Van Nostrand Reinhold.

Kalish, R. A., & Reynolds, D. K. (1976). *Death and ethnicity: A psychocultural study.* Los Angeles: University of Southern California Press (reprinted 1981, Baywood Publishing Co, Farmingdale, NJ).

Kallman, D. A., Plato, C. C., & Tobin, J. D. (1990). The role of muscle loss in the age-related decline of grip strength: Cross-sectional and longitudinal perspectives. *Journals of Gerontology: Medical Sciences, 45,* M82–88.

Kalmijn, M. (2003). Shared friendship networks and the life course: An analysis of survey data on married and cohabiting couples. *Social Networks, 25,* 231–249.

Kalmuss, D. (2004). Nonviolational sex and sexual health. *Archives of Sexual Behavior, 33,* 197–209.

Kaltiala-Heino, R., Kosunen, E., & Rimpela, M. (2003). Pubertal timing, sexual behavior and self-reported depression in middle adolescence. *Journal of Adolescence, 26,* 531–545.

Kalyanasumdaram, A., & Shirani, J. (2010). *Acute coronary syndromes.* Retrieved August 27, 2010 from http://emedicine.medscape.com/article/164525-overview.

Kandler, C., Bleidorn, W., Riemann, R., Spinath, F., Thiel, W., & Angleitner, A. (2010). Source of cumulative continuity in personality: A longitudinal multiple-rater twin study. *Journal of Personality and Social Psychology, 98,* 995–1008.

Kane, C. (1998). Differences in family of origin perceptions among African American, Asian American and Hispanic American college students. *Journal of Black Studies, 29,* 93–105.

Kane, T., Staiger, P., & Ricciardelli, L. (2000). Male domestic violence: Attitudes, aggression and interpersonal dependency. *Journal of Interpersonal Violence, 15,* 16–29.

Kanemura, H., Aihara, M., Aoki, S., Araki, T., & Nakazawa, S. (2004). Development of the prefrontal lobe in infants and children: A three-dimensional magnetic resonance volumetric study. *Brain and Development, 25,* 195–199.

Kang, S., Basham, R., & Kim, Y. (2013). Contributing factors of depressive symptoms among elderly Korean immigrants in Texas. *Journal of Gerontological Social Work, 56,* 67–82.

Kann, L., Olsen, E., McManus, T., Kinchen, S., Chyen, D., Harris, W., & Wechsler, H. (2011). Sexual identity, sex of sexual contacts, and health-risk behaviors among students in grades 9–12: Youth risk behavior surveillance, Sselected Ssites, United States, 2001–2009. *Surveillance Summaries, 60,* 1–133.

Kannayiram, A. (2012). *Vascular dementia.* Retrieved July 16, 2013, from http://emedicine.medscape.com/article/292105-overview.

Kannel, W. B., & Gordon, T. (1980). Cardiovascular risk factors in the aged: The Framingham study. In S. G. Haynes & M. Feinleib (Eds.), *Second conference on the epidemiology of aging,* U.S. Department of Health and Human Services NIH Publication No. 80–969 (pp. 65–89). Washington, DC: U.S. Government Printing Office.

Kanto, L., Huttunen, K., & Laakso, M. (2013). Relationship between the linguistic environments and early bilingual language development of hearing children in deaf-parented families. *Journal of Deaf Studies and Deaf Education, 18,* 242–260.

Kaphingst, K., & Story, M. (2009). Child care as an untapped setting for obesity prevention: : State child care licensing regulations related to nutrition, physical activity, and media use for preschool-aged children in the United States. *Prevention of Chronic Diseases, 6,* 1–13.

Kaplan, G. (1992). Health and aging in the Alameda County study. In Schaie, K., Blazer, D., & House, J. (Eds.), *Aging, health behaviors, and health outcomes* (pp. 69–88). Hillsdale, NJ: Erlbaum.

Kaplan, H., & Sadock, B. (1991). *Synopsis of psychiatry* (6th ed.). Baltimore, MD: Williams & Wilkins.

Kaplowitz, P. (2010). *Precocious puberty.* Retrieved August 13, 2010 from http://emedicine.medscape.com/article/924002-overview.

Kaplowitz, P. (2013). *Precocious puberty.* Retrieved July 13, 2013, from http://emedicine.medscape.com/article/924002-overview#a0199.

Kaplowitz, P., & Oberfield, S. (1999). Reexamination of the age limit for defining when puberty is precocious in girls in the United States: Implications for evaluation and treatment. *Pediatrics, 104,* 936–941.

Karreman, A., de Haas, S., Van Tuijl, C., van Aken, M., & Dekovic, M. (2010). Relations among temperament, parenting, and problem behavior in young children. *Infant Behavior & Development, 33,* 39–49.

Kaslow, F. (2004). Death of one's partner: The anticipation and the reality. *Professional Psychology: Research & Practice, 35,* 227–233.

Katz, P., & Bartone, P. (1998). Mourning, ritual and recovery after an airline tragedy. *Omega, 36,* 193–200.

Kauffman, J. (2005). *Characteristics of emotional and behavioral disorders of children and youth.* Upper Saddle River, NJ: Prentice Hall.

Kaufman, A., Kosberg, J., Leeper, J., & Tang, M. (2010). Social support, caregiver burden, and life satisfaction in a sample of rural African American and White caregivers of older persons with dementia. *Journal of Gerontological Social Work, 53,* 251–269.

Kaufman, G., & Elder, G. (2003). Grandparenting and age identity. *Journal of Aging Studies, 17,* 269–282.

Kaur, K. (2012). *Hormone therapy.* Retrieved July 21, 2013, from http://emedicine.medscape.com/article/276104-overview#a1.

Kawabata, Y., Tseng, W., Murray-Close, D., & Crick, N. (2012). Developmental trajectories of Chinese children's relational and physical aggression: Associations with social-psychological adjustment problems. *Journal of Abnormal Child Psychology, 40,* 1087–1097.

Keefe, S. E. (1984). Real and ideal extended familism among Mexican Americans and Anglo Americans: On the meaning of "close" family ties. *Human Organization, 43,* 65–70.

Keen, R. (2003). Representation of objects and events: Why do infants look so smart and toddlers look so dumb? *Current Directions in Psychological Science, 12,* 79–83.

Keen, R., Berthier, N., Sylvia, M., Butler, S., Prunty, P., & Baker, R. (2008). Toddlers' use of cues in a search task. *Infant and Child Development, 17,* 249–267.

Keene, J., Hope, T., Rogers, P., & Elliman, N. (1998). An investigation of satiety in ageing, dementia, and hyperphagia. *International Journal of Eating Disorders, 23,* 409–418.

Keith, P. M. (1981/1982). Perception of time remaining and distance from death. *Omega, 12,* 307–318.

Keizer, R., & Schenk, N. (2012). Becoming a parent and relationship satisfaction: A longitudinal dyadic perspective. *Journal of Marriage and Family, 74,* 759–773.

Kellehear, A., & Lewin, T. (1988/1989). Farewells by the dying: A sociological study. *Omega, 19,* 275–292.

Kelleher, C. C., Friel, S., Gabhainn, S., & Tay, J. B. (2003). Socio-demographic predictors of self-rated health in the Republic of Ireland: findings from the National Survey on Lifestyle, Attitudes and Nutrition, SLAN. *Social Science & Medicine, 57,* 477–486.

Keller, M. (2012). Moral developmental science between changing paradigms. *International Journal of Developmental Science, 6,* 65–69.

Keller, S., Maddock, J., Laforge, R., Velicer, W., & Basler, H. (2007). Binge drinking and health behavior in medical students. *Addictive Behaviors, 32,* 505–515.

Kelley-Gillespie, N. (2012). A secondary analysis of perceptions of quality of life of older adults residing in a nursing home and assisted living setting using an integrated conceptual model of measurement. *Applied Research in Quality of Life, 7*, 137–154.

Kemmelmeier, M., Wieczorkowska, G., Erb, H., & Burnstein, E. (2002). Individualism, authoritarianism, and attitudes toward assisted death: Cross-cultural, cross-regional, and experimental evidence. *Journal of Applied Social Psychology, 32*, 60–85.

Kendall, P., & Comer, J. (2010). *Childhood disorders* (2nd ed.). New York: Psychology Press.

Kendall, P., & Comer, J. (2010). *Childhood disorders* (2nd ed.). New York, NY, USA: Psychology Press.

Kendler, K., Kessler, R., Walters, E., MacLean, C., Neale, M., Health, A., & Eaves, L. (1995). Stressful life events, genetic liability, and onset of an episode of major depression in women. *American Journal of Psychiatry, 152*, 833–842.

Kendler, K., Thornton, L., Gilman, S., & Kessler, R. (2000). Sexual orientation in a U.S. national sample of twin and nontwin sibling pairs. *American Journal of Psychiatry, 157*, 1843–1846.

Kensinger, E., Clarke, R., & Corkin, S. (2003). What neural correlates underlie successful encoding and retrieval? A functional magnetic resonance imaging study using a divided attention paradigm. *Journal of Neuroscience, 23*, 2407–2415.

Kent, L., Doerry, U., Hardy, E., Parmar, R., Gingell, K., Hawai, Z., Kirley, A., Lowe, N., Fitzgerald, M., Gill, M., & Craddock, N. (2002). Evidence that variation at the serotonin transporter gene influences susceptibility to attention deficit hyperactivity disorder (ADHD): Analysis and pooled analysis. *Molecular Psychiatry, 7*, 908–912.

Keown, L. (2012). Predictors of boys' ADHD symptoms from early to middle childhood: The role of father—child and mother—child interactions. *Journal of Abnormal Child Psychology, 40*, 569–581.

Kercsmar, C. (1998). The respiratory system. In R. Behrman & R. Kliegman (Eds.), *Nelson essentials of pediatrics* (3rd ed.). (pp. 459–500). Philadelphia: Saunders

Kerr, C., McDowell, B., & McDonough, S. (2007). The relationship between gross motor function and participation restriction in children with cerebral palsy: An exploratory analysis. *Child: Care, Health and Development, 33*, 22–27.

Kesselring, T., & Müller, U. (2011). The concept of egocentrism in the context of Piaget's theory. *New Ideas in Psychology, 29* 327–345.

Kessler, R., Berglund, P., Demler, O., Jin, R., Merikangas, K., & Walters, E. (2005). Lifetime prevalence and age-of-onset distributions of *DSM-IV* disorders in the national comorbidity survey replication. *Archives of General Psychiatry, 62*, 593–602.

Kessler, R., McGonagle, K., Zhao, S., Nelson, C., Hughes., M., Eshleman, S., Wittchen, H., & Kendler, K. (1994). Lifetime and 12-month prevalence of DSM-III-R psychiatric disorders in the United States: Results from the National Comorbidity Survey. *American Journal of Psychiatry, 51*, 8–19.

Khanna, G., & Kapoor, S. (2004). Secular trend in stature and age at menarche among Punjabi Aroras residing in New Delhi, India. *Collegium Antropologicum, 28*, 571–575.

Kiecolt-Glaser, J. (2000, August). *Friends, lovers, relaxation, and immunity: How behavior modifies health. Cortisol and the language of love: Text analysis of newlyweds' relationship stories.* Paper presented at the annual meeting of the American Psychological Association. Washington, DC.

Kiecolt-Glaser, J. K., & Glaser, R. (1995). Measurement of immune response. In S. Cohen, R. C. Kessler, & L. U. Gordon (Eds.), *Measuring stress: A guide for health and social scientists* (pp. 213–229). New York: Oxford University Press.

Kiel, E., & Buss, K. (2012). Associations among context-specific maternal protective behavior, toddlers' fearful temperament, and maternal accuracy and goals. *Social Development, 21*, 742–760.

Kilic, C., & Ulusoy, M. (2003). Psychological effects of the November 1999 earthquake in Turkey: An epidemiological study. *Psychiatrica Scandinavica, 108*, 232–238.

Killen, M., Mulvey, K., Richardson, C., Jampol, N., & Woodward, A. (2011). The accidental transgressor: Morally-relevant theory of mind. *Cognition, 119*, 197–215.

Kilpatrick, S. J., & Laros, R. K. (1989). Characteristics of normal labor. *Obstetrics & Gynecology, 74*, 85–87.

Kim, E., (2013). *Erectile dysfunction.* Retrieved July 17, 2013, from http://emedicine.medscape.com/article/444220-overview.

Kim, G., Walden, T., & Knieps, L. (2010). Impact and characteristics of positive and fearful emotional messages during infant social referencing. *Infant Behavior & Development, 33*, 189–195.

Kim, S. (1997). Relationships between young children's day care experience and their attachment relationships with parents and socioemotional behavior problems. *Korean Journal of Child Studies, 18*, 5–18.

Kim, S., Chen, Q., Wang, Y., Shen, Y., & Orozco-Lapray, D. (2013). Longitudinal linkages among parent—child acculturation discrepancy, parenting, parent—child sense of alienation, and adolescent adjustment in Chinese immigrant families. *Developmental Psychology, 49*, 900–912.

Kim, Y., Petscher, Y., Schatshneider, C., & Foorman, B. (2010). Does growth rate in oral reading fluency matter in predicting reading comprehension achievement? *Journal of Educational Psychology, 102*, 652–667.

Kim-Spoon, J., Cicchetti, D., & Rogosch, F. (2013). A longitudinal study of emotion regulation, emotion lability—negativity, and internalizing symptomatology in maltreated and nonmaltreated children. *Child Development, 84*, 512–527.

Kimura, M., Hjelmborg, J., Gardner, J., Bathum, L., Brimacombe, M., Lu, X., Christiansen, L., Vaupel, J., Aviv, A., & Christiansen, K. (2008). Telomere length and mortality: A study of leukocytes in elderly Danish twins. *American Journal of Epidemiology, 167*, 799–806.

King, P., & Kitchener, K. (2004). Reflective judgment: Theory and research on the development of epistemic assumptions through adulthood. *Educational Psychologist, 39*, 5-18.

Kingma, B., Frijns, A., Saris, W., van Steenhoven, A., & van Marken Lichtenbelt, W. (2010). Cold-induced vasoconstriction at forearm and hand skin sites: The effect of age. *European Journal of Applied Physiology, 109*, 915–921.

Kins, E., & Beyers, W. (2010). Failure to launch, failure to achieve criteria for adulthood? *Journal of Adolescent Research, 25*, 743–777.

Kirkcaldy, B.D., Siefen, G., Surall, D., & Bischoff, R.J. (2004) Predictors of drug and alcohol abuse among children and adolescents. *Personality and Individual Differences, 36*, 247-265.

Kitson, G. C. (1992). *Portrait of divorce: Adjustment to marital breakdown.* New York: Guilford Press.

Kitzan, L., Ferraro, F., Petros, T., & Ludorf, M. (1999). The role of vocabulary ability during visual word recognition in younger and older adults. *Journal of General Psychology, 126*, 6–16.

Kiuru, N., Aunola, K., Torppa, M., Lerkkanen, M., Poikkeus, A., Niemi, P., Viljaranta, J., Lyyra, A., Leskinen, E., Tolvanen, A., & Nurmi, J. (2012). The role of parenting styles and teacher interactional styles in children's reading and spelling development. *Journal of School Psychology, 50*, 799–823.

Kivlighan, K., DiPietro, J., Costigan, K., & Laudenslager, M. (2008). Diurnal rhythm of cortisol during late pregnancy: Associations with maternal psychological well-being and fetal growth. *Psychoneuroendocrinology, 33*, 1225–1235.

Klaczynski, P., Fauth, J., & Swanger, A. (1998). Adolescent identity: Rational vs. experiential processing, formal operations, and critical thinking beliefs. *Journal of Youth & Adolescence, 27*, 185–207.

Klar, A. (2003). Human handedness and scalp hair-whorl direction develop from a common genetic mechanism. *Genetics, 165*, 269–276.

Klaus, D. (2009). Why do adult children support their parents? *Journal of Comparative Family Studies. 40*, 227–241.

Kleemeier, R. W. (1962). Intellectual changes in the senium. *Proceedings of the Social Statistics Section of the American Statistics Association, 1*, 290–295.

Klein, R., Mannuzza, S., Olazagasti, M., Roizen, E., Hutchison, J., Lashua, E., & Castellanos, F. (2012). Clinical and functional outcome of childhood attention-deficit/hyperactivity disorder 33 years later. *JAMA Psychiatry, 69*, 1295–1303.

Kliegl, R., Smith, J., & Baltes, P. (1990). On the locus and process of magnification of age differences during mnemonic training. *Developmental Psychology, 26*, 894–904.

Kliegman, R. (1998). Fetal and neonatal medicine. In R. Behrman & R. Kliegman (Eds.), *Nelson essentials of pediatrics* (3rd ed., pp. 167–225). Philadelphia: Saunders.

Kliegman, R. (1998). Fetal and neonatal medicine. In R. Behrman & R. Kliegman (Eds.), *Nelson essentials of pediatrics* (3rd ed., pp. 167–225). Philadelphia:-Saunders.

Klimstra, T., Luyckx, K., Hale, W., Frijns, T., van Lier, P., & Meeus, W. (2010). Short-term fluctuations in identity: Introducing a micro-level approach to identity formation. *Journal of Personality and Social Psychology, 99*, 191–202.

Kline, D. W., & Scialfa, C. T. (1996). Visual and auditory aging. In J. E. Birren & K. W. Schaie (Eds.), *Handbook of the psychology of aging* (4th ed., pp. 181–203). San Diego, CA: Academic Press.

Kline, D. W., & Scialfa, C. T. (1996). Visual and auditory aging. In J. E. Birren & K. W. Schaie (Eds.), *Handbook of the psychology of aging* (4th ed., pp. 181–203). San Diego, CA: Academic Press.

Kline, D. W., Kline, T. J. B., Fozard, J. L., Kosnik, W., Schieber, F., & Sekuler, R. (1992). Vision, aging, and driving: The problem of older drivers. *Journals of Gerontology: Psychological Sciences, 47*, P27–34.

Kline, G., Stanley, S., Markman, H., & Olmos-Gallo, P. (2004). Timing is everything: Pre-engagement cohabitation and increased risk for poor marital outcomes. *Journal of Family Psychology, 18*, 311–318.

Klingberg, T., Fernell, E., Olesen, P., Johnson, M., Gustafsson, P., Dahlstrom, K., Gillberg, C., Forssberg, H., & Westerberg, H. (2005). Computerized training of working memory in children with ADHD: A randomized, controlled trial. *Journal of the American Academy of Child and Adolescent Psychiatry, 44*, 177–186.

Klomsten, A., Skaalvik, E., & Espnes, G. (2004). Physical self-concept and sports: Do gender differences still exist? *Sex Roles: A Journal of Research, 50*, 119–127.

Knickmeyer, R., & Baron-Cohen, S. (2006). Fetal testosterone and sex differences in typical social development and in autism. *Journal of Child Neurology, 21*, 825–845.

Kobak, R., Zajac, K., & Smith, C. (2009). Adolescent attachment and trajectories of hostile/impulsive behavior: Implications for the development of personality disorders. *Development and Psychopathology, 21*, 839–851.

Kochanska, G. (1997a). Multiple pathways to conscience for children with different temperaments: From toddlerhood to age 5. *Developmental Psychology, 33*, 228–240.

Kochanska, G. (1997b). Mutually responsive orientation between mothers and their young: Implications for early socialization. *Child Development, 68*, 94–112.

Kochanska, G., Murray, K., Jacques, T., Koenig, A., Vandegeest, K. (1996). Inhibitory control in young children and its role in emerging internalization. *Child Development, 67*, 490–507.

Koenen, K., Moffitt, T., Poulton, R., Martin, J., & Caspi, A. (2007). Early childhood factors associated with the development of post-traumatic stress disorder: Results from a longitudinal birth cohort. *Psychological Medicine, 37*, 181–192.

Koenig, A., Cicchetti, D., & Rogosch, F. (2004). Moral development: The association between maltreatment and young children's prosocial behaviors and moral transgressions. *Social Development, 13*, 97–106.

Koenig, H. (2007). Religion and depression in older medical inpatients. *American Journal of Geriatric Psychiatry, 15*, 282–291.

Koenig, H., George, L., Hays, J., Larson, D., Cohen, H., & Blazer, D. (1998). The relationship between religious activities and blood pressure in older adults. *International Journal of Psychiatry in Medicine, 28*, 189–213.

Kohlberg, L. (1966). A cognitive-developmental analysis of children's sex-role concepts and attitudes. In E. E. Maccoby (Ed.), *The development of sex differences* (pp. 82–172). Stanford, CA: Stanford University Press.

Kohlberg, L. (1976). Moral stages and moralization: The cognitive developmental approach. In T. Lickona (Ed.), *Moral development and behavior: Theory, research, and social issues* (pp. 31–53). New York: Holt.

Kohlberg, L. (1981). *Essays on moral development, Vol. 1: The philosophy of moral development.* New York: Harper & Row.

Kohlberg, L., & Elfenbein, D. (1975). The development of moral judgments concerning capital punishment. *American Journal of Orthopsychiatry, 54*, 614–640.

Kohlberg, L., & Kramer, R. (1969). Continuities and discontinuities in childhood and adult moral development. *Human Development, 12*, 3–120.

Kohlberg, L., & Ullian, D. Z. (1974). Stages in the development of psychosexual concepts and attitudes. In R. C. Friedman, R. M. Richart, & R. L. Vande Wiele (Eds.), *Sex differences in behavior* (pp. 209–222). New York: Wiley.

Kohlberg, L., Levine, C., & Hewer, A. (1983). *Moral stages: A current formulation and a response to critics.* Basel, Switzerland: S. Karger.

Kok, H., van Asselt, K., van der Schouw, Y., Peeters, & Wijmenga, C. (2005). Genetic studies to identify genes underlying menopausal age. *Human Reproduction Update, 11*, 483–493.

Kolb, B., Mychasiuk, R., Muhammad, A., Li, Y., Frost, D., & Gibb, R. (2012). Experience and the developing prefrontal cortex. *PNAS Proceedings of the National Academy of Sciences of the United States of America, 109*, 17186–17193.

Komur, M., Ozen, S., Okuyaz, C., Makharoblidze, K., & Erdogan, S. (2013). Neurodevelopment evaluation in children with congenital hypothyroidism by Bayley-III. *Brain & Development, 35*, 392–397.

Konold, T., & Canivez, G. (2010). Differential relationships between WISC-IV and WIAT-II scales: An evaluation of potentially moderating child demographics. *Educational and Psychological Measurement, 70*, 613–627.

Konstantareas, M. (2006). Social skill training in high functioning autism and Asperger's disorder. *Hellenic Journal of Psychology, 268*, 66–73.

Kopala-Sibley, D., Mongrain, M., & Zuroff, D. (2013). A lifespan perspective on dependency and self-criticism: Age-related differences from 18 to 59. *Journal of Adult Development, 20*, 126–141.

Koppenhaver, D., Hendrix, M., & Williams, A. (2007). Toward evidence-based literacy interventions for children with severe multiple disabilities. *Seminars in Speech and Language, 28*, 79–90.

Korobov, N., & Thorne, A. (2006). Intimacy and distancing: Young men's conversations about romantic relationships. *Journal of Adolescent Research, 21*, 27–55.

Korula, G., & Kamath, M. (2005). Fertility and age. *Journal of Human Reproductive Science, 3*, 121–123

Koskinen, P., Blum, I., Bisson, S., Phillips, S., et al. (2000). Book access, shared reading, and audio models: The effects of supporting the literacy learning of linguistically diverse students in school and at home. *Journal of Educational Psychology, 92*, 23–36.

Koskinen, P., Blum, I., Bisson, S., Phillips, S., et al. (2000). Book access, shared reading, and audio models: The effects of supporting the literacy learning of linguistically diverse students in school and at home. *Journal of Educational Psychology, 92*, 23–36.

Kost, K. (1997). The effects of support on the economic well-being of young fathers. *Families in Society, 78*, 370–382.

Koster, A., Bosma, H., Boese van Groenou, M., Kempen, G., Penninx, B., van Eijk, T., & Deeg, D. (2006). Explanations of socioeconomic differences in changes in physical function in older adults: Results from the Longitudinal Aging Study Amsterdam. *BMC Public Health, 6*, 244.

Kozma, A., Stones, M., & Hannah, T. (1991). Age, activity, and physical performance: An evaluation of performance models. *Psychology and Aging, 6*, 43–49.

Kramer, J., Mungas, D., Reed, B., Wetzel, M., Burnett, M., Miller, B., Weiner, M., & Chui, H. (2007). Longitudinal MRI and cognitive change in healthy elderly.

Krampe, R. (2002). Aging, expertise and fine motor movement. *Neuroscience & Biobehavioral Reviews, 26*, 769–776.

Krause, N., Ingersoll-Dayton, B., Liang, J., & Sugisawa, H. (1999). Religion, social support, and health among the Japanese elderly. *Journal of Health Behavior & Health Education, 40*, 405–421.

Krebs, D., & Denton, K. (2006). Explanatory limitations of cognitive-developmental approaches to morality. *Psychological Review, 113*, 672–675.

Krebs, N., & Primak, L. (2011). Pediatric nutrition and nutritional disorders. In K. Marcdante, R. Kliegman, H. Jensen, & R. Behrman (Eds.), *Nelson's essentials of pediatrics* (pp. 103–122). New York: Elsevier Health Publishers.

Kreider, R. (2008). Living arrangements of children: 2004. *Current Population Reports P70–114.* Washington, DC: U.S. Census Bureau.

Kristensen, P., & Bjerkedal, T. (2007). Explaining the relation between birth order and intelligence. *Science, 316*, 1717.

Kristenson, H., Österling, A., Nilsson, J., & Lindgärde, F. (2002). Alcoholism: Clinical and experimental research. *Alcoholism: Clinical and Experimental Research, 26*, 478–484.

Kroger, J., Martinussen, M., & Marcia, J. (2010). Identity status change during adolescence and young adulthood: A meta-analysis. *Journal of Adolescence, 33*, 683–698.

Kronenberg, F. (1994). Hot flashes: Phenomenology, quality of life, and search for treatment options. *Experimental Gerontology, 29*, 319–336.

Krueger-Lebus, S., & Rauchfleisch, U. (1999). Level of contentment in lesbian partnerships with and without children. *System Familie, 12*, 74–79.

Kubzansky, L., Cole, S., Kawachi, I., Vokonas, P., & Sparrow, D. (2006). Shared and unique contributions of anger, anxiety, and depression to coronary heart disease: A prospective study in the normative aging study. *Annals of Behavioral Medicine, 31*, 21–29.

Kuhn, D. (1992). Cognitive development. In M. H. Bornstein & M. E. Lamb (Eds.), *Developmental psychology: An advanced textbook* (3rd ed., pp. 211–272). Hillsdale, NJ: Erlbaum.

Kuhn, D., Kohlberg, L., Languer, J., & Haan, N. (1977). The development of formal operations in logical and moral judgment. *Genetic Psychology Monographs, 95*, 97–188.

Kumabe, C. (2006). Factors influencing contemporary Japanese attitudes regarding life and death. *Japanese Journal of Health Psychology, 19*, 20–24.

Kung, S., Rummans, T., Colligan, R., Clark, M., Sloan, J., Novotny, P., & Huntington, J. (2006). Association of optimism-pessimism with quality of life in patients with head and neck and thyroid cancers. *Mayo Clinic Proceedings, 81*, 1545–1552.

Kunkel, S. R., & Applebaum, R. A. (1992). Estimating the prevalence of long-term disability for an aging society. *Journals of Gerontology: Social Sciences, 47*, S253–260.

Kuntoro, I., Saraswati, L., Peterson, C., & Slaughter, V. (2013). Micro-cultural influences on theory of mind development: A comparative study of middle-class and pemulung children in Jakarta, Indonesia. *International Journal of Behavioral Development, 37*, 266–273.

Kurdek, L. (1997). Relation between neuroticism and dimensions of relationship commitment: evidence from gay, lesbian, and heterosexual couples. *Journal of Family Psychology, 11*, 109–124.

Kurdek, L. (2000). The link between sociotropy/autonomy and dimensions of relationship commitment: Evidence from gay and lesbian couples. *Personal Relationships, 7*, 153–164.

Kurdek, L. A. (2003). Differences between gay and lesbian cohabiting couples. *Journal of Social & Personal Relationships, 20*, 411–436.

Kurdek, L. A., & Fine, M. A. (1994). Family acceptance and family control as predictors of adjustment in young adolescents: Linear, curvilinear, or interactive effects? *Child Development, 65*, 1137–1146.

Kushi, L., & Giovannucci, E. (2002). Dietary fat and cancer. *American Journal of Medicine, 113*, 63S–70S.

Kuttler, A., LaGreca, A., & Prinstein, M. (1999). Friendship qualities and social-emotional functioning of adolescents with close, cross-sex friendships. *Journal of Research on Adolescence, 9*, 339–366.

Kyriacou, D., Anglin, D., Taliaferro, E., Stone, S., Tubb, T., Linden, J., Muelleman, R., Barton, E., & Kraus, J. (1999). Risk factors for injury to women from domestic violence. *New England Journal of Medicine, 341*, 1892–1898.

Kyser, K., Morriss, F., Bell, E., Klein, J., & Dagle, J. (2012). Improving survival of extremely preterm infants born between 22 and 25 weeks of gestation. *Obstetrics & Gynecology, 119*, 795–800.

la Cour, P., Avlund, K., & Schultz-Larsen, K. (2006). Religion and survival in a secular region. A twenty year follow-up of 734 Danish adults born in 1914. *Social Science & Medicine, 62*, 157–164.

Labouvie-Vief, G. (2006). Emerging structures of adult thought. In J. Arnett & J. Tanner (Eds.). *Emerging adults in America: Coming of age in the 21st century* (pp. 59–84). Washington, DC: American Psychological Association.

Lacey, J., Mink, P., Lubin, J., Sherman, M., Troisi, R., Hartge, P., Schatzkin, A., & Schairer, C. (2002). Menopausal hormone replacement therapy and risk of ovarian cancer. *Journal of the American Medical Association, 288*, 334–341.

Lachman, M. (2004). Development in midlife. *Annual Review of Psychology, 55*, 305–331.

Lachman, M., & Weaver, S. (1998). Sociodemographic variations in the sense of control by domain: Findings from the MacArthur studies of midlife. *Psychology & Aging, 13*, 553–562.

LaFontana, K., & Cillessen, A. (2010). Developmental changes in the priority of perceived status in childhood and adolescence. *Social Development, 19*, 130–147.

Laird, R., Marrero, M., Melching, J., & Kuhn, E. (2013). Brief report: Improving the validity of assessments of adolescents' feelings of privacy invasion. *Journal of Adolescence, 36*, 227–231.

Laird, R., Pettit, G., Dodge, K., & Bates, J. (1999). Best friendships, group relationships, and antisocial behavior in early adolescence. *Journal of Early Adolescence, 19*, 413–437.

Lakatos, K., Nemoda, Z., Birkas, E., Ronai, Z., Kovacs, E., Ney, K., Toth, I., Sasvari-Szekely, M., & Gervai, J. (2003). Association of D4 dopamine receptor gene and serotonin transporter promoter polymorphisms with infants' response to novelty. *Molecular Psychiatry, 8*, 90–97.

Lakatta, E. (1990). Heart and circulation. In Schneider, E., & Rose, J. (Eds.). *Handbook of the biology of aging* (3rd ed.). (pp. 181–216). San Diego, CA: Academic Press.

Lam, R., Pacala, J., & Smith, S. (1997). Factors related to depressive symptoms in an elderly Chinese American sample. *Gerontologist, 17*, 57–70.

Lamb, M. (1981). *The role of the father in child development* (2nd ed.). New York: Wiley.

Lamb, M. E., Sternberg, K. J., & Prodromidis, M. (1992). Nonmaternal care and the security of infant-mother attachment: A reanalysis of the data. *Infant Behavior & Development, 15*, 71–83.

Lamb, M., & Lewis, C. (2010). The development and significance of father-child relationships in two-parent families. In M. Lamb & C. Lewis (Eds.), *The role of the father in child development* (pp. 94–152). New York: John Wiley & Sons.

Lamb, M., & Lewis, C. (2011). The role of parent-child relationships in child development. In M. Bornstein & M. Lamb (Eds.), *Developmental science: An advanced textbook* (6th ed., pp. 469–518). New York: Psychology Press.

Lamborn, S. D., Mounts, N. S., Steinberg, L., & Dornbusch, S. M. (1991). Patterns of competence and adjustment among adolescents from authoritative, authoritarian, indulgent, and neglectful families. *Child Development, 62*, 1049–1065.

Landes, S., & Ardelt, M. (2011). The relationship between spirituality and death fear in aging adults. *Counselling and Spirituality, 30*, 87–111.

Landis, M., Peter-Wight, M., Martin, M., & Bodenmann, G. (2013). Dyadic coping and marital satisfaction of older spouses in long-term marriage. *GeroPsych: The Journal of Gerontopsychology and Geriatric Psychiatry, 26*, 39–47.

Landolt, M., & Dutton, D. (1997). Power and personality: An analysis of gay male intimate abuse. *Sex Roles, 37*, 335–359.

Landry, S. H., Garner, P. W., Swank, P. R., & Baldwin, C. D. (1996). Effects of maternal scaffolding during joint toy play with preterm and full-term infants. *Merrill-Palmer Quarterly, 42*, 177–199.

Langer, G., Arnedt, C., & Sussman, D. (2004). *Primetime Live poll: American sex survey analysis*. Retrieved June 22, 2007 from http://abcnews.go.com/Primetime/PollVault/story?id=156921&page=1

Langlois, J. H., Ritter, J. M., Roggman, L. A., & Vaughn, L. S. (1991). Facial diversity and infant preferences for attractive faces. *Developmental Psychology, 27*, 79–84.

Langlois, J. H., Roggman, L. A., & Rieser-Danner, L. A. (1990). Infants' differential social responses to attractive and unattractive faces. *Developmental Psychology, 26*, 153–159.

Lansford, J., Costanzo, P., Grimes, C., Putallaz, M., Miller, S., & Malone, P. (2009). Social network centrality and leadership status: Links with problem behaviors and tests of gender differences. *Merrill-Palmer Quarterly: Journal of Developmental Psychology, 55*, 1–25.

Lansford, J., Putallaz, M., Grimes, C., Schiro-Osman, K., Upersmidt, J., & Coie, J. (2006). Perceptions of friendship quality and observed behaviors with friends: How do sociometrically rejected, average, and popular girls differ? *Merrill-Palmer Quarterly: Journal of Developmental Psychology, 52*, 694–720.

Lapierre, M., Piotrowski, J., & Linebarger, D. (2012). Background television in the homes of U. S. children. *Pediatrics, 130*, 2011–2581.

Larson, L. (2012). Worklife across the lifespan. In E. Altmaier, E., & J. Hansen, J. (Eds.), *The Oxford handbook of counseling psychology*. Oxford library of-psychology (pp. 128–178). New York, NY, USA: Oxford University Press.

Larson, R. (2000). Toward a psychology of positive youth development. *American Psychologist, 55*, 170–183.

Larson, R., & Brown, J. (2007). Emotional development in adolescence: What can be learned from a high school theater program? *Child Development, 78*, 1083–1099.

Larson, R., & Verma, S. (1999). How children and adolescents spend time across the world: Work, play, and developmental opportunities. *Psychological Bulletin, 125*, 701–736.

Larson, R., Mannell, R., & Zuzanek, J. (1986). Daily well-being of older adults with friends and family. *Psychology & Aging, 1*, 117–126.

Lasley, M., & Heterington, K. (2011). Allergy. In K. Marcdante, R. Kliegman, H. Jensen, & R. Behrman (Eds.), *Nelson's essentials of pediatrics* (6th ed., pp. 309–354). New York: Elsevier Health Publishers.

Latimer, W. & Zur, J. (2010). Epidemiologic trends of adolescent use of alcohol, tobacco, and other drugs. *Child and Adolescent Psychiatric Clinics of North America, 19*, 451–464.

Laumann, E. O., Gagnon, J. H., Michael, R. T., & Michaels, S. (1994). *The social organization of sexuality: Sexual practices in the United States*. Chicago: University of Chicago Press.

Lauriello, J., McEvoy, J., Rodriguez, S., Bossie, C., & Lasser, R. (2005). Long-acting risperidone vs. placebo in the treatment of hospital inpatients with schizophrenia. *Schizophrenia Research, 72*, 249–258.

Laursen, B. (1995). Conflict and social interaction in adolescent relationships. *Journal of Research on Adolescence, 5*, 55–70.

Lawrence, R. H., Bennett, J. M., & Markides, K. S. (1992). Perceived intergenerational solidarity and psychological distress among older Mexican Americans. *Journals of Gerontology: Social Sciences, 47*, S55–65.

Lawrence, V., Houghton, S., Douglas, G., Durkin, K., Whiting, K., & Tannock, R. (2004). Children with ADHD: Neuropsychological testing and real-world activities. *Journal of Attention Disorders, 7*, 137–149.

Lawton, L., Silverstein, M., & Bengtson, V. (1994). Affection, social contact, and geographic distance between adult children and their parents. *Journal of Marriage & the Family, 56*, 57–68.

Layton, L., Deeny, K., Tall, G., & Upton, G. (1996). Researching and promoting phonological awareness in the nursery class. *Journal of Research in Reading, 19*, 1–13.

Leaper, C. (1991). Influence and involvement in children's discourse: Age, gender, and partner effects. *Child Development, 62*, 797–811.

Leatherman, S., & McCarthy, D. (2005). *Quality of health care for Medicare beneficiaries: A chartbook.* Retrieved August 31, 2010 from http://www.cmwf.org.

Lecovich, E., & Lankri, M. (2002). Title attitudes of elderly persons towards receiving financial support from adult children. *Journal of Aging Studies, 16*, 121–133.

Lederman, R., & Mian, T. (2003). The Parent-Adolescent Relationship Education (PARE) program: A curriculum for prevention of STDs and pregnancy in middle school youth. *Behavioral Medicine, 29*, 33–41.

Lee, I.-M., Hsieh, C., & Paffenbarger, R. S. (1995). Exercise intensity and longevity in men. *Journal of the American Medical Association, 273*, 1179–1184.

Lee, J., Manson, J., Hennekens, C., & Paffenbarger, R. (1993). Body weight and mortality: A 27 year follow-up of middle-aged men. *Journal of the American Medical Association, 20*, 2823–2828.

Lee, M., Law, C., & Tam, K. (1999). Parenthood and life satisfaction: A comparison of single and dual-parent families in Hong Kong. *International Social Work, 42*, 139–162.

Lee, S. & Keith, P. (1999). The transition to motherhood of Korean women. *Journal of Comparative Family Studies, 30*, 453–470.

Leemann, R. (2002). Transitions into research careers in Switzerland. *Education & Training, 44*, 185–198.

Legerstee, M., Pomerleau, A., Malcuit, G., & Feider, H. (1987). The development of infants' responses to people and a doll: Implications for research in communication. *Infant Behavior & Development, 10*, 81–95.

Lehman, D., & Nisbett, R. (1990). A longitudinal study of the effects of undergraduate training on reasoning. *Developmental Psychology, 26*, 952–960.

Leman, P., & Lam, V. (2008). The influence of race and gender on children's conversations and playmate choices. *Child Development, 79*, 1329–1343.

Lemery-Chalfant, K., Kao, K., Swann, G., & Goldsmith, H. (2013). Childhood temperament: Passive gene-environment correlation, gene-environment interaction, and the hidden importance of the family environment. *Development and Psychopathology, 25*, 51–63.

Lenhardt, A., & McCourt, B. (2000). Adolescent unresolved grief in response to the death of a mother. *Professional School Counseling, 3*, 189–196.

Leo, R., Narayan, D., Sherry, C., Michalek, C., et al. (1997). Geropsychiatric consultation for African-American and Caucasian patients. *General Hospital Psychiatry, 19*, 216–222.

Leong, F., Hartung, P., & Pearce, M. (2014). Work and career development: Theory and research. In F. Leong, F., L. Comas-Diaz, L., G. Nagayama Hall, G., V. McLloyd, V., & J. Trimble, J. (Eds.), *APA handbook of multicultural psychology, Volume 1: Theory and research* (pp. 451–469). Washington, DC, USA: American Psychological Association.

Lerner, R. (2008). The contributions of Paul B. Baltes to the transformation of the field of child development: From developmental psychology to developmental science. *Research in Human Development, 5*, 69–70).

Lerner, R., Lewin-Bizan, S., & Warren, A. (2011). Concepts and theories of human development. In M. Bornstein & M. Lamb (Eds.), *Developmental science: An advanced textbook* (6th ed., pp. 3–50). New York: Psychology Press.

Lester, D. (1990). The Collett-Lester fear of death scale: The original version and a revision. *Death Studies, 14*, 451–468.

Leung, Y., Grewal, K., Gravely-Witte, S., Suskin, N., Stewart, D., & Grace, S. (2011). Quality of life following participation in cardiac rehabilitation programs of longer or shorter than 6 months: Does duration matter? *Population Health Management, 14*, 181–188.

Levendosky, A., Bogat, G., Huth-Bocks, A., Rosenblum, K., & von Eye, A. (2011). The effects of domestic violence on the stability of attachment from infancy to preschool. *Journal of Clinical Child and Adolescent Psychology, 40*, 398–410.

Levine, D. (2011). Growth and development. In K. Marcdante, R. Kliegman, H. Jensen, & R. Behrman (Eds.), *Nelson's essentials of pediatrics* (6th ed., pp. 13–44). New York: Elsevier Health Publishers.

Levine, D. (2011). Growth and development. In Marcdante, K., Kliegman, R., Jenson, H., & Behrman, R. (Eds.) *Nelson essentials of pediatrics* 6th ed. (pp. 13–44). Philadelphia, PA, USA: Saunders Elsevier.

Levine, L., & Bluck, S. (1997). Experienced and remembered emotional intensity in older adults. *Psychology & Aging, 12*, 514–523.

Levinson, C., & Rodebaugh, T. (2013). Anxiety, self-discrepancy, and regulatory focus theory: Acculturation matters. *Anxiety, Stress, and Coping, 26*, 171–186.

Levinson, D. J. (1978). *The seasons of a man's life.* New York: Knopf.

Levinson, D. J. (1990). A theory of life structure development in adulthood. In C. N. Alexander & E. J. Langer (Eds.), *Higher stages of human development* (pp. 35–54). New York: Oxford University Press.

Levy, G. D., & Fivush, R. (1993). Scripts and gender: A new approach for examining gender-role development. *Developmental Review, 13*, 126–146.

Levy, L. H., Martinkowski, K. S., & Derby, J. F. (1994). Differences in patterns of adaptation in conjugal bereavement: Their sources and potential significance. *Omega, 29*, 71–87.

Levy, P., & Marion, R. (2011). Human genetics and dysmorphology. In Marcdante, K., Kliegman, R., Jenson, H., & Behrman, R. (Eds), *Nelson essentials of pediatrics* (6th ed., pp. 167–186). Philadelphia, PA, USA: Saunders Elsevier.

Lewis, C. C. (1981). How adolescents approach decisions: Changes over grades seven to twelve and policy implications. *Child Development, 52*, 538–544.

Lewis, C., & Lamb, M. E. Fathers' influences on children's development: The evidence from two-parent families. *European Journal of Psychology of Education, 18*, 211–228.

Lewis, D. (2011). Neurology. In K. K. Marcdante, R. Kliegman, H. Jensen, & R. Behrman (Eds.), *Nelson's essentials of pediatrics.* (6th ed., pp. 671–712). New York: Elsevier Health Publishers.

Lewis, D. (2011). Neurology. In Marcdante, K., Kliegman, R., Jenson, H., & Behrman, R. (Eds.), *Nelson essentials of pediatrics* (6th ed., pp. 671–712). Philadelphia, PA, USA: Saunders Elsevier.

Lewis, M. (1990). Social knowledge and social development. *Merrill-Palmer Quarterly, 36*, 93–116.

Lewis, M. (1991). Ways of knowing: Objective self-awareness of consciousness. *Developmental Review, 11*, 231–243.

Lewis, M. D. (1993). Early socioemotional predictors of cognitive competence at 4 years. *Developmental Psychology, 29*, 1036–1045.

Lewis, M., & Brooks, J. (1978). Self-knowledge and emotional development. In M. Lewis & L. A. Rosenblum (Eds.), *The development of affect* (pp. 205–226). New York: Plenum.

Lewis, M., & Carmody, D. (2008). Self-representation and brain development. *Developmental Psychology, 44*, 1329–1334.

Lewis, M., Allesandri, S. M., & Sullivan, M. W. (1992). Differences in shame and pride as a function of children's gender and task difficulty. *Child Development, 63*, 630–638.

Lewis, M., McBride, C., Pollak, K., Puleo, E., Butterfield, R., & Emmons, K. (2006). Understanding health behavior change among couples: An interdependence and communal coping approach. *Social Science & Medicine, 62*, 1369–1380.

Lewis, M., Sullivan, M. W., Stanger, C., & Weiss, M. (1989). Self development and self-conscious emotions. *Child Development, 60*, 146–156.

Li, S., Lindenberger, B., Aschersleben, G., Prinz, W., & Baltes, P. (2004). Transformations in the couplings among intellectual abilities and constituent cognitive processes across the life span. *Psychological Science, 15*, 155–163.

Li, Z., Connolly, J., Jiang, D., Pepler, D., & Craig, W. (2010). Adolescent romantic relationships in China and Canada: A cross-national comparison. *International Journal of Behavioral Development, 34*, 113–120.

Lichtenthal, W., Neimeyer, R., Currier, J., Roberts, K., & Jordan, N. (2013). Cause of death and the quest for meaning after the loss of a child. *Death Studies, 37*, 311–342.

Lickona, T. (1978). Moral development and moral education. In J. M. Gallagher & J. A. Easley (Eds.), *Knowledge and development* (Vol. 2, pp. 21–74). New York: Plenum.

Lickona, T. (1994). *Raising good children.* New York: Bantam Books.

Lieberman, M. A. (1965). Psychological correlates of impending death: Some preliminary observations. *Journal of Gerontology, 20*, 182–190.

Lieberman, M. A., & Coplan, A. S. (1970). Distance from death as a variable in the study of aging. *Developmental Psychology, 2*, 71–84.

Ligaray, K., & Isley, W. (2010). *Diabetes mellitus, Type 2.* Retrieved August 27, 2010 from http://emedicine.medscape.com/article/117853-overview.

Li-Grining, C. (2007). Effortful control among low-income preschoolers in three cities: Stability, change, and individual differences. *Developmental Psychology, 43*, 208–221.

Lillard, A. (2006). The socialization of theory of mind: Cultural and social class differences in behavior explanation. In A. Antonietti, O. Sempio-Liverta, & A Marchetti (Eds.), *Theory of mind and language in developmental contexts* (pp. 65–76). New York: Springer Science & Business Media.

Lillard, A. S., & Flavell, J. H. (1992). Young children's understanding of different mental states. *Developmental Psychology, 28*, 626–634.

Lillard, A., Lerner, M., Hopkins, E., Dore, R., Smith, E., & Palmquist, C. (2013). The impact of pretend play on children's development: A review of the evidence. *Psychological Bulletin, 139*, 1–34.

Lim, K., Zipursky, R., Watts, M., & Pfefferbaum, A. (1992). Decreased gray matter in normal aging: An in vivo magnetic resonance study. *Journal of Gerontology, 47*, B26-30.

Lincourt, A., Rybash, J., & Hoyer, W. (1998). Aging, working memory, and the development of instance-based retrieval. *Brain & Cognition, 37*, 100–102.

Lindahl, K., Clements, M., & Markman, H. (1997). Predicting marital and parent functioning in dyads and triads: A longitudinal investigation of marital processes. *Journal of Family Psychology, 11*, 139–151.

Lindau, S., Schumm, P., Laumann, E., Levinson, W., Muircheartaigh, C., & Waite, L. (2007). A study of sexuality and health among older adults n the United States. *New England Journal of Medicine, 357*, 762–774.

Lindgren, C., Connelly, C., & Gaspar, H. (1999). Grief in spouse and children caregivers of dementia patients. *Western Journal of Nursing Research, 21*, 521–537.

Lindsay, D. S., & Read, J. D. (1994). Psychotherapy and memory of childhood sexual abuse: A cognitive perspective. *Applied Cognitive Psychology, 8*, 281–338.

Lindsay, R. (1985). The aging skeleton. In Haug, M., Ford, A., & Sheafor, M. (Eds.). *The physical and mental health of aged women* (pp. 65–82). New York: Springer.

Lindstrom, T. (1997). Immunity and somatic health in bereavement. A prospective study of 39 Norwegian widows. *Omega, 35*, 231–241.

Lineweaver, T., & Hertzog, C. (1998). Adults' efficacy and control beliefs regarding memory and aging: Separating general from personal beliefs. *Aging, Neuropsychology, & Cognition, 5*, 264–296.

Linnenbrink, M. (2010). *Transition to the middle school building and academic achievement in Iowa.* Retrieved August 16, 2010 from http://intersect.iowa.gov/admin/ckfinder/userfiles/files/Intersect%20Middle%20Sch.pdf.

Liossis, P., Shochet, I., Millear, P., & Biggs, H. (2009). The Promoting Adult Resilience (PAR) program: The effectiveness of the second, shorter pilot of a workplace prevention program. *Behaviour Change, 26*, 97–112.

Lippa, R. (2005). *Gender, nature, and nurture.* Hillsdale, NJ: Lawrence Erlbaum Associates.

Lippé, R., Perchet, C., & Lassonde, M. (2007). Electrophysical markers of visocortical development. *Cerebral Cortex, 17*, 100–107.

Lips, H., & Hastings, S. (2012). Competing discourses for older women: Agency/leadership vs. disengagement/retirement. *Women & Therapy, 35*, 145–164.

Lissner, L., Bengtsson, C., Björkelund, C., & Wedel, H. (1996). Physical activity levels and changes in relation to longevity: A prospective study of Swedish women. *American Journal of Epidemiology, 143*, 54–62.

Liu, A., Wollstein, A., Hysi, P., Ankra-Badu, G., Spector, T., Park, D., Zhu, G., Larsson, M., Duffy, D., Montgomery, G., Mackey, D., Walsh, S., Lao, O., Hofman, A., Rivadeneira, F., Vingerling, J., Utterlinden, A., Martin, N., Hammond, C., & Kayser, M. (2010). Digital quantification of human eye color highlights: Genetic association of three new loci. *Public Library of Science: Genetics, 6*, e1000934.

Liu, J., & Richardson, P. (2012). Successful aging in older adults with disability. *OTJR: Occupation, Participation and Health, 32*, 126–134.

Liu, W., & Aaker, J. (2007). Do you look to the future or focus on today? The impact of life experience on intertemporal decisions. *Organizational Behavior and Human Decision Processes, 102*, 212–225.

Liubicich, M., Magistro, D., Candela, F., Rabaglietti, E., & Ciairano, S. (2012). Physical activity, fine manual dexterity and a coach's self-efficacy in a physical activity program for older persons living in residential care facilities. *Psychology, 3*, 384–392.

Livesley, W. J., & Bromley, D. B. (1973). *Person perception in childhood and adolescence.* London: Wiley.

Livingstone, S., & Helsper, E. (2006). Does advertising literacy mediate the effects of advertising on children? A critical examination of two linked research literatures in relation to obesity and food choice. *Journal of Communication, 56*, 560–584.

Lobel, T., Slone, M., & Winch, G. (1997). Masculinity, popularity, and self-esteem among Israeli preadolescent girls. *Sex Roles, 36*, 395–408.

LoBue, V., Coan, J., Thrasher, C., & DeLoache, J. (2011). Prefrontal asymmetry and parent-rated temperament in infants. *Public Library of Science ONE, 6*. e22694.

Locuniak, M, & Jordan, N. (2008). Using kindergarten number sense to predict calculation fluency in second grade. *Journal of Learning Disabilities, 41*, 459.

Loeb, S., Fuller, B., Kagan, S., & Carrol, B. (2004). Child care in poor communities: Early learning effects of type, quality, and stability. *Child Development, 75*, 47–65.

Loewy, J., Stewart, K., Dassler, A., Telsey, A., & Homel, P. (2013). The effects of music therapy on vital signs, feeding, and sleep in premature infants. *Pediatrics, 131*, 902–918.

Lofquist, D., Lugalla, T., O'Connell, M., & Feliz, S. (2012). *Households and families: 2010.* Retrieved July 19, 2013, from http://www.census.gov/prod/cen2010/briefs/c2010br-14.pdf.

Lohan, J., & Murphy, S. (2001/2002). Parents' perceptions of adolescent sibling grief responses after an adolescent or young adult child's sudden, violent death. *Omega, 44*, 195–213.

Longino, C. (2003). A first look at retirement migration trends in 2000. *The Gerontologist, 43*, 904–907.

Longino, C., Bradley, D., Stoller, E., & Haas, W. (2008). Predictors of non-local moves among older adults: A prospective study. *The Journals of Gerontology: Series B, 63*, S7–S14.

Lorant, V., Kunst, A., Huisman, M., Bopp, M., & Mackenbach, J. (2005). *Social Science & Medicine, 60*, 2431–2441.

Lorenz, K. (1935). The companion in the bird's world. The fellow-member of the species as releasing factor of social behavior. *Journal for Ornithology, 83*, 137–213.

Losh, M., Martin, G., Klusek, J., Hogan-Brown, A., & Sideris, J. (2012). Social communication and theory of mind in boys with autism and fragile X syndrome. *Frontiers in Psychology, 3*, 266.

Love, J., Harrison, L., Sagi-Schwartz, A., van IJzendoorn, M., Ross, C., Ungerer, J., Raikes, H., Brady-Smith, C., Boller, K., Brooks-Gunn, J., Constantine, J., Kisker, E., Paulsell, D., & Chazan-Cohen, R. (2003). Child care quality matters: How conclusions may vary with context. *Child Development, 74*, 1021–1033.

Low, C., Bower, J., Moskowitz, J., & Epel, E. (2011). In K. Sheldon, K., T. Kashdan, T., & M. Steger, M. (Eds.), *Designing positive psychology: Taking stock and moving forward* (pp. 41–50). New York, NY, USA: Oxford University Press.

Low, C., Bower, J., Moskowitz, J., & Epel, E. (2011). Positive psychological states and biological processes. In K. Sheldon, KT., Kashdan, T., & M. Steger, M. (Eds.), *Designing positive psychology: Taking stock and moving forward* (pp. 41–50). New York, NY, USA: Oxford University Press.

Lowenstein, D., Acevedo, A., Czaja, S., & Duara, R. (2004). Cognitive rehabilitation of mildly impaired Alzheimer disease patients on cholinesterase inhibitors. *American Journal of Geriatric Psychiatry, 12*, 395–402.

Lucas, J., & Heady, R. (2002). Flextime commuters and their driver stress, feelings, of time urgency, and commute satisfaction. *Journal of Business and Psychology, 16*, 565–572.

Luiselli, J., & Hurley, A. (2005). The significance of applied behavior analysis in the treatment of autism spectrum disorders (ASD). *Mental Health Aspects of Developmental Disabilities, 8*, 128–130.

Lumbiganon, P., Laopaiboon, M., Bulmezoglu, A., Souza, J., Taneepanichskul, S., Ruyan, P., Attygalle, D., Shrestha, N., Mori, R., Hinh, N., Bang, H., Rathavy, T., Chuyun, K., Cheang, K., Festin, M., Udomprasertgul, V., Germar, M., Yanqiu, G., Roy, M., Carroli, G., Ba-Thike, K., Filatova, E., & Villar, J. (2010). Method of delivery and pregnancy outcomes in Asia: The WHO global survey on maternal and perinatal health 2007–08. *The Lancet, 375*, 490–499.

Luthar, S. S., & Zigler, E. (1992). Intelligence and social competence among high-risk adolescents. *Development & Psychopathology, 4*, 287–299.

Lynn, R. (1998). New data on black infant precocity. *Personality and Individual Differences, 25*, 801–804.

Lynne-Landsman, S., Graber, J., & Andrews, J. (2010). Do trajectories of household risk in childhood moderate pubertal timing effects on substance initiation in middle school? *Developmental Psychology, 46*, 853–868.

Lyons, D., Parker, K., & Schatzberg, A. (2010). Animal models of early life stress: Implications for understanding resilience. *Developmental Psychobiology, 52*, 402–410.

Lytton, H., & Romney, D. M. (1991). Parents' differential socialization of boys and girls: A meta-analysis. *Psychological Bulletin, 109*, 267–296.

Ma, H. (2003). The relation of moral orientation and moral judgment to prosocial and antisocial behaviour of Chinese adolescents. *International Journal of Psychology, 38*, 101–111.

Ma, H. (2012). Internet addiction and antisocial internet behavior of adolescents. *International Journal of Child Health and Human Development, 5*, 123–130.

Ma, H., Shek, D., Cheung, P., & Oi Bun Lam, C. (2000). Parental, peer, and teacher influences on the social behavior of Hong Kong Chinese adolescents. *The Journal of Genetic Psychology: Research and Theory on Human Development, 161*, 65–78.

Maakaron, J. (2013). *Sickle cell anemia.* Retrieved July 5, 2013, from http://emedicine.medscape.com/article/205926-overview#a0156.

Maas, H. S., & Kuypers, J. A. (1974). *From thirty to seventy.* San Francisco: Jossey-Bass.

Macaluso, M., Wright-Schanpp, T., Chandra, A., Johnson, R., Satterwhite, C., Pulver, A., Berman, S., Wang, R., Farr, S., & Pollack, L. (2008). A public health focus on infertility prevention, detection, and management. *Fertility and Sterility, 93*, 16.e1–16.e10.

Maccoby, E. E. (1980). *Social development: Psychological growth and the parent-child relationship.* New York: Harcourt Brace Jovanovich.

Maccoby, E. E. (1988). Gender as a social category. *Developmental Psychology, 24*, 755–765.

Maccoby, E. E. (1990). Gender and relationships: A developmental account. *American Psychologist, 45*, 513–520.

Maccoby, E. E. (1995). The two sexes and their social systems. In P. Moen, G. H. Elder, Jr., & K. Lüscher (Eds.), *Examining lives in context: Perspectives on the ecology of human development* (pp. 347–364). Washington, DC: American Psychological Association.

Maccoby, E. E., & Jacklin, C. N. (1987). Gender segregation in childhood. In H. W. Reese (Ed.), *Advances in child development and behavior, Vol. 20* (pp. 239–288). Orlando, FL: Academic Press.

Maccoby, E. E., & Martin, J. A. (1983). Socialization in the context of the family: Parent-child interaction. In E. M. Hetherington (Ed.), *Handbook of child psychology: Socialization, personality, & social development, Vol. 4* (pp. 1–102). New York: Wiley.

Maccoby, E., & Lewis, C. (2003). Less day care or different day care? *Child Development, 74*, 1069–1075.

MacDorman, M., & Atkinson, J. (1999). Infant mortality statistics from the 1997 period linked birth/infant death data set. *National Vital Statistics Reports, 47*(23). Hyattsville, MD: National Center for Health Statistics.

MacDorman, M., Hoyert, D., & Mathews, M. (2013). Recent declines in infant mortality in the United States, 2005—2011. *NCHS Data Brief, 120*, 1–8.

Mackey, E., & La Greca, A. (2007). Adolescents' eating, exercise, and weight control behaviors: Does peer crowd affiliation play a role? *Journal of Pediatric Psychology, 32*, 13–23.

Mackintosh, N. (2007). Review of race differences in intelligence: An evolutionary hypothesis. *Intelligence, 35*, 94–96.

Macrae, C., & Bodenhausen, G. (2000). Social cognition: Thinking categorically about others. *Annual Review of Psychology, 51*, 93–120.

MacWhinney, B. (2011). Language development. In M. Bornstein & M. Lamb (Eds.), *Developmental science: An advanced textbook* (6th ed., 389–424). New York: Psychology Press.

Madan-Swain, A., Brown, R., Foster, M., Verga, R., et al. (2000). Identity in adolescent survivors of childhood cancer. *Journal of Pediatric Psychology, 25*, 105–115.

Madden, M. (2010). *Older adults and social media.* Retrieved September 1, 2010 from http://www.pewinternet.org/~/media//Files/Reports/2010/Pew%20Internet%20-%20Older%20Adults%20and%20Social%20Media.pdf.

Madigan, S., Atkinson, L., Laurin, K., & Benoit, D. (2013). Attachment and internalizing behavior in early childhood: A meta-analysis. *Developmental Psychology, 49*, 672–689.

Maeda, D. (2004). Societal filial piety has made traditional individual filial piety much less important in contemporary Japan. *Geriatrics & Gerontology International, 4*, S74–S76.

Mäenpää, E., & Jalovaara, M. (2013). The effects of homogamy in socio-economic background and education on the transition from cohabitation to marriage. *Acta Sociologica, 56*, 247–263.

Maglione, J., & Ancoli-Israel, S. (2012). Sleep disorders in the elderly. In C. Morin, C., & C. Espie, C. (Eds.), *The Oxford handbook of sleep and sleep disorders* (pp. 769–786). New York, NY, USA: Oxford University Press.

Mah, L., Arnold, M., & Grafman, J. (2005). Deficits in social knowledge following damage to ventromedial prefrontal cortex. *The Journal of Neuropsychiatry and Clinical Neurosciences, 17*, 66–74.

Main, M., & Hesse, E. (1990). Parents' unresolved traumatic experiences are related to infant disorganized attachment status: Is frightened and/or frightening parental behavior the linking mechanism? In M. T. Greenberg, D. Cicchetti, & E. M. Cummings (Eds.), *Attachment in the preschool years: Theory, research, and intervention* (pp. 161–182). Chicago: University of Chicago Press.

Main, M., & Solomon, J. (1990). Procedures for identifying infants as disorganized/disoriented during the Ainsworth Strange Situation. In M. T. Greenberg, D. Cicchetti, & E. M. Cummings (Eds.), *Attachment in the preschool years: Theory, research, and intervention* (pp. 121–160). Chicago: University of Chicago Press.

Mainemer, H., Gilman, L. C. and Ames, E. W. (1998) Parenting stress in families adopting children from Romanian orphanages. *Journal of Family Issues, 19*, 164–180.

Maitel, S., Dromi, E., Sagi, A., & Bornstein, M. (2000). The Hebrew Communicative Development Inventory: Language-specific properties and cross-linguistic generalizations. *Journal of Child Language, 27*, 43–67.

Majzoobi, M., Momeni, K., Amani, R., & Khah, M. (2013). The effectiveness of structured group reminiscence on the enhancement of the elderly's life quality and happiness. *Journal of Iranian Psychologists, 9*, 189–202.

Maki, P., Veijola, J., Rantakallio, P., Jokelainen, J., Jones, P., & Isohanni, M. (2004). Schizophrenia in the offspring of antenatally depressed mothers: A 31-year follow-up of the Northern Finland 1966 Birth Cohort. *Schizophrenia Research, 66*, 79–81.

Malabonga, V., & Pasnak, R. (2002). Hierarchical categorization by bilingual Latino children. Does a basic-level bias exist? *Genetic, Social, & General Psychology Monographs, 128*, 409–441.

Malarcher, A., Dube, S., Shaw, L., Babb, S., & Kaufmann, R. (2011). Quitting smoking among adults: United States, 2001—2010. *Morbidity and Mortality Weekly Report, 60*, 1513–1519.

Malchiodi, C. (2012). Creativity and aging: An art therapy perspective. In C. Malchiodi, C. (Ed.), *Handbook of art therapy* (2nd ed., pp. 275–287). New York, NY, USA: Guilford Press.

Malchiodi, C. (2012). Creativity and aging: An art therapy perspective. In C. Malchiodi, C. (Ed.), *Handbook of art therapy* (2nd ed., pp. 275–287). New York, NY, USA: Guilford Press.

Malkinson, R., & Bar-Tur, L. (1999). The aging of grief in Israel: A perspective of bereaved parents. *Death Studies, 23*, 413–431.

Mallet, P., Apostolidis, T., & Paty, B. (1997). The development of gender schemata about heterosexual and homosexual others during adolescence. *Journal of General Psychology, 124*, 91–104.

Malo, J., & Tremblay, R. (1997). The impact of parental alcoholism and maternal social position on boys' school adjustment, pubertal maturation and sexual behavior: A test of two competing hypotheses. *Journal of Child Psychology & Psychiatry & Allied Disciplines, 38*, 187–197.

Malone, J., Cohen, S., Liu, S., Vaillant, G., & Waldinger, R. (2013). Adaptive midlife defense mechanisms and late-life health. *Personality and Individual Differences, 55*, 85–89.

Maniecka-Bryla, I., Gajewska, O., Burzynska, M., & Bryla, M. (2013). Factors associated with self-rated health (SRH) of a University of the Third Age (U3A) class participants. *Archives of Gerontology and Geriatrics, 57*, 156–161.

Mann, S., Hazlett, E., Byne, W., Hof, P., Buchsbaum, M., Cohen, E., Goldstein, K., Haznedar, M., Mitsis, E., Siever, L., & Chu, K. (2011). Anterior and posterior cingulate cortex volume in healthy adults: Effects of aging and gender differences. *Brain Research, 1401*, 18–29.

Manson, J., Willett, W., Stampfer, M., Colditz, G., Hunter, D., Hankinson, S., Hennekens, C., & Speizer, F. (1995). Body weight and mortality among women. *New England Journal of Medicine, 333*, 677–685.

Manson, J., Willett, W., Stampfer, M., Colditz, G., Hunter, D., Hankinson, S., Hennekens, C., & Speizer, F. (1995). Body weight and mortality among women. *New England Journal of Medicine, 333*, 677–685.

Manzoli, L., Villari, P., Pironec, G., & Boccia, A. (2007). Marital status and mortality in the elderly: A systematic review and meta-analysis. *Social Science & Medicine, 64*, 77–94.

Mao, H. (2003). The relationship between voluntary employer changes and perceived job stress in Taiwan. *International Journal of Stress Management, 10*, 75–85.

Maratsos, M. (1998). The acquisition of grammar. In W. Damon (Ed.), *Handbook of child psychology, Vol. 2: Cognition, perception, and language* (5th ed., pp. 421–466). New York: Wiley.

Maratsos, M. (2000). More overregularizations after all: New data and discussion of Marcus, Pinker, Ullman, Hollander, Rosen, & Xu. *Journal of Child Language, 27*, 183–212.

March of Dimes. (2010). *Environmental risks and pregnancy.* Retrieved July 4, 2010 from http://www.marchofdimes.com/professionals/14332_9146.asp.

Marcia, J. (2010). Life transitions and stress in the context of psychosocial development. In T. Miller (Ed.), *Handbook of stressful transitions across the lifespan* (pp. 19–34). New York: Springer Science & Business Media.

Marcia, J. E. (1966). Development and validation of ego identity status. *Journal of Personality & Social Psychology, 3*, 551–558.

Marcia, J. E. (1980). Identity in adolescence. In J. Adelson (Ed.), *Handbook of adolescent psychology* (pp. 159–187). New York: Wiley.

Market Wire. (2003). *Research from Quality Planning Corporation shows elderly drivers involved in more accidents, fewer violations than younger drivers.* Retrieved July 31, 2007 from http://findarticles.com/p/articles/mi_pwwi/is_200309/ai_mark446110727.

Markey, C., Markey, P., & Tinsley, B. (2003). Personality, puberty, and preadolescent girls' risky behaviors: Examining the predictive value of the Five-Factor Model of personality. *Journal of Research in Personality, 37,* 405–419.

Markides, K. S., & Lee, D. J. (1991). Predictors of health status in middle-aged and older Mexican Americans. *Journals of Gerontology: Social Sciences, 46,* S243–249.

Marks, N., & Lamberg, J. (1998). Marital status continuity and change among young and midlife adults. *Journal of Family Issues, 19,* 652–686.

Marroun, H., Tiemeier, H., Steegers, E., Jaddoe, V., Hofman, A., Verhulst, F., & Huizink, B. (2009). Intrauterine cannabis exposure affects fetal growth trajectories: The Generation R study. *Journal of the American Academy of Child and Adolescent Psychiatry, 48,* 1173–1181.

Marsh, H., & Yeung, A. (1997). Coursework selection: Relations to academic self-concept and achievement. *American Educational Research Journal, 34,* 691–720.

Marsh, H., Craven, R., & Debus, R. (1999). Separation of competency and affect components of multiple dimensions of academic self-concept: A developmental perspective. *Merrill-Palmer Quarterly, 45,* 567–601.

Marshall, V. W. (1975). Age and awareness of finitude in developmental gerontology. *Omega, 6,* 113–129.

Marshall, V. W., & Levy, J. A. (1990). Aging and dying. In R. H. Binstock & L. K. George (Eds.), *Handbook of aging and the social sciences* (3rd ed., pp. 245–260). San Diego, CA: Academic Press.

Marshall, W. A. & Tanner, J. M. (1986). Puberty. In F. Falkner, J. M. Tanner (Eds.), *Human growth: A comprehensive treatise* (pp. 171–209). New York: Plenum Press.

Martin, C. L. (1991). The role of cognition in understanding gender effects. In H. W. Reese (Ed.), *Advances in child development and behavior, Vol. 23* (pp. 113–150). San Diego, CA: Academic Press.

Martin, C. L., & Little, J. K. (1990). The relation of gender understanding to children's sex-typed preferences and gender stereotypes. *Child Development, 61,* 1427–1439.

Martin, C. L., Wood, C. H., & Little, J. K. (1990). The development of gender stereotype components. *Child Development, 61,* 1891–1904.

Martin, C., & Ruble, D. (2002). Cognitive theories of early gender development. *Psychological Bulletin, 128,* 903–933.

Martin, C., & Ruble, D. (2004). Children's search for gender cues: Cognitive perspectives on gender development. *Current Directions in Psychological Science, 13,* 67–70.

Martin, C., & Ruble, D. (2010). Patterns of gender development. *Annual Review of Psychology, 61,* 353–381.

Martin, C., Kornienko, O., Schaefer, D., Hanish, L., Fabes, R., & Goble, P. (2013). The role of sex of peers and gender-typed activities in young children's peer affiliative networks: A longitudinal analysis of selection and influence. *Child Development, 84,* 921–937.

Martin, J., & D'Augelli, A. (2003). How lonely are gay and lesbian youth? *Psychological Reports, 93,* 486.

Martin, J., Hamilton, B., Sutton, P., Ventura, S., Mathews, T., Kirmeyer, S., & Osterman, M. (2010). Births: Final data for 2007. *National Vital Statistics Report, 58,* 1–125.

Martin, J., Hamilton, B., Sutton, P., Ventura, S., Menacker, F., Kirmeyer, S., & Mathews, T. (2009). Births: Final data for 2006. *National Vital Statistics Reports, 57,* 1–102.

Martin, J., Hamilton, B., Sutton, P., Ventura, S., Menacker, F., & Munson, M. (2005). Births: Final data for 2003. *National Vital Statistics Reports, 54,* 1–116.

Martin, J., Hamilton, B., VeEntura, S., Osterman, M., Wilson, E., & Mathews, T. (2012). Births: Final data for 2010. *National Vital Statistics Reports, 61,* 1–71.

Martin, J., Hamilton, B., Ventura, S., Osterman, M., Wilson, E., & Mathews, T. (2012). Births: Final data for 2010. *National Vital Statistics Reports, 61,* 1–71.

Martin, J., Hamilton, B., Ventura, S., Osterman, M., Wilson, E., & Mathews, T. (2012). Births: Final data for 2010. *National Vital Statistics Reports, 61,* 1–71.

Martin, J., Hamilton, B., Ventura, S., Osterman, M., Wilson, E., & Mathews, T. (2012). Births: Final data for 2010. *National Vital Statistics Reports, 61,* 1–71.

Martinez-Schallmoser, L., Telleen, S., & MacMullen, N. (2003). Effect of social support and acculturation on postpartum depression in Mexican American women. *Journal of Transcultural Nursing, 14,* 329–338.

Martorano, S. C. (1977). A developmental analysis of performance on Piaget's formal operations tasks. *Developmental Psychology, 13,* 666–672.

Maruyama, M., Arai, H., Ootsuki, M., Okamura, N., Matsui, T., Sasaki, H., Yamazaki, T., & Kaneta, T. (2003). Biomarkers in subjects with amnestic mild cognitive impairment. *Journal of the American Geriatrics Society, 51,* 1671–1672.

Marwick, H., Doolin, O., Allely, C., McConnachie, A., Johnson, P., Puckering, C., Golding, J., Gillberg, C., & Wilson, P. (2013). Predictors of diagnosis of child psychiatric disorder in adult—infant social-communicative interaction at 12 months. *Research in Developmental Disabilities, 34,* 562–572.

Mascolo, M. F., & Fischer, K. W. (1995). Developmental transformations in appraisals for pride, shame, and guilt. In J. P. Tangney & K. W. Fischer (Eds.), *Self-conscious emotions: The psychology of shame, guilt, embarrassment, and pride* (pp. 64–113). New York: Guilford Press.

Mason, B., Goodman, A., Chabac, S., & Lehert, P. (2006). Effect of oral acamprosate on abstinence in patients with alcohol dependence in a double-blind, placebo-controlled trial: The role of patient motivation. *Journal of Psychiatric Research, 40,* 383–393.

Mason, W., & Spoth, R. (2012). Sequence of alcohol involvement from early onset to young adult alcohol abuse: Differential predictors and moderation by family-focused preventive intervention. *Addiction, 107,* 2137–2148.

Mast, B., Azar, A., MacNeill, S., & Lichtenberg, P. (2004). Depression and activities of daily living predict rehospitalization within 6 months of discharge from geriatric rehabilitation. *Rehabilitation Psychology, 49,* 219–223.

Masten, A., & Coatsworth, D. (1998). The development of competence in favorable and unfavorable environments: Lessons from research on successful children. *American Psychologist, 53,* 205–220.

Maszk, P., Eisenberg, N., & Guthrie, I. (1999). Relations of children's social status to their emotionality and regulation: A short-term longitudinal study.

Mathew, A., & Cook, M. (1990). The control of reaching movements by young infants. *Child Development, 61,* 1238–1257.

Matorras, R., Matorras, F., Exposito, A., Martinez, L., & Crisol, L. (2010). Decline in human fertility rates with male age: A consequence of a decrease in male fecundity with aging? *Gynecology and Obstetrics Investigations, 71,* 229–235.

Mattis, J., & Grayman-Simpson, N. (2013). Faith and the sacred in African American life. In Pargament, K., Exline, H. J., & Jones, J. (Eds.) *APA handbook of psychology, religion, and spirituality (Vol. 1): Context, theory, and research* (pp. 547–564). Washington, DC: American Psychological Association.

Matz, A., Wells, J., Minor, K., & Angel, E. (2013). Predictors of turnover intention among staff in juvenile correctional facilities: The relevance of job satisfaction and organizational commitment. *Youth Violence and Juvenile Justice, 11,* 115–131.

Matzen, L., & Benjamin, A. (2013). Older and wiser: Older adults' episodic word memory benefits from sentence study contexts. *Psychology and Aging, 28,* 754–767.

Matzen, L., & Benjamin, A. (2013). Older and wiser: Older adults' episodic word memory benefits from sentence study contexts. *Psychology and Aging, 28,* 754–767.

Maughan, B., Pickles, A., & Quinton, D. (1995). Parental hostility, childhood behavior, and adult social functioning. In J. McCord (Ed.), *Coercion and punishment in long-term perspectives* (pp. 34–58). Cambridge, UK: Cambridge University Press.

Mauldin, J. (2005). *The new retirement model.* Retrieved July 7, 2007 from www.agewave.com/media_files/ota.htm.

Mayo Clinic. (2005). *Dietary fiber: An essential part of a healthy diet.* Retrieved July 4, 2007 from www.mayoclinic.com/health/fiber/NU00033.

Mayseless, O., & Scharf, M. (2007). Adolescents' attachment representations and their capacity for intimacy in close relationships. *Journal of Research on Adolescence, 17,* 23–50.

McAlister, A., & Peterson, C. (2006). Mental playmates: Siblings, executive functioning and theory of mind. *British Journal of Developmental Psychology, 24,* 733–751.

McBride-Chang, C., & Ho, C. (2000). Developmental issues in Chinese children's character acquisition. *Journal of Educational Psychology, 92,* 50–55.

McCall, B., Cavanaugh, M., Arvey, R., & Taubman, P. (1997). Genetic influences on job and occupational switching. *Journal of Vocational Behavior, 50,* 60–77.

McCall, R. B. (1993). Developmental functions for general mental performance. In D. K. Detterman (Ed.), *Current topics in human intelligence, Vol. 3: Individual differences and cognition* (pp. 3–30). Norwood, NJ: Ablex.

McChristian, C., Ray, G., Tidwell, P., & LoBello, S. *(2012). The Journal of Genetic Psychology: Research and Theory on Human Development, 173,* 463–469.

McCrae, R., & Costa, P. (2013). Introduction to the empirical and theoretical status of the five-factor model of personality traits. In T. Widiger, T., & P. Costa, P. (Eds.), *Personality disorders and the five-factor model of personality* (3rd ed.), (pp. 15–27). Washington, CD, USADC: American Psychological Association.

McCrae, R., Costa, P., Ostendord, F., & Angleitner, A. (2000). Nature over nurture: Temperament, personality, and life span development. *Journal of Personality & Social Psychology, 78*, 173–186.

McCrae. R. R., & Costa, P. T. Jr. (1990). Personality in adulthood. New York:

McCune, L. (1995). A normative study of representational play at the transition to language. *Developmental Psychology, 31*, 198–206.

McDonald, L. (2004, April 28). China may grow old before it gets rich. *Sydney Morning Herald.* Retrieved September 10, 2004, from http://www.smh.com.au/articles/2004/04/27/1082831569621.html?from=storyrhs&oneclick=true.

McElwain, A., Korabik, K., & Rosin, H. (2005). An examination of gender differences in work-family conflict. *Canadian Journal of Behavioural Science, 37*, 283–298.

McFalls, J. A., Jr. (1990). The risks of reproductive impairment in the later years of childbearing. *Annual Review of Sociology, 16*, 491–519.

McGrath, M., & Sullivan, M. (2002). Birth weight, neonatal morbidities, and school age outcomes in full-term and preterm infants. *Issues in Comprehensive Pediatric Nursing, 25*, 231–254.

McGregor, K., Sheng., L., & Smith, B. (2005). The precocious two-year-old: Status of the lexicon and links to the grammar. *Journal of Child Language, 32*, 563–585.

McHale, S., Crouter, A., & Tucker, C. (1999). Family context and gender role socialization in middle childhood: Comparing girls to boys and sisters to brothers. *Child Development, 70*, 990–1004.

McHugh, M. (2005). Understanding gender and intimate partner abuse. *Sex Roles: A Journal of Research, 52*, 717–724.

McIntosh, B. R., & Danigelis, N. L. (1995). Race, gender, and the relevance of productive activity for elders' affect. *Journals of Gerontology: Social Sciences, 50B*, S229–239.

McLanahan, S., & Sandefur, G. (1994). *Growing up with a single parent: What hurts, what helps.* Cambridge, MA: Harvard University Press.

McLoyd, V. C. (1998). Socioeconomic disadvantage and child development. *American Psychologist, 53*, 185–204.

McNeal, C., & Amato, P. (1998). Parents' marital violence: Long-term consequences for children. *Journal of Family Issues, 19*, 123–139.

McPherson, J. (2010). *Coronary artery disease: Atherosclerosis.* Retrieved August 27, 2010

Mediascope Press. (1999). *Substance use in popular movies and music: Issue Brief Series.* Studio City, CA: Mediascope Inc.

Meece, D., & Mize, J. (2010). Multiple aspects of preschool children's social cognition: Relations with peer acceptance and peer interaction style. *Early Child Development and Care, 180*, 585–604.

Meerkerk, G., van den Eijnden, R., Franken, I., & Garretsen, H. (2010). Is compulsive internet use related to sensitivity to reward and punishment, and impulsivity? *Computers in Human Behavior, 26*, 729–735.

Mehta, M., Goodyer, I., & Sahakian, B. (2004). Methylphenidate improves working memory and set-shifting in AD/HD: Relationships to baseline memory capacity. *Journal of Child Psychology and Psychiatry, 45*, 293–305.

Mehta, P., & Beer, J. (2010). Neural mechanisms of the testosterone-aggression relation: The role of orbitofrontal cortex. *Journal of Cognitive Neuroscience, 22*, 2357–2368.

Mehta, P., & Strough, J. (2009). Sex segregation in friendships and normative contexts across the life span. *Developmental Review, 29*, 201–220.

Meisenhelder, J., & Chandler, E. (2000). Faith, prayer, and health outcomes in elderly Native Americans. *Clinical Nursing Research, 9*, 191–203.

Melby, J. N., & Conger, R. D. (1996). Parental behaviors and adolescent academic performance: A longitudinal analysis. *Journal of Research on Adolescence, 6*, 113–137.

Melby-Lervåg, M., Lyster, S., & Hulme, C. (2012). Phonological skills and their role in learning to read: A meta-analytic review. *Psychological Bulletin, 138*, 322–352.

Melnick, M., Miller, K., Sabo, D., Barnes, G., & Farrell, M. (2010). Athletic participation and seatbelt omission among U.S. high school students. *Health Education & Behavior, 37*, 23–36.

Melnick, M., Miller, K., Sabo, D., Barnes, G., & Farrell, M. (2010). Athletic participation and seatbelt omission among U.S. high school students. *Health Education & Behavior, 37*, 23–36.

Melot, A., & Houde, O. (1998). Categorization and theories of mind: The case of the appearance/reality distinction. *Cahiers de Psychologie Cognitive/Current Psychology of Cognition, 17*, 71–93.

Meltzoff, A. N. (1988). Infant imitation and memory: Nine-month-olds in immediate and deferred tasks. *Child Development, 59*, 217–225.

Meltzoff, A. N. (1995). Understanding the intentions of others: Re-enactment of intended acts by 18-month-old children. *Developmental Psychology, 31*, 838–850.

Meltzoff, A. N., & Moore, M. K. (1977). Imitation of facial and manual gestures by human neonates. *Science, 198*, 75–78.

Menaghan, E. G., & Lieberman, M. A. (1986). Changes in depression following divorce: A panel study. *Journal of Marriage & the Family, 48*, 319–328.

Menesses, K., & Gresham, F. (2009). Relative efficacy of reciprocal and nonreciprocal peer tutoring for students at-risk for academic failure. *School Psychology Quarterly, 24*, 266–275.

Menna, L., Fontanella, M., Santaniello, A., Ammendola, E., Travaglino, M., Mugnai, F., DiMaggio, A., & Fioretti, A. (2012). Evaluation of social relationships in elderly by animal-assisted activity. *International Psychogeriatrics, 24*, 1019–1020.

Merikangas, K. R., & Angst, J. (1995). The challenge of depressive disorders in adolescence. In M. Rutter (Ed.), *Psychosocial disturbances in young people: Challenges for prevention* (pp. 131–165). Cambridge, UK: Cambridge University Press.

Merrill, D. (2007). *Mothers-in-law and daughters-in-law: Understanding the relationship and what makes them friends or foe.* Westport, CT: Praeger Publishers.

Merrill, D. (2011). *When your children marry: How marriage changes relationships with sons and daughters.* New York, NY: Rowan & Littlefield Publishers, Inc.

Merson, M. (2006). The HIV/AIDS pandemic at 25: The global response. *New England Journal of Medicine, 354*, 2414–2417.

Merz, E., & McCall, R. (2010). Behavior problems in children adopted from psychosocially depriving institutions. *Journal of Abnormal Child Psychology, 38*, 459–470.

Meyer, J. (2012). *Centenarians.* Retrieved July 16, 2013, from http://www.census.gov/prod/cen2010/reports/c2010sr-03.pdf.

Meyer-Bahlburg, H. F. L., Ehrhardt, A. A., Rosen, L. R., Gruen, R. S., Veridiano, N. P., Vann, F. H., & Neuwalder, H. F. (1995). Prenatal estrogens and the development of homosexual orientation. *Developmental Psychology, 31*, 12–21.

Michael, R. T., Gagnon, J. H., Laumann, E. O., & Kolata, G. (1994). *Sex in America.* Boston: Little, Brown.

Miech, R., & Shanahan, M. (2000). Socioeconomic status and depression over the life course. *Journal of Health & Social Behavior, 41*, 162–176.

Mikulincer, M., & Shaver, P. (2011). Attachment, anger, and aggression. In P. Shaver & M. Mikulincer (Eds.), *Human aggression and violence: Causes, manifestations, and consequences* (pp. 241–257). Washington, DC: American Psychological Association.

Milkie, M., Bierman, A., & Schieman, S. (2008). How adult children influence older parents' mental health: Integrating stress-process and life-course perspectives. *Social Psychology Quarterly, 71*, 86–105.

Miller, B. C., & Moore, K. A. (1990). Adolescent sexual behavior, pregnancy, and parenting: Research through the 1980s. *Journal of Marriage & the Family, 52*, 1025–1044.

Miller, B., Benson, B., & Galbraith, K. (2001). Family relationships and adolescent pregnancy risk: A research synthesis. *Developmental Review, 21*, 1–38.

Miller, P., Wang, S., Sandel, T., & Cho, G. (2002). Self-esteem as folk theory: A comparison of European American and Taiwanese mothers' beliefs. *Science & Practice, 2*, 209–239.

Miller, R. (1990). Aging and immune function. *International Review of Cytology, 124*, 187–216.

Miller, T. Q., Turner, C. W., Tindale, R. S., Posavac, E. J., & Dugoni, B. L. (1991). Reasons for the trend toward null findings in research on Type A behavior. *Psychological Bulletin, 110*, 469–495.

Mills, D., Coffey-Corina, S., & Neville, H. (1994). Variability in cerebral organization during primary language acquisition. In G. Dawson & K. Fischer (Eds.) *Human behavior and the developing brain.* New York: Guilford Press.

Minkler, M., & Fadem, P. (2012). Successful aging: A disability perspective. In I. Marini, I., & M. Stebnicki, M., (Eds.), *The psychological and social impact of illness and disability* (6th ed., pp. 395–404). New York, NY, USA: Springer Publishing Co.

Minkler, M., Fuller-Thomson, E., & Guralnik, J. (2006). *New England Journal of Medicine, 355*, 695–703.

Minnes, S., Lang, A., & Singer, L. (2011). Prenatal tobacco, marijuana, stimulant, and opiate exposure: Outcomes and practice implications. *Addiction Science and Clinical Practice, 6*, 57–70.

Minzi, M. (2010). Gender and cultural patterns of mothers' and fathers' attachment and links with children's self-competence, depression and loneliness in middle and late childhood. *Early Child Development and Care, 180*, 193–209.

Mischel, W. (1966). A social learning view of sex differences in behavior. In E. E. Maccoby (Ed.), *The development of sex differences* (pp. 56–81). Stanford, CA: Stanford University Press.

Mischel, W. (1970). Sex typing and socialization. In P. H. Mussen (Ed.), *Carmichael's manual of child psychology, Vol. 2* (pp. 3–72). New York: Wiley.

Mitchell, P. R., & Kent, R. D. (1990). Phonetic variation in multisyllable babbling. *Journal of Child Language, 17*, 247–265.

Mohan, J. (2006). Cardiac psychology. *Journal of the Indian Academy of Applied Psychology, 32*, 214–220.

Mohanty, A. & Perregaux, C. (1997). Language acquisition and bilingualism. In J. Berry, P. Dasen, & T. Saraswath (Eds.), *Handbook of cross-cultural psychology, Vol. 2*. Boston: Allyn & Bacon.

Mohsin, M., Wong, F., Bauman, A., & Bai, J. (2003). Maternal and neonatal factors influencing premature birth and low birth weight in Australia. *Journal of Biosocial Science, 35*, 161–174.

Moksnes, U., Moljord, I., Espnes, G., & Byrne, D. (2010). The association between stress and emotional states in adolescents: The role of gender and self-esteem. *Personality and Individual Differences, 49*, 430–435.

Moldzio, R., Radad, K., Krewenka, C., Kranner, B., Duvigneau, J., & Rausch, W. (2013). Protective effects of resveratrol on glutamate-induced damages in murine brain cultures. *Journal of Neural Transmission, 120*, 1271–1280.

Monarch, E., Saykin, A., & Flashman, L. (2004). Neuropsychological impairment in borderline personality disorder. *Psychiatric Clinics of North America, 27*, 67–82.

Monroy, T. (2000, March 15). Boomers alter economics. *Interactive Week.* Retrieved March 21, 2000, from http://www.ZDNet.com.

Montemayor, R., & Eisen, M. (1977). The development of self-conceptions from childhood to adolescence. *Developmental Psychology, 13*, 314–319.

Montero, I., & De Dios, M. (2006). Vygotsky was right: An experimental approach to the relationship between private speech and task performance. *Estudios de Psicológáia, 27*, 175–189.

Montgomery, M., & Sorell, G. (1998). Love and dating experience in early and middle adolescence: Grade and gender comparisons. *Journal of Adolescence, 21*, 677–689.

Moon, J., Kondo, N., Glymour, M., & Subramanian, S. (2011). Widowhood and mortality: A meta-analysis. *Public Library of Science Online, 6*, e23465.

Mooney, L., Knox, D., & Schacht, C. (2000a). *Social problems.* Belmont, CA: Wadsworth.

Mooney, L., Knox, D., & Schacht, C. (2000b). *Understanding social problems* (2nd ed.). Thousand Oaks, CA: Wadsworth.

Moore, C. (2007). Maternal behavior, infant development, and the question of developmental resources. *Developmental Psychobiology, 49*, 45–53.

Moore, C., Barresi, J., & Thompson, C. (1998). The cognitive basis of future-oriented prosocial behavior. *Social Development, 7*, 198–218.

Moore, J., & Moore, C. (2010). Talking to children about death-related issues. In C. Corr & D. Balk (Eds.), *Children's encounters with death, bereavement, and coping* (pp. 277–291). New York: Springer Publishing.

Moore, K. L. (1998). *The developing human: Clinically oriented embryology* (6th ed.). Philadelphia, PA, USA: Saunders.

Moore, K. L., & Persaud, T. V. N. (1993). *The developing human: Clinically oriented embryology* (5th ed.). Philadelphia: Saunders.

Moorman, S., & Inoue, M. (2013). Persistent problems in end-of-life planning among young- and middle-aged American couples. *The Journals of Gerontology: Series B: Psychological Sciences and Social Sciences, 68B*, 97–106.

Mor, V. (1987). *Hospice care systems: Structure, process, costs, and outcome.* New York: Springer.

Morales, J., Calvo, A., & Bialystok, E. (2013). Working memory development in monolingual and bilingual children. *Journal of Experimental Child Psychology, 114*, 187–202.

Morgan, C. (2012). Toward a more nuanced understanding of intercoupling: Second-generation mixed couples in Southern California. *Journal of Family Issues, 33*, 1423–1449.

Morgan, C., Covington, J., Geisler, M., Polich, J., & Murphy, C. (1997). Olfactory event-related potentials: Older males demonstrate the greatest deficits. *Electroencephalography & Clinical Neurophysiology, 104*, 351–358.

Morgan, J. L. (1994). Converging measures of speech segmentation in preverbal infants. *Infant Behavior & Development, 17*, 389–403.

Mork, J., Lie, K., Glattre, E., Clark, S., Hallmans, G., Jellum, E., Koskela, P., Moller, B., Pukkala, E., Schiller, J., Wang, Z., Youngman, L., Lehtinen, M., & Dillner, J. (2001). Human papillomavirus infection as a risk factor for squamous-cell carcinoma of the head and neck. *New England Journal of Medicine, 344*, 1125–1131.

Morris, D., Kritchevsky, S., & Davis, C. (1994). Serum cartonoids and coronary heart disease. The Lipid Research Clinics Coronary Primary Prevention Trial and Follow-up Study. *Journal of the American Medical Association, 272*, 1439–1441.

Morrison, C., & Gore, H. (2010). The relationship between excessive internet use and depression: A questionnaire-based study of 1,319 young people and adults. *Psychopathology, 43*, 121–126.

Morrison, N., Qi, J., Tokita, A., Kelly, P., Crofts, L., Nguyen, T., Sambrook, P., & Eisman, J. (1994). Prediction of bone density from vitamin D receptor alleles. *Nature, 367*, 284–287.

Morrow, D., Menard, W., Ridolfo, H., Stine-Morrow, E., Teller, T., & Bryant, D. (2003). Expertise, cognitive ability, and age effects on pilot communication. *International Journal of Aviation Psychology, 13*, 345–371.

Mortimer, J. T., & Finch, M. D. (1996). Work, family, and adolescent development. In J. T. Mortimer & M. D. Finch (Eds.), *Adolescents, work, and family: An intergenerational developmental analysis* (pp. 1–24. Thousand Oaks, CA: Sage.

Mortimer, J. T., Finch, M. D., Dennehy, K., Lee, C., & Beebe, T. (1995, March). *Work experience in adolescence.* Paper presented at the biennial meetings of the Society for Research in Child Development, Indianapolis, IN.

Mortimer, J., & Harley, C. (2002). The quality of work and youth mental health. *Work & Occupations, 29*, 166–197.

Mortimer, J., Zimmer-Gembeck, M., Holmes, M., & Shanahan, M. (2002). The process of occupational decision making: Patterns during the transition to adulthood. *Journal of Vocational Behavior, 61*, 439–465.

Mott, J., Crowe, P., Richardson, J., & Flay, B. (1999). After-school supervision and adolescent cigarette smoking: Contributions of the setting and intensity of after-school self-care. *Journal of Behavioral Medicine, 22*, 35–58.

Mounts, N. S., & Steinberg, L. (1995). An ecological analysis of peer influence on adolescent grade point average and drug use. *Developmental Psychology, 31*, 915–922.

Mueller, K., & Yoder, J. (1999). Stigmatization of non-normative family size status. *Sex Roles, 41*, 901–919.

Mueller, U., Overton, W., & Reene, K. (2001). Development of conditional reasoning: A longitudinal study. *Journal of Cognition & Development, 2*, 27–49.

Müller, U., & Giesbrecht, G. (2008). Methodological and epistemological issues in the interpretation of infant cognitive development. *Child Development, 79*, 1654–1658.

Mullins, L. C., & Mushel, M. (1992). The existence and emotional closeness of relationships with children, friends, and spouses. The effect on loneliness among older persons. *Research on Aging, 14*, 448–470.

Munakata, Y. (2006). Information processing approaches to cognitive development. In W. Damon, R. Lerner, D. Kuhn, & R. Sieglers (Eds.), *Handbook of child psychology, Vol. 2, Cognition, Perception, and Language* (6th ed., pp. 426–465). New York: John Wiley & Sons.

Mundy, G. (1994) Osteoporosis: Boning up on genes. *Nature, 367*, 216–217.

Muniz-Terrera, G., van den Hout, A., Piccinin, A., Matthews, F., & Hofer, S. (2013). Investigating terminal decline: Results from a UK population-based study of aging. *Psychology and Aging, 28*, 377–385.

Munroe, R. H., Shimmin, H. S., & Munroe, R. L. (1984). Gender understanding and sex role preference in four cultures. *Developmental Psychology, 20*, 673–682.

Muris, P., Meesters, C., & Timmermans, A. (2013). Some youths have a gloomy side: correlates of the dark triad personality traits in non-clinical adolescents. *Child Psychiatry and Human Development, 44*, 658–665.

Murnen, S., Smolak, L., Mills, J., & Good, L. (2003). Thin, sexy women and strong, muscular men: Grade-school children's responses to objectified images of women and men. *Sex Roles, 49*, 427–437.

Murphy, S., Braun, T., Tillery, L., Cain, K., Johnson, L., & Beaton, R. (1999). PTSD among bereaved parents following the violent deaths of their 12- to 28-year-old children: A longitudinal prospective analysis. *Journal of Traumatic Stress, 12*, 273–291.

Murphy, S., Xu, J., & Kochanek, K. (2013). Deaths: Final data for 2010. *National Vital Statistics Reports, 61*, 1–168.

Murray, J., Liotti, M., Ingmundson, P., Mayberg, H., Pu U., Zamarripa, F., Liu, Y., Woldorff, M., Gao, J., & Fox, P. (2006). Children's brain activations while viewing televised violence revealed by MRO. *Media Psychology, 8*, 25–37.

Murray, L., Sinclair, D., Cooper, P., Ducournau, P., et al. (1999). The socio-emotional development of 5-year-old children of postnatally depressed mothers. *Journal of Child Psychology & Psychiatry & Allied Disciplines, 40*, 1259–1271.

Murrell, S. A., & Himmelfarb, S. (1989). Effects of attachment bereavement and pre-event conditions on subsequent depressive symptoms in older adults. *Psychology & Aging, 4*, 166–172.

Musick, M., Koenig, H., Hays, J., & Cohen, H. (1998). Religious activity and depression among community-dwelling elderly persons with cancer: The moderating effect of race. *Journals of Gerontology, Series B: Psychological Sciences & Social Sciences, 53B*, S218–S227.

Must, O., te Njienhuis, J., Must, A., & van Vianen, A. (2009). Comparability of IQ scores over time. *Intelligence, 37*, 25–33.

Mutch, L., Leyland, A., & McGee, A. (1993). Patterns of neuropsychological function in a low-birth-weight population. *Developmental Medicine & Child Neurology, 35*, 943–956.

Muzi, M. (2000). *The experience of parenting.* Upper Saddle River, NJ: Prentice Hall.

Mwamwenda, T. (2999). Undergraduate and graduate students' combinatorial reasoning and formal operations. *Research and Theory on Human Developmenti, 106*, 503–506.

Myyry, L, Juujärvi, S., & Pesso, K. (2013). Change in values and moral reasoning during higher education. *European Journal of Developmental Psychology, 10*, 269–284.

Nagamine, S. (1999). Interpersonal conflict situations: Adolescents' negotiation processes using an interpersonal negotiation strategy model: Adolescents' relations with their parents and friends. *Japanese Journal of Educational Psychology, 47*, 218–228.

Nagumey, A., Reich, J., & Newsom, J. (2004). Gender moderates the effects of independence and dependence desires during the social support process. *Psychology & Aging, 19*, 215–218.

Naito, A. (2007). Internet suicide in Japan: Implications for child and adolescent mental health. *Clinical Child Psychology and Psychiatry, 12*, 583–597.

Namka, L. (2002). *What the research literature says about corporal punish-ment.* Retrieved June 15, 2007 from http://www.angriesout.com/parents10.htm.

Narvaez, D. (1998). The influence of moral schemas on the reconstruction of moral narratives in eighth graders and college students. *Journal of Educational Psychology, 90*, 13–24.

National Cancer Institute (NCI). (2000). *Questions and answers about smoking cessation.* Retrieved July 4, 2007 from www.cancer.gov/cancertopics/factsheet/Tobacco/cessation.

National Cancer Institute (NCI). (2006). *Breast cancer and the environment research centers chart new territory.* Retrieved June 21, 2007 from http://www.nci.nih.gov/ncicancerbulletin/NCI_Cancer_Bulletin_081506/page9

National Center for Education Statistics (NCES). (2006c). *How many students with disabilities receive services?* Retrieved June 19, 2007 from http://nces.ed.gov/fastfacts/display.asp?id=64

National Center for Education Statistics (NCES). (2008). *Issue brief: 1.5 million homeschooled children in the United States.* Retrieved July 10, 2013, from http://nces.ed.gov/pubs2009/2009030.pdf.

National Center for Education Statistics (NCES). (2010). *The condition of education.* Retrieved August 24, 2010 from http://nces.ed.gov/programs/coe/.

National Center for Education Statistics (NCES). (2013). *The condition of education 2011.* Retrieved July 10, 2013, from http://nces.ed.gov/programs/coe/.

National Center for Education Statistics. (2010). *Trends in undergraduate Stafford Loan borrowing: 1989–90 to 2007–2008.* Retrieved August 26, 2010 from http://nces.ed.gov/pubs2010/2010183.pdf.

National Center for Education Statistics. (2013). *Digest of education statistics.* Retrieved October 8, 2013 from http://www.nces.ed.gov/Programs/digest/.

National Center for Health Statistics (NCHS) (2010). *Health United States, 2009.* Retrieved July 9, 2010 from http://www.cdc.gov/nchs/data/hus/hus09.pdf.

National Center for Health Statistics (NCHS). (2007). *Prevalence of over-weight among children and adolescents: United States 2003–2004.* Retrieved June 19, 2007 from www.cdc.gov/nchs/products/pubs/pubd/hestats/overweight/overwght_child_03.htm

National Center for Health Statistics (NCHS). (2009). *Health, United States 2008 with special report on the health of young adults.* Retrieved August 29, 2010 from http://www.cdc.gov/nchs/data/hus/hus08.pdf.

National Center for Health Statistics (NCHS). (2013). *Health, United States 2012.* Retrieved June 15, 2013, from http://www.cdc.gov/nchs/data/hus/hus12.pdf.

National Center for Health Statistics (NCHS). (2013). *Health, United States, 2012.* Retrieved July 17, 2013, from http://www.cdc.gov/nchs/data/hus/hus12.pdf#018.

National Center for Health Statistics (NCHS). (2013). *Health, United States, 2012.* Retrieved July 17, 2013, from http://www.cdc.gov/nchs/data/hus/hus12.pdf#018.

National Center for Health Statistics (NCHS). (2013). *Underlying cause of death 1999—2010.* Retrieved July 15, 2013, from http://wonder.cdc.gov/controller/datarequest/D76;jsessionid=DD32A469D781F7C71F5D8ED8B605D6F0.

National Center for Health Statistics. (2000). *CDC growth charts.* Retrieved August 23, 2000, from http://www.cdc.gov/nchs.

National Center for Injury Prevention and Control (NCIPC). (2007), *Suicide.* Retrieved July 3, 2007 from www.cdc.gov/ncipc/factsheets/suifacts.htm.

National Center on Elder Abuse (NCEA). (2005). *Fact sheet: Elder abuse prevalence and incidence.* Retrieved September 1, 2010 from http://www.ncea.aoa.gov/ncearoot/Main_Site/pdf/publication/FinalStatistics050331.pdf.

National Council for Injury Prevention and Control (NCIPC). (2000). *Fact book for the year 2000.* Washington, DC: Author.

National Hospice and Palliative Care Organization (NHPCO). (2012) *Factors and figures: Hospice care in America.* Retrieved July 15, 2013, from http://www.nhpco.org/sites/default/files/public/Statistics_Research/2012_Facts_Figures.pdf.

National Institute for Literacy. (2008). *Developing early literacy.* Retrieved September 27, 2013 from http://lincs.ed.gov/publications/pdf/NELPReport09.pdf.

National Institute of Child Health and Human Development (NICHD) Early Child Care Research Network. (1998). The effects of infant child care on mother-infant attachment security: Results of the NICHD study of early child care. *Child Development, 68*, 860–879.

National Institute of Child Health and Human Development (NICHD). (2013). *Safe to sleep public education campaign.* Retrieved June 15, 2013, from http://www.nichd.nih.gov/SIDS/Pages/sids.aspx.

National Institute of Child Health and Human Development. (2006). *The NICHD study of early child care and youth development.* Retrieved October 21, 2010 from http://www.nichd.nih.gov/publications/pubs/upload/seccyd_06.pdf

National Institute on Aging (NIA). (2000a). *Depression: A serious but treatable illness.* Retrieved February 7, 2001, from http://www.nih.gov/nia.

National Institute on Aging (NIA). (2000b). *Sexuality in later life.* Retrieved February 7, 2001, from http://www.nih.gov/nia.

National Institute on Alcohol Abuse and Alcoholism. (2006). *Young adult drinking.* Retrieved August 24, 2010 from http://pubs.niaaa.nih.gov/publications/aa68/aa68.htm.

National Middle School Association (NMSA). (2004). *Small schools and small learning communities.* Retrieved June 22, 2007 from http://www.nmsa.org/About-NMSA/PositionStatements/SmallSchools/tabid/293/Default.aspx

National Vital Statistics System. (2006). *Death rates by 10-year age groups: United States and each state 2004.* Retrieved July 9, 2007 from www.cdc.gov/nchs/data/statab/mortfinal2004_worktable23r.pdf.

Naudé, H., & Pretorius, E. (2003). Investigating the effects of asthma medication on the cognitive and psychosocial functioning of primary school children with asthma. *Early Child Development and Care, 173*, 699–709.

Neff, L., & Karney, B. (2009). Stress and reactivity to daily relationship experiences: How stress hinders adaptive processes in marriage. *Journal of Personality and Social Psychology, 97*, 435–450.

Neild, R. (2009). Falling off track during the transition to high school: What we know and what can be done. *The Future of Children, 19*, 53–76.

Neild, R., & Balfanz, R. (2006). An extreme degree of difficulty: The educational demographics of urban neighborhood high schools. *Journal of Education for Students Placed at Risk, 11*, 123–141.

Neill, M. (1998). *High stakes tests do not improve student learning.* Retrieved September 27, 2013 from http://www.fairtest.org/high-stakes-tests-do-not-improve-student-learning-0.

Neimeyer, R., Prigerson, H., & Davies, B. (2002). Mourning and meaning. *American Behavioral Scientist, 46*, 235–251.

Neisser, U., Boodoo, G., Bouchard, T. J., Jr., Boykin, A. W., Brody, N., Ceci, S. J., Halpern, D. F., Loehlin, J. C., Perloff, R., Sternberg, R. J., & Urbina, S. (1996). Intelligence: Knowns and unknowns. *American Psychologist, 51*, 77–101.

Neitzel, C., & Stright, A. (2003). Mothers' scaffolding of children's problem solving: Establishing a foundation of academic self-regulatory competence. *Journal of Family Psychology, 17*, 147–159.

Nelson, D., Robinson, C., Hart, C., Albano, A., & Marshall, S. (2010). Italian preschoolers' peer-status linkages with sociability and subtypes of aggression and victimization. *Social Development, 19,* 698–720.

Nelson, E. A., & Dannefer, D. (1992). Aged heterogeneity: Fact or fiction? The fate of diversity in gerontological research. *The Gerontologist, 32,* 17–23.

Nelson, K. (1977). Facilitating children's syntax acquisition. *Developmental Psychology, 13,* 101–107.

Nelson, M. E., Fiatarone, M. A., Morganti, C. M., Trice, I., Greenberg, R. A., & Evans, W. J. (1994). Effects of high-intensity strength training on multiple risk factors for osteoporotic fractures. *Journal of the American Medical Association, 272,* 1909–1914.

Nelson, S. (1980). Factors influencing young children's use of motives and outcomes as moral criteria. *Child Development, 51,* 823–829.

Neshat-Doost, H., Taghavi, M., Moradi, A., Yule, W., & Dalgleish, T. (1998). Memory for emotional trait adjectives in clinically depressed youth. *Journal of Abnormal Psychology, 107,* 642–650.

Netherlands Twin Register. (2013). *Netherlands twin register: Twin and family research.* Retrieved June 7, 2013, from www.tweelingenregister.org/index_uk.html.

Neuburger, E. (2001). *Home computers and internet use in the United States: August 2000.* Retrieved August 12, 2010 from http://www.census.gov/prod/2001pubs/p23-207.pdf.

Neugarten, B. L. (1979). Time, age, and the life cycle. *American Journal of Psychiatry, 136,* 887–894.

Newcomb, A. F., & Bagwell, C. L. (1995). Children's friendship relations: A meta-analytic review. *Psychological Bulletin, 117,* 306–347.

Newman, D., Caspi, A., Moffitt, T., & Silva, P. (1997). Antecedents of adult interpersonal functioning: Effects of individual differences in age 3 temperament. *Developmental Psychology, 33,* 206–217.

Ng, A., Ying, P., Phillips, D., & Lee, W. (2002). Persistence and challenges to filial piety and informal support of older persons in a modern Chinese society: A case study in Tuen Mun, Hong Kong. *Journal of Aging Studies, 16,* 135–153.

Ni, Y. (1998). Cognitive structure, content knowledge, and classificatory reasoning. *Journal of Genetic Psychology, 159,* 280–296.

Nichikawa, S., Hägglöf, B., & Sundbom, E. (2010). Contributions of attachment and self-concept on internalizing and externalizing problems among Japanese adolescents. *Journal of Child and Family Studies, 19,* 334–342.

Nichols, A. (2006). *Understanding recent changes in child poverty.* Retrieved June 20, 2007 from http://www.urbaninstitute.org/UploadedPDF/311356_A71.pdf

Nichols, D., & Melov, S. (2004). The aging cell. *Aging, 3,* 1474–1497.

Nicolis, H. (2007). Nonlinear dynamics and probabilistic behavior of adolescent suicidal outbreaks. *Nonlinear Dynamics, Psychology, and Life Sciences, 11,* 451–472.

Nikolich-ŽugichZugich, J. (2005). T-cell aging: Naïve but not young. *Journal of Experimental Medicine, 201,* 837–840.

Nilsson, E., Gillberg, C., Gillberg, I., & Rastam, M. (1999). Ten-year follow-up of adolescent-onset anorexia nervosa: Personality disorders. *Journal of the American Academy of Child & Adolescent Psychiatry, 38,* 1389–1395.

Nisan, M., & Kohlberg, L. (1982). Universality and variation in moral judgment: A longitudinal and cross-sectional study in Turkey. *Child Development, 53,* 865–876.

Niska, K., Snyder, M., & Lia-Hoagberg, B. (1998). Family ritual facilitates adaptation to parenthood. *Public Health Nursing, 15,* 329–337.

Nolen-Hoeksema, S., & Girgus, J. S. (1994). The emergence of gender differences in depression during adolescence. *Psychological Bulletin, 115,* 424–443.

Nomaguchi, K. (2006). Maternal employment, nonparental care, mother-child interactions, and child outcomes during preschool years. *Journal of Marriage and Family, 68,* 1341–1369.

Norboru, T. (1997). A developmental study of wordplay in preschool children: The Japanese game of "Shiritori." *Japanese Journal of Developmental Psychology, 8,* 42–52.

Norboru, T. (1997). A developmental study of wordplay in preschool children: The Japanese game of "Shiritori." *Japanese Journal of Developmental Psychology, 8,* 42–52.

Norman, S., Norman, G., Rossi, J., & Prochaska, J. (2006). Identifying high- and low-success smoking cessation subgroups using signal detection analysis. *Addictive Behaviors, 31,* 31–41.

Norris, F. H., & Murrell, S. A. (1990). Social support, life events, and stress as modifiers of adjustment to bereavement by older adults. *Psychology & Aging, 5,* 429–436.

Norwood, T. H., Smith, J. R., & Stein, G. H. (1990). Aging at the cellular level: The human fibroblastlike cell model. In E. R. Schneider & J. W. Rowe (Eds.), *Handbook of the biology of aging* (3rd ed., pp. 131–154). San Diego, CA: Academic Press.

Nussbaum, A., & Steele, C. (2007). Situational disengagement and persistence in the face of adversity. *Journal of Experimental Social Psychology, 43,* 127–134.

Nuttall, A., Valentino, K., Borkowski, J. (2012). Maternal history of parentification, maternal warm responsiveness, and children's externalizing behavior. *Journal of Family Psychology, 26,* 767–775.

Oakland, T. (2009). How universal are test development and use? In E. Grigorenko (Ed.), *Multicultural psychoeducational assessment* (pp. 1–40). New York: Spring Publishing Co.

O'Brien, C. (1996). Recent developments in the pharmacotherapy of substance abuse. *Journal of Consulting and Clinical Psychology, 64,* 677–686.

O'Brien, E., Wu, K., & Baer, D. (2010). *Older Americans in poverty: A snapshot.* Retrieved September 1, 2010 from http://assets.aarp.org/rgcenter/ppi/econsec/2010-03-poverty.pdf.

O'Brien, E., Wu, K., & Vaer, D. (2010). *Older Americans in poverty: A snapshot.* Retrieved October 23, 2013 from http://assets.aarp.org/rgcenter/ppi/econsec/2010-03-poverty.pdf.

O'Connor D.L., Khan S., Weishuhn K., Vaughan J., Jefferies A., & Campbell D.M. (2008) Growth and nutrient intakes of human milk-fed preterm infants provided with extra energy and nutrients after hospital discharge. *Pediatrics 121* 766–76.

O'Connor, B. P. (1995). Identity development and perceived parental behavior as sources of adolescent egocentrism. *Journal of Youth & Adolescence, 24,* 205–227.

O'Connor, M., Shear, M., Fox, R., Skritskaya, N., Campbell, B., Ghesquiere, A., & Glickman, K. (2013). Catecholamine predictors of complicated grief treatment outcomes. *International Journal of Psychophysiology, 88,* 349–352.

O'Leary, A. (1990). Stress, emotion, and human immune function. *Psychological Bulletin, 108,* 363–382.

O'Neill, D. K., Astington, J. W., & Flavell, J. H. (1992). Young children's understanding of the role that sensory experiences play in knowledge acquisition. *Child Development, 63,* 474–490.

Oakland, T. (2009). How universal are test development and use? In E. Grigorenko (Ed.), *Multicultural psychoeducational assessment* (pp. 1–40). New York: Spring Publishing Co.

Oatley, K., & Jenkins, J. (1996). *Understanding emotions.* Cambridge, MA: Blackwell Publishers.

Odgers, C., Caspi, A., Russell, M., Sampson, R., Arsenault, L., & Moffitt, T. (2012). Supportive parenting mediates neighborhood socioeconomic disparities in children's antisocial behavior from ages 5—12. *Development and Psychopathology, 24,* 705–721.

Offenberg, R. M. (2001). The efficacy of Philadelphia's K-to-8 schools compared to middle grades schools. Middle School Journal, 32(4), 23–29.

Office of Minority Health. (2012ab). *Heart disease.* Retrieved July 17, 2013, from http://minorityhealth.hhs.gov/templates/browse.aspx?lvl=3&lvlid=6.

Office of Minority Health. (2012ba). *Diabetes.* Retrieved July 17, 2013, from http://minorityhealth.hhs.gov/templates/browse.aspx?lvl=3&lvlid=5.

Ofiesh, N., Hughes, C., & Scott, S. (2004). Extended test time and postsecondary students with learning disabilities: A model for decision making. *Learning Disabilities Research & Practice, 19,* 57–70.

Ogbu, J. (1990). Cultural models, identity and literacy. In J. W. Stigler, R. A. Shweder, & G. Hendt (Eds.), *Cultural psychology: Essays on comparative human development* (pp. 520–541). Hillsdale, NJ: Erlbaum.

Oh, J., & Fuligni, A. (2010). The role of heritage language development in the ethnic identity and family relationships of adolescents from immigrant backgrounds. *Social Development, 19,* 202–220.

Okamoto, K., & Uechi, Y. (1999). Adolescents' relations with parents and friends in the second individuation process. *Japanese Journal of Educational Psychology, 47,* 248–258.

Olin, J., & Zelinski, E. (1997). Age differences in calibration of comprehension. *Educational Gerontology, 23,* 67–77.

Olino, T., Durbin, C., Klein, D., Hayden, E., & Dyson, M. (2013). Gender differences in young children's temperament traits: Comparisons across observational and parent-report methods. *Journal of Personality, 81,* 119–129.

Oliván, G. (2003). Catch-up growth assessment in long-term physically neglected and emotionally abused preschool age male children. *Child Abuse & Neglect, 27,* 103–108.

Oller, D. K. (1981). Infant vocalizations: Exploration and reflectivity. In R. E. Stark (Ed.), *Language behavior in infancy and early childhood* (pp. 85–104). New York: Elsevier North-Holland.

Oller, D., Cobo-Lewis, A., & Eilers, R. (1998). Phonological translation in bilingual and monolingual children. *Applied Psycholinguistics, 19,* 259–278.

Olson, M., Krantz, D., Kelsey, S., Pepine, C., Sopko, G., Handberg, E., Rogers, W., Gierach, G., McClure, C., & Merz, C. (2005). Hostility scores are associated with increased risk of cardiovascular events in women undergoing coronary angiography: A report from the NHLBI-sponsored WISE study. *Psychosomatic Medicine, 67,* 546–552.

Olweus, D. (1995). Bullying or peer abuse at school: Facts and intervention. *Current Directions in Psychological Science, 4,* 196–200.

Oman, D., Thoresen, C., & McMahon, K. (1999). Volunteerism and mortality among the community-dwelling elderly. *Journal of Health Psychology, 4,* 301–316.

Omiya, A., & Uchida, N. (2002). The development of children's think-ing strategies: The retrieval of alternatives based on the categorization with conditional reasoning tasks. *Japanese Journal of Psychology, 73,* 10–17.

Ompad, D., Strathdee, S., Celentano, D., Latkin, C., Poduska, J., Kellam, S., & Ialongo, N. (2006). Predictors of early initiation of vaginal and oral sex among urban young adults in Baltimore, Maryland. *Archives of Sexual Behavior, 35,* 53–65.

Onen, S., Onen, F., Mangeon, J., Abidi, H., Courpron, P., & Schmidt, J. (2005). Alcohol abuse and dependence in elderly emergency department patients. *Archives of Gerontology and Geriatrics, 41,* 191–200.

Onrust, S., & Cuijpers, P. (2006). Mood and anxiety disorders in widowhood: A systematic review. *Aging & Mental Health, 10,* 327–334.

Operario, D., Adler, N., & Williams, D. (2004). Subjective social status: reliability and predictive utility for global health. *Psychology & Health, 19,* 237–246.

Orenstein, W., Paulson, J., Brady, M., Cooper, L., & Seib, Katherine. (2012). Global vaccination recommendations and thimerosal. *Pediatrics, 131,* 149–151.

Orth-Gomér, K., Rosengren, A., & Wilhelmsen, L. (1993). Lack of social support and incidence of coronary heart disease in middle-aged Swedish men. *Psychosomatic Medicine, 55,* 37–43.

Osofsky, J. D. (1995). The effects of exposure to violence on young children. *American Psychologist, 50,* 782–788.

Österbacka, E., & Zick, C. (2009). Transition to adulthood in Finland and the United States. *Social Indicators Research, 93,* 131–135.

Ostrom, T., Carpenter, S., Sedikides, C., & Li, F. (1993). Differential processing of in-group and out-group information. *Journal of Personality & Social Psychology, 64,* 21–34.

Ouellette, G., & Sénéchal, M. (2008). Pathways to literacy: A study of invented spelling and its role in learning to read. *Child Development, 79,* 899–913.

Overby, K. (2002). Pediatric health supervision. In A. Rudolph, R. Kamei, & K. Overby (Eds.), *Rudolph's fundamental of pediatrics* (3rd ed., pp. 1–69). New York: McGraw-Hill.

Oweis, A., Gharaibeh, M., & Alhourani, R. (2010). Prevalence of violence during pregnancy: Findings from a Jordanian survey. *Maternal and Child Health Journal, 14,* 437–445.

Owen, P. (1998). Fears of Hispanic and Anglo children: Real-world fears in the 1990s. *Hispanic Journal of Behavioral Sciences, 20,* 483–491.

Owens, C. (2009). Of mamothers and behmothers-in-law: Toward a twenty-first-century bestiary. In A. Hall & M. Bishop (Eds.), *Mommy angst: Motherhood in American popular culture* (pp. 63–79). Santa Barbara, CA: Praeger Publishers.

Paden, S. L., & Buehler, C. (1995). Coping with the dual-income lifestyle. *Journal of Marriage & the Family, 57,* 101–110.

Paffenbarger, R. S., Hyde, R. T., Wing, A. L., & Hsieh, C. (1987). Physical activity, all-cause mortality, and longevity of college alumni. *New England Journal of Medicine, 314,* 605–613.

Pagani, L., Boulerice, B., Tremblay, R., & Vitaro, F. (1997). Behavioural development in children of divorce and remarriage. *Journal of Child Psychology & Psychiatry & Allied Disciplines, 38,* 769–781.

Painter, K. (2013). *Parents say they feel positive about young adult kids.* Retrieved July 21, 2013, from http://www.usatoday.com/story/news/nation/2013/05/06/parents-young-adults-survey/2138727/.

Pajares, F., & Graham, L. (1999). Self-efficacy, motivation constructs, and mathematics performance of entering middle school students. *Contemporary Educational Psychology, 24,* 124–139.

Pajares, F., & Valiante, G. (1999). Grade level and gender differences in the writing self-beliefs of middle school students. *Contemporary Educational Psychology, 24,* 390–405.

Panepinto, J., & Scott, J. (2011). Hematology. In K. Marcdante, R. Kliegman, H. Jensen, & R. Behrman (Eds.), *Nelson's essentials of pediatrics* (6th ed., pp. 555–584). New York: Elsevier Health Publishers.

Pang, T., & Lam, C. (2002). The widowers' bereavement process and death rituals: Hong Kong experiences. *Illness, Crisis, & Loss, 10,* 294–303.

Parault, S., & Schwanenflugel, P. (2000). The development of conceptual categories of attention during the elementary school years. *Journal of Experimental Child Psychology, 75,* 245–262.

Parent, S., Tillman, G., Jule, A., Skakkebaek, N., Toppari, J., & Bourguignon, J. (2003). The timing of normal puberty and the age limits of sexual precocity: Variations around the world, secular trends, and changes after migration. *Endocrine Review, 24,* 668–693.

Park, C., Edmondson, D., & Mills, M. (2010). Religious worldviews and stressful encounters: Reciprocal influence from a meaning-making perspective. In T. Miller (Ed.), *Handbook of stressful transitions across the lifespan* (pp. 485–501). New York: Springer Science+Business Media.

Park, J., & Roh, S. (2013). Daily spiritual experiences, social support, and depression among elderly Korean immigrants. *Aging & Mental Health, 17,* 102–108.

Park, N. (2009). The relationship of social engagement to psychological well-being of older adults in assisted living facilities. *Journal of Applied Gerontology, 28,* 461–481.

Parke, R. (2004). The Society for Research in Child Development at 70: Progress and promise. *Child Development, 75,* 1–24.

Parke, R. D., & Tinsley, B. R. (1981). The father's role in infancy: Determinants of involvement in caregiving and play. In M. E. Lamb (Ed.), *The role of the father in child development* (2nd ed., pp. 429–458). New York: Wiley.

Parmley, M., & Cunningham, J. (2008). Children's gender-emotion stereotypes in the relationship of anger to sadness and fear. *Sex Roles, 58,* 358–370.

Parsons, J., Starks, T., Garnarel, K., & Grov, C. (2012). Non-monogamy and sexual relationship quality among same-sex male couples. *Journal of Family Psychology, 26,* 669–677.

Pascarella, E. (1999). The development of critical thinking: Does college make a difference? *Journal of College Student Development, 40,* 562–569.

Pascarella, E., & Terenzi, P. (1991). *How college affects students: Findings and insights from twenty years of research.* San Francisco: Jossey-Bass.

Patel, S., Gaylord, S., & Fagen, J. (2013). Generalization of deferred imitation in 6-, 9-, and 12-month-old infants using visual and auditory contexts. *Infant Behavior & Development, 36,* 25–31.

Patterson, C. (2006). Children of lesbian and gay parents. *Current Directions in Psychological Science, 15,* 241–244.

Patterson, G. R. (1980). Mothers: The unacknowledged victims. *Monographs of the Society for Research in Child Development, 45* (Serial No. 186).

Patterson, J. (1998). Expressive vocabulary of bilingual toddlers: Preliminary findings. *Multicultural Electronic Journal of Communication Disorders, 1.* Retrieved April 11, 2001, from www.asha.ucf.edu/patterson.html.

Pauen, S. (2002). The global-to-basic level shift in infants' categorical thinking: First evidence from a longitudinal study. *International Journal of Behavioral Development, 26,* 492–499.

Pearson, P., & Cervetti, G. (2013). The psychology and pedagogy of reading processes. In Reynolds, W., Miller, G., & Weiner, I. (Eds). *Handbook of psychology, Vol. 7: Educational psychology* (2nd ed.). (pp. 257–281). Hoboken, NJ, John Wiley & Sons Inc.

Pederson, D. R., Moran, G., Sitko, C., Campbell, K., Ghesquire, K., & Acton, H. (1990). Maternal sensitivity and the security of infant-mother attachment: A Q-sort study. *Child Development, 61,* 1974–1983.

Pediatric Nutrition Surveillance System. (2012). *Summary of health indicators.* Retrieved July 8, 2013 from http://www.cdc.gov/pednss/pednss_tables/pdf/national_table2.pdf.

Pegg, J. E., Werker, J. F., & McLeod, P. J. (1992). Preference for infant-directed over adult-directed speech: Evidence from 7-week-old infants. *Infant Behavior & Development, 15,* 325–345.

Peigneux, P., & van der Linden, M. (1999). Influence of ageing and educational level on the prevalence of body-part-as-objects in normal subjects. *Journal of Clinical & Experimental Neuropsychology, 21,* 547–552.

Pelletier, L., Dion, S., & Levesque, C. (2004). Can self-determination help protect women against sociocultural influences about body image and reduce their risk of experiencing bulimic symptoms? *Journal of Social & Clinical Psychology, 23,* 61–88.

Penedo, F., Dahn, J., Kinsinger, D., Antoni, M., Molton, I., Gonzalez, J., Fletcher, M., Roos, B., Carver, C., & Schneiderman, N. (2005). Anger suppression mediates the relationship between optimism and natural killer cell cytotoxicity in men treated for localized prostate cancer. *Journal of Psychosomatic Research, 60,* 423–427.

Peoples, C. E., Fagan, J. F., III, & Drotar, D. (1995). The influence of race on 3-year-old children's performance on the Stanford-Binet: Fourth edition. *Intelligence, 21,* 69–82.

Peplau, L. A. (1991). Lesbian and gay relationships. In J. C. Gonsiorek & J. D. Weinrich (Eds.), *Homosexuality: Research implications for public policy* (pp. 177–196). Newbury Park, CA: Sage.

Pérez-Edgar, K., Schmidt, L., Henderson, H., Schulkin, J., & Fox, N. (2008). Salivary cortisol levels and infant temperament shape developmental trajectories in boys at risk for behavioral maladjustment. *Psychoneuroendocrinology, 33,* 916–925.

Perho, H., & Korhonen, M. (1999). Coping in work and marriage at the onset of middle age. *Psykologia, 34,* 115–127.

Perkins, K., Malone, K., & Barabino, G. (2013). Missed encounters: A qualitative study of views of faculty on mentoring and student narratives on race science education. In M. Paludi, M. (Ed.), *Psychology for business success, Volume 3: Managing, leading, and developing employees* (pp. 91–118). Santa Barbara, CA, USA: Praeger/ABC-CLIO.

Perry, W. (1968). *Forms of intellectual and ethical development in the college years.* New York: Holt, Rinehart & Winston.

Persson, A., & Musher-Eizenman, D. (2003). The impact of a prejudice-prevention television program on young children's ideas about race. *Early Childhood Research Quarterly, 18,* 530–546.

Pesonen, A., Raikkonen, K., Strandberg, T., Kelitikangas-Jarvinen, & L., Jarvenpaa, A. (2004). Insecure adult attachment style and depressive symptoms: Implications for parental perceptions of infant temperament. *Infant Mental Health Journal, 25,* 99–116.

Petersen, A. C., Compas, B. E., Brooks-Gunn, J., Stemmler, M., Ey, S., & Grant, K. E. (1993). Depression in adolescence. *American Psychologist, 48,* 155–168.

Peterson, B. (2002). Longitudinal analysis of midlife generativity, intergenerational roles, and caregiving. *Psychology & Aging, 17,* 161–168.

Peterson, C. (1999). Grandfathers' and grandmothers' satisfaction with the grandparenting role: Seeking new answers to old questions. *International Journal of Aging & Human Development, 49,* 61–78.

Peterson, C., Seligman, M., & Vaillant, G. (1988). Pessimistic explanatory style is a risk factor for physical illness: A thirty-five-year longitudinal study.

Petitto, L., Katerelos, M., Levy, B., Gauna, K., Tetreault, K., & Ferraro, V. (2001). Bilingual signed and spoken language from birth: Implications for the mechanisms underlying early bilingual language acquisition. *Journal of Child Language, 28,* 453–496.

Petrill, S., Hart, S., Harlaar, N., Logan, J., Justice, L., Schatschneider, C., Thompson, L., DeThorne, L., Deater-Deckard, K., & Cutting, L. (2010). Genetic and environmental influences on the growth of early reading skills. *Journal of Child Psychology and Psychiatry, 51,* 660–667.

Pettingale, K. W., Morris, T., Greer, S., & Haybittle, J. L. (1985). Mental attitudes to cancer: An additional prognostic factor. *Lancet,* 85.

Peverly, S., Ramaswamy, V., Brown, C., Sumowski, J., Alidoost, M., & Garner, J. (2007). What predicts skill in lecture note taking? *Journal of Educational Psychology, 99,* 167–180.

Pew Research Center. (2010). *Religion among the Millennials.* Retrieved September 3, 2010 from http://pewforum.org/uploadedFiles/Topics/Demographics/Age/millennials-report.pdf.

Pezdek, K., Blandon-Gitlin, I., & Moore, C. (2003). Children's face recognition memory: More evidence for the cross-race effect. *Journal of Applied Psychology, 88,* 760–763.

Philip, P., Sagaspe, P., Prague, M., Tassi, P., Capelli, A., Bioulac, B., Commenges, D., & Taillard, J. (2012). Acute versus chronic partial sleep deprivation in middle-aged people: Differential effect on performance and sleepiness. *Sleep: Journal of Sleep and Sleep Disorders Research, 35,* 997–1002.

Phillips, A., Wellman, H., & Spelke, E. (2002). Infants' ability to connect gaze and emotional expression to intentional action. *Cognition, 85,* 53–78.

Phillips, E. (2013). A case study of questioning for reading comprehension during guided reading. *Education 3-13, 41,* 110–120.

Phillips, S. K., Bruce, S. A., Newton, D., & Woledge, R. C. (1992). The weakness of old age is not due to failure of muscle activation. *Journals of Gerontology: Medical Sciences, 47,* M45–49.

Phillipson, C. (2013). Commentary: The future of work and retirement. *Human Relations, 66,* 143–153.

Phinney, J. (2008). Ethnic identity exploration in emerging adulthood. In D. Browning (Eds.), *Adolescent identities: A collection of readings* (pp. 47–66). New York: The Analytic Press.

Phinney, J. S. (1990). Ethnic identity in adolescents and adults: Review of research. *Psychological Bulletin, 108,* 499–514.

Phinney, J. S., & Rosenthal, D. A. (1992). Ethnic identity in adolescence: Process, context, and outcome. In G. R. Adams, T. P. Gullotta, & R. Montemayor (Eds.), *Adolescent identity formation* (pp. 145–172). Newbury Park, CA: Sage.

Piaget, J. (1932). *The moral judgment of the child.* New York: Macmillan.

Piaget, J. (1952). *The origins of intelligence in children.* New York: International Universities Press.

Piaget, J. (1954). *The construction of reality in the child.* New York: Basic Books. (Originally published 1937.)

Piaget, J. (1965). *The moral judgment of the child.* New York: Free Press.

Piaget, J. (1970). Piaget's theory. In P. H. Mussen (Ed.), *Carmichael's manual of child psychology* (Vol. 1, 3rd ed.) (pp. 703–732). New York: Wiley.

Piaget, J. (1977). *The development of thought: Equilibration of cognitive structures.* New York: Viking.

Piaget, J., & Inhelder, B. (1969). *The psychology of the child.* New York: Basic Books.

Pianta, R. C., & Egeland, B. (1994). Predictors of instability in children's mental test performance at 24, 48, and 96 months. *Intelligence, 18,* 145–163.

Pickhardt, C. (2009). Parental divorce and adolescents. *Psychology Today.* Retrieved August 1, 2010 from http://www.psychologytoday.com/blog/surviving-your-childs-adolescence/200908/parental-divorce-and-adolescents.

Pierce, L. (2001). Caring and expressions of spirituality by urban caregivers of people with stroke in African American families. *Qualitative Health Research, 11,* 339–352.

Pierce, M., & Leon, D. (2005). Age at menarche and adult BMI in the Aberdeen children of the 1950s cohort study. *American Journal of Clinical Nutrition, 82,* 733–739.

Pies, R. (2009). Should DSM-V designate "internet addiction" a mental disorder? *Psychiatry, 6,* 31–37.

Pillemer, K., & Suitor, J. (1992). Violence and violent feelings: What causes them among family caregivers? *Journal of Gerontology Social Sciences, 47,* S165–172.

Pillemer, K., & Suitor, J. J. (1990). Prevention of elder abuse. In R. Ammerman & M. Hersen (Eds.), *Treatment of family violence: A sourcebook* (pp. 406–422). New York: Wiley.

Pillow, B. (1999). Children's understanding of inferential knowledge. *Journal of Genetic Psychology, 160,* 419–428.

Pinker, S. (1994). *The language instinct: How the mind creates language.* New York: HarperCollins.

Pinker, S. (2002). *The Blank Slate.* New York: Viking.

Pinquart, M., & Soerensen, S. (2000). Influences of socioeconomic status, social network, and competence on subjective well-being in later life: A meta-analysis. *Psychology & Aging, 15,* 187–224.

Pinquart, M., & Sorensen, S. (2006a). Gender differences in caregiver stressors, social resources, and health: An updated meta-analysis. *Journals of Gerontology: Series B: Psychological Sciences and Social Sciences, 61B,* P33–P45.

Pinquart, M., & Sorensen, S. (2006b). Helping caregivers of persons with dementia: Which interventions work and how large are their effects? *International Geriatrics, 18,* 577–595.

Placek, P., Taffel, S., & Moien, M. (1983). Cesarean section delivery rates: United States, 1981. *American Journal of Public Health, 73,* 861–862.

Plomin, R. (1990). *Nature and nurture: An introduction to behavior genetics.* Pacific Grove, CA: Brooks/Cole.

Plomin, R., Emde, R. N., Braungart, J. M., Campos, J., Corley, R., Fulker, D. W., Kagan, J., Reznick, J. S., Robinson, J., Zahn-Waxler, C., & DeFries, J. C. (1993). Genetic change and continuity from fourteen to twenty months: The MacArthur longitudinal twin study. *Child Development, 64,* 1354–1376.

Plomin, R., Reiss, D., Hetherington, E. M., & Howe, G. W. (1994). Nature and nurture: Genetic contributions to measures of the family environment. *Developmental Psychology, 30,* 32–43.

Pluess, M., & Belsky J. (2009). Differential susceptibility to rearing experience: The case of childcare. *Journal of Child Psychology and Psychiatry, 50*(4): 396–404 (2009).

Poeschla, B., Strachan, E., Dansie, E., Buchwald, D., & Afari, N. (2013). Chronic fatigue and personality: A twin study of causal pathways and shared liabilities. *Annals of Behavioral Medicine, 45,* 289–298.

Polka, L., & Werker, J. F. (1994). Developmental changes in perception of nonnative vowel contrasts. *Journal of Experimental Psychology: Human Perception & Performance, 20,* 421–435.

Pollack, J. M. (1979/1980). Correlates of death anxiety: A review of empirical studies. *Omega, 10*, 97–121.

Pollett, T., & Nettle, D. (2009). Birth order and adult family relationships: Firstborns have better sibling relationships than laterborns. *Journal of Social and Personal Relationships, 26*, 1029–1046.

Pomerantz, E., & Ruble, D. (1998). The role of maternal control in the development of sex differences in child self-evaluative factors. *Child Development, 69*, 458–478.

Pomerleau, A., Scuccimarri, C., & Malcuit, G. (2003). Mother-infant behavioral interactions in teenage and adult mothers during the first six months postpartum: Relations with infant development. *Infant Mental Health Journal, 24*, 495–509.

Ponds, R., Commissaris, K., & Jolles, J. (1997). Prevalence and covariates of subjective forgetfulness in a normal population in the Netherlands. *International Journal of Aging and & Human Development, 45*, 207–221.

Popham, L., Kennison, S., & Bradley, K. (2011). Ageism and risk-taking in young adults: Evidence for a link between death anxiety and ageism. *Death Studies, 35*, 751–763.

Population Resource Center. (2004). *Latina teen pregnancy: Problems and prevention.* Retrieved October 27, 2004, from http://www.prcds.org/summaries/latinapreg04/latinapreg04.html.

Posner, M., & Rothbart, M. (2007). Expertise. In M. Posner & M. Rothbart (Eds.), *Educating the human brain* (pp. 189–208). Washington, DC: American Psychological Association,

Posthuma, D., de Geus, E., & Boomsma, D. (2003). Genetic contributions to anatomical, behavioral, and neurophysiological indices of cognition. In R. Plomin, J. DeFries, I., Craig, & P. McGuffin (Eds.), *Behavioral genetics in the postgenomic era* (pp. 141–161). Washington, DC: American Psychological Association.

Postrado, L., & Nicholson, H. (1992). Effectiveness in delaying the initiation of sexual intercourse in girls aged 12–14. *Youth in Society, 23*, 356–379.

Poulson, C. L., Nunes, L. R. D., & Warren, S. F. (1989). Imitation in infancy: A critical review. In H. W. Reese (Ed.), *Advances in child development and behavior, Vol. 22* (pp. 272–298). San Diego, CA: Academic Press.

Powell, R. (May 31, 2006). *The $400 billion income shortfall: Baby-boomer women have tougher road to retirement.* Retrieved August 2, 2007 from www.marketwatch.com/News/Story/Story.aspx?guid=%7B107BAF88-C68D-473E-B022-6C3533D216AD%7D.

Powers, C. & Bierman, K. (2013). The multifaceted impact of peer relations on aggressive-disruptive behavior in early elementary school. *Developmental Psychology, 49*, 1174–1186.

Powlishta, K. K. (1995). Intergroup processes in childhood: Social categorization and sex role development. *Developmental Psychology, 31*, 781–788.

Prager, E. (1998). Men and meaning in later life. *Journal of Clinical Geropsychology, 4*, 191–203.

Prasthani, J., Dasari, B., Marwarha, G., Larson, T., Chen, X, Geiger, J., & Ghribi, O. (2010). Caffeine protects against oxidative stress and Alzheimer's disease-like pathology in rabbit hippocampus induced by cholesterol-enriched diet. *Free Radical Biology and Medicine, 49*, 1212–1220.

Prat-Sala, M., Shillcock, R., & Sorace, A. (2000). Animacy effects on the production of object-dislocated descriptions by Catalan-speaking children. *Journal of Child Language, 27*, 97–117.

Pratt, M., Arnold, M., & Pratt, A. (1999). Predicting adolescent moral reasoning from family climate: A longitudinal study. *Journal of Early Adolescence, 19*, 148–175.

Premack, D. (1959). Toward empirical behavior laws: I. Positive reinforcement. *Psychological Review, 66*, 219–233.

Prepavessis, H., Cameron, L., Baldi, J., Robinson, S., Borrie, K., Harper, T., & Grove, J. (2007). The effects of exercise and nicotine replacement therapy on smoking rates in women. *Addictive Behaviors, 32*, 1416–1432.

Pressley, M., & Dennis-Rounds, J. (1980). Transfer of a mnemonic keyword strategy at two age levels. *Journal of Educational Psychology, 72*, 575–582.

Price, C., & Kunz, J. (2003). Rethinking the paradigm of juvenile delinquency as related to divorce. *Journal of Divorce & Remarriage, 39*, 109–133.

Prichard, E., Propper, R., & Christman, S. (2013). Degree of handedness, but not direction, is a systematic predictor of cognitive performance. *Frontiers in Psychology, 4*, 9.

Prigerson, H., Bierhals, A., Kasl, S., Reynolds, C., et al. (1997). Traumatic grief as a risk factor for mental and physical morbidity. *American Journal of Psychiatry, 154*, 616–623.

Prigerson, H., Bridge, J., Maciejewski, P., Beery, L., Rosenheck, R., Jacobs, S., Bierhals, A., Kupfer, D., & Brent, D. (1999). Influence of traumatic grief on suicidal ideation among young adults. *American Journal of Psychiatry, 156*, 1994–1995.

Prince, M., Bryce, R., Albanese, E., Wimo, A., Ribeiro, W., & Ferri, C. (2013). The global prevalence of dementia: A systematic review and meta-analysis. *Alzheimer's and Dementia, 9*, 63–75.

Propopenko, S., Mozheyko, E., Petrova, M., Koryagina, T., Kaskaeva, D., Chernykh, T., Shvetzova, I., & Bezdenezhnih, A. (2013). Correction of post-stroke cognitive impairments using computer programs. *Journal of the Neurological Sciences, 325*, 148–153.

Proulx, C., & Snyder-Rivas, L. (2013). The longitudinal associations between marital happiness, problems, and self-rated health. *Journal of Family Psychology, 27*, 194–202.

Provasi, J., Dubon, C., & Bloch, H. (2001). Do 9- and 12-month-olds learn means-ends relation by observing? *Infant Behavior & Development, 24*, 195–213.

Provasnik, S., & Gonzales, P. (2009). *Condition of education, special analysis 2009.* Retrieved August 8, 2010 from http://nces.ed.gov/programs/coe/2009/analysis/.

Pulkkinen, L. (1982). Self-control and continuity from childhood to late adolescence. In P. Baltes & O. G. Brim, Jr. (Eds.), *Life span development and behavior, Vol. 4* (pp. 64–107). New York: Academic Press.

Pungello, E., Kainz, K., Burchinal, M., Wasik, B., Sparling, J., Ramey, C., & Campbell, F. (2010). Early educational intervention, early cumulative risk, and the early home environment as predictors of young adult outcomes within a high-risk sample. *Child Development, 81*, 410–426.

Purnine, D., & Carey, M. (1998). Age and gender differences in sexual behavior preferences: A follow-up report. *Journal of Sex & Marital Therapy, 24*, 93–102.

Purugganan, O., Stein, R., Johnson Silver, E., & Benenson, B. (2003). Exposure to violence and psychosocial adjustment among urban school-aged children. *Journal of Developmental & Behavioral Pediatrics, 24*, 424–430.

Qi, C., & Kaiser, A. (2003). Behavior problems of preschool children from low-income families: Review of the literature. *Early Childhood Special Education, 23*, 188–216.

Quick, H., & Moen, P. (1998). Gender, employment and retirement quality: A life course approach to the differential experiences of men and women. *Journal of Occupational Health Psychology, 3*, 44–64.

Quitmann, J., Krison, L., Romer, G., & Ramsauer, B. (2012). The capacity to see things from the child's point of view—Aassessing insightfulness in mothers with and without a diagnosis of depression. *Clinical Psychology & Psychotherapy, 19*, 508–517.

Raaijmakers, Q., Verbogt, T., & Vollebergh, W. (1998). Moral reasoning and political beliefs of Dutch adolescents and young adults. *Journal of Social Issues, 54*, 531–546.

Rabasca, L. (1999, October). Ultra-thin magazine models found to have little negative effect on adolescent girls. *APA Monitor Online 30.* Retrieved January 16, 2001, from http://www.apa.org/monitor/oct99.

Rabinowitz, P. (2000). Noise-induced hearing loss. *American Family Physician, 61*, 1053.

Radford, S., & Bloch, P. (2013). Consumers' online responses to the death of a celebrity. *Marketing Letters, 24*, 43-55.

Radmacher, K., & Azmitia, M. (2006). Are there gendered pathways to intimacy in early adolescents' and emerging adults' friendships? *Journal of Adolescent Research, 21*, 415–448.

Raffaelli, M., & Ontai, L. (2004). Gender socialization in Latino/a families: Results from two retrospective studies. *Sex Roles, 50*, 287–299.

Ragnarsdottir, H., Simonsen, H., & Plunkett, K. (1999). The acquisition of past tense morphology in Icelandic and Norwegian children: An experimental study. *Journal of Child Language, 26*, 577–618.

Rahman, O., Strauss, J., Gertler, P., Ashley, D., & Fox, K. (1994). Gender differences in adult health: An international comparison. *The Gerontologist, 34*, 463–469.

Raj, A.. & Bertolone, S. (2010). *Sickle cell anemia.* Retrieved June 27, 2010 from http://emedicine.medscape.com/article/958614-overview.

Raja, S. N., McGee, R., & Stanton, W. R. (1992). Perceived attachments to parents and peers and psychological well-being in adolescence. *Journal of Youth & Adolescence, 21*, 471–485.

Rajkumar, A., Mohan, T., & Tharyan, P. (2013). Lessons from the 2004 Asian tsunami: Epidemiological and nosological debates in the diagnosis of post-traumatic stress disorder in non-Western post-disaster communities. *International Journal of Social Psychiatry, 59*, 123–129.

Ralston, S., & Lorenzo, M. (2004). ADORE: Attention-Deficit Hyperactivity Disorder Observational Research in Europe. *European Child & Adolescent Psychiatry, 13*, i36–i42.

Ramchandani, P., Domoney, J., Sethna, V., Psychogiou, L., Vlachos, H., & Murray, L. (2013). Do early father—infant interactions predict the onset of externalizing behaviours in young children? Findings from a longitudinal cohort study. *Journal of Child Psychology and Psychiatry, 54*, 56–64.

Ramey, C. T. (1993). A rejoinder to Spitz's critique of the Abecedarian experiment. *Intelligence, 17*, 25–30.

Ramey, C. T., & Campbell, F. A. (1987). The Carolina Abecedarian Project: An educational experiment concerning human malleability. In J. J. Gallagher & C. T. Ramey (Eds.), *The malleability of children* (pp. 127–140). Baltimore: Paul H. Brookes.

Randall, K. (2007). Examining the relationship between burnout and age among Anglican clergy in England and Wales. *Mental Health, Religion, & Culture, 10*, 39–46.

Rao, G., & Rao, S. (1997). Sector and age differences in productivity. *Social Science International, 13*, 51–56.

RäsänenRasanen, O. (2012). Computational modeling of phonetic and lexical learning in early language acquisition: Existing models and future directions. *Speech Communication, 54*, 975–997.

Raskind, M. A., & Peskind, E. R. (1992). Alzheimer's disease and other dementing disorders. In J. E. Birren, R. B. Sloane, & G. D. Cohen (Eds.), *Handbook of mental health and aging* (2nd ed., pp. 478–515). San Diego, CA: Academic Press.

Rasmussen Reports. (April 10, 2010). *58% of Americans have been on a diet.* Retrieved August 16, 2010 from http://www.rasmussenreports.com/public_content/lifestyle/general_lifestyle/april_2010/58_of_americans_have_been_on_a_diet.

Rauer, A., Pettit, G., Lansford, J., Bates, J., & Dodge, K. (2013). Romantic relationship patterns in young adulthood and their developmental antecedents. *Developmental Psychology 49*, 2159–2171.

Ray, B. (2010). Academic achievement and demographic traits of homeschool students: A nationwide study. *Academic Leadership Journal, 8.* Retrieved July 10, 2013, from http://contentcat.fhsu.edu/cdm/compoundobject/collection/p15732co114/id/456.

Raz, N., & Rodrigue, K. (2006). Differential aging of the brain: Patterns, cognitive correlates and modifiers. *Neuroscience and Biobehavioral Reviews, 30*, 730–748.

Raz, N., Rodrigue, K., Kennedy, K., & Acker, J. (2007). Vascular health and longitudinal changes in brain and cognition in middle-aged and older adults. *Neuropsychology, 21*, 149–157.

Reczek, C. (2012). The promotion of unhealthy habits in gay, lesbian, and straight intimate partnerships. *Social Science & Medicine, 75*, 1114–1121.

Reed, M. (1998). Predicting grief symptomatology among the suddenly bereaved. *Suicide & Life-Threatening Behavior, 28*, 285–301.

Rego, A. (2006). The alphabetic principle, phonics, and spelling: Teaching students the code. In J. Schumm (Ed.), *Reading assessment and instruction for all learners* (pp. 118–162). New York: Guilford Press.

Reich, J. W., Zautra, A. J., & Guarnaccia, C. A. (1989). Effects of disability and bereavement on the mental health and recovery of older adults. *Psychology & Aging, 4*, 57–65.

Reichle, B., & Gefke, M. (1998). Justice of conjugal divisions of labor—you can't always get what you want. *Social Justice Research, 11*, 271–287.

Reid, P., & Roberts, S. (2006). Gaining options: A mathematics program for potentially talented at risk adolescent girls. *Merrill-Palmer Quarterly, 52*, 288–304.

Reijntjes, A., Vermande, M., Goossens, F., Olthof, T., van de Schoot, R., Aleva, L., & van der Meulen, M. (2013). Developmental trajectories of bullying and social dominance in youth. *Child Abuse & Neglect, 37*, 224–234.

Reinehr, T., & Toschke, A. (2009). Onset of puberty and cardiovascular risk factors in untreated obese children and adolescents: A 1-year follow-up study. *Archives of Pediatric Adolescent Medicine, 163*, 709–715.

Reiner, W., & Gearheardt, J. (2004). Discordant sexual identity in some genetic males with cloacal extrophy assigned to female sex at birth. *The New England Journal of Medicine, 350*, 333–341.

Renati, R., Berrone, C., & Zanetti, M. (2012). Morally disengaged and unempathic: Do cyberbullies fit these definitions? An exploratory study. *Cyberpsychology, Behavior, and Social Networking, 15*, 391–398.

Rendell, P., & Thomson, D. (1999). Aging and prospective memory: Differences between naturalistic and laboratory tasks. *Journals of Gerontology, 54B*, P256–P269.

Repetto, P., Caldwell, C., & Zimmerman, M. (2004). Trajectories of depressive symptoms among high risk African-American adolescents. *Journal of Adolescent Health, 35*, 468–477.

Reskin, B. (1993). Sex segregation in the workplace. *Annual Review of Sociology, 19*, 241–270.

Reynolds, C. R., & Brown, R. T. (Eds.). (1984). *Perspectives on bias in mental testing.* New York: Plenum.

Reynolds, C., & Shaywitz, S. (2009). Response to intervention: Ready or not? Or, from wait-to-fail to watch-them-fail. *School Psychology Quarterly, 24*, 130–145.

Reynolds, M., Schieve, L., Martin, J., Jeng, G., & Macaluso, M. (2003). Trends in multiple births conceived using assisted reproductive technology, United States, 1997–2000. *Pediatrics, 111*, 1159–1162.

Rezende, T., Coimbra, A., Costallat, L., & Coimbra, I. (2010). Factors of high impacts on the life of caregivers of disabled elderly. *Archives of Gerontology and Geriatrics, 51*, 76–80.

Rhee, S., & Waldman, I. (2011). Genetic and environmental influences on aggression. In P. Shaver, M. Mikulincer (Eds.), *Human aggression and violence: Causes, manifestations, and consequences.* Washington, DC: American Psychological Association.

Rhodes, J., van Praag, H., Jeffrey, S., Girard, I., Mitchell, G., Garland, T., & Gage, F. (2003). Exercise increases hippocampal neurogenesis to high levels but does not improve spatial learning in mice bred for increased voluntary wheel running. *Behavioral Neuroscience, 117*, 1006–1016.

Rholes, W. S., & Ruble, D. N. (1984). Children's understanding of dispositional characteristics of others. *Child Development, 55*, 550–560.

Ribarska, T., Klaus-Marius, B., Koch, A., & Schulz, W. (2012). Specific changes in the expression of imprinted genes in prostate cancer—Implications for cancer progression and epigenetic regulation. *Asian Journal of Andrology, 14*, 436–450.

Ricciardelli, L., & Mellor, D. (2012). Influence of peers. In N. Rumsey, N., & D. Harcourt, D. (Eds.), *The Oxford handbook of the psychology of appearance.* (pp. 253–272). New York, NY, USA: Oxford University Press.

Richardson, J. L., Zarnegar, Z., Bisno, B., & Levine, A. (1990). Psychosocial status at initiation of cancer treatment and survival. *Journal of Psychosomatic Research, 34*, 189–201.

Rich-Edwards, J., Manson, J., Hennekens, C., & Buring, J. (1995). The primary prevention of coronary heart disease in women. *New England Journal of Medicine, 332*, 1758–1766.

Rideout, V., Foehr, U., & Roberts, D. (2010). *Generation M2: Medial in the lives of 8- to 18-year-olds.* Retrieved August 12, 2010 from http://www.kff.org/entmedia/upload/8010.pdf.

Ridgway, C., Ong, K., Tammelin, T., Sharp, S., Ekelund, U., & Marjo-Ritta, J. (2009). Infant motor development predicts sports participation at age 14 years: Northern Finland Birth Cohort of 1966. *Public Library of Science ONE, 4*, e6837.

Ridolfo, H., Chepp, V., & Milkie, M. (2013). Race and girls' self-evaluations: How mothering matters. *Sex Roles, 68*, 496–509.

Riegle-Crumb, C., Farkas, G., & Muller, C. (2006). The role of gender and friendship in advanced course taking. *Sociology of Education, 79*, 206–228.

Ries, L., Melbert, D., Krapcho, M., Mariotto, A., Miller, B, Feuer, E., Clegg, L., Horner, M., Howlader, N., Eisner, M., Reichman, M., Edwards, B. (2007). *SEER cancer statistics review.* Retrieved July 6, 2007 from http://seer.cancer.gov/csr/1975_2004/.

Riggle, E., Rostosky, S., & Horne, S. (2010). Psychological distress, well-being, and legal recognition in same-sex couple relationships. *Journal of Family Psychology, 24*, 82–86.

Riggs, A. (1997). Men, friends, and widowhood: Towards successful aging. *Australian Journal on Ageing, 16*, 182–185.

Riley, B. (2010). GLB adolescent's "coming out." *Journal of Child and Adolescent Psychiatric Nursing, 23*, 3–10.

Rinaldi, P., Polidori, M., Metastasio, A., Mariani, E., Mattioli, P., Cherubini, A., Catani, M., Cecchetti, R., Senin, U., & Mecocci, P. (2003). Plasma antioxidants are similarly depleted in mild cognitive impairment and in Alzheimer's disease. *Neurobiology of Aging, 24*, 915–919.

Rique, J., & Camino, C. (1997). Consistency and inconsistency in adolescents' moral reasoning. *International Journal of Behavioral Development, 21*, 813–836.

Risch, H., Jain, M., Marrett, L., & Howe, G. (1994). Dietary fat intake and risk of epithelial ovarian cancer. *Journal of the National Cancer Institute, 86*, 1409–1415.

Riskind, R., & Patterson, C. (2010). Parenting intentions and desires among childless lesbian, gay, and heterosexual individuals. *Journal of Family Psychology, 24*, 78–81.

Rispoli, K., McGoey, K., Koziol, N., & Schreiber, J. (2013). The relation of parenting, child temperament, and attachment security in early childhood to social competence at school entry. *Journal of School Psychology 51*, 643–658.

Rivera, D., & Frye, R. (2010). *HIV infection*. Retrieved June 27, 2010 from http://emedicine.medscape.com/article/965086-overview.

Rivera-Nivar, M., & Pomales-Garcáa, C. (2010). E-training: Can young and older users be accommodated with the same interface? *Computers & Education, 55*, 949–960.

Rizzi, T., & Posthuma, D. (2013). Genes and intelligence. in Reisberg, D. (Ed.). *The Oxford handbook of cognitive psychology* (pp. 823–841). New York, NY, USA: Oxford University Press.

Robards, J., Evandrou, M., Falkingham, J., & Vlachantoni, A. (2012). Marital status, health and mortality. *Maturitas, 73*, 295–299.

Robb, M., Richert, R., & Wartella, E. (2009). Just a talking book? Word learning from watching baby videos. *British Journal of Developmental Psychology, 27*, 27–45.

Robbins, A. (2001). *Quarterlife crisis: How to get your head around your twenties.* New York: Penguin Putnam.

Roberts, R. E., & Sobhan, M. (1992). Symptoms of depression in adolescence: A comparison of Anglo, African, and Hispanic Americans. *Journal of Youth & Adolescence, 21*, 639–651.

Robinson, N., Lanzi, R., Weinberg, R., Ramey, S., & Ramey, C. (2002). Family factors associated with high academic competence in former Head Start children at third grade. *Gifted Child Quarterly, 46*, 278–290.

Robinson-Whelen, S., & Kiecolt-Glaser, N. (1997). The importance of social versus temporal comparison appraisals among older adults. *Journal of Applied Social Psychology, 27*, 959–966.

Roche, A. F. (1979). Secular trends in human growth, maturation, and development. *Monographs of the Society for Research in Child Development, 44*(3–4, Serial No. 179).

Roderick, M., & Camburn, E. (1999). Risk and recovery from course failure in the early years of high school. *American Educational Research Journal, 36*, 303–343.

Rodgers, W., Murray, T., Selzler, A., & Norman, P. (2013). Development and impact of exercise self-efficacy types during and after cardiac rehabilitation. *Rehabilitation Psychology, 58*, 178–184.

Rodkin, P., & Berger, C. (2008). Who bullies whom? Social status asymmetries by victim gender. *International Journal of Behavioral Development, 32*, 473–485.

Rodkin, P., Farmer, T., Pearl, R., & Van Acker, R. (2000). Heterogeneity of popular boys: Antisocial and prosocial configurations. *Developmental Psychology, 36*, 14–24.

Rodkin, P., Ryan, A., Jamison, R., & Wilson, T. (2013). Social goals, social behavior, and social status in middle childhood. *Developmental Psychology, 49*, 1139–1150.

Rodrigo, M., Janssens, J., & Ceballos, E. (1999). Do children's perceptions and attributions mediate the effects of mothers' child rearing actions? *Journal of Family Psychology, 13*, 508–522.

Roehling, P., Roehling, M., & Moen, P. (2001). The relationship between work-life policies and practices and employee loyalty: A life course perspective. *Journal of Family & Economic Issues, 22*, 141–170.

Roer-Strier, D., & Rivlis, M. (1998). Timetable of psychological and behavioural autonomy expectations among parents from Israel and the former Soviet Union. *International Journal of Psychology, 33*, 123–135.

Rogers, R. L., Meyer, J. S., & Mortel, K. F. (1990). After reaching retirement age physical activity sustains cerebral perfusion and cognition. *Journal of the American Geriatric Society, 38*, 123–128.

Rogoff, B. (1990). *Apprenticeship in thinking: Cognitive development in social contexts.* New York: Oxford University Press.

Roisman, G., Masten, A., Coatsworth, J., & Tellegen, A. (2004). Salient and emerging developmental tasks in the transition to adulthood. *Child Development, 75*, 123–133.

Roland, P. (2012). *Presbycusis*. Retrieved July 16, 2013, from http://reference.medscape.com/article/855989-overview.

Röll 2012 aggression, J., Koglin, U., & Petermann, F. (2012). Emotion regulation nd childhood aggression: Longitudinal associations. *Child Psychiatry and Human Development, 43*, 909–923.

Rollins, B. C., & Feldman, H. (1970). Marital satisfaction over the family life cycle. *Journal of Marriage & the Family, 32*, 20–27.

Rolls, E. (2000). Memory systems in the brain. *Annual Review of Psychology, 51*, 599–630.

Roos, S. (2013). The Kübler-Ross Model: An esteemed relic. *Gestalt Review, 17*, 312–315.

Root, M. (2004). *Mixed race identities: Theory, research, and practice implications*. Workshop presented at the annual meeting of the American Psychological Association. Honolulu, HI, August, 2004.

Rosario, M., Schrimshaw, E., & Hunter, J. (2004). Ethnic/racial differences in the coming-out process of lesbian, gay, and bisexual youths: A comparison of sexual identity development over time. *Cultural Diversity and Ethnic Minority Psychology, 10*, 215–228.

Rosario, M., Schrimshaw, E., Hunter, J., & Braun, L. (2006). Sexual identity development among lesbian, gay, and bisexual youths: Consistency and change over time. *Journal of Sex Research, 43*, 46–58.

Rose, A., Schwartz-Mette, R., Smith, R., Asher, S., Swenson, L., Carlson, W., & Waller, E. (2012). How girls and boys expect disclosure about problems will make them feel: Implications for friendships. *Child Development, 83*, 844–863.

Rose, D. (1993). Diet, hormones, and cancer. *Annual Review of Public Health, 14*, 1 17.

Rose, S. A., & Ruff, H. A. (1987). Cross-modal abilities in human infants. In J. D. Osofsky (Ed.), *Handbook of infant development* (2nd ed., pp. 318–362). New York: Wiley-Interscience.

Rosenberg, J., Pennington, B., Willcutt, E., & Olson, R. (2012). Gene by environment interactions influencing reading disability and the inattentive symptom dimension of attention deficit/hyperactivity disorder. *Journal of Child Psychology and Psychiatry, 53*, 243–251.

Rosenberg, M. (2003). Recognizing gay, lesbian, and transgender teens in a child and adolescent psychiatry practice. *Journal of the American Academy of Child and Adolescent Psychiatry, 42*, 1517–1521.

Rosenblatt, J., & Elias, M. (2008). Dosage effects of a preventive social-emotional learning intervention on achievement loss associated with middle school transition. *Journal of Primary Prevention, 29*(6), 535–555.

Rosenblith, J. F. (1992). *In the beginning* (2nd ed.). Thousand Oaks, CA: Sage.

Rosenfield, R., Lipton, R., & Drum, M. (2009). Thelarche, pubarche, and menarche attainment in children with normal and elevated body mass index. *Pediatrics, 123*, 84–88.

Rosenkrantz, S., Aronson, S., & Huston, A. (2004). Mother-infant relationship in single, cohabiting, and married families: A case for marriage? *Journal of Family Psychology, 18*, 5–18.

Rosenman, R. H., & Friedman, M. (1983). Relationship of Type A behavior pattern to coronary heart disease. In H. Selye (Ed.), *Selye's guide to stress research* (Vol. 2) (pp. 47–106). New York: Scientific and Academic Editions.

Rosenthal, R. (1994). Interpersonal expectancy effects: A 30-year perspective. *Current Directions in Psychological Science, 3*, 176–179.

Rosenthal, S., & Gitelman, S. (2002). Endocrinology. In A. Rudolph, R. Kamei, & K. Overby (Eds.) *Rudolph's fundamentals of pediatrics* (3rd Ed.). New York: McGraw-Hill (pp. 747–795).

Ross, H., Ross, M., Stein, N., & Trabasso, T. (2006). How siblings resolve their conflicts: The importance of first offers, planning, and limited opposition. *Child Development, 77*, 1730–1745.

Ross, M., & Mansano, R. (2010). *Fetal growth restriction*. Retrieved July 4, 2010 from http://emedicine.medscape.com/article/261226-overview.

Rossouw, J., Anderson, G., Prentice, R., LaCroix, A., Kooperberg, C., Stefanick, M., Jackson, R., Beresford, S., Howard, B., Johnson, K., Kotchen, J., & Ockene, J. (2002). Risks and benefits of estrogen plus progestin in healthy postmenopausal women: Principal results from the Women's Health Initiative randomized controlled trial. *Journal of the American Medical Association, 288*, 321–333.

Rossow, I., & Amundsen, A. (1997). Alcohol abuse and mortality: A 40-year prospective study of Norwegian conscripts. *Social Science & Medicine, 44*, 261–267.

Rostosky, S., Owens, G., & Zimmerman, R., & Riggle, E. D. (2003). Associations among sexual attraction status, school belonging, and alcohol and marijuana use in rural high school students. *Journal of Adolescence, 26*, 741–751.

Rotenberg, K., McDougall, P., Boulton, M., Vaillancourt, T., Fox, C., & Hymel, S. (2004). Cross-sectional and longitudinal relations among peer-reported trustworthiness, social relationships, and psychological adjustment in children and early adolescents from the United Kingdom and Canada. *Journal of Experimental Child Psychology, 88*, 46–67.

Roth, M. (2003). Validation of the Arnett Inventory of Sensation Seeking (AISS): Efficiency to predict the willingness towards occupational change, and affection by social desirability. *Personality & Individual Differences, 35*, 1307–1314.

Rothbart, M., (2012). Advances in temperament: History, concepts, and measures. In M. Zentner, M., & R. Shiner, R. (Eds.), *Handbook of temperament.* (pp. 3–20). New York, NY, USA: Guilford Press.

Rotter, J., (1990). Internal versus external control of reinforcement: A case history of a variable. *American Psychologist, 45,* 489–493.

Rovee-Collier, C. (1993). The capacity for long-term memory in infancy. *Current Directions in Psychological Science, 2,* 130–135.

Rovee-Collier, C., & Cuevas, K. (2009). The development of infant memory. In M. Courage & N. Cowan. (Eds.), *The development of memory in infancy and childhood* (2nd ed.). New York: Psychology Press.

Rowe, D. (2002). IQ, birth weight, and number of sexual partners in White, African American, and mixed race adolescents. *Population & Environment: A Journal of Interdisciplinary Studies, 23,* 513–524.

Rowe, J., & Kahn, R. (1998). *Successful aging.* New York: Pantheon.

Rowland, D., & Tai, W. (2003). A review of plant-derived and herbal approaches to the treatment of sexual dysfunctions. *Journal of Sex & Marital Therapy, 29,* 185–205.

Roy, E., Bryden, P., & Cavill, S. (2003). Hand differences in pegboard performance through development. *Brain & Cognition, 53,* 315–317.

Rubin, K. H., Fein, G. G., & Vandenberg, B. (1983). Play. In E. M. Hetherington (Ed.), *Handbook of child psychology: Socialization, personality, and social development* (Vol. 4) (pp. 693–774). New York: Wiley.

Rubin, K. H., Hymel, S., Mills, R. S. L., & Rose-Krasnor, L. (1991). Conceptualizing different developmental pathways to and from social isolation in childhood. In D. Cicchetti & S. L. Toth (Eds.), *Internalizing and externalizing expressions of dysfunction: Rochester Symposium on Developmental Psychopathology* (Vol. 2) (pp. 91–122). Hillsdale, NJ: Erlbaum.

Rubin, K., Burgess, K., & Hastings, P. (2002). Stability and social-behavioral consequences of toddlers' inhibited temperament and parenting behaviors. *Child Development, 73,* 483–495.

Rubin, K., Burgess, K., Dwyer, K., & Hastings, P. (2003). Predicting preschoolers' externalizing behaviors from toddler temperament, conflict, and maternal negativity. *Developmental Psychology, 39,* 164–176.

Rubin, K., Coplan, R., Chen, X, Bowker, J., & McDonald, K. (2011). Peer relationships in childhood. In M. Bornstein & M. Lamb (Eds.), *Developmental science: An advanced textbook* (6th ed., pp. 519–570). New York: Psychology Press.

Rubin, K., Wojslawowica, J., Rose-Krasnor, L., Booth-LaForce, C., & Burgess, K. (2006). The best friendships of shy/withdrawn children: Prevalence, stability, and relationship quality. *Journal of Abnormal Child Psychology, 34,* 143–157.

Rubin, S., & Schechter, N. (1997). Exploring the social construction of bereavement: Perceptions of adjustment and recovery in bereaved men. *American Journal of Orthopsychiatry, 67,* 279–289.

Rubinstein, R. L. (1986). *Singular paths: Old men living alone.* New York: Columbia University Press.

Ruble, D., & Dweck, C. (1995). Self-conceptions, person conceptions, and their development. In N. Eisenberg (Ed.), *Social development.* Thousand Oaks, CA: Sage.

Rudd, M., Viney, L., & Preston, C. (1999). The grief experienced by spousal caregivers of dementia patients: The role of place of care of patient and gender of caregiver. *International Journal of Aging & Human Development, 48,* 217–240.

Rudolph, K., & Troop-Gordon, W. (2010). Personal-accentuation and contextual-amplification models of pubertal timing: Predicting youth depression. *Development and Psychopathology, 22,* 433–451.

Runyan, C., Vladutiu, C., Schulman, M., & Rauscher, K. (2011). Parental involvement with their working teens. *Journal of Adolescent Health, 49,* 84–86.

Rushton, J., & Jensen, A. (2006). The totality of available evidence shows the race IQ gap still remains. *Psychological Science, 17,* 921–922.

Rushton, J., & Rushton, E. (2003). Brain size, IQ, and racial-group differences: Evidence from musculoskeletal traits. *Intelligence, 31,* 139–155.

Rushton, J., Skuy, M., & Fridjhon, P. (2003). Performance on Raven's Advanced Progressive Matrices by African, East Indian, and White engineering students in South Africa. *Intelligence, 31,* 123–137.

Rutgers, A., Bakermans-Kranenburg, M., Van IJzendoorn, M., & Van Bercklelaer-Onnes, I. (2004). Autism and attachment: A meta-analytic review. *Journal of Child Psychology and Psychiatry, 45,* 1123–1134.

Rutter, M., Sonuga-Barke, E., Beckett, C., Castle, J., Kreppner, J., Kumsta, R., Schlotz, W., Stevens, S., & Bell, C. (2010). Deprivation-specific psychological patterns: Effects of institutional deprivation. *Monographs of the Society for Research in Child Development, 75,* 1–231.

Ryan, A., & Sackett, P. (2013). Stereotype threat in workplace assessments. In Geisinger, K., Bracken, B., Carlson, J., Hansen, J., Kuncel, N., Reise, S., & Rodriguez, M. (Eds.). *APA handbook of testing and assessment in psychology, Volume 1: Test theory and testing and assessment in industrial and organizational psychology* (pp. 661–673). Washington, DC, USA: American Psychological Association.

Rydell, R., Shiffrin, R., Boucher, K., Van Loo, K., & Rydell, M. (2010). Stereotype threat prevents perceptual learning. *Proceedings of the National Academy of the Sciences, 107,* 14042–14047.

Saavedra, M., Ramirez, A., & Contreras, C. (1997). Interactive interviews between elders and children: A possible procedure for improving affective state in the elderly. *Psiquiatricay Psicologica de America Latina, 43,* 63–66.

Sackett, P., Hardison, C., & Cullen, M. (2004a). On interpreting stereotype threat as accounting for African American–White differences on cognitive tests. *American Psychologist, 59,* 7–13.

Sackett, P., Hardison, C., & Cullen, M. (2004b). On the value of correcting mischaracterizations of stereotype threat research. *American Psychologist, 59,* 38–49.

Sackett, P., Hardison, C., & Cullen, M. (2005). On interpreting research on stereotype thread and test performance. *American Psychologist, 60,* 271–272.

Saddler, B. (2007). Improving sentence construction skills. In S. Graham, C. MacArthur, & J. Fitzgerald (Eds.), *Best practices in writing instruction* (pp. 163–178). New York: Guilford Press.

Sagi, A, Koren-Karie, N, Gini, M, Ziv, Y, & Joels, T. (2002). Shedding further light on the effects of various types and quality of early child care on infant-mother attachment relationship: The Haifa Study of Early Child Care. *Child Development, 73,* 1166.

Sagiv, M., Vogelaere, P., Soudry, M., & Shrsam, R. (2000). Role of physical activity training in attenuation of height loss. *Gerontology, 46,* 266–270.

Salkeld, L., & Koster, O. (2008). *Coroner launches probe into 'internet suicide cult' after seven youngsters in one town hang themselves.* Retrieved September 3, 2010 from http://www.dailymail.co.uk/news/article-509727/Coroner-launches-probe-internet-suicide-cult-SEVEN-youngsters-town-hang-themselves.html.

Sallquist, J., Eisenberg, N., Spinrad, T., Eggum, N., & Gaertner, B. (2009). Assessment of preschoolers' positive empathy: Concurrent and longitudinal relations with positive emotion, social competence, and sympathy. *The Journal of Positive Psychology, 4,* 223–233.

Salovey, P., & Mayer, J. (1990). Emotional intelligence. *Imagination, Cognition, and Personality, 9,* 185–211.

Salthouse, T. (2004). What and when of cognitive aging. *Current Directions in Psychological Science, 13,* 140–144.

Salthouse, T. (2011). What cognitive abilities are involved in trail-making performance? *Intelligence, 39,* 222–232.

Salthouse, T. (2012). Consequences of age-related cognitive declines. *Annual Review of Psychology, 63,* 201–226.

Salthouse, T. A. (1993). Speed mediation of adult age differences in cognition. *Developmental Psychology, 29,* 722–738.

Saltz, R. (1979). Children's interpretations of proverbs. *Language Arts, 56,* 508–514.

Sampson, R. J., & Laub, J. H. (1994). Urban poverty and the family context of delinquency: A new look at structure and process in a classic study. *Child Development, 65,* 523–540.

Sanchez, B., Reyes, O., & Singh, J. (2006). A qualitative examination of the relationships that serve a mentoring function for Mexican American older adolescents. *Cultural Diversity & Ethnic Minority Psychology, 12,* 615–631.

Sanders, C. M. (1989). *Grief: The mourning after.* New York: Wiley-Interscience.

Sanders, M., & Mazzucchelli, T. (2013). The promotion of self-regulation through parenting interventions. *Clinical Child and Family Psychology Review, 16,* 1–17.

Sandman, C., Wadhwa, P., Hetrick, W., Porto, M., & Peeke, H. (1997). Human fetal heart rate dishabituation between thirty and thirty-two weeks. *Child Development, 68,* 1031–1040.

Sandnabba, N., & Ahlberg, C. (1999). Parents' attitudes and expectations about children's cross-gender behavior. *Sex Roles, 40,* 249–263.

Sands, L. P., & Meredith, W. (1992). Blood pressure and intellectual functioning in late midlife. *Journals of Gerontology: Psychological Sciences, 47,* P81–84.

Sands, L. P., Terry, H., & Meredith, W. (1989). Change and stability in adult intellectual functioning assessed by Wechsler item responses. *Psychology & Aging, 4,* 79–87.

Sandvig, C. (2006). The Internet at play: Child users of public internet connections. *Journal of Computer-Mediated Communication, 11,* 932–956.

Sanford, K., & Madill, L. (2006). Resistance through video game play: It's a boy thing. *Canadian Journal of Education, 29,* 287–306.

Santelli, J., Ott, M., Lyon, M., Rogers, J., Summers, D., & Schleifer, R. (2006). Abstinence and abstinence-only education: A review of U.S. policies and programs. *Journal of Adolescent Health, 38,* 72–81.

Sapienza, P., Zingales, L., & Maestripieri, D. (2009). Gender differences in financial risk aversion and career choices are affected by testosterone. *Proceedings of the National Academy of Sciences of the United States of America, 106,* 15268–15273.

Saslari, S., & Zhang, W. (2006). Kin keepers and good providers: Influence of gender socialization on well-being among USA birth cohorts. *Aging & Mental Health, 10*, 485–496.

Sato, S., Shimonaka, Y., Nakazato, K., & Kawaai, C. (1997). A life-span developmental study of age identity: Cohort and gender differences. *Japanese Journal of Developmental Psychology, 8*, 88–97.

Sattler, J. (2001). *Assessment of children: Cognitive applications*. San Diego, CA: Jerome M. Sattler Publishers, Inc.

Saudino, K. J., & Plomin, R. (1997). Cognitive and temperamental mediators of genetic contributions to the home environment during infancy. *Merrill-Palmer Quarterly, 43*, 1–23.

Savage, M., & Holcomb, D. (1999). Adolescent female athletes' sexual risk-taking behaviors. *Journal of Youth & Adolescence, 28*, 583–594.

Savage, S., & Gauvain, M. (1998). Parental beliefs and children's everyday planning in European-American and Latino families. *Journal of Applied Developmental Psychology, 19*, 319–340.

Savina, N. (2009). Endogenous factors of juvenile delinquency and the perspectives of its prognosing. *International Journal of Academic Research, 1*, 195–198.

Sax, L., & Bryant, A. (2006). The impact of college on sex-atypical career choices of men and women. *Journal of Vocational Behavior, 68*, 52–63.

Sax, L., Lindholm, J., Astin, A., Korn, W., & Mahoney, K. (2002). *The American freshman: National norms for fall 2002*. Los Angeles, CA: Higher Education Research Institute UCLA.

Sbarra, D. (2012). Marital dissolution and physical health outcomes: A review of mechanisms. In L. Campbell, L., J. La Guardia, J., Olson, J., & M. Zanna, M. (Eds.), *The science of the couple* (pp. 207–229). New York, NY, USA: Psychology Press.

Scarr, S. (1997). Why child care has little impact on most children's development. *Current Directions in Psychological Science, 6*, 143–147.

Scarr, S., & Eisenberg, M. (1993). Child care research: Issues, perspectives, and results. *Annual Review of Psychology, 44*, 613–644.

Scarr, S., & McCartney, K. (1983). How people make their own environments: A theory of genotype/environment effects. *Child Development, 54*, 424–435.

Scarr, S., & Weinberg, R. A. (1983). The Minnesota adoption studies: Genetic differences and malleability. *Child Development, 54*, 260–267.

Schaan, B. (2013). Widowhood and depression among older Europeans: The role of gender, caregiving, marital quality, and regional context. *The Journals of Gerontology: Series B: Psychological Sciences and Social Sciences, 68B*, 431–442.

Schachar, R. (2010). *Presbyopia—Cause and treatment*. Retrieved August 27, 2010 from http://emedicine.medscape.com/article/1219573-overview.

Schadt, D. (1997). The relationship of type to developmental issues of midlife women: Implications for counseling. *Journal of Psychological Type, 43*, 12–21.

Schaffer, H., & Emerson, P. (1964). The development of social attachments in infancy. *Monographs of the Society for Research in Child Development, 29* (3, Serial No. 94).

Schaie, K. (2009). "When does age-related cognitive decline begin?" Salthouse again reifies the "cross-sectional fallacy." *Neurobiology of Aging, 30*, 528–529.

Schaie, K. (2013). *Developmental influences on adult intelligence: The Seattle Longitudinal Study* (2nd ed.). New York, NY, USA: Oxford University Press.

Schaie, K. (2013). *Developmental influences on adult intelligence: The Seattle Longitudinal Study* (2nd ed.). New York, NY, USA: Oxford University Press.

Schaie, K. W., Nguyen, H., Willis, S., Dutta, R., & Yue, G. (2001). Environmental factors as a conceptual framework for examining cognitive performance in Chinese adults. *International Journal of Behavioral Development, 25*, 193–202.

Schaie, K., & Hertzog, C. (1983). Fourteen-year cohort-sequential analyses of adult intellectual development. *Developmental Psychology, 19*, 531-543.

Schaie, W., & Willis, S. (2005). *Mind alert: Intellectual functioning in adulthood: Growth, maintenance, decline, and modifiability*. Lecture presented at the Joint Conference of the American Society on Aging and the National Council on Aging as part of the Mind-Alert Program. Retrieved June 10, 2006 from http://geron.psu.edu/sls/publications/MindAlert.pdf.

Scheibel, A. B. (1992). Structural changes in the aging brain. In J. E. Birren, R. B. Sloane, & G. D. Cohen (Eds.), *Handbook of mental health and aging* (2nd ed., pp. 147–174). San Diego, CA: Academic Press.

Scheibner, G., & Leathem, J. (2012). Memory control beliefs and everyday forgetfulness in adulthood: The effects of selection, optimization, and compensation strategies. *Aging, Neuropsychology, and Cognition, 19*, 362–379.

Scheier, M. F., Matthews, K. A., Owens, J. F., Magovern, G. J., Lefebvre, S., Abbott, R. A., & Carver, C. S. (1989). Dispositional optimism and recovery from coronary artery bypass surgery: The beneficial effects on physical and psychological well-being. *Journal of Personality & Social Psychology, 57*, 1024–1040.

Schleiss, M. (2010). *Cytomegalovirus infection*. Retrieved June 27, 1010 from http://emedicine.medscape.com/article/963090-overview

Schlosser, L., Safran, D., & Sbaratta, C. (2010). Reasons for choosing a correction officer career. *Psychological Services, 7*, 34–43.

Schmidt, M., DeMulder, E., & Denham, S. (2002). Kindergarten social-emotional competence: Developmental predictors and psychosocial implications. *Early Child Development & Care, 172*, 451–461.

Schmitt, D., Shackelford, T., & Buss, D. (2001). Are men really more "oriented" toward short-term mating than women? A critical review of theory and research. *Psychology, Evolution, & Gender, 3*, 211–239.

Schmitz, S., Fulker, D., Plomin, R., Zahn-Waxler, C., Emde, R., & DeFries, J. (1999). Temperament and problem behavior during early childhood. *International Journal of Behavioral Development, 23*, 333–355.

Schneider, B., Hieshima, J. A., Lee, S., & Plank, S. (1994). East-Asian academic success in the United States: Family, school, and community explanations. In P. M. Greenfield & R. R. Cocking (Eds.), *Cross-cultural roots of minority child development* (pp. 323–350). Hillsdale, NJ: Erlbaum.

Schneider, M. (2004). The intersection of mental and physical health in older Mexican Americans. *Hispanic Journal of Behavioral Sciences, 26*, 333–355.

Schneider, R. (2006). Group bereavement support for spouses who are grieving the loss of a partner to cancer. *Social Work with Groups: A Journal of Community and Clinical Practice, 29*, 259–278.

Schneider, W. (2010). Metacognition and memory development in childhood and adolescence. In H. Waters & W. Schneider (Eds.), *Metacognition, strategy use, and instruction* (pp. 54–81). New York: Guilford Press.

Scholle, S., Buranosky, R., Hanusa, B., Ranieri, L., Dowd, K., & Valappil, B. (2003). Routine screening for intimate partner violence in an obstetrics and gynecology clinic. *American Journal of Public Health, 93*, 1070–1072.

Schonert-Reichl, K. (1999). Relations of peer acceptance, friendship adjustment, and social behavior to moral reasoning during early adolescence. *Journal of Early Adolescence, 19*, 249–279.

Schothorst, P., & van Engeland, H. (1996). Long-term behavioral sequelae of prematurity. *Journal of the American Academy of Child and Adolescent Psychiatry, 35*, 175–183.

Schraf, M., & Hertz-Lazarowitz, R. (2003). Social networks in the school context: Effects of culture and gender. *Journal of Social & Personal Relationships, 20*, 843–858.

Schreiber, M., Lutz, K., Schweizer, A., Kalveram, K., & Jaencke, L., (1998). Development and evaluation of an interactive computer-based training as a rehabilitation tool for dementia. *Psychologische Reitraege, 40*, 85–102.

Schreiber, M., Schweizer, A., Lutz, K., Kalveram, K., & Jaencke, L. (1999). Potential of an interactive computer-based training in the rehabilitation of dementia. An initial study. *Neuropsychological Rehabilitation, 9*, 155–167.

Schroeder, D., & Salthouse, T. (2004). Age-related effects on cognition between 20 and 50 years of age. *Personality and Individual Differences, 36*, 393-404.

Schuler, M., Nair, P., & Black, M. (2002). Ongoing maternal drug use, parenting attitudes, and a home intervention: Effects on mother-child interaction at 18 months. *Journal of Developmental & Behavioral Pediatrics, 23*, 87–94.

Schull, W., & Otake, M. (1997). Cognitive function and prenatal exposure to ionizing radiation. *Teratology, 59*, 222–226.

Schultz, N. R., Jr., Elias, M. F., Robbins, M. A., Streeten, D. H. P., & Blakeman, N. (1986). A longitudinal comparison of hypertensives and normotensives on the Wechsler Adult Intelligence Scale: Initial findings. *Journal of Gerontology, 41*, 169–175.

Schwartz, C. (2010). Pathways to educational homogamy in marital and cohabiting union. *Demography, 47*, 735–753.

Schwartz, P., Maynard, A., & Uzelac, S. (2008). Adolescent egocentrism: A contemporary view. *Adolescence, 43*, 441–448.

Schweizer, T., Schnegg, M., & Berzborn, S. (1998). Personal networks and social support in a multiethnic community of southern California. *Social Networks, 20*, 1–21.

Scott, C., & Temporini, H. (2010). Forensic issues and the Internet. In E. Benedek, P. Ash, & C. Scott (Eds.), *Principles and practice of child and adolescent forensic mental health* (pp. 253–263). Arlington, VA: American Psychiatric Publishing.

Sebanc, A. (2003). The friendship features of preschool children: Links with prosocial behavior and aggression. *Social Development, 12*, 249–268.

Sedney, M. (1999). Children's grief narratives in popular films. *Omega, 39*, 314–324.

Segatto, B., & Di Filippo, L. (2003). Vita relazionale ed emozioni nelle coppie in fase di pensionamento e/o nido vuoto. *Eta Evolutiva, 74*, 5–20.

Seidman, A. (2005). Minority student retention: Resources for practitioners. In G. Gaither (Ed.) *Minority retention: What works?* (pp. 7–24). San Francisco, CA: Jossey-Bass.

Seidman, E., Allen, L., Aber, J. L., Mitchell, C., & Feinman, J. (1994). The impact of school transitions in early adolescence on the self-system and perceived social context of poor urban youth. *Child Development, 65*, 507–522.

Seiffge-Krenke, I., & Connolly, J. (2010). Adolescent romantic relationships across the globe: Involvement, conflict management, and linkages to parents and peer relationships. *International Journal of Behavioral Development, 34*, 97.

Seligman, M. (2006). *Learned optimism: How to change your mind and your life.* New York: Vintage Books.

Sellers, A., Burns, W., & Guyrke, J. (2002). Differences in young children's IQs on the Wechsler Preschool and Primary Scale of Intelligence-Revised as a function of stratification variables. *Neuropsychology, 9*, 65–73.

Selman, R. L. (1980). *The growth of interpersonal understanding.* New York: Academic Press.

Serpell, R., & Hatano, G. (1997). Education, schooling, and literacy. In J. Berry, P. Dasen, & T. Saraswathi (Eds.), *Handbook of cross-cultural psychology. Vol. 2: Basic processes and human development.* Boston: Allyn & Bacon.

Serpell, R., & Jere-Folotiya, J. (2008). Developmental assessment, cultural context, gender, and schooling in Zambia. *International Journal of Psychology, 43*, 88–96.

Shanahan, T., (2006). *The national reading panel report: Practical advice for teachers.* Retrieved July 10, 2013, from http://www.learningpt.org/pdfs/literacy/nationalreading.pdf.

Shapiro, E. (2002). Family bereavement after collective trauma: Private suffering, public meanings, and cultural contexts. *Journal of Systemic Therapies, 21*, 81–92.

Share, D., & Leiken, M. (2004). Language impairment at school entry and later reading disability: Connections at lexical versus supralexical levels of reading. *Scientific Studies of Reading, 8*, 87–110.

Shaver, P., & Mikulincer, M. (2012). An attachment perspective on morality: Strengthening authentic forms of moral decision making. In M. Mikulincer, M., & P. Shaver, P. (Eds.), *The social psychology of morality: Exploring the causes of good and evil.* (pp. 257–274). Washington, CD, USADC: American Psychological Association.

Shaw, D. S., Kennan, K., & Vondra, J. I. (1994). Developmental precursors of externalizing behavior: Ages 1 to 3. *Developmental Psychology, 30*, 355–364.

Sheng, L., Bedore, L., Pena, E., & Fiestas, C. (2013). Semantic development in Spanish–English bilingual children: Effects of age and language experience. *Child Development, 84*, 1034–1045.

Sher, L. (2004). Type D personality, cortisol and cardiac disease. *Australian and New Zealand Journal of Psychiatry, 38*, 652–653.

Sherman, A., Lansford, J., & Volling, B. (2006). Sibling relationships and best friendships in young adulthood: Warmth, conflict, and well-being. *Personal Relationships, 13*, 151–165.

Sherrod, A., (2012). Review of *Ttotal engagement: An arts-based guide to providing meaningful activities* (2nd ed.). *Educational Gerontology, 38*, 824–825.

Shi, J. (2004). Diligence makes people smart. In R. Sternberg (Ed.), *The international handbook of intelligence* (pp. 325–343). New York: Cambridge University Press.

Shih, K., & Pyke, K. (2010). Power, resistance, and emotional economies in women's relationships with mothers-in-law in Chinese immigrant families. *Journal of Family Issues, 31*, 333–357.

Shiner, R., & Caspi, A. (2012). Temperament and the development of personality traits, adaptations, and narratives. In M. Zentner, M., & R. Shiner, R. (Eds.), *Handbook of temperament* (pp. 497–516). New York, NY, USA: Guilford Press.

Shochat, L. (2003). Our neighborhood: Using entertaining children's television to promote interethnic understanding in Macedonia. *Conflict Resolution Quarterly, 21*, 79–93.

Shock, N. W. (1984) Normal Human Aging: The Baltimore Longitudinal Study of Aging (National Institutes of Health, Bethesda, MD), NIH Publ. No. 84-2450.

Shockley, K., & Allen, T. (2012). Motives for flexible work arrangement use. *Community, Work, & Family, 15*, 217–231.

Shore, C. (1986). Combinatorial play, conceptual development, and early multiword speech. *Developmental Psychology, 22*, 184–190.

Siegal, M. (1987). Are sons and daughters treated more differently by fathers than by mothers? *Developmental Review, 7*, 183–209.

Siegel, B. (1996). Is the emperor wearing clothes? Social policy and the empirical support for full inclusion of children with disabilities in the preschool and early elementary grades. *Social Policy Report, Society for Research in Child Development, 10(2–3)*, 2–17.

Siegler, I. C. (1983). Psychological aspects of the Duke Longitudinal Studies. In K. W. Schaie (Ed.), *Longitudinal studies of adult psychological development* (pp. 136–190). New York: Guilford Press.

Siegler, R. (1994). Cognitive variability: A key to understanding cognitive development. *Current Directions in Psychological Science, 3*, 1-5.

Siegler, R., & Chen, Z. (2002). Development of rules and strategies: Balancing the old and the new. *Journal of Experimental Child Psychology, 81*, 446–457.

Siegler, R., & Lin, X. (2010). Self-explanations promote children's learning. In H. Waters & W. Schneider (Eds.), *Metacognition, strategy use, and instruction* (pp. 85–112). New York: Guilford Press.

Sigman, M., Neumann, C., Carter, E., Cattle, D. J., D'Souza, S., & Bwibo, N. (1988). Home interactions and the development of Embu toddlers in Kenya. *Child Development, 59*, 1251–1261.

Sijtsema, J., Rambaran, A., & Ojanen, T. (2013). Overt and relational victimization and adolescent friendships: Selection, de-selection, and social influence. *Social Influence, 8*, 177–195.

Sijuwade, P. (2003). A comparative study of family characteristics of Anglo American and Asian American high achievers. *Journal of Applied Social Psychology, 33*, 445–454.

Silver, R., & Wortman, C. (2007). The stage theory of grief. *Journal of the American Medical Association, 297*, 2692.

Silverman, J., Ciresi, G., Smith, C., Marin, D., & Schnaider-Beeri, M. (2005). Variability of familial risk of Alzheimer's disease across the late life span. *Archives of General Psychiatry, 62*, 565–573.

Silverstein, M., & Long, J. (1998). Trajectories of grandparents' perceived solidarity with adult grandchildren: A growth curve analysis over 23 years. *Journal of Marriage & the Family, 60*, 912–923.

Simons, R. L., Robertson, J. F., & Downs, W. R. (1989). The nature of the association between parental rejection and delinquent behavior. *Journal of Youth & Adolescence, 18*, 297–309.

Simonton, D. (2000). Creativity: Cognitive, personal, developmental, and social aspects. *American Psychologist, 55*, 151–158.

Simonton, D. K. (1991). Career landmarks in science: Individual differences and interdisciplinary contrasts. *Developmental Psychology, 27*, 119–130.

Simpkins, S., Davis-Kean, P., & Eccles, J. (2006). Math and science motivation: A longitudinal examination of the links between choices and beliefs. *Developmental Psychology, 42*, 70–83.

Simpson, J., Collins, W., Tran, S., & Haydon, K. (2008). Developmental antecedents of emotion in romantic relationships. In J. Forgas & J. Fitness (Eds.), *Social relationships: Cognitive, affective, and motivational processes* (pp. 185–202). New York: Psychology Press.

Skelton, J., Cook, S., Auinger, P., Klein, J., & Barlow, S. (2009). Prevalence and trends of severe obesity among US children and adolescents. *Academic Pediatrics, 9*, 322–329.

Skinner, B. F. (1953). *Science and human behavior.* New York: Macmillan.

Skinner, B. F. (1980). The experimental analysis of operant behavior: A history. In R. W. Riebes & K. Salzinger (Eds.), *Psychology: Theoretical-historical perspectives.* New York: Academic Press.

Skoe, E., Hansen, K., Morch, W., Bakke, I., Hoffman, T., Larsen, B., & Aasheim, M. (1999). Care-based moral reasoning in Norwegian and Canadian early adolescents: A cross-national comparison. *Journal of Early Adolescence, 19*, 280–291.

Skulachev, V. (2009). New data on biochemical mechanism of programmed senescence of organisms and antioxidant defense of mitochondria. *Biochemistry (Moscow), 74*, 1400–1403.

Skwarchuk, S., & Anglin, J. (2002). Children's acquisition of the English cardinal number words: A special case of vocabulary development. *Journal of Educational Psychology, 97*, 107–125.

Slaby, R. G., & Frey, K. S. (1975). Development of gender constancy and selective attention to same-sex models. *Child Development, 46*, 849–856.

Slaughter, V., & Lyons, M. (2003). Learning about life and death in early childhood. *Cognitive Psychology, 46*, 1–30.

Slaughter, Va. (2005). Young children's understanding of death. *Australian Psychologist, 40*, 179–186.

Slining, M., Adair, L., Goldman, B., Borja, J., & Bentley, M. (2010). Infant overweight is associated with delayed motor development. *Journal of Pediatrics, 157* (27–31).

Sloan Center on Aging & Work at Boston College. (2009). *Timing of retirement and the current economic crisis.* Retrieved September 1, 2010 from http://www.bc.edu/research/agingandwork/meta-elements/pdf/publications/FS25_TimingofRetirement.pdf.

Smetana, J. (2006). Social-cognitive domain theory: Consistencies and variations in children's moral and social judgments. In M. Killen & J. Smetana (Eds.), *Handbook of moral development* (pp. 119–153). Mahwah, NJ: Lawrence Erlbaum Associates.

Smetana, J., Jambon, M., Conry-Murray, C., & Sturge-Apple, M. (2012). Reciprocal associations between young children's developing moral judgments and theory of mind. *Developmental Psychology, 48,* 1144–1155.

Smetana, J., Schlagman, N., & Adams, P. (1993). Preschool children's judgments about hypothetical and actual transgressions. *Child Development, 64,* 202–214.

Smith, D., & Moen, P. (2004). Retirement satisfaction for retirees and their spouses: Do gender and the retirement decision-making process matter? *Journal of Family Issues, 25,* 262–285.

Smith, D., Xiao, L., & Bechara, A. (2012). Decision making in children and adolescents: Impaired Iowa Gambling Task performance in early adolescence. *Developmental Psychology, 48,* 1180–1187.

Smith, E. (1982). Exercise for prevention of osteoporosis: A review. *Physican & Sportsmedicine, 10,* 72–83.

Smith, G., & Palmieri, P. (2007). Risk of psychological difficulties among children raised by custodial grandparents. *Psychiatric Services, 58,* 1303–1310.

Smith, J. (2006). Examining the long-term impact of achievement loss during the transition to high school. *Journal of Secondary Gifted Education, 17,* 211–221.

Smith, M., Sharit, J., & Czaja, S. (1999). Aging, motor control, and the performance of computer mouse tasks. *Human Factors, 41,* 389–396.

Smith, P., & Slonje, R. (2010). Cyberbullying: The nature and extent of a new kind of bullying, in and out of school. In S. Jimerson, S. Swearer, & D. Espelage (Eds.), *Handbook of bullying in schools: An international perspective* (pp. 249–262). New York: Routledge/Taylor & Francis Group.

Smith, P., Smees, R., & Pelligrini, A. (2004). Play fighting and real fighting: Using video playback methodology with young children. *Aggressive Behavior, 30,* 164–173.

Smith, P., White, J., & Holland, L. (2003). A longitudinal perspective on dating violence among adolescent and college-age women. *American Journal of Public Health, 93,* 1104–1109.

Smith, S. (2011). Infectious diseases. In K. Marcdante, R. Kliegman, H. Jensen, & R. Behrman (Eds.), *Nelson's essentials of pediatrics* (6th ed., pp. 355–462). New York: Elsevier Health Publishers.

Smith, S., Howard, J., & Monroe, A. (1998). An analysis of child behavior problems in adoptions in difficulty. *Journal of Social Service Research, 24,* 61–84.

Smith, S., Maas, I., & van Tubergen, F. (2012). Irreconcilable differences? Ethnic intermarriage and divorce in the Netherlands, 1995-2008. *Social Science Research, 41,* 1126-1137.

Smith, Y., van Goozen, S., Kuiper, A., & Cohen-Kettenis, P. (2005). Sex reassignment: Outcomes and predictors of treatment for adolescent and adult transsexuals. *Psychological Medicine, 35,* 89–99.

Smock, P. J. (1993). The economic costs of marital disruption for young women over the past two decades. *Demography, 30,* 353–371.

Snarey, J. (1995). In communitarian voice: The sociological expansion of Kohlbergian theory, research, and practice. In W. M. Kurtines & J. L. Gerwitz (Eds.), *Moral development: An introdution* (pp. 109–134). Boston: Allyn & Bacon.

Snarey, J. R. (1985). Cross-cultural universality of social-moral development: A critical review of Kohlbergian research. *Psychological Bulletin, 97,* 202–232.

Snarey, J. R., Reimer, J., & Kohlberg, L. (1985). Development of social-moral reasoning among kibbutz adolescents: A longitudinal cross-sectional study. *Developmental Psychology, 21,* 3–17.

Snarey, J., Son, L., Kuehne, V. S., Hauser, S., & Vaillant, G. (1987). The role of parenting in men's psychosocial development: A longitudinal study of early adulthood infertility and midlife generativity. *Developmental Psychology, 23,* 593–603.

Sneed, R., & Cohen, S. (2013). A prospective study of volunteerism and hypertension risk in older adults. *Psychology and Aging, 28,* 578–586.

Snider, T., & Dillow, S. (2012). *Digest of education statistics, 2011.* Retrieved July 10, 2013 from http://nces.ed.gov/pubs2012/2012001.pdf.

Snieder, H., MacGregor, A., & Spector, T. (1998). Genes control the cessation of a woman's reproductive life: A twin study of hysterectomy and age at menopause. *Journal of Clinical Endocrinology and Metabolism, 83,* 1875–1880.

Snow, C. E. (1997, April). Cross-domain connections and social class differences: Two challenges to nonenvironmentalist views of language development. Paper presented at the biennial meetings of the Society for Research in Child Development, Washington, DC.

"Social Security: More going out than coming in." (August 5, 2010). Retrieved October 20, 2013 from http://money.cnn.com/2010/08/05/news/economy/social_security_trustees_report/.

Soken, N., & Pick, A. (1999). Infants' perception of dynamic affective expressions: Do infants distinguish specific expressions? *Child Development, 70,* 1275–1282.

Sola, A., Rogido, M., & Partridge, J. (2002). The perinatal period. In A. Rudolph, R. Kamei, & K. Overby (Eds.), *Rudolph's fundamental of pediatrics* (3rd ed., pp. 125–183). New York: McGraw-Hill.

Solano, L., Costa, M., Salvati, S., Coda, R., Aiuti, F., Mezzaroma, I., & Bertini, M. (1993). Psychosocial factors and clinical evolution in HIV-1 infection: A longitudinal study. *Journal of Psychosomatic Research, 37,* 39–51.

Soldo, B. J., Wolf, D. A., & Agree, E. M. (1990). Family, households, and care arrangements of frail older women: A structural analysis. *Journals of Gerontology: Social Sciences, 45,* S238–249.

Somers, M. D. (1993). A comparison of voluntarily childfree adults and parents. *Journal of Marriage & the Family, 55,* 643–650.

Sommer, B., Avis, N., Meyer, P., Ory, M., Madden, T., Kagawa-Singer, M., Mouton, C., Rasor, N., & Adler, S. (1999). Attitudes toward menopause and aging across ethnic/racial groups. *American Psychosomatic Society, 61,* 868–875.

Soori, H., & Bhopal, R. (2002). Parental permission for children's independent outdoor activities: Implications for injury prevention. *European Journal of Public Health, 12,* 104–109.

Sophian, C. (1995). Representation and reasoning in early numerical development: Counting, conservation, and comparisons between sets. *Child Development, 66,* 559–577.

Sørensen, T., Lien, L., Holmen, J., & Danbolt, L. (2012). Distribution and understanding of items of religiousness in the Nord-Trøndelag Health Study, Norway. *Mental Health, Religion, & Culture, 15,* 571–585.

Sorkhabi, N., & Mandara, J. (2013). Are the effects of Baumrind's parenting styles culturally specific or culturally equivalent? In R. Larzelere, Morris, A., & A. Harrist (Eds.), *Authoritative parenting: Synthesizing nurturance and discipline for optimal child development* (pp. 113–135). Washington, DC, USA: American Psychological Association.

Sotelo, M., & Sangrador, J. (1999). Correlations of self-ratings of attitude towards violent groups with measures of personality, self-esteem, and moral reasoning. *Psychological Reports, 84,* 558–560.

Sowell, E., Peterson, B., Thompson, P., Welcome, S., Henkenius, A., & Toga, A. (2003). Mapping cortical change across the human life span. *Nature Neuroscience, 6,* 309–315.

Sparrow, P., & Davies, D. (1988). Effects of age, tenure, training, and job review of three components of a death concept. *Child Development, 55,* 1671–1686.

Spearman, J., & Harrison, L. (2010). *Real role models: Successful African Americans beyond pop culture.* Austin, TX, USA: University of Texas Press.

Spelke, E. S. (1982). Perceptual knowledge of objects in infancy. In J. Mehler, E. C. T. Walker, & M. Garrett (Eds.), *Perspectives on mental representation* (pp. 409–430). Hillsdale, NJ: Erlbaum.

Spelke, E. S. (1991). Physical knowledge in infancy: Reflections on Piaget's theory. In S. Carey & R. Gelman (Eds.), *The epigenesis of mind: Essays on biology and cognition* (pp. 133–169). Hillsdale, NJ: Erlbaum.

Spelke, E., & Hespos, S. (2001). Continuity, competence, and the object concept. In E. Dupoux (Ed.), *Language, brain, and cognitive development: Essays in honor of Jacques Mehler* (pp. 325–340). Cambridge, MA: MIT Press.

Spence, J. T., & Helmreich, R. L. (1978). *Masculinity and femininity.* Austin: University of Texas Press.

Spiegel, D., Bloom, J. R., Kraemer, H. C., & Gottheil, E. (1989, October 14). Effect of psychosocial treatment on survival of patients with metastatic breast cancer. *Lancet,* 888–901.

Spieler, D., & Griffin, Z. (2006). The influence of age on the time course of word preparation in multiword utterances. *Language and Cognitive Processes, 21,* 291–321.

Spittle, A., Spencer-Smith, M., Eeles, A., Lee, K., Lorefice, L., Anderson, P., & Doyle, L. (2013). Does the Bayley-III Motor Scale at 2 years predict motor outcome at 4 years in very preterm children? *Developmental Medicine & Child Neurology, 55,* 448–452.

Spokane, A., & Cruza-Guet, M. (2005). Holland's theory of vocational personalities in work environments. In S. Brown & R. Lent (Eds.). *Career development and counseling: Putting theory and research to work* (pp. 24–41). Hoboken, NJ: John Wiley & Sons.

Sprang, G., & McNeil, J. (1998). Post-homicide reactions: Grief, mourning and post-traumatic stress disorder following a drunk driving fatality. *Omega, 37,* 41–58.

Springer, K. (2009). Masculinity can make you sick. *Health and Society News, 5,* 1.

Springer, S. (2010). *The fetus as a patient, prenatal diagnosis and fetal therapy.* Retrieved June 27, 2010 from http://emedicine.medscape.com/article/947706-overview.

Srivastava, S., John, O., Gosling, S., & Potter, J. (2003). Development of personality in early and middle adulthood: Set like plaster or persis-tent change? *Journal of Personality and Social Psychology, 84,* 1041–1053.

St. Pierre, T., Mark, M., Kaltreider, D., & Aikin, K. (1995). A 27-month evaluation of a sexual activity prevention program in boys and girls clubs across the nation. *Family Relations, 44,* 69–77.

Stack, S. (1992a). The effect of divorce on suicide in Finland: A time series analysis. *Journal of Marriage & the Family, 54,* 636–642.

Stack, S. (1992b). The effect of divorce on suicide in Japan: A time series analysis, 1950–1980. *Journal of Marriage & the Family, 54,* 327–334.

Stack, S., & Wasserman, I. (1993). Marital status, alcohol consumption, and suicide: An analysis of national data. *Journal of Marriage & the Family, 55,* 1018–1024.

Stacks, A., Oshio, T., Gerard, J., & Roe, J. (2009). The moderating effect of parental warmth on the association between spanking and child aggression. *Infant and Child Development, 18,* 178–194.

Stainback, S., & Stainback, W. (1985). The merger of special and regular education: Can it be done? A response to Lieberman and Mesinger. *Exceptional Children, 51,* 517–521.

Stampfer, M., Hennekens, C., Manson, J., Colditz, G., Rosner, B., & Willett, W. (1993). Vitamin E consumption and the risk of coronary disease in women. *New England Journal of Medicine, 328,* 1444–1449.

Standley, J. (2002). Meta-analysis of the efficacy of music therapy for premature infants. *Journal of Pedistric Nursing, 17,* 107–113.

Stanford, E. P., Happersett, C. J., Morton, D. J., Molgaard, C. A., & Peddecord, K. M. (1991). Early retirement and functional impairment from a multi-ethnic perspective. *Research on Aging, 13,* 5–38.

Steele, C., & Aronson, J. (1995). Stereotype threat and the intellectual test performance of African Americans. *Journal of Personality & Social Psychology, 69,* 797–811.

Steele, C., & Aronson, J. (2004). Stereotype threat does not live by Steele and Aronson (1995) alone. *American Psychologist, 59,* 47–48.

Steele, J., & Mayes, S. (1995). Handedness and directional asymmetry in the long bones of the human upper limb. *International Journal of Osteoarchaeology, 5,* 39–49.

Steele, M., Hodges, J., Kaniuk, J., Hillman, S., & Henderson, K. (2003). Attachment representations and adoption: Associations between maternal states of mind and emotion narratives in previously maltreated children. *Journal of Child Psychotherapy, 29,* 187–205.

Steffens, D., Artigues, D., Ornstein, K., & Krishman, K. (1997). A review of racial differences in geriatric depression: Implications for care and clinical research. *Journal of the National Medical Association, 89,* 731–736.

Stein, C., Wemmerus, V., Ward, M., Gaines, M., Freeberg, A., & Jewell, T. (1998). "Because they're my parents": An intergenerational study of felt obligation and parental caregiving. *Journal of Marriage & the Family, 60,* 611–622.

Stein, H. (2007). Review of *Wake-up call: The political education of a 9/11 widow. Psychiatric Services, 58,* 722–723.

Steinberg, L., Blatt-Eisengart, I., & Cauffman, E. (2006). Patterns of competence and adjustment among adolescents from authoritative, authoritarian, indulgent, and neglectful homes: A replication in a sample of serious juvenile offenders. *Journal of Research on Adolescence, 16,* 47–58.

Steinberg, L., Elmen, J. D., & Mounts, N. S. (1989). Authoritative parenting, psychosocial maturity, and academic success among adolescents. *Child Development, 60,* 1424–1436.

Steinberg, L., Fletcher, A., & Darling, N. (1994). Parental monitoring and peer influences on adolescent substance use. *Pediatrics, 93,* 1060–1064.

Steinberg, L., Lamborn, S. D., Dornbusch, S. M., & Darling, N. (1992). Impact of parenting practices on adolescent achievement: Authoritative parenting, school involvement, and encouragement to succeed. *Child Development, 63,* 1266–1281.

Steinberg, L., Mounts, N. S., Lamborn, S. D., & Dornbusch, S. D. (1991). Authoritative parenting and adolescent adjustment across varied ecological niches. *Journal of Research on Adolescence, 1,* 19–36.

Steinhauser, K., Christakis, N., Clipp, E., McNeilly, M., Grambow, S., Parker, J., & Tulsky, J. (2001). Preparing for the end of life: Preferences of patients, families, physicians, and other care providers. *Journal of Pain & Symptom Management, 22,* 727–737.

Stemler, S, Chamvu, F., Chart, H., Jarvin, L., Jere, J., Hart, L., Kaani, B., Kalima, K., Kwiatkowski, J., Mambwe, A., Kasonde-N'gandu, S., Newman, T., Serpell, R., Sparrow, S., Sternberg, R., & Grigorenko, E. (2009). Assessing competencies in reading and mathematics in Zambian children. In Grigorenko, E. (Eds.), *Multicultural psychoeducational assessment* (pp. 157–185). New York: Springer Publishing.

Sternberg, R. (1988). *The triarchic mind: A new theory of intelligence.* New York: Viking Press.

Sternberg, R. (2002). A broad view of intelligence: The theory of successful intelligence. *Consulting Psychology Journal: Practice and Research, 55,* 139–154.

Sternberg, R. J. (1987). Liking versus loving: A comparative evaluation of theories. *Psychological Bulletin, 102,* 331–345.

Sternberg, R., Wagner, R., Williams, W., & Horvath, J. (1995). Testing common sense. *American Psychologist, 50,* 912–927.

Stetson, B. (2002). *Living victims, stolen lives: Parents of murdered children speak to America about death value, and meaning.* New York: Baywood Publishing Company.

Stevenson, B., & Wolfers, J. (2007). Trends in marital stability. *Journal of Economic Perspectives, 21,* 27–52.

Stevenson, D., & Bramson, J. (2009). Hospice care in the nursing home setting: A review of the literature. *Journal of Pain and Symptom Management, 38,* 440–451.

Stevenson, H. (1994). Moving away from stereotypes and preconceptions: Students and their education in East Asia and the United States. In P. M. Greenfield & R. R. Cocking (Eds.), *Cross-cultural roots of minority child development* (pp. 315–322). Hillsdale, NJ: Erlbaum.

Stevenson, H. W., & Lee, S. (1990). Contexts of achievement: A study of American, Chinese, and Japanese children. *Monographs of the Society for Research in Child Development, 55* (1–2, Serial No. 221).

Stewart, A., & Ostrove, J. (1998). Women's personality in middle age: Gender, history, and midcourse corrections. *American Psychologist, 53,* 1185–1194.

Stewart, K. (2009). Dimensions of the voice: The use of voice and breath with infants and caregivers in the NICU. In R. Azoulay & J. Loewy (Eds.), *Music, the breath and health: Advances in integrative music therapy* (pp. 235–250). New York: Satchnote Press.

Stigler, J. W., & Stevenson, H. W. (1991). How Asian teachers polish each lesson to perfection. *American Educator* (Spring), 12–20, 43–47.

Stigler, J. W., Lee, S., & Stevenson, H. W. (1987). Mathematics classrooms in Japan, Taiwan, and the United States. *Child Development, 58,* 1272–1285.

Stilberg, J., San Miguel, V., Murelle, E., Prom, E., Bates, J., Canino, G., Egger, H., & Eaves, L. (2005). Genetic environmental influences on temperament in the first year of life: The Puerto Rico Infant Twin Study (PRINTS). *Twin Research and Human Genetics, 8,* 328–336.

Stiles, J., & Jernigan, T. (2010). The basics of brain development. *Neuropsychological Review, 20,* 327–348.

Stimpson, J., Kuo, Y., Ray, L., Raji, M., & Peek, K. (2006). Risk of mortality related to widowhood in older Mexican Americans. *Annals of Epidemiology, 17,* 313–319.

Stipek, D., Gralinski, J., & Kopp, C. (1990). Self-concept development in the toddler years. *Developmental Psychology, 26,* 972–977.

Stoller, E. P., Forster, L. E., & Duniho, T. S. (1992). Systems of parent care within sibling networks. *Research on Aging, 14,* 28–49.

Stoolmiller, M., Gerrard, M., Sargent, J., Worth, K., & Gibbons, F. (2010). R-rated movie viewing, growth in sensation seeking and alcohol initiation: Reciprocal and moderation effects. *Prevention Science, 11,* 1–13.

Stormshak, E., Bierman, K., McMahon, R., Lengua, L., et al. (2000). Parenting practices and child disruptive behavior problems in early elementary school. *Journal of Clinical Child Psychology, 29,* 17–29.

Strawbridge, W. J., Camacho, T. C., Cohen, R. D., & Kaplan, G. A. (1993). Gender differences in factors associated with change in physical functioning in old age: A 6-year longitudinal study. *The Gerontologist, 33*, 603–609.

Strayer, F. (1980). Child ethology and the study of preschool social relationships. In Foot, H., Chapman, A., & Smith, J. (Eds.). *Friendship and social relations in children* (pp. 235–265). Piscataway, NJ, USA: Transaction Publishers.

Striano, T., & Rochat, P. (1999). Developmental link between dyadic and triadic social competence in infancy. *British Journal of Developmental Psychology, 17,* 551–562.

Stroebe, M. (2002). Paving the way: From early attachment theory to contemporary bereavement research. *Mortality, 7*, 127–138.

Stroebe, M., & Schut, H. (1999). The dual process model of coping with bereavement: Rationale and description. *Death Studies, 23*, 1–28.

Stroebe, M., Folkman, S., Hansson, R., & Schut, H. (2006). The prediction of bereavement outcome: Development of an integrative risk factor framework. *Social Science & Medicine, 63*, 2440–2451.

Stroebe, M., Schut, H., & Stroebe, W. (2005). Attachment in coping with bereavement: A theoretical integration. *Review of General Psychology, 9*, 48–66.

Stroebe, M., van Son, M., Stroebe, W., Kleber, R., Schut, H., & van den Bout, J. (2000). On the classification and diagnosis of pathological grief. *Clinical Psychology Review, 20*, 57–75.

Stroganova, T., Posikera, I., Pushina, N., & Orekhova, E. (2003). Lateralization of motor functions in early human ontogeny. *Human Physiology, 29*, 48–58.

Stroud, C., Durbin, C., Saigal, S., & Knobloch-Fedders, L. (2010). Normal and abnormal personality traits are associated with marital satisfaction for both men and women: An actor-partner interdependence model analysis. *Journal of Research in Personality, 44*, 466–477.

Stroud, R. (2004). The strain of the occasional athlete. *Orthopedic Technology Review, 6*. Retrieved July 4, 2007 from www.orthopedictechreview.com/issues/mayjun04/pg24.htm.

Stunkard, A. J., Harris, J. R., Pedersen, N. L., & McClearn, G. E. (1990). The body-mass index of twins who have been reared apart. *New England Journal of Medicine, 322*, 1483–1487.

Sturm, J., & Seery, C. (2007). Speech and articulatory rate of school-aged children in conversation and narrative contexts. *Language, Speech, and Hearing Services in Schools, 38*, 47–59.

Substance Abuse and Mental Health Services Administration. (2006). *Suicidal thoughts, suicide attempts, major depressive episode, and substance use among adults.* Retrieved August 24, 2010 from http://www.oas.samhsa.gov/2k6/suicide/suicide.htm.

Sugisawa, H., Liang, J., & Liu, X. (1994). Social networks, social support, and mortality among older people in Japan. *Journals of Gerontology: Social Sciences, 49*, S3–13.

Sulkes, S. (1998). Developmental and behavioral pediatrics. In R. Behrman & R. Kliegman (Eds.), *Nelson essentials of pediatrics* (3rd ed., pp. 1–55). Philadelphia: Saunders.

Sullivan, K., Zaitchik, D., & Tager-Flusberg, H. (1994). Preschoolers can attribute second-order beliefs. *Developmental Psychology, 30*, 395–402.

Sullivan, M., Ormel, J., Kempen, G., & Tymstra, T. (1998). Beliefs concerning death, dying, and hastening death among older, functionally impaired Dutch adults: A one-year longitudinal study. *Journal of the American Geriatrics Society, 46*, 1251–1257.

Sumner, M., Bernard, K., & Dozier, M. (2010). Young children's full-day patterns of cortisol production. *Archives of Pediatrics & Adolescent Medicine, 164*, 567–571.

Super, C. (1976). Environmental effects on motor development. *Developmental Medicine & Child Neurology, 18*, 561–567.

Super, D. (1990). A life-span, life-space approach to career development. In D. Brown & L. Brooks (Eds.). *Applying contemporary theories to practice.* (2nd ed.) (pp. 197–261). The Jossey-Bass management series and the Jossey-Bass social and behavioral science series. San Francisco, CA: Jossey-Bass.

Suryadevara, V., Storey, S., Aronow, W., & Ahn, C. (2003). Association of abnormal serum lipids in elderly persons with atherosclerotic vascular disease and dementia, atherosclerotic vascular disease without dementia, dementia without atherosclerotic vascular disease, and no dementia or atherosclerotic vascular disease. *Journals of Gerontology, Series A: Biological Sciences & Medical Sciences, 58A*, 859–861.

Susser, E., St. Clair, D., & He, L. (2008). Latent effects of prenatal malnutrition on adult health. *Annals of the New York Academy of Sciences, 1136*, 185–192.

Suzuki, L., & Aronson, J. (2005). The cultural malleability of intelligence and its impact on the racial/ethnic hierarchy. *Psychology, Public Policy, & Law, 11*, 320–327.

Swaim, K., & Bracken, B. (1997). Global and domain-specific self-concepts of a matched sample of adolescent runaways and nonrunaways. *Journal of Clinical Child Psychology, 26*, 397–403.

Swanson, H., & Alloway, T. (2012). Working memory, learning and academic achievement. In Harris, K., Graham, S., Urdan, T., McCormick, C., Sinatra, G., & Sweller, J. (2012). *APA educational psychology handbook, Volume 1: Theories, constructs, and critical issues* (pp. 327–366). Washington, DC, USA: American Psychological Association.

Sweeting, H., & West, P. (2002). Gender differences in weight related concerns in early to late adolescence. *Journal of Family Issues, 23*, 728–747.

Swendsen, J., & Mazure, C. (2000). Life stress as a risk factor for postpartum depression: Current research and methodological issues. *Clinical Psychology, 7*, 17–31.

Symister, P., & Friend, R. (2003). The influence of social support and problematic support on optimism and depression in chronic illness: A prospective study evaluating self-esteem as a mediator. *Health Psychology, 22*, 123–129.

Syska, E., Schmidt, R., & Schubert, J. (2004). The time of palatal fusion in mice: A factor of strain susceptibility to teratogens. *Journal of Cranio-mascillofacial Surgery, 32*, 2–4.

Szymanski, L., & Bacon, J. (2008). *Estrogen therapy.* Retrieved August 27, 2010 from http://emedicine.medscape.com/article/276107-overview.

Tach, L., & Halpern-Meekin, S. (2012). Marital quality and divorce decisions: How do premarital cohabitation and nonmarital childbearing matter? *Family Relations, 61*, 571–585.

Taga, K., Markey, C., Friedman, H. (2006). A longitudinal investigation of associations between boys' pubertal timing and adult behavioral health and well-being. *Journal of Youth and Adolescence, 35*, 401–411.

Takahashi, K., Tamura, J., & Tokoro, M. (1997). Patterns of social relationships and psychological well-being among the elderly. *International Journal of Behavioral Development, 21*, 417–430.

Takata, T. (1999). Development process of independent and interdependent self-construal in Japanese culture: Cross-cultural and cross-sectional analyses. *Japanese Journal of Educational Psychology, 47*, 480–489.

Takei, W. (2001). How do deaf infants attain first signs? *Developmental Science, 4*, 71–78.

Tam, H., Jarrold, C., Baddeley, A., & Sabatos-De Vito, M. (2010). The development of memory maintenance: Children's use of phonological rehearsal and attentional refreshment in working memory tasks. *Journal of Experimental Child Psychology, 107*, 306–324.

Tam, K. (2013). Existential motive underlying cosmetic surgery: A terror management analysis. *Journal of Applied Social Psychology, 43*, 947–955.

Tan, A., Wang, J., Rochtchnia, E., & Mitchell, P. (2006). Comparison of age-specific cataract prevalence in two population-based surveys 6 years apart. *BMC Opthalmology, 6*, 17.

Tang, S., Chang, W., Chen, J., Want, H., Shen, W., Li, C., & Liao, Y. (2013). Course and predictors of depressive symptoms among family caregivers of terminally ill cancer patients until their death. *Psycho-Oncology, 22*, 1312–1318.

Tanner, J. M. (1990). *Foetus into man* (revised and enlarged ed.). Cambridge, MA: Harvard University Press.

Tanner, J. M. (1990). *Foetus into man* (revised and enlarged ed.). Cambridge, MA: Harvard University Press.

Tan-Niam, C., Wood, D., & O'Malley, C. (1998). A cross-cultural perspective on children's theories of mind and social interaction. *Early Child Development & Care, 144*, 55–67.

Tanski, S., Cin, S., Stoolmiller, M., & Sargent, J. (2010). Parental R-rated movie restriction and early-onset alcohol use. *Journal for the Study of Alcohol and Drugs, 71*, 452–459.

Tapanya, S., Nicki, R., & Jarusawad, O. (1997). Worry and intrinsic/extrinsic religious orientation among Buddhist (Thai) and Christian (Canadian) elderly persons. *International Journal of Aging and Human Development, 44*, 73–83.

Tardif, T., & Wellman, H. (2000). Acquisition of mental state language in Mandarin- and Cantonese-speaking children. *Developmental Psychology, 36*, 25–43.

Tardif, T., So, C., & Kaciroti, N. (2007). Language and false belief: Evidence for general, not specific, effects in Cantonese-speaking preschoolers. *Developmental Psychology, 43*, 318–340.

Tatzer, V., van Nes, F., & Jonsson, H. (2012). Understanding the role of occupation in ageing: Four life stories of older Viennese women. *Journal of Occupational Science, 19*, 138–149.

Taveras, E., Gillman, M., Kleinman, K., Rich-Edwards, J., & Rifas-Shiman, S. (2010). Racial/ethnic differences in early-life risk factors for childhood obesity. *Pediatrics, 125*, 686–695.

Taylor, L., & Gaskin-Laniyan, N. (2007). Sexual assault in abusive relationships. *National Institute of Justice Journal, 256*, 1–3.

Taylor, P., & Kopelman, M. (1984). Amnesia for criminal offences. *Psychological Medicine, 14*, 581–588.

Taylor, P., Funk, C., & Clark, A. (2007). *Generation gap in values, behaviors: As marriage and parenthood drift apart, public is concerned about social impact.* Pew Research Center. Retrieved July 5, 2007 from http://pewresearch.org/assets/social/pdf/Marriage.pdf.

Taylor, P., Funk, C., Craighill, P., & Kennedy, C. (2006). *Families drawn together by communication revolution.* Retrieved August 2, 2007 from http://pewresearch.org/assets/social/pdf/FamilyBonds.pdf.

Taylor, P., Passel, J., Fry, R., Morin, R., Wang, W., Velasco, G, & Dockterman, D. (2010). *The return of the multi-generational family household.* Retrieved August 29, 2010 from http://pewsocialtrends.org/assets/pdf/752-multi-generational-families.pdf.

Teachman, J. (2003). Premarital sex, premarital cohabitation and the risk of subsequent marital dissolution among women. *Journal of Marriage & the Family, 65*, 444–455.

Teasell, R., & Kalra, L. (2004). What's new in stroke rehabilitation. *Stroke, 35*, 383–385.

Temko, N. (2005). *Anti-bullying protests force policy u-turn.* Retrieved June 20, 2007 from www.guardian.co.uk/child/story/0,7369,1557999,00.html

Terashima, K., Mikami, A., Tachibana, N., Kumano-Go, T., Teshima, Y., Sugita, Y., & Takeda, M. (2004). Sleep characteristics of menopausal insomnia: A polysomnographic study. *Psychiatry & Clinical Neurosciences, 58*, 179–185.

Terman, L. (1916). *The measurement of intelligence.* Boston: Houghton Mifflin.

Terman, L., & Merrill, M. A. (1937). *Measuring intelligence: A guide to the administration of the new revised Stanford-Binet tests.* Boston: Houghton Mifflin.

Terracciano, A., McCrae, R. R., Brant, L. J., & Costa, P. T., Jr. (2005). Hierarchical linear modeling analyses of the NEO-PI-R scale in the Baltimore longitudinal study of aging. *Psychology and Aging, 20*, 493–506.

Tershakovec, A., & Stallings, V. (1998). Pediatric nutrition and nutritional disorders. In R. Behrman & R. Kliegman (Eds.), *Nelson essentials of pediatrics* (3rd ed.). (pp. 56–92). Philadelphia: Saunders.

Tervo, S., Kivipelto, M., Hänninen, T., Vanhanen, M., Hallikainen, M., Mannermaa, A., & Soininen, H. (2004). Incidence and risk factors for mild cognitive impairment: A population-based three-year follow-up study of cognitively healthy elderly subjects. *Dementia & Geriatric Cognitive Disorders, 17*, 196–203.

Tharenou, P. (1999). Is there a link between family structures and women's and men's managerial career advancement? *Journal of Organizational Behavior, 20*, 837–863.

Tharp, R. G., & Gallimore, R. (1988). *Rousing minds to life.* New York: Cambridge University Press.

The Wedding Report, Inc. (2012). *2013 U.S. Wedding Market Insight Report.* Retrieved October 13, 2013 from http://www.theweddingreport.com/wmdb/index.cfm?action=reports.index&rpt=2013mireport.

Thelen, E. (1995). Motor development: A new synthesis. *American Psychologist, 50*, 79–95.

Thelen, E., & Adolph, K. E. (1992). Arnold L. Gesell: The paradox of nature and nurture. *Developmental Psychology, 28*, 368–380.

Thobaben, M., & Duncan, R. (2003). Domestic elder abuse by health care providers. *Home Health Care Management & Practice, 15*, 168–169.

Thomas, A., & Chess, S. (1977). *Temperament and development.* New York: Brunner/Mazel.

Thomas, M. (2005). *Comparing theories of child development* (6th ed.). Pacific Grove, CA: Wadsworth/Cengage.

Thomas, R. M. (Ed.). (1990). *The encyclopedia of human development and education: Theory, research, and studies.* Oxford, UK: Pergamon Press.

Thommessen, S., & Todd B. (2010). *Revisiting sex differences in play: Very early evidence of stereotypical preferences in infancy.* Paper presented at the annual meeting of the British Psychological Society. Stratford-upon-Avon, UK, April, 2010.

Thompson, B., Brough, P., & Schmidt, H. (2006). Supervisor and subordinate work-family values: Does similarity make a difference? *International Journal of Stress Management, 13*, 45–63.

Thompson, G., & Joshua-Shearer, M. (2002). In retrospect: What college undergraduates say about their high school education. *The High School Journal, 85*, 1–15.

Thompson, R. (2009). Early foundations: Conscience and the development of moral character. In D. Narvaez & D. Lapsley (Eds.), *Personality, identity, and character: Explorations in moral psychology* (pp. 159–184). New York: Cambridge University Press.

Thompson, R., & Newton, E. (2010). Emotion in early conscience. In W. Arsenio & E. Lemerise (Eds.), *Emotions, aggression, and morality in children: Bridging development and psychopathology* (pp. 13–31). Washington, DC: American Psychological Association.

Thompson, R., Winer, A., & Goodvin, R. (2011). The individual child. In M. Bornstein & M. Lamb (Eds.), *Developmental science: An advanced textbook* (6th ed., 427–468). New York: Psychology Press.

Thompson, W. (2013). *Alcoholism.* Retrieved July 17, 2013, from http://emedicine.medscape.com/article/285913-overview.

Thompson, W., & Lande, R. (2007). Alcoholism. Retrieved July 2, 2007 from www.emedicine.com/med/topic98.htm.

Thompson, W., Lande, R., & Kalapatapu, R. (2010). *Alcoholism.* Retrieved August 27, 2010 from http://emedicine.medscape.com/article/285913-overview.

Thorn, A., & Gathercole, S. (1999). Language-specific knowledge and short-term memory in bilingual and non-bilingual children. *Quarterly Journal of Experimental Psychology: Human Experimental Psychology, 52A*, 303–324.

Thorne, B. (1986). Girls and boys together…but mostly apart: Gender arrangements in elementary schools. In W. W. Hartup & Z. Rubin (Eds.), *Relationships and development* (pp. 167–184). Hillsdale, NJ: Erlbaum.

Thorson, J. A., & Powell, F. C. (1992). A revised death anxiety scale. *Death Studies, 16*, 507–521.

Tice, R. R., & Setlow, R. B. (1985). DNA repair and replication in aging organisms and cells. In C. E. Finch & E. L. Schneider (Eds.), *Handbook of the biology of aging* (2nd ed., pp. 173–224). New York: Van Nostrand Reinhold.

Tiedemann, J. (2000). Parents' gender stereotypes and teachers' beliefs as predictors of children's concept of their mathematical ability in elementary school. *Journal of Educational Psychology, 92*, 144–151.

Tincoff, R., & Jusczyk, P. (2012). Six-month-olds comprehend words that refer to parts of the body. *Infancy, 17*, 432–444.

Tolar, T, Lederberg, A., & Fletcher, J. (2009). A structural model of algebra achievement: Computational fluency and spatial visualisation as mediators of the effect of working memory on algebra achievement. *Educational Psychology, 29*, 239–266.

Tolomio, S., Ermolao, A., Lalli, A., & Zaccaria, M. (2010). The effect of a multicomponent dual-modality exercise program targeting osteoporosis on bone health status and physical function capacity of postmenopausal women. *Journal of Women & Aging, 22*, 241–254.

Tomás, J., Sancho, P., Gutiérrez, M., & Galiana, L. (2013). Predicting life satisfaction in the oldest-old: A moderator effects study. *Social Indicators Research, 17*, 94–101.

Tomasello, M. (1999). *The cultural origins of human cognition.* Cambridge, MA: Harvard University Press.

Tomasello, M. (2009). *Why we cooperate.* Cambridge, MA: MIT Press.

Tomassini, C., Kalogirou, S., Grundy, E., Fokkema, T., Martikainen, P., van Groenou, M., & Karisto, A. (2004). Contacts between elderly parents and their children in four European countries: Current patterns and future prospects. *European Journal of Ageing, 1*, 54–63.

Tomasuolo, E., Valeri, G., Di Renzo, A., Pasqualetti, P., & Volterra, V. (2013). Deaf children attending different school environments: Sign language abilities and theory of mind. *Journal of Deaf Studies and Deaf Education, 18*, 12–29.

Tomita, T., Ohta, Y., Ogawa, K., Sugiyama, H., Kagami, N., & Agari, I. (1997). Grief process and strategies of psychological helping: A review. *Japanese Journal of Counseling Science, 30*, 49–67.

Tomlinson-Keasey, C., Eisert, D. C., Kahle, L. R., Hardy-Brown, K., & Keasey, B. (1979). The structure of concrete operational thought. *Child Development, 50*, 1153–1163.

Toomela, A. (1999). Drawing development: Stages in the representation of a cube and a cylinder. *Child Development, 70*, 1141–1150.

Torgesen, J., Wagner, R., Rashotte, C., Rose, E., Lindamood, P., Conway, T., & Garvan, C. (1999). Preventing reading failure in young children with phonological processing disabilities: Group and individual responses to instruction. *Journal of Educational Psychology, 91*, 579–593.

Tortora, G., & Grabowski, S. (1998). *Principles of anatomy and physiology*. New York, NY, USA: John Wiley & Sons.

Tottenham, N., Hare, T., Quinn, B., McCarry, T., Nurse, M., Gilhooly, T., Millner, A., Galvan, A., Davidson, M., Eigsti, I., Thomas, K., Freed, P., Booma, E., Gunnar, M., Altemus, M., Aronson, J., & Casey, B. (2010). Prolonged institutional rearing is associated with atypically large amygdala volume and difficulties in emotion regulation. *Developmental Science, 13*, 46–61.

Trautner, H., Gervai, J., & Nemeth, R. (2003). Appearance-reality distinction and development of gender constancy understanding in children. *International Journal of Behavioral Development, 27*, 275–283.

Trehub, S. E., & Rabinovitch, M. S. (1972). Auditory-linguistic sensitivity in early infancy. *Developmental Psychology, 6*, 74–77.

Treyvaud, K., Anderson, V., Howard, K., Bear, M., Hunt, R., Doyle, L., Inder, T., Woodward, L., & Anderson, P. (2009). Parenting behavior is associated with the early neurobehavioral development of very preterm children. *Pediatrics, 123*, 555–561.

Trichpoulou, A., Costacou, T., Bamia, C., & Trichpoulou, D. (2003). Adherence to a Mediterranean diet and survival in a Greek population. *New England Journal of Medicine, 348*, 2599–2608.

Trivers, R. (1972). Parental investment and sexual selection. In B. Campbell (Ed.), *Sexual selection and the descent of man: 1871–1971* (pp. 136–179). Chicago: Aldine.

Tronick, E. Z., Morelli, G. A., & Ivey, P. K. (1992). The Efe forager infant and toddler's pattern of social relationships: Multiple and simultaneous. *Developmental Psychology, 28*, 568–577.

Tsang, P. (1998). Age, attention, expertise, and time-sharing performance. *Psychology & Aging, 13*, 323–347.

Tsang, W., & Hui-Chan, C. (2003). Effects of Tai Chi on joint proprioception and stability limits in elderly subjects. *Medicine & Science in Sports & Exercise, 35*, 1962–1971.

Tsang, W., & Hui-Chan, C. (2004). Effects of exercise on joint sense. *Medicine and Science in Sports and Exercise, 36*, 658–667.

Tufvesson, E., Melander, O., Minthon, L., Persson, M., Nilsson, P., Struck, J., & Nagga, K. (2013). Diabetes mellitus and elevated copeptin levels in middle age predict low cognitive speed after long-term follow-up. *Dementia and Geriatric Cognitive Disorders, 35*, 67–76.

Turnage, B. (2004). African American mother-daughter relationships mediating daughter's self-esteem. *Child & Adolescent Social Work Journal, 21*, 155–173.

Twenge, J., Campbell, W., & Foster, C. (2003). Parenthood and marital satisfaction: A meta-analytic review. *Journal of Marriage & the Family, 65*, 574–583.

Twohig, M., & Crosby, J. (2010). Acceptance and commitment therapy as a treatment for problematic Internet pornography viewing. *Behavior Therapy, 41*, 285–295.

Twohig, M., Crosby, J., & Cox, J. (2009). Viewing Internet pornography: For whom is it problematic, how, and why? *Sexual Addiction & Compulsivity, 16*, 253–266.

Twyman, K., Saylor, C., Taylor, L., & Comeaux, C. (2010). Comparing children and adolescents engaged in cyberbullying to matched peers. *Cyberpsychology, Behavior, and Social Networking, 13*, 195–199.

U. S. Census Bureau. (1990). *Statistical abstract of the United States*. Washington, DC: U. S. Government Printing Office.

U. S. Census Bureau. (2007). *The American community: American Indians and Alaska natives 2004*. Retrieved September 27, 2013 from http://www.census.gov/prod/2007pubs/acs-07.pdf.

U. S. Census Bureau. (2012). *Income, poverty, and health insurance coverage in the United States: 2011*. Retrieved July 11, 2013, from http://www.census.gov/newsroom/releases/archives/income_wealth/cb12-172.html.

U.S. Bureau of Labor Statistics. (2009). *Work-at-home patterns by occupation*. Retrieved August 26, 2010 from http://www.bls.gov/opub/ils/pdf/opbils72.pdf.

U.S. Bureau of Labor Statistics. (2013). *American time use survey summary*. Retrieved July 21, 2013, from www.bls.gov/news.release/atus.nr0.htm.

U.S. Bureau of Labor Statistics. (2013). *Employment characteristics of families summary*. Retrieved June 20, 2013, from www.bls.gov/news.release/famee.nr0.htm.

U.S. Bureau of Labor Statistics. (2013). *Employment characteristics of families summary*. Retrieved June 20, 2013, from www.bls.gov/news.release/famee.nr0.htm.

U.S. Census Bureau. (2009b). American Community Survey, 2006–2008 data. Retrieved August 28, 2010 from http://factfinder.census.gov/servlet/DatasetMainPageServlet?_program=ACS&_submenuId=datasets_2&_lang=en&_ts=.

U.S. Census Bureau. (2010a). *Income, poverty, and health insurance in the United States: Tables and figures*. Retrieved August 12, 2010 from http://www.census.gov/hhes/www/poverty/data/incpovhlth/2008/tables.html.

U.S. Census Bureau. (2010b). *Statistical abstract of the United States*. Retrieved August 31, 2010 from http://www.census.gov/compendia/statab/.

U.S. Census Bureau. (2012). *2012 national population projections: Summary tables*. Retrieved July 16, 2013, from http://www.census.gov/population/projections/data/national/2012/summarytables.html.

U.S. Census Bureau. (2012). *Family households by number of own children under 18 years of age: 2000 to 2010*. Retrieved July 9, 2013, from http://www.census.gov/compendia/statab/2012/tables/12s0065.pdf.

U.S. Census Bureau. (2013). *Median age at first marriage, 2011 American Community Survey 1-year estimates*. Retrieved July 19, 2013, from http://factfinder2.census.gov/faces/tableservices/jsf/pages/productview.xhtml?pid=ACS_11_1YR_B12007&prodType=tablehttp://factfinder2.census.gov/faces/tableservices/jsf/pages/productview.xhtml?pid=ACS_11_1YR_B12007&prodType=table.

U.S. Department of Health & Human Services. (2010). *Child maltreatment, 2008*. Retrieved July 21, 2010 from http://www.acf.hhs.gov/programs/cb/pubs/cm08/cm08.pdf.

U.S. Department of Health and Human Services. (1998c). *National initiative to eliminate racial and ethnic disparities in health: Diabetes*. Retrieved October 11, 2000, from http://www.raceandhealth.omhrc.gov.

U.S. Department of Health and Human Services. (2007). *Choosing long-term care*. Retrieved August 2, 2007 from http://www.ahrq.gov/consumer/qnt/qntltc.htm.

U.S. Department of Human Services. (2012). *Child maltreatment 2011*. Retrieved July 8, 2013, from http://www.acf.hhs.gov/sites/default/files/cb/cm11.pdf...

Udell, J., Fischer, M., Brookhart, M., Solomon, D., & Choudhry, N. (2006). Effect of the Women's Health Initiative on osteoporosis therapy and expenditure in Medicaid. *Journal of Bone and Mineral Research, 21*, 765–771.

Udry, J. R., & Campbell, B. C. (1994). Getting started on sexual behavior. In A. S. Rossi (Ed.), *Sexuality across the life course* (pp. 187–208). Chicago: University of Chicago Press.

Uemura, N., Okamoto, S., Yamamoto, S., Matsumura, N., Yamaguchi, S., Yamakido, M., Taniyama, K., Sasaki, N., & Schlemper, R. (2001). *Helicobacter pylori* infection and the development of gastric cancer. *New England Journal of Medicine, 345*, 784–789.

Ulmer, J., Desmond, S., Jang, S., & Johnson, B. (2012). Religious involvement and dynamics of marijuana use: Initiation, persistence, and desistence. *Deviant Behavior, 33*, 448–468.

Underwood, M. (1997). Peer social status and children's understanding of the expression and control of positive and negative emotions. *Merrill-Palmer Quarterly, 43*, 610–634.

Underwood, M. K., Coie, J. D., & Herbsman, C. R. (1992). Display rules for anger and aggression in school-age children. *Child Development, 63*, 366–380.

Ungerer, J. A., & Sigman, M. (1984). The relation of play and sensorimotor behavior to language in the second year. *Child Development, 55*, 1448–1455.

Uno, D., Florsheim, P., & Uchino, B. (1998). Psychosocial mechanisms underlying quality of parenting among Mexican-American and White adolescent mothers. *Journal of Youth & Adolescence, 27*, 585–605.

Upadyaya, K., & Salmela-Aro, K. (2013). Development of school engagement in association with academic success and well-being in varying social contexts: A review of empirical research. *European Psychologist, 18*, 136–147.

Updegraff, K., & Obeidallah, D. (1999). Young adolescents' patterns of involvement with siblings and friends. *Social Development, 8*, 52–69.

Urberg, K., Değirmencioğlu, S., Tolson, J., & Halliday-Scher, K. (1995). The structure of adolescent peer networks. *Developmental Psychology, 31*, 540–547.

Utz, R., Caserta, M., & Lund, D. (2012). Grief, depressive symptoms, and physical health among recently bereaved spouses. *The Gerontologist, 52*, 460–471.

Uylings, H. (2006). Development of the human cortex and the concept of "critical" or "sensitive" periods. *Language Learning, 56*, 59–90.

Vachon, M. (1998). Psychosocial needs of patients and families. *Journal of Palliative Care, 14*, 49–56.

Vaeisaenen, L. (1998). Family grief and recovery process when a baby dies. *Psychiatria Fennica, 29*, 163–174.

Vaillant, G. (2012). *Triumphs of experience: The men of the Harvard Grant Study*. Cambridge, MA, USA: Belknap Press of Harvard University Press.

Vaillant, G. E. (1977). *Adaptation to life: How the best and brightest came of age*. Boston: Little, Brown.

Valdez-Menchaca, M. C., & Whitehurst, G. J. (1992). Accelerating language development through picture book reading: A systematic extension to Mexican day care. *Developmental Psychology, 28,* 1106–1114.

Valentino, K., Nuttall, A., Comas, M., Borkowski, J., & Akai, C. (2012). Intergenerational continuity of child abuse among adolescent mothers: Authoritarian parenting, community violence, and race. *Child Maltreatment, 17,* 172–181.

Valenza, E., Leo, I., Gava, L., & Simion, F. (2006). Perceptual completion in newborn human infants. *Child Development, 77,* 1810–1821.

van Beijsterveldt, C., Bartels, M., Hudziak, J., & Boomsma, D. (2003). Causes of stability of aggression from early childhood to adolescence: A longitudinal genetic analysis in Dutch twins. *Behavior Genetics, 33,* 591–605.

Van Beijsterveldt, T., Hudziak, J., & Boomsma, D. (2005). Short- and long-term effects of child care on problem behaviors in a Dutch sample of twins. *Twin Research and Human Genetics, 8,* 250–258.

Van Boxtel, M., Paas, F., Houx, P., Adam, J., Teeken, J., & Jolles, J. (1997). Aerobic capacity and cognitive performance in a cross-sectional aging study. *Medicine & Science in Sports & Exercise, 29,* 1357–1365.

Van den Broek, P., Lynch, J., Naslund, J., Ievers-Landis, C., & Verduin, K. (2004). The development of comprehension of main ideas in narratives: Evidence from the selection of titles. *Journal of Educational Psychology, 96,* 707–718.

van den Hoonaard, D. (1999). "No regrets": Widows' stories about the last days of their husbands' lives. *Journal of Aging Studies, 13,* 59–72.

van der Leij, A., Bekebrede, J., & Kotterink, M. (2010). Acquiring reading and vocabulary in Dutch and English: The effect of concurrent instruction. *Reading and Writing, 23,* 415–434.

van der Molen, M., Molenaar, P. (1994). Cognitive psychophysiology: A window to cognitive development and brain maturation. In G. Dawson & K. Fischer (Eds.), *Human behavior and the developing brain* (pp. 456–492). New York: Guilford Press.

van Doorn, C., Kasl, S., Beery, L., Jacobs, S., & Prigerson, H. (1998). The influence of marital quality and attachment styles on traumatic grief and depressive symptoms. *Journal of Nervous & Mental Disease, 186,* 566–573.

van Doornen, L., Snieder, H., & Boomsma, D. (1998). Serum lipids and cardiovascular reactivity to stress. *Biological Psychology, 47,* 279–297.

Van Duuren, M. Kendall-Scott, L. & Stark, N. (2003) Early aesthetic choices: infant preferences for attractive premature infant faces. *International Journal of Behavioral Development, 27,* 212–219.

van IJzendoorn, M. (2005). Attachment at an early age (0–5) and its impact on children's development. In Centres of Excellence for Children's Well-Being (Eds.), *Encyclopedia on Early Childhood Development.* Retrieved June 13, 2007, from www.excellence-earlychildhood.ca/documents/van_IJzendoornANGxp.pdf

van IJzendoorn, M. H., & Kroonenberg, P. M. (1988). Cross-cultural patterns of attachment: A meta-analysis of the Strange Situation. *Child Development, 59,* 147–156.

van IJzendoorn, M., & Sagi-Schwarz, A. (2008). Cross-cultural patterns of attachment: Universal and contextual dimensions. In J. Cassidy & P. Shaver (Eds.), *Handbook of attachment: Theory, research, and clinical applications* (2nd ed.) (pp. 880–905). New York: Guilford Press.

van IJzendoorn, M., Bakermans-Kranenburg, M., Pannebaker, F., & Out, D. (2010). In defence of situational morality: Genetic, dispositional and situational determinants of children's donating to charity. *Journal of Moral Education, 39,* 1–20.

Van Impe, A., Coxon, J., Goble, D., Doumas, M., & Swinnen, S. (2012). White matter fractional anisotropy predicts balance performance in older adults. *Neurobiology of Aging, 33,* 1900–1912.

Van Solinge, H. (2007). Health change in retirement: A longitudinal study among older workers in the Netherlands. *Research on Aging, 29,* 225–256.

van Wormer, K., & McKinney, R. (2003). What schools can do to help gay/lesbian/bisexual youth: A harm reduction approach. *Adolescence, 38,* 409–420.

Vandell, D., Belsky, J., Burchinal, M., Steinberg, L., & Vandergrift, N. (2010). Do the effects of early child care extend to age 15 years? Results from the NICHD study of early child care and youth development. *Child Development, 81,* 737–756.

Vandewater, E., Shim, M., & Caplovitz, A. (2004). Linking obesity and activity level with children's television and video game use. *Journal of Adolescence, 27,* 71–85.

Varner, F., & Mandara, J. (2009). Marital transitions and changes in African American mothers' depressive symptoms: The buffering role of financial resources. *Journal of Family Psychology, 23,* 839–847.

Vartanian, L. (2001). Adolescents' reactions to hypothetical peer group conversations: Evidence for an imaginary audience? *Adolescence, 36,* 347–380.

Vazsonyi, A., & Huang, L. (2010). Where self-control comes from: On the development of self-control and its relationship to deviance over time. *Developmental Psychology, 46,* 245–257.

Veenstra, R., Lindenberg, S., Munniksma, A., & Dijkstra, J. (2010). The complex relationship between bullying, victimization, acceptance, and rejection: Giving special attention to status, affection, and sex differences. *Child Development, 81,* 480–486.

Vega, W. A. (1990). Hispanic families in the 1980s: A decade of research. *Journal of Marriage & the Family, 52,* 1015–1024.

Velásquez, A., Santo, J., Saldarriaga, L., Lopez, L., & Bukowski, W. (2010). Context-dependent victimization and aggression: Differences between all-girl and mixed-sex schools. *Merrill-Palmer Quarterly: Journal of Developmental Psychology, 56,* 283–302.

Venkatraman, M. M. (1995). A cross-cultural study of the subjective wellbeing of married elderly persons in the United States and India. *Journals of Gerontology: Social Sciences, 50B,* S35–44.

Ventura, S., Curtin, S., & Abma, J. (2012). Estimated pregnancy rates and rates of pregnancy outcomes for the United States, 1990—2008. *National Vital Statistics Reports, 60,* 1–22.

Verbrugge, L. M. (1989). Gender, aging, and health. In K. S. Markides (Ed.), *Aging and health* (pp. 23–78). Newbury Park, CA: Sage.

Verbrugge, L. M., & Wingard, D. L. (1987). Sex differentials in health and mortality. *Women & Health, 12,* 103–145.

Verhaegen, P. (2013). Cognitive aging. In D. Reisberg, D. (Ed.), *The Oxford handbook of cognitive psychology.* (pp. 1014–1035). New York, NY, USA: Oxford University Press.

Verkooijen, K., de Vries, N., & Nielsen, G. (2007). Youth crowds and substance use: The impact of perceived group norm and multiple group identification. *Psychology of Addictive Behaviors, 21,* 55–61.

Vermeer, H., & van IJzendoorn, M. (2006). Children's elevated cortisol levels at daycare: A review and meta-analysis. *Early Childhood Research Quarterly, 21,* 390–401.

Viallon, P. (2012). Retired snowbirds. *Annals of Tourism Research, 39,* 2073–2091.

Vig, E., & Pearlman, R. (2003). Quality of life while dying: A qualitative study of terminally ill older men. *Journal of the American Geriatrics Society, 51,* 1595–1601.

Villar, J., Valladares, E., Wojdyla, D., Zavaleta, N., Carroli, G., Velazco, A., Shah, A., Campodonico, L., Bataglia, V., Faundes, A., Langer, A., Narvaez, A., Donner, A., Romero, M., Reynoso, S., Simonia de Padua, K., Giordano, D., Kublickas, M., & Acosta, A. (2006). Cesarean delivery rates and pregnancy outcomes: The 2005 WHO global survey on maternal and perinatal health in Latin American. *The Lancet, 367,* 1819–1829.

Villegas, J., Castellanos, E., & Gutiérrez, J. (2009). Representations in problem solving: A case study with optimization problems. *Electronic Journal of Research in Educational Psychology, 17,* 279–308.

Viner, R. (2002). Is puberty getting earlier in girls? *Archives of Disease in Childhood, 86,* 8–10.

Vinokur, A. D., & van Ryn, M. (1993). Social support and undermining in close relationships: Their independent effects on the mental health of unemployed persons. *Journal of Personality & Social Psychology, 65,* 350–359.

Virtala, A., Kunttu, K., Huttunen, T., & Virjo, I. (2006). Childbearing and the desire to have children among university students in Finland. *Acta Obstetricia et Gynecologica Scandinavica, 85,* 312–316.

Vitaro, F., Tremblay, R., Kerr, M., Pagani, L., & Bukowski, W. (1997). Disruptiveness, friends' characteristics, and delinquency in early adolescence: A test of two competing models of development. *Child Development, 68,* 676–689.

Voelcker-Rehage, C., Godde, B. & Staudinger, U.B. (2010) Physical and motor fitness are both related to cognition in old age. *European Journal of Neuroscience, 31,* 167–176.

Vogin, J. (2005). *Taking medication while pregnant.* Retrieved June 7, 2007 from http://www.medicinenet.com/script/main/art.asp?articlekey=51639

Volkers, A., Westert, G., & Schellevis, F. (2007). Health disparities by occupation, modified by education: A cross-sectional population study. *Public Health, 7,* 196.

Volz, J. (2000). Successful aging: The second 50. *Monitor, 31,* 24–28.

Von Marées, N., & Petermann, F. (2010). Bullying in German primary schools: Gender differences, age trends and influence of parents' migration and educational backgrounds. *School Psychology International, 31,* 178–198.

Vuchinich, S., Bank, L., & Patterson, G. R. (1992). Parenting, peers, and the stability of antisocial behavior in preadolescent boys. *Developmental Psychology, 28,* 510–521.

Vuorenkoski, L., Kuure, O., Moilanen, I., & Peninkilampi, V. (2000). Bilingual-ism, school achievement, and mental wellbeing: A follow-up study of return migrant children. *Journal of Child Psychology & Psychiatry & Allied Disci-plines, 41,* 261–266.

Wagner, C. (2009). *Counseling the breastfeeding mother.* Retrieved July 7, 2010 from http://emedicine.medscape.com/article/979458-overview.

Waldinger, R., & Schulz, M. (2010). What's love got to do with it? Social functioning, perceived health, and daily happiness in married octogenarians. *Psychology and Aging, 25,* 422–431.

Walker, L. J. (1980). Cognitive and perspective-taking prerequisites for moral devel-opment. *Child Development, 51,* 131–139.

Walker, L. J. (1989). A longitudinal study of moral reasoning. *Child Development, 60,* 157–160.

Walker, L. J., de Vries, B., & Trevethan, S. D. (1987). Moral stages and moral orienta-tions in real-life and hypothetical dilemmas. *Child Development, 50,* 042–050.

Walker-Andrews, A. S. (1997). Infants' perception of expressive behaviors: Differen-tiation of multimodal information. *Psychological Bulletin, 121,* 437–456.

Walker-Andrews, A. S., & Lennon, E. (1991). Infants' discrimination of vocal expres-sions: Contributions of auditory and visual information. *Infant Behavior & Development, 14,* 131–142.

Walker-Andrews, A., & Kahana-Kalman, R. (1999). The understanding of pretence across the second year of life. *British Journal of Developmental Psychology, 17,* 523–536.

Wallerstein, J., & Lewis, J. (1998). The long-term impact of divorce on children: A first report from a 25-year study. *Family & Conciliation Courts Review, 36,* 368–383.

Wallerstein, J., Lewis, J., & Packer Rosenthal, S. (2013). Mothers and their children after divorce: Report from a 25-year longitudinal study. *Psychoanalytic Psy-chology, 30,* 167–184.

Wallien, M., & Cohen-Kettenis, P. (2008). Psychosexual outcome of gender-dysphoric children. *Journal of the American Academy of Child & Adolescent Psychiatry, 47,* 1413–1423.

Walters, M., Chen, J., & Breiding, M. (2013). *The National Intimate Partner and Sexual Violence Survey (NISVS): 2010 findings on victimization by sexual orientation.* Retrieved July 18, 2013, from http://www.cdc.gov/violenceprevention/pdf/nisvs_report2010-a.pdf.

Walton, G. E., Bower, N. J. A., & Bower, T. G. R. (1992). Recognition of familiar faces by newborns. *Infant Behavior & Development, 15,* 265–269.

Walusinski, O., Kurjak, A., Andonotopo, W., & Azumendi, G. (2005). Fetal yawning: A behavior's birth with 4D US revealed. *The Ultrasound Review of Obstetrics & Gynecology, 5,* 210–217.

Wang, C., & Chou, P. (1999). Risk factors for adolescent primigravida in Kaohsiung county, Taiwan. *American Journal of Preventive Medicine, 17,* 43–47.

Wang, C., & Phinney, J. (1998). Differences in child rearing attitudes between immi-grant Chinese mothers and Anglo-American mothers. *Early Development & Parenting, 7,* 181–189.

Wang, D., Kato, N., Inaba, Y. & Tango, T. (2000). Physical and personality traits of preschool children in Fuzhou, China: Only child vs. sibling. *Child: Care, Health & Development, 26,* 49-60.

Wang, L., & Xu, R. (2007). The effects of perinatal protein malnutrition on spatial learning and memory behaviour and brain-derived neurotrophic factor con-centration in the brain tissue in young rats. *Asia Pacific Journal of Clinical Nutrition, 16,* 467–472.

Wang, Q. (2006a). Culture and the development of self-knowledge. *Current Direc-tions in Psychological Science, 15,* 182–187.

Wang, Q. (2006b). Relations of maternal style and child self-concepts to autobio-graphical memories in Chinese, Chinese immigrant, and European American 3-year-olds. *Child Development, 77,* 1794–1809.

Wang, X., Dow-Edwards, D., Anderson, V., Minkoff, H., & Hurd, Y. (2004). In utero marijuana exposure associated with abnormal amygdala dopamine D-sub-2 gene expression in the human fetus. *Biological Psychiatry, 56,* 909–915.

Wang, Y. (2002). Is obesity associated with early sexual maturation? A comparison of the association in American boys versus girls. *Pediatrics, 110,* 903–910.

Wang, Y., & Lobstein, T. (2006). Worldwide trends in childhood overweight and obesity. *International Journal of Pediatric Obesity, 1,* 11–25.

Wang, Y., & Ollendick, T. (2001). A cross-cultural and developmental analysis of self-esteem in Chinese and Western children. *Clinical Child & Family Psychology Review, 4,* 253–271.

Ward, S. L., & Overton, W. F. (1990). Semantic familiarity, relevance, and the devel-opment of deductive reasoning. *Developmental Psychology, 26,* 488–493.

Wark, G. R., & Krebs, D. L. (1996). Gender and dilemma differences in real-life moral judgment. *Developmental Psychology, 32,* 220–230.

Warr, P., Jackson, P., & Banks, M. (1988). Unemployment and mental health: Some British studies. *Journal of Social Issues, 44,* 47–68.

Warren, S., Gunnar, M., Kagan, J., Anders, T., Simmens, S., Rones, M., Wease, S., Aron, E., Dahl, R., & Sroufe, A. (2003). Maternal panic disorder: Infant tem-perament, neurophysiology, and parenting behaviors. *Journal of the American Academy of Child & Adolescent Psychiatry, 42,* 814–825.

Wartner, U. B., Grossman, K., Fremmer-Bombik, E., & Suess, G. (1994). Attachment patterns at age six in south Germany: Predictability from infancy and implica-tions for preschool behavior. *Child Development, 65,* 1014–1027.

Waskowic, T., & Chartier, B. (2003). Attachment and the experience of grief follow-ing the loss of a spouse. *Omega, 47,* 77–91.

Watamura, S., Donzella, B., Alwin, J., & Gunnar, M. (2003). Morning-to-afternoon increases in cortisol concentrations for infants and toddlers at child care: Age differences and behavioral correlates. *Child Development, 74,* 1006–1020.

Waters, E., Treboux, D., Crowell, J., Merrick, S., & Albersheim, L. (1995, March). *From the Strange Situation to the Adult Attachment Interview: A 20-year lon-gitudinal study of attachment security in infancy and early adulthood.* Paper presented at the biennial meetings of the Society for Research in Child Devel-opment, Indianapolis, IN.

Waters, H., & Waters, T. (2010). Bird experts: A study of child and adult knowledge utilization. In H. Waters & W. Schneider (Eds.), *Metacognition, strategy use, and instruction* (pp. 113–134). New York: Guilford Press.

Watson, A., Nixon, C., Wilson, A., & Capage, L. (1999). Social interaction skills and theory of mind in young children. *Developmental Psychology, 35,* 386–391.

Watson, J. B. (1930). *Behaviorism.* New York: Norton.

Webster-Stratton, C., & Reid, M. (2003). Treating conduct problems and strength-ening social and emotional competence in young children: The Dina Dino-saur treatment program. *Journal of Emotional & Behavioral Disorders, 11,* 130–143.

Wechsler, D. (2002). *The Wechsler preschool and primary scale of intelligence* (3rd ed.). San Antonio, TX: The Psychological Corporation.

Wee, C., Hamel, N., Davis, R., & Phillips, R. (2004). Assessing the value of weight loss among primary care patients. *Journal of General Internal Medicine, 19,* 1206–1211.

Wee, D. (2012). *China's rocketing elderly population prompts a rethink on pen-sions.* Retrieved July 21, 2013, from http://www.guardian.co.uk/global-devel-opment/2012/oct/01/china-elderly-population-pensions-rethink.

Weeks, J. (2004). Same-sex partnerships. *Feminism & Psychology, 14,* 158–164.

Weil, L., Fleming, S., Dumontheil, I., Kilford, E., Weil, R., Rees, G., Dolan, R., & Blakemore, S. (2013). The development of metacognitive ability in adoles-cence. *Consciousness and Cognition: An International Journal, 22,* 264–271.

Weimer, B., Kerns, K., & Oldenburg, C. (2004). Adolescents' interactions with a best friend: Associations with attachment style. *Journal of Experimental Psychology, 88,* 102–120.

Weinberg, R. A. (1989). Intelligence and IQ: Landmark issues and great debates. *American Psychologist, 44,* 98–104.

Weinberg, R. A., Scarr, S., & Waldman, I. D. (1992). The Minnesota transracial adoption study: A follow-up of IQ test performance. *Intelligence, 16,* 117–135.

Weinfield, N., & Egeland, B. (2004). Continuity, discontinuity, and co-herence in attachment from infancy to late adolescence: Sequelae of organization and disorganization. *Attachment & Human Development, 6,* 73–97.

Weisse, C. (1992). Depression and immunocompetence: A review of the literature. *Psychological Bulletin, 111,* 475-489.

Weitoft, G., Hjern, A., Haglund, B., & Rosén, M. (2003). Mortality, severe morbidity, and injury in children living with single parents in Sweden: A population-based study. *The Lancet, 361,* 289–295.

Welford, A. T. (1993). The gerontological balance sheet. In J. Cerella, J. Rybash, W. Hoyer, & M. L. Commons (Eds.), *Adult information processing: Limits on loss* (pp. 3–10). San Diego, CA: Academic Press.

Wellman, H. M. (1982). The foundations of knowledge: Concept development in the young child. In S. G. Moore & C. C. Cooper (Eds.), *The young child: Reviews of research, Vol. 3* (pp. 115–134). Washington, DC: National Association for the Education of Young Children.

Wellman, H., Cross, D., & Watson, J. (2001). Meta-analysis of theory-of-mind devel-opment: The truth about false belief. *Child Development, 72,* 655–684.

Wentzel, K. R., & Asher, S. R. (1995). The academic lives of neglected, rejected, popular, and controversial children. *Child Development, 66,* 754–763.

Werker, J., Pons, F., Dietrich, C., Kajikawa, S., Fais, L., & Amano, S. (2007). Infant directed speech supports phonetic category learning in English and Japanese. *Cognition, 103*, 147–162.

Werner, E. E., & Smith, R. S. (1992). *Overcoming the odds: High risk children from birth to adulthood*. Ithaca, NY: Cornell University Press.

Wesson, D., Stephens, D., Lam, K., Parsons, D., Spence, L., & Parkin, P. (2008). Trends in pediatric and adult bicycling deaths before and after passage of a bicycle helmet law. *Pediatrics, 122*, 605–610.

West, A., & Weinstein, S. (2012). Bipolar disorder: School-based cognitive-behavioral interventions. In R. Mennuti, R. Christner, & A. Freeman. (Eds.) *Cognitive-behaviorral interventions in educational settings: A handbook for practice* (2nd ed., pp. 239–274). New York, NY, USA: Routledge/Taylor & Francis Group.

West, A., Schenkel, L., & Pavuluri, M. (2008). Early childhood temperament in pediatric bipolar disorder and attention deficit hyperactivity disorder. *Journal of Clinical Psychology, 64*, 402–421.

West, P., Sweeting, H., & Ecob, R. (1999). Family and friends' influences on the uptake of regular smoking from mid-adolescence to early adulthood. *Addiction, 97*, 1397–1411.

West, R. L., & Crook, T. H. (1990). Age differences in everyday memory: Laboratory analogues of telephone number recall. *Psychology & Aging, 5*, 520–529.

Westerhof, G., Katzko, M., Dittmann-Kohli, F., & Hayslip, B. (2001). Life contexts and health-related selves in old age: Perspectives from the United States, India and Congo/Zaire. *Journal of Aging Studies, 15*, 105–126.

Wetzel, N., Widmann, A., Berti, S., & Schröger, E. (2006). The development of involuntary and voluntary attention from childhood to adulthood: A combined behavioral and event-related potential study. *Clinical Neurophysiology, 117*, 2191–2203.

Wharton, A., & Blair-Loy, M. (2006). Long work hours and family life: A cross-national study of employees' concerns. *Journal of Family Issues, 27*, 415–436.

White, J. (2006). Multiple invalidities. In J. Schaler (Ed.), *Howard Gardner under fire: The rebel psychologist faces his critics* (pp. 45–72). Chicago, IL: Open Court.

White, M., Wilson, M., Elander, G., & Persson, B. (1999). The Swedish family: Transition to parenthood. *Scandinavian Journal of Caring Sciences, 13*, 171–176.

White, W. H. (1992). G. Stanley Hall: From philosophy to developmental psychology. *Developmental Psychology, 28*, 25–34.

Whitehurst, G. J., Arnold, D. S., Epstein, J. N., Angell, A. L., Smith, M., & Fischel, J. E. (1994). A picture book reading intervention in day care and home for children from low-income families. *Developmental Psychology, 30*, 679–689.

Whitehurst, G. J., Falco, F. L., Lonigan, C. J., Fischel, J. E., DeBaryshe, B. D., Valdez-Menchaca, M. C., & Caulfield, M. (1988). Accelerating language development through picture book reading. *Developmental Psychology, 24*, 552–559.

Whitehurst, G. J., Fischel, J. E., Crone, D. A., & Nania, O. (1995, March). *First year outcomes of a clinical trial of an emergent literacy intervention in Head Start homes and classrooms*. Paper presented at the biennial meetings of the Society for Research in Child Development, Indianapolis, IN.

Wicki, W. (1999). The impact of family resources and satisfaction with division of labour on coping and worries after the birth of the first child. *International Journal of Behavioral Development, 23*, 431–456.

Wiederman, M., & Allgeier, E. (1992). Gender differences in mate selection criteria: Sociobiological or socioeconomic explanation? *Ethology & Sociobiology, 13*, 115–124.

Wilde, C. (2000). The new workplace: Telework programs are on the rise. *Information Week, 781*, 189.

Willcox, B., Curb, J., & Rodriguez, B. (2008). Antioxidants in cardiovascular health and disease: Key lessons from epidemiologic studies. *American Journal of Cardiology, 101*, 75D–86D.

Willett, W., Hunter, D., Stampfer, M., Colditz, G., Manson, J., Spiegelman, D., Rosner, B., Hennekens, C., & Speizer, F. (1992). Dietary fat and fiber in relation to risk of breast cancer: An 8-year follow-up. *Journal of the American Medical Association, 268*, 2037–2044.

Williams, G., Keigher, S., & Williams, A. (2012). Spiritual well-being among older African Americans in a midwestern city. *Journal of Religion and Health, 51*, 355–370.

Williams, J. E., & Best, D. L. (1990). *Measuring sex stereotypes: A multination study* (rev. ed.). Newbury Park, CA: Sage.

Williams, K., Frech, A., & Carlson, D. (2010). Marital status and mental health. In T. Scheid & T. Brown (Eds.), *A handbook for the study of mental health: Social contexts, theories, and systems* (2nd ed.). New York: Cambridge University Press.

Williams, R. (2013). Overview of the Flynn effect. *Intelligence, 41*, 753–764.

Wilmore, J., Stanforth, P., Gagnon, J., Rice, T., Mandel, S., Leon, A., Rao, D., Skinner, J., & Bouchard, C. (2001). Cardiac output and stroke volume changes with endurance training: The HERITAGE Family Study. *Medical Science & Sports Exercise, 33*, 99–106.

Wilson, H., & Donenberg, G. (2004). Quality of parent communication about sex and its relationship to risky sexual behavior among youth in psychiatric care: A pilot study. *Journal of Child Psychology & Psychiatry & Allied Disciplines, 45*, 387–395.

Wilson, R., Boyle, P., Segawa, E., Yu, L., Begeny, C., Anagnos, S., & Bennett, D. (2013). The influence of cognitive decline on well-being in old age. *Psychology and Aging, 28*, 304–313.

Wilson, W. J. (1995). Jobless ghettos and the social outcome of youngsters. In P. Moen, G. H. Elder, Jr., & K. Lüscher (Eds.), *Examining lives in context: Perspectives on the ecology of human development* (pp. 527–543). Washington, DC: American Psychological Association.

Wimmer, H., Mayringer, H., & Landerl, K. (1998). Poor reading: A deficit in skill-automatization or a phonological deficit? *Scientific Studies of Reading, 2*, 321–340.

Winter, B., Breitenstein, C., Mooren, F., Voelker, K., Fobker, M., Lechtermann, A., Krueger, K., Fromme, A., Korsukewitz, C., Floel, A., & Knecht, S. (2007). High impact running improves learning. *Neurobiology of Learning and Memory, 87*, 597–609.

Winter, R. (1999). A Biblical and theological view of grief and bereavement. *Journal of Psychology & Christianity, 18*, 367–379.

Wintre, M., & Yaffe, M. (2000). First-year students' adjustment to university life as a function of relationships with parents. *Journal of Adolescent Research, 15*, 9–37.

Wolfle, L., & List, J. (2004). Locus of control is fairly stable over time but does change as a result of natural events, such as the acquisition of college education. *Structural Equation Modeling, 11*, 244–260.

Wolpe, J. (1958). *Psychotherapy by reciprocal inhibition*. Palo Alto, CA: Stanford University Press.

Wong, B., Iam, S., Wong, W., Chen, J., Zheng, T., Feng, R., Lai, K., Hu, W., Yuen, S., Leung, S., Fong, D. Ho, J., Ching, C., & Chen, J. (2004). Helicobacter pylori eradication to prevent gastric cancer in a high-risk region of China: A randomized controlled trial. *Journal of the American Medical Association, 127*, 344–346.

Wong, C., & Tang, C. (2004). Coming out experiences and psychological distress of Chinese homosexual men in Hong Kong. *Archives of Sexual Behavior, 33*, 149–157.

Wong, D. (1993). *Whaley & Wong's essentials of pediatric nursing*. St. Louis, MO: Mosby-Yearbook, Inc.

Wong, T. (2002). Aging of the cerebral cortex. *McGill Journal of Medicine, 6*, 104–113.

Woo, M., & Oei, T. (2006). The MMPI-2 gender-masculine and gender-feminine scales: Gender roles as predictors of psychological health in clinical patients. *International Journal of Psychology, 41*, 413–422.

Wood, C., & Terrell, C. (1998). Pre-school phonological awareness and subsequent literacy development. *Educational Psychology, 18*, 253–274.

Wood, W., & Eagly, A. (2007). Social structure origins of sex differences in human mating. In Gangestad, S., & Simpson, J. (Eds.), *The evolution of mind: Fundamental questions and controversies* (pp. 383–390). New York: Guilford Press.

Woodhouse, S., Ramos-Marcuse, F., Ehrlich, K., Warner, S., & Cassidy, J. (2010). The role of adolescent attachment in moderating and mediating the links between parent and adolescent psychological symptoms. *Journal of Clinical Child & Adolescent Psychology, 39*, 51–63.

Woodward, M., & Tunstall-Pedoe, H. (1995). Alcohol consumption, diet, coronary risk factors, and prevalent coronary heart disease in men and women in the Scottish heart health study. *Journal of Epidemiology & Community Health, 49*, 354–362.

World Health Organization (WHO). (2010). *Maternal mortality*. Retrieved July 4, 2010 from http://www.who.int/making_pregnancy_safer/topics/maternal_mortality/en/index.html.

World Health Organization. (2000). *Violence against women*. Retrieved September 1, 2000, from http://www.who.int.

World Health Organization. (2013). *Global and regional estimate of violence against women*. Retrieved July 18, 2013, from http://apps.who.int/iris/bitstream/10665/85239/1/9789241564625_eng.pdf.

Worrell, F. (1997). Predicting successful or non-successful at-risk status using demographic risk factors. *High School Journal, 81*, 46–53.

Wortman, C. B., & Silver, R. C. (1989). The myths of coping with loss. *Journal of Consulting & Clinical Psychology, 57*, 349–357.

Wortman, C. B., & Silver, R. C. (1990). Successful mastery of bereavement and widowhood: A life course perspective. In P. B. Baltes & M. M. Baltes (Eds.), *Successful aging: Perspectives from the behavioral sciences* (pp. 225–264). New York: Cambridge University Press.

Wortman, C. B., Silver, R. C., & Kessler, R. C. (1993). The meaning of loss and adjustment to bereavement. In M. S. Stroebe, W. Stroebe, & R. O. Hansson (Eds.), *Handbook of bereavement* (pp. 349–366). Cambridge, UK: Cambridge University Press.

Wortman, C., & Boerner, K. (2007). Beyond the myths of coping with loss: Prevailing assumptions versus scientific evidence. In H. Friedman, H., & R. Silver, R. (Eds.), *Foundations of health psychology* (pp. 285–324). New York, NY, USA: Oxford University Press.

Wrenn, K., & Maurer, T. (2004). Beliefs about older workers' learning and development behavior in relation to beliefs about malleability of skills, age-related decline, and control. *Journal of Applied Social Psychology, 34*, 223–242.

Wright, C., & Birks, E. (2000). Risk factors for failure to thrive: A population-based survey. *Child: Care, Health & Development, 26*, 5–16.

Wright, M., Battista, M., Pate, D., Hierholzer, R., Mogelof, J., & Howsepian, A. (2010). Domain-specific associations between burden and mood state in dementia caregivers. *Clinical Gerontologist: The Journal of Aging and Mental health, 33*, 237–247.

Wright, T., & Bonett, D. (2007). Job satisfaction and psychological well-being as nonadditive predictors of workplace turnover. *Journal of Management, 33*, 141–160.

Writing Group for the Women's Health Initiative Investigators. (2002). Risks and benefits of estrogen plus progestin in healthy postmenopausal women: Principal results from the Women's Health Initiative randomized controlled trial. *Journal of the American Medical Association, 288*, 321–333.

Wu, P., Liu, X., & Fan, B. (2010). Factors associated with initiation of ecstasy use among US adolescents: Findings from a national survey. *Drug and Alcohol Dependence, 106*, 193–198.

Wu, T., Mendola, P., & Buck, G. (2002). Ethnic differences in the presence of secondary sex characteristics and menarche among U.S. girls: The Third National Health and Nutrition Examination Survey, 1988–1994.

Wu, T., Yeh, K., Cross, S., Larson, L., Wang, Y, Tsai, Y. (2010). Conflict with mothers-in-law and Taiwanese women's marital satisfaction: The moderating role of husband support. *The Counseling Psychologist, 38*, 497–522.

Wyatt, G., Axelrod, J., Chin, D., Carmona, J., & Loeb, T. (2000). Examining patterns of vulnerability to domestic violence among African American women. *Violence Against Women, 6*, 495–514.

Wyatt, J., & Carlo, G. (2002). What will my parents think? Relations among adolescents' expected parental reactions, prosocial moral reasoning and prosocial and antisocial behaviors. *Journal of Adolescent Research, 17*, 646–666.

Wylie, B., & Mirza, F. (2008). Cesarean delivery in the developing world. *Clinics in Perinatology, 35*, 571–582

Xie, H., Cairns, R., & Cairns, B. (1999). Social networks and configurations in inner-city schools: Aggression, popularity, and implications for students with EBD. *Journal of Emotional & Behavioral Disorders, 7*, 147–155.

Xu, F., Sternberg, M., Gottlieb, S., Berman, S., & Markowitz, L. (2010). Seroprevalence of herpes simplex virus type 2 among persons aged 14–49 years, United States, 2005–2008. *Morbidity and Mortality Weekly Report, 59*, 456–459.

Xu, J., Kochanek, K., Murphy, S., & Tejada-Vera, B. (2010). Deaths, final data for 2007. *National Vital Statistics Reports, 58*, 1–73.

Xu, M., Sun, W., Liu, B., Feng, G., Yu, L., Yang, L., He, G., Sham, P., Susser, E., St. Clair, D., & He, L. (2009). Prenatal malnutrition and adult schizophrenia: Further evidence from the 1959–1961 Chinese famine. *Schizophrenia Bulletin, 35*, 568–576.

Xuncià, M., Badenas, C., Domínguez, M., Rodríguez-Revenga, L., Madrigal, I., Jiménez, L., Soler, A., Borrell, A., Sánchez, A., & Milà, M. (2010). Fragile X syndrome prenatal diagnosis: Parental attitudes and reproductive responses. *Reproductive Biomedicine Online, 21*, 560–565.

Yager, J., (2013). *Bulimia nervosa*. Retrieved July 13, 2013, from http://emedicine.medscape.com/article/286485-overview.

Yamada, A., & Singelis, T. (1999). Biculturalism and self-construal. *International Journal of Intercultural Relations, 23*, 697–709.

Yaman, A., Mesman, J., van IJzendoorn, M., & Bakermans-Kranenburg, M. (2010). Parenting and toddler aggression in second-generation immigrant families: The moderating role of child temperament. *Journal of Family Psychology, 24*, 208–211.

Yang, H., Lu, S., Liaw, Y., You, S., Sun, C., Wang, L., Hsiao, C., Chen, P., Chen, D., & Chen, C. (2002). Hepatitis B/e antigen and the risk of hepatocellular carcinoma. *New England Journal of Medicine, 347*, 168–174.

Yang, H., Youm, Y, Sun, Y., Rim, J., Galban, C., Vandanmagsar, B., & Dixit, V. (2009). Axin expression in thymic stromal cells contributes to an age-related increase in thymic adiposity and is associated with reduced thymopoiesis independently of ghrelin signaling. *Journal of Leukocyte Biology, 85*, 928–938.

Yellowlees, P., & Marks, S. (2007). Problematic internet use or internet addiction? *Computers in Human Behavior, 23*, 1447–1453.

Yerkes, M. (2010). Diversity in work: The heterogeneity of women's employment patterns. *Gender, Work and Organization, 17*, 696-720.

Yeung, A., Chui, H., & Lau, I. (1999). Hierarchical and multidimensional academic self-concept of commercial students. *Contemporary Educational Psychology, 24*, 376–389.

Yi-Bing, Y, & Ming-Gui, G. (2005). Social status of children aged 3–6 and its relation to problematic behavior. *Chinese Mental Health Journal, 19*, 682–684.

Yildiz, A., & Arikan, D. (2012). The effects of giving pacifiers to premature infants and making them listen to lullabies on their transition period for total oral feeding and sucking success. *Journal of Clinical Nursing, 21*, 644–656.

Yonas, A., Elieff, C., & Arterberry, M. (2002). Emergence of sensitivity to pictorial depth cues: Charting development in individual infants. *Infant Behavior & Development, 25*, 495–514.

Yordanova, J., Kolev, V., & Basar, E. (1998). EEG theta and frontal alpha oscillations during auditory processing change with aging. *Electroencephalography & Clinical Neurophysiology: Evoked Potentials, 108*, 497–505.

Young, A. (1997). I think, therefore I'm motivated: The relations among cognitive strategy use, motivational orientation and classroom perceptions over time. *Learning & Individual Differences, 9*, 249–283.

Young, L. M., Baltes, B. B., & Pratt, A. (2007). Using selection, optimization, and compensation to reduce job/family stressors: Effective when it matters. *Journal of Business and Psychology, 18*, 1–29.

Yu, C., & Ballard, D. (2007). A unified model of early word learning: Integrating statistical and social cues. *Neurocomputing: An International Journal, 70*, 2149–2165.

Yu, Z., & Liu, A. (2007). Self-awareness and social anxiety in elementary school students with different social status. *Chinese Mental Health Journal, 21*, 598–601.

Yuill, N. (1997). English children as personality theorists: Accounts of the modifiability, development, and origin of traits. *Genetic, Social & General Psychology Monographs, 123*, 5–26.

Zaeiden, R. (2013). *Hemophilia A*. Retrieved July 5, 2013, from http://emedicine.medscape.com/article/779322-overview#a0156.

Zakriski, A., & Coie, J. (1996). A comparison of aggressive-rejected and nonaggressive-rejected children's interpretation of self-directed and other-directed rejection. *Child Development, 67*, 1048–1070.

Zamboni, B. (2006). Therapeutic considerations in working with the family, friends, and partners of transgendered individuals. *The Family Journal, 14*, 174–179.

Zeidán-Chuliá, F., Rybarczyk-Filho, J., Slmina, A., Neves de Oliveira, B., Noda, M., & Moreira, J. (2013). Exploring the multifactorial nature of autism through computational systems biology: Calcium and the Rho GTPase RAC1 under the spotlight. *NeuroMolecular Medicine, 15*, 364–383.

Zelazo, N. A., Zelazo, P. R., Cohen, K. M., & Zelazo, P. D. (1993). Specificity of practice effects on elementary neuromotor patterns. *Developmental Psychology, 29*, 686–691.

Zelazo, P., Helwig, C., & Lau, A. (1996). Intention, act, and outcome in behavioral prediction and moral judgment. *Child Development, 67*, 2478–2492.

Zelinski, E., & Burnight, K. (1997). Sixteen-year longitudinal and time lag changes in memory and cognition in older adults. *Psychology & Aging, 12*, 503–513.

Zero Poverty. (2010). *Ten facts about poverty in Europe*. Retrieved August 12, 2010 from http://www.zeropoverty.org/userupload/10+Facts+About+Poverty+In+Europe-1.pdf.

Zhang, R., & Yu, Y. (2002). A study of children's coordinational ability for outcome and intention information. *Psychological Science* (China), *25*, 527–530.

Zhao, Y., Montoro, R., Igartua, K., & Thombs, B. (2010). Suicidal ideation and attempt among adolescents reporting "unsure" sexual identity or heterosexual identity plus same-sex attraction or behavior: Forgotten groups? *Journal of the American Academy of Child & Adolescent Psychiatry, 49*, 104–113.

Zhong, C., Bohns, V., & Gino, F. (2010). Good lamps are the best police: Darkness increases dishonesty and self-interested behavior. *Psychological Science, 21*, 311–314.

Zhou, L., Dawson, M., Herr, C., & Stukas, S. (2004). American and Chinese college students' predictions of people's occupations, housework responsibilities, and hobbies as a function of cultural and gender influences. *Sex Roles, 50,* 463.

Zhou, M., Yao, L., & Xu, J. (2002). Studied the influence of Taoist education on the subjective well-being of the elderly. *Chinese Mental Health Journal, 16,* 175–176.

Zhou, W., He, G., Gao, J., Yuan, Q., Feng, H., & Zhang, C. (2012). The effects of group reminiscence therapy on depression, self-esteem, and affect balance of Chinese community-dwelling elderly. *Archives of Gerontology and Geriatrics, 54,* e440–e447.

Zhou, X., Huang, J., Wang, A., Wang, B., Zhao, Z., Yang, L., & Zhengzheng, Y. (2006). Parent-child interaction and children's number learning. *Early Child Development and Care, 176,* 763–775.

Zhou, Z., & Boehm, A. (2004). American and Chinese children's understanding of basic relational concepts in directions. *Psychology in the Schools, 41,* 261–272.

Zick, C., & Holden, K. (2000). An assessment of the wealth holdings of recent widows. *Journal of Gerontology, 55B,* S90–S97.

Zigler, E., & Styfco, S. J. (1993). Using research and theory to justify and inform Head Start expansion. *Social Policy Report, Society for Research in Child Development, VII* (2), 1–21.

Zimmer-Gembeck, M. (1999). Stability, change and individual differences in involvement with friends and romantic partners among adolescent females. *Journal of Youth & Adolescence, 28,* 419–438.

Zimmerman, C. (2000). The development of scientific reasoning skills. *Developmental Review, 20,* 99–149.

Zimmerman, F., Christakis, D., & Meltzoff, A. (2007). Television and DVD/video viewing in children younger than 2 years. *Archives of Pediatric and Adolescent Medicine, 161,* 473–479.

Zimmerman, M., Copeland, L., Shope, J., & Dielman, T. (1997). A longitudinal study of self-esteem: Implications for adolescent development. *Journal of Youth & Adolescence, 26,* 117–141.

Zimmerman, S., Scott, A., Park, N., Hall, S., Wetherby, M., Gruber-Baldini, A., & Morgan, L. (2003). Social engagement and its relationship to service provision in residential care and assisted living. *Social Work Research, 27,* 6–18.

Zimmermann, P. (2004). Attachment representations and characteristics of friendship relations during adolescence. *Journal of Experimental Child Psychology, 88,* 83–101.

Zisook, S., Chentsova-Dutton, Y., & Shuchter, S. (1998). PTSD following bereavement. *Annals of Clinical Psychiatry, 10,* 157–163.

Zisook, S., Paulus, M., Shuchter, S., & Judd, L. (1997). The many faces of depression following spousal bereavement. *Journal of Affective Disorders, 45,* 85–94.

Zmyj, N., Buttelmann, D., Carpenter, M., & Daum, M. (2010). The reliability of a model influences 14-month-olds' imitation. *Journal of Experimental Child Psychology, 106,* 208–220.

Zola, S., & Squire, L. (2003). Genetics of childhood disorders: Learning and memory: Multiple memory systems. *Journal of the American Academy of Child and Adolescent Psychiatry, 42,* 504–506.

Zucker, A., Ostrove, J., & Stewart A. (2002). College-educated women's personality development in adulthood: Perceptions and age differences. *Psychology & Aging, 17,* 236–244.

Zunker, V. (2006). *Career counseling: A holistic approach* (7th ed.). Belmont, CA: Brooks/Cole Publishing.

Zunzunegui, M., Alvarado, B., Del Ser, T., & Otero, A. (2003). Social networks, social integration, and social engagement determine cognitive decline in community-dwelling Spanish older adults. *Journals of Gerontology, Series B: Psychological Sciences & Social Sciences, 58B,* S93–S100.

Zuurbier, L., Nikolova, Y., Ahs, F., & Hariri, A. (2013). Uncinate fasciculus fractional anisotropy correlates with typical use of reappraisal in women but not men. *Emotion, 13,* 385–390.

Zysset, S., Schroeter, M., Neumann, J., & von Cramon, D. (2007). Stroop interference, hemodynamic response and aging: An event-related fMRI study. *Neurobiology of Aging, 28,* 937–946.

Credits

Source: Montemayor, R., & Eisen, M. (1977). The development of self-conceptions from childhood to adolescence. Developmental Psychology, 13, p. 317. Reprinted with permission, *Source:* Montemayor, R., & Eisen, M. (1977). The development of self-conceptions from childhood to adolescence. Developmental Psychology, 13, pp. 317–318. Reprinted with permission: p. 245 CLEO PHOTOGRAPHY/PhotoEdit ; p. 246, *Source:* Livesley, W. J., & Bromley, D. B. (1973). Person perception in childhood and adolescence. London: Wiley, p. 213; p. 247 Myrleen Pearson/PhotoEdit, Livesley, W. J., & Bromley, D. B. (1973). Person perception in childhood and adolescence. London: Wiley, p. 217; p. 249 Iofoto/Shutterstock; p. 251 Courtesy of Denise Boyd. Used with permission; p. 252 CREATISTA/Shutterstock, Tom Prettyman/PhotoEdit; p. 253 Tim Hall/cultura/Corbis; p. 254 Bill Aron/PhotoEdit, Inc.; p. 256, *Source:* Galanaki, E. (2004). Teachers and loneliness: The children's perspective. School Psychology International, 25, 92–105; p. 257 Getty Images, *Source:* Galanaki, E. (2004). Teachers and loneliness: The children's perspective. School Psychology International, 25, 92–105; p. 259, *Source:* Data from Rideout, V., Foehr, U., & Roberts, D. (2010). Generation M2: Medial in the lives of 8- to 18-year-olds. Retrieved August 12, 2010 from http://www.kff.org/entmedia/upload/8010.pdf; p. 260 Lunamarina/Fotolia; p. 265 Maskot/Getty Images; p. 267 Will Hart/PhotoEdit; p. 271 Darrin Klimek/Lifesize/Getty Images; p. 272 Eric McCandless/ABC Family via Getty Images; p. 273 Maria Taglienti-Molinari/Corbis; p. 278, *Source:* http://www.monitoringthefuture.org/data/12data/fig12_6.pdf. Monitoring the Future, Institute for Social Research, University of Michigan; p. 279 Tony Freeman/PhotoEdit, Inc.; p. 283 James Shaffer/PhotoEdit, Inc.; p. 284, *Source:* Martorano, S. C. (1977). A developmental analysis of performance on Piaget's formal operations tasks. Developmental Psychology, 13, p. 670. Copyright by the American Psychological Association. Reprint with permission; p. 287 Daniel R. Patmore/AP Images; p. 289 Lawrence Migdale/Science Source; p. 295 get4net/Fotolia; p. 296 Adams Picture Library t/a apl/Alamy; p 297 *Source:* Based on Marcia, J. E. (1980). Identity in adolescence. In J. Adelson (Ed.), Handbook of adolescent psychology (pp. 159–187). New York: Wiley; p. 298 Bill Aron/PhotoEdit, Inc., Carl & Ann Purcell/Corbis;p. 299 p. 299, *Source:* Montemayor, R., & Eisen, M. (1977). The development of self-conceptions from childhood to adolescence. Developmental Psychology, 13, p. 318., *Source:* Based on Montemayor, R., & Eisen, M. (1977). The development of self-conceptions from childhood to adolescence. Developmental Psychology, 13, 314–319. from Table 1, p. 316; p. 301 Myrleen Pearson/PhotoEdit, Inc; p. 303 Kris Timken/Getty Images, Comstock/Thinkstock; p. 304, *Source:* Kohlberg, L., & Elfenbein, D. (1975). The development of moral judgments concerning capital punishment. American Journal of Orthopsychiatry, 54, p. 621; p. 305, *Source:* Republished with permission of John Wiley and Sons Inc., from Colby, A., Kohlberg, L., Gibbs, J., & Lieberman, M. (1983). A longitudinal study of moral judgment. Monographs of the Society for Research in Child Development, Vol. 48, Nos. 1 and 2, Fig. 1, p. 46, 1983; permission conveyed through Copyright Clearance Center, Inc.; p. 305, *Source:* Kohlberg, L. (1976). Moral stages and moralization: The cognitive developmental approach. In T. Lickona (Ed.), Moral development and behavior: Theory, research, and social issues (pp. 31–53). New York: Holt; Lickona, 1978; p. 306 Based on Walker, L., de Vries, R., & Trevethan, S. (1987). Moral stages and moral orientations in real-life and hypothetical dilemmas. Child Development, 58, 842–858. (Table 1, p. 849), *Source:* Snarey, J. R. (1985). Cross-cultural universality of social-moral development: A critical review of Kohlbergian research. Psychological Bulletin, 97, p. 221; p. 307 Bettmann/Corbis; p. 311 John Neubauer/PhotoEdit, Inc.; p. 313 Steve Debenport/Getty Images; p. 315 Myrleen Pearson/Alamy; p. 321 James Woodson/Photodisc/Getty Images; p. 324 Mark Richards/PhotoEdit, Inc.; p. 325, *Source:* Bartoshuk & Weiffenbach, 1990; Blatter et al., 1995; Braveman, 1987; Briggs, 1990; Brock, Guralnik, & Brody, 1990; Doty et al., 1984; Fiatarone & Evans, 1993; Fozard, 1990; Fozard, Metter, & Brant, 1990; Gray, Berlin, McKinlay, & Longcope, 1991; Hallfrisch, Muller, Drinkwater, Tobin, & Adres, 1990; Hayflick, 1994; Ivy, MacLeod, Petit, & Marcus, 1992; Kallman, Plato, & Tobin, 1990; Kline & Scialfa, 1996; Kozma, Stones, & Hannah, 1991; Lakatta, 1990; Lim, Zipursky, Watts, & Pfefferbaum, 1992; McFalls, 1990; Miller, 1990; Mundy, 1994; Scheibel, 1992, 1996; Shock et al., 1984; Weisse, 1992; p. 327 Dr. Yorgos Nikas/Science Source; p. 329 Travel Pictures Ltd/SuperStock; p. 330 Gary Conner/PhotoEdit, Inc.; p. 333, *Source:* Data from World Health Organization. (2000). Violence against women. Retrieved September 1, 2000, from http://www.who.int; p. 334 Jonathan Nourok/PhotoEdit, Inc.; p. 337, *Source:* Data from World Health Organization. (2000). Violence against women. Retrieved September 1, 2000, from http://www.who.int; p. 341 Jeff Greenberg/PhotoEdit, Inc.; p. 342, *Source:* Schaie, K. W. (1983). The Seattle longitudinal study: A 21-year exploration of psychometric intelligence in adulthood. In K. W. Schaie (Ed.), Longitudinal studies of adult psychological development (pp. 64–135). New York: Guilford Press; p. 343 Corbis; p. 344, *Source:* National Center for Education Statistics (NCES). (2010). The condition of education. Retrieved August 24, 2010 from http://nces.ed.gov/programs/coe/; p. 349 Payless Images, Inc./Alamy; p. 350 michaeljung/Shutterstock, Gallo Images/Hayley Baxter/Getty Images; p. 353, *Source:* Lofquist, D; Lugalla, T; O'Connell, M; Feliz, S. (2012). Households and families: 2010. Retrieved July 19, 2013 from http://www.census.gov/prod/cen2010/briefs/c2010br-14.pdf; p. 355 FancyVeerSet/Alamy, JUPITERIMAGES/Brand X/Alamy; p. 357 Permission is granted to use the requested material, provided that such use does not in any way imply that Pew Research Center endorses a cause, candidate, issue, party, product, business or religion. To view our Use Policy and Citation Guidelines please visit http://www.pewresearch.or/about/use-policy/; p. 360 Lisa F. Young/Fotolia; p. 361 Thinkstock Images/Getty Images, *Source:* The Quotable Woman, p. 53. Pennsylvania: Running Press, 1991, *Source:* Bill Cosby; p. 362 JUPITERIMAGES/Thinkstock/Alamy; p. 366 Mark Wilson/Getty Images; p. 367 Jack Hollingsworth/Getty Images, *Source:* Holland, J. L. (1973). Making vocational choices: A theory of careers. Englewood Cliffs, NJ: Prentice-Hall.; Holland, J. L. (1992). Making vocational choices: A theory of vocational personalities and work environments (2nd ed.). Odessa, FL: Psychological Assessment Resources; p. 368 Ariel Skelley/Corbis; p. 369 Diego Cervo/Shutterstock, laviejasirena/Fotolia; p. 375 VStock LLC/Tanya Constantine/Getty Images; p. 378 Monkey Business Images/Shutterstock; p. 380 bikeriderlondon/Shutterstock.com; p. 381 Assembly/Blend Images/Getty Images, *Source:* Duursma et al., 1991; Gambert, Schultz, & Hamdy, 1995; Goldberg & Hagberg, 1990; Gordon & Vaughan, 1986; Lindsay, 1985; Morrison et al., 1994; Smith, 1982; p. 382 Monkey Business Images/Shutterstock; p. 384, *Source:* Centers for Disease Control, 1994; Dwyer et al., 2004; Gaziano & Hennekens, 1995; Hunter et al., 1996; Lee, Manson, Hennekens, & Paffenbarger, 1993; Manson et al., 1995; Manson et al., 2002; Morris, Kritchevsky, & Davis, 1994; Rich-Edwards, Manson, Hennekens, & Buring, 1995; Risch, Jain, Marrett, & Howe, 1994; Rose, 1993; Stampfer et al., 1993; Trichopoulou, Costacou, Bamia, & Trichopoulou, 2003; Willett et al., 1992, 1995; Woodward & Tunstall-Pedoe, 1995; p. 385 Tim Boyles/Getty Images; p. 390, *Source:* Xu, J; Kochanek, K; Murphy, S; Tejada-Vera, B. (2010). Deaths, final data for 2007. National Vital Statistics Reports, 58, 1–73; CDC, 1998c; U.S. Bureau of the Census, 1990, 1995; National Center for Health Statistics (NCHS). (2013). Health, United States, 2012. Retrieved July 17, 2013 from http://www.cdc.gov/nchs/data/hus/hus12.pdf#018, *Source:* Xu, J; Kochanek, K; Murphy, S; Tejada-Vera, B. (2010). Deaths, final data for 2007. National Vital Statistics Reports, 58, 1–73; CDC, 1998c; U.S. Bureau of the Census, 1990, 1995; National Center for Health Statistics (NCHS). (2013). Health, United States, 2012. Retrieved July 17, 2013 from http://www.cdc.gov/nchs/data/hus/hus12.pdf#018; p. 391 Tom Stewart/CORBIS; p. 392 Jeff Greenberg/The Image Works; p. 394, *Source:* Thomas Edison; p. 399 Corbis/SuperStock; p. 400 Ronnie Kaufman/Larry Hirshowitz/Getty Images, *Source:* Erikson, E. H. (1963). Childhood and society (2nd ed.). New York: Norton. p. 267; p. 401 Manuel Balce Ceneta/AP images; p. 403 wavebreakmedia/Shutterstock, Paul Avis/Photodisc/Getty Images; p. 404 Sean Justice/Cardinal/Corbis; p. 405, *Source:* Data from Bumpass, L. L., & Aquilino, W. S. (1995). A social map of midlife: Family and work over the middle life course. Report of the MacArthur Foundation research network on successful midlife development, Vero Beach, FL. Data from Tables 11, 12, 25, and 26; p. 406 JGI/Tom Grill/Blend Images/Getty Images, *Source:* Cherlin, A., & Furstenberg, F. F. (1986). The new American grandparent. New York: Basic Books. P. 55; p. 407 Robert Voets/CBS Photo Archive/Getty Images, Vibe Images/Fotolia; p. 409 Monkey Business/Fotolia; p. 411 Sara D. Davis/AP images; p. 412 Ocean/Corbis; p. 417 John Donegan/AFP/Newscom; p. 419 Mark Richards/PhotoEdit, *Source:* Federal Interagency Forum on Aging Statistics (FIFARS). (2012). Older Americans: Key indicators of well-being. Retrieved July 16, 2013 from http://www.agingstats.gov/Main_Site/Data/2012_Documents/docs/EntireChartbook.pdf; p. 421 Federal Interagency Forum on Aging Statistics (FIFARS). (2012). Older Americans: Key indicators of well-being. Retrieved July 16, 2013 from http://www.agingstats.gov/Main_Site/Data/2012_Documents/docs/EntireChartbook.pdf.; p. 422 Rubberball Productions - Mike Kemp/Getty Images; p. 424 Steve Mason/Photodisc/Getty Images; p. 427 PNC/Brand X Pictures/Getty Images; p. 432 Stewart Cohen/Pam Ostrow/Blend Images/Corbis, *Source:* Federal Interagency Forum on Aging Statistics (FIFARS). (2012). Older Americans: Key indicators of well-being. Retrieved July 16, 2013 from http://www.agingstats.gov/Main_Site/Data/2012_Documents/docs/EntireChartbook.pdf.; p. 433 Enid Alvarez/NY Daily News Archive/Getty Images; p. 434 Frida Marquez/Blend Images/Getty Images; p. 435, *Source:* FIFARS, 2006; p. 436, *Source:* Data from West, R. L., & Crook, T. H. (1990). Age differences in everyday memory: Laboratory analogues of telephone number recall. Psychology & Aging, 5, 520–529. From Table 3, p. 524, *Source:* Adapted from R. Kliegel, J. Smith, and P. B. Baltes, On the Locus and Process of Magnification of Age Differences During Mneumonic Training, *Developmental Psychology, Vol. 26*, Fig. 2, p. 899. Copyright 1990 by the American Psychological Association. Adapted with permission; p. 437 Paul Panayiotou/Paul Panayiotou/Corbis, Camille Tokerud/The Image Bank/Getty Images; p. 442 Blinkbox/Splash News/Newscom; p. 444 imageshunter/Shutterstock; p. 446, *Source:* Guse, L., & Masesar, M. (1999). Quality of life and successful aging in long-term care: Perceptions of residents. Issues in Mental Health Nursing, 20, 527–539; p. 447 Rana Faure/Corbis; p. 448 Kelly Redinger/Age Fotostock; p. 450 MANCEAU/BSIP/Superstock, Federal Interagency Forum on Aging Statistics (FIFARS). (2012). Older Americans: Key indicators of well-being. Retrieved July 16, 2013 from http://www.agingstats.gov/Main_Site/Data/2012_Documents/docs/EntireChartbook.pdf.; p. 452 Best View Stock/Getty Images; p. 454 Digital Vision/Getty Images; p. 455 Syracuse Newspapers/Maria Salatino/The Image Works; p. 456 Bill Aron/PhotoEdit, Tom & Dee Ann McCarthy/corbis/Glow Images; p. 458 John S Lander/LightRocket/Getty Images, Tom Carter/PhotoEdit; p. 460, Federal Interagency Forum on Aging Statistics (FIFARS). (2012). Older Americans: Key indicators of well-being. Retrieved July 16, 2013 from http://www.agingstats.gov/Main_Site/Data/2012_Documents/docs/EntireChartbook.pdf.; p. 462 A. Ramey/PhotoEdit; p. 466 xmasbaby/Fotolia; p. 467, *Source:* National Center for Health Statistics. (2013). Underlying cause of death 1999–2010. Retrieved July 15, 2013 from http://wonder.cdc.gov/controller/datarequest/D76;jsessionid=DD32A469D781F7C71F5D8ED8B605D6F0; p. 468 Bill Aron/PhotoEdit; p. 469 RubberBall Productions/the Agency Collection/Getty Images; p. 471 GL1 WENN Photos/Newscom; p. 472, Lester, D. (1990). The Collett-Lester fear of death scale: The original version and a revision. Death Studies, 14, 451–468, Thorson, J. A., & Powell, F. C. (1992). A revised death anxiety scale. Death Studies, 16, 507–521; p. 475, *Source:* Kubler-Ross, E. (1969). On death and dying. New York: Macmillan. p. 83; p. 476 Ken Glaser/Corbis, Judy Bellah/Alamy; p. 480, Bowlby, J. (1980). *Attachment and Loss, Vol. 3:* Loss, sadness, and depression. New York: Basic Books. p. 481 *Source:* Bowlby, J. (1980). Attachment and loss, Vol. 3: Loss, sadness, and depression. New York: Basic Books; Sanders, C. M. (1989). Grief: The mourning after. New York: Wiley-Interscience; p. 483 Philip Gould/Documentary Value/Corbis, Steve Skjold/Alamy, Bruno Morandi/Alamy; p. 485 Evan Vucci/AP images.

Name Index

Subject Index

Continuity-discontinuity debate, 7, 20
Continuity theory, 445
Contraction, 73
Control group, 14
Conventional morality, 306
Conventional reasoning, 306
Conventional stage (moral development stage), 305t
Cooing, 117
Copycat suicide, Internet (impact), 470
Corpus callosum, 154
Correlational studies, 18t
Correlations, 13
C-reactive protein (CRP) levels, measurement, 384
Creativity
    enhancement, 438
    middle adulthood, 393–395
    stages (Cohen), 438
    wisdom, relationship (late adulthood), 437–439
Critical consumer, 14
Critical period, 8
Cross-cultural differences, achievement
        (relationship), 229–231
Cross-cultural research, 17, 18t
    importance, 17, 20
Cross-gender behavior, 190
Cross-linking, 426
Cross-race effect, 181
Cross-sectional design, 15, 18t
    advantages/disadvantages, 20
    example, 16f
Crowds (reputation-based group), 315
CRP. See C-reactive protein
Crying, increase (cross-cultural studies), 86
Crystallized intelligence, 342
Cultural beliefs, 230
Cultural context (macrosystem), 40
Cultures
    language development, 121–122
    moral reasoning, relationship, 309
    theory of mind, 163–164
Curriculum flexibility, importance, 224
CVD. See Cardiovascular disease
CVS. See Chorionic villus sampling
Cyberbullying, 310
Cytomegalovirus (CMV), 68

D

Darwin, Charles, 3
Day-care center, selection, 146
Day-care experience, 143
Death
    adolescents, understanding, 469–470
    adult meaning, 470–472
    brain death, 467
    children, understanding, 469–470
    clinical death, 467
    experience, 467–468, 488
    fear, 472–473
    meaning, 469–474, 488
    preparation, 473–474
    religious beliefs, 472–473
    responses, 477–479
    rituals, psychosocial functions, 483–484

Decentration, 218
Deception, 19
Deductive logic, 218
Defense mechanisms, 25
Deferred imitation, 108
    studies, 110
Degree completion rates (United States), 344f
Delayed retirement, 458
Delinquency, 310
Delusion of grandeur, 337
Delusions, 337
Dementia, 429–431
Dendrites, 62
Denial (dying diagnosis grouping), 477
Denial (dying stage), 475
Denney, Nancy (model of physical and cognitive
        aging), 390
Deoxyribonucleic acid (DNA), 49
Dependent variable, 14
Depressants, 339t
Depression
    adolescents, 280–282
    grief-related depression, 484
    late adulthood, 432–434
    mothers, 135
    postpartum depression (PPD), 362
    prevalence, 432–433
    risk factors, 432–434
    therapy/medication/prevention, 434
Desires, understanding, 162–163
Despair, ego integrity (differences), 27, 443–444
Development. See Human development; Prenatal
        development
    Diabetes, 387–388
Dialectical thought, 341
Diet, impact, 68–69
Dilation (birth), 73
Diphtheria/tetanus/pertussis (DTP), 91
Disabilities, 231–233
Disengagement theory, 444–445
Dishabituation, 97
Disruptive behavior, 255–256
Disruptive mood dysregulation disorder, 185
Divorce, 200–201
    coping (middle-aged women), 403
    early adulthood, 358
    effects, understanding, 201–202
    inevitability, 201
Dizygotic twins, 50
DNA. See Deoxyribonucleic acid
Domains of development, 4–5
Dominance hierarchies, 204
Dominant disorder, 78
Dominant genes, 51–52
Dominant-recessive pattern, 51–52
Down syndrome (trisomy 21), 56
Drugs
    adverse effects, 66–67, 79
    causal links, studying, 72–73
    statin drugs, administration, 384
    teratogens, types, 65t
    tolerance, 338
DTP. See Diphtheria/tetanus/pertussis

Dynamic systems theory, 87–88
Dyslexia, 231–232

E

Early adulthood
    anxiety, 336–337
    educational influences, 366
    family, influences, 366
    health, 328–340, 345–346
        habits, 328–329
    mental health problems, 335–338
    personality disorders, 337
    postsecondary education, 343–345, 346
    sexually transmitted diseases (STDs), 331–333
    smoking, cessation, 330
    social support, 439
    strength/speed, change, 326
    substance use/abuse, 338–340
Early childhood, 5
Early retirement, 459
Eating disorders (adolescence), 279–280
Eating patterns, 155–156
Eclecticism, 43–44
Ecological theories, 38–41, 45
Ectopic pregnancy, 58
Edison, Thomas, 394
Effacement (birth), 73
Effortful control/task persistence (temperament
        dimension), 138
Ego, 24, 28
Egocentric empathy, 185t
Egocentrism, 159–160
Ego-integrity-versus-despair stage (Erikson), 443
Elder abuse, 454
Elderly, ethnicity/poverty rates, 460f
Elders, respect (moral principle), 309
Electra, 25
Electrical activity patterns, production, 61
Embryo, development, 57
Embryonic stage, 59, 60t
    critical periods, 65
Emerging adulthood, 352–353
    neurological changes, 352
Emotional availability, 135
Emotional characteristics, genetic components, 51
Emotional intelligence, 227
Emotional regulation, 184
    acquisition process, 184–185
Emotional relationships, requirement, 39
Emotional responses (learning), classical
        conditioning (usage), 112
Emotional responsiveness, 135
Emotional self, 141–142, 184–185
Empathy, 185
    development stages, 185t
Empiricism, 3
Empiricists, 101
Empowered trailblazers, 412
Empty nest, 404
Encore phase (creativity stage), 438
Endocrine system, development, 59
Energy expenditure, 391
English as a Second Language (ESL), programs, 224